International Directory of
COMPANY
HISTORIES

International Directory of

COMPANY

HISTORIES

VOLUME 25

Editor
Laura E. Whiteley

ST. JAMES PRESS

AN IMPRINT OF GALE

DETROIT • NEW YORK

STAFF

Laura E. Whiteley, *Editor*

Miranda H. Ferrara, *Project Manager*

Joann Cerrito, David J. Collins, Nicolet V. Elert, Kristin Hart,
Margaret Mazurkiewicz, Michael J. Tyrkus, *Contributing Editors*

Peter M. Gareffa, *Managing Editor, St. James Press*

Library of Congress Catalog Number: 89-190943

British Library Cataloguing in Publication Data

International directory of company histories. Vol. 25
I. Laura E. Whiteley
338.7409

ISBN 1-55862-367-1

Printed in the United States of America
Published simultaneously in the United Kingdom

St. James Press is an imprint of Gale

Cover photograph: The Philadelphia Stock Exchange, Philadelphia, Pennsylvania
(courtesy Philadelphia Stock Exchange)

10 9 8 7 6 5 4 3 2 1

CONTENTS _____

Company Histories

PREFACE

The St. James Press series *The International Directory of Company Histories (IDCH)* is intended for reference use by students, business people, librarians, historians, economists, investors, job candidates, and others who seek to learn more about the historical development of the world's most important companies. To date, *IDCH* has covered over 3,500 companies in 25 volumes.

Inclusion Criteria

Most companies chosen for inclusion in *IDCH* have achieved a minimum of US$50 million in annual sales and are leading influences in their industries or geographical locations. Companies may be publicly held, private, or non-profit. State-owned companies that are important in their industries and that may operate much like public or private companies also are included. Wholly owned subsidiaries and divisions are profiled if they meet the requirements for inclusion. Entries on companies that have had major changes since they were last profiled may be selected for updating.

The *IDCH* series highlights 10% private and non-profit companies, and features updated entries on approximately 40 companies per volume.

Entry Format

Each entry begins with the company's legal name, the address of its headquarters, its telephone, toll-free, and fax numbers, and its web site. A statement of public, private, state, or parent ownership follows. A company with a legal name in both English and the language of its headquarters country is listed by the English name, with the native-language name in parentheses.

The company's founding or earliest incorporation date, the number of employees, and the most recent sales figures available follow. Sales figures are given in local currencies with equivalents in U.S. dollars. For some private companies, sales figures are estimates. The entry lists the exchanges on which a company's stock is traded and its ticker symbol, as well as the company's principal Standard Industrial Classification codes.

Entries generally contain a *Company Perspectives* box which provides a short summary of the company's mission, goals, and ideals, a list of *Principal Subsidiaries*, *Principal Divisions*, *Principal Operating Units*, and articles for *Further Reading*.

American spelling is used throughout *IDCH*, and the word "billion" is used in its U.S. sense of one thousand million.

Sources

Entries have been compiled from publicly accessible sources both in print and on the Internet such as general and academic periodicals, books, annual reports, and material supplied by the companies themselves.

Cumulative Indexes

IDCH contains two indexes: the **Index to Companies**, which provides an alphabetical index to companies discussed in the text as well as companies profiled, and the **Index to Industries**, which allows researchers to locate companies by their principal industry. Both indexes are cumulative and specific instructions for using them are found immediately preceding each index.

Suggestions Welcome

Comments and suggestions from users of *IDCH* on any aspect of the product as well as suggestions for companies to be included or updated are cordially invited. Please write:

The Editor
International Directory of Company Histories
St. James Press
27500 Drake Rd.
Farmington Hills, Michigan 48331-3535

ABBREVIATIONS FOR FORMS OF COMPANY INCORPORATION

A.B.	Aktiebolaget (Sweden)
A.G.	Aktiengesellschaft (Germany, Switzerland)
A.S.	Atieselskab (Denmark)
A.S.	Aksjeselskap (Denmark, Norway)
A.Ş.	Anomin Şirket (Turkey)
B.V.	Besloten Vennootschap met beperkte, Aansprakelijkheid (The Netherlands)
Co.	Company (United Kingdom, United States)
Corp.	Corporation (United States)
G.I.E.	Groupement d'Intérêt Economique (France)
GmbH	Gesellschaft mit beschränkter Haftung (Germany)
H.B.	Handelsbolaget (Sweden)
Inc.	Incorporated (United States)
KGaA	Kommanditgesellschaft auf Aktien (Germany)
K.K.	Kabushiki Kaisha (Japan)
LLC	Limited Liability Company (Middle East)
Ltd.	Limited (Canada, Japan, United Kingdom, United States)
N.V.	Naamloze Vennootschap (The Netherlands)
OY	Osakeyhtiöt (Finland)
PLC	Public Limited Company (United Kingdom)
PTY.	Proprietary (Australia, Hong Kong, South Africa)
S.A.	Société Anonyme (Belgium, France, Switzerland)
SpA	Società per Azioni (Italy)

ABBREVIATIONS FOR CURRENCY

Abbr.	Currency	Abbr.	Currency
DA	Algerian dinar	M$	Malaysian ringgit
A$	Australian dollar	Dfl	Netherlands florin
Sch	Austrian schilling	Nfl	Netherlands florin
BFr	Belgian franc	NZ$	New Zealand dollar
Cr	Brazilian cruzado	N	Nigerian naira
C$	Canadian dollar	NKr	Norwegian krone
RMB	Chinese renminbi	RO	Omani rial
DKr	Danish krone	P	Philippine peso
E£	Egyptian pound	Esc	Portuguese escudo
Fmk	Finnish markka	SRls	Saudi Arabian riyal
FFr	French franc	S$	Singapore dollar
DM	German mark	R	South African rand
HK$	Hong Kong dollar	W	South Korean won
HUF	Hungarian forint	Pta	Spanish peseta
Rs	Indian rupee	SKr	Swedish krona
Rp	Indonesian rupiah	SFr	Swiss franc
IR£	Irish pound	NT$	Taiwanese dollar
L	Italian lira	B	Thai baht
¥	Japanese yen	£	United Kingdom pound
W	Korean won	$	United States dollar
KD	Kuwaiti dinar	B	Venezuelan bolivar
LuxFr	Luxembourgian franc	K	Zambian kwacha

International Directory of
COMPANY HISTORIES

A & W Brands, Inc.

P.O. Box 869077
Plano, Texas 75086-9077
U.S.A.
(972) 527-7096
Fax: (972) 673-7171

Wholly Owned Division of Cadbury Schweppes PLC
Incorporated: 1950 as A&W Root Beer Company
Employees: 120
Sales: $65 million (1997 est.)
SICs: 8053 Beverages

A&W Brands, Inc. is best known for its famous A&W Root Beer beverage. Historically one of the most popular soft drinks in the United States, the A&W Brands, Inc. root beer concoction retains a leading share of the market in the late 1990s, despite strong competition from Barq's, Dad's, and Hires root beer products. Ownership of the well-known beverage, however, and the franchise restaurants that serve it, have undergone many changes since the 1960s. In 1993, Cadbury Schweppes PLC, a prominent beverage company in Great Britain, purchased A&W Brands, Inc. to strengthen its growing presence both in the United States and international beverage markets. Now independent from A&W Brands, Inc. are A&W Restaurants, which is in the business of licensing franchises not only in the United States but around the world, and A&W Food Services of Canada, managed by a group of businessmen who are building a beverage and restaurant empire across North America.

Early History

The driving force behind A&W Root Beer was Roy Allen, an ambitious entrepreneur who at the turn of the 20th century became widely known throughout the southwestern United States for buying, renovating, and selling older hotels and motels. Having become acquainted with a recipe for root beer that a pharmacist had given him at a soda fountain while he was arranging a hotel deal in Tucson, Arizona, Allen impetuously purchased the recipe and opened a hamburger and root beer stand in Lodi, California, in June 1919.

With an innate sense of what was popular among the people at the time, Allen knew that by playing on the name of "root beer" he could attract alcohol drinkers into his establishment, especially since he decorated it as an old, well-worn saloon, complete with bar and barstools. The Volstead Act of 1919 had prohibited the sale and consumption of alcoholic beverages, so soldiers returning from the World War I battlefields in France flocked to Allen's root beer stand, finding the beverage a palatable substitute. By the summer of 1920, in order to meet the growing demand for his product, Allen opened a second root beer stand in Stockton, California.

With more and more people clamoring for his product, Allen formed a partnership with Frank Wright, one of his employees, in order to establish five more outlets in the Sacramento area. After formally naming their product "A&W Root Beer" (the name reflecting the initials of the two partners), more outlets were opened in Houston, Texas, in 1922. Capitalizing on the increasing mobility of the American public, and the fact that more people were purchasing automobiles, Allen came up with the idea of transforming the root beer stands into drive-in restaurants. As people headed downtown in their cars on steamy summer evenings, Allen attracted them to his root beer stand by providing "car hop" services. Modeled after the bell hops of exclusive hotels, "tray boys" were hired to deliver root beer to customers while they sat in the comfort of their automobiles.

By 1924, with the popularity of his soft drink and drive-in outlet assured, Allen decided to buy Wright's share of the business. At the same time, Allen registered the name "A&W Root Beer" and the A&W logo with the United States Patent and Trademark office, and began a comprehensive strategy to expand his business throughout the western United States. His first move was to establish a franchise restaurant chain for A&W Root Beer Stands. Selling the rights to franchises in Oregon, California, Washington, Nevada, and Arizona to two businessmen, H.C. Bell and Lewis Reed, the outlets within these states were renamed "Reed & Bell Root Beer."

Then Allen moved to Salt Lake City, Utah and restarted his business. By selling A&W franchises throughout the United States, except for the five states where he had sold the rights to Bell and Reed, Allen created the very first restaurant chain in

America. Demanding and meticulous in his franchise agreements, Allen stipulated in each contractual arrangement the precise design and floorplan of each root beer drive-in restaurant, the design and weight of the mugs his root beer was to be served in, and the mixture of the brew that had established his reputation and had given him a fortune. By the end of the 1920s, the A&W Root Beer Drive-In was becoming a common sight to many Americans.

The Great Depression and World War II

The crash of the stock market in the autumn of 1929 had profound effects for the entire American economy and the population across the country. Depending on the area of the country, A&W Root Beer Drive-Ins either thrived or closed down. Due to the drought in the southern part of the country, and the dust bowls across the Plains States, many A&W Drive-Ins were forced to cease operations. In general, however, the franchise drive-ins continued to increase in number throughout the 1930s, and in 1933 Allen happily reported that there were over 170 A&W outlets in the United States.

By the end of 1941, when the United States entered World War II, more than 260 A&W outlets were in operation. Unfortunately, the advent of the war had a deleterious impact on A&W Root Beer Drive-Ins. Not only was there a shortage of employees, caused by young men going to the war and young women taking jobs to fuel the production of wartime materials, but the essential ingredients to make root beer were simply not available. Sugar and extract were scarce commodities, rationed carefully to the American public for consumption. Not a priority business for the success of the American war effort, A&W Root Beer Drive-Ins began closing at a rapid rate. When the war ended in 1945, nearly 80 of the A&W outlets across the country had been forced to close due to the shortages resulting from the war.

Growth and Prosperity in the Postwar Era

When Reed and Bell's franchise agreement expired in 1945, the A&W rights reverted to Allen, along with all the outlets run by the two men. With soldiers returning from overseas, and the government's offer of easy-to-obtain GI loans, hundreds of new A&W outlets opened across the United States. By 1950, over 450 A&W outlets were in operation. However, Allen suddenly decided to sell the business he had founded due to the illness of wife. A businessman from Nebraska, Gene Hurtz, became the new owner and immediately incorporated his holdings as the A&W Root Beer Company.

Hurtz's management style allowed individual franchisees to run their business as they pleased, including marketing and public relations functions. In addition, Hurtz maintained an extremely small staff at his corporate headquarters, having no intention of providing extended support system for the franchisees he had contracted. Although franchisees grew more displeased with Hurtz's management style as the 1950s progressed, the number of A&W outlets continued to grow. Perhaps Hurtz's most important decision during his time as leader of the company was to allow the franchisees to serve food and develop their outlets as drive-in restaurants. By the end of the decade, there were more than 1,900 A&W restaurants through-

out the United States, and the first outlet outside the country had opened in Canada.

Growing discontent among the franchisees led Hurtz to sell the company in 1963 to the J. Hungerford Smith Company, the firm which had been brewing the root beer extract and bottling it since 1919. Hungerford was acquired by the United Fruit Company just three years later, and in 1970 management at United Fruit Company decided to merge with AMK Corporation in order to form United Brands Company. During these years of changing ownership, the A&W Root Beer Company was changed to A&W International, to reflect the firm's growing international operation, and a new marketing strategy was implemented which focused less on the root beer brand and more on the drive-in restaurant. Thus the promotion and success of the A&W outlet became more important than the promotion and sale of the root beer extract itself, a decision that would dramatically affect the viability of the company.

Growth and Transition in the 1970s–80s

United Brands management decided to bottle A&W Root Beer for distribution to retail stores during the early 1970s. Despite the somewhat altered flavor effected by the difference in packaging, the introduction of the beverage was successful and the company introduced Sugar Free A&W Root Beer in 1974. In conjunction with the development of these two products for the retail market, the company formed A&W Beverages, Inc., a wholly owned subsidiary with the purpose of selling the root beer to consumers apart from the restaurant chain. By 1976, A&W Root Beer had become the leading root beer sold in bottles and cans within the United States, surpassing long-time leader Hires. In 1978, company management at United Brands decided to form another wholly owned subsidiary, A&W Restaurants, Inc., to manage the growing number of restaurant franchises. The separation of the beverage from the restaurant chain, however, as distinctively administered entities and operations, gave rise to the prospect of each one becoming a takeover or acquisition target.

In 1982, in a move that surprised no one, United Brands Company sold A&W Restaurants, Inc. to a well-known and enterprising real estate developer, A. Alfred Taubman. The new owner of the A&W Restaurant chain immediately relocated company headquarters to Michigan and implemented a comprehensive reorganization strategy. One year later, management at United Brands sold A&W Beverages, Inc. to a consortium which was formed to create A&W Brands, Inc., a new company with the purpose of managing the production, marketing, and sale of the regular and sugar-free root beer beverages. In 1986, the management team at A&W Brands, with the assistance of an investment firm, bought the company from the consortium for approximately $74 million. Losing no time in consolidating its market position, A&W Brands introduced A&W Cream Soda and A&W Diet Cream Soda in 1986, reformulated Sugar Free A&W Root Beer in 1987 using NutraSweet and renamed it Diet A&W Root Beer, and purchased Squirtco, the producer of Squirt soft drink. One year later, A&W Brands acquired Vernors, Inc., the manufacturer of Vernors ginger ale.

Under management at A&W Brands, all of the company's product line prospered enormously. Diet A&W Root Beer soon accounted for approximately one-third of the firm's total sales volume. By 1989, the company's cream soda had captured more than 40 percent of the total market share for that beverage. Without having to focus on the development of the restaurant business, management at A&W Brands was pleased to see profits rise dramatically. At the same time, A&W Restaurants, Inc. was experiencing a resurgence after its reorganization had been completed. Management at A&W Restaurants had standardized a menu for all franchisees to follow, and aggressively expanded its operations. In 1989, the company reached a major agreement with Carousel Snack Bars to redesign nearly 200 mall and food court outlets and convert them to "A&W Hot Dogs and More" over a period of two years.

The 1990s and Beyond

A&W Brands entered the 1990s in a comfortable position: all the its product lines—root beer and non-root beer beverages—were selling well, and prospects for future growth seemed assured. Then, in 1993, management received an offer from Cadbury Schweppes PLC and decided to sell the company, including all of its assets and operations, for $334 million. Cadbury Schweppes, created during 1969 out of the merger of two famous companies, had already established itself as one of the leaders in the food, beverage, and personal hygiene markets. During the early 1990s, Cadbury Schweppes decided to focus on and expand upon its two related core businesses, beverages and confectionery products, while selling off all the non-core business operations. Having already purchased Crush International, a carbonated soft drinks producer, in 1989, which significantly enhanced its hold on the market, in 1990 Cadbury Schweppes purchased Oasis soft drinks brand in France, and Aguas Minerales in Mexico, which gave the firm leading shares of the market in their respective segments in both France and Mexico. Moving into the United States market appeared to be the next natural step, and thus Cadbury Schweppes purchased A&W Brands, Inc. to immediately gain a prominent position in the soft drinks sector. In 1996, Cadbury Schweppes bought Dr.

Pepper/Seven-Up, Inc., based in Plano, Texas, and merged it with A&W Brands, Inc., relocating A&W to Texas and thereby consolidating its leading position within the American soft drinks market.

In 1994, A&W Restaurants, Inc. was purchased by Sagittarius Acquisitions. The president of Sagittarius, Sidney Feltenstein, had formerly worked as a vice-president of marketing for Burger King Worldwide, and acquired A&W Restaurants in order to revitalize the company's operations in the United States. Despite the separation of the beverage business from the restaurant chain, it is the tradition and legacy of the root beer beverage that most people are attracted to, and what people continue to drink through the myriad changes in ownership of the brand-name product. Under management at Cadbury Schweppes since 1993, all of the A&W Brand products have sold well, with A&W root beer competing directly with Coca-Cola, Seven-Up, Dr. Pepper, and Pepsi. Although it is unlikely that A&W root beer will ever increase its share of the soft drink market, the 30 percent share of the root beer market that it retains is more than enough to keep management at Cadbury Schweppes happy.

Further Reading

"An American Tradition, The History of A&W," corporate typescript, Plano, Tex.: A&W Brands, Inc., 1992.
Giltenan, Edward, "Bubbling," *Forbes,* January 20, 1990, p. 12.
——, "Root Beer Gloat," *Forbes,* December 11, 1989, p. 156.
"History of A&W Restaurants, Inc.: The Taste America Loves To Remember," corporate typescript, Plano, Tex.: A&W Restaurants, Inc., 1995.
Marcial, Gene G., "A Root-Beer Biggie with Lots of Fizz," *Business Week,* April 23, 1990, p. 114.
Winters, Pat, "A&W Goes Bowling, Leaves Larry Behind," *Advertising Age,* December 4, 1989, p. 40.
——, "Cream Of The Smaller Crop," *Advertising Age,* August 18, 1988, p. S-10.

—Thomas Derdak

A.M. Castle & Co.

3400 North Wolf Road
Franklin Park, Illinois 60131-1319
U.S.A.
(847) 455-7111
Fax: (847) 455-7136
Web site: http://www.amcastle.com

Public Company
Incorporated: 1904
Employees: 1,850
Sales: $754.9 million (1997)
Stock Exchanges: American
Ticker Symbol: CAS
SICs: 5051 Metal Service Centers & Offices

A.M. Castle & Co. is one of North America's largest independent operators of metals distribution centers, offering quick delivery of specialty metals to a large variety of industrial companies. These metals come in many forms, including round and flat bars, plates, tubing, sheets, and coils. The company also distributes a wide variety of industrial plastics.

The First 85 Years: 1890–1975

The company was founded in Chicago in 1890 by A.M. Castle, as a distributor and jobber of steel manufactured products, including plates, rivets, beams, and similar structural materials. By 1920, when W.B. Simpson was its president and the founder's descendant A.C. Castle a vice-president, the company was reporting assets of $2.6 million. Its Chicago plant consisted of a fabricating factory, two fireproof warehouses, and two office buildings. Net sales reached $7.2 million in 1927, and net earnings a pre-Depression peak of $987,042 in 1929. By then the company was active on the Pacific Coast as well as in the Middle West, with steel warehouses in San Francisco, Los Angeles, and Seattle, as well as in Chicago. During this time, Simpson moved up to the position of chairman, and A.C. Castle became the company's president.

Although profits were leaner in the 1930s, A.M. Castle lost money only in 1932 and suspended its dividend only in 1932 and 1933. The company had a record net profit of $1 million on net sales of $12.8 million in 1941. Net profit reached a peak of $1.6 million in 1946, on sales of $14.8 million. A.M. Castle purchased Biggs Steel Co. of Milwaukee in 1945. By 1950 the company had added steel warehouses in Berkeley, California, and North Kansas City, Missouri, as well as in Milwaukee, to its roster. It had net profit of $1.3 million on net sales of $18.7 million in that year.

During the 1950s business surged and contracted according to the vagaries of the national economy, with A.M. Castle's net sales climbing from a low of $18.5 million in 1954 to a high of $44.2 million in 1959 and net profit from a low of $547,520 in the former year to $1.8 million in 1956. During this time, the company moved its headquarters and main warehouse to Franklin Park, a suburb of Chicago and also added warehouses in Rockford, Illinois, and Baltimore—its first location in the East—and began distributing aluminum and plastic pipe as well as steel products. In 1958 the company acquired Nottingham Steel & Aluminum Co. for about $1.5 million, thereby adding warehouses in Cleveland and Galion, Ohio.

By the mid-1960s A.M. Castle, along with other companies in its field, preferred to call its warehouses "service centers." Each of its ten service centers (now including one in Salt Lake City) carried an inventory specially tailored to the needs of its customers in that area. The company also provided financial counseling to its smaller customers, introducing some of them to banks. About 20 percent of all steel from U.S. mills was finding its way to users via companies like A.M. Castle, and only the auto manufacturers were taking a larger volume.

In 1965 A.M. Castle purchased the West Coast metals-distributing businesses of Pacific Metals Co., a subsidiary of Bangor Punta Alegre Sugar Corp. At the same time Bangor Punta acquired a substantial interest and managerial responsibility in Amcodnye Corp., an Ohio subsidiary of Castle that was fabricating sewage systems and steel swimming pools. In 1967 A.M. Castle had some 20,000 sizes, shapes, and grades of metals stockpiled, mainly in steel but also in aluminum, copper, brass, bronze, and many specialized alloys and exotic metals.

Orders ranged from a few pounds of high-temperature alloys for jet aircraft to carloads of plate for ship repair. Castle was processing some 75 percent of its shipments for its customers through such operations as flame-cutting, shearing, sawing, grinding, and slitting.

A.M. Castle's net sales reached $109.2 million in 1969, when its net income was $1.5 million. By the end of 1970 its roster included service centers in Phoenix, Sacramento, and Fresno, California. In addition to metals, the company was stocking and distributing abrasives, saw blades, wire rope, and industrial tapes. John M. Simpson, company chairman, owned 19 percent of the shares, and trustees for the benefit of the Simpson family members owned another 20 percent. Hy-Alloy Steels Co. was acquired in 1973 for $3.45 million and made a subsidiary.

Transition to Specialty Product Lines: 1976–90

In 1976, as the nation's heartland began turning into the "Rust Belt," A.M. Castle initiated an effort to become less dependent on basic carbon steel. "We were trying to be all things to all people and weren't doing a very good job on any of them," Michael Simpson, who had succeeded to the chairmanship, later recalled. The company decided to concentrate on products in which it could be competitive by building its inventory of specialty lines of steel such as stainless and co-finished bars and alloy plates. It also resolved to diversify into some metal products with higher profit margins than steel, such as nickel and titanium.

In 1978 A.M. Castle's sales increased 17 percent in volume, to 288,000 tons. The following year was even better, with net sales surging to $306.2 million and net income to $6.4 million. Between 1970 and 1980, the company cut low-margin carbon steel's share of its sales from 58 to 43 percent, while volume of higher-margin carbon alloy steel rose from three percent in 1971 to 18 percent in 1980. The company's 21 warehouses in 1980 included recent additions in Santa Clara, California; Pocatello, Idaho; Davenport, Iowa; Wichita, Kansas; Tulsa, Oklahoma; and Erie, Pennsylvania.

A.M. Castle closed its Baltimore service center in 1979 but established one in Seattle in the early 1980s. (The earlier Seattle warehouse was shuttered in the 1960s.) The company continued to seek sales for high-technology metals such as nickel alloys and duplex stainless steels in place of garden-variety carbon-steel product lines. It was adopting "just in time" inventory management to combat the rising cost of borrowing money in order to carry inventory, developing a customer database that it considered a first in the metals-distribution industry, and becoming more active in cutting and shaping parts for its customers. In 1983 A.M. Castle acquired George F. Blake Inc. of Worcester, Massachusetts, a major New England steel and aluminum service center. All told, the company's service centers were now reaching into markets accounting for more than 80 percent of the metals used in the United States.

A.M. Castle boosted its sales volume in 1984 by 30 percent, to $325 million. Although the Blake acquisition accounted for some of this gain, the company also benefited in part by carrying more metals with high temperature tolerances and light weights that were useful to, for example, the aerospace and electronics industries. It became one of the few national service centers to carry titanium after making a distribution deal with RMI, a large producer, in 1984. To service new markets, Castle had spent more than $10 million on new equipment for pre-heating, annealing (softening), and precisely cutting metals. After having established its metal-usage database in the early 1980s, the company opened service centers in Philadelphia; Worcester, Massachusetts; Charlotte, North Carolina; and the Rochester, New York metropolitan area during 1983–86.

A.M. Castle's expansion ended in 1985, when unfavorable conditions nationally in its field led to a revenues slump to $307.2 million, down from the previous year's $328.4 million. Net earnings fell 48 percent to $3.7 million. Castle responded by curbing inventory still further to contain costs. Performance goals, tied to Castle's overall return-on-investment objective, required managers at every level to focus on cost control and asset management as well as sales and margin. A resurgence of business brought net income to $13.7 million in 1988 on net sales of $499.3 million. In 1990 the company purchased Norton Steel Co., Ltd. of Canada for $9.3 million, thereby adding four distribution centers in Quebec, Ontario, and Manitoba.

A.M. Castle in the 1990s

Richard Mork, a 33-year veteran of the company, became president and chief executive officer in 1990, A.M. Castle's centennial year. He was the company's seventh president, all of whom had risen through the ranks. With profits having slumped from 1988's peak, and revenues beginning to fall from 1989's record of $501.1 million, there was little to celebrate at the time, however. The outlook became even worse as the national economy fell into recession, and in 1991 Castle earned only $200,000 on revenues of $436 million. By 1993, however, sales and profits had begun to recover. Castle was first, second, or third in most of its product lines, and its Hy-Alloy Steels division in 1992 became the first major U.S. broad-line metals distributor to attain the coveted ISO 9002 international standard of quality assurance.

The 1994–96 period was outstanding for A.M. Castle, with revenues rising from $537 million in 1994 (a $63-million gain from 1993) to $673 million in 1996. Net income, a record $15.4 million in 1994, rose to $26.8 million in 1995 and was $26.1 million in 1996. A share of common stock, still hovering at about $10 in early 1995, reached $30 in the summer of 1996. Hundreds of customers, including Du Pont, Boeing, Ingersoll Rand, and Raytheon, were allowing the company to manage their metal inventories, making Castle, in effect, a raw-materials consultant as well as a distributor.

Buoyed by these results, A.M. Castle entered a new field in 1996, purchasing Total Plastics Inc. of Kalamazoo, Michigan, a company engaged in preprocessing, fabricating, and distributing plastics in four states. Castle decided to add plastics to its products because some of its customers were having corrosion problems with steel. Total Plastics was doing about $25 million a year in sales, as was Cutter Precision Metals, Inc., a Pacific Northwest-based high-technology metals processor and distributor that Castle also acquired in 1996. Also in 1996, A.M. Castle, in a joint venture with a Swiss partner, acquired a one-third interest in Chicago-based Kreher Steel Co., a distributor with $110 million in annual sales. The company founded a joint-venture operation, Castle de Mexico, in Monterrey, Mexico, in 1994 and established a British subsidiary in 1996.

In 1997 A.M. Castle purchased Keystone Tube Inc., a specialty distributor of tubular products and processor of mechanical tubing and chrome-plated bars based in Titusville, Pennsylvania. This company had sales of about $60 million in 1996. Castle reported sales of $754.9 million in 1997 and net income of $23.8 million. Its Chicago, Los Angeles, and Cleveland distribution centers combined accounted, in 1997, for about half of all its sales, which consisted 73 percent of carbon and stainless steel and 27 percent of nonferrous metals. The company's long-term debt was $90.7 million at the end of the year.

At the end of 1997, Castle Metals was maintaining 17 service centers with nearly 2.2 million square feet in floor area. The Hy-Alloy Steels division had its facility in Bedford Park, Illinois, and the H-A Industries bar-processing center, opened in 1993, was in Hammond, Indiana. Cutter Precision Metals had two service centers. A.M. Castle's Canadian subsidiary had five service centers and the British subsidiary one, in Manchester, England. Keystone Tube had three facilities, and Total Plastics had six. Michael Simpson was still chairman of A.M. Castle in 1997. The Simpson family owned 35 percent of the company's common stock that year—about the same as it had in 1965.

Principal Divisions

Cutter Precision Metals; H-A Industries; Hy-Alloy Steels Co.

Principal Subsidiaries

A.M. Castle & Co. (Canada), Inc.; A.M. Castle & Co. Limited (United Kingdom); Keystone Tube Company; Total Plastics, Inc.

Further Reading

"A.M. Castle to Buy Keystone Honing," *American Metal Market,* October 14, 1997, p. 4.

Byrne, Harlan S., "A.M. Castle," *Barron's,* November 1, 1993, p. 50.

Carey, David, "Smart Fish Amid the Barracuda," *Financial World,* April 1, 1986, pp. 40–41.

"Defiance Industries Group Buys Interest in A.M. Castle; Says It Seeks Acquisition," *Wall Street Journal,* November 12, 1965, p. 6.

Hoeffer, El, "A.M. Castle: Chicago Skyrocket," *American Metal Market,* May 17, 1965, pp. 17, 38.

Lawton, Clark, "Castle a Vital Link Between Metal Users and Mills," *Investment Dealers' Digest,* August 7, 1967, pp. 32–33.

Riggs, Larry, "Service Centers Elude the Steel Trap," *Sales & Marketing Management,* September 9, 1985, pp. 47–48.

Rosenbaum, Michael, "Proving Its Mettle," *Barron's,* May 25, 1981, pp. 38–39.

Roush, Matt, "Kalamazoo Company Buys a Revived Pontiac Plastics," *Crain's Detroit Business,* March 25, 1996, p. 16.

Sebastian, Pam, "Castle Shifting Market Strategy to Build Up Specialty Products," *American Metal Market,* May 17, 1977, pp. 1, 20.

"Sharper Edge," *Barron's,* March 12, 1984, pp. 62–63.

Simpson, Michael, "Opportunities for Innovation in the Metals Industry," *Journal of Business Strategy,* Summer 1986, pp. 84–87.

Thompson, Donald B., "Simpson's New Castle," *Industry Week,* November 14, 1983, p. 25.

Young, David, "Diverse Steels Building Castle," *Chicago Tribune,* March 20, 1997, Sec. 3, pp. 1, 3.

—Robert Halasz

Abitibi-Consolidated, Inc.

1155 Metcalfe Street
Sun Life Building
Montreal, Quebec H3B 1Y9
Canada
(514) 875-2160
Fax: (514) 875-6284

Public Company
Incorporated: 1912 as Abitibi Pulp & Paper Co. Limited
Employees: 14,000
Sales: C $4.16 billion (1997)
Stock Exchanges: New York Toronto Montreal
Ticker Symbols: ABY; A
SICs: 5111 Printing & Writing Paper; 5113 Industrial &
   Personal Service Paper; 2621 Paper Mills; 2671
   Packaging Paper & Plastics Film, Coated &
   Laminated; 0811 Timber Tracts

Abitibi-Consolidated, Inc. is the world's largest newsprint and uncoated groundwood producer. It was formed in May 1997 by a merger of Abitibi-Price, Inc. and Stone-Consolidated Corporation. The two companies, which had been competitors, expected to achieve savings of $100 to $200 million annually just by eliminating duplications in the selling and administrative areas. Abitibi-Consolidated began operations with a total of 18 paper mills: 14 in Canada, three in the United States, and one in Great Britain, plus seven wholly owned or affiliated sawmills in Canada. The combined company had a market capitalization of C $4.1 billion, and annualized sales for 1997 were C $4.16 billion.

Early History

Along with much of the Canadian paper industry, Abitibi-Price owed its existence to the bitter squabbling that developed in the latter part of the 19th century between U.S. manufacturers and consumers of newsprint. Ever since the newspaper industry had converted from rag-based paper to paper made from the pulp of trees in the 1870s, it had been troubled by recurring overcapacity and disastrous price wars. These were usually followed by attempts to moderate competition through mergers and combinations. The most ambitious of these consolidations was the creation in the 1890s of International Paper Company from the assets of 19 U.S. paper concerns. In the first decade of the 20th century International Paper controlled nearly 75 percent of the U.S. newsprint market, a situation that elicited charges of monopoly and price gouging from the publishers of newspapers.

Newspaper publishers were able to publicize their accusations, sometimes coupling them with warnings about the need to protect freedom of the press from coercive economic forces. They eventually convinced the U.S. Congress to remove a long-standing tariff on imported paper products. The lifting of the tariff in 1913 prompted a rush to build plants in Canada, where abundant forests and water power made it a natural site for pulp and paper manufacturing. In the year 1911 alone, some 81 new forestry companies were created in Canada in anticipation of the lifting of the tariff. It was in the midst of this stampede that Abitibi Pulp & Paper Company Limited was established.

Abitibi's founder was an American named Frank H. Anson, born in 1859 in Niles, Michigan. Before coming to the paper business, Anson had worked as a railroad ticket agent, rubber prospector, exporter, and as general superintendent of Ogilvie Flour Mills in Montreal. While at Ogilvie, Anson became interested in the mining wealth of Ontario's northern reaches, and in 1909 Anson hired two young men from McGill University to prospect for him in that remote part of Canada. The students found no minerals but did recommend that Anson start a paper mill along the Abitibi River, from whose swift current electrical and mechanical power could be generated to run such an operation.

With the abolition of the U.S. paper tariff drawing closer every day, Anson enlisted the financial backing of Shirley Ogilvie, son of the Ogilvie Flour Mills family. In 1912 he incorporated Abitibi Pulp & Paper Company Limited. In 1913 he built the company's first mill on the Abitibi River, some 300 miles north of Toronto at Iroquois Falls. In 1914 Abitibi Pulp & Paper changed its name and reincorporated as Abitibi Power & Paper Company Limited, since the firm also sold electric power from its hydroelectric facility. Anson's timing was very good:

Company Perspectives:

We are a leading Canadian-based manufacturer and global marketer of newsprint and uncoated groundwood papers. Operating 18 mills throughout North America and the United Kingdom, our vision is to be the world's preferred marketer and manufacturer of papers for communication.

World War I soon drove up the price of newsprint to an all-time peak of US $65 per ton, and the new Canadian paper companies enjoyed unrestricted access to the immense U.S. markets.

Antitrust Investigations into Newsprint Association, 1917

So successful were the paper companies on both sides of the border that another round of investigations of the industry was launched, and in 1917 the U.S. Department of Justice began antitrust prosecution of the members of an industrywide cooperative group called the News Print Manufacturers Association. The association's membership pleaded no contest, paid US $11,000 in fines, and dissolved the organization. Still, the price of newsprint nearly doubled by 1920 to a new record of US $112.60 per ton.

The newsprint industry's history of antitrust allegations and cyclical depressions seemed to be a result of three factors: the enormous cost of building new plant capacity; the relative inelasticity of demand for newsprint (sales do not tend to increase when the price drops); and the highly vocal and influential nature of the product's consumers, the newspaper community. Since competition often proved fatal, newsprint manufacturers tried to curb competition, resulting in well-publicized accusations by the newspapers of antitrust violations.

Decade of Expansion, 1920s

The postwar price peak encouraged a full decade of nonstop expansion in the Canadian paper industry, which nearly doubled its capacity by the year 1930. The consequence of this expansion was a long decline in the price of newsprint. By the end of the decade, it had fallen to about US $62 per ton. There was also a growing overcapacity, which threw the industry into a premature depression of its own as early as 1928.

Abitibi Power & Paper had participated enthusiastically in the decade of expansion. It entered the fine-paper business with the purchase of a sulfite pulp mill at Smooth Rock Falls, Ontario; acquired substantial interests in Manitoba Paper Company and Sainte Anne Paper Company; and built its own mills. It became one of the industry's more important competitors.

Faced with the problems of increased capacity and falling prices, Abitibi and other paper manufacturers concluded that their best chance for collective survival was to amalgamate their holdings. Accordingly, in 1928 Abitibi engineered a quintuple merger, buying up the remainder of Manitoba Paper and Sainte Anne Paper and adding three others—Spanish River Pulp and Paper Mills, Fort William Power Company, and Murray Bay Paper Company. These, and a number of subsequent purchases

by Abitibi, proved disastrous; but at the time it was hoped that by consolidating the industry could prevent price competition and increase production efficiency. That strategy might have succeeded in a thriving economy, but instead Abitibi was hit by the Great Depression of the 1930s and soon was in desperate straits.

Abitibi Goes into Receivership, 1932

By 1932 sales had dropped to a fraction of their earlier levels, while the company's C $50 million debt was more than four times what it had been in 1927. This combination could not be sustained long, and on June 1, 1932, Abitibi defaulted on interest payments and was thrown into receivership. For the next 14 years Abitibi was directed by a court-appointed receiver, whose task it was to stabilize the company's finances, pay down the outstanding debts, and return the company to its shareholders at some future date.

By 1933 the price of newsprint finally stabilized, allowing Abitibi to begin the long road back to solvency. The remainder of the 1930s was not a bad period for Abitibi, which managed to earn a fairly steady operating income to reduce its debt and maintain its physical assets. World War II revived the economy, and in 1940 Abitibi sales jumped immediately and remained between C $25 million and C $30 million for the duration of the war, providing the company with an excellent return and setting the stage for an end to receivership.

In 1943 the premier of Ontario appointed a committee for the purpose of designing a plan to take Abitibi out of receivership. After the committee's recommendations were accepted by all the creditors in 1946, the company was formally independent once again. Abitibi's 14-year receivership was the longest and most important in the history of Canadian industry, a trauma that would leave its mark in the form of a conservative corporate philosophy and deep skepticism about future expansion of capacity. Abitibi's experience during the Depression was only an extreme example of the Canadian paper industry as a whole. When a remarkable postwar surge in demand for newsprint raised and prompted U.S. demands for increased capacity, the Canadian producers generally chose to increase production speed at existing plants rather than add new ones.

Company Rebounds After World War II

Abitibi Chief Executive Douglas W. Ambridge strongly concurred with the prevalent conservatism, guiding Abitibi through two postwar decades of bountiful sales and profit increases while avoiding unnecessary capital expenditures. In this he was helped by the extraordinary expansion the company had undertaken in 1928, which provided Abitibi with a reserve of production capacity so great that corporate assets did not surpass those of 1928 until 30 years afterward. Abitibi thus merely made use of what plants it had to meet the rapidly growing demand of the 1950s, and Ambridge was able to keep debt low and earnings per share extremely high. After the years of receivership, the 1950s were a new golden age.

Name Changed in 1965

In 1965 Abitibi Power & Paper Company Limited changed its name to Abitibi Paper Company Ltd. Abitibi had been feeling the effects of the new U.S. presence as early as 1962, when, together with the rest of the Canadian industry, it entered a decade of declining net income and diminished share of the critical U.S. market. To counteract this trend, Abitibi overcame its habitual reluctance to expand with the 1968 purchases of Cox Newsprint, Inc. and Cox Woodlands Company for US $36.58 million. Cox, located in Augusta, Georgia, added 150,000 tons per year of newsprint capacity to Abitibi's Canadian holdings of 1.1 million tons and gave the company a presence in the booming southern U.S. industry.

Acquires Majority Interest in The Price Company Limited in 1974

A new generation of leaders at Abitibi, headed up by Chief Executive Officer Tom Bell and Chief Operating Officer Harry Rosier, became increasingly aggressive in the search for additional capacity. Three exceptionally lean years were followed by an upsurge in 1973–1974, when Abitibi sales soared from C $307 million to C $552 million. The company's capacity was strained, and Rosier suggested that it would be cheaper for the company to buy existing mills than to build them from scratch. After a brief search for likely targets, Bell and Rosier gained control of 54 percent of the outstanding common shares of The Price Company Limited, another Canadian paper concern with 1974 sales of C $335 million.

Like Abitibi, Price was strongest in newsprint and kraft production, but it had no fine-paper and building-materials divisions. It recorded a significantly higher proportion of its sales outside North America than did Abitibi. Both companies had modest but profitable base-metal mining operations in Canada, and together they controlled rights to about 50,000 square miles of forest land—an area somewhat smaller than the state of Illinois. Price was a company much older than Abitibi, dating back to the early 19th century and the British navy's need for a new source of lumber for its masts. In 1910, William Price had been sent by a leading London lumber merchant to Canada to organize the new operation, and Price subsequently started the company bearing his name.

No sooner had Abitibi completed its 22-day, C $130.11 million conquest of The Price Company than the newsprint market collapsed, cutting the combined companies' 1975 net sales by two-thirds at a time when its debt had nearly doubled. Once again, Abitibi's poor timing led indirectly to a change in ownership. Caught in a cash squeeze, Abitibi tried to placate union demands with big pay hikes and thereby avoid a disastrous strike; instead the unions pushed their advantage and forced the strike anyway. The walkout was bitter and lasted for months, and by the time the economy rebounded in 1977 Abitibi was still trying to put its shaken house in order. In October 1978 Abitibi agreed to buy about ten percent of Price's outstanding stock from Consolidated-Bathurst—a Canadian company that had bid against Abitibi for control of Price in 1974 and still held ten percent of Price's stock. Later that month, Abitibi purchased Price's remaining shares. Abitibi paid about C $95 million for the 46 percent interest outstanding.

Owned by Olympia & York During the 1980s

In December 1978 Consolidated-Bathurst bought ten percent of Abitibi's stock and set off a prolonged bidding war for control of the company. When the dust settled 15 months later, Abitibi-Price—which had changed its name in October 1979—was owned by Olympia & York, a Toronto-based real estate holding company run by the Reichmann family. Olympia & York, whose holdings were so vast that Abitibi-Price figured as a footnote in their annual reports, paid C $670 million for 92 percent of Abitibi-Price's stock. Olympia & York appeared to be the ideal silent partner for Abitibi-Price's management, offering great financial strength when needed but never meddling in the affairs of a business about which it knew little.

During the 1980s Abitibi-Price made a concerted effort to lessen its dependence on the brutally cyclical newsprint business. It sold off plants, streamlined operations, and focused its efforts on markets where it felt it could be a leader. By the end of the decade the company's diversified group operated the largest network of paper distributors in Canada, the largest envelope manufacturer and largest school and office supplies maker, and one of the leading producers of building materials in the United States. The diversified group in 1990 accounted for approximately half of all corporate revenue, with the remainder generated by the paper group's two divisions of newsprint and printing papers. Newsprint remained the most profitable segment, however, and was the heart of Abitibi-Price's various holdings. After four straight years of bullish profits, the bottom dropped out once again in 1989, and in 1990 Abitibi-Price lost C $45 million.

Newsprint Market Suffers in the Early 1990s

In 1989–90 the newsprint industry entered its worst period since the Great Depression. From 1990 to 1995, Abitibi-Price lost hundreds of millions of dollars. In 1991 a global newspaper glut forced Abitibi-Price to close or sell mills and decentralize its operations to regain profitability. Ronald Oberlander became the company's new CEO. He adopted a new strategy to become the world's finest paper company rather than the world's largest. He also began shifting profit responsibilities away from corporate headquarters to the managers at the company's plants and mills.

In spite of falling pulp prices, Abitibi-Price managed to report an operating profit for the first six months of 1991. A C $20 million restructuring charge left the company with a net loss of C $11.2 million on revenue of C $1.46 billion for the first half of 1991. That was an improvement over the same period of 1990, when the company lost C $15 million on revenue of C $1.59 billion. The 1990 loss was affected by a one-time charge of C $42.6 million. Operating profits for the first half of 1990 were a strong C $45.5 million compared with C $2.6 million for the first half of 1991.

In June 1992 Abitibi-Price announced that it would sell its U.S. building products division for US $100 million (C $120 million) to two separate buyers. Three of the four units involved were sold to an investment group formed by New York-based investment banker Kohlberg & Co. and George T. Brophy. The fourth unit, a national supplier of interior wood products from facilities in Hiawatha, Kansas and Lumberton, North Carolina, was sold to an investment group led by Alan J. Gitkin of Wayne, New Jersey. It would change its name to Flair Fold.

For 1992 Abitibi-Price reported a loss from continuing operations of C $200 million, compared with a loss of C $58 million for 1991. Overall, the company reported an after-tax loss of $219 million for 1992 after discontinuing some of its noncore assets. That compared with an after-tax loss of $76 million in 1991. Severe price erosion, caused by a continued oversupply of the company's paper products, was blamed for the poor results. Sales improved marginally to C $1.7 billion in spite of an almost ten percent increase in tonnage sold. Included in the loss for 1992 was a charge of C $60 million relating to the permanent closure of the Thunder Bay newsprint mill. Ownership of a second mill in Thunder Bay was in the process of being transferred to its employees. The company was continuing to focus on its core business, the manufacture and marketing of groundwood papers. Other divisions included office products and converted products.

In 1992 Olympia & York, which held a controlling interest in Abitibi-Price, filed for protection from its creditors. It owned some 54.5 million shares of Abitibi-Price, an 82 percent stake. With Olympia & York's bankruptcy filing, the shares came under the control of a banking syndicate led by Hong Kong & Shanghai Banking Corporation Ltd., who appointed Salomon Brothers of New York and RBC Dominion Securities of Toronto to advise on their disposal.

In spring 1993 Abitibi-Price was targeted by the Energy and Paperworkers Union of Canada (CEP), which counted 4,000 Abitibi-Price employees among its 35,000 members in eastern Canada. Nationwide, CEP represented about 137,000 workers. Among the union demands were job security, significant wage hikes, cost-of-living indexing, and improved pensions. Abitibi-Price's labor force had been cut back from some 14,000 in 1990 to 8,600 at the end of 1992. Closing one of the Thunder Bay mills in 1992 eliminated 400 jobs.

For the first quarter of 1993, Abitibi-Price reported its first quarter-to-quarter improvement since 1988 when it cut losses from continuing operations by 24 percent. The company would not have a profitable quarter until 1995, when it reported annual net income of C $273 million on net sales of C $2.8 billion.

To cope better with the newsprint industry's cyclical downturns, Abitibi-Price developed what it called a "Cornerstone Strategy." Criteria were established for each mill that would enable it to turn a profit in even the most severe cyclical downturn. As part of its new cornerstone strategy, mills that did not meet those criteria were put up for sale. In early 1997 the company put up for sale its 75-year-old Fort Williams newsprint mill in Thunder Bay, Ontario, and associated timberlands.

Abitibi-Price and Stone-Consolidated Corp. Merged in 1997 To Form Abitibi-Consolidated, Inc.

In February 1997 Abitibi-Price and Stone-Consolidated Corporation announced plans to merge operations and become the world's largest newsprint and uncoated groundwood producer. The new company, to be called Abitibi-Consolidated Inc., would be created by a tax-free amalgamation following an exchange of stock. The combined company would have market capitalization of C $4.1 billion, almost double the capitalization of C $2.2 billion of the industry's largest producer, MacMillan Bloedel Ltd. Shareholders of Abitibi-Price and Stone-Consolidated each would receive approximately one share of the new company for each share they held. The merger was completed in May 1997.

At the time of the merger, it was expected that Chicago-based Stone Container Corporation, which owned about half of Stone-Consolidated, would hold on to its shares and vote in favor of the transaction. Stone Container would own about 25 percent of the new company. Before the end of 1997, however, Stone Container sold its 48.8 million shares of Abitibi-Consolidated to raise cash needed to reduce its long-term debt of US $4 billion. Following the disposal in the early 1990s of the 54.5 million shares previously held by Olympia & York, Abitibi-Price shares were held widely, with two U.S. institutions holding about 20 percent of the stock between them.

Abitibi-Price CEO Ronald Oberlander became the operating chairman of the new company, and Stone-Consolidated CEO James Doughan became Abitibi-Consolidated's new president and CEO. The two expected to achieve savings of $100 million annually—later revised to $200 million—just by eliminating duplications in the selling and administrative areas. At the time of the merger, Abitibi-Price was planning to sell its Fort Williams facility in Thunder Bay and was seeking to sell other noncore assets. Including those mills, Abitibi-Consolidated would start operations with a total of 18 paper mills: 14 in Canada, three in the United States, and one in Great Britain, plus seven wholly owned or affiliated sawmills in Canada.

Analysts seemed to agree that the merger made sense, given the deeply cyclical nature of the North American newsprint industry. The emergence of stronger players through consolidations such as this one was seen as leading to more rational markets. Analysts expected shareholders to benefit as a result of the merger.

In terms of output, Abitibi-Consolidated was expected to have a total capacity of 2.8 millions tons for newsprint, exceeding current world leader Fletcher Challenge Ltd. of New Zealand's capacity of 1.8 million tons. For uncoated groundwood, Abitibi-Consolidated would have a capacity of 1.5 million tons, more than leader UPM-Kymmene of Finland's capacity of 1.2 million tons. Overall, Abitibi-Consolidated would become the world's eleventh largest pulp and paper producer in terms of tonnage and would rank seventeenth internationally in sales. It would have about a 15 percent share of the world's paper market.

Following the merger, Abitibi-Consolidated announced that its headquarters would be in Montreal, where Stone-Consolidated was headquartered, rather than in Toronto, where Abitibi-Price's main office was located. About half of Abitibi-Price's 220-person headquarters staff in Toronto was expected to relocate to Montreal. The goal was to make the Montreal headquarters equally balanced between employees of the two former rivals.

Although the merger was completed in May 1997, results for the new company were annualized for 1997. Abitibi-Consolidated reported a net loss of C $121 million after amalgamation and restructuring charges. Annualized net sales were C $4.16 billion. It reported an upbeat fourth quarter, however, posting net income before restructuring charges of C $57 million. For 1998, the company planned on keeping a tight lid on costs and capital spending to achieve profitability.

In March 1998 Abitibi-Consolidated was unsuccessful in its hostile takeover attempt of one of its major competitors, the Montreal-based newsprint producer Avenor Inc. Its bid of C $2.8 billion was surpassed by a C $3.5 billion bid by U.S.-based Bowater Inc. Abitibi-Consolidated's bid was a sign that it was in an acquisition mode. Investor interest appeared to be increasing in the company, which saw the value of its stock rise by some C $500 million after it announced its bid for Avenor.

As part of its strategy to eliminate or sell off noncore assets, Abitibi-Consolidated announced in April 1998 that it had completed the sale of the U.S. and Mexican operations of its Office Products Division to United Stationers Inc. for approximately US $110 million. The three business units that were sold were Azerty, which distributed computer supply consumables, peripherals, and accessories in the United States and Mexico; Positive ID, which distributed bar-code scanning products; and AP Support Services, which provided outsourcing services in direct marketing, telemarketing, and other areas. The three units had combined annual sales of about US $350 million.

For the future, it appeared likely that Abitibi-Consolidated would continue to focus on its core business and seek to achieve profitability through tight controls on costs and capital spending. On the other hand, it has announced that it will continue to look for acquisition opportunities to achieve further economies of scale. According to Operating Chairman Ronald Oberlander, "Our plan in North America is to search out acquisitions which are the best fit and the best value."

Further Reading

"Abitibi, 35,000 Workers Square Off for Pact Fight," *Toronto Star,* February 26, 1993, p. 7.

Foot, Richard, "Bigger Is Better, Says Abitibi Chairman," *Calgary Herald,* January 31, 1998, p. E7.

Fowlie, Laura, "Abitibi-Price Pact May Bring Peace," *Financial Post,* May 26, 1993, p. 5.

Gibbens, Robert, "Abitibi-Consolidated Headquarters Will Be in Montreal," *Financial Post-Toronto,* March 11, 1997, p. 8.

——, "Abitibi Shows a Profit as It Keeps a Tight Lid on Costs," *Financial Post-Toronto,* February 12, 1998, p. 9.

——, "Stone Stays Cool Despite Rumors," *Financial Post-Toronto,* April 12, 1997, p. 5.

——, "Stone To Sell Its Stake in Abitibi," *Financial Post-Toronto,* October 28, 1997, p. 8.

Hill, Bert, and Lewis, Michael, "Avenor Sold to Bowater for $3.5B: U.S. Bid Is 20% Higher Than One by Abitibi-Consolidated," *Ottawa Citizen,* March 10, 1998, p. B1.

Kennedy, Peter, "Abitibi Picture Brightens," *Financial Post,* April 20, 1993, p. 17.

Langevin, J. Raymond, "Abitibi-Price Continues Focus on Core Businesses," *PR Newswire,* June 22, 1992.

Leger, Kathryn, "Abitibi Hunting Acquisitions," *Financial Post-Toronto,* April 28, 1998, p. 3.

——, "Merger Creates Paper Giant," *Financial Post-Toronto,* February 15, 1997, p. 1.

McGovern, Sheila, "Abitibi Merger 'Doing Well,' " *Montreal Gazette,* November 5, 1997, p. C1.

McHugh, Michael, "Abitibi's Riding Out Pulp Slump," *Financial Post,* July 20, 1991, p. 20.

Mercier, Eileen, "Abitibi-Price Records Loss of $219 Million as Continued Oversupply Erodes Paper Prices in 1992," *PR Newswire,* February 15, 1993.

"Merger Creates Paper Giant," *Northern Ontario Business,* March 1997, p. 3.

Mills, Patricia, "Abitibi-Price Selling Off Its Assets in Northwestern Ontario," *Northern Ontario Business,* March 1997, p. 22.

Parker, Wendy, "New Direction at Abitibi-Price," *Northern Ontario Business,* September 1987, p. 35.

Reguly, Eric, "Abitibi Discards Big Dreams," *Financial Post,* June 13, 1991, p. 5.

"United Stationers Acquires the U.S. and Mexican Operations of the Office Products Division of Abitibi-Consolidated Inc. and Announces Financing Transactions," *PR Newswire,* April 3, 1998.

—updated by David Bianco

ABM Industries Incorporated

50 Fremont Street, Suite 2600
San Francisco, California 94105
U.S.A.
(415) 597-4500
Fax: (415) 597-7160
(800) 470-4357
Web site: http://www.abm.com

Public Company
Incorporated: 1909 as American Building and
   Maintenance Company
Employees: 52,000
Sales: $1.25 billion (1997)
Stock Exchanges: New York
Ticker Symbol: ABM
SICs: 7349 Building Cleaning & Maintenance Services;
   7521 Automobile Parking; 7382 Security Systems
   Services

ABM Industries Incorporated is one of the nation's largest suppliers of janitorial and other services to the owners of commercial, industrial, and institutional buildings. Started by one man with a mop and a bucket, the company now offers a wide range of functions including cleaning; elevator maintenance; air conditioning, heating, engineering, and energy conservation services; lighting and electrical sign maintenance; building security; parking garage management; and janitorial supplies. Much of ABM's operations take place on the West Coast, where the company first began. However, the company established a strong nationwide presence in its industry by acquiring companies in other geographical areas and in other industries throughout the 1960s, 1970s, and 1980s.

Humble Beginnings

ABM got its start in San Francisco in 1909, when Morris Rosenberg found himself out of work after his restaurant and hotel business failed in a general economic downturn. Sensing an opportunity in the dusty store windows of San Francisco's commercial district, Rosenberg invested $4.50 in a bucket, mop, sponge, broom, and brush, and began calling on merchants, offering to wash their windows for whatever pay they thought the job was worth. At the end of the first day, Rosenberg had earned back the money he spent, plus an additional $3.50 in profit. From this modest start, Rosenberg founded the industry of contract janitorial services.

Soon, however, Rosenberg encountered competition: a man who called himself the Chicago Window Cleaning Company and transported his supplies in a Ford Model T car. When it became clear that there was not enough demand for cleaning services to sustain both companies, Rosenberg bought out his competitor for $300, acquiring both the company's name and its vehicle.

Encouraged by his new capabilities, Rosenberg began offering annual cleaning contracts to San Francisco merchants. He signed his first contract with the Hotel St. Francis. Optimistic that his business would provide a steady income, Rosenberg opened an office in the Phelan Building and set out to win other clients. Soon, the Joseph Magnin Company, Praeger & Company, the Union Trust Company, and others had signed on.

With new clients, Rosenberg needed capital to add new equipment, supplies, and employees, so he sought a bank loan. After being turned down for lack of collateral at the first institution he tried, Rosenberg made inquiries to the Bank of Italy, which not only lent him the money he needed but also employed him to clean its buildings throughout San Francisco. With this development, Rosenberg's business broadened its offerings from simple window cleaning to full janitorial services. In April 1913 Rosenberg named his company American Building and Maintenance Company (ABM), reflecting its wide range of activities.

Prewar Expansion

By 1920 ABM had expanded its activities throughout San Francisco and across the bay to Oakland. In addition, the company had opened offices in Los Angeles, Portland, and Seattle. ABM entered the lucrative business of cleaning theaters where popular movies were shown. The company had contracts with 15 cinemas in San Francisco, as well as with the Grauman's chain in Los Angeles and the Loew's theater systems in Oregon and Washington.

In the following year, ABM entered another area of the cleaning business when it signed a contract to clean Stanford University in Palo Alto, California, its first educational or institutional client. Throughout the 1920s, ABM continued to expand by offering customers cheaper services than they themselves could provide. It was this cost effectiveness that allowed the company to survive the stock market crash of 1929 and the ensuing Great Depression without losing ground and, in fact, with a slight increase in business.

ABM expanded to the East Coast in 1932, when the company won yet another movie theater contract—a $250,000 assignment from RKO to maintain properties it owned on both coasts. Morris Rosenberg's son Theodore was dispatched to New York to follow up on this success and solicit other eastern business. A year and half later Theodore Rosenberg returned to San Francisco in time for his father's retirement from the business as a result of ill health. In 1935 Morris Rosenberg died, leaving ABM to Theodore, then 26 years old. At the time, ABM's annual revenue had reached $750,000.

During this period ABM also acquired an electrical services subsidiary, the Alta Electric Company, which provided electrical wiring for the Golden Gate Bridge, the San Francisco Bridge, and the city's opera house. When the United States entered World War II in 1941, ABM also entered the temporary business of cleaning military ships, joining the war effort by maintaining U.S. Navy carriers and destroyers that put into West Coast ports. Because the military had called up many of the company's employees, ABM began employing women on its cleaning crews. All-female janitorial teams cleaned the buildings of the company's clients throughout the war.

Postwar Boom

In the 1940s ABM slightly altered its corporate name to American Building Maintenance Company and began to prepare for aggressive future growth by inaugurating a management training program for college graduates. At that time, the company had expanded into Canada and had operations in a total of 17 cities.

By the end of the 1950s, ABM had offices in 45 cities across North America and employed 6,000 people. In 1962 the company offered stock to the public for the first time in the over-the-counter market. One year later, revenue was reported at $31 million for operations in 74 towns in 13 states and two Canadian provinces. With the capital it raised through its stock offering, ABM set out on a policy of rapid expansion into all 50 states through the acquisition of other janitorial services companies. The company had already branched out into related industries with the purchase of the Easterday Supply Company, a cleaning equipment and supplies distributor. In addition, ABM bought Advance Chemical Company, a manufacturer and vendor of sanitation chemicals.

Although ABM had attained a leading place in the contract janitorial services industry by the early 1960s, much of the market for its services remained untapped, with building owners handling cleaning chores through their own staff. The company set out to expand its market share by enhancing awareness of its industry and the benefits of contract cleaning. By 1965 over 50 percent of the nation's commercial buildings had switched to professional cleaning services. ABM's list of clients had grown to include 4,500 customers, and its sales exceeded $40 million.

In addition to its acquisition of cleaning services in new territories, ABM also set out to enter complementary fields in order to offer clients comprehensive maintenance services. Toward that end, the company purchased Commercial Air Conditioning of Northern California in 1967 and established its CommAir Division to provide equipment maintenance. ABM also bought the largest public parking company in San Jose, California. This became the foundation of AMPCO Auto Parks, Inc., which ran public parking facilities.

In the following year the company added to these divisions when it bought American Air Conditioning, located in Los Angeles, and Mr. Maintenance, another equipment upkeep firm based in Denver. ABM also branched out further when it bought four-fifths of the Rose Exterminator Company, a pest control firm. In 1969 the company purchased the General Elevator Corporation, located in Southern California, adding yet another concern to its array of integrated maintenance services, which also included security services and lighting maintenance by that time.

Growth Through Acquisitions in the 1970s and 1980s

ABM developed and implemented a two-part strategy for growth, involving sales efforts to gain a larger share of the markets in which it already operated, and acquisitions to open up opportunities in new markets. By 1970 these efforts had garnered the company $75 million in annual revenue; the company bought six other firms in that year alone. In the following year, ABM stock made its debut on the New York Stock Exchange. The company continued with its acquisitions program when it bought SMI Industries, specialists in the maintenance of illuminated signs.

In 1974 ABM's revenue topped $100 million for the first time. In the next few years, the company's sales accelerated dramatically as ABM continued to acquire new companies. In 1977 ABM bought the Jones Janitor Service of Memphis, Tennessee; Beverly Pest Control, a California firm; and Real Estate Maintenance, located in Philadelphia. Two years later ABM purchased the American Janitor Service. By that time earnings had more than doubled—in just a five-year period—to $213 million.

At the start of the 1980s, ABM announced plans to offer its full range of services in each major American city. At that time, only Los Angeles and San Francisco had the entire range of ABM operations. In addition, the company announced ambitious plans to again double its revenue in just five years. A key element of that expansion was ABM's increased involvement in ancillary, nonjanitorial services, which promised a much higher profit margin than its traditional functions. The janitorial services industry was heavily fragmented and highly competitive, which kept earnings down. To gain a more diverse earnings base, the company moved aggressively into the energy management business, from which it expected high growth in the coming years. In 1981 ABM created the American Technical Services Company, abbreviated Amtech, by combining its air conditioning, elevator, lighting, and energy services operations into one division. With its operations consolidated, the company was better able to respond to innovations in technology and energy conservation.

By 1982, sales exceeded $300 million, and ABM had offices in over 190 locations. In the mid-1980s, ABM arranged its activities into three groups: Janitorial Services, which handled cleaning and building engineering; Public Services, made up of the security, parking, pest control, and Janitorial Supplies Division; and Amtech, its energy-related branch.

ABM's earnings continued to rise throughout the second half of the 1980s, reaching $7.1 million in 1988. In the following year Sydney and Theodore Rosenberg, the founder's sons, who controlled approximately 30 percent of the company's stock, announced that they were involved in discussions about the possible sale of the company. In February of 1990 ABM began to explore different ways of restructuring itself and rearranging its financing, including the possibility of buying out its stockholders and becoming privately held. Eight months later, the company announced that a plan on the part of its management and other investors for a leveraged buy-out to take ABM private had foundered on the opposition of the Rosenberg brothers. Subsequently, the company's president left ABM, and several lawsuits were filed in the wake of the collapsed deal. Despite this turmoil, the company reported an extraordinary gain in revenue and earnings at the close of 1990.

In October of the next year ABM streamlined its operations by selling its residential extermination service, Rose Pest Control, to Terminix, one of its competitors. All of the company's other divisions provided services in commercial, industrial, or institutional settings; the residential nature of the pest control division made it an inappropriate fit with the rest of ABM's operations.

Strong Growth in the 1990s

In the following month, ABM rearranged its corporate structure somewhat, moving several departments out of the Janitorial Services Division and into other areas of the company. ABM Engineering Services became a stand-alone division, and the Property Services Division was merged with the company's security, parking, and cleaning supplies operations, under the heading "Other Services." Although Sydney Rosenberg had ceded his position of chief executive officer when he was named chair of the board in 1984, he reclaimed the CEO position in 1992. That same year the company exceeded three-quarters of a billion dollars in sales.

The company continued its program of steady acquisition by purchasing System Parking West. The acquisition, which bolstered ABM's nonjanitorial business, was merged into ABM's existing parking subsidiary, AMPCO Auto Parks. The new entity was named Ampco System Parking. The company's diversification into a variety of facilities services other than building maintenance had made the name American Building Maintenance Industries obsolete. To better represent the diversity of its services, the company changed its name to ABM Industries Incorporated in 1994.

Also in 1994, Sydney Rosenberg again stepped down from the CEO position, although he remained chair of the board. Bill Steele, president of ABM Industries, was promoted to chief executive officer and also retained his duties as president.

ABM's strong growth broke several company records in 1996. Revenue surpassed the $1 billion mark, reaching $1.09 billion for fiscal 1996. The 13 percent revenue gain over the previous year was exceeded by the 21 percent gain in earnings, to over $38 million. Earnings per share also hit an all-time high, reaching $1.05, a 14 percent increase over the previous year.

The company's financial health helped fuel further expansion in 1997. ABM made two major acquisitions that year. The first, the purchase of the assets of Polaris Inc., added to the company's Janitorial Services Division. According to Steele, "The acquisition of the Polaris business allows our janitorial division to better serve our national client base. The Midwest is a key market for ABM Janitorial Services, and Polaris Inc. is clearly one of the most visible and highly respected janitorial service companies servicing that area." The second acquisition, of Ogden Corp.'s building maintenance and on-site engineering operations, gave ABM a greater foothold in New York City.

Sydney Rosenberg stepped down as chair of the company's board in 1997, although he accepted the positions of chairman emeritus and honorary director of the company. His departure marked the end of family control of the company founded by his father almost a century earlier. When he handed over the reins to Martinn Mandles, the company was in excellent health: revenue hit a new high in fiscal 1997, exceeding $1.25 billion.

Principal Subsidiaries

Easterday Supply Company, Inc.; AMPCO Auto Parks, Inc.; American Building Service Company; CommAir; ABMI Security Services, Inc.; Associated Building Maintenance of Canada, Ltd.; Elevator Engineering Company; Amtech Energy Services Company; Amtech Light Service Company; American Technical Services Company; Servall Mechanical Contractors, Inc.

Further Reading

"ABM Industries Acquires 'Big Apple' from Ogden Corp.," *Business Wire,* August 1, 1997.
"ABM Industries Acquires Polaris of Indianapolis," *Business Wire,* May 1, 1997.
75 Years of American Building Maintenance Industries, San Francisco: American Building Maintenance Industries, 1985.
Troxell, Thomas N., Jr., "Cleaning Up," *Barron's,* March 2, 1981.

—Elizabeth Rourke
—updated by Susan Windisch Brown

Books, Music & More

Amazon.com, Inc.

1516 Second Avenue, Fourth Floor
Seattle, Washington 98108-0387
U.S.A.
(206) 622-2335
Fax: (206) 622-2950
(800) 201-7575
Web site: http://www.amazon.com

Public Company
Incorporated: 1997
Employees: 256
Sales: $147.8 million (1997)
Stock Exchanges: NASDAQ
Ticker Symbol: AMZN
SICs: 5961 Catalog & Mail-Order Houses

Amazon.com, Inc. is the world's biggest book and music store, offering more than 3 million book and music titles over the internet. The leading online shopping site by the end of the 1990s, Amazon.com possesses virtually unlimited online shelf space and offers its vast selection of retail items to customers through efficient search and browse features. A pioneer in the relatively new business of internet commerce, Amazon.com offers customers features such as 1-Click ordering, secure credit card payment, and direct shipping.

The Beginnings of Amazon.com

Throughout the 1990s, the popularity of the world wide web and the internet swept across the world, and personal computers in most businesses and households got hooked up in some form or another to internet providers and web browser software. As use of the internet became more prevalent in society, companies began looking to the web as a new avenue for commerce. Selling products over the internet offered a variety of choices and opportunities. One of the pioneers of business on the internet was Jeff Bezos, founder of Amazon.com.

In 1994, Bezos left his job as vice-president of the Wall Street firm D.E. Shaw, moved to Seattle, Washington, and began to work out a plan for the company that would become Amazon.com. After reading a report that projected annual web growth at 2,300 percent, Bezos drew up a list of twenty products that could be sold on the net. He narrowed the list to what he felt were the five most promising: compact discs, computer hardware, computer software, videos, and books. Bezos eventually decided that his venture would sell books over the web, due to the large worldwide market for literature, the low price that could be offered for books, and the tremendous selection of titles that were available in print. He chose Seattle as the company headquarters due to its large high-tech workforce and its proximity to a large book distribution center in Oregon. Bezos then worked to raise funds for the company while also working with software developers to build the company's web site. The web site debuted in July 1995 and quickly became the number one book-related site on the web.

In just four months of operation, Amazon.com became a very popular site on the web, making high marks on several internet rankings. It generated recognition as the sixth best site on Point Communications' ''top ten'' list, and was almost immediately placed on Yahoo's ''what's cool list'' and Netscape's ''what's new list''. The site opened with a searchable database of over one million titles. Customers could enter search information, prompting the system to sift through the company database and find the desired titles. The program then displayed information about the selection on a customer's computer screen, and gave the customer the option to order the books with a credit card and have the books shipped to them in a just a few days.

Unlike its large competitors, such as Barnes & Noble and Borders, Amazon.com carried only about 2,000 titles in stock in its Seattle warehouse. Most orders through Amazon.com were placed directly through wholesalers and publishers, so no warehouse was needed. Amazon.com would simply receive the books from the other sources, then ship them to the customer. At first, the company operated out of Bezos' garage, until it was clear that it was going to be a success and the company decided to move to a Seattle office, which served as the customer

Company Perspectives:

We opened our virtual doors in July 1995 with a mission to use the Internet to offer products that educate, inform, and inspire. We decided to build an online store that would be customer-friendly and easy to navigate and would offer the broadest possible selection.

support, shipping and receiving area. It was interesting that such a small venture realized such a broad scope so quickly; for example, within a month of launching the web site, Bezos and Amazon.com filled orders from all fifty states and 45 other countries. This feat was attributed to the large geographic range that the internet gave access to a retailer such as Bezos.

Making the Site Customer Friendly

As a pioneer in the world of Internet commerce, Amazon.com strived to set the standard for web businesses. With that goal in mind, Bezos went to work on making the web site as customer friendly as possible, and relating the site to all types of customers. For those people who knew what book they were looking for and just wanted quick performance and low cost, Amazon.com offered powerful search capabilities of its expanded 1.5 million-title database. The company also began offering ten to thirty percent discounts on most titles, making the prices extremely affordable. For other customers who were just looking for something to read in a general area of interest, Amazon.com offered topic areas to browse, as well as lists of Bestsellers, Award winners, and titles that were recently featured in the media. Finally, for people who were just in the mood to read anything, Amazon.com offered a recommendation center. There a customer could find books based on his or her mood, reading habits, or preferences. The recommendation center also offered titles based on records of books the customer had purchased in the past, if they were return customers to the site.

Other hits with customers were the little touches, such as optional gift wrapping of packages, and the ''eye'' notification service, which acted to send customers e-mails alerting them when a new book in their favorite subject or by their favorite author came into stock. The site also offered the ability for customers not only to write their comments about different books and have them published on the site, but to read other customers' comments about books they were interested in buying.

Public Offering in 1997

After less than two years of operation, Amazon.com became a public company in May 1997 with an initial public offering of 3,000,000 shares of Common Stock. With the proceeds from the IPO, Bezos went to work on improving the already productive web site and on bettering the company's distribution capabilities.

To help broaden the company's distribution capabilities, and to ease the strain on the existing distribution center that came from such a high volume of orders, in September 1997 Bezos announced that Amazon.com would be opening an East Coast

distribution center in New Castle, Delaware. There was also a seventy percent expansion of the company's Seattle center. The improvements increased the company's stocking and shipping capabilities and reduced the time it took to fill customers' orders. The Delaware site not only got Amazon.com closer to East Coast customers, but also to East Coast publishers, which decreased Amazon.com's receiving time. With the new centers in place, Bezos set a goal for the company of 95 percent same-day shipping of in-stock orders, getting orders to the customers much faster than before.

Another growth area for Amazon.com was the success of its 'Associate' program. Established in July 1996, the program allowed individuals with their own web sites to choose books of interest and place them on their own sites, then allowed visitors to purchase those books. The customer was then connected to Amazon.com, who took care of all the orders. Associates were sent reports on their sales and made a three to eight percent commission from books sold on their sites. The Associates program really began to take off in mid-1997 when Amazon.com formed partnerships with Yahoo, Inc. and America Online, Inc. Both companies agreed to give Amazon.com broad promotional capabilities on two of the most visited sites on the Web. As the success continued, Amazon also struck deals with many other popular sites, including Netscape, GeoCities, Excite, and AltaVista.

As the company continued to grow in 1997, Bezos announced in October that Amazon.com would be the first Internet retailer to reach the milestone of one million customers. With customers in all fifty states and now 160 countries worldwide, what had started in a Seattle garage was now a company with $147.8 million in yearly sales.

Further Expansion in 1998

As Amazon.com ventured into 1998, the company continued to grow. By February, the Associates program had reached 30,000 members, who now earned up to 15 percent for recommending and selling books from their web sites. Four months later, the number of associates had astonishingly doubled to 60,000.

The company's customer database continued to grow also, with cumulative customer accounts reaching 2,260,000 in March, an increase of 50 percent in just 3 months, and of 564 percent throughout the previous year. In other words, it took Amazon.com 27 months to serve its first million customers and only six months to serve the second million. This feat made Amazon.com the third largest bookseller in the United States.

Financed by a $75 million credit facility secured in late 1997, Amazon.com continued to reshape its services in 1998. To its catalog of over 2.5 million titles, the company added Amazon.com Advantage, a program to help the sales of independent authors and publishers, and Amazon.com Kids, a service providing over 100,000 titles for younger children and teenagers.

Amazon.com also expanded its business through a trio of acquisitions in early 1998. Two of the companies were acquired to expand Amazon.com's business into Europe. Bookpages, one of the largest online booksellers in the United Kingdom, gave Amazon.com access to the U.K.'s market. Telebook, the largest online bookseller in Germany, added its German titles to the mix. Both companies not only gave Amazon.com access to new customers in Europe, but it also gave existing Amazon.com customers access to more books from around the world. The Internet Movie Database, the third acquisition, was used to support plans for an eventual move into online video sales. The tremendous resources and information of the IMD served as a valuable asset in the construction of a customer-friendly and informative web site for video sales.

Another big change in 1998 was the announcement of the company's decision to enter into the online music business. Bezos again wanted to make the site as useful as possible for his customers, so he appealed to them for help. Several months before officially opening its music site, Amazon.com asked its bookstore customers and members of the music profession to help design the new Web-site.

The music store opened in June 1998, with over 125,000 music titles available. The new site, which opened at the same time that Amazon.com had also redesigned it book site, offered many of the same helpful services available at the company's book site. The database was searchable by artist, song title, or label, and customers were able to listen to more than 225,000 sound clips before making their selection.

Amazon.com ended the second quarter of 1998 as strong as ever. Cumulative customer accounts broke the three million mark, and as sales figures for Amazon.com continued to rise, and more products and titles were added, the future looked bright for this pioneer in the internet commerce marketplace. With music as a part of the company mix, and video sales on the horizon, Bezos seemed to have accomplished his goal of gathering a strong market share in the online sales arena. As Bezos told *Fortune* magazine in December 1996, "By the year 2000, there could be two or three big online bookstores. We need to be one of them." As it approached the end of the decade, Amazon.com already appeared to be one of the biggest online retail operations, if not the biggest of all.

Further Reading

Green, Lee, "Net Profits," *Spirit Magazine,* March 1998, pp. 52–54, 126–128.

Haines, Thomas, "Amazon.com Sales Grow While Loss Widens," The Seattle Times, January 23, 1998, p. C1.

Hazleton, Lesley, "Jeff Bezos: How He Built a Billion Dollar Net Worth Before His Company Even Turned A Profit," *Success,* July 1998, pp. 58–60

"Jeffrey Bezos," *Chain Store Age Executive,* December 1997, p. 124.

Jeffrey, Don, "Amazon.com Eyes Retailing Music Online," *Billboard,* January 31, 1998, pp. 8–9.

Martin, Michael, "The Next Big Thing: A Bookstore," *Fortune,* December 9, 1996, pp. 168–170.

Perez, Elizabeth, "Store On Internet Is Open Book: Amazon.com Boasts More Than 1 Million Titles On The Web," *The Seattle Times,* September 19, 1995, p. E1.

Rose, Cynthia, "Site-Seeing," *The Seattle Times,* March 10, 1996.

—Robert Alan Passage

American Software Inc.

470 E. Paces Ferry Rd.
Atlanta, Georgia 30305
U.S.A.
(404) 261-4381
Fax: (404) 264-5514
(800) 726-2946 (SCM-2-WIN)
Web site: http://www.amsoftware.com

Public Company
Incorporated: 1970
Employees: 630
Sales: $84.7 million (1997)
Stock Exchanges: NASDAQ
Ticker Symbol: AMSWA
SICs: 7372 Prepackaged Software

Atlanta-based American Software Inc. produces, sells, and offers customer support for a line of business-based software applications. Its products, made to be used on IBM mainframes, and compatible with either Windows or UNIX client/server architecture, assist companies in maintaining control not only over finances, but over the myriad details of logistics—supply, inventory, and distribution. Its Flow Manufacturing applications, for instance, help businesses to optimize the flow of goods, reducing the period of time a supplier has to wait for new product to fill orders, and freeing marketing teams to concentrate more on sales and less on managing their customers' needs. Through the Logility subsidiary, established in 1997, American Software offers a comprehensive package which assists retailers, distributors, and manufacturers in coordinating their efforts. In the late 1990s, American became a leader in efforts to deal with the computer software "Year 2000 Problem," and thus a number of investment consultants predicted strong growth for the company.

The Highs and Lows of the First Two Decades

In 1970, two employees of Management Science America, James Edenfield and Thomas Newberry, established a small Atlanta company called American Computer Systems. Though computers had first appeared just after World War II, the industry's period of most explosive growth—which followed the advent of microprocessors in the early 1980s—lay more than a decade in the future. For example, the computers which operated the spacecraft used for the abortive Apollo 13 mission, launched the year Edenfield and Newberry started their company, were far inferior in memory to an ordinary household personal computer (PC) in the 1990s. Likewise, American Computer Systems was a tiny enterprise compared to the giant it would become during the next two decades.

The new company soon found its niche with the textile industry—particularly West Point-Pepperell—for which American Computer Systems developed a sales-forecasting program. Such forecasts, which involved detailed and complicated statistical calculations, had previously been created by teams of human analysts whose computations were often imperfect and sometimes became obsolete before they were completed. American's program, however, made it possible to feed data into a computer regarding past sales and production, and in a matter of minutes receive output that would assist in setting accurate quarterly production goals.

Though their software application was originally geared toward the textile industry, Edenfield and Newberry soon realized that production was production, whether the item produced was cloth, canned food, or computers. Therefore, they began marketing their software applications to a wide range of industries.

Within seven years of the company's creation, the founders changed the its name and increased its size through a merger. American Software and Computer had been founded a year after American Computer Systems, and in 1978 the two joined forces to become American Software Inc. In 1983 the company went public, with stock traded on NASDAQ. Growth was slow at first, but American received a significant boost following a 1987 agreement with IBM whereby it supplied software for the AS/400 mainframe computer.

Troubled Times in the Early 1990s

On August 2, 1991, GTE Corporation brought a lawsuit against American Software in the Boston U.S. District Court, seeking $17.3 million in damages due to what it claimed was

Company Perspectives:

American Software's suite of business solutions represents the most comprehensive line of integrated applications available today for multi-platform client/server processing environments.

"nearly total failure of a multi-million dollar computer software system" designed by American. According to a lawyer for GTE, the alleged failure had put his client "substantially beyond the time they expected to devote to the project."

American responded with a statement in which it "suggest[ed] that individuals at GTE wish to avoid responsibility for their own failures by blaming American Software. American Software products are performing well and up to specifications at sites all over the world." Neal Miller, a spokesman for American Software, told *Newsbytes News Network*, an industry information source, "This is all new to us. It hasn't happened before. Our clients have always expressed satisfaction with our products and services." Miller went on to speculate that the problems GTE was experiencing were due to hardware capacity, rather than software error. He stated his understanding that GTE had downsized its computer system from IBM mainframe to AS/400, and his belief that the smaller computer system apparently could not handle the application effectively.

Although the legal entanglement with GTE was problematic, of greater significance to American Software was a slump in profitability experienced by the company during the early- to mid-1990s. As product development slowed, sales began to drop off; in 1994 and 1995, losses reached 30 cents a share, and by 1996, 44 cents per share. In 1994, the company underwent a reshaping of its corporate structure, installing new officers and expanding its markets. It also clarified its area of focus, which it identified as producing UNIX- and Windows-based client/server products.

By 1997, The *Atlanta Journal and Constitution* reported that American Software had shown a profit of 10 cents per share that year—a figure which analysts predicted would grow to 42 cents in 1998. "In essence," the publication stated, "American Software suffered—and recovered—from an erosion in revenue and profits while retooling its products to meet the changing demands and improvements of computer hardware technology." Now, according to Edenfield—who along with Newberry remained owner of nearly three-quarters of the company—"the transition is complete and new products are in the pipeline." Management's goal became to double the size of the company by the end of the century.

Strategic Alliances and Diversification

In the late-1990s, American Software created strategic alliances with computer-industry enterprises such as Rijnhaave Information Systems. It also developed strong marketing ties with leading companies such as Nestle and Heineken, and further built on its core mission of supply chain planning. The latter, sometimes called supply chain management or inventory

management, simply equates to business management practices—ordering, production, storing, and shipping of products from one place to another, accompanied by the relevant billing and bookkeeping. American Software made these tasks its business by creating software applications which led computers to shorten the process, making it more efficient and less costly.

Further diversification occurred with the introduction of new product lines. In November of 1996, the company presented Warehouse P&RO (parts and reusable objects), a system for managing warehouses. Warehouse P&RO incorporated the advanced tools necessary for a company's computer system to track incoming and outgoing items, as well as receive and locate products in real time. This capability would enable warehouse managers to know precisely when and where an item is received, stored, moved, picked, packed, or shipped.

Another software solution was released by American Software in December of 1996—Resource Chain Voyager. The company introduced the supply chain planning software so that it could be used on the Internet or on a company's intranet—or even in an "extranet" set up for the purpose of managing a supply chain. The software package would make it possible for customers, wholesalers, retailers, and distributors to interact via the browser capabilities of either Netscape Navigator or Microsoft Internet Explorer. These browsers, by offering a medium for exchange of information, would overcome the problem posed by incompatible software platforms.

An example of a successful American Software supply chain management application at work was the one that was developed for Heineken, the world's second-largest beer manufacturer. Called HOPS (Heineken Operation Planning System), the system cut down on lag time between orders from a retailer and the actual shipment of the product. Reported Charles Waltner of *Communications Week*, the $6.5 billion Dutch-based company "couldn't do much to cut the two to five weeks it took shipments to reach America." So instead it worked to facilitate a faster relay of information between its approximately 450 U.S. distributors, the headquarters of Heineken USA, and the parent company headquarters in Holland. HOPS taps the Internet to create a comprehensive and easily deployable network for coordinating the exchange of crucial business information about such operational matters as orders. Heineken expected its new system to reduce the order cycle from an average of thirteen weeks to an average of five. Under the old way of inventory management, during the two months' extra lag time, beer aged and the distributors' money remained tied up in orders; under the new system, a distributor reported, "We can now focus on what is going to happen in the marketplace."

The Birth of Logility

In September of 1996, American Software reported that it was considering the creation of a new company to handle its supply chain planning solutions. At that time, a software package called Supply Chain Planning (SCP) was the leading product family in American Software's line of supply chain management systems. SCP was a software suite that included planning capabilities for demand, requirements, replenishment, constraint-based manufacturing, and scheduling.

American desired to expand its presence within this growing market, and the solution was the creation of a new company. In the early weeks of 1998, the parent company unveiled its new subsidiary: Logility. With headquarters also in Atlanta, Logility was formed to develop, market, install, and support software applications designed to optimize operations throughout the value chain from manufacturer to retailer. Logility Value Chain Systems make use of a trademarked implementation methodology called ROI to achieve results quickly. Among Logility's clients, in addition to Heineken USA, are Eastman Chemical, Newell, Pharmacia & Upjohn, Reynolds Metals, Sony Electronics, Timex, and VF Corporation.

At that time, American Software announced the initial public offering (IPO) of 2.2 million shares of Logility on NASDAQ, where it carried the ticker symbol "LGTY." Selling shares at $14.50 each, the company collected some $29 million in the IPO—funds it intended to invest in research and development, as well as on sales and marketing efforts. Some 330,000 of the shares went to the underwriters, and after the sale, American retained slightly more than eight out of ten shares in the new company. In a June, 1998 review of American Software's earnings in the fourth quarter of 1997, the *Atlanta Journal and Constitution* reported "better-than-expected results" for Logility.

The Year 2000—Opportunities for Expansion

By the end of the decade, the business world as a whole—and the software industry in particular—was abuzz with discussion of the "Year 2000 Problem," or "Y2K." When growth in the software industry exploded during the early 1980s, the end of the twentieth century still lay nearly two decades in the future, and programmers did not take it into account in creating date-related logic for their software. For dates, most programs use a two-number system to designate years; hence "98" would mean 1998. Had the programmers used a three-digit system, this would not have solved the problem: the end of the millennium would bring a change in all four digits, from 1999 to 2000. Because of the inefficient system, computers would assume that "00" meant 1900, not 2000—and this could lead to untold havoc in calculating interest and other functions.

The problem might have seemed simple, but it was anything but: large programs and networks such as those in place on corporate intranets use millions upon millions of lines of code. One industry analyst compared a programmer's efforts to adjust date-related logic with those of a plumber attempting to find a leaky pipe—but instead of searching the plumbing system of a single house, the plumber would have to inspect all the pipes in a city. Research by the Gartner Group indicates that approximately thirty percent of all computer applications would not be Year 2000-compliant by the end of 1999, and the same study indicated that companies worldwide would spend between $300 billion and $600 billion to convert their software.

American Software was not slow to see the growth opportunity offered by the Year 2000 challenge. "It's a business problem, not a technical problem," Vice President Ron Harris told the *Atlanta Journal and Constitution.* "This has the potential for shutting down your business." As for American Software's role in dealing with the crisis, Harris said, "In addition to being an enormous service opportunity, this is a huge licensing opportunity." To meet the needs of its clients, American Software has developed a seven-step process to discover, adjust, and test all date-related logic in software and interfaces between programs.

To begin the process, American Software technicians spend between one and four weeks on-site, conducting an in-depth study of the client's software. From this results a detailed printed assessment of the problem, identifying critical dates on which the software may stop functioning. Having mapped out a strategy, the technicians move on to analyze codes, convert them, test the unit's date calculations, convert all data, conduct verification testing, and implement post-conversion activities. In April of 1998, American Software reported that it was assisting Harley-Davidson, Bausch & Lomb, and other companies with Year 2000 issues. As the turn of the century drew closer, American Software was a company truly prepared for the next millennium.

Principal Subsidiaries

Logility (82%)

Further Reading

"American Software Sets Up Seven-Step Plan for Year 2000," *Newsbytes News Network,* January 13, 1997.
"American Puts Supply Chain on the Net," *Electronic Buyer News,* December 16, 1996.
Bond, Patti, "New Jersey Firm, American Software Enter Joint Venture," *Atlanta Journal and Constitution,* July 18, 1995.
DeVoe, Deborah, "Top of the News: Case Study," *InfoWorld,* December 30, 1996.
"Earnings Report: Georgia: American Software," *Atlanta Journal and Constitution,* June 10, 1998.
"Inside Wall Street: 'American Is a Bargain,' " *Business Week,* December 22, 1997.
Kannell, Michael E., "Software Firm Tackling 'Millennium Bug'," *Atlanta Journal and Constitution,* January 11, 1997.
McMullen, Barbara E. and John F. McMullen, "More on GTE vs. American Software Lawsuit," *Newsbytes News Network,* August 7, 1991.
McKeefry, Hailey Lynn, "American Software Offers Managed Warehouse System," *Electronic Buyer News,* November 25, 1996.
Trommer, Diane, "American Considering New Supply Chain Planning Co.—Unit Would Focus on Burgeoning SCP Market," *Electronic Buyer News,* September 30, 1996.
Walker, Tom, "Spotlight on Georgia Stocks: American Software Is Starting to Click with Investors," *Atlanta Journal and Constitution,* August 6, 1997.
Waltner, Charles, "Case Study: Heineken Taps Internet's Utility Orders System," *Communications Week,* May 19, 1997.

—Judson Knight

ASSOCIATED ESTATES
REALTY CORPORATION

Associated Estates Realty Corporation

5025 Swetland Court
Richmond Heights, Ohio 44143
U.S.A.
(216) 261-5000
Fax: (216) 289-9600
(800) 440-2372
Web site: http://www.aecrealty.com

Public Company
Incorporated: 1964 as Associated Estates Group
Employees: 1,200
Sales: $108.8 million (1997)
Stock Exchanges: New York
Ticker Symbol: AEC
SICs: 6798 Real Estate Investment Trusts; 6513 Operators
of Apartment Buildings; 6512 Operators of Nonresiden-
tial Buildings; 6531 Real Estate Agents & Managers

For the first 30 years, Associated Estates Realty Corporation
was a family-owned business that built, managed, and owned
apartment communities in the Cleveland, Ohio area. When it
became a publicly traded real estate investment trust (REIT) on
the New York Stock Exchange in November 1993, all of its
holdings were located in northeast Ohio. Over the next four
years it expanded into other states but kept its focus on the
Midwest. At the end of 1997, it was the only one of some 30
publicly traded multifamily apartment REITs that was focused
on the Midwest. About half of the company's portfolio was
located in northeast Ohio, with four percent in northwestern
Ohio, 22 percent in central Ohio, one percent in southern Ohio,
15 percent in Michigan, three percent in Indianapolis, and three
percent in Pittsburgh. With the acquisition of MIG Realty Advisors, Inc. in 1998, the company's focus expanded beyond the
Midwest into multiple markets across the United States, including higher growth cities in the Southeast and Southwest.

Established in 1964 as Associated Estates Group

The company was established in 1964 as Associated Estates
Group to build, manage, and own apartment communities in

Cleveland, Ohio. It was a family-owned business focused on
generating profits by owning, developing, and managing apartment
communities. When it went public in 1993, it still owned practically every property it ever developed or purchased. It referred to
its apartments as "suites" and to its tenants as "residents."

Associated Estates was involved mainly in the Cleveland
and Akron markets in northeastern Ohio. During the mid-1970s,
when apartment building was not justified because of economic
conditions, the company explored existing government programs and decided to provide housing to senior citizens and
families through government-assisted programs. Associated Estates did not expect to expand this area in the 1990s, but its
existing portfolio of government-assisted housing provided
continued and steady growth. The company also managed properties owned by nonprofit and other owners, but again this was
not perceived as an area for further acquisitions.

The company's growth strategy was focused on conventional,
or market-rate, apartments that could be purchased at below
replacement costs and at rental rates that had not yet been hit by
inflation. Taking a conservative approach to controlling expenses
and generating rental income, management realized this was not a
quarter-to-quarter business, but rather one of long-term growth.
Northeastern Ohio was particularly attractive because of its large
employer base and revitalization efforts in the region.

Initial Public Offering Raised $144.8 Million in 1993

Associated Estates Realty Corporation was formed in 1993
to continue the business of the Associated Estates Group. In
addition to properties in northeastern Ohio, the company owned
properties in the Columbus area in central Ohio, all of which
were built since 1988. They ranged from newly constructed,
single-story brick apartments to luxury townhomes.

On November 19, 1993, the initial public offering (IPO) of
Associated Estates Realty Corporation consisted of 7.25 million
shares of common stock offered at $22 per share. Net proceeds
to the company were $144.8 million, of which $86.7 million
was used to repay some of the company's debt. The reserved
proceeds from the IPO were used for acquisitions in early 1994
rather than to pay down the company's long-term, fixed-rate
debt, as originally planned. Associated Estates planned to fi-

nance its growth through a balanced combination of debt and equity. It believed that long-term debt was the best source of financing for real estate.

At the time Associated Estates went public, Chairman, President, and Chief Executive Officer (CEO) Jeffrey I. Friedman and his family owned more than 33 percent of the company's common stock. The company elected to be taxed as a self-administered and self-managed real estate investment trust (REIT). An REIT is basically a corporation that pools funds from investors and invests the funds in real estate. So long as Associated Estates met the Internal Revenue Service's requirements for an REIT, its net income would not be subject to federal income tax. Most states honor this federal tax treatment and do not require REITs to pay state income tax, either.

One of the requirements Associated Estates had to meet was that it had to distribute to its shareholders 95 percent of its income that would otherwise be taxable. In addition, the company could not engage or pay for an REIT advisor. It managed all of its properties itself. Of the 55 multifamily properties it owned as of March 1994, it had developed 39 of them and acquired 16 of them. Many of the acquired properties were rehabilitated substantially. Ten of the 16 acquired properties were acquired after the IPO. In addition, Associated Estates managed 7,155 multifamily property suites and eight commercial properties not owned by the company.

Increased Real Estate Holdings by 38 Percent in 1994

In the five months following the IPO, Associated Estates grew its portfolio by 15.5 percent, from 8,704 suites to 10,056 suites. From January to March 1994, it acquired ten properties with 1,352 suites. Nine of those properties were located in central Ohio in the Columbus area. The other property was located in northeastern Ohio near the company's headquarters. A Columbus office was established to handle management tasks and situations on-site at the company's properties.

Of the company's 10,056 suites, 7,801 were in conventional high-rise, mid-rise, and garden apartments. A total of 2,085 suites were contained in multifamily properties with rents subsidized by the U.S. Department of Housing and Urban Development (HUD). The latter were called government-assisted properties, with tenants consisting of a mix of senior citizens, physically impaired individuals, and lower-income families or individuals. Also included in the company's portfolio were some 170 suites in apartment communities for elderly persons that provided them with a personal service package.

All of the company's properties were held for long-term investment. Ongoing property improvement programs included

an annual review of each property to determine budgets for renovation and other improvements. The company also conducted routine preventive maintenance as a way of reducing operating costs over the life of each property. Costs associated with such improvements and maintenance were expensed rather than capitalized by the company to the extent permitted by generally accepted accounting principles.

In August 1994 Associated Estates completed a secondary offering of three million common shares at $20.625 per share, with net proceeds of $58.5 million. Substantially all of the proceeds from this secondary offering were applied to pay off the company's credit facility.

With access to capital markets, Associated Estates could capitalize on situations where liquidity or management problems created favorable opportunities to acquire existing properties. During 1994 the company acquired 21 properties consisting of 3,349 suites. It also completed construction on its 40-suite addition to a central Ohio property. The acquisitions represented a 38 percent increase in the company's portfolio, bringing the total number of suites owned to 12,093. Much of the acquisition activity was focused on the Columbus area, which had a variety of employers in addition to being the state capital and home to the Ohio State University. The company owned 17 properties in the Columbus area. Rents ranged from $440 to $700 per month, providing a measure of diversification that would help weather various real estate cycles. In December it established its newest region in southern Michigan.

For 1994 Associated Estates had total revenue of $55.5 million, including rental revenue of $48.9 million. Net income was $13.5 million, and funds from operations (FFO) were $22.9 million. FFO per common share were $1.92. At the end of the year, the company had 658 employees. About 104 of them worked at the company's headquarters, with the rest being employed at the company's respective properties. In December the company relocated its corporate headquarters from Mayfield Village, where it had been located for almost 20 years, to Richmond Heights.

Experienced Steady Growth, 1995–96

During 1995 Associated Estates acquired 15 apartment properties containing 2,276 suites and three parcels of land. It added 132 suites to three existing properties, including properties in Rochester Hills, Michigan and in Medina, Ohio. In March 1995 it acquired Arrowhead Station, a 102-suite property in Columbus, bringing to 70 the number of properties the company owned and managed.

For 1995 Associated Estates had total revenue of $77.1 million, which included $70 million in rental revenue. Net income was $16.2 million, and funds from operations were $28.3 million, or $2.04 per share. For 1996 total revenue increased by 23 percent to $94.5 million, and rental revenue was up 26 percent to $88.0 million.

Lower Than Expected Growth in 1997

Associated Estates experienced lower than expected growth in 1997. Management felt it was a disappointing year. Rent growth was lower than expected, and the average economic occupancy for its core market-rate portfolio was the lowest posted in several years. The company had a four to five percent rental growth objective. For the year, rental income was $101.6 million, up 15.5 percent over 1996, and total revenues were $108.8 million. Net income was $20.7 million, up 7.3 percent over 1996.

In an effort to improve customer satisfaction, the company introduced a 24-hour maintenance guarantee at 12 of its properties. Under this program, a portion of a resident's monthly rent would be refunded for each day or portion of a day that passed with no response after 24 hours from the submission of a written maintenance request. The company found that the 24-hour response time was met or exceeded 99 percent of the time.

In 1997 Associated Estates entered two new markets, Indianapolis, Indiana and Cincinnati, Ohio. In Indianapolis, it acquired The Gables at White River and Waterstone Apartments. In Cincinnati, it acquired Remington Place Apartments. It also expanded its presence in Toledo and Columbus with the acquisition of Hawthorne Hills in Toledo and Oak Bend Commons and Saw Mill Village Apartments in Columbus. The company expanded its presence in Michigan with the acquisition of Clinton Place Apartments in Clinton Township and Spring Valley Apartments in Farmington Hills. All told, Associated Estates added eight properties in 1997 containing a total of 1,762 suites at a cost of $105.1 million.

Whereas most of the company's growth in 1997 came through the acquisition of existing properties, it also had extensive experience with new construction. In 1997 it completed construction of the 324-suite Bradford at Easton development in Columbus, Ohio. Two other properties were scheduled for completion in 1998, and expansions to three Michigan properties were under way.

At the end of 1997 the company's market capitalization exceeded $750 million. During the year it filed with the Securities and Exchange Commission a $368.8 million proposed shelf registration to raise funds through debt securities, preferred shares, depositary shares, common shares, and common share warrants. A total of 71 of the company's 81 wholly owned properties were unencumbered. The company enjoyed an average economic occupancy rate of 94 percent. Its turnover rate was 49 percent, well below the national average of 65 percent.

Acquired MIG Realty Advisors, Inc. in 1998

In January 1998 Associated Estates announced plans to acquire the privately owned MIG Realty Advisors, Inc. (MIG), a leading multifamily asset manager and pension fund advisor, for $306 million in cash, stock, and assumed debt. Associated Estates would acquire the property management and advisory business of MIG as well as 11 properties managed by MIG. In addition, it would acquire three properties under development in Florida that would contain 1,216 suites upon completion.

Founded in 1982 and based in West Palm Beach, Florida, MIG managed 36 multifamily apartment communities containing more than 11,000 suites for institutional clients. The 11 MIG-managed properties that Associated Estates would acquire contained 2,734 suites located in Arizona, California, Florida, Georgia, Maryland, Missouri, North Carolina, and Texas. In February 1998, Associated Estates acquired three of the properties, which contained 1,004 suites located in Florida, Georgia, and Maryland. With 350 employees, MIG would remain headquartered in West Palm Beach, Florida, and operate as a wholly owned subsidiary of Associated Estates. MIG Chairman Larry Wright would become an executive vice-president of Associated Estates and, probably, would be elected to the company's board of directors.

In February 1998 Associated Estates acquired the 316-suite Country Club Apartments in Toledo. The three MIG properties and the Toledo acquisition cost a total of $74.4 million. These acquisitions increased Associated Estates' portfolio of owned and managed properties to 92 multifamily properties containing 18,920 suites. Once the MIG acquisition was completed, Associated Estates would own or manage properties containing more than 35,000 suites, making it the fourth largest multifamily REIT property manager.

Continued Growth Projected for the Future

Associated Estates' growth strategy involved two distinct markets. One, which the company called continuous markets, included those that had a diversified economy, a long trend of growth, and a deep apartment market. Included in this type of market were Columbus, Ohio; Atlanta, Georgia; south Florida; and the greater Washington, DC area. Associated Estates planned to seek new properties in those markets continuously.

The second type of market in which the company was interested was opportunistic markets. Those would include places that had potential growth and good buying opportunities. Acquisitions would be concentrated in shorter time periods while opportunities existed.

Principal Subsidiaries

MIG Realty Advisors, Inc.

Further Reading

"Associated Estates Realty Corporation To Acquire MIG Realty Advisors, Inc.," *PR Newswire*, January 29, 1998.
Ball, Brian R., "Cleveland Investor Group Snaps Up Multifamily Complex on East Side," *Business First-Columbus*, June 20, 1997, p. 7.
Flint, Troy, "Associated Estates Buys Company," *Cleveland Plain Dealer*, January 30, 1998, p. 1C.

—David Bianco

Auto Value Associates, Inc.

14351 Blanco Road
San Antonio, Texas 78216-7723
U.S.A.
(210) 492-4868
Fax: (210) 492-4890
Web site: http://www.autovalue.com

Private Company
Incorporated: 1976
Employees: 85
Sales: $85 million (1997 est.)
SICs: 3465 Automotive Stampings

Auto Value Associates, Inc. is an organization made up of 39 U.S. and Canadian automotive parts warehouse distributors, which own and operate over 100 distribution centers and facilities from the eastern shores of Canada to the islands of Hawaii. Although directly competing with such strong firms as Pep Boys, AutoZone, and Western Auto, Auto Value Associates is a leader in the field of automotive parts distribution. One of the reasons for the associations's success has been its ability to implement a highly effective and thoroughly comprehensive jobber support system, whereby affiliated auto parts installers display the Auto Value identification sign and take advantage of a full range of marketing programs, store merchandising materials, personnel training, seasonal promotions, advertising assistance, and quality automotive replacement parts. One of the most important factors that set Auto Value warehouse distributors and affiliated jobbers apart from the competition is that all decisions regarding products, pricings, promotions, and advertising methods are made regionally and in light of the prevailing local market conditions. In the late 1990s, Auto Value Associates decided to expand its activities and enter into the Mexican auto parts distribution and jobber markets.

Early History

During the early and mid-1970s, a number of leading automotive parts distributors began to form groups or consortiums in order to compete on a more equal basis with mass merchandisers, chain stores, such organizations as NAPA and APS, and various other participants in the automotive parts aftermarket. These ''marketing groups'' or ''programmed distributor systems,'' as they called themselves, were initially formed to promote a common identification and to standardize advertising methods. However, within a short time of their formation, it became clear that these groups had come to represent a highly organized and significant degree of buying power, which possessed enormous potential in the marketplace. The ability of such groups to negotiate prices and terms of purchase gave them a distinct advantage over non-affiliated warehouse distributors.

Recognizing the developing importance and advantage of these marketing groups, four major warehouse owners arranged to meet in order to discuss and formulate a solution for warehouse distributors whose preference was to retain individual control over their marketing programs. As the meeting progressed, it soon became apparent that the four principal owners not only had a great deal in common, but also agreed on many issues related to marketing programs, automotive parts distribution centers, pricing systems, and purchasing strategies. The camaraderie and congenial relations, not to mention common business interests, that were a result of the meeting led to the creation of Auto Value Associates, Inc. in 1976, an organization established exclusively for the purpose of implementing combined purchase activities.

After forming a board of directors, S. R. Downey of Chattanooga, Tennessee, was elected as the association's first chairman. Downey brought extensive experience in the automotive parts aftermarket to the association and guided it through its initial stages of incorporation, organization, and systemization. Downey convinced the board of directors to headquarter Auto Value Associates in his hometown of Chattanooga and immediately went to work establishing a firm legal foundation for the association's activities. Paying particular attention to the possible liabilities of group buying, Downey contracted one of the most talented antitrust lawyers practicing in the United States and gave him the task of developing a stringent set of operating guidelines that would guarantee compliance with all the appropriate laws within the industry. Downey understood the need for credibility within the association, and the requirement that its success depended largely on forging on honest and open relationship with the general public. Pricings, vendor agreements, marketing campaigns, automotive parts warranties had to be clearly formulated and legally agreed upon. Within a few years, the chairman had developed the association into one of the most promising and fastest growing associations within the automotive parts aftermarket.

One of the important factors for the association's early success was its marketing and advertising program. Initially based in Springfield, Missouri, the original administrator of all marketing and advertising activities was Ozark Automotive, a firm highly committed to the growth of Auto Value Associates. Within two years, the marketing and advertising efforts of the group had expanded so quickly that the board of directors at Auto Value Associates decided to relocate the program to its headquarters in Chattanooga, Tennessee. By the end of the 1980s, the number of warehouse distributors belonging to Auto Value Associates had grown to over 30.

Growth and Expansion in the 1990s

During the early and mid-1990s, Auto Value Associates added a number of programs that significantly enhanced their share of the automotive parts aftermarket. The North American parts warranty program was one of the first of its kind within the industry. The warranty arranged by Auto Value Associates included coverage for all parts warranted by the original manufacturer, under the exact same conditions and terms, and period of the warranty, initially offered by the manufacturer. The attraction of the Auto Value Associates warranty program was that every customer could exercise his right to the warranty at all of the Auto Value stores, no matter where they were located. The store providing the warranty service would provide a brand new part in exchange for the defective or damaged part, and subsequently receive full credit for the part from its automotive parts warehouse distributor, which was part of the Auto Value Associates system. Since the association had expanded by this time to cover a broad geographical area, encompassing all of the United States, a large region of Canada, and certain portions of Mexico, a customer could get warranty service almost anywhere in North America.

A short time later, Auto Value Associates established the University of Auto Value jobber and installer training program. The purpose of the University was to provide current information and training programs for affiliated parts stores throughout North America. Management at Auto Value Associates was well aware of the pressure on installers to keep abreast of the continuously changing technology within the automotive parts aftermarket, and the introduction of the Installer Training Guide was instrumental in the development of this program. The Training Guide provided the phone number of manufacturers' technical service hotlines so that any participating installer could have access to information that was necessary in diagnosing or repair a difficult problem in a customer's vehicle. An additional section provided a listing and summary of manufacturer's warranty programs, so that an installer would be certain as to what he could or could not repair cost free to the customer. And finally, the Training Guide contained a lengthy list of videotapes that each Auto Value warehouse distributor kept in stock for installers to refer to in case there was more information needed on a specific automotive part or diagnostic problem.

In 1994, a new president of Auto Value Associates was chosen to lead the organization. Richard H. Morgan assumed his responsibilities as president having had many years of experience in the automotive part aftermarket. One of the first decisions that he made was to relocate the entire administrative operation of the group from Chattanooga, Tennessee, to San Antonio, Texas. The reason for this move was to take advantage of the dramatic growth in the automotive parts aftermarket throughout the southern and southwestern part of the United States. In addition, the move also facilitated the organization's expansion into Mexico, which was regarded by Morgan as one of the largest potential markets in the world.

Recognizing the importance of advertising, and the revenues it could produce if directed at the appropriate audience, Morgan implemented an aggressive strategy to put the name of Auto Value Associates at the forefront of the sports world. Working diligently since he was appointed president, within a short period of time Morgan was able to reach an agreement for Auto Value Associates to co-sponsor the Bondo/Mar-Hyde Super Car Racing Series of the Automobile Club of America. Held at many of the most prestigious racing tracks across the country, the Automobile Club of America sponsored races typically held a day before a major race such as the Winston Cup Series. Since the events were held at the same track and one day after the other, both events enjoyed and took advantage of comprehensive, worldwide press coverage. TNN, ESPN, and TBS provided national television coverage of all the Bondo/Mar-Hyde Super Car Races, for example, with significant excerpts shown on other televised sports programs across the United States. Morgan was able to arrange for Auto Value to be viewed in an innovative way; the name Auto Value would be placed on a stripe across the windshield of every car in the race. Thus in any publicity photo for the race, the name Auto Value was not only visible but prominent. The results of this advertising campaign were impressive. Auto Value figured that, after the first race of the series on February 12, 1995 at Daytona International Speedway in Daytona, Florida, the association had received a 24 percent return on its entire investment as a sponsor of the event.

The next step in the association's growth involved the development of a service center concept. In 1995, members of the association, with Morgan leading the discussion at the national marketing meeting in Salt Lake City, Utah, decided to develop an Auto Value Service Center to heighten the group's identification program. The program was designed to include interior and exterior identification elements, such as signs, awnings, mats, window-posters, and also personnel identification items, including uniforms, caps, and tee-shirts. Other components of the service center program involved cleanliness standards and the requirement to hire at least one ASE-certified technician. Cautious about its image, but committed to helping affiliated installers become more competitive in the marketplace, the association members agreed to develop a prototype before the actual program was implemented.

Competition and Success

By 1995, the number of warehouse distributors within the association had grown to 39, and the number of affiliated jobbers operating under the name of Auto Value Stores had grown to 1,500. By the middle of 1997, the number of affiliated jobbers had increased to over 1,800. The 39 warehouse distributors operated more than 100 distribution centers across the United States and Canada, with new locations in Hawaii and Mexico. By 1997, the number of distribution centers operated by warehouse distributors had also grown to more that 120 locations.

Although Auto Value Associates had implemented an aggressive campaign to attract new warehouse distributors and new affiliate jobbers, the automotive parts aftermarket remained a highly competitive industry. Nevertheless, the association's emphasis on marketing, with price savings for warehouse distributors and assistance for each new affiliated jobber to advertise his services, continues to attract new members within a rapidly consolidating market.

Further Reading

"ASE Scholarships, Service Center Program Lead Marketing Mix," *Automotive Marketing,* June 1997, p. 30.

"Auto Value Develops Service Center Concept," *Automotive Marketing,* June 1995, p. 29.

"Auto Value Goes Racing," *Automotive Marketing,* June 1995, p. 24.

"Auto Value Plans For Steady Growth At Jobber Level," *Automotive Marketing,* June 1995, p. 22.

"Auto Value Shifts Focus, Plans New Growth," *Automotive Marketing,* July 1997, p. 21.

"Entrepreneurship Attracts," *Automotive Marketing,* June 1997, p. 22.

"Motorsports Builds Customer Relations," *Automotive Marketing,* June 1997, p. 29.

"O'Reilly Likes Group Flexibility," *Automotive Marketing,* June 1997, p. 27.

"University of Auto Value Founded," *Automotive Marketing,* June 1995, p. 26.

—Thomas Derdak

B. Dalton Bookseller Inc.

122 Fifth Avenue
New York, New York 10011
U.S.A.
(212) 633-3300
Fax: (212) 807-6105

Wholly Owned Subsidiary of Barnes & Noble, Inc.
Incorporated: 1966
Employees: 12,000
Sales: $504.9 million (1997)
SICs: 5942 Book Stores

B. Dalton Bookseller Inc. is the second-largest operator of shopping-mall bookstores in the United States. This subsidiary of Barnes & Noble, Inc., the world's largest bookstore chain, also oversees the operations of two smaller bookstore chains, Doubleday Book Shops and Scribner's Bookstores.

Suburban-Mall Specialist: 1966–78

B. Dalton Bookseller was founded in 1966 by Dayton Co., an expanding retailer best known for its Minneapolis department store. Company president Bruce Dayton later explained the decision to enter the fragmented retail book trade in this way: "Sears, Roebuck, and Penney's, our typical competitors, weren't strong on books. And on the other hand, we saw nonpublishers like General Electric and Xerox making books and saw no reason why a previously non-bookseller like Dayton's couldn't sell them." He went on to add, "We felt that what the book business needed was merchandising knowhow, the kind of selling that 'mom-and-pop' stores don't do. Naturally, our emphasis was on salesmanship rather than bookmanship."

Accordingly, Dayton had no qualms about hiring Richard N. Hagen, a former department store buyer specializing in women's hosiery, as the first president of B. Dalton. Hagen targeted well-educated, middle-class suburbanites 20 to 35 years of age, the customers whom market research indicated spent the most money on books. The first B. Dalton store opened in a shopping center in Edina, a suburb of Minneapolis.

By April 1968 there were nine B. Daltons, all in suburban shopping centers.

These outlets of 4,000 to 7,000 square feet were uncluttered, with parquet flooring, wide aisles, and an unrestricted approach to the book displays so customers did not have to squint or stand on tiptoe to read titles. The average store carried 20,000 titles, including a hardcover list of 8,000 adult books and 3,000 to 4,000 juveniles, with the rest in paperback. Their stock was 85 percent books; stores also carried greeting cards, adult games, phonograph records, den decorations, and various novelty items. A furniture section displayed Bank of England chairs and Williamsburg decks, and a $1,200 world globe was featured in the window.

B. Dalton could count on vital support from the parent company, which became Dayton Corp. in 1967 and then Dayton Hudson Corp. in 1969, after it acquired Detroit's J. L. Hudson department store. By adopting the use of Dayton's NCR315 computer system, B. Dalton became the first completely computerized book operation in the country, with each sale recorded on tape and the tapes shipped to the computer center on weekends so that the new inventory figures were back in the stores by Monday. As a volume buyer, B. Dalton could afford to place large, preseason orders with publishers at an advantageous discount. At this time, however, an estimated 75 percent of sales volume was in backlist books rather than best-sellers.

By mid-1968 there were 12 B. Dalton bookstores in Arizona, California, Kansas, Minnesota, Missouri, Ohio, and Wisconsin. Just two years later there were 27, including outlets in Indiana and Nevada as well. By 1974 there were about 125 B. Dalton stores in operation, each of them stocking about 25,000 titles. By then the chain had converted to a high-volume, mass-marketing approach, catering to a broader class of reader than before. The walls were now covered with books piled to the ceiling, with more stacked on the floors at the ends of display islands (a strategy later described as "pile 'em high and watch 'em fly"). Many of the outlets displayed hardcover books and paperbacks side by side, an unusual method for the time. By late 1976 there were some 360 B. Dalton stores in existence, with store space ranging from 1,400 to 9,000 square feet.

In 1976 another Dayton Hudson subsidiary, Pickwick Book Shops, Inc., was merged into B. Dalton. Founded by Louis

Epstein, Pickwick was operating seven stores in southern California when it was acquired by Dayton in 1968 for $8 million. The main store, opened in 1938 on Hollywood Boulevard, had attracted among its customers (or browsers) such authors as Bertolt Brecht, Theodore Dreiser, William Faulkner, F. Scott Fitzgerald, Aldous Huxley, and Thomas Mann. Among the film colony in attendance were Charlie Chaplin (who complained about the prices) and Marlene Dietrich (whom one customer reportedly mistook for a clerk). The Pickwick chain grew to 16 by 1972. After merger with B. Dalton, it became B. Dalton/Pickwick. The main store—later B. Dalton Hollywood—closed in 1995.

By the end of fiscal 1978 there were 357 B. Dalton outlets in 43 states, with combined annual sales of $174 million, making the chain the largest in sales in the country and second only to Waldenbooks in store number. During that year the company sold 47 million books, including about one-tenth of all hardcover books published. Some of its stores offered such services as reproducing out-of-print books and ordering from foreign publishers. The centralized computer system enabled Dalton's 20-odd buyers to spot popular books early and restock the best-selling ones quickly.

Mass Marketing: 1978–86

In November 1978 B. Dalton opened a 25,000-square-foot, two-story flagship store on Manhattan's Fifth Avenue that carried 100,000 titles and 300,000 books, making it one of the largest in the world. There were other B. Dalton outlets in central business districts and also in freestanding buildings in strip shopping centers, but most remained in suburban malls. Sites were chosen using demographic studies of 36,000 communities with information broken down into census tracts. The chain's research had found that the heaviest readers were between 21 and 49 years old, were generally in managerial or professional positions, and were predominantly female. However, not all locations and offerings were aimed at this kind of reader; an outlet in a working-class neighborhood of Troy, Michigan, for example, stocked almost triple the number of home-improvement books and auto-repair manuals found in a store five miles away.

Whatever the location, B. Dalton stores tended to bear a close resemblance to one another. The parquet floors and heavy fixtures once typical of the bookseller were phased out; dangling pieces of cardboard signage suspended from the ceiling, some showing smiling green worms chewing on books, were introduced. All outlets fed their cash-register data into the company computer—now an IBM 158—so that headquarters could immediately dictate what should be stocked and how it should be displayed. Book sales were broken down into 100 categories, ranging from philosophy to rocks and gems. "Given a lot of display, any book will sell," said a buyer for the chain, adding "The trick is to find out what book will sell best and put it where people can see it." New titles selling more than 80 copies a week were placed on what a store called its "hot list," entitling them to special display on racks near the front. If such a book moved to the chain's best-seller list, it qualified for front-window display.

This kind of commercial appeal, however, found no favor among those with eclectic taste in literature. In a 1979 issue of

Saturday Review, a college journalism director complained that among the 40,000 titles in Edina—the original B. Dalton store—"serious readers would look in vain for anything of real interest. Most ... fall in such categories as pop-psychology, how-to, cookery, and gothic romances; the store has the best selection of 'me-first' books in Christendom.... 'Hitler,' the Edina store manager told him, 'is very big this year'." B. Dalton rarely considered stocking a book with a printing of fewer than 10,000 copies.

By the end of fiscal 1981 there were 579 B. Dalton stores in operation nationwide. Late that year the chain introduced a buy-by-category policy, under which money was budgeted to spend on each category, rather than, as previously, by publisher. This system, according to a publisher's sales manager, was similar to the way in which department stores operated, as it better controlled cash flow and proved more efficient for administration. However, the manager noted, it affected reorders adversely "because there's usually no money available to capitalize on the fast-moving titles." Nevertheless, in 1986, B. Dalton's chairman called the change to category buying "the single best thing we've ever done.... I know it creates problems for publishers, but it has improved service 100%."

In 1983 B. Dalton opened Pickwick Books as a discount chain, establishing three outlets on a trial basis in Columbus, Ohio. The number of outlets had reached 22 by the end of fiscal 1984, each carrying some 7,500 titles. Pickwick Books offered a 40 percent discount on hardcover best-sellers and an across-the-board ten percent on all other titles. The number of Pickwick stores reached 37 by June 1986, when B. Dalton announced that the chain would be discontinued. Dalton, which had begun its own discounting program in 1984, said it would convert 17 of the stores to its own chain and close the rest. Store surveys had shown that when B. Dalton lost customers it was to other stores discounting the top ten titles.

Still expanding, B. Dalton had 777 stores, averaging 3,000 to 5,000 square feet in size, at the end of fiscal 1984 and sales of $539.1 million for the year, but its profit margin fell to little more than four percent, compared to a peak of 10.5 percent in 1981. This was the result of a book market increasingly driven by discounters such as Crown Books Corp., which was established in 1978. In addition, the chain's growth prospects were being adversely affected by a slowdown in the construction of shopping malls, and its profits were further threatened by rising rental costs in the existing ones. One promising area for B. Dalton, however, was computer software; the company was, in 1986, testing software "stores within a store" at more than 30 of its locations. Another new foray was into leased book departments; the chain had opened them in eight Dayton Hudson department stores and was actively pursuing other such locations.

A Barnes & Noble Subsidiary: 1986–97

B. Dalton had 798 outlets in November 1986, when Dayton Hudson sold the company for around $300 million to a corporation owned by Barnes & Noble Bookstores Inc., the nation's third-largest bookseller, and two other parties—Leonard Riggio and the Dutch retailer Vendex International, N.V. Operations for both Barnes & Noble and B. Dalton were consolidated, with all back-office operations moved to Westbury, Long Island, and

B. Dalton's buying office moved to New York City. "Under Dayton Hudson, B. Dalton was fairly bureaucratic," a publishing executive said in 1991. "Under Lenny's direction," he continued, "it's a lot more entrepreneurial."

One of the parent company's first moves was to eliminate home-video products from the 550 B. Dalton outlets that regularly carried the category. The chain had repeatedly failed to devise a program to match the success that Waldenbooks enjoyed in video operations. B. Dalton continued to carry audio tapes, including the self-hypnosis/subliminal-persuasion type that dominated this category. By the summer of 1988 Riggio, the chief of both Barnes & Noble and B. Dalton, was spending $5 million a year on spot television commercials in which "Books Dalton," a bookish-looking, bespectacled, suspenders-wearing character, promoted the chain's best-selling titles. Nevertheless, backlist titles kept in print because of steady demand made up about 70 percent of B. Dalton's business and were higher-profit items than best-sellers because they were rarely discounted.

B. Dalton opened another chain of bookstores after acquiring the Scribner's bookstore name and the Scribner's bookstore in Costa Mesa, California, in 1989. (The publishing house Charles Scribner's Sons, acquired in 1984 by Macmillan Inc., continued to be held by that company.) In 1990 B. Dalton gained the resources of another chain when its parent company purchased 39-outlet Doubleday Book Shops Inc. from Bertelsmann A.G. for about $20 million. (Bertelsmann, which had also purchased the publisher Doubleday & Co. in 1986, retained what had become Bantam Doubleday Dell Publishing Group.) B. Dalton continued to position Scribner's and Doubleday as upscale rather than mass-market chains. A few months later Barnes & Noble bought a Texas and Florida chain of discount bookstores called Bookstop and about this time opened a mall-based retail chain called Software Etc.

As the construction of shopping malls slowed in the late 1980s, B. Dalton cast around for new ways to stimulate sluggish sales growth. In 1990 it introduced a "Booksavers Club," which, for a $10-membership fee, offered discounts and mailed newsletters and coupons to its enrollees. Also that year, the chain introduced a "Discover Great New Writers" program promoting 29 novels by unknown or little-known authors, some of whom were published by small presses. A *Wall Street Journal* article reported that a string of fiction and nonfiction books had become surprise best-sellers in the past years without the chains paying much attention. As a result, according to a small-press founder, "The chains like B. Dalton are trying to pick up on what has made some independents so successful."

In September 1990 B. Dalton opened the first of what it said would be a series of large stores stocking more than 100,000 titles. The chain had, in 1989, begun closing more than 50 outlets a year because of disappointing sales while also seeking better sites for others within the malls. A prototype store was developed in 1993, and over the next three years B. Dalton fielded more than 100 new or converted stores. At the same time, however, the number of B. Dalton outlets continued to shrink—from 698 in 1994 to 639 in 1995, 577 in 1996, and 528 in 1997. Sales volume for the combined Dalton, Scribner's, and Doubleday chains fell from a peak of $732 million in 1991 to $707 million in 1993, then to $646.7 million in 1994, $603.2 million in 1995, $564.9 million in 1996, and $509.4 million in 1997.

At the end of fiscal 1997 B. Dalton's 528 stores in 45 states and the District of Columbia included 18 Doubleday Book Shops (down from a peak of 40) and nine Scribner's Bookstores, both of which were in higher-end shopping malls and placed a greater emphasis on hardcover and gift books than the B. Dalton outlets. B. Dalton stores ranged in size between 2,800 and 6,000 square feet and were stocking between 15,000 and 25,000 titles. About 90 percent were located in enclosed regional shopping malls.

The B. Dalton store on Manhattan's Fifth Avenue closed in May 1997, a victim of the high rents in that part of midtown. One month later, the last remaining Doubleday Book Shop on the avenue closed its doors after 36 years. There had been at least one Doubleday bookstore on Fifth Avenue since 1916.

Principal Subsidiaries

Doubleday Book Shops, Inc.

Further Reading

"B. Dalton Discontinues Pickwick Discount Chain," *Publishers Weekly,* July 4, 1986, p. 13.

"B. Dalton's Book Superintendent," *Chain Store Age Executive,* November 1976, pp. 40, 44.

Cohen, Roger, "B. Dalton, in a Radical Shift, to Open Large Bookstores," *New York Times,* September 6, 1990, p. D19.

Cox, Meg, "B. Dalton Bookstore Chain Launches Program to Spur Sales of Serious Books," *Wall Street Journal,* April 30, 1990, p. B6C.

"Dayton Turns Its Talent to Books," *Business Week,* September 7, 1968, pp. 68–70.

Epstein, Louis, "Memoirs of Mr. Pickwick, L.A.'s Literary Godfather," *Los Angeles Times,* November 28, 1976, Book Sec., p. 3.

Foderaro, Lisa W., "Another Fifth Ave. Bookshop Is Felled by High Rents," *New York Times,* June 17, 1997, pp. B1, B6.

"Mass Marketing Hits the Bookstores," *Business Week,* February 9, 1974, pp. 80–81, 83.

McDowell, Edwin, "Doubleday Book Shops Sale Is Seen," *New York Times,* February 14, 1990, p. D1.

——, "Scribner Name and Store Are Sold to B. Dalton," *New York Times,* May 12, 1989, p. D15.

Moss, Linda, "The Super Story at Barnes & Noble," *Crain's New York Business,* February 18, 1991, pp. 1, 21.

Mutter, John, "B. Dalton Bookseller," *Sales & Marketing Management,* May 14, 1979, pp. 49–51.

Porter, Bruce, "B. Dalton: The Leader of the Chain Gang," *Saturday Review,* June 9, 1979, pp. 53–54, 56–57.

Potts, Mark, "Competition Thickens at 3 Bookstore Chains," *Washington Post,* March 6, 1990, pp. D1, D7.

Richards, Bill, "Dayton Hudson Agrees to Sell B. Dalton Unit," *Wall Street Journal,* November 28, 1986, p. 4.

Schmuckler, Eric, "Full Color and In Motion," *Forbes,* August 8, 1988, pp. 98–99.

Spain, Tom, "Dalton Drops Troubled Video Program in Back-to-Basics Push," *Publishers Weekly,* April 3, 1987, pp. 39–40, 42.

Symons, Allene, "Barnes & Noble to Buy B. Dalton," *Publishers Weekly,* December 12, 1986, pp. 17, 23.

——, "Dalton's Progress, Part 2," *Publishers Weekly,* December 26, 1986, pp. 32, 34–35.

Yen, Marianne, "What Troubles B. Dalton?," *Publishers Weekly,* October 17, 1986, pp. 16–17.

—Robert Halasz

Baan Company

Galvanistraat 9
P.O. Box 250
6710 BG Ede
The Netherlands
(31) 318-691691
Fax: (31) 318-691690
Web site: http://www.baan.com

Public Company
Incorporated: 1978 as Financieel Management
    Begeleidingsbureau Baan
Employees: 3,500
Sales: US$ 684 million (1997)
Stock Exchanges: NASDAQ; Amsterdam
Ticker Symbol: BAANF
SICs: 7372 Prepackaged Software; 6719 Holding
    Companies

The Baan Company is one of the world's top producers of enterprise business management and client/server software systems, with more than 3,000 customers at 5,000 sites around the world. From its dual headquarters in The Netherlands and in Reston, Virginia, Baan oversees a global organization of subsidiary and partnership companies, both for product development and for distribution and implementation of the company's products. Baan's 20 years of experience developing automated software solutions for manufacturing and business systems has placed it in a strong position to meet the 1990s boom in client/server systems technology. The company has grown from being a US $35 million company in the early 1990s to earning nearly US $700 million in 1997 sales. Since going public in 1995, Baan's market capitalization of some $7 billion has won it a place on the Fortune 500.

Baan has long been a pioneer in offering open-ended, platform-independent Enterprise Resource Planning (ERP) tools to companies. Under the umbrella name ''BaanSeries'', the company's products feature a modular architecture, enabling the company to offer client-specific solutions using standardized components developed by Baan and its partners. This feature sets Baan apart from its competitors' systems, offering a flexibility of deployment and development to meet customers' current and future needs. Baan components span the entire range of manufacturing and business systems, from inventory and ordering, to sales and customer support services, to financial system and forecasting processes. In addition, Baan products offer multi-lingual support with translations of its software in more than 20 languages, and a distribution and support presence in some 60 countries as well as multi-currency support. Furthermore, the company offers Internet and World Wide Web functionality, and support for Unix, Windows, and Microsoft BackOffice and FrontOffice applications.

Modest Beginnings in the late 1970s

Jan Baan seemed far from the most likely candidate to head one of the world's leading information technology companies. Born in 1946 in Rijssen, Baan's father was a carpenter, and his grandfather was originally a farmer and later an owner of a bus company. Baan himself left school at the age of sixteen, going to work in a meat packing plant. After fulfilling his mandatory military service, Baan found work in an administrative services office. In 1970, Baan went to work for a building materials supply firm. In 1972, after the death of his supervisor, Baan was appointed head of the company's administrative services department. At that time, the company was automating its systems, and Baan's position introduced him to emerging computer technology, as he became responsible for automating the company's bookkeeping functions.

By the mid-1970s, Baan had begun working as a management consultant to an accounting firm, where he gained new experience that would prove central to his later career. It was then that Baan, with a family of five children, decided to set out on his own. In 1978, Baan formed his own management consulting firm, Financieel Management Begeleidingsbureau Baan (FMBB), renting an office in Barneveld. FMBB's original focus was on providing models to assist companies in their financial planning; Baan sought to provide tools, in the form of information, to enable companies to make calculated decisions. Using a programmable calculator, Baan worked on refining his models.

A year later, Baan had succeeded in building up a list of clients, and had hired his first employee, Centinus van Haberden. Baan's work had shown him that there was a need among small businesses for better record-keeping tools. A turning point for the company came when one of FMBB's clients, a computer importer, paid Baan with an early computer, a Durango, one of the first small computers to be based on the Intel 086 processor. No Dutch-language software yet existed for the Durango, so Baan decided to design the software himself, hiring programmers to write software that would enable him to offer record-keeping and other administrative services to his clients as well. In this way, FMBB expanded its services beyond consulting toward an early systems management approach. By late 1980, Baan had brought in his own programmer to create programs tailor-made for each of the firm's clients.

Baan was determined to offer a complete automation solution to his customers, which by then included a growing number of administrative services firms. FMBB became an authorized dealer for Durango computers in the Netherlands; thus, in addition to the company's consulting and administrative services, FMBB could offer its clients tailor-made computer hardware and software solutions. The Durango sales quickly took on a central role for the company, and Baan sold off FMBB's administrative services activities to van Haberden, who was then starting out on his own. The changing focus of the company led to the adoption of a new name: Baan Automation. The company also moved its offices to a farm in Terschuur, which also served as the Baan family home.

Computer software of the period remained hardware-specific. Most programs were written for a particular brand of computer, in that computer's specific language, and would work only on that computer. Programs tended to be created from the ground up and tailored to a single client's needs. Baan's insight was to see the need for what he referred to as an 'industrial' approach to software programming. Instead of taking the tailor-made approach, Baan instead sought to create a standard program that could then be easily adapted to each client's requirements. The resulting software would be less expensive to produce, and less expensive to the company's clients. The off-the-shelf concept would continue to mark the Baan Company's products through the 1990s.

By the summer of 1981, Baan had determined to develop his company into a full-fledged system house. At this time, he brought in two new partners—his younger brother, Paul Baan, and Tom Bakker, a former colleague from the building materials supply firm. Each of the three set up an office, with Jan Baan remaining in Terschuur, Paul Baan opening an office in Rijssen, and Bakker setting up an office in Middelburg. In that way, Baan established itself as a national company in The Netherlands. Paul Baan became his brother's partner, with each man owning 50 percent of the company, and serving as co-directors, a relationship that would continue up until the company's 1995 public offering.

The three Baan branches quickly developed particular areas of expertise, with the Terschuur office specializing in accounting and production firms, Rijssen focused on the building and construction market, and Middelburg on the trade industry. The company's client list—chiefly small and mid-sized companies—was growing rapidly, and achieving a national scale. By 1984, Baan decided to group its activities into a single location, centralizing the firm in Terschuur. A year later, the company's

growing number of employees led Baan to construct a new building in Barneveld. By 1985, the company employed more than 120 people.

Independence in the 1980s

In the early 1980s, Baan's software, as with most of the computer industry at the time, remained dependent on a single platform. This system, however, was soon feeling the strain of rapid developments being made in computing technology—particularly the introduction of what would become the first personal computers. On a trip to California in 1981, Baan had discovered an emerging operating system, called Unix, which promised platform-independence—that is, the capability to run on any type of computer hardware. Unix, moreover, offered the ability to control several computer-clients from a central computer, the server, which linked the system to share resources, such as printers and other network operations. While this latter ability would not take on its full importance until the early 1990s, Baan was attracted to the possibilities of platform-independence, and became among the first to bring Unix to the Netherlands.

Working with Unix required Baan to convert all of its software from the Durango's proprietary language to the Unix's code. The company created its own set of tools, computerizing the conversion process. Baan, meanwhile, continued to supply Durango-based systems to a client base reluctant to embrace the new operating system. But Baan's early interest in Unix positioned the company to become the Netherlands' premier Unix systems provider in the second half of the decade. The company also found itself perfectly positioned to bridge the demise of the Durango and other proprietary hardware systems.

By the mid-1980s, Baan, now known as Baan Info Systems, had succeeded in building a strong library of tools, including its own Unix shell, that the company could implement for its clients' needs. While the company had successfully broken the 'built-to-order' mold, its software nevertheless represented an evolutionary process—the software would be expanded, and otherwise adapted, for each new client's needs. The company's three areas of specialization had, in fact, led to the development of three separate software systems, each with its own architecture, making it impossible for the company to offer a fully integrated package. The fact that the company had become the Netherland's premier Unix systems supplier did not prevent Baan from recognizing its own limited future. The Netherlands remained a small market, and the company's software—despite being translated into English and German during the 1980s—was not suited for an international market composed of large-scale and increasingly global businesses. While the company managed to score several successes—including an implementation order from Italy's Olivetti in 1988, and a similar OEM agreement with France's Bull in 1989—Baan looked forward to a scenario of continuing to sell its MRP (manufacturing resource planning) software for another couple of years, then abandoning software development to become a third-party vendor for other systems.

Instead, in 1985 Baan decided to risk stepping backwards. While continuing to develop its existing package, the company set to work developing a new software system, beginning from scratch. The new system, dubbed Triton, would not be ready until 1989. The new product's launch would also coincide with a drastic reorganization of the company.

A World Leader in the 1990s

In 1989, Baan suffered a dramatic drop-off in new orders. The company's reliance on its first-generation software had meant that it had fallen behind its competitors. The company had been attempting an aggressive domestic and international expansion, opening a series of sales offices—including US offices in Grand Rapids, Michigan and in Menlo Park, California. The stock market crash of October 1987 and the long slump of the high technology industry through much of the 1980s, however, provided limited perspective for the type of financial backing Baan required for its expansion. The company, forced to fund itself, had meanwhile become bloated with a variety of additional services and activities, including technical maintenance, and even tools supplies. The company became determined to regroup around its core software development operations. The 1989 reorganization slashed the company's payroll—from 400 down to 215—and exposed Baan to a great deal of criticism in the Netherlands.

Emerging from its reorganization, Baan had now become a holding company for two operations: Baan Info Systems was placed under Paul Baan's leadership, and focused on distribution activities to the company's domestic market, while Baan International was led by Jan Baan, and continued the company's software development while serving its distribution needs on the international front. Through the first half of the 1990s, Baan continued to experience revenue losses, as customers proved reluctant to return.

By the end of 1990, Baan showed signs that it had weathered the crisis. Aiding the company was a new policy of seeking OEM agreements providing Baan software to companies to sell under their own name. Agreements with companies including IBM and ASK Computer Systems in the early 1990s helped add some $10 million to Baan's till. The company also began to develop an international distribution network, this time turning to third-party and other partnerships, instead of developing a more capital-intensive, company-owned network. The distribution network—which the company would later gradually dismantle in favor of direct ownership—helped the company survive the early years of the 1990s. The company remained extremely small. In 1991, it's revenues amounted to just US $35 million.

Baan's turning point came with the 1991 introduction of its Triton software. If the company had been lagging the competition, Triton now gave Baan an advance of several years over its competitors. Triton also represented the fulfillment of Baan's 'industrial' vision. Featuring a truly modular concept, Triton customers could purchase a system tailored to their needs from among a hundred or more components, all designed to work interactively. With a modular system, moreover, the client discovered a new flexibility: where competing systems required clients to determine the current and future needs at the time of the purchase contract, Triton would enable clients to add-on and otherwise evolve their systems processes as their needs evolved or changed.

Baan's system quickly attracted the attention of the investment firm General Atlantic Partners, which foresaw the coming boom in client/server technology rapidly becoming an essential component in the increasingly globalized economy. General Atlantic Partners offered to invest in Baan—an offer Jan Baan initially rejected. Yet Baan's international customers were increasingly demanding worldwide support directly from Baan, requiring the company to develop a company-owned distribution and support network. In 1993, Baan agreed to sell 34 percent of the company to General Atlantic Partners, in exchange for their investment of $18 million. With this capital, Baan was able to begin building a new direct sales and distribution network, including establishing a second US headquarters in California's Silicon Valley. At the same time, the company phased out its OEM sales.

Soon Baan was attracting large-scale customers. Among the first were the US's Snap-On Tools and Northern Telecom. Baan's success was solidified, however, with a $20 million contract from Boeing in 1994, which helped it edge out more than 60 competitors, including industry leaders Oracle and SAP. The contract gave Baan instant name recognition and boosted its revenues for that year to nearly US $123 million. In order to consolidate its reputation in the U.S.—which alone accounted for more than 41 percent of worldwide software sales—Baan next turned to the stock exchange. Listing as a public company would give the company's image the added stability and maturity necessary for attracting the world's large-scale, globally-based organizations.

Baan's 1995 listing proved to be among the year's most successful IPOs. The initial offer price was adjusted up from $12 per share to $16 per share before trading even began; the offering, oversubscribed by some 40 times, would top $25 per share by the end of its first trading day. Two years later, and after a stock split, the company's stock price would soar past $61 per share—giving the company a market capitalization of nearly US $7 billion and placing it among the world's leading software developers. At the same time, Jan Baan, recognizing this new development in the modest business he had founded nearly 20 years before, brought in Tom Tinsley, formerly with McKinsey & Company, to serve as the company's president—and later chairman—in order to lead Baan's future growth. Jan Baan remained involved in the company's operations as its CEO.

In the late 1990s, Baan continued to play a leading role in the development of client/server and ERP systems, including being among the first to develop systems for the Microsoft BackOffice and FrontOffice lines. In 1997 and 1998, Baan introduced its next generation of products, grouped under the name BaanSeries, including its Dynamic Enterprise Modeling-Strategy Execution (DEMSE), a graphical interface enabling clients to expand and re-deploy their Baan-based systems in real-time, and an enhanced version of the company's Orgware products, developed specifically for the needs of globally-operating enterprises. Baan was poised to increase its share of the industry. Its future plans called for the company to advance from its 5 percent market share (in 1997) to becoming a US $1 billion company among the top five software developers in the world by the year 2000.

Further Reading

Hutheesing, Nikhil, "Auto-Baan," *Forbes,* October 6, 1997.
Post, Henk A., *Ongoing Innovation: The Way We Built Baan,* Barneveld: Baan Business B.V. 1996.

—M.L. Cohen

BALDWIN ®

Baldwin Technology Company, Inc.

One Norwalk West
40 Richards Avenue
Norwalk, Connecticut 06854
U.S.A.
(203) 838-7470
Fax: (203) 852-7040
Web site: http://www.baldwintech.com

Public Company
Incorporated: 1984
Employees: 1,047
Sales: $244.1 million (1997)
Stock Exchanges: American
Ticker Symbol: BLD
SICs: 3555 Printing Trades Machinery and Equipment

With more than $244 million in sales in fiscal 1997, Baldwin Technology Company, Inc., is the leading manufacturer of accessories, controls, and material handling technology for the printing, publishing, and packaging industries worldwide. The company's products are designed to improve workplace productivity, improve print quality, reduce press down time, reduce paper waste, and reduce VOC emissions, especially in the cleaning process. The company has manufacturing, sales, and service facilities around the world, in the United States, China, Japan, Australia, Sweden, France, the United Kingdom, and Germany, and its sales are equally distributed across the Americas, Europe, and Pacific Asia. Customers include magazine and catalog printers, newspaper publishers, book and insert printers, and packaging houses.

Founding in 1918

Baldwin Technology was started in 1918 and remained a fairly small company until 1950. It was begun by ex-printer and press service technician William Gegenheimer in his garage in Baldwin, New York. He invented a device, the Baldwin Press Washer, that unlocked the potential of offset printing by reduc-

ing the time required to clean printing presses from hours to minutes. A patent was granted for The Baldwin Press Washer in 1927, and in 1929 the company moved to Brooklyn, New York.

Over the coming decades, Baldwin's innovations would make offset lithography more efficient and profitable, accelerating the industry's growth and expanding its own market. Baldwin developed a reputation for listening to the needs of printers and developing innovative products to meet those needs.

Sales of $1 Million in 1950

Baldwin began to expand its product line when Harold W. Gegenheimer, son of the founder, joined the company in 1950. Harold Gegenheimer was a press designer and engineering manager. Sales reached the $1 million mark in 1950, and during the 1950s the company began to license its products for manufacture abroad.

Harold Gegenheimer became president of the company in 1961, chairman in 1971, and chairman of the executive committee in 1982. He retired in 1986. In 1987 the Harold W. Gegenheimer Endowment was established at Rochester Institute of Technology's School of Printing Management and Sciences. The endowment would enable students and faculty to pursue field research into the technological challenges facing the printing industry.

Wendell Smith joined the company in the 1960s, and in 1966 the company's headquarters was moved to Stamford, Connecticut. Together with Gegenheimer, Smith helped grow the company by expanding its product lines further and penetrating international markets. In the 1960s overseas affiliates were set up. Baldwin Japan was established when the company entered into a joint venture agreement in Japan in 1968, and Baldwin Gegenheimer GmbH was established in 1971 with offices in Augsburg, Germany. Japan and Germany would become Baldwin's strongest overseas markets.

In 1969 Baldwin began an aggressive program of acquisitions to expand its product lines. It acquired Korthe Engineering, which became the basis for Baldwin's web break detection and protection product line. In 1971 Baldwin added a signature

35

handling and stacking product line when it acquired Graphic Engineers. In 1974 it acquired Sun Chemical Co.'s web control product line. In 1976 the Automatic Blanket Cleaner was introduced in Europe. Levimatic Packaging Systems was acquired in 1978, and in 1981 Baldwin acquired D&R Engineering's gluer product line.

Sales Exceed $50 Million in the 1980s

In the early 1980s Baldwin was generating sales of $40 to $50 million. Through acquisitions and internal growth, sales approached $200 million by 1990. In 1983 Baldwin received a patent for an improved version of its Automatic Blanket cleaner, and in the following year the product won the InterTech Award from the Graphic Arts Technical Foundation (GATF). The award was given for a product expected to have a significant impact on the printing industry over the next five years.

Baldwin incurred its first-ever loss in 1983, the result of losses at a computer software company, which was sold the next year, and a large investment in establishing a manufacturing plant in Ireland. That same year a management buyout established Wendell Smith and his group as owners of the company. Smith became chairman of the board, president, and CEO. The following year Baldwin returned to the black, reporting a small profit on sales of $46 million. In November 1984 the Baldwin Technology Company, Inc., was organized as a holding company to purchase the assets of Baldwin Technology Corporation and its wholly owned subsidiary, NB Technology Corporation (NBT). In March 1985 NBT was merged with Baldwin Technology Corporation, with Baldwin Technology Corporation surviving as a wholly owned subsidiary of Baldwin Technology Company. For FY1985 (ending June 30) Baldwin reported net income of $1.2 million on sales of $53 million. The next year net income improved to $1.9 million on sales of $61 million.

Going Public, 1987

Baldwin became a publicly traded company on January 15, 1987. The initial public offering raised approximately $10 million, which together with the company's record year in 1987 enabled it to pay off the $9 million in debt it had incurred during the management buyout of 1983. Sales improved dramatically to $75 million, while net income jumped to $3.2 million. Both were company records. Sales for 1988 were projected at $90 million. Following its IPO, Baldwin experienced a period of growing sales and income as well as new product development and a stronger market position.

Baldwin was enjoying strong demand for its products from European and Far Eastern markets as well as a slight improvement in the U.S. market, which had been flat in recent years. Growth in the overseas market was due in part to Baldwin's becoming an increasingly important parts supplier to press manufacturers in Germany and Japan. The majority of the world's sheet-fed presses were produced in those two countries.

Non-U.S. operations were starting to contribute significantly to operating income. In 1985, non-U.S. operations contributed only $580,000 to operating income, while in 1987 they contributed $6.7 million, with U.S. operations contributing $4.3 million to operating profits. Sales were about evenly divided between the United States and overseas markets. International sales would continue to become more important to Baldwin. In 1988, 59 percent of the company's profits and 69 percent of its sales came from Japan and Germany. Additional areas for international growth included France, the Soviet Union, and China.

Growth Through New Products and Acquisitions

In early 1987 Baldwin introduced a patented newspaper blanket cleaner (NBC) that operated at full press speed, eliminating the need for costly shutdowns to clean the press blankets. Baldwin also introduced an automatic signature bundler (ASB), which gathered high-speed press output to allow efficient handling in binding operations. The ASB solved a long-standing problem associated with high-volume, high-speed printing. It was aimed at directory and publications printers.

In late 1987 Baldwin acquired the Ultrasonic web break detection system from Beaudreau Electronic Inc, which detected web breaks. During the year Baldwin introduced a new family of newspaper press protection products and systems. These new on-press sensors and computer systems would guarantee that presses with the most complex web leads were fully protected from damage due to paper breaks.

For the past 25 years, Baldwin had enjoyed a compound annual growth rate of about 15 percent. The company was dependent on overall economic conditions and the changing levels of capital spending. For many customers, price was less of a consideration than such factors as a company's staying power, product quality, and level of customer support, areas in which Baldwin was strong.

Factors at work in the printing industry were also contributing to Baldwin's growth. Advances in press technology were resulting in higher press speeds, which created a need for more and better accessories and attachments to reduce down time and paper waste and to lower other costs. According to a 1988 analyst's report, Baldwin enjoyed a dominant 42 percent market share in press accessories and had room for growth in controls and material handling systems. Most of the companies competing against Baldwin were much smaller. Baldwin's new product development program was characterized by one analyst as "aggressive." In 1988 the company spent $1.9 million on research and $5.3 million on engineering and applications work. The company was spending about 10 percent of revenue on research and development efforts.

70th Anniversary, 1988

Sales for 1988 rose to $95.5 million, and net income nearly doubled to $6.1 million. It was the company's 70th anniversary. In October 1988 Baldwin announced plans to acquire the Kansa Corp, based in Emporia, Kansas. Kansa manufactured newspaper inserters, padding machines, and other equipment for newspaper and commercial printers worldwide. The acquisition was completed in early 1989 for $4.5 million in cash and 400,000 shares of common stock valued at $2.9 million. Baldwin also opened a new 30,000-square-foot facility in Naugatuck, Connecticut, devoted to manufacturing the company's growing line of fountain solution control products and the Accu Spray Dampener, a newly developed product used on double-width newspaper presses. Fountain solution control systems controlled the supply, temperature, cleanliness, chemical composition, and other characteristics of water used in offset printing.

During 1988 Baldwin entered the thermographic and forms handling equipment business with the acquisition of Ecamo, S.A., a French corporation, for $1.6 million. It acquired its U.S. counterpart, Specialized Printing Machinery (SPM), in 1990. These operating units served small printers, a segment that would be particularly hard hit during the economic recession of the early 1990s. In 1992 both units were put up for sale.

In Baldwin's Pacific Asian market, company representatives attended ChinaPrint '88, a printing machinery exhibition, and made contacts with Chinese press manufacturers. A letter of intent was signed with China National Machinery and Equipment Import and Export Corporation and a proposed joint venture partner, Beijing Small Compressor Factory, to enter into a 75 percent company-owned joint venture for the manufacture of Baldwin products in the People's Republic of China.

In 1989 sales rose to $125.5 million, up 31.4 percent, and net income increased to $9.2 million, up 50.6 percent. Overall, the printing industry was continuing to expand into more sophisticated material handling as well as accessory and control equipment. Worldwide, printing was also continuing to grow. Baldwin Japan was the company's fastest-growing segment. It enjoyed a 51.1 percent increase in sales, mainly through existing product lines. In Europe, business grew by 29.8 percent, with the strongest segment being sheetfed presses. After four years of stable sales, business in the United States also grew through new product introductions. These included additions to Baldwin's automatic blanket cleaners, web break detectors, rotary cutters, high-speed stackers, and other products. Baldwin's 15 percent annual compound growth rate was outpacing the growth of the printing industry.

During the year Baldwin acquired the remaining 29.4 percent interest in its Japanese subsidiary. Enkel Corporation of Sweden was acquired for $10 million in cash and $12.3 million worth of stock. Enkel made machinery for splicing and handling huge rolls of paper for web printers and converters. Stobb, Inc., a manufacturer of stacker/bundlers based in Clinton, New Jersey, was acquired for $3.7 million, which included the assumption of $2.4 million in liabilities.

During 1989 Baldwin was reorganized into three geographic sectors based on the worldwide printing market: the Americas, Europe Consolidated (including Africa), and Asia Pacific. Each geographic sector would have its own product development, manufacturing, and marketing capabilities. The new regional structure was designed to help the company keep in close touch with its customers. During 1989 the company applied for 44 patents.

In 1990 Baldwin's sales rose 45.8 percent to $183 million, and net income increased 31.4 percent to $12.1 million. While U.S. market conditions remained soft, the company was able to continue reporting record sales and income because of strong performance in its Asia Pacific and European regions. Each geographic segment of the business—Europe, the Americas, and Asia Pacific—accounted for about one-third of the company's sales. Business was also equally balanced between press manufacturers and printers. New product development was equally split between internal R&D and outside acquisitions.

Acquisitions in 1990 included Misomex AB of Stockholm, Sweden, and its North American subsidiary, Misomex of North America, Inc. The company was an international manufacturer of platemaking and other pre-press equipment for the printing industry. It was headquartered in Sweden and also had operations in Germany, Great Britain, and the United States. Baldwin completed the acquisition on July 27, 1990, for $44 million in cash. The acquisition was financed through bank loans. Other acquisitions included Specialized Printing Machinery, which became Baldwin SPM, the U.S. sales counterpart to Ecamo.

During 1990 Baldwin raised $24 million in capital through a sale of stock, and the company's geographic reorganization was completed. Trading companies were established in the different regions to facilitate the exchange of product ideas and make importing and exporting products easier. During the year operating subsidiaries were established in Hong Kong and Beijing, China. An Australian subsidiary was established in 1991.

In 1991 Baldwin achieved its eighth straight year of record sales through recent acquisitions. Sales were $221.3 million, up 21 percent, but net income declined 43 percent to $6.9 million. While the decline in net income was attributed to a sluggish economy, the increase in sales was due primarily to the acquisition of Misomex.

Recession, 1990s

In 1992 a severe recession in global printing markets continued to impede Baldwin's financial performance. Sales rose one percent to $221.5 million. Income from continuing operations was $770,000, but the company took a special charge of $7.6 million for restructuring and discontinuing certain operations, resulting in a net loss of $6.9 million for the year. The recession was limiting the sales of new presses that might have been equipped with Baldwin products. The company was also experiencing intense pricing pressures that reduced and in some cases eliminated profitability on some products. Sales of new web presses, for example, were 50 percent below their 1989 level.

As a result of those recessionary conditions, Baldwin's recent acquisitions, Ecamo, Enkel, and Misomex, had to be downsized and restructured. Ecamo and its U.S. sales operation Baldwin SPM were discontinued at a cost of $5.9 million. Both units lost $1.8 million in 1992. These losses were offset somewhat by a 16 percent increase in net sales for Baldwin Asia Pacific in spite of a 30 percent decline in the Japanese printing press and accessory market. In an effort to trim costs, the company's workforce was reduced to 1,148 in 1992, down from a high of 1,390 employees in July 1990.

With the effects of the recession wearing off, Baldwin reported net income from continuing operations of $3.8 million for 1993, up from $770,000 for 1992. However, net sales declined by 2.6 percent to $215.8 million in 1993 from $221.5 million in 1992. In 1992 the company took a charge of $7.7 million for discontinued operations, which resulted in a net loss of $7.0 million for the year. Worldwide, the printing market was still a difficult one, according to chairman Wendell Smith.

At the end of 1993, Gerald Nathe was elected president. Wendell Smith retained chairmanship of the board and the title of CEO. In 1994 net income was $4.1 million, an increase of nine percent over net income of $3.8 million for 1993. Net sales declined by eight percent to $198 million. Asian operations were hampered by a strong yen and weak economic conditions in Japan. Order rates in Europe were improving, and the North American market was showing signs of increased business activity.

In 1995 net income rose 37 percent to $5.7 million on record sales of $222.3 million. Baldwin's financial performance reflected continuing economic recovery in the company's key markets. The company was in the process of acquiring the Acrotec group of companies, which was expected to add about ten percent to Baldwin's sales. The Acrotec acquisition was completed in October 1995, and its German operations would be merged with Baldwin Gegenheimer GmbH.

In 1996 net income was $2.4 million on sales of $259.3 million. It was a year of mixed results. Net sales set a new record, up 17 percent, but net income fell short of expectations due largely to restructuring charges. While the Americas and Asia Pacific operations were strong, sales in Europe were disappointing. The German operation was being restructured.

Several streamlining measures were taken during the year. In the United States, two Baldwin Graphic Products operations were consolidated in a single facility in Shelton, Connecticut, and two separate facilities were closed in Stamford, Connecticut. In Europe, the acquisition of Acrotec allowed the company to combine three sales operations for accessories and controls in the United Kingdom into one location. Other operations moved into new locations in Malmo, Sweden, and Tokyo, Japan.

In April 1997 Baldwin divested its Misomex unit, which was acquired in 1990. In the face of strong competition and a difficult technology to master, Misomex consistently lost money. Once the company decided to sell the unit, its stock price began to rise to the $5 per share range. The sale of Misomex to Kaber Imaging Inc. of Hudson, New Hampshire, was completed in July 1997 for $4 million and the assumption of certain liabilities. In other moves, the company downsized its German workforce by 15 percent and merged two separate businesses there, reducing plant capacity by 25 percent.

In 1997 Baldwin changed organizationally from a geographic orientation to a product market orientation. It reorganized its operations management from three geographic regions into two business areas: the Graphic Products and Control Group (press accessories and controls) and the Material Handling Group (splicer, in-line finishing, inserter and stacker bundler product lines). Baldwin companies from around the world with similar products, markets, and customer bases were put into similar groups. The reorganization was expected to facilitate technology transfers between business units and to enable the company to provide better customer service and respond more quickly to market changes.

Improved Sales Forecast for 1998

For 1997 Baldwin reported a net loss of just under $38 million on sales of $244.1 million, which included a one-time charge of $42.4 million for the Misomex sale. However, changes implemented during the year resulted in positive growth figures toward the end of the fiscal year. The company also had a higher order backlog than at the end of 1996. Improved sales were forecast for 1998 in Europe and Japan, where markets were expected to emerge from a prolonged recession.

In April 1997 Wendell Smith resigned as chairman of the board. President and CEO Gerald Nathe was elected to succeed him as chairman. Nathe had joined Baldwin Technology in 1990 as president of Baldwin Americas. In 1993, he became president of Baldwin Technology Company Inc., while continuing to serve as president of Baldwin Americas, and in 1995 he was elected CEO.

For the future, Baldwin identified print-on-demand, or distributed printing, as a new opportunity to be exploited through joint ventures. It would involve shorter print runs and printing only in black and white. Baldwin Technology was working with manufacturers of electronic printing engines, such as IBM, OCE, and Xerox, to build this area.

In an April 1998 interview in the *Wall Street Transcript*, Nathe was optimistic regarding the growth of print throughout the world. He said that Baldwin was also looking at new markets, such as packaging and print-on-demand. Nathe noted, ''Packaging is a market that's changing to require more and more information on the package,'' and printing quality was becoming more important.

Among the trends Baldwin was watching was the rise of alternative media, to see whether they would replace printed material or generate the need for additional printed products. Software, for example, while it may displace some print products, requires additional catalogs, magazines, and manuals. Baldwin was also carefully monitoring the growth rate of printing in lesser developed countries, which was generally outpacing the overall growth rate of such countries.

Principal Subsidiaries

Baldwin Graphic Products; Baldwin Dampening Systems; Baldwin Web Controls; Baldwin Enkel Corporation; Baldwin

In-Line Finishing; Baldwin Kansa Corporation; Baldwin Stobb; Baldwin Davlin Finishing Systems, Inc.; Baldwin Graphics Equipment Pty. Ltd. (Australia); Baldwin Japan Ltd.; Baldwin Printing Control Equipment (Beijing) Company, Ltd.; Baldwin Printing Controls Ltd. (Hong Kong); Baldwin France Sarl; Baldwin Grafotec GmbH (Germany); Baldwin UK Ltd.

Further Reading

"Baldwin Earnings Triple in Third Quarter," *Business Wire,* May 6, 1998.

"CEO Interview: Baldwin Technology Company Inc. (BLD), Gerald Nathe," *Wall Street Transcript,* April 20, 1998.

Dzikowski, Don, "Norwalk's Baldwin Technology on Rebound after Shedding Unit," *Fairfield County Business Journal,* September 29, 1997, p. 7.

Mastandrea, John, "Market-Dominant Baldwin Looks at Foreign Opportunities," *Fairfield County Business Journal,* November 21, 1988, p. 1.

Oster, Helen P., "Baldwin Reports Improved 1993 Earnings," *Business Wire,* August 26, 1993.

——, "Baldwin Reports Improved 1994 Earnings," *Business Wire,* August 22, 1994.

——, "Baldwin to Withdraw from Business Segment and Record Special Charge in Fourth Quarter," *PR Newswire,* June 25, 1992.

——, "Gerald A. Nathe Named Chief Executive Officer of Baldwin Technology Co. Inc.," *Business Wire,* October 18, 1995.

——, "Gerald A. Nathe Named President of Baldwin," *Business Wire,* August 5, 1993.

Troxell, Tom, "Baldwin Tech Makes Mark with Major Printers," *Intercorp,* May 27, 1988, p. 36.

—David Bianco

Bally Total Fitness Holding Corp.

8700 West Bryn Mawr Avenue
Chicago, Illinois 60631
U.S.A.
(773) 380-3000
Fax: (773) 693-2982
Web site: http://www.ballyfitness.com

Public Company
Incorporated: 1995
Employees: 12,600
Sales: $661 million (1997)
Stock Exchanges: NYSE
Ticker Symbol: BFT
SICs: 7991 Physical Fitness Facilities; 7997 Membership
   Sports & Recreation Clubs

Bally Total Fitness Holding Corp. is the largest commercial operator of fitness centers in the United States. The Company has close to four million members and operates 325 facilities in 27 states and Canada. Bally Total Fitness offers a variety of services in their fitness centers, including personal training services and BFIT Rehab, a physical rehabilitation service. They also sell a variety of health, fitness, and nutritional products—including their own BFIT Nutritionals—at BFIT Essentials retail stores located inside several of the fitness centers. Facilities offer the latest in cardiovascular and strength training, as well as a variety of aerobic programs, from spinning and step, to low impact and yoga. Club members may purchase either single club memberships or premier memberships, allowing the use of Bally Total Fitness Centers nationwide.

The Beginnings of Bally Total Fitness

Bally Total Fitness has roots that extend all the way back to 1931 and a company by the name of Lion Manufacturing. Lion Manufacturing, which later became Bally Manufacturing, was formed as and expanded as one of the largest producers of coin-operated amusement games. Bally Manufacturing continued its growth in the entertainment industry for the next fifty years, developing and producing products such as slot machines, video games, and pinball machines. Bally Manufacturing also entered into the casino business by becoming the owner of a series of a few different gaming hotels.

In a push to become a leader in the recreation industry, Bally Manufacturing later purchased Health and Tennis Corporation of America in 1983, creating Bally Health and Tennis Corporation, which became a subsidiary of the Bally parent company, now named Bally Entertainment. Bally also acquired Lifecyle, Inc., an exercise bike manufacturer, renaming it Bally Fitness Products, Corporation. With this expansion, Bally became the world's largest owner and operator of fitness centers by the year 1987. With the purchase of the American Fitness Centers business and 19 Nautilus Fitness Centers, Bally Health and Tennis Corp. continued to grow throughout the remainder of the 1980's and into the 1990's, at one point operating a total of almost 400 fitness centers in the United States and Canada.

The Bally Total Fitness name was developed in 1995, as Bally Health and Tennis Corp. consolidated all of its various health clubs under one name. Before the consolidation, the Bally clubs were operated under several different names, such as Bally's Health and Fitness, Vic Tanny, and Jack LaLanne. The move to consolidate under the Bally Total Fitness name was done in an attempt to unify the clubs and to increase Bally's already recognizable national image. Bally's marketed this change with a promotional campaign featuring the slogan ''Turn on Your Life'' and television's Terri Hatcher, from the hit show 'Lois and Clark'.

New Leadership for Bally Total Fitness in 1996

In January 1996, Bally Total Fitness Holding Corporation emerged from Bally Health and Tennis Corp. after being spun off from Bally Entertainment. This move completely separated the health and fitness arm of the Bally operation from that of the Bally gaming and entertainment arm. Now on its own, Bally Total Fitness Holding Corp. began to institute a strong campaign to improve its operations and head into the next century as a leader in the fitness center industry.

Company Perspectives:

Bally Total Fitness is committed to offering its members the best resources to help them achieve their personal fitness and health goals at an affordable price.

In October 1996, Lee Hillman was named president and Chief Executive Officer of Bally Total Fitness, and was put in charge of paving the way for Bally's growth. Hillman took over for the retiring Michael Lucci Sr., who had decided to step down after leading the company through the early 1990's. Hillman, who was in charge of making Bally Total Fitness profitable—after years of muddled fitness and gaming operations had eroded profitability somewhat—had worked in a similar situation under Bally Entertainment CEO Arthur Goldberg, who had turned that company around several years earlier. Hillman's main focus now was to increase the shareholders' value, through efforts at expansion, increasing revenues per square foot, and increasing operating margins.

The company already operated over 340 fitness centers in the United States and Canada, so the focus of Bally's expansion was not to increase the number of fitness centers, but to expand the variety of products that the company had to offer. Selling only one product—memberships—the company had well over 120 million visitors each year. With the desire to sell a variety of products, Hillman looked to his customers for ideas. He noticed that the customers all came into the fitness centers with T-shirts, sweatsuits, shoes, and socks, yet Bally did not sell any of those items. He also noticed the tremendous opportunity in the market of vitamins, nutritional supplements, and protein bars. He saw all of these items as avenues for increased product offerings from Bally Total Fitness.

Another avenue for increased exposure of the Bally name became the use of strategic partnerships. Bally entered into a deal with Florida-based ContinueCare Corporation to operate physical rehabilitation services in its fitness centers. The partnership was a perfect match for Bally's, because the fitness centers already had the necessary equipment and the demand for physical therapy often comes between 10:00am and 5:00pm, the least busy time for Bally's fitness centers.

Another partnership was developed with Metris Companies to deliver a co-branded MasterCard to Bally's customers. The MasterCard, another step by Hillman to expand the products and services, offered a competitive interest rate, and customers who used the card could take advantage of significant travel benefits and savings, while also collecting valuable savings on Bally's memberships.

The last of the initial changes started by Hillman was to shift the company's marketing focus away from heavily discounting memberships to attract new customers. Instead, the company began focusing more on people who were serious about their health. Bally stopped offering deep discounts to customers who paid cash up front for long term memberships and they soon actually saw new membership revenue begin to rise.

Building a Strong Foundation for Growth in 1997

Bally Total Fitness returned a profit of $2.5 million for the first quarter of 1997. According to Hillman, the profit was not so much a sign of the changes starting to take effect, but more a sign that the company was still solid. He felt that the changes made would only serve to further increase profitability. With bright days ahead, the income earned during that quarter marked an important step for Bally Total Fitness.

With initial plans working well, Bally continued to expand its operations in step with Hillman's five-year plan. Part of this included closing some of the less profitable fitness centers, redesigning other existing centers, and building newly designed facilities. New clubs were built with more space for weight machines and cardiovascular areas and less space for the lesser-used swimming pools and basketball and racquetball courts. The new design cost 60 percent less to build, while providing space for 40 percent more people.

Also introduced in 1997 were 40 'BFIT Essentials' retail stores. These stores operated right inside the fitness centers, and offered items ranging from vitamins to T-shirts to gym bags. The fitness centers could now offer the products that customers traditionally had been purchasing away from the Bally Total Fitness Centers, which was yet another step toward increasing overall profits.

Despite all of the new changes, Bally Total Fitness still showed a net loss for the overall year of 1997. Several signs pointed in the right direction, however, as membership revenues continued to increase. The company's goal for the following year was not only to increase revenue, but also to introduce new profit centers. With the addition of personal training centers in the facilities, BFIT Essentials retail stores, and the rehabilitative services, Bally built those strong profit centers that were ready to show results in the future.

The Return to Profitability in 1998

The start of 1998 marked the real move of Bally Total Fitness toward becoming a profitable entity. Bally Total Fitness once again experienced growth in membership fees, bolstered by sales of all-club premier memberships. These memberships allowed customers to use their Bally memberships at any Bally location around the country, which was a very appealing feature to business people who tended to travel a lot but did not want to sacrifice their work-out schedules to do so. Continued growth in revenues from personal training, BFIT Nutritionals, and BFIT Essentials retail stores also helped the centers to raise profits.

In early 1998 Bally Total Fitness introduced its new BFIT Energy Bar, a snack bar designed to act as an energy source during and after workouts. This product became the twelfth in a growing line of BFIT Nutritionals, including BFIT-RX, a meal replacement shake, BFIT for men and women, a daily multivitamin, and SnackFit—snack crackers that acted to reduce between-meal cravings. Sales of these nutritional products reached nearly $1 million per month after fewer than eighteen months in existence.

Now solid within the fitness centers themselves, Bally's next move was to increase brand visibility and perception. Bally signed an agreement with Baywatch Production Company, owner of *Baywatch,* the most watched television show in the world. The deal included several promotions throughout the year, including an episode to be filmed at a Bally Total Fitness Center. Bally also penned an agreement with Quintana Roo to become the official sponsor of the United States Triathalon Series, in an effort to attract the serious athlete to the fitness centers.

As growth continued, Bally looked to outside sources to fund the development. In May 1998, Bally sold 2.8 million shares of common stock, with the proceeds of $83 million being used to build new fitness centers and acquire club-related real estate. The expansion came fast as Bally acquired nine new clubs, including entering into the densely-populated San Francisco bay area with the acquisition of the Pinnacle Fitness and Gorilla Sports Club chains.

As new centers were acquired through construction and aggressive acquisition, and the new programs and services became successful, Bally Total Fitness announced revenues of $365.4 million for the first half of 1998. Revenues from the new products—personal training services, BFIT Nutritionals, BFIT Essentials retail stores, and BFIT Rehab Centers—also surpassed 1997 levels.

Plans for the future included opening close to 110 new BFIT Essentials retail stores by the end of 1999, while also continuing to expand the number of BFIT Rehab Centers to over 100 and building more fitness centers in the coming years. With these plans in place, and with revenues from memberships and other products continuing to grow while the fitness centers operated more effectively and efficiently, Bally Total Fitness moved closer to being the biggest operator of fitness centers in not only quantity, but in quality as well.

Further Reading

Borden, Jeff, "Bally Total Fitness CEO Flexed Product, Partnership Muscles," *Crains Chicago Business,* February 24, 1997, p. 6.
Curtis, Richard, "For-Profit Facilities Set Counterattack," *Cincinnati Business,* March 31, 1997, p. 6.
Kirk, Jim, "Bally's Brand Workout," *Adweek,* June 6, 1995, pp. 1–2.
——, "Bally Total Fitness Gets New President," *Chicago Sun-Times,* October 9, 1996, p. 64.
Pauly, Heather, "Bally Total Fitness CEO Gets Firm Back In Shape," *Chicago Sun-Times,* December 9, 1997, p. 57.

—Robert Alan Passage

Baltimore Gas and Electric Company

39 West Lexington Street
Baltimore, Maryland 21201
U.S.A.
(410) 234-5000
Fax: (410) 234-5999
(800) 561-9145
Web site: http://www.bge.com

Public Company
Incorporated: 1906 as Consolidated Gas Electric Light
    and Power Company of Baltimore
Employees: 8,000
Sales: $3.3 billion (1997)
Stock Exchanges: New York Midwest Pacific Boston
    Cincinnati Philadelphia
Ticker Symbol: BGE
SICs: 4939 Combination Utilities, Not Elsewhere
    Classified

Baltimore Gas and Electric Company (BGE) is an investor-owned utility with diversified operations in energy and environmental projects, real estate, and investments. BGE's principal business as of the late 1990s was the purchase, production, and sale of electricity and gas to business and residential customers in Baltimore and ten central Maryland counties. At that time, the company provided electrical service to over one million customers and gas service to over half a million customers.

Company Origins

Baltimore Gas and Electric Company dates back to 1816, when Rembrandt Peale, William Gwynn, and three other partners formed the Gas Light Company of Baltimore. Peale was the son of the painter Charles Willson Peale, and was himself a well-known painter of portraits and historical scenes. Gwynn was a local businessman. Another of the partners was a wealthy merchant, William Lorman. Within a week of a successful demonstration of gas lighting in what is now the Peale Museum, the new company secured a franchise to light the streets and homes of Baltimore, Maryland, with gas. The Gas Light Company was the first gas utility in the United States. Lorman was the company's first president, serving from 1816 to 1832. The Gas Light Company set to work laying pipes throughout Baltimore, bringing the new method of lighting to more neighborhoods. The company's first seven years were hard, producing no profit. The new company faced several problems of a technical nature. The method of gas manufacturing it had adopted proved inadequate for large-scale production, and there were no means of measuring the quality of the gas produced. And gas meters, although they existed in England, were not available in the United States. Since there was no method for measurement of gas used, the company had to charge a flat annual rate.

The Gas Light Company continued to lose money, and by 1818 the company had exhausted its capital. To raise the money necessary to continue operating, the company made an initial public stock offering in 1818. The capital raised by the offering was to be used to buy equipment to expand the number of customers Gas Light Company served. By increasing its customer base, the company could sell more gas and thus increase profit. Between 1818 and 1821, Baltimore, in common with other U.S. cities, was rocked by financial panic. The company's new influx of capital saw it through this period. In 1822, using a process already established in England, the company began manufacturing gas from coal. Previously tar was the raw material used. Coke, the by-product of this process, was a salable commodity. The company paid its first dividends in 1826.

In 1832 Columbus O'Donnell became president of the company and served until 1871. By 1830 the company was again running low on capital and was unable to continue to grow as quickly as the city of Baltimore. Much of the capital raised in 1818 had been spent on experimentation and on pipes and equipment of unsatisfactory quality. In 1833 the company issued new stock to raise capital.

The use of gas meters was underway in some homes by 1834, despite widespread opposition by members of the public, who did not trust the accuracy of gas meters. In fact, the meters lowered rates for most consumers.

Meanwhile, the city was still inadequately lit due to the cost of laying pipes, and by 1850 critics of the company, including Baltimore's mayor, voiced complaints. In 1860 Gas Light's first local competitor, Peoples' Gas Light Company, was formed. The organizers of Peoples' capitalized on Gas Light Company's unpopularity in persuading members of the Maryland state legislature to charter their company. Peoples' did not begin to operate until 1871, however, due first to internal disagreements among its founders, then to the Civil War.

Post-Civil War Competition

In 1861 the Civil War broke out, imposing difficulties and setbacks, especially in railroad traffic. The war ended in 1865, but the higher cost of living, and thus of doing business, that it produced continued. Peoples' Gas Light Company began to operate in 1871, after reaching an agreement with Gas Light Company to divide the city. Also in 1871, William Sinclair assumed the presidency of Gas Light Company, serving until 1880. In 1876 another contender in the increasingly profitable industry was formed—Consumers Mutual Gas Light Company of Baltimore. Fierce price wars between the three gas companies were waged until 1880 when the companies merged to become Consolidated Gas Company of Baltimore City. John W. Hall served as president for the next 20 years.

During the mid-1880s Consolidated Gas faced competition in some areas from the Chesapeake Company, another provider of gas for lighting. In areas where both companies provided service, they slashed prices. In 1886 the Maryland legislature restricted competition among gas companies by making it more difficult to establish a new company. In 1881 two electric light companies, Brush Electric Light Company and the United States Electric Light and Power Company, appeared in the city. Consolidated Gas was not yet involved in electric light, which was still fairly experimental at this time. When Thomas Edison's incandescent light bulb came into common use during the late 19th century, however, electric light became the standard. Electricity became the new competitor to gas.

In 1904 the city was devastated by the Great Baltimore Fire. Company employees labored to protect exposed mains from exploding. Despite the loss of property and the disruption of commerce, the company emerged prosperous and on solid ground and began to attract New York financiers.

By 1906 it had become clear to the leaders of Consolidated Gas that most homes and businesses favored electricity over gas for lighting. It was also clear that both gas and electric companies could operate more cheaply and efficiently if they did not duplicate services. In 1906, therefore, Consolidated Gas Company of Baltimore City merged with Consolidated Gas Electric Light and

Power Company to form Consolidated Gas Electric Light and Power Company of Baltimore. The new company provided fully integrated gas and electric service in Baltimore. Chairman S. Davies Warfield made good use of New York investors' capital and thus launched the direct predecessor of BGE. General Ferdinand C. Latrobe became president, serving until 1910. Its capital shortages behind it, Consolidated grew at a healthy pace. During the financial panic and depression of 1907–1908, the new company managed a small increase in sales.

The Public Service Commission of Maryland was created in 1910 to regulate utilities. Also during this time, natural gas was becoming a popular substitute for manufactured gas. Warfield wanted to bring natural gas to Baltimore but did not succeed in doing so. Between 1906 and 1910, gross income increased by 31 percent, and in 1910 Warfield resigned and was succeeded by J.E. Aldred as chairman. Aldred embarked upon vigorous expansion. Much of the company's electricity was supplied by hydroelectric plants on the Susquehanna River, and Consolidated owned several gas generating plants. With production in place, the company could offer more competitive rates.

The domestic economy, especially manufacturing, was boosted when World War I started in Europe. After the United States entered the war in 1917, demand for fuel rose. Soon a coal shortage developed, coincident with a severe cold wave. This period of strain and high prices did not end after the war. Two rate increases were granted and cost-cutting measures enforced to make up for the increased cost of labor and of coal, oil, and gas manufacture. In 1921 a contract was formed between Consolidated, United Railways & Electric Company and Pennsylvania Water & Power Company, under which all of Baltimore's electric power was organized under one management. It was another year of depressed earnings, but Consolidated began to recover in 1922 and 1923.

Due to several years of low water levels in the Susquehanna, the company began relying more heavily on its Baltimore steam plants in 1923, and Consolidated ordered two large turbine generators. By 1924 electric refrigerators and other appliances had become increasingly popular. The company was expanding to the north for power supplies. It entered an entirely new field in 1925 with the establishment of WBAL, a radio station that was sold to the American Radio News Corporation in 1935. In 1926, the use of gas was still growing. The company's Gould Street generating station began service in 1927, and was the first of the city's power plants to burn pulverized coal. In 1928 the company further diversified with the purchase of the Terminal Freezing & Heating Company. Steam heating was related to Consolidated's gas and electric interests, but the purchased system still had to be overhauled.

Lean Years During the Depression

In 1928, to simplify its corporate structure, a number of companies held by Consolidated were dissolved and absorbed. The company contracted to buy two-thirds of the energy generated by the Safe Harbor Water Power Company in 1931. Safe Harbor produced hydroelectricity at a plant on the Susquehanna River. In the early 1930s there was a boom in air conditioning, and population and industry increased in Baltimore as well. But these factors did not entirely offset the effects of the Depression.

By 1936 the company's lean years were abating. That year it signed a long-term contract for electricity supply with Bethlehem Steel Company. Between 1929 and 1936 the company's operating revenue increased by more than 18 percent. In 1939 Consolidated benefited from a number of newly established large industrial plants in Baltimore. And within two years, World War II began to have an impact on the U.S. economy. War and the defense industry stimulated production, and Consolidated was called upon to meet higher demands. Charles M. Cohn became president of Consolidated in 1942, serving four years. During the war, the company had to use lower quality fuels to meet the demands of increased production. Electric and gas sales soared.

In 1946, the year after the war's end, William Schmidt, Jr., was elected president and chairman. At this time, gas use was still in steady decline nationwide, while the cost of manufacturing gas had risen nearly 300 percent in two decades. Consolidated was still expanding its capacity to provide service to new customers. In 1948 its third 60,000-kilowatt generating unit was completed and a fourth was ordered. Another, larger plant was under way at the company's Westport, Maryland site. The company set a record for new property expenditures in 1948—more than $21 million.

With revenues and energy demands on the rise, net earnings declined. The company had been working to discontinue the production and sale of manufactured gas and to convert to natural gas, and the conversion was completed in 1950. It was an enormous undertaking that involved changes in equipment from pipelines to appliances; the total cost of the conversion to the company was $9 million. The benefits were many: natural gas is less expensive, more efficient, and cleaner burning than manufactured gas. The lower cost of natural gas led to increased consumption. Also in 1950, Charles P. Crane became president, with Schmidt continuing as chairman. In 1951 the 20-year effort to convert Baltimore's electric system from direct current (DC) to alternating current (AC) was completed.

In 1955 the company's name was changed to Baltimore Gas and Electric Company. The following year, BGE formed one of the world's largest fully integrated power pools when it signed a contract with seven other electricity distributors to inaugurate the Pennsylvania–New Jersey–Maryland Interconnection.

1960s–1980s: Steady Growth

The 1960s saw more steady growth, marked by construction of a new BGE headquarters in 1964 and the announcement in 1967 that BGE would build Maryland's first nuclear-powered generating plant. The two-unit facility was built at Calvert Cliffs, about 60 miles south of Baltimore, and represented an enormous investment. The first of these units was in operation by 1975. In its first year, it produced more than a third of the company's generation and reduced customer fuel rate adjustment charges by more than $50 million. The second unit began operation in 1977.

Demand had continued to grow, and in 1981 the Safe Harbor Hydroelectric Project started a four-year expansion project. In an effort to improve profitability, BGE trimmed its operating budget in 1982 and 1983 and sought diversification into other businesses. In 1983 however, the Maryland Public Service Commission turned down BGE's application to form a holding company, stating that Maryland law forbids such a structure for utilities. The holding company reorganization would have enabled BGE to diversify freely.

The Brandon Shores Unit Number 1—a coal-burning electricity-generating plant—opened in 1984, helping to eliminate the company's dependence on foreign oil. A second Brandon Shores unit started up in 1991. In 1983 about 60 percent of the company's operating revenue was in electric power sales, and around the same time gas sales began to slump. In 1986 BGE formed Constellation Holdings, Inc., a subsidiary through which it planned to expand its nonutility interests, despite being denied the right to form a holding company.

By the mid-1980s, problems with the Calvert Cliffs nuclear power plant began to emerge. The Nuclear Regulatory Commission (NRC) fined the company for procedural and equipment violations at the plant in 1985. The NRC proposed further fines for alleged violations at the Calvert Cliffs plant in 1988. By year's end, the NRC placed Calvert Cliffs on its watch list of plants "warranting close agency monitoring" because of "declining performance." In 1988 these units were providing 40 percent of BGE's fuel mix and were the company's lowest-cost producers of power.

Calvert Cliffs' second unit was shut down in 1989, after stress and erosion cracks were discovered. The NRC identified a number of equipment and managerial problems at the plant, and the first unit was also closed for inspection.

The shutdown of Calvert Cliffs forced BGE to purchase more expensive electricity from other utilities. The cost incurred by the idled plant ran to $300,000 a day, and BGE sought numerous rate increases that were held up by debate. In addition, the NRC fined BGE for safety-related violations, one of which involved a worker's death. Startup of Calvert Cliffs' first unit eased somewhat the expense of purchased—rather than produced—electricity, but the facility's second unit was closed until May 1991.

BGE's credit ratings were lowered in 1990, the result of financial deterioration brought on by the extended Calvert Cliffs outage, cost of energy replacements, and uncertainty about approval of rate increases. In December 1990 Maryland regulators approved base rate increases totaling $201 million annually and authorized BGE to apply for surcharges to recover a portion of its purchased power costs.

With the startup of Calvert Cliffs' second unit in 1991, BGE's prospects improved. A second coal-fired unit at Brandon Shores also went into operation early in 1991. Debate was ongoing among regulatory officials regarding how much of the costs of the Calvert Cliffs failure could be passed on to customers. The company estimated total replacement power costs ran to $415 million.

Deregulation in the 1990s

In 1992 the company faced a dramatic shift in the way it did business when Congress passed the Federal Energy Policy Act. The act permitted competition in the wholesale power market and, by allowing retail competition, signaled the end of regulated, regional monopolies. Although its relatively small size and regional coverage would work against it in a competitive market, analysts felt BGE's customer mix could be a benefit. Because it had few industrial customers, BGE would not be so much at the mercy of large manufacturers who would set one supplier against another in a bidding war. However, BGE apparently felt the disadvantage of its size and responded to the act's passage by looking for a partner that would help cut costs through economies of scale.

In the mid-1990s, the electricity market was growing at a rate of only two percent a year. BGE focused on expanding its gas customer base and managed to increase that division's profits 25 percent in 1995. However, the company's real estate investments were performing poorly, which pulled down overall company earnings that year.

BGE forged an agreement to merge with Washington, D.C.-based Potomac Electric Power Co. (PEPCO) in 1995. The two companies anticipated making substantial staff cuts to reduce overlapping jobs; those cuts and savings from eliminating related redundancies were expected to save $1.3 billion over 10 years. Stockholders approved the deal in 1996, and the Federal Energy Regulatory Commission gave its okay in 1997. Maryland followed suit with conditional approval, but the process was held up by conditions placed on the merger by the District of Columbia. BGE and PEPCO had proposed splitting the expected savings from the merger evenly between customers and shareholders. D.C. regulators, however, wanted customers to get a larger share, and made that a condition of the merger. BGE and PEPCO would not agree to that condition, and the two companies called off the merger in December 1997. The companies had invested more than two years and $100 million in arranging the merger. Analysts considered both companies as

likely candidates for other merger or takeover deals in the coming years.

In 1998 BGE began a major organizational restructuring that split the company into three discrete units: utility operations, power generation, and unregulated subsidiaries. "All the rules under which we operate are being rewritten," Christian H. Poindexter, BGE's chairman and CEO, said to *Baltimore Sun* correspondent Kevin McQuaid. "That's what's driving this." Part of the reorganization entailed the creation of Constellation Enterprises Inc., a holding company for the utility's unregulated subsidiaries. The company expected to continue to make management and organizational changes in 1998 as part of its preparation for competition, which Maryland had slated to begin in 2002.

Principal Subsidiaries

Constellation Enterprises Inc.; BGE Energy Projects & Services, Inc.; BGE Home Products and Services, Inc.; BGE Commercial Building Systems; Constellation Energy Source.

Further Reading

Hamilton, Martha M., "PEPCO, Baltimore Gas Cancel Two-Year-Old Plan to Merge," *Washington Post,* December 23, 1997, p. 1.

King, Thomson, *Consolidated of Baltimore: 1816–1950,* Baltimore, Md.: Consolidated Gas Electric Light and Power Company of Baltimore.

McQuaid, Kevin L., "BGE to Split Itself into Three Parts," *Baltimore Sun,* March 7, 1998, p. 16C.

Sparks, Debra, "Baltimore Gas & Electric: Time to Unplug," *Financial World,* August 1, 1995, pp. 20–21.

—Carol I. Keeley
—updated by Susan Windisch Brown

BANANA REPUBLIC

Banana Republic Inc.

1 Harrison Street
San Francisco, California 94105-1602
U.S.A.
(415) 777-0250
Fax: (415) 896-0322

Wholly Owned Subsidiary of The Gap, Inc.
Incorporated: 1978 as Banana Republic Travel and
    Safari Clothing Company
Employees: 3,800
Sales: $282 million (1997 est.)
SICs: 5651 Family Clothing Stores

A subsidiary of The Gap, Inc. since 1983, Banana Republic Inc. "has long been to khaki what Levi's was to denim," according to Mel Ziegler, who, along with his wife, Patricia, founded the company in 1978. Part of a growing wave of national retailers, Banana Republic has, in recent years, branched out to sell housewares, personal care items, footwear and dressy as well as casual clothes and is one of The Gap's most successful ventures in the specialty fashion market. Banana Republic's niche is with high-income, over-25, white-collar professionals, 32 percent of whom have an annual household income of more than $100,000. Another 22 percent of the company's customers earn at least $75,000, and yet another 19 percent are in the $50,000 to $75,000 range.

The Early Years: Selling a Concept As Well As Clothing

The company owes it origins to Mel Ziegler's search for a replacement for his well-worn military surplus jacket. Ziegler finally purchased a British Burma jacket in a Sydney "disposal" store, which his wife altered to downplay the garment's military look and "play up its sensibility as a comfortable, utilitarian, everyday garment," as stated in Banana Republic's historical documents. Family and friends admired the jacket's look, prompting the couple to create and open the Banana Republic Travel and Safari Clothing Company in Mill Valley, San Francisco.

From the start, Banana Republic sold a concept as well as clothing; the look was unique, and trade dress identity strong. The company's original catalogues stood out for their ink and watercolor drawings of flight jackets, photo-journalist's vests, paratrooper briefcases, and gurkha shorts—all of which were accompanied by travelogue-type copy highlighting the theme of travel and adventure. All items were constructed of natural fibers. As the premier outfitters of travel and safari wear from 1978–1983, Banana Republic was a forerunner in the specialty fashion market which appealed to the 25–44 year old crowd of young professionals.

Acquired By The Gap in the 1980s

By late 1983, when The Gap—under president Millard S. Drexler and chairman Donald G. Fisher—acquired Banana Republic, there were five Banana Republic stores in California, and the company's annual sales had grown to $10 million. The new subsidiary was an immediate boon to the then-floundering Gap, which was struggling to broaden its market beyond a well-established teenage customer base. Banana Republic experienced meteoric sales growth and rapid expansion for the next three years, with sales per square foot peaking in 1986 at about $750, compared to an industry average of about $235. New stores were opened whose interiors were designed to recreate the adventurous setting of the outback. Bush planes hung from ceilings; thatched-roofed huts, jeeps and ersatz wild animals were arranged on the display floor. Catalogue publications increased. The Zieglers stayed on as president and vice president of the new Banana Republic subsidiary, with creative autonomy to run the company.

But beginning in 1986, amid a period of apparel industry slump, Banana Republic's safari and khaki concept began to lose its appeal. In-store sales, which had been at 15 percent of The Gap totals and 20 percent of its profits, shrank as the product line rapidly lost popularity. Gap stock sold at a "liar's discount," with a price-earnings ratio more than 10 percent below the industry's. *Trips*, a travel magazine intended to promote the Banana

Republic line, was launched and discontinued after its first issue and the resignation of two associate editors. The Gap gave the management at Banana Republic most of 1987 to make adjustments, but sales continued to slide. Only 15 new stores were opened in 1987, instead of the planned 25.

Banana Republic, which had been the hottest retail concept around, was eating away at its parent company's profits, showing a loss for 1988 despite the opening of many new stores. Sales totaled only between 10 and 15 percent of The Gap's totals in 1987 and 1988. In an attempt to shift the company from a purveyor of safari wear to traditional travel and casual wear, Drexler took on the additional role of CEO of Banana Republic, succeeding Fisher—who remained chairman and chief executive of The Gap. The Gap's management decided to get away from Banana Republic's basics look, and tried out new items in new colors, but the unpopularity of the new merchandise, coupled with inadequate inventories, continued to hobble Banana Republic. In April of 1988, Mel and Patricia Ziegler resigned, citing "fundamental creative and cultural differences with the management of The Gap," according to an April 1988 article which appeared in the *Daily News Record*.

The Turn of the Decade and A New Corporate Identity

The search for a solid corporate identity began to take shape in 1988, when The Gap brought in a new management team, including Tasha Polizzi, formerly of Ruff Hewn and Polo/Ralph Lauren, as vice-president and director of design and product at Banana Republic. Although Polizzi stayed in the post for only a year, citing creative differences in updating the direction of the chain's merchandise, the new team made some successful moves, including a decisive shift away from the safari motif. In an effort to maintain traffic in the chain's then-100 stores, it knocked down prices substantially to clear out old merchandise and to develop and test new merchandise. The new lines, which included brighter-colored casual wear and cruise line apparel, were moved to the front of the stores, while the more traditional khaki and safari apparel were placed in the back. Stores were refurbished to reflect a more sophisticated, modern sensibility. In 1989, the catalogue was discontinued.

The early nineties saw a positive turn-around for Banana Republic, under the direction of Richard L. McNally, its executive vice-president and top official. Menswear sales were much improved with the first comparable-sales increase in five quarters occurring in the first quarter of 1990. The chain generated same-store sales growth in line with The Gap's total of 5 percent beginning in 1991, a time during which yearly sales at Banana Republic were estimated at about $300 million. Banana Republic's operating income was higher in 1992 than the previous year, and the chain expanded to include 162 stores nationwide. The company began further efforts at diversifying its product lines, and innerwear, sleepwear and accessories were added to the men's and women's lines as well as a variety of looks suitable for the office. Advertising campaigns were adopted to sell the company's new relaxed, urban lifestyle image. Two received notoriety for their exceptional quality, including one which specifically targeted the gay community.

Continuing Growth in the 1990s

By 1994, Banana Republic was racking up the biggest gains of any subsidiary at The Gap, and formulated plans to open 20 new stores a year for the next several years. In 1995, it opened its first store outside the U.S. in Alberta, Canada, and rolled out its Body Care collection. In 1996, it introduced separate gender-specific concept stores, Banana Republic Men and Banana Republic Women. The women's mix had by then grown to include career suiting, casual wear, shoes, belts, handbags, lingerie, and luggage. In keeping with its story line, all items in the body care collection were perfumed with a scent called "Classic."

By 1996, there were more than 200 Banana Republic stores in the U.S., as well as five in Canada; they had a total estimated sales volume of more than $500 million. Menswear still accounted for 50 percent of all sales, and stores had begun to offer free alterations and personal shopping assistants. Home merchandise items were introduced into a handful of stores during the holiday season, such as formally dressed tables and beds in fabrics popular from the men's and women's clothing collections. Some negative press was garnered when Banana Republic ran an ad campaign featuring Senator Ben Nighthorse Campbell at a time when Fisher had legislative business before the Senate, and again when several articles appeared citing the fact that Banana Republic employed maquiladora workers to produce some of their goods. But the company took both criticisms in stride, without compromising its positive trend. In 1997, "BR Athletic" was introduced, adding athletic clothing and footwear, a move mirrored by mall favorites and competitors such as Eddie Bauer, L.L. Bean and J. Crew. Donald Fisher was named National Retail Federation's Gold Medal winner, and Jeanne Jackson moved into the position of chief executive officer mid-year, while at the same time announcing the company's intent to open 30 stores a year to add to the 226 then in existence.

By early 1998, that number had grown to 40, according to Jackson, who said that the company was planning 20 percent growth a year. Among these new stores, there were plans for a new type of store, the flagship, first introduced in San Francisco, Chicago and Waikiki in 1997. Flagship stores were larger than previous Banana Republic retail locations, averaging 25,000 to 35,00 square feet and featuring all of the company's merchandise lines under one roof. Their interior design reflected the look and feel of their distinctive communities, while incorporating the chain's signature features—super-sleek fixtures, lots of polished metal, neoclassical arches, and an overall spare design. The Chicago store, for example, incorporated the glass and steel staircase from the original Michigan Avenue store, had a facade whose vertical lines pay tribute to the city's modern architecture, and showcased art from local artists. In San Francisco, the unit was designed to replicate an upscale home, with separate rooms used to display the different styles of clothing.

Additional flagships were planned for New York, Boston and Philadelphia in 1998, while some of the smaller retail locations were slated to grow in size from around 10,000 square feet to units that were twice as large or larger. The number of stores was projected to break the three hundred mark, and there were plans to reintroduce the company's catalogue. As the end of the century approached, Banana Republic was poised to remain a strong presence in the chain store apparel market, an innovator in the area of specialty merchandise, and the marketer of a lifestyle.

Further Reading

Barrett, Joyce, "Banana Republic ad Ignites Ethics Question," *Women's Wear Daily,* April 4, 1996, p. 9

Busillo, Teresa, "Banana Republic Makes Home in New York," *Home Textiles Today,* September 22, 1997, p. 2.

Dunn, Brian, "Banana Republic Starts Opening in Canada," *Women's Wear Daily,* February 9, 1995, p. 2.

Edelson, Sharon, "Banana Republic Said in Talks for Space in Rockefeller Center," *Women's Wear Daily,* March 6, 1998, p.6.

——, "Banana Republic's 34th Street Flourish," *Women's Wear Daily,* April 2, 1998, p. 19.

Finkelstein, Anita J., "Banana Republic Brings Miami Beach its Own Style," *Women's Wear Daily,* February 22, 1996, p. 17.

Hammond, Teena and Kristi Ellis, "High Tech and High Design; Gap, Banana Republic; New Store Strategies," *Women's Wear Daily,* November 26, 1997, p. 4.

Herbert, Bob, "In America; Sweatshop Beneficiaries," *The New York Times,* July 24, 1995, p. A13.

Kagan, Cara, "Banana Republic to Launch Bath Bunch," *Women's Wear Daily,* February 17, 1995, p. 5.

Palmieri, Jean E., "The Makeover on 34th Street," *Daily News Record,* April 8, 1998, p. 5.

Ruben, Howard, "Gap Sees $2B Sales; Men's the Backbone," *Daily News Record,* May 30, 1990, p. 2.

Sheridan, Mary Beth, "Riding the Ripples of a Border Boom; Foreign Factories are Moving Deeper into Mexico," *Los Angeles Times,* June 9, 1997, p. A1.

Turk, Rose-Marie, "Banana Republic Launches its Third Store for Women," *Women's Wear Daily,* October 7, 1996, p. 20.

—Carrie Rothburd

BANYAN®

Banyan Systems Inc.

120 Flanders Road
P.O. Box 5013
Westborough, Massachusetts 01581-5013
U.S.A.
(508) 898-1000
Fax: (508) 898-1755
Web site: http://www.banyan.com

Public Company
Incorporated: 1983
Employees: 410
Sales: $74.3 million (1997)
Stock Exchanges: NASDAQ
Ticker Symbol: BNYN
SICs: 7372 Prepackaged Software; 7379 Computer
    Related Services, Not Elsewhere Classified

Banyan Systems Inc. designs, develops, and markets standards-based computer-network directory and messaging products. In the late 1990s it was describing itself as the premier provider of enterprise directory products and services, enabling organizations to integrate diverse computing resources into unified, global networks. The company estimated that it had about 7,000 customers in 1997, with about seven million users worldwide. After a decade of success with its VINES network software package, Banyan lost market share to Windows-supported software and saw its revenues fall by half in three years. The company expected to be profitable again in 1998, however, and it was expanding its service arm.

Private Company: 1983–92

Banyan Systems was founded in 1983 by David Mahoney, a Data General Corp. manager involved in building computer software that focused on communications problems, and two associates, Lawrence Floryan and Anand Jagannathan. The three men sublet the office in Westborough, Massachusetts, where Jonathan Sachs had recently developed the Lotus 1-2-3 electronic spreadsheet. Within 40 days after leaving Data General, Mahoney had secured $2.5 million in financing from Greylock Management Corp. and Chatham Venture Corp. (The company was named for the tropical tree that drops vines which then grow their own roots; VINES was the name of Banyan's first product.)

In October 1984 Banyan Systems began shipping its "virtual networking system" (VINES) to link IBM and IBM-compatible personal computers. The software-driven system enabled office workers to retrieve information stored in any of the linked PCs, without having to know exactly where such information lay and without having to learn new instructions. A 32-bit computer called a network server directed the electronic traffic. The system also included StreetTalk, software that allowed users to issue computer commands in plain English and to use shared computer peripherals such as printers and data-storage devices. Besides the network server, the only hardware needed was a circuit board placed in the PC. The VINES system, which retailed for $17,000, could also be connected to other office networks.

One of Banyan Systems' first customers was Continental Grain Co., which in 1985 bought VINES to wire together 800 PCs. Most companies, however, eschewed the UNIX-based system and purchased simpler, DOS-based networking products. Banyan, according to one critic in a 1991 *Forbes* article, did a terrible job of marketing, relying on word of mouth, while IBM, Novell Inc., and Microsoft Corp. spent millions of dollars publicizing their own networks. In 1990 Banyan abandoned further development of its network server and said it would lay off about 40 of its 550 employees.

Even with its problems, however, Banyan Systems had sales of $80 million and net income of $3.8 million in 1989. This grew to $98.2 million and $4.7 million, respectively, in 1990, and by the end of the year the VINES system was being supported by more than 40 hardware platforms. Because this system could seamlessly attach PCs to minicomputers and mainframes of differing makes across a wide area, Banyan was well-positioned to profit in the coming era of bigger, more complex networks. By contrast, its name-brand competitors had been selling systems suitable only for smaller, local area networks.

In 1991 Banyan Systems introduced a VINES version for computers running IBM's OS/2 operating system. These computers were also able to use StreetTalk software, the company's global naming service that allowed a user anywhere on a VINES network to communicate directly with other computers without having to know their location or specify access routes to them. VINES allowed users to find and communicate with each other in seconds, a technically sophisticated feature that Novell's rival NetWare lacked.

Banyan Systems enjoyed its fifth successive profitable year in 1991. Software sales now outpaced hardware sales by two to one (compared to 50–50 in 1990), and the company held 7.5 percent of the $1.2-billion market for network software. While this represented only one-eighth of Novell's share of the market, Banyan, according to Mahoney, had a share of the market equal to Novell's for large networks of 300 to 600 personal computers. Also in 1991, the Marine Corps used VINES during the Persian Gulf War to link 350 PCs in the region, transmitting almost immediately the equivalent of 300 pages of orders that until recently had taken hours to deliver electronically.

Transition from VINES to ENS: 1992–96

Banyan Systems went public in August 1992, raising $28 million by selling common stock at $10.50 a share. The following month the company announced its Enterprise Network Services (ENS) server and software, aimed at integrating previously incompatible computer networks into a single, manageable, global, enterprise-wide network. The company became a supplier as well as a competitor of Novell by offering ENS for NetWare so that this local area network operating system could become much more powerful, linking an entire corporation's computers, including minicomputers and mainframe systems as well as PCs. ENS for NetWare retailed initially for $3,995, plus an additional amount based on the number of users, from $295 for five users to $3,495 for 250 users.

Banyan Systems reported record revenues of $113.5 million and record net income of $8.2 million in 1992. The following year it raised these figures to $127.8 million and $13 million, respectively. Some of the revenue came from fees paid by the vendors of the more than 400 hardware platforms and more than 3,000 software packages certified by the company as "VINES-compliant." In February 1994 Banyan purchased Beyond Inc., a producer of sophisticated offerings for electronic mail, for

$17.5 million in cash. Beyond's key product was BeyondMail, considered one of the best electronic-mail programs for managing work flow.

Although seemingly healthy, Banyan Systems was entering a more challenging era in 1994 because recent versions of Novell's NetWare and Microsoft's new Windows NT operating system included far greater capability for managing large networks of computers and peripherals. While Banyan's revenues set a new record of $150.1 million in 1994, net income dropped to $5 million. In February 1995 the company conceded the network operating-system market to Novell and Microsoft and officially recast itself as a network-services provider, centered around key components of its ENS: StreetTalk; Intelligent Messaging, a message transport engine; Distributed Enterprise Management Architecture, a network-management suite; and security and system-administration tools. However, revenues slipped to $129.7 million for the year, and the company lost $21.4 million. In November 1996 Mahoney resigned as chairman, president, and chief executive of Banyan.

Banyan Systems retained a number of assets, based on the technical superiority and power of VINES. VINES required only about one-third the number of network administrators as competing products in late 1995, and its users almost unanimously hailed the StreetTalk, intelligent-messaging, and security capabilities. A Banyan executive, citing the superiority of StreetTalk to other directories, suggested in 1996 that, rather than migrating to the Windows NT platform, its customers should use Windows NT as an operating system within a Banyan VINES network. This advice found little favor, however, among customers who feared the company and its products would simply disappear; as one systems administrator put it, "We liked VINES, but we didn't want to be the last dopes using the product."

Banyan Systems in the Late 1990s

Banyan Systems' revenues dropped to $105.4 million and its losses to $27 million in 1996, despite laying off about a quarter of its work force. William Ferry, the new president and chief executive officer hired in February 1997, cut the number of employees by another 22 percent. By mid-year, the majority of the company's software revenues were coming from sales of StreetTalk for Windows NT, which was introduced in September 1996 as the first corporate-wide directory system for Windows NT.

A promising new product at Banyan was Switchboard, a White and Yellow pages directory for the Internet, which it introduced in February 1996 and made available free on a Web site. Switchboard enabled Internet users to locate individuals or businesses nationwide from a database of more than 100 million listings. This site also provided free e-mail, free Web pages, and a directory of Web sites. Banyan also introduced, in 1997, Intranet Connect, Intranet-service software to access network files, printers, and e-mail using a standard Web browser, and Intranet Protect, a Web-server software solution enabling organizations to easily protect and share intranet information over their enterprise network. Still, revenues plunged to $74.3 million in 1997. The net loss of $16.9 million included a pretax charge of $8 million to provide for severance costs. Banyan's stock, as high as $26.50 a share in 1993, fell below $2 a share in the spring of 1997.

These figures concealed some good news. The last half of 1997 was profitable, and the company's service business grew. Switchboard was among the top 25 destinations in 1997 for both home and business users and the tenth most visited Web site by home users in January 1998. VINES still had 3,000 customers, with seven million users, and one study estimated that it would cost up to 15 times more per user to switch to NT machines than to integrate new NT servers into VINES. Banyan ended the year with $11 million in the bank and a new $15-million credit line. Moreover, in March 1998 HarbourVest Partners LLC, a Boston venture-capital firm, bought a 13 percent stake in the company for $10 million. Banyan made money in the first quarter of 1998, its third consecutive quarter of profit. Furthermore, as of September 1997 the company had no long term debt and hence, virtually no interest expenses.

Banyan Systems' products in 1997 fell into two major categories: network operating system products and intranet products. The former were integrating mainframes, minicomputers, workgroup networks, and personal computers into a unified computing environment and were based on enterprise directory services such as StreetTalk and Intelligent Messaging (for both Windows NT and VINES). All of the company's enterprise directory services were integrated with the StreetTalk directory, including messaging, management, security, local and wide area communications, and host connectivity. Banyan's intranet products, Intranet Connect and Intranet Product, enabled its customers to utilize Internet standards to allow people to contact other people and information in a reliable and secure manner over the Intranet. All these products were fully integrated with Year 2000 solutions by mid-1998.

Banyan Systems was also offering upgrade and subscription programs for enhanced versions of StreetTalk and other product offerings and was selling and supporting several network application programs that were integrated with its enterprise network services. It was actively encouraging independent software vendors, system integrators, and system vendors to develop and market application software for use with StreetTalk, VINES, and BeyondMail and provide developers with development tools to assist them in producing programs integrated with Banyan's enterprise networking program. To aid these companies in marketing their products to Banyan's customer base, the company was publishing an application directory that included more than 5,000 software programs running in Banyan environments.

Banyan Systems was maintaining technical-response centers in Westborough, Tokyo, Sydney, and Crawley, England, and it was also engaged in consulting and professional services. Of its 1997 revenues, software accounted for 78 percent and services for 21 percent. International sales, made by distributors in 75 countries, accounted for 29 percent of the total. Banyan had

about 50 sales and support offices in major cities in the United States, Canada, Great Britain, France, Germany, the Netherlands, Australia, Malaysia, and Japan.

In February 1997 Banyan Systems announced a new user-based pricing program providing greater flexibility of platform deployment and a simplified purchasing process, with user-based licensing as an alternative to the company's server-based licensing. This was intended to provide customers with the flexibility to choose the pricing model that best suited the needs of their particular computing environment. In 1998 Banyan products were installed in nearly half of all Fortune 1000 companies.

Principal Subsidiaries

Banyan Enterprise Networks (South Africa); Banyan Securities Corp.; Banyan Systems (Deutschland); Banyan Systems do Brasil Ltda.; Banyan Systems (France) S.A.R.L.; Banyan Systems (Holland) B.V.; Banyan Systems (Korea) Co., Ltd.; Banyan Systems S.A. de C.V. (Mexico); Banyan Systems (Taiwan), Inc.; Banyan Systems (UK) Ltd.; Banyan Systems Asia-Pacific Inc.; Banyan Systems Asia Pacific Ltd. (Hong Kong); Banyan Systems International Inc.; Beyond Inc.; Coordinate.com Inc.; Nihon Banyan Systems K.K. (Japan); Switchboard Inc.

Further Reading

Bailey, Steve, and Steven Syre, ''Banyan Site Is a Hit, But Misses on Profits,'' *Boston Globe,* May 20, 1998, pp. C1, C5.
Burns, Christine, ''Banyan Continues Quest to Stay Afloat,'' *Network World,* April 13, 1998, p. 12.
Churbuck, David, ''Wider Area Networks,'' *Forbes,* February 18, 1991, p. 106.
Day, Charles R., Jr., ''New Tacks Make It Easier to Tie PCs,'' *Industry Week,* November 26, 1984, pp. 86, 88.
DiDio, Laura, ''Vines Loses Grip,'' *Computerworld,* November 20, 1995, pp. 1, 127.
DiDio, Laura, and Stewart Deck, ''Mahoney Shaken from Banyan Tree,'' *Computerworld,* November 11, 1996, p. 16.
McCright, John S., ''David C. Mahoney: Can't Sit Still,'' *Boston Business Journal,* March 10, 1995, p. 19.
Miller, Stephen C., ''Managing Systems with Thousands of Users,'' *New York Times,* September 27, 1992, Sec. 3, p. 8.
Morrisey, Jane, ''Banyan to Drop Its LAN Hardware Development,'' *PC Week,* October 15, 1990, p. 4.
Rifkin, Glenn, ''Little Software Maker with a Loud Voice,'' *New York Times,* December 26, 1991, pp. D1, D7.
Senolof, Marcie, ''Users, Developers Riled by Banyan,'' *Communications Week,* February 22, 1993, pp. 1, 56–57.
Smith, Joel, ''PC Users Can Look Up to 'Net—Via Switchboard,'' *Detroit News,* April 8, 1996, p. F9.
Wexler, Joanie M., ''Banyan Set to Ensnare OS/2 in Vines,'' *Computerworld,* March 25, 1991, pp. 1, 96.

—Robert Halasz

Bausch & Lomb Inc.

One Lincoln First Square
Rochester, New York 14601
U.S.A.
(716) 338-6000
Fax: (716) 338-6007
(800) 828-6974
Web site: http://www.bausch.com

Public Company
Incorporated: 1853 as Bausch & Lomb Optical Co.
Employees: 13,000
Sales: $2 billion (1997)
Stock Exchanges: New York
Ticker Symbol: BOL
SICs: 3851 Ophthalmic Goods; 2834 Pharmaceutical
　　Preparations; 3842 Surgical Appliances & Supplies

Bausch & Lomb Inc. is the United States' leading ophthalmic goods firm and stands as one of the premiere contact lens manufacturers in the world. The company also produces Ray-Ban sunglasses, the best-selling line of sunglasses in the world, as well as several other brands of high-end sunglasses. As of the late 1990s, the company was restructuring to focus on products related to the eye. It sold such unrelated units as its skin care products and its oral care business and directed acquisitions toward high-margin eye care products, such as those for ophthalmic surgery. The company's pharmaceutical unit was also narrowing its focus to prescription and over-the-counter ophthalmics.

Early History

Bausch & Lomb Optical Co., an eyeglass store and manufacturer of eyeglass frames, was founded in 1853 by two German immigrants, John Jacob Bausch and Henry Lomb, in Rochester, New York. Bausch's son Edward learned to make microscopes, and the company prospered after it began to manufacture them. In 1890 Edward Bausch contacted Carl

Zeiss, a German optics firm, and soon arranged for Bausch & Lomb to license Zeiss's patents, with the exclusive rights to the U.S. market. The most important patents were to Zeiss's new photographic lens and its first prism binoculars. Bausch & Lomb expanded, opening offices in Chicago, Boston, New York City, and Frankfurt, Germany. Bausch & Lomb gradually became a leading name in optics in the United States, supplying microscopes to schools and laboratories and manufacturing the U.S. Navy's first telescopic gun sights.

In the early 1900s, Zeiss perfected the military range finder. Impressed by U.S. manufacturing expertise, Zeiss eventually decided that, rather than build its own factory, it would allow Bausch & Lomb to manufacture range finders in the United States. In 1907 Zeiss bought 20 percent of Bausch & Lomb, granting the company free use of Zeiss patents in the United States. Zeiss, on the other hand, sold to the rest of the world and was paid in dividends rather than royalty payments. Bausch & Lomb also sent technicians to Germany for training at Zeiss laboratories. Military products accounted for only a small amount of Bausch & Lomb's production, but as the only U.S. manufacturer of many optical products, production was nevertheless vital to the U.S. military. As a result, the U.S. Navy stationed technical experts in the company's plant in 1912.

Bausch & Lomb's arrangement with Zeiss unraveled after the outbreak of World War I. The company had sold the Allies equipment without Zeiss's approval in Europe, which was not one of Bausch & Lomb's markets. In 1915 Zeiss sold its 20 percent share back to Bausch & Lomb, and until 1921, the two companies had no dealings with one another (although Bausch & Lomb continued to use Zeiss patents). Because of the war, Bausch & Lomb became the major U.S. supplier of scientific precision glass, from which the lenses used by the military were ground. After the war, the other U.S. companies that had learned to make the glass stopped production, making Bausch & Lomb the only producer of scientific precision glass in the Western Hemisphere. In 1921 Zeiss made all of its military patents exclusively available to Bausch & Lomb for use in the United States.

In 1926 John Jacob Bausch died, and Edward Bausch became chairman of the board. In the 1937 Bausch & Lomb went public, selling $3.6 million worth of stock to raise working capital. At the time the company made 17,000 products, from eyeglasses to spectroscopes. Bausch & Lomb made 28 percent of U.S. eyeglass lenses and a large percentage of the country's microscopes and binoculars. Even after the offering, the company was still closely held, with family members owning significant percentages of Bausch & Lomb stock and holding most top management positions.

Preparing for World War II

During the late 1930s, as Europe once again headed toward war, Bausch & Lomb focused on becoming self-sufficient by searching for U.S. sources of most materials to make optical glass and by stockpiling two year's worth of foreign supplies. During this time, the firm emerged as a leading provider of professional photographic lenses, particularly for the film industry. Bausch & Lomb's Cinephor coated projection lenses were used by almost all U.S. movie houses, while its high-speed lenses were used for projecting background scenes. Bausch & Lomb was awarded an honorary Oscar for these contributions. With help from these new products, company sales increased from $16.2 million in 1938 to about $21 million in 1940.

Despite these accomplishments, Bausch & Lomb's image was tarnished somewhat by a 1940 federal suit regarding its relationship with Zeiss. The U.S. Justice department charged both companies with antitrust violations because of their agreed-upon division of world markets. The government alleged that this resulted in inflated prices and also questioned the propriety of a German company dictating the sales of optical products by a U.S. company. While denying any wrongdoing, Bausch & Lomb paid a fine and again severed its relationship with Zeiss. The company was expanding for a new rearmament program and bidding on navy contracts, and industry analysts assumed that Bausch & Lomb wanted the incident put behind it as quickly as possible.

During World War II Bausch & Lomb produced optical instruments, including range finders and field scopes. As one of the earliest manufacturers of high-quality sunglasses, the company also benefited from the use of Ray-Ban sunglasses by U.S. Army Air Corps pilots and General Douglas MacArthur.

During the war, the percentage of company output relating to the military soared, but by the early 1950s, military sales had fallen to 15 percent of the total. Sales had increased to about $48.5 million, and the firm had more than 150 prescription labs for grinding and polishing glass lenses throughout the United States. Bausch & Lomb spent less than 2 percent of sales on research and development. Meanwhile, as Japanese firms recovered from the war, they became competitive. In 1951 Bausch & Lomb realized it was slowly losing its competitive edge and began allocating more money—some of it borrowed—into research and development. As a result, the company moved into the growing electronic optics field in 1954. By the early 1960s the firm was spending approximately 6.5 percent of sales on research and development. Bausch & Lomb also upgraded its marketing department to determine customer demand prior to developing new product lines.

In 1959 William McQuilken became the first president not related to the families of Bausch & Lomb's founders. The firm dropped Optical from its title in 1961, reflecting its move into other technologies and measurements. Sales reached $70 million in 1962. The company moved into the school market, which was growing quickly and required inexpensive, rugged instruments. In 1963 the firm released a $12 microscope targeted at the elementary and secondary school market. The instrument, with features usually reserved for expensive models, was made of tough plastics. Bausch & Lomb released two additional school microscopes priced under $50. Company earnings were static for much of the 1960s, however, because low-margin ophthalmic products such as eyeglass lenses and frames still accounted for a sizable portion of its sales.

Development of Soft Contact Lenses in the 1960s

In 1966 Bausch & Lomb made its most important decision since World War II when it negotiated a license to make and sell contact lenses made from a fluid-absorbing hydrophilic plastic. The material had been invented in Czechoslovakia and Western Hemisphere rights were purchased by National Patent Development Corp., from whom Bausch & Lomb licensed them. Bausch & Lomb spent $3.3 million on research and development, learning how to make viable soft contact lenses from the material. Many people experienced so much discomfort with hard contact lenses that they refused to wear them. The company hoped soft contact lenses would garner a huge share of the contact lens market. Bausch & Lomb encountered a few difficulties at the beginning. Because soft contact lenses conformed to the shape of the cornea, people with irregularly shaped corneas initially could not wear them. Other problems cropped up, including eye infections. Further, the U.S. Food and Drug Administration (FDA) classified soft contact lenses as a drug, which meant that Bausch & Lomb's product encountered numerous regulatory hurdles. Nonetheless, many doctors greeted the new lenses with enthusiasm. The firm's Softlens contacts were released in 1971 and sold about 100,000 pairs that year.

Because of the excitement generated by soft contact lenses, Bausch & Lomb's stock tripled in value in less than a year and at one point sold for 75 times annual earnings. At that time, approximately 44 percent of Bausch & Lomb's sales came from scientific instruments, mostly optical instruments sold to medical, industrial, military, film, and educational customers. The company served as the major supplier of lenses for Xerox

Corp.'s copy machines. Bausch & Lomb also sold consumer goods, such as microscopes, binoculars, and rifle scopes.

By 1973 Softlens contact lenses accounted for 14 percent of company earnings and 51 percent of revenue. Bausch & Lomb had little competition and made roughly $14 per pair of contact lenses sold. The market for lenses was enormous; surveys found that more than 50 percent of Americans wore prescription glasses or contact lenses, and industry analysts predicted that large numbers of them might eventually get soft contact lenses. Yet the price of soft contacts—more than $300 including prescription and doctor's visit—held down sales. There was also slow acceptance of lenses among some doctors who had been offended by Bausch & Lomb's initial, high-pressure marketing. Additionally, certain doctors and lens wearers were disappointed with the slim selection of lenses offered. Bausch & Lomb worked hard to correct this, spending $3.5 million a year on Softlens research and development and hoping to offer at least five lenses. Despite these problems, trade sources estimated that 350,000 patients throughout the world bought Bausch & Lomb's soft contacts in 1973, and an additional 500,000 customers were added in 1974.

Competitors, however, were eager to enter such a large, untapped market. In 1974 Soft Lenses Inc. won FDA permission to produced soft lenses for vision correction. Warner-Lambert Co. received approval to produce lenses for therapeutic reasons and also applied to furnish vision-corrective lenses. Bausch & Lomb managed to maintain a large portion of its market share because of a three-year lead, name identification, and marketing strategies that reduced retailers' inventory costs. The company also cut wholesale prices by 25 percent, reducing retail of lenses by between $25 and $30 a pair. Despite price cuts, soft lenses accounted for 27 percent of company sales in 1979 and 63 percent of profits. By 1979 Bausch & Lomb still had a 55 to 65 percent share of the soft contact lens market, which had grown to $400 million a year. The firm was also selling gallons of lens cleaning and soaking solutions. Its saline solution had a 56 percent market share, its lens lubricant had 50 percent, and its daily cleaner 32 percent. In 1979 Bausch & Lomb began a lens fitting system that allowed 90 percent of new lens wearers to be fit with the firm's new Ultra Thin lenses with a single visit. The company also introduced a prescription version of its AmberMatic sunglasses, which darkened as light levels increased.

Diversification in the 1980s

In 1980 Daniel Gill, a former marketing specialist with Abbott Labs, became Bausch & Lomb's company chairman. He felt that the company was too dependent on contact lenses and too bloated by low-performance products. Gill restructured the company by selling off low-profit businesses. One of the first to go was prescription eyeglasses. Gill justified this change because the firm had missed a trend to plastic lenses and was also being pinched by cheaper imported lenses. Yet with its traditional business gone, the company went into upheaval, and many top managers left.

The market for soft contact lenses continued to grow more competitive as it grew larger. By 1982 competitors included such large companies as Johnson & Johnson, Revlon, and Ciba-Geigy. Although Bausch & Lomb continued to hold nearly half of the market, new competitors were introducing products Bausch & Lomb either did not have or had no lead on, such as gas-permeable hard lenses, extended-wear soft lenses, bifocal contacts and color-tinted contacts. The competitors pushed these products with expensive television advertising campaigns. While Bausch & Lomb's cost for producing soft contacts had dropped to $1.50 to $2 each, American Hydron reported that it was nearly finished with a system that would produce contacts for $1.

Bausch & Lomb moved quickly into the extended-wear lens market, an area in which it had been losing new lens wearers. While waiting for FDA approval of its own lens, Bausch & Lomb leased an extended-wear system from American Medical Optics. The lenses were lathe cut, not spin cast like the Softlens, and cost $7 to $8 a pair to manufacture. When FDA approval came in 1984, Bausch & Lomb displayed its marketing power by supplying new lenses to 90 percent of the U.S. outlets selling contact lenses within a month. Within four months the company's extended-wear lenses had 37 percent of the market and stood as the leading brand. Part of that success came through aggressive pricing. The lenses wholesaled for $20 a pair, while the industry average was $30. As a result, Bausch & Lomb was soon embroiled in a price war with rival CooperVision.

Sunglasses sales were also improving. The firm had signed a $50,000-a-year agreement with Unique Product Placement in 1982 to feature Ray-Bans in films. The Ray-Ban Wayfarer line did particularly well. The company sold 16,000 pairs in 1982, but after Tom Cruise wore them in the 1983 film *Risky Business*, sales jumped to 360,000. Wayfarers were also worn by actors on the *Miami Vice* and *Moonlighting* television series. By 1986 sales reached 1.5 million, and Ray-Ban's 40 lines accounted for one-third of the $500 million U.S. market for premium sunglasses.

Meanwhile restructuring within Bausch & Lomb continued. In 1983 the company entered a new business when it bought the Charles River Laboratory, the world's largest supplier of laboratory mice and rats, for $108 million in stock. Though the business was not related to optics, it offered a steady supply of cash and operating profit margins of more than 20 percent. In 1984 most of the $217 million instrument business was sold to its management, except for microscopes and telescopes. The unit had lost $16 million over the two preceding years.

Bausch & Lomb earned $74.7 million on sales of $698.9 million in 1986, despite a leveling off of soft contact lens sales. The market was damaged by reports of people wearing extended-wear lenses and subsequently developing eye infections. The biggest market for contacts, women between the ages of 18 and 25, began shrinking. The firm fought to maintain sales and market share by introducing new contact lens technologies. In 1987 it won FDA approval to sell lenses with a Teflon-like surface that protected against protein buildup and made the lenses more comfortable. Bausch & Lomb also tried new marketing strategies such as introducing disposable contact lenses meant to be worn for a week or two and then thrown out. The primary difference between the disposable and regular soft lenses was the packaging, which was less expensive and durable for the disposables. Bausch & Lomb faced tough competition for this niche, however. Johnson & Johnson beat them to market by introducing its Acuvue lenses before Bausch & Lomb's SeeQuence.

Despite the leveling off of the contact lens market, Bausch & Lomb continued to expand by moving into businesses using similar distribution methods, especially ear, mouth, and skin care products. The company's strategy was to offer technologically advanced products that had few competitors and therefore high margins. Bausch & Lomb also began focusing on sales outside of the United States, an area which accounted for only 17 percent of sales in 1984. In 1986 the firm agreed to a joint venture with Beijing Contact Lens Ltd. to produce contact lenses and solutions in China. Bausch & Lomb then bought Dr. Gerhard Mann Pharma, an ophthalmic drugs company based in West Germany, for $97 million. The firm also began designing and marketing products specifically for countries in Europe, Asia, and Latin America. For example, Bausch & Lomb had mainly sold adjustable metal-frame sunglasses in Japan because the firm's more popular plastic models did not offer comparable fit. In 1987 Bausch & Lomb redesigned its plastic sunglasses and sales took off.

In 1988 Bausch & Lomb bought Dental Research for $133 million. Included in this sale was Interplak, a patented, sophisticated electric toothbrush used to remove plaque. The device had been sold on the retail market, but Bausch & Lomb used dentists to let consumers know about it, and its sales climbed to approximately $110 million by 1989. In 1989 the firm acquired 80 percent of Voroba Hearing Systems, a maker of hearing aids. Bausch & Lomb also announced plans to introduce a line of sunglasses containing a synthetic version of melanin, the pigment that protects the skin from ultraviolet rays.

Rapid Growth in the Early 1990s

By 1990, sales outside of the United States accounted for 40 percent of the firm's total sales. When Bausch & Lomb began concentrating on international sales, it gave local managers more flexibility. One result was that European sales managers pushed for flashier styles of Ray-Ban sunglasses. These styles proved popular and fetched higher prices than in the United States. Partly due to this, operating income doubled in Europe between 1987 and 1990. In 1991 half of Ray-Ban's new styles were developed for international markets, and by 1992 Ray-Bans accounted for 40 percent of premium international sunglasses sales. Managers in China advised making contact lenses there inexpensive, in order to make money from volume rather than sales margin. As a result, lens sales in China were third in the world in 1992, after the United States and Japan.

By the early 1990s, Gill's restructuring seemed a clear success. Sales were growing more than 10 percent a year, the company was expanding internationally, and it had moved away from its dependence on contact lens sales. The company's pharmaceuticals were beginning to pay off their start-up costs, and the firm's debt was relatively low. By 1994 the company's stock price had tripled since 1981, including two stock splits. Gains in earnings had averaged almost 14 percent over the previous ten years. Gill boasted in 1994 to *Financial World* "I think the bulk of the world would give us credit for having moved the company from the Bausch & Lomb of the 1980s to

today." However, in a startling reversal, Gill was forced to resign in shame only a year later.

Sunglasses sales had begun to slow in 1992 and 1993, and the growth of disposable contact lenses (a market that Bausch & Lomb had declined to enter) had eaten into both B&L's sales of traditional contact lenses and its sales of contact lens solutions, which are not needed by users of disposable contact lenses. However, earnings in the mid-1990s continued to meet Gill's ambitious goal of 15 percent, a fact that seemed to reassure edgy analysts. The bubble burst a short time later when SEC investigations in 1994 and 1995 forced the company to restate their 1993 and 1994 sales and earnings figures, which led in turn to a lawsuit by the shareholders. Around the same time a class-action lawsuit was filed against Bausch & Lomb by customers upset about the company's practice of marketing one type of contact lens as several different products with a range of prices. Eventually, 17 states initiated deceptive-trade investigations.

Redirecting Efforts in the Late 1990s

In 1995 Gill resigned and was replaced by outsider William Waltrip, who set about restoring the company's tarnished image and boosting its faltering growth. The following year, the class-action suit was settled when Bausch & Lomb agreed to pay $68 million in restitution to customers. In 1997, the company ended the deceptive-trade investigations by agreeing to pay $100,000 to each of the states involved.

In 1996, Bausch & Lomb began to refocus on its eye-related products in earnest. It sold both its dental implant business and its oral care business, the former to a group of investors and the latter to Conair Corp. Although the company continued to acquire new businesses, its purchases all related to eye care. In 1996 it purchased the sports sunglasses producer Arnette Optic Illusions and a manufacturer of daily wear disposable contact lenses, Award plc. The following year, it acquired the sunglasses brand Killer Loop Eyewear from Benetton Sportsystem. Late in 1997 the company made two related acquisitions: the $300 million purchase of Chiron Vision Corporation, a manufacturer of equipment used in cataract and refractive surgery and products used to treat progressive eye disease, and the $380 million purchase of Storz Instrument Company, a manufacturer of ophthalmic surgical instruments, diagnostic equipment, intra-ocular lens implants, and ophthalmic pharmaceuticals. Early in 1998 the company combined the product lines of the two companies to form a new division: Bausch & Lomb Surgical. The pharmaceutical line of Storz was placed in Bausch & Lomb's pharmaceutical division.

In keeping with the company's efforts to divest its non-eye-related businesses, Bausch & Lomb announced its intention to sell its skin care business to the Andrew Jergens Company in 1998. Jergens agreed to pay $135 million cash and to assume certain liabilities for the Curel and Soft Sense brands.

Principal Divisions

Bausch & Lomb Pharmaceutical Division; Eyewear Division; Thin Film Technology Division; Vision Care Division; Bausch & Lomb Surgical.

Principal Subsidiaries

Arnette Optic Illusions, Inc.; Charles River Laboratories, Inc.; Dahlberg, Inc.; Polymer Technology Corp.; Revo, Inc.

Further Reading

"Back in Focus," *Financial World,* November 1, 1979.

"Bausch & Lomb," *Fortune,* October 1940.

"Bausch & Lomb to Acquire Chiron Vision for $300 Million," *Business Wire,* October 21, 1997.

"Bausch & Lomb: Hardball Pricing Helps it to Regain its Grip on Contact Lenses," *Business Week,* July 16, 1984.

Benoit, Ellen, "Through a Glass, Slowly," *Financial World,* November 28, 1989.

Du Bois, Peter C., "The Old Fish Eye," *Barron's,* November 25, 1974.

"Getting One-Up on the Japanese," *Business Week,* October 19, 1963.

Hirsch, James S., "Bausch & Lomb Applies an Above-die Neck Strategy," *Wall Street Journal,* February 27, 1990.

Jacob, Rahul, "Trust the Locals, Win Worldwide," *Fortune,* May 4, 1992.

Leinster, Colin, "A Tale of Mice and Lens," *Fortune,* September 28, 1987.

"Long Grind," *Time,* January 24, 1938.

Maremont, Mark, "Judgment Day at Bausch & Lomb," *Business Week,* December 25, 1995, p. 39.

"Optical Restraint of Trade?" *Time,* April 8, 1940.

Phalon, Richard, "Bausch & Lomb's Myopia," *Forbes,* December 5, 1994, p. 14.

Reingold, Jennifer, "Above the Neck: Can Bausch & Lomb Maintain Its Focus by Broadening Its Scope," *Financial World,* January 18, 1994, pp. 30–33.

——, "Bausch & Lomb: Clouded Vision," *Financial World,* May 23, 1995, pp. 16–17.

Reynes, Roberta, "New Contact Lens Competition Focuses on Bausch & Lomb," *Barron's,* August 1, 1983.

Troxell, Thomas N., Jr., "Broader Focus," *Barron's,* August 18, 1986.

Wilner, Richard, "Outlook Dimming for Bausch & Lomb," *New York Post,* April 24, 1997.

—Scott Lewis
—updated by Susan Windisch Brown

Bell Atlantic Corporation

1095 Avenue of the Americas
New York, New York 10036
U.S.A.
(212) 395-2121
Fax: (212) 466-2416
Web site: http://www.bellatlantic.com

Public Company
Incorporated: 1983
Employees: 141,600
Operating Revenues: $30.2 billion
Stock Exchanges: New York
Ticker Symbol: BEL
SICs: 3651 Household Audio & Video Equipment; 3661
    Telephone & Telegraph Apparatus; 3663 Radio & TV
    Communications Equipment; 4812 Radiotelephone
    Communications; 4813 Telephone Communications,
    Except Radiotelephones; 6719 Holding Companies;
    7372 Prepackaged Software

Bell Atlantic Corporation is growing ever-more prominent in U.S. and international telecommunications with assets of almost $54 billion. The company's 1997 merger with NYNEX made it the second largest telephone company in the United States with nearly 40 million telephone access lines, 5.4 million wireless customers, and 4.4 million miles of fiber optic cabling. Additionally, Bell Atlantic is the world's largest publisher of Yellow Pages directories, with over 80 million copies distributed annually, while its global telecommunications services include investments and state-of-the-art ventures in 21 countries.

The Breakup of AT&T: 1982–84

In January 1982 the U.S. Department of Justice ended a 13-year antitrust suit against the world's largest corporation, the American Telephone and Telegraph Company (AT&T). Pursuant to a consent decree, AT&T maintained its manufacturing and research facilities, as well as its long-distance operations.

On January 1, 1984, AT&T divested itself of 22 local operating companies, which were divided among seven regional holding companies (RHCs).

Thus Bell Atlantic was free of AT&T; the company served the northern Atlantic states and oversaw seven telephone subsidiaries. AT&T as a tough competitor rather than a parent company proved an immediate and ever-present challenge for Bell Atlantic. On January 2, 1984, Federal Justice Harold Greene ordered Bell Atlantic to transfer a $30 million contract with the federal government to AT&T, ruling that AT&T was granted the contract pre-divestiture. Bell Atlantic claimed that many terms of the contract—which included the sale of 200,000 telephones, a year-long maintenance contract worth $6 million involving approximately 275 employees—were made directly with Bell Atlantic, not AT&T. Bell Atlantic argued, also unsuccessfully, that the transfer of employees would give AT&T knowledge of Bell Atlantic's advanced voice and data communications Centrex system, so that AT&T could conceivably design and market a system to underprice Bell Atlantic.

Nevertheless, Bell Atlantic bounced back from its court loss, acquiring a 40 percent interest in A Beeper Company Associates in January 1984. The following month the company announced the formation of Bell Atlanticom Systems, a systems and equipment subsidiary, to market traditional, cordless, and decorator telephones, wiring components, and home security and healthcare systems. Bell Atlantic Mobile Systems took off early from the starting gate: in March 1984 the company introduced Alex, a cellular telephone service to commence a month later in the Washington, D.C., and Baltimore, Maryland, markets. Bell Atlantic Mobile Systems invested $15.1 million in the fledgling cellular service.

During this time, skirmishes continued between the RHCs, AT&T, and Justice Harold Greene. Greene asserted that the RHCs were more concerned with entering new business markets than in improving the local networks. In an effort to restrain RHCs from using regulated business profits to finance non-telephone ventures, the consent decree ruled that new endeavors may comprise no more than ten percent of the RHCs' yearly revenues and that there be a strict financial separation between regulated telephone business and new ventures. Justice Greene set a March

23, 1984 deadline for all RHCs to submit specific requests for waivers or further explanation of the original consent decree.

In April 1984 Bell Atlantic went to court over the Federal Communications Commission's (FCC) delay in charging tariffs for customers accessing the local network. Delaying implementation of the access fee not only violated the consent decree, Bell Atlantic charged, but it also caused Bell Atlantic and its sibling RHCs to cover some of AT&T's service costs in the interim. To make matters worse, because Bell Atlantic was the lowest-cost provider of all the RHCs, it was losing the most money. (The FCC system was one of allocation, with access-fee funds collected first, then distributed to RHCs based on the company's cost.) Bell Atlantic planned to succeed in spite of the access fee tangle and subsequently allotted more than half of its construction budget for improvement of the network. Bell Atlantic became the first RHC to employ the use of digital termination systems, a microwave technology for local electronic message distribution. The company experimented with a local area data transport system, and planned to install 50,000 miles of optical fiber within a year.

Carving a Niche: Late 1984

Bell Atlantic made several major acquisitions in its first year of operation. The purchase of Telecommunications Specialists, Inc. (TSI), a Houston-based interconnect firm with offices in Dallas, San Antonio, and Austin, was completed in October 1984, and Bell Atlantic planned to let TSI retain its marketing and sales staff and continue operations. TSI, a marketer of private branch exchange (PBX) and key systems, also offered financing for equipment-leasing customers.

In December 1984 Bell Atlantic bought New Jersey's Tri-Continental Leasing Corporation (Tri-Con), a computer and telecommunications equipment provider. As Tri-Con supplied TSI with financing, Bell Atlantic seemed to be vertically integrating its acquisitions. Another big Tri-Con customer was Basic Four Information Systems, owned by Management Assistance Inc. (MAI). Early in 1985 Bell Atlantic completed the purchase of MAI's Sorbus Inc. division, the second-largest U.S. computer service firm, with 187 locations and 2,200 employees, for $180 million. Bell Atlantic also bought a related company, MAI Canada Ltd. With the Sorbus acquisition Bell Atlantic hoped to strengthen its position with the federal government; as the company's largest customer, the federal government provided three percent of total company revenues in the first year of operation.

With the most aggressive diversification of all the RHCs, Bell Atlantic planned to be a full-service company in the increasingly related merging telecommunications and computer sectors. As a struggle for large customers was inevitable, and because the larger customers could potentially set up their own information systems, the company decided to target medium-sized customers. Bell Atlantic offered this customer base everything from information services equipment and data processing to computer maintenance.

Because the original consent decree was drawn to strictly regulate RHC activity and allow long-distance carriers equal access to local networks, fledglings such as Bell Atlantic faced competition on all levels. On the national level, the FCC approved a $2 end-user fee for all subscribers to basic telephone service, another tactic to give the RHCs a cushion in large-business markets. The institution of this fee coincided with the availability of rapidly evolving technology; thus the fee merely encouraged larger customers to create their own information networks, a process termed "bypass." To help keep Bell Atlantic competitive in the large-customer markets—those most vulnerable to bypass—several states in its region granted the company considerable flexibility in pricing.

Baby Bell Legal Skirmishes in 1985

Of all the unregulated businesses Bell Atlantic was just entering, competition threatened to be even stiffer in the private branch exchange (PBX) market. By early 1985 IBM and Digital Equipment were offering maintenance for their mainframe users, a large portion of Bell Atlantic's recently acquired Sorbus customer base. Larger than many competing companies nonetheless, Bell Atlantic took advantage of the buyer's market that the tough competition created; in June 1985 it acquired CompuShop Inc., a retail computer company with $75 million in sales annually, for $21 million. With the acquisition, Bell Atlantic joined siblings NYNEX (the New England and New York RHC), and Pacific Telesis (the West Coast RHC), as surprise competitors in a market that, in spite of a recent surge in sales, was in decline. The retail computer slump was marked by smaller companies' rapid entry into, and exit from, a market with high overhead costs. The entrance of big names such as Bell Atlantic, retail computer experts argued, could provide just the shot in the arm the market needed to take off.

A year-and-a-half after divestiture, Bell Atlantic, along with its sibling RHCs and other companies, realized that convergence of telephone hardware and computer data processing was a huge business. Over the next several years the RHCs repeatedly petitioned the Department of Justice for business waivers to become more competitive in not only the national but international telecommunications market. Back in July 1984 Bell Atlantic had requested the government waive a body of rules prohibiting the RHCs from supplying their own telephone hardware. Unable to provide equipment for its own Centrex system, Bell Atlantic stood to lose a huge federal government contract to competitors—nearly 370,000 Centrex lines coming up for bid. Having already lost 48,000 Centrex lines due to restrictions of the past year, Bell Atlantic officials thought it was time to confront the issue.

Since divestiture, the FCC allowed AT&T to resell basic services, and it considering letting the company provide customer premises equipment as well. IBM, strengthened by its recently acquired Rolm Corporation and Satellite Business Systems, was not restricted in its marketing efforts, but Bell Atlantic was. By the end of 1985 Bell Atlantic earnings were $1.1 billion on revenues of $9.1 billion. Rated against its competitors, Bell Atlantic was the only RHC close to turning a profit on its unregulated businesses, worth $600 million in revenues. While profits remained strong in Bell Atlantic's local phone service, its Yellow Pages directory publishing division, due to a disagreement, would be competing with Reuben H. Donnelly Corporation, its previous publisher.

In the meantime, the long-distance market moved uncomfortably close to the RHCs' local turf. AT&T and other carriers began competing to carry toll calls in local areas. While this would seem to benefit the residential consumer, it did not; outside competitors cutting into RHC profits merely threatened the very profit margin that helped subsidize the cost of local service. Ending its second year in operation, Bell Atlantic's chairman and CEO, Thomas Bolger, described the restrictions on RHCs as "the most significant problem in the telecommunications industry" in *Telephone Engineer & Management*'s mid-December 1985 issue and requested the Justice Department come to a decision before the scheduled January 1, 1987 date. If the purpose of the breakup was to promote maximum competition in the industry, the RHCs reasoned that they, the most likely competitors of industry leaders AT&T and IBM, shouldn't be prohibited from fully competing.

Diversification & More Legal Battles: 1986–88

Continuing to expand its unregulated businesses in spite of, or perhaps because of, line-of-business restrictions as outlined in the consent decree, in September 1986 Bell Atlantic acquired the real estate assets of Pitcairn Properties, Inc. In October the company followed with the $140-million purchase of Greyhound Capital Corporation, since renamed Bell Atlantic Systems Leasing International, Inc. Bell Atlantic then had a firm position in the financial and real estate markets. One month later, Bell Atlantic became the first RHC to propose a new cost allocation plan under recently outlined requirements to the FCC. The corporation also opted, if allowed, to begin planning its comparably efficient interconnection (CEI) system. By March 1987 Bell Atlantic filed its CEI plan asking for the provision of message storage, hoping to get a jump on offering enhanced services. Due to several regulatory restrictions, development of the service was halted. Continuing to acquire attractive companies, Bell Atlantic acquired Pacific Computer Corp., in June 1987 and Jolynne Service Corp. several months later.

In July 1987 Bell Atlantic announced a restructuring plan, combining operations of basic telephone service and unregulated businesses under one newly-created position, chief operating officer (COO). The plan also called for all staff of separate Bell Atlantic telephone companies to report to their respective presidents. Raymond Smith, a Bell employee since 1959, was named COO, reporting directly to Bolger. In September of that year, Judge Greene ruled to uphold the manufacturing and long-distance restrictions on RHCs, while allowing only limited information services. The RHCs all objected, but none as strongly as Bell Atlantic. The corporation alleged that the judge alluded to information discussed during the original consent decree

settlement, which claimed that the Bell operating companies, pre-divestiture, had been accused of engaging in anticompetitive practices—remarks not relevant to the case at hand.

The tables turned rather quickly for Bell Atlantic. In January 1988 the company found itself, along with BellSouth, accused of misconduct in bidding attempts to win government contracts. Senator John Glenn of Ohio led the accusations that the two RHCs had been given confidential price information by a General Services Administration chief. Bell Atlantic disputed the charges entirely, claiming that the senator's report was inaccurate. Despite the legal battles, business transpired as usual with Bell Atlantic selling MAI Canada Ltd., and some of the assets of Sorbus Inc., for $146 million. Following that divestiture, the company purchased the European computer maintenance operations of Bell Canada Enterprises, Inc. Next Bell Atlantic's Sorbus subsidiary acquired Computer Maintenance Co., Inc., and in 1988, following Judge Greene's approval of its CEI plans, Bell Atlantic announced the introduction of four new information services: an electronic message storage system (allowing subscribers to record messages for consumers to play back); a telephone answering service; a voice mail service; and a videotex gateway service, through which data bases and customers communicated. All services involved monthly surcharges for customers, as well as an hourly fee for videotex and a one-time user's fee for message storage.

Juggling its assets a bit more, Bell Atlantic completed the sale of its retail computer CompuShop in June and acquired the assets of CPX Inc., a company specializing in Control Data Corporation equipment in July. Bell Atlantic also acquired the assets of Dyn Service Network.

A New Era in the Late 1980s

Bolger announced his retirement as CEO, effective in January 1989, and COO Smith became the new chief executive officer. Bolger, formerly a vice-president of AT&T in business services and marketing, had led Bell Atlantic through divestiture into a leading position in telecommunications, real estate and leasing finance, and computer maintenance. A strong critic of consent decree restrictions on RHCs, Smith and Bell Atlantic were also active in helping establish international standards for telecommunications. On the national level, however, Judge Greene kept his eye on RHC activities. A Bell Atlantic proposal to conduct a trial involving interstate phone traffic was rejected because it was not deemed a necessity, but rather an advanced, competitive service. Bell Atlantic wanted to cut costs by using a central processor for state-to-state traffic rather than having separate facilities perform the same tasks, and thus held that the judge's decision was against the public interest.

Bell Atlantic implemented another reorganization in 1989, trimming its management staff by 1,700 through voluntary retirement and other incentive plans. Significant parts of the restructuring included closing the Washington, D.C., Chesapeake, and Potomac Telephone Company headquarters and merging employees into other locations; refinancing various debts; reassessing computer holdings; and outlining a plan to cover future retirees.

During this time, Bell Atlantic invested $2.3 billion in network services to upgrade telephone facilities. Signaling System 7 (SS7), a high-speed information exchange system, was operating on more than 60 percent of Bell Atlantic's telephone lines. To compete in mobile communications, the company marketed an extremely lightweight cellular telephone; at the same time, Bell Atlantic Paging's customer base grew, with a 16 percent increase. In partnership with GTE, Bell Atlantic Yellow Pages increased its customer base through a new subsidiary, the Chesapeake Directory Sales Company. Bell Atlantic Systems Integration was formed in 1989 to research and explore marketing capabilities in voice and data communications, as well as in artificial intelligence.

Perhaps the biggest opportunity for Bell Atlantic came at year-end 1989, when it stepped up activity in the international arena. Economic changes in the Soviet Union and eastern Europe opened up entirely new possibilities in global telecommunications. Slowly exploring opportunities abroad since divestiture, Bell Atlantic was, by 1989, assisting in the installation of telephone software systems for the Dutch national telephone company, PTT Telecom, B.V., as well as for the national telephone company in Spain. A Bell Atlantic German subsidiary was awarded a contract to install microcomputers and related equipment at U.S. Army locations in Germany, Belgium, and the United Kingdom. With consultants located in Austria, France, Italy, and Switzerland, Bell Atlantic planned a European headquarters, Bell Atlantic Europe, S.A., to be located in Brussels, Belgium.

Bell Atlantic kept running into challenges stateside, however. In April 1990 the company's Chesapeake and Potomac Telephone Company was charged with fraud and barred from seeking federal contracts. Bell Atlantic fought back, citing a double standard in that the U.S. Department of Treasury allowed AT&T to win contracts without necessarily having all the required equipment immediately available, while it had barred the Chesapeake and Potomac Telephone Company from doing so. Undaunted by its squabbles with the government, Bell Atlantic had created the world's largest independent computer maintenance organization by 1990, able to service some 500 brands of computers. With the January 1990 purchase of Control Data Corporation's third-party maintenance business, Bell Atlantic sealed its position as the leader in maintenance of both IBM and Digital Equipment Corporation systems.

Other Bell Atlantic acquisitions of 1990 included Northern Telecom's regional PBX operations and Simborg Systems Corporation. Through the latter purchase, renamed Bell Atlantic Healthcare Systems, the company provided software for hospital computer networks. Aggressive as ever, in June 1990 Bell Atlantic, along with sibling U S West became the first two Baby Bells to upgrade systems with synchronous optical fiber through the use of Sonet-based equipment. In addition, Bell Atlantic poured over $2 billion into a host of upgrades, including SS7 and ISDN capabilities. In sum, Bell Atlantic offered more choices by year-end 1990 than any information transmission competitor, and its revenues had reached $12.3 billion with earnings of $1.3 billion.

In the early and mid-1990s Bell Atlantic's international division thrived. In 1990 alone the corporation made several significant ventures, which included teaming up with the Korean Telecommunications Authority in a variety of research, marketing, and information exchanges; joining U S West to modernize Czechoslovak telecommunications; and partnering with Ameritech and two New Zealand companies to acquire the Telecom Corporation of New Zealand. For its $105 million investment in the Czech deal, Bell Atlantic gained 24.5 percent of both the cellular and public data network; in the New Zealand venture, where the network was already digitally-advanced and in a relaxed regulatory environment, the RHCs' initial investment of $1.2 billion was considered a boon to all involved. Additionally, Bell Atlantic and NORVANS, a Norwegian telecommunications company, jointly applied for a license to develop and operate an independent cellular network in Norway and next came an agreement with the Republic of China to consult in marketing, research, and information exchanges.

Distinguishing Itself: 1991–96

Continuing international expansion, Bell Atlantic joined Belle Meade International Telephone, Inc. in early 1991 to set up a communication system in the Soviet Union; other big news was Telecom Corp. in New Zealand's successful initial public offering on the New York Stock Exchange in July, and its subsequent announcement to have ISDN capabilities for 90 percent of its customers within three years. Stateside, Bell Atlantic was also on the lookout for complementary businesses and merged its own Bell Atlantic Knowledge Systems, Inc. with Technology Concepts Inc. to form Bell Atlantic Software Systems Inc. Metro Mobile, the second largest independent cellular radio telecommunications provider in the United States, was acquired in 1992. This particular transaction gave Bell Atlantic the most extensive cellular phone coverage on the East Coast, while a joint venture with NYNEX and GTE to combine their respective cellular networks into one huge national service made news from coast to coast.

In 1993 Bell Atlantic bought 23 percent of Mexico's second largest telecommunications company, Grupo Iusacell, and set to work on a number of projects. On the legal front, Bell Atlantic finally won one, when the U.S. Court of Appeals upheld its right to provide video programming and other services over its established telephone lines. The ruling was a significant win in the cable programming business, as Bell Atlantic was now free to develop video-on-demand, home shopping, and educational programs over telephone wires. The next year, Bell Atlantic and NYNEX moved forward in this area by investing $100 million in CAI Wireless Systems to help in their quest for video programming innovations. Yet before this deal went through, Bell Atlantic made headlines on the legal front again, joining with three other Baby Bells to break the consent decree that had kept them from competing in the long-distance services market.

1995 proved pivotal for Bell Atlantic's future. A long-awaited ruling in the federal courts gave the company a sweet victory; a federal judge finally ruled in favor of the Baby Bells to offer long-distance services. Bell Atlantic wasted little time, becoming the first Baby Bell to jump into the long distance market by recruiting customers in Florida, Illinois, North and South Carolina, and Texas in early 1996. Bell Atlantic had also been busy overseas as well. The company and Italian conglomerate Ing. C. Olivetti & Co. formed a joint venture in preparation for the breakup of Italy's telecommunications monopoly three years hence. Telecom Italia SpA, the state-owned company, was due for regulation in 1998, and Bell Atlantic, as well as several other joint ventures, including one from France Telecom, Duetsche Telekom AG, and Sprint Corp., were ready to offer Italians a myriad of choices. Another global venture, Iusatel S.A., Bell Atlantic's partnership in Mexico with Grupo Iusacell S.A., was given the green light to provide both national and international long-distance services to at least three dozen Mexican cities by the year 2000.

Another major development in 1996 was the announcement that Bell Atlantic and NYNEX would merge and become the nation's second largest telephone company. Though the official announcement came as a surprise to few (rumors had been swirling for months), the deal was at once controversial and ironic—once-struggling Baby Bells were beginning to rival their old parent company. Soon after news of the merger was made public, a new operating unit called Bell Atlantic Internet Solutions debuted, giving customers in Washington, D.C., Philadelphia, and New Jersey a wide range of both business and residential Internet-based products and services.

The New Bell Atlantic: 1997 and Beyond

Bell Atlantic's merger with NYNEX was completed in early 1997. The new company's assets serviced 25 percent of the overall U.S. market in 13 states and accounted for about 140-billion minutes of long distance traffic; the region not only held one-third of the Fortune 500's headquarters, but the U.S. government's nerve center as well. South of the border, Bell Atlantic continued its varied international coups, this time investing another $50 million in its Mexican venture to gain controlling interest in Grupo Iusacell, of which it had previously owned 42 percent.

By early 1998, the new Bell Atlantic had 39.7 million domestic access lines, 5.4 million domestic wireless customers, 6.3 million global wireless customers, and services in 21 countries worldwide. The company was also the world's largest publisher of both print and electronic directories, with over 80 million distributed annually. After a rocky road as Bell Atlantic's local markets were forced open to competitors, the company was taking advantage of new opportunities in the $20 billion long-distance market and the $8 billion video market, and was continuing to expand globally.

Principal Divisions

Bell Atlantic-Delaware, Inc.; Bell Atlantic-Maryland, Inc.; Bell Atlantic-New Jersey, Inc.; Bell Atlantic-Pennsylvania, Inc.; Bell Atlantic-Virginia, Inc.; Bell Atlantic-Washington, D.C., Inc.; Bell Atlantic-West Virginia, Inc.; Bell Atlantic-Massachusetts, Inc.; Bell Atlantic-Vermont, Inc.; Bell Atlantic-Rhode Island, Inc.; Bell Atlantic-New Hampshire, Inc.; Bell Atlantic-Maine, Inc.; Bell Atlantic-New York, Inc.; Bell Atlantic Network Services; Bell Atlantic Data Solutions Group; Bell Atlantic Information Services Group; Bell Atlantic Internet Solutions; Bell Atlantic Mobile.

Further Reading

Barrett, Paul M., ''Legal Beat: Justices Questions Congress' Ban on Phone Concerns Offering Cable,'' *Wall Street Journal,* December 7, 1995, p. B10.
Cauley, Leslie, ''Bell Atlantic and NYNEX Discuss Merger to Form Second-Biggest Phone Firm...,'' *Wall Street Journal,* December 18, 1995, p. A3.
——, ''Bell Atlantic and NYNEX Merger Talks Highlight Roles of Smith and Seidenberg,'' *Wall Street Journal,* December 19, 1995, p. A3.
——, ''Technology & Telecommunications: Baby Bells Square Off Against AT&T on Calling Cards, U S West Agreement,'' *Wall Street Journal,* October 27, 1995, p. B3.
''The Foreign Invasion: New Zealand Discovered the Benefits of Letting Global Companies Be a Part of Reform,'' *Wall Street Journal,* October 2, 1995, p. R16.
Gold, Howard, ''Tom Bolger's One-Stop-Shop,'' *Forbes,* March 25, 1985.
Lannon, Larry, ''Bell Atlantic's Bolger Demands His Freedom,'' *Telephony,* July 14, 1986.
Lavin, Douglas, ''European Phone Giants Challenge Italy,'' *Wall Street Journal,* November 16, 1995, p. A14.
Mason, Charles, ''RHC Barred Federal Contracts,'' *Telephony,* April 16, 1990.
Naik, Gautam, ''Technology & Telecommunications: Bells Venture Likely to Place Cellular Order,'' *Wall Street Journal,* November 10, 1995, p. B2.
Tell, Lawrence J., ''Footloose and Fancy Free,'' *Barron's,* November 12, 1984.

—Frances E. Norton
—updated by Taryn Benbow-Pfalzgraf

BFC Construction Corporation

3660 Midland Avenue
Scarborough, Ontario M1V 4V3
Canada
(416) 754-8735
Fax: (416) 754-8736
Web site http://www.bfc.ca

Public Company
Incorporated: 1969 as Banister Continental Corp.
Employees: 571
Sales: C$606.8 million (US$438.1 million) (1997)
Stock Exchanges: American Alberta Montreal Toronto
Ticker Symbol: BFC
SICs: 1522 General Contractors—Residential Buildings,
    Other than Single-Family; 1541 General
    Contractors—Industrial Buildings & Warehouses;
    1542 General Contractors—Nonresidential Buildings,
    Other than Industrial Buildings & Warehouses; 1611
    Highways & Street Construction, Except Elevated
    Highways; 1622 Bridge, Tunnel & Elevated Highway
    Construction; 1623 Water, Sewer, Pipeline &
    Communications & Power Line Construction; 3511
    Steam, Gas & Hydraulic Turbines & Turbine
    Generator Set Units

BFC Construction Corporation is one of Canada's largest construction companies. Its areas of operation in the 1990s included building large-scale energy developments; commercial, retail, industrial, and residential buildings; and subways, bridges, dams, tunnels, highways, and airports in Canada, the United States, and certain foreign countries. It was also managing construction, procurement of equipment, commissioning, and related services for overseas nuclear-power projects; designing and manufacturing steam generators, mostly for power generation and cogeneration; engaging in underground utilities work in Ontario; and operating in all phases of oil and gas pipeline construction in Canada.

The First 30 Years: 1948–78

The company was founded as Banister Pipelines in 1948, a year after Ronald Banister, a native of the oil-rich Canadian province of Alberta, began laying pipeline with a second-hand ditching machine. He also founded Banister Construction. The parent firm, Banister Cos., was acquired in early 1969 by Continental Computer Associates, Inc. The merged companies were renamed Banister Continental Corp., with Banister as chairman and executive offices in Wyncote, Pennsylvania.

At this time Banister Continental was engaged in all phases of oil and gas pipeline contracting, specializing in projects performed under severe winter conditions. It was operating primarily in the Canadian provinces of Alberta, Saskatchewan, Manitoba, and Ontario, and to a lesser extent in other parts of Canada and in parts of the northern contiguous United States and Alaska. The company was leasing a plant in Edmonton, Alberta, and regional offices in Minneapolis and Anchorage, Alaska. It also, through Continental Computer Associates, owned 60 computer systems, principally IBM System 360 computers, which were available for leasing, along with various other pieces of equipment necessary for the operation of such systems.

In fiscal 1969 (the year ended March 31, 1969), the consolidated company had total income of $9.2 million—about half from pipeline construction and half from computer rentals—and net income of $459,266. Income from pipeline construction grew much faster than that from computer rentals and in fiscal 1973 accounted for nearly 90 percent of Banister Continental's revenues of C$67.2 million. Net income came to $8 million. (At this time U.S. and Canadian dollars were close to equivalent in value.)

Banister Continental subsequently moved its headquarters to Minneapolis, but in 1973 it moved again to Edmonton, where it purchased a three-story office building and maintained an equipment-repair terminal. It reincorporated there as Banister Continental Ltd. The action was taken to comply with guidelines laid down by the Canadian government so the company could participate in oil and gas projects in Canada. Banister's son Rodger became both chairman and president of Banister Continental in 1975. By this time the company was also operating in Saudi Arabia, through a joint venture with H.C. Price Co. In addition, it had formed a civil engineering division that, in 1973, began construction of Toronto's CN Tower, the world's tallest free-standing structure. This project was completed in 1976. Despite these activities, Banister Continental's revenues slumped sharply in fiscal 1974 and again in 1975, when the company lost $1.4 million on revenues of only $27.5 million.

In 1976 Banister Continental was ruled Canadian-controlled, allowing it to develop and expand without restrictions in Canada. The ruling also allowed the firm to acquire control of Canadian enterprises or establish new businesses in Canada without being required to give notice or apply for government approval. The outlook for large-diameter pipeline construction in Canada and Alaska was not good at the time, but one Banister Continental executive noted that the company had $27 million in cash and short term deposits and was exploring investment opportunities in the energy services areas. During the fiscal year the company was again profitable on record revenues of $80.5 million.

In 1978 Banister Continental sold its computer-leasing subsidiary for $5.75 million and acquired the remaining half-share in the Middle East joint venture. The company also purchased Pitts Engineering Construction Ltd. of Toronto, a civil engineering firm, for $41 million. This put Banister into the business of building highways, bridges, subways, and dams, as well as its prior energy related activities such as pipeline, marine, gas-distribution, and underground utilities storage facility construction. Severe cutbacks in energy development had reduced Banister Continental's revenues in fiscal 1978 to C$33.6 million (about $30.2 million in U.S. dollars).

Many Acquisitions, Mixed Results: 1978–90

To keep its employees and equipment working during this slack period, Banister Continental bid low in order to win pipeline contracts in Louisiana, Oregon, and Virginia. As a result the company lost money despite record revenues during the next three years, culminating in a C$14.5 million loss ($12.3 million U.S.) on revenues of C$146.5 million ($124.5 million U.S.) in fiscal 1981. Losses from pipeline projects came to C$26 million (about $22 million U.S.) in that period. Banister Continental's problems worsened after Pitts, in 1979, became the sponsor and half-partner for the $320 million Revelstone dam and powerhouse on the Columbia River in British Columbia, the largest publicly tendered construction project in Canadian history. The company bid too low for this project, partly because it failed to foresee sharply rising interest rates on the loans needed. As a result it lost $40.8 million on the job, which was not completed until 1984.

By mid-1981 Banister Continental was in severe financial trouble. It was selling off its U.S. pipeline division, wrapping up its involvement in the Middle East, and seeking relief in the form of as much as $30 million in loss-settlement payments for the Oregon project from Northwestern Utilities Ltd. and for the Louisiana project from the federal government, which had failed to provide vital rights-of-way for the project to proceed. The company's long-term debt had climbed to C$40 million ($32.8 million U.S.) in this period, and it was having trouble meeting payments on its C$140 million ($115 million U.S.) share of the dam project.

Ronald Banister returned from retirement in the Bahamas in early 1981 to assume the chairmanship of the company, in which a family corporation held nearly 25 percent of the common stock. A few months later he also became president and chief executive officer, following the resignation of his son Rodger. In 1982 Trimac Ltd., a Calgary-based energy and transportation concern, agreed to buy about another quarter of the stock at C$7.50 ($6.08 U.S.) a share. (The stock had traded as high as C$24.50 a share in 1980.) Banister Continental returned to profitability in 1984. In 1986 the company enjoyed record net income of C$15.7 million ($11.3 million U.S.). These results were greatly enhanced by a $12.8 million award from Northwest Pipeline Corp. on the Oregon project and a C$12 million ($8.6 million U.S.) claims settlement for the joint venture that built the Revelstone project.

Banister Continental purchased a half-interest in Nicholls-Radtke Ltd., an industrial-construction firm, in 1985. Two years later it purchased The Foundation Co. of Canada Ltd., paying for the acquisition by selling shares of stock to Skanska AB, a Swedish contracting company. This transaction resulted in Skanska holding 48 percent of Foundation and 15 percent of Banister Continental, the parent company. Foundation, a construction firm established in 1910, was specializing in the commercial, institutional, and resources market and was doing business on four continents. The civil engineering divisions of the two companies were integrated, with Foundation management holding most operating responsibility. Also in 1987, Banister Continental acquired The Jackson-Lewis Co., Ltd., a builder of commercial buildings in Canada dating from 1913, and Frontier Construction Co., which was doing the same kind of work in the United States.

The Banister family sold its remaining 16 percent stake in Banister Continental in 1989 for C$14 a share ($11.90 U.S.), or C$13.1 million ($11.1 million U.S.), to Churchill Corp., an Edmonton-based investment-holding concern. Ronald Banister was then replaced as chairman and chief executive officer by Allan S. Olson, president of Churchill. All was not well, however, with the company, which became Banister Inc. in 1990. The firm fell in the red in 1989 because of a C$7.8 million ($6.6 million U.S.) loss on pipeline construction. In 1990 it also lost money on civil engineering and, despite record revenues of C$700.4 million ($598.6 million U.S.), lost C$8.5 million ($7.3 million U.S.) in total.

Banister/BFC in the 1990s

Olson resigned in 1990 because he was unable to agree with the board on the future direction of Banister Inc. Churchill then sold its stake in Banister to Trimac and Skanska for C$9.78 a share ($8.36 U.S.). The new president was William M. Bateman, who had previously been president of Banister Continental during 1985–86. Revenue fell sharply in 1991, but the firm returned to profitability. That year it sold its 51 percent interest in Pitts International Inc. and completed construction of the ultramodern Terminal III of Toronto's Pearson International Airport, a project begun in 1988.

In 1993 Banister acquired Majestic Contractors Ltd., which it merged into a new subsidiary called Banister Majestic Inc., which was now the largest pipeline contractor in Canada. The parent company was renamed Banister Foundation Inc. in 1994 and moved its headquarters from Edmonton to Scarborough, Ontario, one of the boroughs that make up the municipality of metropolitan Toronto. The firm remained profitable in spite of a Canadian economic slump and some bad contracts during 1994–95. At its 1994 annual meeting the company reported a record backlog of C$750 million ($547 million U.S.) in orders. That year the company became a major contractor for the construction of Ontario's Highway 407, a $1 billion project. Also in 1994, Skanska (USA) Inc. sold the parent company's entire remaining stake (7.9 percent) in Banister Foundation for about C$8.2 million ($6 million U.S.).

Banister Foundation raised its stake in Nicholls-Radtke to 75 percent in 1995 and took full ownership in 1996. By 1997 the parent company, which was renamed BFC Construction Corp. that year, had lined up big projects in China, Hungary, India, and Israel. Net income reached C$9.1 million ($6.7 million U.S.) in 1996 on record revenues of C$715.6 million ($526.2 million U.S.). Of this revenue, civil, industrial, and building construction accounted for 73 percent and utility and pipeline construction for 27 percent. In 1997 BFC's revenues slumped to C$606.8 million ($438.1 million U.S.) and its net income to only C$1 million.

At the beginning of 1997, Foundation (which had recently absorbed Banister Majestic), Jackson-Lewis, and Cliffside Utility Contractors—another subsidiary—were amalgamated into a new subsidiary named BFC Construction Group Inc. Driver Ltd., a mechanical- and electrical-construction contractor, was purchased that year and placed in a subsidiary called BFC Industrial-Driver Ltd. Nicholls-Radtke was reorganized as BFC Industrial-Nicholls Radtke Ltd. Both these subsidiaries were engaged in industrial construction in Canada, but the latter included Innovative Steam Technologies, a division that was designing and building steam generators. Frontier, which became BFC Frontier, was active in building construction, primarily in the state of Washington, and also had a design-build service for its clients through 50 percent-owned Group West Associates Inc.

BFC Civil, a division of the parent company, was specializing in the construction of large scale energy developments, complex building structures, subways, bridges, highways, dams, tunnels, and airports in Canada, the United States, and internationally. BFC Buildings was constructing commercial, retail, and industrial buildings, including residential condominiums, in Canada. BFC Nuclear Managers (formerly Foundation Nuclear Managers) was active in services for overseas nuclear-power projects, currently in China and South Korea.

BFC Utilities (formerly Cliffside Utility Contractors) was engaged in underground utilities work throughout Ontario. BFC Traffic Technology, a new unit, was engaged in the construction and installation of traffic-signal and freeway traffic-management systems and highway lighting. BFC Pipelines (formerly Banister Majestic) was operating in all phases of oil and gas pipeline construction in Canada. The parent company also held a 25 percent interest in Bantrel Inc., which was performing services in the petroleum sector in Canada, the United States, and overseas.

BFC Construction's chief stockholders at the end of March 1997 were Trimac, with 22 percent of the shares of common stock, and Mackenzie Financial Corp., with 11 percent. The company's long-term debt was C$48.4 million at this time. In addition to its Toronto headquarters, the company had major facilities in Ellerslie, Alberta, and Cambridge, Ontario.

Principal Subsidiaries

BFC Construction Group Inc.; BFC Frontier (United States); BFC Industrial-Driver Ltd.; BFC Industrial-Nicholls Radtke Ltd.

Principal Divisions

BFC Buildings; BFC Civil; BFC Nuclear Managers; BFC Pipelines; BFC Traffic Technology; Innovative Steam Technologies.

Further Reading

"Banister Founders Plan to Sell Shares," *Financial Post,* November 20, 1989, p. 6.
"Banister Given Status as Canadian-Controlled," *Globe and Mail,* September 24, 1976, p. B6.
Barnes, Angela, "Banister Looking at Domestic and Foreign Investment Opportunities," *Globe and Mail,* October 14, 1976, p. B6.
Chianello, Joanne, "Banister Builds on Business," *Financial Post,* November 22, 1994, p. 14.
Cuff, Daniel F., "Reshuffling at Banister Brings Back President," *New York Times,* October 23, 1990, p. D4.
Gherson, Giles, "Tough Times for Pipelining at Banister," *Financial Post,* May 23, 1981, pp. 1–2.
Marcial, Gene G., "Leaning Hard on Banister," *Business Week,* March 17, 1997, p. 110.
"Renamed Banister Moves to Toronto," *Toronto Star,* May 20, 1994, p. B7.
Stinson, Marian, "Canadian Construction Firms Join Forces," *Globe and Mail,* March 28, 1987, p. B4.
"Trimac Agrees to Buy Holding in Banister," *Wall Street Journal,* February 11, 1982, p. 36.

—Robert Halasz

Big V Supermarkets, Inc.

176 Main Street
Florida, New York 10921
U.S.A.
(914) 651-4411
Fax: (914) 651-7048

Private Company
Incorporated: 1942 as Victory Supermarket
Employees: 5,100
Sales: $762.9 million (1997)
SICs: 5411 Grocery Stores

Operator of a leading supermarket chain in the northeastern United States, Big V Supermarkets, Inc. owns 32 grocery stores in New Jersey, New York, and Pennsylvania that operate primarily under the ShopRite name. Big V began as a family-owned business with one store, then grew robustly under the guidance of the founders' son, J. Arthur Rosenberg, who took the company public in 1972. Two leveraged buyouts in the late 1980s and early 1990s returned the company to the private sector. Big V's greatest physical presence during the 1990s was in the mid-Hudson Valley, north of New York City, where its stores earned a reputation for astute merchandising. A member of the Wakefern Food Corp., the largest cooperative food wholesaler in the United States, the company enjoyed an entrenched position in many of its markets, successfully withstanding the relentless pressure of competing supermarkets encroaching upon its home turf.

1940s Origins

A family-owned business for many years, Big V began operating in 1942, when husband and wife William and Viola Rosenberg opened their first grocery store in upstate New York. The first store operated under the name Victory Supermarket, and stood for many years as the sole business supporting the Rosenbergs. Neither of the pair intended to nurture that single store into a chain of supermarkets, but their son, J. Arthur Rosenberg, had other ideas. The younger Rosenberg was re-sponsible for transforming a single supermarket into a tightly knit chain of supermarkets anchored in the mid-Hudson Valley. Under his direction, professional managers were brought in who shaped the family business into a genuine corporation, one that made its debut as a publicly-traded company on the American Stock Exchange in 1972, thirty years after the first store had opened.

With the proceeds netted from the issuance of stock, J. Arthur Rosenberg (who by this point completely presided over Big V's operations) gained the financial resources to accelerate expansion. He opened a number of new stores, though never straying far from the company's headquarters in Orange County, New York, and operated the chain under the ShopRite banner. Supporting the company, aside from its own senior management and employees, was an important partner—the Wakefern Food Corp.—a retailer-owned cooperative based in Elizabeth, New Jersey that served as the wholesale distribution and merchandising arm for Rosenberg's ShopRite supermarkets. With the help of Wakefern, which ranked as the largest cooperative food wholesaler in the United States, Big V carved a lasting territory for itself in the state of New York. The resiliency of its grip on its operating territory, however, was seriously tested in the years following Rosenberg's departure.

Ownership Changes Begin in Late 1980s

The first major change in Big V's ownership after its 1972 conversion to a publicly-held company occurred in 1987. First, Boston Corp., a New York-based investment banking organization that paid approximately $170 million for Big V, led a leveraged buyout (LBO) in 1987. With the purchase, First Boston gained control of the company's 33 stores, which collected $600 million in sales a year, and began making moves to ensure that its investment paid a respectable return.

After a comparatively inactive 1988, there was a flurry of activity in 1989. Ten stores underwent thorough renovation, while less substantial changes were made to three other stores. Three new stores were established in upstate New York during the year—a store in Fishkill, another in Chester, and a third in Vails Gate—all of which were an average of 12,000 square feet larger than Big V's other stores. At the same time the chain was expanding, it was also contracting, losing seven stores in the Albany, New York, market. Company executives, still led by Rosenberg, had decided to retreat from the Albany area and concentrate on their core territory, ceding ground in order to secure a stronger hold over its major markets. The sale of the seven Albany stores in the spring of 1989, coupled with the addition of three new stores during the year, was reflective of the operating strategy embraced by Big V officials.

The progress of the company was not measured by annual leaps of its store count, but instead by the performance of its existing fleet of stores. In the years ahead, new stores would be opened, to be sure, but the aim was not on developing a chain of supermarkets that ultimately would sweep across the country in great numbers. Instead, the focus was on fine-tuning the stores, both in terms of square footage and merchandising, to perfectly match the particular demands of a particular market. Accordingly, the emphasis was on the renovation or relocation of existing stores rather than the geographic expansion of the company's corporate banner. For the next decade, Big V concerned itself with identifying its markets and tailoring its stores to the desires of the people residing in its core operating territory.

Management Changes in the 1990s

As the company headed into the 1990s, it did so—for the first time in its history—without a Rosenberg in charge. In 1990, a second LBO was completed, passing ownership of the company to an investment group that included members of Big V's senior management and was led by a Boston investment firm called Thomas H. Lee Company. Thomas H. Lee paid $212 million for Big V, which after the expansion and contraction of the chain in 1989, comprised 27 ShopRite stores which were collecting $630 million in annual sales. The change in ownership resulted in one important management change: the resignation of Rosenberg. He was succeeded by David G. Bronstein, who added the chairman title in addition to the president and chief executive officer position he held before the LBO. Aside from Rosenberg, there were no management changes in the wake of the "friendly" buyout. The change of ownership occurred without disruption, and its arrival was viewed as a positive event, particularly by Bronstein. "In our case," he effused, shortly after taking command, "LBO stands for Love Being Owners. Being owners has really helped to energize the company, and to do things worthwhile, whether one is a public company, private company, or LBOed or not."

Under the stewardship of Bronstein, there was promise of progress amid what the new leader described as "the largest expansion period in the company's history." Typically, progress at Big V did not mean a proliferation of new stores, but instead the renovation or relocation of the company's existing stores. According to Bronstein's plans, by 1993 or 1994 more than 80 percent of the chain's stores would either be new or remodeled since 1985, part of a sweeping facelift to rejuvenate the appeal of the company's supermarkets. With this remodeling effort as its goal, the company tackled the 1990s, concentrating its efforts in the Hudson Valley, and particularly in affluent Westchester County, immediately north of New York City.

New Challenges at the End of the Century and Beyond

Forces within the company's major trading areas and forces stemming from industry-wide trends dictated, to a certain degree, the new "look" that Big V would assume during the 1990s. Within the eight-county region in the Hudson Valley that represented the heart of Big V's territory, competitive forces intensified as the 1990s progressed. Although the pressure of competition was not a new phenomenon in the company's experience, the ardor with which competitors entered Big V's markets did assume a more aggressive nature during the 1990s. The type of competition the company faced was relatively new as well—a retail concept born in the 1980s that was thriving in the 1990s: the "superstore." Sprawling, 80,000-square-foot stores were inundating markets throughout the country, forcing much smaller competitors out of business and making second-tier retailers devise a response to the encroachment.

For its part, Big V concentrated on nonfood merchandise within its stores, placing a particular emphasis on videotape rentals. As the company busied itself with remodeling the majority of its existing stores, "video areas" were replaced with "video centers," the main difference between the two being the number of videos offered to customers. Instead of stocking 800 videos, remodeled Big V stores featuring video centers carried more than 2,000 tapes, enabling the company to offer a greater selection of movie titles. By the beginning of 1992, 11 of Big V's supermarkets were being outfitted with video centers, with a continued emphasis in this direction promised in the years ahead.

Another early response to the heated competition that characterized the 1990s was the opening of a warehouse membership store. In October 1992, Big V opened a "test pilot" Price Rite store in Fishkill, New York, as an experimental effort to fight competition in the Hudson Valley. The store, which measured 30,000 square feet, was far smaller than competing warehouse stores that reached upwards of 100,000 square feet, but Big V's version of the warehouse store operated in much the same way that competing warehouse stores operated. For $19 a year, a membership card was issued to a customer, enabling him to shop at discount prices for a broad assortment of merchandise, including grocery products, frozen foods, fresh meat, produce, dairy, health and beauty care items, and electronics. Despite being billed as a test pilot store, the Price Rite store did not signal the beginning of a concerted push into warehouse store expansion. From the earliest days of Price Rite's operation, Big V officials explained that they had no expansion plans for the concept. In the years ahead, the store in Fishkill would stand as the sole warehouse store within Big V's operations.

As the company tinkered with finding the best strategy to carry it forward through the contentious 1990s, management changes at corporate headquarters provided a backdrop for Big V's efforts out in the field. In August 1993, Stuart A. Rosenthal was named president and chief operating officer, succeeding Bronstein, who had narrowed his executive duties to the responsibilities assigned to the company's chief executive officer and chairman posts. Working together with Bronstein, Rosenthal ranked as the number two executive, but less than 16 months later Rosenthal resigned, allegedly quitting because he was convinced he would never be promoted to the chief executive office. A future promotion to chief executive was contingent upon Bronstein's retirement, which was something Bronstein himself declared he had no plans for in "the foreseeable future." With Rosenthal gone, Joseph V. Fisher, the company's senior vice president of operations and marketing, took his place as chief operating officer, but the title of president remained vacant. Less than ten months after Rosenthal's departure, Bronstein announced his retirement, paving the way for Fisher to be named president and chief executive officer. Fisher, subsequently, assumed day-to-day control over the company, while Bronstein served as a consultant, retaining his chairman title.

As the management shuffle took place between December 1994 and September 1995, competition in Big V's operating territory stiffened discernibly. Along one 10-mile stretch of road, for instance, six new stores opened in a matter of months, spurring Big V officials to take action. As a response to the encroachment of superstores, Big V accelerated the pace of its long-term strategy of matching a store with the area in which it operates. As before, the company sought to fine-tune its stores, striving to identify the right-sized store for the right location and the right product offering. Executives opted for stores ranging in size between 48,000 square feet and 58,000 square feet, purposely avoiding building the 80,000-square-foot superstores that were fast circling its stores. In certain markets, the company believed the mammoth stores were not in touch with the clientele they were supposed to serve, a perspective articulated by Bronstein before his retirement when he remarked, "You're not going to into an 80,000-square-foot store for a loaf of bread."

With Big V's smaller version of the conventional superstore selected as the store type for the years ahead, the company moved quickly to install "replacement" stores—stores that were remodeled to reflect management's prevailing strategy. "We're at the beginning of the greatest expansion program in the history of the company," Bronstein had declared in 1994, reiterating his words of three years earlier. "Between now and 1996, we see a major transformation. If less than half of our units are superstores now, we predict three-quarters of them, or more, will be superstores by then." To finance its accelerated replacement program, the company took on additional debt. The company entered the mid-1990s with no plans to move outside its boundaries in the Hudson Valley.

By the late 1990s, a new twist to the format of Big V's supermarkets was beginning to emerge. The concept was taken from the company's store in Vails Gate, New York, which in 1996 began experimenting with a prototype christened Market Fresh Cafe. The cafe was a self-service buffet featuring prepared meals such as brick-oven pizza, submarine sandwiches, and fried seafood. The original operation at Vails Gate served as the training ground for managers to become acquainted with the concept so that they could then carry the concept to other stores. At the opening of the company's new store in Montague, New Jersey, in late 1997 (a 59,000-square-foot replacement of a 31,000-square-foot store), the prototype Market Fresh Cafe was unveiled, a debut that most likely promised the establishment of additional self-service buffets in the future. "We've been working on a Market Fresh Cafe concept for about a year and a half," Fisher explained shortly after the Montague store opening, "and this is the first store to get it full-blown. This is our prototype." With the blueprint set for the company's remodeling efforts in the future, Big V moved forward with its strategy, striving to keep competitors at bay as the company prepared for the 21st century. Early reports of the performance of the prototype, disclosed in mid-1998, exceeded the company's expectations, instilling confidence for the future.

Further Reading

Alaimo, Dan, "Big V's Commitment: The Chain Is Carving Out a Solid Niche in Video with Aggressive Merchandising and Pricing," *Supermarket News,* May 31, 1993, p. 28.
"Big V Appoints President," *Supermarket News,* August 16, 1993, p. 6.
"Big V Taps Fisher as President," *Supermarket News,* September 25, 1995, p. 6.
Elson, Joel, "Big V Strikes Back to Protect Nonfood Turf," *Supermarket News,* November 13, 1995, p. 6.
Gutman, Barry, "Big V ShopRites Expand, Remodel Video Centers," *Supermarket News,* February 10, 1992, p. 18.
Harper, Roseanne, "Self Centered: Big V ShopRite's Prototype Is Offering a Mix of Broadly Defined Service to Complement Its Help-Yourself Buffet," *Supermarket News,* November 3, 1997, p. 25.
Liebeck, Laura, "Price Rite Club Takes a Bite Out of Warehouse Competition," *Discount Store News,* November 2, 1992, p. 5.
Merrefield, David, "A Traditional Strategy," *Supermarket News,* April 4, 1994, p. 2.
"Rosenthal Resigns as Big V's President and Operating Chief," *Supermarket News,* December 5, 1994, p. 6.
Turcsik, Richard, "Getting Some Leverage," *Supermarket News,* April 29, 1991, p. 1.
Zweibach, Elliot, "Big V Supermarkets Is Sold in Second LBO," *Supermarket News,* January 14, 1991, p. 1.

—Jeffrey L. Covell

Binney & Smith Inc.

1100 Church Lane
Easton, Pennsylvania 18042
U.S.A.
(610) 253-6271
Fax: (610) 250-5768
(800) 272-9652
Web site: http://www.crayola.com

Wholly Owned Subsidiary of Hallmark Cards, Inc.
Incorporated: 1902 as Binney & Smith Co.
Employees: 2,100
Sales: $600 million (1997)
SICs: 3998 Manufacturing of Art Supplies

Binney & Smith Inc. (B&S) was incorporated in 1902 and in 1984 became a wholly owned subsidiary of privately held Hallmark Cards, Inc. B&S operates manufacturing facilities in the United States, Canada, England, Mexico, and Germany; the company also maintains sales and marketing facilities in these countries as well as in France, Spain, Singapore, Australia, Italy, and Germany. The Crayola name brand for colored crayons is the company's most widely known and recognized name in this country (98 of every 100 Americans know the name) and in more than 60 other countries abroad, from Iceland to Belize. Annually, B&S produces 120 shades of some two billion crayons, labeled in 12 different languages. All Crayola products are certified for nontoxicity by the Art & Creative Materials Institute. The Crayola brand has branched into the stationery segment with its markers, crayons, and chalk, into the arts and crafts category with its paint sets, and into a licensed interior paint category with its co-branded Benjamin Moore line of children's paints. Moreover, B&S offers other major brands among its products: namely, Liquitex, Silly Putty, Magic Marker, and Revell-Monogram. Liquitex brand art materials are known and respected worldwide as the technical leaders in fine artists' acrylic paints. Generations of children have played with Silly Putty; the Magic Marker brand is perhaps the best known name in markers for adults; for more than 50 years, modelers

have chosen the Revell-Monogram brand for its high quality and attention to detail. B&S sees the visual arts as vital for teaching all subjects and is an avid supporter of arts-in-education initiatives around the country.

The Early Years: 1864–1902

Joseph W. Binney left England in 1860 for upstate New York, where he founded, in 1864, Peekskill Chemical Works for the grinding, packaging, and distribution of ground charcoal and lamp black. In 1880 he set up headquarters in New York City and was joined by his son Edwin Binney and his nephew C. Harold Smith. They were responsible for products in the black and red color ranges, such as lamp black, charcoal, and a red iron oxide paint often used to coat the barns in rural America. Joseph trained the young men in salesmanship for the various pigments and colors he developed. When Joseph retired in 1885, Edwin Binney and Harold Smith formed the partnership of Binney & Smith. Meanwhile, a new and valuable black pigment had been developed from natural gas deposits discovered during the oil rush in Pennsylvania. This pigment was more intensely black and stronger than any other pigment in use at the time; it soon became the main ingredient in printing ink, stove and shoe polish, marking inks, and black crayons. B&S played an active role in the development and production of carbon black from the factories that sprang up in Pennsylvania, Indiana, Ohio, and West Virginia when other natural gas deposits were discovered in those states. B&S sold the greater part of the total production of carbon black, bought an interest in some of the operations, and stayed in touch with many new methods of production.

Edwin Binney and Harold Smith proved to be complementary partners. Binney kept busy expanding the company's presence in the United States, developing new applications for carbon black and other pigments, and forming alliances that ensured the solid growth of the company. Binney also took care of the company's finances, thereby allowing Smith to exercise his talent as a master salesman. Smith traveled throughout most countries of the world to introduce the new American gas carbon and demonstrate its advantages over the local pigments in use during the 19th century for most of the paints, varnishes, and other protective finishes. The Chinese, for instance, collected the smoke and soot from the incomplete combustion of camphor leaves to make their stick inks and black lacquer finishes. By the end of the century, in China and in many other countries, practically all printing inks, polishes, and paints were made from the American black. B&S thrived and was incorporated in 1902 in Easton, Pennsylvania.

In 1900 B&S bought an old water-powered stone mill on Bushkill Creek, near Easton, Pennsylvania, and used the mill to grind the scrap slate from the region's quarries. The ground slate was mixed with additional materials to create a superior slate pencil. Distribution of the slate pencils introduced B&S to the needs and potential of the educational market; the company listened and responded to teachers' needs for better materials, especially for chalk that did not crumble and good, affordable colored crayons. In 1902 experiments at the Easton mill resulted in the production of An-Du-Septic, a white dustless chalk made by an extrusion process to "weight" dust particles. Two years later An-Du-Septic chalk won a gold medal at the St. Louis World Exposition. Meanwhile, an experiment consisting of mixing dry carbon black with various waxes led to replacing the company's Eclipse Marking Ink, a black liquid used on barrels and boxes, with trouble-free black crayons called Staonal (that is, "Stay-on-all"), because they worked well on many types of surfaces, such as wood and paper.

Successful sales of Staonal triggered experiments for another product: the colored wax crayons schoolteachers needed to replace the poor-quality crayons children were using in their one-room schoolhouses. Artists did have access to high-quality colored crayons but these were imported and far too expensive for children's use. B&S chemists, aware that most of the pigments available at the time were highly toxic, developed synthetic, nontoxic pigments to replace organic colors. Furthermore, the company wanted to match the color uniformity and consistency of fine imported crayons while keeping costs low. In 1903 B&S produced its first box of eight Crayola crayons (red, orange, yellow, green, blue, violet, brown, and black); the box sold for a nickel. Edwin Binney's wife, a former schoolteacher who recognized the significance of colored crayons in terms of child development, took particular interest in the new product. In fact, it was she who coined the name *Crayola* from *craie* (the French word for chalk or stick of color) and *ola* (from *oleaginous,* a word referring to the oily characteristic of liquid petroleum before it is distilled into the paraffin used for

crayons). Thus B&S established itself in the avant-garde of suppliers for educational and artistic products.

Two Business Divisions: 1904–54

During the next half century the company added many new products. The various carbon blacks were increasingly in demand for more and more manufactured materials. This part of the business (later known as the Pigment Division) continued to be handled by the New York office; business that was to form the Crayon Division produced its items at Easton, but all sales were made from the New York office. The company's fortunes rose and ebbed with the conditions of the times—World War I, the 1920s postwar slump, the depression of the early 1930s—but gathered enough steam during the good times to sail through the bad times. It is noteworthy that during the Great Depression, and for many years after that, B&S hired local farm families to hand-label crayons to supplement their winter incomes.

For the Pigment Division, the highlight of this period was a 1911 request from Akron-based B.F. Goodrich Company for an annual supply of one million pounds of carbon. Why? In the early years of the automobile, tires were white because of the zinc oxide in the rubber compound. Goodrich, however, experimented with "Silvertown" tires brought from England and discovered that the tread rubber wore considerably longer than that of the older white tire. The London manufacturer said he used a small amount of B&S carbon black to give his tires a distinguishing gray tint. Goodrich experimented with tires containing varying amounts of No. 40 black mixed with rubber and found that increasing the amount of carbon bound the rubber particles together to a greater degree than ever known and considerably prolonged the life of the tire. B&S met the Goodrich challenge by forming the Columbian Carbon Company and fulfilled its contract in due time. The downside of dispersing carbon black into rubber in its dry state was that it created much dust, compared with the dust-free addition of carbon black to liquid bases, such as paints and inks. B&S technicians, however, developed and patented a formula for putting the black into the form of pellets and practically eliminated the dust.

The rapid development of many varieties of carbon black also spurred important advances in other industries. In the graphic arts, printing inks required the proper carbons for application to various new surfaces, such as highly finished papers, cellophane, and different plastic materials. Carbon black gave printing inks the special qualities needed for efficient operation at the rapid rate used to print modern newspapers. Furthermore, carbon black made it possible to develop the special lacquers required for automobiles. And carbon black was used for shading or tinting cement to eliminate the glare of an untreated finish.

While the Pigment Division was experiencing rapid growth, the Crayon Division was quietly learning how to produce a superior crayon for both the retail trade and the education field. The first Crayola crayons were made in 16 colors; the eight-stick box sold for five cents and the 16-stick box sold for ten cents. Crayola Rubens crayons for art students and Perma Pressed fine-art crayons that could be sharpened were added to the product line. A new Crayola 48-stick box introduced in 1949 featured new colors, such as *bittersweet, burnt sienna, periwin-*

kle, and *prussian blue.* Nine years later, *prussian blue* was renamed *midnight blue* in response to teachers' observations that students were no longer familiar with Prussian history. (Note: The small *p* was an intentional grammatical error to keep the word consistent with the way all Crayola crayon names appeared on labels. Tests had shown that words written in lowercase letters were easiest for elementary school children to read.) By 1955 B&S had placed some 464 different items on the market.

Crayola Takes Over: 1955–92

Sales in the Crayon Division increased steadily while the Pigment Division grew rapidly in size and products. Over the years the Pigment Division had relied more and more on the Columbian Carbon Company for carbon black, bone black, iron oxides, new inks, and other products that accompanied developments in the oil and gas fields. Columbian became much larger than B&S; it was one of the important U.S. corporations and was listed on the New York Stock Exchange. Wanting to own and direct its own sales activities, Columbian bought the B&S Dispersion Division and the Pigment Division in 1955. Consequently, B&S turned its attention to developing the business of the Crayola Division through relevant acquisitions and new products to carry out what it later identified as its unique mission: "to bring hands-on products for creative personal development and fun to consumers of all ages, at home and away from home."

In 1958 the Crayola 64-crayon box, which included 16 new colors and a built-in sharpener, makes its debut on the "Captain Kangaroo Show." According to B&S archives, this Crayola box "became part of the collective history and experiences of generations of Americans, and a symbol of the color and fun of childhood." Partially as a result of the U.S. Civil Rights Movement, in 1962 Crayola changed its crayon color named *flesh* to *peach,* in recognition of the fact that not everyone's skin is the same shade. With the 1964 purchase of Permanent Pigments Inc., maker of Liquitex, B&S established its brand of fine art and decorative art supplies. As a world leader in acrylic paints, Liquitex provided artists with technically advanced, high quality, versatile products in a broad range of colors, textures, and media. Thirteen years later B&S acquired the manufacturing rights for Silly Putty, which had started as a wartime experimental replacement for rubber and became one of the world's best-loved toy classics. Craft and activity kits became a vital part of the company's business. Then, Hallmark Cards, Inc., the world's largest greeting card manufacturer and a privately owned corporation, in 1984 acquired B&S as a wholly owned subsidiary.

That same year marked the introduction of Crayola's Dream-Makers, an art education program for the nation's elementary schools. To the great delight of children, mothers, and teachers, in 1987 Crayola placed *washable* markers on the market. This event was followed by the 1989 acquisition of the manufacturing rights for the Magic Marker brand of markers. In 1990 eight Crayola crayons—maize, raw umber, lemon yellow, blue gray, orange yellow, orange red, green blue, and violet blue—were retired into the Crayola Hall of Fame in Easton, Pennsylvania.

Two years later Crayola showed its leadership in the development of art products that emphasized international diversity by launching Crayola My World multicultural crayons. The company hoped that by using crayons, markers, paints, and modeling compounds that reflected the variety of skin tones, children would build a positive sense of self as well as respect for cultural diversity. By 1992 Crayola crayons came in 80 colors.

Toward the 21st Century: 1993 and Beyond

To celebrate Crayola brand's 90th anniversary, in 1993 B&S offered 16 new colors in the largest assortment of crayons to date: the Crayola 96 Big Box. Departing from the Crayola tradition of having company color experts name the new shades, B&S asked the public to name the new colors. Until then, most Crayola crayon color names were taken from the U.S. Commerce Department's National Bureau of Standards book, *Color: Universal Language and Dictionary of Names.* Newspapers throughout the nation publicized Crayola's "Name the New Colors Contest." One of the goals was to have this new generation of 16 crayons indicate the insights and interests of a new generation of users.

From January through August 1993, nearly two million suggestions came in from crayonists young and old. Five-year-old Laura Bartolomei-Hill, who submitted *razzmatazz* for the raspberry-red crayon, was the youngest winner. The eldest winner was 89-year-old Mildred Sampson, who submitted *purple mountain's majesty* for a purple crayon. Many other names—such as *pacific blue, tropical rain forest* (blue-green), *robin's egg blue, shamrock* (green), *wisteria* (lavender), *tumbleweed* (tan), and *timber wolf* (gray)—reflected growing interest in the environment. Some names, such as *tickle me pink* and *mauvelous* (mauve, destined to become the favorite color of comedian Billy Crystal, who made a living out of "looking maahvelous"), connoted the fun associated with using crayons. Other names referred to foods: *asparagus* (green), *granny smith apple* (green), and *macaroni and cheese* for the orange color of cheddar cheese melting on macaroni. Another winning entry, *cerise* (the French word for cherry, bright red), exposed children to a foreign language, as did the name *denim* (blue), which acknowledged the French source (*de Nîmes*) of a fabric that remained popular. Soon thereafter, in 1993, Crayola acquired Revell-Monogram, a world leader in the manufacture of model kits, die-cast models, and modeling accessories. From authentically detailed military aircraft to striking replicas of classic cars, Revell-Monogram kits had been favorites of modelers around the world for 50 years.

Comforting memories of a childhood "color-full" rite of passage were rekindled for baby boomers everywhere when, in 1998, B&S celebrated the classic Crayola 64-crayon box's 40th anniversary by the reintroduction of the original packaging, complete with built-in sharpener and original package graphics. More than 185 million of these Crayola boxes had been sold since 1958; undeniably, the 64-crayon box was one of the most enduring and identifiable symbols of American youth culture. For instance, the company estimated that the average U.S. child wore down 730 crayons by age ten. And, in the same spirit, the Smithsonian Institution's National Museum of American History placed an actual 1958 Crayola 64-crayon box and an assortment of 20th century Crayola advertising in the permanent collection of the Division of Cultural History.

Another form of recognition occurred in February 1998 when the U.S. Postal Service included Crayola crayons in its "Celebrate the Century" program, which honored memorable and significant people, places, events, and trends for each decade of the 20th century. The commemorative stamp depicted the original eight-count Crayola crayon box introduced in 1903.

As Binney & Smith approached its 100th anniversary in the 21st century, it had grown from its roots as a local supplier of pigment to a worldwide marketer of products to educate and entertain people of all ages. Judging from its uninterrupted, successful operation for nearly a century, there was reason to believe that the company would sensitize many more genera-tions to the wonder of color and to the enjoyment of educational hobbies, crafts, and the fine arts.

Further Reading

Cardona, Mercedes M., "Crayola Breaks Ad Effort To Target Parents' Nostalgia," *Advertising Age,* July 21, 1997, p. 35.

Goldstein, Seth, "Hallmark Inks Kid Vid Deal," *Billboard,* February 22, 1997, pp. 8–10.

Kitchel, A.F., *The Story of the Rainbow,* Easton, Penn.: Binney & Smith (company archives), 1961.

Mehegan, Sean, "Brand Builders: The Color of Money," *Brandweek,* September 15, 1997, p. 22.

—Gloria A. Lemieux

BJ Services Company

5500 NorthWest Central Drive
P.O. Box 21106
Houston, Texas 77092
U.S.A.
(713) 462-4239
Fax: (713) 895-5897
Web site: http://www.bjservices.com

Public Company
Incorporated: 1872 as Byron Jackson Company
Employees: 8,453
Sales: $1.47 billion (1997)
Stock Exchanges: New York
Ticker Symbol: BJS
SICs: 1389 Oil & Gas Field Services

BJ Services Company is a major provider of specialized oil-field services, ranking second worldwide. Its chief competitors are Halliburton and Schlumberger, which provide similar services to the petroleum industry. BJ's services primarily relate to pressure pumping activities at new and remediated oil and gas well sites, and include well stimulation, commissioning, sand control, cementing, and casing and tubing services. It also provides inspection and leak-detection services and, in selected geographic regions, markets specialized chemicals. In addition, in the North Sea, Gulf of Mexico, and South America, the company operates, owns, or leases several stimulation vessels. It thus maintains a high industry profile in major onshore and offshore oil fields, including those of the Gulf of Mexico, Texas, California, Canada, the North Sea, much of Latin America, Indonesia, and the Middle East. The company has divisional offices and branches at or near many of these sites, all networked to its central corporate office in Houston, Texas.

BJ Services began to take its current shape in 1990, after it was reorganized and incorporated as a public company and commenced aggressive expansion through acquisitions and consolidation. Its major additions in the following years included the Western Company of North America, acquired in July 1995, and

Nowsco Well Services Ltd., bought in June 1996. Nowsco, headquartered in Calgary, Alberta, is BJ Services' Canadian subsidiary and provides all the core pumping services of the parent company. Other subsidiaries are Unichem (the production and refinery chemicals unit), BJ Process and Pipeline Services, and BJ Tubular Services. Unichem, with headquarters in Houston, specializes in fouling and corrosion problems. It helps gas and oil operators, refineries, and petrochemical producers reach maximum production levels by minimizing the cost of treating these problems. BJ Process and Pipeline Services, headquartered in Aberdeen, Scotland, offers leak detection and commissioning services plus a complete range of services and equipment for the global oil industry, including refineries, process plants, and pipelines. It includes Pipeline Cleaners, a division headquartered in Houston, and a plant in Iowa. Also headquartered in Scotland, BJ Tubular Services provides casing and tubing services and sends highly experienced, veteran crews to drilling sites in Europe, the North Sea, and the Pacific Rim. These various divisions operate within a subsidiary arrangement, which, in 1997, supported over 80 divisional and branch offices throughout the world.

Byron Jackson and the Origin of BJ Services

The man whose initials remain part of the company name was Byron Jackson, a pioneer-inventor who, in 1872, founded the Byron Jackson Company. The firm designed and manufactured pumps and other equipment for miners and farmers, including the Jackson Feeder, a major labor-saving device.

In 1879, the company moved to San Francisco, where, as the Byron Jackson Machine Works, it manufactured prototypes of both deep-well turbine and submersible pumps. The growing business had one major setback in 1906, when San Francisco's great earthquake and fire destroyed the plant, but Jackson rebuilt his factory, and before his retirement in 1913, he helped design and engineer a new fire prevention and protection system for San Francisco. The system included the first use of fire trucks and fire boats equipped with efficient, high-pressure centrifugal pumps.

Other companies that would figure in the early history of BJ Services were the Independent Torpedo Company of Findlay,

Ohio, and the Dunn Manufacturing Company of Oxnard, California. Independent Torpedo was formed in 1905, with a primary aim of ''shooting'' wells with explosives to induce fracturing in oil reservoirs. Dunn, in 1911, began marketing a new type of casing wrench, an early version of tongs, a major oil-field device. Expansion followed, particularly in the case of Independent Torpedo, which began servicing oil fields of the southwest from its plant in DeLeon, Texas, which opened in 1917. In 1928, Independent merged with the Eastern Torpedo Company.

BJ Expansion Through the Great Depression

In 1929, at the start of the Great Depression, the company established the Byron Jackson Oil Tool Division after acquiring the Dunn Manufacturing Company and some other, smaller companies engaged in manufacturing oil-field tools. It also purchased the Pacific Cementing Company and commenced servicing drilling operations in the Los Angeles Basin in southern California. Three years later, in 1932, it put the Chemical Process Company in operation in Breckenridge, Texas, where it specialized in oil-well acidizing. Then, in 1938, with new oil-field strikes in the Mid-Continent and Permian Basin regions, BJ built a new manufacturing plant in Houston, its future home base. Two years later, amidst World War II, it also entered into an arrangement with Baker Oil Tools, Schlumberger, and Dowell to provide joint oil-field cementing services under the conglomerate name International Cementers Inc.

New Technologies in the Post-World War II Boom

In 1945, BJ developed the first practical air-powered drilling device, the BJ Power Slip, and in the following year jointly developed a prototype jet-shaped charge, making it the first to jet perforate concrete casings for oil wells. It also developed the PL-7 pump truck, a cementing unit with a 10,000 psi capacity. In 1948, BJ introduced a new system for handling drill pipe, ultimately to become the Type V Pipe Racking System, which is still widely used in the industry.

The company's innovations led to success and inevitable expansion. In 1951, BJ acquired International Cementing. Then, in 1956, it became a subsidiary of Borg-Warner, one of the

largest and most innovative industrial complexes in the country. In that same year, BJ purchased the Chemical Process Company, which earlier had merged with the Eastern/Independent Torpedo Company. The move strengthened BJ's role in fracturing and acidizing services, and opened up new markets, both domestic and foreign.

Expansion Through the 1960s

BJ's reputation also strengthened as it expanded. The company created 40 service districts to service all the major oil fields in the United States and also established overseas operations in over 20 countries, notably in Canada, Argentina, and Australia.

Clearly, BJ had become a leading oil-field service company, noted for its development of new technologies and equipment. In 1959, Phillips Petroleum used tools developed by BJ to drill a well in Pecos, Texas, to over 25,000 feet, at the time the deepest drilled well in the world. In 1962, the company introduced the Pacemaker, a triplex pump that became the prototype for compact pumping skids, which, by 1967, were being used on offshore rigs and various remote locations. These light weight skids could be broken down quickly for transport by helicopter, then reassembled at inaccessible sites for both cementing and drilling services.

Other important innovations followed. During 1967 and 1968, the company introduced new systems, both for handling mud and automatically controlling its density as well as creating cement slurry additives and verifying cement blends. It also developed the BJ Subsea Cementing Plug System, making offshore cementing both more efficient and safer.

Name and Ownership Changes with the Oil Slowdown of the 1970s and 1980s

After the oil boom of the early 1970s, there was a long cooling off in the petroleum industry that reached a nadir in the mid-1980s. During that time, the company went through some restructuring and name changes. First, in 1974, Hughes Tool Company purchased the concern, changing its name to BJ-Hughes Inc. A decade later, in 1985, a subsidiary of Dresser Industries named Titan Services formed a partnership with Hughes, using the name BJ Titan Services, but the partnership dissolved in 1989. That breakup allowed the company to evolve into an independent corporation, BJ Services, formed on May 13, 1990. In July of that same year, the company went public. It became totally independent of Hughes by 1991, when Baker Hughes Inc. sold all its remaining interest in the company.

The 1990s: Rapid Growth Through New Technologies and Major Acquisitions

The newly reorganized BJ Services Company immediately entered a period of expansion in both size and technological development. In 1991, it developed two computer monitoring systems that allowed users precise control over cement slurry mixtures and fracturing fluids. It also began marketing an offshore cementing unit, the RAM (Recirculating Averaging Mixer), and introduced newly developed fracturing fluids (including Spectra Frac, Medallion Frac, and Spartan) as well as

CEMFACTS PLUS, a computer software program for design, realtime data control, and post-use analysis in cementing applications. Additional innovative products followed over the next few years, including, in 1993, a proprietary enzyme breaker known as Enzyme G SM, designed to increased the efficiency of fracturing fluid systems, and, in 1995, BJ Sandston Acid, a formula allowing deep oil reservoir penetration for enhancing recovery and production speed.

These technological developments went hand in hand with BJ Services growth through the purchase of other oil-field suppliers, starting with Salvesen Oilfield Technology, Ltd., in 1992. Salvesen, renamed BJS Oilfield Technology Limited, provided casing, tubing, and leak-detection services in the North Sea/U.K. fields and provided BJ with a growing presence in those markets.

In April 1995, after some other minor acquisitions, BJ purchased the Western Company of North America, a Texas company that had developed hydraulic fracturing for oil well stimulation. This acquisition boosted BJ's domestic revenue base by over 100 percent and improved its competitiveness in both national and international markets. It increased BJ's share of the domestic oil pumping service to about 30 percent and provided BJ with highly skilled personnel who helped develop more efficient and versatile fracturing fluid systems from the two companies' diverse products. The consolidation reduced BJ's inventory costs, saving the company over $40 million annually.

In the next year, BJ bought Nowsco Well Services Ltd., a company, formed in 1962, which developed coil tubing and innovative technologies. Nowsco, whose acronym stands for "Nitrogen Oil Well Service Company," started from a single office in Red Deer, Alberta, and quickly expanded operations into the United States, the United Kingdom, and Europe, and its purchase gave BJ new domestic, Canadian, and overseas markets. As a subsidiary of BJ Services, Nowsco has made BJ the primary pumping service provider in Canada and, worldwide, a major coiled tubing and leak detection service provider. The operational integration of BJ and Nowsco has resulted in an expanding coiled tubing business and increased cost reductions of over $22 million.

One additional acquisition was the Top Tool Company, Inc., purchased in July 1997. Top Tool provides oil-field tools for rigs drilling along the coast of Louisiana. The purchase has provided BJ with a greater servicing capacity, expanded its downhole tool operations, and improved its tool proficiency.

These major acquisitions have allowed BJ Services to offer increased synergistic services around the world and rapidly increase its sales. Between 1992 and 1996, BJ almost tripled its total sales, from $330 million to $965 million, and it achieved another 50 percent increase the next year, nearly reaching $1.5 billion.

Company prospects appeared excellent, although always to some degree contingent on the price of oil in a volatile market that largely outside BJ's control. Yet, even during oil price slides and industry slow-downs, the diversification of BJ Services made it a strong, virtually fail-safe enterprise. In the spring of 1998, oil prices slipped lower than anticipated, with a negative impact on oil production in the United States, Canada, and Latin America. However, BJ's CEO, J. W. Stewart, was able to claim that, thanks to the continuing need to drill for natural gas in the United States, the company's growth initiatives in stimulation, coiled tubing, downhole tool, and pipeline inspection services were still on target. The company's reported earnings through the first half of 1998 supported Stewart's optimistic analysis. Revenues increased by 19 percent and net income by 106 percent over the same period of the previous year.

The core businesses of BJ Services remained what they had been for several years: cementing, stimulation, and coiled tubing services offered across the globe. But, through its acquisitions over the decade of the 1990s, it made strong advances into ancillary, pressure-pumping services, including casing and tubular supply, inspection, and industrial commissioning services. The company took pride in its global, synergistic technologies that allowed it to provide an array of services to even the most remote oil-production sites. It should continue as an industry leader well into the 21st century.

Principal Subsidiaries

BJ Services Company, U.S.A.; BJ Services Company Middle East; BJ Services Company Overseas; BJ Services Company Limited (U.K.); Nowsco Well Service Ltd. (Canada); Unichem; BJ Process and Pipeline Services (U.K.); BJ Tubular Services (U.K.).

Further Reading

"BJ Service Inc., Houston, Won a Bidding War with a $788 Million (Canadian) Offer for Nowsco Well Service Ltd., Calgary," *Oil and Gas Journal*, 94, December 4, 1995, p. 71.

"BJ Services Announces Increase in Stock Repurchase Program," http://www.prnewswire.com/cgi-bin/stories.pl?ACCT = 105&STORY = /www/story/05-29-1998/0000668401&EDATE = .

"BJ Services Co. (Marvin Wade, President)," *Oil and Gas Journal*, 93, June 17, 1996, p. 23.

"BJ Services Reports 53% Increase in Earnings Per Share on Record Revenue and Profits," http://www.prnewswire.com/cgi-bin/stories.pl? ACCT = 105&STORY = /www/story/51098 &EDATE = .

"BJ Services Reports Record Results with a 112% Increase in EPS," http://www.prnewswire.com/cgi-bin/stories.pl?ACCT = 105&STORY = /www/story/1-20-98/397344&EDATE = .

Eichenwald, Kurt, "Information Was the Key in the Selloff of BJ Services Stock," *New York Times* (Late Edition), August 27, 1993, p. D4.

Norman, James R., "Cloud over Baker," *Forbes*, 149, May 11, 1992, pp. 220–21.

———, "Hot Potato? (Parker & Parsley Brings Suit Against Baker Hughes, Dresser and BJ-Titan on Charges of Shortchanging)," *Forbes,* July 9, 1990, pp. 38–39.

Schwartz, Nelson D., and John Lovoi, "How Did Oil Services Get So Hot?" http://www. pathfinder.com/fortune/pfortune/1124por.html.

—John W. Fiero

BLAIR®

Blair Corporation

220 Hickory Street
Warren, Pennsylvania 16366-0001
U.S.A.
(814) 723-3600
Fax: (814) 726-6376

Public Company
Incorporated: 1924 as New Process Company
Employees: 2,300
Sales: $486.6 million (1997)
Stock Exchanges: American
Ticker Symbol: BL
SICs: 5961 Catalog & Mail Order Houses, Retail

Blair Corporation sells women's and men's apparel and home furnishings by mail. Its product lines are geared toward low- and middle-income buyers, emphasizing quality at a reasonable price. Women's clothing represents approximately 60 percent of Blair's sales, followed by menswear at 25 percent. The remaining portion of its sales is taken up by home furnishings. Blair mainly solicits customers through direct mailings of letters and circulars, though in recent years the company has added a catalog as well. Blair has no manufacturing facilities of its own. The company maintains a merchandise distribution center and a mail processing plant in Irvine, Pennsylvania, close to its administrative headquarters in Warren. Blair also runs two outlet stores and two retail stores, all of which are located in Pennsylvania and Delaware.

Early History

Blair Corporation was founded by John L. Blair, a law student from Warren, Pennsylvania. In 1910, while he was in the last year of law school at the University of Pennsylvania, he took up a business venture with a classmate who had recently inherited a raincoat factory. The classmate asked Blair to market the coats for him. Thus, while on his spring break, Blair dutifully tried to sell the black coats to merchants in the towns between Philadelphia and his hometown. In one town, he sold one of the black raincoats to an undertaker, but he could not

persuade any store to buy his black stock, because tan was the color in fashion at that time. Blair decided to contact undertakers directly by mail. He borrowed $500 and used the money to print and mail flyers. He solicited 10,000 undertakers, and in no time had sold the entire first batch of 400 black raincoats.

Blair decided to pursue this business, and named his company the New Process Rubber Company, after the process of sandwiching rubber between two layers of cloth to make the raincoats waterproof. But the firm quickly expanded beyond its first product line, and offered other goods by mail as well. In consequence, "Rubber" was dropped from the company name in 1916. John Blair's New Process Company sought out all kinds of low-cost apparel and advertised it by mailing letters and flyers to its growing customer list.

The company outgrew its quarters several times, starting in the basement of a Warren furniture store, moving next to a third floor loft above a dry goods store, and in the 1920s expanding into a string of brick buildings along Hickory Street. Blair's two younger brothers, Harold and Lester, joined the company, and even Blair's father worked with him for a time. New Process pioneered a seven-day free trial approval for its goods, letting customers test their purchases for a week, with the right to return anything unsatisfactory. The simple flyer that had advertised black raincoats gave way to more sophisticated mailings featuring photos of professional models, or else spirited drawings. Value was the key to all of New Process's goods; they were bargains that could be obtained only by mail.

By the 1920s, the company was offering a gamut of goods, from silk stockings and pearl necklaces to motor oil and Gladstone bags. Cigars, pajamas, dolls, shoes, furs and footballs all found a place in the New Process line. For a while, the company also offered a three-volume *Book of Success*, penned by the successful president of the company, John L. Blair, and several of his co-executives. In 1924, New Process incorporated as a public company, and listed its stock on the American Stock Exchange.

Through the Depression into Postwar Expansion

New Process expanded its customer list rapidly in the 1920s, at a time of growing consumerism. In 1927, the company built a large brick three-story building behind its Hickory Street complex, the first building it had constructed for itself. When the stock market crashed in 1929, leading into the Great Depression, many of New Process's customers were hard hit. The company struggled to keep afloat. Net sales for the period 1930–1934 dipped to about half what they had been from 1925–1929. Nevertheless, net income averaged over the two periods to about the same. New Process continued to search for new customers, and was on its way to becoming one of the largest mail order companies in the world. The company's resilience was tested in 1933, when an early morning fire gutted all of New Process's Hickory Street buildings. Workers salvaged what inventory they could, and moved it to the building the company had built in 1927. Remarkably, the company was operating again in ten days, and within a year New Process had erected a new, more modern building at the site of the fire.

By the end of the 1930s, New Process was expanding again, with sales figures equal to or better than those of the late 1920s. The company purchased additional warehouse space and expanded and modernized its existing facilities. Presumably because the company offered bargain goods, its stock sold well during the years of war-time scarcity. After World War II ended, sales boomed at New Process. Items such as nylon stockings, unavailable during the war, were big sellers. The company added an automated conveyor system to its packaging department in 1950, and added footage to it in 1952 and 1954. The conveyor belt grew to nearly half a mile long, and a large staff packed, taped, weighed and addressed the outgoing orders.

New Process continued to build and modernize. In 1965, the company installed its first computers. First typewriters and then specialized machines called addressographs had been used previously to print the thousands of labels for the company's direct mailings. Using computers, New Process's workers could turn out address labels significantly faster and less laboriously. The company also gained storage space. The old addressograph system used metal plates for each customer address, and by 1965 there were six million of these plates, taking up thousands of square feet of floor space. In contrast, the tape reels used by the computer occupied a only a closet-sized space. But the growing company was still in need of storage, and throughout the 1960s continued to build and purchase warehouses.

1970s and 1980s

Both founder John L. Blair and his younger brother Lester died in 1962. The remaining brother, Harold, had retired from the company in 1960, and passed away in 1971. Blair family members retained a large percentage of the firm's stock. But in the early 1970s institutional investors suddenly discovered the

company, and apparently fell in love with its long record of rising sales, low debt, and consistent dividend payments. On Wall Street, money managers deemed New Process a "one-decision" stock, meaning that once the decision had been made to buy it, there was no second decision coming up regarding whether or not to sell. New Process stock became so hot that it soared from around $20 a share in 1971 to over $70 a year later. This frenzy for the stock was not encouraged by New Process's management, which was famous for not taking calls from Wall Street analysts. The company published no earnings projections, and so did nothing to prepare its adherents for a bump that came in 1973. Profits dipped, and the "one-decision" buyers were apparently so dismayed that they forgot their philosophy and bailed out. The stock dropped as low as $3 in 1974.

Nevertheless, the company was in very good shape financially. By 1976, New Process had over 11 million customers across the U.S., employed close to 1700 people, and had sales of just under $200 million. After expending capital on building expansions in the early 1970s, the company was essentially free of debt by 1976. Its sales fluctuated some in the late 1970s, with some losses attributed to the passing of the leisure suit fad. But one strength of the company was that it tended to have higher sales during recessions. Because it catered to cost-conscious consumers, it found more customers during economic downturns. So in 1979, a disastrous year for many industries, New Process had record sales, and seemed to be an enviably stable company.

By 1984, New Process was the largest publicly-held direct mail business in the U.S. The company, now run by John Blair Jr., the son of founder John L. Blair, was using its computers to generate mailings every two weeks to over 12 million targeted customers. The company sometimes took in as many as 40,000 orders a day. New Process's inventory control, order routing, and much of its packaging was now automated, so orders were turned around very quickly.

In the mid-1980s the company was still virtually free of debt. A home furnishings division, begun in 1977, was contributing a substantial portion of earnings to the company's profits by 1985, and overall earnings were at a record high. Sales grew at a rate of over 10 percent annually throughout the 1980s, and the company seemed able to adjust quickly to financial challenges. For example, when increased postal rates ate into profits, the company researched its potential market more thoroughly, and targeted its mailings to get a higher response rate. As a result, New Process attracted more orders with fewer mailings, and its postal costs as a percentage of sales dropped.

Into the 1990s

In April, 1989, the New Process Company formally changed its name to Blair Corporation, after its founder. The Blair family still retained over 30 percent of the stock, and there was much about the company that was old-fashioned. For instance, where most mail order businesses relied on catalogs, Blair persisted in its old formula of mailing circulars and fabric swatches stuffed in envelopes. But the old-fashioned image belied a company that was always willing to modernize where needed. For example, Blair spent approximately $18 million in the early 1990s to build a new mail facility.

The 1990s, however, were a time of transition for the company. Though sales rose steadily year by year, profits were up and down. Blair's customers were very sensitive to price increases, and it was difficult for the company to pass on its own rising costs. The company tried to get out of its difficulties by extending more credit to customers. In 1996 Blair launched an aggressive program to boost sales through liberal credit, and ended up collecting a lot of bad debt. Though customers responded to Blair's generous credit policy by buying more, the company found it difficult to collect payment in many instances. The push for higher sales ultimately hurt the company. Profits in 1995 stood at over $25 million on sales of over $560 million; the next year sales dropped slightly to $544 million, but profits sank to $14.7 million.

Because its new credit policy was clearly not working, Blair's management agreed to change course, and the company instituted a new strategy in 1997. In order to get the best possible results from its mailings, the company resolved to develop a more sophisticated information system. Blair began to test databases that would give it more in-depth and accurate information about its products and customers. The new computer programs could analyze customers' seasonal buying patterns and product preferences. An accounts receivable database allowed the company to extend credit selectively, targeting good customers and avoiding risky ones. Blair also decided to purchase demographic and lifestyle databases from outside sources, to supplement its own customer databases.

The company made other changes too. Blair's traditional customer base had been over 50 years old. In 1997, Blair decided to actively pursue a little younger age group, people aged 40 and over. This group was larger, and with broader tastes. And while many of its customers preferred the circular mailers Blair had always sent out, the company was aware that many younger consumers preferred to buy from catalogs. So Blair began developing catalogs for its womenswear, menswear and home products lines. The company did not want to shift over entirely to catalogs, but tried to offer different consumers the marketing format they were most comfortable with.

Sales and earnings fell in 1997, further emphasizing the importance of getting the new business strategies working. By early 1998, the company seemed to be in a better position regarding its bad debts. Earnings in the first quarter of 1998 were better than in the previous quarter. All in all, it seemed that Blair was cognizant of the problems which had caused its earlier difficulties, and was on the way to correcting them. The company had a long history of economic stability and a rich knowledge of the mail order industry. With these strengths, Blair appeared ready to continue its growth into the next century.

Principal Subsidiaries

Blair Holdings, Inc.

Further Reading

Abelson, Alan, "Up and Down Wall Street," *Barron's,* December 23, 1985, p. 31.
Blyskal, Jeff, "Mail Order for the Masses," *Forbes,* July 16, 1984, pp. 35–36.
Cochran, Thomas N., "Check's in the Mail," *Barron's,* September 19, 1988, p. 46.
Jaffe, Michael, "Stocking Stuffers?" *Forbes,* November 26, 1990, p. 316.
Lazo, Shirley A., "Speaking of Dividends," *Barron's,* May 18, 1992, p. 44.
New Process Company 75th Anniversary Book. Warren, Penn.: New Process Company, 1985.
Tenreiro, Michael, "Blair Corp," *Value Line,* February 20, 1998, p. 1681.
Troxell, Thomas N. Jr., "Aggressive Merchandiser," *Barron's,* March 8, 1982, p. 46.

—A. Woodward

THE BOC GROUP

BOC Group plc

Chertsey Road
Windlesham, Surrey GU20 6HJ
England
(0276) 77222
Web site: http://www.boc.com

Public Company
Incorporated: 1886 as Brin's Oxygen Co., Ltd.
Employees: 41,000
Sales: £4.0 billion (1997)
Stock Exchanges: London New York
Ticker Symbol: BOC
SICs: 2813 Industrial Gases; 2834 Pharmaceutical
    Preparations; 3841 Surgical & Medical Instruments &
    Apparatus; 8742 Manufacturing Management,
    Physical Distribution, & Site Location Consulting

BOC Group plc is one of the world's largest producers of industrial gases essential to almost every manufacturing process. It supplies a variety of gases to the petroleum, electronic, steel manufacturing, metal producing and fabricating, construction, ceramic, and food and beverage industries. Its principal related companies operate in over 60 countries across the globe. The company also owns subsidiaries that provide vacuum technology and distribution services.

Company Origins

Although oxygen had been used in an extremely limited capacity since the late 18th century as a respiratory agent, the development of chemically produced oxygen was hampered by costly methods, yielding only small amounts of relatively impure gases. Commercially produced oxygen was largely confined to "limelight," used to illuminate the stages of theaters and music halls, and that popular means of entertainment and enlightenment, the lantern lecture.

In 1885 two French brothers and chemists, Arthur and Leon Quentin Brin, traveled to the Inventions Exhibition in South Kensington, London, and erected a demonstration of their recently patented method of making oxygen by heating barium oxide, with a view to attracting financial support. They found it in Henry Sharp, an English stoneware manufacturer. In January of 1886 the brothers established Brin's Oxygen Company Limited.

In the spring of 1886 the fledgling company hired its first foreman, a young Scotsman by the name of Kenneth Sutherland Murray. A man of remarkable mechanical ingenuity, Murray redesigned the plant in his first year on the job. In 1888 the new plant went into operation and production increased from nearly 145,000 to 690,000 cubic feet of oxygen. One year later the plant installed an automatic gear, invented by Murray, and improved Brin's production to nearly a million cubic feet of oxygen a year.

From the beginning, however, limelight was a limited market, and so the company board members searched for new ideas to develop oxygen sales. They promoted the use of oxygen in preserving milk, bleaching sugar, manufacturing saccharine, vinegar and linoleum, maturing whisky, and in the production of iron and steel. They hired a horse and carriage for the express purpose of "pushing business."

As a result, sales of oxygenated water in any form, flavored or not, increased dramatically. Moreover, the beverage found favor among temperance groups. The company published signed physicians' testimonials extolling the virtues of this new "health" drink, prescribing it as a sort of universal remedy.

The company then turned its attention to the means of gas containment and distribution. The early method of storing and distributing gas, the gas bag, was an inefficient method which resulted in a significant loss of both gas and profit, and was soon replaced by the sturdier iron cylinder. However, even with this vast improvement over the gas bag, the new method of containment was cumbersome and costly. The cylinder itself weighed and cost more than the gas it held, making the product economically impractical to distribute over a large geographical area.

Consequently, in 1887, under the guiding hand of Henry Sharp, Brin's began granting licenses to a handful of independent companies throughout Great Britain to produce oxygen under the

Company Perspectives:

The BOC Group is built around its customers. Whatever the industry or interest, our goal is to respond to their needs as quickly and effectively as possible. Their ever-changing requirements are the driving force behind the development of all our products, technologies and support services. We recognize that BOC people are our most important asset, and through them we ensure that we play a full and active role in communities around the world and are committed to the highest standards of safety and environmental practice. At the same time, we believe that the best way we can assist any of the communities in which we operate is to build a successful business. That's why, as the BOC Group continues to expand and develop, one thing will never change. We will always remain built around our customers.

patented Brin process. In 1890 Brin's introduced another improvement in containment, a steel cylinder, which soon became the standard of gas containment worldwide, and expanded its production to related products, such as valves and fittings.

At the same time, in a move that marked the beginning of the company's international growth, Brin's began exporting oxygen in cylinders to Australia for medical use, and developed plants in France, Germany and the United States, granting them sole rights to operate under the Brin process.

In the decade that followed, Brin's did little more than consolidate its operations and improve its market share. The company took over two of the British companies which had been granted licenses earlier to produce its product. The company also elected its second chairman, Edward Badouin Ellice-Clark. After several years into his chairmanship, Ellice-Clark expressed some regret that the industry had produced no advances in the application of industrial oxygen.

By 1900, however, a new method of producing oxygen by converting air to liquid had been devised independently in Britain, the United States and Germany. The German scientist reached a patent office first, and the patent went to Dr. Carl von Linde. Brin's almost immediately negotiated an agreement to use the Linde patents and within several years abandoned both its now dated barium oxide method of oxygen production and the company name. In 1906 Brin's Oxygen Company Limited became the British Oxygen Company Limited, or BOC.

Early Twentieth Century Expansion

There followed steady expansion spurred by development of new technologies using oxygen in metal cutting and welding. In 1914 Britain declared war on Germany, and business increased significantly. No previous war had equaled the output of munitions, and the essential element of oxygen was apparent in almost every aspect of munitions production. Every means of transport, including ships, tanks and trucks, involved either metal cutting or welding, usually both.

BOC continued to grow in the immediate post-World War I years through acquisitions and through development in the commercial use of products such as acetylene and the rare gases. These various gases, with their exotic sounding names of argon, krypton, helium, neon and xenon, were developed and marketed for use in such products as the neon light, fog lamps, miner's lamps, respiratory gas in obstetric analgesia, and as protection for divers against the "bends."

In 1920 BOC acquired a London company called Sparklets Ltd. A major producer of small arms munitions during World War I, Sparklets had originally formed for the purpose of manufacturing small bulbs of carbon dioxide for carbonated drinks. Ten years later, BOC merged with Allen-Liversidge Ltd., a South African company with whom BOC had collaborated throughout the 1920s in further developing the acetylene welding process. In 1925 Kenneth Sutherland Murray, the company's first foreman, was appointed chairman.

Technological Advances in the mid-1900s

As an adjunct to its admittedly limited production of medical oxygen, and in response to a request by the National Birthday Trust Fund, BOC designed a machine for use by midwives in 1935 called the "Queen Charlotte's Gas-Air Analgesia Apparatus." Soon afterwards, BOC introduced an improved anesthetic gas, called "Entonox," used extensively to ease pain in childbirth and which was available in ambulances for use during emergencies.

That same year, in a pioneering accomplishment, the company set up a separate medical division equipped to install oxygen which would be available "on tap" by means of an extensive circuit of copper pipes connecting hospital wards and operating theaters to a battery of cylinders usually located in the basement of a hospital. Four years later, the company developed a machine which was the forerunner of surgical anesthetic equipment in use today. In an effort to further increase its welding interests, during 1936 BOC acquired the Quasi-Arc Company, a British company which had a refined welding electrode instrument that improved the process of arc welding.

With the onset of World War II, BOC produced gases for munitions and for medical needs. The Air Ministry enlisted the assistance of the company to produce oxygen and equipment designed to withstand high pressures for the Royal and allied Air Forces. Sparklets again began producing a variety of its unique bulbs, including bulbs used to inflate lifejackets; bulbs filled with insecticide, used to protect soldiers against malaria; bulbs used to lower landing gear in emergencies; and larger bulbs filled with ether, enabling engines to quick-start in the below-freezing Russian temperatures.

By 1950 BOC had formed subsidiary companies in over 20 countries. It was a decade that brought with it a revolution in the manufacture of steel as an increased demand for automobiles also led to increased productivity in both the steel and the gases industries. The common method of tanking liquid oxygen to various industries to be evaporated, pressurized and then fed to furnaces proved inadequate to the new demands of steel-making. The search for a new method gave rise to the production of "tonnage" oxygen.

A variation of medical oxygen on tap, tonnage oxygen is, as the name suggests, the production of oxygen by the ton. Rather than tank in the oxygen, and then have it converted, tonnage plants were built on or near the customer site to pump in the already converted oxygen by pipeline. Toward the end of the 1950s BOC was supplying tonnage oxygen to Wimpey for use in rocket motor testing and liquid oxygen for the launching sites of the Thor and Blue Streak missiles. For use in manufacturing semiconductor devices, BOC began supplying argon to Texas Instruments.

In 1957 the British Monopolies and Restrictive Practices Commission published a report stating that the company's prices for oxygen and dissolved acetylene were "unjustifiably high" and operated "against the public interest." According to the report, BOC had deliberately set out to build a monopoly. Successfully so, it would seem, as by this time the company had managed to secure 98 percent of the British market. The commission disclosed BOC's practice of providing plant equipment under highly restrictive conditions, and stated that BOC had concealed ownership of several of its subsidiaries while at the same time pretending to be in competition with them in a deliberate effort to drive up prices.

The report was the most scathing ever produced by the commission, according to one reporter. However, at the same time, the commission admitted there was nothing to suggest that BOC was operating under substandard levels of efficiency in any area, as might otherwise be expected in a company of similar standing and resources. The commission also noted that not one of the company's customers had actually complained about the high prices.

BOC drew criticism again in 1962 when the Board of Trade released the company from some of its obligations to the Monopolies and Restrictive Practices Commission. In response to the board's action, and immediately following a recent 6 percent price raise, the British division of Air Products of America noted that BOC still controlled 95 percent of the British market and argued that the action would restore the company to a monopoly.

Diversification in the 1960s and 1970s

New applications for liquid nitrogen prompted the company to develop new markets in refrigeration, food preservation and packaging, preserving medical tissues, and storing and transporting bull semen for artificial insemination. Along these lines, BOC set up BOC-Linde Refrigeration Ltd., with Linde A.G. of Germany in 1968, acquired Ace Refrigeration Ltd., and J. Muirhead Ltd., quick frozen food suppliers, in 1969, and held Batchelors Ltd., Ireland, a food processor, from 1969 to 1973.

The 1960s and 1970s were marked by an accelerated program of diversification at BOC. Under Chairman Leslie Smith, the company began planning for the 1980s, particularly with an eye to expansion in the Far East, by setting up British Oxygen (Far East) Ltd., in Tokyo. Diversification took BOC even farther afield into such areas as fatty acids, resins, and additives produced for paints, inks, and adhesives. In 1970 the company began producing cutting and welding machines which incorporated sophisticated techniques using lasers and electron beams.

The company also began developmental work on underwater welding techniques, producing DriWeld, a system that made structural welds possible at depths of 600 feet. Factories, joint ventures and new holdings were established in Jamaica, Holland, South Africa, Sweden and Spain for a variety of products, including transformers, magnetizing equipment, frozen foods, stable isotopes and radioactively labeled compounds and cryogenic systems. Furthermore, in 1971 the company installed the largest mainframe computer in Britain, linking a network of computers throughout the country. In a move characteristic of BOC, the company sold computer time to outside customers and, as a result, BOC found itself suddenly in the computer business.

In the wake of the 1973–74 oil crisis, BOC reassessed its portfolio and decided to divest itself of its more peripheral interests in order to concentrate on its primary business, especially the gases and health care markets. This was done with the intention of expanding production in these areas, particularly in Europe, the Americas and the Far East.

Perhaps the most important and far-reaching move in the history of BOC involved the acquisition of one of America's major industrial corporations, Airco, a company whose history, in terms of products and growth, nearly mirrored that of BOC. It was an acquisition that came after 11 years of litigation in which the U.S. Federal Trade Commission instigated antitrust proceedings against BOC in order to force the company to divest itself of all Airco stock. The decision was appealed and then delayed, but in 1978 Airco became a wholly owned subsidiary of BOC. This doubled the size of the company, and consequently the British oxygen company changed its name to the BOC Group.

Expansion into Home Health Care

Although secondary to its gas production, BOC's health care division was a world leader in the 1980s in researching and manufacturing completely integrated anesthesia systems, including the Modulus II Anesthesia System, one of the most technologically sophisticated anesthesia devices ever produced. Indeed, the bulk of the group's health care effort was concentrated in its anesthetic pharmaceuticals and equipment and in critical care and patient monitoring. The group's health care market was largely concentrated in the United States. Encouraged by the U.S. government's determination to contain hospital costs, the company was aggressively promoting home health care services.

In 1982 BOC acquired a U.S. company called Glasrock Home Health Care, which provided oxygen therapy and medical equipment to chronically ill and elderly patients at home. In 1986 Glasrock became the exclusive national distributor of the first portable defibrillator designed for home use and of the Alexis computer-controlled, omnidirectional wheelchair. And the company anticipated a growing need for long-range in-home care for AIDS patients, whom hospitals were often not equipped to handle.

BOC's chairman and chief executive officer, Richard Giordano, who came to the Group along with the acquisition of Airco, noted in 1987 that the likely future markets for further development in health care services would be in wealthier countries, such as the United States and Germany, followed by Sweden and Switzerland. In the United Kingdom, he stated, home health care was ''in the hands of the politicians,'' and he complained that ''the health service is absolutely Neanderthal.'' Japan was an additional possibility for the expansion in health care services, according to Giordano, since it was a country burdened with an aging population.

The group's third important area of business in the 1980s, the graphite division, which principally made graphite electrodes for furnaces, was described as a ''slow leak in BOC's earnings performance.'' This was a business that, like Giordano, came to BOC along with the Airco acquisition. During 1980, in an act that was described as a fit of misguided loyalty, Giordano invested in two new U.S. graphite plants; in 1985 the group experienced a loss of six million British pounds.

Under the leadership of Giordano, the BOC Group streamlined its portfolio through divestments and liquidations, concentrating on its two strongest businesses of gases and health care. Thirty of the companies acquired during the 1960s and 1970s diversification program had been sold by the late 1980s, and the work force trimmed by about 20,000.

Expansion in the Early 1990s

Having divested numerous unrelated subsidiaries in the 1980s, BOC resumed its expansion efforts, this time focusing on adding to its principal business units. Although this new direction was initiated under the leadership of Giordano, it was primarily executed by Patrick Rich, who became chief executive officer in 1991 and chairman in 1992.

In particular, the company invested in the first half of the 1990s in numerous gas companies. In 1990 BOC purchased the remaining shares of Commonwealth Industrial Gases in Australia, and the following year doubled its investment in the Nigerian company Industrial Gases Lagos, bringing its stake to 60 percent. In 1992 BOC formed a gases joint venture with Hua Bei Oxygen in northern China and in 1993 purchased Huls A.G., a German hydrogen business, as well as a 70 percent stake in one sector of Poland's state industrial gases business. The company spent $50 million in 1995 to purchase a 41 percent stake in Chile's leading industrial gases company, Indura SA Industria Y Commercio.

BOC made similar investments in its health care unit in the early 1990s. The company initiated a medical equipment joint venture with Japan's NEC San-ei and purchased the home medical businesses of Healthdyne Inc., both in 1990. The following year, BOC purchased Delta Biotechnology Ltd. for $23 million. In 1993 BOC combined its health care businesses, giving them the name Ohmeda. Acquisitions continued in 1994 with the purchase of the Calumatic Group, a Dutch manufacturer of filling, sterilizing, and packaging equipment for injectable pharmaceuticals.

BOC also expanded into the distribution business in the 1990s, becoming one of Britain's largest logistics operations. In 1990 the company purchased the U.K. distribution facilities of SmithKline Beecham consumer brands, and in 1993 acquired the Dutch distribution company Kroeze and the distribution operations of Gaymer Group. The following year BOC purchased the French distribution company TLO and the London Cargo Group, an airside cargo-handling specialist based in Heathrow.

BOC's finances in 1996 seemed strong, despite a slide in the performance of its health care business Ohmeda. Overall, the company reported record profits, up 11 percent from the previous year to $745 million. Sales had also risen, up 7 percent to $2.5 billion. In 1997, Ohmeda revenues were again down, this time by 6 percent. Profits declined even further, to 16 percent below 1996 levels. Overall, BOC revenues increased somewhat, to £4.0 billion from £3.75 billion in 1996. Profits also rose slightly, to £288 million.

In the late 1990s BOC increased its focus on its core gas business, both by expanding investment in that area and divesting other areas of the company. The first business to go was the underperforming health care subsidiary Ohmeda. In January 1998 the company announced it had reached an agreement to sell Ohmeda to a group of companies that comprised the Finnish business Instrumentarium Corporation and the U.S. businesses Becton, Dickinson & Company and Baxter International Inc. The $1050 million cash sale was due to be completed by April 4, 1998. In mid-1998 BOC announced its intention to exit the carbide industry by selling Odda Smelteverk A/S. The company was to be sold to Philipp Brothers Chemicals, Inc., for £11.5 million cash.

BOC's core gas business was performing strongly in the late 1990s, with growth in each major region of the world. The company commissioned ten new plants in the United States in 1997 to meet its long-term contracts and began construction on several large plants in Europe in 1998. In a joint venture with Foster Wheeler, BOC built the largest hydrogen plant in South America, which began operation in late 1997. Several other new plants were either under construction or began operations in the late 1990s in Africa and the Asia-Pacific region; both regions saw double digit rates of growth in their profits in 1997.

Principal Subsidiaries

BOC Gases Australia Ltd.; BOC Cylinder Gas NV (Belgium); BOC Canada Ltd.; BOC Distribution Services Ltd.; BOC Ltd.; BOC Overseas Finance Ltd.; BOC Technologies Ltd.; Edwards High Vacuum International Ltd.; BOC Gaz SA (France); BOC Group Ltd. (Hong Kong); BOC Japan Ltd.; BOC Gases Ireland Ltd.; BOC AG (Switzerland); The BOC Group, Inc.

Further Reading

''BOC's Record Profits Dispel Gloom,'' *Reuter Business Report,* November 29, 1996.
''Foster Wheeler/BOC Gases Will Celebrate Start-Up of the Largest Hydrogen Plant in South America,'' *Business Wire,* October 6, 1997.
Newman, Judy, ''Ohmeda Foresees a Painless Transition,'' *Wisconsin State Journal,* February 8, 1998.
Oliver, Judith, ''Patrick Rich,'' *Management Today,* August 1993, pp. 32–35.

—updated by Susan Windisch Brown

Bongrain SA

42 rue Rieussec
78223 Viroflay Cedex
France
(33) 1.01.34.58.63.00
Fax: (33) 1.01.30.24.03.83

Public Company
Incorporated: 1920 as Fromagerie d'Illoud; 1970 as
    Bongrain-Gérard
Employees: 8,549
Sales: FFr 11.583 billion (US $1.99 billion) (1997)
Stock Exchanges: Paris
SICs: 5143 Dairy Products Except Dried or Canned;
    2022 Cheese—Natural & Processed; 6719 Holding
    Companies, Not Elsewhere Classified

In France, cheese is spelled with a "B"—for Bongrain, Besnier, and Bel, the country's top three cheese and dairy producers, together responsible for more than 50 percent of all cheeses sold in that country. Bongrain SA counts among the world leaders in cheese and dairy product sales, with an extensive international presence, including a strong position in the United States through its subsidiaries Zausner and Aita Dena and such brands as Real Fresh, which together provide some 16 percent of the company's annual sales. In South America, Bongrain has built a leading presence in Brazil and Argentina, with production facilities in Chile and Uruguay as well. Bongrain also has maintained a continued presence in the developing Asian countries—for the day when these vast consumer markets adopt a taste for cheese.

Yet sales in Europe, and especially France, continue to account for more than 80 percent of Bongrain's annual revenues, with France alone providing some 48 percent of revenues. Outside of France, Bongrain's principal European markets include Germany, which provides some 13 percent of sales, with Italy, Spain, and Portugal figuring among Bongrain's major European markets as well. In addition, the company has made strong moves into the emerging Eastern European markets, with

a focus on Hungary, the Czech Republic, and Poland. With the mature French market—which counts more than 500 cheese specialties—providing limited opportunities for future growth, Bongrain has stepped up its international expansion in the 1990s.

Unlike rivals Besnier and Bel, which tend toward a centralized focus especially on single-brand sales (President and La Vache Qui Rit, respectively), Bongrain long has operated as a holding company for an extensive portfolio of subsidiaries and individual brand development—with some 40 brands, including the company's flagship Caprice des Dieux brand, in France alone. Since the 1950s Bongrain has maintained an intensive research and development wing, providing for the regular introduction of new cheese brands, enabling the company to establish positions in nearly every market segment. The company also has exhibited a flair for marketing and packaging that has enabled it to reinforce its new product launches, producing an enviable record of successes. Among the company's top-selling brands are Saint-Agur, P'tit Louis, Tartare, Fol Epi, Alouette (for the U.S. market), and Vieux Pané.

Decentralization is the key to the Bongrain organization. Built through acquisition, the company maintains an extensive list of subsidiaries, grouped principally under its European and International divisions. Many of the company's subsidiaries long have been responsible for production of single brands or types of cheeses—important in a country where cheese production remains in large part a matter of regional specialties. A vast program of capital expenditures for the opening of new plants and the renovation of existing plants begun in the 1990s, however, has converted many, if not most, of the company's production facilities into multi-type plants. In addition to the subsidiaries listed under parent Bongrain SA, the company's 10.3 percent share (through Bongrain family shareholding arm Soparind) of Compagnie Laitière Européenne (CLE, the former Union Laitière Normande) gives it operating control of that producer of an extensive line of dairy products and raw materials. The struggling CLE, however, remains unconsolidated with the Bongrain group's activities.

Bongrain continues to be led by founder Jean-Noël Bongrain. In late 1997, however, the 72-year-old Bongrain led a restructuring of the company, giving operating control of the company to long-time friend Bernard Lacan, while looking toward the family's succession by placing sons Armand and Alex in directorship positions. Through the Bongrain shareholding company Soparind, the Bongrain family holds nearly 51 percent of the company. After a difficult period in the mid-1990s, Bongrain appears to be back on course, with 1997 revenues rising past FFr 11.5 billion (nearly US $2 billion), for net profits of more than FFr 313 million.

Inspired by the Gods in the 1950s

Bongrain was founded as a small family-run cheese-making farm in the 1920s in Illoud, a village in the Haute Marne (Ardennes-Champagne) region of eastern France. Jean-Noël Bongrain formed part of the second generation to operate the family business, together with his older brother. But after Bongrain's brother was killed as a member of the Resistance during the Second World War, the family company came entirely under the then 19-year-old Jean-Noël Bongrain's leadership. Bongrain soon began to seek a new dimension for the small Fromagerie d'Illoud, one that would break the mold of the postwar French dairy industry, which was characterized chiefly by small or mid-sized independent companies, each concentrating on regional varieties. Among a single cheese variety, quality and other characteristics, such as flavor and texture, could vary widely, even when produced by the same company. The idea of "nationally" branded cheeses was still barely known—with Bel's La Vache Qui Rit forming one of the few exceptions.

By the start of the 1950s Bongrain, too, began searching for his own unique cheese. Together with employees, Bongrain spent some five years in research and experimentation, perfecting a formula that would provide not only a unique taste, but also the consistency of quality needed to break out of the regional boundaries. By the mid-1950s Bongrain had found his cheese: a molded cheese, with a firm outer skin yet with a soft, fresh-tasting center. Wedding modern production methods with traditional French cheese-making craftsmanship, Bongrain was able to provide the quality consistency needed to win over the French consumer, while maintaining an appealing flavor and texture.

Inventing the cheese was only part of the company's victory. Bongrain quickly proved himself an intuitive master of the art of marketing. Rather than package his new cheese in the common shape of the day (typically, round molds), Bongrain chose an oval form, instantly recognizable among the others. The cheese required a name, too: Bongrain chose *Caprice des Dieux* ("caprice of the gods"). The cheese's label also was chosen carefully, although the original portrayal of Zeus and Poseidon would give way to a longer lasting "angel" motif in the 1960s, while maintaining a tri-color scheme (blue for freshness, white for purity, red for passion) emulating the French flag. The company proved equally adept at inventing marketing slogans to appeal to the French consumer, including the early "un amour de fromage." Bongrain also made ready use of radio and television and other advertising venues. With such techniques—unusual for the French cheese industry of the time—Bongrain sought to build the brand beyond simply another cheese variety. *Caprice des Dieux* proved a quick success, launching Bongrain on a national scale.

Bongrain soon began to look over the French border. By the end of the 1950s *Caprice des Dieux* had begun to captivate German consumers as well. In the following decade the company moved into other European markets as well, including Switzerland, Austria, Italy, and Spain. The company also established subsidiaries in each country to provide for distribution. In the 1960s Bongrain began to look for further domestic expansion opportunities. Growing demand for *Caprice des Dieux* required the company to develop a more extensive supplier and production network. At the same time Bongrain sought to expand the company beyond its already famous single product. During the 1960s the company established a steady supply of milk with a regional network of dairy producers. The company also began buying other small cheese makers, for the time centered in the same region. The first wave of conglomeration in the food and dairy industries was already under way. Yet Bongrain resisted this trend, instead operating its acquisitions as small-sized, "human-scale" subsidiaries linked to the regional dairy network. Production of the new acquisitions, however, was converted toward products supporting the company's plans to expand its portfolio of cheese varieties.

An early addition was *Tartare,* produced by the company's Fromarsac subsidiary in 1964. The new brand again displayed the company's care for packaging: *Tartare* became one of the first cheeses to be packaged in portions. In 1967 the company acquired Fromageries des Chaumes, launching the company into that cheese variety as well. This acquisition was followed the next year by that of the Compagnie Fromagère de la Vallée de l'Ance. During the same period the company also had begun a similar policy in its foreign markets, acquiring a string of cheese producers in each country.

Building Scale in the 1970s and 1980s

The 1970s would see Bongrain's company emerge as one of France's premier national cheese producers. In 1970 three major acquisitions, of Laiterie Centrale Krompholtz, Grand'Ouche, and especially Gérard, gave the company a new boost in size. In that year Fromagerie d'Illoud changed its name to Bongrain-Gérard. More French acquisitions followed, including those of the Laiterie de la Vallée du Dropt in 1971, Siclet in 1973, and Rambol in 1975, accompanied by the creation of another subsidiary, Société Savoyarde des Fromagers du Reblochon. Each acquisition would strengthen Bongrain's line of cheese varieties.

In the mid-1970s the company also began to look beyond Europe. In 1975 Bongrain entered South America, with the purchase of Polenghi, in Brazil, the first of a series of Brazilian acquisitions that would establish Bongrain as that country's leading specialty cheese producer. The following year Bongrain made a move into the U.S. market with the takeover of Colombo. Bongrain was quick to adapt its technical and marketing strengths to the new market—and the taste buds of Americans—launching a line of successful products, including frozen yogurt, before branching out into other food products, including sauces.

By 1979 the company had firmly established itself as one of France's top cheese producers, as well as a leading specialty cheese maker worldwide. In that year the company reorganized, before going public the following year and adopting the new name, Bongrain. The company's plans for the 1980s continued its ambitious expansion. In 1980 the company set up new production facilities in Australia and New Zealand, complementing this development the following year with the acquisition of Australia's Lactos. These moves were made with an eye on positioning itself to enter the rapidly developing Asian markets—for the day when consumers in those countries might adopt more Western eating habits, including the consumption of cheese products.

Bongrain marked the 1980s with a long series of acquisitions, including Martinus in the Netherlands; Johnston, Kolb-Lena, and Real Fresh in the United States; Skandia and Campo Lindo in Brazil, and Horizons Laitiers in France. In 1989 alone, the company acquired nine companies, adding Italy's Ludovico and Faprena; the United States' Alta-Dena; Hirz, of Switzerland; Millway Foods, of Great Britain; Aiuruoca, of Brazil; and three French concerns, La Cloche d'Or, La Fromagerie du Velay, and Fauquet. Among the products launched by Bongrain were the successful P'tit Louis and Fol Epi cheeses. By then, the company's annual sales neared FFr 6 billion.

During the same period the company also attempted to diversify, principally through the Bongrain family shareholding group, Soparind, through a separate company, IFM, which established a strong position in the prepared meat products market. The company met with more limited success as it attempted to enter the confectionery market; in the early 1990s the company would sell off these activities to the foods giant BSN, later known as Danone. Together, these activities, which remained private and separate from Bongrain SA, were estimated to contribute an additional FFr 6 billion in yearly sales.

Squeezed in the 1990s

Bongrain started the 1990s with several new strategic moves, including the 1990 acquisition of Fromagerie Paul Renard and an alliance with the Union des Coopératives Bressor, which added that company's popular *Bresse-Blue* and *Grièges* brands. In 1992 rivals Bongrain and Besnier—itself continuing a long acquisition spree, including the acquisition of dairy producer Bridel, which had placed it as the country's leading dairy and cheese producer—went head to head for the control of the Union Laitière Normande (ULN). Bongrain won, taking a ten percent share and operating control of the subsidiary, renamed Compagnie Laitière Européenne (CLE). CLE, however, would enter a difficult period, posting losses into the late 1990s.

Meanwhile, Bongrain was entering a new market: Eastern Europe. As these countries were opening up to foreign invest-

ment and establishing free markets with the end of Soviet dominance, Bongrain established positions in Hungary, with the acquisition of Veszpremtej, and in the Czech Republic, with the acquisition of Pribina, while also adding production facilities in Poland. The company also expanded its South American presence by moving into Chile and Uruguay in the mid-1990s. During this time the company embarked on an intensive capital investment program, designed to modernize its French production plants, including the building of new plants and the renovation of existing plants. The company's subsidiaries now were converted from single-product facilities to being capable of producing multiple cheese varieties.

The cost of these investments, coupled with a continuing recession, losses from the ULN, and pressure from elevated French milk prices, combined to put the squeeze on Bongrain. Revenues, which had risen to FFr 9.7 billion in 1992, fell to FFr 9.6 billion in 1993. Although the company's revenues would climb again in the mid-1990s, topping FFr 10.4 billion in 1996, its profitability was faltering, with net earnings dropping from FFr 366 million in 1994 to just FFr 300 million in 1996. In response—and as well as to ensure the company's succession, as Jean-Noël Bongrain turned 72 years old—the company restructured its organization in September 1997. While sons Armand and Alex Bongrain took directorships in the company, actual operating leadership of the company fell to long-time family friend Bernard Lacan, former CEO for Nestlé subsidiary Findus.

In 1998 Bongrain's difficulties appeared to be in the past as the company posted its results for the 1997 fiscal year. Sales had risen strongly to more than FFr 11 billion, and net earnings regained slightly to FFr 313 million. While certain of the company's markets remained under pressure, Bongrain was poised to continue its thrust to become an international cheese leader.

Further Reading

Chirot, Françoise, ''Bongrain: des profits sur un plateau,'' *Le Monde,* September 29, 1989, p. 29.

Denis, Anne, ''Bongrain prépare la relève en modifiant ses statuts,'' *Les Echos,* September 9, 1997, p. 10.

——, ''Bongrain reste confiant pour l'avenir malgré une rude année 1996,'' *Les Echos,* April 30, 1997, p. 15.

——, ''Le groupe fromager Bongrain à la conquête de l'Amérique,'' *Les Echos,* April 26, 1995, p. 9.

Jicquel, Jean-Luc, ''Gros plan sur Bongrain,'' *RIA,* May 1997, p. 25.

''Le Bongrain nouveau est arrivé,'' *Le Figaro Economie,* September 29, 1997, p. 3.

''Le resultat d'exploitation de Bongrain a augmenté de 22.9% en 1997,'' *Les Echos,* March 6, 1998, p. 12.

Sinchet-Lassabe, Ghislaine, ''Bongrain maintient le cap,'' *Linéaires,* June 1997, p. 52.

—M.L. Cohen

Boole & Babbage, Inc.

3131 Zanker Road
San Jose, California 95134-1933
U.S.A.
(408) 526-3000
Fax: (408) 526-3055
(800) 544-2152
Web site: http://www.boole.com

Public Company
Incorporated: 1967
Employees: 900
Sales: $197 million (1997)
Stock Exchanges: NASDAQ
Ticker Symbol: BOOL
SICs: 7372 Prepackaged Software

Boole & Babbage, Inc. is the oldest independent software vendor in the systems management industry. A worldwide leader among providers of software for managing computer networks and mainframe systems, Boole sells more than 40 products in North America, Europe, Asia, Australia, and Latin America. The company's 6,000 customers across the globe include most of the Fortune 500 list and about two-thirds of the world's largest commercial banks. Boole's COMMAND/Post network management software is the market leader among all solutions of its type.

The Early Years

Boole & Babbage was founded in 1967 by two men, but neither of them were named Boole or Babbage. The company was started by Ken Lolence, a physicist and software specialist, and David Katch, an expert in computer software monitoring. These two computer professionals decided to join forces to create software for measuring and managing the performance of mainframe computer systems. They named the company after two earlier geniuses whose work had made computers possible: mathematician George Boole, the inventor of Boolean algebra, and Charles Babbage, inventor of the first computer engine. To bankroll their project, Lolence and Katch found the Asset Management Company, led by venture capitalist Franklin "Pitch" Johnson. Previously, Johnson had provided seed capital for a number of pioneering Silicon Valley companies.

Boole's mainframe monitoring package, which could track how many hours a day big, expensive computers and peripherals were up and running, was the first software of its kind, and as such it set the industry standard for years to come. By late 1968 the company had collected its first million dollars in sales. In spite of the special niche Boole was creating, however, the company had difficulty remaining profitable. In 1972 Boole made Bruce Coleman, a Harvard graduate who had been with the company less than two years, president. From his previous position as head of the sales and finance department, Coleman saw that Boole's expenses were far too high for the revenue it was generating. As president, Coleman went to work on the problem. By the following year Boole was breaking even. In 1978 Boole earned a pretax profit of more than 15 percent.

By 1978 Coleman felt ready to run a bigger company. He left Boole to join another software developer, Informatics General. He later went to work for Walker Interactive Systems, a San Francisco-based producer of accounting software packages. In Coleman's absence, Boole fell on hard times. As the IBM computers on which Boole's software ran evolved, the company's product line started to become obsolete. An ill-advised investment in another software company made matters worse. By 1980 Boole was teetering on the brink of bankruptcy.

To right the ailing company, Boole brought in Jack van Kinsbergen as president in 1980. Van Kinsbergen was seen as an ideal candidate for the job because of his background at IBM—where he had helped develop the mainframe computers that ran Boole's software, and at Hughes Aircraft—where the software was put to practical use. When describing what it was that Boole & Babbage provided, Van Kinsbergen was fond of resorting to an automotive analogy. "If you bought a car and all you had was a steering wheel, pedals and an ignition but no gauges," he was quoted as saying in a 1986 *Business Journal* article, "you could drive the car but you'd probably have some difficulty figuring out how far you'd gone, how many miles you

Company Perspectives:

Through its large international customer base, Boole & Babbage transparently manages business applications that touch the lives of millions of people each day. Working behind the scenes, we're there during point-of-sale transactions at shopping malls, gas stations, restaurants and convenience stores. We keep passenger reservation systems available for the world's largest air carriers. We ensure the availability of ATM networks serving banking customers everywhere. At major public utility companies, our software helps keep households supplied with electricity and natural gas. We help the global telecommunications industry connect the world with quality phone service. We protect the availability of online consumer services accessed via the Internet. And much, much more. In every instance, Boole & Babbage is there, supplying the advanced enterprise management solutions that keep these kinds of key business applications available to their end users, keeping information moving, ensuring customer satisfaction.

could get out of your gas tank, how much gas was left, etc.'' Boole's software provided the computer's metaphorical driver with just that sort of information.

In 1982 Boole made what investor Johnson—chairman of Boole's board since 1970—described in *Boole & Babbage Magazine* as ''the single most important acquisition we've ever made'' in the purchase of The European Software Company (TESC). The leading independent software distribution company in Europe at the time, TESC became a wholly owned subsidiary of Boole and was renamed Boole & Babbage Europe in 1990. The addition of TESC gave Boole a presence in all of Europe's most important markets, including England, France, Germany, Spain, Italy, and the Scandinavian countries.

Ups and Downs in the 1980s

Boole enjoyed a couple of strong years in the early 1980s. New mainframe management products were added, and the company went public in 1984. The following year, however, IBM threw Boole a curve by changing its operating system, leaving the company with a batch of out-of-date software products on its hands. Reeling from IBM's move, Boole was forced to discard nine of its 25 products and lay off 100 employees. For fiscal 1985 the company lost $6 million on sales of $28.5 million. Still smarting from this turn of events, Boole looked to former president Coleman to turn things around. Coleman returned as president and CEO, while van Kinsbergen stayed on as chief technical officer, allowing him to focus on the technological end of the business, where he had always been most comfortable.

Coleman saw that Boole's problems went beyond events at IBM. ''The changes in the IBM operating systems had hurt, but the company had over-expanded, too,'' he was quoted as saying in a 1986 *Industry Week* article. ''It got a little too optimistic about its ability to generate revenues.'' Coleman quickly took

measures to cut expenses, and he placed a renewed emphasis on sales and marketing. Three new products that supported the new IBM systems were added by the end of fiscal 1986, and plans were made for two more to debut the following year. For 1986, Boole's sales grew comfortably to $34 million.

Boole's revenue grew steadily through the rest of the 1980s, reaching $41.7 million in 1987 and $56 million in 1988. In 1988, Johannes Bruggeling succeeded Coleman as president and chief executive of Boole. By the following year Boole was selling 40 products, all of them software packages for mainframe computers, in the United States, Europe, Asia, and Latin America. Those products, part of the MainView systems management architecture, included monitoring systems, automated operations products, and advisers. Sales at Boole climbed to $74.8 million for 1989.

Challenges in the 1990s

As the 1990s began, the company faced a gigantic challenge. Boole had staked its entire operation on the primacy of mainframe computers. By 1990 it was beginning to look as though mainframes were going the way of the dinosaurs. Throughout the business world, large central computers were being replaced by networks of small, personal computers all fed by a powerful ''server''—a system known as ''client/server.'' Boole began working on its first client/server software in 1990. COMMAND/Post was described in company literature as a product for ''managing availability and service levels in complex distributed environments.''

Even with the introduction of COMMAND/Post, however, the transition to client/server was a traumatic one for Boole. The company's health was still dependent in large part on that of IBM and the mainframe. The entire mainframe industry began to bottom out in 1991. Mainframe manufacturers such as IBM and Amdahl Corporation saw their sales go into freefall, and Boole joined them in their descent. For 1991 the company reported a loss of $11 million on sales of $101 million. Boole's products were becoming obsolete so fast that some of them did not even generate enough revenue to cover the cost of selling them.

To help stop the bleeding, Boole brought in a new president, Paul Newton, a veteran of software pioneers University Computing Corp. and Ingres Corporation. Newton immediately took measures to bring Boole into the 1990s. The first thing he did was to fire 11 percent of the company's employees. A large portion of those layoffs came from the sales force, which had doubled in size during predecessor Bruggeling's tenure. Next, Newton began to scrutinize the company's product line. He determined that the best course of action was to narrow Boole's focus. His goal was to concentrate on just a couple of products and to make them very well.

The company began selling only two kinds of products: software that minimized computer downtime and software that helped customers minimize operating costs. Their target customers would be the same as they had always been—namely, companies that used lots of computers. The only difference was that these companies were now relying overwhelmingly on client/server setups rather than mainframes. In many ways, the transition away from mainframes could now work to Boole's advantage, since client/server systems are much more complex and, therefore, prone to foul-ups than are mainframe systems.

COMMAND/Post quickly became Boole's flagship product. Another step in the company's rebound was a marketing blitz based on a *Star Trek* theme. Boole was able to purchase a two-year license to use *Star Trek* imagery from Paramount Pictures for a mere $75,000 a year. *Star Trek* star Jonathan Frakes served as the company's pitch man for the campaign.

Newton had Boole back in excellent shape within a couple of years. In 1994 COMMAND/Post was "enhanced with intelligent agent technology for event management, operations and administration of UNIX, Novell NetWare and Windows NT server," according to company literature, making Boole software useful to an even greater portion of network-reliant corporations. For the fiscal year ending in September of 1994 the company earned $8 million on sales of $132 million. There was also $35 million cash on hand and no debt to service. Meanwhile, Boole stock tripled in value. By this time the company's top layer of executives and most of its sales force had turned over since the dark days of 1991. Boole's fortunes continued to improve as it pressed on with the transition from mainframe to client/server automation software. By 1995 the company's $150 million in revenue was split about 50–50 between mainframe and client/server products.

In spite of the shift in focus, however, Boole maintained its commitment to making high-quality mainframe products. As a result, the company's MainView line has retained a solid share of the mainframe monitoring market, at a time when many companies have abandoned that market completely. In 1996 Boole introduced Command MQ, which was, according to the company's own description, "one of the first solutions for managing the availability of distributed (IBM) MQSeries networks . . . in terms of automation, performance, administration and configuration."

The End of the Century and Beyond

Toward the end of 1996, Boole made the bold move of acquiring one of its chief rivals, the McLean, Virginia-based Maxm Systems Corp., maker of the Max/Enterprise network automation software. The purchase of Maxm put Boole at the head of the class among companies producing software for enterprise event management, a market worth an estimated $300 million and expected to triple by the end of the century. By 1997 nearly 500 corporations and telecommunications pro-

viders were running Boole's network server software, including both COMMAND/Post and MAX/Enterprise. Next, the company began working on a new network concept called Desired-State Management. Desired-State Management means, according to a 1997 *Computerworld* article, that "one policy could describe all adverse conditions and steps required to keep the entire . . . system available during business hours." Meanwhile, as the company worked toward a projected mid-1998 debut of its Desired-State product, enhancements were added to its existing network management tools. With sales approaching the $200 million mark in 1997 and networks everywhere growing in number and complexity, Boole seemed poised to finish the 20th century in a desired state, indeed.

Principal Subsidiaries

Boole & Babbage Europe; Joint Systems and Technology (Japan).

Principal Divisions

International Operations; North American Field Operations.

Further Reading

"Boole & Babbage," *Business Journal—San Jose,* February 19, 1990, p. 26.
"Boole & Babbage," *Business Journal—San Jose,* March 13, 1989, p. 25.
Dryden, Patrick, "Making Policy for the Network," *Computerworld,* October 27, 1997, p. 49.
——, "Rivals Manage Merger," *Computerworld,* December 16, 1996, p. 32.
Garber, Joseph R., "How To Repair a Train Wreck," *Forbes,* January 16, 1995, p. 92.
Hostetler, Michele, "Boole Well Along on Turnaround from Dark Days of 1991," *Business Journal,* May 29, 1995, p. 9.
Musich, Paula, "B&B Enhances Service," *PC Week,* February 23, 1998, p. 115.
Patterson, William Pat, "Ex-Chief Returns to Ailing Company," *Industry Week,* November 24, 1986, p. 64.
Privett, Cyndi, "Company President Comes and Goes, and Comes Again," *Business Journal,* February 10, 1986, p. 37.
Taber, Mark, "Future Quest: Boole & Babbage Inc.," *Datamation,* September 15, 1992, p. 44.
"30 Years of Excellence," *Boole & Babbage Magazine,* Autumn 1997, p. 4.

—Robert R. Jacobson

Bozell Worldwide

Bozell Worldwide Inc.

40 West 23rd Street
New York, New York 10010
U.S.A.
(212) 727-5000
Fax: (212) 645-9173
Web site: http://www.bozell.com

Private Subsidiary of True North Communications, Inc.
Incorporated: 1921
Employees: 2,695
Gross Billings: $3 billion (1997)
SICs: 7311 Advertising Agencies; 8743 Public Relations
Services

Bozell Worldwide Inc. is one of the preeminent advertising agencies in the world. With the merger between Bozell & Jacobs and Kenyon & Eckhardt in 1986, Bozell Worldwide is presently ranked as the 14th largest advertising agency across the globe. The company is famous for its highly successful advertising campaigns, including the persuasive Jeep Cherokee ads, the Milk Mustache ads with well-known celebrities, and other ads for Hush Puppies, Merrill Lynch, Mutual of Omaha, Chrysler, Excedrin, and the National Pork Producers Council. During the 1990s, Bozell Worldwide has implemented a comprehensive expansion strategy and presently has offices in 51 countries throughout the world.

Early History

The history of Bozell Worldwide can be traced back to its origin in Omaha, Nebraska. Morris Jacobs, who worked as the night police reporter on the *Omaha Bee-News,* and Leo Bozell, a former editor at the *Omaha Daily News,* combined their scant resources and decided to start a part-time advertising and public relations agency. The two men had become acquainted with one another while Jacobs wrote about local business and Bozell was his editor at the *Daily News.* Incorporating their business as Bozell & Jacobs in 1921, the young entrepreneurs worked part-time and contracted a few small accounts until they were

noticed by Nebraska Power Company, the largest utilities firm in the state. With one of the largest accounts under contract, Bozell & Jacobs, Inc. opened its doors as a full-time operation in 1923.

Throughout the decade of the 1920s, Bozell & Jacobs was known as an agency that specialized in advertising campaigns and public relations work for regional utility companies. As the firm's reputation grew, however, more contracts were signed with utility companies in other states, such as Midland United, the holding company of Public Service Co. of Indiana. Along with this increasing business, the company decided to expand its operations to meet the needs of a growing client list, so new offices were opened in Indianapolis, Indiana; Chicago, Illinois; and Houston, Texas. By the end of the 1930s, Bozell & Jacobs was one of the most widely respected and well-known advertising agencies working in the Midwest. Perhaps the most striking fact about the company's accomplishment was that it occurred during the height of the Great Depression, when many other businesses in the United States were affected by distressing economic conditions that often resulted in bankruptcy and foreclosure.

In addition to the advertising campaigns designed for utilities and a handful of consumer firms such as Amling Co., a regional floral retailer, and Roper, Inc., a manufacturer of kitchen ranges, Bozell & Jacobs provided pro bono work for Boys Town, the home and school for boys located in Omaha, Nebraska. Founded by Father Flanagan and established in Omaha during the 1920s, Bozell & Jacobs contributed their services to publicize the good work Father Flanagan had achieved at Boys Town. By the mid-1930s, through the efforts of Bozell & Jacobs, Boys Town had become famous throughout the United States and Father Flanagan was a hero to adults and children alike. The growing publicity led to the filming of a major motion picture in 1938 called *Boys Town,* for which Spencer Tracy's warm and generous portrayal of Father Flanagan won an Oscar for Best Actor.

By the end of the 1930s billings for Bozell & Jacobs amounted to approximately $5 million, not a small achievement for an advertising agency operating in Omaha, Nebraska, far away from the major metropolitan areas of the United States where most corporations had established their headquarters.

Slow but steady growth occurred throughout World War II and the postwar era, with new offices established in Shreveport, Louisiana; Seattle, Washington; Minneapolis, Minnesota; Los Angeles, California; New York, New York; and Washington, D.C. The agency's largest and most prominent account, contracted in 1949, was Mutual of Omaha, the sponsor of the long-running television show "Wild Kingdom."

Growth and Expansion During the Postwar Era

From 1951 to 1956, Bozell & Jacobs increased its billings from $9.3 million to $20 million. Yet the billings rested upon an unstable client base amounting to 350 accounts, all companies with modest budgets and not immune to the fluctuations of the U.S. economy. Leo Bozell had died in 1946, but Morris Jacobs, still a driving force at the company, grew apprehensive about the future. Fortunately, he found the right man for the right job—his son-in-law, Charles Peebler, Jr.

Jacobs convinced his son-in-law, a dropout from Drake University who had previously worked at the management level of a department store, to join Bozell & Jacobs in the production department. Bozell, of course, was grooming Peebler to assume control of company operations, and in 1965 at the tender age of 28 Peebler became president of the company. As the new president, Peebler set extremely ambitious goals to increase the company's billings, and within the first year of his tenure billings jumped from $20 million to $23 million. But this effort was just the first indication of Peebler's talent.

In 1967, in what was later regarded as a major turning point in the history of Bozell & Jacobs, Peebler purchased Emerson Foote, Inc. Emerson Foote, one of the founders of the famous advertising agency Foote, Cone, & Belding, and the man who originated the legendary Lucky Strike cigarette campaign, had fallen out with his partners and formed his own company. But Foote was in need of cash, and Peebler not only hired Foote as a consultant but acquired his company for $500,000. Foote's company had billings of $7 million, and when combined with Bozell & Jacobs's New York office billings, Peebler had built an East Coast base of nearly $10 million in billings. When Morris Jacobs retired during the same year and sold his controlling interest to Peebler and a group of close associates, Peebler became CEO and immediately relocated the agency's headquarters to the Lexington Avenue offices of Emerson Foote's company in New York City.

Working out of the New York City office, with a solid base of clients on the East Coast and no longer dependent upon Midwestern customers, Peebler implemented one of the most aggressive campaigns to increase billings in the advertising industry. By 1971 his efforts had been rewarded when Bozell & Jacobs announced that billings amounted to approximately $50 million for that year alone. But Peebler was not content to rest on his laurels, and he continued to pursue aggressively ever larger and larger accounts. His strategy included the purchase of Glenn Advertising Agency, a firm located in Dallas, Texas whose clients included American Airlines and Quaker Oats Company. In 1975, Peebler purchased Knox Reeves Advertising Agency, a Minneapolis-based company that had a large account with General Mills. With these acquisitions and the new accounts they brought to the company, Bozell & Jacobs

reached the $100 million billing milestone by 1975. By 1979 billings had skyrocketed to $287 million, and Bozell & Jacobs entered the elite and prestigious list of the top 20 advertising agencies in the United States.

The 1980s: A Decade of Transition

As the company continued to add new accounts and increase its billings during the early 1980s, Peebler arrived at the conclusion that Bozell & Jacobs had grown as large as it possibly could in the U.S. market. The time to expand into the international sector had come, and Peebler began to look for a candidate with worldwide contacts and foreign accounts with which Bozell & Jacobs could merge. Lorimar Telepictures, a holding company for television productions such as "Knots Landing," "The Waltons," and "Dallas," had purchased Kenyon & Eckhardt Advertising in 1983. When Peebler was approached by executives from Lorimar, he happily agreed to merging with Kenyon & Eckhardt. In 1985 Lorimar purchased Bozell & Jacobs, with billings of $808 million, merged it with Kenyon & Eckhardt, whose billings amounted to $412 million, and formed the 14th largest advertising agency in the world.

The merger between Bozell & Jacobs and Kenyon & Eckhardt was a good one, both philosophically and operationally. Kenyon & Eckhardt had its roots in an agency founded by Ray D. Lillibridge in New York City in 1899. Otis Kenyon and Henry Eckhardt worked for Lillibridge at the small firm and, when the founder decided to retire in 1929, Kenyon and Eckhardt purchased the company and transformed it into an advertising agency. The firm grew rapidly during its first decade in business, with the client list including Kellogg Company, Abercombie & Fitch, Munsingwear, Stetson, and Quaker State Oil. In 1948 Kenyon & Eckhardt Advertising Agency won its largest account up to that time, Ford's Lincoln-Mercury Automotive Division, which pushed the firm's billings to more than $20 million for the year. By 1956 billings had increased to $81 million, and in 1975 Kenyon & Eckhardt reported billings amounting to $100 million.

The largest and most important account in the company's history, however, was signed in 1979 when Lee Iacocca, the president of the near-bankrupt Chrysler Corporation, handed over the car firm's entire advertising budget of $120 million to Kenyon & Eckhardt. Billings skyrocketed overnight to $328 million but, most important, Kenyon & Eckhardt garnered a reputation within the industry as the firm that helped turn Chrysler around and make Lee Iacocca one of the most recognized and admired personalities in the United States. When Lorimar purchased Kenyon & Eckhardt, both companies saw the acquisition as an opportunity for growth. And when Lorimar merged Bozell & Jacobs with Kenyon & Eckhardt, the former gained access to a worldwide office network, while the latter gained an astute and experienced management team that was regarded widely as one of the best in the advertising industry.

At first sight, everything appeared to be developing smoothly for Lorimar's new wholly owned subsidiary BJK&E. In 1986 a major account was won when Merrill Lynch and Company contracted the company to manage its advertising, and one year later BJK&E unveiled its soon to be famous "Pork—the other white meat" campaign for the National Pork

Producers Council. Yet the high-level executives at both Bozell & Jacobs and Kenyon & Eckhardt were dissatisfied with Lorimar's management approach. Rather than strong direction coming from the parent company, the two agencies discovered that they were both left to operate autonomously. In addition to the lack of a strategic vision and strong management, BJK&E became increasingly suspicious about Lorimar's ventures into wholly unrelated businesses, such as real estate and theme parks, and concluded that management at the parent company had lost its focus.

BJK&E was determined to extricate itself from an unhealthy situation and, since Lorimar began losing money on its wide array of investments, bought itself back for a mere $133 million in cash. The two agencies, which had entered the merger as medium-sized, well-respected firms within the industry, came out on the other side as an independent company on the threshold of becoming one of the top international advertising firms in the world.

The 1990s and Beyond

BJK&E started out the decade of the 1990s in an auspicious manner when it won the $80 million J.C. Penney account in 1991. Additional accounts such as Bristol-Myers' Excedrin, PepsiCo's Taco Bell, Chrysler's Jeep, Bell Atlantic/Nynex Mobile, and the famous "Milk mustache" ads soon followed. Along with its success in garnering new and lucrative accounts, BJK&E implemented a comprehensive reorganization plan that combined the company's international and national divisions into Bozell Worldwide and appointed David Bell as its president. Charles Peebler, Jr. became the president and CEO of BJK&E, a communications holding company for the various advertising efforts of the entire firm, and still remained a driving force behind the scenes. From 1993 through 1996, BJK&E achieved a growth rate of 20 percent per year and had developed into a company with billings of more than $3 billion.

A significant amount of this growth occurred during the early and mid-1990s when Bozell Worldwide pursued an aggressive expansion policy. In Asia the company formed a close association with Dentsu, the premier advertising agency in Japan, resulting in Dentsu's purchasing large amounts of Bozell Worldwide media. In India the company managed to jump into seventh place among the top ten advertisers in that country, and in China Bozell Worldwide made significant, long-term investments in a potential blockbuster market. Europe provided the company with its largest revenues from overseas, but the market grew increasingly competitive, especially in France and Germany. By the end of fiscal 1997, BJK&E had offices in 51 countries across the globe, with an international headquarters located in London and world headquarters situated in New York City.

In 1997, BJK&E was the holding company for a total of eight divisions and 30 operating units, including, among others: Bozell Wellness Worldwide, the third largest health care marketing services firm in the United States; Bozell Sawyer Miller Group, a public relations and medical communications firm; Poppe Tyson, a company specializing in interactive advertising and web site development; and Temerlin McClain, a full-service advertising agency with high profile accounts such as J.C. Penney, Sara Lee Corporation, American Airlines, GTE,

and NationsBank. In 1997 alone, still adhering to its aggressive growth strategy, the company acquired Terre Lune in France, Direct Friends in Germany, McCracken Brooks in the United States, and Charles Barker, plc in England.

In January of 1998 an unexpected development occurred when True North Communications, Inc., an advertising and communications agency located in Chicago, Illinois with approximately $2 billion in billings and the owner of Foote, Cone & Belding, acquired BJK&E in a brief courtship. True North, looking for a White Knight to help it resist a hostile offer from Publicis SA, one of France's most prominent ad agencies, found the perfect partner in BJK&E. The combination of the two agencies created the sixth largest advertising firm in the world. Charles Peebler, Jr., once again the mastermind behind the scenes, assumed the position of president at True North Communications and immediately set about the task of reorganizing the entire company. Many industry analysts predicted not only a comprehensive restructuring of the new agency, but the spin-off of many operating units.

Since tying the knot with True North Communications, the opportunities for BJK&E's continued growth seem limitless. The new company's combined resources include astute management, a high degree of creativity, and a worldwide network of offices to attract new accounts. One of the major advertising agencies in the world, BJK&E is thoroughly prepared for the 21st century.

Principal Subsidiaries

O'Connell, Norton and Partners.

Principal Divisions

Food Marketing Division of Bozell Worldwide.

Further Reading

Bell, David, "Bozell's Bell Paints Active Future for 4A's," *Advertising Age,* April 7, 1997, p. 26.
Cardona, Mercedes M., and Petrecca, Laura, "Combined True North, Bozell in a Buying Mood," *Advertising Age,* August 4, 1997, p. 1.
Cardona, Mercedes M., "Publicis Votes No, But True North BJK&E Tie Knot," *Advertising Age,* January 5, 1998, p. 1.
Cuneo, Alice Z., "Wine Group Huddles with Bozell Over Generic Push," *Advertising Age,* September 15, 1997, p. 14.
Gleason, Mark, "Bozell's New CEO Sees More Room for Growth," *Advertising Age,* April 15, 1996, p. 38.
Kelly, Keith J., "Media Mavens: Lauded Milk Print Campaign Has Publishers Raising Their Glasses," *Advertising Age,* September 16, 1996, p. S1.
McDonough, John, "Midwest Roots Meld Well with Big City: Omaha Shop That Found Glamour Merger Partner Creates Leader in Agency World" (Bozell at 75: A Commemorative), *Advertising Age,* April 8, 1996, p. C2.
"Peebler Picks Targets, Then Devotes Shop's Total Resources" (Bozell at 75: A Commemorative), *Advertising Age,* April 8, 1996, p. C8.
Schulberg, Jay, "Sell the Client's Product, Not Just the Creativity" (Bozell at 75: A Commemorative), *Advertising Age,* April 8, 1996, p. C18.

—Thomas Derdak

Budget Group, Inc.

Suite 210
125 Basin Street
Daytona Beach, Florida 32114
U.S.A.
(904) 238-7035
Fax: (630) 955-7799
Web site: www.teamrental.com

Public Company
Incorporated: 1987 as Team Rental Group Inc.
Employees: 12,000
Sales: $1.30 billion (1997)
Stock Exchanges: New York
Ticker Symbol: BD
SICs: 4119 Local Passenger Transportation, Not
    Elsewhere Classified; 5271 Mobile Home Dealers;
    5521 Motor Vehicle Dealers (Used Only); 5561
    Recreational Vehicle Dealers; 5571 Motorcycle
    Dealers; 6719 Holding Companies, Not Elsewhere
    Classified; 7513 Truck Rental & Leasing without
    Drivers; 7514 Passenger Car Rental; 7515 Passenger
    Car Leasing; 7519 Utility Trailer & Recreational
    Vehicle Rental

Budget Group, Inc., is a holding company that, through subsidiary companies and their franchisees, operates Budget Car and Truck Rental, which in 1997 was the world's third-largest automobile and truck rental system, operating in more than 120 countries. A subsidiary, Budget Car Sales, was one of the largest independent retailers of late model vehicles in the United States. Budget Group also was also operating parking facilities, leasing vans for pooling operations, and renting and selling recreational vehicles, including motor homes, truck campers, and motorcycles.

Private Budget Franchisee, 1987–93

Budget Group got its start as Team Rental Group, which was founded in 1987 by Sanford ''Sandy'' Miller. Miller entered the car rental business in 1976 as an Avis management trainee in Providence, Rhode Island. After two years, he and Jeffrey Congdon decided to buy Fordham Rent A Car, an independent, severely undercapitalized outlet in the Bronx. Miller got a quick education about doing business in the inner city when his first customer stole the car rented to him.

Miller and Congdon—who later served as chief financial officer of Team Rental, from 1991 to 1997—sold Fordham to Dollar Rent a Car and helped Dollar expand to New York's airports. From there Miller moved on to run a Budget Rent a Car Corp. franchise in Florida and then to become regional field operation manager for the company in the Northeast. During 1980 and 1981, Miller and Congdon became executive officers and principal stockholders of corporations that owned and operated 30 Budget Rent a Car franchises which were sold to the company in 1989.

Miller and Congdon founded Team Rental Group in 1987 with the acquisition of a Budget Rent a Car franchise for the San Diego metropolitan area. Team Rental had operating revenues of $16.5 million in 1990 and lost $246,000 that year. In 1991 revenue fell to $15.1 million, and the company lost $1.3 million. Despite its slow start, Team Rental borrowed money in 1991 to acquire Budget rental franchises in Albany and Rochester, New York, and Richmond, Virginia. It was operating at 18 locations by the end of 1992. That year the company had net income of $558,000 on operating revenue of nearly $22 million. The next year it earned $428,000 on revenue of $22.3 million.

Headlong Expansion, 1994–96

In August 1994 Team Rental purchased foreclosed Budget rental operations in Cincinnati, Philadelphia, and Pittsburgh, paying for these acquisitions and refinanced vehicles by issuing $104 million in five-year notes and by going public, offering 3.3 million shares of common stock at $12 a share. Team Rental now was renting 7,400 cars, trucks, and passenger cars at 52 locations and believed itself to be the largest Budget franchise group in the United States in terms of payment of royalty fees. Team Rental added Fort Wayne, Indiana, to its operations in November 1994. That year its revenues reached $38.6 million, but it earned only $250,000 after taxes and interest payments.

Company Perspectives:

Management's long term strategy is to create a network of transportation-related companies, which leverage the asset base and expertise of Budget Group. Budget Group's assets include a trade name recognized around the world, locations for the rental, sale and maintenance of vehicles; a workforce that is proficient in acquiring, financing, monitoring, maintaining and selling vehicles; and advanced information systems to support these operations. Increasing the utilization of these assets by acquiring related businesses delivers economies of scale and increases profitability.

At the end of 1994 about 90 percent of the vehicles in Team Rental's fleet were subject to repurchase by automobile manufacturers under guaranteed buy-back programs. Although this greatly lessened the company's risks, auto manufacturers were reducing the number of cars in repurchase programs and had trimmed or eliminated cash rebates and other financial incentives for these arrangements. Accordingly, Team Rental decided to go into the used car business, opening a San Diego lot in November 1994 and stocking the lot partly with retired Budget rental autos. By the end of March 1996 the company was selling cars at seven locations in five states. Congdon, Team Rental's second-largest shareholder, was running the company's used car business from offices in Indianapolis, where he made his home. Miller, the chairman and chief executive officer of the parent company, was running it from headquarters in Daytona Beach, Florida.

Team Rental's main effort continued to be directed toward extending its rental operations by acquiring still more Budget franchises. In January 1995 it completed a deal for seven Budget rental locations in Dayton and Springfield, Ohio, and Richmond, Virginia. During the same month it added Charlotte, North Carolina, to its roster, and in March, Hartford, Connecticut. And in April 1995 Team Rental made its largest acquisition, purchasing BRAC-OPCO, Inc., for stock. This company was a wholly owned subsidiary of Budget Rent a Car of Southern California, with 49 locations, a fleet in excess of 5,500 cars and trucks, and annual revenue (in 1994) of about $65 million.

Team Rental had operating revenue of $149.7 million in 1995, of which vehicle sales, rather than rentals, accounted for 28 percent. In expanding, it more than doubled its total debt, to $319 million and had net income of only $337,000 for the year after paying $14.5 million in interest. This did not keep Team Rental from completing its eighth acquisition since going public 19 months earlier, by purchasing Arizona Rent-A-Car Systems Inc. in March 1996. This Budget franchisee had 24 locations in the Phoenix area and annual revenues of about $60 million. By the end of March 1996 Team Rental had 157 Budget rental locations in 13 metropolitan areas, and its 14,259 vehicles made it Budget's largest franchise in terms of fleet size as well as royalty fees.

Team Rental also expanded into a new area in February 1996, when it purchased VPSI, Inc., from Chrysler Corp. VPSI owned Van Pool Services, the market-share leader in van pool-ing, operating in 22 states with annual revenue of about $36 million. For 1996, Team Rental raised its revenues to $375.4 million, of which sales, rather than rentals, accounted for 38 percent. For the first time the company had significant net income—$4.5 million—although its long term debt rose to $454.1 million.

Budget and Cruise America Acquisitions, 1997

In a deal that one observer described as "the mouse swallowing the elephant," Team Rental purchased Budget Rent a Car, the nation's third-largest rental car firm, from its owner, Ford Motor Co., in January 1997 for about $1.95 billion in cash and stock. Budget, which also was selling used cars at 23 locations, had annual revenue of $1.5 billion but had lost more than $100 million in 1995 and was said to have been only marginally profitable in 1996. As part of the agreement, Team Rental agreed to continue featuring Ford vehicles in the Budget rental fleet. With the completion of the transaction, Team Rental owned 80 percent of Budget's U.S. fleet, with the other 20 percent continuing to be owned by other franchisees. After completing the purchase, Team Rental renamed itself Budget Group.

Team Rental apparently outbid larger rivals HFS Inc. (owner of Avis) and Republic Industries Inc. (owner of National Car Rental and Alamo) to acquire Budget Rent a Car, even thought it had no available cash. An innovative financial package organized by Credit Suisse First Boston (CSFB) involved more than 40 lawyers and bankers, representing Team Rental, CSFB, and five law firms. A CSFB banker recalled, "We took an entire floor of a New York law firm and closed everything in four hours. When you have enough people scared of the consequences of failure, it's amazing what can happen."

This blockbuster purchase did nothing to dull Budget Group's voracious appetite for still more acquisitions in the motor-vehicle field. In July 1997 the company purchased Premier Car Rental LLC, which was serving the insurance replacement market through a network of 150 locations in 17 major U.S. markets. Three months later it announced plans to acquire Cruise America Inc., a dealer of recreational vehicles with annual sales of $95.6 million in fiscal 1997. Based in Mesa, Arizona, Cruise America had a network of 91 locations and a fleet of more than 4,300 recreational vehicles, including motor homes, vans, campers, and motorcycles.

In making the announcement, Scott White, a Budget Group vice-president, declared, "Our strategy is to be a company that owns these kinds of automotive services that have operating synergies between them. The common theme between the companies is we borrow money more cheaply so we can finance our fleets more cheaply. . . . We want to leverage this fixed asset base and acquire companies like Cruise America where we can take our costs in the back office and behind the scenes and grow revenues through cross marketing." The Cruise America acquisition was completed in January 1998 for $61 million in stock and the assumption of $76 million in debt.

Ryder Acquisition, 1998

Budget Group went a step further in March 1998 when it purchased Denver-based Ryder TRS Inc. from Questor Partners L.P. for $706 million in cash, stock, and other considerations, a sum that included assumption of $441 million of debt. Ryder, the second-largest company in the drive-it-yourself truck rental field, had 4,200 locations worldwide, a fleet of 30,500 vehicles and annual revenue of about $550 million. Miller said Budget and Cruise America's truck rental operations would be consolidated with Ryder in Denver. With the acquisition, about 40 percent of Budget Group's revenues were expected to come from truck rentals, which an analyst said were yielding higher profit margins than car rentals.

The acquisition of Budget Rent a Car and other companies enabled Budget Group's revenues to reach $1.3 billion in 1997. Its net income rose to $36.9 million. Investors applauded these results, bidding the company's stock as high as $39.50 a share in early 1998. Of the company's 1997 income, vehicle rentals accounted for 78 percent and car sales for 18 percent. Company debt came to $2.6 billion at the end of the year.

Budget Group's Budget Car and Truck Rental system had more than 3,200 locations in 1997 and a peak fleet size during the year of 283,000 cars, 22,500 trucks, and 5,100 pick-ups. Of the 964 Budget System (which included car-sales lots) locations in the United States, 509 were owned by Budget Group and the others by franchisees. Of the 2,242 locations in other countries, only 71 were owned by the company. Budget Car Sales was operating 26 retail car-sales facilities. Cruise America was renting and selling recreational vehicles at 92 North American locations. Premier Car Rental had a network of 150 locations in 16 major U.S. markets. Van Pool Services was leasing vans for pooling operations in 28 cities in 18 states and the District of Columbia. Budget Airport Parking was operating airport parking facilities at certain locations.

Miller, Congdon, and John P. Kennedy, who was the company's president and chief operating officer from August 1994 to May 1997, held, combined, about 8 percent of the company's Class A shares of common stock in February 1998. In addition, they held all of the company's Class B shares, giving them 48 percent of the voting power.

Principal Subsidiaries

Budget Car Sales, Inc.; Budget Rent A Car Corporation; Budget Rent A Car Systems, Inc.; Cruise America, Inc.; Premier Car Rental LLC; VPSI, Inc.

Further Reading

Andrews, Greg, "Budget Car Franchisee Accelerates Expansion," *Indianapolis Business Journal,* September 16, 1996, p. 1.

Ellison, Evelyn, "Budget Rental Car Deal Drives up Team Stock," *Indianapolis Business Journal,* January 20, 1997, p. 11.

Keates, Nancy, and Stern, Gabriella, "Budget Group Expected to Buy Ryder TRS," *Wall Street Journal,* March 4, 1998, p. A4.

Miller, Lisa, and Stern, Gabriella, "Ford Is Expected to Shed Budget Rent a Car Unit," *Wall Street Journal,* January 8, 1997, p. A3.

Rosato, Donna, "Team Rental Tunes up Strategy as Budget Rent a Car Owner," *USA Today,* January 27, 1997, p. B5.

Schmeltzer, John, "Budget Gets Keys to Ryder This Time," *Chicago Tribune,* March 5, 1998, p. C1.

——, "Budget Rent a Car Settling into Driver's Seat of RV Firm," *Chicago Tribune,* October 23, 1997, Sec. 3, p. 1.

"Team Rental Group," *Barron's,* August 8, 1994, p. 44.

"Team Rental's Audacious Bid Sets the Trend," *Corporate Finance,* December 1997, p. 63.

—Robert Halasz

Business Objects S.A.

Tour Chantecoq
5, rue Chantecoq
92800 Puteaux
France
(33) 1.41.25.21.21
Fax: (33) 1.41.25.31.00
Web site: http://www.businessobjects.com

Public Company
Incorporated: 1991
Employees: 757
Sales: US $114.25 million (1997)
Stock Exchanges: NASDAQ
Ticker Symbol: BOBJY
SICs: 7372 Prepackaged Software

France's Business Objects S.A. is a leading provider of software-based enterprise decision support tools to mid-sized and large-scale corporations. Business Objects' client/server software focuses on providing an intuitive "semantic layer" between the end user and the often arcane protocols needed to access corporate databases, data warehouses, and other data repositories. Using their own natural language criteria, Business Objects' clients can perform sophisticated interrogative analysis procedures, producing rapid and specific reports to aid in the decision-making process. By placing the tools to access information in the hands of the end user, Business Objects enables corporations to achieve greater speed and accuracy in decision making and greater competitiveness in the global marketplace.

The company targets four primary market segments. In addition to its principal market of providing front-end support to data warehouses and data marts, the company adds third party decision support services to packaged software applications, such as Microsoft Excel; Internet-based database and data warehouse reporting functionality using the World Wide Web; and decision support services to corporate and third party custom-built relational database management system (RDBMS) applications. Business Objects' client/server software can be adapted for use in corporations ranging from 100 to 10,000 or more licensed stations.

The heart of the company's product line is its Business-Objects client/server platform, which entered its version 4.1 in late 1997. BusinessObjects's chief function is to provide a company-patented "semantic layer" meant to shield the end user from the need to formulate data query requests using the highly technical Standard Query Language (SQL) demanded by most data repositories. Instead, a corporation's Information Services department creates a series of graphical "objects" representing SQL search commands, providing the end user with a point-and-click interface tailored to the user's commercial language needs. Objects can be combined to provide highly specific data requests; the results can be presented in graphical charts and diagrams and exported to other decision support software.

Available for use with most major operating systems, including Unix and Windows, BusinessObjects is comprised of separate, combinable component modules. Reporter forms the software's core, providing the graphical query engine with which the end user constructs an object-based data request; resulting data is submitted to a report generator, which produces editable, template-based reports, and a graph generator to create a variety of two-dimensional and three-dimensional charts, graphs, and other graphical report tools. An add-on to Reporter is the analysis-oriented Explorer, with which the end user submits the Reporter-generator base report to multidimensional analytic criteria. Reader and Driller function as separate components. Reader enables read-only viewing of previously generated reports; Driller allows users to read and conduct "data mining" analysis on previously generated reports. A fifth component, which began shipping in December 1997, is the company's thin-client, Java applet, WebIntelligence, enabling World Wide Web-based, real-time querying, reporting, and analysis not only within the corporation but also for the corporation clients, suppliers, and partners.

In addition to these core components, Business Objects provides a series of add-on products, including BusinessQuery for Excel, which provides BusinessObjects querying abilities and reporting directly integrated into that Microsoft application. BusinessMiner is a Reporter add-on that provides additional "decision tree" graphical formulation for identifying data trends. The company licenses BusinessMiner from a third party developer. Information Services support is provided by the company's suite of BusinessObjects environment tools, including Designer; the security and access management module Supervisor; the query request router Document Agent Server; Data Access Drivers for use with major relational database systems; and pre-prepared Rapid Deployment Templates for use with major database applications from SAP, Oracle, Baan, People-Soft, and others.

Although based in France, Business Objects has from the start taken a distinctly international approach. With subsidiary operations in 14 countries and sales to more than 60 countries, foreign sales represent some 70 percent of Business Objects' revenues. The United States, which alone accounts for more than 30 percent of the company's annual sales, plays a key role in Business Objects' development and future strategy. Whereas research and development are maintained at the company's Paris area headquarters, the company's sales and marketing are governed by its San Jose, California headquarters. Business Objects has also adopted a business model similar to its Silicon Valley counterparts, including an aggressive, internationally oriented recruitment policy, salaries boosted by stock options, and an early opening to investment capital. Since 1994 the company has been listed on the NASDAQ stock exchange.

Business Objects' client list reads as a Who's Who among the world's leading corporations. The company boasts more than 6,200 clients with more than 780,000 licensed products, with clients including Texas Instruments, 3M, France Telecom, Sollac, ATT, and Shell. The company also has strategic partnership and distribution agreements with major industry forces such as Microsoft, Oracle, Sun, Silicon Graphics, IBM, Sybase, and Hewlett-Packard, among others.

While posting steady revenue gains throughout the 1990s, including a 34 percent increase in 1997 to top US $114 million in sales, Business Objects has struggled to maintain profitability—posting a net income of less than US $3 million for 1997, a drop of nearly 50 percent from the previous year. This is in part because of the intensive nature of the company's software sales process, which often involves three to six months of prototype setup and testing before the conclusion of a sale. Nonetheless, the company holds a key position in the booming client/server technology market, which has been growing steadily since the mid-1990s. Business Objects continues to be led by co-founder, Chairman, President, and CEO Bernard Liautaud.

Liautaud, who had traveled to California to obtain a Master's in Management from Stanford University before working for the French subsidiary of database leader Oracle in the 1980s, joined with Oracle colleague Denis Payre, who had been responsible for Oracle France's strategic accounts department, to form Business Objects in 1990. With start-up capital of merely FFr 100,000 (approximately US $18,000), the two partners set up shop in a small office in the Parisian suburb of Puteaux. Already steeped in the Silicon Valley culture, Liautaud and Payre had come across a software program written by an independent developer, Jean-Michel Cambot, that provided a simpler means of working with Oracle database systems. Liautaud and Payre, then aged 29 and 28, respectively, immediately recognized the program's potential. As Payre told *Les Echos:* "No one had seen this market."

Purchasing the program from Cambot, Liautaud and Payre were able to start business with a product already in hand. Their experience with Oracle's database systems, as well as their understanding of the outstandingly successful Silicon Valley business model, would mark Business Objects' development from the beginning. The partners hired an international team, many of whom also had worked for Oracle, giving the company not only a strong technical and commercial base, but a working knowledge of its target customers' needs. Business Objects also would benefit from Oracle's disinterest in pursuing this new market with its own resources, giving its tacit support to the development of a product that, by making Oracle's systems more accessible, would also make them more attractive. The company's international focus was apparent immediately, as development of the software, soon dubbed BusinessObjects, and its introduction in 1991, was done simultaneously in English and French.

Liautaud and Payre adopted another particularity of the Silicon Valley business model—a distinctly non-French opening up of the company's capital. Almost immediately after opening Business Objects' offices, Liautaud and Payre began making the rounds of investment firms in New York, Paris, and San Francisco. Aided by Liautaud's father-in-law, former American Electronic Association President Arnold Silverman, the pair succeeded in attracting investment interest not only in France, but among the crucial Silicon Valley community. Within seven months after starting out, Business Objects had succeeded in raising some US $1 million in investments, principally among France's Paribas Technologies (subsidiary of major banking group Paribas) and Innovacom (a France Telecom subsidiary), Dutch-American investors Atlas Ventures, and the United States's Donald Lucas and Silverman, both leading figures in the California investment community. The internationalization of the company's capital would prove critical for enabling Business Objects to penetrate the crucial U.S. market.

That market readily embraced Business Objects and its ground-breaking product. By 1993 the company was in the black, having already wooed more than 1,000 clients worldwide. With revenues of FFr 51 million (approximately US $10 million) and profits of FFr 5.6 million, Business Objects had achieved a growth of more than 400 percent since 1991. At the same time, with the growth of new client/server technology in the early 1990s, analysts had begun estimating that the niche market Business Objects had created, then worth some US $90 million worldwide, could near US $800 million by the late 1990s.

Indeed, Business Objects' product had come at the right time. The collapse of the international economy during the 1990s and the lingering effects of the recession, which would last into the middle of the decade, coupled with the increasing globalization of business competition, had driven corporations to search for new means not only to increase efficiency but also to achieve more accurate business forecasting models. By placing the tools to conduct database queries and generate reports in the hands of the corporate end user, Business Objects had created an important—and eagerly embraced—tool for these corporations.

The company quickly expanded, opening offices in the United States, England, the Netherlands, and Germany, as well as in Tokyo (where it began translating its software into Japanese). In 1994 Business Objects took the next step toward corporate respectability. In that year Business Objects went public, listing on the NASDAQ stock exchange, becoming the first independent French company ever to do so. The choice to go public, and to list on an American exchange, would give the company the appearance of stability necessary to attract the world's largest corporations to its product line. At the same time, the company's initial public offering (IPO) garnered favorable publicity for its products. The public offering for US $8.5 per share was one of the year's big successes: the company, with revenues of US $30 million and a net income of US $2.3 million in 1994, was valued at some US $200 million.

One year later Business Objects continued to build on its promise. By 1995 more than 70 percent of its sales were made internationally and 35 percent of its revenues came from the United States alone. Sales had doubled over the previous year, topping US $60 million, for a net income of more than US $8 million. The company, though maintaining its headquarters and, in particular, its development activities in France, was nonetheless shifting more and more of its efforts to the all-important American market. By the end of 1995 the company's stock had continued to climb, reaching US $53.5 per share and placing the company's value at nearly US $1 billion.

By the end of 1996, however, Business Objects stock had crashed, plunging to just US $11 per share. The company had overestimated its first quarter's sales totals—the fault of one of its subsidiaries, which had included a prospective sale in its revenue statement—forcing the company to adjust its revenues for its second quarter. The second half of the year proved equally difficult: the launch of the new version 4.0 of the BusinessObjects suite was delayed, crippling the development of sales. Porting the software to a 32-bit platform, necessary to run the software under the WindowsNT operating system, led to a further drag on sales. Although the new version was compatible with Windows95, it now was incompatible with the previous version of Windows (which is a 16-bit platform), still widely in use in the corporate world. A 16-bit version of BusinessObjects (4.5) was not readied until November 1996. In addition, problems with BusinessObjects 4.0 caused the company to prepare an updated version (4.1) within months of its release.

The company, which had been doubling sales each year, saw its revenue growth slip dramatically, closing the year at just US $80 million. More troubling was the slip in profits, which fell back to just US $5 million in 1996. The company's difficulties would continue into 1997, which saw its profits slip again, to US $2 million, despite an increase in revenues to US $114 million. Business Objects' competitors—notably Cognos and Brio Technology—also had made inroads into the business-decision market, taking market share from Business Objects. Nevertheless, the company—and market analysts—found cause to remain optimistic. In 1997 the company began preparing the launch of several new products, including Miner, developed in partnership with France's ISoft, and WebIntelligence, which allowed use of BusinessObjects's functions through the World Wide Web and through corporate intranets.

Business Objects was preparing another transition. In November 1996, Denis Payre, then 34 years old, "retired" from active leadership of the company. Years of commuting between France and the United States had taken its toll, and Payre announced his decision as a means to spend more time with his family. Although Payre kept a position on Business Objects' administrative board, his new interest turned to investing his fortune and his experience into new European computer industry start-up companies. Meanwhile, Business Objects itself seemed to be looking to end its commuter relationship with the United States. The company replaced Payre with the American David Ellett, former division chief with Oracle, whose offices were to be not in France, but in San Jose; another American took a position in the company's top executive ranks, when Tom Weatherford was named CFO in early 1998. Accompanying these appointments was the shift of the company's marketing department to its San Jose headquarters.

The company's increasing emphasis on its U.S. operations was seen as a necessity for the company's future growth. As Bernard Liautaud explained to *Le Monde:* "The time has come to shift more to the United States. More and more, our largest clients are Americans. That's where the influential financial analysts are." Yet, despite its American ingredients, Business Objects remained a distinctly French success story.

Further Reading

"Business Objects: l'activité progresse, mais pas le résultat," *Les Echos,* February 12, 1998, p. 13.

Constanty, Hélène, "Business Objects: un nouveau-né déjà multinational," *Le Nouvel Economiste,* June 16, 1995, p. 6.

Leparmentier, Arnaud, "Le tandem fondateur de l'entreprise informatique Business Objects se sépare," *Le Monde,* November 20, 1996, p. 19.

Perez, Alain, "La réussite à l'américaine de Business Objects," *Les Echos,* June 8, 1994, p. 2.

Robert, Virginie, "Business Objects: une offensive aux Etats-Unis," *Les Echos,* April 25, 1997, p. 13.

—M.L. Cohen

Cable and Wireless plc

New Mercury House
26 Red Lion Square
London WC1R 4UQ
United Kingdom
(071) 315 4000
Fax: (071) 315 5000
Web site: http://www.cwplc.com

Public Company
Incorporated: 1929 as Imperial and International
    Communications Company Limited
Employees: 37,488
Sales: $10.37 billion (1997)
Stock Exchanges: London New York Tokyo Hong
    Kong Frankfurt Geneva Basel Zürich
Ticker Symbol: CWP
SICs: 3661 Telephone & Telegraph Apparatus; 4813
    Telephone Communications, Except Radiotelephone;
    4841 Cable & Other Pay Television Services

As a provider of telecommunications services in more than 50 countries around the globe, Cable and Wireless plc is a leading player in a rapidly growing and evolving industry. Its operations in the late 1990s were concentrated in three major areas: the United Kingdom, the Caribbean, and Asia. The company, whose fortunes once depended on telegraphic connections between the various parts of the British Empire, operated in the late 20th century all over the world, using equipment that even Guglielmo Marconi, the inventor of the wireless and one of the company's first directors, could not have imagined.

Early History

The history of the companies that became Cable and Wireless plc began in 1852, when a Manchester cotton merchant named John Pender joined other businessmen from the north of England on the board of the English and Irish Magnetic Telegraph Company, set up to run a telegraph cable service between London and Dublin. This was only two years after the first submarine cable had been laid, between England and France, and coincided with the first laying of cables in India, then Britain's largest overseas possession. Pender next became a director of the Atlantic Telegraph Company, whose first cable to the United States was laid in 1858 but failed to function properly. Six years later, when it became clear that the company could not afford to make a second attempt with its own resources, he was instrumental in creating the Telegraph Construction and Maintenance Company (Telcon) through a merger of the two leading cable-making companies, under Pender's chairmanship. However, the second cable broke and fell into the Atlantic during the laying stage in 1865. Pender and his colleagues had to set up a successor to the Atlantic Telegraph Company, the Anglo-American Telegraph Company Ltd., on behalf of which Telcon not only retrieved the 1865 cable but successfully constructed and laid a transatlantic cable in 1866.

In 1868 the British government decided to buy up all the inland telegraph companies, including English and Irish Magnetic, a process completed in 1870, but left overseas telegraphy in private hands. In 1869 John Pender created three more companies. The British-Indian Submarine Telegraph Company and the Falmouth, Gibraltar and Malta Telegraph Company completed the cable system between London and Bombay in 1870, while the China Submarine Telegraph company set about connecting Singapore and Hong Kong, Britain's main possessions in East Asia. Pender's other company, Telcon, supplied cable not only for these ventures but also for a cable from Marseilles to Malta, which provided France with a link to its colonies in North Africa and Asia. When the governments of South Australia and Queensland, Australia, decided that the monthly steamships between Australia and Britain were too slow a means of communication, it was John Pender whom they invited to fill the telegraphic gap between Bombay and Adelaide, Australia. The All-Sea Australia to England Telegraph, supplied by Telcon, was opened in 1872. It was operated in two sections, Bombay to Singapore by the British India Extension Telegraph Company and Singapore to Adelaide by the British Australian Telegraph Company, both under Pender's control.

Pender now set about reorganizing his cable interests. First, in 1872, came the amalgamation of British Indian Submarine, Falmouth, Gibraltar and Malta, and the Marseilles, Algiers, and

Malta companies with the Anglo-Mediterranean, which had been created in 1868 to link Malta, Alexandria, and the new Suez Canal. Pender became chairman of the Eastern Telegraph Company that resulted from their merger. Next, in 1873, he presided over the merger of his Australian, Chinese, and British India Extension companies into the Eastern Extension Australasia and China Telegraph Company. It was also in 1873 that Pender created a holding company, the Globe Telegraph and Trust Company. The holding company's investors received portions of shares in the operating companies, chiefly the Eastern Telegraph and the Anglo-American. All the companies so far named remained within the Eastern Telegraph group, except Anglo-American, which was taken over in 1910 by a U.S. firm, Western Union. Finally, 1873 also saw the creation of the Brazilian Submarine Telegraph Company, which had several directors and shareholders in common with Eastern Telegraph and opened a cable from Lisbon, Portugal, to Pernambuco, Brazil, in 1874.

Between 1879 and 1889 Pender's group added Africa to its list of cable routes through three companies, African Direct, a joint venture with Brazilian Submarine; West African, incorporated into Eastern Telegraph; and Eastern and South African. In 1892, following the expiration of the telegraph concession operated by Brazilian Submarine, that company and its main rival, Western and Brazilian, formed a new venture, the Pacific and European Telegraph Company, to renew the concession and link Brazil with Chile and Argentina. Having helped to arrange this operation, Pender became chairman of Brazilian Submarine in 1893, further reinforcing his position as the leading figure in the worldwide cable business. John Pender died in 1896; his successor as chairman of Eastern Telegraph and Eastern Extension was Lord Tweeddale, while Pender's son John Denison-Pender, later Sir John, continued as managing director. The last stage in restructuring the set of companies Pender had been so instrumental in creating came in 1899, when Brazilian Submarine, having absorbed two other London-based telegraph companies operating in South America, was renamed the Western Telegraph Company.

The first confrontation between cable and the new medium of wireless ended in acrimony. Guglielmo Marconi's success in sending a signal from Cornwall to Newfoundland in 1901 was soured when the Anglo-American Telegraph Company, part of the Pender group, forbade any further experiments, since they would infringe on the Pender group's monopoly of communications in Newfoundland. Marconi moved his work to Nova Scotia, and found Americans and Canadians generally more receptive to his achievement than Europeans. Certainly the Eastern Telegraph group remained unimpressed, citing lack of privacy, lack of speed, interruptions, and mixing of messages as decisive disadvantages of wireless compared with cable. Even so, the management was cautious enough to have a mast secretly installed at its Cornwall station with which to listen in on Marconi's experiments and, on at least one occasion, to disrupt a demonstration of wireless transmission.

Early 20th Century Expansion

In 1900 the governments of Britain, Australia, New Zealand, and Canada had agreed on the joint financing of a Pacific Cable, for which the construction contract was won by Telcon. The project began 21 years after it had first been proposed by Sandford Fleming, the chief engineer of the Canadian Pacific Railway. It eventually involved the laying of the largest single piece of cable so far—4,000 miles, out of a total Pacific Cable length of 7,836 miles—but was completed ahead of schedule, in October 1902. Alarmed by this competition from public enterprise, the Eastern Telegraph group reduced rates on its cables in 1900, and laid a cable across the Indian Ocean to serve the three Australian states—South Australia, Western Australia, and Tasmania—which had refused to join the Pacific project.

Throughout World War I all cable services out of Britain were controlled by the government. The Eastern Telegraph group profited enormously from the diversion of business to India and East Asia away from the German-owned overland routes and from the general use of telegrams in preference to letters, which were delayed by lack of civilian shipping. For the first time cables became targets of warfare in themselves. Eastern Telegraph, the British Royal Navy, and the British General Post Office collaborated on cutting all cable links between Germany and North America. The Germans temporarily disabled both the Pacific Cable and the cable across the Indian Ocean, by attacking island stations in each ocean. However, the most spectacular event of the first "cable war" came in 1917, when, following the United States' entry into the war, the German cable that had been cut three years before was lifted out of its position between New York and Emden, Germany, moved to a new position between Nova Scotia and Cornwall, and taken over by the British government as a prize of war, to be operated by the General Post Office. In 1920 the government decided to keep this cable, despite U.S. protests, and to purchase a second line, the two together being renamed Imperial Cable.

The wartime boom in Eastern Telegraph group's business gave way to slack trading in the early 1920s, as government telegrams declined in number and length, overland rivals got back to work, and the Pacific and Imperial Cables became direct competitors for communications with North America and Australia. However, the biggest blow to the whole cable business was struck once again by Marconi when he succeeded, in 1924, in telephoning Australia from England on short-wave radio equipment. This latest kind of wireless worked faster, cost less, and used less energy than either long-wave radio transmission or cable, and offered a flexibility its rivals did not then have, since it transmitted both telephony and telegraphy. Five years later the Marconi-Wright facsimile system added picture transmission to wireless's advantages. Within six months of its establishment, the General Post Office's system of short-wave stations had taken 65 percent of the Eastern Telegraph group's business, as well as more than 50 percent of Pacific Cable's, and its service cost a fraction of the price of cabling. In the meantime, however, the cable systems were given a new lease on life, from 1925 onwards, as manual re-transmission of messages, at points where the signals weakened with distance, gave way to far less time- and labor-intensive automatic regeneration, using a system devised by Telcon.

1929 Merger Created Cable and Wireless

At the suggestion of the private Marconi company, which operated separately from the G.P.O. but under a G.P.O. license, Sir John Denison-Pender met its chairman, Lord Inverforth, in December 1927, to decide on a joint response to the Imperial Wireless and Cable Conference called for the following month.

In March 1928 they both signed a letter to the conference proposing a merged holding company, owned 56.25 percent by the Eastern Telegraph group's shareholders and 43.75 percent by Marconi's. This was against the wishes of the father of wireless himself, who had lost the chairmanship of his own company the year before. But the conference accepted this plan. On April 8, 1929, two new companies began trading. One, Cable and Wireless Limited, had two functions: first, to control all the nontraffic interests, such as patent rights and manufacturing, and secondly to hold all the shares in the cable companies and Marconi. They, in turn, were exclusive owners of the second company, Imperial and International Communications Limited, which owned and operated the actual cable and radio stations, cables, ships, and other assets of Eastern Telegraph and Marconi, as well as the U.K. government's Imperial and Pacific Cables and, on lease, the Post Office transmitting stations. In 1934 the companies were renamed, respectively, Cable and Wireless (Holding) Limited and Cable and Wireless Limited. From the outset they were controlled by a single board, known, on the model of the Bank of England, as the Court of Directors, as Cable and Wireless's board still was in the early 1990s. Since Sir John Denison-Pender had died one month before the companies started up, it was his son John Cuthbert who became governor, and Lord Inverforth sole president of the Court.

The Great Depression hit the new companies badly. Between 1929 and 1935 the number of chargeable words carried fell by more than half, and net profits, just over £1 million in 1929, declined to £75,000 in 1931 and reached only £625,000 in 1934. By 1933 the work force had been reduced by about a third and the introduction of telex in 1932 helped to cut operating costs. Competition was intensifying, as U.S.-owned International Telephone and Telegraph Corporation (ITT) expanded worldwide and Imperial Airways built up its inexpensive air mail service with subsidies from the same governments whose 1928 conference had led to the creation of Imperial and International. Some expansion of the cable and wireless businesses did occur, however, with the acquisition of wireless concessions in Southern Rhodesia—(now Zimbabwe), Singapore (replacing the old Bombay-Rangoon cable), Turkey, and Peru, as well as domestic telephone services in Turkey, Cyprus, and Hong Kong. The structure agreed for Cable and Wireless in 1928 was altered slightly ten years later. In return for giving the company ownership, rather than rental, of the short-wave radio system created by the General Post Office, the British government took shares in the company for the first time, although for the time being it waived its right to appoint a director to the Court. At the same time an empire flat rate scheme was introduced, cutting the company's prices to the public and improving its finances.

World War II revived the cable war of 1914–1918. In 1939 German-owned cables across the Atlantic were cut once again, and in 1940 Italian cables to South America and Spain were cut in retaliation for Italian action against two of the five British cables linking Gibraltar and Malta. Electra House, the company's head office and central cable station, was damaged by German bombing in 1941. However, the company made a considerable contribution to the Allied war effort, supplying, for instance, the wireless equipment with which the North African campaign was conducted in 1942, and sending staff, in army uniforms marked with Telcon flashes, into several campaigns, starting in Italy in 1943. In Britain the end of the European war was followed by the election of a Labour government on a program that included expanding state ownership of leading industries. With the consent of the governments of the other independent countries in the Commonwealth—as the former British Empire was then to be known—Cable and Wireless was put on the shopping list, although the holding company and the main assets—cables, ships, and wireless stations—were not. All shares in Cable and Wireless were transferred to the government on January 1, 1947, while Cable and Wireless (Holding) became an investment trust. In 1948 the company made an agreement with the government of Hong Kong to provide external telecommunications for the colony.

In 1950, following another agreement among the Commonwealth governments, most of Cable and Wireless's U.K. assets and staff were transferred to the General Post Office, just as parts of its assets overseas were acquired by governmental bodies in the other countries involved. Even so, Cable and Wireless remained the largest single international telegraphy enterprise in the world, with 186,000 miles of submarine cable still converging on a station at Porthcurno in Cornwall, England, that had been opened in 1870. By the time the station closed in 1970, the company's business had been transformed. As telegraphy became obsolete in the 1950s, the development of coaxial voice transmission offered the chance to switch over to telephone cables. The company's first venture into this new field was its participation, with American Telephone and Telegraph Company (AT&T) and the Canadian Overseas Telecommunications Corporation, in the laying of TAT-1, the first telephone cable across the Atlantic, completed in 1956. The transmission of the high frequencies needed for telephone links under the sea had been technically possible for 30 years, but plans to lay such a cable in 1928 had been aborted by the Depression. TAT-I was followed by the opening, in 1961, of CANTAT, a telephone cable between Scotland and Canada which, in a departure from its own traditions, Cable and Wireless helped to lay and owned half of but took no part in operating. CANTAT was a single cable, capable of transmitting communication simultaneously in both directions. The completion of the projected Commonwealth round-the-world cable continued in stages, with COMPAC, a system that could provide capacity of at least 60 channels over distances of several hundred miles, linking Canada to Australia, New Zealand, and Fiji, being finished in 1963; and SEACOM, linking Singapore to Australia, in 1967. Cable and Wireless retained its participation in COMPAC and SEACOM, but sold its half of CANTAT to the British Post Office in 1971.

Throughout the 1960s more and more U.K. overseas possessions became independent states. In many cases their external telecommunications systems had been operated by Cable and Wireless, which then became junior partner, with the various new governments, in East African External Communications Limited (1964), Sierra Leone External Telegraph Limited (1964), Trinidad and Tobago External Telecommunications Company (1970), and other such joint ventures. Nigeria's decision, in 1966, to take 100 percent ownership was thus unusual.

Diversification: 1970s through 1990s

By 1972 Cable and Wireless' largest operation was in Hong Kong, where the international telephone service it operated provided 88 percent of its profits, and it was here that it launched Cable and Wireless Systems Limited as a subsidiary offering specialized services. In its first few years these included microwave systems—high frequency radio links for transmission over line-of-sight routes—for customers in Hong Kong, Brunei, and Thailand, a satellite earth station in Nauru, an island in the Pacific Ocean near the equator, and airline communications in the Persian Gulf. Diversification was made even more imperative in 1973, when the Brazilian government withdrew the concession first granted 100 years earlier. Another subsidiary, Eurotech BV, was set up that year as a holding company for projects in the European community, and through participation in supplying the communications network for the U.K. sector of the North Sea oil fields. By 1978 Cable and Wireless' specialized projects included electronic systems for hotels, security systems, marine telex, and, under the largest contract in its history, communications systems for the Saudi Arabian National Guard. Cable and Wireless' reconstruction as an international telecommunications company had been entirely self-financed. While it received no assistance at all from U.K. taxpayers, its profits went to its sole shareholder, the U.K. government. However, a new administration came into office in 1979, determined to privatize as much of the state-owned sector as possible, and in 1981 it decided to sell just less than half of the shares in Cable and Wireless. By 1985 all of the shares in the company had been sold to the private sector apart from a single ''golden share'' retained by the government. The company's franchise to provide Hong Kong's international telecommunications was renewed in 1981, when Cable and Wireless (Hong Kong) was formed. The acquisition of Hong Kong Telephone in 1984 added the domestic services to the company's portfolio. These two companies were restructured in 1988 with the formation of Hong Kong Telecom which, by 1990, still provided half of Cable and Wireless' profits.

The 1980s saw a further transformation in the company's business, from dependence on service concessions from governments to a more varied range of governmental and commercial ventures. To take just one example, in 1981 it launched its subsidiary Mercury Communications Ltd.—initially a joint venture with Barclays Bank and British Petroleum—to compete against British Telecom, which then held a monopoly in providing telephone services in the United Kingdom. By 1990 Cable and Wireless had invested more than £1 billion in Mercury, which was estimated to have taken 3 percent of the U.K. telephone market from British Telecom. This was a more impressive result than it may sound; a great deal of Mercury's business was in the more profitable areas of long-distance and business communications, so that it was able to generate about 25 percent of Cable and Wireless' turnover. In 1991, with the entry of new competitors into the industry looking more and more likely, Cable and Wireless decided to continue Mercury's specialization in business and international services and to develop further its mobile telephone venture, Mercury PCN. Lord Young, the erstwhile trade and industry secretary, became chairman of Cable and Wireless in October 1990.

Between April 1989 and March 1990, Cable and Wireless formed new companies in Yemen and the Seychelles to continue telecommunications services. In Pakistan, a subsidiary set up a mobile telephone network, while in the Caribbean the company extended the list of countries where it provided both domestic and international services. The company's presence in the Caribbean was enhanced in 1990 by its further purchase of shares in Telecommunications of Jamaica Ltd. from the Jamaican government and raising its holding from 59 percent to 79 percent. Cable and Wireless also owned 70 percent of Grenada Telecommunications. In spite of diversification, the company's Hong Kong businesses remained central to its profitability. The company endeavored to cooperate with the Chinese government, to prepare for its takeover of Hong Kong in 1997.

This cooperation took various forms. First, in March 1990 the China International Trade and Investment Corp. (CITIC), the Chinese Government's international investment body, bought 20 percent of the shares in Hong Kong Telecom from Cable and Wireless, having already invested in Cable and Wireless' subsidiary in Macao. Cable and Wireless' own holding in Hong Kong Telecom was subsequently increased from 55.1 to 58.5 percent. Secondly, April 1990 saw the launch of AsiaSat, the first privately financed domestic telecommunications satellite in Asia, from a site in China into an orbit covering half the population of the planet from the China Sea to the Mediterranean. Ownership of the satellite was shared equally by Cable and Wireless, the Hong Kong company Hutchison Whampoa, and CITIC. Thirdly, in June 1990 the Chinese government decided to make Guangzhou its third point of entry for telecommunications, after Beijing and Shanghai, thus further boosting the importance of Hong Kong Telecom to the Chinese economy. Hong Kong Telecom then began to construct fiber optic cable links to southern China. When opened in March 1991, these doubled the telecommunications capacity between the crown colony and the People's Republic of China.

The company's main objective for the 1990s was the completion of what it called the global digital ''highway,'' linking the centers of the world economy through fiber optic cables. The highway included the private transatlantic telecommunications cable, which came into operation in the autumn of 1989. It linked customers of Cable and Wireless and of its U.S. partner, US Sprint, in the United Kingdom and the United States with the European mainland, Bermuda, and many other Atlantic countries too. The highway also included the North Pacific Cable, which opened one year later as a joint venture between Cable and Wireless, U.S. company Pacific Telecom, and Japanese company IDC, of which Cable and Wireless owned more than 16 percent.

Fighting Competition in the 1990s

In 1993 the company initiated another joint venture, this time with U S West: Mercury One2One, which provided digital cellular service in the United Kingdom. As a second-tier telecom operator, Mercury was having trouble wresting territory away from British Telecom. By 1994 it held only 13.5 percent of the British telecommunications market and faced increased competition from newcomers scrambling for market share after the 1991 deregulation. Cable and Wireless had entered numerous other markets as a second-tier player, most notably with Optus in Australia and Tele2 in Sweden, but as one of the smaller international firms it was vulnerable to finding itself spread too thin and pushed out by larger telecom concerns. Outside of Britain, its largest and strongest bases remained the

Caribbean and Hong Kong, where Cable and Wireless held monopolies in providing telecom service.

Profits in 1994 rose over 18 percent from the year before to $1.6 billion. However, Mercury's trouble in the newly open market in Britain contributed to the underperformance of the company's stock in 1995. Over the previous year, the stock had fallen from a high of 540 pence to a low of 354. Another factor in the stock's weakness was uncertainty over the future of the company's Hong Kong subsidiary when Hong Kong reverted to Chinese rule in 1997. Already Hong Kong Telecommunications, which provided two-thirds of Cable and Wireless' profits, had lost its monopoly. By 1995 three rivals had been granted licenses to provide fixed-wire telephone services and they were proceeding to cherry-pick Hong Kong Telecom's choicest customers.

To add to the company's problems, infighting between CEO James Ross and chairman Lord Young led the board to fire both in late 1995. The board's decision in 1996 to hire American Dick Brown as the permanent CEO replacement caused an uproar because of his nationality and his lack of international experience. The same year, merger talks with British Telecom fell apart. However, Cable and Wireless' plans to merge its Mercury Communications subsidiary with cable television operators Nynex CableComms, Bell Canada International, and Videotron solidified in 1996. Cable and Wireless owned a 53 percent stake in the new venture, dubbed Cable and Wireless Communications.

In early 1997, Cable and Wireless dissolved its alliance with Veba AG and Rheinisch Westfaelisches Elektrizitaetwerk AG, two German utilities, to provide telecom services in European Union countries. In the opposite direction, Cable and Wireless increased its investment in the Australian telecom provider Optus Communications by purchasing an additional 24.5 percent stake for $735 million. In addition, it announced its intention to acquire 49 percent of Panama's state-owned telephone company for $652 million. After its failed proposal to merge with British Telecom, Cable and Wireless also appeared to be looking for another major partner. Rumors were circulating in 1997 that Cable and Wireless was bidding for the 80 percent of Sprint Corp. not owned by France Telecom and Deutsche Telekom AG.

With the reversion of Hong Kong to Chinese rule in mid-1997, Cable and Wireless had little choice but to sell a stake in Hong Kong Communications to a mainland Chinese company. Considered by the Chinese government as part of a ''strategic'' industry, Hong Kong Communications was required to be held in part by a Chinese firm. China Telecom acquired a 5.5 percent stake in the company for $1.2 billion. Cable and Wireless hoped that by sacrificing a portion of its cash cow, it would gain access to mainland China, where the telecommunications market promised to boom in the coming years.

Principal Subsidiaries

Mercury Communications Ltd.; Hong Kong Telecommunications Ltd. (58.5%); Hong Kong Telephone Company Ltd.; Hong Kong Telecom International Ltd.; Telecommunications of Jamaica Ltd. (79%); Cable & Wireless North America Inc. (U.S.A.); Companhia de Telecomunicacoes de Macau SARL (51%, Macao); Barbados External Telecommunications Ltd. (85%).

Further Reading

Barty-King, Hugh, *Girdle Around the Earth,* London: Heinemann, 1979.
''Casting around for a Line,'' *The Economist,* November 25, 1995, p. 58.
''EC Approves Pay TV and Telecom Merger,'' *InfoWorld,* January 13, 1997, p. TW3.
Girard, Kim, and Kristi Essick, ''Sprint Taking Suitor's Call?'' *Computerworld,* March 24, 1997, p. 33.
Kupfer, Andrew, ''A Yank Takes over at Cable & Wireless,'' *Fortune,* August 5, 1996, pp. 18–19.
''Panda on Hong Kong's line,'' *The Economist,* May 10, 1997, pp. 57–58.
''Poacher or Gamekeeper: Cable & Wireless,'' *The Economist,* May 28, 1994, pp. 62–64.
Reier, Sharon, ''Cable & Wireless: Can It Capture the Sum of Its Parts?,'' *Financial World,* April 25, 1995, pp. 20–21.
Schonfeld, Erick, ''The World of Telecom Is Calling,'' *Fortune,* January 13, 1997, p. 166.
''Unravelled,'' *The Economist,* February 8, 1997, p. 7.

—Patrick Heenan
—updated by Susan Windisch Brown

Coflexip S.A.

23, avenue de Neuilly
75116 Paris
France
(33) 1.40.67.60.00
Fax: (33) 1.40.67.60.03
Web site: http://www.coflexipstenaoffshore.com

Public Company
Incorporated: 1971
Employees: 3,899
Sales: FFr 7.14 billion (US $1.22 billion)
Stock Exchanges: NASDAQ Paris
Ticker Symbol: CXIPY
SICs: 1623 Water, Sewer, & Utility Lines; 1629 Heavy
  Construction, Not Elsewhere Classified; 3569 General
  Industrial Machinery, Not Elsewhere Classified; 1731
  Electrical Work

France's Coflexip S.A. is the holding company for the operations of Coflexip Stena Offshore and subsidiaries, one of the world's leading subsea contractors. Coflexip designs, manufactures, and implements systems and products that enable offshore and deepwater oil exploration and drilling, the laying and protection of telecommunications cables, and other subsea construction products, and is the world leader in the design and manufacture of subsea robotics systems. The company also provides turnkey design, engineering, and construction services. One of the pioneers in its field, Coflexip has played a prominent role in the development of ultra-deepwater projects; the inventor of flexible pipe is the world's leading producer of systems permitting oil exploration companies to tap the vast oil reserves of the world's oceans. In 1998 Coflexip has continued to break its own world depth records, laying flexible pipe at a depth of 1,709 meters and rigid pipe at 1,373 meters, both off the Brazilian coast. Coflexip expects to be able to break the 2,500-meter mark by the year 2000.

Coflexip's primary activities are grouped under three interrelated divisions: Integrated Subsea Services; Engineering and Technology; and Deepwater and Ultra-Deepwater. The company's subsea services include integrated, turnkey engineering, development, and project management services for new offshore installations and their activation, as well as the decommissioning and dismantling/abandoning of existing offshore facilities. The company designs, manufactures, and installs riser systems, flexible and rigid reeled pipe, and umbilical support systems and other subsea systems; Coflexip also designs and constructs offshore oil platforms and other floating production and mooring systems. In addition to these activities, the company's Subsea Services division provides general subsea construction services and maintenance, repair, and inspection services to existing offshore wells and other offshore facilities. Coflexip continues to play a leading role in the design, development, and manufacture of new subsea systems, including the manufacture of flexible pipe capable of withstanding the corrosive and high-pressure environment of deepwater and ultra-deepwater installations.

In 1997 the company introduced its flexible Teta pipe design, developed at the company's Le Trait, France engineering facility. The Product Engineering Division, based in Le Trait, and its Offshore Engineering Division, based in Aberdeen, Scotland, coordinate Coflexip's new product design and development, with a particular focus, in the late 1990s, on supporting the company's deepwater and ultra-deepwater activities. New technologies developed by this division in the late 1990s include the Teta pipe technology and Coflexip's ground-breaking Flexconnect system, which enables the remote-controlled connecting of subsea pipe and umbilical systems. Flexconnect was developed in cooperation with the company's Perry Tritech subsidiary, itself the world's leading designer and developer of subsea and other robotics systems. The system permits the remote-controlled connection of pipe and other systems at depths beyond the limits of human diver abilities.

In the late 1990s Coflexip has increasingly focused on the booming deepwater and ultra-deepwater exploration and drilling activities of the world's oil and energy companies. The creation of new technology, including the Teta flexible pipe design and the Flexconnect system, has enabled Coflexip to take a leading position in the world market for deepsea construction, as the search for petroleum products has brought the industry

---

Company Perspectives:

Our mission is to support oil and gas companies worldwide through the provision of strategic products and services for the development and implementation of innovative subsea solutions to increasingly complex field development situations.

---

into the most profound depths of the world's oceans. The company expects deepsea construction and services to provide a strong motor for its future growth.

Coflexip supports its services with an impressive fleet of pipelaying and ocean construction vehicles, permitting the company to fulfill simultaneous contracts throughout the world. With four pipelaying ships and seven equipped for in-water construction, Coflexip's fleet is among the market's largest, with capacities ranging from shallow sea waters to the deepest oil fields in the Gulf of Mexico and Brazil. Coflexip continues to expand its fleet, with an emphasis especially on increasing its ultra-deepwater capability. The company's pipelaying vessels also are equipped with trenching equipment, permitting the company to fulfill both activities. The company's chief areas of activity are in the North Sea, especially in the United Kingdom and Scandinavian countries; North America, including a participation in the Terra Nova field development in Canada and in the Gulf of Mexico; Brazil, chiefly in conjunction with the company's exclusive contracts with the Brazilian government's Petrobras group; and to a more limited extent in the Asia Pacific and African regions. Long present in the United States, Coflexip increased its U.S. activities in 1997, with the purchase of a 25.6 percent stake in Houston, Texas's Cal-Dive International; in 1998 Coflexip and Cal-Dive created the joint venture Quantum Offshore Contractors, focusing on the booming oil and gas field developments in the Gulf of Mexico.

Coflexip has been listed on the NASDAQ stock exchange since 1993 and on the Paris stock exchange since 1994. After a restructuring in the mid-1990s, the company is led by chairman and CEO Pierre Valentin, who led Coflexip to sales of FFr 7.32 billion in 1997, from 1996 sales of FFr 4.9 billion, an increase of 49 percent. The company's 1997 net profit reached FFr 553 million (US $92 million). Approximately 65 percent of the company's sales are provided through its contracting services. Some 60 percent of the company's revenues are provided by its activities in the North Sea.

Subsea Pioneer in the 1970s

Flexible pipelines, which would revolutionize the offshore oil industry, were introduced by the French Petroleum Institute in 1971. During the 1950s, the French government, under the leadership of Charles de Gaulle, had begun an ambitious program to develop the country's oil and gas exploration and supply capacity, to counter the country's lack of domestic petroleum resources. This program would inspire the creation of two leading oil companies, Elf and Total, as well as massive research efforts into new technologies under the French Petro-

leum Institute. The introduction of flexible pipeline technology led to the creation of Coflexip in 1971.

Coflexip's original charter was to manufacture flexible pipe. The success of the new technology was given a strong boost in 1973 with the Arab Oil Embargo. Forced to recognize their dependence on the Middle Eastern oil wells, Western countries initiated renewed oil exploration efforts. Flexible pipelines enabled the exploitation of an entirely new part of the world—the vast petroleum fields located beneath the world's oceans. To meet the growing demand, Coflexip began establishing a network of subsidiaries and branch offices to bring the company closer to worldwide developments in subsea oil exploration. In 1974 the company established its U.S. subsidiary in Houston, Texas. Coflexip had already expanded its manufacturing capacity to include, beginning in 1972, the production of umbilicals, or pipeline support systems. The flexible pipeline technology also was adapted to provide short-length and small-diameter piping used for general exploration and refining activities.

The most natural market for Coflexip's technology was France's North Sea coastline, which would undergo intensive development in the 1970s and 1980s. The North Sea region would remain the company's principal market into the 1990s, accounting for more than 60 percent of the company's 1997 revenues; its implantation in North America, however, soon was expanded to include South America as well. Coflexip formed its Brazilian subsidiary in 1977; in the mid-1980s the company opened a Brazilian-based manufacturing facility, in Vittoria, for the production of flexible pipelines for the growing Brazilian oil exploration market.

In the late 1970s and 1980s Coflexip developed beyond its original manufacturing mandate by adding support services to the petroleum exploration industry, including design, engineering, construction, and pipelaying services. These developments would lead the company to building its own fleet of vessels capable of serving the principal oil exploration markets throughout the world. In 1987 the company opened a new subsidiary in London, followed two years later by a branch office in Oslo, which permitted Coflexip to extend its operation further into the North Sea market. In 1990 Coflexip formed a joint venture partnership with the United Kingdom's Dunlop Ltd. to create Dunlop Coflexip Umbilicals Ltd., later renamed Duco Ltd., which brought the company's manufacturing capacity to Newcastle, England. Coflexip would acquire 100 percent control of Duco in 1995. By 1992 the company's revenues topped FFr 1.8 billion.

Acquisitions in the 1990s

In the 1990s Coflexip stepped up the expansion of its services. Although its earlier development had come in large part through internal growth, the company began an engagement of acquisitions, adding new products and services capabilities that would more than triple the company's sales in just five years. In 1992, the company, in joint acquisition with L.D. Canocéan, part of France's Louis Dreyfus group, acquired another French company, Travocéan, which specialized in trenching and installation of trans-ocean power cables for the telecommunications industry. Later that same year Coflexip acquired Perry Tritech, based in Florida, the world's leading designer and manufacturer of submarine robotic systems.

Further fueling its acquisition drive, Coflexip listed its shares on the NASDAQ stock exchange in 1993 and became one of the first French companies to introduce their stock on this market. The NASDAQ initial public offering (IPO) was followed a year later by a listing on the Paris stock exchange. The success of its public offerings enabled the company's next (and largest) acquisition. In 1994 Coflexip agreed to purchase Stena Offshore N.V., a unit of the Swedish Stena AB conglomerate, principally in exchange for some 2.8 million Coflexip shares at US $40 per share, giving Stena nearly 18 percent of Coflexip's stock. Stena Offshore specialized in the submarine petroleum installations; its focus on rigid and rolled rigid pipelines, as well as its geographical implantation, complemented Coflexip's own flexible pipeline specialty.

The Stena acquisition would double Coflexip's sales, which topped FFr 4 billion in 1995. Yet the merger of the two companies' operations, begun in 1995, proved less than smooth. Adding to the companies' difficulties that year was a number of technical difficulties, resulting in a drop in revenue growth. Meanwhile, the company began operations of a new manufacturing facility in Freemantle, Australia. The facility for production of flexible pipeline for the Asian market would face a struggle from the start, as the region's weak oil exploration activity failed to bring the plant to full operational capacity. At the same time, Coflexip faced problems on another front. Among its acquisitions in the first half of the 1990s had been a number of principally France-based manufacturers of composite materials. Although composite materials were used in Coflexip's primary subsea petroleum markets, the synergy between these activities remained difficult to achieve. By 1995 the company made the decision to exit the composite materials market, selling its newly added subsidiaries and forcing writedowns on these sales. By the end of 1995 the company posted a loss of more than FFr 100 million.

Coflexip's difficulties proved short-lived, however. By 1996 the company was posting profits again, because of a reorganization of the company under new Chairman and CEO Pierre Valentine. Once again focused on its core subsea market, Coflexip also determined to step up its research and development into providing deepwater and ultra-deepwater capacity, as this category was poised to begin a worldwide expansion. The

company soon would show initiative on several fronts, introducing its Flexconnect system, in conjunction with its Perry Tritech subsidiary, as well as a new pipelaying technology, and the Teta technology, which provided for stronger and larger riser systems. With a new steel production facility opened in Houston by its Duco Ltd. subsidiary and a new production facility in La Trait, Coflexip finished the 1996 year with revenues of FFr 4.9 billion and profits of FFr 70 million.

The company's reorganization and refocus on its core activities, however, would show its full impact in 1997, as the company's sales increased by 49 percent to top FFr 7 billion, placing Coflexip firmly among the world leaders in its market. Aiding this growth was the company's acquisition of a 25 percent interest in Houston's Cal-Dive International Inc., a submarine construction specialist operating in the Gulf of Mexico. In 1997 and 1998, Coflexip continued to show its technological leadership, establishing worldwide depth and pressure records for its pipeline installations. Although deepwater and ultra-deepwater pipelines remained a small percentage of the company's sales, Coflexip clearly marked these areas for its future growth.

Principal Subsidiaries

Coflexip Stena Offshore International (France); Coflexip Développement (France); Coflexip Stena Offshore N.V. (Netherlands); Coflexip Stena Offshore Ltd. (U.K.); Coflexip Stena Offshore Services Inc. (U.S.A.); DUCO Ltd. (U.K.); Coflexip Stena Offshore Norge A/S (Norway); DUCO Inc. (U.S.A.); Perry Tritech Inc. (U.S.A).; Flexservice N.V. (Dutch Antilles); Brasflex (Brazil); Flexibras (Brazil); Sigma (Brazil); Coflexip Stena Offshore Asia Pacific PTY Ltd. (Australia); Cal Dive International (U.S.A.; 25.5%); Travocéan (France; 50%).

Further Reading

Cosnard, Denis, "Coflexip renoue avec les profits," *Les Echos,* March 27, 1997, p. 9.
Jemain, Alain, "Coflexip se prépare à l'offshore ultra-profond," *L'Usine Nouvelle,* October 2, 1997, p. 37.
Remoué, Agathe, "Une connexion à très grande profondeur," *L'Usine Nouvelle,* October 9, 1997, p. 86.
"Sur la bonne voie dans des marchés porteurs," *Petrole Informations,* February–March 1997, p. 52.

—M.L. Cohen

Commonwealth Telephone Enterprises, Inc.

100 CTE Drive
Dallas, Pennsylvania 18612-9774
U.S.A.
(717) 674-2700
Fax: (717) 675-0900
Web site: http://www.ct-enterprises.com

Public Company
Incorporated: 1907 as Commonwealth Telephone Co.
Employees: 1,081
Sales: $196.6 million (1997)
Stock Exchanges: NASDAQ
Ticker Symbols: CTCO CTCOB
SICs: 4813 Telephone Communications, Except
    Radiotelephone; 4841 Cable & Other Pay Television
    Services; 4899 Communications Services, Not
    Elsewhere Classified

Commonwealth Telephone Enterprises, Inc. is the 13th-largest independent local-exchange carrier in the United States. Its core market consists of 19 counties in northeastern Pennsylvania, including areas where it has been a monopoly service provider for a century. The company, on a competitive basis, also began in 1997 to offer a variety of telephone services in adjacent areas, including high-speed data transmissions and interactive videoconferencing. It also became an Internet access provider in 1994 and was offering telecommunications engineering and technical services.

Commonwealth Telephone Through the 1970s

The company dates its beginnings to 1897, when Bert Stroh constructed a telephone line linking his home in Center Moreland, Pennsylvania, to that of a neighbor. His further linkups resulted in the organization of the Center Moreland Telephone Co. in 1902. Three years later this company merged with the Northern Lackawanna Telephone Co. to form Commonwealth Telephone Co. In 1912 Commonwealth Telephone signed a

contract with the Bell Telephone Co. that gave it exclusive territorial rights. In return, Commonwealth was linked to the American Telephone & Telegraph long-distance lines and the New York Telephone Co. In 1924 Commonwealth had assets of $961,393 and net income of $21,353 on gross earnings of $180,876.

Andrew J. Sordoni, a state senator, acquired a controlling interest in Commonwealth Telephone in 1928 through Public Service of Pennsylvania, Inc. and assumed the presidency of the corporation. Headquarters were in Forty Fort, Pennsylvania. In 1930 the company was supplying telephone service in Wyoming, Sullivan, and Susquehanna countries and parts of Luzerne, Lackawanna, and Bradford counties. Commonwealth made money throughout the Great Depression, although it stopped paying dividends in 1932 and net income fell to as low as $1,163 in 1937. In 1940 Commonwealth lost $29,857 on gross earnings of $402,734, but the company thereafter became profitable again. Dividends on common stock resumed in 1950, and stock was sold to the public for the first time in 1952.

By 1953 Commonwealth Telephone was providing service in eight Pennsylvania counties, with 27,186 telephones in service and corporate headquarters in Dallas, Pennsylvania. Sordoni had moved up to chairman, while Andrew J. Sordoni, Jr. had become president in 1950. Commonwealth acquired Tioga County Bell Telephone Co. in 1953, adding more than 6,000 telephones to its system, and Pennsylvania Community Telephone Co., with over 15,000 telephones in service, in 1954. The number of counties covered, in 1960, had reached 16, with 75,046 telephones in service. Net income that year came to $896,551 on operating revenues of $5.9 million.

Commonwealth Telephone was the third-largest independent telephone company in Pennsylvania and about the 15th-largest in the nation in 1966, when it installed its 100,000th telephone in service. Sixty percent of its customers still had only minimum basic service on a four-party line, but the company's operating area, once predominantly rural, was changing rapidly. With the emergence of the interstate highway system, northeastern Pennsylvania, only three hours from New York City by expressway, had become the site of facilities established by a number of large industrial corporations.

Commonwealth Telephone introduced touch-tone dialing in 1969 and completed nationwide direct distance dialing in the same year for all its subscribers, 60 percent of whom now had one- or two-party service. The number of telephones now had reached 124,102. The company had net income of $2.4 million in 1970 on operating revenues of $14.7 million. Commonwealth acquired Leesport Telephone Co. in 1971, Lewisberry Telephone Co. in 1977, and Sullivan County Telephone Co. in 1980, bringing the number of counties being served to 19 and the number of phones in service to more than 200,000. A digital microwave network was completed in 1976 and the nation's first commercial fiber-optic application in 1979. Net income in 1980 came to $5.4 million on operating revenues of $45.8 million.

Expanded Services in the 1980s

Although doing well as a telephone company, Commonwealth Telephone was looking at new services for further growth. In 1979 it formed a holding company, Commonwealth Telephone Enterprises Inc. (CTE), to preside over newly created nonregulated communications-related endeavors as well as the traditional telephone business. Established in 1978, the first of these new companies was Commonwealth Telephone Technologies Corp. (CTTC), which began selling business communications systems to markets outside of the telephone company's franchised service area, as well as management and engineering services to customers who included operating telephone companies and the cable television industry. This enterprise was enhanced by the acquisition of Sterling Telecommunication Supply Co., a leading full-service supplier to telephone, interconnect, and cable-TV companies.

After completion of its fiber-optic system, CTE formed, in 1980, Commonwealth Cable Systems, making available to its customers 52 television channels. This company was not free to operate within the telephone company's regulated area, but by the end of 1985 it was providing cable television to 27,100 subscribers in 20 New York and New Jersey communities, all within 50 miles of New York City. CTTC introduced cellular mobile telephone service to three Pennsylvania counties in 1984 and soon added radio paging operations. The following year it purchased Business Systems Inc. of Greenville, South Carolina, a supplier of turnkey computer-management systems—especially cable television—with 150 clients worldwide. Between 1981 and 1985 parent CTE almost doubled its revenues and raised its net income by 169 percent.

CTE had moved its headquarters to Wilkes-Barre, Pennsylvania, by the end of 1984, but Commonwealth Telephone remained in Dallas, Pennsylvania. This regulated telephone subsidiary, which added to its operations by acquiring Coopersburg Telephone Co. in 1984, was still responsible for 75 percent of the parent company's $110 million in revenues in 1985, when it was serving 155,000 customers. The following year, however, CTE changed its name to C-Tec Corp. to underline its commitment to diversification. "In the broadest context, we're interested in businesses in the information transport field," a senior executive explained.

In 1989 C-Tec added 108,000 cable subscribers by purchasing the Michigan operations of Centel Corp. for $206.6 million. Also that year, C-Tec's communications group began offering technical services to third parties. In 1990 a new subsidiary began offering long-distance services.

Major Changes: 1990–97

C-Tec's expenses were, however, outstripping its expansion. The Michigan acquisition brought its long-term debt to $365 million in 1990, compared to only $100 million two years later. That year C-Tec's interest expenses reached $31.9 million, and it lost nearly $10 million despite revenues and sales of $200.4 million. In 1991 the company's long-term debt reached $437 million, its interest payments $37.5 million, and its net loss $12.4 million. C-Tec also lost money in 1992 and 1993. Commonwealth Telephone completed a 15-year project of analog equipment replacement in 1993 and became one of the first telephone companies in the United States to institute a fully digital network.

RCN Corp., a subsidiary of Peter Kiewit Sons Inc., purchased a controlling interest in C-Tec from the Sordoni family in 1993 for $196.5 million. In making the purchase for 34 percent of the stock but 57 percent of the voting power, RCN paid $34.50 a share for the Sordoni stock, double the market price at the time. Some ten percent of the acquired stock was purchased by David McCourt, RCN's president, who became C-Tec's chairman and chief executive officer. In 1994 C-Tec sold its deficit-ridden cellular properties to Independent Cellular Network Inc. for $182.5 million in order to focus on its wire-based operating businesses.

McCourt moved the parent company's cable operation, C-Tec Cable Systems Inc., to Princeton, New Jersey, from where in October 1994 it was offering cable TV to more than 250,000 subscribers in New York, New Jersey, and Michigan. Three months later C-Tec acquired 40 percent of Megacable, the second-largest cable-television operation in Mexico, for $84 million. Megacable was serving 174,000 subscribers in 12 cities, including Guadalajara.

Parent company C-Tec, which by 1995 also had moved its headquarters to Princeton, raised about $217 million in December 1994 by selling 10.9 million shares of newly issued stock, much of which was purchased by Kiewit. For 1994 C-Tec earned its first profit since 1989, registering net income of $2.8 million on revenues of $269 million. The following year was much better, with revenues rising to $325 million, net income to $22.7 million, and long-term debt (which had reached a high of $432 million in 1991 and was still $409 million in 1993) reduced to $263 million.

The Telecommunications Act of 1996 substantially reduced regulatory barriers to new markets for telecommunications providers, encouraging new service offerings by multiple providers allowing telephone, cable, and television companies to compete and combine more freely. An executive for Commonwealth Telephone said the law would most likely provide the company's customers with a "one-stop-shop" for all communications needs. Commonwealth also in 1994 introduced Pennsylvania's first direct Internet service, through its Eastern Pennsylvania Internet Exchange ("epix"). With epix, Commonwealth was providing both business and residential customers toll-free, dial-up, and full-period access to the Internet.

Returning to its Roots in 1997

In February 1997 C-Tec announced it would divide into three companies. Spun off to shareholders was Cable Michigan, Inc. and RCN Corp., the parent company's unit for a variety of residential telecommunications services on the East Coast and the Megacable investment. These two units had accounted for 53 percent of C-Tec's revenues of $367.3 million in 1996, when net income came to $12.5 million. After the breakup was completed in September, C-Tec was renamed Commonwealth Telephone Enterprises, Inc. and headquarters returned to Dallas, Pennsylvania. McCourt, who remained the company's chairman and chief executive officer, said C-Tec's combination of geographically disparate businesses had kept the stock undervalued by confusing investors who "want to hear a single, straightforward story."

With the disposition of RCN and Cable Michigan, the new Commonwealth Telephone Enterprises (CTE) was now organized into two principal operating segments: Commonwealth Telephone Co. (CT), a local-exchange carrier still operating as a monopoly service provider in Pennsylvania, and Commonwealth Telecom Services (CTSI), Inc., a competitive local-exchange carrier that began operations in 1997 in markets adjacent to CT's traditional service area. In addition, CTE was operating three support businesses providing expertise to its two principal operating segments. These businesses were Commonwealth Communications (CC),, epix (TM) Internet Services (epix), and Commonwealth Long Distance (CLD). CC was designing, installing, and managing telephone systems for corporations, hospitals, and universities, mainly in Pennsylvania. CLD was operating only in CT's service area.

CT was providing service to 258,803 main access lines at the end of 1997 in a 19-county, 5,191-square-mile territory in Pennsylvania. These services including not only local and long-distance telephone services but also complex communications services such as interactive videoconferencing and high-speed data transmission. Under contract with the Northern Tier Rural Distance Learning Consortium, it was providing videoconferencing services to about 36 schools in three states.

CTSI was beginning to provide local and all-distance telephone service, offering flat-rate and bundled telephone packages in a service area including about 2.1 million people. It had 25,890 customer connections at the end of 1997. CC was providing telecommunications engineering and technical services to CT and, since 1989, to third parties. Epix was offering flat-rate access to the Internet and had more than 30,000 customers in Pennsylvania and New York at the end of 1997.

Commonwealth Telephone Enterprises had sales (excluding those of the spinoff businesses) of $196.6 million in 1997. Of this total, CT accounted for 73 percent, CTSI for three percent, and other operations (CC, epix, and CD) for 24 percent. The company reported a net loss of $14 million for the year after taking a $36.1 million charge for discontinued operations. Its long-term debt was $167.3 million at the end of 1997.

Principal Subsidiaries

Commonwealth Long Distance Company; Commonwealth Telecom Services, Inc.; Commonwealth Telephone Company; C-TEC Cable Holdings, Inc.; C-TEC Cellular Centre County, Inc.; epix Internet Services, Inc.; Mobilefone, Inc.; Mobile Plus, Inc.; Mobile Plus of Iowa, Inc.; Mobile Plus Services, Inc.; Mobile Plus Services of PA, Inc.; SRHC, Inc.; TMH, Inc.

Further Reading

Booker, Ellis, "C-Tec Corp.—More Than a Telco," *Telephony,* June 30, 1986, pp. 32, 36, 38.

"Commonwealth Tel Rings the Bell in Its Resurging Service Territory," *Barron's,* June 16, 1969, pp. 31–32.

Cullen, Jean V., "Commonwealth Telephone Hits All-Time Highs," *Investment Dealers' Digest,* March 28, 1966, pp. 34–35.

"Dial T for Takeover?" *Barron's,* January 2, 1989, pp. 6–7, 22.

Helzner, Jerry, "Imaginative Independent," *Barron's,* December 2, 1985, p. 71.

Kirkpatrick, David D., "C-Tec Corp. Plans to Divide Itself Into 3 Companies," *Wall Street Journal,* February 14, 1997, p. B5.

Lysiak, Fran Mateo, "Commonwealth Telephone Co.: Advanced Technology Keeps Customers Connected," *Northeast Pennsylvania Business Journal,* September 1996, p. SS3.

Puhalla, Marianne Tucker, "Fiber Optics: Officials Tout Technology as a Key Component for Economic Development," *Northeast Pennsylvania Business Journal,* February 1992, pp. 1+.

Sloan, Allan, "Main Street Scores One Over Wall Street in Rights Offer by C-Tec Corp.," *Los Angeles Times,* November 6, 1994, p. D2.

Umphred, William J., "How Commonwealth Tel Jumped into New Markets," *Telephone Engineer & Management,* August 1, 1981, pp. 48–51.

Werner, Thomas, "New Name, Big Game," *Barron's,* February 23, 1987, pp. 57–58.

—Robert Halasz

CompHealth

COMPREHENSIVE
HEALTHCARE STAFFING

CompHealth Inc.

4021 South 700 East, Suite 300
Salt Lake City, Utah 84107-2184
U.S.A.
(801) 264-6400
Fax: (801) 264-6464
Web site: http://www.comphealth.com

Wholly Owned Subsidiary of HealthSouth Corporation
Incorporated: 1979
Employees: 350+
SICs: 7361 Employment Agencies; 7363 Medical Help
    Service

CompHealth was the nation's first and is the nation's largest firm providing temporary staffing of medical doctors and other health care professionals. Although conceived to serve rural areas of the Intermountain West, CompHealth now serves a wide variety of clients in both rural and urban areas, ranging from large metropolitan medical centers to small clinics and individual practices. Its clients are found in all 50 states. Although such firms as Kelly Services, Inc. and Manpower, Inc. had pioneered the temporary staffing concept, CompHealth was the first to apply that concept in the medical staffing industry. Given the tremendous growth in America's health care field, CompHealth and its numerous competitors play an important role in keeping the nation healthy.

1970s Origins

Although the United States leads the world in many areas of modern medicine, it has struggled with an overconcentration of physicians in cities and not enough working in rural areas. To help remedy this persistent problem, in the early 1970s the University of Utah College of Medicine started new programs to help rural areas gain the services of medical doctors. With the help of a federal grant, the medical school's Department of Family and Community Medicine attempted to recruit and train doctors through its Rural Outreach Physician Education (ROPE) program. Rural doctors considering leaving their prac-

tices were brought to the university for specially designed continuing education courses lasting from three weeks to three months. At the same time, the medical school provided temporary physicians to cover those rural practices left vacant.

A network resulted of doctors willing to relocate temporarily while physicians took time to upgrade their knowledge and training or simply take a vacation from the heavy burdens of often single-handedly serving small towns and rural clinics. The University of Utah's pilot program worked so well that hospital administrators around the nation started asking for help.

The key person in these developments was Dr. Therus C. Kolff, who was born in Holland in 1949. In 1950 his father Dr. Willem J. Kolff moved with his family to work at the Cleveland Clinic. Then in 1967 the Kolff family moved to Salt Lake City, where Willem Kolff became famous for his work on artificial organs. Not only Therus Kolff's father, but also his grandfather, an uncle, and two brothers became doctors. While still a medical student at the University of Utah, Therus participated in the federally funded temporary staffing grant. In 1974 he received his degree and then worked for Intermountain Health Care (IHC) as part of the Health System Research Institute, which was developing programs to improve rural health care. Kolff in 1977 first personally covered for another doctor in *locum tenens,* or temporary physician staffing. After leaving IHC, he went to Boston for his masters in public health, a joint program between the Harvard Business School and Harvard's School of Public Health. After graduating in June 1979 with his MPH degree, Kolff returned to Utah and later in the year started his new firm called CompHealth.

Temporary work offered by CompHealth proved attractive to physicians for several reasons. Some doctors liked to work in different geographical areas before deciding on a permanent place to practice. Others liked to sample hospitals, HMOs, or other types of medical practices before making a long-term commitment. Physicians just out of residency programs were attracted to *locum tenens* before settling down. Military doctors moving into civilian life appreciated the opportunity to try different options. Older MDs who wanted to combine both travel and part-time work found CompHealth's programs beneficial. Of course, the travel advantages appealed to many doctors of any age. The bottom line was that many doctors liked the freedom to choose where, when, and how much they would work, a flexibility which gave them time to balance work with family responsibilities, hobbies, and civic activities.

Kolff originally knew most if not all his employees, clients, and temporary doctors. At first, CompHealth provided temps for general or family practitioners, but soon the company was working for numerous specialists. In any case, CompHealth screened its doctors carefully so that its clients felt comfortable accepting them.

Expansion in the 1980s

Initially CompHealth provided temporary coverage for just a short period of time, an average of two weeks, and it supplied physicians in Utah, Wyoming, Nevada, Montana, and Colorado. However, by the mid-1980s the firm had taken responsibility for providing different medical specialists in much longer assignments in other parts of the nation. For example, in 1985 CompHealth took over staffing for Duke University's Radiation Oncology Department, a 36-month contract.

Around 1982 CompHealth started its first branch office in Atlanta, Georgia. There, the company had become involved with Health Corp., which was developing freestanding cancer centers. Health Corp. had additional space available, so CompHealth took this opportunity to start an office in the Southeast.

Since its temporaries depended on CompHealth's medical malpractice insurance, the company became quite concerned in 1983 when its carrier, a Montana firm called Glacier, went broke. Kolff later remarked that it was very difficult to get such insurance in the early 1980s since few carriers were in business. His company replaced its Glacier coverage with a two-year policy from St. Paul Insurance, one of the few large medical malpractice firms, but eventually CompHealth ended up with Chicago's MMI as its insurance carrier.

One of the company's vice-presidents created CompHealth's first subsidiary called Group One Anesthesia and started a branch office in Grand Rapids, Michigan, where he had grown up. Group One provided certified registered nurse anesthetists (CRNAs) to hospitals and clinics.

In 1985, CompHealth's employees purchased the company. In the process, however, they were inheriting a debt of $800,000. To improve the firm's finances, the new owners acquired a new computer database system, expected to improve operating efficiencies. These changes fueled CompHealth's expansion in the late 1980s. Revenues increased 350 percent from about $10 million in 1985 to $45 million in 1989. In 1989 the firm provided over 57,000 days of temporary doctor staffing for clients in every state. In the late 1980s CompHealth added physical therapists, registered nurses, and certified nurse anesthetists to its list of temporaries.

Growth in the 1990s

CompHealth started the 1990s by moving its Salt Lake City headquarters from 155 South 300 West to the new Woodlands Tower II building located at 700 East 4021 South. The company leased 28,000 square feet for its 100 employees who worked to place approximately 1,200 doctors and other healers in temporary positions around the nation. Those physicians represented 14 medical specialties.

One of CompHealth's orthopedic physicians made media headlines in February 1990 after he helped save the life of a Utah man named Randy Lewis. While fishing near Ketchikan, Alaska, Lewis seriously injured his leg and then fell into the cold water. At the same time, Dr. Ben Gilson, a substitute for the only practicing orthopedic physician between Seattle and Juneau, Alaska, flew overhead in his float plane. Gilson flew Lewis to the Ketchikan hospital, where he worked on the leg wound and prepared Lewis to transfer to a Salt Lake City hospital. After returning to work, Lewis praised CompHealth's ability to make sure its temporaries like Gilson were qualified to handle such emergencies.

By 1990 CompHealth had spent about $220,000 per month on malpractice insurance, which relieved its physicians of this growing burden. The firm's monthly expenses also included $50,000 for licensing physicians in new states, $120,000 for air travel, and $48,000 for rental cars.

In the early 1990s the nation prepared to enter the Gulf War, and many U.S. doctors and nurses were called on to leave their regular jobs as their reserve units were mobilized. Meanwhile, hospitals juggled schedules of their remaining staff and cut back on elective surgery and other routine procedures. During this time, CompHealth helped by providing at least 100 physicians to the hospitals by December 1990.

Although CompHealth started the temporary physician staffing industry, other firms entered the fray, including one that was started by former employees. In March 1990 three CompHealth middle managers, Mark Brouse, Kathryn Hoffman Abby, and Clark Shaw, left CompHealth to found Vista Staffing Solutions in Salt Lake City. In a telephone interview, Vista's president and CEO Mark Brouse said leaving CompHealth was a difficult decision. "CompHealth was a good place to work," he remarked, adding "we owed a lot to Dr. Therus Kolff for starting this industry." Brouse believed that the fact that only one firm had spun off from CompHealth bespoke the generally good relations CompHealth maintained with its work force. While Vista Staffing continued to focus on *locum tenens* for physicians, CompHealth diversified into staffing other health care professions.

In 1991 CompHealth was the Utah winner in the Blue Chip Enterprise Initiative Competition, an effort sponsored by the U.S. Chamber of Commerce, the Connecticut Mutual Insurance Company, and *Nation's Business* magazine to recognize the nation's best small businesses.

That year CompHealth management worked with Alex Brown, a Baltimore investment banking group, to find a purchaser. Working with his attorney, Daniel Littlefield of Salt Lake City, Kolff met with the first company on the Alex Brown list, Continental Medical Systems (CMS). Based in Pennsylvania, CMS was one of the nation's two largest providers of rehabilitation services, a rapidly growing field due to the increasing number of senior citizens. In November 1991 CMS acquired CompHealth, which continued to operate independently under Kolff, its chief executive officer.

Continental Medical Systems in February 1993 acquired Kron Medical Corporation, a North Carolina-based rival of CompHealth, and merged the two temporary medical staffing firms to meet the growing demands for such services. Kolff reported that CompHealth/Kron in its first year together brought in about $100 million in annual revenues.

Dr. Kolff left the company in January 1994, going on to start another firm called Cancer Carve Out, a disease management company, which he later sold to Value Health. In May 1994 Jeffrey F. Poore, DDS, became CompHealth's new president and chief operating officer. Poore previously had worked on mergers and development as FHP International's CEO. Poore's stay at CompHealth, however, lasted just one year. In 1995 Christopher Slayter became CompHealth's interim president, until he was chosen as the firm's president in June 1997.

In Kolff's last months at CompHealth, the firm began looking at a general credentialing service for other organizations. CompHealth had to verify the credentials of its own personnel, so Kolff reasoned that this service could be expanded as a way to save others the bother. Eventually credentialing expanded to become a complete CompHealth division.

In 1996 CompHealth's credentialing service was certified by the National Committee for Quality Assurance (NCQA), an independent nonprofit organization. Renewed in 1997 for three more years, CompHealth's certified credentialing included verification of medical school graduation, license to practice, hospital privileges, Drug Enforcement Agency certification, residency completion, specialty board certification, malpractice claims history, National Practitioner Data Bank, state licensing sanctions, and Medicare/Medicaid sanctions.

The importance of this detailed process of background checking was emphasized when *The Wall Street Journal* on June 2, 1994 reported that half of all large United States employers refused to sign HMO (health maintenance organization) contracts unless the HMO had verified its providers credentials according to NCQA or JCAHO (Joint Commission on the Accreditation of Healthcare Organizations) standards.

In November 1997 HealthSouth Corporation acquired CompHealth from Horizon/CMS Healthcare Corporation, the parent of Continental Medical Systems. Based in Birmingham, Alabama, HealthSouth was Continental's main competitor in the 1990s. HealthSouth had acquired several other firms, such as National Medical Enterprises in 1993 and ReLife in 1994. After purchasing Caremark International's rehabilitation services in 1995, HealthSouth had about 440 outpatient facilities and 40 percent of the rapidly growing rehabilitation market. Under the leadership of HealthSouth's CEO and chairperson Richard M. Scrushy, the firm provided not only outpatient and inpatient rehabilitation, but also home health care and outpatient surgery. Since CompHealth provided temporary physical and occupational therapists, it was a logical target for HealthSouth, a rapidly growing public corporation with $3 billion in annual revenues in 1997.

By late 1997 CompHealth was staffing some 5,000 physicians, therapists, and other health care providers for temporary assignments with its 1,700 clients in all 50 states. CompHealth had exclusive contracts to provide temporary physician staffing for Walter Reed Hospital in Washington, D.C.; Kaiser Permanente in California; and Las Vegas' Veterans Administration Hospital.

To promote its services, CompHealth sent representatives to national conferences in every major medical specialty and included notices of its services in over 100 medical journals. The company annually made educational/recruiting presentations at over 200 residency programs around the nation. It contacted 500,000 doctors and other health care professionals by direct mail and maintained a database with information on about 140,000 physicians and other healers.

In 1997 and 1998 CompHealth consolidated some of its operations, closing small offices in Dallas and Phoenix in March 1998 and in June shuttering its Atlanta office. Offices in Seattle and Denver had been closed earlier. CompHealth decided the Salt Lake City office could more effectively handle needs of those various areas.

CompHealth also consolidated its therapy staffing operations. In October 1997 it closed its Pro Therapy office in Detroit, moving it to Grand Rapids, Michigan, where Group One was based. Group One provided physical and occupational therapists and assistants, as well as speech and language pathologists, for traveling positions around the country. It also supplied some therapists who preferred to work temporary assignments in their local areas. Pro Therapy also provided the services of physical and occupational therapists. However, Pro Therapy accepted therapists with or without experience who had been trained in other countries. Those therapists were willing to take just about any assignment to gain experience, while Group One therapists, who had at least two years experience, usually expected better positions. CompHealth in 1998 was also working to integrate the services of Health Providers Inc., another therapy provider, already under the parentage of HealthSouth before it acquired CompHealth in late 1997.

Although the largest firm in its industry, CompHealth faced plenty of competitors in an unconsolidated new field. A consulting study by Bernstein-Rein, CompHealth's advertising agency, found 108 other companies doing similar temporary medical staffing. CompHealth accounted for approximately 22 percent of that market, while the next top ten firms provided 49 percent and other firms handled the remaining 29 percent.

CompHealth's major competitors in the late 1980s included Atlanta's Medical Doctor Associates; Jackson & Coker, also of Atlanta; Daniel & Yeager; Cross Country Staffing; Therapists Unlimited, a division of CareerStaff Unlimited; TravCorps-Clinical Staffing Solutions; ATC Healthcare Services, a division of Staff Builders; Olsten Health Services, part of Olsten Corporation; and Interim HealthCare. Although temporary medical staffing accounted for less than ten percent of the total staffing industry revenues in 1998, that figure was growing rapidly. The *locum tenens* industry was estimated at about $1 billion annually.

CompHealth's leadership in the health care temporaries industry allowed it to do some things its smaller competitors could not. For example, in March 1998 CompHealth announced it had hired Christopherson Business Travel to establish an on-site office at its Salt Lake City headquarters. CompHealth typically provided travel tickets to and from a temporary assignment and also paid for a rental car and housing.

In April 1998 CompHealth gained the leadership of Michael R. Weinholtz, who had worked 13 years in the temporary medical staffing industry. He left his position as president and CEO of CareerStaff Unlimited, a CompHealth competitor in Houston, Texas, to become the president of CompHealth's Locum Tenens Division, and in June 1998 he was promoted to become the president of the entire firm.

Weinholtz's firm enjoyed continual growth as the new millennium approached, partly because of its own abilities and track record, but also due to overall trends in the American economy. A Bureau of Labor Statistics study released in 1998 found that Americans in their 30s had held an average of nearly nine jobs between the ages of 18 and 32. Moreover, some experts have suggested that the concept of lifetime career placement is obsolete, part of an industrial revolution now superseded in America by the post-industrial era or Information Age. According to a 1996 article in *The Futurist,* "about 20% of all professionals now work as temps, including lawyers, doctors, and even executives." With that trend expected to continue,

CompHealth's future indeed looked promising as a new century approached.

Further Reading

Halal, William E., "The Rise of the Knowledge Entrepreneur," *The Futurist,* November–December 1996, p. 13.

Jacobsen-Wells, JoAnn, "S.L. Firm Fills in When Physicians Need a Break," *Deseret News* (Web Edition), February 8, 1990.

"Local Company Leads in Physician-Staffing Services," *Salt Lake Tribune—Advertising Supplement,* October 19, 1997, p. 31.

"Medical Staffing's Window of Opportunity," *Staffing Industry Review,* June 1998, pp. 43–54.

Pusey, Roger, "4 Utah Firms Honored for Resourcefulness," *Deseret News* (Web Edition), May 30, 1991.

"S. L. CompHealth Gets New President," *Salt Lake Tribune,* April 2, 1998, p. B1.

Studt, Ward B., et. al., *Medicine in the Intermountain West: A History of Health Care in Rural Areas of the West,* Salt Lake City: Olympus Publishing Company, 1976, pp. 325–326.

Wilson, Anne, "Military Call-Ups Force VA to Close 36 Beds," *Salt Lake Tribune,* December 7, 1990, p. B1.

——, "Nursing Newborns Is Challenge for Working Moms," *Salt Lake Tribune,* October 30, 1994, p. F1.

—David M. Walden

Cullen/Frost Bankers, Inc.
A Family of Texas Banks

Cullen/Frost Bankers, Inc.

100 West Houston Street
P.O. Box 1600
San Antonio, Texas 78296
U.S.A.
(210) 220-4011
Fax: (210) 220-4791
(800) 562-6732
Web Site: http://www.frostbank.com

Public Company
Incorporated: 1977
Employees: 2,550 (1977)
Total Assets: $6.43 billion (1998)
Stock Exchanges: New York
Ticker Symbol: CFR
SICs: 6712 Bank Holding Companies; 6021 National
Commercial Banks

Cullen/Frost Bankers, Inc. is a bank holding company consisting of two wholly owned banking subsidiaries: Frost National Bank (Frost)—the largest independent bank in Texas—and United States National Bank of Galveston. Each subsidiary bank is a separate entity that operates under the day-to-day management of its own board of directors and officers. Frost accounted for approximately 97 percent of the bank holding company's 1997 consolidated assets and 98 percent of its loans and deposits. Cullen/Frost operates 76 financial centers dispersed throughout San Antonio, Austin, Boerne, Corpus Christi, the Fort Worth/Dallas area, the Galveston/Houston area, McAllen, New Braunfels, and San Marcos. The company provides policy direction to its two member banks for asset and liability management, accounting, budgeting, planning and insurance; capitalization; and regulatory compliance. The subsidiary banks offer services related to commercial banking, consumer banking, international banking, trusts, correspondent banking, and discount brokerage. Cullen/Frost, with trust assets totaling $10 billion and a market capitalization of over $1 billion, ranks among the 60 largest trust banks in the nation. According to

September 30, 1997 data from the Federal Reserve Board, Cullen/Frost is the largest of the 93 unaffiliated bank holding companies headquartered in Texas.

The Beginnings of Frost National Bank in the Late-1800s

The early history of Frost National Bank is rooted in that of Texas. Its founder, Thomas Claiborne Frost, was born in Alabama in 1833 and graduated from Irving College in Tennessee. He then settled in Texas as an assistant professor at Austin College, studied law in Sam Houston's office, and was admitted to the bar in 1856 by Judge R.E.B. Baylor. The young lawyer played an active role in community and state affairs: in 1857 he served with the Texas Rangers to protect citizens against Indian raids and was elected district attorney for Comanche County. In 1861 he was a delegate to the Secession Convention in Austin and, when Texas seceded from the Union, served as a lieutenant colonel in the Confederate Army.

After the Civil War, due to Reconstruction regulations against former Confederate officers, Colonel Frost could not resume his law practice. Thus, he instead established a freight business between San Antonio and the Gulf port of Indianola. Soon afterwards, John Frost (his brother) and J. L. Fitch (John's partner) asked him to join their mercantile and auction business. As a partner of Fitch, Frost and Bro., the Colonel anticipated the needs of post-war Texas and stocked the hard merchandise—such as axes, rifles, pistols, ammunition, boots, harnesses, saddles, and plows—that men would need to finish taming the land. He bought Fitch's share of the business and the store operated as Frost & Bro. until 1881.

Recognizing the difficulty Texas wool producers experienced in getting their goods to market during the poor economy of the postwar period, Colonel Frost formulated a plan to help. He contracted with haulers to collect the wool, built a large warehouse, and stored the wool until market conditions became favorable. The Colonel made loans (based on the wool stocks he was holding) to the producers. Thus began the state's first merchandising, financing, and marketing program. Proceeds of wool shipments made to eastern markets were deposited in New

Company Perspectives:

Cullen/Frost Bankers, Inc. is committed to relationship banking, that is, to combining a high level of professional competence and personal service with financial products that answer to the needs and interests of its customers.

York bank accounts that accumulated increasingly large balances, against which Colonel Frost ordered supplies of silver and gold from mints for his own trade and to supply silver to bankers and merchants in nearby Texas towns. Growers became accustomed to leaving some of their money on deposit with him in order to draw against them during periods between sales.

In 1896 Colonel Frost abandoned his wool-commission business and applied for a national bank charter. In February 1899 the bank's official name became Frost National Bank of San Antonio, with assets of $1.3 million. Upon the death of Colonel Frost in 1903, T.C. Frost, Jr. was named president, a position he held until 1926 when he became chairman and his younger brother, J.H. Frost, was named president.

Frost's Success in Weathering the Depression

During this period, the U.S. population tripled and the gross national product rose sharply from $6 billion a year to $70 billion. Banks played a primary role in supporting this growth through loans, investments, and community involvement. Due to the boom in construction and real estate, during the early 1920s both individuals and institutions invested heavily in the stock market. In 1928 Frost Bank—in a fortuitous move that created a financial institution strong enough to survive the hardships that were to come—merged with the city's oldest bank, Lockwood National Bank.

As bank customers continued to withdraw funds to fuel their investments, the real-estate boom came to a halt. The stock market crashed, and nearly 5,000 banks failed. During the first several years of the 1930s, additional banks failed and some states declared bank holidays. Recognizing the urgency of the situation, President Franklin D. Roosevelt declared a mandatory bank holiday to give Congress time to vote on an emergency banking bill. Frost Bank records attest to the fact that, except for the government-decreed bank holidays, the bank never closed its doors during these troubled times.

In an effort to pull the nation and financial institutions out of the depression, the U.S. Congress passed The Banking Act of 1933 to establish federal insurance of deposits and, hopefully, prevent further runs on banks. But the economy recovered slowly until it was fueled by the job market created by the defense industry during World War II. After the war, military personnel returned home to find jobs plentiful. Having survived a depression and the restrictions imposed by another war, U.S. citizens were quick to demand new housing, appliances, automobiles and other tangible goods. During the 1950s and 1960s, American industry expanded—and banks prospered. For the

first time, banks began to offer consumer loans that could be repaid in installments, replacing the old "call loan" method.

During the 1970s, Frost Bank began a period of steady expansion. Assets climbed 12 percent in 1972 to reach $667 million, while loans increased to $312 million—a 31 percent leap that boosted operating profits by more than 50 percent. In 1973, the FrostBank Corporation was formed as a bank holding company and opened three additional banks. Frost entered the Corpus Christi market in 1974 by acquiring Parkdale State Bank. About this time, a gradual—and then sudden—decline occurred in the national economy. Climbing interest rates began to choke economic activity, triggering increased loan defaults. Equities markets continued to slide, and real-estate trusts—created by many bank holding companies as ancillary vehicles—reported severe losses. With loan demand steadily diminishing, banks across the country began to shift into government and municipal securities. It was a period of lingering inflation and a stagnant economy but, thanks to conservative operating policies, Frost Bank continued to prosper.

Cullen's Texas Roots

While FrostBank Corporation had been sinking its roots deep into Texas soil during the 1920s and '30s, two native Texas oil wildcatters—Hugh Roy Cullen and Robert E. Smith—built a fortune and invested some of it in serving the Houston community. Cullen wanted to build an office center in downtown Houston similar to that of Rockefeller Center in order to house a family-controlled bank. He died in 1957 but his dream was realized in part when his sons-in-law began the development of seven blocks of land in the south part of downtown Houston.

Over the years, the Cullen Center complex grew to include the 20-story Marathon Building that served as Cullen Bank headquarters, three other office buildings, the Whitehall Hotel, and a multi-story parking garage. In 1968, Smith and V.F. Neuhaus joined members of the Cullen family to obtain a charter for the Cullen Center Bank & Trust of Houston. Deposits of $29 million on July 1, 1969—the opening day—exceeded the founders' projections for the first three years of the bank's operation. Within five years, Cullen Center Bank & Trust held deposits of $210 million and was the county's ninth-largest bank. In 1974 the holding company of Cullen Bankers, Inc. was formed and acquired both Cullen Center Bank & Trust of Houston and Citizens National Bank of Dallas.

Cullen/Frost Bankers, Inc: 1977–90

On July 7, 1977, Cullen Bankers, Inc. merged into FrostBank Corporation to form Cullen/Frost Bankers, Inc. In the early 1920s, Frost Bank had issued stock to non-family members to fund its new 12-story bank building; brokers conducted over-the-counter market trading of the bank's stock. Later, in 1977, Cullen/Frost stock was quoted and traded on NASDAQ.

Mergers followed apace. In 1982 Cullen/Frost entered the Galveston market by acquiring United States National Bancshares, expanded in the Houston area with the acquisition of Sugar Land State Bank, and entered the Austin market through a merger agreement with Chase National Bank. The growth market looked promising but difficult times were ahead. An unexpected drop in the price of oil, the real-estate crash and the demise of the savings and loan industry resulted in a severe economic downturn. Problem loans increased and many financial institutions struggled to survive. Nevertheless, Frost Bank remained healthier than many other institutions and, ultimately, was the only one of Texas' 10 largest banking companies of the 1980s to survive without federal assistance or acquisition by an out-of-state institution.

The Texas banking picture began to change when new legislation allowed the banks to open branches in the state, thereby capturing a large segment of the retail market previously dominated by credit unions, and savings and loans institutions. Fortunately for Frost Bank, sound credit analysis apparently ran in the Frost family's genes. "While many of Frost's Texas rivals piled up loans to speculative real-estate ventures in the early and mid-1980s, Frost concentrated on making commercial loans to longtime customers and well-secured mortgage loans to owners of existing residential and commercial property," wrote Graham Button in a 1992 issue of *Forbes*. "By 1987 Cullen/Frost was the only Texas bank with assets of more than $1.5 billion to show a profit. 'In the land of the blind,' Frost told *Forbes* in 1988, 'the one-eyed man is king.' " And despite the perpetually volatile behavior of the stock markets during the 1980s, the total trust assets of Frost Bank's Trust Division regularly outperformed Standard and Poor's 500-stock index.

During the 1990s, Cullen/Frost continued to make strategic acquisitions, thereby strengthening its position in established markets and securing a presence in new locations. In August 1997, the company was listed on the New York Stock Exchange and traded under the symbol CFR. By June 30, 1998, the bank holding company operated 76 financial centers across Texas through 17 locations in San Antonio, five in Austin, two in Boerne, 10 in Corpus Christi, 14 in the Fort Worth/Dallas area, 22 in the Galveston/Houston area, two in McAllen, one in New Braunfels, and three in San Marcos.

Relationship Banking in the 1990s

Through its two banking subsidiaries, Cullen/Frost provided commercial banking services for corporations and other business clients, on both a national and an international basis. Loans were made for a wide variety of purposes, including interim-construction financing, and financing on recapitalizations and turnaround situations. The subsidiary banks offered a full range of consumer banking services, international banking, trust services, correspondent banking, and discount brokerage.

Keeping alive the Frost commitment to staying close to customers in order to understand and serve their needs, the subsidiary banks continually introduced, developed and updated products according to the latest available banking technologies. In fact, in a 1996 issue of the *Houston Business Journal*, industry analyst Steve Didion commented that "Cullen/Frost is perceived as a 'super community bank' because it serves more than one market, but in every market, it targets that middle market and upper market customer."

For example, Cullen/Frost participated in the introduction of automatic teller machines (ATMs) in the mid-1970s and in their continuing deployment through its markets. By November 1997 the Frost ReadyBank card carried the Visa/PLUS ATM Network symbol and could be used to access not only the bank's Texas ATMs but also the 250,000 ATMs in the Visa network. It could be used as a debit card wherever the Visa symbol was found, that is, in more than 13 million places around the world. By June 1998, Cullen/Frost operated ATMs throughout central and southern Texas. Other electronic services included Ready-Bank Touch-Tone Bill Pay and ReadyBank Online.

In May 1996, Frost National Bank launched a series of new products designed to answer the needs of small businesses in Texas. The Frost Bank Business CreditLine provided a credit line of up to $50,000 with interest payable monthly and a maximum maturity term of three years; long-term, fixed rate financing from $100,000 to $1 million for the purchase of owner-occupied premises, with up to 15-year amortization tied to the 10-year and 5-year treasury rates. Additionally, long-term, fixed-rate financing was available for loans between $1 million and $2.5 million. With this option, there was a 15-year amortization term; the rate was fixed for the first seven years; a floating rate was in effect for the remaining eight years.

Cullen/Frost's business did not stop at the state border. As a leader in Texas' growing international–banking market, the company had correspondent banking relationships throughout Mexico—where it had begun to do business in the 1930s—and in Canada. The company's customers had access to confirmation of foreign letters of credit, clearance of foreign drafts drawn on Frost Bank accounts, over-the-counter exchange of foreign currency, and international wiring of funds through S.W.I.F.T. (Society for Worldwide Interbank Financial Telecommunications), the global network that member banks used to exchange various transaction types in standardized, language-independent format.

Cullen/Frost further implemented its commitment to relationship banking by forming the Frost Financial Management Group to consolidate all the bank's financial management services, including the previously separate trust and brokerage services of the bank. In this way, the company built upon the longstanding Frost reputation for sound financial management and integrity, becoming one of the 60 largest trust banks in the United States. The Group enabled customers to combine their investment and banking relationships in a single institution that offered a wide range of products at highly competitive rates. Financial Management Services combined trust investments, financial management, and brokerage services in a single entity. Private trust services provided new and former trust clients with revocable and irrevocable trusts. Retirement services brought new expertise, products and services to the employee benefits function and offered customers a broader range of investment and savings opportunities.

Additionally, Cullen/Frost owned three non-banking companies. In April 1981 Cullen/Frost had purchased Daltex General Agency, Inc., a managing general-insurance agency. As a wholly owned non-banking subsidiary, Daltex provided vendor's single-interest insurance for the subsidiary banks. Another non-banking subsidiary, Main Plaza Corporation, held real estate for future expansion of certain subsidiary banks, and occasionally made loans to qualified borrowers. Loans were funded with borrowings against Cullen/Frost's current cash or borrowings against credit lines. Finally, the New Galveston Company, Inc. was a second-tier bank holding company subsidiary which held all shares of each banking and non-banking subsidiary.

As the 20th century came to a close, Cullen/Frost Bankers, Inc. had reaffirmed its commitment to relationship banking, especially through the decentralization strategy implemented in its "family of Texas banks." In the new millennium, Cullen/Frost—the largest unaffiliated bank holding company headquartered in Texas—would continue to grow while offering its customers the personal and efficient service that nurtured its roots.

Principal Subsidiaries

The Frost National Bank; United States National Bank of Galveston; Daltex General Agency, Inc.; Main Plaza Corporation; The New Galveston Company, Inc.

Further Reading

Bamford, Janet and Suzanne Woolley, "The Prize Catches Being Eyed by Big Banks," *Business Week,* July 27, 1992, pp. 64–65.

Button, Graham, "One-Eyed King," *Forbes,* November 9, 1992, p. 13.

Chase, Brett, "In the Heart of Texas, Cullen/Frost Buying Overton for $254 Million in Stock," *American Banker,* February 18, 1998, pp. 1–2.

Lowe, Sandra, "Cullen/Frost Restructures in Quest for Growth," *San Antonio Business Journal,* September 10, 1993, pp. 1–3.

Martin, Steven, "Processing Move Pays Off for Cullen/Frost Bankers," *Bank Systems & Technology,* June 1997, p. 48.

Perin, Monica. "Several Companies Try but Fail to Reach Wall Street in 1997," *Houston Business Journal,* January 2, 1998, p. 7.

Pybus, Kenneth R., "Bull Markets Boost Prices of Bank Company Stocks," *Houston Business Journal,* July 12, 1996, p. 32.

Willis, Belinda, "Overton Bank Acquisition Hits Texas High," *The Business Press,* February 20, 1998, pp. 3–4.

—Gloria A. Lemieux

Cybermedia, Inc.

Suite 2001
3000 Ocean Park Boulevard
Santa Monica, California 90405
U.S.A.
(310) 664-5000
Fax: (310) 664-4720
(800) 721-7824
Web site: http://www.cybermedia.com

Public Company
Incorporated: 1996
Employees: 285
Sales: $78.6 million (1997)
Stock Exchanges: NASDAQ
Ticker Symbol: CYBR
SICs: 7372 Prepackaged Software

Cybermedia, Inc. is a developer of computer software products that work with each other to automatically diagnose, fix, update, clean and protect personal computers from a wide array of potential problems. Using Cybermedia's ActiveHelp technology—a large database of problem-solving information—the programs access solutions through the internet with solutions and/or updates automatically delivered to the computer. Cybermedia's products are distributed through more than 10,000 retail stores in the United States, as well as internationally in Canada, Australia, and most of Western Europe. The products are also available on the internet at the company's web site.

Cybermedia's Beginnings: The Early 1990s

The idea for Cybermedia was developed in 1991 by a multicultural group of software engineers. The founders, Unni Warrier and Srikanth Chari from India, Anne Lam and Jonathan Tran from Vietnam, Chi Chi Chang from Taiwan, and Art Puryear from the United States, joined together to produce software that worked to provide support and service for users of the Microsoft Windows operating system. The six founders all met through connections at computer companies in California. Lam and Warrier first met at a company called Systems Development Corp. From there, they went on to start their own company, NetLabs, which is where they were introduced to the four other eventual founders of Cybermedia.

The funding for Cybermedia's start-up costs came from the six founders themselves. Initially, they scraped together just enough money to get by, but soon found outside sources that helped get the company off the ground. For their first influx of outside funds, they took advantage of a United States foreign aid program which financed Indian companies in joint venture with U.S. companies. Partnered with Cybermedia, an Indian firm received a $318,000 grant from the U.S. government, and then invested those funds in Cybermedia. That money helped the founders work on the development of the company's first product and was added to in 1993, when the group received another $250,000 from a few venture capitalists. The company was further bolstered by the additional help of Unni Warrier's countryman Suhas Patil, a founder of Cirrus Logic, and of Kanwal Rekhi of Novell, both of whom helped give Cybermedia its first big break.

In 1993, the team spent $40,000 for a booth at Comdex, a big computer industry expo in Las Vegas. At the expo, the founders gave away dozens of free copies of their product, which at that time was named Win Win. Many of the free copies were sent back to Cybermedia after the expo because people did not like the way that the program functioned, but the concept was a hit and the founders went back to the drawing boards to redesign and fix the program.

In 1994, the company re-released the program as ''First Aid.'' The company shipped 300,000 copies of First Aid that year as the program gradually began to develop sales. While this was happening, Cybermedia began working on a new version of the program to be used with Microsoft's new ''Windows 95.''

Mid-1990s Expansion: New Products and New Status

With the success of First Aid spreading and the release of Windows 95 on the horizon, Cybermedia went to work to

117

Company Perspectives:

Cybermedia's mission is to help computer users, anytime, anywhere with a complete set of products and services that provide the highest quality of immediate help to computer users at home and work, all over the world.

---

develop not only a new version of First Aid, but also a new product called Oil Change. While First Aid helped to detect and resolve software and configuration errors, the purpose of Oil Change was to automatically detect and download updates of Cybermedia's programs over the internet. With the rapidly changing environment in the computer industry and the number of software conflicts that were caused by Windows 95, the two programs quickly became valuable resource for personal computer owners. Cybermedia's role became to clean up the problems that were caused by all of the new software that was being released. And clean up they did. First Aid sold 1.5 million copies in its first year of release and accounted for 90 percent of Cybermedia's revenues during that time period.

Buoyed by the success of its First Aid products and the emergence of Oil Change, Cybermedia entered the public arena with an initial public offering of 2,500,000 shares of Common Stock in October of 1996. As the leading producer of software providing automatic service and support to owners of personal computers, Cybermedia fed off of the energy of the IPO to release a new version of First Aid. First Aid 97 for Windows 95 was released in November 1996. The new version worked with Windows 95 and was designed for the scheduled, but never released, Windows 97. Some changes that went into the new version ranged from more customer friendly toolbars and functions to other added capabilities. With the new version, the software not only resolved problems when they occurred, it was also able to help prevent them from ever becoming a problem in the first place. Customers loved this preventative, rather than reactive, approach to personal computer management, and the product was a big hit.

Cybermedia also introduced the Tech Support Yellow Pages in June of 1996. The Yellow Pages consisted of a 300-page book and a CD-ROM, both containing listings for over 2,000 technical support resources. It included the phone numbers and web addresses for manufacturers of a wide variety of computer software, devices, and systems, as well as tips on troubleshooting and a glossary of computer terms. Now, if Cybermedia software could not fix your problem, they offered help finding someone who could.

With the IPO complete and the release of First Aid 97 under its belt, Cybermedia posted third quarter revenue growth of 734 percent over the third quarter of 1995. Cybermedia's products comprised 11.2 percent of the top 25 business titles sold in 1996, with the company's three software titles all ranking in the top fifteen business software titles. Not satisfied with their position, despite all of the success, the founders continued to work on updating the current products and on developing new software.

Continued Growth in 1997

As a major factor in the business software industry, Cybermedia began looking for ways to improve its already award-winning product line. First the company released its first improved version of Oil Change in mid-1997. By increasing its knowledge base, allowing for the scheduling of automatic updates, and gaining technology to notify users when updates were available, Oil Change became even more of a valuable resource for personal computer owners. Cybermedia also continued to add partners to its Oil Change product. Companies like Broderbund Software and Hewlett-Packard signed agreements with Cybermedia to use the Oil Change program as a way for their own customers to get updates easier and more effectively.

Another development for Cybermedia was a partnership with ServiceWare, Inc., a leading provider of knowledge management products for customer support and help desk operations. This helped build Cybermedia's problem-solving knowledge base, which in turn made its products, when combined with Cybermedia's already existing ActiveHelp technology, even more effective.

To further help users of personal computers, Cybermedia soon developed Guard Dog, a software product designed to provide personal internet security. Initially named ''Cyberwall'' during its development, the Guard Dog program blocked harmful viruses and internet programs from damaging the users' hard drives by monitoring the users' systems and automatically removing harmful properties from downloaded files and e-mail attachments. Using technology the company received through the acquisition of Walk Softly, Inc., a leading internet privacy and security company, the program was also designed to defend against ActiveX and Java intruders from the web.

Also in 1997, Cybermedia acquired the worldwide distribution rights to Microhelp Uninstaller from Luckman Interactive. Safely and easily removing applications from personal computers to avoid costly system problems, the program fit very nicely into Cybermedia's line of fix-it products. The company repackaged and renamed the program as Cybermedia Uninstaller and released it into its own product line in mid-1997.

While the company was working on improving their offerings for PC owners, they also began a major project to design products for the networked business environment. While crashes and delays could cause problems for an individual user, they could mean disaster for a business connected to a company network. To help with this, Cybermedia released CSS Repair Station for Workgroups, the first product of the new Cybermedia Support Services (CSS) line.

Cybermedia ended 1997 as strong as ever. Revenues for the year increased 104 percent to $78.6 million in 1997. With the release of First Aid 98 and Guard Dog, the start of CSS, and the combined success of older versions of First Aid and Oil Change, Cybermedia remained strong heading into the new year.

The Future of Cybermedia

The company had continued to prosper since the release of its first version of First Aid back in 1994, but things started to change at Cybermedia in the start of 1998. As Cybermedia continued to roll out new and improved products, such as Repair Engine for Small Business, the second product of the CSS line, the company was going through a shift in management and structure. Revenues for the first quarter of 1998 were $4.7 million, down from $16.8 million during the same period the previous year. At the same time, the company issued a statement that fourth quarter 1997 revenues would have to be adjusted to show a $6–8 million increase in return reserves. This prompted several fraud lawsuits by investors claiming that Cybermedia had issued false statements of earnings.

In management changes, Jeffrey Beaumont resigned as chief financial officer and was replaced by Kanwal Rekhi, a Cybermedia director and investor in the early development of the company. One of the founders, President and Chief Executive Officer Unni Warrier, also resigned. Rekhi was named as a temporary replacement for Warrier before being hired as CEO in May, with James R. Tolonen becoming president and chief operating officer.

With a new management structure now in place, the focus turned to getting the company back to the top of its industry. The Cybermedia products remained solid, with First Aid 98 and Uninstaller winning PC Magazine's Best Buy Awards. The company also announced partnerships with Gateway and Microsoft, helping to demonstrate the respect that the young company had earned in the computer software market.

The strength of Cybermedia in the marketplace was further increased with its merger agreement with Network Associates. With the completion of the merger in July 1998, Cybermedia became part of the McAfee Software Division of Network Associates. Combined with the help of Network Associates' tremendous marketing and sales services, the products offered by Cybermedia would have greater access to the computer software marketplace. With strong leadership reestablished, its product line continuing to win awards, and improved marketing and sales capabilities, Cybermedia had the potential to continue growing as a subsidiary of Network Associates.

Further Reading

Bisson, Giselle, "Cybermedia Announces New First Aid 97," *Business Wire,* October 29, 1996, p. 1

"Cybermedia, Inc. Announces Initial Public Offering," *Business Wire,* October 23, 1996, p. 1.

Darlin, Damon, "A Needed Import: Entrepreneurial Spirit," *Forbes,* November 4, 1996, pp. 210–218.

Deady, Tim, "International Corps Scores With Software," *Los Angeles Business Journal,* June 24, 1996.

—Robert Alan Passage

Cygne Designs, Inc.

1372 Broadway
New York, New York 10018
U.S.A.
(212) 354-6474
Fax: (212) 921-8318

Public Company
Incorporated: 1975
Employees: 887
Sales: $254.3 million (1996)
Stock Exchanges: NASDAQ
Ticker Symbol: CYDS
SICs: 5137 Women's/Children's Clothing; 5136 Men's/
   Boys' Clothing

Cygne Designs, Inc. is a private label manufacturer of women's apparel, including woven and knit career and casual apparel. A private label merchandiser and manufacturer, Cygne Designs, Inc. produces apparel based on retailer's orders, which are then sold with the retailer's own label. Cygne does not have a label of its own. In recent years, Cygne's single biggest customer has been The Limited, Inc., of which sales to the company account for a majority of Cygne's annual sales figures. Despite a long-established relationship with this key customer, Cygne does not have a long-term contract with any of its customers. As a private label manufacturer, filling high volume orders from a small number of customers, Cygne is dependent on its key customers and is sensitive to changes in the highly competitive and dynamic women's apparel market. Recently, retailers are moving away from ordering private label products from outside vendors and sourcing those products in-house. Due to the fact that Cygne is not involved in contract arrangements with its customers, this trend has led to the cessation of Cygne's supply of apparel to a few key customers in recent years.

The Early Years

Cygne Designs Ltd. was founded by clothing designer Irving Benson in 1975. With its beginnings as an importer of designer clothes from Europe, the company eventually began manufacturing its own silk blouses and skirts. By the early 1980s, Cygne had built a solid business designing private lines for companies like AnnTaylor, The Limited, and Talbots. In October 1984, Mast Holdings, a wholly owned subsidiary of The Limited, Inc., acquired 80 percent of Cygne; four years later, however, The Limited began selling off all companies that did not produce exclusively for its chains. Unable to buy Cygne back on his own, Benson approached an acquaintance named Bernard Manuel, who was then working for the French investment bank Amvent Inc. In March 1988, Amvent organized a leveraged buyout of Cygne, with Amvent and its investors receiving 71 percent of the company and Benson receiving the other 29 percent.

Despite the return of the company's control to its founder, in 1989 Cygne was mired in serious quality and delivery problems. The company had sales of $30 million, losses of $6 million, and was facing bankruptcy. The Amvent-led investment group sold its interest. Manuel, however, decided to remain with Cygne. In exchange for a 33 percent interest in the firm, he took over as CEO, with Irving Benson as president and chief designer. Under Manuel, Cygne was reorganized. "The company we acquired was not a complete company," Manuel told *Forbes* in November 1994. "It had great design capabilities and good sales, but, buried in The Limited group, it had no abilities in systems, sourcing and manufacturing. It could sell very well, but it couldn't deliver." Manuel had to re-establish the infrastructure once provided by The Limited, while at the same time reducing the number of Cygne's foreign production facilities and placing Cygne personnel there to monitor quality.

A Turn For the Better in the 1990s

Cygne's business was booming between 1990 and 1993. In that four year period, Manuel told Forbes, Cygne "never solicited a single customer." The clients came to Cygne, including The Limited, Victoria's Secret Catalogue, and Compagnie Internationale Express. Business with AnnTaylor Stores, in particular, flourished. In June 1992, the two companies formed a joint venture—CAT—to produce casual wear exclusively for AnnTaylor stores, with Cygne owning 60 percent and Ann-

The results of the offering highlighted Cygne's successful year—ten months earlier its stock had sold for $10 a share, but by June 1994 it went for $18.25 a share.

Company Perspectives:

The manufacture of private label apparel is characterized by high volume sales to a small number of customers at competitive prices. Although private label gross margins are lower than in the brand name apparel industry, marketing expenses and collection and markdown costs are typically commensurably lower, and inventory turns are generally higher. Inventory risks are also reduced because the purchasing of fabric and other supplies begins only after purchasing commitments have been obtained from customers. The Company believes that retailers, including customers of the Company, are increasingly sourcing private label products themselves rather than utilizing outside vendors like the Company.

Expansion Efforts and Trying Times in the Mid-1990s

Cygne's mid-year figures in 1994 seemed to indicate a healthy company. New customers had helped to more than double sales during the first six months of the year, from $96.6 million to $198.8 million. CEO Manuel stated that Cygne's successful integration of Fenn, Wright & Manson had also helped contribute to the positive results. In order to establish itself more firmly, Cygne announced its intent to reduce its dependence on AnnTaylor and The Limited, which together accounted for 83 percent of company sales. This decision reflected the company's understanding of the problems that would be posed if Cygne lost either company as a customer.

Branching out, the company signed contracts with American Eagle Outfitters and Casual Corners. The two contracts combined were expected to be worth $60 million a year, and Manuel was also working on placing Cygne designs in mass outlets like Kmart and Target.

Cygne continued its wave of acquisitions in late 1994, purchasing GJM International Ltd. for a total estimated at about $13.3 million. Like Cygne, the Hong Kong-based GJM was a private label apparel manufacturer whose largest customer, Victoria's Secret Stores, accounted for 67 percent of its $100 million in sales the previous year. In purchasing the company, Cygne hoped to broaden its product lines through the addition of intimate apparel. As part of a fifteen year non-compete agreement, Cygne paid $3 million to Glynn Manson, GJM's chairman and CEO. Manson had helped found Fenn, Wright & Manson, the company Cygne had acquired the previous spring. Under the terms of the deal, Manson retained his positions at GJM.

It was around this time that Cygne's success story began to unravel. After it was announced that third quarter earnings were expected to fall well below earlier estimates, Cygne stock plunged to a 52 week low of $14; bad expectations were confirmed by figures released in December. The company blamed a variety of factors. Depressed retail sales had led some customers to cancel orders. Suppliers had postponed deliveries, as well as delivering substandard knitwear which Cygne's customers had often refused to accept. Despite the disappointing earnings, sales were up significantly from the same quarter the previous year, and the company had grown in 1994 as a whole. *Women's Wear Daily* reported that "analysts were particularly impressed with the strength of Cygne's core apparel business, driven by strong sales of career and casual wear to AnnTaylor," and they predicted increases of 50 percent or more in 1995. The lower-priced AnnTaylor Lofty line Cygne was working on was considered to be particularly promising. Manuel told the publication "Despite the current soft retail environment, which we expect to continue into the first half of 1995, we feel that Cygne Designs is uniquely positioned to take advantage of growth opportunities, particularly with new customers."

The value of Cygne shares continued to drop, however, and by spring the downward spiral had steepened. Sales fell to

Taylor the other 40 percent. In April 1993, CAT actually became a subsidiary of Cygne, who owned 60 percent of the operation with AnnTaylor owning the remaining 40 percent interest.

Sales in 1993 rose 77 percent, from $70.4 million to $124.7 million. Two customers accounted for the lion's share of those sales—AnnTaylor, and The Limited Stores and Express. At the beginning of August 1993, in an effort to repay outstanding debts, the company made an initial public offering of 2.4 million shares. Helped by a previous commitment from The Limited to purchase a 10.2 percent interest, the offering raised approximately $21.4 million. A month later, Cygne reported a sales increase of 142 percent for the first half of 1993, from $39.8 million to $96.6 million, and sales and profits continued to climb for the remainder of the year.

Cygne made a number of acquisitions in 1993. It purchased JMB Internacionale S.A., a company that supervised the manufacture of apparel in Guatemala. Cygne also paid $500,000 and 150,000 shares of Cygne common stock for T. Wear Company S.r.l. and M.T.G.I. Textile Manufacturers Group (Israel), both of which were women's apparel companies. In September 1993, Cygne announced plans to issue 2 million new shares of its stock in order to purchase Fenn, Wright & Manson, a private sportswear manufacturer. Irving Benson told *Women's Wear Daily*, "The combined company will offer well-balanced strength in all categories of woven and knit casual and career sportswear for women." Fenn, Wright & Manson's casual sportswear, sweaters and woven silk products were expected to complement Cygne's woven career sportswear lines, while also introducing a brand new element. The acquisition was completed on April 6, 1994. In addition to the stock, Cygne paid cash for Fenn, Wright & Manson. The total value of the purchase was estimated at $44 million. Fenn, Wright & Manson's CEO became a vice-chairman and chief operating officer at Cygne.

Another public stock offering was mounted by Cygne in June 1994. Two million new shares were issued, and raised $34 million, with $6 million of the proceeds slated to repay debt incurred through the acquisition of Fenn, Wright & Manson.

levels that were 10 percent under earlier Wall Street projections. At the end of April 1995, Cygne stock reached an all-time low of $6¼, and in June the company reported first quarter losses of $4.7 million. The company called the decline "a temporary stumble" and blamed a slump affecting the entire women's apparel market. Cygne also admitted that there had been more problems integrating its Fenn, Wright & Manson unit than were initially apparent. Finally, the company had to write off a bad debt of approximately $1.1 million "from a customer which is experiencing financial difficulties," as reported to *Women's Wear Daily*.

Some analysts believed Cygne's problems began with its two large acquisitions the previous year. The company announced plans to lay off a number of Fenn, Wright & Manson employees, and told its shareholders at its June meeting that it was implementing an austerity program.

The problems did not go away, however and losses continued to plague the company. In the first half of 1995 Cygne had $9.7 million in losses compared to $3.6 million in profit during the same period the previous year. By the end of the year, the value of its stock had dropped once again, this time to $4⅛. In November, as a result of a $53 million deficit, The Hong Kong & Shanghai Bank suspended the company's line of credit. With the possibility looming that the bank could call in its outstanding loans, Cygne began negotiations for a new payment schedule and the restoration of credit.

Challenges at the Turn of the Century and Beyond

In the wake of its rapidly compounding financial problems, Cygne was hit with two law suits in the latter half of 1995, both of which maintained that the company had lied about its financial situation during the preceding year. The first was a suit for $5.6 million brought by a former Cygne vice-president. Richard M. Kramer had been recruited by Cygne from The Leslie Fay Co., but was fired just three months after he joined the company. Kramer alleged that Cygne officials had failed to make him aware of the fact that Cygne was in serious financial trouble. Kramer also charged that he had been persuaded to accept much of his compensation in the form of stock options, although Cygne officials were aware that the value of the stock would "drop significantly" as soon as the poor upcoming quarterly results were made public.

Late that year, after the company's stock had dropped to a dismal $1¼, a Cygne shareholders group brought suit against the company, Irving Benson, Bernard Manuel, company accountants, and the investment companies that underwrote the Fenn, Wright & Manson acquisition. The suit, according to *The Wall Street Journal*, charged Cygne with "disseminating false and misleading information about Cygne's business, finances and prospects that damaged purchasers of Cygne stock" when the company purchased Fenn, Wright & Manson. The suit also maintained that Cygne was "riddled with huge losses, massive operational and management problems and is threatened with bankruptcy." Manuel maintained that the company would not be filing for bankruptcy, and said that in order to satisfy its bank the company was considering the sale of various assets.

The first item put on the Cygne sales block was GJM, the company's sleepwear division. In February 1996, the Warnaco Group paid Cygne $12.5 million in cash and assumed all liabilities connected with GJM. In addition to GJM's other assets, Warnaco acquired its private label accounts, including Victoria's Secret. Cygne took a loss of $33 million on the sale.

In September 1996 the company completed a major deal with AnnTaylor Stores Corp. Cygne gave up its 60 percent interest in CAT, the joint venture that the two companies had established in 1992. It also sold off its AnnTaylor woven division. Cygne received $9.76 million in cash and 2.35 million shares of AnnTaylor common stock, a deal estimated to be worth $50 million. The sale put AnnTaylor Stores, also hurt by the overall decline in the women's apparel market, on firmer footing by reducing their dependence on outside sourcing—in particular, it reduced their dependence on the troubled Cygne. For Cygne, the deal, once completed, meant the restoration of its credit lines. On the other hand, giving up the two divisions meant giving up its largest customer. The previous year, AnnTaylor had accounted for 54 percent of the company's sales.

Between October 1996 and January 1997, the company sold all of its AnnTaylor stock to pay its $8.9 million in outstanding debt. Incidental to the sale, both Irving Benson and Bernard Manuel received three-year $225,000 consulting contracts with AnnTaylor which went into effect if their employment with Cygne was for any reason terminated.

Around the same time, Cygne signed two five-year contracts with Kenzo, a French manufacturer that hoped to break into the U.S. market. Under the deal, Cygne was to design for the 1997–1998 Kenzo Studio bridge line and the Kenzo Jeans collection. The deal marked the first major new customer for Cygne in nearly a year, and the company viewed it as an upturn. Manuel stated his belief that the company had weathered the crisis; he also made clear Cygne's intent to move slowly in looking for new customers. Cygne's primary focus, he said, would be to maintain the private label business and attempt to expand it.

In November 1996, Cygne's founder, Irving Benson, resigned suddenly from the company. Without offering any reasons to the press, he announced that he planned to form a consulting company which would continue to work with Cygne on various projects. In addition, Benson entered into a consultant relationship with AnnTaylor.

In January 1997, Cygne shareholders were awarded $5.75 million in damages when federal court in New York City found the company guilty of security violations. Cygne said afterwards it would pay $2.1 million of the settlement; insurance and other litigants paid the remainder. When the settlement was reached Cygne stock had dropped to 1 3/16 on the over the counter market.

Meanwhile, Cygne losses continued. In the spring of 1997, the company announced that it expected a net loss for the fiscal year. The extent of the loss, Cygne said, depended on the start-up costs entailed by its Kenzo contracts. In June, however, that deal fell through altogether when the two companies came to a mutual agreement to terminate the arrangement. Kenzo stressed that there were no problems with design or production; the company had simply decided that in order to gain a foothold in the U.S. market, it would have to use top-level, not mid-level, lines. For Cygne, the cancellation was disastrous. The company was left with a single major customer, The Limited, and Cygne's sales to them had fallen $7 million between 1996 and 1997. By the end of June, Cygne stock had plummeted to $⅜.

In an attempt to cut costs further, Cygne discontinued its design studio in New York City during the 1997 fiscal year. It also moved its corporate offices to a significantly smaller office space. In April 1998 the NASDAQ National Market notified Cygne that its stock was scheduled for delisting. NASDAQ requires that shares maintain a minimum price of at least $1 a share, a requirement Cygne had not met for the better part of a year. The stock was officially delisted by NASDAQ on June 6, 1998.

The company's disastrous past few years, coupled with expenses actually resulting from attempts to downsize in order to deal with the crisis, led to a net loss of $14.5 million in 1997. Furthermore, the company was forecasting another net loss for 1998. As the decade came to a close, Cygne's future was anything but steady. Its ability to stay afloat would depend upon continued orders from The Limited, Inc., the attraction of new customers, and the success of the company's reorganization.

Further Reading

Agins, Teri and Laura Bird, "Cygne Designs Accused of Fraud in Shareholder Suit," *Wall Street Journal,* December 21, 1995.

"AnnTaylor alters pact with Cygne," *Women's Wear Daily,* August 29, 1996.

"Benson steps down as Cygne head," *Women's Wear Daily,* December 2, 1996.

"Companies to Watch: Cygne Designs," *Fortune,* January 24, 1994.

"Cygne buys GJM for cash plus shares," *Women's Wear Daily,* October, 11, 1994.

"Cygne inks deal to buy Fenn Wright & Manson," *Daily News Record,* December 14, 1993.

"Cygne raises $34.07M in secondary offering," *Women's Wear Daily,* June 10, 1994.

"Cygne takes a $33M loss in deal with Warnaco," *Women's Wear Daily,* February 13, 1996.

"Cygne's initial public offering raises $21.5M," *Women's Wear Daily,* August 3, 1993.

Feldman, Amy, "Ugly Duckling into Swan," *Forbes,* November 7, 1994, p. 170.

"FTC clears AnnTaylor to buy sourcing operation from Cygne," *Women's Wear Daily,* July 10, 1996.

Ryan, Thomas J., "Cygne to buy Hong Kong intimate apparel maker," *Women's Wear Daily,* August 5, 1994.

Seckler, Valerie, "AnnTaylor to buy Cygne out of CAT," *Women's Wear Daily,* April 9, 1996.

Siegel, Jeff, "Former exec sues Cygne for $5.6M," *Women's Wear Daily,* August 31, 1995.

Weisman, Katherine, "Kenzo inks deal with Cygne for jeans, bridge," *Women's Wear Daily,* September 17, 1996.

—Evelyn Hauser

Dairy Mart Convenience Stores, Inc.

210 Broadway East
Cuyahoga Falls, Ohio 44222
U.S.A.
(330) 342-6000
Fax: (330) 923-0488
Web site: http://www.dairymart.com

Public Company
Incorporated: 1972 as Snow White Dairies Inc.
Employees: 3,500
Sales: $501 million (1998)
Stock Exchanges: American
Ticker Symbol: DMCa
SICs: 5411 Grocery Stores

Dairy Mart Convenience Stores, Inc. is one of the largest convenience store chains in the United States with approximately 600 stores in seven states in the Midwest and Southeast. In the late 1990s, the company pursued dominance in the midwestern convenience store market and expansion internationally.

Company Origins

Dairy Mart's origins date back to 1949, when Charles Nirenberg began selling ice cream from the back of his truck in the back lot of a Springfield, Massachusetts, gas station. Four years later Nirenberg had more than 60 ice cream trucks operating in various locations, as well as a winter business that sold coffee and doughnuts.

The success of these businesses showed Nirenberg there was money to be made by offering consumers convenience. In order to cash in on this opportunity, he opened his first store in 1957 with $1,500. Nirenberg first named the shop Dairy Land, but soon changed it after receiving complaints from another retailer using the same name. To save money, Nirenberg settled on the name Dairy Mart so he would only have to change three of the letters on his sign. Despite saving money on new signage,

the store went bankrupt a year later. Nirenberg blamed the failure on the store's location next to a high-rise apartment building. Initially he reasoned the location would guarantee him plenty of customers, but many of the residents were elderly with smaller budgets for food and impulse items.

Instead of giving up, Nirenberg opened two more stores soon after, and by 1972 he was running a chain of 37 outlets with sales of $6 million. The stores were incorporated under the name Snow White Dairies Inc.

Nirenberg decided the success of the company warranted a public offering, but before any stock could be issued, the company attracted the interest of Giant Stores, Inc., a retail chain based in Chelmsford, Massachusetts, which sought to acquire the company. Nirenberg decided he couldn't turn the offer down, and he sold his company for Giant stock. "They made . . . a deal to give me 86,000 shares of Giant stock, which at the time was selling for $18.60 a share, and within a matter of weeks it hit $26 a share," Nirenberg told *New England Business* correspondent Gregory Sandier. "[Giant] quickly made me a paper millionaire. Except the problem was the following year, they went bankrupt and I became a paper pauper." Undaunted, Nirenberg borrowed $250,000, bought back the 37 Dairy Mart outlets from Giant in 1974 and started again.

In 1975 Dairy Mart Convenience Stores, Inc. relocated to Enfield, Connecticut. In addition, the company built a $2.6 million milk processing plant in order to expand its business. The plant produced ice cream, frozen desserts, and other dairy items for Dairy Mart outlets. Milk, orange juice, and fruit drinks were also processed in the facility.

Aggressive Expansion in the 1980s

By 1980 Dairy Mart was poised for bigger and better things, and top management set a goal to build the company into a 1,000-store chain. To meet this objective, Dairy Mart began an aggressive plan of acquisition. In 1981 the company purchased Sunnybrook Farms and its 66 stores, followed in 1983 by the acquisition of Dutchland Farms' 32 stores, and IPO with 143 stores. Still far from the goal, Dairy Mart found itself in need of more capital. Spearheading the aggressive growth period was

Company Perspectives:

Our mission is to provide superior convenience and service to help make our customers' lives easier.

then-vice-president of real estate/corporate development Frank Colaccino. To help fund its growth, the company went public in 1983. Sales stood at $60.3 million and net income was $439,000. The stock offering raised $3 million.

Two years later, Dairy Mart was ready to expand beyond its stronghold in the Northeast. The company made this bold move with the acquisition of The Lawson Co. from Sara Lee Corp. The 779-outlet chain, based in Ohio, was three times the size of Dairy Mart, and the $45 million deal included a dairy plant and a distribution center. While such competitors as Circle K were buying stores for as much as $350,000, Dairy Mart estimated its cost per Lawson store somewhere between $40,000 and $50,000.

Dairy Mart soon began to feel the effects of its rapid growth. Three months after Dairy Mart bought the company, workers at the Lawson dairy plant went on strike when their demands for higher wages were turned down. Replacement workers were hired to fill the jobs, sparking more controversy. Consumers organized a boycott, some stores were damaged, one security guard was shot, and rumors were spread about poisoned milk. Dairy Mart suffered yet another boycott in 1986, this time by the American Family Association, an antipornography group upset with Dairy Mart's decision to continue selling adult magazines.

The Lawson acquisition still was not enough to put Dairy Mart over the 1,000-store mark, and in 1986 the company bought CONNA Corp., the Louisville, Kentucky, franchiser of the Convenient Food Mart chain with 369 stores. The $25 million purchase gave Dairy Mart a total of 1,207 stores in 11 states. Negotiating the purchase was not an easy task, however. Convenient Food Mart Inc. (CFMI), a group of Chicago-based franchisers and owners of Convenient Food Marts, also wanted to buy CONNA, though Dairy Mart would be required to pay franchiser's fees to CFMI if the acquisition went through. After extensive negotiations, the two parties agreed to divide the outlets. CFMI retained the stores in its region, as well as 72 stores in New England, while Dairy Mart received the balance. Now Dairy Mart had three divisions: one in Connecticut, another in Kentucky, representing the former CONNA stores, and the third in Ohio, overseeing the Lawson interest.

Under the terms of the CONNA acquisition, Dairy Mart was paying CFMI a substantial annual fee for its franchise of Convenient Food Marts. However, with a 1987 court ruling that stated "convenient" is a generic name, Dairy Mart took the opportunity to buy its way out of the franchise agreement with CFMI and give the former CONNA stores the Dairy Mart name. Those stores, however, proved to be well worth the trouble it took to get and keep them. That division was considered the most

profitable part of the company, due in large part to the stores' high gasoline sales.

Weakened Company Ripe for Takeover in the Late 1980s

Dairy Mart's aggressive acquisition and expansion strategy since going public began to take its toll in the late 1980s. Financial performance was shaky, and the company's stock fluctuated from 15 points to 6 and $\frac{1}{8}$. Dairy Mart's 1,207 stores garnered $482 million in sales in 1987, but the company still posted a $3.5 million loss because of a $3.3 million pension settlement and a slide in store margins. The company also carried a high debt to equity ratio. In fiscal year 1987, the rate was 2.86 to 1 compared to 1.4 to 1 the year before. Dairy Mart began to move forward again in 1988, however, with a leap in sales to $723 million and a net income of $4 million. Though some stores identified as weak performers were closed, and sales dropped to $717 million, this was offset with $3 million from the sale of Dairy Mart's Midwest distribution center. In all, the company ended the year with a net income of $4.1 million.

In 1989 a team led by Nirenberg, which included four senior managers and the Salomon Brothers Holding Co., formed DCMS Holdings Inc. to attempt a leveraged buyout of Dairy Mart and take it private. The move would put Nirenberg and his managers in control of the firm and give Salomon Bros. a hefty 37.5 percent share. Charlie and Jan Nirenberg, who owned 35 percent of Dairy Mart's outstanding shares along with 60 percent of the voting power, stood to make a profit of $22 million. They would also have the opportunity to pay just $5 per share of the newly private Dairy Mart. Armed with an $80 million loan commitment from the Bank of Boston, Salomon's promise to sell $35 million in junk bonds, and another $35 million in bonds that were already in place, DCMS Holdings offered shareholders $14.50 for each of their Dairy Mart shares, which were then trading at $8. The value of the buyout would have been about $150 million.

The deal, however, was challenged by United Acquisitions—a New York company that owned Red Apple supermarkets—when they countered with an offer of $15 a share. DCMS quickly raised its offer to match it. When United tried again with a $16 a share offer, DCMS had already signed a definitive merger agreement, and the offer was ignored.

But DCMS still was not in the clear, as it turned out. The deal collapsed when the Bank of Boston pulled back its financing support. The bank blamed Dairy Mart's weak first-quarter earnings, but Nirenberg surmised that the bank was abandoning the risky leveraged buyout business, particularly in light of the federal regulatory pressures on the struggling New England banking system at the time. Rather than increase its reliance on junk bonds or eat into its low buyout price, DCMS Holdings dropped its goal of once again making Dairy Mart a private company.

The failed deal turned out to be a blessing in disguise and helped the firm avoid the heavy debt burdens of its competitors, including Circle K, the Southland Corp., operators of the 7-Eleven chain, and Convenient Food Mart Inc., which filed for bankruptcy in 1989. Without the debt burden, in 1990 Dairy Mart went on to purchase 137 "Stop N Go" stores from the Sun Company, Inc. for $16.2 million. The stores were located in Ohio, Kentucky, and Michigan, rounding out the company's presence in the Midwest.

Even after buying Stop N Go, Dairy Mart retained its strong position. Fiscal year 1991 was the company's best ever, with sales reaching $809 million, up from $742 million the previous year. Net income was $3.8 million versus $682,000 the year before. The 1991 figures were especially healthy in light of the fact that the country was suffering from a recession, and gasoline sales had been hurt by the high prices caused by the Persian Gulf War.

Modernizing Stores in Early 1990s

After its acquisition fervor calmed down somewhat, Dairy Mart turned its attention to modernizing its stores. In 1991, the company began testing a point-of-sale system in ten stores, hoping to reduce the paperwork burdens of store managers and increase store margins by half of a percent. The system, scheduled for a company-wide roll-out in 1993, provided an electronic link between each site's personal computer, cash register, gas consoles, and money-order dispenser. The computer tallied all of the day's transactions, including sales and deposits, deliveries, and accounts payable, bundled the information, and sent it to Dairy Mart's headquarters for processing. With little or no paperwork, store managers could then focus more closely on their customers and other needs. The second phase of the project involved installing the technology to give stores price scanning capability.

Dairy Mart also began to focus more on customer relations. In 1991 the company started a new program called MAGIC, or Make A Good Impression on the Customer. Store employees were trained in customer service skills and rewarded for providing good service through a recognition system.

In 1992, Charlie and Jan Nirenberg decided to sell their controlling interest to a limited partnership headed by Frank Colaccino, Dairy Mart's president. Nirenberg abdicated his position as chief executive officer but remained as chairman of the board. Colaccino, who had long been groomed by Nirenberg for the job, took the title of CEO. In addition to Nirenberg, the limited partnership also included several other members of Dairy Mart's senior management team. News of the transition came as Dairy Mart entered its fifth consecutive year of profitability. Sales were $795 million, a decline from the year before due to the closing of another 62 low-volume stores and a drop in the price of gasoline. Pretax earnings were $7 million and net income was $4 million.

The changing of the guard at Dairy Mart coincided with a major step in ensuring the company's future growth. Dairy Mart entered into a joint venture agreement with two international firms to establish a network of convenience stores in Mexico. The venture, called Dairy Mart de Mexico, was the company's new strategy for growth in the 1990s. While the company had consulted with and licensed its name to convenience store operators in Japan, England, France, Australia, Germany, and Korea, it had done so for a one-time fee, payable at the outset of

the arrangements. The Mexican deal represented the first time that Dairy Mart, with a one-third stake in the business, would hold equity in a foreign operation. Dairy Mart's partners in the deal were Grupo Corvi S.A. de C.V., a Mexican food distributor, and Filles S.A. de C.V., a distribution, canning, and real estate company. Unlike their U.S. counterparts, Mexican Dairy Marts would not be designed around its driving customers and would be geared, instead, to walk-in traffic.

In 1992 the company unveiled the prototype of a new outlet combining gasoline service and a convenience store. The prototype emphasized the gasoline islands, which are sometimes ignored by consumers more comfortable filling their tanks at a regular gas station. Earmarked for 432 stores, the design called for T-shaped canopies to be placed over extended gas dispensers, more closely linking the area to the convenience store. By placing emphasis on the gas pumps, the company hoped to increase its already significant gasoline volume. In 1990, for example, the 420 Dairy Marts that sold gas contributed 35 percent of the company's total revenue. The prototype building also served to highlight the company's food service and beverage programs. In addition to popcorn, pizza, and fried chicken, the site also included a counter for store-made, shrink-wrapped sandwiches.

By 1992, Dairy Mart's dairy operations also saw some new developments. In addition to the 400,000 gallons of milk the company's two processing plants produced every week, the Cuyahoga Falls, Ohio, facility began production of a low-fat line of frozen yogurt and ice milk. The increased product line, combined with expanded distribution of Dairy Mart brand ice cream to its southeast stores, helped increase the plant's distribution by 25 percent.

Dairy Mart's uneven performance continued in the mid-1990s. In 1993, the company reported a substantial loss of $6.8 million on revenue of $580 million. The following year, Dairy Mart moved slightly into the black, with profits of $866,000 on revenue of $592 million. However, the company slipped back into the red in 1995 with a loss of $11.2 million on revenue of $597 million.

Refocusing the Company in the Late 1990s

In 1995 Dairy Mart made a couple of strategic decisions designed to refocus the company and move it onto solidly profitable ground. The first decision, accomplished in April 1995, was to sell its dairy processing business. Operating at only 40 percent of capacity, the dairy was a drain on the company's resources rather than a profit-generating unit. "This is a segment of the business that has not been effective for us, and we think can be better served if outside people do it," explained Robert Stein, Dairy Mart's president. "We have focused on identifying those areas of the company which have the strongest and weakest earnings potential, and concluded that our strongest earnings potential will come from retail operations."

Those retail operations were under scrutiny also. By the middle of 1995 the company had sold 80 stores it considered unproductive and closed 30 others. The closings and accelerated sales contributed to the company's loss for that year, but analysts agreed dumping the unprofitable stores and divesting the dairy operations would strengthen the company in the long run. Store sales and closings continued, until Dairy Mart owned approximately 900 stores in late 1995, down from its high of over 1,200 stores.

New store construction continued, but under a lease deal with Realty Investment Group that lowered the Dairy Mart's real estate investment. Realty Investment put up the money for construction costs, and Dairy Mart paid for equipment, furnishings, and other expenses. Dairy Mart planned to add 20 new stores each year for the next five years and to renovate about 100 stores.

Also in 1995 founder Nirenberg attempted to regain the CEO position. But eventually he and his partners in DM Associates Limited Partnership agreed to sell their interest in the company for $10 million. Nirenberg accepted an additional $2.3 million for agreeing not to compete with the company and for allowing Dairy Mart to continue to use his name and likeness in advertising campaigns.

Although Dairy Mart experienced losses for both fiscal 1996 and 1997, Stein was pleased with the progress of his long-term strategic plan. Store closings ate into profits by $2.7 million in 1997, contributing to a loss of $1.9 million. However, same-store sales were rising, indicating that weeding out unprofitable stores would eventually pay off. In addition, the company sold its headquarters in Connecticut and moved to Ohio, a decision that cost the company $1.2 million but positioned the headquarters in the greatest concentration of Dairy Mart stores.

The final part of Stein's plan to redirect the company was to focus its operations in the Midwest. To that end, the company sold its Northeastern stores in mid-1997 for $39.7 million to DB Cos. By eliminating the inefficiencies associated with operating two groups of stores 600 miles apart, Dairy Mart was free to concentrate its efforts on expansion in the Midwest. The sale left Dairy Mart with 400 stores in Ohio and 250 more in Kentucky, Michigan, Pennsylvania, Indiana, North Carolina, and Tennessee.

In addition to expanding in the midwestern United States, Dairy Mart was increasing its international presence in the late 1990s. In 1997 the company received royalties from 200 stores in South Korea and 20 stores in Malaysia. In addition, Dairy Mart consulted with the Malaysian Petronas Dagangan Berhad on adding convenience stores to its gas stations. Dairy Mart was working to expand this consulting business to other countries in Asia and Latin America, with plans to increase its percentage of revenue derived from international business from its 1997 level of 5 percent to 20 percent in three years.

Principal Subsidiaries

Dairy Mart, Inc.; Dairy Mart Farms, Inc.; The Lawson Company; CONNA Corporation.

Further Reading

Anderer, Charles, "Dual Purpose Prototype," *Convenience Store News,* August 31, 1992.
"Charlie Nirenberg, Running With the Bulls," *Convenience Store People,* June 1991.
"Dairy Mart Announces Fiscal 1997 Fourth-Quarter and Full-Year Financial Results," *Business Wire,* April 30, 1997.
"Dairy Mart Lists Losses for Quarter, Fiscal Year," *Hartford Courant,* May 16, 1995, p. F2.
Geehern, Christopher, "New Dairy Mart CEO Describes Chain's Foreign Plans," *Union-News,* June 10, 1992.
Hardin, Angel Y., "Overseas Mission: Dairy Mart Seeks Foreign Appeal," *Crain's Cleveland Business,* June 23, 1997, p. 3.
Kauffman, Matthew, "Dairy Mart to Sell Northeast Stores to Providence Firm," *Hartford Courant,* March 7, 1997, p. F1.
Krachevsky, David, "Dairy Mart Buys out Founder," *Manchester Journal Inquirer,* December 2, 1995.
"Retailing's Entrepreneurs of the Year," *Chain Store Age Executive,* December 1991.
Sandler, Gregory, "Ahead of the Herd," *New England Business,* October 1990.
Segel, Dee, "Dairy Mart to Sell Dairy Operations, Concentrate on Its Stores," *Hartford Courant,* April 27, 1995, p. F1.
——, "Expansion, More Convenience in Dairy Mart's CEO's Plans," *Hartford Courant,* September 30, 1995, p. F1.
"Transition at Dairy Mart," *Convenience Store People,* March 1992.

—Julie Monahan
—updated by Susan Windisch Brown

Dames & Moore, Inc.

911 Wilshire Boulevard
Los Angeles, California 90017
U.S.A.
(213) 683-1560
Fax: (310) 628-0015
Web site: http://www.dames.com

Public Company
Incorporated: 1992
Employees: 5,300
Sales: $690.1 million (1997)
Stock Exchanges: New York
Ticker Symbol: DM
SICs: 8711 Engineering Services

A pioneer in civil engineering, Dames & Moore, Inc. represents a global network of companies known as the Dames & Moore Group. Dames & Moore specializes in a variety of civil engineering and environmental and earth sciences disciplines, providing consulting services to corporate and government customers. With 197 offices in major U.S. cities and in countries throughout the world, the company is recognized as an international leader in its field. Roughly 14 percent of Dames & Moore's revenues are derived from government projects.

1930s Origins

The history of Dames & Moore parallels the development of a new discipline in engineering, the science of soils and foundation engineering. Before the birth of Dames & Moore, little was known of soil mechanics and foundation engineering, and what was known rested in the minds of the company's pioneering founders, Trent R. Dames and William W. Moore. Dames was born in Brooklyn, New York, in 1911 and at age seven moved with his family to southern California, where he attended San Diego High School and developed an abiding interest in civil engineering. Moore was a native Californian, born in Pasadena

three months after his future, Brooklyn-born business partner. Dames and Moore met for the first time at the California Institute of Technology (Cal Tech), where each earned his Bachelor of Science degree in 1933 and stayed on to pursue post-graduate work in civil engineering. Both Dames and Moore had developed an affinity for a particular aspect of civil engineering—the study of soil mechanics and foundation engineering—but their chosen academic paths led to uncharted territory. Much like the pair would be forced to do in the business world, Dames and Moore had to break new ground just to get started.

Their main obstacle—and it was a formidable one—was that Cal Tech did not offer any courses in soils and foundation engineering. Few engineering schools included such courses in their curriculum, but Dames and Moore were undaunted and, along with several of their classmates, they lobbied Cal Tech officials to include soil mechanics as part of the university's post-graduate engineering studies. Dames and Moore prevailed, but without any textbooks on the subject in existence, the first students of the course had to search for available research on soil mechanics and pool their discoveries. Pursuing their academic studies in this manner, Dames and Moore were scientific pioneers early in their careers. When they left Cal Tech in 1934 with master's degrees in civil engineering, each possessed expertise in a field few others had ever heard of. As they had done at Cal Tech, Dames and Moore would share their knowledge in the business world; the resultant joint effort materialized as Dames & Moore.

It took several years before Dames and Moore realized that their best chance to put their academic training to work in the business world was to form their own company. After leaving Cal Tech, Moore worked as a staff member of the U.S. Coast and Geodetic Survey organization, while Dames joined the U.S. Bureau of Reclamation as a junior engineer. The two were friends, however, and remained in contact with each other, eventually working together for R. V. Labarre and Fred Converse, two of the West Coast's first soil mechanics consultants. Because of the infancy of their shared specialty, Dames and Moore found little opportunity to use their skills in the existing

Company Perspectives:

Our mission is to be the best consulting, full-service engineering and construction management firm in the world. Our purpose is to create value for our clients by always anticipating and satisfying their environmental and engineering needs in a cost-effective and innovative manner.

marketplace; the obstacle that had confronted them at Cal Tech assumed a similar form outside the confines of academia. Consequently, in 1938 they decided to form a partnership. At the inception of the company, however, optimism concerning their business future was a luxury neither could afford. Moore kept a job with the Corps of Engineers, working on weekends and during the evenings, while Dames worked out of his home in Pasadena. Optimism and a more sharply focused daily work schedule did not arrive until the two entrepreneurs developed their first major innovation.

When the patented Dames & Moore Type U underwater sampler was created, the two Cal Tech graduates could begin to imagine a future filled with steady business. Prior to the development of the Type U, soil exploration was conducted either by drilling a large hole or a number of small holes. The large-diameter borings were big enough to permit an individual to descend into the opening and record findings gleaned from the exposed strata, while the much smaller drillings offered loose or disturbed samples. Neither method was satisfactory: the former was impractical; the latter was inaccurate, creating a great need for an efficient, reliable method of determining soil dynamics. Dames & Moore had developed such a method. The Type U drove the sampler ahead of the boring, enabling engineers to obtain undisturbed samples taken from below the water table, which only rarely had been achieved. As a result, the partnership could point to its first advantage over the paltry few competitors it faced, the realization of which instilled a consistent commitment to technical research in the decades ahead.

After the success of the Type U and the clientele it attracted, the founders invested a considerable portion of their income into developing soil samplers, soil containers, and field and laboratory testing equipment. The fruits of their labor were more clients, clients who offered brief but telling descriptions of the two pioneer engineers they dealt with. To the company's clients, Dames was known as "Mr. Inside," the half of the duo adept at the administrative and managerial side of running the company's operations from its Los Angeles headquarters. Moore was regarded as "Mr. Outside," the person clients met face-to-face. It was, then, the complementary mixture of two different personalities that described the union of Dames and Moore. As the two looked ahead after the development of the Type U, everything about their business was still in question. Much would be determined in the years ahead. Fortunately for "Mr. Inside" and "Mr. Outside," the future held great promise.

Post-World War II Expansion

The outbreak of World War II and the United States' entrance into the global conflict in 1941 proved to be a boon to Dames & Moore's development. A second office was opened in San Francisco in 1941, as the company worked on a series of projects for the U.S. Navy and Army, using its soils and foundation engineering skills to assist in the construction of military facilities, as well as devoting its expertise to the development of field soils kits for the U.S. Navy Sea Bees. World War II business also pushed Dames & Moore overseas for the first time, setting the stage for the firm's expansion into European markets after the war. In 1943, when the German Army occupied most of North Africa and maintained an entrenched position in Europe, the Allied forces were in desperate need of fuel. To help supply the demand, decision-makers resolved to construct an oil refinery at Ras Tanura, Saudi Arabia, and called upon "Mr. Outside" to conduct soils investigations at the site. Moore flew to Saudi Arabia and supervised the construction of testing equipment and the ensuing soils investigation, gathering information that provided foundation design recommendations for the refinery.

In the decades following the war, the national economy expanded mightily, creating an unprecedented need for engineers of all types to assist in the nation's strident growth. Construction activity throughout the country occurred at a dizzying pace, companies—Dames & Moore clients included—expanded ambitiously, while nearly every sector of the economy, after a decade-long depression and five years of war, awoke from dormancy to record robust growth. In the economic boom period following the war, Dames and Moore found themselves operating in a business environment primed for their services, and they moved resolutely forward to take advantage of the prosperous times. Their company expanded into Europe for the first time in 1948, undertaking a detailed foundation investigation for an oil refinery in Rotterdam. Domestically, Dames & Moore expanded its geographic presence, opening offices in Portland, Oregon, and Seattle, Washington, in 1947, and an office in New York one year later. Further expansion followed, precipitated by the expansion of the company's mainstay clients. As oil companies extended their geographic reach, so did Dames & Moore, giving the company a payroll of 100 consultants working in eight offices by the end of the 1940s.

Burgeoning growth in the late 1940s reached full stride during the 1950s, as Dames & Moore not only continued to physically expand but also began to broaden the scope of its engineering services. Engineering projects were undertaken in the Far East, South America, and Australia, extending the company's reach around the globe, and its services were diversified. Until 1952, Dames & Moore had focused exclusively on soils and foundation engineering, but as consultants with backgrounds in geology and geophysics joined the company's growing roster of experts, capabilities increased commensurately. Midway through the 1950s, Dames & Moore's services included engineering geology, ground-water development, mineral exploration, and other areas in the applied earth sciences. By the 1960s, further maturation added new services that represented new scientific disciplines, including environmental engineering, earthquake engineering, and marine services. With the addition of these new services, Dames & Moore could perform its traditional soils mechanics and foundation work, such as the foundation investigation the company completed for Dodger Stadium in the 1950s, and it also could participate in a bevy of different projects that required expertise in the other engineering disciplines. Accordingly, the company was involved in a number of high-profile projects during the 1960s. It was involved in the construction of the BART rapid transit system in San Francisco. Dames & Moore consultants completed the geotechnical investigation for the 606-foot-high Seattle Space Needle, constructed for the 1962 World's Fair. The company investigated the 8.5 magnitude Alaska earthquake in 1964, conducted the foundation investigation of the Ala Moana shopping center and office building project in Honolulu, Hawaii, and it provided foundation specifications for a massive parcel of wetlands in Orlando, Florida, where Walt Disney World was erected.

The 1960s also marked the emergence of two new important areas of business for Dames & Moore: scientific investigations related to environmental concerns and nuclear power concerns. Well before the promulgation of the National Environmental Policy Act (NEPA) of 1969, the company began providing environmental services to its clients, mainly major utilities, oil companies, and industrial companies. These services, distinct from foundation analysis, enabled customers to assess the affect a particular project would have on the environment, which became mandatory with the establishment of the NEPA and the U.S. Environmental Protection Agency. In the regulation-driven era that ensued, Dames & Moore stood poised as one of the diversified experts capable of assuring that utilities and companies were in compliance with federal mandates. On the nuclear power front, Dames & Moore made an early entry into what would prove to be a lucrative business area. In 1963, the company began one of its first major environmental projects related to nuclear power, an evaluation of the site for Niagara Mohawk Power Corporation's Nine Mile One nuclear power plant near Oswego, New York. Aside from providing its typical foundation engineering and geological services, the company performed an examination of regional seismology, groundwater flow patterns, water-use patterns, and surface-water hydrology. During the 1970s, this aspect of Dames & Moore's business grew strongly, as the company developed new talents that kept pace with the changing conditions in its marketplace.

By the late 1960s and early 1970s, Dames & Moore's entry into environmental and nuclear power related business was beginning to pay big dividends. A surge of business arrived with the increased demand by utilities for studies required to license proposed nuclear power plants, both at home and abroad. Concurrently, there was another prodigious increase in business related to the construction of offshore platforms, processing facilities, and pipeline systems undertaken by the petroleum industry, long a source of business for Dames & Moore. As the company entered the 1980s, its environmental services took the form of waste management consultations for companies endeavoring to deal with hazardous substances and toxic waste. By 1984, roughly a third of Dames & Moore's new business in the United States was derived from projects related to waste management. Again, the company had demonstrated its ability to change with the times; a talent that would be put to an extreme test in the years ahead.

Revamped in the 1990s

Dames & Moore celebrated its 50th anniversary in 1988, when the company employed more than 1,400 professional consultants and staff in more than 50 cities across the globe, collecting more than $115 million in revenues. The half-century celebrations occurred at a propitious juncture in Dames & Moore's history, for the festivities offered an opportunity for all those associated with the company to reflect on the past before sweeping changes entirely reshaped the company for its second half-century of business. The late 1980s marked a signal turning point in Dames & Moore's development, ushering in a new breed of company designed to compete in a different business environment. The growth of Dames & Moore's mainstay markets had flattened out as the 1980s drew to a close, prompting management to seriously reconsider the company's future. The actions company officials took after this period of self-reflection produced a new, greatly diversified company, the Dames & Moore of the 1990s.

The first significant move toward the company's wholesale transformation occurred in 1992, when Dames & Moore, a limited partnership since its inception, incorporated and converted to public ownership. The organizational change created Dames & Moore, Inc., a corporate entity comprising a global network of companies that would become known as the Dames & Moore Group. Within the Dames & Moore Group, a name that was adopted in 1997, were a handful of operating companies Dames & Moore, Inc. had obtained through acquisitions. The bulk of these companies were acquired in 1995, when Dames & Moore purchased Walk Haydel & Associates, Inc., O'Brien Kreitzberg, Inc., and DecisionQuest, Inc. Founded in 1959 and headquartered in New Orleans, Louisiana, Walk Haydel offered program management services for major construction projects such as the U.S. Department of Energy's Strategic Petroleum Reserve storage facility at Big Hill, Texas. DecisionQuest, a company formed in 1991, employed experts in behavioral research and the science of persuasion, lending its expertise to law firms and corporate attorneys preparing for trial or special presentations. The third company acquired in 1995, O'Brien Kreitzberg, was similar to Walk Haydel. O'Brien Kreitzberg provided project and construction management services for large-scale projects such as the GSA Federal Building in Oakland, California, for which the company identified $11 million in engineering savings.

Two more additions to Dames & Moore Group occurred in 1996, as the company neared the completion of its reconstruction for the 21st century. The BRW Group, founded in 1970 and based in Minneapolis, Minnesota, gave Dames & Moore a seasoned veteran to provide preliminary site planning and final site design to large corporate clients. Next, the company formed Dames & Moore Ventures, a company created to identify and fund investment opportunities connected to its parent company's technical practice. As part of this effort, Dames & Moore Ventures was involved in a joint venture company that repaired and redeveloped environmentally impaired property.

Organized as such, the Dames & Moore of the late 1990s stood as a vastly different company than the enterprise that had existed a decade earlier. Whether the changes effected would translate into continued success during the company's second half-century of business remained to be determined in the years ahead. The company's solid background in civil engineering and the pioneering achievement of its founders, however, was a fact the future could not erase. As Dames & Moore headed into the 21st century, this immutable strength represented the company's foundation for future success.

Principal Subsidiaries

Walk Haydel & Associates, Inc.; O'Brien Kreitzberg, Inc.; BRW Group; DecisionQuest, Inc., Dames & Moore Ventures.

Further Reading

Lillard, Judith, "Dames & Moore Celebrates 50 Years of Practice," Los Angeles: Dames & Moore, Inc., 1988, 10 p.

——, "Trent R. Dames and the Consulting Firm He Founded 50 Years Ago Are Still Models for the Profession," Los Angeles: Dames & Moore, Inc., 1988, 4 p.

——, "William W. Moore Still a Vital Influence After 50 Years in the Consulting Engineering Profession," Los Angeles: Dames & Moore, Inc., 1988, 4 p.

—Jeffrey L. Covell

Dassault Systèmes S.A.

9, quai Marcel Dassault
BP 310
92156 Suresnes Cedex
France
(33) 1 40 99 40 99
Fax: (33) 1 42 04 45 81
Web site: http://www.dsweb.com

Public Company
Incorporated: 1981
Employees: 1,672
Sales: FFr 1.96 billion (US$ 335 million) (1997)
Stock Exchanges: Paris NASDAQ
Ticker Symbol: DASTY
SICs: 7372 Prepackaged Software; 7371 Computer
    Programming Services; 5045 Computers, Peripherals,
    and Software

Dassault Systèmes S.A. is the world's leading developer of CAD/CAM/CAE (computer-assisted design, manufacturing, engineering) software, with a product family of more than 120 interrelated component software packages enabling the implementation of design, analysis, manufacturing, and post-production support systems tailored to clients' specific needs. Dassault's CATIA and CADAM software products permit engineering and product design teams, generally working across a network, to develop prototype products, as well as to provide software-based modeling, assembly, testing, analysis and other procedures using three-dimensional images, eliminating the expense of building physical models and prototypes during a product's initial design phase. Beyond the design and engineering of a product, the company's software enables clients to develop and implement full-scale manufacturing systems, while also providing post-production support capacity, including quality assurance and product data generation.

One of the originators of the three-dimensional CAD/CAM/CAE market, Dassault has sold some 100,000 'seats,' or licenses, of its CATIA and CADAM software products, to more than 10,000 clients worldwide. In the 1990s, the company's software has been used to develop seven out of every ten new airplanes and four out of every ten new cars worldwide, including those from such corporations as Dassault Aviation, Boeing, Aerospatiale, BMW, Chrysler, Peugeot, Honda, Lockheed Martin, and others. CATIA has been used to design such products as Chrysler's Voyager minivans, RAM pickups, and Viper and Neon automobiles. Aircraft designed using CATIA include the Boeing 777, the Falcon 2000 business jet, and the Rafale jet fighter plane from Dassault Aviation. In addition to the aerospace and automotive/transportation industries, Dassault's primary markets include consumer goods, with clients such as Black & Decker, Electrolux, and Sony; plant design and shipbuilding, with clients including General Dynamics and Technip; and fabrication and assembly, with clients including ABB, Staubli, and Valmet.

Dassault's CATIA and CADAM product family forms the core of the company's development efforts. Users of the linked CATIA and CADAM system can achieve an end-to-end product development process from initial product specification, design and testing, through engineering analysis, to full-scale manufacturing utilizing a sole systems-wide interface, database, and programming set. Product development employs simultaneous solid-body, surface, and wireframe rendering. The use of both parametric modeling—in which the entire process responds to a series of fixed parameters—and variation modeling, which enables the ability to apply changes to individual components—for example, for customization purposes—without being required to redefine the entire parameter set, offers users sophisticated 'next-generation' flexibility in the design and post-design processes. The integration of CAE and CAM processes within the CAD process enable not only sophisticated stress and meshing analysis, but also the concurrent definition of the manufacturing process. The fully integrated CAD/CAM/CAE system enables manufacturers to eliminate costly physical modeling steps, improve quality control procedures, and achieve a more efficient and faster design–to–product development system. In addition, the integration of manufacturing processes in the design phase provides the ability to avoid the need to retool the production process, as the early design phase of a product can be adapted to the manufac-

132

turer's existing machine park. Finally, CATIA and CADAM users have access to the system's knowledge base capacity, providing access to product and specification history, as well as the integration of industry standards, regulatory requirements, and the client's own specifications throughout the design and manufacturing process.

In addition to its CATIA-CANAM product families, Dassault also develops and distributes CATWEB Navigator, a real-time intranet and web-based browser allowing worldwide access to clients' database and product development systems. Other products include Enovia, a computer-assisted design application supporting the emerging PDM II (product data management) and extended enterprise markets. The acquisition of Deneb adds that company's principally Unix- and Windows NT based products to the Dassault's traditional IBM, Hewlett Packard, and Silicon Graphics platform focus. Similarly, Solid-Works, acquired in 1997, adds that company's set of CAD products, enabling Dassault to extend its product solutions to the Windows-based PC market. Both Deneb and Solidworks continue their independent operations. The company also operates direct subsidiaries in the United States and Japan.

Since its inception, Dassault Systèmes has been partnered with IBM, which provides the company's primary marketing, distribution, and support services through IBM's Engineering Technology Solutions and Business Partners organizations. Apart from providing Dassault with a combined sales staff of some 1,500, the IBM partnership arrangement has also enabled Dassault to gain a broad penetration of the world's leading industrial markets. Dassault also maintains its own sales force of approximately 200, with which it markets its products and offers support directly to a growing number of clients. Europe continues to account for the company's primary market, with nearly 60 percent of Dassault's installed product base, compared to 23 percent in the United States, and 14 percent in the Asian market. Industry-wide, Dassault has captured an estimated 16 percent of the total CAD/CAM/CAE market.

Dassault Systèmes has been a public company since its 1996 introduction to the Paris and NASDAQ stock exchanges. More than 60 percent of the company's stock continues to be held by former parent Dassault Aviation, and ultimate parent Dassault Industries.

Pioneering the Third Dimension in the 1970s

Dassault Systèmes grew directly out of the aerospace industry's search for more sophisticated drafting tools that could not only aid in streamlining the development process, but also respond to the increasing complexity of aviation design. Computer technology had already entered the manufacturing process, offering numerical-controlled tooling functions and the first CAM systems. The appearance of the microcomputer in the 1970s offered broader applications of computer technology, particularly for product design. One of the earliest efforts to replace hand-drawn drafting with computer-assisted design software was a program developed by Lockheed, called CADAM, for Computer-Augmented Drafting and Manufacturing. CADAM enabled drafters and engineers to automate much of the two-dimensional drafting process, using the computer to perform the necessary calculations. Among the first CADAM

customers was Marcel Dassault, one of the pioneers of the French aviation industry, and head of Avions Marcel Dassault, the forerunner to Dassault Aviation.

Dassault purchased CADAM licenses in 1975. Yet, despite the advantages offered by CADAM and similar packages of the period, the software functioned more or less as an electronic drafting board and remained limited in its applications for the complex demands of aeronautical design. Dassault sought software that would add the third-dimension to the computer screen. Finding no such software to suit its needs, the company formed its own development team in 1977; by the end of the 1970s, Dassault's programmers had developed the predecessor to CATIA, becoming the first to bring three-dimensional modeling to the design process. CATIA (for Computer-Aided Three Dimensional Interactive Application) represented an industry breakthrough. The addition of a third plane to the drafting process eliminated many of the errors encountered when attempting to translate a two-dimensional drawing into a physical model, offered greater interaction among drafters and engineers, while reducing—and eventually all but eliminating—the expense of building models and prototypes for each step of the product development process.

At the beginning of the 1980s, Avions Marcel Dassault decided to market CATIA to other aerospace manufacturers. In 1981, the company created Dassault Systèmes, transferring its 15-member development staff and the CATIA program to the new independent subsidiary, which could concentrate its efforts on improving the software. Instead of forming its own sales force, Dassault Systèmes reached an agreement with IBM, then at the height of its computer industry dominance, to market, distribute, and provide technical support for CATIA. The agreement called for IBM to receive some 50 percent of revenues generated by CATIA sales; in turn, the partnership brought CATIA to IBM's worldwide customer base. Demand for CATIA was immediate, not only in France, but throughout the world. CATIA was quickly translated into English and German and then other languages. While the initial target market had been the aviation industry, the powerful new capabilities offered by CATIA were quickly adopted throughout the manufacturing world; the automobile industry became one of Dassault Systèmes most important markets. CATIA also found clients among the consumer goods and shipbuilding industries.

The initial commercial version of CATIA, presented in 1982, was offered as an add-on program to existing two-dimensional drafting programs, adding 3D design, surface modeling, and numerical-control tool programming functions. By then Dassault Systèmes was already working to incorporate drafting tools into its software, which would allow CATIA to function independently of CADAM and similar software. This next version of CATIA was readied by 1984 and launched commercially the following year. In addition to drafting functions, CATIA Version 2 also incorporated robotics functions, extending the program's reach into the computer-aided manufacturing field, offering linked CAD and CAM functionality. These new feature additions enabled CATIA to capture the leading share of the aeronautical design market.

The next step in CATIA's development was the addition of computer-assisted engineering capabilities. CATIA Version 3, launched in 1988, was among the first to include CAE functions; at the same time, Dassault Systèmes introduced compatibility with IBM's Unix-based workstations. By the end of the decade, CATIA had become the worldwide market leader among the automotive industry as well.

Expansion and Independence in the 1990s

Throughout the 1980s, CADAM, which had been purchased by IBM from Lockheed, and CATIA continued to be developed independently, while reaching a complementary customer base—including Dassault Aviation itself. In 1992, IBM agreed to transfer future development of CADAM to Dassault Systèmes, with the creation of a new independent subsidiary, Dassault Systems of America. In exchange the transfer agreement gave IBM a ten percent share of Dassault Systèmes. The first integrated version of the two industry-leading programs appeared in 1993. Now dubbed CATIA-CADAM Solutions, the system brought the various software programs developed under each product family into a single package, featuring an open architecture adaptable to each customer's requirements. CATIA-CADAM was now capable of performing simultaneously the variety of tasks in the CAD/CAM development process, providing the design, engineering, manufacturing, and other departments of a manufacturer with access to the same data and the same user interface.

Also in 1993, the company moved to deepen its penetration into the booming Asian market, forming a wholly owned Japanese subsidiary, Dassault Systèmes Kabushiki Kaisha (Dassault Systèmes KK) and translating its software into Japanese and Korean. By year-end 1993, Dassault Systèmes's revenues had reached FFr 914 million, for a net profit of FFr 117 million. The following year, the company's relationship with IBM was strengthened, when IBM initiated a separate sales force, Engineering Technology Solutions, which would grow to some 800 employees, dedicated to marketing, sales, and support of the CATIA-CADAM product family.

The next version of CATIA-CADAM, introduced in 1995 and called CATIA-CADAM CAE Plant Solutions, brought enhanced engineering functionality—particularly with the incorporation of knowledge-based capacity—to the software suite. In that same year, Dassault Systèmes moved beyond its long-time IBM workstations base, offering compatibility with the Hewlett Packard 9000 Series 700 workstations. Compatibility with the fast-growing Silicon Graphics workstations market followed in 1996. By 1997, IBM's Engineering Technology Solutions department agreed to market and support CATIA-CADAM for third-party hardware platforms. Another IBM sales department, Business Partners, had also begun to market and support the Dassault Systèmes products.

By the end of 1995, Dassault Systèmes had posted revenues of more than FFr 1.1 billion, with net earnings of FFr 221 million. The following year, the company poised to begin a new expansion, which brought it to the stock market. The company's initial public offering (IPO), performed simultaneously on the Paris and NASDAQ stock markets, was one of the year's successes, with the 17.5 percent of the company on offer oversubscribed by some 35 times. The IPO enabled the company to acquire, in 1997, 100 percent of SolidWorks, a California-based company specializing in Windows-based mechanical design software. The acquisition not only strengthened the company's 2D drafting capacity, but also gave it an entry into the Windows market, which, with the rapid development in processor power for personal computers, had begun to impose itself on markets which had traditionally depended on the larger workstation environments. The acquisition raised a few eyebrows; the purchase price, through a stock swap, came to $310 million—for a company that had posted only $25 million the previous year.

The SolidWorks acquisition was joined at the end of 1997 by another acquisition, that of Deneb, which added that company's digital manufacturing software to the Dassault Systèmes product line. Both companies continued to operate as independent subsidiaries. They also pointed the way to the next step in Dassault Systèmes quest to provide a total manufacturing system. In 1998, the company, together with IBM, announced the formation of a new Dassault Systèmes subsidiary, ENOVIA, releasing the ENOVIA PM suite of software. Designed for the PDM II, extended-enterprise market, ENOVIA enabled the access of data across the spectrum of manufacturing processes, while remaining independent of the CAD environment. While Dassault Systèmes faced increasing competition during the 1990s, particularly from Waltham, Massachusetts-based Parametrics Corp., the company's expansion enabled it to maintain its leadership position among the worldwide CAD/CAM/CAE market. In 1997, the company's revenues neared FFr 2 billion, providing net earnings of more than FFr 460 million.

Principal Subsidiaries

SolidWorks; Deneb; Enovia Corp. (United States); Dassault Systèmes of America; Dassault Systèmes KK (Japan); Dassault Data Services.

Further Reading

"Dassault Systèmes Runs into a Hitch in a Bid to Rule Computer-Aided Design," *Wall Street Journal (Europe),* June 3, 1997, p. S32.

Haas, Patrick, "Dassault Systèmes vole de ses propres ailes," *Le Figaro Economique,* July 8, 1996, p. 12.

Lucas, Thierry, "Dassault Systèmes prend place dans le PC," *L'Usine Nouvelle,* July 3, 1997, p. 29.

Vidal, François, "Dassault Systèmes séduit par le 'pooling of interests'," *Option Finance,* November 1997, p. 19.

—M.L. Cohen

DAW TECHNOLOGIES, INC.
Ultraclean Manufacturing Environments

DAW Technologies, Inc.

2700 South 900 West
Salt Lake City, Utah 84119
U.S.A.
(801) 977-3100
Fax: (801) 973-6640
Web site: www.dawtech.com

Public Company
Incorporated: 1987
Employees: 324
Sales: $52 million (1997)
Stock Exchanges: NASDAQ
Ticker Symbol: DAWK
SICs: 3564 Blowers & Fans; 1711 Plumbing, Heating &
Air Conditioning

Daw Technologies, Inc., is the leading American supplier of ''cleanrooms,'' or ultra-clean manufacturing facilities, for the semiconductor industry. The company originates the design, engineers and manufactures the components, installs the environment, and provides comprehensive maintenance service for all the systems included in a cleanroom. Daw Technologies' integrated approach allows its customers to reap huge benefits from its accelerated design, installation, and project maintenance. Critical to the semiconductor manufacturing process, cleanrooms control contamination levels and environmental variables, including such factors as humidity, gases, electromagnetic fields, and temperature. Competition and shorter product life cycles within the semiconductor industry have enabled Daw Technologies to carve out its own niche by providing fully operational cleanrooms in the shortest possible timeframe. During the mid-1990s, company management has embarked on an aggressive expansion strategy and, in addition to its existing U.S. facilities, opened new sales and design offices in Livingston, Scotland; Aix-en-Provence, France; and Hsin-Chu City, Taiwan. In 1998 Daw Technologies won the largest contract in its history when the company reached an agreement with the People's Republic of China to provide a cleanroom system for a semiconductor manufacturing facility in Tianjin, China.

Early History

The founder and moving force behind Daw Technologies is Ronald W. Daw. Born and raised in the mountain air of Utah, Ronald Daw spent his childhood days like many other American children raised during the decade of the 1950s, with lots of room to play and unbridled optimism in the future. After graduating from high school, he attended the University of Utah, where he received a Bachelor of Science degree in the field of accounting. His did well at university, and was welcomed into corporate life in Salt Lake City. During his early career, Daw learned about corporate organization, people management, and financial operations. Extremely talented, with an acute sense of product development and marketing, by the time Daw reached his mid-30s he was running his own company, Daw Incorporated, an interior finish construction firm.

Having started his first company in 1984, Ronald Daw negotiated the difficulties of the construction industry and its cyclical nature with decisive action and a sharp sense of what the market required. Within four years he had built a sizeable firm that provided high-quality interior finishing. Always looking for bigger and better opportunities, the entrepreneur decided to enter into the cleanroom business after discovering the demand for ultra-clean manufacturing environments in the semiconductor industry. Formed and incorporated in 1987, DTI was one of the first companies to provide comprehensive services for all the principal components of a cleanroom environment. Of course, by the late 1980s, the semiconductor industry was already fully developed, with a number of small companies designing and installing cleanroom environments. But Daw's vision included a more thorough approach involving not only the design and installation of cleanroom manufacturing facilities, but also the manufacture and maintenance of the entire cleanroom, including its ceiling systems, wall systems, floor systems, and recirculating air-handling systems, as well as testing, certification, tool fit-up, and continuous on-site maintenance and repair.

Unfortunately, the firm was hit hard by the cyclical nature of the semiconductor industry during the late 1980s. Demand dropped precipitously, and, in light of the fact that a large supply of semiconductors was readily available from earlier

Company Perspectives:

There are always lessons to be learned and improvements to be made in a business. The Company's management team has been and remains open to learn from these lessons. So what have we learned over the past two years? We have been reminded that the semiconductor industry is cyclical and that our business has been solely dependent on this industry. As a result, management is working to diversify the business operations without compromising our current position within the semiconductor industry. Further, we have found it much easier to deal with the challenges of growth than with the challenges of an industry downturn. The management group will continue to monitor our cost structure through the current downturn while staying ready for expected and anticipated growth. Lastly, our shareholders' investment remains our number one concern. The changes we are making and the opportunities we are pursuing are directed specifically at increasing shareholder value and providing for overall growth and profitability.
—Letter to the Shareholders, Daw Technologies, Inc.,
    1997 Annual Report

production schedules, services provided by companies such as DTI were either canceled or placed on indefinite postponement. The severity of this particular cycle was intense, and resulted in a decision to downsize company operations. The most important lesson Daw learned from the detrimental effects of the cycle was to prepare for the next one.

Growth and Development During the Early 1990s

Before the 1990s, semiconductor manufacturers contracted a number of vendors to provide them with cleanroom systems and related maintenance services. Much like the approach in a wide range of industries, a request for a price quote for either cleanroom component systems and/or maintenance services was issued, competitors submitted their initial designs and estimated budgets, and, after review, revised both their designs and budgets in light of the needs made explicit by the contracting semiconductor manufacturer. This process of design and budget submission and revision would repeat itself until the semiconductor company made its final vendor selection. After the completion of this process, which might take as much as a year, the vendor would prepare its final design and initiate the cleanroom project. The final design might be installed by the vendor that submitted the original bid, but it might also be sub-contracted by the vendor to an independent firm for installation.

The pace of competition, innovation, and technological development within the semiconductor industry increased rapidly during the late 1980s and early 1990s, however, and resulted not only in briefer semiconductor product cycles but also in shorter cleanroom facility cycles. Semiconductor manufacturers strove to bring their products to market more quickly, with cleanroom design and construction time both shortened as much as possible. A higher product volume, in conjunction with smaller wafer sizes, increased chip densities, and the growing number of steps in the manufacturing process led to a heightened emphasis on the control and manipulation of environmental variables within the cleanroom setting. More than ever before, the elimination of even the slightest deviations in environmental parameters within the cleanroom was the only way to assure a higher product yield.

Ronald Daw understood the changing nature of the semiconductor industry, and, using his broad experience in cleanroom environments gleaned from some difficult years leading DTI, he decided to reorganize the company, refine its vision, and create a new approach to the business. Renaming his company Daw Technologies, Inc., in 1992, the entrepreneur took advantage of the pace of competition within the semiconductor industry. In direct contrast to the traditional approach of submitting designs and budgets, revising them, and then resubmitting a bid, under the leadership of Daw the company offered fully integrated services for cleanroom environments, including the design, engineering, manufacture, installation, testing, evaluation, product development, and continuous maintenance service. Daw was convinced that his integrated approach not only gave customers greater control over the design and installation of a cleanroom environment by eliminating the number of vendors and subcontractors involved in the process, but also led to a higher product volume.

Continued Growth During the Mid-1990s

By the mid-1990s, Daw Technologies, Inc., was selling its products and services to some of the world's largest and most prominent disk drive, semiconductor, and flat panel display manufacturers. Sales had increased dramatically since the company's reorganization in 1992, with $30 million in sales in 1993 jumping to more than $70 million in 1995 and $112 million in 1996. Along with the increase in sales came an increase in the number of employees, amounting to more than 300 by 1995. Much of this success was due to the company's ability to patent various components of its cleanroom wall systems, floor systems, and air handling systems, which constituted some of the most sophisticated technology ever developed for cleanroom environments.

Each cleanroom that is constructed requires a variety of systems that provide an uninterrupted flow of filtered air circulating from the ceiling to the floor with the purpose of eliminating or flushing out every possible contaminant and particle. Within each cleanroom, the air pressure is slightly higher than in the surrounding rooms so that any leak or open door results in clean air escaping rather than contaminated air entering the environment. Cleanliness within a cleanroom environment cannot be compromised for any reason whatsoever; consequently, all wiring, piping, and movement of materials and personnel are considerations in the design of such an environment. To meet the stringent requirements for cleanroom environments, Daw Technologies patented systems including the following: the Stratus Air Handling System, which provides a source of recirculated air that reduces noise, vibration, and power consumption and adapts to changes in humidity, temperature, and pressure variations by employing specialty sensors; the Air Frame Ceiling System, which provides ultra-clean air filtration and an airflow that is unidirectional for the cleanroom environment; the Network Wall System, which separates cleanroom environments into distinct, individual airflow zones; and Matrix Raised Access Flooring, which provides removable panels that meet the exacting industry requirements for air flow, cleanliness, and structural design.

In 1997 the company was once again hit hard by the cyclical nature of the semiconductor industry. Although management tried its best to prepare for the downturn, the variables of the marketplace were overwhelming, and Daw Technologies lost a significant number of contracts. Sales, or contract revenue, dropped precipitously to a low of $52 million in 1997, and management was forced to lay off employees. To compensate for the downturn in the U.S. semiconductor industry, management at Daw Technologies, under the leadership of Ronald Daw, decided to launch a strategic international expansion program that would minimize the effects of cyclical downturns in the future.

In April 1998, Daw Technologies secured a major contract from an American-based semiconductor manufacturer to provide airhandling systems for the company's new cleanroom under construction in mainland China. Even though the worsening economic situation in Southeast Asia resulted in lower sales for personal computers in Thailand, Korea, Malaysia, Indonesia, and the Philippines, the Chinese market was growing at a rate of approximately 40 percent. Daw Technologies also secured another major contract from a Japanese semiconductor manufacturer to design and install a cleanroom for the company's growing operation in the United States. In June 1998 the company won two more contracts to provide fully integrated design and installation services for major semiconductor firms located in Western Europe.

In an additional move to strengthen its position within the industry, in April 1998 Daw Technologies purchased Intelligent Enclosures Corporation, a leading American provider of contamination control solutions and high-performance controlled environments. Located in Norcross, Georgia, the new acquisition was an innovator in the field of process equipment enclosures and tool isolation environment technology.

Soundly managed, Daw Technologies, Inc., is considered a prime candidate for significant growth within the next five to ten years. Having found its niche in a highly specialized field, the company should reap the benefits of its plan to expand overseas and acquire other firms that provide similar services.

Further Reading

Beinglass, Israel, ''Integrated Processes Reduce Set-up Time,'' *Electronic Business Today,* July 1996, p. 49.
Billat, Susan H., ''Productivity Gains Leverage Fab Investment,'' *Electronic Business Today,* July 1996, p. 44.
Haystead, John, ''Making the Right Moves,'' *Electronic Business Today,* February 1997, p. 52.
Johnson, Brock, ''How to Set up a Clean Room,'' *Plastics World,* April 1996, p. 23.
''Labor Shortage Could Squeeze Chip Industry,'' *Electronic Business Today,* December 1996, p. 20.
Ristelhueber, Robert, ''Wafer Fabs: Getting More Bang for the Buck,'' *Electronic Business Today,* July 1996, p. 37.
Young, Lewis H., ''Getting the Biggest Bang for Your Billion,'' *Electronic Business Today,* October 1996, p. 105.

—Thomas Derdak

DC Comics Inc.

1325 Avenue of the Americas
New York, New York 10003
U.S.A.
(212) 636-5400
Fax: (212) 484-2849
Web site: http://www.dccomics.com

Wholly Owned Subsidiary of Time Warner Inc.
Founded: 1935 as National Allied Publications
Employees: 200
Sales: $75 million (1997 est.)
SICs: 2721 Periodicals Publishing & Printing, 6794
   Patent Owners & Lessors

DC Comics Inc. is the world's largest comic book company and is perhaps best known for publishing the adventures of Superman and Batman. The history of DC is in many ways the history of American comic book publishing; its dominance during the 1990s is a testament to the enduring appeal of comic book superheroes, whose marketability in a variety of formats—including the big screen, television, video games, and CD-ROM—appeared to be boundless.

Progenitors, 1934–37

In 1934, Eastern Color Printing (ECP) began publishing news-strip comics reproductions in *Famous Funnies*. Imitators soon included *King Comics* and *Popular Comics*. In 1935, Malcolm Wheeler-Nicholson published *New Fun: The Big Comic Magazine* #1, the first all-original comic book. Wheeler-Nicholson founded National Allied Publications (NAP), attracting such talent as Vin Sullivan and Whitney Ellsworth. By 1938, Wheeler-Nicholson sold to Liebowitz/Donenfeld; Ellsworth left; and only Sullivan remained at NAP.

Superman Appears, 1938

Donenfeld traveled, building distribution. Liebowitz released 200,000 copies of *Action Comics* #1/1938, in which Sullivan published the first appearance of Siegel and Shuster's Superman and Fred Guardineer's Zatara. Created by two "kids" from Cleveland, Superman solidified the industry. The comic, selling for a dime then, was worth six figures in the 1990s.

Initially created in 1932 for *Science Fiction*, a fanzine the two published, Superman coincided with Hitler's rise to power and vow to create a race of Nietzschean "supermen." The first Superman was a bald villain! The second was *sans* cape but a crime-fighter. The "real" Superman came in 1934, with alter-ego Clark Kent named for Clark Gable. Superman reappeared on the cover of 500,000 copies of *Action Comics* #7, and was selling a million copies by 1939. Siegel and Shuster opened a studio, and Superman got his own title, becoming a McClure-syndicated news-strip in 1939, appearing in 300 daily newspapers worldwide by 1941, and then appearing regularly until 1966.

Batman Debuts, 1939

In May 1939, Bob Kane's Batman—created from such images as da Vinci's flying machine, *The Bat Whispers* (1930), *The Mark of Zorro* (1921), and *Dracula* (1931)—debuted in "The Case of the Chemical Syndicate" (*Detective Comics* #27). Sullivan promptly bought the character, though left later that year to start his own company.

Everyone Else, 1939

Liebowitz rehired Ellsworth and also hired Weisinger and Jack Schiff from the pulps. But the comics flood was only beginning. NAP accountant Victor Fox quit, opened offices, and hired Will Eisner for Wonder Man (*Wonder Comics*, 1939). NAP sued and the title was canceled after one issue. Fox created The Blue Beetle later that year.

Liebowitz, with M(axwell) C(harles) Gaines, created All American. Gaines, who, in 1933 at ECP, helped develop the first comic books, thought to sell them at newsstands, and also worked at The McClure Syndicate repackaging news-strips into comic books with Sheldon Mayer, the two who recommended Superman to NAP in 1938. Mayer would also create Scribbly for *All-American Comics* and hire Joe Kubert. All American also featured Jon L. Blummer's Hop Harrigan and Bud Fisher's Mutt and Jeff.

The Golden Age: 1939–50

By 1940, the distinctive DC circular logo (for *Detective Comics*) was appearing on NAP and All American comics. NAP created Superman Inc.—a licensing company—turning out hundreds of merchandise items and promotions. That year, Johnny Thunder and Gardner Fox creations The Flash and Hawkman debuted.

When Fawcett Publications debuted Captain Marvel (*Whiz Comics*), NAP promptly sued for similarities to Superman, fighting through 1953 before Fawcett settled, canceling Captain Marvel. In 1973 NAP acquired the rights to Captain Marvel, resurrecting him in *Shazam!*.

In 1941, *The Adventures of Superman* radio program began. Batman and Robin visited in 1945, beginning regular appearances, and the show ran until 1951.

A seven-minute animated film—*Superman* (1941)—appeared from Paramount Pictures. The first of 17, this Academy Award-nominated film was suggested to producer Max Fleischer, whose studio had created Betty Boop and Popeye.

Meanwhile, Jack Kirby and Joe Simon created Captain America for Marvel and Jack Cole's Plastic Man and Will Eisner's Blackhawk debuted for Quality Comics Group, both characters which NAP acquired (1956). Weisinger created Johnny Quick, Aquaman, and Green Arrow, the three moving to *Adventure Comics*.

William Moulton Marston, best known for creating the lie detector, due to an article the psychologist wrote attacking comics, was approached by Mayer to write comics. Marston agreed and Wonder Woman debuted in *All Star Comics* #8/1941, becoming lead character in *Sensation Comics* #1/1942 and graduating to *Wonder Woman* #1/1943.

After Pearl Harbor, Weisinger enlisted; Bert Christman (*Sandman*) died with The Flying Tigers; Superman and Batman promoted war bonds; Simon and Kirby created Boy Commandos before ending up in uniform themselves; and before Siegel joined up, he and Hal Sherman created The Star-Spangled Kid, who debuted in *Star Spangled Comics* #1, a series which also featured Liberty Belle and Siegel's Robotman.

In 1942, Superman villain The Prankster appeared; Random House published the first Superman novel; Wildcat debuted (*Sensation Comics*); and Hop Harrigan appeared on a radio show which ran until 1948.

Batman became McClure-syndicated in 1943. Wonder Woman and Hop Harrigan also had newspaper runs. Superman villain The Toyman debuted. Batman finally beat Superman to the punch, becoming the first NAP superhero with a live-action film. Columbia Pictures released a 15-part serial entitled *Batman*.

In 1944, DC hired Julius Schwartz—literary agent for H. P. Lovecraft—as story editor. Concurrently, Liebowitz bought out Gaines's share of All American, merging it with NAP. Gaines went with his son Bill to create EC Comics—which would release *Tales from the Crypt*, *Mad* (1952), and *Mad Magazine* (1955; sold to Premier Industries, 1962). The Three Mousketeers also debuted that year.

Superboy debuted in *More Fun Comics* #101/1945, graduated to *Adventure Comics* (1946), and got his own title (1949), the last of the important superhero titles of The Golden Age. *Superboy* introduced Lana Lang, but created contradictions (Supe was not a superhero until adulthood, did not meet Lois until Metropolis). Siegel and Shuster did not like the character, suing NAP (1947) for royalties, which they received, but left the company, creating a rift until 1975, when they were awarded compensation, pensions, and credit again on their creations.

From 1946 to 1949, NAP published *Real Fact Comics* to promote education through comics (with Pearl S. Buck among the writers). That year, NAP, All American, and other DC predecessors combined to form National Comics Publications (NCP).

Marston died in 1947; Kirby and Simon created a new Sandman; Mayer quit to return to drawing, and after World War II interest in superheroes began to slump. NCP canceled *More Fun Comics*, *Flash Comics*, *All-Flash Comics*, and dropped costumed characters from *All Star Comics*, *Sensation Comics*, and *Star Spangled Comics*. *Action Comics*, *Detective Comics*, and *Adventure Comics* continued with Superman, Batman, and Superboy.

In 1948, Superman debuted in film, appearing in Columbia's 15-chapter serial *Superman*, produced by Sam Katzman, who also produced *Batman and Robin* (1949) and *Atom Man vs. Superman* (1950).

Other NCP characters appearing as Columbia serials included *Hop Harrigan* (1946), *The Vigilante* (1947), and *Congo Bill: King of the Jungle*.

The impact of TV and film was felt in comics, as evinced by such titles as *The Adventures of Ozzie and Harriet* and *The Adventures of Alan Ladd* (1949); *Feature Films* and *The Adventures of Bob Hope* (1950); *The Adventures of Dean Martin and Jerry Lewis* (1952–57); *Jackie Gleason*, (1956–58); *Sgt. Bilko*, (1957–60); *The Adventures of Jerry Lewis* (1957–71); *The Many Loves of Dobie Gillis* (1960–64); and *Welcome Back, Kotter* (1976).

George Reeves played Superman in the superhero's first feature film, *Superman and the Mole Men* (1951), serving as the pilot for the television series *Adventures of Superman* (1951–57).

In the 1940s and 1950s, westerns and animals gained popularity, with debuts of *Western Comics, Tomahawk,* and *The Dodo and the Frog*; and name changes from *All-American Comics* to

All-American Western, *All Star Comics* to *All Star Western*, *Funny Folks* to *Nutsy Squirrel*, and *Animal Antics* to *The Raccoon Kids*. Dell Publishing bought Walt Disney, Walter Lantz, and Warner Bros. characters. NCP acquired *The Fox and The Crow*, based on Columbia's 1941 cartoon *The Fox and the Grapes,* and Superman's pal Jimmy Olsen got his own title in 1954.

Mysteries and horror boomed, with Gleason's *Crime Does Not Pay* (1942), followed by DC's *Gangbusters* (1947), *Mr. District Attorney* (1948), *Big Town* (1950), *House of Mystery* (1951), and *House of Secrets* (1956); and EC's *Tales from the Crypt*. Science fiction also grew, with debuts of *Strange Adventures* (1950) and *Mystery in Space* (1951); war stories abounded, with *Our Army at War*, *Star Spangled War Stories*, and *All-American Men of War* (all 1952); and romance and teen comics popped up, with Prize Comics/Simon and Kirby's *Young Romance* (1947; acquired by DC, 1963), and DC's *A Date with Judy* (1947), *Leave It to Binky*, *Here's Howie*, *Romance Trail* (1949), *Girls' Love Stories* (1949), *Secret Hearts*, *Girls' Romances*, *Falling in Love*, and *Heart Throbs* (bought from Quality, 1955).

Attack on Comics, 1954

In 1954, with a booming comics industry, Dr. Fredric Wertham of Bellevue launched a Congressional inquiry when he blamed comic books and their gruesome, lurid covers for growing juvenile delinquency, and asserted that Batman, Robin, and Wonder Woman were homosexual. Though the industry created the self-governing Comics Code Authority, EC Comics was essentially destroyed, as were other comics publishers.

The Silver Age Begins, 1956

Schwartz inaugurated The Silver Age of Comics when he revived Flash in 1956. In 1958, Lois Lane got her own title—*Superman's Girlfriend Lois Lane*—as did *The Challengers of the Unknown* (April–May). Two years later *The Justice League of America* debuted. In 1961, Kirby and Stan Lee released *The Fantastic Four*; Donenfeld died; his son Irwin replaced him; and NCP changed its name to National Periodical Publications (NPP).

Getting their own titles were Hawkman (1964), Metamorpho The Element Man (1965), and Teen Titans (1966). In 1966, Superman hit Broadway with *It's A Bird . . . It's A Plane . . . It's Superman!* and returned to a cartoon series (1966–70), going on to Hanna-Barbera's *Super Friends* (1973–86). The superhero icon was also immortalized in paintings by both Andy Warhol and Roy Lichtenstein. Concurrently, Batman debuted on television, appeared in a film and two animated TV series (1966, 1977), plus novels, collections of kids' letters to Batman, and every merchandise item imaginable.

NPP and Warner Bros. were purchased in 1968 by Kinney National Services. In 1972, NPP debuted Len Wein and Bernie Wrightson's innovative horror title *Swamp Thing*—which would become a cult hit movie (1982) and sequel (1989), as well as a spinoff TV series (1990), and animated miniseries (1991). That same year Tarzan came to DC.

In 1973, *Prez*, *Plop!*, and *The Shadow* appeared in print, and Aquaman launched a cartoon television series (1973–86),

which included solo appearances by The Atom, The Flash, Green Lantern, Hawkman, The Teen Titans, and The Justice League. Marvel's Dr. Strange appeared, and *Captain America* and *The Punisher* were shot, but never released. Wonder Woman debuted in a TV movie (1974), followed by a series (1975–79), and *Jonah Hex* got his own title (1976).

The Path of Kahn, 1976

Jenette Kahn became publisher in 1976 and president five years later, and was credited with revamping the entire company. She changed the name NPP to DC Comics Inc. in 1977, fashioned a new logo, and led DC to become the first comics company to pay royalties in 1981.

Christopher Reeve took over in *Superman: The Movie* (1978), *Superman II* (1980), *III* (1983), and *IV: The Quest for Peace* (1988)—spinning off a *Supergirl* film (1984)—before moving to videocassette.

In 1982, DC's *Camelot 3000*, became the first original offset series sold through direct-sales market, followed by Frank Miller's *Ronin* (1983) and *Sun Devils* (1984). Spinoffs from games began with *Atari Force* (1984) and Dick Grayson transformed from Robin to Nightwing. Graphic novels began appearing, with DC's *Star Raiders* (1983), *Metalzoic* (1986), and *Tell Me, Dark* (1992), as well as Ray Bradbury's *Frost and Fire*, Harlan Ellison's *Demon with a Glass Hand*, and Jack Kirby's *Hunger Dogs*.

In 1985, DC cleaned house, consolidating all of its universes (including those acquired from Fawcett, Charleton, and Quality), but some heroes—Supergirl, Silver Age Flash, and Nighthawk—paid the ultimate price. A second housecleaning came in 1994, with Hal Jordan's Green Lantern becoming the victim.

In 1986, Miller's *Batman: The Dark Knight Returns* sophisticatedly redefined Batman; John Byrne's Superman—updated in *Man of Steel*—became the first million-copy seller since The Golden Age, and had three top-100 titles; and *Watchmen*, which would become the most-honored comic series in history, debuted.

Mickey Mouse, Betty Boop, and Peanuts made comebacks in the 1980s, joined by Wonder Woman, The Justice League of America, and The Flash (1987). That summer, DC outsold Marvel for the first time in years.

During the 1970s–80s, industry birthday parties abounded, with Mickey Mouse, Donald Duck, and Snow White and the Seven Dwarfs all hitting the golden mark (1978, 1984, and 1987, respectively). February 29, 1988 marked Superman's 50th birthday and DC Comics started a year-long celebration beginning on Memorial Day 1987, when an exhibition opened at The Smithsonian Institute; *Superman IV* debuted; Superman joined The White House and U.S. Department of Education in The Drug-Free America Balloon Launch; CBS had a one-hour prime-time special on Supe; a weekend birthday party occurred in New York City; and The Grand Finale occurred in Cleveland that June, with a ticker-tape parade and a statue of Supe.

In 1988, Superboy appeared in a live-action TV series (1988–91); Jason Todd as Robin died, being replaced by Tim Drake. In 1989, Warner Communications merged with Time

Inc. to form Time Warner Inc., making DC part of the largest media company in the world, and Neil Gaiman created a third version of Sandman. Simultaneously, Marvel was sold by struggling New World Pictures to MacAndrew & Forbes, a holding company of financier Ronald Perelman.

That year also marked Batman's 50th birthday. *Batman: Arkham Asylum* became the bestselling hardcover comic ever; and *Batman* became the largest-grossing Warner film ever, with domestic box-office sales of $251 million (sixth in film history), total sales at over $400 million, and the videocassette was the bestselling ever.

Analysts estimated the comics industry went from $130 million in 1986 to $400 million in 1990 as Clark Kent and Lois Lane got engaged. Superman died in *Superman #75* (1993), the most widely read comic book ever, selling over six million copies. However, he was resurrected in 1993 and married Lois in 1996.

The Flash starred in a TV series (1991), but DC was hard-pressed to catch industry leaders Marvel and Malibu. In 1992 DC's *The Human Target* ran six episodes; *Batman: The Animated Series* debuted, winning an Emmy award; Superman and Batman appeared in *The New Batman/Superman Adventures*; *Batman Returns* (1992) became the only film to date beating *Batman*'s opening weekend box office record; and Bill Gaines died.

In 1989, seemingly only Kool-Aid advertised in comics. But in 1993, an upsurge occurred. DC and others suddenly had attracted such advertisers as Sega, Nordic Trak, Warner Bros., Crunch 'N Munch, and Stridex; Marvel characters promoted Pizza Hut (X-Men) and Burger King; and Malibu introduced its Ultraverse on MTV and Nickelodeon—the first time a comic publisher used national advertising—and a merger with Acme Interactive triggered Malibu's tie-in package, with a live-action video portion of the story, and the rest in the comics. *Lois and Clark: The New Adventures of Superman*, an hour-long prime-time series, also appeared.

DC debuted a new line—''Vertigo''—offering innovative graphic stories to adult readers of nontraditional comics. The psychologically compelling, cutting-edge titles ranged from science fiction to horror to dark fantasy.

July 1994 saw year-old Milestone Media—publishers of *Icon, Static, Kobalt, Rocket, Shadow Cabinet,* and *Xombi*—team characters from *Hardware* and *Blood Syndicate* with Superman, Superboy, and Steel in the ''Worlds Collide'' cross-over series, following Superman/Spiderman (1970s), Batman/Hulk (1980s), and Teen Titans/X-Men (1990s). Also appearing in 1994 were *Looney Toons* and Paradox Press—with such titles as *Brooklyn Dreams, La Pacifica, Beautiful Stories for Ugly Children, Urban Legends, The Big Book of Weirdos,* and *Stuck Rubber Baby.*

Batman Forever was the top-grossing film of 1995, and DC comics appeared in Waldenbooks. In 1996, Superman joined Snuggle Bear, WB, Kids WB Network, and Six Flags' Magic Mountain in Best Western promotions. *Batman and Robin* debuted in 1997.

By mid-1998, *Action Comics* and *Detective Comics* were still appearing, along with numerous other titles. Rumors abounded of a *Superman V* film; and, with Marvel/Malibu bankrupt, DC became sole survivor of The Golden Age of comics and the largest comics publisher in the world.

Further Reading

Barmann, Timothy C., ''Rhode Island Internet Provider Engages in Battle with Comic Giant,'' *Knight-Ridder/Tribune Business News*, February 18, 1998, p. 218B1051.

Boughton, Victoria, ''Wonder Woman,'' *Working Woman*, March 1982, p. 71.

Daniels, Les, *DC Comics: Sixty Years of the World's Favorite Comic Book Heroes*, Boston and New York: Little, Brown and Company, 1995, 256 p.

Fenner, Austin Evans, ''Manhattan Publisher Milestone Media Celebrates 16 Months in Business,'' *Knight-Ridder/Tribune Business News*, July 19, 1994, p. 07190074.

Flatow, Sheryl, ''Leaps and Bounds,'' *Public Relations Journal*, February 1988, p. 13.

Fost, Dan, ''Comics Age with the Baby Boom,'' *American Demographics*, May 1991, p. 16.

Frank, Jerome P., ''DC Comics Is Serious About Production; Using an In-House Electronic System, the Comic Book Publisher Saves Money and Improves Quality,'' *Publishers Weekly*, October 7, 1988, p. 91.

Grimm, Matthew, ''Marvel Comics Strikes Back: Beaten Badly by Archrival DC in the Cross-Marketing Arena, the Industry Leader Vows to Flex Its Muscles in Licensing, Promotion and Hollywood,'' *ADWEEK's Marketing Week*, January 1, 1991, p. 13.

''Holy Suit, Batman!: Owners of Copyright Sue Stores,'' *Philadelphia Business Journal*, February 26, 1990, p. 28.

Jensen, Jeff, ''Dead Superman May Revive DC Comics,'' *Advertising Age*, November 23, 1992, p. 13.

Ketzenberger, John, ''Holy Bootleg, Batman!: Warner, DC Comics File Suit Here to Stop 'Caped Crusader' Rip-Offs,'' *Indianapolis Business Journal*, September 4, 1989, p. 1A.

Lehrman, Celia Kuperszmid, ''Superman Faces Midlife Crisis,'' *Public Relations Journal*, September 1986, p. 15.

McCoy, Frank, and Alfred Edmond, Jr., ''Serious Business,'' *Black Enterprise*, September 1989, p. 86.

Miller, Cyndee, ''Comic Book Publishers Battle for Market Share, Advertisers,'' *Marketing News*, October 11, 1993, p. 1.

Morris, Chris, ''Winters Show Discontent Over DC Comics Depiction,'' *Billboard*, March 23, 1996, p. 95.

Reid, Calvin, ''500 Walden Stores to Feature DC Comics,'' *Publishers Weekly*, February 27, 1995, p. 32.

Rigg, Cynthia, ''Upstarts Aim to Be Comic Book Heroes,'' *Crain's New York Business*, April 6, 1992, p. 1.

''Swamp Thing's Quagmire,'' *Time*, July 10, 1989, p. 47.

Underwood, Elaine, and Betsy Spethmann, ''Superman, WB Fly at Best Western,'' *BRANDWEEK*, May 27, 1996, p. 4.

''Will Superman Fly?'' *Chain Store Age—General Merchandise Trends*, June 1987, p. 69.

Zinn, Laura, ''It's a Bird, It's a Plane—It's a Resurrection; Superman Returns on Apr. 15, But No One Knows What Form He'll Take,'' *Business Week*, April 12, 1993, p. 40.

—Daryl F. Mallett

Dollar Thrifty Automotive Group, Inc.

5330 East 31st Street
Tulsa, Oklahoma 74135
U.S.A.
(918) 660-7700
Fax: (918) 669-2934
Web sites: http://www.dollar.com
http://www.thrifty.com

Public Company
Incorporated: 1989 as Pentastar Transportation Group,
   Inc.
Employees: 5,200
Sales: $843.94 million (1997)
Stock Exchanges: New York
Ticker Symbol: DTG
SICs: 7614 Passenger Car Rentals

Dollar Thrifty Automotive Group, Inc. (DTAG), formerly known as Pentastar Transportation Group, Inc., a Chrysler Corporation subsidiary, owns two separate vehicle-rental companies, Dollar Rent A Car Systems, Inc. (Dollar) and Thrifty Rent-A-Car System, Inc. (Thrifty). These two companies function as separate vehicle-rental systems and also license independent franchisees to rent cars under the Dollar and Thrifty brand names. The businesses of Dollar and Thrifty complement each other but differ in their approach to the vehicle-rental market. Dollar and its licensees have suburban locations and on-airport locations at most major airports across the nation; their main focus is serving the leisure and international tour business. Dollar has more than 370 worldwide locations in 26 countries, including more than 230 locations in the United States. It is also significantly present in Australia, Canada, the Caribbean region, and Latin America. Through its alliance with Europcar International Corporation, Limited, one of the major European car-rental groups, Dollar offers services in 96 additional countries in Europe, the Middle East, Africa, and the Asia-Pacific regions. Thrifty, the only car-rental company with a franchising focus, derives its revenues primarily from franchising fees in both local markets and airports; it is a leading leaser of rental

vehicles in North America. Thrifty offers its franchisees a full line of services and products not easily or cost-effectively available from other sources. Thrifty operates in 63 countries and territories in nearly 1,200 locations throughout the Americas, Africa, Europe, the Middle East, and the Caribbean and Asia-Pacific regions. The Dollar and Thrifty brands represent a value-priced rental vehicle meant to appeal to a cost-conscious, value-sensitive market: leisure and discretionary customers (who typically are spending their own money), domestic and foreign tourists, small businesses, and independent business travelers. DTAG's two subsidiaries administer a combined fleet of approximately 100,000 vehicles.

Background: 1989–97

During the 1980s and early 1990s Detroit's Big Three automakers—Ford Motor Company, General Motors Corporation, and Chrysler Corporation—raced into diversification to prop up meager income from flat sales of cars. According to Dave Phillips's story in the April 14, 1996 issue of the *Detroit News,* the automakers soon built and sold almost everything. For instance, a Chrysler marine division made boats and outboard motors; General Motors manufactured earth-moving equipment; and Ford produced lawn and garden tractor equipment. The automakers' varied assets ranged from ownership of a data processing company and a credit card company to missile launchers, software developers, and car-rental companies.

Automakers initially acquired rental-car companies because they were a substantial portion of fleet sales, gave added exposure to some car models, kept the manufacturers' assembly plants running during times of slow car sales, and were a convenient place to unload cars that did not sell. In 1989 Chrysler formed the Pentastar Transportation Group, Inc. to operate its rental-car subsidiaries, which included General Rent-a-Car and Snappy Car Rental, Inc. Then Chrysler strengthened its stake in the car-rental business with the purchase of Thrifty Rent-A-Car System, Inc. in 1989 and of Dollar Rent A Car Systems, Inc. in 1990.

Automakers soon discovered, however, that side businesses occasionally provided new automotive technologies and often improved the bottom line but they also diverted management's time and attention away from the main business of focusing solely on cars and trucks. Consequently, during the latter part of the 1990s, shareholder pressure, booming stock prices, and a desperate need for capital to expand overseas prompted Detroit's Big Three auto manufacturers to sell their noncore businesses, including their car-rental companies. General Motors sold its interest in National Car Rental in 1995 and divested itself of Avis in 1997. When Ford sold its interest in Budget Rent a Car in 1997 to a group of franchise holders and kept only a minor stake in the Hertz Corporation, Chrysler became the last of the Big Three to own car-rental companies.

In 1993 Chrysler merged the operations of its General Rent-a-Car subsidiary into those of Dollar and in 1994 sold Snappy Car Rental, Inc. Unable to find a buyer for Thrifty and Dollar as separate entities, Chrysler reorganized the two car-rental companies into the Dollar Thrifty Automotive Group, Inc. (DTAG), a wholly owned subsidiary of Pentastar Transportation Group, Inc. (itself a wholly owned subsidiary of Chrysler). Pentastar then was merged into DTAG, which became the surviving subsidiary corporation. In November 1997 Chrysler announced that DTAG had filed with the U.S. Securities and Exchange Commission to offer its common stock. On December 23, 1997 DTAG completed its initial public offering (IPO). The company was traded on the New York Stock Exchange under the ticker symbol DTG.

DTAG Business Strategy: 1997

Data from publicly held U.S. car-rental companies and DTAG's experience indicated that until 1995 their industry had not kept pace with rising fleet costs. Furthermore, several of the domestic automotive manufacturers of the major U.S. vehicle-rental companies had been sold and were now publicly held. These changes in ownership led to higher car-rental rates, as a result of increased industry focus on profitability and shareholder returns rather than on transaction volume and market share. How would DTAG succeed as a company? It developed and began to implement a six-point strategy to increase revenues and improve profitability by strengthening its value-priced brands.

First, to capitalize on the changing industry dynamics described above, DTAG identified the benefits that would accrue to smaller independent and regional rental operators that became franchisees of national brands, such as those of Dollar or Thrifty. These benefits included better access to vehicle supply, more attractive financing, national marketing programs, and new technology. Second, DTAG expanded the market niches

already established by the national brands of its two subsidiaries, Dollar and Thrifty. Third, DTAG took advantage of the operating efficiencies resulting from its joint ownership of Dollar and Thrifty; namely, volume discounts for advertising, insurance, and information systems as well as the consolidation of some administrative functions and the sharing of facilities. Additional benefits resulted from the coordinated disposal of used cars, the transfer of vehicles between fleets to adjust to variations in regional demands, the development of joint training programs, and the referral of overflow customers from one system to the other.

Fourth, joint investments in strategic information and reservation systems enabled Dollar to introduce, and Thrifty to improve, customer-frequency and loyalty programs. Fifth, international operations were expanded by having Dollar and Thrifty accept rental reservations for each other in their respective geographical areas. In addition, both Dollar and Thrifty licensed foreign vehicle-rental companies as master franchisees for specific countries or regions. Sixth, to develop opportunities for business expansion into related areas, DTAG applied its experience in fleet leasing and management, used car disposal, and franchising. The company entered into joint ventures with new car dealer groups and used its existing telecommunications capacity to provide telemarketing services. Seventh, DTAG encouraged growth by linking incentive compensation to operating performance. DTAG implemented its business strategy through its two subsidiaries, Dollar and Thrifty.

Dollar Rent A Car Systems, Inc.: 1965–97

Dollar was incorporated in 1965 in Los Angeles, was acquired by Chrysler in 1990, moved its executive offices to Tulsa, Oklahoma in August 1994, and became part of DTAG in 1997. Focusing mainly on the leisure market and on tour operators, in 1997 Dollar had an average fleet of some 61,336 vehicles, compared with an average fleet of 52,571 cars in 1995. About 76 percent of Dollar's 1997 rental revenues came from operations in Florida, California, Hawaii, and Nevada. The company also provided a high level of service to foreign-tour operators, especially those in the United Kingdom. Dollar realized significant income from rentals to tour customers because they reserved vehicles for longer periods and canceled reservations less frequently. The many tourist attractions of central Florida made this area the most important leisure destination for rentals. Dollar operated a company-owned store at Orlando International Airport and a facility at the Orlando Sanford International Airport, located 25 miles north of Orlando. This facility, designed to serve mainly charter flights and to handle tour customers, had 42 rental stations and parking for approximately 1,600 vehicles.

Dollar's line of services and products included fleet leasing, centralized reservations, insurance, supplies (such as ski racks, mobile telephones, baby seats), and operational support. At year-end 1997 Dollar's vehicle rental system included 255 U.S. and Canadian locations consisting of 103 company-owned stores and 152 franchised stores. Dollar's total 1997 revenue was $617.53 million (of which 91 percent came from company-owned stores), compared with $499.17 million in 1996. Vehicle rentals by customers of foreign and domestic tour operators generated approximately 35 percent of these rental revenues. In

1997 Dollar was the exclusive U.S. car-rental company for three of its five largest tour-operator accounts.

To determine rental demand based on historical reservation patterns and adjust its rental rates accordingly, Dollar had an agreement with The SABRE Group, Inc. (SABRE), a leader in electronic-distribution systems for the travel industry. SABRE managed and monitored Dollar's data center network and its daily information processing. All of Dollar's key systems were housed in an Oklahoma underground SABRE facility designed to withstand disasters.

In December 1997 Dollar inked an alliance with Europcar International, one of the major European car-rental groups, to allow rental locations in the United States and in Europe to use both names, that is, that of Dollar Rent A Car and that of Europcar. In addition, Europcar agreed to reserve Dollar vehicles for its customers travelling to the United States, Canada, and Latin America. Dollar had operated under the name of EuroDollar in Europe, Africa, and the Middle East; however, the alliance with Europcar, effective February 1, 1998, ended the EuroDollar relationship and enabled travelers wanting to reserve rental cars in these countries to contact Dollar for Europcar rentals.

Thrifty Rent-A-Car System, Inc.: 1958–97

Thrifty (in this section, also referred to as the company) was founded in 1958 and in 1989 completed an IPO of common stock. Chrysler acquired Thrifty in 1991 and divested it as part of an IPO completed by DTAG. In contrast to major competitors who focused almost exclusively on the airport market, Thrifty concentrated on offering franchising and franchise-support services but it operated some company-owned stores in a few U.S. and Canadian cities. Typically, Thrifty established company-owned stores only upon the financial failure of a franchisee.

The company's approach to serving both the airport and the local markets within each territory enabled many of its franchisees and company-owned stores to have multiple locations: fleet utilization and profit margins could thereby be improved by moving vehicles among locations for better administration of differences in demand among their markets. As of year-end 1997, Thrifty's car-rental system comprised 636 U.S. and Canadian rental locations, of which 600 were franchised locations and 36 were company-owned stores. The Thrifty system also included 359 franchised locations in 63 other countries. In 1997 the company's total revenue reached $225.25 million, compared with $204.94 in 1996.

In addition to its U.S. suburban locations, Thrifty maintained a relationship with Montgomery Ward and operated rental facilities in many of the retailer's Auto Express Centers. In Canada, Thrifty had a similar relationship with Canadian Tire Corporation, Limited, a nationwide retail chain selling automotive products, sporting goods, home and garden hardware, and plumbing supplies. Thrifty Truck Rental and Ryder Consumer Truck Rental formed a North American alliance to recruit Ryder dealers as Thrifty franchise owners and vice-versa. Thrifty also functioned as the official car-rental company of the Black Coaches Association, an organization of minority basketball and football coaches, and of the United States Figure Skating Association, the national governing body for figure skating.

This agreement expanded both companies' core services, access to new customers, and opportunities for location growth.

Although Thrifty operated company-owned stores in a few U.S. and Canadian cities, its main focus was on franchising and franchise-support services. In fact, franchises were essential to its profitability and growth. For example, franchisees paid Thrifty an initial franchise fee based on such factors as population, number of airline passengers, total airport vehicle-rental revenues, and level of any other car-rental activity in the franchised territory. During the past few years, the company's average annual turnover rate for franchisees was approximately ten percent, with an average of 17 terminations and 25 new sales. For 1997, Thrifty's five largest U.S. franchisees generated administrative, fleet-leasing, reservation, and other fees that accounted for about 18 percent of Thrifty's total revenue. Fleet also offered franchisees a fleet-leasing program that provided them with a competitive and flexible source of fleet vehicles. For 1997, fleet-leasing fees accounted for about 58 percent of Thrifty's total revenue. Approximately 70 percent of Thrifty's revenue came from its franchises.

Thrifty's franchisees benefited from the company's continuously staffed worldwide reservation center headquartered in Tulsa, Oklahoma. In 1997 that center processed more than 4.4 million telephone calls and 1.6 million reservations. The center was linked to all of the major U.S. airline reservation systems and, through them, to worldwide travel agencies. Like Dollar, its companion subsidiary, Thrifty engaged SABRE to manage and monitor its data center network and daily information processing. The company also negotiated national account programs to allow its franchisees to take advantage of volume discounts for materials and services, such as tires, glass replacement, long distance telephone service, and overnight mail. Thrifty helped new franchisees to develop revenue opportunities, such as airport parking, used car sales, and truck rentals. Thrifty locations across the United States offer customers access to more than 14,000 airport parking spaces.

DTAG: 1997 and Beyond

At year-end 1997, DTAG total revenue peaked at $843.94 million, an increase of 20 percent over 1996 total revenue of $705.59 million in 1996. Without sacrificing the separate operating and brand identities of Dollar and Thrifty, DTAG planned to continue making investments in reservation, tour, and other information system improvements during 1998.

In only a few years the $16.4 billion rental-car business had changed a great deal. "The big automakers, which owned the rental companies, realized that their subsidiaries made ideal captive customers for cars they couldn't sell, and they dumped vehicles on them. With so much excess inventory, the rental companies launched into a bloody round of competitive price cutting. Losses rocketed, reaching an estimated $150 million in 1995," wrote reporter Alex Taylor III in the May 25, 1998 issue of *Fortune* magazine. The automakers were also losers; the rental fleets on used car lots stole new car sales. The Detroit Big Three, among others, sold their car-rental companies, which became independent public companies who could no longer depend on subsidies and "remodeled their businesses along the lines of airlines and hotels by using yield management," Taylor commented.

In short, whereas between 1986 and 1996, car-rental companies had focused mainly on market share, they were now independent public companies that had to assure profits for their shareholders. DTAG, therefore, faced a formidable challenge: not only that of increasing the revenues and improving the profitability of Dollar and Thrifty, whose loss of consolidated net income had gone from $40.48 million in 1993 to $146.28 million in 1996, but also that of keeping their individual identities. Analyzing DTAG's performance during its first year as a public company, one can say that DTAG was ready to drive into the 21st century at a steady, profitable rate.

Principal Subsidiaries

Dollar Rent A Car Systems, Inc.; Thrifty Canada, Ltd.; Thrifty Rent-A-Car System, Inc.

Further Reading

"Dollar Opens 4 New Locations," *Journal Record,* June 16, 1998.

Hildebrand, Steven, "Dollar Thrifty Automotive Group, Inc.," *Wall Street Journal,* February 25, 1998, p. B5.

King, Sharon, "Hoping To Follow in Others' Tread Marks," *New York Times*, December 14, 1997, p. 8.

Peltz, James F., "Car Rental Agencies Driving Up Profits with Higher Prices," *Los Angeles Times,* April 25, 1998.

Phillips, Dave, "Big 3 Shopping Spree Over; Now Comes the Yard Sale," *Detroit News,* April 14, 1996.

——, "Chrysler To Unload Thrifty, Dollar Rentals," *Detroit News,* November 7, 1997.

Taylor III, Alex, "Back in the Driver's Seat," *Fortune,* May 25, 1998.

Yung, Katherine, "Big 3 Existing Car Rental Business," *Detroit News,* January 15, 1997.

—Gloria A. Lemieux

Emery Worldwide Airlines, Inc.

One Lagoon Drive
Suite 400
Redwood City, California 94065
U.S.A.
(650) 596-9600
(800) 367-3592
Web site: http://www.emeryworld.com

Wholly owned subsidiary of CNF Transportation Inc.
Incorporated: 1946 as Emery Air Freight, Inc.
Employees: 7,000
Sales: $2.27 billion (1997)
SICs: 4213 Trucking; 4513 Air Courier Services; 4522
   Air Transportation, Nonscheduled; 4731 Arrangement
   of Transportation of Freight and Cargo; 4225 General
   Warehousing and Storage; 8742 Management
   Consulting Services

Emery Worldwide Airlines, Inc., commonly known as Emery Worldwide, is an integrated air freight carrier that provides services to 229 countries, carrying mainly business-to-business commercial parcel, package, and freight shipments over five pounds for next-day or second-day arrival. Other important Emery business units in the late 1990s were ocean freight transportation, logistics management, and customs brokerage. A pioneering company in air freight forwarding and for decades an acknowledged industry leader, Emery returned from a downward slide in the late 1980s to profitability and renewed prominence in the 1990s.

Rough Beginnings

Emery Air Freight was founded in 1946 as a freight-forwarding operation by navy veteran John Colvin Emery, Sr., who rejoined civilian life with experience in military air transport service. He would have returned to the Railway Express Agency (REA), where he had worked since 1937, if REA had shown interest in his air freight-forwarding ideas. But REA was not interested, so he began his own operation with three employees, two used trucks, $125,000 in borrowed money, and one customer—the Federal Reserve Bank of New York.

The first year, Emery moved 50 tons of air freight for $30,000. John C. Emery, Jr. served as Emery Air Freight's sales vice-president from the company's inception until 1956. Prior to joining the family business, he had spent one year with United Airlines and one year at National Airline.

Forwarders connected shippers with airlines, tracked shipments' progress from airport to airport, and then moved the cargo from final airport to final ground destination, using trucks or any other ground transportation deemed necessary. John, Sr. entered a niche market as part of the burgeoning air freight industry, which many armed forces veterans such as himself were creating. Such businesses included all-freight airlines like Slick Airways and the Flying Tiger Line, or forwarders of Emery Air Freight's caliber, which transported cargo to other freight lines as well as to regular passenger lines. The industry's potential was great, but obstacles loomed at every turn for the newcomers. For instance, when Slick—the nation's largest freight carrier in the late 1940s—and 18 other all-cargo carriers achieved common-carrier status in 1947, they were no longer permitted to give forwarders a rate break on the consolidated less-than-planeload shipment, one of the forwarders' bread-and-butter items.

The forwarders were a parvenu lot, as was the air freight industry as a whole, prompting the trade magazine Aviation Week to publish articles entitled ''Give Air Freight Its Chance'' in May of 1949 and ''Why Sneer at Air Freight?'' in December of 1950. References were made to air freighters' uphill battle against the passenger lines, for whom freight carriers were competitors and forwarders were barely-tolerated middle men.

Mid-Century Challenges

By 1951 half the forwarders were losing money, but among those who were succeeding, Emery was setting the pace. In a 1954 report citing wide variances in the scope of freight forwarding services, the national air-transport regulatory body, the Civil Aeronautics Board (CAB), commended Emery as the only

146

Company Perspectives:

Our goal is to exceed our customers' expectations by ensuring quality and excellence in every aspect of our business. We do this by providing complete global logistics services, multi-modal transportation, and customs brokerage for our customers. By placing emphasis on employee satisfaction, we will ensure our success in market leadership, shareholder value, and most importantly, customer satisfaction.

United States air freight forwarder operating nationwide. Emery had 30 branches in 18 states, plus another in the District of Columbia. Emery neither owned nor operated aircraft, and leased its automotive equipment. The company was moving 14,000 tons each year and grossing $7.2 million annually.

The advantage was speed at a premium price—or even savings—when air shipment reduced inventory. Emery could field an occasional call to get around surface shipment bottlenecks to keep a Detroit assembly line running, or regular calls to keep down inventory of parts to be assembled.

As the 1950s closed, any early industry disappointments had been forgotten and air cargo was scoring "impressive gains," according to *Business Week*. Though the company remained based in New York City, Emery's operations spread abroad to include eight European offices, including one office in London and two in Canada. The company had 29 U.S. offices by 1960. Gross revenues had reached $13.6 million in 1959, up $3 million from 1958's gross.

The jet age was approaching, meaning air freight would carry considerably more than small items like fresh fruit, vegetables, and flowers. The jets brought much greater capacity, but even then cargo was considered by the passenger lines as something to fill unused baggage space. American Airlines was the first passenger airline to go beyond that mindset by investing in "flying warehouses," or planes without windows designated for cargo-carrying purposes; other airlines followed suit soon thereafter.

Domination of the Market in the 1960s

By 1965 Emery Air Freight was "the tallest midget" among air freight-forwarders, John Emery, Sr. told *Business Week*. One hundred of those midgets were licensed by the CAB, and of those, only 50 were active. Forwarders now ferried freight by truck from shipper to airline, functioning as a carrier to the shipper and as a shipper to the airline. Airlines resented the need for a middle man, but air freight was growing faster than passenger service and forwarders could capitalize without investing in trucks, terminals, or aircraft. Emery leased its trucks, built a terminal, and booked space on passenger airlines.

Investors were impressed. In 1965 Emery's stock was almost 40 times greater than its earnings. The nearest competitor was the Air Express division of John Emery's former employer, Railway Express, but Emery's $38.5 million in reve-nues for 1964 exceeded those of the four nearest competitors combined. Emery had a strong international presence with agents everywhere in the world except South America. One of the passenger airlines's best customers—second only to the U.S. government—Emery could demand space otherwise unavailable.

Not everyone in the company had endorsed the high-speed, high-cost service which had become Emery's specialty, as opposed to the high-volume, low-margin approach generally typical of freight forwarding. But John Emery, Sr. had decided that competition with surface rates was out of the question.

Emery's revenues hit $46 million in 1965, and net profit rose nearly 50 percent to $2.7 million. Emery averaged 20 percent yearly growth in volume and had experienced an amazing 38 percent growth in profits since the early 1950s. The firm was forwarding 10 percent of the $600-million air freight volume—all without owning a single plane—and hauling more than 1.5 million shipments a year, totaling well over 100 million pounds for 20,000 customers.

In 1961, the year Emery relocated headquarters to a leased office building in Wilton, Connecticut, Emery acquired ground facilities at Bradley Air Field in Hartford, Connecticut. Emery had 50 U.S. offices and, in addition to Europe, was reaching the Middle East, Japan, the Philippines, Hong Kong, South Africa, Australia, and New Zealand from points in the United States. Likewise, Emery's service connected the United States, Canada, Japan, Australia, New Zealand, and South Africa from points in Europe. Emery owned airport terminal buildings in New York City, Chicago, and Detroit, and was building one in Los Angeles. The company used working capital to construct terminals and only built upon leased land.

John, Sr. resigned in 1961; he died eight years later. In the interim period from 1963 to 1969 John, Jr. acted as executive vice-president of Emery. He had become president upon his father's death; veteran Emery operations director James J. McNulty remained chairman. The company's revenues were pushing $100 million. Emery had 2,000 employees in 96 offices around the world and served some 350 cities with airports and ten times as many within airport "trading centers."

Changes in the 1970s

In the early 1970s, not long after John Emery, Sr.'s death, the air freight world began to change considerably. Passenger airlines, hit by rising fuel costs, cut back on freight-only schedules. At first, Emery rode high as usual with revenues of $142 million in 1972 and $175 million in 1973. Emery's bicycle fleet, riding the teeming streets of big cities, was beefed up. Emery also employed a strategy of using alternate carriers—primarily chartered planes. This "air taxi" service became important for Emery, which depended on such obscure operations as the Des Moines-based Sedalia-Marshall-Boonville Stage Line, which nightly carried machinery, auto parts, and the like in vintage World War II DC-3s along the Omaha-Chicago route.

Emery improvised to counter the slipping economy by drumming up more business for late-night shipping. The company supported freight rate increases for the major airlines. John C. Emery, Jr. testified before the Civil Aeronautics Board for United Airlines, Emery Air Freight's biggest supplier. Emery knew a market existed for overnight service—which businesses used to maintain tight inventory control in the poor economic climate—higher priced or not. John Emery's company could afford the higher rates as his business was booming.

The number of U.S. offices grew to 77 in 1975 and Emery had 112 offices worldwide; the company was providing service almost everywhere. John, Jr. became chief executive officer of Emery that year, as revenues and profits rose steadily. REA Express Inc., John Emery Sr.'s former company, went out of business in 1975, leaving the field open to Emery and a newcomer, Federal Express Corporation.

Competition with Federal Express in the 1980s

In 1978, two years after Federal Express became profitable under the leadership of its president, Arthur C. Bass, Emery started a small-package business. The creation of Emery Express required making major investments in equipment, a move that violated the debt-avoidance formulas of the company's early history. The coming of Federal Express had proved ominous for Emery, however, as the two firms dueled in the new business of small-package delivery. Investments were necessary in order to compete.

Under newly-appointed board chairman John Emery, Jr., Emery moved from freight forwarding with other parties' planes in the 1970s to freight transportation in the 1980s using its own. Emery was forced to do this, in part, by the passenger airlines's reluctance and/or inability to carry freight as was done in the 1970s. Emery was literally using fly-by-night taxi services, but in order to compete with Federal Express the corporation needed more access to air transportation than was available—the airlines were no longer an option.

In 1981 Emery, rechristened Emery Worldwide, bought 24 Boeing 727 freighters and leased 40 other planes, taking on a long-term debt of $130 million—more than 60 percent of the company's total capital. Emery mimicked the Federal Express national-hub system, constructing a "superhub" in Dayton, Ohio, to which all intercity packages were directed for sorting and reshipment no matter their size or U.S. point of origin. These costly adaptations were temporarily successful. Profits rose 145 percent in 1983 to a record $25 million and yielded record revenues of $683 million.

In 1985 Emery opened a European hub in the Netherlands, leasing cargo planes to fly there nonstop from Dayton. The company was, therefore, competing in two markets—the small-package market in which Federal Express was the clear leader, and the heavyweight market in which Emery had traditionally performed well. The heavier-weight market grew sharply as companies began to emulate the Japanese "just-in-time" inventory system. Air freight, once considered just an emergency service, became an everyday procedure. John Emery, Jr. predicted in *The Economist* that only half of the air freight in 10 years would be made up of emergency service.

But the "steep climb" of air express, as air freight was now called in deference to its faster-growing segment, was reaching altitudes that proved dizzying for some. By mid-1986 Purolator Courier Corporation, the fourth-largest ground-only company among U.S. carriers, was losing money badly. Emery, third behind Federal Express and United Parcel Service (UPS), was suffering losses too—but not as damaging.

Losses in the Late 1980s

The problem was, in part, a maturing market. An estimated 95 percent of U.S. cities and towns had air express service. At least eight companies, not including the U.S. Postal Service, were competing for what had become a limited market. Federal Express and UPS were cash-rich, but Emery, whose income plummeted in 1986 from nearly $40 million to $18 million, was doing worse than expected. *Fortune* even revealed that John Emery, Jr. had been calling major customers to say, "I'm John Emery and I care." By 1988 Emery Air Freight was in financial trouble.

Seeking a way out of carrying both large and small items by air and conducting less than half its business as overnight delivery, Emery turned to a small-package specialist, Purolator, a company also having difficulties. Emery bought Purolator for $323 million in April of 1987 to handle small-package capacities, but the purchase was too late. A limping company had bought a sick—if not mortally wounded—company, and the relationship did not thrive. Emery had simply failed to capitalize on previous heavy investments in overnight capabilities, and was losing out to Federal Express.

Seeking to integrate Purolator's operations, Emery closed Purolator's Indianapolis hub and rerouted Purolator's more than 50,000 packages a day to Dayton. Unable to handle the added load, the Dayton location had to be remodeled. Months after the acquisition, Emery and Purolator were still competing with each other on many routes. Operating costs rose sharply for the now-parent Emery. Talk of a takeover erupted, but even that seemed inopportune because Emery stock, though depressed, was not low enough.

The upshot was an apparent "palace revolt" staged by Emery directors in late December of 1988, in which John C. Emery, Jr. was removed as chief executive and replaced by an Emery director—retired Xerox Corp. executive William F. Souders. Emery's stock price doubled in one month as takeover artists bought up shares. Among suspected bidders were Federal Express, Emery's archrival; a California-based trucking company called Consolidated Freightways, Inc.; and a separate group headed by former Federal Express president Arthur C. Bass.

But Emery was not selling. Indeed, Emery may have bought Purolator precisely to fend off a takeover. Instead, Emery ended up paying much of the Purolator-induced debt by selling Purolator's auto-parts business. The company was madly cutting costs and prices to stay in business. Emery also hinted at filing for voluntary bankruptcy. Both Arthur Bass and Consolidated Freightways, Inc., apparently gave up plans for buying Emery.

Takeover by Consolidated Freightways

Consolidated then changed its mind, however. The California company bought Emery on April 3, 1989, for $478 million. Consolidated's chief executive, Lary Scott, had a history of going against the dictates of conventional wisdom, as exemplified when he built the first national long-haul freight delivery system in the mid-1970s, and when he set up a series of regional truckers specializing in next-day delivery in the early 1980s. Under his leadership and that of the company's chairman, Raymond F. O'Brien, Consolidated had become the top hauler of less-than-truckload—or under 10,000 pounds of freight in the United States. Both Consolidated's revenues and profits had doubled in the 1980s.

With Emery, however, Scott faced a losing proposition which to many looked hopeless; $32 million in losses were incurred the two quarters following Consolidated's acquisition. The venture gave Consolidated instant capability in the international arena. "This global thing is not a fad," Scott insisted in *Business Week*, as he looked to European and Asian traffic.

Scott placed at the head of Emery Worldwide a 19-year Consolidated veteran, Donald Berger, the head of Consolidated's CF AirFreight, with which Emery's operations were merged. Berger withdrew Emery from competition with Federal Express, virtually limiting the company's business to industrial freight averaging over 300 pounds. Major new contracts with the U.S. Postal Service and IBM gave Berger and Scott confidence. But the announced intent to specialize in heavy freight gave a mixed signal to customers whom Emery could not afford to lose. In the third quarter of 1989, Emery withstood a 20 percent loss in shipping volume, consisting mostly of the small freight which Berger had declared unwelcome. Emery's operating loss—$40 million by the year's end—decimated Consolidated's earnings, which sank from $113 million to $12 million. In addition, Emery's billing mistakes overstated revenues forcing a $19-million write-off.

On July 30, 1990, Scott, yet another casualty in the ongoing effort to revive Emery's success, resigned as CEO of Consolidated Freightways, Inc. after 23 years with the company, including two years with Emery in tow. Business Week reported that Consolidated was "in sorry shape, thanks to Emery," which had suffered $100 million in operating losses within six months. Corporate parent Consolidated had lost $37.5 million in the same period and stock had dropped from 37¾ to almost 15 in a slide that had reduced its market capitalization by almost $800 million.

Chairman Raymond O'Brien, 68 years old and a former Consolidated CEO, returned to the helm; a 69-year-old Consolidated director was assigned the presidency. Talk arose of selling Emery. Five weeks after Scott's departure, Arthur Bass, the former Federal Express president who had once wanted to buy Emery, was hired to head the sinking flagship, but he lasted only five months.

Stemming Losses in the Early 1990s

Bass was replaced in March of 1991 by W. Roger Curry as part of a new Consolidated management team headed by new president and CEO, retired former chief financial officer Donald E. Moffitt. Moffitt directed his efforts at Emery, which was dragging Consolidated down with losses that averaged $97 million a year. Moffitt and Curry decided to pull Emery from direct competition with Federal Express. Emery had traditionally emphasized heavy freight delivery, business-to-business,

on the same or second day. In renewed pursuit of this old goal, Emery's average shipment weight rose to 124 pounds in 1991 from an average of 45 pounds in 1990. The company more than doubled its fleet of DC-8 jet airplanes during the year, adding 17 for a total of 30; all but two of them were leased.

In addition to this shift to overnight delivery of mid- and heavyweight freight, Emery needed to cut costs. Moffitt and Curry directed managers to reduce expenses in whatever way necessary. Over the next year and a half, Emery's costs were reduced by $200 million by laying off 2,000 employees, giving up terminal space, and making other such cuts.

The company also expended money in order to make money. It instituted a new incentive program for salespeople that offered substantial bonuses for signing on new clients. Sales increased 37 percent over the first two years of the program. A profit-sharing program was also begun to motivate employees to work for the company's turnaround. In 1994 nonunion workers and management divided approximately $20 million in profit.

Emery still lost money in 1991, but only $83 million compared to $127 million in 1990. A contract with the U.S. Postal Service to fly express and priority mail to 32 U.S. cities helped the company's bottom line, and increased stockholders' and customers' confidence. Additional contracts with the government to ship Desert-Storm-related supplies for the military also pushed up Emery's revenues. Other nongovernmental contracts followed, such as a "primary carrier" contract with General Motors.

In the first quarter of 1992, Emery lost less than it had during the same period the previous year, and this achievement came without the onetime $10 million gain from Desert Storm work. In September 1992 Emery reported its first monthly profit since being acquired by Consolidated. Emery remained part of a Consolidated strategy to go international. Consolidated's customers were operating globally, and without Emery, Consolidated could not serve them fully. With Emery, Consolidated could reach 88 countries. As part of this international plan, Emery created a logistics subsidiary, Emery Global Logistics, in 1992. The subsidiary's custom logistics solutions provided customers with warehousing, inventory management, order fulfillment, and distribution.

Turnaround Assured in Mid-1990s

Cutting costs and refocusing on mid- and heavyweight freight brought Emery firmly back into the black. In 1993 the company reported $1.3 billion in revenues. More important, profits for the year reached $16.6 million, the first annual profit for Emery in seven years. The turnaround seemed secure when Emery won a ten-year contract from the U.S. Postal Service to operate its Express Mail air transportation system, a contract valued at $1 billion.

By 1994, the company's operating profits had risen to $77 million. In addition, the company had captured 24 percent of the over-70-pound freight market, placing it in front of its nearest competitor by 11 points. From this secure position, Emery raised its rates 7.2 percent in October 1994.

In 1995 the company launched Emery Expedite! to provide quick-response, door-to-door service using trucks, aircraft charters, and next-flight-out air transport. The following year parent Consolidated Freightways divested its long-haul motor carrier unit. As part of the spin-off, the parent company was renamed CNF Transportation Inc.

In 1997 an extended strike at United Parcel Service threw Emery into a turmoil. Emery's shipping counts tripled during the strike and the company added approximately 100 temporary workers and nine flights to meet this new demand. Because of the high cost of temporarily leasing additional aircraft and trucks, Emery did not necessarily profit from the rush of business. However, the strike did offer Emery the opportunity to permanently expand its customer base, by winning away disgruntled UPS customers.

Emery's goal of increasing international business had made good progress by 1997. In 1993 international business contributed about 20 percent of Emery's revenues. By 1997 that figure had risen to 43 percent. The company planned to increase that to 50 percent in 1998.

Profits continued to rise at the rejuvenated Emery: operating income rose in 1997 to 109.3 million on revenues of $2.27 billion. The good times looked to continue, in part because Emery won another important contract from the U.S. Postal Service. A $1.7 billion contract to run the USPS Priority Mail service on the east coast was awarded to Emery in 1997.

Principal Divisions

Airlines; Ocean Services; Customs Brokers; Global Logistics; Emery Expedite!

Further Reading

"Air Freight Forwarder Finds Ceiling Unlimited," *Business Week,* October 16, 1965.

"Air Freight: The Passenger Lines Are Winning Out," *Business Week,* December 11, 1954.

"Anything to the Ends of the Earth by Air Freight," *Newsweek,* January 19, 1953.

Beauchamp, Marc, "This Global Thing Is Not a Fad," *Business Week,* December 11, 1989.

Biesada, Alexandra, "Con Freight's Coming U-Turn," *Financial World,* April 30, 1991, p. 17.

"The Big Guns Aiming at Emery Air," *Business Week,* February 1, 1988.

Colodny, Mark M., "A Rolling Stone Is Freight Firm Boss," *Fortune,* October 22, 1990.

Dumaine, Brian, "Turbulence Hits the Air Couriers," *Fortune,* July 21, 1986.

"The Emery Overnight Express," *Business Week,* September 25, 1978.

Hamilton, Joan O'C., "Emery Is One Heavy Load for Consolidated Freightways," *Business Week,* March 26, 1990.

——, "Is Emery Too Heavy for Consolidated Freight?" *Business Week,* August 13, 1990.

Hoffman, Thomas, "Strike Chokes Delivery Systems," *Computerworld,* August 11, 1997, pp. 1–2A.

"Holding Pattern," *Forbes,* August 24, 1987.

"How Emery Lives with Airline Cutbacks," *Business Week,* January 19, 1974.

"Keep On Truckin'," *Forbes,* August 20, 1990.

King, Resa W., "Will the Palace Revolt Deliver Emery from Red Ink?" *Business Week,* January 18, 1988.

Krause, Kristin S., "CNF Subsidiary Widens Its Lead over BAX Global," *Traffic World,* February 9, 1998.

Levy, Robert, "Hourglass Figure," *Dun's Review,* September, 1966.

Lewis, Kate Bohner, "Full Circle," *Forbes,* March 27, 1995, pp. 56–57.

"Mercurial (Air Freight)," *The Economist,* September 26, 1985.

Norman, James R., Resa W. King and Dean Foust, "Why Emery Is Biting Its Nails," *Business Week,* August 29, 1988.

"Ten Tons in the Morning," *Forbes,* January 18, 1982.

Thruelsen, Richard, "They Deliver the Goods—and Fast!" *Saturday Evening Post,* December 3, 1955.

Tracy, Eleanor Johnson, "Emery Flies High Again," *Fortune,* March 19, 1984.

—Jim Bowman
—updated by Susan Windisch Brown

ENCAD

ENCAD, Incorporated

6059 Cornerstone Court West
San Diego, California 92121
U.S.A.
(619) 452-0882
(888) 436-2347
Fax: (619) 452-0891
Web site: http://www.encad.com

Public Company
Incorporated: 1981
Employees: 455
Sales: $149.04 million (1997)
Stock Exchanges: NASDAQ
Ticker Symbol: ENCD
SICs: 3577 Computer Peripheral Equipment, Not
    Elsewhere Classified

ENCAD, Incorporated is an innovator and market leader in the field of wide-format computer inkjet printers. ENCAD's printers produce high-quality color images on a variety of surfaces for use in the computer-aided design, graphic arts, sign-making, and fashion industries. With distribution to over 67 countries, exclusive manufacturing arrangements with major corporations such as Xerox and Eastman Kodak, and a history of technical leadership, the company is in a strong position to defend its turf against aggressive competition from industry giant Hewlett-Packard.

Beginnings

ENCAD was founded in 1981 by David Purcell and two partners as a maker of pen-plotter printers, devices that were used to print computer-generated images such as blueprints and industrial designs. Purcell had been involved in the formation of several businesses since 1969, the first of which was Celtec, a firm that represented technical manufacturers. In 1976, Purcell cofounded a capacitor manufacturing business, Bishop Electronics, and several years later participated in the formation of

Ryno Electronics, a chip distributor. ENCAD was initially run out of Purcell's home. The new company's first product was introduced in 1982, a pen-plotter printer that featured several improvements over existing designs. ENCAD cofounder Richard Murray, who had worked for several years at Hewlett-Packard, was the company's chief technical officer, and oversaw the creation of its new products. While sales were respectable at first, the company had strong competition from the much larger Hewlett-Packard, which controlled 70 percent of the market.

ENCAD's annual sales reached an early peak of $3 million for fiscal 1983, but a downturn soon followed, and the company was forced to reduce its personnel from 75 to 16. After struggling along for several more years, ENCAD developed a faster, cheaper, and sharper wide-format color pen-plotter, which kept the company alive, if not exactly thriving. During these early years, there were several times when the company appeared to be on the brink of collapse, but Purcell was able to come up with a last-minute strategy that managed to keep the wolf from the door. In early 1991 things looked particularly bleak, with the company being refused a loan of $600,000, which it needed to complete development of a new inkjet printer. Going against the advice of his board of directors, Purcell put up his own personal assets to keep the company alive. His faith in ENCAD paid off within months, however, when the company introduced the NovaJet printer. This newly designed wide-format inkjet printer was the first of its type on the market, and its low price and high-quality printing work made it an instant success. Compared to a pen-plotter device, the NovaJet offered higher-resolution images, a wider range of colors, and was as much as 20 times faster. Within a year ENCAD's annual sales had increased 253 percent, from under $5 million to nearly $15 million. The company's sales of pen-plotters, which had constituted over three-fourths of total revenues, dropped to less than a fifth of total sales.

1993: NovaJet II Introduced; Stock Offered on NASDAQ Exchange

In March 1993, less than two years after its first big leap in sales, ENCAD introduced its second-generation version of the

Company Perspectives:

Our strategy for future growth is to focus on select high-growth markets. We are targeting the signage and textile markets, and may target other high-growth markets in the future. Within the signage and textile markets, we plan to add products with greater productivity and more value-added, technology-driven features.

Our goal is to continue setting new quality and productivity standards as a leader in our targeted markets and to grow ENCAD into a large and highly profitable company. Today, ENCAD offers the best products in the markets we serve, and we plan to continue to offer our customers exciting new imaging products and technologies. We also have in place one of the strongest distribution networks in the industry, and we benefit from the support of more independent software vendors than any of our competitors. Our management team has a well-defined long-term growth strategy and has demonstrated an ability to rapidly innovate and implement strategic initiatives for growth.

NovaJet design. While the original NovaJet had been a significant improvement over pen-plotters, it had still not been able to render photographic images with precision. The new version offered a distinct improvement in this area, with 300 by 300 dot-per-inch (dpi) resolution and streak-free printouts of photographs. The response from buyers was immediate, with users in the graphic arts enthusiastically joining ENCAD's clientele, which already included computer-aided designers such as engineers, architects, surveyors, and map-makers. ENCAD's product line at this time included 36- and 48-inch wide NovaJet printers, and three models of pen-plotters.

Chief competitor Hewlett-Packard, which had been caught off-guard by ENCAD's release of the first NovaJet, introduced its own wide-format inkjet printer in May 1993, and soon gobbled up a majority of the market. Fortunately for ENCAD, sales of wide-format printers were increasing exponentially, and the company did not suffer greatly from this competition. The company's sales had for some time been expanding to overseas markets, with some half of revenues coming from abroad by the start of the 1990s. Over the next few years ENCAD would open sales offices in several important foreign business regions. ENCAD products were being sold through a growing network of over 60 distributors, who supplied hundreds of resellers internationally.

ENCAD's stock was first offered on the NASDAQ exchange in December 1993. The offering was a success, with the price surging over the next several years. At around this time ENCAD began signing a series of "Original Equipment Manufacturer" (OEM) agreements with different companies, starting with LaserMaster and continuing on to Japanese printer manufacturer GraphTec. This type of agreement allowed ENCAD to manufacture specific versions of its products for other companies, who would sell the product under their own brand names. Within several years printers produced under OEM agreements would comprise a quarter of the company's sales. Another

increasing source of revenue for ENCAD was "consumables," or inks and special printing media (such as paper rolls) that were used by owners of its printers. In 1993 this accounted for only five percent of revenues, but the figure grew to eight percent by 1996 and was expected to reach 20 percent in 1998.

As the success of its products gave ENCAD a reputation for quality, it was able to introduce other lines of printers to sell to different segments of the market. The lower-priced CADJet line was introduced in 1994. One of the primary selling points of all ENCAD products, including the NovaJet line, had been affordability. For many of its customers, the NovaJet printer allowed the convenience of doing work in-house that had previously been farmed out to print shops that owned expensive large-format electrostatic or thermal printing equipment. The NovaJet printers were low enough in price to be affordable (costing between $6,000 and $17,000, depending on size and other factors), and their ability to eliminate turnaround times of up to several days was extremely useful to time-dependent customers such as advertising agencies or presentation graphics designers.

ENCAD manufactured its printers using outside companies, who did the injection molding and steel fabrication. The final assembly and testing was done by ENCAD, with the design of products also handled in-house. Hewlett-Packard was one of the companies that ENCAD purchased components from, and this led to the first of several lawsuits initiated by the larger concern against ENCAD. A claim that the company was violating a patent used to produce a metal encoder strip was settled in early 1995, with ENCAD agreeing to make royalty payments. The newer models of NovaJet printers had already been designed around this part, so the problem was not a major one for the company. In mid-1995 an OEM agreement with Xerox was announced, with Xerox to use NovaJet printers as components of products to be sold under the Xerox name. ENCAD's annual sales were growing by leaps and bounds, reaching $65.5 million in 1995 and $107.4 million in 1996, with profits exceeding 10 percent of those figures each year.

1996: Innovative Outdoor Printing Systems Introduced

In addition to signing OEM agreements, ENCAD was also working with other outside companies to come up with ideas for new products. After several years of experimentation, in 1996 the company announced that DuPont had developed newly formulated inks that could be used outdoors, and, with a special coating, would withstand years of exposure to the fading powers of the sun. This brought a significant number of new customers to the company, as sign-making companies snapped up ENCAD products. An OEM agreement with the Japanese GraphTec company led to the development of a specialized printer that could dispense durable inks onto a vinyl surface, then cut the vinyl with great precision, creating another innovative new application for sign makers.

Early in 1997, ENCAD introduced its largest wide-format printer yet, the 60-inch NovaJet PROe model. The company had for some time commanded the majority of the graphic arts wide-format printer market, as its reputation for quality and innovation was widely known. ENCAD also signed an OEM agreement with Kodak to produce some of the new printers to be sold under the Kodak name as part of a specially customized, full-featured imaging system. The new OEM agreement added more fuel to the company's rivalry with Hewlett-Packard, as the larger company had been dumped as Kodak's supplier of wide-format printers in the process. Although sales in ENCAD's Asian markets had experienced a sharp decline for several years running, the company posted another record year for 1997, with $149 million in sales, profits again amounting to more than ten percent of that figure.

While Hewlett-Packard continued to dominate the overall market that ENCAD was a part of, its sights were still set on weakening or eliminating its competitor. Several other patent infringements were claimed, though these were dismissed in August 1997. The larger company (its annual sales amounted to some $38.4 billion in 1996) had the resources to sell its products at a rock-bottom price, which forced ENCAD to cut its own prices (and profits) to compete. Hewlett-Packard also started a trade-in program, offering generous allowances to customers who brought in an ENCAD printer when purchasing a new Hewlett-Packard model. By late 1997 Hewlett-Packard had surpassed ENCAD in sales to the graphic arts market for the first time.

ENCAD continued to introduce innovative products, however, countering the attacks of its competitor by creating new markets for itself. In the spring of 1998 the company introduced an inkjet printer that could print high-resolution images directly onto specially coated fabrics, a concept that appealed greatly to the fashion industry. The standard method of testing new fabric patterns was expensive and could take six to eight weeks, but the ENCAD Digital Textile System offered same-day turn-around. Sales were expected to be brisk, perhaps even surpassing those of the company's previous products within several years. The NovaJet PRO 600e printer was also announced. This latest update of the NovaJet series was ENCAD's first printer with 600 by 600 dpi resolution.

Having gone from being a small, continually struggling concern during the 1980s to a major player in the wide-format printer market of the late 1990s, the success of ENCAD showed that the perseverance of its founders and the company's innovative designs could win it a significant market share despite the efforts of the Goliath-like Hewlett-Packard to vanquish it. Its continued success would likely depend on those same factors, as the competition for market share continued unabated. With the frequent introduction of new products that were likely to find wide acceptance within their target markets, it appeared that the company would hold its own for some time to come.

Further Reading

Aguilera, Mario, "ENCAD Looking for an Encore to Match 1993," *San Diego Daily Transcript*, May 24, 1994, p. 1.

Allen, Mike, "Just Like Magic, Printer Reproducing Itself Too," *San Diego Business Journal*, January 9, 1995, p. 1.

Bauder, Don, "ENCAD Battles a 'Predatory' Hewlett-Packard," *San Diego Union-Tribune*, March 29, 1998, p. I-2.

Bigelow, Bruce, "The Big Picture—Printer Maker Erases Red Ink to Become an Indelible Success," *San Diego Union-Tribune*, June 13, 1995, p. C-1.

——, "ENCAD, H-P Keep Squirting Ink at Each Other," *San Diego Union-Tribune*, August 9, 1997, p. C-1.

——, "ENCAD Unveils Printer for Fabrics," *San Diego Union-Tribune*, March 12, 1998, p. C-1.

——, "H-P Grabs ENCAD Market Share," *San Diego Union-Tribune*, April 24, 1998, p. C-1.

——"Nimble Little ENCAD Must Face Formidable Foe," *San Diego Union-Tribune*, February 21, 1998, p. C-1.

——, "Ranking the Region's Publicly Traded Companies 8: ENCAD," *San Diego Union-Tribune*, April 28, 1998, p. T-7.

Burris, Bill, "ENCAD Going Public on Its NovaJet Success," *San Diego Daily Transcript*, December 3, 1993, p. 1.

"CEO Interview—ENCAD, Inc." *Wall Street Transcript*, May 30, 1994.

"Corporate Profiles 1995: ENCAD Goes Public As Market Eats Up NovaJets I, II & III," *San Diego Daily Transcript*, January 23, 1995, p. 37.

Finnerty, Brian, "The New America: ENCAD, Inc., San Diego, California—Building a New Market in Large Printers," *Investor's Business Daily*, April 28, 1995, p. A4.

——, "New America in Large-Sized Color Printers," *Investor's Business Daily*, July 11, 1994, p. A6.

Karabell, Shellie, "David Purcell, Chairman and CEO of ENCAD" [Interview], *Dow Jones Investor Network*, February 28, 1996.

Krause, Reinhardt, "The New America: ENCAD, Inc., San Diego, California—Printer Maker Faces Off Against Sun, Wind, Rain," *Investor's Business Daily*, September 13, 1996, p. A4.

Levaux, Janet Purdy, "The New America: ENCAD, Inc., San Diego California—Working the Wide Side of Inkjet Color Printing," *Investor's Business Daily*, March 11, 1996, p. A4.

Marsh, Ann, "Picture Perfect," *Forbes*, August 11, 1997, p. 120.

Tarsala, Michael, "Leaders & Success: ENCAD's David Purcell," *Investor's Business Daily*, April 2, 1997, p. A1.

—Frank Uhle

Gets you back where you belong.℠

Farmers Insurance Group of Companies

4680 Wilshire Boulevard
Los Angeles, California 90010
U.S.A.
(213) 932-3200

Wholly Owned Subsidiary of Zurich Financial Services Group
Incorporated: 1927 as Farmers Automobile Inter-Insurance Exchange
Employees: 16,000
Total Assets: $10 billion (1997)
SICs: 6311 Life Insurance; 8741 Management Services

Farmers Insurance Group of Companies was a wholly owned subsidiary of B.A.T. Industries from 1988 until B.A.T.'s merger with Zurich Insurance Company, scheduled to be completed in 1998. The fifth largest property and casualty insurer in the United States in 1997, the company is headquartered in Los Angeles and operates in 30 states with a distribution network of over 16,000 employees. As a reciprocal insurer, the company is an industry leader in auto, fire, truck, and life insurance, as well as other customer services.

Founding Fathers, the 1920s

The company was the brainchild of cofounders John C. Tyler and Thomas E. Leavey, who started Farmers Automobile Inter-Insurance in 1927 to offer preferred insurance rates to rural drivers—an overlooked market. Tyler, the son of an insurance salesman from rural South Dakota, believed that farmers and ranchers, who had better driving rates than urbanites due to the lowered likelihood of accidents, ought to receive lower premiums. His partner, Thomas Leavey, also came from a rural background, and had worked for the Federal Farm Loan Bureau and the National Farm Loan Association prior to founding the company.

From the beginning, Farmers was organized as a reciprocal insurer or inter-insurance exchange. In other words, policy holders function as subscribers, exchanging contracts with each other to provide insurance against certain losses. Tyler became

president and Leavey vice-president of the new company, and a sales manager and secretary completed the original staff of four employees. The company issued three million shares of common stock in 1927, as the Farmers Automobile Inter-Insurance Exchange. Tyler and Leavey convened the first meeting of the board of governors on March 28, 1928. Two weeks later, the company sold its first policy, insuring a 1928 Cadillac Phaeton.

The first two years of business proved the rural niche market to be fruitful. Forty thousand policies were issued, and the staff was expanded from four to 46, with 700 agents working out of 44 district offices. By 1931, the company worked in nine states, and by 1932, the Exchange's assets were $1.08 million with net written premiums of $1.43 million.

Depression Years

The effects of the Depression meant closed doors for over 70 percent of stock insurance companies in the 1930s. Farmers not only survived, but grew stronger during this period. Prior to the bank moratorium declared by President Roosevelt in 1933, Farmers had converted all bank holdings into large cash reserves. Thus, when all national banks were closed, Farmers paid its claims in cash, rather than the non-negotiable paper payments made by other insurers. The company was tested by another disaster in 1933, when southern California was wrecked by a severe earthquake that damaged cars and buildings. Farmers again earned its customers' respect by paying for all earthquake damage to cars under collision coverage, even though no such comprehensive coverage existed at the time.

Expansion and growth continued in the latter half of the 1930s. In 1935, a new reciprocal company, Truck Insurance Exchange, was launched to specialize in truck insurance. Farmers expanded into Kansas City and the midwestern states, and later moved into the Southwest. In 1936, the company was named the leading reciprocal in earned premiums for auto insurance by *National Underwriter.* The next year, premium income was just under $4 million—almost triple growth in just five years. In 1937, Farmers opened its Home Office on Wilshire Boulevard in Los Angeles. By 1940, Farmers was the leading Auto insurance carrier in the Pacific Northwest, with a new regional office open in Portland, Oregon. In 1942, Farmers added a third reciprocal company, the Fire Insurance Exchange.

Gasoline Rationing and Increased Expansion, World War II Era

Gasoline rationing during World War II did not significantly hurt Farmers profits. In 1943, assets reached $9.81 million and direct premiums were $8.82 million, with operations in 19 states. At the end of World War II, gasoline rationing stopped and prewar cars came out of garages and onto the streets. The poor mechanical quality of newly operational vehicles triggered a high rate of insurance claims, causing every insurance writer in the country severe losses. Farmers was able to withstand the claim volume due to its semi-annual renewal system (which allowed the company to adjust its rates to compensate for losses) and its corporate structure.

Growth continued in the late 1940s, with a new regional office in Colorado Springs and expansion of the Los Angeles home office. In 1948, when the company celebrated its 20th anniversary, the three Exchanges' policies had reached 693,610 with assets of $30 million. Annual auto insurance claims almost reached 200,000, with over 22,000 truck claims. Farmers boasted a 90-day-or-less settlement rate for 79 percent of bodily injury claims and 74 percent of truck claims. Between 1949 and 1954, the company expanded into Wyoming, Texas, Illinois, Michigan, and Indiana. The role of regional offices was expanded to respond to growing business, and six more regional offices were added.

Two more companies were added to the Exchange in the 1950s. In 1950, the Mid-Century Insurance Company was organized as a multi-line carrier and a wholly owned subsidiary of the Farmers Insurance Exchange. In addition to services provided by the existing three Exchanges, Mid-Century offered coverage for Inland Marine, robbery, felony, burglary, personal lines, plate glass, selected bonds, and floaters. In 1953, Farmers acquired the Seattle-based New World Life Insurance Company, with assets of $27 million.

New Programs and Diversification, 1950s and 1960s

In 1958, written premiums reached $158 million for the Exchange as a whole. Between 1948 and 1958, the Fire Exchange grew from $575,000 in written premiums to $7.3 million, and the Truck Exchange quadrupled from $9 million to $36 million. In the late 1950s and early 1960s, the company built upon this growth by diversifying and adding new programs, including the 30/60 policy for mature drivers and the Truck Exchange's Sentinel policies (among the first comprehensive commercial packages), the first monthly pay plan that was not a finance plan (1961), and the first drive-in claims office

(1962). In 1959, Farmers began what would be annual participation in the Pasadena Rose Parade, launching its involvement in parades and community events nationwide.

The company's fourth decade saw even greater growth than its third. Written premiums skyrocketed to almost $400 million by 1968, well over two times the achievement of 1958. The company continued to introduce new types of coverage, including discounts for non-smokers and the Alpha and Omega Plans (predecessors of the Universal Life Plan).

End of an Era, 1970s

In 1973, founder and CEO John Tyler died at the age of 86. Cofounder Thomas Leavey stepped up to the post of CEO. Five years later, Leavey retired in the 50th anniversary year of the organization he had cofounded, continuing to serve as an adviser until his death in 1980.

At the time of Leavey's retirement in 1978, the company had exceeded $2 billion in written premiums, exceeding the 1968 figure more than five times over. Almost 7.5 million policies were in force, and the agency employed 8,778 full-time and 3,220 reserve workers. Nine new regional offices opened in the 1980s, bringing the total to 19. Customer files were directly computer-accessible from agents' offices to maximize efficiency. By 1987, written premiums reached $5 billion and policies-in-force grew to over 10 million. Farmers was operational in 26 states, employing over 14,000 agents.

Earthquakes, Fire, and Acquisition, 1980s and 1990s

Sixty years of growth and innovation prefaced the most challenging decade in Farmers' history in the 1980s and 1990s, including major acquisition and reorganizations and three disasters in California. In December 1988, Farmers was acquired by the United Kingdom-based British American Tobacco (B.A.T.) Industries, which became the sole stockholder of the company's 68 million shares of common stock. Under B.A.T.'s parentage, Farmers continued its expansion, moving into Tennessee, Alabama, and Virginia, and becoming the number three property/casualty insurer in the United States.

Although auto, fire, and life insurance continued to bring profits to the company, losses were incurred in commercial policy sales. The 1989 San Francisco earthquake, the 1991 Oakland fire, and the 1994 Northridge, California, earthquake posed major financial challenges to the company, as claims increased. Farmers' members companies operated at a net loss in 1989 on Proposition 103 lines in California, and—according to *National Underwriter* (Haggerty, January 2, 1995)—record losses from the Northridge earthquake alone were estimated at $1.3 billion in 1995. In auto insurance, the leading four companies—Farmers, State Farm, Allstate, and Nationwide Group—together had added one percent of the market to their annual share between 1987 and 1991. However, in 1992, the "big four" only claimed .1 percent of the $5 billion market, and specialized underwriters began to compete for market share growth.

To respond to these threatening circumstances, a number of organizational adjustments were made. Farmers changed the way it wrote commercial policies, establishing a Commercial Qualified Agent program and identifying commercial niches for whom the company created custom products. Emphasis on the expansion of the life insurance market was bolstered with new products, and several new annuities programs were announced as well. Farmers introduced new services to reduce the cost and inconvenience of auto claims: allowing approved auto shops to repair car damage, quick and inexpensive repair of auto windows, and the Farm Tow program were all introduced in the early 1990s. To keep its finger on the pulse of changing market conditions and state insurance regulations and needs, Farmers established state offices. By 1995, the company reorganized its core business operations into separate units for personal lines, commercial, and life insurance. In 1996, a special partnership with Citibank offered auto loans through Farmers insurance agents. That year, the company realized the top 10's largest increase of 14.5 percent, with premiums of $8.55 billion. Such growth—largely due to the low 1994 premiums due to the Northridge earthquake—allowed Farmers to overtake Nationwide, becoming number four in the industry (from number six).

Legal Issues and Community Involvement

Several legal issues surrounded Farmers in the 1990s. Farmers' Truck Insurance Exchange affiliate was the subject of a legal investigation in the late 1980s and early 1990s. Marmac, a California engineering firm, sued Farmers and its affiliate for allegedly refusing to defend a third-party lawsuit. A $58 million judgment against the company launched an investigation to determine whether the conduct of the affiliate was present in all Farmers' companies. In 1994, the original decision against Truck Insurance Exchange was reversed by the California Court of Appeals. That same year, both Farmers and State Farm were accused by California Insurance Commissioner John Garamendi of discrimination in homeowners' insurance sales in low-income and minority areas of Los Angeles. In 1995, Garamendi ordered Farmers to pay $183 million in Proposition 103 refunds (Farmers was one of 20 companies ordered to pay a total of $1.2 billion). In 1996, Allstate and Farmers were named in a "double rounding" class action suit (alleging that auto insurance premiums were illegally rounded up twice annually).

During the 1990s, the company sought to increase its community profile through involvement in programs such as Partners in Pride, the March of Dimes, the Youth Education and Safety (Y.E.S.) program, and "The American Promise" public television series. The Farmers Action for Communities of Tomorrow (FACT) program brings the company's services to underserved urban markets. FACT was jointly announced by Farmers and California Insurance Commissioner John Garamendi after the 1992 Los Angeles riots, and was intended to serve the needs of inner-city residents and businesses who could not afford property insurance because of redlining by insurance companies (declining to offer coverage in high-risk areas). By the company's 70th anniversary in 1998, written premiums exceeded $10 billion with over 16.5 million policies-in-force and 8.5 million customers.

The Zurich Merger, 1997–98

After a decade under the ownership of B.A.T., Farmers was poised for another major ownership transition in the late 1990s.

In 1997, B.A.T. and Zurich Insurance Company initiated a merger. Creating a new company to be called Zurich Financial Services Group, this merger resulted in the world's fifth largest insurance group, with aggregate gross premiums of $45 billion, and worldwide market presence. This merger most likely signaled continued expansion for Farmers—the largest U.S. member of the ZF group—since the Zurich company offered mutual fund and other asset-growth products. Farmers was expected to develop new programs in auto, fire, life, and commercial lines, along with new financial products including auto loans and leasing, home loans, and education loans. With a solid history of managed relationships with affiliates, subsidiaries, and parent companies, Farmers would be an important partner of the new and powerful Zurich Financial Services Group.

Principal Subsidiaries

Farmers Direct; Fire Underwriters Association; Truck Underwriters Association; Farmers New World Life Ins. Co.; Property and Casualty Insurance Subsidiaries (Mid-Century and Domestics).

Principal Divisions

Farmers Texas County Mutual; Farmers Insurance Exchange; Fire Insurance Exchange; Truck Insurance Exchange.

Further Reading

Banks, Howard, "A Zurich in Your Future?" *Forbes,* April 20, 1998, pp. 85–86.
"Calif. Insurers Face Redlining Charges As Texas Pilot Begins," *Best's Review,* November, 1994, p. 10.
"Court Decision Prompts Calif. Probe of Farmers," *National Underwriter,* November 29, 1993, p. 16.
"Farmers Insurance: Over Seventy Years of Superior Service, The Story of the Farmers Insurance Group of Companies," Los Angeles: Farmers Group, Inc., 1998.
"Farmers Plan Targets Calif. Inner Cities," *National Underwriter,* May 16, 1994.
Haggerty, Alfred G., "Court Reverses $58M Judgment Against Farmers," *National Underwriter,* August 29, 1994, p. 7.
——, "Farmers Ins. Group to Fight $183M Prop. 103 Refund Order," *National Underwriter,* January 2, 1995, pp. 2, 29.
——, "Farmers, State Farm See Ratings Cut," *National Underwriter,* May 8, 1995, p. 23.
Jennings, John, "European Giants in Flurry of Merger Activity," *National Underwriter,* October 20, 1997, pp. 3, 23.
Otis, L. H., "Allstate, Farmers Fight 'Double-Rounding' Ruling," *National Underwriter,* July 15, 1996, p. 12.
Pasher, Victor Sonshine, "Farmers Joins with Citibank on Auto Loans," *National Underwriter,* June 16, 1997, pp. 1, 30.
Sciafane, Susanne, "Farmers Adding Agents in 'Underserved' Areas," *National Underwriter,* October 2, 1995, p. 6.
——, "Top-20 Company Premium Growth Better Than P-C Industry Average," *National Underwriter,* July 21, 1997, pp. 9, 40.
Sullivan, Brian P., "Are the Big Four Running Out of Gas?" *Best's Review,* October, 1993, pp. 43–48+.
Sweeney, Patrick M., "A Year of Modest Premium Growth," *Best's Review,* July, 1997, pp. 28–31.

—Heidi Feldman

Finnair Oy

Tietotie 11 A
Helsinki-Vantaa Airport
P.O. Box 15
01053 Finnair
Finland
+358 9 81 881
Fax: +358 9 818 4401

State-Controlled Public Company
Incorporated: 1923 as Aero O/Y
Employees: 10,836
Sales: FMk 8.06 billion (US$1.48 billion) (1997)
Stock Exchanges: Helsinki London
Ticker Symbol: FIA
SICs: 4516 Air Transportation, Scheduled; 4522 Air
   Transportation, Nonscheduled

Based in Helsinki, Finnair Oy is the national airline of Finland and the sixth-oldest airline in the world. Operating passenger and air freight services throughout Finland and the Baltic region, Finnair also provides regular and seasonal service to Europe, North America, and Asia.

An Early Start

Finnair was established in 1923 as Aero O/Y. The small company was the creation of a small circle of financiers, including Gustav Snellman, Fritiof Ahman, and Bruno Otto Lucander, formerly a Belgian vice-consul. Lucander became involved in aviation in 1918 as the general manager of Finland Spedition, a managerial group that oversaw the Finnish operations of an airline based in Tallin, Estonia, known as Aeronaut.

At that time, the local aviation industry was dominated by German interests, including the aircraft manufacturer Junkers, a company experienced with aircraft designs that were capable of enduring the extreme physical demands of northern European weather. Aero purchased several seaplanes from Junkers, inaugurating airmail service between Helsinki and Tallin with a single-engine, four-passenger model F 13. In exchange for the aircraft and technical advisors, Junkers was given a 50 percent financial interest in Aero. The airline operated out of a seaplane ramp in the Katajanokka district of Helsinki. The company's aircraft were fitted with water floats in the summer and skis in the winter.

Aero began services to Stockholm on June 2, 1924, in conjunction with the airline Swedish ABA. With rail connections from Tallin and Stockholm, travelers were afforded quick passage to Copenhagen, Konigsberg, and Berlin. While the route system remained small, Aero launched a campaign to promote air travel. In 1925 alone, it operated 833 sight-seeing tours.

Also in 1925, Junkers amalgamated its Nord Europa Union and Trans Europa Union air transport subsidiaries into a single company consisting of 16 airlines in nine countries. This new company, Europa Union, was then combined with another German airline interest, Aero Lloyd, to form Deutsche Lufthansa.

Aero remained outside this consortium, but received less support from Junkers, which gave priority to the new German air consortium. Aero turned to the Finnish government for financial assistance to acquire new aircraft, and in 1926 the airline took delivery of its first Junkers G 24, a three-engine, nine-passenger seaplane.

Aero was reluctant to switch to land-based aircraft. In a country with more than 60,000 lakes, the trouble and expense of building runways remained prohibitive as long as Aero continued to operate seaplanes. Additionally, Aero could establish new destinations virtually anywhere there was a lake. With the 1929 death of Lucander, Aero appointed Gunnar Stänhle, who was trained as an engineer, general manager. Aero also ended its financial relationship with Junkers in 1929, when Finnish investors completed a buyout of the German company's interest. In 1930 Aero began to establish a closer relationship with other Scandinavian airlines. The company ran night airmail services in cooperation with Swedish, Danish, and later, Dutch airline companies. Junkers, however, remained the company's aircraft supplier, providing five 14-passenger Ju 52s during the decade.

With the opening of an airport at Turku in 1935 and Stockholm in 1936, pressure mounted to establish a landing strip in Helsinki. Land operations began at Malmi airport later that year, although the airport remained officially closed until May 1938. Aero converted its aircraft to wheel landing gear and operated its last seaplane service on December 15, 1936.

In 1937 Aero took delivery of its first non-Junkers aircraft, two twin-engine DH 89A Dragon Rapides. These planes were operated on domestic routes to northern Finland. The following year, the Tallin route was extended to Berlin, via Riga, Latvia, and Kaunas, Lithuania. In anticipation of increased air traffic for the 1940 Helsinki Olympic Games, Aero ordered two 26-passenger Condor aircraft from Focke-Wulf.

World War II

Due to a complex history of financial and cultural ties with Germany, Finland at this time was politically allied with the fascist Nazi-installed government in Germany. German Chancellor Adolph Hitler made one of his few international trips to Finland to lend support to the Finnish government, which by 1939 had fallen into acrimonious relations with the government of Hitler's archenemy, Josef Stalin.

Tensions between Finland and the Soviet Union mounted. In October 1939 all civilian aviation was placed under Finnish military control. On November 30 hostilities broke out. Finnish troops held off Soviet advances for several months. Aero ceased operation from Helsinki but continued to operate to Stockholm from Vaasa and Turku, despite sporadic air attacks. Of the 3,900 passengers it ferried to Sweden, 1,500 were children who were being evacuated to safety. The Helsinki Olympics were canceled, and Aero never took delivery of the Condors it had ordered.

By the following spring the Soviets had achieved a hard-won victory in Finland. As part of its peace treaty with Stalin, Finland was forced to cede land in its eastern Karelian sector to the Soviet Union. Aero, however, was free to reestablish air services, and in April 1940 resumed flights to Tallin and Stockholm. On the domestic front, the company began a "Lapland Express" to the northern city of Petsamo, in addition to more than a dozen other destinations.

As a result of the Molotov-Ribbentrop pact, in which Germany and the Soviet Union partitioned Poland and occupied Latvia, Lithuania, and Estonia, Finland was afforded an opportunity to reestablish stronger links with Germany. In 1941 Aero acquired two Douglas DC-2s from Lufthansa. The aircraft had been seized from Czechoslovakia when Germany invaded the country two years earlier.

On June 25 of the previous year, the war between Germany and Britain and France broke out. This war, which Finns call the "Continuation War," forced the Finnish government to once again place civilian air resources under government control. Aero ceased its operations from Helsinki and Turku and relocated temporarily to the city of Pori. Even after the United States and the Soviet Union became involved in hostilities during the Continuation War, and in spite of fuel shortages, Aero continued to operate air services to Rovaniemi, Stockholm, and even Berlin.

For Finland, a nominal German ally, the Continuation War ended on September 19, 1944, after Soviet troops had again overrun Helsinki. Malmi airport was placed under allied military control. Aero, however, was allowed to resume operations to Turku, Maarianhamina, and Stockholm from Hyvinkaa.

The Allies banned all commercial aviation from March to August of 1945, when Aero was permitted to resume only domestic schedules. Gunnar Stänhle, however, was forced to resign by order of the Allied Control Commission, which cited the director's sympathies to Nazi Germany during the war. Stänhle was replaced by C. J. Ehrnrooth, who shortly afterward was succeeded by Uolevi Raade. The company was also reorganized during this period, and a board of directors was established.

Post-War Expansion

Finnish investment capital was scarce after the war, and Aero was forced to turn to the government to fund new equipment. In return for its backing, the Finnish government was allowed to acquire 70 percent of Aero's shares. The remainder were held by banks, other companies, and private citizens.

Through the Finnish Ministry of Supply, Aero purchased several surplus American C-47s and commissioned the Dutch aircraft company Fokker to convert them to their civilian equivalent, the DC-3. These aircraft entered service in May of 1947, emblazoned with the title Finnish Air Lines and featuring Aero's first flight attendants.

The following year, Aero resumed international services and by 1949 had retired all of its DC-2s, Rapides, and Junkers aircraft. In preparation for the Helsinki Olympic Games, which were rescheduled for 1952, Aero reconfigured its DC-3s and designed the new Helsinki Airport near Seutula. After transporting more than 100,000 passengers in 1952, Aero began to investigate a need for larger, more modern aircraft and decided on the Convair 340, a 44-passenger aircraft with a pressurized cabin, and the more advanced Convair 440 Metropolitan.

In 1953 the company introduced the name Finnair in its advertising materials and on its aircraft, partly out of concern that the name Aero had become outdated and generic. The company's official name, however, did not change. By 1957 Finnair operated one of the densest domestic route structures in Europe. The short-term nature of this structure led the company to plan for a new generation of aircraft to replace its Convairs and DC-3s on long-distance flights. Aero chose the 73-passenger Sud Aviation Caravelle twin jet, which entered the fleet in 1960.

The Caravelles were later deployed on winter charter flights to Majorca, the Canary Islands, and Rimini. At the time, International Air Traffic Association (IATA) regulations prevented Aero from directly operating charter and student flights. Instead, the company created a subsidiary, Polar Air, to handle this business. In 1963, however, Aero acquired a 27 percent interest in another Finnish airline, Kar Air, which took over Polar Air's operations.

In 1960, after 13 years of leadership under Leonard Grandell, an economist named Gunnar Korhonen was appointed managing director of Aero O/Y. Several changes occurred under Korhonen's leadership. In addition to introducing the

Caravelles, Aero opened its Finnair Aviation College to train pilots who could be recruited out of the Finnish air force. The company's route structure continued to expand, adding flights to Leningrad, Athens, Dubrovnik, and Brussels.

Early in 1968 the company officially adopted Finnair Oy as its new corporate name and laid plans to expand into the hotel and travel agency businesses as part of an effort to achieve greater control over all aspects of the tourism industry. The company took delivery of its first 189-passenger DC-8 the following year, placing it into service on a new route to New York. Two years later, continuing its association with Douglas Aircraft, Finnair added somewhat smaller DC-9 aircraft to its fleet and opened new routes to Lisbon and East Berlin.

In 1975 Finnair began operating wide-body DC-10 aircraft, opening routes to Bangkok and numerous destinations in the Middle East. Four years later the airline created a subsidiary to handle domestic charter operations and general aviation maintenance and repair services. In 1982 Finnair revived the Aero Oy name for another subsidiary handling technical services and aircraft leasing and sales activities. Forced to close both its service to Baghdad, because of the war between Iran and Iraq, and its Amman route, due to low demand, Finnair opened routes to Seattle and Los Angeles in 1981 and to Tokyo via the North Pole in 1983.

Like many other Finnish businesses, Finnair benefited greatly from its government's unusual relationship with the former Soviet Union. Finland shared many parallel interests with the Soviet government. As an agent of the Finnish government, and because of its proximity, Finnair was afforded greater access to Eastern Bloc cities and airspace than Western airline companies, and it succeeded in using this as a corporate asset.

One result of this relationship was a growth in air freight, which compelled the company to invest heavily in a new air cargo facility at Helsinki Vantaa Airport in 1986. Political changes in the Soviet Union after 1986 opened Eastern Europe to more Western airlines and shifted Soviet business alliances to Germany, where greater investment capital was available. In addition, Finnair was faced with high cost structures, which led the company's chairman, Antti Potila, to undertake a series of cost-cutting moves and reduce the number of employees by ten percent beginning in 1990.

Kar Air and Finnaviation were reorganized as independent subsidiaries and made responsible for their own productivity. Finnair, however, managed to retain its position as the gateway airline to the Soviet Union and the Baltic states. This position was strengthened in 1989 after Finnair backed the opening of Strand Inter-Continental in Helsinki and the Savoy Hotel in Moscow. Also maintaining its close relationship with aircraft manufacturer McDonnell-Douglas, Finnair has added advanced MD-11, Airbus A-300, and ATR planes to its fleet.

Finnair shares were first listed on the Helsinki Stock Exchange in May 1989. By this time the carrier was flying about five million passengers per year.

Finding a Place in the New World Order

In the early 1990s Finnair teamed with Scandinavian Airlines System (SAS), Austrian Airlines, and Swissair to pool financial resources for future aircraft purchases. The European Quality Alliance collapsed, however, as Chairman Antti Potila felt Finnair was losing its independence. Finnair then concentrated on an alliance with Lufthansa beginning in 1991.

After the Soviet Baltic states gained their independence from Moscow in 1990, Finnair stepped in to help establish an Estonian airline company. The airline soon had distinguished service and air safety records, and maintained one of the most modern air fleets in Europe. It existed under the majority control of the government of Finland, with the remaining share in the hands of banks and other institutional investment interests.

Finnair launched some cost-cutting measures in 1991. It pulled back flights from the Mediterranean in response to the Persian Gulf crisis, but found that Portugal increased in popularity as a tourist destination.

New Horizons

The onset of glasnost not only opened up new routes with Russia but also allowed more direct flights to the Far East. However, the airline also had to deal with an economic recession during this time, accumulating losses of FIM 576 million between 1991 and 1993. A recovery came in 1994, both within the Finnish economy and in regards to business traffic in particular. Still, the company continued to reduce its work force as a means of remaining profitable.

Another part of the company's strategy in the mid-1990s was to reduce the number of aircraft types it operated. Finnair began replacing its DC-9s with used McDonnell Douglas MD-80 aircraft. A stock offering in January 1995 helped fund the purchases. This offering received much attention from European investment institutions and raised foreign ownership of the company from 5 to 16 percent.

In 1997, Finnair's board voted to replace the MD-80 airliners on its European routes with Airbus aircraft, the order to be worth FIM 2 billion. Finnair still operated a dozen DC-9 aircraft and in June 1998 announced it was retrofitting them with newly available hush kits. The company also leased several Boeing 757s.

Finnair completed expansion work on its cargo terminal late in 1997. The company carried approximately 80,000 tons of mail and cargo, providing about FIM 900 million, or 13 percent, of the company's total turnover. The Far East accounted for 30 percent of its business.

Finnair terminated its partnership with Lufthansa after the German carrier teamed with SAS in 1997. Finnair then installed a second hub in Stockholm—the site of SAS's headquarters but not its operating center, which was Copenhagen. Finnair fed the hub via code shares with other Scandinavian carriers and declared itself Stockholm's official airline. It also teamed with Maersk Air to compete on one of SAS's most lucrative routes, Copenhagen-Stockholm, after SAS began flying from Frankfurt into Maersk's home base of Billund, Denmark. Meanwhile, competitors were slowly taking away from Finnair's domestic market share.

Early in 1998, Finnair and SAS rival British Airways announced a new alliance, which offered travelers the prospect of reduced fares. The cooperation was intended to help both carriers cope with competing alliances such as the Star Alliance created in 1997 of SAS, Lufthansa, United, Thai International, Varig, and Air Canada. Code sharing agreements with Delta, Braathens, Swissair, Austrian Airlines, Sabena, and Maersk Air were in force as well. Flights outside of Europe remained a low priority for the carrier; however, the company planned to triple its flights to Russia.

In 1998, Finnair celebrated its 75th anniversary. Demand increased in all sectors while costs were contained. Passenger growth boomed in early 1998 and Finnair carried nearly four million passengers. The government of Finland owned 59.80 percent of Finnair shares in March 1998. Management hoped to see a decrease in this figure and to retain more capital within the company.

Principal Subsidiaries

Malmilento Oy; Area Travel Agency Ltd.; Area Baltica Reisibüroo AS (Estonia); ZAO Norvista (Russia); Estravel AS (Estonia; 72%); BMR Balti Meediareklaami AS (Estonia; 72%); Finlandia Agence de Voyages S.A.R.L. (France; 99.8%); Finlandia Travel Agency Ltd. (United Kingdom); Mikkelin Matkatoimisto Oy (51%); Norvista Travel AB (Sweden); Finland Travel Bureau Ltd. (99.8%); Kuopion Matkatoimisto Oy; Varkauden Matkatoimisto Oy (69.6%); Oy Aurinkomatkat—Suntours Ltd Ab (97.1%); Finnair Travel Services Oy; Oy Finnmatkat—Finntours Ltd Ab; Norvista Travel Ltd. (Canada); Norvista Ltd. (United States); Norvista S.R.L. (Italy); Norvista Reisen GmbH (Germany); Finnair Gateway Ravintolat Oy; Finncatering Oy; Amadeus Finland Oy (95%).

Further Reading

The Art of Flying Since 1923, Finland: Finnair Oy, 1983.

Elliot, Tom, "In Pole Position," *Airfinance Journal*, April 1995, pp. 36–38.

"The European Skies," *New York Times*, June 7, 1992.

Feldman, Joan M., "The Nordic Airline War," *Air Transport World*, November, 1997, pp. 85–89.

Finnair 1923–1986: Blue-White Wings—Over Sixty Years of Operation, Finland: Finnair Oy, November 26, 1986.

"Helsinki to Miami," *Aviation Week & Space Technology*, June 29, 1992.

Lefer, Henry, "Small is Beautiful," *Air Transport World*, December 1991, pp. 30–35.

Malkin, Richard, "Air Cargo: Looking for a Niche in the World," *Distribution*, March, 1994, p. 62.

O'Dwyer, Gerard, "Finnish Privatisation Train Stays on Course," *The European*, May 19, 1995, p. 17.

Shifrin, Carole A., "Finnair's MD-80 Plan Reflects Stronger Traffic, Finances," *Aviation Week and Space Technology*, December 12–29, 1994, p. 39.

"Small Is Beautiful," *Air Transport World*, December 1991.

—John Simley
—updated by Frederick C. Ingram

FORE Systems, Inc.

1000 FORE Drive
Warrendale, Pennsylvania 15086
U.S.A.
(724) 742-4444
(800) 884-0040
Fax: (724) 742-7777
Web Site: http://www.fore.com

Public Company
Incorporated: 1990
Employees: 1,360
Sales: $458.37 million (1998)
Stock Exchanges: NASDAQ
Ticker Symbol: FORE
SICs: 3577 Computer Peripheral Equipment, Not
    Elsewhere Classified; 7372 Prepackaged Software

FORE Systems, Inc. is a major player in the niche market of Asynchronous Transfer Mode (ATM) computer network switches, and was the first company to commercially develop such a switch, in 1992. Since that time FORE has broadened its product range, partly through acquisitions of other companies, to include a variety of different types of switch and networking products, with the company's emphasis remaining on ATM technology. Having experienced dramatic growth every year since its founding, FORE has become a large and established force in the still-expanding field of computer network switching equipment.

1990 Founding by Carnegie-Mellon Researchers

FORE Systems was the creation of four computer science research colleagues at Carnegie-Mellon University in Pittsburgh, Pennsylvania. The founders, Francois Bitz, Onat Menzilcioglu, Robert Sansom, and Eric Cooper, had been working in the late 1980s on developing a custom high-speed computer network and decided that a business that marketed the Asynchronous Transfer Mode (ATM) switches they were using

could be profitable. ATM is a technology in which identical-sized packets of information are routed across a computer network in a way that allows efficient use of network bandwidth, and is also capable of great speed, allowing simultaneous transmission of different types of information including data, video, and audio. Taking the first letters of each of their names to name the corporation, the four founders started their new business in April 1990 with a minimal amount of capital. Eric Cooper would be chosen to serve as the company's president, while the other founders focused on development of the company's products. Reportedly, the partners were so frugal that they sometimes scavenged computers and office furniture from dumpsters. FORE's first product, a network interface adapter card for Sun Microsystems computers, was introduced in late 1991. Sales during the company's first year amounted to only slightly more than $100,000.

FORE signed its first development contract in 1991, with the U.S. Navy, and delivery of the company's first ATM switch came in June 1992. The Navy's response was enthusiastic, and word soon spread to other potential customers, with new orders coming from universities and other owners of large computer networks. FORE's ForeRunner brand of ATM switches were much faster than other types of data switching devices in use at the time, such as Ethernet, which used data packets of varying, rather than fixed, length, and which was then unable to handle multimedia input. Other products from the company, in addition to the ATM switches and interface cards, included the software which was needed to operate the ATM equipment. Early on, FORE began distributing its products to foreign markets, and within several years over one-third of sales came from overseas, with particularly strong interest shown in Japan.

The company soon began opening sales offices in a number of key locations. Although several other companies had begun developing ATM switches, the initial lead established by FORE enabled it to continue to control the majority of the market. The company's ATM switches were expensive items, priced anywhere from the low five figures range to over $100,000, depending on the application, with sales amounting to only a few hundred switches over a span of several years. In many cases, early sales were made as part of pilot programs, with customers

---

Company Perspectives:

FORE Systems, a leading global supplier of networking solutions based on an Intelligent Infrastructure, *designs, manufactures and sells products designed to handle the networked applications of today and tomorrow. FORE's* Networks of Steel *deliver the increased capacity, reduced complexity and unparalleled flexibility and scalability necessary to build networks that last.*

---

often taking only a single switch at first. Once the company learned the benefits of ATM, FORE would end up selling the customer additional units.

In January 1993 FORE received an infusion of $5 million from a venture capital group to expand the company's sales, manufacturing, and marketing efforts. Soon thereafter, the company was able to triple its number of employees. Around this time FORE also had begun establishing partnerships with other companies, including US Sprint, the long-distance telephone carrier, and Cabletron Systems, Inc., a large developer of computer local area network (LAN) systems. In January 1994 FORE signed a $10 million, three-year agreement with Cabletron to develop components for Cabletron's computer network hubs.

1994: IPO and a Second Generation of ATMs

Having seen its annual sales leap to $1 million in 1992, $5.5 million in 1993, and $23.5 million for the fiscal year ending in 1994, the next logical step for FORE was to issue stock to raise money to fuel further growth. The stock was offered on the NASDAQ exchange in May 1994, and the price quickly soared. At the time, the company was selling its switches to a variety of customers, including the U.S. government, universities, and other users of LANs and wide area networks (WANs) such as health care providers, computer-aided design and modeling firms, telephone companies, and more.

In mid-1994 FORE also released its second generation of ATM products, and sales of the updated ForeRunner ASX-200 series of switches were strong. FORE products won a number of computer industry awards for excellence, a trend that would continue in the future. The company also lowered its prices frequently, which it would continue doing over time, as more competitors began to enter the ATM market. The increase in sales volume was great enough that revenues, as well as profits, continued to increase dramatically. In fact, FORE was named the fourth fastest growing company of 1994 by *Fortune* magazine.

As FORE grew, it also continued to become involved with other companies through partnerships and acquisitions. The ForeThought Partners program was started to create strategic alliances with a number of companies involved in different aspects of computer networking, with almost three dozen signing on within the first year.

FORE also began a series of acquisitions. In early 1995 the company bought both Applied Network Technology, Inc., a maker of Ethernet switches, and RainbowBridge Communica-

tions, Inc., a routing software developer. A few months later CellAccess Technology, Inc., a maker of digital access products for ATM and Frame Relay networks, was added. The company's largest acquisition followed in February 1996, when ALANTEC Corporation was merged into FORE. ALANTEC, a designer and manufacturer of intelligent switching hubs for Ethernet and Fiber Distributed Data Interface (FDDI) local area networks, was almost half the size of FORE, and it, along with the other acquisitions, greatly broadened the scope of FORE's operations. As FORE had grown, the company had recognized the need to offer a variety of ways to integrate ATM-based products with Ethernet, FDDI, and Token Ring systems, to allow the company's customers to preserve their investments in existing technology while making use of the advantages offered by ATM. The new companies FORE had bought provided it, and its customers, with an improved "on-ramp" from existing technologies to ATM.

FORE's revenues were continuing to grow dramatically, with annual sales of $75.6 million in the 1994–95 fiscal year, almost four times that of the previous year, climbing to $235.2 million in the fiscal year ending in March 1996. The company's pilot programs and pricing strategies were paying off. International sales continued to account for one-third or more of total revenues, and the company was responsible for nearly two-thirds of global ATM product sales. While competition from Cisco Systems, IBM, 3Com and other large companies was increasing, the rapidly expanding market ensured that there was still room for multiple players. The company began planning a new corporate headquarters, a dramatic building to be located in the Pittsburgh suburb of Warrendale. The ForeRunner line of switches had now been through several generations of design improvements and was still being cited in computer industry publications, along with other products from FORE, as being among the best of their type.

The Later 1990s: Further Growth

FORE Systems continued its aggressive growth with the rapid-fire acquisition of three companies in late 1996. In November it announced agreements to purchase Nemesys Research Ltd. of England, a developer of ATM video conferencing products, and Scalable Networks, Inc., makers of Fast Ethernet connections. Soon thereafter, in December, Cadia Networks, Inc., a WAN technology company, was also acquired.

As FORE's international sales continued to be a major part of its business, the company opened a manufacturing plant in Dublin, Ireland, in May 1997. FORE's manufacturing process consisted generally of final assembly of components purchased from third party manufacturers. Research and Development efforts were a priority, with as much as 12 to 14 percent of revenues turned back into this area. The second-largest category of employees, after sales, was engineering, with only about one-third of this number employed in the actual manufacturing process.

Among the many users of FORE's ATM switches were such industry giants as Microsoft (which used ATM switches for their own internal data network), several large cable television companies and newspapers, and a number of movie industry editing and special effects houses. For the latter, the need to process and transfer huge amounts of video and audio information required the use of the fastest, most capacious network backbone switches that could be had, with ATM considered the best choice available. FORE even received onscreen credit in several major Hollywood films for the assistance it provided.

At the start of 1998, with FORE just moved into its new headquarters building in Warrendale, the company installed a new president and CEO: Thomas Gill, formerly the company's chief financial officer and chief operating officer. Exiting CEO Eric Cooper retained his role of chairman of the board. Of the company's other founders, only Francois Bitz had left the company, with former company president Onat Menzilcioglu still on the company's Board, and Robert Sansom continuing in his position of senior vice-president and chief technology officer.

FORE also announced two new marketing strategies, Intelligent Infrastructure and Networks of Steel. Intelligent Infrastructure highlighted the company's concept of a network design which could be flexible and expandable without requiring major re-tooling or ''ripping out and replacing'' of components. Networks of Steel was the company's first major advertising campaign, and included television spots and newspaper ads. Playing on the Pittsburgh area's renown as the center of the American steel industry, FORE sought to tie in its own reputation for reliability in a bid for wider recognition among the mainstream of computer users, and not just with networking experts. In conjunction with the advertising, the company was expanding its sales efforts and offering hands-on seminars to potential customers.

As it neared the end of its first decade in business, FORE Systems had seen incredible growth, widespread acceptance of its products, and virtually continuous profitability. The company offered a wide range of computer network switching products, but still focused on the ATM standard which it had started with. As more and more customers worldwide turned to ATM as the backbone of their computer networks, FORE became more deeply entrenched in its position as the leader in its field, despite strong competition from a number of latecomers. With the potential market for its products far from saturated, the company seemed certain to continue to prosper for the foreseeable future.

Further Reading

''At the FORE Front of the Network,'' *Computer Business Review,* September 1, 1994.

Bates, Daniel, ''Big Blue Skies Ahead,'' *Pittsburgh Business Times & Journal,* August 9, 1993, p. 1.

——, ''FORE Systems Fattens Coffers with $5 Million Stock Deal,'' *Pittsburgh Business Times & Journal,* January 11, 1993, p. 3.

——, ''FORE Systems Ready for Public Offering to Bankroll Growth,'' *Pittsburgh Business Times & Journal,* March 7, 1994, p. 1.

Duffy, Jim, ''FORE Reloads ATM Cannon,'' *Network World,* July 27, 1998.

Higgins, Steve, ''The New America: FORE Systems Inc.—Setting the Pace in ATM Network Products,'' *Investor's Business Daily,* July 7, 1994, p. A4.

Hostetler, Michele, ''Computers & Technology: FORE Systems Irons Out Bugs for a Film Studio's Network,'' *Investor's Business Daily,* November 25, 1997, p. A8.

Krause, Reinhardt, ''Leaders & Success: FORE Systems' Eric Cooper,'' *Investor's Business Daily,* June 10, 1996, p. A1.

——, ''The New America: Up With ATM,'' *Investor's Business Daily,* July 24, 1996, p. A4.

Massey, Steve, ''For(e)ging Ahead: Acquisition a 'Stepping Stone' for Area High-Tech Company,'' *Pittsburgh Post-Gazette,* December 12, 1995, p. B14.

——, ''Pittsburgh Post-Gazette Top 50: A Challenge for FORE: More Growth,'' *Pittsburgh Post-Gazette,* March 7, 1995, p. D14.

Mencke, Claire, ''The New America: FORE Systems Inc.—Pioneering New Methods of Communication,'' *Investor's Business Daily,* January 13, 1995, p. A4.

Newman, Michael, ''Before & After,'' *Pittsburgh Post-Gazette,* October 7, 1997, p. D1.

——, ''Steeling Itself FORE Systems Hopes to Generate High-Tech Buzz with a Low-Tech Image Campaign,'' *Pittsburgh Post-Gazette,* January 28, 1998, p. C1.

Parets, Robin Taylor, ''The New America: FORE Systems Inc.—Turbocharging Computer Network Engines,'' *Investor's Business Daily,* October 26, 1995, p. A6.

Roberts, Erica, ''Leading a LAN Revolution,'' *LAN Times,* July 11, 1994, p. 1.

Samuelson, James, ''A Switch in Time,'' *Forbes,* May 5, 1997, p. 174.

Tascarella, Patty, ''FORE Systems Pending IPO Piques Local Investor Interest,'' *Pittsburgh Business Times & Journal,* May 16, 1994, p. 4.

—Frank Uhle

Fruit of the Loom, Inc.

5000 Sears Tower
233 South Wacker Drive
Chicago, Illinois 60606
U.S.A.
(312) 876-1724
Fax: (312) 993-1749
(800) 888-2600
Web site: http://www.fruit.com

Public Company
Incorporated: 1955
Employees: 30,000
Sales: $2.1 billion (1997)
Stock Exchanges: American Chicago Pittsburgh Pacific
Ticker Symbol: FTL
SICs: 2211 Broadwoven Fabric Mills, Cotton; 2252
   Hosiery Not Elsewhere Classified; 2253 Knit
   Outerwear Mills; 2254 Knit Underwear and
   Nightwear Mills; 2321 Men's and Boy's Shirts; 2322
   Men's/Boys' Underwear & Nightwear; 2329 Men's/
   Boys' Clothing Not Elsewhere Classified; 2341
   Women's/Children's Underwear

Fruit of the Loom, Inc., a global manufacturer and marketer of family apparel, is America's biggest seller of men's briefs. The company's products also include underwear for men, women, and children, as well as T-shirts, activewear, casualwear, and clothing for children. As of the late 1990s, the company's brands, which included BVD, Munsingwear, Gitano, and the namesake Fruit of the Loom, were among the best known in the world. In addition to these popular brands, the company licensed characters for children's apparel—such as Winnie the Pooh and Batman—and the names, logos, and trademarks of colleges, universities, and professional sports teams. With more than 60 manufacturing and distribution facilities, the company had operations in ten states and in various countries around the world, including Canada, Mexico, and Germany.

Brand Introduction in the Mid-Nineteenth Century

The history of the company involves two separate entities: the B. B. & R. Knight Brothers textile company and The Union Underwear Company. The Knight Brothers established a textile company in Pontiac, Rhode Island, in the mid-nineteenth century. Their high quality broadcloth was recognized as some of the best fabric for the homemade clothing and linens that were common at the time. In 1851, when trademarking was still in its infancy, the brothers gave their cloth the imaginative name "Fruit of the Loom."

Rufus Skeel, one of the merchants who sold the Knight brothers' cloth commercially, operated a dry goods store in New York's Hudson Valley, and his daughter, an artist, painted pictures of local apple varieties. Over time, her paintings became associated with the Fruit of the Loom name. Soon, the apple accompanied the name on printed labels that identified the Knight brothers' increasingly popular cloth. The serendipitous combination of the two components helped make Fruit of the Loom the first branded textile product in the United States. When the federal patent and trademark office opened in 1871, the trademark (which had grown to include a cluster of fruits) received the United States' 418th patent.

As long as women made their own clothing and linens, Fruit of the Loom textiles remained in demand. But the development of the manufactured apparel industry in the early twentieth century considerably diminished the fabric market. The market for piecegoods declined as homemakers did less sewing and began to favor ready-made clothing and linens. Although the original product's market dwindled, the trademark still enjoyed popularity. Thus, in 1928, the Fruit of the Loom Company began to license the brand to manufacturers of finished garments.

At about the same time that Fruit of the Loom lost its direct consumer market, a young immigrant named Jacob (Jack) Goldfarb decided to start his own clothing business. Goldfarb learned about the apparel industry through his work with the Ferguson Manufacturing Company. There he noticed that Ferguson only made low-priced "sale items" available to those retailers who also purchased the company's higher priced goods. Goldfarb reasoned that if he could provide retailers with strictly lower-priced, quality undergarments, he could establish a popular business.

He decided to concentrate on the most popular style of men's underwear of the nineteenth century—the unionsuit—and named his endeavor The Union Underwear Company. Like the term "unionsuit" itself, there is some controversy about the origin of the company name. Some historians assert that the term unionsuit referred to the "union" of a top and bottom, while others maintain that the name grew out of the fact that members of the Civil War-era Union Army wore the garment. Whether the name for The Union Underwear Company alluded to the United States or the construction of its clothing remains a mystery.

Oddly enough, Goldfarb started his manufacturing business without a factory. He purchased cloth from one supplier, had it delivered to a cutter, then sent the parts to a sewing shop for finishing and shipping. Union Underwear's first garments were sewn by nuns in and around Indianapolis, Indiana, the site of the company's first finishing plant.

Goldfarb continued to work within this complex system even through the onset of the Great Depression. Then, in 1930, he was approached by some promoters from Frankfort, Kentucky, who were looking for an industry that would provide employment and increase the city's tax base during the lengthy depression. The municipality offered to build a plant for the business, which would bring all of Union's operations to a single location. Goldfarb agreed to the lucrative offer, and within five years employed 650 people at the new location.

Union Underwear and Fruit of the Loom's fortunes converged near the end of the decade. In his quest to become a national marketer, Goldfarb purchased a 25-year license for the Fruit of the Loom trademark in 1938. He was certain that the well-known brand would propel his products to national prominence.

Union Underwear built a second plant—which produced broadcloth "boxer" shorts—in Bowling Green, Kentucky, on the eve of World War II. When America joined the Allied effort in 1941, the company was enlisted to manufacture millions of pairs of G.I. shorts. Union Underwear received numerous commendations from the government for its contribution on the homefront.

Postwar Brand Extensions and Innovations

Goldfarb made several promotional innovations in the postwar era that set Union Underwear and the Fruit of the Loom label apart from other undergarment manufacturers. Before World War II, underwear was usually sold separately, but in the late 1940s, Goldfarb introduced a printed cellophane bag with three pair of shorts inside. The new packages were displayed separately to call attention to Union's branded undergarments. The move established a trend that has become an industry standard for most basic underwear. And even though Goldfarb was only a licensee of the trademark, he became the only licensee to invest his own funds in consumer advertising.

The company expanded its product line from unionsuits and boxer shorts to include knit underwear in 1948, and opened its third plant in Campbellsville, Kentucky, in 1952. The plant provided internal knitting and bleaching facilities for Union

manufacturing for the first time, helping the company to gain more vertical control of production and facilitating the production of a wider variety of men's and boy's undergarments.

Goldfarb continued his promotional innovations when Union became the first underwear company to advertise on network television in 1955. The company purchased spots during Dave Garroway's "Today Show." Union also utilized banners, posters, signs, price tickets, newspaper slicks, and a cooperative advertising program to support Fruit of the Loom sales. Consumer advertising campaigns were coordinated with such seasonal events as Father's Day, Back-to-School, and Christmas to maximize the company's advertising dollar.

Around the same time, Union allied itself to the mass merchandisers that were beginning to spring up in the mid-1950s. The company's growth was soon tied to these new retailer's success: by the early 1990s, 45 percent of men's basic underwear was sold by discount stores.

Structural Changes in the 1950s and 1960s

The mid-1950s saw the start of a string of acquisitions that would place Union Underwear in several different hands over the next three decades. In 1955, Union Underwear was taken over by the Philadelphia & Reading Corporation, a newly-formed conglomerate. The new corporate structure provided Union with additional resources, enabling it to extend its manufacturing operations.

At that point, Union Underwear had grown to become Fruit of the Loom's dominant licensee, and to most people, the name had come to mean underwear more than fabric. The licensee, in fact, had grown larger than Fruit of the Loom. In order to assure the availability of its well-known trademark, Philadelphia & Reading acquired the Fruit of the Loom Licensing Company in 1961.

In 1968, Union Underwear's parent was purchased by Northwest Industries. The consolidation furnished new capital which further facilitated the company's growth. That same year, Goldfarb stepped down from the chair to be replaced by Everett Moore, who had joined the company in 1932 at the Frankfort plant.

Advertising in the 1960s and 1970s

Union Underwear strove to energize advertising for men's underwear in the late 1960s and early 1970s. In 1969 the company contracted sportscaster Howard Cosell to appear in five television commercials over three years. Next, British comedian Terry Thomas was named spokesperson, as advertisers hoped that an English representative would lend an air of quality and endurance to their commercials. The use of celebrity spokespersons brought more public attention to Fruit of the Loom underwear, but the company continued to seek more brand recognition and market share.

In 1975, Union made advertising history with the first "Fruit of the Loom Guys" campaign. The commercials featured three men in costume as a bunch of grapes, an Autumn leaf, and an apple, all elements of the brand's trademark. The characters helped propel the Fruit of the Loom brand to 98 percent recognition and doubled Union's share of the market for men's and boy's underwear.

Also that year, Moore retired and was succeeded by John Holland. In 1976 Union acquired the century-old BVD trademark. The company began to merchandise BVD as a completely separate line of underwear aimed at the more upscale department store market. Union also began to expand its product line in 1978 to include "Underoos"—decorated underwear for boys and girl—and began to supply blank T-shirts for the screen print market during the 1970s. The expansion into plain T-shirts soon evolved into a huge business known as Screen Stars, which sold unbranded T-shirts, sweatshirts, and sweatpants to wholesalers who imprinted them for promotional uses.

Mid-1980s Leveraged Buyout and Reorganization

Union did not escape the trend toward leveraged buyouts of the 1980s. In 1984, William F. Farley acquired Union Underwear when he bought Northwest Industries for $1.4 billion. Farley privatized the parent company and renamed it Farley Industries. In the 1980s tradition of leveraged buyouts and junk bonds, Farley parlayed his acquisitions into larger and larger conquests until, by the end of the decade, he had fashioned a textile and apparel conglomerate with $4 billion in annual sales and 65,000 employees worldwide.

In 1985, the conglomerate was restructured, $260 million in shares were sold, and Union Underwear was renamed Fruit of the Loom, Inc. to relate the business more closely to its famous trademark. Farley, a former encyclopedia salesperson, worked to improve Fruit of the Loom's operational efficiency and squeeze more profits out of the company's number-one status as the holder of a 35 percent share of the undergarment market. Farley proceeded to sell the bulk of Northwest Industries' other businesses and cut costs at Fruit of the Loom. The proceeds of the asset sales were combined with revenues from bond issues to finance domestic modernization and expansion into Europe.

Over the course of the 1980s, those manufacturing changes facilitated Fruit of the Loom's evolution from an underwear manufacturer into an apparel company. Farley and Chief Executive Holland decided to expand into men's fashion underwear, women's underwear, and socks over the course of the decade, putting the Fruit of the Loom label on sportswear in 1987. Women's panties became one of the brand's most popular extensions. The company launched that division in 1984 and led the category with a ten percent share within four years. Fruit of the Loom also made apparel history with its popular pocket T-shirt. Produced in a rainbow of colors, the wardrobe staple's flexibility made it a consumer favorite for decades.

In 1982, sales of men's and boy's white underwear accounted for 80 percent of the company's revenues, but by 1988, brand extensions comprised more than 40 percent of revenues. The activewear market also grew much more rapidly than the underwear category: activewear sales tripled in the 1980s, while the underwear market grew only about six percent annually.

Losses in the Late 1980s

Capital improvements had enabled Fruit of the Loom to expand into newer, faster-growing markets, but they also left the company saddled with debt. Fruit's debt-to-equity ratio of 3.5-to-1 contributed to three out of four years of losses before the decade was over. Interest expenses also consumed ten percent of annual sales revenues in 1989. At the same time, Fruit of the Loom was threatened on two fronts: low priced imports began to eat into Fruit of the Loom's 38 percent market share of basic men's undergarments, and the company's largest competitor, Sara Lee Corp.'s Hanes Knit Products, was raising the ante in the "underwars."

In an effort to promote its move from department stores to discount merchandisers, Hanes introduced "Inspector 12" into its advertising campaigns in 1982. The curmudgeonly quality-control character claimed that her brand fit better and shrank less than Fruit of the Loom's. Fruit of the Loom fired back with promotions that featured the tagline, "Sorry, Hanes, you lose!" The war escalated into a legal battle that ended with an out-of-court settlement wherein the two competitors agreed to pull the offensive ads.

The Fruit of the Loom Guys were phased out when the company launched its more modern "We fit America like we never did before" campaign in 1988. The television spots featured family scenes, including a mother dropping her daughter off at the school bus, and also included the first views of a woman in a pair of panties on network television. The $25 million campaign, created by Grey Advertising, Inc., emphasized Fruit of the Loom's move into basic apparel for both sexes and all ages.

The brand extensions, expanded capacity, advertising blitz and years of debt paid off in 1988 when Fruit of the Loom made its first profit since its acquisition by Farley. The mid-1980s capital investments had pumped up domestic operating margins to 20 to 25 percent, and European plants began earning profits in the early 1990s. Sales had actually grown 13 percent annually since 1976 to $1 billion in 1988, but debt had consumed all of the income.

In 1990, Fruit of the Loom unveiled the underwear industry's first network advertisements that featured a male model sporting the flagship white briefs. The commercials asked the musical question, "Whose underwear is under there?" The answer was provided by hunky celebrities Ed Marinaro, Patrick Duffy, and James DePavia. Lawyers for Grey Advertising spent two weeks battling one of the big three networks to air the commercials that would have been banned just three years earlier. Over the next two years, Fruit of the Loom's celebrity "underwearers" would include soap-opera star Don Diamont, action-adventure hero David Hasselhoff, and sitcom dad Alan Thicke.

Continued Challenges in the 1990s and Beyond

In 1991, Fruit of the Loom introduced the "It's your time," campaign for its growing line of casualwear, which was extended to include garments for infants and toddlers. The company enlarged its array of brands that year through a licensing agreement with the upscale Munsingwear brand in the hopes of expanding Fruit of the Loom's retail distribution.

The company's financial restabilization continued. Debt was reduced by more than $332 million with the help of sales totaling $1.4 billion, a stock offering of $100 million, a decline in capital expenditures, and the conversion of $60 million of debt into equity. Fruit of the Loom's European sales surged 43 percent in 1990 as these divisions hit stride.

Despite a lingering recession in the United States, the company once again found its capacity constrained. Farley and Holland predicted that Fruit of the Loom would invest $125 million in new equipment and increase the workforce by 3,000 at plants in the United States, Canada, and Europe in 1992. With strong ties to mass merchandisers, major product launches, and line extensions, Fruit of the Loom hoped to increase sales 15 percent each year, decrease debt load, and grow per share earnings by one third annually in the 1990s.

However, Fruit of the Loom's optimism led to manufacturing overcapacity in 1993. Management responded by cutting back production; unfortunately, customer spending was starting to rebound then from the recession of the early 1990s. In 1994, cotton prices unexpectedly rose and exacerbated the company's problems. Fruit of the Loom's stock price fell 50 percent between 1993 and 1995.

The company took several steps to correct its problems. In an effort to reduce its dependency on low-margin briefs and boxers, Fruit of the Loom focused on developing activewear and casualwear products, both by continuing to broaden the product lines of its traditional brands and by purchasing new brands. In 1993 the company acquired Salem Sportswear and arranged a licensing agreement to manufacture and market athletic wear under the Wilson logo. The following year it acquired sports logo clothing makers Artex Manufacturing Inc. and Pro Player. Also in 1994 it bought the bankrupt sportswear maker Gitano Group, Inc., for $100 million. By 1995, only 25 percent of the company's revenues derived from sales of men's and boys' underwear.

Fruit of the Loom also addressed operating inefficiencies in the early and mid-1990s. It invested in modernizing its manufacturing facilities, from spinning the yarn to assembling the finished clothing. However, in 1995 the company took more drastic measures to cut costs: It closed nine manufacturing facilities in the United States and laid off 6,000 employees. With the hope of cutting costs through lower-cost offshore labor, the company began moving its sewing operations—a labor-intensive step in manufacturing clothing—to the Caribbean and Central America. One-time charges related to the plant closings and relocations added to Fruit of the Loom's losses for 1995, which tallied in at $227 million.

The following year, Fruit of the Loom helped fund its manufacturing relocations by selling the operating assets of its hosiery division to Renfro Corp. for $90 million. In 1997 the company laid off an additional 4,800 workers and closed another U.S. plant. By that time, over 60 percent of the company's production was taking place internationally, with plans for it to reach 80 percent by 1999.

Although the company returned to the black in 1996, with approximately $147 million in net earnings, in 1997 the company saw another loss. The net loss of $488 million was due in part to continuing costs of moving sewing operations offshore, and to a charge of $102 million made to pay a legal judgment against Fruit of the Loom. The court judgment ended litigation dating from 1984 related to the Fruit of the Loom subsidiary Universal Manu-

facturing (which the company sold in 1986). However, sales were also down to $2.1 billion from $2.4 billion in 1996.

The company's reduction in labor expenses seemed to be reaping rewards early in 1998. First quarter profits were up 38 percent, and a price increase in men's underwear in April 1998 indicated potentially higher margins in a traditionally low-margin area for Fruit of the Loom. CEO William Farley expressed confidence in a press release in February 1998: ''We feel strongly that the company can affect a strong recovery in 1998. Inventories are expected to decline while capital spending will continue to be restrained. These factors should help to improve cash flow and, along with better operating performance, result in improved shareholder returns.'' However, similar optimism had been expressed earlier in the decade and the predictions did not materialize. The company's performance over the next couple of years would tell if such confidence was warranted.

Principal Subsidiaries

NWI Land Management Corp.; Union Underwear Co., Inc.; Fruit of the Loom GmbH; Russell Hosier Mills, Inc.; Camp Hosiery Company, Inc.; Union Sales, Inc.; Union Yarn Mills, Inc.; FOL International; Fruit of the Loom International, Ltd.; Fruit of the Loom Investments, Ltd.; Fruit of the Loom Trading Company.

Further Reading

Applebaum, Cara, ''Fruit of the Loom Sticks with Stars,'' *Adweek's Marketing Week,* February 4, 1991, p. 8.
''Bill Farley Could Lose His Shirt and His Underwear,'' *Business Week,* March 11, 1991, p. 86.
''Boyswear Brightens the Apparel Picture,'' *Discount Merchandiser,* December 1991, p. 52.
''Commanding Lead in Men's Underwear,'' *Discount Merchandiser,* August 1992, p. 38.
Corwin, Pat, ''More Options in Men's Underwear,'' *Discount Merchandiser,* September 1990, pp. 36–39.
Esquivel, Josephine R., ''The Pains and Gains of '91,'' *Bobbin,* June 1992, pp. 50–60.
Fannin, Rebecca, ''Underwear: Inspector 12 Takes on the Fruits,'' *Marketing & Media Decisions,* April 1988, pp. 55–56.
''Fruit of the Loom, Hanes Stretch from Skivvies into Active Wear,'' *Adweek's Marketing Week,* December 2, 1991, p. 7.
Greising, David. ''Bill Farley in on Pins and Needles,'' *Business Week,* September 18, 1989, p. 58.
Laing, Jonathan R., ''Love that Leverage!'' *Barron's,* May 1, 1989, p. 6.
Levine, Joshua, ''Marketing: Fantasy, Not Flesh,'' *Forbes,* January 22, 1990, pp. 118–120.
Oneal, Michael, ''Fruit of the Loom Escalates the Underwars,'' *Business Week,* February 22, 1988, p. 114.
''Profit Surges 38% on Moves to Reduce Labor Expenses,'' *Wall Street Journal,* April 16, 1998, p. A8.
Schifrin, Matthew, ''Matchmaker Leon?'' *Forbes,* March 28, 1994, p. 20.
Stark, Ellen, ''The Underwear King Could Snap Back for a 43 % Gain,'' *Money,* February 1995, p. 57.
Zipser, Andy, ''Cherry-picking Fruit of the Loom,'' *Barron's,* May 20, 1991, pp. 30–31.

—April S. Dougal
—updated by Susan Windisch Brown

GATX Corporation

500 West Monroe Street
Chicago, Illinois 60661-3676
U.S.A.
(312) 621-6200
Fax: (312) 621-6698
(800) 428-8161
Web site: http://www.gatx.com

Public Company
Incorporated: 1902 as German-American Car Company
Employees: 6,000
Sales: $1.7 billion (1997)
Stock Exchanges: New York
Ticker Symbol: GMT
SICs: 3743 Railroad Equipment; 4741 Rental of Railroad
   Cars; 6159 Miscellaneous Business Credit; 7359
   Equipment Rental and Leasing Not Elsewhere
   Classified

GATX Corporation's business is to provide capital equipment to its customers—usually other companies—enabling them to transport, store, distribute, or finance their own products. GATX is divided into five segments: railcar leasing and management, terminals and pipelines, logistics and warehousing, financial services, and Great Lakes shipping. As of the late 1990s, the company's principal business was the leasing of tank and other specialty cars to railroads and shippers. The dominant tank-leasing company in the United States, GATX's fleet of railcars is one of the largest in the world, including the fleets owned by railroads. To support this fleet of railcars, the company maintains an extensive system of maintenance facilities. Its second-largest operation is that of GATX Capital Corporation, whose primary business is the leasing of aircraft. Other principal businesses include the operation of an extensive network of bulk liquid storage facilities through GATX Terminals Corporation; shipping on the Great Lakes through American Steamship Company; and leasing and managing different communication technology assets—such as desktop computer sys-

tems and local area networks—through Centron DPL Company, Inc. and Sun Financial Group, Inc.

Early History

GATX was founded by Max Epstein in 1898. At that time, the Duquesne Brewery of Pittsburgh, Pennsylvania, was in need of refrigerator cars in which to ship beer. Epstein, then working in the Chicago stockyards, connected Duquesne with Armour and Co., which had 48 old cars to dispose of. Before Duquesne representatives came to view the cars, Epstein had their florid company logo emblazoned on one. At first sight, the Duquesne reps thought the car was a giant billboard for their company and purchased 20 cars.

Epstein purchased the other 28 cars on a mortgage, using as down payment his $1,000 commission from the Duquesne sale. He began leasing cars under the name The Atlantic Seaboard Dispatch. Three years later, in 1902, the company incorporated as the German-American Car Company, a name taken after a Chicago packing firm. Although other companies also rented out cars as needed, Epstein originated the idea of leasing specialty cars to shippers on a long-term basis. The continuing mainstay of the business was the leasing of tank and other specialty cars to railroads and shippers that cannot bear the cost and upkeep of maintaining such complex cars year round.

By 1907, with 360 tank cars and 73 refrigerator cars, the company had shifted its focus to tank cars and established itself as a prominent lessor. The same year, it moved its repair facilities from a bit of rail trackage in Chicago, Illinois, to a larger site in East Chicago, Indiana.

The company was able to attract certain customers by creating custom-designed cars for their products. Among its early specialty cars were chromium steel-lined cars to transport nitric acid; rubber-lined cars for phosphoric and muriatic acid; high pressure cars, which were developed in 1914; nickel-lined cars for transport of caustic substances; and air-tight cars for dry-ice transport. By 1916 the business merited a stock offering, and stock was listed under the name General American Tank Car Company (GATC), which served as a holding company for its subsidiaries.

In 1925 the company officially entered into the field of bulk liquid storage, sowing the seeds for what would become the GATX Terminals Corporation, an operation that reached international proportions by the early 1990s with 27 terminals in the United States, 7 in the United Kingdom, and a world-wide daily throughput capacity of 69 million barrels.

In 1928 GATC purchased Sharon Tank Car Corporation, whose manufacturing facilities in Sharon, Pennsylvania, became GATC's second building site.

Expansion During the Depression

In 1929, the year Black Friday's stock market crash ushered the United States into the Great Depression, the company posted its best earnings to date. The following year, profits were over $6.5 million, or $8.03 per share, exceeding those of 1929 by 13 percent. Assets reached $90 million for General American and its subsidiaries, and the company operated a fleet of 50,000 cars.

Epstein's company weathered the Great Depression well, increasing profits each year despite the general financial malaise permeating the country. The three qualities that maintained the business during the Depression years are those that have continually kept earnings on a steady incline to the present day. First, the company transported products such as petroleum and food; during an economic depression, the price of these items may fall, but demand remains constant, thus ensuring the need for their transport. Second, the company ran its leases over relatively long periods—usually three or four years—enabling it to ride out tough times on the cushion of old leases. Finally, the constant repair and maintenance work needed for the cars was a continual source of work for its manufacturing facilities, even when new car orders were low.

In 1932, Epstein, shortly after he became chairman and Lester Selig was appointed president, declared that "a time of depression is the best time to make mergers. You can make better deals then." While the company made only three acquisitions before 1926, it made thirteen between 1926 and 1931, with five of these coming after 1929. These included the company's first foreign subsidiary in 1928, Allegmeine Transpotmittel Aktiengesellschaft.

In 1936 the assets and property of most of the subsidiaries were transferred to GATC, and the subsidiaries dissolved into the larger company. GATC would later become a portion of a larger holding company, GATX Corporation, which remains in present day as the parent company for all remaining businesses

discussed. GATC took over the management of the Pressed Steel Car Co., the United States' third-largest car builder. By 1940, the company was operating 60,000 various kinds of freight cars, making it the country's largest freight car leasing system. The company's bulk liquid storage system had also grown in its first 14 years to become the country's largest public liquid storage terminal facility.

By the end of World War II, the company's two main enterprises remained the leasing of railcars and their manufacture. The company, however, was interested in diversifying, principally into the transportation-related fields. It had made some significant outside acquisitions in the 1930s, but many of them—such as a plastics facility and a bus manufacturing operation—would soon be sold off as unprofitable.

Diversification through the Mid-Century

The most portentous diversification came in 1939, when the company acquired about 50 percent interest in Barkley-Grow Aircraft Corporation, a Detroit aircraft builder. By the early 1940s, GATC was also operating cargo ships on the Great Lakes, foreshadowing its later domination of that trade. By 1952, the company ranked as the country's fourth-largest manufacturer of freight cars, as well as the largest lessor. The terminal and storage business continued to grow slowly and steadily, contributing 15 percent of 1952's net earning.

In 1954, having earned profits every year since its incorporation, the company acquired Fuller Co., a business that built turnkey cement plants. Fuller was a wise investment that yielded steady profits until its sale in 1986. In 1959 came the purchase of Traylor Engineering & Manufacturing Company, a producer of cement machinery to complement Fuller's operations. In addition to other projects, the company constructed a cement plant in the Philippines in 1960 and an industrial waste treatment plant for Whippany Board Co. in 1962.

In 1960, the company earned record profits of $3.44 per share, despite the fact that the railroad industry in general was a dark spot on the national economy. By the early 1960s, leasing of capital equipment had become a popular way of doing business in several fields, including trucking, airplanes, and tugboats. Automation developments in the 1960s made hauling less labor-intensive, and so the company developed several products that were more mechanized, including a 20,000-gallon wine tank and side-loading device for transferring 20-foot containers.

In 1961 GATC set up its two Sharon, Pennsylvania, manufacturing plants as a separate division of the company, and T. M. Thompson moved into the position of chairman. In 1963 there was a huge boom in orders because the railroads were stepping up their competition with trucking and barges due to changes in the federal tax laws which made capital equipment purchases desirable. As a result, the company reported the biggest backlog of rail flat-car orders in its history up to that point. Equipment lease demand remained strong through 1965, and the company ranked fifth among builders as well. Both of the company's main areas of business were booming. By 1968, as sales of freight cars dropped significantly throughout the industry, GATC stopped producing freight cars, although it continued to build tank cars. Design and development of freight cars continued, but the company began relying on outside manufacturers to increase its fleet-size.

With the down-sizing of manufacturing facilities, the company entered into a somewhat unfocused period of diversification, which yielded both weak and strong investments. Among the profitable ventures was the formation in 1967 of GATX Leasing, which focused on the leasing of airplanes. This was the core of the contemporary GATX Capital Corporations, one of the country's oldest non-bank capital equipment leasing companies.

Also profitable was the 1973 acquisition of American Steamship Company (ASC), which considerably expanded the company's trade in the Great Lakes Shipping market. By 1977, ASC carried 15 percent of the growing Great Lakes cargo trade. By the early 1990s it operated the largest self-unloading fleet on the Great Lakes.

Among the less profitable acquisitions was the purchase in 1968 of Chicago's LaSalle National Bank, which subsequent holding company legislation forced GATX to divest by 1980. In addition, a particularly burdensome acquisition was made in 1979, when the company purchased an ocean-tanker business from Chinese entrepreneur C. Y. Chen for $65 million. GATX anticipated similarity between tank-leasing and ocean ship-leasing because the two industries serve the same customers and haul similar cargo. The company did not consider, however, that the cost of building an ocean-going ship is hundreds of times what it costs to build a train car. Nor did the company realize that the industry was in a state of overcapacity and would take a drastic downturn in the 1980s, rendering it weaker than it had been during the Great Depression. The confluence of these trends led the ocean shipping subsidiary to lose a hefty $7 million in 1976.

Restructuring in the 1970s and 1980s

The cost of GATX's diversification errors was a few years of declining income from 1974 through 1977, a period in which it posted a $40 million loss provision, based mostly on losses and difficulties in the ocean shipping business. The company changed to its current name of GATX Corporation in 1975, becoming a holding company for its various subsidiaries, and in 1977 GATX began restructuring. In terms of management changes, this meant the replacement of five of the ten board members between 1977 and 1980. By choosing outsiders, GATX freed key managers to work in operating units. Fran Theis was appointed president and James Glasser became chairman and chief executive officer.

GATX redefined itself as a business concerned with providing equipment and services for extracting, processing, and distributing dry and liquid bulk commodities. This resulted in the sale of most of the company's insurance operations, a drastic reduction in its ocean shipping, and the sale of an 84 percent interest in the LaSalle National Bank. The company posted growth in 1978 and 1979, and the remaining sectors began gaining strength.

In the early 1980s GATX narrowed its focus even more, centering on its service business and divesting its manufacturing operations. Expecting a diminishing demand for railcars at least through 1990, it completely closed its manufacturing facil-

ities in 1984. It retained, though, its perennially profitable Fuller Co. until 1986. In 1981 the company blundered by acquiring the manufacturing facilities of Tech Specialty, a concern that lost money every year after its acquisition. By 1986 it was finally sold, as the company also completely shed its ocean shipping lines, which became Marine Transport Line, Inc.

The restructuring resulted in some financial ups and downs for GATX. In 1984 its profit was $36.7 million due to a $78 million write down, and the following year the company lost $45.5 million. The instability, combined with some solid business, attracted some unwanted suitors for GATX. Leucadia National, a New York finance and insurance company, led a bidding war when it made an unsolicited offer to GATX to purchase the rest of its stock at $38 per share. GATX immediately turned down the offer, but Adler & Shaykin, a New York investment firm that specialized in leveraged buyouts, stepped in the next week with an offer of $40 per share. Leucadia matched the offer, and in the third week Gabelli & Co., another New York investment firm, topped the offers with a proposal of $42 per share.

GATX chose Leucadia, but the firm backed out of the deal less than two hours before their midnight deadline. Leucadia had previously provided a letter from Merrill Lynch supporting its ability to find adequate financial backing, and it had full access to GATX books. Nevertheless, its abrupt withdrawal was based, it said, on unforeseen financial obligations stemming from GATX debts. After the takeover war, GATX fortified itself against a repeat performance by repurchasing 30 percent of its stock and adopting certain defensive measures concerning the distribution of shareholder rights. In 1986 it sold both Fuller and Al Tech, completing its withdrawal from manufacturing.

In 1988 GATX Capital forged a joint venture with Credit Lyonnais, one of Europe's largest banks, to do all future aircraft leasing. By 1989, the two companies sold 40 percent of the interest to four other financial backers. GATX was left with 40 percent interest as manager of the operation. The company concentrated on leasing high-demand, medium-range craft. By the early 1990s, however, the airplane market had taken a downturn, causing lower-than-expected earnings.

Within the financial division of GATX, a real estate division was established in 1985 that did not fare well. The company reduced its real estate investment from $204 million at the end of 1989 to $170 million at the end of 1990. Heading into the 1990s, GATX Capital Corporation's portfolio of investments were 44 percent in commercial jet aircraft, 14 percent in railroad equipment, 13 percent in real estate, 7 percent in production equipment, and 5 percent in golf equipment, with a remaining 17 percent in other fields.

Rapid expansion of GATX Terminals in the late 1980s and early 1990 included the purchase of a 60 percent interest in WYCO pipeline and the acquisition of the Calney Pipeline. In 1989 it announced a joint venture to build a major petroleum facility in Singapore. Also in 1989 GATX acquired Associated Unit Companies, whose name was changed in 1990 to The Unit Companies, Inc. Although it operated at a $400,000 loss in 1990 and a $700,000 loss in 1991, the company was the largest provider of warehousing and distribution in the United States with 127 locations in 35 cities. The subsidiary's name was again changed a short time later to GATX Logistics, Inc.

General Expansion in the 1990s

Although some of its businesses were experiencing reduced profits, GATX headed into the 1990s looking strong. From 1986 to 1991 its income expanded at a 24 percent compound annual growth rate, and it could boast that it had paid a dividend every quarter since 1919. It continued to design new railcars such as the Arcticar, a cryogenically cooled jumbo car for frozen food transport. It also continued to supply industry-specialized cars, such as the Airslide car—used in the flour industry—and its interconnected tank cars, in which a string of cars can be filled or emptied from a single hook-up point. It stood as a market leader in each of its diverse yet focused operating sectors, and still dominated the backbone industry it helped create: the leasing of tank cars.

In the early and mid-1990s GATX focused its expansion efforts internationally. In 1993 the company purchased the Scottish Sealand Oil Services Ltd. The following year it formed GATX EnviroLease Corp., a joint venture with EnviroLease, Inc. to provide capital equipment for the transport of wastes and recyclable materials by rail. The new company would provide lease financing for special-purpose containers, chassis, railcars, and other material- and container-handling equipment, which would provide safe transport of such materials as municipal solid waste, incinerator and coal ash, industrial sludge, and contaminated soil.

In 1995 GATX formed another international joint venture by teaming its GATX Rail Europe, Inc., with AAE Ahaus Alstatter Eisenbahn Holding AG, Switzerland. The venture company, AAE Ahaus Alstatter Eisenbahn Cargo AG, would provide services to government-owned railways and rail transportation companies across Europe with an initial fleet of over 2,000 freight cars. The same year the company expanded its presence in Mexico by leasing 1,200 tank cars to the state railroad. In 1996 GATX acquired 65 percent ownership of a bulk-liquid storage facility in Altamira, Mexico.

Sales climbed steadily for GATX in the early and mid-1990s, rising from $870 million in 1990 to $1.1 billion in 1993 to $1.4 billion in 1996. Net income faltered somewhat in the early 1990s, but by 1994 had reached $92 million, surpassing the company's previous high of $83 million in 1990. In 1996, net income reached $103 million. In 1995 the company added 5,300 new and used railcars to its fleet.

GATX Capital, which had begun leasing information technology equipment in the mid-1980s, increased its commitment to this market in the mid-1990s. Having established joint ventures with lessors of various equipment types, GATX acquired full ownership of Centron DPL Company, Inc. in 1996 and Sun Financial Group, Inc. in 1997. The goal of GATX's Technology Services Group was to provide "one-stop" solutions to customers' information technology needs.

Although the company achieved record sales of $1.7 billion in 1997, restructuring costs resulted in a net loss of $51 million. Most of the restructuring charges were attributed to changes implemented in GATX Terminals, including the sale or closing of the company's Staten Island terminal and certain U.K. terminal assets. Other charges could be traced to GATX Logistics' writing off of past acquisitions in the public warehousing sector, an area the company had decided to abandon as unprofitable. Without these charges, 1997 consolidated income would have been a healthy $112 million. With these one-time charges behind them, the company expected their profitability to rebound in 1998, their 100th anniversary year.

Principal Subsidiaries

General American Transportation Corp.; GATX Terminals Corporation; GATX Financial Services, Inc.; GATX Capital Corp.; American Steamship Company; GATX Logistics, Inc.

Further Reading

Altschul, Selig, "General American's Diversified Business," *Barron's,* April 8, 1940.
Byrne, Harlan S., "GATX Corp.: Despite the Economy's Slowdown, Record Profits Are in Store," *Barron's,* December 24, 1990.
"Business Turns to Equipment Leasing," *Financial World,* February 1, 1961.
"Car-Builder's Net Propped by Leasing," *Barron's,* April 3, 1950.
Deveny, Kathleen, "GATX Is in Play—And It Doesn't Seem to Mind," *Business Week,* March 17, 1986.
"EMD and GATX Form Joint Leasing Venture," *Railway Age,* June 1996, p. 24.
Epstein, Ralph C., *GATX: A History of the General American Transportation Corporation, 1898–1948,* New York: North River Press, 1948.
"GATX Capital Corp. and EnviroLease, Inc. Form GATX EnviroLease Corp. Joint Venture," *Railway Age,* May 1994, p. 28.
"GATX Capital Corp.," *Railway Age,* March 1997, p. 8.
"GATX Corp. Agrees with LaSalle National on Divestiture Plan," *Wall Street Journal,* October 21, 1976.
"GATX Corp. Creates European Freight Car Joint Venture," *Railway Age,* February 1995, p. 60.
"GATX Earnings," *New York Times,* April 29, 1998, p. B15.
"GATX to Stop Making Freight Cars: Leasing, Tank-Car Output to Continue," *Wall Street Journal,* April 24, 1968.
"Increase in Earnings Seen for Railroad Car Company," *Barron's,* March 22, 1954.
Richards, Bill, "GATX Board Clears Leucadia Merger Offer," *Wall Street Journal,* March 24, 1986.
"They Shudda Stayed on Dry Land," *Forbes,* July 15, 1977.
" 'This Is the Time for Mergers,' Says General American Tank Car," *Business Week,* March 25, 1931.
"Transportation Company Net Stabilized at High Level," *Barron's,* March 31, 1952.
Troxell, Thomas N., Jr., "Boxcar Power," *Barron's,* August 20, 1979.
Williams, John D., "Freight Car Boom," *Wall Street Journal,* February 21, 1963.

—Elaine Belsito
—updated by Susan Windisch Brown

Gaumont SA

30, avenue Charles de Gaulle
92522 Neuilly-Sur-Seine CEDEX
France
(33) 1.46.43.20.00
Fax: (33) 1.47.38.12.18
Web site: http://www.gaumont.fr

Public Company
Incorporated: 1895 as Société Léon Gaumont et Cie
Employees: 900
Sales: FFr 1.908 billion (US $329 million) (1997)
Stock Exchanges: Paris
SICs: 7812 Motion Picture & Video Production; 7832
   Motion Picture Theaters Except Drive-In

With one of the most illustrious names in motion picture history, Gaumont SA has developed into one of Europe's leading motion picture production and distribution houses. Gaumont's activities are grouped under three principal divisions: the production of films (Film and Television) and their distribution (Circuit) both worldwide and through the exploitation of the company's France-based network of multiplex cinemas.

Through its Circuit division, Gaumont owns and operates more than 300 cinemas—almost all multiplex—throughout France, as well as, to a more limited extent, in Belgium (Antwerp), Switzerland (Geneva), and the United States (New York). Many Gaumont theaters feature at least one so-called "Grand Ecran," that is, a screen measuring at least 14 meters (45.5 feet) tall and reaching proportions of 24 by 10 meters (78 by 32.5 feet). All new Gaumont theaters and all recently renovated Gaumont theaters feature a Grand Ecran. In addition, Gaumont has an exclusive agreement to operate Imax theaters in France. Legislation adopted by the French government in 1996 limiting the development of multiplex theaters has encouraged Gaumont to look beyond France for future growth. In 1997 the company opened or acquired theaters in Geneva and Antwerp; the company also has developed a partnership with the Czech Republic's Bonton to extend its distribution activities to that country and neighboring Slovakia. In addition to operating cinemas, Gaumont acts as a worldwide distributor for its own and other films, including, through subsidiary Gaumont Buena Vista, certain Walt Disney Company productions. The company also distributes its catalog (both archives and new productions) to television.

Typically, the company's Circuit activities represent the largest part of its revenues—in 1997 that division generated FFr 797 million of the company's total FFr 1.9 billion in sales. Yet, in 1997, revenues from the company's Film division topped its distribution revenues for the first time, more than doubling over the previous year to reach FFr 914 million. The motor for this growth was the international success of Luc Besson's *The Fifth Element (Le Cinqième Elément)*, the most expensive production ever made by a European production house. That film marked a turning point of sorts for Gaumont: while the company continues to produce French-language films and television programs, it has adopted a strategy of increasing the number of its English-language productions, with the view of competing with the Hollywood giants on the international scene. In its production catalog the company also includes such internationally seen television programs as "The Highlander." Gaumont also has entered the multimedia arena, producing computer and video games based on its film titles.

Pioneers of Film at the Turn of the Century

A brilliant engineering student, Léon Gaumont was forced nonetheless to leave school at the age of 16 when his father was unable to continue to pay his tuition. Gaumont apprenticed to a maker of binoculars, while continuing to study in the evenings. At the age of 28, Gaumont became the director of the Comptoir Général de la Photographie, a maker of optical and photographic equipment. A dispute among the owners of the company gave Gaumont the opportunity to buy the company and its equipment in 1895. Gaumont renamed the company Léon Gaumont et Cie.

At first producing equipment for still photography, Gaumont was quick to recognize the potential of the Cinématographe, introduced by the Lumière brothers in 1895 and inaugurating the era of motion pictures. Gaumont began working on his own motion picture camera; the following year the company brought out the Chrono. To sell the camera, Gaumont needed a means to demonstrate its usefulness. Film production was added quickly to the Gaumont enterprise and would establish the company worldwide as a leading manufacturer and production house. Yet Gaumont's primary interest lay in his company's technical—not artistic—development. Much of the company's film production activity was placed in the hands of Gaumont's secretary, Alice Guy, with the agreement that her film work would not interrupt her other duties. Guy became the first female director and one of the originators of the scenario-based film.

Between Gaumont's cameras and Guy's films, the Gaumont name became one of the most important in the turn-of-the-century film industry. The decision by the Lumière brothers to stop production of films in 1900 provided a new boost to Gaumont. With the American film industry still in its infancy, primarily based in New York, Gaumont became a principal supplier of moving pictures. Its chief competitor was another French firm, Pathé. Although much of the company's film work took place in natural settings, the company soon opened its first studio, the Théâtre Cinématographique in Buttes-Chaumont, in 1905. Gaumont also became among the first studios to offer multifilm contracts to its directors and actors. By 1912 the company began adding the names of actors to its publicity, as the cinema began to produce its first stars.

By 1904 the company's revenues had grown to 900,000 francs. The expansion of Gaumont's activities called for increased capital. Already associated with La Banque Suisse et Française (later, the Crédit Commercial de France) and with industrialist investors including Gustave Eiffel, Gaumont reorganized the company in 1906. Now known as Société des Etablissements Gaumont, the company's capital was raised to 2.5 million francs. A year later the company raised its capital base to three million francs.

For the first decade of the new century, Gaumont remained a manufacturer of cinema equipment and a producer of films. Distribution was added in 1910, following the move made two years earlier by Charles Pathé. Whereas films had previously been sold outright to the rising numbers of cinema operators, Pathé had introduced the concept of distributorships, renting films instead of selling them. Gaumont founded its own distributor group, called the Comptoir Ciné-location, which soon began exploiting cinemas as well. Owning the cinemas provided Gaumont not only with a means to distribute its films, but also the profits from the vast audiences flocking to the new entertainment form. At the time, most cinema houses in France had been converted from former theaters and vaudeville houses. Gaumont took the cinema concept a step further, converting the Hippodrome, a structure built for the 1900 Paris Expo, into the Gaumont-Palace. Opened in 1911, the Palace was the world's largest cinema, with 3,400 seats, setting a new standard for cinema comfort and opulence.

In the years leading to the First World War, the company constructed a second studio in Nice, taking advantage of that region's natural light and mild climate. In Paris, meanwhile, the company had continued to expand its operations, building a complex of workshops, studios, and processing laboratories that became known as the Cité Elge (the pronunciation of Gaumont's initials) and eventually would cover some 25,000 square meters. Gaumont recorded a film first, with the presentation of the world's first animated film, *Fantasmagorie*, in 1908. The company soon launched its own string of serial films, including the famous *Fantomas* series directed by Louis Feuillade, who had succeeded Alice Guy in 1907. In 1910 Gaumont also began producing a cinema magazine, *Gaumont Actualités,* the forerunner to the newsreel. By 1914, with revenues of some three million francs per year, Gaumont neared full vertical integration, not only producing film cameras and projectors, but developing and processing film, operating studios, and building its own decors and storehouses for its sets, props, and costumes. The company also had established a worldwide presence, with offices, agencies, and studios in cities including New York, London, Moscow, Vienna, Budapest, Calcutta, Saigon, Barcelona, Casablanca, Buenos Aires, Montreal, and elsewhere. Gaumont had become one of the world's foremost providers of motion pictures and equipment, with production reaching as high as 145 films per year.

World War Setbacks

The consequences of the First World War were dramatic for the French and European film industry and for Gaumont. Not only did Gaumont lose as much as 15 percent of its work force to wartime casualties, but the war had disrupted its international distribution. Emerging from the war, the film industry had undergone a drastic change: Hollywood had begun to conquer the worldwide motion picture scene. Meanwhile, the loss of Gaumont's Axis audiences extended beyond the war years; even among allied countries, the rise of national film industries throughout Europe during the war years resulted in the end of their dependence on the French filmmakers for product. Although the company had continued to produce films during the war, the loss of the company's international market forced Gaumont to cut back severely on production. In 1919 its total production was a mere 11 films.

Gaumont began losing money, forcing it to turn to its investors. By 1921 its capital investment had reached ten million francs. The company soon passed under the control of the Crédit Commercial. Although Léon Gaumont remained at the head of the company until 1932, the bank imposed its own members on the company's direction, eventually taking over Gaumont's operations entirely. The company attempted to shore up its position by forming strategic distribution partnerships with international film producers, including Italy's UCI, Sweden's Svenska, and the United States' Metro Goldwyn. The company also reopened many of its foreign agencies and offices. But there was little the company could do against the enormous success of Hollywood. By 1925 Gaumont's production had fallen to just three films, competing against as many as 400 Hollywood imports, which combined to account for more than 80 percent of the French box office. In that year Gaumont took the drastic step of abandoning nearly all of its film production efforts.

Gaumont fared little better on the technical side. The film industry was turning to so-called talking pictures, which required a new generation of film recording and projection equipment. Gaumont developed its own version of sound equipment, succeeding in outfitting a strong percentage of France's cinemas with its designs. To impose the Gaumont equipment on the cinema circuit, the company began forming alliances, merging with other cinema network operators to form Gaumont-Franco-Film-Aubert in 1930. The company also began looking to acquire other French cinema equipment manufacturers, including Constinsouza. But the technical progress made by the company's American and German competitors proved to be too much competition for Gaumont.

In 1932, Gaumont, under a new director, Paul Keim, ended its film and projection equipment manufacturing activities. The company again closed down its foreign branches; also shut down were its costly Paris and Nice film studios. At the same time, Gaumont took steps to bring its distribution network under centralized control, taking over programming for its theater network. Although the company had stepped up film production in that year, to nine films, its debt was growing even faster. Exacerbated by the Depression, Gaumont's debt would reach some 320 million francs by mid-decade. Finally, in 1935, the company declared bankruptcy. Its only consolation was that its chief French rival, Pathé, had declared bankruptcy several months before.

By 1937 Gaumont suspended all operations but its distribution and theater circuit. In 1938, however, the company found a new owner, the French media giant Havas. Renamed the Société Nouvelle des Etablissements Gaumont, the company was placed under charge of Alain Poiré, grandson of Havas President Léon Rénier. Under Poiré, Gaumont would regain much of its international renown.

Gaumont was aided, paradoxically, by the German occupation of France during World War II. With British and, soon, American film imports banned, French filmmakers once again took a central place at the box office. Yet the uplift was short-lived. By the end of the war, with the French and European economies in ruins, with large numbers of the French theater circuit destroyed by bombs, and with a shortage of both film stock and personnel, Gaumont was forced to suspend production again. Meanwhile, the Hollywood invasion had returned in force.

Postwar Allure

Production resumed in 1947, inaugurating a period of renewed success for the French cinema. In the early 1950s Gaumont discovered a novel method of competing against the American film juggernaut. The 1953 film, *Caroline Chérie,* had proved a great success for Gaumont, paying back its production costs within months. The reason for the film's success was its willingness to portray nudity, a feature the American film industry, under tight and puritanical censor, was forbidden to exploit. The success of the film sparked a series of sequels and made its lead actress, Martine Carol, a star.

At the same time, Gaumont was pursuing another strategy, that of buying up many of France's cinemas and renovating all of its theaters to provide a new level of comfort to the audience. These audiences also were treated to a new era of filmmakers and their films that would place France once again at the pinnacle of international film. The French New Wave cinema, including directors such as François Truffaut, Alain Resnais, Jean-Luc Godard, and Claude Chabrol, gave new allure to Gaumont and the country's film industry. In the early 1960s, with the creation of subsidiary Gaumont International, the company began engaging in coproduction activities with Italian producers, where such directors as Fellini, Antonioni, and Pasolini were making their marks on world cinema.

In the mid-1960s Gaumont formed a distribution alliance with rival Pathé, giving the two companies a network of 150 theaters, for a total of 120,000 seats, and a virtual monopoly on the French cinema industry. The alliance would last nearly 20 years, until it was broken by French government intervention. In the late 1960s and early 1970s the company began installing automatic projection booths, and then began converting its theaters into a new multiplex concept, which, giving a greater programming flexibility, proved a hit with audiences. During the 1970s Gaumont's production arm would have a string of successes, including the *Tall Blonde Man* series.

In 1975 a new director arrived at Gaumont. Through share purchases, Nicolas Seydoux, grandson of industrial leader Marcel Schlumberger and brother of later Pathé owner Jérôme Seydoux, had succeeded in gaining control of the company. Under Seydoux and his CEO Daniel Toscan du Plantier, the company, renamed simply Gaumont, began an ambitious expansion program. Apart from forming distribution alliances, among others, with the United States' Fox, Seydoux and Toscan moved to expand Gaumont's operations internationally by opening production and distribution subsidiaries in Brazil and Italy, forming Gaumont Inc. in the United States, founding Triumph Films in a partnership with Columbia, opening two Gaumont-owned theaters in New York City, and taking a 50 percent share of Téléfrance, a cable channel meant to bring French-language programming to U.S. audiences. Beyond film, the company sought to expand into publishing, purchasing Editions Ramsay and the weekly magazine *Le Point.*

Retreat and Rebuilding in the 1980s and 1990s

The ambitions of these plans proved too much for Gaumont. By the early 1980s, with losses of FFr 245 million on revenues of FFr 1.3 billion, the company was forced to abandon many of its new projects, closing down its Italian and Brazilian subsidiaries and its U.S. cable venture. The company later would sell off its money-losing publishing activities as well. Gaumont regrouped around its distribution and network and its production activities. The latter found a new market in the opening of the French television system to private broadcasters in the mid-1980s. The new competition not only produced a greater demand for programming, but also boosted prices. Gaumont now extended its production activities to include programs and films for television, while finding a ready market for its vast archives of films and film footage.

The inauguration of a new theater concept—that of the giant screen—would help revive the dwindling cinema audiences. In the 1990s Gaumont would begin incorporating giant screens into each of its new and renovated multiplexes—which themselves were reaching as many as 15 theaters. A series of hits also would provide a boost to the company, including the international success of Luc Besson's *The Big Blue* and the 1993 smash hit, *Les Visiteurs,* which set a French audience record of 14 million tickets sold. In the mid-1990s Gaumont would take a new risk, producing for a record European budget of FFr 500 million another Luc Besson feature, *The Fifth Element*. The production capped a developing Gaumont strategy of returning to the international production stage. Filmed in English and released in 1997, *The Fifth Element* would prove a resounding success worldwide. That film alone was enough to double the company's cinema revenues for the year, pushing its sales to nearly FFr 2 billion.

The company opened 1998 with a new hit on its hands, *Les Visiteurs II,* affirming the company's commitment to French-language production, even as it pursued its English-language aims. While Hollywood continued to dominate the world's cinemas, Gaumont seemed ready to reassert its position as a major player in the international film scene.

Further Reading

Garçon, Françoise, *Gaumont: Un Siecle de Cinéma,* Paris: Gallimard, 1992.

Les Echos, "Gaumont Va Produire Plus de Films en Anglais," *Les Echos,* May 7, 1997, p. 50.

Leventer, Martine, "Gaumont: Un Nouveau Montage," *Le Point,* December 10, 1984, p. 120.

Meyer, Phillipe, "Gaumont: Le Retournement," *L'Express,* December 14, 1984, p. 107.

Normand, Clarisse, "Si Gaumont Nous Etait Compté," *Journal des Finances,* July 27, 1996, p. 6.

—M.L. Cohen

GC Companies, Inc.

27 Boylston Street
Chestnut Hill, Massachusetts 02167
U.S.A
(617) 278-5600
Fax: (617) 277-2787
(800) 325-6027
Web site: http://www.generalcinema.com

Public Company
Incorporated: 1922 as Philip Smith Theatrical Enterprises
Employees: 7,200
Sales: $447 million (1997)
Stock Exchanges: New York
Ticker Symbol: GCX
SICs: 7832 Motion Picture Theaters, Except Drive-Ins;
    6799 Investors, Not Elsewhere Classified

Although it invests in industries as diverse as optical superstores and cable television operators, GC Companies, Inc., considers its core business to be that of General Cinema Theaters, one of the leading movie exhibitors in the United States. As of 1997, General Cinema Theatres operated 175 theaters in 24 states in the United States, and 5 theaters in Mexico and Argentina. Having closed dozens of unproductive theaters in the mid-1990s, the company was expanding in the late 1990s—both internationally and through the construction of domestic multiplexes.

Company Origins

Philip Smith founded the precursor to GC Companies in 1922 when he bought the National Theater in Boston. The 23-year-old businessman was familiar with the infant movie industry: his father had owned two silent movie theaters in New York a couple of decades earlier, and his uncle, Serge Smith, had created one of the biggest movie studios in France. Although the National Theater was shabby and unprofitable when he purchased it, Philip Smith saw its potential. He immediately dropped ticket prices from 25 cents to 10 cents, and then developed an exhibition schedule that featured a variety of movies with several show times. This innovative plan not only helped restore the National Theater's profitability, but it soon became the industry standard. Smith named his new project Philip Smith Theatrical Enterprises.

The success of the National Theater led Smith to purchase 11 more theaters in the Boston area by 1925. Smith had created and was operating the Boston area's first independent exhibition circuit. However, the Depression forced Smith to cut back his burgeoning chain: in an effort to weather the hard times, Smith sold nine of his theaters.

By 1935, however, the Depression had ended and Smith was ready to expand once again. He took advantage of the boom in automobile ownership by opening drive-in theaters in Detroit and Cleveland. Described as the first successful drive-ins in the United States, Smith's newest twist on the exhibition circuit incorporated oversized screens and advanced speaker systems. Some of Smith's drive-ins could accommodate as many as 2,000 cars per show. To reflect the changed geographic focus of his enterprise, Smith called his new business Midwest. The drive-ins were dubbed Midwest Drive-In Theaters, as the circuit expanded into Illinois and other neighboring states by the 1940s. By the 1950s, the company had built 53 drive-in theaters throughout the United States, all of which were modestly profitable.

Mall Theaters in the 1950s

Smith was well aware of the fact that box office receipts in large urban movie houses were dwindling rapidly because of the rise of television and a reluctance on the part of suburban dwellers to travel into the city for entertainment. Throughout the 1950s population growth in the cities of the United States had been predominantly in their suburbs. More people lived farther from the central city and its movie houses than ever before. In the late 1940s, 90 million Americans viewed a film every week; the money they spent amounted to $1.7 billion in 1948. By 1958, the average weekly movie attendance was down to 39.6 million, and box office receipts had slipped below $1.2 billion.

Once again Smith led the movie exhibition industry with another innovative idea. He decided in 1951 to open a theater in a newly-constructed suburban shopping center—the suburban equivalent of "downtown." The first shopping center-based movie theater in the nation, the new Massachusetts theater benefitted from the free mall parking. The mall increasingly became the equivalent of a town square, acting as the center for both shopping and entertainment, and business boomed for Midwest. Soon, the mutually-beneficial relationship between retail stores and movie theaters was too promising for Midwest's competitors to resist. Of the approximately 180 indoor theaters built in 1961 and 1962, one-third were in shopping malls. To reflect the shifting focus of its operations, the company was renamed General Cinema Corporation in 1964. By 1970, the company was the largest shopping center theater chain in the country.

Philip Smith viewed the company's prosperity in the 1950s as an invitation to move into new industries. In an interview with the *Boston Sunday Post* in 1956, Smith explained his desire to diversify the company's holdings: "You have it good in one line and then something happens and you have to change." To protect the company from a potential downturn in the cinema industry, Smith opened a chain of restaurants called Richard's Drive-Ins, and a series of coffee shops called Amy Joe's Pancake Houses. Late in the decade, General Cinema also opened several bowling alleys.

Diversification in the 1960s–1980s

In 1960 the company went public on the New York Stock Exchange, although Smith retained a controlling interest. The next year, Philip Smith died, and his son Richard became chief executive officer. Richard oversaw a period of great diversification and expansion for the company. In the late 1960s the firm began acquiring bottling franchises, including a Pepsi bottling operation it purchased in 1968 for less than $20 million. Soon, General Cinema was the largest independent bottler in the United States, in addition to its theater operations. The company also expanded within its traditional industry. It acquired the Mann Theatres Chain of Minneapolis for $6.6 million in cash and notes in 1970. Two years later, the company purchased an interest in 47 indoor theaters located in Louisiana and Florida from Loews Corporation for nearly $16 million.

General Cinema's bottling division prospered throughout the 1970s, but in 1979, Herb Paige, the head of the division, was accused of embezzling millions of dollars from the company

and was forced to resign. He later spent two years in prison, and in the mid-1980s, was reportedly ordered by a judge to pay General Cinema over $26 million in damages.

Despite this isolated difficulty, General Cinema was known for its efficient and dependable management team. Richard Smith had a reputation for hiring businessmen with proven talent for solving financial, legal, and managerial problems. Two of his most notable "finds" were Robert J. Tarr and J. Atwood Ives. Tarr, who arrived at the company in 1976 after a career as an investment banker at PaineWebber, was named president and chief operating officer in 1985. Ives, who also joined the company after a stint at PaineWebber, became chairman and chief financial officer in 1985. These appointments seemed to signify Smith's plan to change General Cinema's reputation from that of a one-man company to that of a company in which decisions were made collectively among top executives. Yet it was hard to downplay Smith's own business acumen. According to one investor, "You're not really betting on soft drinks or movies. You're betting that Dick Smith is going to make another smart deal."

In fact, General Cinema was doing remarkably well in Smith's hands. Fiscal 1985 marked the 12th consecutive year, and the 24th out of its 25 years as a public company, in which General Cinema posted record operating results. Throughout the 1980s the beverage division, rather than the theater operation, was the strongest cash generator; it accounted for more than 70 percent of the company's annual operating earnings.

General Cinema's forays into the larger marketplace also proved rewarding. With its characteristic low profile, the company began purchasing stock in Heublein Inc. Attempting to thwart a perceived takeover by General Cinema, Heublein was finally forced to seek a higher-priced bid from another company. The result—Smith sold his holdings in Heublein for a significant profit.

In 1984 General Cinema diversified into yet another industry with the purchase of a controlling interest in Carter Hawley Hale, which was at the time the tenth largest clothing retailer in the United States, with Bergdorf Goodman and Neiman-Marcus under its control. Prior to the purchase by General Cinema, the Los Angeles-based Carter found its market share eroding in the competitive environment of California, and was soon confronted with an unwanted takeover bid from a clothing store chain. To prevent that, Carter Hawley Hale issued one million shares of preferred stock, which General Cinema purchased for $300 million. This provided General Cinema with a 37 percent interest in Carter, and helped Carter avoid a full-blown takeover. Furthermore, General Cinema's interest in Carter actually caused Carter's share value to increase dramatically, despite the fact that the company's profits were well below what had been expected on Wall Street.

Reorganization in 1990s

After having built up its bottling division over the previous two decades, General Cinema sold it in 1989 for $1.75 billion. With the vast influx of cash, the company went shopping. In 1991 it purchased the well-known but financially-ailing publishing company Harcourt Brace Jovanovich for $1.5 billion. Saddled with debt, Harcourt saw the buyout as a new lease on life. "Instead of owing $2 billion in debt, it's gone away," CEO

Peter Jovanovich said to *Publishers Weekly,* "Our balance sheet is healthy and HBJ will grow, maybe even make some acquisitions." General Cinema increased HBJ's budget for 1992 by 10 percent over the 1991 budget, to help the publisher invest in new authors and books.

Two years later, in 1993, General Cinema Corporation split itself in two portions. Harcourt General took the publishing business and the controlling interest in the Neiman-Marcus Group. The movie theater division became GC Companies, Inc., in which the Smith family retained a 28 percent controlling interest.

In the mid-1990s, GC Companies initiated a plan to weed out unproductive theaters. In 1994 the company sold a group of 14 theaters with a total of 61 screens for $14 million. The company also sold or closed several other theaters that year, reducing its holdings by 37 theaters and 133 screens. Although the loss of these theaters led to a drop in patronage and revenue, net earnings actually rose that year to $13.6 million, an occurrence which was indicative of the profitability problems the divested theaters had been causing. The following year the company sold or closed an additional 12 theaters, with 31 screens, continuing the decline in patronage. Also hurt by a net investment loss of $2.3 million, GC Companies saw a decline in net earnings to $8.7 million. Over the next couple of years, the company continued to sell or close unproductive theaters. Revenues held almost steady through 1996 and 1997 and, combined with substantial investment income, net earnings rose to $17.2 million and $14.8 million respectively.

In addition to dumping unprofitable theaters, GC Companies sought productive new theater ventures. Amidst an industry atmosphere of almost frenzied building of multiplex and megaplex theaters with up to 30 screens in each theater, GCC was cautiously expanding in the United States. It began constructing state-of-the-art megaplexes in areas where they would have the greatest impact—namely highly-populated urban and suburban areas. The new megaplexes featured amenities not found in traditional movie theaters, such as sit-down cafes for patrons to enjoy before and after viewing a movie, auditoriums with their own cafes for seat-side service, "loveseats," gourmet foods and coffees, and even liquor. Part of this strategy included selling well-known brands at the concession stands; in 1998 GCC had associations with Starbucks, Pepsi, Taco Bell, and Pizzeria Uno. The $250-million expansion plan included the construction of over 300 new screens by 1999.

New Ventures in the Late 1990s

In late 1997 GC Companies announced an alliance with the Sundance Institute to build theaters dedicated to exhibiting independent films. What megaplexes are to the Hollywood blockbuster, the new Sundance Cinemas were to be to the independent film. "Sundance Cinemas is the logical extension of our efforts over the past 18 years," said actor Robert Redford, Sundance Institute founder, in a statement quoted in *Variety.* "I also believe filmgoers are starved for new ideas, voices and visions. By joining with General Cinema, we hope to create a unique circuit that will bring audiences across the country together with the work of independent filmmakers." According to GCC chairman Paul Del Rossi, the theaters would be built in metropolitan areas or college towns and would feature six to ten screens. Each screen would provide bigger-than-usual, more comfortable seating for 75 to 200 people. The new cinemas would not show mainstream Hollywood movies—only independent films, including documentaries and experimental works.

GC Companies moved into another new area in 1997, expanding for the first time outside the United States. The company spent $36 million to acquire five theaters in Mexico and Argentina from United Artists Theater Circuit. Committed to even greater expansion in Central and South America, GCC enjoyed an immediate presence in the region due to the acquisition of the theaters. Construction on some additional theaters in Mexico was completed in 1998. The company hoped to ride a boom in movie theater construction in Central and South America, with plans to expand not only in Mexico and Argentina, but also into Brazil. "We consider ourselves the best in the country in service and design," Carlos Walther, president and CEO of the new GC Mexico said in *Variety.* "We have the aggressiveness to become the largest chain in Mexico." The company planned to show predominantly U.S. films, although Walther said good Mexican and South American films would also be featured.

Celebrating its 75 years of exhibiting movies in 1998, GC Companies seemed solidly positioned in the competitive market of movie exhibition. It was combining cautious construction of the popular new luxury multiplexes in the United States—where analysts were warning of overcapacity—with rapid expansion in markets outside of the United States, where run-down theaters and newly loosened price restrictions combined with unparalleled demand to create tremendous opportunities for U.S. exhibitors.

Principal Subsidiaries

General Cinema Theatres, Inc.; GCC Investments, Inc.

Further Reading

Grove, Christopher, "Showbiz Runs in the Family," *Variety,* December 22, 1997, pp. 38–39.
"HBJ Holders Approve General Cinema Takeover," *Publishers Weekly,* December 6, 1991, p. 10.
Kramer, Pat, "More than Just Popcorn and Pop," *Variety,* December 22, 1997, p. 50.
Mack, Walter and Peter Buckley, *No Time Lost,* New York: Atheneum, 1982.
Rechtshaffen, Michael, "Five Star General: General Cinema 75th Anniversary Salute," *Hollywood Reporter,* March 6, 1998, pp. S1–3.
Roberts, Jerry, "Latin American Growth Part of Agenda," *Variety,* December 22, 1997, p. 40.
——, "Sundance, GCC Build Home for Indie Pix, *Variety,* December 22, 1997, p. 38.

—Susan Windisch Brown

Godfather's Pizza Incorporated

9140 W. Dodge Road
Omaha, Nebraska 68114
U.S.A.
(402) 391-1452
Fax: (402) 255-2685
Web site: http://www.godfathers.com

Private Company
Incorporated: 1973
Sales: $265.0 million (1997)
SICs: 2038 Frozen Specialties, Not Elsewhere Classified

Godfather's Pizza Incorporated (Godfather's) is the nation's fourth largest pizza chain, with more than 500 corporate and franchised restaurants located in 40 states. The company initially prospered based on its introduction of thick crust pizzas with multiple toppings. Its primary competitors include Pizza Hut, Domino's Pizza, Little Caesar's, and Pizza Inn.

The 1970s: Godfather's Heritage

In 1973 Godfather's was founded in Omaha, Nebraska. While operating under the ownership of Diversified Foods Inc., a period of rapid growth ensued. The Pillsbury Company, the Minneapolis-based giant food corporation whose products include flour, baking goods, Green Giant foods, and Haagen-Dazs ice cream, bought Godfather's and operated it as a subsidiary. Pillsbury also owned numerous restaurants, including Quick Wok, Bay Street, Key West Grill, Steak and Ale, Bennigan's, and Burger King. From 1977 to 1979 Godfather's was the fastest growing food chain in the United States in terms of sales growth. Development of the chain continued until its peak in 1984, when the company amounted to 911 Godfather's restaurants, generating annual sales of $365 million.

Following that growth period, intense competition within the pizza business and the failure of many of its stores to open in prime locations resulted in declining sales and profits. In 1986 Pillsbury appointed Herman Cain, an employee of Pillsbury

Company since 1977, as the new Godfather's president. Cain had earned an impressive reputation previously with the Burger King restaurant chain division in the Philadelphia region, where he had rescued several of their operations. At the outset of his efforts to enhance stability for Godfather's, Cain worked to settle several lawsuits filed by franchise owners, disposed of money-losing units, arranged for many of its units to provide home-delivery service, and introduced new products such as bacon-cheese-burger pizzas. Under his management the company showed profits for the first time in three years, according to Stephen Madden of *Fortune*.

In January of 1988 Pillsbury announced that, because of weakening corporate profits and difficulties in competing with McDonald's, the fast food industry giant, the company planned to sell or close approximately 103 of its fast food and full-service restaurants. The company's stock had plummeted approximately 62 cents on the New York Stock Exchange prior to the announcement, but began a steady climb after the restructuring announcement was made. Calvin Sims reported in the *New York Times* that "the restaurants that Pillsbury plans [ed] to divest itself of have been a $150 million drain on operating revenues and about $20 million drain on profits." Pillsbury reported that it primarily intended to refocus attention on its Burger King restaurant operations, which had proven more successful than the others.

As part of the restructuring—and prompted by takeover rumors—Pillsbury encouraged a leveraged buyout of Godfather's by a group of senior managers, led by President and CEO Herman Cain and Executive Vice-President and COO Ronald B. Gartlan. The purchase price was not disclosed, but was estimated by some analysts at $100 million. At that point, Godfather's ranked fifth in the pizza segment lineup, having slipped from its third place ranking in 1985. The chain continued to face considerable competitive challenges and reported that although most of the company-owned businesses were profitable, many of its 420 franchisees, which paid royalties to the parent company, were not. Cain told James Scarpa of *Restaurant Business Magazine* that Godfather's aim over the next several years was to move from fifth to fourth place in the ranking. Staffing levels were expected to remain the same, but

---

Company Perspectives:

The mission of Godfather's Pizza Incorporated is to profitably provide consistently good food and great service.

---

to help finance the purchase, which was provided by Citibank, certain assets were sold. Cain stressed, "The easiest way for a big public company like Pillsbury to meet its goals to compound earnings per-share-growth is by opening more units and making investments that are bigger, bigger, bigger. . . . Opening units is a nice short-term way to help increase earnings." Cain continued, "But long-term, if you don't have people and resources to do that as effectively as you run your existing units, you can get into trouble." He emphasized that their goal was not to surpass the competition in the number of units (Pizza Hut, for example, had 5,800 units at that time). Rather, he explained, ". . . our goal instead is to surpass them in average unit sales, which relates back to quality." Cain reasoned that the ranking was misleading because Godfather's average per unit volume of $429,000 almost matched the $466,000 per unit volume of Domino's Pizza, and in their strongest regions Godfather's outperformed the competition in unit volumes.

The company decided to concentrate on saturating several strong regional pockets, like the Seattle, Washington area, rather than trying to establish a larger national presence. Other strongholds included market areas such as Omaha, Nebraska; Kansas City, Missouri; Minneapolis, Minnesota; and Salt Lake City, Utah. Before looking to new markets, the company initiated a company store remodeling program and then planned for future expansion outside of existing markets. Under consideration were the vicinities of San Francisco, San Diego, and Pittsburgh; international markets also were suggested. Rather than relying heavily on passive income from the franchisees, Godfather's anticipated maintenance of a core of 20 to 30 percent company-owned stores.

Delivering Convenience in the 1980s

In 1986 Godfather's initiated a one-number pizza delivery system as a trial in the Seattle region, hoping that the one-number convenience would give the company a competitive edge at a time when the home delivery of pizzas was on the rise. According to company reports, home deliveries had grown to account for 60 percent of the pizza business, up from 40 percent a few years earlier. The company expanded the one-number program to the more than 60-unit Spokane and Yakima Washington markets, before considering the extension of the program systemwide. Menu development was another area undergoing changes. Specialty pizzas, including apple and cherry dessert pizzas topped with fruit fillings, were introduced. The company originally had eliminated their salad bars in favor of "Walk Away Salads," in an attempt to focus on cost control, but found that since most of their restaurants were in strip malls, the prepackaged salads were not adaptive to that type of customer traffic. They opted to reinstate the salad bars in the form of luncheon buffets that included all-you-can-eat pizza slices.

In an attempt to catch up with the enormous advertising campaigns of its competitors, Cain also implemented a new media thrust soon after taking over the company. Godfather's hired the ad agency Buckley/DeCerchio New York and created a humorous TV character called "Spooner Wiggins, Godfather of the Airwaves." Scarpa described Wiggins as "an irreverent call-in radio show host who mixes good-natured barbs with plugs for Godfather's Pizza." The spots, he said, were "designed to boost awareness and create a 'fun halo' for the concept, much as the successful Noid character did for Domino's." In addition to TV advertising, Godfather's became one of many corporations to introduce its products into the public schoolroom. Following the lead of Everything Yogurt, in particular, Godfather's developed pizza-related games that elementary school teachers could use to "target" second and third grade children to master the basics of addition, subtraction, and fractions. Students were rewarded for good performance with certificates of achievement that could be redeemed for pizza coupons. Cain told John Soeder of *Restaurant Hospitality,* "When we tested this concept in classroom settings, we discovered that students not only worked harder when pizza was used as an incentive, but they also displayed more interest in the subject and learned basic mathematical facts more quickly." He continued, "Kids love pizza. We wanted to channel their interest and enthusiasm in a positive way." Cain's industry-related accomplishments were rewarded by the International Foodservice Manufacturers Association, who presented him with the 1991 Gold Plate Award, naming him "Foodservice Operator of the Year."

In October of 1992 Godfather's started a new TV and print advertising campaign with the introduction of a new pizza product called the "Jumbo Combo." Touted as oversized and price-friendly, the more than five-pound, 18-inch-diameter pizza sold for $13.99 and featured six toppings: beef, pepperoni, sausage, black olives, mushrooms, and onions. The company's standard large pizza measured 14 inches. In addition, the company released the specialty "Super Hawaiian" pizza, a combination of "tropical" tasting ham, pineapple, bacon, green pepper, and mozzarella cheese, offered as a buy-one-get-one-free promotion.

1992: Testing the Supreme Court Concept

In response to consumer demand for convenience and quality, Godfather's became one of several branded chains who entered into the supermarkets. Cain told Louise Kramer of *Supermarket News,* "Brands create a certain expectation for the consumer. They say 'quality.' Shoppers know what they are going to get." The partnership of the two food sectors was initiated because it was determined that 45 percent of the food dollar was going to restaurant and food service, while 55 percent went to supermarkets. In 1992 it was expected that five percent of Godfather's business would be located in supermarkets within the following five years, and the company had already identified a large number of potential locations. The restaurant-within-supermarket food court concept was dubbed the "Supreme Court" and was implemented on a trial basis in the fall of 1991. The first was located inside the Price Chopper units of two Kansas City Ball's Super Food Stores. The other Supreme Court was placed in a Riser Foods Rini-Rego Supermarket, but was pulled later because of lackluster performance, according to Roseanne Harper of *Supermarket News.* Godfather's management was hoping to draw in customers who might be skeptical about trying a supermarket pizza. Independent concept managers felt that it was important to offer variety by having several restaurant choices, with three as the minimum, rather than operating as a stand-alone operation. Other branded restaurant programs moving into the supermarket courts included Chi Chi's, Bennigan's, and Ricky Shaw's Oriental Express, but they were less successful than Godfather's, whose officials claimed that new management of the Supreme Court concept by Philadelphia-based ARA Services (one of the country's largest foodservice contract companies) had improved efficiencies on site. Godfather's fine-tuned their supermarket menus after experimentation showed that small pies and pizza by the slice were not selling, so they switched to offering only medium and large sizes. Supermarkets were hoping that alliances with restaurateurs who could share their experience would add to long-term profitability. According to a *Supermarket News* interview with Mike Clifford, a spokesman for Godfather's, the company succeeded where others had failed because "we spent a lot of time developing products that fit the needs of those particular consumers. For example, we developed fresh-baked, topped pizza for self-service. That required modifying our formulation to give it some shelf-life." After having made a major investment in the Supreme Court and having learned from ARA's organization and trainers, the company found that they could do better by running a program of their own, called the Fresh-To-Go Shoppe.

An Offer He Couldn't Refuse: 1994

Herman Cain, whose academic background included a B.S. in mathematics from Morehouse College and an M.S. from Purdue University in computer science, became the 73rd president of the National Restaurant Association (NRA) and began his active political career as a speaker and lobbyist for the food industry, while maintaining his title as chairman of Godfather's. His CEO duties were handed over to President Ron Gartlan. As the new NRA spokesman, Cain announced that he would focus his attention on "reforming the tax code, elevating the image of the industry and increasing the size of the association," according to Amy Zuber of *Nation's Restaurant News.* Cain was recognized as an active Republican who campaigned for U.S. presidential candidate Bob Dole during the 1996 race. "His stature in the field led Jack Kemp to anoint him the Colin Powell of the restaurant industry—and then to seek his support during the November election," reported Peter Romeo in *Restaurant Business.* Romeo also stated that some in the industry worried that Cain's "highly publicized face-off" over President Bill Clinton's health care plan could hamper the industry under the Democratic administration. Cain had toured the country in a grass roots effort to warn those in the industry of the potential ill effects of Clinton's health reform initiatives, positioning himself as a leader on those issues and bringing the food industry into the forefront of media attention. He argued that Clinton's health care proposal would cost his business more than the 2.5 percent of sales that the administration had estimated, claiming that Godfather's would have to increase the volume of sales by 16 percent to generate enough to cover the proposed mandated costs. He also argued that government intervention in the form

of increasingly costly entitlement programs such as Medicare and Welfare were putting an overwhelming strain on the industry. Cain further established his leadership abilities when he was named deputy chairman and a director of the Kansas City branch of the Federal Reserve Bank, of which 12 branches exist nationwide, and when Nabisco Holdings Corporation named Cain chairman and chief executive officer to their board of directors.

As a leader for Godfather's, Cain's "empowerment" approach, which gives managers a vested state in store performance, has helped to keep the crew and management turnover at approximately half the industry average. He stated in a 1995 interview with Teresa Howard of *Nation's Restaurant News,* "My next goal is for Godfather's to reach its goal of financial independence." He further stated, in reference to the company's heavily leveraged debt, "I want to retire debt in order to allow us to grow the way we want to."

Further Reading

Allen, Robin Lee, "Can to Industry: Unite To Battle Government," *Nation's Restaurant News,* October 10, 1994, p. 56.
Berg, N. Eric, "Godfather's Pizza Sold by Pillsbury," *New York Times,* September 20, 1988, p. D5.
Cain, Herman, "If the White House Won't Listen . . . Senators Must," *Nation's Restaurant News,* June 6, 1994, p. 24.
Farkas, David, "Herman Cain," *Restaurant Hospitality,* May 1994, p. 36.
"Godfather's Introduces Jumbo Combo," *Nation's Restaurant News,* October 19, 1992, p. 12.
Hanry, Harry, "Employee Benefits? You Get What You Pay For," *Nation's Restaurant News,* August 1, 1994, p. 70.
Harper, Roseanne, "Retail Judgment: One Supreme Court Survives Trial by Use," *Supermarket News,* May 9, 1994, p. 40.
Howard, Teresa, "Herman Cain: President, National Restaurant Association, Godfather's Pizza, Omaha, Nebraska," *Nation's Restaurant News,* January 1995, p. 38.
Kramer, Louise, "Godfather's CEO Says Partnerships Essential," *Supermarket News,* June 29, 1992, p. 49.
——, "The Jury Is Still Out on Supreme Court," *Supermarket News,* August 24, 1992, p. 37.
Lee, Robin Allen, "Industry Reps Rally in DC, Vow To Aid Welfare Reform; NRA President Cain Leads 250 Operators, Execs in Presenting Pledge to Gingrich," *Nation's Restaurant News,* January 23, 1995, p. 1.
Madden, Stephen, "Pizza To Go," *Fortune,* October 24, 1988, p. 209.
"Nabisco Holdings Adds Directors," *Supermarket News,* September 18, 1995, p. 36.
"Pillsbury's Pizza Unit To Be Sold," *New York Times,* March 18, 1988, p. D1.
"Praising Cain," *Restaurant Hospitality,* July 1991, p. 32.
Romeo, Peter, "Raising Cain: Who Thought He'd Get to Washington This Way?," *Restaurant Business,* December 10, 1996, p. 27.
Scarpa, James, "Godfather's Newest Challenge," *Restaurant Business Magazine,* February 10, 1989, p. 180.
Sims, Calvin, "Pillsbury Restaurant Cutbacks Set," *New York Times,* January 8, 1988, p. D1.
Soeder, John, "Hit Those Books," *Restaurant Hospitality,* April 1991, p. 27.
Zuber, Amy, "Mr. Cain Goes to Washington; Named To Replace Fisher, Will Serve as NRA President, Chief Executive," *Nation's Restaurant News,* November 18, 1996, p. 1.

—Terri Mozzone

Graphic Industries Inc.

2155 Monroe Drive Northeast
Atlanta, Georgia 30324
U.S.A.
(404) 874-3327
Fax: (404) 874-7589

Wholly Owned Subsidiary of Wallace Computer Services, Inc.
Incorporated: 1970
Employees: 3,200
Sales: $437.1 million (1997)
SICs: 2752 Commercial Printing—Lithographic; 2754 Commercial Printing—Gravure; 2759 Commercial Printing, Not Elsewhere Classified; 6719 Holding Companies, Not Elsewhere Classified

One of the ten highest-volume commercial printing operations in the United States, Graphic Industries was founded in Atlanta in 1970. The company has grown far beyond its original base, to include a network of twenty-two printing and related service businesses stretching from Texas to Connecticut. Known for an aggressive strategy of growth through acquisition, Graphic Industries itself became the target of an acquisition by Wallace Computer Services, Inc. in 1998. After the merger was completed, Graphic Industries and its operations were integrated into those of Wallace, and the company took on the Wallace name.

The Old Roots of a Young Company

Graphic Industries, Inc. was born in Atlanta in 1970, but the roots of some of its subsidiaries are much older. Among the twenty-two companies which make up the Graphic Industries network, one was founded ninety-nine years before Graphic, in 1871. Four other companies in the network were started near the end of World War II.

As for the Atlanta roots of Graphic Industries, these lie in Williams Printing Company, which continues to operate as a subsidiary. In fact, its facilities near Georgia Tech—clearly visible to travelers passing through Atlanta on the Downtown Connector created by interstates 75 and 85—are more visible than those of the parent. Founded in 1922 by Jesse R. Williams, Williams Printing began as a one-man enterprise. Williams persevered during the difficult years of the Great Depression, gradually expanding his printing business. By the 1940s, when Mark C. Pope III went to work for him, Williams Printing was an Atlanta institution.

In 1955, Pope—just thirty years old at the time—became president of Williams Printing. He would hold that position until 1970, at which time Graphic Industries was created to bring Williams Printing together with six smaller companies. Within a decade, the newly-formed enterprise had grown to become the largest full-line printer in the southeastern United States, with the most diversified line of services in the region.

By 1984, however, Graphic Industries had begun to expand beyond the Southeast. That year, it acquired W. E. Andrews Co., Inc., of Bedford, Massachusetts. Over the next thirteen years, the company acquired numerous businesses in Connecticut, Florida, Maryland, New York, North Carolina, Ohio, Pennsylvania, South Carolina, Tennessee, Texas, and metropolitan Atlanta. It was a period of aggressive growth, and soon Graphic Industries was one of the largest commercial printers in the United States.

The "Urge to Merge" in the 1990s

In 1994, M. Richard Vinocur of *American Printer* cited a number of trends within the commercial printing industry, the first of which was a strategy of mergers and acquisitions. This he traced to Graphic Industry's mid-1980s purchase of W. E. Andrews, "the beginning of a trend line that has seen hundreds of mergers and acquisitions during the past 10 years." Vinocur would return to the topic in 1996, with an editorial in which he asked "What's Behind the Urge to Merge?" He offered many reasons, including the desire to economize, which drove mergers and acquisitions in many other industries as well.

In an environment conducive to growth through mergers and acquisitions, Graphic Industries grew rapidly through a series of company or division purchases, as well as strategic alliances with large corporate customers. In April 1993, for instance, its IPD Printing & Distributing unit bought the Equifax Supply Service Center division from Equifax, Inc. In December 1995,

Graphic Industries bought the in-house printing operations of lensmaker Bausch & Lomb, an enterprise generating annual revenues of $8 million at the time of the sale.

In May of 1996, Imaging Technologies—a Graphic Industries company headed by Pope's son, Carter D. Pope—undertook the purchase of Spire, Inc. The latter, an Atlanta-based division of First Financial Management Corporation (FFMC), produced some $1.2 million annually in its CD-ROM Service Bureau and Multimedia Resale Group. Graphic Industries intended to add the Spire CD multimedia training software to a line of multimedia products offered by Imaging Technologies. According to the April 1996 edition of the *Atlanta Business Chronicle*, "The acquisition is part of Graphic's strategy to grow by expanding into broader communications and core commercial printing."

In fiscal 1994, Graphic Industries ranked seventeenth in sales among commercial printing enterprises—and it continued to move up. Pope told the *Atlanta Journal and Constitution* in August 1995 that upcoming acquisitions would help the company reach the $500 million mark in annual revenues during the year that followed. Pope, who was actually the subject of a 1993 *Business Week* profile which singled him out as a particularly astute judge of stocks, would miss his prediction by about thirteen percent. Nonetheless, Graphic Industries remained an expanding company.

Changes in 1996

The year 1996 brought with it a number of changes which, though not necessarily strong setbacks, certainly represented challenges to be overcome. Among these was an event that many other Atlanta businesses—particularly lodging and food-service establishments—treated as a bonanza: the 1996 Summer Olympics, which were held in Atlanta. Spanning seventeen days from July 19 to August 4, the Olympic Games would bring in millions of visitors to attend sporting events at a number of locations around the city, and to mingle in Centennial Park at the heart of downtown. By any estimate, the sudden increase in traffic would bring normal daily operations to a halt. Because Graphic's business was not something that would necessarily benefit from tourism, the company predicted that the Olympics would actually throw a loop in its ability to operate effectively.

Whereas other companies with offices downtown were able to allow their employees to work at home, using telephone lines to communicate with their supervisors and coworkers, Graphic Industries faced a more difficult situation. Typically, before a print supervisor can give the final okay to do a large run for a customer, the customer needs to view proofs and give final approval. With the city facing disastrous traffic conditions, however, the employees themselves—let alone customers—

would have a hard time getting back and forth to the printing plants, which were located right in the heart of the mayhem.

The Olympics, as it turned out, did not create the panicked situation that Atlanta residents had feared—in part because most of the city's residents, terrified to even attempt driving after six years of dire traffic predictions, stayed home during the Games. Nonetheless, Graphic Industries dealt with a number of changes and challenges over the course of the year. On May 15, it announced plans to sell Graphic Direct, Inc. of Elmhurst, Illinois. The company, a direct mail unit, had not been profitable for years. In addition, the company closed one of its Atlanta printers, Stein Printing Company.

In September, Pope's son, Mark Pope IV, resigned as president of Graphic Industries. Forty-six years old at the time, he had served as president since 1989, during a period of rapid and aggressive growth. With his departure, his father would temporarily add the job of president to his responsibilities, along with his existing roles as chairman and chief executive officer. Two other sons, John Pope and Carter Pope, remained as presidents of other companies within the Graphic Industries network. Predictable questions concerning a possible rift between father and son were denied, and all parties involved assured the public and the media that the departure had been the younger Pope's wish, and that there were no hard feelings.

The end of the year brought with it both good and bad news for Graphic Industries. The bad news was the fact that on November 5 its stock had hit a fifty-two-week low of $6.25, though it rebounded by more than $1.50 before the close of the business day. Pope believed that the heavy trading could be explained by the fact that a number of companies wanted "to clean up their portfolios" before year's end. The good news, on the other hand, was that of yet another acquisition—Presstar Printing of Silver Spring, Maryland, which gave Graphic Industries access to the extremely lucrative Washington, D.C. commercial printing market.

Continued Growth in 1997

The setbacks of 1996 were minor, and Graphic Industries would fully rebound in 1997. By the end of that year, in fact, the company would show such a strong balance sheet that it would become the focus of a bidding war between two would-be purchasers.

On September 15, 1997, the *Atlanta Business Chronicle* published its list of "The Market Millionaires," Atlanta's richest denizens. Headed by media mogul Ted Turner and Coca-Cola chairman Roberto C. Goizueta, the list included Pope and his sons. The father, Mark III, owned some 939,000 shares of Graphic Industries stock, with a value of approximately $17.8 million. His son Carter owned another chunk of the company worth $4 million, and John R. Pope, president of Williams Printing, held nearly $1 million.

As for Mark Pope IV, he had cashed in his 99,000 shares and given up a $298,000 annual salary when he resigned. It was soon reported that the younger Pope had gone to work at a local competitor, Geographics, Inc. "We literally started talking the second day after I left," Pope said of Geographics CEO Norvin C. Hagan. The new employer, with only $24 million in annual sales, was much smaller than Graphic Industries. But Hagan—who professed great admiration for Pope's father's company—said "I didn't bring him here to run a $24 million printing company.'' Hagan had big plans for his company and its expansion possibilities, and had penciled in the young Pope to help spearhead the project. Pope's father endorsed his son's desire to grow his career along with the company, where he could help a small entity build equity and expand—something that he could not have done at Graphic, which was an already-established entity.

Graphic Industries continued to apply the growth principle in its own operations. It restructured its management in April 1997, decentralizing according to a regional plan whereby it appointed vice-presidents over the southeast, northeast, and southwest regions of the United States. Also in April, the company struck a deal with computer software giant Microsoft, whereby Graphic Industries' Wetmore subsidiary would print documents and compact discs for Microsoft Information. The agreement made Graphic Industries one of five commercial printers in the United States authorized to print Microsoft data and market it directly to firms with licensed Microsoft technology. For Graphic Industries, this meant that it could sell directly to Compaq Computer, an extremely lucrative account, instead of having to sell to an authorized Microsoft Information dealer who acted as go-between.

Just months later, Graphic, whose stock had formerly been traded on NASDAQ, switched to the New York Stock Exchange, where it would gain greater visibility. Pope projected that Graphic was soon going to be a billion-dollar company. Among the issues standing in the company's way was the fact that the president's seat still had not been filled. The company leadership had considered a number of candidates—most notably John and Carter Pope. Most of these concerns, however—as well as Pope's predictions for future growth—would soon appear in an entirely different light.

Wallace Computer Systems Takeover: 1998 and Beyond

On September 29, 1997, Wallace Computer Services, Inc. announced that it had offered to purchase Graphic Industries for $260 million in cash, or $18.50 a share. By acquiring Graphic Industries, according to the *Wall Street Journal*, executives at Wallace—a $906 million Lisle, Illinois-based company specializing in business forms—hoped to further the objective of making their corporation a ''fully integrated supply manager.'' Graphic's wide geographic and customer bases made it an attractive property for Wallace. Following the acquisition, Graphic would constitute thirty-eight percent of profits in a company of 8,000 employees and $1.4 billion in assets.

Though the deal appeared to be done, it was not. Two weeks later, in early October, Mail-Well, Inc. of Englewood, Colorado presented its own offer of ''at least $20 per share,'' according to a statement by Graphic Industries. In addition to the payment, amounting to $282 million, the Colorado firm would assume $127 million of Graphic Industries' debt—a $387 million offer. Suddenly there was a heated battle for the chance to own Graphic, and Wallace was quick to respond. Three days after the announcement of the Mail-Well offer, an Atlanta newspaper reported that Graphic Industries had been sold to Wallace—for $21.75 a share, along with $104.9 million in debt.

As for the future, Pope told the *Atlanta Journal and Constitution* that Wallace planned ''to keep growing Graphic. That's the reason I went with them. That and the price, which I thought was great for the stockholders.'' He would remain with the company as a consultant, and it appeared that most employees and subsidiaries would continue as well. It also seemed likely that Graphic Industries—even if under the Wallace Computer Systems name—would continue to do what it had done so well for more than a decade: to grow.

Principal Subsidiaries

W.E. Andrews Co., Inc.; Baum Printing, Inc.; Carpenter Reserve Printing Co.; Central Press of Miami, Inc.; Craftsman Printing Co.; Heritage Press, Inc.; Hoechstetter Printing Co., Inc.; IDP Printing & Distributing, Inc.; Imaging Technology Services (Atlanta Blue Print Company; Atlantic Reprographics; Executive Courier, Inc.; 10 other companies); Mercury Printing Co., Inc.; Monroe Litho, Inc.; Quadras, Inc.; Southern Signatures, Inc.; State Printing Co., Inc.; Stein Educational Marketing Group; Wallace Integrated Graphics (formerly Presstar Printing Corp.); Wetmore & Co.; Williams Printing Co.

Further Reading

Chambers, Rob, ''New Suitor in the Picture: Colorado Firm Tops Current Offer for Graphic Industries,'' *Atlanta Journal and Constitution,* October 11, 1997.

Coleman, Zach, ''Pope Finds New Home After Graphic Industries,'' *Atlanta Business Chronicle,* May 19, 1997.

Ezell, Hank, ''Graphic Industries Sold to Illinois Firm: Founder Makes Deal to Stay as Consultant,'' *Atlanta Journal and Constitution,* October 14, 1997.

Gramig, Mickey H., ''Graphic Industries Acquired: $260 Million Deal,'' *Atlanta Journal and Constitution,* September 30, 1997.

Greene, Kelly, ''Industry's Summertime Blues,'' *Atlanta Business Chronicle,* April 19, 1996, p. 1A.

——, ''Graphic Industries Buying Part of an FFMC Spinoff,'' *Atlanta Business Chronicle,* May 10, 1996, p. 18A.

Kanell, Michael E. and Robert Luke, ''Graphic Industries, Microsoft Sign Pact,'' *Atlanta Journal and Constitution,* April 11, 1997.

Lewis, Al, ''Mail-Well Bids for Atlanta Print Chain, Offering $283 Million in Unsolicited Offer for Graphic Industries,'' *Rocky Mountain News,* October 11, 1997.

——, ''Mail-Well Adds $132 Million to Assets with 5 Companies, Hopes to Grow More,'' *Rocky Mountain News,* December 21, 1997.

Luke, Robert, ''Graphic Industries Pops Up as a Leading Market Gainer,'' *Atlanta Journal and Constitution,* August 2, 1997.

McNaughton, David, ''Founder's Son Leaving Graphic Industries,'' *Atlanta Journal and Constitution,* September 14, 1996.

Miller, James P., ''Wallace Computer Agrees to Acquire Graphic Industries,'' *Wall Street Journal,* September 29, 1997, p. 9K.

Mitchell, Cynthia, ''Printing: Acquisitions Put Stamp of Approval on Metro Properties,'' *Atlanta Journal and Constitution,* December 8, 1997.

Murphy, H. Lee, ''Wallace Diversifies with Printing Buy,'' *Crain's Chicago Business,* November 17, 1997, p. 26.

Smith, William, ''When Familiarity Breeds Impressive Returns,'' *Business Week,* May 31, 1993, p. 68.

Vinocur, M. Richard, ''Spotting a Trend,'' *American Printer,* May 1, 1994.

——, ''What's Behind the Urge to Merge?,'' *American Printer,* November 1, 1996.

''Wallace Computer Acquiring Graphic Industries,'' *Reuters Business Report,* September 29, 1997.

—Judson Knight

Habersham Bancorp

Highway 441 North
Cornelia, Georgia 30531
U.S.A.
(706) 778-1000
Fax: (706) 778-6886
Web site: http://www.habcorp.com

Public Company
Incorporated: 1984
Employees: 261
Assets: $328.1 million (1997)
Stock Exchanges: NASDAQ
Ticker Symbol: HABC
SICs: 6712 Bank Holding Companies; 6022 State
    Commercial Banks; 7374 Data Processing and
    Preparation

Established as a holding company in 1984, Habersham Bancorp combines Habersham Bank—a northeast Georgia financial institution incorporated eighty years earlier—with a number of other bank and non-bank holdings. In addition to Habersham Bank itself, Habersham Bancorp's banking subsidiaries include Security State Bank, a financial institution chartered in 1988 in Cherokee County, Georgia; and BancMortgage Financial Corp., a full-service mortgage and construction lending company located in the northern part of the Atlanta metropolitan area. Non-bank subsidiaries include The Advantage Group, Inc., which manages a children's banking program called Kids' Advantage, and develops personal computer software and other services; Appalachian Travel Service, Inc., a travel agency in Cornelia, Georgia; and Advantage Insurers, a Cornelia insurance agency. With its base in a fast-growing part of the country, Habersham Bancorp places a large portion of its lending dollars in home mortgages and construction.

Beginnings in the Back of a Store

Habersham County is located in the northeast corner of Georgia, near the North and South Carolina state lines. Named after Georgia statesman Joseph Habersham, the county was founded in 1818, and for many decades thereafter, it was relatively removed from the life of Atlanta or of the cotton-growing lowlands. The Civil War had little effect on the area, whose soil was not suited to large crops. Even with the coming of the automobile age, the county was several hours' drive north of Atlanta. Nonetheless, Habersham County built its financial base on an unlikely combination of tourism and recreation on the one hand, and manufacturing and processing on the other. The county's two principal towns long represented these seemingly contradictory trends: Clarkesville, the county seat in the north which serves as a gateway to the mountains; and Cornelia in the south, which would one day become home to a number of manufacturing companies. Among these companies was Fieldale Farms Corporation, a chicken-processing operation owned by the Arrendale family, who would come to retain an almost 40 percent share in the eventual Habersham Bancorp almost a century later. At the time that Habersham Bank was founded, however, the establishment of Fieldale Farms—which would become Habersham County's largest business—lay two generations in the future.

One night in the early part of the twentieth century, many of the prominent men of the area gathered to discuss Habersham County's greatest need. Their names—West, Asbury, Burns, Erwin, Furr, Mauldin, Bass, and McMillan—would remain prominent for many years to come in Clarkesville. These community leaders agreed that Habersham County was in need of a bank. Putting together their funds, they began to hammer out a charter, which Robert McMillan, an attorney, formalized and presented to the Georgia Secretary of State.

On May 13, 1904, Secretary of State Phillip Cook granted a charter to Habersham Bank (the founders chose the name to signify its mission of serving the entire county), and the bank commenced operations. With the pooled assets of its founders and others, the new bank had $25,000, and offered stock at $100 a share. Its location, however, was not very bank-like: one of the founders, Dr. E. P. West, had a store on the county square in Clarkesville, and the new financial institution operated out of the back of his shop.

Growing Through the Depression and Boom Years

Three years after its founding, in 1907, the bank was moved across the square to a structure known as the Martin Building,

---

Company Perspectives:

The mission of Habersham Bank is to become the financial services company of choice in the community which it serves. Its vision is to be a regional and multifaceted financial services company which provides superior customer service, innovative products, and consistent growth of investment for its shareholders.

---

which remained standing nearly a century later. Ten years later, the United States entered World War I, and in the years following the Armistice, Habersham Bank experienced rapid growth. During that period, as the county welcomed a number of new residents, the bank made numerous agricultural loans.

This boom period, however, came to a halt with the stock market crash of 1929 and the Great Depression that followed. In the aftermath of the Wall Street crash, Habersham Bank experienced considerable losses. Yet the citizens of the county, much like the residents of the fictional Bedford Falls in Frank Capra's *It's a Wonderful Life* (1946), rallied around their local bank, and purchased shares of stock. Just as Jimmy Stewart's character in the film managed to keep the Bailey Building and Loan open during a period of widespread bank closings, Habersham Bank's customers saw to it that their bank stayed closed only for a few days. On February 13, 1934, the bank's charter was renewed, this time under the newly-established Federal Deposit Insurance Corporation (FDIC), which protected depositors against possible future bank failures.

Soon thereafter came the advent of World War II, and the United State's involvement in it. When the war ended, Habersham County—like much of the nation—experienced a period of economic growth that was greater and much longer in duration than the one that followed World War I. Habersham bank flourished.

In the 1960s, W. F. Holcomb became bank president, inaugurating a period in which the bank expanded significantly. In 1964, Clarkesville lawyer Steve Frankum, like Robert McMillan submitting the original charter sixty years before, submitted a petition for its renewal, which the state granted. During the 1960s, the bank finally acquired air-conditioning, along with something entirely new in Habersham County: a drive-through window.

Expansion in the 1970s and 1980s

In 1969, the bank moved into a new facility it had built on Washington Street in Clarkesville, vacating the location it had held since 1907. Toward the end of the 1960s, the fortunes of the Arrendale family grew. Tom Arrendale became bank president and chairman of the board, and the Arrendale brothers—Tom and Lee—established Fieldale with a third partner in 1972. Late in 1972, Habersham Bank opened its second office in Baldwin, at the extreme southern end of the county. Physical expansion continued in 1975, with the enlarging of the loan department at the Clarkesville main branch. The growth of the

1970s, however, would be dwarfed by that which occurred in the 1980s, when Habersham Bancorp was established.

Even in the 1970s, when interstates 75 and 85 crisscrossed Georgia, Atlanta seemed a long way from Habersham County. Travellers had to take a two-lane highway for many miles, and could seldom make the journey in less than two and a half hours. But with the opening of I-985 and Georgia Highway 365 in the late 1970s and 1980s, the psychological distance to Atlanta—as well as the time it actually took to get there—was much reduced. Habersham County, semi-isolated from the larger world for many years, found itself increasingly linked to the growing hub of metropolitan Atlanta.

Symbolic of this shift was the establishment in 1980 of a central Habersham Bank location in Cornelia, overlooking Highway 365. With the extension of 365 past Cornelia in the late 1980s and 1990s, the county became part of a corridor from Atlanta to North Carolina, and tourist traffic increased manyfold. In May of 1989, Habersham Bank opened a hospitality center in its original 1907 office. In addition to offering tourist information, the Hospitality Center served as headquarters of the bank's Golden Advantage Club and marketing department.

Another change, both symbolic and actual, was the establishment of Habersham Bancorp on December 31, 1984. In 1987, The Advantage Group became the holding company's first subsidiary. The first merger came on June 30, 1995, when Habersham Bancorp paid $9.2 million for Security Bancorp, based in Canton, Georgia. Security Bancorp owned Security State Bank in Canton and Waleska, both towns of which are located on the northwest fringes of the Atlanta metropolitan sprawl—several counties away from Habersham. "Habersham's acquisition of Security represents a very significant expansion for Habersham," Arrendale stated in a company press release. "We are confident that we now have the best group of community bankers in Cherokee County, which is one of the best markets in the country."

Such growth occurred in spite of state laws which, in the eyes of many, hampered the growth of small banks while failing to prevent takeovers by rapacious super-corporations such as North Carolina's NationsBank. Among those who held this view was Habersham Bancorp President and CEO David D. Stovall, quoted in a *Wall Street Journal* article on the subject: "In the next few days, Georgia lawmakers will close out their legislative year having once again retained barriers to widespread banking in the state—protecting the interests of the protectionists ... But while everybody's talking, Georgia bankers, increasingly competing in a national interstate-banking environment, are left with a remnant from 1960 ..."

This "remnant" dictated that a bank wishing to expand beyond county borders could only establish a branch in a county where it possessed a charter; or else it had to purchase an existing bank. Both options are "expensive and painstaking processes," and the law was particularly detrimental in a state which has 159 counties—the second-largest number in the nation, after Texas. Moreover, according to the *Wall Street Journal,* the law failed to offer small-town bankers protection against acquisition by greedy superbanks; "Instead, the losers are people like David D. Stovall, who runs Habersham Bank in

Clarkesville, a town of about 1,150 in northeast Georgia. Seven counties touch Habersham County and Mr. Stovall, who boasts that 'I call my customers by name,' wants to bring his community-banking spirit to those markets.''

Commenting on the current state laws governing bank expansion, Stovall said, ''Let's get real . . . Everything is for sale at a price. But I can't afford to pay two times book [value] to grow my market. On the other hand, if BankAmerica wants to come into Georgia, they have the capital to pay that.'' Bankers such as Stovall were opposed by the State Community Bankers Association, whose chief executive, Julian Hester, offered an ''if its not broken, don't fit it'' explanation of his position. An interesting footnote to this disagreement between Stovall and Hester: Hester had once held Stovall's job, having served as president of Habersham Bank in the 1970s.

The Late 1990s and Beyond

Against challenges to expansion, Habersham Bancorp continued to grow. On May 6, 1994, it celebrated its ninetieth birthday with a party on the lawn of its Cornelia office, complete with birthday cake, ice cream, fireworks, and entertainment by country and western singer Larry Stewart. ''On May 4, 1904,'' noted a brochure announcing the event, ''Habersham Bank opened its doors to its first customers in Dr. E. P. West's store in Clarkesville, now Carey's Department Store . . . In those days, all our entries were done by hand. Interests and dividends were figured on paper.. . . Now, we are serving the great-grandchildren of some of our original customers.''

A little more than a year later, in July 1995, Habersham Bancorp stock began trading on NASDAQ. On January 2, 1996, when it acquired BancMortgage, a full-service mortgage lender in the northern part of metro Atlanta, Habersham Bancorp grew even further from its Cornelia base than it had with the purchase of Security Bancorp the previous year. Calling Habersham Bancorp ''growth-minded,'' the *Atlanta Journal and Constitution* reported that the mortgage company would open an office in the north Atlanta suburb of Dunwoody, and planned to take on some thirty employees in the next year.

The acquisitions continued. On September 9, 1996, Habersham Bancorp acquired a travel agency, Appalachian Travel Services of Cornelia. A few months later, in February 1997, it purchased Advantage Insurers, formerly Cornelia Insurance Agency. ''Our company's vision is to be a regional and multifaceted financial service company,'' Stovall observed in a press release, ''and this acquisition is an opportunity to expand our

company's operations in order to provide customers a broader base of services while increasing our shareholders' value.'' Also in 1997, Habersham Bank opened a branch in the nearby town of Cleveland, in White County—the first Habersham Bank location outside of Habersham County. Finally, on October 23 of that year, it bought Prestwick Mortgage Group and established BancFinancial Services Corporation in Alexandria and McLean, Virginia. Thus, it spread for the first time outside the borders of its home state.

In its May 18, 1997 edition, the *Atlanta Journal and Constitution* recognized Habersham Bancorp as one of the top 100 companies in Georgia. The company ranked tenth in the banking size category, twenty-fourth among companies in revenue growth, and twenty-fifth in stock value gain among public companies. Clearly the company was, in accordance with a slogan echoed by Stovall in his letter to shareholders in 1998, ''Reaching New Horizons.'' Among other developments, mortgage operations had grown to $422 million in loan closings, and BancMortgage had opened new offices at Town Center in Cobb County outside Atlanta, and in Gainesville. Between its various mortgage operations, including those in Virginia, the bank would end the year with $600,000 in net deferred earnings. Clearly Habersham Bancorp, which started life with a little more than four percent of that figure in total assets, had come a long way since its beginnings in the back of Dr. West's store.

Principal Subsidiaries

Habersham Bank; Security State Bank; The Advantage Group, Inc.; BancMortgage Financial Corp.; Appalachian Travel Service, Inc.; Advantage Insurers, Inc.

Further Reading

Habersham Bancorp, ''History of Habersham Bank,'' Cornelia, GA: Habersham Bancorp, 1998.
Higginbotham, Mickey, ''Business Report on Financial Services: Seasoned Bankers in New Venture,'' *Atlanta Journal and Constitution,* January 5, 1996, p. E2.
Salwen, Kevin G., ''Georgia's Banking Laws Protect the Protectionists,'' *Wall Street Journal,* March 15, 1995, p. S1.
Stovall, David D., ''Habersham Bancorp Acquires Security Bancorp Inc.,'' *PR Newswire,* July 12, 1995, p. 1.
——, ''Habersham Bancorp Announces Pending Acquisition of Cornelia Insurance Agency,'' *PR Newswire,* February 28, 1997, p. 1.

—Judson Knight

Halliburton Company

3600 Lincoln Plaza
500 North Akard Street
Dallas, Texas 75201-3391
U.S.A.
(214) 978-2600
Fax: (214) 978-2611
Web site: http://www.halliburton.com

Public Company
Incorporated: 1924 as Halliburton Oil Well Cementing
    Company
Employees: 70,750
Sales: $8.82 billion (1997)
Stock Exchanges: New York Zürich Geneva Basel
    Lausanne
Ticker Symbol: HAL
SICs: 1389 Oil & Gas Field Services, Not Elsewhere
    Classified; 1629 Heavy Construction, Not Elsewhere
    Classified; 2892 Explosives; 2899 Chemicals &
    Chemical Preparations, Not Elsewhere Classified;
    3533 Oil & Gas Field Machinery & Equipment; 6719
    Offices of Holding Companies, Not Elsewhere
    Classified; 8711 Engineering Services

Halliburton Company is a world leader in energy services, as well as engineering and construction. The company has two main business segments: the Energy Group, which offers a broad range of services and products used in the exploration, development, and production of oil and gas; and the Engineering and Construction Group, which designs and constructs major projects, including chemical plants, refineries, and paper mills. Halliburton, which has operations in more than 100 countries, announced in early 1998 that it would merge with Dresser Industries, Inc. to create the number one energy services firm in the world.

Early History

One of Halliburton's numerous service operations is oil well cementing. This process protects oil from contamination by underground water, strengthens the walls of a well, lessens the danger of explosions from high pressure oil and gas, and protects fresh water veins from contamination by oil. It was the first service offered by company founder Erle Palmer Halliburton.

Erle Halliburton learned the cementing technique in California, during a period of employment with the Perkins Oil Well Cementing Company that began and ended in 1916. Fired for suggesting too many method changes, he decided to utilize the engineering and hydraulics he had learned in the U.S. Navy, and go into the cementing business on his own. He borrowed a pump and wagon, pawned his wife's wedding ring to finance his venture, and moved to Burkburnett, Texas, to introduce his services to the oil industry. Halliburton's method met with little interest in Texas.

Undaunted, he transferred his operation to Oklahoma. Here his luck soon changed, bringing the need for additional equipment, a patent for his process, and efficient management. To cope with these needs and increasing demands for his service, in 1920, Halliburton organized the Halliburton Oil Well Cementing Company. One year later, 17 trucks carried his crews and equipment to drilling sites in Louisiana, Arkansas, and other oil-rich areas from a base in Wilson, Oklahoma, as well as from the new company headquarters in Duncan, Oklahoma. Part of this growing reputation came from uncompromisingly reliable service, which was enhanced by new equipment invented by Halliburton to meet the needs of each project. One creation that revolutionized the oil industry was the jet mixer, a mechanized mixer that did away with hand-mixing of the minimum 250 bags of cement and water slurry needed for each well. Because it could control the proportions of cement and water, it eliminated wasted slurry that would harden before it could be poured.

By 1922 the company owned $14,000 worth of equipment and was paying some of its cementers $300 monthly. Two years later, Halliburton with his wife, Vida, as his partner, set out to expand. To finance this they converted their partnership into a corporation and offered a substantial interest in their business to other oil companies. Their trump card lay in their meticulous patenting of all new processes and devices, which had left the oil companies unable to have oil wells cemented without using Halliburton services. Company patents also covered processes designed for well recementing, a maintenance necessity that gave the Halliburtons relative independence from competitors.

In 1924 the Halliburton Oil Well Cementing Company became a corporation in Delaware. The Halliburtons held 52 percent of the stock, and the Magnolia, Texas, Gulf, Humble, Sun, Pure, and Atlantic oil companies jointly held 48 percent. So as to retain equal voting rights with their partners, the Halliburtons placed 4 percent of their stock in a voting trust.

By the time the company reached its ten-year milestone in 1929, research and development had improved processes and equipment to the point where a mixture made up of 2,500 sacks of cement could be injected into a well in 48 minutes. By 1929 the use of four new company planes made for speedy contract completion. Marking this important anniversary was the Halliburton entry into Canada, as well as offering for sale a wide range of oil well apparatus.

The 1930s saw automobile production soar from 2.3 million vehicles in 1931 to 4.5 million by 1940. Domestic oil heating became more popular, growing from 100,000 homes supplied in 1929 to 2 million by 1940. Both circumstances benefited the oil industry. As the decade ended, oil and gas were supplying 44.5 percent of the U.S. total energy requirements.

Halliburton's expansion kept pace with demand. In 1932, it opened four new branches, enabling it to send 75 cementing and well-testing crews to sites in seven states. The company introduced bulk cementing to replace hand moving of heavy cement sacks. Eager to participate in the marine oil exploration taking place in the Gulf of Mexico, Halliburton also began to mount equipment on ships and barges.

In 1940 the Halliburtons bought Perkins Cementing Company, extending operations to the West Coast and the Rocky Mountain region. In the same year, the company established its first South American subsidiary, in Venezuela. These two moves were profitable; just one year later, earnings reached $13.5 million, of which $2 million was net profit.

Soon after the Japanese attack on Pearl Harbor, the company began to make gun-mount bearings for the U.S. Navy at its Duncan shops. Other war material manufactured included parts for the B-29 bomber, and jigs, fixtures, and dies for the Boeing airplane plant in Wichita, Kansas. Wartime contracts were lucrative, and when World War II ended in 1945, annual earnings reached $25.7 million.

In 1948 Halliburton shares were offered on the New York Stock Exchange for the first time. Having split its shares on a four-to-one basis a year earlier, Halliburton was able to offer 600,000, to which the Atlantic Refining Company added a further 80,000 shares. Of these, 50,000 shares were offered to employees before the balance were offered to the public.

By the end of the 1940s, although well cementing and bulk cement sales accounted for about 70 percent of company revenues, there were other profitable undertakings, all supported by specially designed equipment. Electrical well services provided information on the types of formations penetrated by a drill; acidizing of geological formations increased oil flow; and specialized equipment deposited various cements and chemicals into wells. Most profitable of all was a new process called Hydrafrac, licensed exclusively to Halliburton for a period of time by its developer, the Stanolind Oil and Gas Company. Designed to increase well productivity, this method used jellied gasoline, which was pumped under pressure into the bottom of a well to split the rock formation. The resulting crack was then propped open with quantities of sand, making penetration of tight rock formations easier. The Hydrafrac process made it possible to rejuvenate many dwindling oil wells, and reduced the number of sites necessary to drain a field. A surge in annual revenues showed Hydrafrac's great success: $57.2 million in 1949, increasing to $69.3 million the following year, and leaping to $92.6 million by 1951.

Diversifying and Expanding in the 1950s

Between 1950 and 1955 the company expanded in all directions. Drilling activity increased dramatically. The company had 7,000 employees, and drills probed to more than 4,000 feet in an average well, as compared to 3,600 feet five years earlier. Offered for rental as well as for sale, equipment then included formation testing tools to obtain fluids and pressure readings from oil-bearing rock, plus other new equipment used in well completion operations. Wall cleaners, depth measuring equipment, and production packers were other lines that drillers could rent or buy. Services provided by the company included electronic logging and sidewall wellcoring, and the transporting of cement and fracturing sands to drilling sites from nearby Halliburton storage areas. Oil exploration in the Texas and Louisiana Gulf Coast areas was flourishing; 23 vessels as well as about $10 million worth of other equipment were available for offshore drilling purposes. There were almost 200 operating centers in the United States, as well as 32 service locations in Canada, and subsidiaries in Venezuela and Peru. The company also had operations in Mexico, Saudi Arabia, Sumatra, Italy, Germany, Australia, and Cuba.

Research and development kept the company at the forefront of oil exploration technology. Costing $3 million in 1956 alone, it rewarded the company's efforts with a new composition for cementing deep wells and a method for making the fracturing sand radioactive, among other innovations. All of this was reflected in the annual sales figures, which reached $152.4 million by the end of 1955, and produced net profits of $16.3 million.

Erle Halliburton died in 1957, after 28 years as company president and ten as chairman. Cited by the *New York Times* as one of the richest people in the United States, he left behind a fortune estimated at between $75 and $100 million—the days of a pawned wedding ring long gone.

The same year saw the acquisition of Welex Jet Services. Originally based in Fort Worth, Texas, Welex broadened the Halliburton line of electronic testing and logging services. Other companies were acquired during this time, including Jet Research Center and FreightMaster, a maker of rail car couplings.

The end of the war had brought an increased demand for oil. Due partly to freedom from wartime price controls and partly to the technological advancement that brought plastics, synthetic fibers, fertilizers, and other petrochemical products into daily life in the United States, these demands were willingly fed by the oil drillers. Production almost doubled between 1945 and 1954, reaching a level of 2.3 million barrels daily. Such overexpansion came to a head in 1957 when a slump followed, bringing with it a corresponding decrease in the demand for exploration equipment. The company's annual sales figures showed the trend of the time: its net income before taxes, $38 million in 1957, decreased to $27.6 million in 1958, rallied to $33.9 million the following year, only to sink once again to $26.9 million by 1960. Because Halliburton was chiefly a supplier of drilling-related services, however, recovery was relatively swift. These services, plus the equipment required to implement them, were needed both for the deeper wells then being drilled, and for stimulation of existing sites.

Acquiring Brown & Root in 1962

Offsetting the oil exploration slump, Halliburton continued with its acquisition program. Otis Engineering Corporation joined the company in 1959. Brown & Root, Inc. became a Halliburton subsidiary in 1962. A firm internationally known for the construction of military bases, petrochemical plants, and offshore platforms, Brown & Root was a private subsidiary of the Brown Foundation. Other Brown subsidiaries acquired at the same time were Southwestern Pipe, a manufacturer of explosives and thin-walled pipe; Joe B. Hughes, a trucking business; and Highlands Insurance Company, chiefly concerned with casualty insurance. Together, the four new subsidiaries broadened Halliburton's product and service lines, giving the company entry into many overseas markets and providing ways to adapt Halliburton skills to new purposes. Two company staples quickly found new uses: blended cement was now sold for building projects and thin-walled pipes for playground equipment and bicycles.

By 1965 Halliburton's acquisitions program resulted in 16 units that were autonomous but closely coordinated into three main areas. One division was oil-field services and sales. The second was the engineering segment headed by Brown & Root, the focus of which were such international construction projects

as bases in Saigon and parts of NASA's Manned Spacecraft Center near Houston. The third division, specialty sales and services to general industry, included power supply units and transformers for the electronics industry, missile cleaning for defense, and, through two subsidiaries, insurance. Earnings reflected the company's steady growth. 1960's total earnings of $181.5 million rose to $525.7 million by 1965.

In the 1960s, offshore oil exploration became a major activity. Successfully undertaken in the Gulf of Mexico since 1938, offshore drilling produced about 12,500 wells by 1970, accounting for approximately 15 percent of U.S. oil and ten percent of its gas. Anticipating its participation in offshore activities, Halliburton equipped Brown & Root well, spending $100 million to ensure competitiveness. The company had developed an automated mixing system for drilling mud, used in offshore operations. Designed to cut costs by monitoring and controlling fluid density, the new system came in tandem with a 50-percent interest in IMC Drilling Mud, a company with special emphasis on overseas expansion.

In 1968 the company's marine capabilities were broadened further by the acquisition of Jackson Marine Corporation, a Texas company specializing in the construction of vessels for offshore petroleum exploration, and the purchase of an 80-percent interest in New Orleans-based Taylor Diving and Salvage Company. The latter company proved its worth within a year by developing an underwater chamber that could be lowered to depths of 600 feet, then pumped dry. It was used for the undersea repair of damaged pipes.

Offshore exploration proved lucrative, and by 1970 the company's net income reached $46.3 million, up from $33.1 million in 1965. Other profitable ventures were hydraulic cushioning for railroad cars; electronics and explosives for the defense and aerospace industries; plant and road construction; transportation; and pollution control.

Destined for permanent importance, concern for the environment had attracted national attention a year earlier, after a well eruption in California's Santa Barbara channel spilled 10,000 barrels of oil. Outrage over the resulting 200-mile-square oil slick hampered offshore exploration, as well as the construction of oil refineries—and nuclear power plants. As could be expected, oil imports rose.

Continuing to Prosper in the 1970s

Halliburton, nevertheless, prospered. Total revenues of $1 billion in 1970 grew to $2.1 billion by 1973, despite the Arab oil embargo that led to huge OPEC price increases in 1974. Acquisitions giving the company new entry into overseas markets encouraged industrial variety. The reconditioning and stimulation of older wells then became more profitable than it had ever been before, especially as the equipment the company used for its own projects was not available on the open market. Lucrative as oil-field services were, however, they were now contributing a smaller proportion to the company's total revenues. A larger part came from construction projects like steel mills, municipal construction, and paper mills.

The Halliburton corporate structure was relatively simple. In the 1970s, although the company had 55,000 employees worldwide, the Dallas headquarters housed fewer than 30 people, and day-to-day activities were handled by each segment. Operations were still divided into three main segments: oil-field services and products, producing 46 percent of 1975's total earnings; engineering and construction, contributing a 51 percent share; and specialty services and products, responsible for the remaining three percent. Each of these three groups had several internal divisions, themselves divided into several hundred profit centers run by field managers. Headquarters kept in touch with these field managers in a monthly reporting system that monitored specified financial goals.

By 1975 Halliburton had 40 subsidiaries in all parts of the world, most of which were smoothly fitted into their appropriate company segments. The exception was Ebasco Services, acquired along with Vernon Graphics from Boise Cascade in 1973. Like Brown & Root, Ebasco's main business was the engineering and construction of fossil fuel and nuclear electric power plants. Its merger led to a Justice Department antitrust suit, claiming unfair competition. Ebasco was, therefore, sold in 1976.

By 1977, price controls had drained enthusiasm for domestic oil exploration. Imports now cost a total of $45 million, as against $7.7 billion in 1973. Two years later the situation changed. Instability in Iran and the higher prices imposed by OPEC countries now stimulated domestic production, to alleviate international oil shortages. Beginning in June 1979, price controls were to be phased out over 28 months, although they were replaced with a windfall-profits excise tax to keep prices high, a method of encouraging oil conservation.

All these developments as well as the slowdown of offshore exploration in the North Sea, where most major discoveries had already been made, affected the oil supply business. Halliburton's total income, in 1977, $660.2 million, reached $717.5 in 1978, sinking slightly to $648.2 in 1979.

Joint ventures in construction fields helped to offset the oil-field slowdown. In 1976 Brown & Root and Raymond International, a competitor, teamed up in a $22 million bridge construction project in Louisiana. A similar arrangement the same year paired Brown & Root and Norwegian Petroleum Consultants.

Competition Increases in the 1980s

It was the company's old faithful, however, oil well cementing, that formed the basis for post-slump recovery; by 1980 Halliburton was servicing 60 percent of the market. Its service of stimulation of existing wells to retrieve remaining oil was garnering a 50 percent share. In early 1981 all oil price controls were eliminated and well drilling increased proportionally. That year 77,500 new wells appeared, as compared to about 48,500 in 1978.

The upward trend brought competition for Halliburton, when Dresser Industries, Schlumberger Limited, and other industry giants began to diversify into the traditional Halliburton strongholds of cementing and stimulation. By keeping service prices at competitive levels, Halliburton's market share remained at its usual high level, however, and company strength in drilling muds and well logging operations continued to be a flexible guard against competition.

By 1980 the company's total revenues reached $8.3 billion. In 1982, an economic recession plus sharply lower oil prices began to affect the oil exploration industry and its suppliers. The slowdown showed in the total income figure for 1983, which was down to $1.2 billion. While many smaller companies were unable to withstand the hard times, Halliburton merely downsized, slashing its employee roll from 115,000 to 65,000 by 1986, to an eventual 48,600 workers by 1988. Nevertheless, this was not a smooth time for the company. A lawsuit alleging that Brown & Root had mismanaged a south Texas nuclear power plant construction project cost a 1985 settlement of $750 million, producing a $340 million loss for the year.

The acquisitions program continued unabated. A 60-percent share of Geophysical Services, a maker of seismic analysis systems for oil exploration, was bought from Texas Instruments. Gearhart Industries joined the company lineup; within a year its wireline services consolidated with Welex, and its geophysical operations with Geophysical Services.

Research and development became even more active including the development of horizontal drilling techniques. Spearheaded by the Geophysical Services unit, other research focused on continuous three-dimensional control for seismic surveys in offshore exploration.

As the 1980s drew to a close, Halliburton was engaged in about 40 other research and development projects. Streamlining for profitability, it had divested itself of its life insurance subsidiary, plus two other non-oil businesses. In 1989 its total revenues, showing assets of $4.2 billion, were $5.66 billion.

Restructuring and a Major Merger in the 1990s

Under the leadership of CEO Thomas Cruikshank, Halliburton in the early 1990s was contending with the effects of the sustained downturn in the U.S. oil industry, which had begun in 1986. After net income fell from $197 million in 1990 to $27 million in 1991, the company began a multiyear restructuring in 1992. A special charge of $264.6 million was recorded in 1992 for the first stages of the restructuring, which included the elimination of 3,000 jobs, including 26 vice-president slots. In July 1993 Halliburton merged its ten semiautonomous energy services units, including Halliburton Services and Otis Engineering, into a single group called Halliburton Energy Services, in a significant act of streamlining. Also created in 1993 was Brown & Root Energy Services, which combined all of Brown & Root's upstream oil and gas engineering and construction services. Later in the 1990s Halliburton Energy Services and Brown & Root Energy Services were tied more closely together when they were placed within a newly formed Energy Group. Halliburton's engineering and construction activities (with the exception of upstream oil and gas) were likewise consolidated under a new Construction and Engineering Group.

At the same time, Halliburton shed additional noncore or underperforming units. It sold its health care cost management company for $24 million in September 1992; its troubled geophysical services and products unit to Western Atlas International Inc. for $190 million in January 1994; and its natural gas compression business to Tidewater Compression Service for $205 million in November 1994. In relation to its sale of the geophysical unit, Halliburton recorded a $301.8 million charge in 1993. In January 1996, in the last major divestment, the company spun off to shareholders Highlands Insurance, finally ridding itself of its last insurance unit. The only major acquisition of this period came in March 1993 when Smith International, Inc.'s Directional Drilling Systems and Services business was added for about $247 million in stock.

In late 1995 Dick Cheney, who had served as U.S. Secretary of Defense under President George Bush, was named chairman, CEO, and president of Halliburton, taking over the helm from the retiring Cruikshank. Cheney inherited a much leaner and more profitable company thanks to the Cruikshank-led restructuring (net income was $178 million in 1994), and quickly launched another round of acquisitions, perhaps the most ambitious in company history. In October 1996 Halliburton acquired Landmark Graphics Corp. for about $550 million in stock. Landmark, which became part of the Energy Group, was a provider of petroleum exploration and production information systems, software, and services. In April 1997 the company acquired OGC International plc—provider of engineering, operations, and maintenance services, mainly to North Sea petroleum production companies—for about $118.3 million. And in September 1997 Halliburton spent about $360 million for NUMAR Corporation, a manufacturer of magnetic resonance imaging tools that evaluate subsurface rock formations in newly drilled oil and gas wells.

But these deals paled in comparison to the $7.7 billion merger between Halliburton and Dresser Industries announced in February 1998. If consummated, the combination would create the world's largest oil services firm in the world, surpassing previous leader Schlumberger. The company, which would operate under the Halliburton name and be headquartered in Dallas, would also combine the two companies engineering and construction units, creating a very strong player in that sector. Dresser would also add to Halliburton a third unit in the area of energy equipment. The new Halliburton, whose revenues would exceed $16 billion, would be led by William E. Bradford (Dresser's chairman and CEO) as chairman and Cheney as CEO.

Principal Operating Units

Energy Group (Halliburton Energy Services, Brown & Root Energy Services, Landmark Graphics Corporation, Halliburton Energy Development); Engineering and Construction Group (Brown & Root Engineering and Construction, Brown & Root Government Services).

Further Reading

Basralian, Joseph, "Reveille in Dallas," *Financial World,* January 31, 1995, pp. 32–33.
Brown & Root Engineering, Houston: Brown & Root, Inc., 1990.
Dittrick, Paula, "Halliburton to Combine 10 Business Units to Create New Energy Services Organization," *Oil Daily,* June 17, 1993, p. 3.
Haley, J. Evetts, *Erle P. Halliburton: Genius with Cement,* Duncan, Okla., 1959.
"Halliburton Agrees to Buy Numar Corp. in $360 Million Deal," *Wall Street Journal,* June 11, 1997, p. C13.
Halliburton Company: Seventy-Five Years of Leadership, Dallas: Halliburton Company, 1994, 32 p.
Hogan, Rick, "Halliburton to Buy Landmark Graphics in $557 Million Deal," *Oil Daily,* July 2, 1996, pp. 1 +.
Hudson, Rex, "A Brief History of Halliburton Services (1916–1977)," Halliburton corporate typescript, 1977.
Lipin, Steven, and Peter Fritsch, "Halliburton Agrees to Acquire Dresser," *Wall Street Journal,* February 26, 1998, p. A3.
Mack, Toni, "A Piece of the Action," *Forbes,* August 11, 1997, p. 60.
McWilliams, Gary, "Dick Cheney Ain't Studyin' War No More," *Business Week,* March 2, 1998, pp. 84–85.
Reifenberg, Anne, "Halliburton Co. Selects Cheney for 3 Top Posts," *Wall Street Journal,* August 11, 1995, p. B8.
Rodengen, Jeffrey L., *The Legend of Halliburton,* Fort Lauderdale, Fla.: Write Stuff Syndicate, 1996, 208 p.
Scism, Leslie, "Halliburton to Spin Off Insurance Unit in Plan Values at Up to $250 Million," *Wall Street Journal,* October 12, 1995, p. A8.

—Gillian Wolf
—updated by David E. Salamie

Hardinge Inc.

1 Hardinge Drive
Elmira, New York 14902-1507
U.S.A.
(607) 734-2281
Fax: (607) 732-4925
(800) 843-8801
Web site: http://www.hardinge.com

Public Company
Incorporated: 1931 as Hardinge Brothers Inc.
Employees: 1,510
Sales: $246.6 million (1997)
Stock Exchanges: NASDAQ
Ticker Symbol: HDNG
SICs: 3541 Machine Tools, Metal Cutting Types; 3545
Machine Tool Accessories; 3546 Power-Driven
Handtools; 3599 Industrial Machinery, Not Elsewhere
Classified

Hardinge Inc., located in the city of Elmira, in Chemung County, New York, which is on the south-central border of upstate New York, was founded more than 100 years ago. The company is an international leader in the machine tool industry, designing, manufacturing, and selling metal cutting lathes, grinding machines, EDM machines, machining centers, turning machines, and related tooling and accessories throughout the world. The majority of Hardinge's sales are made principally in the United States and Western Europe, but Hardinge also numbers customers in Canada, China, Mexico, Japan, Australia, and other countries. A substantial portion of the company's sales are to small- and medium-sized independent job shops, which in turn sell machined parts to their industrial customers. The company also offers option packages with each of its machines to meet specific customer requirements and turnkey services through which it will engineer complete systems for customers. The company has subsidiaries located in Canada, China, Germany, Spain, and the United Kingdom, with distributors located worldwide.

The company markets its machine tools under the ''Hardinge'' and ''Hardinge Super Precision'' names directly to manufacturers in the demanding industries of automotive, aerospace, communications, computers, dental equipment, electronics, medical equipment, and photographic equipment, as well as in the construction equipment, defense, energy, farm equipment, recreational equipment, and transportation industries. Major competitors have included Bridgeport Machines Inc., Cincinnati Milacron, Giddings & Lewis, Hurco Companies, Monarch Machine Tool Co., and Newcor Inc.

Early Days, 1890–1930s

Hardinge Brothers was founded in 1890 and organized in Illinois, where it began manufacturing industrial-use, super-precision, and general precision turning machine tools.

There are two principal methods for producing a metal part or finished product: metal cutting and metal forming. All of the machines produced by the company are metal cutting machines.

Turning machines, commonly known as lathes, are one of the most commonly used power-driven machine tools used to remove material from a rough-formed part by moving multiple cutting tools arranged on a turret assembly against the surface of a part rotating at very high speeds in a spindle mechanism. The multi-directional movement of the cutting tools allows the part to be shaped to the desired dimensions. On parts produced on Hardinge machines, those dimensions are often measured in millionths of inches. Hardinge produces: horizontal turning machines, where the spindle is aligned horizontally to the base of the machine; vertical turning machines, where the spindle is aligned perpendicularly to the base; and Swiss-type lathes, where rotating bar stock is fed through a bushing past stationary turning tools. Each of these designs provides unique advantages to the user.

The company was reincorporated in New York in March 1931, as Hardinge Brothers Inc., a successor to the previous company. Several years later, in December 1937, Hardinge Brothers Inc. merged with Morrison Machine Products Inc., itself founded in December 1925, but kept the Hardinge name.

The company established Hardinge Machine Tools Ltd. (HMT) in the United Kingdom in 1939. HMT became a wholly owned subsidiary of the company in 1981 when it redeemed the shares previously held by other investors.

Mid-Stride, 1940s–70s

In 1958, the company established a subsidiary called Canadian Hardinge Machine Tools Ltd., located near Toronto, Ontario.

In the late 1970s, the company began producing computer numerically controlled (CNC) machines and machining centers, which used commands from an on-board computer to control the movement of cutting tools and rotation speeds of the part being produced. The computer control enabled the operator to program operations such as part rotation, tooling selection, and tooling movement for a specific part, and then store that program in memory for future use. The machine would be able to produce parts while left unattended when connected to automatic bar-feeding or robotics equipment designed to supply raw materials. Because of this ability, as well as superior speed of operation, CNC machines are able to produce the same amount of work as several manually controlled machines, as well as reduce the number of operators required. Since the introduction of CNC turning machines, continual advances in computer control technology have allowed for easier programming and additional machine capabilities.

Fight for Survival, 1980s

The decade of the 1980s was a fight for survival in the turning industry. According to the U.S. Census Bureau, in 1982 there were 865 metal cutting machine tool companies in the United States operating 942 manufacturing facilities. By 1986, foreign machine tool manufacturers accounted for more than 66 percent of the U.S. market for horizontal CNC lathes, forcing the U.S. government to negotiate Voluntary Restraint Agreements (VRAs) with Japan (57 percent) and Taiwan (three percent), which were effective from January 1987 through December 1993, limiting Japanese and Taiwanese manufacturers to their 1981 market share levels of various machine tools. By 1992, the number of American metal cutting machine tool companies had declined to 393 operating 423 manufacturing facilities and, by 1994, imports once again accounted for an estimated 66 percent of U.S. sales of horizontal CNC lathes—in addition to huge sections of CNC machining center (51 percent), vertical CNC lathe (79 percent), manual lathe (69 percent), and grinding machine (55 percent) sales.

In 1987, the company started implementation of "Total Quality" at its facilities. The process for Hardinge involved three principles: 1) Meet the Requirements; 2) Manage by Prevention; and 3) Error Free Work, resulting in continuous im-

provement in all areas of the company. Also that year, the company created a subsidiary called Hardinge GmbH, located in Germany.

Roaring into the 1990s

The first several years of the 1990s were decent, but not great, for the company, with revenue for 1990 reaching $102.9 million and net income reaching $4.6 million. The following year, revenues dropped to $82.6 million, with net income slipping to $2.7 million. In 1992, revenue reached $84.8 million, with a net loss of $1.2 million. From 1993 to 1998, the company would introduce 21 new machine models across its product line, bouncing back with total revenues in 1993 climbing again to $98.4 million, with a net income of $5.2 million.

In 1994, the company expanded its machine tool line to include CNC vertical turning machines and vertical machining centers, the first sales of which occurred during the first quarter of 1995. Prior to that, all of the company's turning machines were horizontal, which meant that the spindle holding the rotating part and the turret holding the cutting tools were arranged on a horizontal plane. On a vertical turning machine, the spindle and turret are aligned on a vertical plane, with the spindle on the bottom, allowing the customer to produce larger, heavier, and more oddly shaped parts on a machine that uses less floor space when compared to a traditional horizontal turning machine.

A vertical machining center cuts material differently than a turning machine. These machines were designed to remove material from stationary, prismatic (box-like) parts, usually held in a vise on a table, of various shapes with rotating tools capable of milling, drilling, tapping, reaming, and routing. The table is also able to move in various planes. Machining centers have mechanisms that automatically change tools based on commands from a built-in computer control without the assistance of an operator. Machining centers were generally purchased by the same customers as turning machines and were marketed by the company on the basis that a customer would be able to obtain machining centers with the same quality and reliability as the company's turning machines and would be able to obtain its turning machines and machining centers from a single supplier.

In 1994, revenue and net income reached $117.3 million and $6.7 million, respectively, with the machine tool industry in the United States estimated at $5.2 billion, of which $3.6 billion (69 percent) was in the metal cutting category.

The company's name was changed from Hardinge Brothers Inc. to Hardinge Inc. in May 1995. The company further extended its machine offerings into the grinding machine sector of the metal-cutting machine tool industry in November 1995 with the acquisition of St. Gallen, Switzerland-based L. Kellenberger & Co. AG for approximately $19 million.

Founded in 1917, Kellenberger designed, manufactured, and sold high-precision manual and CNC straight, angular, and universal cylindrical grinders with the highest degree of precision and reliability available in the market. The grinding machines of Kellenberger were used to grind the inside and outside diameters of round, cylindrical parts. Such grinding machines were typically used to provide for a more exact finish on a part partially completed on a lathe. The grinding machines of Kellenberger were manufactured in both CNC and manually controlled models, were generally purchased by the same type of customers as other Hardinge equipment, and furthered the ability of the company to be a sole source supplier for its customers.

During 1997, Kellenberger and Hardinge combined their respective skills to introduce a new jointly developed line of grinders, the Kel-Vision. Revenue for the year hit $180.6 million, with a net income of $14.9 million.

During 1996, the company took yet another step to address a new market segment with the introduction of its Cobra 42 CNC Lathe. A basic, no frills, yet very reliable and accurate lathe, the Cobra provided a relatively inexpensive product offering for potential customers with limited financial resources. Additional models were added to this product line in 1997. Further refining its ability to provide products aimed at particular types of customer applications, Hardinge also introduced two new ''long bed'' lathes in 1996, specially designed to manufacture parts of greater length than would normally be possible using smaller, more conventional lathes.

By August, the turning industry was growing again due to the adoption of total quality management and successful turning machinery manufacturers were focusing on self-managed work teams, continuous learning, transformational leadership, and customer satisfaction, and looking forward to the utilization of artificial intelligence and investments in technology and flexible manufacturing.

That year, the company established its Hardinge Shanghai Company Ltd. subsidiary near the city of Shanghai in The People's Republic of China. The facility was created to assemble machinery for deliveries to customers located throughout Asia.

Additionally, the company received its third consecutive Supplier of the Year Award from General Motors; was honored as one of the top 50 companies in America by The National Association of Manufacturers; and total revenue for the company reached $220 million, with a net income of $17.3 million.

In April 1997, the company entered the market for electrical discharge machines (EDM) with its acquisition of privately held, Urbana, Illinois-based Hansvedt Industries Inc., the largest manufacturer of EDMs and related equipment in the United States, via a stock purchase. The acquisition of the $8 million company added another high-quality new member to the growing Hardinge family of metal cutting machines.

EDMs are used to produce complex metal parts through a process of erosion with electricity using either a cutting wire or electrode, essentially, removing metal with sparks. Many of the same customers who purchased other Hardinge products also purchased EDMs, adding a new dimension to the company's product lines without moving beyond its core businesses, and broadening the market for Hansvedt products to be sold outside the United States for the first time.

In May 1997, the company released the new Kellenberger KEL-VISION URS Universal and RS Angular OD Cylindrical Grinders for precision grinding of medium to small lot sizes. In June, the company opened new facilities in both Germany and Britain to expand sales support and customer service capabilities in the two countries, and to increase the amount of space available for the display and demonstration of products. That month also featured the introduction of Hardinge's second generation CONQUEST Swiss-Turn CNC lathes, for turning, milling, drilling, and threading for high-speed production of complex parts for industries such as aerospace, computer, medical, precision instruments, and audio/video equipment.

August of that year saw the company open a Tech Center in Charlotte, North Carolina to provide improved customer support. Additionally, the center was created to provide live demonstrations of machines, support customer's specific applications requests, provide direct service support, and conduct on-site programmer's and hands-on training classes. Also that month, the company introduced the CONQUEST GT27 Precision Gang Tool Lathe, a product which provided precise, JIT (just-in-time) machining and an exclusive interchangeable pretooled top plate, each holding up to ten tools, which are able to be removed and interchanged within .0002" in under one minute. Additionally, General Motors Corporation bestowed the company with its third consecutive Supplier of the Year Award, chosen on the basis of quality, service, and price. Net sales for 1997 reached $247 million, with net income inching up to $17.9 million.

In April 1998, the company's common stock split three-for-two. In June, the company opened a Tech Center in Cleveland, Ohio. That month also saw the addition of a new 12-inch, 3-jaw power chuck to the company's lineup of Sure-Grip Power Jaw Chucks.

By the end of 1998, the company was looking ahead to improving uptime, just-in-time, faster cycle time, waste reduction, setup reduction, lot-size reduction, multipurpose machines and tooling, CNC, hard turning, 24-hour production, product life cycle management, and vertical integration, so that it could continue to be a profitable company well into the future.

Principal Subsidiaries

Canadian Hardinge Machine Tools Ltd. (Canada); Hansvedt Industries Inc.; Hardinge GmbH (Germany); Hardinge Machine Tools Ltd. (U.K.); Hardinge Shanghai Company Ltd. (China); L. Kellenberger & Co. AG (Switzerland); Kellenberger Incorporated.

Further Reading

Agan, Robert E., ''Making a Living in the Turning World,'' *Tooling & Production*, August 1996, p. 107.
''Hardinge Inc.,'' *New York Times*, April 24, 1998, p. C5(N)/D5(L).
''Hardinge Inc.,'' *Wall Street Journal*, February 3, 1998, p. B10(E).
''Hardinge Inc.,'' *Wall Street Journal*, April 28, 1998, p. B17(W)/ B19(E).
''Hardinge Reports Increased Sales, Increased Earnings in First Quarter of 1998,'' *PR Newswire*, April 23, 1998 p. 0423CGTH005.
''Lathe Design Meets High Volume Demands,'' *Tooling & Production*, December 1997, p. 79.

—Daryl F. Mallett

Harley-Davidson, Inc.

1700 West Juneau Ave.
P.O. Box 653
Milwaukee, Wisconsin 53201
U.S.A.
(414) 342-4680
Fax: (414) 935-4806
(888) 4HD-95TH (443-9584)
Web site: http://www.harley-davidson.com

Public Company
Incorporated: 1903 as Harley-Davidson Motor Company
Employees: 5,300
Sales: $466.52 million (1997)
Stock Exchanges: New York
Ticker Symbol: HDI
SICs: 3751 Motorcycles, Bicycles & Parts; 3711 Motor
  Vehicles & Car Bodies; 3443 Fabricated Plate
  Work—Boiler Shops; 6719 Holding Companies, Not
  Elsewhere Classified; 3089 Plastics Products, Not
  Elsewhere Classified; 2900 Petroleum & Coal
  Products; 2389 Apparel & Accessories, Not
  Elsewhere Classified; 3714 Motor Vehicle Parts &
  Accessories; 3716 Motor Homes; 3792 Travel Trailers
  & Campers; 2522 Office Furniture Except Wood;
  2521 Wood Office Furniture; 3524 Lawn & Garden
  Equipment; 3519 Internal Combustion Engines, Not
  Elsewhere Classified; 5651 Family Clothing Stores

The only motorcycle manufacturer in the United States, Harley-Davidson, Inc. has been designing heavyweight machines for bike enthusiasts for almost a century. The company is legendary for the great loyalty its vehicles have inspired in generations of cyclists.

Early 20th-Century Origins

The first Harley-Davidson motorcycle was built in Milwaukee, Wisconsin—still the location of the company's headquarters—in the early 1900s. The Davidson brothers—William, Walter, and Arthur—along with William S. Harley, designed and developed the bike and its three horsepower engine in their family shed. The machine went through many refinements until 1903, when the men established the Harley-Davidson Motor Company and produced three of their motorcycles for sale. Over the next several years both demand and production grew at a healthy rate, and by 1907 the company had begun to advertise.

Two years later the company produced a new model featuring a V-twin engine that produced a low, deep rumble now identified as the signature Harley-Davidson sound. The revolutionary engine—still a company standard—enabled riders to reach speeds of 60 miles per hour, which until that time had been believed impossible. Such capabilities served to set the company's motorcycles apart from the competition; by 1911 there were 150 other companies manufacturing the vehicles.

Growth During and Following World War I

The onset of World War I was actually a boon for Harley-Davidson. The motorcycle, having done well in its utilization by police, was commissioned for use by the military. It proved especially useful on the U.S.-Mexico border, which was suffering incursions by the forces of Mexican revolutionary leader Pancho Villa. In all, 20,000 of the company's machines were employed by the U.S. infantry during the war.

The battlegrounds of the war also served as proving grounds for the motorcycles. After resuming normal production, Harley-Davidson was able to begin incorporating improvements into its new machines. The 1920s saw the company taking the lead in innovative engineering with such features as the Teardrop gas tank and the front brake. In 1921, the winner of the first race in which motorists reached average speeds of more than 100 miles per hour was riding a Harley-Davidson machine. Only Harley-Davidson and Indian would survive the grueling years of the Great Depression. However, a strong dealer network, continued use by the military and police, as well as the U.S. Postal Service, and strong exports to Canada and Europe, allowed Harley-Davidson to weather the economic disaster.

Henry Ford's introduction of the assembly line, on which he could quickly and inexpensively produce his Model T automobile, had a profound effect on the motorcycle industry. While motorcycles had traditionally been used by workers and businesspeople, the more affordable car became their vehicle of choice. The motorcycle, in the meantime, was gradually becoming a recreational vehicle.

World War II: Military Demand Again Spurs Growth

Military procurement during World War II proved as helpful to Harley-Davidson as it was during World War I. In 1941 the company turned its entire manufacturing effort toward supplying U.S. and Allied troops going into battle, shipping nearly 100,000 machines overseas. Harley-Davidson's efforts earned them the Army-Navy "E" award, an honor bestowed upon companies that excelled at production during wartime. The healthy postwar economy found consumers with money to spend on recreation. To meet burgeoning demand, the company purchased additional manufacturing capacity in 1947.

The Superbike Era: 1950s and 1960s

As the second generations of the founding families began moving into management positions at the company, Harley-Davidson found itself "king of the road"—with the shutdown of Indian in 1953, the company became the sole American motorcycle manufacturer. Continuing to prove itself a design innovator, the company introduced its Sportster model in 1957, heralding the era of the all-powerful, throaty "superbikes." An entire subculture began to grow up around these motorcycles, and leather jackets and riding boots became as much a statement of one's desire for a life of freedom on the open road as a necessity for motorcycling. Unfortunately, the film *The Wild One*, starring Marlon Brando, depicted biker gangs riding Harley-Davidson motorcycles as packs of lawless renegades. The stereotype that grew out of this is one the company still actively strives to dispel.

In 1965 Harley-Davidson went public when the two families decided to give up control and put the company's shares on the market. Four years later the company was bought by the American Machine and Foundry Co. (AMF), a leisure equipment manufacturer headed by Harley-Davidson fan Rodney C. Gott. The arrangement proved, at least initially, to be a good one for Harley-Davidson, for it was also in the 1960s that the company experienced its first competition since Indian went out of business. The financial resources and stability that AMF was able to

provide helped the company battle Japanese motorcycle manufacturers, who had begun exporting their vehicles around the world, placing themselves in direct competition with Harley-Davidson.

Problems and Corrective Measures: The 1970s and 1980s

Demand for motorcycles continued to grow through the early 1970s, and, in an effort to keep up, the company opened an assembly plant in York, Pennsylvania, in 1974. While engines would still be made in the Milwaukee facilities, the bikes themselves would be assembled in the new plant. In 1975 AMF put Vaughn Beals at the head of Harley-Davidson, and Jeff Bleustein was named chief engineer. Bleustein was charged with making manufacturing improvements, which were becoming increasingly necessary as production grew.

These efforts added an extra $1,000 in costs to each bike, however, and the profit line suffered as a result. To compensate, AMF management began to apply pressure for greater sales volume, with the result that quality began to suffer. The production standards that customers had come to count on were being lowered, and there were chronic shortages of parts, with the result that as many as 30 percent of the vehicles coming off the assembly line were incomplete. This, in turn, meant extra manpower searching for spare parts to finish outfitting the machines, a task that even fell to dealers on those occasions when incomplete bikes were accidentally shipped.

Such problems took their toll on the company, especially in light of rising Japanese competition. In 1969 Harley-Davidson had enjoyed an 80 percent share of the U.S. motorcycle market for super heavyweight machines—bikes with engines over 850 cubic centimeters (cc). Ten years later, just when Honda Motor Co. was opening a plant in Marysville, Ohio, that share had dropped sharply to 20 percent. While there were still some riders who would settle for nothing but a Harley-Davidson motorcycle, newcomers to the motorcycle market were opting for Japanese affordability and dependability.

To make matters worse, the 1981 recession severely threatened Harley-Davidson's share of the market for heavyweight bikes—motorcycles with engine capacities of 700–850 cc—nearly finishing the company off as a manufacturer. Soon AMF began to lose interest in keeping the struggling business afloat. To save the company, and to effect a turnaround, 13 Harley-Davidson executives, led by Vaughn Beals, put together a plan for a leveraged management buyout. With the financial support of Citicorp, the management team succeeded in taking control of Harley-Davidson from AMF on June 16, 1981, at a cost of $81.5 million.

The group's turnaround strategy called for getting back on the quality track through new management and manufacturing techniques. Unable to beat them, Harley-Davidson instead decided to join their Japanese competition, adopting such management techniques as decentralized quality discussion groups and "just-in-time" inventory control. After the company's top management toured Honda's Marysville plant in 1981, Vaughn Beals noted in *Fortune*, "We were being wiped out by the Japanese because they were better managers. It wasn't robotics, or culture, or morning calisthenics and company songs—it was professional managers who understood their business and paid attention to detail.'' In an effort to do likewise, management at the York plant developed three principles for change: worker involvement, manufacturing materials available as needed, and statistical operator control.

One of the first steps Harley-Davidson took was to group the employees in a plant-wide network to ensure their input in improving the manufacturing process. The York plant management met with workers' representatives for months in 1981 to achieve a consensus on what was sought and also to ease skepticism. The increases in productivity stemming from these measures were deemed to be the effects of effective communication, shop floor enthusiasm, and increased recognition.

The second point of the revitalization program involved managing the company's inventory. A program of just-in-time inventory control called MAN—Material As Needed—was developed, based on Toyota Motor Corporation's Toyota Production System. The plan called for the use of expanded communication in monitoring the flow of inventory. Harley-Davidson also introduced a statistical operator control system to improve quality control. The aim was to reduce defects and scrap by reworking machines right on the assembly line. The process began with the operators, who established parameters for quality using statistical methods. Then workers along the assembly line would chart actual quality and introduce improvements where warranted.

During the early 1980s, the company began making cosmetic changes to its motorcycles, prompted by Vice-president William G. Davidson, grandson of the founder. Davidson, who felt it was important to remain close to the bike maker's customers and their needs, would often mingle with Harley devotees at gatherings, sporting his own beard, black leather, and jeans. As he explained in *Fortune,* ''They really know what they want on their bikes, the kind of instrumentation, the style of bars, the cosmetics of the engine, the look of the exhaust pipes, and so on. Every little piece on a Harley is exposed, and it has to look right. A tube curve or the shape of a timing case can generate enthusiasm or be a turn-off. It's almost like being in the fashion business.'' In addition to changing the look of established models, the company began to design new motorcycles to appeal to a broad range of consumers.

Meanwhile, the competition was moving ahead. Though the recession of the early 1980s had depressed demand for heavyweight bikes, Japanese manufacturers swamped the U.S. market with their surplus inventory, driving average market prices down still further. In 1982, however, the company won an anti-dumping judgment from the International Trade Commission (ITC). This led then-U.S. President Ronald Reagan to impose additional tariffs on imported heavyweight Japanese models, as allowed by the ITC.

The additional tariffs—45 percent on top of an existing 4.4 percent measure—were meant to decrease gradually over five years, until April 1988. These measures would give Harley-Davidson the opportunity to effect its revitalization plans. Predictably, as the company's market share began to increase, so, too, did its profits. Harley-Davidson had lost $25 million in 1982, but rebounded into the black again in 1983 before posting

$2.9 million in profits on sales of $294 million in 1984. Though Japanese bike makers were able to elude some of the tariffs by building more machines in the United States, by 1986 Harley-Davidson's share of the U.S. super heavyweight market had crept back up to 33.3 percent, ahead of Honda for the first time since 1980.

During this time, Harley-Davidson began placing more emphasis on its marketing efforts. In a.1983 public relations move, the company established the Harley Owners Group (HOG), a club with its own newsletter for fans of the motorcycle. By the end of the 1980s, membership in HOG had grown to 100,000 members. The company developed the SuperRide promotion, several years later; it was designed to attract large numbers of new buyers from an upscale niche. Television commercials invited people to visit one of Harley-Davidson's 600 dealers across the United States to test ride a new bike. Over 40,000 people took Harley-Davidson up on its offer. Though immediate sales did not cover the promotion's $3 million price tag, the effort did result in increased sales over the course of the next several years, and many of the new buyers were owners of rival Japanese models.

Although Harley-Davidson was making great strides, the company suffered yet another blow in 1984. Citicorp—nervous that the economy was headed back into a recession, especially in light of the 1988 deadline on import tariffs—informed Harley-Davidson that in future years they would no longer provide overadvances—money over and above the conservative lending limits set as part of the company's business plan. Taking this as an indication that Citicorp wanted out of its arrangement with the company, Beals and Richard Teerlink, who was then the finance officer, began searching for another lender. Once word concerning Citicorp's plans got out, however, other banks showed little interest in making the commitment. By October 1985 Beals and his management team had contacted the investment firm Dean Witter Reynolds in order to begin Chapter 11 bankruptcy proceedings.

Before those plans were finalized, Beals and Teerlink were approached by an interested lender. After weeks of hard bargaining, Heller Financial Corporation—whose second in command, Bob Koe, was a Harley buff—agreed to supply Harley-Davidson with $49 million to buy out Citicorp's stake in the business. Thus Citicorp was forced to take an $18 million writedown on its original investment. Heller Financial Corporation's faith in Harley-Davidson paid off handsomely. The company's market share began to climb steadily, and profits for 1986 topped $4.3 million on sales of $295 million. That year a revived Harley-Davidson went public, offering two million shares of stock worth $20 million and $70 million worth of unsecured subordinate notes that would mature in 1997.

With the capital raised from these offerings Harley-Davidson purchased the motor home maker Holiday Rambler Corporation. By December 1986 the company had acquired all outstanding Holiday Rambler stock for approximately $156 million, enabling Harley-Davidson to diversify its manufacturing efforts. The company further broadened its business in 1986 when the U.S. government awarded Harley-Davidson a contract to produce military hardware, including casings for 500-pound bombs and liquid-fueled rocket engines for target drone aircraft.

The previous year had proven to be such a successful one for Harley-Davidson that in March 1987 the company asked the ITC to remove the tariffs imposed on Japanese superbike imports a year earlier than scheduled. Even so, Harley-Davidson's share of the super heavyweight market by the end of 1987 had climbed to 47 percent.

Despite the recession taking hold in 1990, Harley-Davidson saw its sales for that year increase to $864.6 million, up from $790.6 million a year earlier. The company also had a 62.3 percent share of the U.S. heavyweight motorcycle market, far and above Honda, its closest competitor with 16.2 percent. Holiday Rambler's sales were somewhat affected, however, by lower consumer spending.

Richard Teerlink, who had become president and CEO of Harley-Davidson, warned in the company's 1990 annual report that "maintaining Harley-Davidson's growth through a recessionary period will be a difficult, but not impossible task. We could easily exploit our worldwide motorcycle popularity for quick profits, a near-fatal mistake we made in the 1970s, but we are committed to a corporate vision that discourages short-term thinking."

The 1990s: Facing the Competition Head-On

The early 1990s brought the company some minor setbacks. Though sales in 1991 rose to $939.8 million, profits fell slightly, marking the first decrease since the 1986 refloatation. In addition, the company's motorcycle division experienced a work stoppage at the York plant, and sales and profits at the Holiday Rambler Corporation continued downwards.

Harley-Davidson instituted new labor and fiscal policies in the late 1990s under the leadership of Jeff Bleustein, policies that revitalized production and sales. The company's stock has grown steadily and attracted many new investors while keeping the old. *Kiplinger's Personal Finance Magazine* reporters Steven T. Goldberg and Nancy Stover declared in May 1998 that "Harley stock is now selling at 23 times this year's estimated earnings. Earnings are expected to grow 15 percent in 1998 and an annualized 18 percent over five years," and named Harley-Davidson, Inc. to their list of 12 stocks "that keep growing & growing & growing." Envisioning Harley-Davidson as a wise stock pick in spite of the motorcycle's rebel image is not misinformed: the company announced in April 1998 that they had realized record sales and earnings for the first quarter of that year. While the company had 32 consecutive quarters of growth, it had to absorb some of the costs of a new Kansas City plant, seen mostly in the decline of the gross margin from 32.4 percent to 32.1 versus the previous year. While company officials warned that further costs would have to be absorbed from plant openings and refurbishings, "the introduction of two new Europe specific Harley-Davidson motorcycle models, a new European marketing campaign, a full year of Buell sales, and additional dealers will result in increased sales for 1998," according to an article on the corporate web site.

There would be no profit without the product, and Harley-Davidson management has explored and incorporated new labor-friendly production techniques that reflect respect for its manufacturers. As the company borrowed management ideas from the Honda plant in Maryland, so also did it take a close look at GM's Saturn plant, with its great success through worker empowerment. Harley-Davidson opened a new plant in Kansas City in January 1998, at a cost of some $85 million, but that was only the tip of the iceberg. For two years, the company interviewed some 2,000 applicants for 300 positions. They were put through hours of rigorous personality and aptitude training. Those few who earned a place with Harley-Davidson enjoyed collective decision-making and a strong voice in the production process. *Dealernews* reported in March 1998 that *Fortune* magazine had named Harley-Davidson as one of the top 100 places to work in the country.

Harley-Davidson wisely selected merchandising that reflected the changing profile of the motorcycle-worshipping customer. "It's one thing to have people buy your products. It's another for them to tattoo your name on their bodies," the web site crows. Harley-Davidson has gone far beyond tattoos in hip merchandising. The *Jacksonville Business Journal* interviewed a third-generation dealership owner who planned to dedicate almost a fourth of his floor space to merchandise including, "Anything from blue jeans and T-shirts to leather jackets and boots. It's not just leather anymore," said Chris Adamec. He pointed to a new and wealthy clientele, the so-called "Rolex" riders, as a new source of demand. VH1, the MTV for yuppies, debuted a commercial in June 1998 raffling off four vintage-style Harleys and leather jackets in their "Chrome on the Range" contest. Smiling mothers holding babies posed in front of the bikes (and the American flag) at the close of the commercial suggested a new generation of Harley riders yet to grasp their first Gold Card.

With the approach of the millennium, Harley-Davidson roared into cyberspace. Besides a Lollapalooza of a party, Harley-Davidson's 95th anniversary was celebrated with a virtual Harley tour online. Visitors to Harley-Davidson's web site were invited to partake of video and audio journals of actual motorcycle mamas and daddies from Washington to Pennsylvania. Harley-Davidson has proved that heavyweight motorcycles are not just about nostalgia, whether for the early days of motorcycles or the freewheeling 1960s; the classic appeal of the Harley-Davidson motorcycle would certainly continue into the next century, and the company was poised to support continued growth.

Principal Subsidiaries

Holiday Rambler Corporation; Utilmaster Corporation; B&B Molders; Creative Dimensions; Nappanee Wood Products.

Further Reading

"Bleustein Appointed Chief Executive Officer of Harley-Davidson, Inc.," http://harley-davidson.com, June 27, 1997.
"Chrome on the Range," http://www.vh1.com, June, 1998.
Gallun, Alby, "Manufacturers Expect Growth to Moderate in '98," *Business Journal Serving Greater Milwaukee*, January 9, 1998.
Goldberg, Steven T., and Nancy Stover, "12 Stocks That Keep Growing & Growing & Growing," *Kiplinger's Personal Finance Magazine*, May 1998, p. 66.
"Harley-Davidson Celebrates First Production Motorcycles in Kansas City," http://harley-davidson.com, January 6, 1998.

"Harley-Davidson, Inc. Announces Record First Quarter Earnings and 32nd Consecutive Quarter of Record Sales," http://www.harley-davidson.com, April 13, 1998.

"Harley-Davidson Inc. Company Briefing Book," *Wall Street Journal,* http://www.interactive.wsj.com/inap-bin/bb, 1998.

"Harley-Davidson Mission," http://www.harley-davidson.com, 1998.

"How Harley Beat Back the Japanese," *Fortune,* September 25, 1989.
"Joe Walsh and the Wallflowers Rock Harley-Davidson's 95th Birthday," http://www.harley-davidson.com, May 4, 1998.

"Maintaining Excellence Through Change," *Target,* Spring 1989.

"95th Anniversary Web Site Cruises the Virtual Highway," http://www.harley-davidson.com, May 11, 1998.

Reid, Peter, *Well Made in America: Lessons from Harley-Davidson on Being the Best,* New York, McGraw Hill, 1990.

"Riding the Road to Recovery at Harley-Davidson," Labor-Management Cooperation Brief No. 15 (April 1988), Washington, D.C., U.S. Department of Labor.

Roth, Stephen, "New Harley Plant Spotlights Training and Empowerment," *Kansas City Business Journal,* January 9–15, 1998.

Stuart, Devan, "Shop's Clothing Sales Ride Motorcycle's Popularity," *Jacksonville Business Journal,* January 16, 1998.

"The Success of Harley-Davidson: 89 Years in the Making," Harley-Davidson News, Milwaukee, Wisconsin, Harley-Davidson, Inc., 1992.

"Top 100 Places to Work," *Dealernews,* March 1998, p. 47.

"Why Milwaukee Won't Die, *Cycle,* June 1987.

—Etan Vlessing
—updated by Christine Ferran

Harmon Industries, Inc.

1300 Jefferson Court
Blue Springs, Missouri 64015
U.S.A.
(816) 229-3345
Fax: (816) 229-0556
Web site: http://www.harmonind.com

Public Company
Incorporated: 1961 as Harmon Electronics, Inc.
Employees: 1,700
Sales: $213.5 million (1997)
Stock Exchanges: NASDAQ
Ticker Symbol: HRMN
SICs: 3669 Communications Equipment, Not Elsewhere
   Classified; 3679 Electronic Components, Not
   Elsewhere Classified

Harmon Industries, Inc. since World War II has played an instrumental part in supplying the nation's railroads with advanced systems for signaling, inspection, and train control and safety. The company designs and manufactures rail/highway grade crossing hardware and related services, such as packaging, installation, and maintenance. Using advanced radio, computer, and infrared technologies, Harmon also provides sophisticated equipment that gives engineers and others the ability to better control today's powerful trains and monitor internal train operations for improved mechanical and electrical reliability. Harmon electronic devices can automatically control train speed and braking if human operators fail. Its contract engineering and asset management services help railroads concentrate on their core functions. Harmon also manufactures circuit boards for its own use and 300 other firms. Harmon serves three markets: domestic freight trains, its core business that accounts for about 85 percent of its annual sales; domestic light rail or mass transit systems; and international freight and rail transit systems. Based in the Kansas City suburb of Blue Springs, Missouri, Harmon Industries operates from several facilities in the United States, Canada, Switzerland, Australia, and England to bring high technology into the rapidly changing railroad industry.

Company Origins

Robert C. "Bob" Harmon, the founder of Harmon Industries, first learned about radio in the 1930s while serving in the Marine Corps. Later he worked as an engineer for the Aireon Manufacturing Company in Kansas City, Kansas, that served the military during World War II. After the war ended, Aireon failed in its attempt to sell two-way radios to the civilian train market, having grown complacent with federal contracts and being generally mismanaged.

Aireon's collapse opened a door for Bob Harmon. To provide work for himself and the many skilled individuals unemployed after the war, Harmon in September 1946 started his own firm, Harmon Electronics, as a sole proprietorship. As Aireon's chief sales engineer, Harmon had made numerous contacts with railroad managers, so he felt he was ready to open his own business. In the company's first two years, it made no profits and survived with the help of a bank loan.

Operating from his first office in an Independence, Missouri, upholstery shop, Harmon set his initial goal as using radio and other electronics to help railroads. For example, he found a better way to inform railroad engineers about overheated axle bearings called hotboxes, which, if ineffective, could lock up wheels and cause trains to derail. Harmon's solution was to transmit data from hotbox detectors, trackside devices that used infrared beams to detect overheated bearings, to a central point using either power or telephone circuits already in place. Once the railroad's central office received the information, it used radio to notify its train engineer of an impending hotbox failure.

With a contract signed with Southern Railway for hot box detector equipment, in 1958 Harmon Electronics moved from its leased building at 11431 Truman Road to its first owned facilities, a new building on farm land next to Bob Harmon's home. The company that year also began replacing vacuum tubes with transistors in its products. Bob Harmon in his company newsletter called 1958 "a memorable year, and a turning point in the business."

In an interview in the January 1990 issue of *Nation's Business,* Bob Harmon's son Robert E. (Gene) Harmon said his father's firm

Company Perspectives:

Harmon Industries will endeavor to provide an adequate rate of return on investment for its SHAREHOLDERS consistent with its long-term growth objectives. It will provide for its CUSTOMERS products and services of the highest quality and value possible while maintaining technological leadership in all product lines. Harmon Industries will provide for its EMPLOYEES a positive and open work environment that will allow everyone to develop to their full potential and provide compensation and incentives competitive with our industry and geographic location. Harmon Industries will strive to be a good corporate citizen within the community while complying with GOVERNMENT regulations.

for 20 years remained a "custom engineering firm" that helped its clients find technical solutions. It employed just two dozen workers and brought in less than $1 million in annual revenues, but change was just around the corner.

Expansion in the 1960s and 1970s

In 1961 Harmon Electronics, Inc. was incorporated with Bob Harmon as president, Gene Harmon as vice-president, and the founder's wife Mildred I. Harmon as secretary-treasurer. After graduating from Georgia Tech, Gene Harmon joined his father's firm on a full-time basis, a decision that proved to be a turning point for Harmon Electronics.

Gene Harmon's first contribution was an electronic switch that improved the timing on railroad crossing gates. Previous devices were quite slow, as the gates would not open to cars until trains had gone 100 feet or more down the track. Gene Harmon's device opened gates after just two feet of clearance. His father liked the idea, and by 1964 the company had a major product to sell.

Sales increased for Harmon Electronics, but the founder reportedly did not enjoy the expansion. "I was primarily an engineer, not a manager," said Bob Harmon in the *Nation's Business* article, adding "I didn't really have any major wish to operate a larger company." Thus, in 1969 Bob Harmon left management while retaining most stock in the still private firm. In 1972 Gene Harmon took Harmon Electronics public.

The company remained profitable through the 1970s, but Gene Harmon thought the firm was complacent and limited with just one major product. Competition and railroads' resistance to price increases led to a dramatic change for Harmon in the 1980s.

Acquisitions, Innovations, and Restructuring

The 1980s began with the Staggers Rail Act, which deregulated the nation's railroads. Deregulation allowed railroads to compete with trucks, although through most of the decade trucks continued to gain market share. The railroads simply had a lot of catching up to do in terms of modernization and investment.

In October 1981 Harmon purchased a line of hot box detectors from General Electric, devices that Harmon Electronics' West Coast operation had started selling in the 1970s. Meanwhile, the company began acquiring complementary firms, including in 1984 Electro Pneumatic Corporation (EPC), which owned a plant in Riverside, California. With its plants for manufacturing and assembling grade crossing hardware in Jacksonville, Florida, and Louisville, Kentucky, Modern Industries was acquired in 1986.

In 1987 Harmon Industries, Inc. was formed as a holding company. Harmon Electronics remained a subsidiary, selling its railroad crossing gate switches, which provided about $20 million in sales out of a total of almost $65 million in 1988. Harmon Electronics ran two manufacturing facilities in Grain Valley, Missouri, and two more in Warrensburg, Missouri. Acquired firms made crossing gates, warning lights, and electronics to control train flow. Under Harmon Industries Chair and President Gene Harmon, things were looking up. In 1985, Harmon was able to repurchase the 51 percent share of its stock bought by SAB Industries AB of Malmo, Sweden, in 1977.

A major train wreck in 1987 led to a Harmon innovation to prevent such tragedies. At Chase, Maryland, a Conrail freight train run by a marijuana-smoking engineer went through a stop signal and was hit by an Amtrak passenger train going over 100 mph, resulting in the deaths of several people. The Federal Railroad Administration began requiring that all freight trains operating between Boston and Washington, D.C., install automatic devices to slow down and stop.

Harmon responded in early 1989 by installing its Locomotive Speed Limiter in its Ultra Cab systems, first on Conrail locomotives and later on locomotives around the nation, including the freight trains of the Florida East Coast line. Instead of engineers watching traffic signals along the track, Harmon's system automatically read electronic pulses traveling through the rails. Even if engineers ignored the Limiter's signals inside the cab, the Harmon device would gradually bring the train to a complete halt. This was particularly important for freight trains, which had to be stopped gradually, as sudden braking tended to derail unstable freight trains.

Harmon Industries in 1987 created a subsidiary called Consolidated Asset Management Company, Inc. (CAMCO) to warehouse inventories of railroad signaling equipment so that it could rapidly put together complete products ready to ship to railroads on demand. CAMCO expanded in the 1990s to provide railroads with comprehensive purchasing and inventory management in a good example of outsourcing. CAMCO benefitted railroads by volume purchasing, saving on inventory costs, and installing and long-term maintenance of a variety of products, such as crossing hardware, track circuitry, and data recording items. CAMCO operated warehouses in Lee's Summit, Missouri, and Riverside, California.

Recovery and Growth in the 1990s

From 1989 to 1991 Harmon Industries suffered economic setbacks. Its earnings per share from continuing operations declined from $.84 in 1989 to $.65 in 1990 and $.57 in 1991. And net income declined from $3.9 million in 1989 to $2.9 million in

1991. One reason for the downturn was the losses from three unprofitable subsidiaries.

First was Harmon's 80-percent-owned subsidiary Cedrite Technologies, Inc. At the Cedrite plant in Kansas City, Kansas, old wooden railroad ties were ground into chips and then mixed with a special resin. Under high pressure, the mixture was baked to produce new ties which were heavier and more durable than regular wooden ties. Cedrite by 1990 had received orders for 200,000 ties each from Union Pacific and Santa Fe, but Harmon in April 1991 shut down this unprofitable operation. Harmon also eliminated another unprofitable subsidiary called Phoenix Data, Inc., a maker of data acquisition and analysis systems for industrial, military, and scientific uses purchased in 1989. Phoenix operations were ended in 1990, and its assets were sold the following year. The third costly subsidiary, Modern Industries, was merged into another Harmon subsidiary in 1990, resulting in reduced labor and overhead costs.

As high technology increased in the railroad industry, the First International Symposium on Advanced Train Control was held in Denver in June 1991. Harmon Industries, along with other firms that provided railroads with communication, signaling, and control technologies, such as General Railway Signal, Safetran, and Union Switch and Signal, took part in this meeting. Issues such as train safety, training personnel to use advanced computerized equipment, and the possibility of creating precision train scheduling of freight deliveries were just a few of the topics discussed.

At about the same time, both the railroads and the federal government began spending more money to upgrade railroads. For example, a new highway bill in 1992 contained $160 million for better train crossing warning systems. Furthermore, more federal money was being spent on mass transit. Such external factors plus Harmon's heavy investment in research and development, about five percent of annual sales, helped Harmon recover.

By the early 1990s, Harmon Industries' products had helped increase safety at railroad-highway crossings. Over 30,000 motion detectors or constant warning time systems had been installed on North American railroads by 1993. In spite of increased auto and train traffic, the Federal Railroad Administration reported fewer accidents and fatalities; there were 6.3 percent fewer accidents and 13.7 percent fewer fatalities in 1991 compared to 1990.

Burlington Northern Railroad emphasized such safety concerns in 1993 when it began installing Harmon's HXP predictor equipment in the busy Chicago area. The HXP system provided constant warnings along a three-track main line used by commuter trains, Amtrak, and local freight trains.

In 1993 Harmon Industries entered the growing mass transit market with a contract to provide the St. Louis MetroLink light rail line with its grade crossings signal devices and its Ultra-Cab II onboard computer-based control system. Harmon reported that entering this new market helped its sales for the first half of 1993 increase 40 percent over the first half of 1992. Harmon won praise from the railway industry for a very successful entry into light rail. Installation went smoothly and almost no prob-

lems bothered the system in 1994. By adapting its freight train technology, Harmon was able to enter a new market.

The company in 1993 received other mass transit orders. In August 1993 the New York City Transit Authority announced a $4.5 million contract to have Harmon install its microcomputer-based speed limiting equipment at 30 points along the transit line. According to Dick Daniels, Harmon's vice-president for transit sales, this New York City contract was quite challenging, partially because the firm was relatively new in the mass transit field, but mainly because of the sheer size of the contract.

Harmon also received a $1.4 million contract for block signaling along Denver's new light rail system, and the Southern California Regional Rail Authority chose Harmon's subsidiary CAMCO to warehouse and assemble track and signal items for its commuter rail system.

Harmon Industries in December 1994 announced it had completed acquiring the transportation division of Hicksville, New York's Servo Corporation of America. Since Servo had competed against Harmon in detecting hot box problems, Harmon gained technical expertise in that area. In addition, Harmon gained Servo's established networks for international sales. The acquisition resulted in the Servo division's manufacturing relocating to Riverside, California, where it began integration with Harmon's subsidiary, Electro Pneumatic Corporation. Harmon also opened in Long Island, New York, a new office to handle sales, engineering, and product management concerning its hot box technology. The following year Harmon acquired Serrmi Services of Atlanta, Georgia, a company with combined office and manufacturing space of 35,360 square feet.

Harmon gained new international contracts in 1995 and 1996. In April 1995 it announced it had gained a $2.4 million agreement with Western Australia's BHP Iron Ore railroad. Harmon agreed to upgrade the railroad's wayside signaling systems using its computer technology and install its advanced Ultra Cab II system, which gave engineers more information and automatically controlled braking. Moreover, in October 1995 the People's Republic of China (PRC) awarded Harmon a $727,000 contract for hot box detectors for its mainline railroads. The following spring the PRC expanded its hot box Harmon contract by another $800,000.

In spite of a $2.2 million contract with Union Pacific to install equipment on UP's Chicago suburban line, Harmon experienced some difficulties in 1995, mainly in integrating its acquired Servo unit. Sales for fiscal year 1995 increased 14 percent to reach $137 million, but net earnings declined ten percent to $6.9 million and earnings per share declined 13 percent.

Harmon enjoyed much better years in 1996 and 1997, based on new acquisitions, contracts, facilities, improved technology, and increased reliability and quality of its products and services. During this time, Harmon Industries acquired the following firms: Vaughan Systems, a U.K.-based maker of train describers and passenger information and modular railway control systems; First Coast Signal Engineering, Inc., a private company with 13 engineers focusing on designing highway train crossings for class one railroads; Omaha Railway Signal, Inc., a Florida-based firm with five experienced engineers in the railway industry; Devtronics, Inc., a firm supplying railroad products and services, including hot box detectors, highway crossing event monitoring and alarm equipment, and stand-alone defect detectors for high and wide loads and dragging equipment; CSS, Inc., and Indiana fir, that installed and maintained railroad equipment, mainly warning systems for highway crossings in the Midwest and Florida.

At the same time, Harmon gained many new or extended contracts. Harmon's Incremental Train Control System (ITCS) was installed and successfully demonstrated in Michigan on the Chicago-Detroit line as part of a joint project with the Federal Railroad Administration, Amtrak, and the Michigan Department of Transportation to allow trains to run at higher speeds with better safety. Improving productivity by increasing the number of trains that safely run on the same track, the ITCS employed Global Positioning System that used radio waves from satellites to determine train position. In 1996, Harmon was selected to provide the signals and control systems for the Florida Overland Express' high-speed route between Miami, Orlando, and Tampa Bay. Moreover, in 1997, Harmon gained two contracts from the Utah Transit Authority for signaling projects along UTA's new light rail system from downtown Salt Lake City to Sandy 15 miles to the south, a route expected to carry 20,000 passengers daily, done in preparation for the 2002 A.D. Winter Olympics.

In 1998 Harmon planned to introduce a new product, the Electro Code 5, an advanced model of signaling technology that electronically replaced pole lines between signals. And the firm intended to start a new training school and a new 24-hour service desk.

To improve the quality of its products and services, Harmon Industries in the 1990s upgraded its facilities and processes to meet International Organization for Standardization (ISO) standards. In 1996 the firm announced ISO-9001 certification with TickIT for its Grain Valley and Warrensburg, Missouri, manufacturing plants and its engineering offices in Omaha, Nebraska; Jacksonville, Florida; Louisville, Kentucky; and Grain Valley. TickIT certification was supported by the Department of Trade and Industry and the British Computer Society to increase quality in developing and producing software. In December 1997 Harmon's Atlanta facility was ISO certified, followed by its Lee's Summit plant also becoming ISO certified in early 1998. In a press release dated April 1, 1998, Harmon President/CEO Bjorn E. Olsson stated, ''With the certification of Lee's Summit, we have completed a major strategic initiative to have every Harmon operation ISO certified. We have increased the standards by which our company operates and will hold all future acquisitions to the same level of quality.''

With these changes in place, Harmon's finances showed considerable improvement in 1996 and 1997. Gross sales increased from $136.1 million in 1995 to $183.9 million in 1996 and then to $214.4 million in 1997. Likewise, net earnings jumped from $6.9 million in 1995 to $9.3 million in 1996 and to $11 million in 1997. Although its international business in 1997 resulted in a small fraction of Harmon's gross sales, it was the fastest growing part of the company, mainly from Vaughan Harmon contracts in the United Kingdom. Harmon at the end of 1997 was creating a Mexican subsidiary and trying to expand its operations in China and India. Its international customers were found in Latin America, the West Indies, Africa, the Middle East, Asia, and New Zealand.

Robert Heggestad, Harmon's vice-president for technology, pointed out a long-term trend helping his company. ''The capability of most new electronic equipment for internal diagnostics, data logging and remote access for diagnostics and data retrieval are very much in tune with the continued downsizing of maintenance staffs on most railroads,'' said Heggestad in the December 1995 *Progressive Railroading*.

In 1998 Harmon Industries operated under the directions of its ten-member Board of Directors chaired by Bob Harmon, the only member of the Harmon family still involved in the firm. The company's president/CEO was Bjorn E. Olsson, who had worked for several Swedish firms before becoming Harmon's president and COO; in 1995 he became president and CEO. Harmon Industries had an impressive track record through most of the 1990s and good prospects for the near future as railroads continue to modernize.

Principal Subsidiaries

Consolidated Asset Management Company, Inc. (CAMCO); Vaughan Harmon Systems Ltd. (United Kingdom); Vale Harmon Enterprises, Ltd. (Canada); Henkes-Harmon Industries, Pty. Ltd. (Australia).

Further Reading

Barrier, Michael, ''Working on the Railroad,'' *Nation's Business,* January 1990, p. 53.

''Harmon Industries Benefits from Revival in Rail Spending,'' *Barron's,* December 14, 1992, pp. 46–47.

Harmon, Robert C., ''SAB Harmon Industries, Inc. History,'' *SAB Harmon Times* (newsletter), July–December 1984, January–May 1985.

Heggestad, Robert E., ''ITCS Will Allow Detroit-Chicago Speed-up,'' *Railway Gazette International,* August 1996.

Judge, Tom, ''Electronic Advances Improve How Railroads Manage,'' *Progressive Railroading,* December 1995.

Kramer, Jerome V., ''MetroLink: Harmon Hits a Home Run,'' *Railway Age,* August 1994.

Pope, Gregory T., ''The Iron Horse Enters the Space Age,'' *High Technology Business,* April 1989, p. 18.

''Tie Tests: Price vs. Cost,'' *Railway Age,* June 1990, p. 41.

Vantuono, William C., ''Transit Signaling: the Next Generation,'' *Railway Age,* October 1993, p. 4.

Welty, Gus, ''FEC [Florida East Coast]: System-Wide with ATC [Automatic Train Control],'' *Railway Age,* February 1988, pp. 28–29.

''Why Crossings Get Safer,'' *Railway Age,* January 1993, p. 33.

—David M. Walden

Helly Hansen ASA

Solgaard Skog 139
N-1539 Moss
Norway
(47) 69 249000
Fax: (47) 69 249290
Web site: http://www.helly-hansen.com

Private Company
Incorporated: 1877
Employees: 476
Sales: NOK 941 million (US $146 million) (1996)
SICs: 2300 Apparel & Other Textile Products; 2381
    Fabric Dress & Work Gloves; 2311 Mens/Boys' Suits
    & Coats; 2339 Womens/Misses' Outerwear, Not
    Elsewhere Classified; 2824 Organic Fibers—
    Noncellulosic; 2329 Mens/Boys' Clothing, Not
    Elsewhere Classified

Helly Hansen ASA is a world-leading designer, manufacturer, and distributor of a branded line of clothing and accessories to marine, outdoor, and other high-performance apparel markets, as well as a range of more fashion-oriented, less technically demanding garments to a growing consumer base. The Helly Hansen hallmark has long been rainwear and other extreme weather gear for the fishing, boating, and other marine industries, a category the company is said to have invented in the late 1800s; since the 1980s, however, the company has expanded its product line to include other industrial and professional markets, as well as the outdoor, ski, and in the late 1990s, snowboarding markets. The company's mid-1990s move into the consumer sportswear apparel market has been inspired in part by the adoption of the Helly Hansen brand by members of the international rap music scene. In the late 1990s, however, the company has indicated that it will be restoring its focus to its core activewear and nautical markets.

While phasing out its manufacturing activities in the late 1990s—instead outsourcing its production requirements to third party manufacturers, chiefly in the Asia Pacific region—Helly Hansen has been developing a chain of flagship retail stores. Located in the U.S. and Canadian markets, which represent more than a third of the company's sales, the Helly Hansen stores are being developed primarily on a licensed basis. The company expects to develop a network of some 50 licensed stores, in addition to the company-owned flagship retail store in Seattle, Washington. In addition to the retail chain, Helly Hansen continues to distribute its products through a network of some 10,000 third party retailers worldwide, as well as operating Helly Hansen ''shop-in-shop'' sales areas in department stores and other retail stores.

The company's headquarters remain in its original Moss, Norway location, where Helly Hansen maintains the research and development activities into new textile technology that have enabled the company to become one of the world's leading suppliers of nautical and other extreme weather gear. Since the 1980s, Helly Hansen has promoted its three-layer Weather-System, designed to provide maximum waterproofing and breathability, consisting of a LIFA (polypropylene) base layer, a Propile (fleece-like) thermal layer, and an outer layer using the company's patented Helly Tech fabric. Helly Hansen products long have been mainstays of the nautical world and have outfitted adventurers from North Pole expeditions to Mount Everest climbs. Continuing the Helly Hansen tradition of innovative technology is the 1998 introduction of illumiNITE, a reflective fabric destined to provide greater safety to mountaineers.

Since April 1997, Helly Hansen has been 70 percent owned by Investcorp, a Bahrain-based investment group that also holds a stake in Saks Fifth Avenue, among others, and previously held positions in such other brand names as Tiffany and Gucci. Longtime principal shareholder, Orkla, of Norway, maintains a 30 percent share in the company. In February 1998, Investcorp named Erik Stensrud, formerly with Adidas, as Helly Hansen's CEO.

The World's First Rainwear Company in the 1870s

When Helly Juell Hansen of Moss, Norway set out to sea in the 1850s, joining the crew of a merchant ship at the age of 15, sailors long had been exposed to the often harsh elements of ocean travel. Hansen, who started his career swabbing the decks, soon would have his fill of the cold and wet conditions found especially in the rough seas of the Northern Hemisphere. Then Hansen hit upon the idea of adding the water-repellant properties of oil to clothing. Hansen fashioned the first ''oil-skin'' using canvas coated with linseed oil (which itself long had been used in paints and other materials, because, unlike other oils, linseed oil dries). The oilskin would become quickly popular among seamen—although stiff and sticky, the oilskin nevertheless helped to protect the sailors from the wet and cold, while also protecting their clothing.

Hansen continued his career at sea, receiving his master's license at the age of 25 and earning a reputation as an able captain. In 1876, however, after surviving a storm (saving his crew and a French vessel as well, for which Hansen was decorated by the French government), Hansen decided to retire to shore. Up until then, Hansen had done little with his oilskin invention. In 1877, however, Hansen and his wife set up shop in Moss, Norway, producing oilskins for the local market and becoming the world's first rainwear manufacturer. The Hansen oilskin was a quick success—in the company's first year, more than 2,000 were sold. By the turn of the century, the Helly Hansen name had already found renown among the world's fishing and marine industries.

Hansen, meanwhile, had continued to develop his invention, enabling the company to outpace a rising number of competitors offering their own oilskins. Among Hansen's innovations was a method of drying the linseed oil so that the oiliness was reduced, while the fabric was made more supple and thus more comfortable to wear. This formula would remain a company secret, and Helly Hansen's oilskins would dominate the industry over the following decades, achieving as much as 65 percent of the worldwide market.

Although Helly Juell Hansen died in 1914, the company, which remained under family control before becoming a wholly owned subsidiary of Norway's industrial giant Orkla, would continue its founder's knack for innovation. The company soon added its own line of garments, to be worn under the oilskin outerwear, to provide greater insulation. In 1950 Helly Hansen attacked the problem of leaking seams with the introduction of its patented MicroWeld process, a method of blending materials using microwaves to create a bonded, 100 percent waterproof fabric. In the 1960s the company became the first to introduce new ''pile'' materials into the outdoor garment industry, providing better insulation properties.

Helly Hansen would prove quick to adapt new materials to its line of nautical wear. The company added polyurethane coating to replace the original oilskin; in the mid-1970s Helly Hansen developed a MultiCoating technique for applying polyurethane in multiple thin layers, as opposed to the single thick layer used by other manufacturers, creating a more durable and pliable material. At the same time, Helly Hansen was quick to recognize the potential of another recently introduced material, the polypropylene-based Lifa, produced by a neighboring Scandinavian manufacturer. Lifa already had found application as a liner for the disposable diaper industry—it is this material that provides the wicking action, drawing moisture away from the skin. Helly Hansen adapted Lifa to its product line in 1975, becoming the first company in the world to manufacture Lifa-based garments to the adult market. Helly Hansen's Lifa underwear would form the primary layer beneath the company's insulation and outerwear garments. Two years later, the company would introduce a line of performance clothing that was among the first to be waterproof and breathable. The company also developed a neoprene-based survival suit that enabled a person to stay warm and float for up to two days in frigid waters.

Expanding Markets in the 1980s and 1990s

Helly Hansen introduced a new insulating fabric, Fibrepile, in 1979. Featuring a patented double-knit construction, the new material boasted not only strong insulation performance, but also high durability, making it ideal for the company's line of work garments. By then, the company had begun to target other markets. The company moved beyond its nautical base into creating clothing for other outdoor industrial applications, including ranching and construction. The boom in outdoor recreation during the 1970s and 1980s would propel Helly Hansen into creating clothing for sports such as skiing and hiking/mountaineering, among others. Along the way the company also expanded its clothing designs to appeal to the growing consumer market, while maintaining its high-end, performance image.

By the beginning of the 1980s, Helly Hansen was established in its Scandinavian and European markets. Until 1981, however, the company's presence in North America remained minimal. In that year the company opened its U.S. headquarters, in Redmond, Washington, with a staff of 15. The following year Helly Hansen also opened a Canadian subsidiary. By 1984 the company's North American subsidiaries employed 130 and sales had topped US $10 million, while total company sales represented some US $100 million, generated by more than 1,600 employees and manufacturing facilities in Canada, Ireland, Portugal, and the United States, in addition to the company's seven Norwegian plants.

The company introduced its Helly Tech fabric coating in 1984, setting a new standard for waterproof, breathable fabric. Helly Tech also would provide the final layer for the 1986 introduction of the Helly Hansen three-layer WeatherSystem, complementing its Lifa-based undergarments, and pile-insulation garments, including the Propile polyester fabric introduced in 1986. North American demand for the company's products, in particular its Lifa-based underwear, caused the company to increase its production, including contracting third party manufacturers.

By the mid-1990s Helly Hansen had made the transition from a sole market supplier—although its nautical products continued to dominate the sports, leisure, and marine segments, the company's ''outdoor'' garments now represented half of its annual sales. As such, Helly Hansen faced an entirely new field of competitors, ranging from L.L. Bean and Timberland to Patagonia and North Face, among others. Yet the company also was struggling through the extended recession of the 1990s; despite rising revenues and operating profits, the company began posting net losses by mid-decade.

In 1995 Helly Hansen's parent Orkla agreed to sell 50 percent of the company to Resource Group International, a Seattle, Washington-based diversified holding group, for NOK 125 million (US $18.6 million). The new partners installed a new management team and effected a dramatic restructuring of the company's operations, including shutting nearly all of the company's manufacturing facilities and instead opening a Hong Kong office to oversee the outsourcing of the company's production requirements to a number of Far East-based contractors. By 1997 nearly 80 percent of the company's clothing products were produced by contract. In this respect, Helly Hansen followed a growing trend, that of transforming itself from a clothing manufacturing company to, as then CEO Johnny Austad wrote in the company's 1996 annual report, "a brand image."

The company stepped up its retailing activities, including expanding its "shop in shop" concept, while also making plans to enter the retail arena with its own retail stores. In the mid-1990s the company received a boost from an unexpected source—rap star L.L. Cool Jay, who had begun sporting Helly Hansen clothes. Before long, Helly Hansen found itself propelled into a new category of street wear, as the rap community quickly adopted the Helly Hansen line. In response, the company expanded its line to include more fashion-oriented, less technologically sophisticated clothing. Helly Hansen also moved to step up its marketing activities. Plans were made as well to create a network of some 50 freestanding Helly Hansen retail stores. By 1998 Helly Hansen had opened its company-owned, flagship Seattle, Washington store, while developing an extensive list of licensed retail stores, primarily located in North America.

The company push to become an international brand name beyond its nautical base led to the agreement to sell a 70 percent stake (Resource Group International's entire 50 percent as well as 20 percent of Orkla's holding) to Investcorp, a Bahrain-based investment group specializing in brand name businesses, for US $112 million. The move was seen as crucial for the company, as its competition now included such international sportswear names as Tommy Hilfiger and Nautica. A further indication of the company's direction came in February 1998 when Investcorp named a new management team; both CEO Erik Stensrud and COO Robert McCulloch had worked previously for major sportswear manufacturer Adidas. Yet despite its moves into the more fashionable sportswear scene, Helly Hansen remained committed to its 120-year tradition of technical innovation and excellence.

Principal Subsidiaries

A/S Helly Hansen (Denmark); Helly Hansen (US) Inc.; Helly Hansen Distributie B.V. (Netherlands); Helly Hansen AB (Sweden); Helly Hansen Spesialprodukter AS (Norway); Helly Hansen Verkaufs GmbH (Germany); Helly Hansen (U.K.) Ltd.; Helly Hansen GmbH (Austria); Helly Hansen Benelux B.V. (Netherlands); Helly Hansen (Suisse) SA; Helly Hansen France SARL; Helly Hansen N.V. (Belgium); FCO Maritim AS (Norway); Oban Wetsuit Ltd. (Scotland); Helly Hansen Leisure Inc. (Canada); Helly Hansen Far East Ltd. (Hong Kong); Retis Ltd. (Iceland); Eurcen Retail (U.K.) Ltd.

Further Reading

Goldsmith, Sarah, "Helly Hansen Poised for US Slalom," *WWD*, December 9, 1996, p. 33.
"Helly Hansen: President Gordon McFadden Steps Down," *Daily News Record*, February 20, 1998, p. 1.
McGowan, Elizabeth, "Behind the Label: Helly Hansen," *Backpacker*, November 1984, p. 26.
"Outdoor Clothier Plans Retail Push," *Marketing News*, March 17, 1997, p. 22.
Piganeau, Joëlle, "Helly Hansen rhabille les rappeurs en marins norvegiens," *Journal du Textile*, January 13, 1997, p. 114.
Spector, Robert, "Helly Hansen's Foul-Weather Gear Being Brought Ashore in US," *Daily News Record*, February 17, 1987, p. 23.

—M.L. Cohen

Hollywood Entertainment Corporation

9275 S.W. Peyton Lane
Wilsonville, Oregon 97070
U.S.A.
(503) 570-1600
Fax: (503) 570-1680

Public Company
Incorporated: 1988
Employees: 20,000
Sales: $500.5 million (1997)
Stock Exchanges: NASDAQ
Ticker Symbol: HLYW
SICs: 7841 Video Tape Rental

Hollywood Entertainment Corp., which operates over 1,000 stores in 43 states under the name Hollywood Video, is the second largest video rental and retailer in the United States. Second only to Blockbuster Entertainment, Hollywood has come a long way in just a decade of existence, boasting larger stores and a wider selection of video titles than its competitors.

Birth of a Video Store Chain: 1988–93

Hollywood Video stores were the brainchild of Mark Wattles, who founded his company in June 1988. Within four months, the 28-year-old Wattles opened his first store in Portland, Oregon. Wattles took his time expanding over the next few years, as the video rental and sales industry took off reaching $9.8 billion in revenues by 1990. By year-end 1991 with a handful of stores, Hollywood Entertainment Corp. generated $5.1 million, with income of $281,000. The following year, Wattles had a total of 15 operational stores in the Pacific Northwest area. Revenues for 1992 were just over $11 million, double the previous year's figures, a pattern Hollywood repeated several times in the next decade. Net income, however, was the bigger story, having gone from 1991's $281,000 to just under $1.2 million in 1992.

By early 1993, Hollywood owned and operated 16 stores in Oregon and Washington. The next big step was taking the company public; in July Hollywood initiated its first offering on the NASDAQ national market. The proceeds netted Hollywood $10.4 million, which helped with its aggressive expansion plans. By the end of the year, there were 25 Hollywood stores in three states and the company's revenues topped $17.3 million and earned net income of $2.1 million or 14 cents per share.

In the five years since Hollywood's founding, videotape rental had become much more commonplace in the United States, as nearly 90 percent of all American households owned at least one VCR, according to the Video Software Dealers Association. Some 60 million videos were rented per week during this time, as consumers came to regard renting videos as an excellent value. The burgeoning presence of video rental outlets was perhaps most influenced by the old real estate adage of "location, location, location." Studies indicated that customers preferred to go the shortest distance to high-traffic, high-visibility locations, and while there was some loyalty to store name, advertising promotions and convenience frequently determined the fate of a video outlet. Rental rates were also subject, naturally, to the whims of the weather, with harsh or inclement weather often keeping consumers at home.

However, perhaps the greatest factor affecting video rental rates was the success or failures of films by the major movie studios that supplied the video outlets. Most consumers did not realize how much major movie studios relied on video sales and rentals, which could account for as much as 45 percent of their annual revenues, higher than the amount generated by the theatrical release of most films. Americans reportedly spent twice as much on videos in a year's time than they did at the theater, which in turn gave big video chains like Blockbuster and Hollywood considerable clout with studios. Most video titles were given to rental stores for an exclusive period of time, usually 45 days, before these same films were offered for viewing via pay-for-view or cable channels such as HBO, Showtime, or Cinemax.

Hitting the Big Time: 1994–96

In February 1994 Hollywood offered a second block of shares to the public, netting $23.6 million. On the heels of the offering came the company's first acquisition: the 33-store

Video Central chain headquartered in Texas. The ink was barely dry on the first purchase when Hollywood moved forward with a second in May 1994, this time buying Eastman Video, based in California. The Eastman deal contributed another 11 stores to Hollywood's growing ranks, as did a third acquisition the next month, of a ten-outlet Nevada and California chain called Video Park. Hollywood completed a third equity offer of shares in August of that year, netting proceeds of $63.6 million, which went to good use funding an expansion that included 33 new "superstores," bringing the total number of Hollywood Video stores to 113 in eight states. Year-end figures were more than encouraging for Hollywood and its high-speed expansion, as revenues leapt to $73.3 million, up from $17.3 million in 1993, and net income reached $8.1 million.

Hollywood began 1995 with an acquisition in the first quarter—this time for a 14-store Minnesota chain called Title Wave. As it had in the previous year, Hollywood brought in funds through another equity offer, its fourth and largest to date, totalling $95.4 million, which in turn made possible its next purchase. In August the company acquired the Midwest-based Video Watch, which oversaw 42 stores. At the same time, Hollywood was also constructing scores of new stores, having added 122 units by the end of the year for a total of 305 in 23 states, a 170 percent increase in size from the year before. In a sampling of eight major cities in the United States, *Video Business* magazine found Hollywood had captured 1.4 percent of the video rental market, to Blockbuster's 32.6 percent. Though progress seemed slow, Hollywood was determined to broaden its consumer base and finished the year with revenues of $149.4 million, double those of the previous year, and net income of $11.8 million.

In the mid-1990s the video rental and retailing industry suffered a slowdown, attributed largely to the activities of industry giant Blockbuster, which was engaged in an effort to become a one-stop shop for a wide range of entertainment products, including such noncore merchandise as music, magazines, and books. In the wake of the industry slowdown, Hollywood's shareholders too watched their stock fall from a high of $22.69 in 1996 to a low of $6.50. Unlike Blockbuster, however, Hollywood stores remained focused on video rentals, which accounted for 85 percent or more of revenues, with candy, gum, and video and other merchandise sales making up the rest. Although Hollywood management knew it routinely took three-to-five years for new outlets to hit their stride and reach optimal sales, they had not banked on an industry-wide slump.

Still, the company bounced back quickly. By the end of 1996, Hollywood was on a roll—during the year it had opened 250 new stores (including the milestone 500th store in December) for a total of 551 nationwide units in 42 states. Moreover, the company had generated $34.7 million from a fifth offering

of stock. Wattles had also created a new infrastructure for the company, dividing operations along four geographic areas (East, West, South, and Midwest) and naming a senior vice-president for each region. Year-end numbers for Hollywood were very healthy, with revenues at $302.3 million, again doubling the previous year's dollars, and net income topping $20.6 million or 59 cents per share.

Taking on Blockbuster: 1997 and Beyond

In 1997 instability in the industry was again prompted by management shakeouts at competitor Blockbuster. Hollywood's stock rollercoastered again, this time climbing to over $25 per share and falling to $8.31 before stabilizing once again. Still, with the video rental and retailing industry in the $10 to $12 billion range and still growing, Hollywood continued to expand, opening a record 356 new superstores in 1997, bringing the chain to 907 units in 42 states. This year also marked the appointment of F. Mark Wolfinger, from Metromedia Restaurant Group, as chief financial officer, and later the hiring of Jeffrey B. Yapp as president, who came to Hollywood from Twentieth-Century Fox Home Entertainment. Near the end of the year, Hollywood commenced a self-tender offer to purchase a minimum of eight million shares up to a maximum of 16 million at $11 per share. The company had doubled its available bank credit to $300 million, and had broken ground on its new 123,000-square-foot headquarters. Finally, Hollywood brought in phenomenal financial results for the year, with $550.5 million in sales.

In January 1998, Hollywood was forced to set aside its self-tender offer, having failed to attain its minimum buy-back of shares. Analysts found the failure comforting; investors apparently had enough confidence in Hollywood's value not to sell for $11 a share, figuring the stock would climb. Though Wattles announced he was disappointed in the self-tender's outcome, he was nonetheless bolstered by the company's stability and said shares would be bought occasionally at the open market price.

Hollywood was still rapidly opening stores in its bid to someday dominate the video rental marketplace: its 1,000th store was opened in April 1998 in a suburb of Dallas, coincidentally the headquarters of the Viacom-owned rival Blockbuster. During this time, Hollywood was opening a new store virtually every day, and nearly 25 percent of this expansion was geared towards smaller geographic areas (with population draws in the 30,000 range) with a somewhat lower output than its larger-market stores.

Hollywood maintained its breakneck expansion speed through a real estate team of 120 who scouted locations throughout the United States and recommended new sites. Once a location was selected, it cost the company in the neighborhood of $475,000 (in 1998 dollars) to complete a 7,500-square-foot store, with nearly $200,000 dedicated to videocassettes, with 10,000 titles, and 16,000 tapes (excluding adult or x-rated titles which Hollywood did not stock) per unit, as well as about $40,000 allotted for sell-through merchandise. While most stores took in an average of $600,000 during their first year, it generally took less than three-and-a-half years to reach the break-even point. Well established stores usually brought in from $700,000 to $900,000 per unit per year, the highest rate in the industry.

By contrast, Blockbuster's average store was smaller, usually less than 6,000-square-feet, with fewer videotapes, and an average unit volume of $650,000. However, Blockbuster ruled the nation, with some 3,300 stores, more than double the number of Hollywood outlets. Competitors in video retail came in the form of such discount chains as Kmart, Wal-Mart, and Target. Other public rental chains included Movie Gallery with nearly 865 outlets; Moovies, with around 270 stores; Video Update, with just over 400 units; and West Coast Video, which had under 300 units. Industry analyst Rosemary Sisson in a NationsBanc Montgomery Securities report found that despite each of its competitors' store number or size, Hollywood still bested them with volume—averaging $735,000 per store, to Moovie's $406,000; Movie Gallery's $305,000; Video Update's $313,000; and West Coast's $406,000. Yet the real story was in same-store sales growth, where Hollywood's numbers grew consistently in each quarter while all of its competitors had minimal growth and/or declines in the same periods.

Hollywood's stores represented three percent of the marketplace to Blockbuster's 15 percent. In revenues, Blockbuster garnered a 31 percent share to Hollywood's five percent, and all the other major public chains combined held a six percent market share. Though Hollywood's numbers were not close to those of Blockbuster, the former had come from nowhere to challenge the giant and had gained a healthy slice of the video pie in under a decade. Industry pundits believed the video market was still expanding, and the competition between Hollywood and Blockbuster was not only good for both of them, but for the smaller chains and independents as well. Increased traffic, brought in by advertising dollars spent by the "big two," served the entire industry by bringing customers out of their homes to rent and buy videos.

Rapid developments in technology presented challenges to both Blockbuster and Hollywood, as videotaped movies were losing ground to pay-per-view TV, direct broadcast satellite TV, video-on-demand cable TV, DVD technology, and the latest, "disposable" DVDs or Zoom TV. However, according to Paul Sweeting in *Video Business* magazine, the "fundamental issue for the video rental business as a whole [was] not its vulnerability to technology but its access to capital."

As a new century approached, there was certainly no dispute that Blockbuster, with its nearly 4,000 domestic stores, was the top video renter in the United States and that Hollywood was a distant though gaining second. Most analysts predicted that further consolidation of the smaller franchises would occur and have a positive effect on the market; the chains Moovies and Video Update were slated to uphold this trend by merging in 1998. Analysts believed Hollywood would break the billion-dollar mark in revenues by 1999, and would reach, at its present breakneck pace, 2,000 stores by the year 2000. The larger question appeared to be how much this growth would affect Hollywood's share of the video rental market.

Further Reading

McMurray, Scott, "Time to Hit the Fast-Forward Button," *U.S. News & World Report,* August 26, 1996, p. 39.
Sender, Isabelle, "Hollywood Video: Will a Store a Day Keep No. 1 Chain Away?," *Chain Store Age,* June 1998.
Sporich, Brett, "On One-a-Day Pace, Hollywood Opens Store No. 1,000 Near Dallas," *Video Business,* April 20, 1998, pp. 1, 8.
Sweeting, Paul, "In-Sight," *Video Business,* October 13, 1997.
——, "When Giants Collide," *Video Business,* October 6, 1997, pp. 1, 8.
"Hollywood Entertainment Corp. Fails to Reach Minimum Number of Shares Required Under Its Self-Tender Offer," *PR Newswire,* January 26, 1998.
"Hollywood Entertainment Corp. Reached Landmark Goal with 1,000th Hollywood Video Superstore," *PR Newswire,* April 16, 1998.

—Taryn Benbow-Pfalzgraf

Home Shopping Network, Inc.

11831 30th Court North
St. Petersburg, Florida 33716
U.S.A.
(813) 573-0339
(800) 284-3900

Wholly Owned Subsidiary of HSN Inc.
Incorporated: 1982
Employees: 4,100
Sales: $1.09 billion (1997 est.)
SICs: 5961 Catalog & Mail-Order Houses

Home Shopping Network, Inc. is perhaps best known for overseeing the operations of the Home Shopping Club, which sells consumer goods and services via a live cable television program during which viewers may make purchases by phoning a toll-free number. Once a public company involved solely in an array of direct marketing activities through its subsidiaries, over time the Home Shopping Network became the hub around which a media empire built by Barry Diller was based.

1970s Origins

The idea for the Home Shopping Network originated in the 1970s, when Lowell W. Paxson owned an AM radio station in Clearwater, Florida, that began to lose listeners to FM alternatives. Paxson also lost advertisers. He decided to try selling merchandise directly over the air, switching from an easy-listening music format to an at-home radio shopping service called The Bargaineers. To finance the new format, Paxson turned to Roy M. Speer, a lawyer and real estate developer. Speer would later become Home Shopping's chairman.

Almost immediately after the switch in format the station's revenues swelled so much that Paxson was eager to try out his home shopping idea on television. Speer liked the idea of expanding to television but wanted to proceed slowly. Speer invested $500,000 for a 60 percent stake and set out to make sure that viewers would not be disappointed before he gave the go-ahead in July 1982.

Speer and Paxson called their local TV program the Home Shopping Club (HSC). Within three months it was turning a profit. After two more Tampa Bay-area cable companies decided to carry HSC, Speer and Paxson began to explore markets in Fort Lauderdale and Miami. By 1985 HSC was so successful that it went national, calling itself the Home Shopping Network. Speer based his decision to expand on the belief that the profiles of Tampa Bay customers would be the same for people all over the United States.

Speer commissioned the development of a computer system that would have the capacity to respond to customers' needs immediately. He acquired a large number of phone lines and hired many operators, all in an effort to make a return customer of that first-time buyer. Within three months Home Shopping had become the world's first network to broadcast live 24 hours a day, and its number of employees had grown from 300 to 1,280. Speer's approach was successful; in just one year he was able to take the company public.

Public Offering in the Mid-1980s

In February 1986 Merrill Lynch underwrote the company's initial public offering at $18 a share. An investment banker who helped with the offering commented on Speer's wisdom in pricing Home Shopping's stock so low, because it was still perceived as a risky company in an untried industry. At that time Home Shopping was still in the process of trying to convince cable operators to carry its show over other alternative programming. Speer's move assured interested stock buyers at the specialist-broker's stand. Home Shopping stock became the fastest rising new issue of 1986, registering a 137 percent gain by the end of the day. Since the initial offering, Home Shopping stock went on to split twice, the first time at three for one, and the second time at two for one.

The Home Shopping Club had developed three formats: Home Shopping Network 1 (HSN 1), Home Shopping Network 2 (HSN 2), and Home Shopping Spree. HSN 1 was available live, 24 hours a day, seven days a week, and was produced exclusively for cable. HSN 2, which offered upscale merchandise, was also available live, 24 hours a day, seven days a week, but was marketed to both broadcast and cable television. Home

Shopping Spree offered limited-time or 24-hour programming to broadcast stations.

Opinions on the quickly increasing popularity of Home Shopping Club's HSN 1 and HSN 2 stations varied. Perhaps viewers were attracted to the fact they automatically became members the first time they placed an order, and that they received a $5 credit applicable to the next purchase. Another reason may have been that the shows' hosts gave no warning as to what items would appear on the TV screen and when. As viewers could only purchase items for as long as the products appeared on their screens, anywhere from two to ten minutes, the typical member would watch the program for several hours each day in an effort to find the best deals on products they wanted.

The hosts of the program, almost all of whom had a background in retail sales, developed personas, complete with nicknames and a fan following. As Home Shopping's success grew, competing stations began popping up, causing host as well as viewer defections. As competition continued to grow, many stations in the industry, including Home Shopping, turned to celebrity endorsements and hosts.

Another more conventional way that Home Shopping ensured that customers kept coming back was by allowing the return of any purchase if for any reason a member was not satisfied. Credit card purchases would be credited, or for a cash sale a refund check would be issued for the whole purchase cost, including shipping and handling. Home Shopping also assured shipment within 48 hours after an order was placed with a credit card, or within 48 hours after a check for payment had been received.

In 1987 Home Shopping acquired Sky Merchant, Inc., a TV shopping service viewed by at least one million subscribers of Jones Intercable, Inc. As Home Shopping grew, so did the companies that supported it. Home Shopping was one of United Parcel Service's largest accounts, and many suppliers owed their success to Home Shopping. A new product could be introduced to the nation on the network and within minutes, thousands of items could be sold. While some of the merchandise sold over Home Shopping came from closeouts, overstocks, or overruns, the company's purchasing clout was evident in the fact that at least 60 percent of the company's sales in 1987 consisted of products made specifically for Home Shopping and sold to them for rock-bottom prices.

Not everything, however, was on the upswing in 1987. In that year alone more than 15 television shop-at-home programs went off the air. Stock market analysts began to question how long Home Shopping could sustain its rapid growth rate. Sales in the period between February and May 1985, for example, were $3.6 million; for the same period in 1986, sales were $42.6 million. Some believed that members would eventually reach their credit card limits. Some thought the company was paying too much for its acquisitions of UHF television stations and burdening itself with excessive debt. Some believed the company would lose market share to its ever-growing number of competitors who offered improvements on Home Shopping's unpredictable format, such as the plan J.C. Penney and Sears announced for Telaction, which would allow customers to use their phone to select items from their screens.

In one year, between March 1987 and March 1988, Home Shopping stock had experienced a market slip of 18.95 percent, compared to a 6.76 percent drop in the Dow Jones Industrial Average. The company lost no time in reacting, however; as early as 1987 it was looking around for better ways to harness its market. In January 1987 Home Shopping announced plans to build a new telecommunications center and corporate headquarters in St. Petersburg, Florida. By September the company had started using the UHF television stations it had been acquiring, and the network began broadcasting from its new 180,000 square-foot telecommunications facility, hoping to beat down its competitors with better reception. In September 1987 Home Shopping announced its plans for a major corporate restructuring with HSN Inc. becoming a holding company for the various subsidiaries conducting its businesses.

Distinctions such as fast delivery and guaranteed products, the ability to process orders rapidly and reduce labor costs, and the higher quality of television reception provided by its own TV stations enabled HSN to preserve its market share, as well as distance itself from all but one of its competitors. It also reported good annual sales gains, passing the $1 billion mark in 1990. However, these distinctions still had not succeeded in recapturing wary investors. There was worry about the stability of the home shopping industry in the face of recession years. HSN stock, nevertheless, moved to the New York Stock Exchange from the smaller American Stock Exchange in 1990, and the company began a stock repurchase program.

New Owners in the 1990s

In May 1993, Liberty Media Corporation acquired HSN. Then a month later HSN experienced some trouble in the forms of civil suits accusing the company of taking kickbacks and unavailable lines of credit. Nonetheless, HSN offered to help R. H. Macy & Company set up its own cable television shopping channel. The channel featured the merchandise found in Macy's stores on a 24-hour, seven-days-a-week basis. HSN provided the technical knowledge to operate the teleshopping operation, as well as offered warehouses and distribution services to the financially challenged Macy's. According to Macy chairman Myron E. Ullman in *WWD*, "HSN has the telephone answering services to respond to customer inquiries and process merchandise orders promptly. Coupled with the merchandising, programming, management and cable distribution expertise already assembled for TV Macy's, HSN fulfillment operations would greatly enhance TV Macy's. We anticipate using HSN systems to process customers' orders, maintain records, control inventory and to facilitate payments."

The following month—in February 1992—the home shopping industry threatened to consolidate when rival company QVC proposed a merger with HSN. The combined company, QVC Network, "would be good for electronic retailing, overall," observed Michael Rourke of QVC in *Communications Daily*. "We'll be more streamlined, and be able to offer the consumer a greater diversity of product, advanced services, and superior convenience. This is going to push the whole evolution of electronic retailing forward, because as a result of our offering better service and product selection and greater convenience, more people will use the service. As we get more people to shop via television, the area will grow and develop." However, by November HSN and QVC ended their merger discussions when QVC decided to pursue the acquisition of Paramount Communications Inc.

HSN began 1994 with global aspirations. The company prepared to partner with Tele-Communications Inc. to launch an international teleshopping service. In August 1993, HSN established an international division, headed by Michael W. D. McMullen, to explore international television opportunities. Known as Home Shopping International, the service countered the international activities of HSN rival QVC, which earlier had established two shopping services in the United Kingdom and Mexico. HSN appointed McMullen to oversee the operations of Home Shopping International.

In an effort to diversity and expand its services, HSN also tested a video-on-demand service through Waterbury, Connecticut's Sammons Communication cable television system early in 1994. MCI also agreed to a three-year $38 million contract providing 800 service to the Home Shopping Network.

HSN launched its first international venture—a home shopping company in Japan—in February 1994. Cable television was not widely available in Japan, but it was available to the wealthy, so HSN planned to develop a home shopping program for more upscale viewers. HSN intended to export products to the Japanese market, but also stated a commitment to developing businesses there, especially for apparel and other products that might depend on native appeal. As McMullen explained in *WWD*: "We will set up buying operations to see whether we can find local products that we can also bring back to the United States. We think it's politically important that we enhance local industries."

About this time, HSN and Prodigy Services Company began working together on an online store to debut in the fall of 1994. Selling housewares, electronics, fashions, jewelry, and other products to personal-computer users, the service was the first to use full-color photos rather than drawings of merchandise. In addition to the shopping aspects, the service also provided a bulletin board for contacting HSN hosts and celebrity guests. HSN also established HSN Interactive, a new division headed by Jeff Gentry.

Beginning in May 1994, HSN worked on expanding its viewer base. The company again entered into an agreement with Tele-Communications Inc. that added 500,000 viewers to its Home Shopping Club in the form of new Tele-Communications Inc. subscribers. The federal government's Cable Act of 1992 ensured that 4.8 million other homes also would be covered through the agreement, since the rules specified that cable operators must carry all broadcasters with signals in the areas. In addition, HSN renewed contracts with ten cable operators with seven million subscribers, including Continental Cablevision, a system with three million subscribers. HSN added 16 million subscribers though agreements with five additional cable television companies that would carry Home Shopping Network programming the following month.

In order to compete financially with the revenues generated by commercials aired on other home shopping networks, HSN initiated a division to produce infomercials and distribute them globally in July 1994. HSN Direct, located at the HSN headquar-

ters in St. Petersburg, Florida, aired its infomercials on cable networks and through broadcast services—excluding HSN's home shopping vehicles, which were not formatted for long commercials. HSN embarked upon a joint venture to produce the infomercials. Headed by Kevin Harrington, a past vice-president at National Media and co-owner of the venture, HSN Direct positioned Home Shopping Network to sell to a European audience. "My primary mission is to begin getting things rolling domestically," Harrington admitted to *WWD*, "but it doesn't take long before you have to start looking internationally. I've done it before and I certainly will be looking into international." Harrington was responsible for developing the infomercial in Europe through Quantum International, a company he formed in 1988. He expected HSN to create infomercials for housewares, exercise equipment, and other products—especially merchandise produced by manufacturers unaware of the infomercial potential of their goods or for products with a history of success on HSN. HSN selected a past executive of Turner Broadcasting—Bob Swift—to serve as chief operating officer of HSN Direct.

During mid-1994, HSN took part in several new ventures. The company assisted the Black Entertainment Television Inc. with establishing a weekly, two-hour home shopping program targeting African-Americans as a test of the viability of a shopping network exclusively for this consumer group. HSN also purchased the online merchandising company Internet Shopping Network, a service first offered in June 1994 for selling computer-related products to consumers. HSN acquired the Internet Shopping Network in an effort to establish an online shopping mall through which to market its products and those of other retailers.

HSN began to sell its merchandise through the online services CompuServe and Prodigy beginning in September 1994. While these services allowed HSN to market its products, they did not facilitate the shopping mall concept that the company wanted to develop. "We hope to be on all of the online services," Gentry explained to *Broadcasting & Cable*. "There will always be a place for live, analog retailing on TV. But you're going to have to learn to be prepared for digital television." During October 1994, HSN allied with Macromedia Inc. to produce software that would "dazzle" consumers browsing on its Internet Shopping Network. The software utilized advanced graphics, animation, and sound.

New Directions in the Mid-1990s

From 1994 to 1995, HSN underwent a transformation. The network redesigned sets, changed the format of programs, and improved the merchandise that it offered. Nevertheless, it remained unprofitable and posted millions of dollars in losses until Barry Diller was named chairman and chief executive at HSN. Diller came to HSN with a proven track record. He successfully managed Paramount Pictures and engineered the creation of the Fox network. Under his direction, QVC, the competing home shopping network, flourished. Diller demonstrated a knack for interesting high-profile investors in his projects, such as John Malone, owner of 39 percent of Silver King Communications, and billionaire David Geffen.

The company pursued growth through technological innovations. HSN's interactive shopping program Global Plaza, for instance, sold electronics and jewelry through the Internet. In May 1995, HSN supplied Global Plaza to Microsoft's Interactive Television service and to Intel's CablePort, which connected personal computers to broadband networks faster than standard modems. (CablePort also offered books and art through HSN's Master-Works and fine jewelry through its Chatelaine program.) HSN then worked with Lockheed Martin Missiles & Space Media Systems Integration on a product for the commercial interactive broadband market. Called the Decision Support System, the software personalized online computer shopping for individual consumers.

Diller became a member of the HSN board in August 1995. His Arrow Holdings recently had purchased a percentage of Silver King Communications, a group of television stations carrying HSN programs. Diller also served as chairman of Silver King Communications, which serviced eight of the larger U.S. markets through 12 television stations. In November of that year, HSN named Diller as its new chairman. The move prompted HSN's president, Gerald Hogan, to resign, and David Dyer, formerly an executive with Lands' End, became the next president.

At the same time, Silver King Communications gained a controlling interest in HSN by trading its stock for that of Liberty Media Corporation, the programming agent of Tele-Communications Inc., owner of 80 percent of HSN stock. Silver King also acquired Savoy Pictures Entertainment Inc. as a wholly owned subsidiary at this time. The merger gave Silver King television stations in New Orleans, Louisiana; Mobile, Alabama; Honolulu, Hawaii; and Green Bay, Wisconsin—enough stations, with Silver King's other 11—to start a new, fifth network. "These steps will add early fiber to the company, quickening our ability to proceed with our ambitions for the development of Silver King," Diller told *WWD*. "Obviously. I did then and do now believe in the future of electronic retailing, just as I did then and do now believe in the future of free, over-the-air broadcasting," he added.

Diller's appointment at HSN created excitement and anticipation within the industry. Janney Montgomery analyst Terry McEvoy observed in *WWD*: "If he [Diller] has a freer hand, maybe he can take home shopping to the next level." Analysts expected Diller to continue to improve programming at HSN and to develop the true value of the company. For example, observers assumed that Diller, well-connected with high-profile designers and celebrities, would utilize his contacts to enhance HSN's offerings and contacts. "Electronic retailing has great potential, and I'm looking forward to what he's [Diller's] going to do with it and what he will do for the whole industry," designer, and Diller's friend, Diana Von Furstenberg said in *WWD*. "With him leaving QVC, the industry kind of flopped a bit. I think he will stir the whole industry. He was not able to do what he wanted to do at QVC and I'm sure this time he will, and will bring everybody out with him," she commented.

Diller sought to purchase the cash-rich Savoy Pictures Entertainment Inc. in December 1995 to add its four VHF television stations to his holdings. However, many industry observers questioned the motives of this move. "People think that you do things for the dumbest reasons," Diller lamented in *Fortune,* explaining "I'm doing this to make this work. I may screw it up, but I have an absolute, clear idea of what businesses I want to build." Part of Diller's strategy included Silver King Communications buying back HSN from Liberty Media Corporation for a $1.3 billion stock exchange in September 1996. A Federal Communications Commission ruling limiting broadcasters from owning more than a 22 percent interest in a cable company, caused the companies to renegotiate an earlier agreement through which Liberty Media would have transferred ownership of HSN to Silver King Communications in exchange for 45 percent ownership. The move allowed Diller to position HSN as a cable network instead of a broadcast-delivered service.

Upon completion of the deal, Silver King controlled more than 80 percent of HSN, leaving Liberty Media with less than 20 percent ownership. HSN common stock converted to .45 of a share of Silver King stock, while HSN Class B stock—"super voting" stock worth ten votes per share and owned in full by Liberty Media—became .54 of a share of Class B Silver King stock.

Silver King Communications' primary source of revenue was the Home Shopping Network programming carried by its 12 UHF broadcast stations. Diller, also this company's chairman, positioned Silver King Communications to purchase HSN in 1995 and initiated a stock swap in 1996. "The companies combined should do wonderfully," Diller revealed in the *Multichannel News.*

Ironically, at one time Silver King Communications was part of HSN. Company founder Roy Speer purchased Silver King in order for its broadcast stations to carry HSN programming. Speer sold the company in 1993 when he needed to divest HSN stock in order to comply with federal laws restricting ownership of cable systems and broadcast stations within the same market. Tele-Communications Inc. purchased HSN.

Stockholders approved the merger of Home Shopping Network, Silver King Communications, and Savoy Pictures on December 19, 1995. Diller continued as the chairman of the new parent company, HSN Inc.

In a stock-for-stock transaction during the summer of 1997, HSN gained control of Ticketmaster, a broker of entertainment tickets. Valued at about $209 million, the merger created opportunities for both companies. HSN greatly expanded its distribution system. "HSN looks at Ticketmaster as a distribution network," noted Mark Hardie, a senior analyst at Forrester Research, adding "and Ticketmaster wants to move away from strictly ticketing." HSN's network provided Ticketmaster with a massive venue through which to market concert, theater, and other entertainment event tickets. "HSN has recognized that Ticketmaster is a great asset," Ticketmaster president Fred Rosen, who maintained his position in the merger, told *Billboard.* "The combination between commercial electronic transactions and broadcasting opens up a world of exciting possibilities," he noted. Founder Paul Allen sold his controlling interest in Ticketmaster in exchange for 11 percent of HSN. He also became a member of HSN's board, as did Frederic Rosen and William Savoy.

Expansion continued after the merger, especially on an international level. Earlier, with Sumitomo Corporation, a large Japanese trading company, HSN brought televised home shopping to

Japan through 30-minute programs broadcast in Tokyo, Osaka, and nearby regions beginning in 1996. Similarly, Jupiter Programming and HSN introduced the SHOP channel in Japan in November 1997. After success in Japan, HSN developed a shopping channel for Germany in conjunction with Quelle, a European catalog company, and Kirch Media Interests of Germany.

Then, with Spanish-language broadcaster Univision, HSN initiated a Spanish-language shopping channel in 1997 for full operations in 1998. "As we looked to develop this venture," McMullen revealed to *Broadcasting & Cable,* "our logical choice was to team with Univision, because they are the strongest Spanish broadcasting group in the United States and because of their partners in Mexico and Venezuela." Univision secured U.S. distribution, and HSN controlled operations of the channel target for seven million Hispanic households in the United States. Since HSN recognized more than 500 million Spanish-speaking consumers worldwide, the company planned to expand the shopping channel into Latin America and Spain, both of which had millions of existing or cable-ready households.

In November 1997, Diller sold an HSN network in Baltimore, Maryland—WHSW—in order to set the groundwork for his Silver King Communications' planned joint venture with the Universal Television Group and the USA Networks. Diller negotiated with the parent company of Universal Studios—Seagram—to join HSN with the television unit of Universal Studios. In exchange for more than $1 million and a 45 percent share of HSN, Seagram, Universal TV's owner, sold its USA Networks and its domestic television business. Diller purchased the lion's share of Universal TV Studios operations in the United States, including production and distribution of such hit television programs as *Law and Order* and *Xena: Warrior Princess,* in a billion-dollar deal. Though Universal Studios retained part ownership in the newly formed company, HSN gained the domestic and some of the international activities of the USA Network (a popular cable station) and the Sci-Fi Network. In addition to the merger on the domestic scene, HSN and Universal worked together on a venture for international television.

Diller remained as chairman of the new company. Executives from Universal TV and its parent company, Seagram, joined the USA Networks board; Diller assumed a seat as a director of Seagram. Shareholders approved HSN's purchase of Universal TV for $4 billion, changing the company's name to USA Networks Inc.

In 1998, HSN joined with the Scandinavian Broadcasting System to bring home shopping to Italy. Distributed by Rete Mia TV, the HSN-SBS Italia network reached 20 million homes. This venture, as HSN's earlier efforts, reinforced its commitment to growth and expansion under the direction of Barry Diller. Diller "would rather die than fail," according to his friend billionaire David Geffen in *Fortune,* adding "He will not fail."

Principal Subsidiaries

Diversified Marketing and Media Services, Inc.; HSN 800/900 Corp.; HSN Health Services Inc.; HSN Telemation Inc.; Home Shopping Club Inc.; Internet Shopping Network; Mistix Corporation; Precision Systems Inc.; Vela Research Inc.

Further Reading

Applefeld, Catherine, "HSN Founder Buys MOR Music TV; Nashville Firm Aims to Build Alternative Distribution, *Billboard,* August 5, 1995, p. 6.

Botton, Sari, "Merger Mania Hits TV Shopping," *HFD—The Weekly Home Furnishings Newspaper,* July 26, 1993, p. 10.

Brodesser, Claude, "Diller Does Station Deal," *MEDIAWEEK,* November 17, 1997, p. 6.

Brown, Rich, "Home Shopping Network Launches Infomercial Unit," *Broadcasting & Cable,* July 18, 1994, p. 22.

——, "It's Everywhere: HSN Gets on the Internet," *Broadcasting & Cable,* September 12, 1994, p. 33.

Colman, Price, "Diller Consolidates Position with HSN Deal," *Broadcasting & Cable,* September 2, 1996, p. 48.

Dickson, Martin, "QVC, Home Shopping Axe Merger," *Financial Post,* November 6, 1993, p. 12.

Edelson, Sharon, "Barry Diller Returns to Home Shopping," *WWD,* November 28, 1995, p. 2.

——, "HSN, BET Slate Shopping Program Targeting Blacks," *WWD,* July 20, 1994, p. 17.

——, "HSN, TCI and Sumitomo Sign Pact for Japan Home Shopping Venture," *WWD,* February 25, 1994, p. 2.

Egan, Jack, "Barry Diller Wheels and Deals," *U.S. News & World Report,* November 3, 1997, p. 62.

Fitzpatrick, Eileen, "Ticketmaster, HSN Deal Opens Options for Both," *Billboard,* May 31, 1997, p. 6.

Harris, Kathryn, "Is Diller Scheming or Just Dreaming?," *Fortune,* December 25, 1995, p. 164.

Hass, Nancy, "Liberty Media: No Need to Shop Around," *Financial World,* May 25, 1993, p. 13.

Higgins, John M., "HSN Takeover Underwhelms Wall Street," *Multichannel News,* September 2, 1996, p. 3.

"Home Shopping Network, Inc.: A History of Growth," Home Shopping Network, Inc. corporate typescript, 1988.

"Home Shopping Network Owner HSN Completed Purchase of Paul Allen's Controlling Interest in Ticketmaster," *Communications Daily,* July 21, 1997, p. 8.

"Home Shopping Network Will Launch Japanese Channel in Joint Venture with Jupiter Programming," *Communications Daily,* November 20, 1996, p. 7.

"HSN Enters Pact to Furnish Intel, Microsoft with Software," *WWD,* May 9, 1995, p. 11.

"HSN to Be a Unit of Silver King," *WWD,* August 27, 1996, p. 8.

James, Ellen L., "So What's a Billion to Roy Speer?" *Venture,* May 1987.

"Merger of Home Shopping Network, Silver King and Savoy Pictures Was Approved by Stockholders of All Three Companies, December 19," *Communications Daily,* December 20, 1996, p. 7.

Moin, David, "Macy and HSN: A TV Marriage in the Making," *WWD,* June 8, 1993, p. 1.

Seagram Joins with Diller's HSN in $4.075-Billion Deal," *Communications Daily,* October 21, 1997, p. 1.

"Ted Turner Is at it Again: The Atlanta-based Entrepreneur Is Eyeing the Home Shopping Network," *Broadcasting & Cable,* April 4, 1994, p. 56.

—Maya Sahafi
—updated by Charity Anne Dorgan

Horton Homes, Inc.

P.O. Drawer 4410
Eatonton, Georgia 31024
U.S.A.
(706) 485-8506
Fax: (706) 485-4446
Web site: http://www.hortonhomes.com

Private Company
Incorporated: 1970
Employees: 1,500
Sales: $294 million (1996)
SICs: 2452 Prefabricated Wood Buildings; 3448
Prefabricated Metal Buildings

Horton Homes, Inc. is the seventh-largest maker of manufactured housing in the world, and the largest privately owned producer of modular homes. Manufactured or modular homes are a far cry from the house trailers of the 1970s, which had a reputation as unattractive and often dangerous dwellings; Horton Homes, by contrast, maintains rigorous quality standards which meet or exceed those for traditional "site-built" housing. The company, located on a 100-acre facility in Eatonton, Georgia, produces between eighty and 100 "floors" (a floor is the equivalent of a single-wide trailer) a day, and applies innovative programs to motivate its workers. In 1996, it had revenues of nearly $300 million, exceeding a 1992 prediction by founder Dudley Horton that the company's annual sales would exceed $250 million by the end of the century.

A Business Born in a Chicken House

In 1987, *Georgia Trend* ran a lengthy profile of the town where Horton Homes is located—Eatonton, Georgia. According to the article, the town "sits in the middle of Putnam County, in a part of the state where dense stands of slash pine and loblolly alternate with the blasted landscapes of clear-cut timber land and pastures dotted with dairy cattle. . . . Seen from U.S. Highway 441, Eatonton consists of a pair of traffic lights, a few strips of aging shops arrayed around an 80-year-old courthouse, and a trio

of newer shopping centers nearby. A statue of Brer Rabbit on the courthouse lawn stakes Eatonton's claim as the hometown of Joel Chandler Harris, who wrote down the recollections of Putnam County's former slaves in his Uncle Remus stories." Another depiction of life in old Eatonton came from Alice Walker in the book—and later movie—*The Color Purple.*

The town, however, more closely echoed the work of another Southern writer, William Faulkner. Like something out of a Faulkner story, Eatonton's businesses were divided between those which supported the venerable old Farmers and Merchants Bank, founded in 1922, and customers of the younger, more brash Peoples Bank—the bank of "outsiders." One such outsider was Dudley Horton, who was born in Eatonton in 1934. Horton's father, a car dealer named N. D. Horton, had moved to Eatonton in 1925. A handsome and dynamic man, he married a girl whose father, a successful cotton merchant, had come to the area from Savannah. Thus the marriage did nothing to solidify the elder Horton's ties to the area; nor did an incident which took place in front of his car dealership in 1939. A lawyer had come after N. D. with a screwdriver, and N. D. shot and killed him in self-defense. According to Mieher, "public opinion on the point is divided even today."

Less ambiguous was the opinion toward N. D. Horton's son. "Outsider" or not, he set up a business called Horton Homes in Eatonton, which later virtually saved the economy of the town. In the mid-1980s, the area was reeling from the closings of two plants, both based in the North. First to go had been a clothing factory, followed by a cookware manufacturer which had employed some 300 people. Horton Homes, with 650 workers at that time, had long been the town's leading employer.

Horton Homes was in no danger of closing, however. The company's founder, a former lawyer and state legislator who had operated as a builder of conventional homes, began the enterprise in 1970 with a few friends and a handful of workers. Working in an abandoned chicken house, Horton and his crew managed to produce between three mobile homes a week and two a day. In 1987, by which time Horton Homes had established its headquarters in an enormous facility that had once been part of the county airport, production had risen to forty homes a day. Horton, a deeply religious man who at one point

216

left Eatonton's First Baptist Church to join a smaller charismatic congregation because he said he needed "a closer walk with the Lord," continued to be a maverick. In the 1980s, his business was just picking up steam, and in the early 1990s, he and other builders would literally change the face of the manufactured housing industry.

Manufactured Housing: Not What It Used to Be

In 1992, Tom Eblen of the *Atlanta Journal and Constitution* reported that Horton had built a 9,000-square-foot home with ten-foot ceilings, hardwood floors, and an enormous swimming pool. That in itself was not so unusual, given the fact that by then he owned a multi-million dollar business. What was significant was the fact that the entire house had been assembled at the Horton Homes plant in eight sixteen-foot-wide prefabricated units. Not only did he save twenty-five percent off the cost of a site-built home, Horton said, construction had taken a third as much time—and the majority of the work had taken place during a period of rain, when an ordinary construction project would have been on hold. "Not bad for a trailer, huh?" quipped the company's purchasing manager as he led a tour of the Horton mansion.

One key to the success of the manufactured housing formula was mass production. "As Henry Ford discovered with automobiles," Eblen wrote, "it's cheaper to build things on an assembly line." The fact that the mass labor took place inside a factory further enabled builders of manufactured housing to gain an edge on their counterparts in the traditional construction industry: there is no rain under the factory roof.

Horton's 9,000 square foot mansion, however, was not necessarily indicative of the future of manufactured housing. Rather, most manufactured homes were made up of two smaller boxes eight feet wide and forty feet long—creating two "halves" of a home. The creation of the product according to

those dimensions represented a coup in packaging and marketing: the boxes were made to exactly fit the regulation ISO (International Standards Organization) shipping container by which freight is sent on oceangoing vessels around the world. Before the company hit upon this solution, it was costing Horton Homes $25,000 to ship a home overseas, which eliminated its profits. With the innovation in sizing, costs dropped to a mere $2,500, and profits soared. Horton suggested that these ready-to-ship houses could provide an answer to the world's housing problems: in 1990, for instance, the State of Israel bought 450 homes from Horton for the use of settlers populating the West Bank of the Jordan River.

Manufactured housing became a Wall Street favorite, but this fact did not necessarily affect Horton Homes, a privately-held enterprise whose owner displayed no intention of ever taking it public (the publicly-owned D. R. Horton construction firm, based in Dallas, Texas, is an entirely different company). Horton had played a part in improving the industry's prestige, however. For years, jokes had persisted about manufactured housing—or rather trailers, sometimes nicknamed "tornado bait." The homes had been considered to be shoddy, unattractive, substandard, and (in the case of a tornado or even of high winds) unsafe. Starting in the 1970s, however, that began to change. In June 1976, the United States Department of Housing and Urban Development (HUD) set new safety standards for mobile home construction. In the wake of hurricanes Hugo (1989) and Andrew (1992), HUD increased its requirements, declaring that manufactured homes should be able to withstand winds of 110 m.p.h. Horton decided that his own product should meet even higher standards, and in 1997 the *Atlanta Business Chronicle* reported that some Horton Homes could sustain winds of 135 m.p.h.

Horton Homes were made of the same quality of material as ordinary houses, but they cost just $26 a square foot in 1996—less than half the cost of a regular site-built home, which averaged $58 a square foot. In the same year, the *Atlanta Journal and Constitution* reported that whereas owners of traditional homes in Georgia paid an average of $765 a month, and renters $487, manufactured housing cost its owners just $323 on average. Hence Mickey Higginbotham of the Atlanta paper quoted the owner of a new 1,300-square foot modular home, whose elation would have been complete if he had realized in advance what he was purchasing: "I didn't know these things were so nice," the new homeowner said. "I could have gotten 2,000 square feet and probably two acres of land" with the money saved. The homeowner, formerly a car salesman, became a manufactured housing salesman.

William I. Weeks, Horton's executive vice-president, gave the *Atlanta Business Chronicle* a very telling piece of evidence that the status of manufactured housing had changed: "In the 1980s and before," he said, "these were temporary homes, financed as temporary housing and personal property, not as real estate." By the late 1990s, however, buyers of manufactured housing could qualify for thirty-year mortgages.

A Boom in Manufactured Housing

Horton's sales experienced a dip in 1991, but ultimately the recession of that period worked to the company's favor, since it meant that more people than ever were looking for inexpensive housing. In 1992, Horton Homes had revenues of $100 million, which Horton predicted would increase to $250 million by the year 2000. Of the latter figure, he predicted that one-fifth would be in exports. As it turned out, he was wrong about the overall sales figure: in 1996, according to *Manufactured Home Merchandiser* magazine, Horton Homes already had revenues of $294 million, with 12,006 homes sold. The *Atlanta Business Chronicle* in 1997 reported that Horton Homes, having opened two new Eatonton facilities in July 1995, had doubled in size since 1992.

Not only was the company itself growing rapidly, so was its environment: Georgia in the early 1990s produced more of the manufactured housing in the United States—fifteen percent—than any other state. Of the 43,369 floors produced in the state in 1994, more than a quarter, or 11,765, were manufactured by Horton. As for the industry itself, manufactured housing had become a $12 billion industry. The future promised only more growth.

With its six production lines and its 7.7-acre manufacturing site, Horton Homes continued rapid production. "While many American industries are struggling to stay afloat," wrote Cheryl Fincher in the *Macon Telegraph,* "Horton Homes Inc. is fighting to keep up with demand." As of September 1995, the company faced an eight-week backlog.

A spokesman for Horton told Fincher that the company's success could be attributed to two simple factors: a strong incentive program, and a quality product. As far as incentives went, the company set a weekly quota, and departments that met or exceeded their quota received bonuses; on the other hand, arriving at work late or missing a day disqualified a worker from receiving a bonus for the week. Likewise, if a dealer had to make a service call due to problems with workmanship, the company traced the error back to the department responsible, and charged a penalty on their bonuses. This led to accountabil-

ity for a quality product and quality service by everyone in the company.

Horton had its own trucking and distribution system, and maintained a large inventory of building supplies at its plant. As of the late 1990s, it sold its product through 212 retailers in 11 states, eighty-nine retailers of whom sold Horton Homes exclusively. With regard to the quality of its housing, using a higher minimum standard than that which applies to site-built homes, the company ensured that its product exceeded federal regulations. "Horton's commitment to quality," according to the Horton Homes World Wide Web page, "is evident in its demand of its employees to build each home as if they were going to live in it themselves. By doing so, Horton Homes represents America at its best, producing a quality product backed with pride."

Further Reading

Eblen, Tom, "Home Sweet Mobile Home: Industry Trying to Shake Its 'Tornado Bait' Image, Grow Into New Markets," *Atlanta Journal and Constitution,* November 22, 1992, p. D1.

Files, Jennifer, "High, Double-Wide & Handsome: Factory-Built Homes Grow in Quality, Appeal, Acceptance," *Dallas Morning News,* July 8, 1996.

Fincher, Cheryl, "Floors on the Go: Horton Homes Expands Manufactured-Housing Capacity, as Sales Surge," *Macon Telegraph,* September 25, 1995, p. D1.

Higginbotham, Mickey, "Dwelling Upon Rapid Growth: The Good Times Roll," *Atlanta Journal and Constitution,* June 25, 1996.

Hotchkiss, Judy, "The Inman Park Mod Squad: Modular-Home Boxes Let Builders Sweat the Details," *Atlanta Journal and Constitution,* March 14, 1996.

"Manufacturing Report," *Manufactured Housing Institute,* http://www.mfghome.org/members/stats/index.html (June 30, 1998).

Mieher, Stuart, "Life Along Main Street," *Georgia Trend,* June 1987, p. 46.

Stoker, Kevin, "Supply of Doublewides Running Deep," *Atlanta Business Chronicle,* January 6, 1997.

—Judson Knight

Hudson's Bay Company

401 Bay Street, Suite 500
Toronto, Ontario M5H 2Y4
Canada
(416) 861-6112
Fax: (416) 861-4720
Web site: http://www.hbc.com

Public Company
Incorporated: 1670 as the Governor and Company of
   Adventurers of England trading into Hudson's Bay
Employees: 61,500
Sales: C $6.45 billion (US $4.45 billion) (1997)
Stock Exchanges: Montreal Toronto
Ticker Symbol: HBC
SICs: 5311 Department Stores; 5621 Women's Clothing
   Stores; 5641 Children's & Infants' Wear Stores

Canada's number one department store retailer, Hudson's Bay Company, is also Canada's oldest corporation. On May 2, 1670, King Charles II granted 18 investors a charter incorporating them as the Governor and Company of Adventurers of England trading into Hudson's Bay. In its first century the company traded with the North American Indians, established forts on Hudson Bay, and successfully fought with U.S. and Canadian competitors to build its fur trade. By the late 1990s, in a coast-to-coast operation accounting for nearly eight percent of Canadian retail sales (excluding food and automobiles) and about 37 percent of department store sales, the company owned and managed about 540 stores in three main retail formats: the Bay fashion department stores, about 100 strong and typically 140,000 to 180,000 square feet in size; Zellers, Canada's leading discount department store, with more than 340 units that average 77,500 square feet; and Fields, a chain in western Canada of more than 100 small clothing stores.

The Early Years

The development of the company is tied to the growth of Canada and settlement of its western region. Those who were important to the development of the company also were important politically and historically to the economic and political growth of the New World. The list of well-known people associated with the company is long and includes Peter Skene Ogden, Solomon Juneau, Henry Kelsey, James Knight, Samuel Hearne, Peter Pond, Alexander Mackenzie, Sir George Simpson, Sir James Douglas, John McLoughlin, and others. The chartering of the company on May 2, 1670, with Prince Rupert—a cousin of Charles II—as the company's first governor, followed the successful fur trading voyage of the ketch *Nonsuch* that brought back beaver pelts for the English market, used by felters and hatters to make the beaver hats that were fashionable at the time.

The Adventurers' charter of 1670 gave it 1.49 million square miles of virgin territory, or nearly 40 percent of today's Canadian provinces, including what would become Ontario, Quebec north of the Laurentian watershed and west of the Labrador boundary, Manitoba, the better part of Saskatchewan, southern Alberta, and much of the Northwest Territories. The group's rights to the lucrative fur trade did not go uncontested, and it was not until 20 years later that the company made its first inland expedition. Henry Kelsey, an apprentice who joined the company in 1677 and who later became a company governor, made the first journey into the prairie in 1690, learning the Cree language and adapting to Indian life. He wished to encourage peace among the Indian tribes so that they could bring beaver pelts to the forts without being attacked. Three forts on James Bay—Rupert's House, Moose, and Albany in the east—and a fourth, York Factory, on the west coast of Hudson Bay were the sites of battles for nearly 30 years between the French and English contesting the territory and the right to conduct trade. The Treaty of Ryswick in 1697 brought peace, but by then the company was near ruin. Most of the company's first century of business was devoted to establishing forts and territorial rights and making peace with the Indians and the French merchants who wanted to be a part of the fur trade in the New World.

Early-1800s: Competition with North West Company

One of the Hudson's Bay Company's fiercest early competitors was North West Company, established in 1779 by a Scottish-Canadian group of nine traders that moved into the Canadian

---

Company Perspectives:

The Company aims to develop its human and material resources and capitalize on its experience in merchandising to anticipate and satisfy the needs of customers for the goods and services they seek at fair prices, and thereby earn a satisfactory return for its shareholders.

---

interior around 1780 and claimed to be the rightful successor to the early French traders who had opened up the land. North West Company had two types of shareholders: the eastern partners, merchants in Montreal and Quebec who supplied the venture capital, and the "wintering" partners, who became responsible for exploratory and sales operations. By 1800 North West became a serious competitor, forcing Hudson's Bay Company to become increasingly more adventurous, pushing the trade boundaries westward from the Hudson Bay, in fear of losing trade with the western Indians. Each company drove the other toward new expeditions, so that by the turn of the century, they each had men trading on the upper Missouri River.

North West's Alexander Mackenzie, who later was knighted, was the most famous fur trader of his day. Mackenzie pushed the trade boundaries farther westward. Several of his trade expeditions were historical achievements: in 1789 he covered 1,600 miles and back in 102 days, and in 1793 he crossed the Rocky Mountains to reach the Pacific Ocean.

Other companies also envied the apparent monopoly of Hudson's Bay Company. U.S. traders wanted a share in the fur trade following the Lewis and Clark expedition of 1804 to 1806. In 1808 Pierre Chouteau, William Clark, and five others established the Missouri Fur Company, and in New York John Jacob Astor, the leading fur dealer in the United States, started the American Fur Company, capitalized at US $300,000, of which he owned all but a few shares.

Peter Skene Ogden, who worked for a time for the American Fur Company, moved to Quebec after being appointed judge of the Admiralty Court in 1788. Ogden wanted to be among the first white men to see the great wilderness. After living in Quebec for six years with his wife and children, he was sent by North West Company into the interior of North America to clerk at the company's post in what is today Saskatchewan Province. Ogden wintered on the prairies for the first time in September 1810, where he met Samuel Black, a Scotsman and also a clerk, who would become a lifelong friend. The two men made a sport of harassing Hudson's Bay men. Among the tales cited by Gloria Cline, author of *Peter Skene Ogden and the Hudson's Bay Company,* was that of the harassment of Peter Fidler of Hudson's Bay Company. Fidler departed in three boats with 16 men for Churchill Factory on Hudson Bay, an important post, and Ogden, with two canoes full of Canadians, taunted the British traders for six days by keeping just ahead of them "to get everything from Indians that may be on the road, as they can go much faster than us," according to Fidler. Ogden was a much valued employee of North West and was promoted as a result of his antics with Black.

Along with Ogden, the North West Company entrusted its goal of westward expansion to David Thompson. In 1807 Thompson had crossed the Rockies and reached the headwaters of the Columbia. In 1809 he again crossed the Rockies and established an outpost in what is now northern Idaho; from there he proceeded into Montana. Directly ahead of Thompson's trading party was the first far-western expedition of John Jacob Astor's Pacific Fur Company, the west coast subsidiary of American Fur Company. Although a U.S. company, it was managed by three Canadians, former Nor'westers—employees of North West. The War of 1812 altered hopes for Astor's company, and the following year Pacific Fur Company sold all of its interests in the region to North West Company.

During the fall of 1818, Ogden took charge of David Thompson's old post, near what is now Spokane, Washington. The following year Ogden returned east. In 1821 the two companies merged under the name of the Hudson's Bay Company after the Nor'westers learned that their company was in poor financial condition. Ogden was excluded from the merger by the company because he had fought so fiercely, although he continued for the new firm as an explorer and trapper.

Gold Rush Difficulties

The next phase of the company's growth was shaped by the 1849 gold fever that caused a great rush westward; almost 40,000 '49ers came west that year. Hudson's Bay Company suffered as a result. Demand made the cost of basic goods skyrocket. Lumber rose from $16 to $65 per thousand feet; unskilled labor received $5 to $10 a day; sailors were paid $150 a month. The steady flow of gold, however, created a favorable balance of trade. With settlement, though, came new tax laws. In 1850 the Treasury Department prohibited trade between Fort Victoria and the English Vancouver Island and Fort Nisqually on the U.S. Puget Sound. This hurt Hudson's Bay Company considerably because it legally tied up all vessels for custom inspection, which took them 350 miles off course, subjected them to twice crossing the hazardous Columbia sandbar, and made them pay heavy piloting fees at the customhouse port. To add to Ogden's troubles in the western outposts of the company, the gold fever created labor difficulties, with many crewmen deserting to seek the possibility of finding gold. After several years of health problems, Ogden returned east for 18 months. Upon returning to his post in the western provinces, the strenuous trip and his advancing age took their toll; Ogden died in 1854.

Equal in importance to the growth of the company was Sir George Simpson, who served as administrator of the company for 40 years following the merger with North West. John McLoughlin, called the Father of Oregon, governed the district under Simpson with wide powers. Sir James Douglas assisted McLoughlin; he later became Governor of the Crown Colonies of Vancouver and British Columbia.

When the westward settlement reached St. Paul, the British government tried to break the Hudson's Bay Company monopoly by charging it with poor administration. A select committee of the House of the Commons investigated the charges, and with Sir George Simpson as one of the principal witnesses, the charges were dismissed. The company's territory and the Northwest Territories became part of the Canadian Confederation through the British North America Act of 1867. The government of Canada transferred to itself the company's chartered territory, Rupertsland, in 1870, in return for farm lands in the prairie provinces, which were sold to settlers over the following 85 years.

Early 20th Century Diversification, Including Retail

Demand for general merchandise increased, and shops were established on the outskirts of the forts. In 1912 a major remodeling and reconstruction of retail trade shops was interrupted by World War I. Following the war, the company diversified, incorporating elements of oil exploration in Alberta, revitalizing its Fur Trade Department, and venturing into the oil business as a favored partner of Hudson's Bay Oil and Gas. After the 1929 stock market crash and Great Depression, the fur department revitalized itself, improving working conditions, and in some areas acted as an agent for Inuit Indian carvings.

Early in the 20th century the company made retail stores its first priority, building downtown department stores (known as the Bay) in each of the major cities of western Canada, moving east through acquisitions, and expanding into the suburbs of major Canadian cities beginning in the 1960s. Hudson's Bay Company acquired Markborough Properties, a real estate company, in 1973; Zellers, a chain of discount department stores, in 1978; and Simpsons, a group of Toronto-area department stores, the following year. Kenneth R. Thomson, representing the family of the late Lord Thomson of Fleet, acquired a 75 percent controlling interest in the company in 1979.

Restructured in the 1980s

In the 1970s the company's governor was Donald McGiverin and George Kosich was chief operating officer. In that decade and into the 1980s, sales and oil prices slipped, while debt from acquisitions piled up. By 1985 the company owed C $2.5 billion and with feeble operating profits wiped out by C $250 million in interest payments, the company suffered its fourth consecutive yearly loss. In response, management shed assets, including the Bay's 179 northernmost stores, some of which could be traced back to the fur trading days of Ogden. The company also divested its fur auction houses, thus cutting its last tie to its fur trading roots. In a strong attempt to survive, Thomson shook up top management, eventually appointing George Kosich, a career merchandiser, president. Thomson revamped retail operations. The combined market share of the three department store chains rose to 33 percent from 29 percent in two years.

Kosich refocused Simpsons to the upscale market and the Bay toward the middle- to lower-priced market. In repositioning the Bay, Kosich put the 300-year-old Canadian giant up against its closest U.S. counterpart, Sears. In 1985 the Bay had ten percent of the market and Sears had 27 percent. Employing an intensive advertising campaign—C $75 million—the Bay produced a bold and aggressive image before Canadians. In the first half of 1986, sales rose 13.2 percent over that of 1985. Operating profit rose to C $31 million in 1985 and to C $83 million on C $1.8 billion in total sales in 1986. Sears was feeling the results, reporting a barely three percent rise in 1986 and a

downturn for the following several years. Zellers was positioned to appeal to the budget shopper as a "junior" department store. Club Z, a frequent-buyer program that allowed customers to accumulate points for prizes, boasted three million members. Hudson's Bay Company reversed a formidable debt picture in 1987 by shedding nonstrategic assets such as its wholesale division and getting out of the oil and gas business. In 1990 it spun off its real estate subsidiary, Markborough Properties, as a separate public company. Shareholders received one share of Markborough for each share they held of Hudson's Bay, with the Thomson family retaining a majority interest in Markborough. Also in 1990, the company bought 51 Towers Department Stores and merged them with Zellers.

In January 1991 Hudson's Bay Company permanently left the Canadian fur trade, an estimated C $350 million market, when it stopped selling fur coats at the Bay stores; the Bay's share of the fur trade had degenerated to a paltry C $7 million by 1990. The company also had been targeted by increasingly vocal antifur groups. Early in 1991 the company sold three million new common shares, with net proceeds of C $72.5 million. It also repurchased slightly more than two million Series A preferred shares for C $42.5 million. Company officials said these transactions would result in a stronger financial position. Because of declines in interest rates in the early 1990s, the Series A shares, with an eight percent dividend, had become more expensive to service than debt. Later in 1991 the company eliminated its Simpsons division, when it sold eight Simpsons stores to Sears Canada Inc. and converted the remaining six stores into the Bay units. Late 1991 also saw the Bay announce a three-year plan to double its purchasing of U.S. brands, a program that aimed at decreasing the number of Canadians seeking bargains in U.S. stores (because of a strong Canadian dollar) and that developed from the passage of the U.S.-Canada free-trade agreement in 1989.

Wal-Mart Challenge in the 1990s

In 1992 Thomson reduced his interest in Hudson's Bay Company to 25 percent through a secondary stock offering; five years later this stake was reduced further through another secondary offering to zero. Meantime, in 1993 Hudson's Bay Company acquired 25 former Woodward's locations in British Columbia and Alberta, converting the sites to company formats. The company also acquired Linmark Westman International Limited, a buying firm in the Far East, that same year.

On the heels of strong 1993 results of C $5.44 billion (US $3.9 billion) and net earnings of C $148 million (US $108 million), Hudson's Bay Company was caught somewhat off-guard when U.S. discounting giant Wal-Mart Stores Inc. entered the Canadian market for the first time in early 1994 through the purchase of 122 stores from Woolworth Corporation's Canadian subsidiary. A price war quickly developed between the new Wal-Mart stores in Canada and the Zellers chain. In a little more than three years, Wal-Mart gained 45 percent of the discount market in Canada, surpassing Zellers, whose market share fell from more than 50 percent to 41 percent. Worse yet, the price war had cut severely into Zellers's and, consequently, Hudson's Bay Company's profits. Net earnings at Zellers fell from a peak of C $256 million in 1993 to C $73 million in 1997, while overall net earnings (after interest and taxes) for the company fell to just $54 million in 1997. Compounding the company's difficulties were reduced earnings at the Bay, which reflected a general downturn in the department store sector.

In responding to the Wal-Mart challenge, the company began to increase the size of its Zellers units, which had averaged 75,000 square feet in comparison with the 120,000-square-foot Wal-Marts. New Zellers that were built now ranged from 90,000 to 125,000 square feet. The company also began to renovate older units. In mid-1997 Hudson's Bay Company hired a new president and CEO, William R. Fields, who had most recently been chairman of Blockbuster Video but was, more important, a 25-year veteran of Wal-Mart. (Kosich initially retired but within days was hired by T. Eaton Company Ltd., a chief rival of Hudson's Bay Company, as president of the Eaton's department store chain. The hiring resulted in Hudson's Bay Company suing Eaton's for stealing other company executives and accusing Kosich of breach of fiduciary duty for joining Eaton's while still employed by Hudson's Bay Company. The suit was settled quickly without terms being disclosed.)

Under Fields's leadership Hudson's Bay Company became much more aggressive in its pursuit of a turnaround. The most dramatic early example of this came in February 1998 when the company bought Kmart Canada Co. for C $240 million (US $167.7 million). The deal eliminated the number three discount retailer from the Canadian market and, in addition, leapfrogged Zellers back ahead of Wal-Mart. Over the next several months, Hudson's Bay Company closed 40 of the 112 Kmart stores it had gained and converted 59 of the units to Zellers stores. Two Kmart stores and one Zellers were changed into Bay units, and 11 Kmart stores and one Zellers were selected to be converted into new specialty retail formats. This new specialty initiative was launched in June 1998 when the first Bed, Bath and More store opened in Newmarket, Ontario; the new chain was the first Canadian-based home category killer. Yet another development in the first few months of the Fields regime was the beginning of the conversion of the Fields chain into small general merchandise discount stores for the mass market, modeled somewhat after the U.S.-based Family Dollar chain. CEO Fields also launched efforts to improve the traditionally poor customer service at the Zellers chain and to make technology upgrades at both Zellers and the Bay aimed at improving inventory control. Finally, Fields made significant changes to the company's management team. And in a move to pare noncore operations, the Linmark Westman subsidiary was divested in mid-1998. This whirlwind of activity in Fields's first year indicated that Hudson's Bay Company had entered into a new era of trailblazing.

Principal Subsidiaries

Hudson's Bay Company Acceptance Ltd.; Zellers Inc.

Principal Divisions

The Bay; Fields Stores.

Further Reading

Burns, John F., "Fur Industry Shrinking with No End in Sight," *New York Times,* February 26, 1991, p. D1.

Cline, Gloria G., *Peter Skene Ogden and the Hudson's Bay Company,* Norman, Okla.: University of Oklahoma Press, 1974.

Fox, Jim, "Fields Getting Hudson's Bay Ready for Battle," *Discount Store News,* June 23, 1997, pp. 3.

Gough, Barry, "Lords of the Northern Forest," *History Today,* September 1991, pp. 49.

Greenberg, Larry M., "Besieged Hudson's Bay Co. Starts To Blaze New Trails," *Wall Street Journal,* February 13, 1998, pp. B1, B2.

——, "Hudson's Bay Faces Challenge from Southern Rival," *Wall Street Journal,* May 24, 1996, p. B4.

——, "Hudson's Bay To Buy Kmart Stores in Canada To Strengthen Position," *Wall Street Journal,* February 9, 1998, p. B2.

Innis, Harold, *The Fur Trade in Canada,* Toronto: University of Toronto Press, 1967.

Matthews, Jan, and Boyd, Greg, "The March of a Retail Martinet," *Canadian Business,* December 1990, pp. 32.

Newman, Peter C., "The Beaver and the Bay," *Canadian Geographic,* August/September 1989, pp. 56.

——, *Company of Adventurers* (3 vols.), Markham, Ontario, and New York: Viking, 1985–91.

——, *Empire of the Bay: An Illustrated History of the Hudson's Bay Company,* edited by John Geiger, Markham, Ontario, and New York: Viking, 1989.

Newman, Peter C., and Fleming, Kevin, "Three Centuries of the Hudson's Bay Company: Canada's Fur-Trading Empire," *National Geographic,* August 1987, pp. 192.

Ray, Auther J., and Freeman, Donald B., *Give Us Good Measure: An Economic Analysis of Relations Between the Indians and the Hudson's Bay Company Before 1763,* Toronto: University of Toronto Press, 1978.

Rich, Edwin Ernest, ed., *Minutes of the Hudson's Bay Company, 1671–1674,* London, Ontario: Hudson's Bay Record Society Publications, 1942.

Scally, Robert, "Hudson's Bay To Buy Kmart Canada, Retool Zellers, and Unveil New Chains," *Discount Store News,* February 23, 1998, pp. 1, 40.

Seckler, Valerie, "Fields's Playbook for Zellers," *WWD,* September 10, 1997, p. 22.

—Claire Badaracco
—updated by David E. Salamie

Hughes Electronics Corporation

P.O. Box 956
El Segundo, California 90245
U.S.A.
(310) 568-7200
Fax: (310) 568-6390
Web site: http://www.hughes.com

Public Subsidiary of General Motors Corporation
Incorporated: 1985 as GM Hughes Electronics
Employees: 14,000
Sales: $5.13 billion (1997)
Stock Exchanges: New York
Ticker Symbol: GMH
SICs: 3663 Radio & TV Communications Equipment; 3669
    Communications Equipment, Not Elsewhere Classified

Hughes Electronics Corporation is one of the world's leading satellite and wireless communications companies. It operates four main areas of business. Its Hughes Space & Communications division manufactures satellites and spacecraft. Its customers are businesses across the globe, and U.S. government agencies including the Department of Defense and NASA (National Aeronautics and Space Administration). Hughes Network Systems builds satellite-based wireless telephone systems, as well as manufactures equipment for satellite-based television service and Internet access service. Hughes's PanAmSat division operates a fleet of 17 satellites, providing service to telecommunications businesses worldwide. Hughes also runs DirectTV, a direct-to-home digital television service offering hundreds of channels. Hughes was formerly a rather different company. Its main areas of business used to be defense electronics, derived from the former Hughes Aircraft, and electronic components for cars, manufactured by its Delco Electronics division. As the satellite and telecommunications areas developed in the 1990s, the company decided to shed its other businesses. Hughes Aircraft and Delco are now owned, respectively, by Raytheon and Delphi.

Early History As Hughes Aircraft

Hughes Electronics was formed in 1985 as GM Hughes Electronics, a company put together by General Motors. The company emerged out of the former Hughes Aircraft, a firm founded by the notorious billionaire recluse Howard Hughes. Howard Hughes inherited control of his father's affluent tool company at the age of 19, in 1924, and subsequently went to Hollywood for a brief career producing and directing movies. Enamored with airplanes, Hughes learned to fly, and founded Hughes Aircraft in 1932. Hughes's personal interest was in faster flight. As a pilot, he set several world speed records in the 1930s, and his company focused on building innovative planes. During World War II, the U.S. government contracted Hughes Aircraft to design and build a large cargo plane. This was envisioned as an alternative to cargo ships, which were vulnerable to submarine attack. Hughes Aircraft did not complete its contract until 1947, two years after the end of the war. Its *Spruce Goose*, a unique wooden plane one-third larger than a jumbo jet, made an extremely short maiden flight before docking forever. During WWII Hughes Aircraft had not produced a successful military or commercial craft.

After the war, Hughes Aircraft became a leader in defense electronics, becoming one of the nation's largest suppliers of weapons systems, missiles, satellites, and lasers. The company made many technical advances as long as it was run by knowledgeable engineers. However, in the 1950s its founder, Howard Hughes, became active in the company's management. Hughes's mental health had begun to deteriorate, and he ran the company as his own fiefdom, arbitrarily making decisions that overrode his directors' wishes. As a result, many top Hughes Aircraft executives quit, and went on to found other top U.S. defense companies. Hughes created the Howard Hughes Medical Institute in 1953, a nonprofit entity, and donated Hughes Aircraft to it so he could run the company tax free. Hughes disappeared from public life around this time, and Hughes Aircraft was run by a competent engineer. After Hughes's death in 1976, the company continued to develop and manufacture weapons, under the aegis of the Medical Institute. However, the company's products were plagued by cost overruns and lack of quality control. Ultimately, the Defense Department refused delivery of Hughes's missiles in 1984. An Air Force auditor uncovered scores of abuses at Hughes, while the Internal Revenue Service questioned the tax-free status of the company. To appease the IRS, the Medical Institute agreed to put Hughes Aircraft up for sale.

Company Perspectives:

Hughes Electronics stands on a threshold of vast telecommunications opportunities around the world. Everywhere we look, we see strong demand for low-cost advanced communications—for networks of telephones, televisions and computers that will handle the boundless flows of conversation, entertainment, information and business data fundamental to modern existence. To tap these global possibilities, we are leveraging the company's leadership in designing and building satellites and wireless systems into delivering innovative communications services to buildings and homes. We are using our rich store of technologies, talents and other assets to lead global markets, build our business and create new value for shareholders.

Growth Under GM in the 1980s

Though the company was obviously troubled, several large corporations were interested in acquiring Hughes. Close to a dozen companies came forward as potential buyers. Finally, five finalists—Allied Corp., Signal Companies, Ford Motor Company, Boeing, and General Motors—entered sealed bids for Hughes. One problem with the process was that aspects of Hughes's finances were secret, because of its defense business. What was supposed to be a simple auction devolved into three weeks of intensive bargaining. GM emerged the winner, shelling out $5 billion in combined cash and stock for Hughes. GM funded the deal through a complex maneuver where it issued some of its common stock as Class H (for Hughes). Holders of GM Class H stock were entitled to a percentage of the company's earnings from its new subsidiary. GM had done the same thing a year earlier when it bought Electronic Data Systems (EDS) and offered Class E stock. GM aimed to offset its slowing auto market with Hughes's defense electronics business, and so it vowed to leave the company essentially intact. It created GM Hughes Electronics as an umbrella over Hughes Aircraft, headquartered in El Segundo, California, and an automotive electronics subsidiary it owned, called Delco Electronics. Delco had originally been a manufacturer of car radios, and also made military navigation equipment and automobile gadgetry such as dashboard computers.

Owning Hughes was supposed to get GM into the lucrative defense business, as well as give it access to breaking technology that might make its cars more competitive. GM's CEO Roger Smith envisioned using Hughes's know-how to make "smart" cars with automatic collision sensors and route-finders. The acquisition of Hughes was key to GM's plans to make "the car of the future" and to bring the company proudly into the 21st century.

Some of these automotive advances did come to pass. Hughes's engineers revamped GM's anti-lock brake system, and the company's advanced computer simulation technology proved useful to its parent in studying things like road-tire interface. Hughes also set to work on the wiring of GM cars, simplifying the number of wires needed with a method called multiplexing. Multiplexing derived from military electronics, and it saved weight, space, and assembly time in GM cars. This was exactly the kind of improvement GM had hoped to get in its cars by linking up with Hughes. Hughes was also a leader in infrared night vision technology, which it had developed for military pilots. In 1987 GM was hopeful that night vision systems could soon be installed in its cars, allowing drivers to see through dark, smoke, fog, and haze. Hughes's partner Delco was also involved in developing a collision-avoidance system and a satellite-based Global Positioning System that would help drivers plot routes.

Despite high hopes, troubles still dogged Hughes. Its satellite business had grown enormously, and by 1988 it was producing over half the communications satellites built in the United States. But that year Hughes's chief executive, Albert Wheelon, resigned after being served with a subpoena from the Justice Department regarding illegal payments to a shell company operated by one of its best satellite customers, Intelsat. Intelsat was a 114-nation satellite consortium that was expected to give Hughes billions of dollars in business. Hughes was suspected of making monthly payments to an Intelsat director, in exchange for access to the satellite company's internal documents. The complicated legal investigation cast a cloud over Hughes.

The company's stock price was going nowhere, and in 1989 General Motors had to work out a new deal with the Howard Hughes Medical Institute about the GM Class H shares the Institute had received when it sold Hughes. GM had guaranteed the Institute a certain price on the stock for a limited time, but it became clear that if the Institute sold its shares after the guarantee was up, the stock price would take a dive as the shares flooded an indifferent market. The two companies restructured their original deal so that each side was happy, but regular shareholders did not seem to be getting much value for the H stock.

Changes in the 1990s

Meanwhile, earnings declined at GM Hughes, falling almost 20 percent in 1989. Though revenue climbed to just over $3 billion, from $2.67 billion the previous year, profits did not keep pace, and the company seemed stagnant. The company needed a new direction, but it was not sure where it should go. Hughes gradually cut its reliance on defense business. This accounted for nearly 70 percent of its sales shortly after GM bought the company, and declined to less than 50 percent by 1991. In 1992 Hughes announced that it would further cut its defense business, and concentrate on automotive electronics and telecommunications. Even while stating this new goal, the company spent $450 million to acquire the missile business of General Dynamics. The impetus behind this purchase was said to come from Michael Smith, vice-chairman of Hughes Aircraft, who was the brother of GM's new CEO Jack Smith. By the end of 1992, GM Hughes was deeply in the red, mostly because of charges associated with laying off thousands of workers and closing facilities.

The company tried to slim down, and in 1994 it announced a significant reorganization. The number of employees had already fallen from 82,000 in 1986 to just 51,000 worldwide in 1994, but Hughes decided to close many of its defense business facilities and lay off more workers. GM Hughes also split into seven different divisions. It put all its defense activities under the heading Hughes Aerospace and Electronics Co., with new headquarters in Washington, D.C. Delco, the automotive electronics division, continued as it was, and the company divided further into a

Commercial Sector, for new start-up technologies, a Telecommunications and Space Sector, for its satellite business, and four smaller groups for radar and communications, electro-optical systems, weapons systems, and information systems.

After all these changes had been put in place, things began to look up for GM Hughes. Its fastest-growing division was its satellite and telecommunications business, which had sales of over $2 billion in 1993. Hughes owned the world's largest fleet of satellites used for television broadcast, and had a large share of the business communications network market. Large companies such as chain stores that had far-flung operations used Hughes's network technology to transmit daily business data, and revenues in this area had been growing by 30 percent a year since 1987. Hughes also developed a new kind of satellite, its HS 601, which had huge potential. It was known as a body-stabilized satellite. Other satellites had to spin like a gyroscope in order to maintain their stability in space, and their solar panels, from which they derived energy, spun with the whole machine. Hughes's HS 601 contained a spinning core within a central box, and its solar arrays remained fixed in an optimum position. The HS 601 was thus more energy efficient and had a lot more broadcast power. In 1993 Hughes put together new digital compression technology with its satellite capabilities and launched DirecTV. This venture used two high-powered satellites to broadcast 150 channels of video programming to customers fitted with a small, inexpensive satellite dish. The DirecTV dish was only 18 inches in diameter, and sold for around $700, so it was far cheaper and less conspicuous than the prevailing dish, which cost upwards of $3,000. DirecTV was totally digital, and so offered a pristine picture and CD-quality sound. Hughes signed up several cable channels to broadcast on DirecTV, and planned to offer pay-per-view movies on 50 or 60 channels. Six months after Hughes began signing up DirecTV customers, it had nearly half a million subscribers. In three years, DirecTV had over three million subscribers in the United States, making it comparable in size to the nation's fifth largest cable company. Hughes called DirecTV the most successful consumer electronic product launch in U.S. history, noting that it had taken the entire cable television industry 20 years to sign up three million customers. In partnership with a Latin American consortium, DirecTV was a leading cable provider in Latin America and the Caribbean by 1997. Hughes joined eight Japanese companies in launching DirecTV in Japan, which was a potential market of 42 million TV households. U.S. subscribers were paying $44 a month for DirecTV in 1997, plus shelling out for the satellite dish and decoder box. Consequently, Hughes's profits took off. Sales were up to almost $15 billion in 1995, and profits had more than doubled since 1991, up to $1.67 billion.

Much of the recent success of Hughes was credited to CEO Michael Armstrong, who took over in 1992. Armstrong set clear goals for the company, demanding that it be either number one or number two in any market it entered. He slashed jobs, backed DirecTV, and focused the company on lucrative commercial business. In 1995, the company changed its name from GM Hughes Electronics to simply Hughes Electronics. Soon after, industry analysts began to speculate that GM might be ready to sell the company. The advances in automotive electronics that GM had hoped for when it bought Hughes in 1985 still had not come to fruition, and there seemed to be little reason for the auto giant to hold on to the company. GM filed a document allowing it to divest Hughes in March 1996. Then in January 1997 news broke that GM was selling the defense portion of Hughes to Raytheon. GM next consolidated the Delco portion of Hughes with another of its automotive electronics companies, Delphi.

What remained of Hughes was only its satellite and telecommunications businesses. These areas were the company's most promising markets. The new structure gave Hughes more focus, and let it use all its resources on the potentially booming telecommunications world of the next century. The company continued to develop new products, working on integrated circuit and electronic memory protection devices, as well as pushing for small, high-speed antennas that could link homes and small businesses with satellites.

Principal Subsidiaries

Hughes Space and Communications Co.; Hughes Network Systems, Inc.; Hughes Communications, Inc.; DirecTV, Inc.; PanAmSat Corporation (71.5%).

Further Reading

Adler, Alan L., "General Motors Announces Breakup of Hughes Electronics Subsidiary," *Knight-Ridder/Tribune Business News*, January 17, 1997, p. 117B0960.
Banks, Howard, "GM's Hidden Treasure," *Forbes*, August 1, 1994, pp. 36–38.
Barrett, Amy, "GM Hughes Electronics: Stempel's Ace in the Hole?" *Financial World*, June 23, 1992, p. 21.
Callahan, Joseph M., "Crash Landing," *Automotive Industries*, December 1992, p. 59.
Grover, Ronald, with Seth Payne and Wendy Zellner, "Is a Big Scandal Brewing at Hughes Aircraft?" *Business Week*, May 23, 1988, p. 58.
Hampton, William J., and Maralyn Edid, "GM Wants Hughes to Help It into the 21st Century," *Business Week*, June 17, 1985, p. 35.
"Hughes Sales Gives GM Even More Options," *Ward's Auto World*, February 1997, p. 23.
Kerwin, Kathleen, and Lawrence J. Tell, "Will It Fly?" *Barron's*, June 10, 1985, pp. 14–22.
Kupfer, Andrew, "Hughes Gambles on High-Tech TV," *Fortune*, August 23, 1993, pp. 90–97.
Levin, Doron P., "Results Mixed for 3 GM Units," *New York Times*, April 20, 1989, p. D4.
McComas, Maggie, "How GM Won the High-Tech Prize," *Fortune*, July 8, 1985, p. 27.
"New-Product Applications Flow from GM-Hughes Linkup," *Automotive News*, July 6, 1987, p. 24.
Schine, Eric, with Larry Armstrong and Kathleen Kerwin, "Liftoff," *Business Week*, April 22, 1996, pp. 136–147.
Schine, Eric, with Kathleen Kerwin, "Digital TV: Advantage, Hughes," *Business Week*, March 13, 1995, pp. 66–68.
Smith, Bruce A., "New Layoffs, Plant Closing at Hughes," *Aviation Week and Space Technology*, September 19, 1994, pp. 28–29.
Taylor, Alex, "GM: Why They Might Break Up America's Biggest Company," *Fortune*, April 29, 1996, pp. 78–84.
Treece, James B., "GM's Alphabet Stocks Spelled Trouble," *Business Week*, March 13, 1989, p. 41.

—A. Woodward

Hungry Howie's Pizza and Subs, Inc.

30300 Stephenson Highway, Suite 200
Madison Heights, Michigan 48071
U.S.A.
(248) 414-3300
Fax: (248) 414-3301
(800) 624-8122

Private Company
Incorporated: 1981
Employees: 6,000
Sales: $154 million (1997)
SICs: 6794 Patent Owners & Lessors; 5812 Eating Places

Hungry Howie's Pizza and Subs, Inc. began in 1973 as a single carryout pizzeria located in Taylor, Michigan, a suburb of Detroit. By the end of the decade it had 12 stores. During the 1980s it began offering franchises and concentrated on opening new locations in Michigan and Florida. It established a niche for itself in a crowded pizza market when it introduced flavored crusts on its pizzas in 1985. In 1990 the company opened its 150th store, and by 1995 it had 300 locations. Only 25 years after the first Hungry Howie's pizzeria opened, the chain had 375 locations and was ranked the ninth largest pizza franchise operation in the United States.

Early History

Steven E. Jackson (born November 1953), president of Hungry Howie's, had his first experience in the pizza business in 1972, when as a teenager he worked as a delivery driver for a local pizzeria owned by James R. Hearn. He worked for Hearn for about a year before taking a job with Ford Motor Company while attending Eastern Michigan University (EMU). Jackson was studying to be an elementary school teacher, but as graduation approached in 1976, jobs for teachers were scarce. Looking for other opportunities, he contacted Hearn, with whom he had remained in touch.

Hearn had opened a successful pizzeria, which he called Hungry Howie's, in 1973 in Taylor, Michigan, making him the founder of Hungry Howie's. It was located in a former hamburger shop that Hearn had converted into a pizzeria. He described it as a "greasy 24-hour hamburger joint." Hearn would later become Hungry Howie's vice-president, secretary, treasurer, and director at various times.

Second Hungry Howie's Opened in 1976

In 1976, just before he was about to graduate, Jackson approached Hearn and proposed they become partners and open a second store. In September 1976, Jackson left EMU, quit his job, and together with his wife Sarah opened the second Hungry Howie's in Southgate, Michigan. The initial investment in the second store was less than $25,000.

Within the next five years, 12 more stores were opened in the metropolitan Detroit area. Many of these were opened by former employees of Hearn or by friends and family. Hearn and Jackson were involved as partners in some of the new stores, but not all of them.

During the late 1970s Hungry Howie's experimented with offering ribs, chicken, shrimp, spaghetti, and ravioli. Jackson later described Hungry Howie's in the late 1970s as a "shoot-from-the-hip" operation. "If somebody wanted to test a new product, we did. And we tested just about anything," he said.

Hungry Howie's was incorporated in 1981. By then, the company was focused entirely on pizza, subs, and salads. The trend in fast food restaurants was toward specialization. Hungry Howie's found that other stores specializing in ribs, chicken, seafood, or pasta could do them better than Hungry Howie's could, so the company returned to its specialty.

Began Offering Franchises in 1983

In 1982 the decision was made to start offering franchises. In January 1983 the first Hungry Howie's franchise was awarded. Jackson was the driving force behind the decision to franchise. He perceived it as necessary for the company to grow. The Hungry Howie's franchise package cost $50,000 to $65,000, which included a $5,000 franchise fee. Franchisees also had to pay a regional advertising fee of three percent and a graduated

226

royalty fee, which started at two percent of sales in the first year and rose to five percent in the fourth year.

Around this time Hearn moved to Florida and began developing Hungry Howie's there, leaving Jackson to develop the rest of the country. Hearn became president and director of Hungry Howie's of Florida, Inc., a sub-franchise that oversees store operations and development in Florida. Hearn eventually developed 140 Hungry Howie's locations in Florida.

Pizza Became Fastest Growing Fast Food Segment in 1984

In 1984 pizza passed hamburgers as the fastest growing segment of the fast food industry, according to a *Restaurant Business* survey. In 1985 franchise pizza sales totaled $5.7 billion and were expected to top $6.7 billion in 1986. Hungry Howie's had 1984 sales of $11 million. In 1985 Hungry Howie's posted sales of $16 million. It projected sales of $22 million in 1986.

Introduced Flavored Crusts in 1985

In September 1985, at the suggestion of a franchisee, Hungry Howie's began offering flavored crusts on its pizzas. Sesame seed, garlic, poppy seed, rye, or butter flavors were offered. These proved quite successful. Almost immediately, more than half the pizzas sold in Florida had flavored crusts. Quarterly sales rose by ten percent. The company later added butter cheese, cajun, and "original" flavors.

Hungry Howie's grew quickly, due in part to its two-for-one offers copied from Little Caesar's "Pizza! Pizza!" campaign. The company was the first to offer two-for-one pizzas in Florida. Jackson told *Crains Detroit Business*, "At first people couldn't even comprehend the concept. They'd say, 'But I don't want two pizzas.'"

The Florida restaurants averaged about $350,000 each in annual sales, and the metro Detroit area stores averaged only $250,000 each. The difference was due to the fact that the Detroit area was a much more competitive pizza market, with pizza giants Domino's Pizza and Little Caesar's headquartered nearby.

By mid-1986 Jackson and Hearn had opened 67 Hungry Howie's restaurants, 33 of them in Florida and 34 in Michigan. Jackson operated out of a one-man office in Plymouth, Michigan, while Hearn had a similarly small office in Clearwater, Florida.

Most of the Hungry Howie's stores were 1,000 to 2,000 square feet. They sold pizza for carryout and delivery. About 90 to 95 percent of the stores were owner-operated. Altogether, the stores had about 650 employees.

Hungry Howie's Distributing Established in 1986

With the company's rapid growth, the need arose for a commissary to control product consistency and pricing. Hungry Howie's Distributing, Inc. was created for that purpose. The first distribution center was opened in Livonia, Michigan, in 1986, and that was where the company located its headquarters. It had about 25,000 square feet of space. A second distribution center was opened in Lakeland, Florida, in 1987. At the same time that the distribution centers were opened, procedures were standardized. Store layouts, signage, promotion, and hiring and accounting procedures were established, making it easier to manage the rapidly growing chain.

In 1986 the company was experimenting with several small, heated trucks that would visit factories and offices during lunch. About half of all the pizzas Hungry Howie's sold were home delivered. The company charged $1.50 for delivery, a charge that Jackson claimed other pizza makers passed on to customers by increasing the cost of their other products.

Sales in 1987 were $31 million, up 40 percent from 1986. In 1988 the company opened its 100th location, with 52 of them located in the metro Detroit area. Hungry Howie's strategy in Michigan was to open franchises in all of the major cities, a strategy it copied from Domino's. Grand Rapids got its first Hungry Howie's franchise in 1988. About 80 percent of the stores were franchises. Although most of the stores were located in Michigan and Florida, Hungry Howie's also had franchises in Georgia, Colorado, California, and North Carolina. By this time Hungry Howie's was offering seven different flavored crusts on its pizzas, and it was using that feature to distinguish itself in a crowded pizza market.

In 1991 sales reached $65 million, making Hungry Howie's the 14th largest pizza chain in the country. It was still far behind the industry's leaders. Pizza Hut had 8,000 restaurants and $5 billion in sales, Domino's operated 5,000 stores, and Little Caesar's had 3,950 stores. Hungry Howie's had 3,200 employees systemwide. During the year the company introduced a desert pizza called Fruzza.

There were 210 Hungry Howie's locations in 1992. The company operated 85 outlets in Michigan and 105 in Florida. Its plans for growth targeted strip malls, where the Hungry Howie's stores would average 1,200 square feet. The ideal location was perceived as being sandwiched between a video rental outlet and a convenience store. Jackson noted in 1992, "Most of our sales are discount-driven. The two-for-one pizza has been very popular." The company also planned to computerize its stores, using computer technology to track customer preferences and record addresses for mailing purposes.

Hungry Howie's grew to 250 stores in 1993. Sales were more than $93 million. In 1994 sales were up 15 percent to $107 million and net revenue was $1.6 million. During the year Howie Wings were introduced.

Moved to New Headquarters in 1995

In 1995 Hungry Howie's moved to a new headquarters and warehouse in Madison Heights, Michigan. With 50,000 square feet, it doubled Hungry Howie's warehouse space and tripled the office space for its 50 corporate employees. The building was located right on I-75 near I-696. Jackson noted, "From a distribution standpoint, from that intersection, you can get just about anywhere from Grand Rapids to Toledo." The I-75 location also provided greater visibility for the corporate name. "It's like a billboard," Jackson said. Jackson once said the company's growth strategy was to grow regionally along I-75 and "then branch out slowly across the nation. That way, we're not scattered all over."

By 1995 the company was the 11th largest carryout and delivery pizza chain. It had 282 stores in 13 states at the beginning of 1995 and planned to open dozens more. Its goal was to open 60 to 75 stores in 1995 and sustain a 20 percent growth rate. Jackson said, "The first 300 stores are the hardest. After that, it jumps—400, 600, 800." Sales for 1995 turned out to be $125 million, with net revenue of $1.57 million.

The whole pizza industry was growing. Little Caesar's now had 4,700 stores and Domino's had 5,100 locations worldwide. Jackson did not believe, however, that the pizza market was saturated. He also was not counting on long-term loyalty from his customers. "You're only as good as your next coupon," he said. Positioning and promotion were the keys to success in the pizza business, according to Jackson. And Hungry Howie's had done a good job of positioning itself with its array of flavored crusts.

Another element in Hungry Howie's positioning was the fact that it charged for deliveries. That put it somewhere between Domino's, with its free delivery, and Little Caesar's, which did not deliver but offered a lower price. When Hungry Howie's customers picked up their pizza, it was priced closer to that of Little Caesar's. When the pizzas were delivered, their cost was closer to that of Domino's.

In terms of new franchises, Domino's and Little Caesar's already had sold most of their prime territory. That made Hungry Howie's more attractive to prospective franchisees, because the company had a wealth of territories available. To fuel future growth, Hungry Howie's sold multiple-unit franchises that clustered units in a single market.

By 1995 the company itself owned none of its stores. Jackson and Hearn individually owned about 50 stores, and the rest were franchised. The company's strong performance in the 1990s was attracting more qualified franchisees, and the company could afford to be selective. It also was achieving a higher profile through recognition awards. *Entrepreneur* magazine ranked Hungry Howie's as the number two pizza carryout and delivery franchise opportunity in 1996 as well as one of the fastest growing franchises in the United States.

Opened 350th Store in 1996

At the beginning of 1996 Hungry Howie's opened its first sitdown, buffet-style restaurant. It was located in downtown Detroit. The franchise was owned by Jeffrey J. Rinke, Hungry Howie's vice-president of marketing and product development, and Mark Mueller. Rinke came to Hungry Howie's in 1987 from R.P.M., Inc., which was Domino's largest franchise organization. Frustrated when he couldn't acquire a Domino's franchise, he was referred to Steve Jackson, who offered him a corporate-level position as well as the opportunity to have his own franchise. Rinke eventually opened a total of six Hungry Howie's franchises.

At the beginning of 1996 Hungry Howie's had more than 300 franchises in the United States and Canada. By the end of the year it had 354 in operation. Sales for 1996 were more than $140 million, with net revenue of $2.27 million. During the year Hungry Howie's introduced its thin-crust and deep-dish pizzas.

By 1997 Hungry Howie's had maintained a ten to 15 percent growth rate for a period of ten years. It had 375 stores by January 1, 1998. Jackson said that the company learned a lot and honed its competitive edge by growing up in the shadow of Domino's and Little Caesar's. After offering two-for-one pizzas for many years, Hungry Howie's adopted a low-price marketing strategy for a single-pizza pickup.

Although most of Hungry Howie's growth came through traditional stand-alone locations, it was exploring the possibility of future growth through nontraditional locations and co-branding. In mid-1997 it had two projects under construction with Burger King in Kentucky and California. It also had 12 nontraditional locations in convenience stores in Florida. It was negotiating to place an outdoor concession at Meadow Brook, an outdoor concert venue in Rochester Hills, Michigan.

In 1997 the company introduced a new, calzone-type sandwich that was made with fresh dough and oven-baked. The hot sandwich was offered with a choice of fillings: Italian; steak, cheese, and mushroom; ham and cheese; turkey; turkey club; pizza; and vegetarian. Hungry Howie's called it an oven-baked sub.

Sales for 1997 totaled $154 million. *Pizza Today* ranked Hungry Howie's as the ninth largest pizza franchise operation. Twenty-five years after the first Hungry Howie's opened in Taylor, Michigan, the company was still growing.

Further Reading

King, R.J., "Pizza Chain's Hungry for Success," *Detroit News*, July 20, 1992, p. 3.

Knorr, David, "Hungry Howie's To Open First GR Franchise," *Grand Rapids Business Journal*, October 10, 1988, p. 3.

Lane-Wilke, Katie, "Howie's Hungers for More Outlets," *Crains Detroit Business*, May 26, 1986, p. 3.

Stopa, Marsha, "Howie's Hungry To Add Growth," *Crains Detroit Business*, February 6, 1995, p. 3.

——, "Hungry for More Growth," *Crains Detroit Business*, June 9, 1997, p. 1.

——, "Hungry Howie's Tries Motown Sitdown Service," *Crains Detroit Business*, December 18, 1995, p. 20.

—David Bianco

Imperial Oil

Imperial Oil Limited

111 St. Clair Avenue West
Toronto, Ontario M5W 1K3
Canada
(416) 968-4111
Fax: (416) 968-5228
Web site: http://www.imperialoil.ca

Public Company, Majority-Owned by Exxon Corporation
Incorporated: 1880 as The Imperial Oil Company,
    Limited
Employees: 7,096
Sales: C $11.12 billion (US$7.46 billion) (1997)
Stock Exchanges: Montreal Toronto American
Ticker Symbol: IMO
SICs: 1311 Crude Petroleum & Natural Gas; 1321
    Natural Gas Liquids; 1382 Oil & Gas Exploration
    Services; 2819 Industrial Inorganic Chemicals, Not
    Elsewhere Classified; 2821 Plastics Materials &
    Resins; 2911 Petroleum Refining; 4412 Deep Sea
    Foreign Transportation of Freight; 5191 Farm
    Supplies; 5989 Fuel Dealers, Not Elsewhere Classified

Imperial Oil Limited is Canada's largest producer of crude oil and a leading producer of natural gas. Imperial, which is 69.6 percent owned by the U.S. corporation Exxon, is Canada's largest refiner of petroleum products, providing the wide variety of products and services that appear under the Esso brand name at more than 2,700 Esso stations across Canada. The company has vast reserves of oil sands, from which it extracts heavy oil (or bitumen), which can be converted to crude oil or used for other purposes. It also produces and markets coal and petrochemicals. Imperial has made itself known for its support of Canadian culture, health, education, and community services.

Founded after 1876 Canadian Oil Bust

In 1880, when Imperial Oil Company was founded in London, Ontario, oil actually did not look like a good business. The Canadian oil boom, triggered in 1857 with the sinking of the first oil well, had gone bust in 1876. Domestic overproduction and liberal free-trade policies had conspired to saturate the Canadian market. The industrial boom and rampant land speculation, begun in the 1850s, were coming to a halt. During the boom many Canadians had jumped to join the oil rush, which contributed to the flooding of the local market. This, coupled with worldwide depression, resulted in deflated oil prices that were one-third of their former value. Thus, in 1876, Canadian refiners who had glutted their own market began to desert their businesses at bailout prices.

It was at this crisis point that 16 well-established Canadian businessmen from London and Petrolia, Ontario, banded together and decided to buy into the petroleum business. On September 8, 1880, with C $25,000, The Imperial Oil Company, Limited was formed. Its charter was "to find, produce, refine and distribute petroleum and its products throughout Canada." With two refineries, one in London and the other in Petrolia, the total capitalization was an impressive C $500,000.

Frederick Fitzgerald, a builder of the London Water Works who also dabbled in furniture, liquor, groceries, and oil, became Imperial's first president. The mastermind of the group's success, however, was its vice president, Jacob Englehart, who by age 33 had 14 years experience in oil, having started his first refinery at age 19. William Spencer and Herman and Isaac Waterman also brought their knowledge of refineries to the association; Isaac Waterman's involvement in municipal politics and the railway, in particular, later proved to be a valuable asset to the group. John Geary, a lawyer-turned-refiner, and John Minhinnik, a plumber-turned-refiner, were more than ready to deal with the business' logistical and physical problems. Thomas Smallman and John Walker brought the experience they had gained when producing sulfuric acid with the first Canadian chemical company, while Walker was also experienced in federal politics. It was no accident that Thomas Hodgens, a former wagon maker, and his brother Edward, a barrel-maker, were brought into the deal. Edward Hodgens in 1879 had also patented a process that sweetened the odor of the rancid-smelling Canadian çrude, making it more competitive with relatively odorless U.S. crude.

The group immediately began trying to set its products apart by improving their quality, as well as by trying to find new uses for the products and to increase distribution. Imperial acquired rights to Hodgens' patent and started deodorizing its oil. It began importing a new kerosene lamp that burned with a brighter, whiter light, from Germany. It sent dealers out into the previously unpenetrated west to hustle up sales. In the space of one year, Imperial was selling to Winnipeg, a frontier town of 8,000, as well as opening up an office in Montreal.

Imperial oil, carried in Imperial's hand-made barrels, rode on Imperial-built wagons across the prairies of the Northwest Territories to Hudson's Bay Company posts. Imperial became so well known for its sturdy oak barrels, that, although the company offered a generous C $1.25 refund for each, most homesteaders chose to keep them and convert them to wash-tubs, rain barrels, and armchairs. By 1883 Walker's position as vice president of Canadian Pacific Railway had helped Imperial to become not only the basic supplier of railroad construction crews, but also of the settlers that squatted along the line as far as British Columbia.

After three years of growth, Imperial Oil suffered a major setback. During a thunderstorm in July, lightning hit an Imperial refinery, sparking a fire that burned its London processing operation to the ground. In 1884, when Imperial requested of the city of London a C $20,000 grant to build a new line to pipe crude from Imperial's Lambton Wells into the city, its political connections were not enough. Londoners had had enough of the flash fires and the stench rising from streams of gasoline that ran from where it was dumped on the streets down to the river. Gasoline, a then-useless by-product of kerosene, created problems elsewhere as well. Some refiners, trying to get the most dollars per barrel, illegally cut kerosene with gasoline, causing lamps not infrequently to explode when ignited. It is believed that gasoline mixed in with lamp kerosene started the Great Chicago Fire. Rather than rebuilding in what it felt to be a now-hostile London, Imperial moved its head offices first to Petrolia and then to Sarnia, Ontario. Within a short time, almost all related industries followed Imperial from London to Sarnia, which was becoming the new oil center.

New Products and Affiliations at the Turn of the Century

By 1893 Imperial had 23 branch offices spread from Halifax to Victoria. Imperial had done such a good job developing new markets that it could no longer supply the demands of the market. Imperial lacked the money necessary to expand to meet its consumers' needs, and feared losing market share to larger U.S. companies. Unable to convince Canadian or British banks or private investors to gamble with large amounts of capital, in 1898 Imperial turned to the U.S. Standard Oil Company of New Jersey, who had offered to purchase Imperial years earlier. On Dominion Day in 1898, Standard Oil (now called Exxon) assumed a majority interest in Imperial. Imperial took over Standard Oil's Canadian assets on February 23, 1899, including its refinery in Sarnia. Standard worked to keep its ownership of Imperial secret, giving Canadian government officials Imperial Oil stock as hush money.

After laying a pipeline to bring in its crude from Petrolia, Imperial was ready to start servicing all of Canada, producing 143 cubic meters per day at its Sarnia plant alone. Imperial's business got another boost with the growing popularity of the automobile. By 1910 there were about 6,000 of these gasoline-consuming machines prowling Canadian streets. Gasoline, a by-product which previously had been thrown away, became a product in such demand that oil companies were not prepared to dispense it quickly enough. People bought gas in open buckets from grocery stores or even went to the oil companies' warehouses.

The first service station got its start when a car pulled up to Imperial's Vancouver warehouse in between the horse-drawn oil wagons, and backfired. By the time the workers had gotten their horses settled, the foreman had banished automobiles forever. C. M. Rolston, Imperial's Vancouver manager, solved the problem the next day when he opened up Canada's first service station, a one-room metal shack with a garden hose and a water tank full of gasoline.

Rapid Growth During and After World War I

Building a service station did not, however, meet all the demands that were awakened by automobiles. The use of automobiles increased so rapidly that Imperial was almost immediately forced to begin looking for ways to increase its supply of crude, simply to produce more gasoline. In 1914 Standard licensed Imperial to use its cracking technique, a process that yielded much more gasoline per barrel of crude, and installed the first units in its Sarnia refineries. Cracking involved the use of heat and pressure coils to chemically decompose the crude. That same year, Imperial formed the International Petroleum Company, Limited, to search for oil in South America; ordered an exploratory geological party to Turner Valley to confirm the discovery of crude near Calgary; laid a pipeline from Sarnia to Cygnet, Ohio, connecting Imperial refineries to some of the most productive oil fields in the United States; and built the first refinery in British Columbia, on Burrard Inlet. Before long, World War I broke out, creating a whole new market hungry for gasoline.

In 1919 the Imperial Oil Company, Limited changed its name to Imperial Oil Limited. To meet the new demands of war, Imperial grew rapidly. Within five years it quintupled the number of its refineries and doubled its refining capacity. By 1920 there were four times as many cars in Canada as five years prior, and once again Imperial began to search for more efficient ways to refine gasoline. In 1923 Imperial obtained Canadian rights to use pressure stills, which enhanced the cracking process, yielding a greater quantity and quality of gasoline.

In 1924 Imperial hired R.K. Stratford, its first research worker. He discovered that sulfur corrosion of the cracking coils could be prevented by adding lime to the crude. He also came up with a way to keep gasoline from gumming up engines by running the cracked product through a slurry of clay.

The 1930s, for Imperial, were full of changes. Previously geologists searching for oil depended on a hammer, a chisel, maybe a pair of field glasses, and a lot of luck. In the 1920s, the rotary drill rig came along, and it became possible to drill deeper beneath the surface. Then, in the 1930s, Imperial started investigating the possibilities of seismology. Its geologist bounced shock waves off of underground rocks, and judging from the waves' reflection, the shape and size of possible oil formations could be determined. Imperial had started implementing these procedures before the outbreak of World War II, when the Allies needed all the fuel they could get.

Contributions to War Effort

Imperial was able to produce a large amount of the 87-octane aviation fuel that the Commonwealth Air Training Plan needed for its training aircraft by selecting crude oils containing the most useful fractions and by modifying its distillation equipment. Imperial also helped to produce 100-octane aviation fuel for combat aircraft. The company aided in the development of portable runways which could be rolled up, taken to a flat field almost anywhere, and laid in place. Imperial was a key player in Operation Shuttle, which kept oil flowing to Great Britain for a full two years before the United States entered the war.

Alaska's importance grew when Japan entered the war, and airports popped up there for U.S. defense. In 1942 the U.S. Army requested that Imperial build a refinery in the Yukon at Whitehorse, to supply the Alaskan airfields. Within two years, a ten-centimeter pipeline snaked out from the Whitehorse refinery to supply the much-needed fuel for a full year before the war ended.

When the war ended, Imperial welcomed back its employees who had served. Throughout the war, the company had made up the difference between military pay and the salaries at Imperial when military pay was lower. On enlistment, Imperial had given its employees one month's salary as a bonus.

In 1946, Imperial sold 6.275 million cubic meters of crude, more than any previous year. The company's officers, realizing that there had been no meaningful field discoveries since 1920, launched a full-scale exploration to assure supplies for the future.

Leduc Strike in 1947

At the end of the 1940s, 90 percent of all crude oil refined in Canada was imported. Imperial drilled 133 consecutive dry holes. The future looked so bad that Imperial was debating the expensive conversion of natural gas to gasoline. If things did not change, the company decided it would have to close its Sarnia refinery and rely on off-shore crude shipped in to Montreal. Before Imperial shut down and began building in Montreal, however, the company's leadership decided to drill once more in the Hinge Belt, south of Edmonton. Seismograph crews picked a sight in Leduc. On February 13, 1947, the Leduc well gushed oil in huge quantities. The extent of Leduc's success is best measured by the fact that the wells that quickly sprouted up in that area provided 90 percent of all oil produced in Canada. With Leduc's success came the call for a neighboring refinery. Imperial dismantled the idled Whitehorse refinery and reassembled it in nearby Edmonton.

With the Leduc oil strike, domestic oil production was so greatly increased that Imperial began searching for ways to export it. To aid in exportation, Imperial and others joined to form Interprovincial Pipe Line Ltd. in 1949. Imperial owned 49.9 percent of Interprovincial's stock. By autumn of 1950, a pipeline had been laid from Edmonton, Ontario, to Superior, Wisconsin. In 1957 the line was extended to Toronto, then in 1976 it stretched to Montreal. Imperial sold its share of Interprovincial in 1990.

The surplus of oil in the 1950s and price wars that ensued led Imperial to analyze gasoline markets, eliminate unprofitable stations, and set up stations in the right places—some were simple gas stations, others were full-service auto "clinics." Imperial was responsible for introducing Canada's first car clinic, complete with electronic diagnosis. It was not long before highway service stations became a familiar sight, offering everything from gas to snacks. In 1970, self-service stations began popping up under the Esso name—Imperial's brand name.

Canadian gas and oil reserves once again had begun to dwindle as demand continued to grow. Imperial began exploring the far northern waters off Canada's eastern coast, which was a costly operation. In January 1970, that extremely expensive search actually paid off when Imperial hit medium-gravity, low-sulfur crude at Atkinson Point, on the Beaufort Sea in the western Arctic, 1,700 meters deep. As a result of this and other offshore searches, Imperial pioneered the artificial island. The first artificial island, Immerl, was built by Imperial at the cost of $5 million, not including the cost of the well, which turned out to be dry. The offshore oil search continued both in the farther north Queen Elizabeth Islands as well as in the Atlantic seabed.

In the 1960s and 1970s, Imperial Oil began developing the vast reserves of oil sands of northern Alberta, considered the world's largest single reserve of crude oil—a trillion and a half barrels worth. Unfortunately, it was extremely difficult and expensive to extract this heavy oil, or bitumen, from the sand to which it was embedded. The oil was extremely viscous and did not flow on its own. Imperial began pilot programs at Cold Lake in the early 1960s. In 1973 the company joined a consortium known as Syncrude Canada Limited, which began production of the Athabasca oil sands in 1978. By 1991 Syncrude had produced 500 million barrels of heavy oil, which could be converted to conventional crude oil or used to produce asphalt for roads, shingles, and roofing tar.

Acquisitions in the 1980s and 1990s

One of Imperial's most important steps toward growth happened in the late 1980s. In 1988, Imperial began talking to

Texaco Canada Inc. about a possible merger, and in February 1989 Imperial bought the company for C $4.96 billion, making it the largest acquisition in Imperial's history and the second-largest in Canada's. The actual merger did not take place until February 1990; it was held up awaiting approval from the Canadian competition authorities, who forced Imperial to sell 638 retail stations, 14 oil terminals, and one refinery. (Following the merger Texaco Canada became known as McColl-Frontenac Petroleum Inc.; this name harkened back to the early history of Texaco Canada, which adopted the name McColl-Frontenac in 1927 upon the merger of McColl Brothers and Frontenac Oil Refineries Limited.)

Two consequences of this merger were immediately noteworthy. The sum of productivity and profits of both companies operating independently was surpassed by those of the two operating together as a whole, creating a synergy. Employees of both companies were looked to for answers to problems of operations and for suggestions about changes. One of the most remarkable features of the merger was the speed with which Imperial was able to reduce the initial debt incurred by the merger, taking it from C $4.96 billion to C $3.1 in 1989.

By this time, Imperial was much more than simply an oil producer, developer, and marketer, although it was now Canada's largest petroleum company. From its beginning, Imperial's interests had branched through all aspects of the business, including the manufacture of wagons, barrels and lamps, as well as chemicals for the treatment plants. Most of Imperial's sales were to industrial customers; it had developed into the leading manufacturer of aviation fuel, marine fuel, railway lubricants, and domestic heating fuels in Canada. In the late 1980s, Imperial stepped up its presence in the natural gas field, through the 1987 purchase of Calgary-based Sulpetro Limited and the 1988 acquisition of the Alberta oil and gas production assets of Ocelet Industries Ltd., and finally with the production capacity and reserves of natural gas gained through the addition of Texaco Canada. By 1989 the company was Canada's third largest producer of natural gas.

Imperial had also developed petrochemical interests, starting as early as 1955, and by the 1970s had developed into one of the largest chemical operations in Canada under the Esso Chemical Canada banner. Fertilizers were added to the manufacturing base in the 1960s, and were bolstered in 1989 with the purchase of Cascade Fertilizers Ltd., a western Canada-based maker of liquid fertilizers. Imperial also developed a natural resources business eventually known as Esso Resources, which at one time mined coal, zinc, and uranium. In the late 1980s all but the coal mining operations were sold off (the company began production of coal in 1981 when Byron Creek Collieries Ltd. of British Columbia was acquired). Also divested in the late 1980s was Building Products of Canada Limited, a manufacturer of a wide variety of building materials that had been acquired in 1964.

Imperial's relationship with the environment had also changed since the early days, when it had dumped gasoline and suffered the flash fires in London. In 1989, its crisis-management team allocated C $8 million to be invested over three years to improve its response to oil spills at its offshore sites. That same year it simulated a large tanker spill to test its response capabilities. Imperial's relationship with the Canadian community was no less impressive. Imperial made news not for oil spills and environmental disasters, but for its support of education and innovative employee assistance programs.

1990s Restructuring

In the early 1990s Imperial Oil was hurt both by continued high debt levels stemming from the acquisition of Texaco Canada and from a worldwide glut on the petroleum market. It consequently suffered the first operating loss in company history in 1991 (C $36 million). Long considered one of the least efficient petroleum companies in North America, Imperial was forced to make drastic changes. In 1992 it cut its workforce by 1,700, closed 1,000 service stations, and restructured its operations, absorbing its Esso Petroleum, Esso Chemical, and Esso Resources divisions into Imperial Oil proper. The following year it shut down its refinery at Port Moody, British Columbia. Imperial sold most of its fertilizer business in 1994 to Canadian mining, chemicals, and materials company Sherritt for $282 million. As a result of these and other moves, Imperial was a much more profitable firm, logging a US $252 million profit in 1995, its largest since 1988. Profits in 1996 were aided by a C $843 million (US $618 million) refund for tax overpayment between 1974 and 1990.

Meanwhile, Imperial was experiencing a steady decline in convention crude oil production as convention sources in Canada were quickly drying up. Rather than invest in the additional equipment required to extract more oil from old fields, Imperial decided to sell off a number of these properties, including the historic Leduc oil field. It was sold in 1997 to Calgary-based Probe Exploration Inc. for more than C $45 million. Also in 1997, the company sold three other Alberta oil fields to Calgary-based Pengrowth Gas Corp. for C $595 million (US $463 million). To replace the loss of this conventional crude, Imperial stepped up production at the Cold Lake heavy oil project. By 1997 almost half of Imperial's net crude oil production came from Cold Lake, with an additional 21 percent deriving from the company's 25-percent interest in Syncrude. Imperial announced in 1997 that it would operate and hold a 58-percent interest in two parallel pipelines to be built for an estimated C $250 million between the Cold Lake area and Hardisty, Alberta, the site of a major pipeline terminal.

For the company's future, an emphasis on expensive-to-extract heavy oil ran the risk of the impact of low oil prices, such as the depressed level of early 1998, which led Imperial to at least temporarily suspend development work at Cold Lake. The company's natural gas operations were concurrently broadened through the May 1998 agreement between Imperial, Shell Canada, and Mobil Oil Canada Properties to explore for natural gas off the coast of Nova Scotia, where about 18 trillion cubic feet of natural gas was estimated to lie. Imperial took a 20-percent stake in the new venture.

Principal Subsidiaries

Imperial Oil Resources Limited; Imperial Oil Resources N.W.T. Limited; Imperial Oil Resources Ventures Limited; McColl-Frontenac Petroleum Inc.; Syncrude Canada Limited (25%).

Further Reading

Boras, Alan, ''Imperial Gets Enormous Tax Refund Check,'' *Oil Daily,* April 1, 1996, p. 3.

——, ''Imperial Gets Hot and Heavy over Plans to Double Spending at Canada's Cold Lake,'' *Oil Daily,* June 11, 1996, p. 2.

Broyles, Karen, ''Imperial Plans $463 Million Property Sale,'' *Oil Daily,* August 21, 1997, p. 1.

MacIsaac, Merle, ''Born-Again Basket Case,'' *Canadian Business,* May 1993, pp. 38–44.

Malone, Mary, ''Imperial Beginnings,'' *London Magazine,* December 1986.

McMurdy, Deirdre, ''Running Out of Gas,'' *Maclean's,* January 13, 1992, p. 26.

Morton, Peter, ''Imperial Oil Ltd. to Lay Off 20% of Employees in Resource Division in Effort to Boost Profit,'' *Oil Daily,* June 29, 1994, p. 3.

——, ''Imperial Switches Focus from Conventional to Heavy Oil,'' *Oil Daily,* April 5, 1995, p. 7.

''The Story of Imperial Oil,'' Toronto: Imperial Oil Limited, 1991, [kp]48 pp.[ke]

—Maya Sahafi
—updated by David E. Salamie

Inserra Supermarkets

20 Ridge Road
Mahwah, New Jersey 07430
U.S.A.
(201) 529-5900
Fax: (201) 529-1189

Private Company
Incorporated: 1961
Employees: 2,300
Sales: $492 million (1997)
SICs: 5411 Grocery Stores

Inserra Supermarkets operates approximately two dozen grocery stores, licensed under the ShopRite name, in New Jersey and New York state. Although it consistently ranks among the 500 largest private companies in the United States, Inserra seldom makes headlines outside of its home area. Nor does it possess a site on the World Wide Web—despite the 1990s trend that led almost all businesses (and many others) to end up with a homepage—and it has no public relations campaign of any note. Thus, the company remains somewhat of a mystery to the outside world. It is apparently a family-owned business—Lawrence R. Inserra is its chairman and chief executive officer (CEO)—and a very successful one at that.

ShopRite and the Growth of Supermarkets

Aspects of Inserra's history can be inferred from a close look at that of the supermarket industry in general, and of the ShopRite network in particular. The concept of a grocery store grew out of specialty stores—such as butcher shops or bakeries—which when combined with the notion of a general store, yielded early grocery chains such as Kroger, founded in 1883. In the period that included the Great Depression, World War II, and the postwar economic boom of the 1950s, grocery stores became a widespread phenomenon in the United States.

During the 1960s, supermarkets—stores which sold at least $2 million a year, and which featured a wide range of products including non-food items—began to make their appearance. The decade also saw the growth of large chains, which helped to bring about the end of many a "mom-and-pop" grocery—that is, an old-fashioned, family-run type business.

Inserra is, according to the public statements of its executives, such a business. It came into being in 1961, during the early part of the supermarket era. But it adopted a strategy common to many independent grocery stores—that of joining a grocery association, which is a network of typically independent stores which operate under the same namesake. IGA is a good example of a well-known grocery association. From the beginning, Inserra was affiliated with Newark, New Jersey-based ShopRite.

ShopRite came into being in 1946, when a Del Monte Foods representative encouraged several Newark grocers to form a cooperative. The seven grocers each invested $1,000, and on December 5, 1946, they created Wakefern Food Corporation. "Wakefern" was an acronym formed from several of the founders' last names, but in 1951 the members of the cooperative agreed to use the name "ShopRite" on their stores.

Despite the change in store names, the cooperative remained the Wakefern Food Corporation. By 1998, it included forty-three member companies, and had become the largest retailer-owned cooperative in the United States, as well as the largest employer in the state of New Jersey. Spread throughout that state, as well as New York, Connecticut, Pennsylvania, and Delaware, were some 190 ShopRite stores. Most of these were family owned.

Inserra Becomes One of New Jersey's Largest Private Companies

As a member of Wakefern Food Corporation, Inserra Supermarkets had the advantages of belonging to a cooperative, which helped the small Inserra enterprise grow. According to ShopRite's corporate information, a cooperative "buys, warehouses and transports produce while providing other support services to ensure customer satisfaction." Wakefern had 2.5 million square feet of warehouse space in Elizabeth, New Jersey, and operated one of the largest private transportation fleets on the East Coast, with some 400 tractors and 2,000 trailers, which travelled more than 23 million miles in 1997. Thus, Inserra could rely on its "big brother" in the grocery industry to take care of the areas that the smaller company was not as well-equipped to do on its own. " 'Volume' buying," ShopRite declared, "enables ShopRite stores to offer their consumers the lowest overall prices, and the greatest value, in the marketplace."

With the cooperative handling wholesale purchases and distribution, Inserra was free to grow, and grow it did. In a November 1992 piece about the seventeen New Jersey corporations that had made the *Forbes* list of the 400 largest private companies for that year, the *Record* led its story with a report on Inserra. Its purchase of a supermarket in Wayne, New Jersey in 1990 had, the newspaper noted, "helped bolster Inserra Supermarkets to the top shelf of private companies." The chain's sales, which reached $463 million in 1991, were "increasing steadily," according to company president Lawrence Inserra.

In January 1995, *Supermarket News* reported that Inserra—which at the time had thirteen stores in New Jersey and five in New York state—purchased five more from Singer Supermarkets, a North Bergen, New Jersey-based ShopRite licensee. At the end of that year, *Forbes* reported that Inserra, with approximately $500 million in annual sales, was the 388th largest privately owned corporation in the United States. Surprisingly, rather than bask in the glory of a job well-done, Inserra kept to its traditional practice of going about business and avoiding the limelight or subsequent media blitz.

But growth slackened in the mid- to late 1990s. By 1997, *Forbes* reported Inserra Supermarkets' sales volume as $492 million, and ranked it 444th, down from its 1996 ranking at 407th place. *Forbes* reported that Inserra owned seven supermarkets and sixteen superstores, all operated under the ShopRite name. The Inserra family maintained control of the company, with Lawrence R. Inserra acting as the chairman and CEO, and Teresa Inserra the company's treasurer.

An Expanded Array of Services

As grocery stores changed in the 1990s, so did the range of Inserra's services. Laura McCafferty of Wakefern Food Corporation told the *Record* in February 1995, "Probably the biggest change is that the size of our stores has gotten larger." This was in part because of what the paper called "lifestyle changes,"—specifically, the fact that more women were working, and fewer spent their days at home maintaining the household. Thus, available time for the family grocery shopping trip was slim, and stores began to carry a more diverse product line so people could get everything they needed in one stop. Also, in response to the success of large wholesalers such as Sam's Clubs and CostCo, ShopRite had begun offering "supersize" packages of such items as paper towels and toilet tissue.

Another change in grocery store operations, and one reflected at Inserra Supermarkets, was the addition of other profit centers under the store roof. The inclusion of facilities such as photo developing centers, coffee shops, banks, and video stores helped to increase profits, and made the supermarket even more of a one-stop store servicing a variety of needs. In October

1995, the *Hudson Valley Business Journal* reported that Poughkeepsie Savings Bank had signed an agreement with Inserra whereby it would place full-service banking centers in three Rockland County, New York Inserra ShopRite stores. The first would open in December at the Spring Valley ShopRite, to be followed with 1996 openings in West Hayerstraw and New City. "In-store banking," Lawrence Inserra told the *Journal,* "will provide our customers with a new array of products and services."

Supermarkets in general, and Inserra in particular, were not merely expanding their non-food offerings in the 1990s. A number of changes in the marketplace likewise dictated new developments at the core of the grocery business: food. Large grocery stores had begun to chip away at the market segments of restaurants, stand-alone delicatessens, specialty food shops, and farmers markets. Hence in December 1995, *Supermarket News* reported that Inserra was "rolling out a program for hearth-baked, crusty breads after successfully testing the concept in two of its units."

According to the company's bakery supervisor, Vinny Lottito, the "breads have taken off slowly, but we knew that would be the case. Now our customers are beginning to accept them." The new line of store-made breads would include walnut raisin, sourdough, rustic, farmer's rye sourdough, mill bread, forrest hill bread, jalapeno pepper-cheddar cheese bread, black forest, sun-dried tomato and black olive baguettine, whole wheat pan au levain, knusperele baguettine and muesli bread. Despite their success in some areas, however, these breads—which were partly-baked by outsourced bakers and finished in-store—would not appear at every Inserra facility: "The breads require the right demographics to sell well, because the prices could be limiting in some areas, [Lottito] said."

Inserra Supermarkets was also becoming involved in an even more ambitious food-service program: catering. "For both [grocery stores] and their customers," Mina Williams wrote in *Supermarket News* in October 1996, "the meaning of catering is broadening to include instances of what used to be just plain eating." Ron Hirt, Inserra's director of appetizing, told her, "We are in the catering business 365 days a year. Catering is no longer spring weddings and Christmas parties. Our customers are seeking more prepared-food items that can be picked up and reheated in the home for a variety of occasions, even in-home entertaining." Inserra Supermarkets' expanding line of catered foods, Williams wrote, included "chicken cordon bleu, chicken stuffed with wild rice or broccoli ... whole rotisserie chickens and chicken parts ... [which] complement the Buffalo-style chicken wings, fried chicken, ribs, macaroni and cheese, lasagna, stuffed shells and ziti as a standard part of the deli department's party options."

A number of Inserra stores had begun accepting custom orders for catered food, and were "aggressively using turkey and ham dinners in a box to capture more deli sales." Inserra's delis were also offering a greater variety of food platters, with smoked fish, shrimp, and sushi added to the traditional meat, cheese, vegetable, and fruit platters. "We are going about capturing catering dollars that are going to small delis and small caterers," Hirt told Williams. Inserra's approach was, as Williams noted, a "holistic" one. Hence she was told by Hirt, "We try not to treat each department as an island, but . . . as one. Our customers work with the appetizing-department manager to place their order across all departments, whether it is meat, seafood, appetizing, bakery or paper goods'' such as napkins.

Nearing the end of the twentieth century, Inserra was attempting to keep pace with both the changing grocery industry and the changing lives and needs of the customers that it served. Rather than resting on its laurels and allowing business to get stagnant, Inserra was proving that it was willing and able to make the changes necessary to carry the company well into the next century.

Further Reading

Bergen, Tom, ''ShopRite Parent Taken Private by Top Managers,'' *Capital Business Review,* November 9, 1987, p. 9.

''Grocery Stores: A Market Basket of Changes,'' *Record* (New Jersey), February 5, 1995, p. 4.

Harper, Roseanne, ''Inserra Rolls Out Crusty Bread After Test,'' *Supermarket News,* December 4, 1995, p. 37.

''Inserra Buys 5 ShopRites,'' *Supermarket News,* January 2, 1995, p. 6.

''Inserra Buys 4 Pharmacies,'' *Supermarket Pharmacy,* February 1995, p. 7.

McGeehan, Patrick, ''Worth a Fortune: N. J. Boasts 17 Companies on Famed List,'' *Record* (New Jersey), November 24, 1992.

''Poughkeepsie Savings to Open Rockland Offices,'' *Hudson Valley Business Journal,* October 30, 1995, p. 5.

''ShopRite Yesterday and Today,'' *ShopRite,* http://www.shoprite.com/ (July 7, 1998).

Williams, Mina, ''Casual Affairs,'' *Supermarket News,* October 14, 1996, p. 25.

—Judson Knight

International Data Group, Inc.

One Exeter Plaza, 15th Fl.
Boston, Massachusetts 02116
U.S.A.
(617) 534-1200
Fax: (617) 262-2300
Web site: http://www.idg.com

Private Company
Incorporated: 1964 as International Data Corporation
Employees: 9,000
Sales: $2.05 billion (1997)
SICs: 2721 Periodicals: Publishing; 2731 Books:
    Publishing; 6719 Holding Companies, Not Elsewhere
    Classified; 7389 Business Services, Not Elsewhere
    Classified; 8732 Commercial Economic, Sociological,
    & Educational Research

Over the course of some 30 years, Patrick J. McGovern has built International Data Group, Inc. (IDG) from a single-publication firm (*Computerworld*) with a research division into the world's leading information technology (IT) media, research, and exposition company. The company is a global leader in periodical publishing, book publishing, online information, research and analysis, conferences and expositions, education and training, and marketing services for the information technology industry.

IDG publishes 285 computer-related magazines and newspapers in 75 countries, of which more than 175 are country-specific editions of five global publication product lines: *Computerworld/Infoworld, Macworld, Network World, PC World,* and *Channel World.* IDG's book publishing subsidiary, IDG Books Worldwide, is the fastest-growing computer book publisher in the world. Its highly successful . . . *For Dummies* series has more than 350 titles and 40 million copies in print worldwide. Online the company offers IDG.net (http://www.idg.net), the largest network of technology specific web sites around the world. Its research subsidiary, International Data Corporation (IDC), has research centers in more than 41 countries and serves

more than 3,900 corporate and government agencies worldwide. Its trade show subsidiary, IDG World Expo, produces more than 110 conferences and expositions in 35 countries annually. Its training subsidiary, ExecuTrain, is the world's largest computer training company, with more than 180 locations worldwide and 320 training courses. IDG also has a marketing services division to help leading IT companies build international brand recognition.

Founder Had Early Interest in Computers

The roots of this enterprise reach as far back as IDG founder Patrick J. McGovern's high school newspaper route. In 1953, with $20 saved from his route, McGovern combined carpet tacks, plywood boards, bell wire, and flashlight bulbs into a computer that was unbeatable at tic-tac-toe. When he found people did not enjoy playing the machine if they were obliged to always lose, McGovern programmed it to make a mistake every 40th move, so contenders could occasionally win. This computer tic-tac-toe champion won McGovern a full scholarship to the Massachusetts Institute of Technology (MIT).

McGovern had gotten the computer bug from reading a book, *Giant Brains: Or, Machines That Think,* while in the tenth grade. McGovern later edited a Boston-based computer magazine published by the author of *Giant Brains.* It was after MIT, while associate publisher of *Computers and Automation*—the first national computer magazine—that McGovern began to witness the information gap between the companies making computers and the people who bought and used them. This was 1964, still fairly early in the computer age.

McGovern Founded International
Data Corporation, 1964

In 1964 McGovern was tapped by rivals of IBM to conduct a market research program to determine where computers were heading and how they were being used. Firms such as Univac, Xerox, and Burroughs paid McGovern for his research, and he established International Data Corporation (IDC) as a research and analysis firm. He hired high school students across the country to help count computers and collect information. Within three years, IDC was grossing $600,000 and growing.

With his experience at *Computers and Automation* and IDC, the next logical step for McGovern was publishing. He got the idea for his first IT publication when his research showed that computer systems managers were not aware of what others were accomplishing with computers, nor were they keeping up with products. In 1967 he launched *Computerworld,* the flagship weekly that is now the cornerstone of IDG's publishing empire. Introduced before the computer boom, the publication's intent was to provide rapid-access information about new products and applications to computer department managers. It went from eight pages to 72 pages within the first year; within five years, *Computerworld* had become the largest specialized business publication in the United States.

International Data Group Established, 1967

With the successful launching of *Computerworld* in 1967, McGovern formed International Data Group, Inc. as a holding company for his publishing and research ventures. IDG Communications, Inc., formerly CW Communications, Inc., became the company's publishing arm, and International Data Corporation was its research subsidiary. The two divisions worked well together, with the research arm locating computer vendors and users as well as potential advertisers and subscribers and IDG Communications pinpointing market opportunities for healthy publications.

In 1972 McGovern began responding to the need for computer information outside of the United States. Recognizing that each country had its own information needs and application problems, McGovern sought to establish local publications in native languages. His first international venture was *Shukan Computer,* a Japanese publication that drew on *Computerworld* while addressing regional needs. IDG developed a reputation for responding to new markets as they emerged. Its global network of magazines and newspapers grew to include more than 285 publications in more than 75 countries by the end of 1997.

Produced First ComNet Trade Show, 1979

The conference and exposition management division of IDG dates to 1976, when McGovern developed Communications Networks in response to the rapid growth of telecommunications technology. In 1979 the first ComNet trade show was held, and it became the premier trade show for large users of communications technology. IDG World Expo Corporation, the company's conference and exposition management subsidiary, has grown to produce a wide range of conferences, seminars, and trade expositions for the information technology industry worldwide, ranging from small regional programs to industry-wide conferences.

In keeping with its ear-to-the-ground timing, IDG announced the publication of *Macworld Magazine* on the same day that the Macintosh computer was introduced in 1984. In 1980 it initiated *China Computerworld,* a joint venture with the People's Republic of China. Within five years it had 100,000 paid subscribers and a 40 percent profit margin. The Beijing-based weekly was China's first computer publication. It would be 1988 before IDG became the first U.S. publisher to enter the Soviet Union with *PC World U.S.S.R.*

Industry Shakeout in Mid-1980s

Having started a stampede, IDG found itself in a crowded computer research market by 1984. When the first shakeout in the computer publishing field hit, magazines were folding or merging on a weekly basis. This was partly a reflection of what was happening in publishing as a whole: in recessions, advertising budgets are often among the first cuts and that immediately affects magazines. But it was also the result of a market glut. By 1985 there were roughly 120 large computer publications fighting over a limited number of readers and ads. Competing head-on with IDG through most of the 1980s was publishing titan Ziff-Davis Communications Company. Ziff-Davis published industry staples *PC Magazine* and *PC Week,* among others and, like IDG, had a research division.

IDG Expanded Internationally

While the market slumped at home, changes abroad opened new doors. The same saturation was reflected in the United Kingdom, which went from a small number of computer magazines in 1981 to a high of more than 150 in 1985. The glut killed off 30 magazines that year alone. So IDG began looking to other parts of the world. In 1985 IDG began its first joint publishing venture in Hungary, producing *Computerworld SZT* and *PC Mikrovilag.* Here again, IDG was ahead of the trend. McGovern recognized the hunger of newly democratized countries to enter the Information Age. "In the former Soviet Union, and in the other Eastern European countries, they see high-tech as their ticket to making their future much brighter," he said in an in-house interview. He claimed that unsold copies of IDG publications were unheard of in Eastern Europe.

In nations that had been without political and economic freedoms, the urge to catch up with the computer world was fierce. Between 1986 and 1989 IDG's revenues doubled as they entered new markets worldwide, including Japan, Taiwan, and the U.S.S.R. In April 1988 IDG forged the first publishing joint venture agreement with the Soviet Union to publish the quarterly *PC World U.S.S.R.* It was the first Soviet magazine on computer technology.

There was another computer magazine industry shakeout in 1989. In that year IDG folded or merged previously robust publications and closed *80 Micro* and *Macintosh Today.* The culprit was flat ad spending again, but this time readers were caught between generations of personal computers. Many publications were tied to aging computer systems such as the Commodore 64 or the Apple II, which were being eclipsed by newer systems. With the dramatic drop in the cost of personal computers in the early 1990s, many new users came into view, bringing with them different application needs. In 1989 the vast technological change within the industry meant consolidation and fallout. The worsening recession was an additional blow to ad revenues.

Continued Expansion During the 1990s

The 1980s ended with the fall of the Berlin Wall, and the floodgates to a new market were opened. In 1990 alone IDG launched new publishing operations in Yugoslavia, Czechoslovakia, Poland, Bulgaria, and Romania. Another magazine, *Manager,* was added to its Russian operations. Later, ventures were started up in Turkey, Slovenia, and Vietnam. In June 1990 IDG and Nigeria-based WENCA Technology began *PC World Africa.* It appeared on newsstands in 20 African nations. At that time, it was estimated that 15 percent of African businesses owned at least one personal computer. Also in 1990, IDG purchased the largest chain of PC-training schools in the United States, an expansion move away from the magazine market that led to the establishment of ExecuTrain, IDG's training subsidiary.

To complement its tradition of starting up magazines in-house, in the 1990s IDG began buying publishing units. The first of these was Lotus Publishing Corporation, based in Cambridge, Massachusetts, with estimated annual revenues of $10 million. Its publications included *Lotus,* a monthly magazine for Lotus customers with a circulation of 368,000, and Lotus books, which were published in conjunction with Simon & Schuster.

Also in 1990, IDG Books Worldwide Inc. was established to publish quality computer books around the world. Within its first 14 months, it had published more than five national bestsellers in its ... *For Dummies* series. In October 1991 it unveiled a new line of books published in association with Compaq Computer Corporation called Compaq Authorized Editions. The books were aimed at technical managers and developers as well as computer users.

For 1990 IDG had annual revenues of $620 million and 3,800 employees. It billed itself as the leading global provider of information services on information technology (IT). IDG Communications, its publishing subsidiary, published more than 150 newspapers and magazines in 49 countries. Its leading titles were *PC World, Infoworld, MacWorld, Lotus,* and *Computerworld.* International Data Corporation, IDG's research subsidiary, was a leading market research and analysis firm covering the computer field. World Expo Corporation, IDG's exposition management subsidiary, ran 48 computer-related exhibitions and conferences in 18 countries. IDG Books Worldwide Inc., established in 1990, was the publisher of the ... *For Dummies* series of books on computers and other topics among its other book publications.

In 1991 annual revenues rose to $770 million, and the company had 4,000 employees. It acquired *Electronic News* from Chilton Co. in 1991. *Electronic News,* launched in 1957, was the leading publication for corporate and operational management in the $100 billion worldwide electronics industry. One year after the acquisition, McGovern acknowledged that it was losing money, as much as $6 million a year according to one source. In 1992 McGovern cut the paper's budget and raised the subscription price.

In 1992 IDG purchased *Electronics International,* a 32-page weekly covering China's electronics industry. The publication began in 1986 with only four pages an issue. The electronics industry in China had been growing at a rate of ten percent a year since 1989. Also in 1992, IDG announced it would be folding *Lotus* into *PC World,* saying it would create the ''nation's largest computer magazine,'' a claim disputed by other publications. Since its acquisition, *Lotus* had not been performing well due to its limited readership. This announcement stiffened the competition between Ziff-Davis and IDG for the dominant position in computer-magazine publishing. Though IDG was ranked ahead of Ziff-Davis in 1992, Ziff-Davis's market share was increasing. When *Lotus* was combined with the much larger circulation magazine *PC World,* readership was boosted to 901,000 for the combined publications. Rival *PC Magazine,* published by Ziff-Davis, offered advertisers a readership of 900,000.

IDG and Ziff-Davis had different marketing styles. Where IDG served many market niches and published in more than 50 countries, Ziff-Davis focused on a few specific markets, such as IBM-compatible computers and mail-order computers, and published several titles for each market. It also operated in only three countries outside the United States—the United Kingdom, France, and Germany—and licensed nearly 20 publications in Asia and other European countries. In terms of advertising dollars, Ziff-Davis claimed a 37 percent share of the computer magazine industry's $871 million in U.S. advertising dollars, while IDG lagged with a 27 percent share. One industry analyst estimated that Ziff-Davis's *PC Magazine* had advertising revenues of $200 million annually, compared with *PC World'* s ad revenue of $60 million.

Combining *Lotus* with *PC World* was part of IDG's response to flat ad sales in 1992. It closed, combined, and sold off other magazines. Many of its periodicals were low-risk, small-circulation computer magazines serving a diversity of markets. The trend among advertisers was to favor large-circulation periodicals, causing IDG to re-examine some of its smaller publications. For example, it sold *Digital News,* a periodical for users of computers made by Digital Equipment Corp. Advertising had been falling at a rate of 20 percent a year. *Computer Buying World* was merged with *Info World,* a magazine aimed at corporate personal-computer professionals.

During 1992 IDG increased its focus on government computer users by forming the Government Information Technology Group. The new group merged Information Strategies Group, an information technology research and consulting firm, and FCW Publishing Corp., which published *Federal Computer Week.* Kenneth Kaplan, CEO of FCW and publisher of *Federal Computer Week,* was named CEO of the new group. At the time of the announcement, McGovern noted that various levels of government in the United States represented a $38 billion information technology business with specialized information needs.

IDG expanded internationally in 1992 by launching three national editions of *PC World* in Asia: *PC World Hong Kong, PC World Singapore,* and *PC World Malaysia.* They brought the total number of publications in the IDG family to 181 periodicals in 58 countries. IDG already published national editions of *Computerworld* in those three locations. Locally written, managed, and produced, the three new editions of *PC World,* like other IDG periodicals, would have access to the IDG News Service, which linked the company's journalists around the world. IDG published about 20 periodicals in Asia with the addition of these three new ones. Later in 1992 it launched *PC World Vietnam.*

In 1993 IDG continued to launch new publications and published a total of 194 computer newspapers and magazines in 62 countries by mid-year. Annual revenues were around $800 million. As was the case for several years, McGovern owned 65 percent of the privately held company, and its employees owned the rest.

Revenues Reached $980 Million in 1994

Fiscal 1994, ending September 30, was the best financial year to date in the company's history. At the end of the fiscal year, Kelly Conlin, formerly with the IDG Marketing Services Division, was promoted to president. James Casella, former president and chief operating officer of *InfoWorld,* was promoted to chief operating officer of IDG. Annual revenues were more than $980 million, and the company's international workforce had grown to 6,800 employees. It published more than 220 newspapers and magazines in 64 countries. The book division, IDG Books Worldwide, was experiencing tremendous growth with its ... *For Dummies* series and had its books translated into more than 25 languages. Toward the end of 1994, IDG Books Worldwide announced the publication of the first Compaq Press book, *The Internet.* It was an easy-to-read guide for computer users. The IDG News Service, which served the staffs of the company's publications, received a boost when IDG and *Business Wire* entered into a strategic marketing alliance whereby *Business Wire* would deliver high-tech news to all of IDG's high-tech publications and research offices throughout the world.

In 1996 revenues exceeded $1.7 billion. The number of company periodicals had increased to 275, and IDG Books had some 450 titles in print. World Expo Corporation produced some 90 computer-related expositions in 35 countries. International Data Corporation had expanded into 51 offices in 43 countries. IDG's operating companies had more than 135 web sites.

In 1997 IDG hoped to expand its periodical base by addressing the emerging digital industry, especially that involving "the intersection of technology, the Internet, entertainment, and media," according to a company announcement. It established a new business unit and hired as its head John Battelle, cofounder of *Wired* magazine and a key executive in the development of that publication. IDG had been building its computer content on the web with more than 140 web sites spanning more than 50 countries. It introduced IDG.net, which gave readers access to content, and IDG Global Web Ad Network, which gave advertisers access to a wide range of computer buyers on the web. New publication launches included *JavaWorld, Netscape World, The Web,* and more than 50 others internationally.

At the same time that Apple Computer Inc. announced it would enter into a partnership with Microsoft Corporation, IDG and Ziff-Davis announced they would restructure *Macworld,* an IDG monthly, and *MacUser,* a Ziff-Davis weekly, under a joint venture called Mac Publications LLC. The consolidation was due in part to falling ad revenues and Apple's declining share of the desktop PC market. *Macworld* claimed a paid audience of 625,000, while *MacUser* controlled a circulation base of 100,000.

For fiscal 1997 IDG announced revenues of $2.05 billion. The company had more than 9,000 employees worldwide. IDG Books Worldwide had more than 500 titles in print in 38 languages. IDG.net had grown to 210 web sites in 52 countries. IDG World Expo was producing more than 110 conferences and expositions in 35 countries. ExecuTrain, the company's training subsidiary, offered more than 320 training courses in more than 180 locations. International Data Corporation, the company's original research arm, had research centers in more than 41 countries and more than 400 research analysts.

There appeared to be no limit to how much IDG could grow. In April 1998 it launched *Industry Standard,* a news magazine of the Internet economy. Developed by Patrick McGovern and John Battelle, it was the newest of IDG's 285 magazines and newspapers. An online version was available at www.thestandard.net.

Principal Subsidiaries

IDG Communications Inc.; IDG Books Worldwide Inc.; IDG.net; International Data Corporation; IDG World Expo Corporation; ExecuTrain; IDG Marketing Services.

Further Reading

Armstrong, David, ''A New Read on the Net,'' *San Francisco Examiner,* April 26, 1998.

Bates, Betsy, ''International Data Group Launches Three Asian Magazines,'' *Business Wire,* May 19, 1992.

Berman, Mike, ''Compaq and IDG Books Launch Computer Book Series with Easy-to-Read Internet Guide,'' *Business Wire,* November 10, 1994.

Berman, Mike, et al., ''Compaq, IDG Books Launch New Book Series to Provide Authoritative Computer Reference Guides,'' *Business Wire,* October 10, 1991.

Creighton, Heidi, ''IDG Appoints Wired Magazine Co-Founder CEO of New Digital Industry Business Unit,'' *PR Newswire,* July 22, 1997.

Day, Kathy, ''IDG Launches IntraNet Magazine in South Africa,'' *PR Newswire,* January 24, 1997.

Dolaher, Mary, ''International Data Group Announces Conlin Is New President; Casella to Be Chief Operating Officer,'' *PR Newswire,* September 26, 1994.

Geoghegan, Joan, and Richard Eckel, ''IDG Purchases Lotus Publishing,'' *Business Wire,* January 11, 1991.

Goldfisher, Alastair, ''Publishers Combine Resources on Mac Magazines,'' *Business Journal-San Jose,* August 18, 1997.

Hemp, Paul, ''The United Nations of Computer Publishing: IDG Has Spawned Family of 194 Titles in 62 Countries,'' *Boston Globe,* June 1, 1993, p. 33.

Hyatt, Josh, ''International Data to Extend Health Benefits,'' *Boston Globe,* December 12, 1992, p. 75.

——, ''Is Boston's Computer Magazine Magnate in a Bind?,'' *Boston Globe,* September 22, 1992, p. 39.

Kaplan, Kenneth N., ''IDG Expands Commitment to Government Market,'' *Business Wire,* September 11, 1992.

Lissauer, Michael, ''Business Wire Announces Strategic Marketing Alliance with IDG International Services,'' *Business Wire,* September 19, 1994.

O'Reilly, Priscilla, and Betsy Bates, ''IDG Acquires Electronic News,'' *Business Wire,* November 4, 1991.

—updated by David Bianco

International Multifoods Corporation

International Multifoods Corporation

200 East Lake Street
Wayzata, Minnesota 55391-1662
U.S.A.
(612) 594-3300
Fax: (612) 340-3338
Web site: http://www.multifoods.com

Public Company
Incorporated: 1892 as New Prague Flouring Mill
Company
Employees: 7,100
Sales: $2.61 billion (1997)
Stock Exchanges: New York
Ticker Symbol: IMC
SICs: 2038 Frozen Specialties, Not Elsewhere Classified;
2053 Frozen Bakery Products Except Bread; 2041
Flour & Other Grain Mill Products; 2045 Prepared
Flour Mixes & Doughs; 2024 Ice Cream & Frozen
Desserts; 5141 Groceries—General Line; 2000 Food
& Kindred Products; 2038 Frozen Specialties, Not
Elsewhere Classified; 2051 Bread, Cake & Related
Products; 2037 Frozen Fruits & Vegetables; 2053
Frozen Bakery Products Except Bread

International Multifoods Corporation was once known as one of the "Big Three" in U.S. flour milling, along with General Mills and Pillsbury. But the company has undergone sweeping restructuring strategies—first diversifying heavily into consumer foods and animal feeds in the 1970s and early 1980s, then divesting itself of such interests (including its stake in the U.S. portion of its original product, Robin Hood flour) and fortifying its stake in the food vending industry in the late 1980s and early 1990s. In the late 1990s, International Multifoods was composed of three business units: Multifoods Distribution Group, North America Foods, and Venezuela Foods. To emphasize its global interests, the company has adopted the signature of "International Multifoods."

The Multifoods Distribution division accounts for 67 percent of all International Multifoods sales and 34 percent of its earn-

ings. Vendors Supply of America, Inc., or VSA, is the most dynamic component of the group—the domestic leader in vending distribution, it has nearly $1 billion in annual sales. Sales are almost evenly divided between foodservice and vending distribution. Since its acquisition in 1984, VSA has grown rapidly in what remains a highly fragmented market; its continuing health is welcome news to International Multifoods shareholders, many of whom consider the bold move by Archer-Daniels-Midland to acquire, in 1990, a 9.4 percent investment in the once floundering company as a singularly auspicious development.

The North America Foods Group is composed of the Robin Hood Foods unit, in Canada, and the U.S. Foods unit which provides frozen bakery items and mixes for various bakeries and foodservice vendors throughout the country. This group employed almost 2,000 people in the late 1990s, and was comprised of more than 45 sales and marketing offices in North America.

The third group in the International Multifoods family is Venezuela Foods. Located in the Caribbean port city of Puerto Cabello and christened Molinos Nacionales, C.A. (MONACA), its wheat mill was established in the mid-1950s. MONACA was initially a subsidiary of Robin Hood Flour Mills, Ltd., of Canada. Under the early direction of Andre Gillet, MONACA quickly became a leading Venezuelan food corporation, branching out into rice processing, corn milling, spices, bakery mixes, oat cereals, and animal feeds. Most importantly, MONACA was eminently profitable from the beginning, typically contributing 20 to 30 percent of total earnings on only eight to ten percent of net sales. In the late 1990s, MONACA accounted for approximately "14 percent of the company's local sales and 25 percent of operating earnings," according to an International Multifoods document. Consumer foods comprised half of the unit's sales, with animal feeds and commercial foods coming in second and third. MONACA was credited with great profitability because of efficiency in production and distribution. Costs were kept low, and brand recognition was high among consumers.

Origins in the 1890s

International Multifoods traces its roots to the Polar Star Milling Company, an initially prosperous southern Minnesota business that was unable to weather the soaring railroad freight rates and plunging flour prices of the early 1890s. When the Faribault-based company declared bankruptcy in 1891, owner Francis Atherton Bean was destitute but not despairing. The following year, with a loan from his brother-in-law, the 50-year-old Bean rented a mill located in New Prague, Minnesota, that had also gone out of business. Due to a close-knit, cooperative atmosphere and the wheat-buying and accounting expertise of Bean's son, F. A. Bean, Jr., the New Prague Flouring Mill Company became a success within a few short years. In 1896, the former owner decided to reclaim and manage the mill; again undaunted, Bean attracted more than $30,000 in capital from local investors and constructed a new mill, which operated under the same name. Increased production and storage capacity as well as an improved location were among the key factors that allowed Bean to expand in the next few years and purchase additional mills in Blue Earth and Wells, Minnesota.

In 1908 the company launched its first, and one of its most successful, international ventures with the purchase of the McLean Mill in Moose Jaw, then the largest city in Saskatchewan, Canada. Given a growing population, rich agricultural land, and dependable railway lines, Bean, Sr., saw considerable potential for the business. The McLean Mill opened the following year as Saskatchewan Flour Mills Ltd., and the parent company now became International Milling and thus commanded heightened status at home, despite its still primarily regional thrust. Bean's vision was confirmed three years later when the company purchased another mill in Calgary, Alberta. Expansion continued and the Canadian operations were soon renamed Robin Hood Flour Mills, Ltd., a designation reflecting the rising popularity of the company's brand name flour which was first introduced around 1910 exclusively for the Canadian markets.

According to several accounts, perhaps the high point for the company's founder came at Christmas time in 1911 when Bean decided to secretly visit, over a two-week period, all the yet unpaid creditors of the failed Polar Star business from back in 1890. Although he had no legal obligation to do so, Bean resurrected and satisfied all the old bills in full, paying both principal and interest for what amounted to more than $200,000. In so doing, he not only ensured himself an unforgettable Christmas, he also secured his place as one of the most loved and respected of all Minnesota entrepreneurs.

The Move to Minneapolis, the 1920s

In 1923 the company moved its headquarters to Minneapolis in order to become a major national competitor in the flour-milling industry. To accommodate the northward flow of Kansas winter wheat, the company acquired mills in Sioux City and Davenport, Iowa. It also realized that other similar-sized Minnesota "interior mills," including the Commander group (later Commander-Larabee Corporation), centered in Montgomery, were quickly gaining a foothold in the Minneapolis flour district. By the mid-1920s, at least 17 such companies had entered this industry center. Equally important to millers, particularly those interested in establishing a presence in the East and a gateway to the European export trade, was Buffalo, New York, which International Milling succeeded in entering by the end of the decade.

The Robin Hood Brand and Mid-Century Growth

Meanwhile in Canada, under the leadership of Charles Ritz, Robin Hood Flour was attaining national distribution, promoting itself as a high quality, "milled from washed wheat" flour and successfully pricing itself above the competition. By 1945, Robin Hood would become the leading consumer flour in Canada, a position it has never since relinquished. This marketing-success-in-the-making inspired Bean's successor, W. L. Harvey, to bring the Robin Hood name to the United States, along with its chief architect. Beginning in 1937, Ritz replaced the company's several regional brands with Robin Hood and then launched a full-scale media blitz, going head-to-head with two chief competitors, Pillsbury's Best Flour and General Mills's Gold Medal Flour. Because of Robin Hood's late entry into the market, results of the long-running campaign were disappointing. As Atherton Bean, grandson of the founder and the company's fifth president later remarked, "There is an adage in the industry. You can be first or second and be confident of success, but if you're third or fourth you're at risk." Unfortunately, that was the position of Robin Hood Flour in the United States. International Milling, nevertheless, became a formidable foe in the industrial flour market, and from the war years through the 1950s, with the purchase of 15 mills, the company spread into a number of new markets in the central and eastern regions of the country. Beginning in 1951, the company also entered the formula feed business and became a major supplier of enriched grains to livestock farmers in the Upper Midwest.

Focus on Venezuela, 1958

In 1958 International Milling, which had been exporting not only to Europe, but also Africa, the Middle East, Asia, and South America, made a momentous decision: to extract itself from markets with political and economic difficulties and focus on one that promised both stability and lucrative returns. The obvious choice at the time was Venezuela, a solid export market—of which the company controlled more than a third—that remained virgin territory for North American investment. The decision was aided by the Venezuelan government's threat in 1956 to close off the import trade; by promising to establish its own wheat mill within the country, the company circumvented the potential loss of market.

Andre Gillet's tenure at MONACA extended until his return to Minneapolis in 1968, and it coincided with Francis Atherton Bean's presidency and chairmanship of the company. The 1960s saw considerable shifts in domestic eating habits and International Milling—with the extra capital supplied by going public in 1964—responded by aggressively entering the consumer foods markets. This policy of expansion and diversification, which was common in the industry, was officially implemented by William G. Phillips, a former president of Glidden-Durkee whom Bean hand-picked to restructure the company. Phillips oversaw some 43 acquisitions during the next decade and soon had a multifaceted company (signified by its new name of International Multifoods, adopted in 1970), operating more than 900 Mister Donuts stores, the Boston Sea Party restaurant chain, a meat-processing plant, several decorative products manufacturers, and a score of small, niche-market food products.

Restructuring During the 1980s

By 1980, the company reported revenues exceeding one billion dollars. Throughout a 15-year period stretching until 1984, the company reported uninterrupted growth in earnings. Yet such signs were misleading. Long before the 1984 decline, the company had become aware of its lagging market shares in nearly all its consumer products; only Kretschmer Wheat Germ represented a market-leading product. International Multifoods' ability to compete with the major food corporations was hampered not only by its relative anonymity among consumers but also by its seemingly indiscriminate purchases.

Restructuring was in order and Phillips appointed Gillet to handle the daunting task of reshaping the now ungainly corporate giant International Multifoods had become. Complicating matters was the looming threat of an unfriendly takeover and the disgruntlement of shareholders, obliged to accept a less than ten percent return on equity while the industry average was close to 20 percent. The metamorphosis that Gillet effected during the next several years was, according to analyst Jim McCartney, "one of the deftest sleight of hand tricks in corporate America's history. By quietly selling off pieces and buying new ones, Gillet gradually transformed Multifoods from a flour milling and consumer foods company into a food service distribution and manufacturing company." Gone was the U.S. portion of Robin Hood Flour, the cornerstone of the company (the U.S. trademark rights were sold to General Mills and the mills themselves to ConAgra, though international Robin Hood operations remained), as well as a host of other less substantial enterprises. In their place was a list of food purveyors that promised a new synergy and direction for the company. The single most important purchase International Multifoods made at the time was the 1984 acquisition of Denver-based Vendors Supply of America. A vending distributor with $900 million in annual sales, VSA was bought for $15 million and then carefully developed into a convenient one-stop supplier to vending operators, with 20 warehouses serving 48 states. The foodservice industry that VSA catered to had by the early 1990s blossomed into a $262 billion market.

The Luiso Years, 1989–96

From 1989 to 1996, Gillet's visionary lead was followed by the cost-conscious programs of CEO Anthony Luiso, a former executive of Beatrice and a veteran of the food trade. Luiso joined International Multifoods in 1986 as head of restaurant supply operations and contributed to a 21 percent rise in revenues, which totaled $1.7 billion; profits for the same year vaulted 82 percent to $33 million. One of the toughest decisions

Luiso faced concerned the fate of MONACA. Despite outstanding earnings in 1990 (25 percent of total operating earnings on only nine percent of net sales), or for that matter a lengthy record of strong performance, MONACA had long been thought to be vulnerable to the inflation-prone economy of Venezuela. In addition, several analysts came to view the flour-and feeds-processor as a cumbersome appendage for International Multifoods. With little fanfare, Luiso resigned from International Multifoods in May 1996. Tony Kennedy of the *Star Tribune* characterized Luiso's seven years of corporate shuffling as "mostly ineffective restructuring.... It has been more than five years since the stock sold for more than $30." Six months after Luiso stepped down as CEO of International Multifoods, Gary Costley came on board, wooed away from a deanship at Wake Forest University's Babcock School of Business. With many years of service at Kellogg's, Costley was not just an ivory tower visionary. The board of directors wanted action taken to boost the stock earnings of International Multifoods, and Costley was going to deliver it.

Looking to the Future

Looking ahead to the 21st century, International Multifoods could be expected to focus increasingly on shareholder value. Once tagged "the wallflower of Wall Street," International Multifoods was by the late 1990s a rejuvenated company, promising a solid commitment to its shareholders. The critical element for Costley was EVA. An invention of the New York consulting firm Stern Stewart & Co., EVA stood for "extra value added." As Costley put it in the *Saint Paul Pioneer Press,* "If an asset doesn't contribute to shareholder value, I get rid of it." To arrive at the EVA figure, one must multiply net assets by return on assets minus the cost of capital. As a business academic Costley had become an EVA disciple, and the chairmanship of International Multifoods might be thought the perfect practical test case. On one of his first days at Multifoods Tower, the old International Multifoods headquarters in Minneapolis, Costley admired a painting in the boardroom. Someone volunteered that it was worth $100,000, to which Costley said, "Sell it." He rounds out his support of EVA by explaining, "Money is not free. If you want to use someone else's money, you have to pay for it," as reported in the *Pioneer Press* article "From Theory to Practice." "If it takes more and more assets to make the same amount of money, you are destroying shareholder value." The new company headquarters made better economic sense to Costley without his losing face. The new building was smaller and smarter, modeled on the English manor style, and set in suburban Wayzata, Minnesota. While the company decided to buy the building, Costley continued to cut corners by vowing to lease any surplus space.

Costley's management style resulted in a more efficient and profitable International Multifoods. Perhaps the best way to evaluate Costley's initial success was to look at annual earnings per share of International Multifoods: bounced up from 15 cents in February 1997 to $1.09 a year later. But Costley reported that in 1998, International Multifoods had a negative EVA of $42 million. Efforts to boost EVA included a realignment of the North American Foods business unit, splicing the VSA and Specialty Distribution into one distribution unit, naming Jeffrey Boies as the president of that new group, and rebranding Multifoods as International Multifoods, complete with a new corporate logo. While Costley hoped to show a rapid EVA improvement to his investors, the price of International Multifoods shares had already soared. The merest mention of EVA "causes investors' hearts to go pitter patter," said Gail MarksJarvis, the *Pioneer Press*'s business columnist. Whether or not EVA would eventually be proven a fad, it was a sign of economic discipline in a corporate chairman, and a tool to provide the shareholders with the best return possible. International Multifoods was now positioned by Costley to be a lean contender well into the 21st century.

Principal Subsidiaries

Fantasia Confections, Inc.; JAC Creative Foods, Inc.; Mexicana de Inversiones FEMAC, S.A. de C.V. (45%); Mixco Intl., S.A. de C.V. (49%); Molinos Nacionales, C.A. (MONACA); Multifoods Bakery Distributors, Inc.; Multifoods Bakery International, Inc.; Prepared Foods, Inc.; Robin Hood Flour Ltd. (Canada); Vendors Supply of America, Inc.

Principal Operating Units

Multifoods Distribution Group; North America Foods; Venezuela Foods.

Further Reading

"Burritos, Anyone?" *Forbes,* March 18, 1991.

Carideo, Anthony, "Food Firm Serves up a Menu of Good News," *Star Tribune,* July 1, 1991.

"Corporate Identity Program Increases Awareness of Multifoods," *Impact* (for Multifoods Employees Worldwide), November 18, 1975.

Egerstrom, Lee, "Multifoods Misunderstood Despite Its Improvements," *St. Paul Pioneer Press,* September 30, 1991.

——, "Multifoods Names Ex-Kellogg Executive As New Leader," *Saint Paul Pioneer Press,* November 5, 1996.

"From Theory to Practice," *Saint Paul Pioneer Press,* September 28, 1997.

Hobart, Randall, "Multifoods Changes Symbol to Reflect Increasing Diversity," *Minneapolis Star,* June 23, 1971.

Houston, Patrick, "Multifoods Is Ditching Its 'Mishmash of Little Businesses'," *Business Week,* September 22, 1986.

"International Multifoods Announces Executive Promotions," April 23, 1998, http://www.wdc.com/new/releases.

"International Multifoods Corp. Company Briefing Book" *Wall Street Journal,* http://interactive.wsj.com/inap-bin/bb, 1998.

"International Multifoods Corporation," *Corporate Report Minnesota,* February, 1992.

Johnson, Ken, "Mixing It Up at Multifoods," *Corporate Report,* March, 1975.

Johnson, Tim, "Multifoods Takes Measures," *CityBusiness,* May 22, 1998.

Kennedy, Tony, "Multifoods Buys Frozen Products Firm in Canada," *Star Tribune,* April 28, 1992.

——, "Multifoods CEO Luiso Resigns," *Star Tribune,* May 18, 1996.

——, "Multifoods Stockholders Want Company to Get Rid of 'Poison Pill'," *Star Tribune,* June 27, 1992.

——, "Multifoods Unveils New Corporate Logo," *Star Tribune,* May 14, 1992.

Kuhlmann, Charles Byron, "The Growth of the Milling Industry After 1890—The Minneapolis District," *The Development of the Flour-Milling Industry in the United States,* Boston and New York, Houghton Mifflin Company, 1929.

Larson, Don W., "Grain and Flour Milling," *Land of the Giants: A History of Minnesota Business,* Minneapolis, Dorn Books, 1979.

Madden, Stephen, "On the Rise: Anthony Luiso, 44," *Fortune,* August 15, 1988.

Marks Jarvis, Gail, "Three Little Words Buoy Multifoods," *Saint Paul Pioneer Press,* April 17, 1997.

Mason, Ralph, "City Firm Building Mill in Venezuela," *Minneapolis Star,* February 28, 1958.

Mattson, Beth, "A Corporate-Image Makeover," *Twin Cities Business Monthly,* December 1997.

McCartney, Jim, "Repackaging International Multifoods," *St. Paul Pioneer Press,* August 14, 1989.

"Multifoods Appoints Costley to Be Its CEO, President, Chairman," *Wall Street Journal,* November 5, 1996.

"Multifoods Attributes 39 Percent Increase in Earnings to Improving Businesses," *Star Tribune,* April 18, 1991.

"Multifoods Beginnings Weren't International," *Skyway News,* May 31, 1983.

Multifoods Today: Building Tomorrow Together, 1892—1992, Minneapolis, International Multifoods, 1992.

"Once Bankrupt Firm Now Second in Field," *Minneapolis Tribune,* October 17, 1954.

Richard, Diane, "Multifoods' New Syllabus," *CityBusiness,* June 20, 1997.

Wieffering, Eric J., "Multifoods Makeover," *Corporate Report Minnesota,* August 1990.

"William Phillips and Andre Gillet Head up International Multifoods," *Skyway News,* April 5, 1983.

Youngblood, Dick, "Multifoods Buys Largest Maker of Wall Accessories," *Minneapolis Tribune,* October 27, 1972.

—Jay P. Pederson
—updated by Christine Ferran

Jalate Inc.

1675 South Alameda Street
Los Angeles, California 90021
U.S.A.
(213) 765-5000
Fax: (213) 765-5020
Web site: http://www.air-shop.com

Public Company
Incorporated: 1987
Employees: 138
Sales: $51.2 million (1997)
Stock Exchanges: American
Ticker Symbol: JLT
SICs: 2253 Knit Outerwear Mills; 2330 Women's & Misses' Outerwear; 2335 Dresses—Women's, Misses, & Juniors; 2339 Womens, Misses, & Jr. Outerwear, Not Elsewhere Classified; 2361 Dresses, Blouses, & Shirts, Girls; 2369 Outerwear Girls, Not Elsewhere Classified

Jalate Inc. is a well-known designer, developer, manufacturer, and marketer of moderately priced women's knit sportswear, dresses, woven sportswear, and other apparel, primarily in junior sizes, under the "Jalate" label; dresses under the "Zanoni" label; and children's apparel under the "Jalate Kids" label. Other labels have included "Lajate," "Pottery," and "Missy." The company also manufactures women's apparel for certain retailers under their own private labels. The company's line consists of baby T-shirts, button-down blouses, halters, vests, trendy cut dresses for all seasons, and hip, high-fashioned jackets in various colors and patterns.

The company's products have been seen on popular television shows such as *Moesha*, *Grace Under Fire*, *Baywatch*, *Sweet Valley High*, *Saved by the Bell*, *7th Heaven*, MTV's *Austin Stories* and *Singled Out*, and movies such as *Scream 2: The Sequel* and *Primary Colors*. Other top women's apparel firms the company has competed against have included Marisa Christina Inc., Norton McNaughton Inc., and The Sirena Apparel Group Inc.

The Beginning of Jalate, 1987

Jalate Ltd. was founded in 1987 by Larry Brahim, Theodore B. Cooper, and Jan Grossman. Beginning in 1992 and continuing on through the end of the 20th century, the women's apparel industry experienced a decline in consumer demand and a continuing trend in consumer preference for value-priced products. The result of such changes was a consolidation among apparel retailers, with a concurrent increase in competition, as well as consolidation in the retail market as department store chains began eating each other up. Total revenue for the following year, 1993, reached $38.3 million, with net income of $1.6 million.

The company had a good year in 1994, with aggressive sales in all product lines (knits, sportswear, and dresses, as well as in its private label segment), and the company moving to utilize more local contractors for manufacturing, allowing better service than overseas production and also holding down costs that would be entailed in building a larger production force. That year, the company also commenced foreign manufacturing of products as a direct response to increased competition by importers for budget-priced products; created a new woven sportswear division called "Pottery"; reduced its reliance upon apparel specialty stores for sales; and expanded its management information systems (MIS) and computerized marketing and grading equipment.

The company became public in March 1994 through the sale of 900,000 shares of stock in an initial public offering, changing its name to Jalate Inc. in the process. First quarter sales grew 59.3 percent to $14.3 million from $9 million. The Jalate knit division accounted for 44 percent of the volume; "Zanoni," the dress line, contributed 37 percent; and the new "Pottery" division accounted for 19 percent.

In November 1994, the company began the development of a manufacturing joint venture in California as equal limited partners with Linroz Manufacturing Company L.P., an affiliate of the company's largest sewing contractor, Lebr Associates

---

Inc., in order to improve efficiency, quality, and cost of its products. Over the next year, the company purchased sewing machines and other ancillary equipment for the joint venture, and operations commenced in May 1995.

Total revenue for 1994 jumped to $63.9 million, with net income of $1.9 million as the Jalate brand knit and kid's sportswear division accounted for 50 percent of sales, with the Zanoni dress division at 33 percent, and private label at 17 percent.

Early in 1995, the company began replacing its "Lajate" brand of sportswear and "Zanoni" brand of dresses with the "Jalate" name. Products began to be manufactured by the company itself in a new 90,000-square-foot cutting and sewing facility, bringing in-house products that, for the most part, had been manufactured in independent cutting and sewing contractors in the Los Angeles area, lowering the company's total operating expenses. The "Zanoni" dress division began importing more and getting better margins, and ended up accounting for some 27 percent of the company's annual sales that year, as compared to the "Lajate" brand name, which brought in nearly 50 percent. Additionally, the company took steps to improve its administrative production, distribution, financial reporting, human resources, and MIS capabilities, and expanded its product development division, which was responsible for designing, developing, and manufacturing under private labels.

But, despite all of the positive steps it took, by September, after poor second quarter results (a loss of $651,000), the company downsized in order to focus on its core "Jalate" and "Zanoni" junior sportswear and dress brands, and changed its manufacturing strategy. The "Pottery" and "Missy" divisions were cut back, and the company cut nearly a third of its full-time work force.

The year would continue to be brutal as the junior market became sluggish and retail conditions weakened, leading to lower gross margins and higher operating expenses throughout the industry. Additionally, since the women's apparel business is driven by season, historically, sales by apparel manufacturers to retailers have been lower in the fourth calendar quarter than in the other three quarters, as a result of reduced purchases by retailers for delivery in the month of December.

All of this, combined with continued consolidation in the retail industry, reflected in the numbers for Jalate, as the company, forced to mark down prices to rouse some competition, took a fourth quarter loss despite a 28 percent sales surge,

ending the year losing $2.9 million, as sales for the entire year advanced 14 percent to $78.5 million.

Despite the rough retail environment, three of the company's competitors—Marisa Christina Inc., Norton McNaughton Inc., and The Sirena Apparel Group Inc.—performed well, attributing their success to strong demand for their brand names and good relationships with their retail customers. Norton McNaughton, a manufacturer of moderate-priced career apparel—saw its sales reach nearly $220 million, up from $168.6 million in 1994. Sirena Apparel Group—with its "Anne Klein," "Kathy Ireland," "Sirena," and other brand names of swimwear and other apparel—had sales reach $49.2 million, up more than 26 percent over 1994.

Plagued by the hard year and quarterly losses, the company needed a change, which it soon received. In December of that year, Vinton W. Bacon (who had been serving the company as a consultant since July of that year, and previously was a principal of The Sonoma Group, a management consulting firm specializing in corporate turnarounds, and chairman and CEO of Safeguard Business Systems), took the helm of the wandering company, being named CEO and president, succeeding Brahim, who remained chairman and became executive vice-president of sales for the company's Zanoni dress division. Additionally, COO Cooper became executive vice-president of sales for the Jalate knit sportswear division.

In 1996, the company started a children's clothing line called "Jalate Kids" which took the retail market by storm. The line of tops, bottoms, and coordinates for ages seven to 14, as well as toddlers, had an initial order of nearly a half million dollars. By the end of the year, orders and backlog would reach nearly $3 million and were available in more than 2,800 outlets representing 12 accounts, such as Penney's, Dillard's, Nordstrom, Macy's, and Bloomingdales.

Also that year, the company implemented improved shipping procedures and managed markdowns; improved gross profit margins; began increasing its total import program; and hired a sweater designer early in 1997 to work on both the sportswear and the dress divisions. The "Pottery" and "Missy" divisions were discontinued as the company attempted to focus on its core product lines. Nevertheless, total revenue for 1996 slipped to $54 million, with a net income of $27,000.

By 1997, the retail market further consolidated, consumer demand dropped, and clothing manufacturers were forced to repeatedly lower their prices to remain competitive. That year, the company continued to develop the "Kids" line of clothing, which ended the year with some $3.9 million in gross sales. Additionally, the company began the installation of an integrated production, shipping, and financial information system. However, troubles continued as the company was forced to close its "Missy" division, as profits in that realm continued to slip, and cofounder, Executive Vice-President, and Director Theodore Cooper resigned in November.

Also in November of that year, Jalate acquired a 40 percent equity interest in the New York-based junior women's apparel design and marketing firm Airshop Ltd., which sold apparel and accessory products through an Internet web site (air-shop.com), and mail-order catalogs. The company also received 100 percent of Airshop's convertible preferred stock.

Jalate invested nearly half a million dollars over the following 18 months for the rights to market the exclusive Airshop private label, including product development, and outside contracting for shipping and telemarketing, all of which had been done in-house by the latter; in addition, the company began the marketing of its own products via the web site and catalogs.

Airshop was incorporated in July 1996, began operations in early 1997, and immediately became the number one site at the virtual mall, fashionmall.com, producing 75 percent of all sales at the mall, receiving nearly 1,500 requests for catalogs per week, with a total of over 1.5 million hits on its web site per month. As requests for print catalogs became overwhelming, Airshop expanded into the direct mail-order catalog business, sending out 50,000 catalogs of its first issue in September 1997 and over 150,000 holiday catalogs in November. With that kind of distribution, Airshop's ''Dollhouse Voyage'' dresses were being marketed as far away as Moscow, and its ''Hula Shaker'' tee shirts were finding their way to Bangkok. But, still in its start-up phase, the subsidiary nevertheless posted a loss of $296,000 on the year, with total revenue for Jalate in 1997 slipping again to $51.2 million, with a net loss of $4.5 million.

February 1998 saw another cofounder and director, Vice-President Jan Grossman, resign. Several months later, in April, the company signed a letter of intent to merge with Los Angeles-based competitor Chorus Line Corp., a privately held $150 million manufacturer of women's dresses, in a transaction which would have created a firm with combined annual sales of approximately $225 million, bringing Chorus Line labels ''Jazz Sport,'' ''All That Jazz,'' ''Molly Malloy,'' ''More Jazz,'' and ''Jazz Kids'' together with the ''Jalate,'' ''Zanoni,'' and ''Jalate Kids'' names. ''Tickets,'' Chorus Line's denim dress division, was closed at the end of 1996. By June, however, the

agreement was terminated, with both sides declining comment as to why the merger fell apart.

By May, the company's Airshop web site was receiving 25,000 requests for catalogs per week, but the company still posted a $398,000 non-operating loss on the subsidiary. First-quarter net sales dropped to $12.2 million (compared to $13.9 the previous year), with a net loss of $119,000.

As the company moved through the end of the 20th century and into the 21st, it continued to seek additional financing from outside sources to fund future operations.

Principal Subsidiaries

Airshop Ltd. (40%).

Further Reading

Brady, Jennifer L., and Thomas J. Ryan, ''3 Makers Bucking the Tide,'' *WWD*, September 18, 1995, p. 30.

''Chorus Line, Jalate Scrap Merger Plan,'' *WWD*, June 2, 1998, p. 2.

''Correction,'' *WWD*, April 16, 1998, p. 2.

Ellis, Kristi, ''Jalate Names New President, CEO,'' *WWD*, December 7, 1995, p. 14.

Ellis, Kristi, and Thomas J. Ryan, ''Jalate Signs Agreement to Acquire Chorus Line,'' *WWD*, April 15, 1998, p. 12.

''Jalate Invests in Airshop,'' *WWD*, November 13, 1997, p. 15.

''Jalate Ltd.,'' *Wall Street Journal*, May 18, 1998, p. C14(W)/B2(E).

''Jalate Ltd.,'' *WWD*, March 4, 1996, p. 23.

''Jalate Net, Sales Rise Sharply in First Quarter,'' *WWD*, May 18, 1994, p. 27.

''Jalate: Net Up, Outlook Uncertain,'' *WWD*, May 18, 1995, p. 8.

''Jalate Notes Quarter Loss, Downsizing Strategies,'' *WWD*, August 17, 1995, p. 13.

—Daryl F. Mallett

Jefferies Group, Inc.

11100 Santa Monica Boulevard
11th Floor
Los Angeles, California 90025
U.S.A.
(310) 445-1199
Fax: (310) 575-5165
Web site: http://www.jefo.com

Public Company
Incorporated: 1962 as Jefferies & Company
Employees: 1,086
Operating Revenues: $764.5 million (1997)
Stock Exchanges: New York
Ticker Symbol: JEF
SICs: 6211 Security Brokers & Dealers; 6719 Holding
   Companies, Not Elsewhere Classified

Jefferies Group, Inc. is a holding company for Jefferies & Company, Inc., a global investment bank focused on capital raising, research, mergers and acquisitions, and advisory and restructuring services for medium-sized companies. The company's reputation is built on successful trading in equity and taxable fixed income securities, convertible bonds, options, futures, and international securities for institutional clients. Situated in "Wall Street West," the company is based in Los Angeles, California, with 19 international offices.

Starting in a Phone Booth, 1962

The company was started in 1962 in a telephone booth at the Pacific Coast Stock Exchange by Boyd Jefferies. Jefferies, who had been a partner at Noble, Tulk, Marsh & Jefferies, borrowed $30,000 to launch his own operation. Jefferies had one employee, whom he directed as floor broker. The year 1962 was not an easy one in which to start a company: the stock market collapsed in June and fell again in August after the Cuban Missile Crisis, with an annual loss of over 79 points (the worst since 1931). Despite this difficult environment, Jefferies' first year was successful, and the company expanded its staff and

opened a real office, using a closed-circuit television and speaker box to link Boyd Jefferies with his office staff.

Jefferies' Niche: Third Market Trading

In the early years, Jefferies was extremely successful in its manipulation of the emerging "third market," which involved trading listed stocks in an over-the-counter style, providing an attractive anonymity to buyers who preferred to keep their interests from becoming public. For these clients, the stock exchange was too public and fixed commission rates were too high. Jefferies' third market offerings, on the other hand, provided privacy and negotiated commissions to banks, mutual funds, and other financial institutions.

In addition to the third market niche, Jefferies pioneered use of the split commission, or "give up," in 1964. The split commission meant that Jefferies could act on behalf of a client, charge full commission, and then share that commission with other brokerage firms that had worked with the client. This commission sharing helped Jefferies build and expand its market. Jefferies joined the Detroit, Midwest, Boston, and Philadelphia stock exchanges by 1965. In 1967, the company joined the New York stock exchange (NYSE), opening a five-person office in New York. From 1967 to 1968, the third market surged 40 percent in volume. The growing third market helped Jefferies become the seventh largest firm in size and trading on the NYSE.

Members of the NYSE were dismayed by the burgeoning third market, and campaigned to eliminate it. Exchange members felt that negotiated commission rates were destructive to free competition, that the third market was irresponsible, and that the market was fragmented. In 1969, a study of the structure of securities markets was conducted by former Federal Reserve Board Chairman William McChesney Martin, who recommended the elimination of the third market and the barring of institutions trading in the market from Big Board membership. The study was followed by SEC hearings on the issue.

The IDS Acquisition, 1969

Meanwhile, Jefferies & Company was acquired in 1969 by the Minneapolis-based Investors Diversified Services, Inc. (IDS), the second largest financial services company in the country at the time. Jefferies saw the acquisition as a means to bypass the restrictions of the NYSE and increase the size of its institutional business through sizeable capital outlay. The details of the acquisition called for an earnout, which meant that Jefferies & Company would receive shares of IDS preferred stock upon the condition that earnings met expectations for four years. If earnings achieved as planned, the deal would be valued at $45 million. Because IDS did not derive at least 50 percent of its gross income from broker-dealer operations, Jefferies had to quit the New York exchange under Exchange Rule 318. Unhampered by the concerns of NYSE members, Jefferies concentrated on third market business.

The economy entered a downturn in the 1970s. While other Wall Street companies made cutbacks, Jefferies actually increased its staff commission rates to 30 percent (the industry standard was 10–20 percent). The result was the attraction and retention of highly qualified staff in a difficult period. Jefferies returned to the regional exchanges, with the exception of New York. Texas became a new site of expansion in 1971, with an office opened in Dallas.

In 1971, the company reapplied for membership in the Big Board of the NYSE. Upon rejection (based on Rule 318), IDS and Jefferies filed an antitrust lawsuit against the exchange, seeking $6 million in damages. Jefferies and its parent company claimed that the NYSE Big Board was an illegal monopoly, and that exclusion had placed the company at a competitive disadvantage. In 1973, the presiding judge informed the NYSE that he planned to rule in Jefferies favor. Membership was opened to brokerage firms owned by other kinds of companies, so long as 80 percent of brokerage was conducted with the public. Jefferies rejoined the exchange in March 1973.

Jefferies had met financial expectations according to its ownership agreement with IDS for the first three years. However, an internal conflict of interest caused an earnings dip in 1973. Almost a third of Jefferies' previous clients were lost due to competition with IDS, which always competed with investment brokerages for the best price. For its part, IDS did not yield the expected capital to Jefferies, nor did it conduct any trades with the firm. In August 1973 Boyd Jefferies bought back his company over dinner for $2.5 million. The story of the Jefferies acquisition was the subject of a later case study at Harvard Business School.

Later that year, Jefferies & Company resigned from the Big Board, only to rejoin the following spring. The NYSE raised its commission rates, and Jefferies reentered the third market in full force. Management salaries and other expenses were cut back, and Jefferies began anew without IDS's parentage.

Rebuilding in the 1970s and 1980s

The mid-1970s marketplace continued to slump, and Congress moved to ease industry restrictions with the Exchange Act of 1975, finally signaling the end of fixed commission rates. As the third market became more attractive to many institutions, Jefferies was poised with familiarity and experience. By the late 1970s, many of Jefferies' clients who had left during the IDS period returned to the firm. In 1977, Jefferies had expanded with offices in Los Angeles, New York, Chicago, Dallas, Boston and Atlanta. The company was a top broker for regional banks including St. Louis Union Trust, Hartford National Bank & Trust, and First National Bank of Minneapolis, and for big volume companies including Citibank, Morgan Guaranty, and Bank of America.

Seeking to expand into the high-net-worth market, Jefferies Group, Inc. (the holding company for Jefferies & Company) took over and reorganized Wagenseller & Durst, a Los Angeles-based retail brokerage. The new company, W&D Securities, first offered secondary stocks and new issues, then became a clearing business for research, and ultimately served as a soft dollar firm, exchanging research activities for commissions.

In 1981, Jefferies achieved its largest transaction ever, a buyback called "the Mighty Mouse of block trading" by *Fortune* magazine. Jefferies assisted drug, food, and liquor conglomerate Foremost-McKesson in a $65 million buyback from industrialist Victor Posner. The company purchased its first computer in 1982, and became accessible 24 hours a day. In December 1982, the company began to take advantage of trading halts. When Warner Communications' Atari division announced losses, Warner trades were closed on the exchange, and Jefferies was the only company moving the stock. In two days, Jefferies traded about six million shares, generating business and new international clients. Later, Jefferies took advantage of similar halts in PepsiCo, Inc. and Alleghany Corporation.

The company went public on October 13, 1983, with an initial offering of 1.75 million shares at $13 per share. By 1984, according to *Business Week,* Jefferies was among the ten most profitable publicly held brokerages. International expansion during trade halts led the company to develop a new overseas office in London, headed by Frank Baxter. In 1986, Baxter became president and chief operating officer, returning to New York to manage the company. Later that year, Jefferies managed the first public trade transfer of ownership, trading 25.8 million shares of Allied Stores for Robert Campeau.

Managing a Crisis, 1987

After 25 years in business, the company reached a potentially disastrous turning point in 1987. Boyd Jefferies, founder and CEO, was charged by the government and the SEC with two securities violations: "parking" stock for customer Ivan Boesky and a customer margin violation. Jefferies pleaded guilty, receiving a fine and a probation barring him from the securities industry for five years. The company itself was not charged, but its brokerage unit was censured by the SEC. Jefferies resigned from the company. To make matters worse, the stock market crashed on

October 19, 1987. Plummeting prices led to a $6.5 million loss on the company's principal holdings. As the new CEO, Frank Baxter had quite a job on his hands.

Baxter's unique leadership style was peppered with personal idiosyncrasy. A disciple of New Age guru Deepak Chopra and an avid practitioner of transcendental meditation, Baxter installed a meditation room in Jefferies' headquarters (which was later closed for lack of use). On his desk sat framed photos of Mahatma Gandhi and Martin Luther King, Jr. Nicknamed "the smiling assassin," Baxter had a New Age demeanor covering a hard-edged business sense.

Baxter's first action was geared toward building staff morale in a time of crisis: he retained the company's name and implemented 20 percent bonuses for the company's 180 traders. The generosity worked: not one trader left the company. To compensate for a dip in business, Baxter cut costs by 15 percent through back office automation, and he limited capital use to $50 million (from $300 million in 1985). What could have been an institutional nightmare was salvaged by Baxter's shrewd managerial techniques. The company earned net income of $6.1 million in 1987, increasing that figure to $16 million (on sales of $145 million) in 1988. Shares rose from $7.50 in 1987 to $14.50 in mid-1989. By 1990, the company traded its highest-ever volume: 3.5 percent of the consolidated NYSE tape.

Rebirth and Diversification, Late 1980s–90s

In its second life, under Baxter's leadership, the company focused on diversification, delving beyond its third market niche. Baxter's expansion plans included global expansion in electronic trading, corporate finance, international convertible sales, and derivative sales (all of which were quick moneymakers). Jefferies moved quickly into the fourth market: off-exchange, computer-based (electronic) trading. In the fourth market, the broker's position was eliminated by the Portfolio System for Institutional Trading (POSIT), which traded portfolios and matched buyers and sellers automatically. POSIT was supplemented with the Quantitative Executive System (QUANTEX), which allowed traders to access buy and sell recommendations throughout the day. The company added a wholly owned subsidiary (Investment Technology Group) in 1987 to run POSIT. Jefferies' fourth market activities resulted in a new role for the firm's account executives, who were now referred to as JeffCAT, or Jefferies Computer Assisted Traders.

The high yield bond trading business was another new area for Jefferies' expansion, made possible by the collapse of Drexel Burnham Lambert. Jefferies hired 18 former Drexel employees and became one of the top three junk bond trading companies. Taxable fixed income (TFI) and corporate finance departments made Jefferies capable of handling bank debt capabilities and products. By 1992, junk bonds became the company's second most profitable sector. That year, the company made plans to open a Hong Kong office. In 1993, the company landed its first public equity-related deal, and 14 employees of Howard Weil Labouisse Friederichs (including the firm's entire corporate finance department) were recruited. With 125 sales traders—the largest institutional equity sales force in the country—Jefferies was well equipped to secure equity deals. In 1992, equity trading comprised almost two-thirds of revenues

($108.2 million). The company that year earned a stunning net of $18.7 million or $3.08 a share.

At this time, the company was the biggest U.S. third market trader, as well as the largest in computer-based trading. Rapid expansion under Baxter's helm, an efficient new accounting method, and the larger boom in securities spelled success for Jefferies in the 1990s. The company's stock price jumped from $11 at the beginning of 1992 to $35 in September 1993—more than a 200 percent gain in less than two years. Since 1989, Jefferies had bought back almost three million shares of its own stock, including Boyd Jefferies' remaining 800,000 shares.

Integration: A Global Investment Bank

In the 1990s, the company positioned itself to entrepreneurial companies as a "custom shop" full investment bank, offering better pricing and financing options than Wall Street.

Beginning in 1993, Baxter sought to maximize earnings per share by integrating the different departments of the firm's diversification effort (business lines, fixed income, and electronic trading). Baxter also continued to explore new industries. In 1993, Jefferies formed a new subsidiary group to compete in the public energy equity market. By 1993, the company had 38 equity analysts, and revenue from investment banking for mid-sized companies had jumped 127 percent over the previous year. In 1994, the company built a new analytical trading division to trade equities and futures. In 1998, Jefferies launched a series of intranet-based data marts to support its transition to investment banking and entry into the corporate, finance, and research markets.

By 1997, it was clear that Baxter had truly saved the company from its potential demise at the time of Boyd Jefferies' indictment. The company had not had a losing year since Baxter took over, and 1997 revenues approached $800 million (a 47 percent increase over 1996), with earnings of $63.6 million. Rumors of a takeover more than doubled 1997 stock prices, which reached an all-time high of $89.63 a share in December. With high employee ownership of stock and an even higher level of personal investment in the newly focused company, Baxter gave no indications of selling. After almost four decades in business, Jefferies Group, Inc. was quite a different company than the one started in a telephone booth in 1962. Resilience, expansion, careful niche market development, and wise leadership allowed the company to weather its storms and remain a leader in the industry.

Principal Subsidiaries

Jefferies & Company, Inc.; Investment Technology Group, Inc.; Jefferies International Limited (U.K.); Jefferies (Japan) Limited; Jefferies Pacific Limited (Hong Kong); Jefferies (Switzerland) Ltd.

Further Reading

"A Brief History of Jefferies," Jefferies & Company, Inc., http://www.jefo.com, 1998.

Hoffman, Thomas, "Intranet Helps Market Shift; Web Data Mart Expands Bank Investment Service," *Computerworld Magazine*, May 25, 1998.

"Making a Difference for 30 Years—1962–1992," Jefferies & Company, Inc., http://www.jefo.com, 1998.

"Overview," Jefferies & Company, Inc., http://www.jefo.com, 1998.

Pratt, Tom, "Jefferies' Equity Effort Expands into New Issues," *Investment Dealers Digest,* April 19, 1993, p. 14.

Schwimmer, Anne, "Something to Cheer About," *Investment Dealers Digest,* September 27, 1993, pp. 16–21.

Sommar, Jessica, "Jefferies Recruits Kipnis to Build Equity Derivatives," *Investment Dealers Digest,* February 4, 1994, p. 6.

Toal, Brian A., "New Jefferies Energy Group Gets Off to Fast 1993 Deal Pace," *Oil & Gas Investor,* October 1993, pp. 16–22.

Vrana, Deborah, "Jefferies' New Age: When Frank Baxter Took Over in the '80s," *Los Angeles Times,* March 22, 1998, p. D-1.

—Heidi Feldman

Jostens, Inc.

5501 Norman Center Drive
Minneapolis, Minnesota 55437–1088
U.S.A.
(612) 830-3300
Fax: (612) 897-4116
Web site: http://www.jostens.com

Public Company
Incorporated: 1906 as Jostens Manufacturing Company
Employees: 6,500
Sales: $742.5 million (1997)
Stock Exchanges: New York
Ticker Symbol: JOS
SICs: 2732 Book Printing; 2752 Commercial Printing,
Lithographic; 3900 Miscellaneous Manufacture; 3911
Jewelry, Precious Metal; 7389 Business Services, Not
Elsewhere Classified

Jostens, Inc. is best known as a manufacturer of high-quality class rings for high school and college students. Since 1960 the company also has produced specially commissioned rings for contestants in the World Series, the Super Bowl, the NBA Championship, and the NHL Stanley Cup. Despite such high-profile coups, however, it is the Jostens $638.8 million school products segment that provides the lion's share of revenues. The company holds more than 40 percent of the combined $1 billion annual U.S. market in graduation products, yearbooks, and class rings and jewelry. After a disappointing end to a promising educational software venture—one that contributed to the interruption of a three-decade-long streak of earnings and revenue increases—Jostens hoped their name-brand appeal would translate to increased sales of products designed to celebrate life events beyond the school walls.

From Small-Town Business to Multimillion-Dollar Corporation: Late 1800s–1960s

Begun in 1897 by Otto Josten, Jostens was originally a small jewelry and watch repair business located in Owatonna, Minne-

sota. In 1900 the founder began manufacturing emblems and awards for nearby schools and in 1906, the year of incorporation, Josten added class rings to his product line, to be sold to schools throughout the Midwest. The company remained small and relatively inconspicuous until Daniel C. Gainey, a former teacher and football coach, was hired in 1922 as the first full-time Jostens ring salesman. The rings at the time carried no gemstones and were all one size. Yet Gainey, with his dynamic and winning personality, secured sales of $18,000 within his first year. The amount was so large that he was forced to return to Owatonna to ensure personally that production demands could be met. By 1923 Gainey had enlisted four more sales representatives—all part-time—and revenues quickly rose to $70,000. Thus class rings became the central concern for the Jostens Manufacturing Company. In 1930 the watchmaking and repair business was sold and the capital was used to construct the company's first ring manufacturing plant. Three years later, with sales approaching the $500,000 mark, Gainey was elected chairman and CEO, positions he held until his retirement in 1968. According to several accounts, Gainey's greatest contribution to the company was his establishment and motivation of a nationwide sales force. Direct sales through independent representatives remain the primary source for the company's virtually uninterrupted growth.

During World War II Jostens contributed to the war effort by adapting its plant and equipment to manufacture precision parts and other materials. Major expansion came following the end of the war. In 1946 the company added graduation announcements to its offerings; in 1950 Jostens launched the American Yearbook Company. Both moves further tapped the education market and made the company less dependent on seasonal sales from rings. In 1958 the company made its first acquisition, purchasing the Ohio-based Educational Supply Company, a manufacturer of school diplomas. Jostens went public the following year and a seemingly unending series of acquisitions, which fortified the company's dominance of the high school and college products markets, characterized the next ten years. Sales for 1962 totaled $26 million; three years later the company obtained its listing on the New York Stock Exchange. In 1968 the company expanded into the Canadian photography market with the purchase of Winnipeg-based National School Studios. By this time Jostens was the undisputed domestic

Company Perspectives:

Jostens provides products and services that help people celebrate achievement, reward performance, recognize service and commemorate experiences.

We provide these achievement and affiliation products in partnership with the diverse organizations people belong to throughout their lives. As a partner, we are committed to delivering value and quality that exceed the needs of the people and organizations we serve. Jostens is a team of employees and independent business partners. Our aim is to be the world leader in providing achievement and affiliation products and to constantly deliver exceptional performance.

leader in both class ring and yearbook sales. Gainey's retirement, however, coupled with Jostens's relocation to Minneapolis in 1969, triggered a tumultuous period that nearly shipwrecked the then nearly $100-million-dollar company.

Rocky Start to Leadership Change: 1970s

Star Tribune columnist Dick Youngblood, reflecting back on this period, wrote: "Jostens had been in turmoil since the late 1960s, when company patriarch Daniel C. Gainey, a major stockholder, pretended to retire as CEO. The trouble was, Gainey remained active enough over the ensuing four years to force the resignation of three chairmen and a president, including his own son." In 1970, amidst the turmoil, a top-performing Jostens salesman and division manager was appointed executive vice-president and effectively became the company's chief operating officer. His name was H. William (Bill) Lurton. Unbeknownst to senior management, however, including Lurton, Gainey had begun negotiations with acquisition-hungry Bristol-Myers. Once Gainey's plan surfaced, several top Jostens officials tendered their resignations; Lurton was among the few who remained. Although Bristol-Myers halted negotiations after the management fallout, Jostens remained in peril under the leadership of replacement CEO Richard Schall. A former top official at General Mills and Metro-Goldwyn-Mayer, Schall, according to *Corporate Report* editor Terry Fiedler, "presided over Jostens for about 18 months before the advent of what amounted to a palace coup." An outsider with little knowledge of the business, Schall had brought in his own management team and radically disrupted the friendly, teamwork-oriented corporate culture and threatened to move the company too quickly into new, uncharted territory. "The Lurton-led old guard demanded that Schall leave, threatening to leave themselves if he didn't. The directors sided with the old guard and in February 1972 Lurton became CEO of Jostens."

Twenty-one years later, Lurton remained in the position, well-liked by his employees and greatly esteemed by his fellow Minnesota CEOs. During his early tenure he moved quickly to reestablish Jostens as a thriving, focused company. Diversification beyond educational products, thought to be the key to the company's future, was renewed only for a short time before being curtailed in large part. In 1974 Lurton divested Jostens of a greeting cards manufacturer and a men's accessories business. Five years later he also rid the company of interests in wedding

rings and library supplies. Jostens Travel, first organized in 1972, also was dissolved before the end of the decade. Jostens did keep at least one peripheral acquisition, Artex Enterprises, for the long term. A manufacturer of custom-imprinted athletic and casual wear, the Artex label survives within the Jostens Sportswear division and is marketed primarily through mass merchants.

Changing Demographics Challenge Lurton: 1980s

Aside from the aftermath of the Gainey debacle, Lurton's greatest challenge as a CEO came in the late 1970s and early 1980s, when demographic studies clearly showed that the last of the baby boom generation had graduated from high school and, therefore, beyond the core products line. According to Jackey Gold in *Financial World*, "Lurton's worry was that declining high school enrollments would shake Wall Street's faith in the company's ability to perform. Jostens' board of directors, too, became infected by such concerns and in August 1982 approved Lurton's proposal for a management buyout." The decision to go private was, for lack of financing, never realized; neither, however, was the company's forecasted decline.

Instead, Lurton launched a concerted campaign to impress Wall Street and counteract potential downswings in profits by boldly entering the proprietary schools business. Beginning in 1983, he acquired San Gabriel Colleges of California and Metridata Education Systems of Kentucky. Three additional private vocational schools were acquired in 1984. That same year Jostens also entered the audiovisual learning and educational software fields by acquiring the Educational Systems Division of Borg-Warner Corporation, which it later renamed Jostens Learning Systems. The new flurry of purchases carried sales to more than $400 million in 1985, when Jostens was accorded Fortune 500 status for the first time. In 1986 the company acquired Illinois-based Prescription Learning Corporation (PLC). A developer of customized computer hardware, software, and support services for the educational market, PLC was merged with Education Systems Corporation three years later to form Jostens Learning Corporation (JLC), a wholly owned subsidiary.

Meanwhile, to the consternation of several analysts, Jostens divested itself of its burgeoning list of proprietary schools, all 36 of them. The company sold the schools to CareerCom Corp. in 1987 for a sizable profit. As then Education Division spokesperson Gary Buckmiller explained, "We didn't view the sale as getting out of the proprietary school business, but rather as changing the way we're involved in the business." The involvement, through JLC, has become one of support and service for, rather than management of, instructors and curriculum. Jostens's one remaining non-educational venture, the Business Products Division, also was sold in 1987, for a gain of $40 million. Now 90 years old, the company had returned to its roots in its service emphasis. By this time Jostens boasted an employee work force of some 9,000, in addition to an independent sales force numbering approximately 1,400.

Brightly Shined Hopes Tarnish: 1990s

Jostens's nearly 27 percent average return on investment between the years 1983 and 1989 brought kudos from all corners for the CEO. *Fortune* magazine highlighted Jostens among its 500 in 1989 as one of the "Companies That Compete Best." In 1990 Lurton was accorded the honor of "Executive of the Year" by *Corporate Report Minnesota;* further recognition came the same year from *Industry Week,* which celebrated Lurton as one of "America's Unsung Heroes." Until fiscal 1992 the news regarding Jostens and Lurton continued to be highly favorable. The 1990 purchase of Gordon B. Miller & Co. (the oldest recognition products company in North America) and Lenox Awards augured well for the company, as did its multimedia agreement with Western Publishing's Little Golden Books. Even the 1992 performance reports were respectable, considering the lingering effects of a recession: net sales increased two percent, while net income showed a four percent decline. The announced consolidation of jewelry manufacturing and photo processing operations were expected to contribute to a quick rebound. The Jostens organizations hoped that rising school enrollment, an improving economy, and a new management team for the Sportswear group would improve the company's performance.

Also fueling hopes for the future was JLC, the leader of the computer-based instructional technology field. Fiscal 1992 revenues for JLC totaled $172 million, or approximately 20 percent of all corporate gross income. JLC, operating in a marketplace that experts estimated as only 15 percent tapped, appeared poised for fast-paced growth, especially considering its August 1992 purchase of chief competitor Wicat Systems and its arrangement with Texas-based Dell Computer to market a Jostens line of 386 and 486 systems. Lurton expected to see an increase of about 25 percent annually. His goal was to return Jostens to "double-digit growth in sales and earnings."

Jostens posted a net loss of $12.1 million in fiscal year 1993. According to an April 1994 Youngblood article, about half of the loss was due to a "poorly managed" consolidation of the photography operation. Compounding problems, JLC missed some key changes in the market, including tightening school budgets and an accompanying shift in demand toward less expensive products and systems.

Lurton announced his retirement as chairman of the board and CEO in October 1993. Robert P. Jensen, a director since 1980, succeeded him as chairman. The combination of missed earnings projections, losses in the earnings column, and nose-diving stock prices had raised the ire of stockholders and Lurton's long, successful tenure ended on a sour note. Yet, under his leadership, the company had put together an enviable succession of sales and earnings increases even while the student population was shrinking.

Robert C. Buhrmaster, a Corning Inc. senior vice-president who came on board as chief of staff in December 1992 and moved into the president's post in mid-1993, succeeded Lurton as CEO and led a revamping of the company. In rapid order, the sportswear division was sold. Veteran executives were replaced. The photography division and JLC were downsized. The corporate culture itself changed as management layers were cut and divisions reported more closely to headquarters. The design and marketing of traditional products such as rings were also re-examined. But losses continued into a second year; underperformance by JLC contributed to the $16.2 million deficit.

Jostens sold JLC to a group led by Boston-based investment firm Bain Capital, Inc. in June 1995 for $90 million in cash and notes. Wicat Systems, the computer-based aviation training division, was sold separately. The sales marked the end of a two-year restructuring and turned emphasis back on traditional business areas of making and marketing class rings, yearbooks, and other recognition products.

Profits for fiscal year 1995 improved in all areas but JLC and net income returned to the plus column with $50.4 million in earnings on $665.1 million in sales. The restructuring and other operational changes resulted in $11 million in cost savings, according to the Jostens annual report. Flush with cash from the JLC sale and the company restructuring, Jostens repurchased seven million shares of stock for $169.3 million in September 1995 through a Modified Dutch Auction tender offer. But the company failed to meet earnings expectations in the later half of fiscal 1996, and Wall Street reacted negatively.

Beginning a Second Century of Business

Buhrmaster continued to fine-tune Jostens in 1997. The company's 100th year in business was celebrated in part with a new logo and identity system. For the first time Jostens consciously worked to extend brand awareness and preference. The effort was part of the larger mission to transform the company from a "ring and yearbook" business to "one that people call upon to help celebrate their most important moments."

The company cut additional costs with the transfer of some ring production to Mexico. In addition, the purchase of the Gold Lance class ring brand from Town & Country Corporation in July 1997 gave Jostens a strong presence in the retail class ring business, which was dominated by companies such as J.C. Penney and Wal-Mart.

Although the retail market accounted for about 33 percent of all U.S. annual class ring sales, Jostens's name-brand appeal helped the company maintain a dominant market share. Scott Carlson wrote in a May 1998 *St. Paul Pioneer Press* article, "Industry observers and Jostens' competitors attribute the company's market strength to making quality products, providing reliable service to students and parents, and hiring enterprising independent sales representatives who build long-term relationships with schools and gain access for in-school marketing." But Jostens's trade practices had drawn fire as well as praise.

Dallas-based Taylor Publishing, one of only two national yearbook companies competing against Jostens (the other was Herff Jones) claimed that the Minnesota company had tried to monopolize the Texas yearbook market. In May 1998 Taylor won a multimillion settlement, which Jostens planned to appeal. Jostens had been under the scrutiny of the attorney general's office of Minnesota in the mid-1990s in regard to "exclusive supply contracts" with schools. And although the company denied that its sales practices were monopolistic, Jostens agreed to avoid using any techniques that would imply that the schools were locked in long-term exclusive deals. Jostens had revamping their sales operations as a part of the general company restructuring.

Buhrmaster, who added the company's chairmanship to his roles as president and CEO in the beginning of 1998, had returned the company to profitability. Yet growth continued to be a concern: total sales for 1997 were up only 4.8 percent. Jostens's mature school market had limited growth opportunities, but the company planned to make the most of those through products such as the "Millennium" ring collection, which capitalized on the interest in the turn of the century. The smaller recognition segment of the business, which primarily served U.S. and Canadian corporations and businesses, directed its focus on the fans of professional sports teams for added sales. Additional plant consolidation and infrastructure improvements that continued into 1998 delayed the implementation of any major expansion plans. The success of Buhrmaster's tenure as the head of the century-old business would be measured by his ability to build markets for Jostens brand-name products while embarking on new business ventures.

Principal Subsidiaries

American Yearbook Company, Inc.; Jostens Canada, Ltd.; Jostens Direct, Inc.; Jostens Photography, Inc.; The Jostens Foundation, Inc.

Further Reading

Benson, Tracy E., "America's Unsung Heroes," *Industry Week,* December 3, 1990, p. 12.

Byrne, Harlan S., "Jostens Inc.: Demographics Offer an Earnings Kick," *Barron's,* October 14, 1991, p. 38.

Carlson, Scott, "Running Rings Around Competition," *St. Paul Pioneer Press,* May 17, 1998, pp. 1D, 3D.

Feyder, Susan, "Jostens' New CEO Rings Out Some Old Concepts," *Star Tribune* (Minneapolis), May 23, 1994, p. 1D.

——, "Jostens Taking Charge for Closing Photo Plant," *Star Tribune* (Minneapolis), May 1, 1998, p. 3D.

——, "Jostens To Buy Back 7 Million Shares for $168 Million in 'Dutch Auction,'" *Star Tribune* (Minneapolis), September 2, 1995, p. 1D.

——, "Longtime Jostens CEO Lurton Says He's Retiring," *Star Tribune* (Minneapolis), October 29, 1993, p. 1D.

——, "Rival Wins Suit Against Jostens over the Selling of Yearbooks," *Star Tribune* (Minneapolis), May 15, 1998, p. 3D.

——, "Still Going for the Brass Ring," *Star Tribune* (Minneapolis), April 20, 1998, p. 1D.

Fiedler, Terry, "H. William Lurton: Modesty That Rings True," *Corporate Report Minnesota,* January 1990, pp. 45–51, 92.

Fierman, Jaclyn, and Rayport, Jeffrey, "How To Make Money in Mature Markets," *Fortune,* November 25, 1985, pp. 46–50.

Foster, Jim, "Jostens Plans Consolidation Moves," *Star Tribune* (Minneapolis), January 29, 1992, p. 3D.

Fredrickson, Tom, "Jostens Tries Staff Buyouts To Ring in Costs," *Minneapolis/St. Paul CityBusiness,* April 22–28, 1994, pp. 1, 30.

Gold, Jackey, "How To Make a Cash Cow Dance," *Financial World,* June 12, 1990, p. 38.

Greenbaum, Jessica, "Lord of the Rings," *Forbes,* May 21, 1984, pp. 108–10.

Gross, Steve, "Jostens Learning Expanding PC Line," *Star Tribune* (Minneapolis), April 15, 1992, p. 3D.

"Highlights from Jostens' History," Minneapolis: Jostens, 1992.

"Jostens Has Lower Earnings, Sales," *Star Tribune* (Minneapolis), January 19, 1993.

Jostens, Inc., *Corporate Report Fact Book 1998,* Minneapolis: Jostens, pp. 337–38.

"Jostens Moves to Head of the Class, *St. Paul Pioneer Press & Dispatch,* October 14, 1985.

Jostens' Today (special 90th anniversary issue: "90 Years of People, Progress and Pride"), Minneapolis: Jostens, August 1987.

Marcotty, Josephine, "Boston Investment Group Is Buying Jostens Learning," *Star Tribune* (Minneapolis), May 24, 1995, p. 1D.

Moylan, Martin J., "Jostens Learning Gives Stock an Edge," *St. Paul Pioneer Press & Dispatch,* August 12, 1991.

Peterson, Susan E., "Lower-Than-Expected Earnings Forecast Drops Jostens Stock," *Star Tribune* (Minneapolis), June 15, 1996, p. 1D.

Raley, Marcia A., "Dain Bosworth Research Capsule: Jostens," January 25, 1988.

Saporito, Bill, "Companies That Compete Best," *Fortune,* May 22, 1989, p. 36.

Spiegel, Peter, "Ringing True," *Forbes,* November 6, 1995, p. 12.

Youngblood, Dick, "Former CEO of Jostens Explains What Went Wrong After 19 Years of Growth," *Star Tribune* (Minneapolis), April 20, 1994, p. 2D.

——, "In a Shrinking Market, He Gently Led Jostens to New World of Growth," *Star Tribune* (Minneapolis), March 18, 1991.

—Jay P. Pederson
—updated by Kathleen Peippo

Kenneth Cole
NEW YORK

Kenneth Cole Productions, Inc.

152 West 57th Street
New York, New York 10019
U.S.A.
(212) 265-1500
Fax: (212) 265-1662
(800) 536-2653 (KEN-COLE)
Web site: http://www.kencole.com

Public Company
Incorporated: 1982
Employees: 600
Sales: $185.3 million (1997)
Stock Exchanges: NYSE
Ticker Symbol: KCP
SICs: 5139 Footwear (primary); 5661 Shoe Stores; 6794
   Patent Owners & Lessors

Kenneth Cole Productions, Inc. (KC) manufactures fashionable men's and women's footwear, handbags, and men's sportswear and tailored clothing, as well as offering accessories and other products under license agreements with other manufacturers. KC products are marketed to more than 2,500 department and specialty stores. The company's Kenneth Cole Catalog reaches more than three million consumers per year, supplementing 47 domestic retail stores, which have expanded to include overseas operations in Amsterdam, Hong Kong, Singapore and Taiwan, and wholesale operations in eight countries. In 1995 *Forbes* named Kenneth Cole Productions 12th of the World's 200 Best Small Companies in America, and in 1996 the company was ranked 21 on this list.

Marketing Footwear in the Early 1980s

The company was founded in 1982 when footwear and accessory designer, Kenneth Cole, debuted a ladies' footwear collection. Cole started the company on a shoestring, with just $300,000, and soon determined that to maintain necessary cash flow he would benefit from acquiring credit from European factories in need of business. Cole contracted with factories in Europe before returning to the United States to offer his first collection of women's shoes. Company records have documented Cole's strategic reasoning: "At the time, a shoe company had two options. You could get a room at the New York Hilton and become one of about 1,100 shoe companies selling their goods [to dealers during market week]. This didn't provide the identity or image I felt necessary for a new company, and it cost a lot more money than I had to spend. The other way was to do what the big companies do and get a fancy showroom in Midtown Manhattan not far from the Hilton. More identity, much more money, too." Instead, he opted to borrow a 40-foot trailer truck from a friend in the trucking business and attempted to get permission from New York City officials to park it in Midtown Manhattan. Cole was informed by officials that the only people getting parking permits were production companies shooting full-length motion pictures and utility companies like AT&T. Not one to be easily dissuaded, Cole responded by changing his company letterhead from Kenneth Cole, Inc. to Kenneth Cole Productions, Inc. and applied for a permit to shoot a full-length film entitled "The Birth of a Shoe Company." The trailer truck was set up across the street from the Hilton Hotel and opened for business with models doubling as actresses. Cole noted, "Sometimes there was film in the camera, sometimes there wasn't." KC sold out 40,000 pairs of shoes in just a few days, earning his reputation as a business maverick.

The man behind the company professes a firm commitment to taking the road less traveled. In a *Los Angeles Times* interview with Mary Rourke, Cole explained, "The more I circumvent the rules, the more successful I become." A Long Island native, the youthful Cole left home to attend Emory University in Atlanta where he earned a degree in political science and planned to go to law school. He abruptly changed his mind when his father's associate resigned, giving the young Cole an opportunity to follow his father's footsteps into the shoe design business. Previously, Kenneth Cole had considered the design of women's shoes to be the most unmasculine career imaginable, but he relented and joined his father in a business called Candies in 1976. He soon learned that the instant gratification of the trade was fulfilling. Within a matter of weeks his designs were rendered into wearable finished products. During the early 1970s their company began importing French and Italian shoes, which led to the fortune they made on "slides," an inexpensive backless sandal with a wedge heel and colored beads strung on a leather strand. In 1987, after selling 14 million pairs of shoes, they sold the business. In the same year Kenneth entered into another partnership when he married philanthropist Maria Cuomo, daughter of former New York Governor, Mario Cuomo.

1994: Initial Public Offering

Cole, who acts as Kenneth Cole Productions' president and CEO, positioned his offices in the prestigious Carnegie Hall Tower above the famous Manhattan concert hall. He told Kathryn Feldman, a writer for *Inside,* "We kept the name Kenneth Cole Productions to remind us of the need to be resourceful." Cole's design and business talents quickly won acclaim within the industry. In 1985 and 1987 he received the Cutty Sark Men's Fashion Award for Outstanding Accessory Design in Men's Footwear. Cole realized that the company would need to respond strongly in a marketplace dominated by the large retailers and that economies of scale and infrastructure were prerequisites to the kind of success he imagined. To grow large quickly the company would need public capital. Cole's company, which had grown from a $5 million operation in 1982 to sales of $84.9 million in 1994, then made its initial public offering, hoping to raise $20 million. KC opened its Bloomingdale's Manhattan flagship concept shop in 1994, followed by 14 concept shops in select Cincinnati-based Federated department stores around the country. KC already had launched its catalogue business, funding it out of the advertising budget. Catalogue sales were intended to promote the KC name and image, rather than serving as a profitable vehicle, although catalogue sales were beginning to improve during this period.

Company profits continued to rise despite lagging performance by many competitors. Cole attributed his success to a philosophy of active listening. He told writer Pamela Reynolds of the *Boston Globe,* "Years ago, I used to think [that] as a designer my responsibility was to determine what a customer should wear. Today I've learned that my responsibility is to give them what they want." His designs in men's fashion were based upon personal preferences—items that he would like to own and wear. Increasingly, the public seemed in favor of reasonably affordable comfort, but not necessarily at the expense of fashionable style. KC shoe lines include Kenneth Cole, the most expensive of his brands, with shoes priced at approximately $100 a pair (in 1996); the Reaction brand, priced around

$60 to $80; and Unlisted, considered a "utility" product (with a name inspired by the trend toward unlisted business phones), selling at $30 to $50. KC's Reaction brand shoes were designed to appeal to those in search of a "utility" shoe, emphasizing comfort with style.

Overall growth profits increased about 35 percent by the third quarter of 1995 on the heels of a secondary stock offering. Approximately 20 percent of business was derived from company-owned retail stores. By 1996 KC operated 17 retail stores in the United States, a store in Amsterdam and another in Singapore. A partnership deal with a Hong Kong firm created a new marketplace in the Pacific Rim, where a series of stores followed featuring KC items.

KC prepared for extensive expansion in 1996 and awarded stockholders a two-for-one stock split. Growth in most areas was attributed to the company's consistent marketing efforts and from opening in-store shops in department stores, which increased sales by as much as 40 percent. The choice of licensing partners was critical since astute retailers carefully inform manufacturers concerning customer brand loyalty and following. The company anticipated continued skyrocketing in royalty income from licensed products—an area where revenues had doubled within the previous year. They held 24 licenses in products such as neckwear, outerwear, belts, eye wear, women's hosiery, briefcases and luggage, and began researching deals for watches, fragrance, jewelry, underwear and men's tailored clothing, sportswear and hosiery, both domestically and internationally. These products were a natural complement to shoes and handbags and allowed those in the industry a broader scope of influence with consumers. Shoe brands that extended into apparel and other areas reinforced customer brand awareness as consumers were identifying KC as the source for "urban-aspirational" fashion, a term coined by company image-makers.

Cause-Marketing a la 1990s

A savvy, risk-oriented marketing approach underlies much of KC's success. Cole's catalogues—which are sent out semi-annually to three million potential customers—and advertisements frequently use vintage black and white photos, combined with a Kenneth Cole quote to captivate his audience. His products were not featured in his early advertisements because he chose to utilize his presence as a forum for raising social awareness. Cole's first public service campaign was in 1984, for AmFAR, the American Foundation for AIDS Research. The issues he spotlighted included supporting the rights of gays in the military, reproductive rights, preservation of rain forests, the rights of the homeless, and the fight against AIDS. One advertisement, for example, depicts a pair of very worn men's boots, captioned: "Have a heart, give a sole." Smaller text beneath the shoes reads: "During the month of February, if you bring an old pair of shoes to any Kenneth Cole store for someone who really needs them, you'll receive 20% off a new pair." Maria Cole chairs HELP, which provides temporary housing in the New York Metropolitan area, and the Coles are associated with a variety of campaigns for the less fortunate. They have challenged corporate America to follow in their socially responsible footsteps.

Other advertisements sport a much lighter tone. For example, a 1936 photo of Ginger Rogers dancing in patent pumps is accompanied by the caption, ''Ginger's footwork left Fred astare.'' Cole does not shy away from political portrayals, which some have called ''irreverent,'' evidenced by an advertisement featuring Dan Quayle, with a goofy expression, smiling above text that reads, ''Don't forget to vot.''—Kenneth Cole alluding to the former vice-president's notorious spelling error. Small print at the bottom of the page reads, ''Come by our Pre-Election Sale going on now.'' Another advertisement quipped: ''Imelda Marcos bought 2,700 pairs of shoes. She could've at least had the courtesy to buy a pair of ours.'' Cole's spoofy ads earned him the 1994 GLADD New York Media Award for Outstanding Achievement in advertising. For his work with AIDS awareness and homeless causes, he received the shoe industry's Man of the Year for 1996. He also received the Humanitarian Leadership Award sponsored by Dom Perignon and presented by the Council of Fashion Designers of America, as well as the Extraordinary Voice Award by Mothers' Voices for his continued efforts in AIDS awareness, among others.

According to a report by Cone Communications and cited by Baber in *Footwear News,* many companies have found that consumers frequently display a loyalty to products associated with one or more charitable issues. Their report showed that when asked to choose between two products of equal price and quality, 76 percent of consumers said they are more likely to select a brand if it is associated with a good cause. Labeled ''cause-marketing,'' the intention is to establish long-term trust relationships with customers, allowing them to feel good about contributing to saving the rain forest, or feeding the homeless, for example, while purchasing items they would have purchased anyway. In discussing the study, Cone stated, ''No one ever bought anything based solely on a cause. Cause-related marketing adds to the brand persona, the character. It's the second tier of influencers.'' A philanthropic image provides another ''edge'' in an increasingly competitive marketplace. The footwear producers, Keds and Reebok, also are counted among the many companies that embrace cause-related marketing, boosting their corporate image and, potentially, boosting long-term revenues, while also benefiting one or more causes.

The company is attempting to make new headway into the boy's footwear market, which had been almost entirely dominated by athletic shoes. A more recent trend suggests that parents are beginning to buy new styles in shoes and boots for their boys, in addition to the athletic footwear popularized by sports stars. KC debuted its children's line in 1997, offering a wide selection of loafers, chunky monk-straps, oxfords, and boots. According to one retail manager, quoted by Boehring in *Footwear News,* ''If the shoes have the comfort of a sneaker, boys aren't a tough sell.''

Kenneth Cole men's tailored clothing (manufactured under a license agreement with Hartmarx) was introduced in the fall of 1997 and men's sportswear (manufactured in partnership with Paul Davril, Inc.) was launched in a debut runway show in early 1998. Like the well-priced, somewhat trendy shoes, the sportswear line appears to fill a niche—a niche defined by the company as urban, fashion-conscious consumers who want designer styles, at a reasonable price. KC's new suits are priced from $395 to $595, a bit less expensive than Calvin Klein and a little costlier than Liz Claiborne, Tommy Hilfiger, and Nautica. The subdued color palate of grays, black, dark blue, and murky violet are consistent with the sophisticated, urbane image. But it may require more than appearances for this clothing to stand out significantly from the crowd, which is where public sentiment concerning brand and image is tested. So far, the combination of product and marketing strategies has worked. Depending upon the success of the 1998 men's lines, KC plans to expand into women's and children's clothing. Except for a second-quarter slide in 1997, revenues at Kenneth Cole Productions have grown steadily.

Further Reading

Boehring, Julie C., ''Boy Wonders; If Today's American Men Grew Up in Nothing But Athletic Shoes, Will Their Sons Wear Anything Else?,'' *Footwear News,* February 2, 1998, p. 82.

——, ''Style Counselors; Should Footwear Companies Take the Nontraditional Accessories Route?,'' *Footwear News,* May 26, 1997, p. SS14.

Campbell, Roy H., ''Kenneth Cole Sizes Up His Success with Shoes: Style and Quality, at a Good Price,'' *The Philadelphia Inquirer,* December 3, 1995, p. H3.

Emert, Carol, ''Kenneth Cole Does About Face; Files IPO,'' *Footwear News,* April 18, 1994, p. 1.

Feldman, Kathryn Levy, ''Sole Man; Head over Heels for Kenneth Cole,'' *Inside,* Fall 1997, pp. 87–89.

Gault, Ylonda, ''Giant Leap for Cole,'' *Crain's New York Business,* January 5–11, 1998, p. 1.

Gellers, Stan, ''Report Kenneth Cole To Ink Suit License with Hartmarx,'' *Daily News Record,* October 1, 1996, p. 2.

Givhan, Robin, ''Kenneth Cole and His Model Citizens,'' *The Washington Post,* February 3, 1998, p. B4.

MacDonald, Laurie, ''Kenneth Cole, Seriously, with Business Growing Beyond $100 Million, the Ads Aren't the Only Things Grabbing Attention,'' *Footwear News,* February 5, 1996, p. 16.

Malone, Scott, ''Footwear IPOs Find Tide Runs High and Low,'' *Footwear News,* May 5, 1997, p. 1.

Reynolds, Pamela, ''Sensible (About) Shoes,'' *The Boston Globe,* June 25, 1996, p. 58.

Rourke, Mary, ''Kenneth Cole's Shoes Grab Our Feet—And His Social Concerns Grab Our Attention,'' *Los Angeles Times,* August 27, 1993.

Sauer, Georgia, ''Shoe-ting Star,'' *Pittsburgh Post-Gazette,* June 9, 1996.

Seo, Diane, ''Stepping into the Future,'' *Los Angeles Times,* January 15, 1998, pp. B5 and B7.

Sohng, Laurie, ''Children's Division Launched by Kenneth Cole,'' *Footwear News,* July 22, 1991, p. 56.

Stronger, Karol, ''Resourcefulness Got Cole's Foot in the Door,'' *Lifestyle and Fashion,* February 7, 1997, p. B3.

—Terri Mozzone

Kewaunee Scientific Corporation

P.O. Box 1842
Statesville, North Carolina 28687-1842
U.S.A.
(704) 873-7202
Fax: (704) 873-1275
Web site: http://www.kewaunee.com

Public Company
Incorporated: 1906 as Kewaunee Manufacturing
   Company
Employees: 500
Sales: $73 million (fiscal 1998)
Stock Exchanges: NASDAQ
Ticker Symbol: KEQU
SICs: 3821 Laboratory Apparatus & Furniture

Since the early 1900s, Kewaunee Scientific Corporation has designed, manufactured, marketed, and installed laboratory furniture. It started out in Kewaunee, Wisconsin, added a plant in Adrian, Michigan, in the 1920s, and then moved all of its manufacturing facilities to Adrian in the 1940s. During the 1950s a wood furniture manufacturing facility was added in Statesville, North Carolina, and in the 1970s Kewaunee added a manufacturing facility in Lockhart, Texas. In the 1980s the company closed its Adrian plant, transferring production to its Statesville and Lockhart facilities.

The company has two primary operating units, the Laboratory Products Group, based in Statesville, North Carolina, and the Technical Products Group, based in Lockhart, Texas. The Laboratory Products Group manufactures quality laboratory furnishings for industrial, government, educational, and healthcare customers. Its product lines include steel and wood laboratory furniture, worksurfaces, flexible systems, and fume hoods. The Technical Products Group is focused on providing modular and durable furniture solutions for high-tech production, technical labs, test and measurement labs, and local area network (LAN) computing centers.

Early History

In 1906 the Kewaunee Manufacturing Company went into the laboratory furniture business. The company first came into existence in 1903 as the Kewaunee Casket and Manufacturing Company in the town of Kewaunee, Wisconsin. In 1906 the same group of local men that started the company reorganized the failed business and dropped "Casket" from the name. At the time, there were only two other manufacturers of laboratory equipment, both based in Chicago, Illinois.

Kewaunee Manufacturing Company was set up as a private company, with four families each having a one-quarter interest. The early years of the company were not profitable, and it was simply making payments against notes payable to the State Bank of Kewaunee to stay in business.

In 1926 the company acquired the plant and equipment of the Economy School Furniture Company, located in Adrian, Michigan. In 1929 the Adrian plant was electrified and a blower system installed. The company produced a profit, but by 1931 falling inventory values resulted in a mere $5,000 profit, barely enough to break even. Then the Great Depression began, and a normal profit was not achieved until 1937. During the Depression, selling prices fell so low that every piece sold resulted in a 25 to 30 percent loss.

Moved from Kewaunee to Adrian, Michigan

During the 1930s several factors combined to cause the company to close its Kewaunee facility and move the entire company to Adrian, Michigan. In 1931 it was decided to equip the Adrian factory for the production of metal furniture, which management felt would experience a growing demand over the next decade. Wood furniture would continue to be manufactured in Kewaunee. By 1932 the Adrian plant was producing metal laboratory furniture. In 1935 the Kewaunee shop became unionized, and by 1939 was fairly militant in its demands. The buildings at Kewaunee were old three- and four-story frame structures. The location was considered a poor one and not conducive to efficient manufacturing. As a result of these factors, all production of wood furniture was moved to Adrian in January 1941. In April 1942 the company rented its empty buildings in Kewaunee to the Kewaunee Shipbuilding and Engineering Corporation, which was beginning to build ships for the war effort. Most of Kewaunee's former employees found employment with the shipbuilding company. The assets of the Wisconsin company were dissolved and transferred to the new Michigan company. The net asset value of the company was $682,400.

During World War II the company received several government contracts. These included making chock blocks, which were used to block airplane wheels. The company also received a top-secret contract to make a certain type of metal enclosure that was used in the Manhattan Project, which led to the development of the atomic bomb.

Sales Increased Dramatically After World War II

After World War II, the company's sales increased dramatically. Sales grew from $2.9 million in fiscal 1947 to $4.1 million in 1948 and $5.1 million in 1949. In 1949 the Adrian plant was expanded with the construction of an engineering building and the establishment of a stainless steel fabricating operation there at a cost of $50,000. An additional $20,000 was spent in 1951 to install water-washed spray booth equipment to prevent paint and lacquer spray from spreading outside the plant.

Sales for 1950 fell back to $4.6 million, and the company reported a profit of $401,000. Around this time the company entered into an agreement with Fisher Scientific Company of Pittsburgh, Pennsylvania, to manufacture a stock line of metal laboratory furniture. Fisher would then warehouse the furniture and sell it to its industrial customers. Kewaunee also began producing its proprietary Kemrock tops, which were made of a natural quarried freestone material impregnated with an acid-resistant coating. Kemrock tops were considered the best available, until Kewaunee introduced the Kemresin top in 1963.

1950s, Growth and Expansion

As the 1950s began, management realized that southeastern Michigan, with its heavy concentration of automobile manufacturers and related suppliers, probably was not the best location for a company making metal and wood laboratory furniture and other scientific equipment. The company began to look for a wood manufacturing facility located in the southern United States.

In 1951 C. G. Campbell became chairman of the company after serving as president for 23 years. J. A. Campbell succeeded him as president. The Campbell family was one of the four families that owned the company. The others were the Bruemmer family (successors to the Borgman estate), the Duvall family, and the Dishmaker family (successors to the Haney estate). John L. Haney, John M. Borgman, and George Duvall were principals in the original Kewaunee Casket and Manufacturing Corporation and held various positions as officers and directors of the company. Throughout the company's early history its board of directors reflected the familial nature of the firm's ownership.

In the spring of 1954 a site for the manufacture of wood furniture was selected in Statesville, North Carolina. A new subsidiary, Technical Furniture, Inc., was formed. Development of the project was financed with $300,000 worth of Kewaunee common stock and term loans totalling $1.2 million. The first phase of construction consisted of 56,000 square feet of office and manufacturing space. The new factory in Statesville began hiring employees and production started in February 1955. In 1959 the name of Technical Furniture, Inc., was changed to Kewaunee Technical Furniture Company, and it became a North Carolina corporation operating as a wholly owned subsidiary of Kewaunee Manufacturing.

In 1956, the company reported sales of $9 million and net income of $622,772. In 1957 sales rose to $11.5 million while net income fell to $602,600. The company was facing increased competition from new companies coming into the laboratory furniture business and from the expansion of existing companies. In October 1957 the Statesville Company was formed to provide warehouse space in Statesville. In 1958 a pilot metal furniture operation was begun in Statesville.

The development of Kemresin began in 1958 with a joint research project with Battelle Laboratories of Columbus, Ohio. Kemresin was a modified epoxy resin product. When production of Kemresin began in Statesville in 1963, the Kemresin factory produced only laboratory sinks. In a couple of years it would be producing the highest quality laboratory tops and sinks available.

1960s: A Decade of Change

By mid-1962 the Statesville operation, with warehouse space expanded to 60,000 square feet, was achieving record sales and profits, while business at the Adrian facility was mediocre at best and labor negotiations were proving difficult. By the end of the year it was decided to discontinue all wood furniture operations at Adrian and re-equip the factory there to produce metal laboratory furniture exclusively. At the same time the Kemresin plant in Statesville was expanded to permit the production of tops as well as sinks.

By 1964 all of the company's metal furniture was being produced in Adrian and all of its wood furniture, plus Kemresin, at Statesville. That year Kewaunee introduced its "Aristocrat" auxiliary air hood and set up a hood demonstration room in Adrian. In 1965 sales topped $20 million, and the company's business remained strong for 1966 and 1967.

In mid-1967 management began discussions with various brokerage houses for a secondary stock offering. The company's name was changed from Kewaunee Manufacturing Company to Kewaunee Scientific Equipment Corporation. Sales for 1967 were $23.2 million, and the company had another $23 million backlog of unfilled orders. The Statesville operations accounted for $16 million of the company's sales. Assets of the Statesville Company were transferred to the Kewaunee Technical Furniture Co. in exchange for 10,647 shares of Kewaunee stock. At the end of the year an underwriting agreement was reached at a special stockholders meeting, and the initial public offering (IPO) of stock was made on February 14, 1968. Kewaunee's IPO was actually a secondary offering, with all proceeds going to the selling stockholders, who generally sold 25 percent of their stock. Some 286,000 shares were sold at a price of $25 per share.

Business Expanded During 1970s

Following the public stock offering, business went into a down cycle for the period, 1970–72. In 1970 the company was reincorporated in Delaware, and Kewaunee Technical Furniture was merged into Kewaunee Scientific Equipment, becoming a division instead of a subsidiary. In 1972 Kewaunee acquired the Angle Steel Division from Gulf and Western Corporation. Angle Steel, located in Plainwell, Michigan, was looked on as a diversification opportunity, and by 1975 it was producing metal farm buildings, or pole barns, as well as other products.

In 1973 the metal furniture operation in Adrian was achieving poor results, and management was becoming concerned whether it would be possible to ever operate profitably in Adrian. By mid-1974 the country was experiencing inflation and a recession, and Kewaunee was having problems profitably fulfilling its long-term fixed-price contracts. In 1974 the company introduced the KemKlad line of plastic laminated particleboard casework for use in arts and crafts and homemaking. By 1975 production levels in Adrian had reached optimum levels.

In 1977 the company purchased a manufacturing facility in Lockhart, Texas, consisting of 30,000 square feet of factory space on 28 acres of land, for $338,000. This location would be the new home of the company's Special Products Division, which was moved from Adrian. In 1978 Kewaunee purchased the assets of Electronic Finishes, Inc. (EFI), a company that had gone bankrupt doing development work in applying acrylic coatings to particleboard and curing the finish with radiation from an electron beam. Kewaunee moved EFI's assets from Plainfield, Illinois, to Statesville, and began working on the electron beam finishing and curing system. After three years of attempting to produce a reliable product, Kewaunee abandoned it.

1980s Began with Recession, Ended with New CEO

The 1979–80 recession strongly affected the company's Angle Steel Division. In 1983, the metal building components part of Angle Steel was sold to another producer, and the Angle Steel Division was renamed the Flexible Furniture Division. It would continue to produce electronic support furniture that could be used with computers, word processors, and other electronic office equipment.

In May 1982 Paul Meech was elected chairman of the board, and William M. Bartlett was elected president. Bartlett had previous experience at American Hospital Supply Company and G.D. Searle Company. Under Bartlett's leadership, Kewaunee moved its corporate headquarters to Wilmette, Illinois, in the Chicago metropolitan area, in May 1984. That same year it acquired the J.M. Manufacturing Corporation of Santa Clara, California, a company that produced high-quality chemical fume hoods and laminar-flow hoods and sinks. It also purchased a 25 percent interest in Triangle Biomedical Sciences, Inc., of Durham, North Carolina. Sales for 1984 were $53.8 million, with net income of $3.1 million.

In 1985 Kewaunee closed and sold its Angle Steel plant in Plainwell, Michigan, and moved production of its Sturdilite product line of flexible furniture to Lockhart, Texas. Management also recommended that the Adrian facility be closed and product lines moved to Statesville and Lockhart. A 57,000-foot expansion to the Lockhart facility was announced. In February 1986, the Adrian plant was closed, and a few months later in August the company changed its name to Kewaunee Scientific Corporation.

A delayed start-up of the transferred operations in Statesville resulted in a net loss of $7.7 million in 1987 (ending April 30). One of the major problems was that North Carolina workers did not have the metal fabrication skills and experience that workers in Adrian had. It took about two years of intensive training programs to bring productivity up to previous levels.

Profits were also negatively affected by the unprofitable instrument distribution business, Scientific Equipment Apparatus Marketing Corporation (known as Seamark), which Kewaunee established in 1985. The subsidiary was formed to import products from the Far East into the United States, but a strong Japanese yen during the period made business difficult. Seamark was sold in 1988.

In 1988 the company was involved in a price war with competitors and the St. Charles division of Whirlpool Corporation. With a well-received new generation of modular workstations, Kewaunee managed to eke out a profit of $786,000 on sales of $68.6 million in 1988. With improved productivity and labor cost savings taking effect at Statesville and Lockhart, Kewaunee saw its net income rise in 1989 to $1.6 million on flat sales of $68.9 million. However, the company still faced difficult circumstances: excess industry capacity and a downturn in prices.

Eli Manchester, Jr., Became President and CEO, 1990

A few months after Kewaunee reported a 70 percent decline in earnings to $472,000 on sales of $74 million (up seven percent) for 1990, William Bartlett resigned unexpectedly. Eli Manchester, Jr., was recruited out of retirement in July 1990 to become Kewaunee's president and CEO. By December Manchester had relocated Kewaunee's corporate headquarters from Wilmette to Statesville. At the company's annual meeting, he told stockholders, "It has become clear that the headquarters office here [in Wilmette] is disassociated from the operations of the rest of the company. It makes more sense to be in North Carolina, closer to our production." The move was expected to save $500,000 annually. Further cost-cutting measures were expected to reduce overhead by another $1 million annually. The company's workforce was 784 employees, its lowest since 1973.

Kewaunee reported net income of $801,000 on sales of $75 million in 1992. For the next three years sales declined, and the company reported net losses of $2.5 million in 1993, $203,000 in 1994, and $1.1 million in 1995. During this period several new programs and strategies were put in place. These included strengthening the company's network of sales agencies and representatives to achieve increased market penetration. Kewaunee wanted not only to increase sales in general, but in particular to increase sales of its higher margin products. A new pricing strategy was introduced to improve profit margins on the low-margin contract-bid portion of the company's business. Additional investments were made in computerized machinery, which helped improve manufacturing efficiencies and reduce costs.

By 1996 Kewaunee was showing signs of revitalization. The company showed a small profit of $361,000 on sales of $57.6 million, the lowest sales level of the decade. In 1997 net earnings increased dramatically by 527 percent to $2.3 million, helped in part by an income tax credit and a 50 percent reduction in interest expense. Sales increased 7.6 percent to $62 million.

By fiscal 1998 (ending April 30), Kewaunee was fully revitalized, with a strong earnings performance and increased sales. Sales rose 18 percent to $73 million. Operating earnings were up 75.8 percent, and pre-tax earnings jumped 95.6 percent to $4.2 million. After-tax net earnings rose 13.3 percent to $2.6 million. Interest expense was again reduced by another 50 percent. During the fiscal year the company's stock price climbed 146 percent, closing at $12.625 per share, up from $5.125 per share at the end of the last fiscal year.

Kewaunee had a particularly strong fourth quarter in fiscal 1998 and entered fiscal 1999 with excellent momentum. President and CEO Eli Manchester, Jr., attributed the company's strong performance not to any one factor or strategy, but to several strategies that had been put in place over the past several years. New product development was contributing to greater sales, with the introduction of the new Research Collection line of steel furniture, a new Alpha System 2000 with modular components, and the Evolution for LANs furniture that supported computer equipment. In addition, the company introduced the Kemresin Lite premium laboratory countertop. Kemresin Lite provided not only chemical resistance, but it had a renewable surface, came in a variety of colors, and was lighter in weight than previous laboratory countertops.

Looking to the future, Kewaunee expected to increase its spending for modern manufacturing equipment. The company spent $1.5 million in fiscal 1998 on capital improvements, and it continued to reduce manufacturing costs and improve productivity through the increased use of computerized manufacturing machinery. These investments were perceived as necessary to meet the expected increased demand for Kewaunee products in the coming years.

Principal Operating Units

Laboratory Products Group; Technical Products Group.

Further Reading

Murphy, H. Lee, ''Kewaunee's Move South: Bumpy Start, Smooth Finish,'' *Crain's Chicago Business,* September 11, 1989, p. 24.
——, ''Kewaunee Turns Corner—Just in Time for Price Wars,'' *Crain's Chicago Business,* September 12, 1988, p. 27.
——, ''New CEO Out to Slash Costs at Kewaunee,'' *Crain's Chicago Business,* September 10, 1990, p. 16.

—David Bianco

K&O·KOO·ROO®
GOOD FOR YOO™

Koo Koo Roo, Inc.

11075 Santa Monica Boulevard, Suite 225
Los Angeles, California 90025
U.S.A.
(310) 479-2080
Fax: (310) 479-8843
Web site: http://www.kookooroo.com

Public Company
Incorporated: 1987
Employees: 3,100
Sales: $68.30 million (1997)
Stock Exchanges: NASDAQ
Ticker Symbols: KKRO
SICs: 5812 Eating Places

Headquartered in Los Angeles, California, Koo Koo Roo, Inc., oversees a restaurant chain specializing in flame-broiled skinless herb chicken, turkey, low-fat sandwiches, and such side dishes as tossed salads, pastas, butternut squash, baked yams, lentil salad, cracked wheat rice, baked goods, and other foods. Doing business as Koo Koo Roo California Kitchens, the company competes with the American Restaurant Group, Boston Market, and Brinker restaurant chains. Seeking to distinguish itself among its competition, Koo Koo Roo restaurants feature a healthy menu of full meals—including a 26-pound turkey dinner with trimmings—and sophisticated decorating schemes. "You walk into a Boston Chicken or a Kenny Rogers Roasters," observed Koo Koo Roo president Michael Mooslin in the *South Florida Business Journal,* "and you're in a chicken place. You walk into a Koo Koo Roo, and you're in a restaurant." Koo Koo Roo California Kitchen outlets offer dining in, carry out, and corporate catering services.

Koo Koo Roo maintains several subsidiaries: Arrosto Coffee Company, which sells primarily to Koo Koo Roo outlets; Color Me Mine paint-your-own ceramic studios; and Hamburger Hamlet, a fast-food chain active in California and Washington, D.C.

Origins on the Corner of Beverly Blvd. and Orlando Ave.

The first Koo Koo Roo outlet opened in Los Angeles in 1988. L.A. restaurateur Mike Badalian founded and co-owned the restaurant with his brother Ray. Within two years, the brothers were operating two outlets in Los Angeles—one on the corner of Beverly Boulevard and Orlando Avenue and one in Koreatown—until one Academy Awards night when the Badalians' chicken caught the attention of Kenneth Berg. Berg saw a long line of people waiting outside Koo Koo Roo to place their orders. "The people in line were raving about how good it was and how healthy," Berg remembered in *Restaurant Business.* "It was a little nothing store down on Beverly and Orlando, but it was filled with Beverly Hills people, in suits and ties and dresses, all eating chicken with their hands," he observed.

Berg, a semi-retired real estate broker from New York, ordered a Koo Koo Roo carry-out dinner to snack on while watching the Academy Awards in his L.A. apartment in 1990 and loved the food. "It was the best chicken I ever had in my life," Berg told the *Los Angeles Business Journal.* He became friends with the Badalian brothers and threw his financial support behind the concept. He first invested $2.5 million as a silent partner. Then, wanting more, he took control of Koo Koo Roo, buying out the Badalians and assembling an expert management team to expand the restaurant chain.

Berg visualized something different for the restaurants than the founding brothers had. "I wanted it to be a real dining experience," Berg explained to *Restaurant Business.* "I wanted the stores to be quick-service and not fast-food. I wanted all the food made fresh. I wanted no butter to be used and all the vegetables to be steamed. I wanted knives and forks and fresh flowers on all the tables."

Kenneth Berg Takes Control in the Early 1990s

Berg first went public with Koo Koo Roo in October 1991, offering stock at $5.00 per share. In less than a year, however, the chain's stock prices reached a low of $0.25 per share, losing

---

Company Perspectives:

Koo Koo Roo appeals to a wide range of people who look for good tasting, freshly prepared, moderately priced food, and who also appreciate menu items that are wholesome and healthy. The sights and smells of fresh food preparation, such as turkey carving and salad tossing, are displayed in glass-enclosed stations featuring 'chefs' in restaurant whites and toques. The restaurants and the food they serve are equally appealing for dining both on and off premise. In the bright, clean dining rooms, guests find fresh flowers at every table, comfortable chairs, and spotless flatware.

$1.9 million in 1991 and $2.5 million during the first part of the following year.

With 15 outlets in 1992, Koo Koo Roo weighed options for its recovery, including consolidation. Less profitable outlets closed in Los Angeles and New York during the year, leaving six stores in operation. Berg then renamed the chain's outlets Koo Koo Roo California Kitchens. He redecorated the restaurants and introduced new products—a deli counter and turkey dinner bar, for example. Berg then began marketing the restaurant's fare as ''home meal replacement.'' ''Perhaps the actual original concept wasn't as good as it could have been,'' noted chief financial officer Morton Wall in the *Los Angeles Business Journal* in 1993. ''We all feel we're going in the right direction now. We're doing dramatic cost reductions to try to turn the company around,'' Wall continued.

Berg cut overhead and provided Koo Koo Roo with $500,000 to aid the company's recovery. He and Badalian became co-chairmen of the company, and Michael D. Mooslin was named chief operating officer and president in March 1993. Their plan for recovery seemed to be working. Koo Koo Roo outlets that sold $7,000 weekly before Berg's changes began averaging $44,000 in weekly sales.

Berg next added new items to Koo Koo Roo's menu. Once in 1993 he sampled some coffee at a single-unit coffee bar in Santa Monica. Impressed, Berg bought 90 percent of Arrosto Coffee and installed the company's coffee bars in Koo Koo Roo outlets to supplement their sales of baked goods during breakfast hours.

Financial Recovery in 1993

Koo Koo Roo's stocks recovered slightly in May 1993. Yet the company still lost $2.9 million that year and $3 million the following year. Despite these losses, the company's unit sales averaged $1.6 million in 1994, an 80 percent increase over the previous year. By 1994, Koo Koo Roo maintained seven restaurants in California, one in New Jersey, and one in Florida—and hoped to expand nationally. Toward the end of the year, the chain's presence in the southern United States finally began to stretch further. In September, Mel Harris, a Miami insurance executive, purchased the chain's franchise rights for the state of Florida after lunching at a Koo Koo Roo with his friend and company chairman Ken Berg. ''I just loved the food,'' Harris told the *South Florida Business Journal* in 1994. ''I thought it was great food at a great price.'' Harris financed his Koo Koo Roo franchises himself. It was his first venture as a restaurateur.

Later that year, Michael Milken offered Koo Koo Roo an infusion of capital from a family trust, giving Milken a majority ownership in the company. Milken, a notorious financier, had pleaded guilty to conspiracy and securities fraud charges in 1990 for his involvement with junk bonds at the Drexel Bernham Lambert brokerage during the 1980s. He was sentenced to U.S. federal prison on six felony counts and was prohibited from any future involvement in the securities industry, from controlling a public company, or from contributing to the buyouts of other investors. In 1994, an agent for the Milken family trust—Archon Capital Partners—offered $55 million for a 51 percent majority share of Koo Koo Roo through a corporation known as Casual Dining Concepts. Stockbroker Bill Scanlon praised the deal, telling the *Los Angeles Business Journal:* ''Now . . . [Koo Koo Roo] will have the capital to expand.''

With news of a possible purchase spreading among investors, Koo Koo Roo's stock doubled from its lowest level. The company's turn around was short-lived, however, as Milken withdrew his investment offer in October owing to disputed terms. Koo Koo Roo's stock plummeted once more.

Plans for Expansion in the Mid-1990s

Nevertheless, the company's expansion plans went on undeterred. In December 1994, the company sold development rights to 23 units in California, with more sites under discussion. Koo Koo Roo also added Arrosto Coffee and Espresso Bars to three more outlets.

Unfortunately, losses also continued—$1.2 million in the quarter ending in September 1995—so expansion for the upcoming year depended on two private placements totaling $18.5 million. Lee Iacocca's Iacocca Capital Partners LP provided $14.3 million, and Iacocca—renowned former president of Ford Motor Company and past chairman of Chrysler Corporation—joined Koo Koo Roo's board of directors.

With 16 outlets in operation at the beginning of 1996, Koo Koo Roo was poised to launch 40 stores on the east and west coasts of the United States. ''We are not trying to compete with the strategy of putting stores everywhere,'' cautioned Koo Koo Roo president John Kaufman in the *San Francisco Business Times,* ''but we are looking for a lot of great sites. We are not doing the Boston Market approach of scattering stores everywhere to blanket a market.'' This round of expansion promised to bring the company into a profitable position.

Four new Koo Koo Roo outlets opened in 1996, with 30 additional restaurant openings planned for the year in California, Nevada, Arizona, Colorado, New Jersey, New York, Maryland, Virginia, and Washington, D.C. Unlike earlier expansions, these new units were company-owned stores; stores franchised earlier closed, or Koo Koo Roo bought them back, electing to franchise no longer. Now active in several U.S. markets, Koo Koo Roo embarked upon a joint venture agreement to start Koo Koo Roo California Kitchens and Arrosto Coffee establishments in Canada. Berg felt that the additional units heralded profitability for the chain. He told *Nation's Restaurant News* that "with the acceleration of the new store openings planned for the third quarter, we expect to achieve a positive net cash flow from operations in the fourth quarter of 1996 or sooner."

In addition to expanding the number of freestanding stores, Berg purchased Color Me Mine, a chain of three craft stores, as a complementary business to Koo Koo Roo restaurants. Color Me Mine patrons designed their own ceramic tiles, which store personnel then baked in kilns. Targeting a high-profile likeness of ceramic tile enthusiasts and Koo Koo Roo chicken lovers, Berg located Color Me Mine units in or near Koo Koo Roo restaurants. "Because the customer profile is similar for Koo Koo Roo California Kitchen restaurants and Color Me Mine, we believe there will be substantial synergy between the concepts both from a sales and a real-estate standpoint," Berg told *Nation's Restaurant News.* Known Koo Koo Roo patrons included such celebrities as talk-show host Jay Leno, comedian Roseanne, and attorneys Marcia Clark and Robert Shapiro. Entertainers Arnold Schwarzenegger, Demi Moore, and Jamie Lee Curtis numbered among Color Me Mine customers.

The expansion of 1996 was not as profitable for Koo Koo Roo as the company's executive management expected, however. The chain lost over $12 million in 1996 and about $20 million total since its initial public offering in 1991.

Undeterred, Koo Koo Roo continued its expansion campaign, acquiring Hamburger Hamlet restaurants in California and Washington D.C. in 1997. The company bought the burger chain hoping to integrate its units in Koo Koo Roo outlets. Despite its newest acquisition, Koo Koo Roo lost $32.8 million in 1997.

Then, in 1998, Koo Koo Roo came under the scrutiny of the Center for Science in the Public Interest (CSPI), a Washington, D.C.-based group founded in 1971 that evaluates food and nutrition in North America. The group had previously derided American fast food, Chinese food, and movie theater popcorn, claiming nutritional deficiencies in these food offerings. The CSPI, however, awarded many Koo Koo Roo menu items its "Best Bite" designation, finding the restaurant's fare better tasting and healthier that its meals-to-go competitors. In its *Nutrition Action Healthletter,* the CSPI claimed that "Koo Koo Roo's dishes have less fat and salt—and more pizzazz and flavor—than the others." Even with this ringing endorsement, the restaurant chain lost money during the year.

Restructuring for the Future

In 1998, Koo Koo Roo adopted a plan for restructuring. The company decided to closed some outlets in the northeastern United States and to exit the Washington, D.C., beltway market, concentrating instead on the California and Nevada markets. In addition, Iacocca, who had become the company's "acting" chairman, assumed responsibility for the sale of Koo Koo Roo's

non-core businesses such as the Arrosto coffee plant and the Color Me Mine outlets. Iacocca was also charged with task of reducing staff. His role, according to Koo Koo Roo's chief executive William Allen in the *Los Angeles Business Journal,* was "to do what a chairman does. A chairman leads the board to govern the company well. I expect that Lee Iacocca will be shoulder to shoulder with management."

According to the company's management discussion and analysis of financial conditions for 1997, Koo Koo Roo management remained optimistic, hoping for improved operating results in the late 1990s. Restructuring of the company and an effort to improve operating efficiencies at the stores were integral to recovery. Management noted that "the company has historically incurred net losses, and the company presently anticipates that it will continue to incur operating losses during 1998. However, the company believes that the net operating losses should begin to decrease during the next calendar year both in the aggregate and as a percentage of sales."

Principal Subsidiaries

Arrosto Coffee Company; Color Me Mine; Hamburger Hamlet.

Further Reading

Carlsen, Clifford, "Chicken Chain Here to Roost; Twenty-five Outlets Sought by Koo Koo Roo," *San Francisco Business Times,* December 20, 1996, p. 1.

Coeyman, Marjorie, "Can This Chicken Fly?," *Restaurant Business,* May 1, 1996, p. 48.

Cole, Benjamin Mark, "Milken Trust to Buy into Radio, Food Companies," *Los Angeles Business Journal,* September 26, 1994, p. 1.

Glover, Kara, "One Night's Takeout Spawns New Career," *Los Angeles Business Journal,* January 15, 1996, p. 13.

Heimlich, Cheryl Kane, "Koo Koo Roo Franchisee Ready to Open First Store," *South Florida Business Journal,* September 30, 1994, p. 6.

"Koo Koo Roo Sells Area Rights for San Francisco and San Diego and Announces Development Plans for 1995," *Business Wire,* December 13, 1994, p. 12131081.

La Franco, Robert C., "Koo Koo Who?," *Forbes,* November 18, 1996, p. 80.

Martin, Richard, "Koo Koo Roo Molds Limited Alliance with Pottery Chain," *Nation's Restaurant News,* June 24, 1996, p. 3.

——, "Koo Koo Roo Plan Plucked as Milken Trust Flies Koop," *Nation's Restaurant News,* October 31, 1994, p. 14.

"Mergers and Acquisitions: Koo Koo Roo, Inc.," *Food Institute Report,* April 28, 1997.

"Mergers and Acquisitions: Koo Koo Roo, Inc.," *Food Institute Report,* June 2, 1997.

Robertiello, Jack, "Koo Koo Roo HRM Is Spreading Its Wings into New York," *Supermarket News,* October 28, 1996, p. 29.

Vrana, Deborah, "Koo Koo Roo Yanks Its Share Price Out of the Fire; New Products, Cutbacks Form Firm's Recipe for Success," *Los Angeles Business Journal,* May 24, 1993, p. 31.

—Charity Anne Dorgan

Koor Industries Ltd.

Four Kaufman Street
Tel Aviv 68012
Israel
(03) 519-5201
Fax: (03) 519-5353
Web site: http://www.koor.co.il

Public Company
Incorporated: 1944
Employees: 31,640
Sales: US $3.56 billion (1997)
Stock Exchanges: Tel Aviv New York London
Ticker Symbol: KOR
SICs: 2834 Pharmaceutical Preparations; 2869 Industrial
    Organic Chemicals, Not Elsewhere Classified; 2879
    Pesticides & Agricultural Chemicals, Not Elsewhere
    Classified; 3241 Cement, Hydraulic; 3253 Ceramic
    Wall & Floor Tile; 3661 Telephone & Telegraph
    Apparatus; 4813 Telephone Communications, Except
    Radio Telephone

Koor Industries Ltd. is the largest industrial holding company in Israel, accounting for seven percent of that nation's industrial output and exports. About half of the company's revenues are derived from telecommunications and electronics operations, principally through holdings in Tadiran Telecommunications Ltd. and Telrad Telecommunications Ltd., which together are the exclusive providers of digital public telephone switching apparatus to Bezeq, Israel's national phone company. Accounting for about 16 percent of sales each are Koor's two other main sectors: agrochemicals, and building and infrastructure. The former includes holdings in Makhteshim Chemical Works Ltd. and Agan Chemical Manufacturers Ltd., while the latter includes holdings in Nesher Israel Cement Enterprises Ltd. (Israel's cement monopoly), United Steel Mills Ltd., and Middle East Tube Co. Publicly traded, Koor is nonetheless controlled by two large shareholders: The Claridge Group, the investment management company of Charles R. Bronfman (co-

chairman of Seagram Company) and his family, which holds almost one-quarter of Koor stock; and Bank Hapoalim, Israel's largest banking and financial services group, which holds nearly 23 percent.

The Early Years: Labor Union Roots

Koor's predecessor was Solel Boneh Construction, founded in British Palestine in 1924 by the Histadrut (the General Federation of Labor) to construct roads and buildings. Through Solel Boneh, the Histadrut provided a livelihood for settlers in an attempt to found a Jewish state in Palestine.

Solel Boneh began planning for independence as early as 1944, when it created an industrial arm called Koor Industries. Koor employed 500 workers at its two plants, Phoenicia Glass and Vulcan Foundries, both in Haifa. Many of Koor's early employees were immigrants who had escaped Europe. After World War II Koor employed many concentration camp survivors and refugees from Arab nations, providing much-needed job training and employment for these immigrants not just in cities but also in remote villages.

Koor formed Nesher Cement in 1945 as a joint venture with private investors. Koor's first exports, Vulcan car batteries, were sold to Syria in 1947. In 1951 Koor entered the telecommunications field through another joint venture called Telrad, which was located in the town of Lod, near Tel Aviv. From this facility and another built at Ma'alot in 1965, Telrad manufactured telephones, PABX switching terminals, and a variety of other electronic devices.

Shortly after Israeli independence was declared in 1948, the state was attacked by Arab nations. In repelling the attack, Israel took additional land and doubled in size. The war, however, left Koor economically isolated within the Middle Eastern region. Without local export markets, the company instead concentrated its sales efforts in Europe, North America, and Africa. But with continuing tensions between Israel and its Arab neighbors came the need for Israel to develop a domestic arms industry. In 1952 Koor, in conjunction with the Finnish company Tampella, established the Soltam artillery manufacturing plant. Koor's arms manufacturing grew over the years as

266

Company Perspectives:

Koor Industries is the partner of choice for international blue chip corporations seeking joint ventures in Israel and the Middle East. In 1997, Northern Telecom, IBM, Carrier, Newbridge Networks, ITT Sheraton, and American Express joined a list of leading multinational corporations which already included Volvo, General Dynamics, Alcatel and others. Cooperation with these global enterprises is a two-way street. They gain access to Israeli high-tech know-how and development, Israeli and Middle Eastern markets and, in turn, are able to reach access to both US and European markets freely. Through its affiliates, Koor benefits from access to new international marketing networks, important research projects, new technologies, and state-of-the-art production methods.

Israel's Arab neighbors acquired increasingly sophisticated weaponry.

Koor opened the Harsah Ceramics plant in Haifa in 1953, and the following year built a steel processing complex in partnership with German interests. In conjunction with American interests, Koor established the Alliance Tire and Rubber Company in 1955. Through these ventures, Koor not only contributed significantly to Israeli import-substitution efforts, but generated valuable foreign exchange, too.

Koor Gains Independence in 1958

By 1958 Koor had grown to 25 plants with 6,000 employees and overshadowed its parent company, Solel Boneh. That year Hevrat Ha'Ovdim, the economic arm of the Histadrut, decided to make Koor a separate entity specializing in industrial products, management and financial services, and foreign trade.

In 1962 Koor created an electronics company called Tadiran, jointly owned by Koor and the Israeli Defense Ministry until 1969. A year after creating Tadiran Koor entered the chemical industry by purchasing Makhteshim. Israel's largest manufacturer of herbicides, pesticides, and insecticides, Makhteshim became an important exporter and source of foreign exchange.

Because it was so closely tied to the Histadrut labor organization, Koor often made business decisions according to workers' welfare rather than profit potential. One of the company's innovations in industrial relations was a joint labor-management committee to discuss production problems. This committee, introduced in 1964 at the Phoenicia Glass plant, raised productivity and minimized labor disputes and was copied later at other plants.

Israeli borders were expanded again in 1967 after another war with its Arab neighbors. The West Bank, formerly a part of Jordan, the Syrian Golan Heights, and Egypt's vast Sinai Peninsula came under Israeli control. Israeli economic influence spread into these occupied territories with the establishment of communal settlements. The development of these largely agrar-

ian frontier regions represented an expansion of the domestic economy and increased demand for many of Koor's industrial and commercial products.

The Israeli Defense Ministry sold its 50 percent interest in Tadiran to America's General Telephone and Electronics Corporation (GTE) in 1969. The new ownership gave Koor access to superior technologies developed by GTE and helped Tadiran to become Israel's largest electronics manufacturer and one of its largest employers. In 1970 Koor purchased Hamashbir Lata'asiya, an integrated food manufacturer that produced edible oils and processed, canned, and frozen foods under the Telma brand name. In consumer goods, the company began manufacturing footwear and later added cosmetics, toiletries, cleaning products, and paper goods.

Foreign Expansion in the 1970s

In 1971 Koor took over the government-owned Elda Trading company and renamed it Koortrade. This new subsidiary promoted Koor products in export markets and represented other manufacturers who could not afford to establish their own trade promotion groups.

Koor also built its international reputation through turnkey projects in developing countries. The first of these was a cotton farm established in Ethiopia in 1972. Additional Koor projects in Nigeria, Togo, and other African nations improved Israeli relations in Africa and elsewhere in the Third World—especially important in light of continued Arab hostility toward Israel.

In 1973, when Israel was attacked by its Arab neighbors, it severely damaged its enemies' air forces in defending itself. Koor now was a more important strategic resource than ever before. The company was called upon to develop new weapons, help increase armament stockpiles, and raise military preparedness. In 1974, as part of an effort to promote more even geographical industrialization, Koor established the Agan Chemical plant in the Negev Desert in southern Israel.

Through peace and war, the company remained highly supportive of its workers, establishing a profit-sharing plan in 1973 and a worker-discount center in 1978. Recognizing the importance of skilled managers, the company also opened a management training school in 1981.

Koor's Telrad subsidiary was awarded the Industrial Development Prize in 1983 for a multiline telephone system it had developed. The award generated greater interest in the system and bolstered both domestic and international sales for the company. Telrad devoted a disproportionately high percentage of earnings to research and development, which led to more sophisticated battle management systems and communication devices as well as "smarter" weapons. In another defense-related project that year, Koor formed a partnership with Pratt & Whitney to build jet engine parts at Carmel Forge in northern Israel.

Despite a lasting peace agreement with Egypt in 1979, Israel endured numerous financial crises that often resulted in a high inflation rate. This in turn compromised the ability of Israeli exporters to remain competitive in world markets. Indeed, because it was in large part an instrument of Israeli labor, Koor devoted much of its excess capital to job creation, leaving it few resources to draw upon in times of economic hardship. Worse yet, a 1986 attempt to attract capital in American markets failed, resulting in losses of $253 million during 1987.

Difficulties in the Late 1980s

A new management team, headed by Benjamin Gaon, took over in May 1988 when Gaon's predecessor resigned in protest over interference from the Histadrut. Gaon's first task was to reorganize the company. Several factories were closed and others were combined. Koor's operations were reorganized into five groups, plus one division for international trade. Each group became an individual profit center, placing the burden of performance on individual group heads, while deep cuts were made in management staff.

But like the economy of which Koor was so much a part, the company's difficulties could not be sorted out overnight. Saddled with a $1.2 billion debt, a third of which was owed to foreign banks, Koor neared bankruptcy in late 1988. In fact, Bankers Trust Co. of the United States tried to force the company into liquidation when it failed to make a $20 million payment on a $175 million loan. After a Tel Aviv court granted the company a temporary stay, Gaon moved quickly to save the company.

Reborn in the 1990s

Gaon responded with an American-style restructuring, slashing the company's work force by 40 percent, from more than 32,000 to 20,000, undeterred by fierce protests from Israeli workers. He also jettisoned numerous noncore subsidiaries, reducing the number of holdings from 100 to less than 30. Three key sectors were retained as the core of the new Koor: telecommunications and electronics, agrochemicals, and building and infrastructure. In 1991 the company's $1.1 billion in debt was restructured. A return to profitability in 1992 signaled the culmination of the turnaround, which also was aided by an influx of Russian immigrants into Israel, who provided a sharp boost to the economy resulting in increased demand for numerous Koor goods and services.

Underlying the restructuring was a fundamental shift in company philosophy away from the pro-labor stance of the past toward a focus on profitability and competitiveness. But perhaps more important, Koor's financial ties to the Histadrut were considerably weakened by the debt restructuring agreement, in which lenders traded debt for equity stakes in Koor. An outgrowth of this deal was that Israeli banks gained significant stakes in Koor—Bank Hapoalim held almost 23 percent by the mid-1990s and Bank Leumi Le-Israel held barely more than six percent. The Histadrut saw its stake decline to only 22.5 percent by 1993. This was reduced to zero in 1995 when Shamrock Holdings, a private investment vehicle of Roy Disney (vice-chairman of Walt Disney) and his family, bought the labor federation's stake. Later in 1995 Koor held a successful international public offering in New York, raising about $120 million in American depository receipts.

By 1997 Shamrock was pushing for a breakup of Koor to enhance shareholder value. Both Gaon and Bank Hapoalim objected to such a move, resulting in Shamrock selling its Koor stake to The Claridge Group, the investment management company of Seagram Company co-chairman Charles R. Bronfman and his family, in mid-1997. Bronfman became chairman of Koor, with Jonathan Kolber, a Claridge Group executive, becoming deputy chairman. In July 1998 Gaon retired as president and CEO and was succeeded by Kolber. With Gaon having successfully established Koor as the largest and most profitable industrial concern in Israel, the stage had been set for the new management team to build upon this solid framework.

Principal Subsidiaries

Tadiran Ltd. (63%); Tadiran Telecommunications Ltd. (50.4%); Telrad Telecommunications Ltd. (80%); ECI Telecom Ltd. (10.7%); Makhteshim Chemical Works Ltd. (68%); Agan Chemical Manufacturers Ltd. (35%); Mashav (50%); Nesher Israel Cement Enterprises Ltd. (50%); United Steel Mills Ltd. (71%); Middle East Tube Co. Ltd. (76%).

Further Reading

"Blimey: Koor," *Economist*, April 3, 1993, pp. 66.

"Claridge Israel Buys Shamrock's Shares in Koor Industries," *Israel Business Today*, July 31, 1997, p. 1.

Dempsey, Judy, "Koor Appoints Kolber as New Chief Executive," *Financial Times*, March 13, 1998, p. 27.

——, "Koor Net Hit by Telecoms Revamp," *Financial Times*, March 31, 1998, p. 33.

——, "Shamrock To Push for Spin-Offs at Koor," *Financial Times*, July 5, 1997, p. 17.

"Gold Fleeced? Israeli Business," *Economist*, July 26, 1997, p. 56.

"Kato to Buy 'Substantial Holdings' in Koor," *Israel Business Today*, January 31, 1997, p. 14.

"Koor Blimey," *Economist*, October 22, 1988, p. 77.

Landau, Pinchas, "Koor Giant Back on Its Feet," *Israel Business Today*, May 15, 1992, pp. 1.

Machlis, Avi, and Dempsey, Judy, "New Owners To Widen Koor's Horizons," *Financial Times*, January 13, 1998, p. 27.

Marcus, Amy Dockser, "Big Israeli Firm and Palestinians Go into Business," *Wall Street Journal*, October 6, 1993, p. A12.

Ozanne, Julian, "Koor Reveals New Strategy for Growth," *Financial Times*, March 29, 1996, p. 30.

——, "Koor's Mr. Turnaround Builds Bridges in the Middle East," *Financial Times*, February 13, 1995, p. 14.

——, "Offering from Koor Draws in Almost $120m," *Financial Times*, November 14, 1995, p. 33.

——, "State Near Completion of Koor Sell-Off," *Financial Times*, December 29, 1993, p. 15.

——, "US Investment Group Agrees To Buy Koor Industries Stake," *Financial Times*, March 8, 1995, p. 25.

Silver, Robert, "Koor Industries: Israel's Conglomerate Restructured," *Multinational Business*, Spring 1989, pp. 28–29.

Waldman, Peter, "Big Brother Is Shown the Door at Koor, Giving Israel's Largest Company a Boost," *Wall Street Journal*, July 3, 1991, p. A4.

—updated by David E. Salamie

KUSHNER·LOCKE
C O M P A N Y

The Kushner-Locke Company

11601 Wilshire Boulevard, 21st Floor
Los Angeles, California 90025
U.S.A.
(310) 481-2000
Fax: (310) 481-2101
Web site: http//www.kushner-locke.com

Public Company
Incorporated: 1988
Employees: 83
Sales: $56.93 million (1997)
Stock Exchanges: NASDAQ
Ticker Symbol: KLOC
SICs: 7812 Motion Picture & Video Production; 7822
   Motion Picture & Tape Distribution

The Kushner-Locke Company is an independent entertainment company based in Los Angeles. The company's primary business is the production and distribution of television programs and feature films for an international market. Kushner-Locke's television programs include series, mini-series, movies, animation, reality, and game show programs for the major networks, cable TV, first-run syndication, and international markets. Feature films are produced for the motion picture, cable, and video markets.

Beginnings in Television Production

The company was founded in 1980 by Peter Locke and Donald Kushner, who had been fraternity brothers at Syracuse University. At first, Kushner-Locke's primary business was syndicated television programs (such as its early production of the five-year series "Divorce Court") and movies, specials and series for cable and network TV. These types of programs generally break even domestically, with potential profits based on international distribution. Kushner-Locke soon developed a reputation for providing reliable, low-budget programming on

time. Managerial decisions exhibited a low-risk philosophy, aimed at reliable niche markets which produced predictably safe returns but few major hits. This conservative strategy contrasted sharply with the excesses of the production industry as a whole, making the company attractive to investors.

For a decade and a half, the company acted as a "producer for hire," by releasing its productions to major networks for a fee. This strategy helped keep risks low, but also deprived the company of its rightful earnings after syndication or resale of its productions. In 1995, to retain more of the financial pot, the company created a joint venture and distribution subsidiary with New City Releasing, Inc.: KLC/New City Ventures (later KLC/New City Televentures), widening its profit margins. Under the auspices of KLC/New City, the company would acquire or produce 107 films between 1996 and 1998, filling the growing cable and pay-per-view markets. KLC productions included many HBO originals and world premieres for pay cable networks (including Oliver Stone's *Freeway* and *Last Time I Committed Suicide* with Keanu Reeves).

Financial Struggles and Feature Films

In 1993, strategically moving beyond TV to increase potential profits, Kushner-Locke had begun producing feature films. The next year, an international distribution subsidiary was established. The company put into place a 12-person foreign distribution staff to bolster international sales, but the results were slow. By 1996, feature films comprised 32 percent of the company's revenues, but none of its earnings. That year, the company produced what it hoped would be its first blockbuster film: *The Legend of Pinocchio,* starring Martin Landau and animatronic puppets. *Pinocchio* was a disappointment, grossing $16 million at the domestic box office (with costs of $29 million). By 1997, *Pinocchio* had made some money for the company through foreign sales, and *André the Seal* (another family title) also showed a slight profit. Deals with directors Oliver Stone and Robert Altman and producer Joel Silver (*Lethal Weapon*) were made, in hopes of producing the successful film *Pinocchio* was to have been. With Altman's production company (Sandcastle 5), Kushner-Locke coproduced "The Gun," an ABC TV series.

Company Perspectives:

The Kushner-Locke Company produces and distributes theatrical, television and video entertainment software, including infomercials and related product sales, throughout the world in all genres and budget ranges. As one of the few surviving independent production companies, we move quickly to seize opportunities in the changing market place, while simultaneously managing our resources in a conservative and prudent manner. Our considerable library of film and television products, which we continue to actively license throughout the world, provides a stable anchor for our continued growth.

Between 1992 and 1996, Kushner-Locke incurred annual losses, which it supported in part by selling stock—five secondary offerings. To finance its losses, the company almost doubled its capitalization by authorizing 70 million new shares of stock. Earnings during this period fluctuated, reflecting changing strategies and activities. In 1993, revenues were $42.5 million, but two years later, in 1995, sales dropped to $20.4 million. In addition to the meager profit margin of TV programs, the company encountered financial problems linked to its amortization strategies. A prime example was the company's decision to take a $7 million write-off in 1994 on a distribution contract to syndicate a 1984 HBO sitcom starring O. J. Simpson. Normally, three-quarters of the company's film production costs were spread over three years, a practice accountants considered with skepticism. In August 1997, with no capital to fund production, the company borrowed $37.7 million on an existing $40 million credit line through Chase Manhattan. By the next month, the credit line was increased to $60 million, causing rumors that Kushner-Locke was preparing for a sell-off. To make the company more attractive to investors, a 1-for-6 reverse stock split was instituted. The company hired Allen & Co., an entertainment investment banking firm, to help assess business strategies, including financing, relationships, and mergers and acquisitions. Again, fluctuating revenue reflected changing strategies. In 1996, revenues reached a record $80.2 million. The next year, sales dropped to $56.9 million, but management of unconsolidated joint ventures resulted in an additional $24.7 million.

Diversification in the Late 1990s

In the late 1990s, Kushner-Locke moved in several directions to raise its profile with major broadcast networks and film studios. The company's initiatives resulted in high Wall Street ratings. Coproduction deals were the rage in 1997, with European companies seeking helping hands to ease their transition into the competitive U.S. market. Granada, Europe's most prolific TV production company, launched a partnership with Kushner-Locke around the release of its British drama "Cracker." The show would air in an extremely competitive time slot on ABC: Thursdays at 9 p.m., opposite NBC's outrageously popular "Seinfeld" and the new, eagerly awaited "Veronica's Closet." International coproduction continued to be a priority with the elaborate filming of *Beowulf,* a big-budget (estimated

at $18–$20 million) Christopher Lambert film shot in Romania and coproduced with Threshold Entertainment and Capitol Films. Post-communist Romania was an extremely cost-effective place to shoot films, and the elaborate sets of *Beowulf* would not have been possible in Los Angeles within budgetary constraints. A castle was created in Romania, combining aspects of many existing castles.

Filming in Romania was not unusual for Kushner-Locke. Between 1993 and 1998, the company had explored numerous international settings, shooting films in Canada, Mexico, Costa Rica, Australia, New Zealand, England, Scotland, Wales, the Czech Republic, Romania, Estonia, Bulgaria, Israel, South Africa, and Mauritius.

The company began to employ a two-tiered approach to the feature film market, producing major releases and low to moderate budget films. *The Adventures of Pinocchio* (1996) and *Basil* (1997) were major releases. Four films in the lower tier premiered at the Sundance Film Festival in 1996–97. In October 1997, K-L International implemented a MIFED slate of five films to expand the company's feature film presence and create more international appeal. These films included: *Susan's Plan,* directed by *Blues Brothers* creator John Landis and featuring *Titanic* star Billy Zane; *Girl,* starring Dominique Swain (of *Lolita*); *A New Life,* with Tom Berenger and directed by John Flynn; *The Point Men,* a Christopher Lambert action film; and *Tax Man,* a Joseph Pantoliano action thriller. Other projects in 1997 included a $20 million action film (*One Man's Hero*), the $4 million comedy *Denial,* and an $8 million period drama (*Basil*). An agreement was made giving Kushner-Locke International foreign rights to Ted Demme's $10 million *Noose,* and another deal was made to cofinance and distribute *Beowulf* and *Mercy* with UK-based Capital Films. Kushner-Locke International also launched a three-year, 15-film agreement with Disney Channel in the United Kingdom. In all, Kushner-Locke's network and studio partners included ABC, NBC, CBS, HBO, Showtime, Disney, Twentieth Century Fox, and Universal. In 1997, the company hired Pascal Borno as president of international distribution operations. Borno's Conquistador Films provided a number of films—including *Basil* and *Double Tap*—which generated over 35 percent of revenues that year.

TV programs generated 40 percent of revenues in fiscal 1997. Major TV sellers were Robert Altman's "Gun," "Cracker" (starring Robert Pastorelli), and "Hammer" (starring Stacy Keach). The company also produced a made-for-TV movie detective series with Brian Dennehy playing Jack Reed. Building upon an existing partnership, Kushner-Locke extended a one-year housing agreement with Robert Altman's Sandcastle 5 Productions. Altman and "Doonesbury" creator Garry Trudeau joined forces to develop a one-hour pilot soap, "Silicon Valley," produced through Kushner-Locke for ABC. The pilot led to a series entitled "Killer App."

Family programming was identified as a lucrative growth area. With Hyperion, Kushner-Locke produced an animated hit called "Brave Little Toaster," which would generate two sequels produced by the company's BLT Ventures for the Disney channel. Between 1996 and 1998, the company produced or acquired 25 family films, including *Pinocchio* and *André.* A highly successful 1998 production was the television series

"Mowgli: The New Adventures of the Jungle Book," which accounted for 44 percent of first quarter revenues. "Mowgli" premiered in February 1998 on the Fox Kids Network, and was the highest rated show in its time slot.

Launching an exploration of new media and interactive television, the company began to distribute Christian music. Through TV First, a Kushner-Locke joint venture, the company produced an infomercial entitled "Keep the Faith," marketing Christian CDs and tapes. A 40-city concert tour took place to support "Keep the Faith" in 1997, and Kushner-Locke oversaw the mass marketing of Christian music in Wal-Mart and other retail stores. In 1998, Kushner-Locke acquired the company 800-US-SEARCH, which provides professional search assistance for friends or relatives.

Looking Backward: A Rerun Library

In addition to successes in the diversified production of new movies and television programs, what really turned the financial picture around for Kushner-Locke in 1997 was its 200-title library of film and TV reruns, valued at approximately $65 million. Library titles included the five-year "Divorce Court" program, the game show "Conniption," and the HBO football comedy "First and Ten." Local and international television station buyers began to patronize the company's library for their reruns, representing between $10 and $13 million in annual sales. At the same time, Hollywood was experiencing a rash of mergers. With most independent companies purchased by larger production houses, Kushner-Locke stood out as one of the only independent companies to sustain its independence.

Looking Forward: New Movies and the Latin Market

In 1998, the company launched a three-year coproduction and foreign distribution deal with Universal Pictures. Under the agreement, Kushner-Locke and Universal would jointly produce, finance, and distribute nine pictures with $35 million or less budgets between 1998 and 2001. The company also premiered Gran Canal Latino, a movie satellite channel aimed at Latin America and Spanish-speaking U.S. markets, and a joint venture with Enrique Cerezo, a company with one of the largest catalogues of classic and contemporary Spanish language feature films. Through Gran Canal Latino, the company planned to air a minimum of 400 movies annually for five years. In January 1998, *Air Bud* was released throughout Latin America, and *Freeway* was shown in Mexico. In April 1998, Kushner-Locke announced that it had closed over $5 million in television deals

in Latin America, with library titles licensed to Diprom (Argentina), Cine Canal and Multivision (pan Latin America), Televisa (Mexico), Caracol (Colombia), and HBO-Olé.

Having survived as one of the few remaining independent production companies in Hollywood, Kushner-Locke managed its longevity by minimizing risk and maximizing effective partnership relationships. Known for its careful, conservative philosophy, the company, despite a lack of blockbusters, remained balanced by its reliable, steady flow of products for an ever-changing media market.

Principal Subsidiaries

Kushner-Locke International; 800-US-SEARCH; TV First; KLC/New City Televentures (82.5%).

Further Reading

Bacal, Simon, "Transylvania Gives Good Grit," *Variety,* February 20, 1998.

Carver, Benedict, "Kushner-Locke Boosts Credit Line," *Screen International,* September 19, 1997.

——, "Landis Joins Kushner-Locke Family," *Screen International,* October 17, 1997.

Chetwynd, Josh, "Zane Makes Post-'Titanic' 'Plan'," *Hollywood Reporter,* April 15, 1998.

De Moraes, Lisa, "Altman's Chips Put on 'Silicon'," *Hollywood Reporter,* November 20, 1997.

Hindes, Andrew, and Benedict Carver, "Kushner Locked Up: U Inks Co-Prod'n, Distrib Deal for up to 9 Pix," *Variety,* May 14, 1998.

Jamgocyan, Nik, "Kushner-Locke Speaks Spanish: Outfit Pacts with Enrique Cerezo to Launch Spanish-Only Channel for Americas," *Screen International,* June 5, 1998.

"The Kushner-Locke Company Reports Results of First Quarter of Fiscal 1998," Los Angeles: Kushner-Locke Company, February 17, 1998.

"The Kushner-Locke Company Sets Strategic Alliances in Latin America with More Than $5 Million in Television Deals," Los Angeles: Kushner-Locke Company, April 1, 1998.

Le Franco, Robert, "Coming to a Stockbroker Near You," *Forbes,* December 30, 1996, pp. 68–69.

Sharkey, Betsy, "Indie on a Fast Track," *Mediaweek,* January 5, 1998.

Stanley, T. L., "Spread the Risk, Share the Riches?", *Mediaweek,* June 2, 1997, pp. 522–24.

Veverka, Mark, "Kushner-Locke Shareholders May Have a Hit on Their Hands," *Wall Street Journal/California,* November 26, 1997.

"What We Do," Los Angeles: Kushner-Locke Company, 1998.

—Heidi Feldman

The L.L. Knickerbocker Co., Inc.

25800 Commercecentre Drive
Lake Forest, California 92630
U.S.A.
(714) 595-7900
Fax: (714) 595-7901
Web site: www.knickerbocker.com

Public Company
Incorporated: 1993
Employees: 598
Sales: $68.3 million (1997)
Stock Exchanges: NASDAQ
Ticker Symbol: KNIC
SICs: 3911 Jewelry, Precious Metal; 3961 Costume
Jewelry and Costume Novelties, Except Precious
Metal; 3942 Dolls and Stuffed Toys; 2731 Books:
Publishing; 6719 Offices of Holding Companies, Not
Elsewhere Classified; 5961 Catalog and Mail-Order
Houses

L.L. Knickerbocker Co., Inc., is a successful manufacturer and marketer of collectibles and jewelry, two growing markets. After the company went public in 1995, its revenues leaped from $7.8 million to $68 million in two years. In addition, LLK makes equity investments in small companies with proprietary technologies in fields such as alternative fuel. As of December 31, 1997, company founders Louis L. Knickerbocker and his wife Tamara Knickerbocker owned approximately 41 percent, or 7.7 million shares, of the company's outstanding common stock.

Early History

Several companies preceded the formation of the L.L. Knickerbocker Co. In 1985 Louis L. Knickerbocker and his wife Tamara Knickerbocker formed a company called International Beauty Supply, Ltd., in California. The company sold a line of cosmetics called Orchid Premium to professional beauty supply houses and later to retail outlets. It began selling collect-ible Knickerbocker products in October 1986 under the Knickerbocker Toy Company brand. In 1987 Louis L. Knickerbocker and Michael Elam co-founded LaVie Cosmetics. It introduced a beauty product called Creme de LaVie for both the I. Magnin and Nordstrom department stores. In October 1988 Creme de LaVie was introduced on the Home Shopping Network with comedienne Phyllis Diller as the product's spokesperson. Then in 1989 the Knickerbockers co-founded MLF Enterprises, with Elam and actress Farrah Fawcett. MLF developed replicas of Farrah Fawcett's jewelry collection and market ed them through television home shopping networks.

The Knickerbockers formed Knickerbocker Creations, Ltd., in 1990 and began developing the products and celebrity endorsement programs that later became part of the L.L. Knickerbocker Co. These included the Kenneth Jay Lane High Society Collection of fashion jewelry (introduced in 1991), the Nolan Miller Glamour Collection of fashion jewelry (introduced in 1992), Marie Osmond fine porcelain collector dolls (introduced in 1991), and Annette Funicello collectible bears (introduced in 1992).

The L.L. Knickerbocker Co., Name Adopted, 1993

In 1993 the Knickerbockers began contemplating making an initial public offering of stock, but Knickerbocker Creations was a Subchapter S corporation and unsuitable for a public offering. In order to facilitate a public offering, the name of International Beauty Supply was changed to the L.L. Knickerbocker Co., Inc., on May 24, 1993. The L.L. Knickerbocker Co. then acquired certain assets of Knickerbocker Creations, including the marketing and distribution rights to the products and programs of Knickerbocker Creations.

In 1994, the year prior to L.L. Knickerbocker's intial public offering, the company reported revenue of $7.8 million, a 50 percent increase over 1993 revenue of $5.2 million.

Initial Public Offering, 1995

L.L. Knickerbocker's initial public offering was completed on January 25, 1995. The company issued 471,500 units, with each unit consisting of two shares of common stock and one common stock purchase warrant. On August 30, 1995, the company approved a five-for-one common stock split and increased the number of authorized shares of common stock to 100 million. The reason for the split was that in July, the share price rose from around $5 to $52 before falling back to $46.75. The split cut the price to make it more affordable to small investors, while increasing the number of outstanding shares to 12.3 million.

The sudden dramatic rise in L.L. Knickerbocker's stock price caused officials at the Securities and Exchange Commission (SEC) and NASDAQ to contact the company to see what it was telling investors. The stock began to rise when an influential broker, Rafi Khan, became interested in the company and introduced Knickerbocker to money managers who began taking big stakes in the company. Daily trading jumped from 20,000 shares to 113,000 shares. Short sellers who borrowed the stock expecting it to fall were caught by surprise. When their lenders became nervous and demanded payment, the short sellers had to purchase the stock at a higher price. The situation, known as a classic short squeeze, caused the stock price to rise even higher. For 1995, LLK reported revenue of $13.1 million.

Acquisitions, 1996

In June 1996 L.L. Knickerbocker acquired Krasner Group, Inc., for $3.2 million in stock and stock purchase warrants. Krasner designed, manufactured, and marketed costume, or fashion, jewelry. In July LLK acquired three companies specializing in fine jewelry: Grant King International, Ltd.; S.L.S. Trading Co., Ltd.; and Harlyn International Ltd. Grant King was merged with S.L.S. Trading, which sourced gemstones and developed proprietary stone cutting technologies. Harlyn was a manufacturer and marketer of fine jewelry. These companies were organized into LLK's Jewelry Division.

In October L.L. Knickerbocker expanded its presence in the collectible market by acquiring an 82 percent interest for $3.2 million in the Georgetown Collection, Inc. Georgetown marketed collectible dolls via direct response catalogs, advertisements, and mail. The acquisition included the Magic Attic Club line of quality vinyl dolls. The Georgetown Collection's main offices were located in Portland, Maine.

During 1996 LLK also made equity investments in two companies with emerging proprietary technologies, Pure Energy Corporation and Ontro, Inc. This was the start of LLK's Investment Division.

Consolidation, 1997

For 1997, revenues increased 62 percent to $68.3 million, as compared to $42.1 million in 1996. Gross profit increased 82

percent to $37.5 million. However, due to costs associated with consolidating the companies acquired in 1996, LLK reported an operating loss of $2.0 million in 1997.

In June 1997 LLK moved to a new corporate headquarters with 50,000 square feet, enough space to accommodate the company's anticipated growth. In Thailand, the company opened a new 3,500-square-foot jewelry showroom. It was also completing its first silver manufacturing plant there.

The Collectibles Division

The company is organized into three divisions: Collectibles, Jewelry, and Investments. The Collectible Division creates precious bears, dolls, and other collectible items, with most of the production being outsourced. In 1997 collectibles accounted for approximately two-thirds of LLK's total revenue. The company began selling collectible toys and teddy bears in October 1986 under the Knickerbocker Toy Company brand, even before the company was called the L.L. Knickerbocker Co. In 1991 it introduced Marie Osmond fine porcelain collector dolls, with singer Marie Osmond acting as the celebrity spokesperson and design director for the collection, which grew to include more than 420 different styles of dolls that sold at retail for $20 to $600. Marie Osmond once sold out $2 million worth of a limited line of her designer dolls in only 13 minutes of air time on the QVC home shopping network.

In 1992 the Collectible Division introduced Annette Funicello collectible bears, with actress Annette Funicello as the celebrity image and design director for the collection. With retail prices ranging from $25 to $200, the collection grew to include more than 325 different styles of collectible teddy bears.

Much of LLK's success in the collectible market was due to its ability to target selected niches. While the largest population for collectibles was the 35–64 year old age group, LLK introduced the Magic Attic Club in 1996 for that age group's children and grandchildren. This line of fine quality vinyl dolls was suitable both for play, which appealed to girls aged 6–11, and for collecting, which appealed to their parents. With vinyl collectibles one of the fastest-growing categories in collectibles, Magic Attic was the second largest catalog retailer in this category, behind the Pleasant Company, a privately held Wisconsin firm with nearly $300 million in annual catalog sales.

Complementing the Magic Attic Club catalog operation was the Magic Attic Press, which published a popular children's book series. In May 1998, the company closed the Magic Attic Press editorial office in New York as part of a consolidation and strategic alliance with Millbrook Press, Inc., which would take over the ongoing production, marketing, sales, and distribution of the Magic Attic Press line. Management, creative, and editorial functions were shifted to the company's Portland, Maine, office.

Strategic alliances were also formed with Eastman Kodak Co. to co-develop and co-promote collectibles for the Marie Osmond line, and with Universal Studios for the Edith Head line. Edith Head was a legendary costume designer who won eight Academy Awards for her designs. In 1997 and 1998 L.L. Knickerbocker launched Kodak Moments by Marie Osmond, Universal Studios Glamour Collection, the Disney Art Classic Collection, and the Richard Simmons Masters Collection. They were expected to be strong brands for the company and to generate significant revenues. Other celebrities associated with LLK collectibles included designer Bob Mackie and Candy Spelling. Three years of development work were typically required for newly introduced collections.

LLK's collectibles were marketed through a variety of distribution channels, including direct response; television shopping sales through networks such as QVC; international distributors; and wholesale sales to retailers via trade shows. LLK was QVC's top-selling collectible vendor.

At the 1998 American International Toy Fair, LLK collectibles received 13 design award nominations. Since 1992 the company had received 51 nominations resulting in 16 awards. The Toy Fair provided LLK with an opportunity to meet new retailers, who accounted for one-third of all of LLK's orders there.

The Jewelry Division

L.L. Knickerbocker's Jewelry Division consists of two categories: fine jewelry and fashion, or costume, jewelry. Fine jewelry is manufactured with precious metals, such as gold, sterling silver, or platinum, with or without gemstones. Fashion, or costume, jewelry, is made with non-precious metals and may be gold-plated.

By the late 1990s L.L. Knickerbocker's fashion jewelry operation was vertically integrated. It exercised control over stone sourcing and cutting, design structures, manufacturing, and marketing. Most of LLK's fashion jewelry lines were managed and produced by its Rhode Island-based subsidiary, the Krasner Group, Inc., which it acquired in 1996.

One of the company's leading fashion lines was the Kenneth Jay Lane brand, which was introduced in 1991. It grew to include 450 different styles of fashion jewelry that sold at retail from $17 to $198. Kenneth Jay Lane is the designer and spokesperson for the collection. In April 1997, several of Mr. Lane's original pieces were sold at Sotheby's Jacqueline Kennedy Onassis auction. The Kenneth Jay Lane Star Brooch and matching earrings sold at the auction for $19,550. In the days immediately following the auction, the Krasner Group supplied nearly 10,000 reproductions of the brooch to QVC, which sold them for $98 each, generating nearly $1 million in sales.

Other celebrities associated with LLK's fashion jewelry included Barbara Mandrell, Pilar Crespi, Wendy Gell, and Nolan Miller. The Nolan Miller Glamour Collection was started in 1992 and grew to include 400 different styles of fashion jewelry priced from $20 to $280 retail. Nolan Miller was the designer and spokesperson for the collection. Several lines of fashion accessories were also marketed with celebrities including Anushka, Albert Capraro, Mary McFadden, and Dennis Basso.

Fashion jewelry accounted for approximately 60 percent of LLK's jewelry sales. Fashion jewelry and accessories were marketed primarily through television retailers such as QVC Network, Home Shopping Network, and TVSN Australia. Fine jewelry accounted for the other 40 percent of LLK's jewelry sales, which were sold mainly in Western Europe and South America through an international distribution network. LLK's fine jewelry was manufactured and marketed by three companies based in Thailand: The L.L. Knickerbocker (Thai) Co., Ltd.; Harlyn International Co., Ltd.; and S.L.S. Trading Co., Ltd. In 1997 combined jewelry sales accounted for 32.1 percent of L.L. Knickerbocker's revenues.

For 1998 LLK planned to complete the integration and consolidation of its recently established Thailand operations. In its first full year of operation, the L.L. Knickerbocker (Thai) Co., Ltd. produced gross sales of $10.3 million and operating profits of $1.2 million in 1997. The Thai subsidiary marketed and manufactured gold, diamonds, emeralds, rubies, and other semi-precious stones worldwide, with its main focus on Western Europe and South America. Its jewelry was produced in a company-owned, 30,000-square-foot manufacturing facility which contained a showroom as well as a design and development division.

The Investment Division

The Investment Division was formed to acquire companies with emerging proprietary technologies. By the end of 1997, LLK was involved with three such investments, in each case providing expertise to help the company reach its potential. As of early 1998, none had yet begun to tap their full market potential.

In 1996 LLK made equity investments in two private companies, Pure Energy Corporation (PEC) and Ontro, Inc. PEC had developed patented alternative fuel and was awaiting U.S. Dept. of Energy certification. A U.S. patent on the fuel was issued in December 1997. PEC held the exclusive, worldwide license from Princeton University to commercialize a cleaner burning alternative fuel consisting of a blend of ethanol, natural gas liquids, and co-solvents derived from renewable resources. LLK held a 30 percent equity interest in PEC.

Ontro Inc., which developed a patented self-heating container for packaging food and beverages, filed for its initial public offering in 1997. Its container design won the 1995 Product of the Year Award at the Invention Convention, and in July 1997 the U.S. Patent Office issued a new patent covering 25 aspects of the container design. In May 1998 the Ontro, Inc., IPO was completed. Some 3.4 million units were sold at $5.50 per unit. Each unit consisted of one share of common stock and one three-year redeemable common stock purchase warrant to purchase one share of common stock at $8.25 per share. Prior to the public offering, L.L. Knickerbocker had a 28 percent equity interest in Ontro, which became a 13 percent interest after the IPO. According to statements made by Louis Knickerbocker at the company's annual meeting in May 1998, ''Our $650,000 investment in Ontro 18 short months ago is valued today at more than $5 million.'' With respect to PEC, he said, ''Our $2.4 million investment in Pure Energy Cor poration a little more than 24 months ago is valued today at more than $50 million.''

L.L. Knickerbocker's third investment venture was with Arkenol Holdings, LLC. In August 1997 LLK teamed with Arkenol Holdings to form a joint venture partnership called Arkenol Asia, Inc. Each company had a half interest in the joint venture, which was formed to use Arkenol's technology to manufacture and sell chemicals, biomass solids, and liquid fuels in selected Asian countries. In December 1997, the joint venture signed a memorandum of understanding with the People's Republic of China (PRC) for the construction of China's first biorefinery. The agreement was expected to lead to the construction of as many as 100 biorefineries over the next 10 to 15 years in China.

At the company's May 1998 annual meeting Louis Knickerbocker announced a new investment. The company traded two percent of its holdings in PEC for a 6.7 percent stake in Phoenix Environmental Ltd. valued at $40 million. Phoenix had a patented, proprietary technology that converted steel mill by-products and other steel-based waste streams into a marketable industrial product.

Positioned for Growth, 1998

In early 1998 LLK introduced cost-saving measures. During the first quarter of 1998 LLK consolidated its global distribution and warehousing operations as well as some U.S. manufacturing operations. The company expected to realize annualized savings of $1 million from these moves. For the future, the company was focused on increasing its sales and marketing efforts for its many branded products.

In the three short years since it went public, L.L. Knickerbocker grew from $7.8 million in sales to $68 million in sales, and its assets increased from $2 million to more than $60 million. The five acquisitions it made in 1996 were turned around from $8 million in losses to $1.5 million in profit in 1997. While lamenting that the company's stock price was undervalued, Louis Knickerbocker emphasized to shareholders that the company was positioned for substantial growth.

Principal Subsidiaries

Georgetown Collection, Inc.; Magic Attic Inc.; Krasner Group, Inc.; TCJC, Inc.; Charisma Manufacturing Co., Inc.; The L.L. Knickerbocker (Thai) Co., Inc.; Harlyn International Co., Inc.; S.L.S. Trading Co., Ltd.

Further Reading

Granelli, James S., ''SEC's Eyes Open Wide at Doll Firm's Success,'' *Los Angeles Times,* August 12, 1995, p. 1.
''L.L. Knickerbocker Announces Completion of Ontro, Inc. Initial Public Offering,'' *PR Newswire,* May 12, 1998.
''L.L. Knickerbocker Subsidiary Magic Attic Press and Publisher Millbrook Join Forces,'' *PR Newswire,* May 21, 1998.
''Our Stock Is Undervalued, Said Louis L. Knickerbocker at Annual Meeting of Stockholders,'' *PR Newswire,* May 17, 1998.
Vrana, Debora, ''Showdown Looms on Knickerbocker Stock,'' *Los Angeles Times,* August 17, 1995, p. 1.

—David Bianco

La Choy Food Products Inc.

901 Stryker Street
P.O. Box 220
Archbold, Ohio 43502
U.S.A.
(419) 445-8015
Fax: (419) 445-2375

Division of Hunt-Wesson, Inc.
Incorporated: 1922
Employees: 350
Sales: $50.8 million
SICs: 2033 Canned Fruits & Specialties

La Choy Food Products Inc. is the oldest and most successful American-based producer of Oriental food products for the grocery or supermarket shelf. The company has a strong hold on more than 40 percent of the shelf-stable Oriental food market in the United States, with its closest rival Chun King maintaining approximately a 20 percent share of the market. La Choy's food product line includes soy sauce, bean sprouts, chow mein noodles, pepper steak dinners, fancy mixed vegetables, chop suey vegetables, and a host of other items. The company has become famous for preparing its products with fresh ingredients: it ships shortening from Indiana; bamboo shoots, water chestnuts, and pineapple from Taiwan, Thailand, and China; mung bean seeds from Oklahoma; pepper and carrots from California and Idaho; and large amounts of chicken, beef, and pork from a number of Midwestern states. Yet, for all its emphasis on high-quality ingredients, the company has experienced difficulty increasing its sales volume during the 1980s and 1990s, because of the introduction of tastier frozen foods and the proliferation of quick-service, Chinese take-out restaurants.

Early History

La Choy Food Products Company was the brainchild of two friends, Wally Smith and Ilhan New. The two men met and developed a close friendship while students at the University of Michigan during the early years of the 20th century, and both had become successful businessmen. Smith, an American who owned his own grocery store in Detroit, Michigan, wanted to sell bean sprouts that were fresh grown to bring a more varied product line to his customers. He thought of his old friend New, a Korean by birth, and asked him whether he had any knowledge or expertise in the matter. New said he was well acquainted with how to grow bean sprouts, and the two men came up with the idea of canning bean sprouts in glass jars. This innovative idea was so successful that Smith and New decided to incorporate their own business, La Choy Food Products Company, in 1922, and to use metal to can a variety of Oriental vegetables in addition to bean sprouts. In just a few years the company was making a tidy sum of money.

Although New left the company for personal reasons in 1930 and Smith was killed by lightning in 1937, the company continued to flourish. By the late 1930s management at the firm had developed a comprehensive line of food products, including bean sprouts, La Choy soy sauce, sub-kum, kumquats, water chestnuts, bamboo shoots, brown sauce, and chow mein noodles. In addition, more than eight million copies of *The Art and Secrets of Chinese Cooking* had been distributed across the United States. Fortunately, the company had capitalized on the growing fascination Americans had with the Orient, including an entirely different type of cuisine. In 1937 the company built its first manufacturing facility in Detroit, Michigan, with 60,000 square feet of production space, and the most sophisticated and modern equipment for processing Oriental food products.

World War II

With America's entry into World War II on December 7, 1941, La Choy Food Products Company was dealt a severe blow by the federal government. The production of Chinese food was deemed as non-essential for the United States war effort and, as a result, the tin-plate that had been used by the company to can its products was no longer available. In addition to the difficulty in procuring container materials for its products, the firm was unable to import ingredients from the Orient because of the Japanese and American conflict spreading throughout the Pacific Ocean. To reduce overhead costs and maintain profitability during the war, management decided to relocate the company from its facility in Detroit, Michigan to new headquarters in Archbold, Ohio. Selling its Detroit plant to the federal government for the production of munitions, the proceeds from the sale enabled the company to start a new era in its history.

La Choy Food Products continued to produce its soy sauce and brown sauce, as well as to package bean sprouts, chow mein noodles, chop suey, and mixed vegetables in a wide variety of containers, including glass, tin, and metal. But the lack of vegetable imports from the Orient was proving hard to overcome. Previous to the war, the company's entire supply of mung beans, which eventually blossomed into bean sprouts, had been imported from different countries in Asia. The inability to import mung beans led the company to engage in its own agriculture project, namely, growing bean sprouts from mung beans. Having relocated from Detroit to Archbold, Ohio, and having addressed the problems surrounding the lack of imports from the Orient, La Choy Food Products began production at its new facility in August of 1942.

In addition to the cultivation of the mung bean, the company discovered that the soil around Archbold was conducive for growing tomatoes. Processing tomatoes at the plant started in 1943, and the company supplied one of the most needed vegetables to the American public during the rest of the war. Unfortunately, however, La Choy Food Products Company was not able to overcome the restrictions caused by the war, and sales began to decline precipitously. In November of 1943 the firm was acquired by Beatrice Food Company, located in Chicago, Illinois, and incorporated into its new parent as an operating division.

Prosperity and Growth During the Postwar Era

With the financial backing of Beatrice Food Company and the growing consumer demand for Chinese foods across the United States during the late 1940s and early 1950s, La Choy Food Products increased both its product line and its revenues. One of the most innovative package designs during the 1950s resulted when La Choy introduced the "family pack," a 34-ounce package of chop suey/chow mein for a family of four. Throughout the 1950s fresh ingredients were used in all of the company's products, requiring a large staff, for example, to debone approximately 14,000 pounds of fresh chicken every day. Locally raised and slaughtered, the amount of chicken used at the Archbold facility indicated the demand for La Choy products.

Another innovation resulted from the increased use of bean sprouts during the 1950s. In the 1940s, because of the war and the firm's inability to import mung beans, the company pioneered the development of a reliable mung bean crop in the United States. By the early 1950s La Choy management had granted significant sums of money to universities and colleges across the United States to conduct research into the development and cultivation of mung beans. The research conducted by academic teams revealed that mung beans grew best in Texas and Oklahoma, where the composition of the soil, the amount of rainfall, and the prevailing harvesting methods combined to produce healthy beans. Yet crop yields tended to vary according to climatic conditions, and company management wanted a

more reliable source of bean sprouts for its product line. Consequently, with the knowledge it had gleaned from the academic research it had funded, La Choy established its own indoor hydroponic garden, where employees harvested bean sprouts from growing mung beans. Raised in an environment of exact temperature and moisture control and irrigated with purified water, the growing period for mung beans amounted to seven days. From that time forward, the company attained its objective for a reliable source of bean sprouts.

With the expansion of its product line and the ever-increasing public demand for Chinese food, the company implemented a three-year, multimillion dollar expansion plan in 1955. By September of 1958 the plan had been completed, and La Choy had double the production capacity of its Archbold facility. Nearly seven and a half acres of space had been added to the plant, with new techniques for producing food that had been developed and designed by company employees. The installation of highly sophisticated cookers and machinery for the quick-cooking process and packing of chow mein, an innovative chow mein noodle production workplace, and the doubling of space devoted to growing and packaging bean sprouts were just a few of the capital improvements that resulted from the expansion plan.

The decade of the 1960s included some of the best years for the company. Not only did La Choy expand its product line to encompass a wide variety of Chinese food, but the firm also expanded its production by purchasing the product lines of other companies. One of its most important acquisitions during this time was the Oriental Show-You product line of Chinese food. As sales for Show-You products continued to increase, La Choy management constructed a new, state-of-the-art soy sauce processing plant in 1963 for the recently acquired product label. By the mid-1960s the company was processing and packaging approximately 300 private-label products.

This increase in product line items necessitated more and more space at the Archbold facility. Large new warehouses were constructed to stock the ever-growing list of products made by the company, as well as bean growing bins that were needed to meet the increasing consumer demand for La Choy Chinese foods. One of the company's major capital investments during this time involved the establishment of a research and development department, formed in 1965. Technicians and scientists in the department began to develop new products, investigate and experiment with the wide range of ingredients used in La Choy foods, and evaluate the technological advances and various methods of processing food with the industry. Following up and augmenting its research and development department, the company also added a bacteriology laboratory in 1969. By combining its own criteria for assessing the quality of ingredients used in the production of its food items with the standards set by the United States government, La Choy assured its customers of a quality control process not often seen in the industry.

During the late 1960s La Choy Food Products Company ventured into the frozen foods business. Marketing research had indicated that frozen food sales would increase rapidly during the next decade, and management at the company decided to invest heavily in this segment of the industry. When construction for new buildings to house frozen food production was completed, La Choy immediately began making different flavors of egg rolls, fruit rolls, soups, dinner entrees, and the innovative boil-in-bag entrees. Not content with its line of frozen Chinese food products, the company made a strategic acquisition by purchasing the Lambrecht line of frozen food items, which included pizzas, pizza rolls, cheesecakes, and other desserts.

The 1970s and 1980s

By the beginning of the 1970s La Choy had become one of the prominent producers of frozen foods and management committed itself to build upon the company's promising entry into this burgeoning market. In 1974 management acquired Temple Frosted Foods, one of the more successful frozen food firms located in New York with an extensive product line that added different types of Chinese soups, egg rolls, and sauces to La Choy's already existing line of frozen food items. By the end of the decade more manufacturing space had been added to the company's frozen food facility in Archbold, along with new administrative offices, employee lockers, and bean growing bins. The decision by management to invest in the frozen foods market was justified clearly by the increasing sales figures for the company's frozen food items.

In 1984 Beatrice Food Company purchased all of the assets and operations of Hunt-Wesson, Inc., a large food products firm located in Fullerton, California. Part of the strategy behind this acquisition was to merge La Choy Food Products Company into Hunt-Wesson. Consequently, La Choy was fully integrated into Hunt-Wesson and the company's administrative operations and offices were relocated from Archbold, Ohio to Fullerton. This reorganization and relocation simultaneously included shifting the responsibility for the marketing and sale of La Choy products from the Archbold facility to Fullerton as well. With all of the La Choy administrative offices and responsibilities moved to Fullerton, the Archbold facility was used solely as a manufacturing plant.

The 1980s were, of course, the years of mergers, hostile acquisitions, and leveraged buyouts, and no company was better at this game than Kohlberg, Kravis, Roberts Company of New York City. In 1986 Kohlberg, Kravis, Roberts purchased Beatrice Food Company and, typical of their targeted acquisitions, sold the company piecemeal to the highest bidders. Along with many other of the food companies Beatrice had purchased over the years, in 1990 Hunt-Wesson, Inc. and La Choy Food Products Company were sold to ConAgra, Inc., a large agricultural

and food products conglomerate located in Omaha, Nebraska. In 1991 ConAgra management decided to decentralize the administration of all Hunt-Wesson business activities, so the company was parceled into what was called "Independent Operating Companies," or IOCs. La Choy Food Products Company was combined with Rosarita Food Company to become La Choy/Rosarita Food Company, a division (or IOC) of Hunt-Wesson, Inc.

The 1990s and Beyond

Although La Choy had a strong hold on approximately 40 percent of the Oriental food products market, amounting to more than $50 million, sales dropped dramatically during the early and mid-1990s. When the frozen foods product line was moved from the Archbold facility to other ConAgra plants in 1994, La Choy lost one of its most stable sources of income. The Chun King label of Chinese foods was purchased by ConAgra during the late 1980s, and some of its product line was merged with La Choy at the Archbold facility. The entire line of Healthy Choice Soups, 19 altogether, was included in the production schedule at Archbold.

La Choy's future appears uncertain. Although the company makes the most complete line of Chinese food products in the United States, canned chop suey, chow mein, and pepper steak are not competing well with easily accessible Chinese takeout food and tastier frozen dinners. Parent company ConAgra has assumed the responsibility of developing new strategies that would enable La Choy to reposition itself within the industry. But the success of such a long-term plan remains to be seen.

Further Reading

"Beatrice Sheds Fat," *Fortune,* October 28, 1985, p. 10.
"Chinese-Style Foods," *Consumer Reports,* January 1981, p. 16.
Henkoff, Ronald, "ConAgra—A Giant That Keeps Innovating," *Fortune,* December 16, 1991, p. 101.
King, Paul, "Branding Out of Control: Who's Driving This Train, Anyway," *Nation's Restaurant News,* March 4, 1996, p. 18.
Koeppel, Dan, "Choy Suey Taipans Ready for War," *Adweek's Marketing Week,* November 26, 1990, p. 14.
"The La Choy Story: A Brief History," *La Choy 75th Anniversary, Archbold (Ohio) Buckeye,* November 1, 1995, p. 3B.
"La Choy Hits Bar Code Target with Labels," *Packaging Digest,* April 1997, p. 42.
" 'You Make The Difference' Makes a Difference in Productivity at La Choy," *Quick Frozen Foods,* October 1981, p. 26.

—Thomas Derdak

Labatt Brewing Company Limited

Labatt House, BCE Place
181 Bay Street, Suite 200
Post Office Box 811
Toronto, Ontario M5J 2T3
Canada
(416) 361-5050
Fax: (416) 361-5200
Web site: http://www.labatt.com

Wholly Owned Subsidiary of Interbrew S.A.
Incorporated: 1911 as John Labatt Limited; 1979 as
    Labatt Brewing Company Limited
Employees: 5,700
SICs: 2082 Malt Beverages; 7941 Professional Sports
    Clubs & Promoters

Labatt Brewing Company Limited, acquired in 1995 by Belgian-based Interbrew S.A., holds the number two position, trailing Molson Companies Ltd., in the Canadian brewing market (by market share). Its Canadian nationwide brands include Labatt Blue (the top-selling beer in Canada), Labatt ICE, Labatt "50," and Labatt Genuine Draft, in addition to such regional brands as Kokanee, "50" Légère, and Keith's I.P.A. Labatt also distributes imported brands, including those of Anheuser-Busch and Carlsberg as well as Guinness Extra Stout. The company exports several of its brands into the United States, commanding 15 percent of the U.S. specialty beer market, and holds a 30 percent stake in Mexico's Formento Económico Mexicano, S.A. de C.V., which through its brewing subsidiary makes such brands as Tecate and Dos Equis. Outside North America—in addition to exporting its brands to and licensing its brands for brewing in Europe, Asia, and Australia—Labatt produces local brands in Venezuela and the Dominican Republic through joint ventures. Worldwide production in 1997 topped 11.5 million hectoliters, equivalent to three billion bottles of beer.

London, Ontario Brewing Beginnings in the Mid-19th Century

Company founder John Kinder Labatt was born in Ireland in 1803. His family heritage can be traced back to the Huguenots in France. Fleeing prosecution, Labatt's ancestors resettled outside Dublin. As a young man Labatt moved to London, England, where he met and married Eliza Kell. Together the couple set sail in 1833 for Canada and arrived in London, Ontario. Labatt became a farmer and sold prize-winning malting barley to the local innkeeper, who had built a small brewery in 1828. Contact with the innkeeper gave Labatt the idea of becoming a brewer himself, an idea in which he became so interested that in 1847 he formed a partnership with Samuel Eccles, an experienced brewer. The two bought the London Brewery from the innkeeper.

Early annual production capacity was 400 barrels. In 1853 Labatt bought his partner's share of the business and increased annual brewing capacity to 4,000 barrels. The newly renamed John Labatt's Brewery had six employees. Despite its remarkable production increase, the young enterprise remained a local operation. The situation changed, however, with the growing presence of the railroads. When the tracks of the Great Western Railway connected London to other cities, Labatt began shipping beer and ale to Montreal, Toronto, and the Maritimes.

John Labatt's third son, John Labatt II, apprenticed as a brewer in Wheeling, West Virginia. Meanwhile, John's two older brothers, Robert and Ephraim, had gone into their own brewery business. Their departure left John Labatt's Brewery without a brewmaster, as it had been assumed that one of the older brothers would eventually fill the position. As a result, at age 26 John Labatt II accepted his father's offer of the post.

In his new capacity, John II was instrumental in establishing a product with international appeal, India Pale Ale, based on a recipe he had learned in Wheeling. By 1878 the ale had earned high marks and honors at the Canada Exposition in Ottawa, the International Centennial in Philadelphia, the Exposition in Australia, and the International Exposition in France.

In 1866, just two years after John II returned to the brewery, the founder died, leaving the company to his wife. Eliza Labatt formed a partnership with her son and renamed the business Labatt & Company. Mother and son operated the brewery together until 1872, when John II bought his mother's interest and became the sole owner.

Before the new company leader had much opportunity to establish himself, fire destroyed the London Brewery. Fortunately, however, insurance coverage enabled Labatt to build a modern facility at the cost of $20,000. Annual production now reached 30,000 barrels.

In addition to introducing an award-winning ale and expanding production, John II is credited with modernizing the company through the use of refrigeration and distribution networks. Labatt products also reached distant Canadian provinces; by 1900 customers in Manitoba and the Northwest Territories could purchase the brewer's products.

At the turn of the century John II's two sons, Hugh and John III, joined the family business. John III had earned a brewmaster's certificate from the brewing academy in New York after graduating from McGill University.

In 1911 John II incorporated his company under the name John Labatt Limited. All but four of the 2,500 shares issued were retained by him. The remainder went to his two sons, a nephew, and his lawyer. Total capitalization amounted to $250,000.

Surviving the Prohibition Era

John Labatt II died in 1915 at age 75, and the company presidency went to John III. At that time the various provinces were debating possible Prohibition laws. Unlike the United States, where the liquor industry was regulated by a blanket federal law, in Canada each province created its own standard. Although almost all of Canada was rendered legally dry by 1916, several provinces allowed the manufacture of alcoholic beverages for export. By the end of Prohibition only 15 of Ontario's 65 breweries still survived. Labatt not only was one of the survivors, but also was the only such firm to have maintained management continuity through the era.

During the 1920s and 1930s the brewery implemented a number of innovative employee policies. In the 1920s Labatt workers became some of the first Canadian employees to receive annual vacation pay. In 1932 Labatt set an industry standard by establishing a group insurance plan for its employees, and six years later an annuity plan was created to build pension benefits.

While the nation struggled through the years of the Depression, the Labatt family underwent its own period of misfortune. On August 15, 1934, John Labatt III, already a widely recognized business and community leader, was kidnapped on the way from his summer home in Sarnia to a company board meeting. Later his empty car was discovered with a note instructing John's brother, Hugh, to pay a ransom of $150,000 for the safe return of the victim. For the next several days the story of the mysterious disappearance appeared in the headlines of major newspapers around the world. The incident was the first kidnap assault in

Canadian history. Detectives concentrated their search around the Detroit, Michigan area as suspicion mounted about the possibility of gangster involvement. During Prohibition, American gangsters had transported alcoholic beverages from Canada into the United States in rowboats down the Detroit River. Authorities believed Labatt had been abducted in a similar fashion. After a few days Labatt was released unharmed at Toronto's Royal York Hotel. The search for his assailants continued over the next several months until the severely shaken Labatt identified a Canadian bootmaker. Labatt retired from public life for the remaining years of his presidency.

Expansion and Public Offering Following World War II

After World War II the company prepared to undertake a major expansion. To raise capital John Labatt Limited became a public company and issued 900,000 shares. Many employees were among the more than 2,000 original shareholders. In 1946 the company completed its first acquisition, the Copland Brewing Company in Toronto, which doubled Labatt's brewing capacity.

The 1950s saw a number of new beverages added to Labatt's product line. The 1950-introduced Fiftieth Anniversary Ale, nicknamed "Annie" or "50," commemorated John and Hugh Labatt's years of activity in the company. It later became Canada's most popular ale. Pilsener Lager Beer debuted in 1951. After its launch in Manitoba this brand gained the nickname "Blue" after the color of its label and because of the company's sponsorship of the Winnipeg Blue Bombers, a Canadian Football League team. The nickname stuck and Labatt Blue gained increasing popularity, becoming the number one beer brand in Canada by 1979.

Also in 1951 the company presidency passed from John III to his brother Hugh, the former vice-president. A year later John died at age 72. The company continued to expand during the decade, most notably with the purchase of Shea's Winnipeg Brewery Ltd., a company dating to 1873. The new subsidiary introduced Labatt into the hotel industry. Labatt also acquired the Lucky Lager Brewing Company of San Francisco. Construction of a $6.5 million brewery in Ville La Salle, Quebec in 1956 marked Labatt's expansion into other provinces.

When Hugh Labatt died in 1956, W. H. R. Jarvis became the first non-family president of Labatt. The following year he oversaw formation of a Feed Products Department, the company's first entrance into an industry outside brewing. The division manufactured animal feed additives using brewing byproducts. In 1958 Lucky Lager Breweries of British Columbia was acquired.

Jarvis died of a heart attack during a board meeting in the early 1960s. John H. Moore assumed the post and supervised the further expansion of Labatt's operations. New breweries were built in Etobicoke, northwest of Toronto, and in Edmonton in the early 1960s. Bavarian Brewing Limited, based in St. John's, Newfoundland, was acquired in 1962. These additions strengthened Labatt's position in the national market.

Major structural changes occurred at Labatt in the next few years. The first came in the mid-1960s when the Milwaukee-based Joseph Schlitz Brewing Company attempted to gain a 40 percent interest in the Canadian brewery. The family trust agreed to sell half of its shares and many public shareholders were also willing to sell, but the acquisition eventually was halted by U.S. antitrust laws. An investigation led by then-U.S. Attorney General Robert F. Kennedy alleged that Schlitz wanted to control the California market through a Labatt subsidiary. In 1967 Schlitz was forced to sell its approximately one million shares to a consortium of three Canadian investment groups.

Expansion of Offerings Beginning in the Mid-1960s

Another major structural change occurred in 1964 when John Labatt Limited became a holding company to manage all of the various company activities. Brewing fell under Labatt Breweries of Canada Ltd. The parent company proceeded to make acquisitions in other areas. Labatt's first purchase in the wine industry was that of Parkdale Wines in 1965. In 1973 Labatt consolidated its many wine holdings under the Chateau-Gai brand name. The Ogilvie Flour Mills Company purchase led Labatt into the dairy and processed food industry. Other food product purchases followed over the next several years. By 1974 company operations fell into three main divisions: brewing, consumer products, and agricultural products. Brewing operations later were divided into the Canadian and International groups.

A major expansion campaign at the London facility in 1965 increased annual capacity to 1.3 million barrels, making it one of the largest breweries in the world. At the same time, Labatt announced plans to form a joint venture with Guinness Overseas Ltd. to produce the famous Irish stout in Canada.

At the end of the decade Moore announced he would leave Labatt to take charge of a company that represented Labatt's largest shareholder. N. E. Hardy, formerly president of Labatt Breweries of Canada Ltd., succeeded Moore. In 1973 Peter Widdrington succeeded Hardy and would lead Labatt into the late 1980s.

In 1971 Labatt purchased Oland & Sons Limited and its Halifax and Saint John breweries and then acquired Columbia Brewery of Creston, British Columbia in 1974. In 1977 the company introduced Canada's first light beer, Labatt Special Light. Labatt participated in the construction of a brewery in Trinidad and purchased an interest in Zambia Breweries and a Brazilian brewing company during the 1970s. It also established Labatt Importers Inc. in New York to develop aggressively Labatt's presence in the U.S. market. The company also acquired a 45 percent interest in the Toronto Blue Jays, an American League baseball franchise. Meanwhile, during this period of diversification, Brascan Ltd., an investment holding company in Peter and Edward Bronfman's corporate empire, gradually built up a significant stake in Labatt—41 percent by the late 1980s.

In 1980 Labatt became the first Canadian brewery to form an international licensing agreement with a major U.S. brewery when it entered into an agreement with Anheuser-Busch Inc. to brew Budweiser and Michelob under license in Canada. The Budweiser brand quickly gained eight percent of the market.

The 1980s and early 1990s were perhaps most noteworthy for additional expansion moves outside of brewing. Many of the purchases were of U.S. food businesses, primarily in the areas of dairy products and fruit juice. Expanding on its ownership of the Blue Jays, Labatt acquired The Sports Network, a cable sports channel, in 1986. Three years later additional entertainment interests were gained in production companies and International Talent Group, a New York City-based rock music talent agency. By the late 1980s only about 30 percent of company revenue came from brewing.

Labatt's brewing operations were not neglected, however, and were themselves the object of expansionary initiatives. In 1987 the Latrobe Brewing Co. of Pennsylvania, brewers of Rolling Rock beer, was acquired. The following year Labatt began to brew the Carlsberg and Carlsberg Light brands under license from Copenhagen, Denmark-based Carlsberg. Labatt purchased a 77.5 percent stake in Italian brewer Birra Moretti in 1989.

Divestments and Sale to Interbrew in the 1990s

The 1990s represented perhaps the most transformational period in Labatt's long history. The company began the decade under the new leadership of Sidney Oland, who had headed Labatt's brewing operations. Oland sought to end the company's diversification drive and quickly sold the wine operations and two unprofitable U.S. dairies. The remaking of Labatt continued under Oland's successor, George Taylor, who took charge in 1992. That year the company sold its remaining food businesses. Bolstered marketing and hot new beer brands revitalized Labatt's brewing side, as the company introduced a cold-filtered draft beer, Labatt Genuine Draft, in 1992, and the following year the very first ice beer, Labatt ICE, which was created through a patented Ice Brewing process—a process Labatt later licensed to other brewers. In the face of increasing competition—fueled by free-trade agreements—from cheap American beers, Labatt introduced a "popular price" beer known as Wildcat in 1993. The company's entertainment division meanwhile celebrated World Series victories in 1992 and 1993 by the Blue Jays.

Also in 1993 Brascan sold its stake in Labatt, leaving the company vulnerable to shareholder discontent and hostile takeover. In July 1994 the company paid C $720 million (US $510 million) for a 22 percent interest in Mexico-based Formento Económico Mexicano, S.A. de C.V. (Femsa), whose brewing subsidiary, Cerveceria Cuahtémoc Moctezuma, boasted of such brands as Tecate and Dos Equis. A few months later Labatt management, concerned about a hostile takeover, proposed a poison-pill plan, but it was rejected by shareholders—the first such defeat in Canadian history—who felt the company had paid too much for the Femsa stake. Shareholders were also adamant that Labatt should divest its entertainment holdings (which by this time also included major stakes in the Toronto Argonauts Canadian Football League team, Toronto's Sky-Dome sports stadium, and cable's The Discovery Channel), a move long promised by management but never delivered. Adding fuel to the fire was the collapse of the peso at the end of 1994, which made what was likely already a premium purchase price even dearer. Labatt was forced to take a C $300 million

(US $219 million) writedown on its Mexican investment in early 1995.

In May 1995 Toronto-based takeover specialist Onex Corp. made a C $2.3 billion (US $1.7 billion) hostile takeover offer for Labatt. Taylor and Labatt's management team rejected this offer as too low, bought some time through a lawsuit in a New York City court, and solicited offers from other friendly suitors. In June Labatt agreed to be acquired for C $2.7 billion (US $2 billion) by Interbrew S.A., a privately held Belgian brewer with a 600-year history. Interbrew planned to divest Labatt of all nonbrewing operations and quickly fulfilled this intention in part when Labatt's broadcasting businesses were sold to a management-led consortium for C $878 million (US $650 million) in July 1995. Interbrew placed the Labatt sports properties up for sale in April 1996 but took the Blue Jays, Argonauts, and SkyDome off the market in October 1997 after failing to secure an acceptable deal with potential local partners.

Labatt's first few years as a subsidiary of Interbrew were also eventful, if not so dramatic. In 1996 the company sold its stake in Birra Moretti. In August 1996 a joint venture in the Dominican Republic launched its first brand, Soberana ("sovereign" in Spanish). The following year saw Labatt enter the fast-growing South American market for the first time through a brewing joint venture with the Cisneros Group of Companies. The first country targeted by this initiative was Venezuela, where a new brewery opened outside of Caracas in 1997. Labatt entered into an agreement in 1997 to brew and sell Lowenbrau beer in North America. In early 1998 Labatt increased its stake in Femsa to 30 percent. In June 1998 Labatt and Anheuser-Busch tightened their relationship in Canada through a new agreement whereby the American company granted Labatt the right to sell Anheuser-Busch brands in Canada in perpetuity. In return Labatt agreed to step up its marketing efforts and to give Anheuser-Busch a larger share of the associated profits. Labatt was clearly a more focused, stronger company, as reflected in all of these developments and in the following facts: earnings for Labatt increased 15 percent in 1997; Labatt Blue celebrated its 20th straight year as the top-selling beer in Canada in 1998;

and this same flagship brand had become the number three import beer in the United States by early 1998.

Further Reading

Barrington, Stephen, "Belgian Owner Gives Labatt New Shot Against Molson," *Advertising Age International,* January 1997, pp. 113, 114.

———, "Labatt Hops Up Canadian Brew Leadership Race," *Advertising Age,* November 13, 1995, p. 12.

Boisseau, Peter, "The Suds Stud," *Canadian Business,* July 1997, pp. 36–43.

Dalglish, Brenda, "Beer Wars: Canadian Brewers Are Competing for Market Share and Investor Interest," *Maclean's,* August 15, 1994, pp. 26.

David, Gregory E., "Strange Brew: The Remaking of John Labatt, Toronto's Beer and Sports Giant," *Financial World,* September 13, 1994, pp. 26.

DeMont, John, "A Global Brew," *Maclean's,* July 24, 1989, pp. 28.

Greenberg, Larry M., "Canada's Top Brewers Draft Ways To Fight New Rivals," *Wall Street Journal,* March 16, 1993, p. B4.

McGee, Suzanne, "Brascan Sells Major Position in Brewer Labatt," *Wall Street Journal,* February 16, 1993, pp. A3, A12.

McMurdy, Deirdre, "Brewing Struggle," *Maclean's,* February 18, 1991, pp. 38.

Prince, Greg W., "The Specialist," *Beverage World,* September 1995, pp. 42.

Smit, Barbara, "Interbrew Avoids Hangover After Canadian Wedding," *European,* July 25, 1996, p. 17.

Stevenson, Mark, "Revving Up the Suds Cycle," *Canadian Business,* September 1993, pp. 53–54.

Symonds, William C., and Flynn, Julia, "Can Labatt Shed Its Belly But Keep the Beer?," *Business Week,* December 14, 1992, p. 70.

Symonds, William C., Malkin, Elisabeth, and Melcher, Richard, "Did Labatt Guzzle Too Much Too Fast?," *Business Week,* May 29, 1995, pp. 55–56.

Terry, Edith, "Canada's Labatt Has Just One Way To Grow: South," *Business Week,* November 9, 1987, p. 70.

Willis, Andrew, "A Bidding Battle: Labatt's Sale of Hot TV and Sports Assets Draws a Crowd," *Maclean's,* June 26, 1995, pp. 24.

———, "Takeover Turmoil," *Maclean's,* June 5, 1995, pp. 42.

———, "The Winning Brew," *Maclean's,* June 19, 1995, pp. 44.

—updated by David E. Salamie

Les Echos
Le Quotidien de l'Economie

Groupe Les Echos

46, rue la Boetie
75381 Paris CEDEX 08
France
(33) 1.49.53.65.65
Fax: (33) 1.45.63.53.33
Web site: http://www.lesechos.fr

Subsidiary of Pearson Group
Incorporated: 1908 as Les Echos de l'Exportation
Employees: 500
Sales: FFr 748 million (US $129 million) (1997)
SICs: 2721 Periodicals; 2731 Book Publishing

A member of British media giant the Pearson Group since 1988, Groupe Les Echos is among France's leading financial and medical information publishers. The company's flagship daily newspaper, *Les Echos,* is France's oldest and most read financial newspaper, with a paid circulation of more than 132,000. The subscription-based, online version of *Les Echos* offers, in addition to the daily, extensive services, including ongoing financial updates and stock market quotations, access to archives and to market sector and business-specific reports. In addition to the daily newspaper, Les Echos publishes the monthly magazine, *Enjeux Les Echos,* France's second largest selling financial and economic magazine. The company's financial branch also publishes various supplements throughout the year, including a yearly report on the 500 leading French corporations.

Les Echos also is a leading publisher of French-language medical information. The company's medical titles include the bimonthly *Revue du Praticien,* the weekly *Revue du Praticien Médecine Générale,* and the bi-weekly *Panorama du Médecin, La Revue du Praticien Gynécologie et Obstétrique,* and *La Revue Française du Dommage Corporel,* as well as a yearly series of supplements and research newsletters.

Guided by editors-in-chief Nicolas Beytout and Emile Favard, *Les Echos* has increased its circulation more than 120 percent since the mid-1980s. The company's financial publications provide more than 60 percent of its revenues, which neared FFr 750 million in 1997.

A Turn-of-the-Century Marketing Tool

Although *Les Echos* would grow into France's premier financial and corporate newspaper, its original purpose was to serve as a marketing brochure for the commercial business of founder Robert Schreiber. A son of Prussian immigrants, Schreiber had joined his parents' import firm selling products from central Europe. Schreiber took over the family business after the death of his father in 1902. Schreiber next formed a partnership with Albert Aronson, locating the commercial firm, Maison de Schreiber and Aronson, in Paris's tenth arrondissement. In 1908, Schreiber, seeking a means to publicize the company's merchandise, began producing a four-page monthly newsletter, *Les Echos de l'Exportation,* with the subtitle, *Bulletin mensuel de la maison Schreiber et Aronson.* This newsletter, among the first of its kind in France, was distributed free of charge not only to the company's prospective and actual customers, but also to its competitors. Beyond simply providing descriptions of the company's products, *Les Echos* provided market, customs, and other shipping information for its primarily import-export sector clients. From the start Schreiber sought advertisers to finance the paper.

The first *Les Echos* appeared in April 1908, in an edition of 1,000 copies. By the end of its first year *Les Echos* had attracted some 135 subscribers. Schreiber was eager to develop the newspaper. In 1909 he sold a portion of *Les Echos* to a Berlin-based equivalent, Confectionaire. The partnership enabled Schreiber to boost *Les Echos* to 16 pages, printing on higher-quality paper and featuring a color cover. Schreiber also changed the now bi-monthly paper's subtitle to *Journal d'information pour le commerce et l'industrie* to reflect its widening scope. The new format proved a quick success. Circulation rose to 5,000 copies, of which some 3,000 were accounted for by subscriptions. The company moved to larger quarters in 1910. The growing success of *Les Echos* also enabled Schreiber to bring brothers Emile and Georges into the company. In the early years of the new decade the growing advertising revenues also would allow Schreiber to buy back full control of the paper from his German partner. Les Echos had offices in London, New York, and Brussels in 1912.

In 1913 the paper made the transition to a weekly 36-page format. The outbreak of the First World War, however, put the paper and Schreiber's commercial firm on hold. Called to service, Schreiber and his brothers would suspend publication for the duration. With the end of the war, Schreiber decided to devote himself fully to his publishing activities, ending his association with Aronson. Reincorporating as Schreiber Frères, the company was now a partnership between Robert, who contributed 20,000 francs and became the company's director, and brother Emile, who contributed 10,000 francs and was placed in charge as editor-in-chief. Emile's participation in the company eventually would reach parity with his brothers, so that by 1938 the brothers were equal partners.

Between the World Wars, Les Echos would continue to develop, both in focus and in revenues. A new subtitle, La Grande Revue Commerciale Française, was adopted, marking Les Echos' position as France's first economic and financial newspaper; the paper's primary focus, however, remained the commercial import-export sector. Circulation rose to 10,000, and the company's increasing advertising revenues enabled it to expand the paper's format to 44 pages. With Emile Schreiber as editor-in-chief and later director, Les Echos also became a vocal proponent of American-style free-market capitalism, while supporting such social initiatives as the five-day work week and paid vacations.

The company's growing revenues prompted it to expand its foreign offices, opening in Vienna, Bucharest, Milan, Warsaw, Frankfurt, and other major European cities. During the 1920s Les Echos began making its first diversifications into other publishing areas. In 1925 the company began producing a second industry-specific paper, Les Echos des Industries d'Art, and began publishing in other languages, including a quarterly in English, Spanish, and German and yearlies in Japanese and Portuguese.

Succeeding the Family in the 1960s

By 1928 Les Echos had grown to a subscriber base of more than 8,000. The increase in revenues permitted the Schreibers to transform the paper into a daily, maintaining the larger weekly paper while adding a daily four-page supplement. The following decade—beginning with the Depression and culminating in the German occupation of France—would spell difficulties for Les Echos. Although the company was able to maintain a circulation of 10,000 copies and a subscriber list of more than 7,000, the shattered economy placed pressure on the company's primary revenue generator, advertising sales. By 1931 the Schreibers were forced to put an end to their other publishing activities to concentrate on keeping Les Echos afloat. The company moved to the Champs Élysées, where rents were lower at the time. A new editor-in-chief, Jacques Rozner, was named, and Robert and Emile turned toward boosting advertising and subscription sales.

The occupation of France by Germany in 1940 forced the company once again to close down its newspaper. The Schreib-

ers—being Jewish—sold their company to a non-Jewish friend to preserve Les Echos from German appropriation. The Schreibers joined the maquis, adopting the surname Servan. Emerging from the war years, the brothers would adopt the surname Servan-Schreiber. Les Echos resumed publication in December 1944. Because of the postwar paper shortage, the newspaper was limited initially to a bi-weekly format, but quickly returned to daily publication. Emile once again took charge of the paper's editorial content, and Robert headed the company's sales activities.

By the end of the decade, Les Echos, boosted by France's burgeoning postwar industrial boom, had reached a circulation of some 30,000 copies, including 25,000 subscribers. The company also had become very much a family operation, with as many as 12 members of the Schreiber family holding positions in the company. This intense family involvement, however, would lead to growing tensions in the next decade, particularly as succession issues began to emerge. Into the 1950s, however, the company's profitability permitted the Schreiber family to prosper.

Prosperity—and politics—would lead to a schism in the Schreiber family. Jean-Claude Schreiber, eldest son of Robert, joined the company's directorship in 1949, followed soon after by the eldest son of Emile, Jean-Jacques Schreiber. With the elder Schreibers approaching retirement (Robert was in his 70s and Emile was in his mid-60s), the younger generation began to vie for control of the company's direction. Their dispute was exacerbated by the success of a new Les Echos project.

In 1953 Jean-Jacques launched L'Express, at a cost of some 30 million ancient francs (FFr 3 million). Subtitled Les Echos de Samedi (Saturday), the new weekly originally formed part of the regular Les Echos subscription, the rate of which was raised by 1,000 ancient francs (100 modern francs) per year to accommodate the new addition. Although L'Express managed to turn a slight profit by 1955, Les Echos itself began to suffer from the experience; in a single year, the company lost some 4,000 subscribers. The political cost of the new weekly was perhaps higher. Under Jean-Jacques, L'Express was formed in part to support the economic and social policies of French Premier Pierre Mendes France, diametrically opposed to the Gaullist initiatives supported by Les Echos and its subscriber base. The legislative elections of 1956 would lead to a break. In September 1955 Jean-Jacques converted L'Express into a daily newspaper, placing his support firmly behind the re-election of Mendes France to the country's premiership. In response, Jean-Claude had his name removed from L'Express, but the paper remained under the co-direction of the two branches of the family. After Mendes France's defeat, L'Express returned to a weekly format. Continued political disputes, centering around the future independence of French colony Algeria, would deteriorate further the relationship between the two sides of the Schreiber family.

Robert Schreiber stepped down from the company's direction in 1958. Under Emile and Jean-Claude, a new dispute emerged. By the late 1950s Les Echos had been stagnating. Its principal readership had been France's merchant and small business community; yet in the 1950s this class was being replaced by new developing industrial and commercial giants.

Jean-Claude sought to rejuvenate *Les Echos,* reorienting its focus and investing in rebuilding the company, whereas Emile preferred to reduce the company's cost above all. The impasse was broken at last in 1960, with the arrival of Emile's youngest son, Jean-Louis, to the leadership of the paper's editorial direction. Under Jean-Louis, *Les Echos* reoriented its focus, now becoming a full-fledged economic newspaper after the model of the *Financial Times* and the *Wall Street Journal.* The redeveloped *Les Echos* appeared in October 1960 and quickly achieved success, raising circulation some 15 percent in its first two years. By the early 1960s the company's revenues had grown to some FFr 12 million.

Joining Pearson in the 1990s

The referendum for the independence of Algeria in 1962 would lead to the final collapse of the relationship between the opposing sides of the Schreiber family. With neither side able to buy out the shares of the other, the family proved unable to provide direction to the company. In 1963 Les Echos ended up in commercial court, which placed the company under a provisional directorship. By the end of that month a solution to the family's problems emerged. Pierre Beytout, a director of the Roussel pharmaceutical concern, and wife Jacqueline, agreed to buy out the Emile Schreiber branch's 50 percent of the company. The price of FFr 3.6 million, however, also included the removal of Jean-Claude Schreiber from the company's direction for a period of 18 months. By the end of that year the Beytouts had succeeded in buying up the 16 percent of Les Echos held by one of Jean-Claude's sisters, Marie-Geneviève. With majority control, Jacqueline Beytout took over the company's direction, continuing the editorial path begun by Jean-Louis Schreiber. In 1965 the Beytouts gained full control of the company, buying up the remaining shares from Jean-Claude and his sister, Marie-France.

Jacqueline Beytout would lead *Les Echos* on a long period of growth. From a circulation of 38,000 at the beginning of the 1960s, the paper would reach 61,000 by the start of the 1980s, with paid subscriptions of 50,000. The 1980s, and the appearance of a new culture embracing the stock market, would lead to even stronger growth—by the end of the decade *Les Echos* had passed the 100,000 mark. Advertising not only provided strong revenue growth, but also healthy margins. Beginning in the early 1980s, Beytout began diversifying Les Echos into the medical publishing field. In 1982 the company acquired the monthly *Panorama du Médecin,* followed by the purchase of publisher Editions Jean-Baptiste Baillière and its *Revue du Praticien.* Les Echos also launched a new medical weekly, *La Revue du Praticien Médecin Générale,* in 1987. In the 1990s the company continued to develop and acquire medical titles, including *Les Archives des Maladies du Coeur et des Vaiseux* and 1997's *Revue du Praticien Gynécologie et Obstétrique.* On the financial side, Les Echos launched a new monthly economic magazine, *Dynasteurs,* in 1986. That magazine was a success, building a circulation of 80,000 by the early 1990s. In 1992 the monthly's name was changed to *Enjeux Les Echos,* a move which helped boost circulation to nearly 130,000 by 1997.

By then the Beytout family began confronting its own succession issues. At the same time the market had been changing, as international conglomerates began replacing many former independent publishers. In 1988 Jacqueline Beytout agreed to sell Les Echos to the Pearson Group for FFr 885 million. The acquisition would give Pearson a strong foothold in France's financial readership, which remained fiercely resistant to non-French publications. The financial clout of the Pearson Group (£2 billion in 1997 sales), meanwhile, assured the future prospects for *Les Echos,* while associating the daily with the venerable *Financial Times.*

Under Pearson, *Les Echos* would continue to build its circulation, passing 120,000 in the early 1990s and, despite the lingering economic crisis in France through the first half of the decade, nearing 140,000 by 1998. Although Jacqueline Beytout left the company in 1989, son Nicolas Beytout remained with the company, becoming editor-in-chief in 1996. Not all of the company's projects proved as successful. The monthly *Argent* magazine, launched in February 1996, was abandoned only five months later, after building losses of FFr 30 million. The company's medical publishing activities also came under threat, after an agreement was reached between the French government and pharmaceuticals companies calling for a reduction in the latter's advertising and promotion budgets.

More promising would be the Les Echos entry into the Internet, with the launch of an online edition of *Les Echos* in 1996. With some two million ''hits'' per month, the site turned commercial in 1997, offering subscription and per-consultation rates for not only the content of the daily newspaper, but also a wide range of value-added services, including consultation of the paper's archives. The French economy slowly emerged from the recession in the mid-1990s, bringing a resurging demand for economic and financial information. Les Echos continued to make strong revenue gains, nearing FFr 750 million for the year 1997.

Further Reading

Eveno, Patrick, ''90 bougies pour Les Echos,'' *Performances,* March 1998, p. 69.

Les Echos, ''Historique du Groupe,'' http://www.lesechos.fr.

Roy, Frédéric, ''Les Echos décide que ses infos valent le même prix on line que sur papier,'' *CB News,* October 27–November 11, 1997, p. 29.

Rusten-Hol, Alain, and Treiner, Sandrine, *La Saga des Servan-Schreiber,* Paris: Editions Seuil, 1993.

—M.L. Cohen

Lincoln National Corporation

200 East Berry Street
Fort Wayne, Indiana 46802-2706
U.S.A.
(219) 455-2000
Fax: (219) 455-3514
Web site: http://www.lnc.com

Public Company
Incorporated: 1905 as Lincoln National Life Insurance
    Company
Employees: 8,120
Total Assets: $77.17 billion (1997)
Stock Exchanges: New York Midwest Pacific London
    Tokyo
Ticker Symbol: LNC
SICs: 6282 Investment Advice; 6311 Life Insurance;
    6351 Surety Insurance; 6371 Pension, Health &
    Welfare Funds; 6411 Insurance Agents, Brokers &
    Services; 6719 Offices of Holding Companies, Not
    Elsewhere Classified; 6726 Unit Investment Trusts,
    Face-Amount Certificate Offices, Closed-End
    Management Investment Offices

With origins in life insurance, Lincoln National Corporation has evolved into a financial services company whose principal offerings include life insurance, annuities, and reinsurance. Additional services include 401(k) plans, mutual funds, institutional investment management, and financial planning. The company continues to maintain its headquarters in the midwestern city of its origin, Fort Wayne, Indiana. Its founders selected the name "Lincoln" as a symbol of integrity in an era when insurance companies were often suspect, and Robert Todd Lincoln quickly authorized the use of his father's image. Through the years the company grew both by internal expansion and by acquisitions, always maintaining stable leadership and highly conservative accounting and investment principles.

Surviving a Troubled Beginning

Lincoln National Corporation traces its origins to the Lincoln Life Insurance Company, which was preceded by a troubled firm in Fort Wayne, Indiana, called the Fraternal Assurance Society of America. Its founder was Wilbur Wynant, who organized a number of supposedly nonprofit fraternal insurance companies which promised to pay benefits by leveling assessments on surviving policyholders. Wynant, who was new to Fort Wayne in 1902, persuaded a number of respected business and professional men to join him in the company, but within two years Wynant had skipped town, and his local associates were left to pick up the pieces or fold the company. The local businessmen reorganized as a legal reserve company to be capitalized at $200,000 but prepared to open for business when $100,000 in stock was sold.

Lincoln National Life Insurance Company was incorporated in Fort Wayne on May 15, 1905. A few months later the New York state investigation of the insurance industry known as the Armstrong Committee exposed widespread abuses and led to much more effective state regulation of the industry. Lincoln National was fully prepared for the more stringent regulations and used the Lincoln name and image to good effect in promoting the new company amid widespread public suspicion of all insurance companies. Arthur Fletcher Hall, formerly an agent for Equitable Life Assurance Society of the United States, was brought in from Indianapolis to serve as secretary and manager, and for practical purposes he was the chief executive officer from the beginning, although a local businessman held the unsalaried office of president. When the company began to write policies in September 1905 it had three agents, including Hall. By 1911 the company had 106 agents and was in sound financial condition.

Arthur F. Hall was the dominant figure at Lincoln National Life Insurance for the company's first 37 years, and he did not hesitate to employ able and determined associates. In 1911 Hall hired Franklin B. Mead, the firm's first full-time actuary. Mead was much more than a numbers man. He devised careful plans for underwriting life insurance policies and for writing reinsurance policies for other companies, and he was a skilled manager. Mead provided statistical support for the company's medical director, Calvin English, and Lincoln National soon achieved a reputation for writing profitable insurance on carefully screened substandard—or undesirable—risks. While the typical insurance company rejected about 11 percent of those who applied for coverage, Lincoln National turned down only about four percent.

In 1916 the company adopted the policy of securing additional insurance in force by taking over other companies. Michigan State Life Insurance Company, acquired in 1916, was even younger than Lincoln Life, but it had grown more quickly. Michigan State Life had been a tool of Frederick L. Apps, who had involved Michigan State Life in a complex fraud. When Lincoln National purchased Michigan State Life, a web of companies set up by Apps to support the insurance company collapsed. Michigan State Life itself was a sound purchase. The merger was so successful that Hall took over another successful midwestern firm in 1917, the Pioneer Life Insurance Company of Fargo, North Dakota. Beyond the additional insurance acquired, these mergers also greatly increased the number of experienced agents selling Lincoln National policies throughout the Midwest.

During World War I the company grew quickly. Between 1913 and 1914 Lincoln National's reinsurance more than doubled, to $2 million. By 1917 reinsurance was bringing in $9.6 million. Lincoln National did not hesitate to pick up business from large German reinsurers at this time; in 1917 the company took over Pittsburgh Life, with its $2.5 million reinsurance business. The great influenza epidemic of 1918–19 had a far greater effect on the company. Death claims almost equaled those the company had paid out over the preceding decade, and extraordinary measures were required to pay benefits. Stockholders went without dividends and the members of the executive committee personally loaned $300,000 to the company, but Mead rightly predicted that deaths attributable to the war or the epidemic would increase the importance of life insurance.

Lincoln National was highly successful throughout the 1920s. The firm built its own offices on the southern edge of downtown Fort Wayne in 1921, part of the site it would continue to occupy into the 1990s, in order to accommodate the growing number of home-office employees. Hall became president in 1923, the year the headquarters building was occupied. Hall was a paternalistic chief executive and encouraged athletic and cultural activities for employees. As was typical in the 1920s, women employees were required to resign when they married, but Hall did sponsor tennis and basketball programs for single women. There was also a nine-hole putting course atop the new building, open to clerical employees as well as to management.

In 1928 Hall employed Louis A. Warren, who was establishing his reputation as a Lincoln scholar, to direct the Lincoln Historical Research Foundation. Hall had only a vague idea of doing something in line with the company's name, but Warren soon persuaded him that the company should sponsor and finance a major research library devoted entirely to the life of Abraham Lincoln. When Warren finally retired 28 years later, the company's library had grown into a national center for Lincoln scholars, called the Louis A. Warren Lincoln Library and Museum and funded entirely by the company.

Under Hall's conservative management Lincoln National avoided the extravagant financial schemes of the late 1920s, although he arranged another successful merger—with Merchants Life Insurance Company of Des Moines, Iowa—in 1928. Hall fought off efforts to sell control of the company to interests based in New York or Chicago and announced his determination to keep Lincoln National in Fort Wayne. Its business was still entrenched in the Midwest and most of its policyholders lived on farms or in small towns. Throughout the 1920s the company had acquired a considerable amount of farm property as a result of defaults on mortgages it held as investments, but Hall worked diligently to make the farms pay, and the company reluctantly found itself raising livestock and distilling mint. The company shifted investment emphasis from mortgages to corporate bonds before the stock market crash of 1929 and began to sell off its farm properties in 1928, sometimes at a loss rather than try to farm the land itself.

Depression and War Pose Significant Challenges

The Great Depression brought unprecedented problems for Lincoln Life and the entire insurance industry. Failed investments were more numerous than ever before, and the company began to be troubled by suicides, often disguised as accidents, among policyholders. There was also an expensive problem resulting from policies written by agents desperate for business on persons who were high risks or simply unable to pay for the insurance. The company's rejection rate increased by 75 percent between 1928 and 1931. Its basic business remained sound and profitable, despite the Depression, and its reinsurance business for some 300 insurance companies was particularly successful.

In 1932 the company unveiled a large statue entitled "Abraham Lincoln, The Hoosier Youth" by sculptor Paul Manship, who received $75,000 for the work. The Lincoln image was a vital theme in the company's advertising during the 1930s. Home-office employment remained stable throughout the Depression, but the proportion of men did increase significantly as the company protected the jobs of family men at the expense of unmarried women. There was not always sufficient work for all of the employees, but the company avoided layoffs and prepared for busier and more prosperous times to come. The Depression also meant opportunities for healthy companies to acquire less successful firms, and Lincoln National took over three smaller life insurance companies between 1932 and 1933: Northern States Life Insurance Company of Hammond, Indiana; Old Line Life Insurance Company of Lincoln, Nebraska; and Royal Union Life Insurance Company of Des Moines, Iowa. The company's business was still primarily midwestern, but Lincoln National reached $1 billion of insurance in force in 1939, a goal that Hall had hoped to reach by 1930.

Franklin Mead had long been the second-ranking executive at Lincoln National and was Arthur Hall's likely successor until Mead's own death in 1933. Mead's successor as chief actuary and prospective president was Alva McAndless, known as "Mac," who had joined the company in 1919. Hall, in failing health, became chairman of the board early in 1939, and McAndless became president and chief executive officer. His primary concern was not in writing insurance policies—that part of the business flourished—but the low yield on the company's investments. Indiana insurance law had been changed to permit greater investment in corporate bonds, but McAndless disliked the high-yielding 30-year obligations of utilities and railroads, while few new mortgages were available on farm property and interest on government bonds slipped as low as 1.9 percent in 1940. The company turned increasingly to mortgages on urban property, particularly homes.

During World War II the company contended with higher federal taxes and a greatly altered investment climate. Labor costs were also a concern. In 1941 the company increased starting salaries for the first time since the onset of the Depression. The tight labor market also persuaded the company to relax its ban on the employment of married women. During the war there was a reduction in automobile accidents, as driving declined as a result of gasoline rationing. Life insurance companies had long escaped most federal income taxes, but wartime demand for revenue led to some changes in the laws in 1942, and the company began to pay a modest level of corporate income tax from 1943 onward.

McAndless also planned for postwar expansion. He particularly hoped to develop Lincoln National's agency force and prod agents to sell more life insurance. By 1945 the company's profits depended more upon its extensive reinsurance business. McAndless also kept dividends moderate and built up extensive cash reserves, both to provide against emergencies—like the Depression—and to take advantage of attractive opportunities. The company had been unable to finance an attractive acquisition during the Depression, and its leadership did not wish to be caught short again. In 1951 Lincoln National purchased the Reliance Life Insurance Company of Pittsburgh from the Mellon National Bank for $27.5 million in cash. Reliance was an exceedingly conservative firm with a strong agency force. Mellon had been forced to sell the operation in order to meet the requirements of the Bank Holding Act. It was a very large merger for the early 1950s, and Lincoln National made the most of it. It retained Reliance employees, as promised; reduced expenses; and greatly improved investment results. Reliance agents were particularly strong in the South, a region in which Lincoln National had been very weak.

McAndless was very much a detail man. He was always tight with the company's money and held a close rein on the company. Under McAndless, Lincoln National's leadership became increasingly shallow as strong managers left for positions of greater authority. His management style was not well-suited for the much larger company that resulted from the Reliance merger, but before any plans were made for a change in leadership, McAndless died of a heart attack early in 1954. McAnd-

less was succeeded by another actuary, Walter O. Menge, who had worked for Lincoln National since 1937. Menge was a systematic chief executive who understood how to manage a large and complex business and could delegate authority. He planned carefully and made effective use of Lincoln National's large capital base while recognizing its problems. Lincoln National faced lagging sales of ordinary life insurance and a decreasing market share in a highly competitive market. He increased efforts in group insurance and continued to seek attractive acquisitions. In 1957 Lincoln National made its first move beyond the United States, acquiring the Dominion Life Assurance Company of Waterloo, Ontario.

New York had long been known for the rigor of its insurance regulation, and only in 1960 did Lincoln National begin to write insurance there, through a new subsidiary. The effort eventually proved unsuccessful. Two years later it acquired American States Insurance Company of Indianapolis—a property and casualty specialist—in an effort to broaden its business beyond life insurance. This was also a defensive acquisition, to help protect Lincoln National's position as the largest reinsurer of life insurance policies in the country. General Reinsurance Corporation, a large non-life reinsurance company had recently entered the life reinsurance market, and Menge believed that his firm should offer a full line of coverage in both the insurance and reinsurance markets in order to remain fully competitive. A year later Lincoln National made its first direct move into the European reinsurance market, although it had long written reinsurance for European firms. The company established a new subsidiary in Paris, the Compagnie de Reassurance Nord-Atlantique, and soon extended its business into Asian and African markets. Lincoln National agents sometimes complained that the firm's extensive reinsurance business only encouraged new competitors in the life insurance field, but reinsurance was a large and very profitable part of Lincoln National's business, more successful in many ways than its agency business.

1960s Reorganization

As Lincoln National grew larger and more complex, becoming a major competitor in the international reinsurance market, Walter Menge and his associates began to plan a reorganization. There was no thought of leaving Fort Wayne, but there were plans for a holding company structure. Before this could be achieved Menge moved up to chairman in 1964, and was succeeded as president by actuary Henry F. Rood. Rood pushed forward with plans to form the holding company, hoping Lincoln National would become a financial department store of sorts. He established subsidiaries in the Philippines and Great Britain. The Lincoln Philippine Life Insurance Company was established for legal reasons in a nation where the company already did business, but the British market was vastly different, and Lincoln National's methods were resented widely.

Henry Rood served as president of Lincoln National for four years before becoming chairman, although he would remain chief executive officer for an additional three years. Thomas A. Watson assumed the office of president in 1968. A marketing expert in group insurance, he had joined the firm in 1945. Rood carried through the 1968 creation of the Lincoln National Corporation as the holding company for all of the firm's operating companies, but Watson had the responsibility for implementing the reorganization.

In 1969 Lincoln National Corporation was listed for trading on the New York Stock Exchange, the new name an appropriate symbol of the new holding company's wider outlook. So too was its acquisition of Chicago Title and Trust Company in 1969. However, this purchase brought unexpected problems. Title insurance was a new line of business for Lincoln National, and far more troublesome was Chicago Title's bond-brokerage subsidiary, Halsey, Stuart & Company. The bond business was completely unfamiliar to Lincoln National, and Halsey Stuart's investment-banking salaries were far higher than those paid in the insurance industry. Thus Halsey, Stuart & Company was sold in 1973. That same year the holding company also divested its British subsidiary, which had never met expectations. Selling insurance in Great Britain was a business which the Fort Wayne executives admitted they had never fully mastered. Watson also withdrew from other overseas operations, for business reasons in France and to avoid local political trouble in the Philippines. At home Watson sharply increased investment in sales agencies in an effort to improve the basic life insurance business.

During this time, Thomas Watson moved to open Lincoln National's offices and agencies to female and African American employees. Commitment to community involvement was evidenced in 1973, when the company established Lincoln Life Improved Housing, to rehabilitate abandoned dwellings near its Fort Wayne headquarters.

Watson planned carefully for an early retirement and in 1977 passed the presidency to Ian M. Rolland, a Fort Wayne native who had joined Lincoln National in 1956. Like most of his predecessors, Rolland was an actuary, although he had a wide range of experience within the company.

Continuing to Expand: Late 1970s and 1980s

As chief executive officer Ian Rolland stressed systematic organization and sophisticated planning as essential for a large and complex corporation. He continued Lincoln National's policy of acquisitions, most notably Security Connecticut Life Insurance Company in 1979. Security Connecticut had no agents of its own and sold its life insurance policies entirely through independent agents and brokers. The combination of company-employed and independent agents has been successful for Lincoln National, despite the potential for conflict between agents. In 1981 Lincoln National acquired First Penn-Pacific Life Insurance Company, an Illinois firm. First Penn-Pacific brought with it growing sales in universal life policies, which quickly became a major part of Lincoln National's life insurance business. By 1983 Lincoln National, through its various subsidiaries, had $100 billion of life insurance in force, and it continued to expand by acquiring both life and property and casualty insurance companies. The larger but less visible reinsurance business grew more by internal expansion, but the firm did acquire National Reinsurance Corporation in 1984, which brought important additions in property and casualty reinsurance. Lincoln National also cautiously reentered the British market in 1984, this time by purchasing an established British company, Cannon Assurance Limited. The following year it sold both its Canadian life insurance subsidiary and

Chicago Title and Trust, withdrawing entirely from the title insurance business.

In the mid- to late 1980s, in response to trends in the medical insurance industry, Lincoln National greatly increased its activity in group health insurance and established its own health maintenance organizations (HMOs) in Indiana and Florida. Despite early problems, the HMOs were profitable by 1990 and had grown in size and in geographical scope, expanding into Texas and California. Also during this time, the company developed a variety of investment programs, particularly individual annuities and corporate pension plans.

By the end of the 1980s Lincoln National—then ranked as the nation's seventh-largest publicly held insurance company—organized its business along five major lines: property and casualty; group life and health; individual life; life, health, and property/casualty reinsurance; and pensions and annuities.

1990s Transformation

The 1990s brought major changes to Lincoln National's mix of businesses, as senior management determined that the company needed to pare back to those core operations in which it excelled. The company thus sold National Reinsurance in May 1990 for $316 million, in the process withdrawing by and large from the property and casualty reinsurance business. Life and health reinsurance continued as a core company offering, however. Also divested were smaller, noncore operations, including Preferred Financial Corporation, sold in 1990; Western Security Life, sold in 1991; and K & K Insurance Agency—an insurer of sports and recreational activities—sold in 1993. Meanwhile, Lincoln National received a boost to its financial strength when Dai-Ichi Mutual Life Insurance Company in 1990–91 purchased a 9.6 percent stake, in new convertible preferred stock, for $312 million. The Japanese firm planned to work closely with Lincoln National and to form several joint ventures but was committed to a long-term holding and pledged not to acquire more than 9.8 percent of the voting shares or to cooperate with any group accumulating shares.

The divestments continued as the 1990s progressed. Next to go were the health insurance businesses, including the HMOs, as the company concluded that it could not compete with the giants of the industry, such as CIGNA and Aetna. In several transactions in 1992, 1994, and 1995 Lincoln National jettisoned its various health insurance units, bringing in an aggregate total of $670 million. The company also sold Security-Connecticut Corporation in 1994 for $238 million.

In 1993 Lincoln National finally began to spend some of the vast sums of money it had accumulated through these sales. That year the company's first major acquisition in six years came in the form of Citibank's life insurance operations in the United Kingdom. Citibank Life was consolidated with Cannon Assurance to form Lincoln National (UK) PLC. This subsidiary was further bolstered in 1995 through the purchase of Liberty Life Assurance Company Limited and Laurentian Financial Group PLC (renamed Lincoln Financial Group PLC), which was bought for $237 million. By this time Lincoln National (UK) had grown into the 12th-largest life insurer in the United Kingdom and also offered investment and retirement products.

In other foreign activity, Lincoln National in 1997 purchased a 49 percent stake in Seguros Serfin S.A., a life insurance company based in Mexico.

Of equal, if not more, importance to these international moves was the company's shift in positioning, from traditional insurer to financial services company, a shift reflecting the impact of deregulation, which had blurred the lines between insurance companies, banks, and investment firms. As evidenced by the 1995 $510 million acquisition of Delaware Management Holdings, Inc., a specialist in mutual funds and institutional money management, Lincoln National intended to focus on asset accumulation businesses—annuities, life insurance, 401(k) plans, mutual funds, and institutional investment management. Subsequent acquisitions aimed to build up these areas: the $72 million purchase of UNUM Corp.'s group tax-sheltered annuity unit in 1996; the $70 million purchase of Voyaguers Fund Managers, Inc., another mutual fund and institutional money management firm, in 1997; the $1.4 billion acquisition of the individual life insurance and annuity businesses of CIGNA Corporation, also in 1997; and the $1 billion purchase of the domestic individual life insurance business of Aetna Inc. in 1998. Meanwhile, Lincoln National exited from property and casualty insurance—which did not fit into the new strategy—when it divested American States Financial through two transactions in 1996 and 1997 that brought in nearly $3 billion. Part of the proceeds from the sale of American States went toward a late 1997 $500 million stock repurchase.

Though the company had divested its property and casualty line, it retained its strong—though seemingly noncore—life and health reinsurance business. Thus, Lincoln National in the late 1990s had four principal business segments: life insurance and annuities, Lincoln UK, reinsurance, and investment management. In 1998 Rolland retired after more than 20 years as CEO. His successor—the man who would lead the new look Lincoln National into the 21st century—was Jon A. Boscia, who had been president of subsidiary Lincoln National Life Insurance. Boscia aimed to increase earnings growth from eight to nine percent per year to 12 percent per year over a three-year period by making additional acquisitions and boosting sales.

Principal Subsidiaries

Delaware Management Holdings, Inc.; LincAm Properties, Inc. (50%); Lincoln Financial Group, Inc.; Lincoln Investment Management, Inc.; Lincoln National Financial Institutions Group, Inc.; Lincoln National Investments, Inc.; The Lincoln National Life Insurance Company; Lincoln National Management Services, Inc.; Lincoln National Realty Corporation; Lincoln National Reinsurance Company (Barbados) Limited; Lincoln National Reinsurance Company Limited (Bermuda); Lincoln National Risk Management, Inc.; Lincoln National Structured Settlement, Inc.; Lincoln National (UK) PLC; Linsco Reinsurance Company; Lynch & Mayer, Inc.; Old Fort Insurance Company, Ltd. (Bermuda); Seguros Serfin Lincoln, S.A. (Mexico; 49%); Servicos de Evaluacion de Riesgos, SRL de CV (Mexico); Underwriters & Management Services, Inc.; Vantage Global Advisors, Inc.

Further Reading

Burton, Thomas M., "Lincoln Agrees to Buy Units from Cigna," *Wall Street Journal,* July 29, 1997, pp. A3, A8.

Byrne, Harlan S., "Lincoln National Corp.," *Barron's,* April 29, 1991, pp. 39–40.

Connolly, Jim, "Lincoln Turns to the Task of Integrating Its Life Purchases," *National Underwriter Life & Health-Financial Services Edition,* June 8, 1998, p. 59.

David, Gregory E., "Emancipation (1994-Style)," *Financial World,* July 5, 1994, pp. 24+.

Fraser, Katharine, "Lincoln Plans New Push in Bank Channel after Buying Cigna Unit," *American Banker,* August 12, 1997, p. 14.

Garcia, Beatrice E., "Japanese Insurer to Pay $312 Million for 9.6% Interest in Lincoln National," *Wall Street Journal,* June 27, 1990, p. A3.

Hawfield, Michael C., *Ninety Years and Growing: The Story of Lincoln National,* Indianapolis: Guild Press of Indiana, 1995, 161 p.

Lohse, Deborah, "Aetna to Sell Some Assets to Lincoln," *Wall Street Journal,* May 22, 1998, pp. A3, A6.

Neely, Mark E., Jr., *Easy to Remember: A Brief History of the Lincoln National Life Insurance Company,* Fort Wayne, Ind.: Lincoln National Corporation, 1980.

Pulliam, Susan, "Lincoln National Seeks to Sell Large Part of Health Maintenance, Insurance Units," *Wall Street Journal,* September 23, 1991, p. A6.

Scism, Leslie, "Lincoln National Seeks Bigger Role in Financial Services," *Wall Street Journal,* June 10, 1997, p. B4.

Skertic, Mark, "When Lincoln Speaks, Fort Wayne Listens," *Indiana Business Magazine,* June 1991, pp. 8+.

—Patrick J. Furlong
—updated by David E. Salamie

Liz Claiborne, Inc.

1441 Broadway
New York, New York 10018
U.S.A.
(212) 354-4900
Web site: http://www.lizclaiborne.com

Public Company
Incorporated: 1976
Employees: 7,000
Sales: $2.41 billion (1997)
Stock Exchanges: New York
Ticker Symbol: LIZ
SICs: 2339 Women's & Misses' Outerwear, Not
Elsewhere Classified; 2335 Women's & Misses'
Dresses; 2389 Apparel & Accessories, Not Elsewhere
Classified; 2329 Men's & Boys' Clothing, Not
Elsewhere Classified; 2311 Mens & Boys Suits &
Coats; 2844 Toilet Preparations; 2331 Women's &
Misses' Blouses and Shirts; 2381 Fabric Dress &
Work Gloves; 2211 Broadwoven Fabric Mills—
Cotton; 3100 Leather & Leather Products: 2337
Women's & Misses' Suits and Coats; 2253 Knit
Outerwear Mills; 5632 Women's Accessory and
Specialty Stores; 3021 Rubber & Plastics Footwear;
3144 Women's Footwear Except Athletic

Liz Claiborne, Inc. is one of America's leading apparel companies. The founders led the company through spectacular growth in the 1980s, but business weathered the doldrums in the early 1990s following their retirement from active management. An aggressive revitalization plan helped put the sheen back on the Liz Claiborne name as it headed toward the new millennium.

Finding a Niche: 1970s

Elisabeth ''Liz'' Claiborne was born in Brussels and raised in Europe and New Orleans. Her natural artistic flair led toward her goal of becoming a fashion designer. At age 20 she got her first break when she won a design contest sponsored by *Harper's Bazaar* magazine. Soon after that, she was employed as a sketcher and model in New York's garment district and worked her way through the ranks at several design firms. After serving for 16 years as the chief designer in Jonathan Logan's Youth Guild division, she realized that the working woman needed more wardrobe options. Unable to sell the concept of stylish, sporty, and affordable clothes for America's working woman to her employer, Claiborne left the company and joined her husband, Arthur Ortenberg, and another partner, Leonard Boxer, to found Liz Claiborne, Inc. in 1976. The three pooled $50,000 in savings and borrowed an additional $200,000 from friends and family to launch the company specializing in fashionable, functional, and affordable women's apparel. Shortly thereafter, Jerome Chazen joined the trio. The company showed a profit its first year and became the fastest-growing, most profitable U.S. apparel company in the 1980s.

Claiborne's timing was perfect; she began providing career clothes to women just as they started entering the work force in record numbers. As Jerome Chazen stated in *Fortune,* ''We knew we wanted to clothe women in the work force. We saw a niche where no pure player existed. What we didn't know was how many customers were out there.'' Clothes designers had not fully exploited one of the largest growing groups in America—women baby-boomers penetrating the labor market. Liz Claiborne ignored the traditional industry seasons of spring and fall, opting instead for six selling periods, including pre-spring, spring I, spring II, summer, fall, and holiday, to provide consumers with new styles every two months. These short cycles allowed more frequent updates of new styles and put clothes on the racks in the appropriate season. By adding cycles, stores cut their inventory costs and overseas suppliers were able to operate more efficiently with the two extra cycles filling their slack periods. Liz Claiborne also made the decision not to field a traveling sales force. This determination, though disregarding conventional industry wisdom, stimulated the company's rapid growth. With virtually no overhead, Liz Claiborne was set for swift growth as sales skyrocketed.

Phenomenal Growth Through the Late 1980s

During the 1980s Liz Claiborne evolved from a basic sportswear business to a multifaceted fashion house. By the early

1990s, it boasted 19 divisions and three licensees, whereas in 1980 it had just one division. The company went public in 1981 at $19 per share, raising $6.1 million. A petite sportswear division was introduced in 1981, and a dress division was added in 1982. A 1984 foray into girls' clothes failed by 1987. Four new divisions were launched in 1985, including Claiborne, the company's expansion into men's clothing. Liz Claiborne discovered that 70 percent of its women customers were also purchasing clothing for their husbands. Also created in 1985 was the accessories division, which was formerly a licensee. Some components of this line included leather handbags, small leather goods, and bodywear.

The company further expanded and introduced its signature scent in September 1986. The cosmetics division began as a joint venture with Avon Cosmetics Ltd., and in 1988 the company regained full rights to the line. (This division has since marketed a new fragrance, Realities, and the Claiborne fragrance for men. In the fall of 1993, the group introduced Vivid, its third women's fragrance.) The year 1988 also marked an important milestone for Liz Claiborne, Inc. After only ten years, the company was on *Fortune*'s list of the top 500 industrial companies. It was one of only two companies started by a woman to achieve that distinction. Also, as an 11-year-old enterprise, it was one of the youngest companies ever to make the cut.

In 1989 the Dana Buchman division was launched. This division specialized in a line of higher-priced women's career clothes created for the bridge market. Its prices spanned the difference between moderately priced ready-to-wear sportswear and designer creations. In mid-1987, however, a slump hit the apparel business. Retail sales stalled in early 1988, inventories increased, and operating margins narrowed. In 1988, for the first time ever, Liz Claiborne's net earnings fell—by an estimated 11 percent, to $102 million. After years of 20 percent increases, sportswear sales increased only about three percent in 1988. Sales gains were getting hard to come by.

Breaking New Ground Through the Early 1990s

Searching for new avenues, Liz Claiborne focused on a long-overlooked group of consumers and introduced its Elisabeth division specializing in apparel for larger women. The line offered everything from career clothing and activewear to social occasion dressing. The line was very well received and gained market leadership. Sales rose 23.4 percent to $161 million in 1992. More importantly, in 1988 the company moved into the retail apparel business when it opened its first retail stores, offering the First Issue brand of casual women's sportswear. This break into apparel retailing was an expensive and highly risky proposition. Thirteen stores were launched that year and the company showed that it could be successful in this type of diversification. It operated 40 First Issue specialty stores throughout the United States and planned to add 16 more stores, mostly in 1993.

The company opened its first Liz Claiborne stores in 1989. These 18 stand-alone stores were placed in affluent suburban malls and served as laboratories for the company to test new designs and product presentations. They provided the company with immediate information regarding market trends through state-of-the-art bar coding and other electronic data interchange systems. Three Elisabeth stores were also opened serving the larger-sized consumer. Overall, sales of the retail division rose 20 percent to $92.9 million in 1992. In addition, the company operated 55 factory-outlet stores that marketed unsold inventory from past seasons. Sales achieved record levels in this area also, up 34.5 percent to $113.9 million. Liz Claiborne positioned these outlets at a distance from the stores where its products were customarily sold.

As profits and volume increased for Liz Claiborne, so did its influence at the manufacturing and retail ends of the business.

In addition to the company stores, Liz Claiborne dominated the selling floors of major department stores—sometimes more than half the allotment for women's apparel. The company did not own any factories, but made all of its merchandise through contracts with independent factories in 50 nations. The company reduced its reliance on Hong Kong, South Korea, and Taiwan in favor of countries like Malaysia, China, and Sri Lanka, where labor was less expensive. Less than ten percent of Liz Claiborne's products were made in the United States. There were drawbacks, though, to not owning the factories. To ensure that goods were produced to the high standards consumers expected, Liz Claiborne employed an overseas staff of almost 700 who regularly visited the factories.

At the retail end, Liz Claiborne commanded extensive clout. The company had a rigid noncancellation policy, meaning that if spring merchandise did not sell well in stores, retailers were still unable to cut summer orders. But Liz Claiborne generated what was known as strong "sell through." Its clothes were rarely marked down—only about five percent of its merchandise versus the industry norm of 15 percent. To reduce the risk of markdowns the company produced fewer goods than the level of demand forecast. Therefore, retailers got better profit margins and allowed Liz Claiborne more space on the floor. But because of limited space in department store floors, the company expanded abroad. In 1988 sales and marketing efforts began in Canada. In January 1991 Liz Claiborne, Inc. entered Great Britain, and later in the year it was introduced into Spain. Merchandise was also sold to stores in the United Kingdom, Ireland, and the Netherlands. Liz Claiborne tailored its strategies when marketing its products outside the United States. In some United Kingdom stores, the company leased space and sold the product itself. In Japan, it marketed through a mail-order catalog, and in Singapore Liz Claiborne granted a retail license for the operation of Liz Claiborne stores. This strategy seemed to work well as international sales totaled $108.1 million in 1992, while only six years earlier $1.4 million of sales came from outside the United States.

The greatest challenge to the company came in 1989, when Liz Claiborne and Arthur Ortenberg announced they would resign from active management in order to pursue philanthropic interests. They established the Liz Claiborne and Art Ortenberg Foundation, a private organization dedicated to protecting wildlife and the environment. This foundation also served the needs of the public through programs in the fields of human services, the environment, healthcare, the arts, and education.

The status quo continued after the founders' departure: Chazen, who had been with the company since the early days, was named chairman. A broad array of new products was introduced, including jewelry and sport shoes. Liz Claiborne further expanded its business to women's and men's optical frames, eyewear (fashion sunglasses and readers), and women's hosiery through licensing, and these revenues continued to climb. Tailored suits for the working woman debuted in 1991. This division was expected to generate sales of $100 million within five years. In May 1992 Liz Claiborne acquired three new labels from the bankrupt Russ Togs Inc. Crazy Horse casual wear was marketed in department and specialty stores. The Russ line offered updated career and casual apparel and was sold in moderate areas of department stores. The Villager line was offered in national and regional chain department stores and focused on career clothing and some casual wear. These and future acquisitions were expected to broaden the company's distribution and allow opportunities to expand clothing lines and create new products.

Although sales for 1992 increased 9.3 percent to a record $2.2 billion and the company's ten percent return on net sales remained one of the highest in the apparel industry, Liz Claiborne faced changing demographics. While the number of working women between the ages of 25 and 54 grew 43 percent in the 1980s, this would increase only about 25 percent during the 1990s. The company needed to become more visible in order to maintain market share. The combination of recession, increased competition in moderately priced sportswear, and the push into new markets led Liz Claiborne to seek a higher profile. In October 1991, the company launched its first print advertising campaign for apparel and accessories.

Liz Claiborne realized that cooperative advertising with retailers and its domination of department store floors was not enough anymore. Instead, the company needed to solidify its fashion image and create a global corporate image. Advertising was critical if the company was to preserve strong relationships with consumers and retailers. Also, Liz Claiborne could not expect to gain a foothold in Europe with an unadvertised fashion brand. Since floor space in Europe was much more limited, a company needed to advertise its image to get into the stores. Liz Claiborne did have an advantage in that the company stood for quality, value, and fit—exactly the standards of the Europeans and Japanese.

Liz Claiborne's $6 million advertising campaign broke in the November 1991 issues of 15 consumer publications, including *HG, Vanity Fair,* and *Elle.* The ad campaign was just part of Liz Claiborne's objective to increase visibility. In the fall of 1991, the company originated Women's Work, a philanthropic enterprise pairing women artists and writers with community groups in projects addressing domestic violence and work/family conflicts. For example, in Chicago, children's author Leah Komaiko collaborated with a group of city kids to write a book on working mothers. It was distributed through Reading Is Fundamental (RIF), schools, libraries, and reading programs.

Liz Claiborne was greatly concerned with listening to its customers. At the company's back-office operation in North Bergen, New Jersey, $10 million worth of IBM computers spit out information on sales trends throughout the country. This automated inventory network allowed quick response to market demand. In addition to this network, Liz Claiborne employed about 150 specialists to solicit feedback from customers at stores around the country and 21 consultants who made sure that clothes and displays were arranged in stores according to company diagrams. Ninety-five customer service telephone operators fielded questions from retailers.

The company that Liz built was noted for its well-organized management, distribution, and sales teams. In an industry where turmoil is a tradition, Liz Claiborne cultivated a strong team to run every aspect of the business. The company met industry challenges by following four guidelines it had instilled from its beginning: listen to consumers; create first-class products addressing their needs; price products with the consumer in mind; and always try to do more, and do it better. In 1992 *Fortune* once again named Liz Claiborne, Inc. as one of the ten most admired corporations in America.

Changing Fortunes During the 1990s

With $2.2 billion in sales and products in over 10,000 stores, Liz Claiborne was the largest women's apparel manufacturer in the world. But the company's fortunes dramatically shifted in 1993. For the first time in the company's history, sales fell for the core Liz Claiborne Collection, Lizsport, and Lizwear lines. Net income fell 42 percent for the year. Some $300 million worth of merchandise went unsold. Business as usual was not working anymore. ''That's too bad, because the old life was pretty good. In its heyday, Claiborne was regarded as the smartest, most efficient apparel outfit around,'' wrote Laura Zinn in a May 1994 *Business Week* article. '' 'When people were hired away from Claiborne, their new employers thought they were getting some magic,' says one ex-executive. Between 1985 and 1991, sales and net income almost quadrupled.''

Critics said Liz Claiborne apparel had gone stale since the departure of the founder. Saks Fifth Avenue dropped the Claiborne core sportswear lines in 1993, and the new mass market lines (Crazy Horse, Russ, and Villager) remained unprofitable. The company depended on just four department stores (Dillards, May, Macy's, and Federated) for nearly half of its sales. Profits fell to $83 million in 1994 from a peak of $223 million in 1991.

Paul R. Charron, who moved from VF Corp. to Liz Claiborne in 1994 and was appointed CEO in 1995, led a restructuring drive: 500 of the company's 8,000 employees were laid of in

1995 and the unprofitable First Issue chain was closed. Charron then implemented a three-year program to cut expenses by $100 million, reduce excess inventory by 40 percent, and shorten production and delivery cycles by 25 percent. A major investment in technology helped the company improve clothing design and track sales more closely.

"Now Liz Claiborne is playing catch-up with a vengeance. The company, which has extremely deep pockets, and no debt, is marketing smartly cut silk suits and cocktail dresses as well as basic blue jeans and khaki pants," wrote Jill Jordan Sieder in a February 1996 *U.S. News & World Report* article. "'They're changing in all the right ways in a very tough environment,' explains Jennifer Black Groves, a retail analyst at Black & Co. 'A few years ago, I would have called their clothes basic, boring, heavy on the polyester. . . . [Now] the word 'dowdy' just isn't fair anymore.'" With its image for fashion flair on the mend, Liz Claiborne rolled out a $25 million advertising campaign in early 1996. Print ads, super models, television commercials, and outdoor advertising dovetailed with an updated in-store marketing program. Charron, who was named chairman in May 1996, had also relaunched product lines, sold off units to licensors, and added new products. Veteran merchandiser Denise V. Seegal came on board as president in October 1996. For the first time since 1992, Liz Claiborne's largest unit, women's sportswear, registered sales increases on the year: up 10.8 percent to $1.23 billion. Dana Buchman's sales were boosted 38.5 percent to $188.7 million thanks to help from the Dana B. and Karan lines introduced in February 1996.

The announcement of a strategic licensing agreement with Donna Karan International Inc. in December 1997 marked the first time Liz Claiborne acted as a licensee rather than a licensor. The 15-year exclusive contract, under which Donna Karan would receive a minimum of $152 million in royalties, gave Liz Claiborne the right to source, distribute, and market DKNY Jeans and DKNY Active trademarks in the Western Hemisphere. Aided by cost reduction measures, operational improvements, and strong sales in core product areas, net sales for 1997 climbed to $2.41 billion and net income reached $185 million.

Trends for the Future

The special markets division, formed in 1996 to encompass the moderate and value-priced brands, marked its first profitable quarter in 1998. The relaunched First Issue line was being sold exclusively in Sears, while the Crazy Horse label was offered by J.C. Penney. The division, which also housed Russ, Emma James, and Villager lines, benefited from Charron's experience with VF—the company moved from department store to a mass merchant focus during his tenure there. Liz Claiborne placed these popular priced products in Wal-Mart and Kmart and regional department stores such as Kohl's and Mervyn's. Special market sales were $104 million in 1997 and expected to increase by 30 percent in 1998. With its DKNY licensing

agreement in place, the company was banking on a variety of brands, from mass to bridge, to drive future growth.

Principal Subsidiaries

Claiborne Limited; Liz Claiborne Cosmetics, Inc.; Liz Claiborne Accessories, Inc.; Liz Claiborne Accessories-Sales, Inc.; Liz Claiborne Export, Inc.; Liz Claiborne Foreign Holdings, Inc.; Liz Claiborne International, Ltd. (Hong Kong); Liz Claiborne (Israel) Ltd.; Liz Claiborne (Italy) Inc.; L.C. Licensing, Inc.; Liz Claiborne Sales, Inc.; Liz Claiborne-Texas, Inc.; LCI Investment, Inc.; LCI Holding, Inc.; Liz Claiborne (Canada) Limited; Liz Claiborne, S.A.; L.C. Caribbean Holdings, Inc.; Liz Claiborne Shoes, Inc.; L.C. Service Company, Inc.; Liz Claiborne Europe; LCI-Claiborne Limited Partnership; Liz Claiborne do Brasil Ltda.; LC/QL Investments, Inc.; L.C. Dyeing, Inc.; L.C. Augusta, Inc.; Textiles Liz Claiborne Guatemala, S.A. : Liz Claiborne (Malaysia) SDN.BHD; Liz Claiborne B.V.; L.C. Special Markets, Inc.; Liz Claiborne Foreign Sales Corporation; Liz Claiborne Operations (Israel); Liz Claiborne Colombia Limitada; Liz Claiborne GmbH; Liz Claiborne De El Salvador., S. A., de C; L.C.I. Fragrances, Inc.; DB Newco, Inc.

Principal Divisions

Liz Claiborne—Apparel; Liz Claiborne—Non-Apparel; Liz Claiborne, Inc.—Additional Brands; DKNY; Special Markets; Liz Claiborne International; Liz Claiborne, Inc. Retail Group.

Further Reading

Appelbaum, Cara, "Stepping Out," *Adweek's Marketing Week*, November 18, 1991, pp. 20–21.

Deveny, Kathleen, "Can Ms. Fashion Bounce Back," *Business Week*, January 16, 1989, pp. 64–70.

D'Innocenzio, Anne, "Claiborne Tells Holders Good Times Ahead," *WWD*, May 15, 1998, pp. 2, 18.

Gannes, Stuart, "America's Fastest-Growing Companies," *Fortune*, May 23, 1988, pp. 28–40.

Hass, Nancy, "Like a Rock," *Financial World*, February 4, 1992, pp. 22–24.

Rotenier, Nancy, "Niki and Me," *Forbes*, January 13, 1997, p. 96.

Ryan, Thomas J., "Dana Buchman Paces Claiborne Gains," *WWD*, April 2, 1997, p. 24.

——, "Karan's Jeanswear Royalties Put at $152M over 15 Years," *WWD*, April 1, 1998, pp. 4, 7.

Sellers, Patricia, "The Rag Trade's Reluctant Revolutionary," *Fortune*, January 5, 1987, pp. 36–38.

Sieder, Jill Jordan, "Liz Claiborne Gets Dressed for Success," *U.S. News & World Report*, February 26, 1996, pp. 55–56.

Zinn, Laura, "Liz Claiborne Without Liz: Steady As She Goes," *Business Week*, September 17, 1990, pp. 70–74.

——, "A Sagging Bottom Line at Liz Claiborne," *Business Week*, May 16, 1994, pp. 56–57.

—Carol Kieltyka
—updated by Kathleen Peippo

Longs Drugs

Longs Drug Stores Corporation

141 North Civic Drive
Walnut Creek, California 94596
U.S.A.
(510) 937-1170
Fax: (510) 210-6886
Web site: http://www.longs.com

Public Company
Incorporated: 1946 as Longs Stores
Employees: 17,300
Sales: $2.95 billion (fiscal 1998)
Stock Exchanges: New York
Ticker Symbol: LDG
SICs: 5912 Drug Stores & Proprietary Stores; 6719
    Offices of Holding Companies, Not Elsewhere
    Classified; 7389 Business Services, Not Elsewhere
    Classified

Longs Drug Stores Corporation is one of the top ten drugstore chains in the United States, with more than 370 stores in six western states: California (about 300 units), Hawaii (32), Nevada, Colorado, Washington, and Oregon. Each Longs Drug Store offers a wide variety of products and services including pharmaceutical products, photofinishing and photo supplies, cosmetics/personal care items, and greeting cards. Longs is also involved in a joint venture with American Stores Company called RxAmerica, which offers pharmacy benefits management services to healthcare plans and employers.

Founded in 1938

Longs Drug Stores Corporation was incorporated in Maryland on May 24, 1985, as a successor to Longs Stores, incorporated in 1946 in California. The company had specialized in the retail drugstore industry since its founding in 1938 by brothers Joseph and Thomas Long, and changed its name from the general Longs Stores to the more specific Longs Drug Stores in 1961. In 1975, at age 62, Joseph Long credited the company's

practice of spreading its wealth among its employees for much of its success. Indeed, a marked decentralization of power not only brought riches to the company's investors but a sense of purpose and handsome financial rewards to its employees. Store managers were paid quarterly bonuses proportional to their unit's profits, and the bonus system extended down through the half dozen assistant department managers that any specific store might employ. By one estimate, a Longs store manager in the late 1980s might have made $80,000 per year.

Longs' expansion began in the late 1960s, when the role of the drugstore began shifting in the U.S. retail market. Its stores, located throughout northern California, with one opened in Hawaii in the 1950s, were typical of the old-fashioned drugstore. Ranging from about 4,000 to 8,000 square feet, they included a pharmacy, soda fountain, and sundry health and beauty products. The drugstores appearing during the late 1960s were often triple that size, dispensed with the soda fountain, and added an array of specialty foods, auto maintenance products, toys, liquor, and stationery, among other products. Many stores set prices below the manufacturer's suggested retail price, pushing them into competition with discount retail department stores. Rather than functioning as the traditional specialty shops, drugstores became discount operations concentrating on health products, and retaining a pharmacist.

In 1967 the industry gained 12.2 percent in revenues, and about 50 percent was estimated to have come from discount chains. In the late 1960s increased prescription drug sales could be traced to an increasing tendency for government subsidy and private insurance to cover the cost of prescription medicines. Longs' 40 stores, located in the center of discount drugstore retailing on the West Coast, saw revenues rise from $78.3 million in 1967 to $95.7 million in 1968.

By the early 1970s chains of 10 or more stores had numbered 180, accounting for more than half of U.S. drugstores. Two- or three-store operations decreased in number, and big supermarkets opened their own drugstore chains. Longs opened its 50th store in 1970, one of eight it opened that year. From 1970 to 1971, sales rose for the first six months from $77.4 million to $90.5 million. Earnings went from $.51 per share to

Company Perspectives:

Our mission is to be "The Best Drug Store in Town." We will provide quality goods and services to customers in our core categories of Pharmacy/Health Care, Photo, Cosmetics/Beauty Care, and Greeting Cards, while also meeting other selected needs of our customers. We will be the leader for prescription services in retail pharmacy. We will always operate with the highest ethical standards and fairness in all of our dealings with customers, employees, suppliers, and shareholders.

$.72 per share. Its stock split two for one following its annual meeting in May 1971.

Longs increased its sales and earnings every quarter since its founding through 1975, at which time it operated 82 stores. For 1965 through 1975, it showed compounded sales growth of 22 percent, and earnings per share growth of 25 percent. With no leverage, Longs earned from 23 to 25 percent on equity from 1970 to 1975.

Expanded Conservatively in the 1970s

Longs expanded conservatively, not only because it thoroughly investigated potential sites but because it preferred to buy the land beneath its stores and did no business on credit. In the early 1970s Longs opened about six stores a year. Most were located in upper-middle-income areas where retail sales were high. It opened outlets mostly in northern California where competition was less keen. In the tougher retail market of southern California, Longs eschewed highly competitive Los Angeles for its affluent suburbs. Despite the tightening economy, Longs increased expansion to about ten stores annually in the mid-1970s. At that time the company's high earnings allowed it to expand from within rather than by acquisition, like most competitors. Longs carried no debt and took out no loans, so rising interest rates did not affect its growth rate. The Long brothers started the company on $15,000 borrowed from Joseph Long's father-in-law, Safeway founder Marion Skaggs. They had seen their father, a general storekeeper in Mendocino County, California, go under in the credit squeeze right before the Great Depression. Vowing to avoid that fate, they operated strictly on cash after their initial loan.

Longs was not affected by 1974's retailing slump. Sales for 1974 were up 22 percent with earnings up 19 percent for the fiscal nine months ended October 1975. Of that rise, 21 percent in sales growth in actual volume, not price increases, accounted for 15 percent. In 1975 each Longs store averaged $4 million in annual sales, versus $500,000 for the industry. Its $250-per-square-foot sales led the industry, where the average was $100. Its gross margin was less than 25 percent in an industry where it was typically 33 percent at that time. Longs stores did about as much business as competing stores twice the size. Decentralized pricing gave Longs an advantage in the inflationary economy of the 1970s, allowing managers to raise prices according to their local costs, instead of waiting for the word from the central office. Its decentralized acquisition of store stock also aided their ability to negotiate in the tough economy. Warehousing costs were nil because it did not maintain a central warehousing system. Most stock was purchased at store level from direct manufacturers or local wholesalers and jobbers. Merchandise was stored in the retail unit, but just briefly, as Longs turned over its inventory eight times a year, about twice the industry standard. The stores in general shied away from costly items such as console TVs. A store might sell such an item, but only stock a few until it proved to be a big seller. This way a unit avoided becoming saddled with unsalable merchandise in an economic downturn.

Doubled in Size in the 1980s

Longs entered Anchorage, Alaska, in 1977, Arizona and Oregon in 1978, and Nevada in 1979. By 1980 it operated 113 outlets in California, 12 in Hawaii, four in Arizona and one each in Alaska, Nevada, and Oregon. The company's rate of expansion increased to 14 to 17 units annually, and over the next decade it would double its total number of stores. Sales per square foot rose to $381 in 1979 from $351 the previous year. Revenue passed the $1 billion mark in 1982. In June 1987 the company acquired 11 Osco drugstores in California and one in Colorado, and sold to the Osco chain 15 of its own Arizona stores. Longs typically closed very few stores.

In addition to its lucrative incentive program, Longs had had profit-sharing since 1956. The company sold $25 million of its stock to the profit-sharing plan in March 1989. The sale provided liquidity and tax benefits, and significantly increased the plan's holding of company stock. In the late 1980s, Longs bought back 2.5 million shares that had been held by outside investors. Of the outstanding 20 million shares, employees owned 12 percent, and the Long family owned about 26 percent. It was speculated that the company was going private, although it announced no such plans, and remained a publicly held company. The family influence remained great. After chairman Joseph Long died in 1990, his son Robert M. Long became chairman and CEO; Thomas Long remained a director until his death in 1993.

Long's outlook was bright as it entered the 1990s, carrying no long-term debt and owning the property housing more than half of its stores. The chain's net income had grown 10 percent a year from 1978 to 1988, and a 28 percent increase in fiscal 1988 put it at $49 million, on sales of $1.8 billion. For 1988 it was still outperforming all large drugstore chains in sales per employee, $147,000; sales per store, $7.8 million; and sales per square foot, $455. In the early 1990s Longs focused on increasing its pharmacy business. In 1989 and 1990 it remodeled 24 pharmacies and promoted its mail-order prescription business. Fiscal 1990 was the fifth consecutive year that pharmacy sales grew more than 20 percent. Company-wide sales surpassed $2 billion for the first time in 1990. Net income grew ten percent from the previous year, to $61.3 million. Per-store sales averaged $8.8 million in 1990.

Centralized Operations Marked 1990s

Longs suffered from declining profits during the early 1990s, even while revenues continued to increase. The early

1990s recession hit Longs particularly hard because so many of its stores were located in California, which suffered a more severe recession. Increasing competition from huge discounters such as Wal-Mart and Costco also cut into profits. While the company's decentralized approach had worked well for many years, the more highly competitive 1990s led Longs to begin moving in the direction of centralization. In 1992 the chain began installing a point-of-sale scanning system in its stores in order to more efficiently control inventory and cut purchasing costs. The following year Longs began to centralize its over-the-counter drug business. The company also began to establish chainwide pricing, breaking with the tradition of store managers setting prices.

In 1993 and 1994 Longs paid $3.1 million to settle charges that it had overbilled the government for Medicaid claims in Nevada and Hawaii. In 1998 the company settled a dispute with the U.S. Department of Labor regarding overtime pay for about 2,000 pharmacists, agreeing to pay millions in back wages. The pharmacists had been paid straight time for hours in excess of 40 in a week. Meanwhile, in 1995 Longs established a subsidiary called Integrated Health Concepts (IHC), a pharmacy benefits management (PBM) company serving employers and healthcare plans. In November 1997 Longs merged ICH with the PBM unit of American Stores Company, creating a joint venture between the two companies known as RxAmerica.

Growth in the 1990s came through both acquisitions and the opening of new stores. In 1993 Longs paid $12 million for the 21-unit Bill's Drugs chain. Two years later six Thrifty PayLess stores in Hawaii were acquired. In 1997 Longs entered the Denver market with one new store and the Las Vegas market with four new stores. Longs announced in July 1998 that it had agreed to acquire Western Drug Distributors, Inc., which ran the 20-unit Drug Emporium chain in Washington and Oregon—with 18 of the stores in western Washington and two in the Portland, Oregon, area.

This last purchase was likely to increase Longs sales past the $3 billion mark. The chain was also closing in on the 400-unit level. Profit levels had improved nicely over those of the early 1990s, with the $58 million of fiscal 1998 a small but significant improvement over the $49 million of fiscal 1995. Per-store sales averaged $8.46 million for fiscal 1998. With its health improving, Longs appeared to be positioned to thrive in the early 21st century.

Principal Subsidiaries

Longs Drug Stores California, Inc.; RxAmerica (50%).

Further Reading

Brookman, Faye, "Drug Chains Shift to Central Control," *Stores,* August 1996, pp. 58–59.

Campanella, Frank W., "Longs' Way Up," *Barron's,* February 11, 1980.

Carlsen, Clifford, "Longs Drug Still Addicted to Its Expansion Plan," *San Francisco Business Times,* November 27, 1992, pp. 1+.

Ginsberg, Steve, "Longs Drug's Rx: $85M Expansion," *San Francisco Business Times,* December 5, 1997, pp. 1+.

Hemmila, Donna, "Longs Writes a Prescription for Its Ailing Profits: New Stores," *San Francisco Business Times,* September 19, 1997, pp. 3+.

Paris, Ellen, "Managers As Entrepreneurs," *Forbes,* October 31, 1988, pp. 62+.

Rosendahl, Iris, "Longs Drug Stores—Pharmacy Chain of the Year," *Drug Topics,* April 25, 1994, pp. 16+.

Westover, Kyle J., *Longs Drugs: A Tradition of Caring, 1938–1988,* Walnut Creek, Calif.: Longs Drug Stores, 1988, 112 p.

Winkler, Connie, "How Longs Got Centralized," *American Druggist,* February 1995, pp. 37+.

—Elaine Belsito
—updated by David E. Salamie

Lotus Development Corporation

55 Cambridge Parkway
Cambridge, Massachusetts 02142
U.S.A.
(617) 577-8500
Fax: (617) 693-1909
Web site: http://www.lotus.com

Subsidiary of IBM
Founded: 1982
Employees: 9,000
Sales: $1.15 billion (1995)
SICs: 7372 Prepackaged Software; 7373 Computer
 Integrated Systems Design; 4822 Telegraph & Other
 Communications; 3600 Electronic & Other Electrical
 Equipment

Lotus Development Corporation, a subsidiary of IBM, is the largest supplier of integrated messaging and groupware products in the world. Its Lotus Notes changed the world of business computing, making it possible for groups of people to share information and ideas through their personal computers at work, using local and wide area networks. As of March 1998, Notes had more than 20 million installed users. The company also produces desktop applications, including SmartSuite integrated software, Organizer time and contact manager, Lotus 1-2-3 spreadsheet, Freelance Graphics, Word Pro word processing, and Approach, a relational database.

Introducing Lotus 1-2-3: 1982–84

Lotus was founded in April 1982 by 32-year-old Mitchell D. Kapor, whose previous experience included writing two business programs for VisiCorp, an early personal computer software company: VisiTrend, which covered statistics, and Visi-Plot, a program for creating business charts. Kapor made $500,000 on the spreadsheet before VisiCorp bought him out for $1.7 million. Setting his sights on a spreadsheet that translated numbers into graphs, Kapor joined forces with Jonathan

Sachs, a programmer who had already envisioned a new spreadsheet and was looking for someone to help him market it. Sachs spent the next ten months writing Lotus 1-2-3 in assembly language for the IBM personal computer. Aside from the graphics, Kapor and Sachs concentrated on making 1-2-3 a fast recalculator. They took advantage of the new personal computers (PCs) with 256K of memory, which enabled the software to far exceed the spreadsheet capabilities of the similar VisiCalc.

Kapor convinced venture capitalist Ben Rosen to invest $600,000 in Lotus and, eventually, brought in other venture capitalists to raise a total of about $5 million, an incredible amount for a software company at that time. Kapor felt that substantial funding was essential to secure the early and abundant press coverage that he saw as necessary to 1-2-3's success. Lotus spent more than $1 million on advertising during a three-month period, and the national financial press extolled the software's virtues before it had even been released.

In the first few days after its official release in November 1982, 1-2-3 received more than $1 million in orders. By January 1983 the new program had surpassed VisiCalc to become the number one selling software package, and during its first nine months on the market nearly 110,000 copies of 1-2-3 were sold at a cost of $495 each. By the end of 1983, 1-2-3 was so popular that Lotus had become the second largest software company, just behind Microsoft, with sales of $53 million. It also had grown to about 250 employees, a figure that doubled to 520 employees by July 1984.

Kapor had started Lotus with an informal management structure, but he was forced to shift toward more traditional management practices by the company's explosive growth. To help him run the growing company, Kapor brought in Jim P. Manzi, a former management consultant, as marketing director. Manzi quickly assumed responsibility for Lotus's daily operations. He hired a team of managers from companies such as IBM to create a more disciplined work environment, displeasing some of the firm's original employees and causing the turnover rate to soar.

Another result of 1-2-3's rapid and widespread success was Lotus's decision to go public in October 1983; the company sold more than two million shares at $18 per share, raising a total of $41 million.

Beyond Lotus 1-2-3: 1984–85

In 1984, the same year that Kapor became chairman and Manzi was named president, sales reached $157 million and the company employed 700 people. Unfortunately, Lotus's well-being was tied closely to 1-2-3, and the firm had little success matching 1-2-3's sales with other products. Trying several different strategies to help it obtain a wider selection of programs, the company invested both in software start-ups begun by former employees and in the creation of completely new programs. One such product was Symphony, an integrated software package that added word processing, a more sophisticated data management system, and the ability to network with other computers, to 1-2-3's features. Although the company put enormous effort into promoting Symphony, sales were disappointing because some users felt the program was difficult to learn, while others preferred the greater power found in single-function applications.

The acquisition of programs through buyouts was also an option that Lotus pursued in diversifying its product base. For example, in early 1985 Lotus purchased a weakened Software Arts for $800,000 and paid its $2.2 million in debt. Software Arts had introduced the first popular spreadsheet, VisiCalc, which had lost its market share to 1-2-3. In addition to VisiCalc, the acquisition brought Lotus a number of other software programs.

The Macintosh Market: 1985–88

When the Macintosh—an Apple computer with a graphic interface—was created, Lotus decided to move into that market with an integrated program of its own called Jazz. Combining a spreadsheet, database, graphics, and word processor into a single program, Jazz was intended to attract the introductory level users at whom Lotus believed the Macintosh was aimed. The company invested in a large-scale advertising campaign introducing Jazz and got Apple to endorse the package. Although Apple executives spoke glowingly of the new software, Lotus's programmers had trouble writing Macintosh-compatible codes, and Jazz's initial introduction date of March 1985 was delayed two months because of programming bugs. Resolving these problems did not spell success for Jazz, however. Once on the market, the program was criticized both for being slow and for being difficult to learn, the same complaint that had been leveled at Symphony.

By this time, Kapor was becoming increasingly dissatisfied with the responsibilities of running a large company. Convinced that he was more of a developer than a manager, he left Lotus in July of 1986 to pursue new projects, with Manzi remaining in charge of the firm. Under Manzi's direction, Lotus continued to build on 1-2-3's success, selling 750,000 copies in 1986, approximately three times as many copies as its nearest competitor, Microsoft's Multiplan. Lotus 1-2-3 had sold more than two million copies since its release, accounting for 17.6 percent of all software sales in the business sector and 60 percent of Lotus's revenues. Manzi, however, recognized the need for the company to break into the market for larger computers and computer networks.

In the meantime, Microsoft was rushing a spreadsheet for the Macintosh to market. Called Excel, the program was more like the powerful 1-2-3 than the slow Jazz package. Excel captured the Macintosh spreadsheet market in much the same way that 1-2-3 had captured the IBM market, becoming a major embarrassment for Lotus. Both the Microsoft and Lotus programs sold for $495, but Excel had the user-friendly graphics-based commands used on the Macintosh and added some features 1-2-3 did not have. A few industry analysts felt that Microsoft had outmaneuvered Lotus, but 1-2-3 had inspired high brand-loyalty, allowing Lotus to hold on to its market share.

To compete better with Excel, Lotus announced improved versions of 1-2-3 that would include some of the advances Microsoft had incorporated into Excel, and it signed an agreement with IBM to develop 1-2-3 for mainframe computers. Lotus also launched a multimillion dollar advertising campaign in late 1986, pushing for a slice of the surging Japanese software market for 1-2-3. These efforts proved successful, and by mid-1987 1-2-3 was outselling Microsoft's Multiplan five to one in Japan.

Success for 1-2-3 was hampered when the upgrade of the program was repeatedly delayed, angering many customers. But despite three delays by late 1988, its share of the $500 million spreadsheet market stood at 70 percent because previous versions of 1-2-3 were powerful enough for most computer users, many of whom still preferred it to other choices. To keep other, less loyal spreadsheet customers from defecting, Lotus offered to give away a program designed by Funk Software Inc. that improved the appearance of 1-2-3's printed reports. The repeated delays hurt company morale, however, and the firm took a beating in the press, with much of the criticism focusing on Manzi. Former IBM manager W. Frank King III was brought on board, therefore, to get the development department back into shape. Lotus 1-2-3 Version 3 was shipped finally in June 1989, relieving the pressure that had depressed employee morale and Lotus's stock price.

Within a year Lotus had released 26 other programs, including the long-promised spreadsheets for mainframes, minicomputers, and workstations. These products were successful, and Lotus's income rose to $68 million in 1989. Lotus also invested in smaller companies like Sybase Inc., a database firm, and Rational Systems Inc., a manufacturer of programming software.

But the move that would have the greatest impact on Lotus in the long run occurred in December 1989, when Lotus shipped the first version of Notes. This was a new category of software called "groupware," designed to allow several computer users to collaborate on documents and other projects from distant locations across a network. Manzi was the exclusive marketer of the new software, developed by Iris Associates, Inc.

Running into Difficulties: 1990–91

Because of the firms' bitter rivalry, Lotus refused for years to develop products for Microsoft's Windows graphic interface program, keeping itself out of a rapidly growing market until early 1990, when it relented and announced Windows programs.

Another drag on Windows development was Lotus's decision to invest in a new operating system called OS/2, developed by IBM and Microsoft and pushed heavily by IBM. OS/2 was not nearly as popular as Windows, and, eventually, Microsoft virtually abandoned it. Unfortunately, Lotus had put effort into developing a version of 1-2-3 for OS/2, which did not sell. 1-2-3, already under pressure from Excel for Windows, faced further competition when Borland International introduced its Quattro Pro spreadsheet. Lotus filed suit against Borland in 1990, claiming Quattro Pro violated Lotus's 1-2-3 copyright. But in 1992 a federal judge rejected both firms' call for a summary judgment, clearing the way for a trial.

In March 1990 Lotus negotiated a merger agreement with Novell Inc., the largest computer networking firm. Lotus wanted access to Novell's networking technology and 1,500 service-oriented dealers, while Novell wanted to tap into Lotus's 1-2-3 customer base, which then stood at about five million. The deal would have created the largest personal computer software company in the world, giving Lotus a competitive advantage over Microsoft at a time when the networking market was growing quickly. The deal also would have gotten Lotus into the lucrative operating systems market, since Novell's Netware ran 65 percent of PC networks. The deal fell apart at the last minute, however, when Novell backed out, reportedly afraid of becoming Lotus's junior partner in the merged company.

Lotus was determined, nevertheless, to become a major player in networking, but it had important obstacles to overcome, including the lack of a service and consulting network similar to that possessed by Novell. Lotus decided, therefore, to join with other companies, including Apple, Novell, and archrival Microsoft, to devise a system to prevent tampering with electronic messages using sophisticated encryption techniques. The goal was to make computerized messages reliable enough to use as contracts and permanent records.

Lotus finally was able to take Microsoft on in the word processing arena with the purchase of Samna Corp. in late 1990. The $65 million deal brought Lotus Ami Pro, a program that had garnered much praise after its 1990 release. Lotus was still a distant third in word processing, however, trailing behind Microsoft and the WordPerfect Corp. As a result of the purchase, Lotus sustained its first quarterly loss in the fourth quarter of 1990, although it still made $23.3 million for the year on sales of $692.2 million.

Lotus faced more problems in 1991. After releasing a version of 1-2-3 for Windows in August, it had to replace it in September because of numerous bugs. By the end of the year, only about 250,000 copies of 1-2-3 for Windows had sold, giving Lotus about a 20 percent market share. With eight million copies of Windows sold, industry analysts had predicted 1-2-3's sales would be closer to one million. Lotus also had delayed repeatedly its release of 1-2-3 for the Macintosh, virtually ceding the Macintosh spreadsheet market to Microsoft. All together, Lotus's market share fell from 75 percent in 1988 to 55 percent. Mostly as a result of this declining share in the spreadsheet market, Lotus's first layoffs occurred in December 1991 when about 400 workers, ten percent of the work force, were cut from the payroll. The firm's stability and morale was shaken further by a management exodus in which ten vice-presidents either resigned or were forced out, including King, who was partially responsible for engineering Lotus's comeback.

Networking and Communications: 1991–94

Moving away from its near-total reliance on spreadsheets, the firm won praise for its continued efforts to diversify. Sales of Ami Pro were predicted at $50 million for 1992, and a graphics program called Freelance Graphics also was released in versions for Windows, OS/2, and DOS, taking Lotus into more new markets. In September 1991 Lotus moved into electronic mail—expected to become a major market—by releasing the mail forwarding software package called Open Messaging Interface. The program, which gave users the ability to send messages without leaving the program in which they were working, was accepted quickly by IBM and Apple.

Meanwhile, Notes was winning strong praise in the computer industry, though some critics felt that Manzi had tied the company's future too closely to its success. Manzi had built Lotus's product strategy around Notes, planning to offer a spectrum of software applications designed to work in a Notes environment. Although it was sold later individually, Notes initially was designed as a huge package, with buyers paying $62,500 for 200 copies of Notes, five days of consulting with Lotus technicians, and six months of free telephone support. Notes sold 112,000 copies in 1991, with major firms like General Motors and Metropolitan Life Insurance deciding to build their computer networks around it.

In March 1991 Lotus bought cc:Mail, Inc. for $32 million. The new subsidiary's product, cc:Mail, was used to send and receive electronic messages and by early 1992 had sold 1.5 million copies. Lotus's networking strategy received an important vote of confidence when IBM adopted Notes and cc:Mail as part of the networking system it recommended to customers. The two products had the largest installed base in their categories and moved Lotus ahead of competitors like Microsoft and Borland International in the networking market, which was expected to be one of the most quickly developing segments of the desktop computer market in the 1990s.

With computer hardware and software sales no longer growing at the explosive rates of the 1980s, Lotus could no longer count on automatic annual sales growth, and it fell far behind Microsoft, the number one software company with 1991 sales of $1.84 billion. With Notes, however, Lotus finally had succeeded in diversifying and seemed well positioned as the personal computer industry moved into an era of constantly shifting alliances.

On a Rollercoaster: 1992–94

In early 1992 Lotus teamed up with Borland, Novell, and Apple to develop electronic message standards for use by those firms and others. An extension of Lotus's Open Messaging Interface, the standards were designed to let different electronic mail systems talk to each other. The move was seen widely as an attempt to keep Microsoft from dominating that market.

That year Lotus bought the Organizer software, a time and contact manager, from Threadz, and in April Lotus introduced

SmartSuite for Windows, a software package that integrated several separate Lotus applications, making it easy for a user to move between Ami Pro (word processing), Lotus 1-2-3 (spread sheet), and Freelance Graphics. With cc:Mail, a user could send mail electronically from any of the SmartSuite applications. But there still was skepticism about this integrated approach. "I don't think the market is ready to buy software this way," Goldman Sachs analyst Rick Sherlund told *PC Week* in 1993. This was seconded, in the same article, by David Watkins of Borland International, "I don't think customers want to sacrifice the capability of one product for the integration. There will always be demand for leading-edge products." Integrated software packages provided another area of competition for Lotus with Microsoft, whose Office suite accounted for more than 60 percent of its application sales in 1993.

By 1993 Lotus's fortunes had apparently turned around, and magazines from *PC Week* to *Investor's Business Daily* were heralding the change. "Lotus has essentially reinvented itself, shifting from being a declining one-product spreadsheet maker to a multi-product leader with highly rated offerings in word processing, electronic mail, graphics, and data base and spreadsheet applications," wrote Glenn Rifkin in the *New York Times*. Sales of Lotus Notes had taken off in the past 12 months, and no one else offered anything like it. In fact, Notes had become the de facto groupware industry standard, as both Microsoft and Borland International announced that their products would run on it.

A big factor in the company's financial health was that with Notes, Lotus had developed a recurring revenue stream from annual maintenance contracts. "It's always been a structural weakness of the packaged software companies that there were no recurring revenues in the business model," Lehman Brothers analyst David Readerman explained in a 1993 *IBD* article. "Notes gets Lotus into the model of a traditional mainframe or minicomputer software maker." That year, recurring sales accounted for 20 percent of the company's total revenue of $981 million, 50 percent from Notes maintenance contracts and 50 percent from upgrade sales.

But the shouting was premature as 1994 sales of the company's spreadsheet and suite software fell sharply. Its late entry into the Windows market continued to hurt sales, particularly in Europe, where Lotus was unable to break Microsoft's dominance in desktop applications. Lotus was in a bind. Analysts were insisting that it should concentrate on its communications software, but desktop applications were needed to push Notes to the level where it established the industry standard. And while posting losses, the company was not able to lower the price of Notes, a step analysts and potential customers thought necessary to get it out and in use.

The company continued to make acquisitions and create partnerships. It bought Iris Associates, whose technology had resulted in Notes; Soft*Switch, which made e-mail switches; and Edge Research, a maker of applications development tools. It also signed a deal with AT&T to use Notes servers on its public network. There were persistent rumors, however, about a possible merger.

Becoming Part of IBM: 1995–97

In June 1995 the acquisition rumors came true when IBM bought Lotus for $3.5 billion in cash in a hostile takeover. The price raised eyebrows and so did the vision of laid-back Lotus, the first company to support an AIDS walk (1986) and to grant benefits for same-sex partners (1992), with its daycare center and family-friendly policies, as part of white-shirt-and-tie, buttoned down IBM.

But the anticipated culture clash did not occur, although Jim Manzi left Lotus three months after the merger and Jeff Papows, who joined Lotus in 1993 as vice-president of the Notes division, became president and CEO. IBM made Lotus the heart of its personal computer software strategy and let it keep its independence and name brand. "Lotus is our desktop people and I don't want to hear any more about it," said IBM Chairman and CEO Lou Gerstner, according to the *Boston Herald*. With access to IBM's financial resources, Lotus dropped the price of Notes three weeks after the merger, and in October 1995 IBM announced an agreement with 11 communications companies, including British Telecom and Nippon Telegraph & Telephone, to carry Notes on their networks.

During 1996 Lotus introduced a Web server add-on for Notes called Domino, the first groupware and e-mail server for the Internet. It allowed developers to build, deploy, and manage applications within Notes, including Web site hosting and authoring. The following year Lotus opened the Soft-Switch Institute to provide hands-on training for companies using Internet-based and proprietary messaging integration systems. Following the merger with IBM, Lotus doubled its sales of Notes each year.

1998 to the Present

In mid-1998 Lotus rolled out the Smart Suite Millennium Edition, with IBM's voice-recognition technology and other improvements, but which, acknowledging reality, was designed so that users could easily exchange documents with Microsoft's Office 97. While Lotus kept its desktop applications current, it was concentrating primarily on products for corporate intranets and new Web technologies.

The company, named for the Hindu spirit of enlightenment, had a "killer app" in 1982 with Lotus 1-2-3, an application that established the business status of the standalone personal computer. PCs were seen as a means of helping people work faster alone. The introduction of Notes began to change that perception; computers and group software now made it easy for people to work faster, and more effectively, together, sharing information. With its acquisition of Data-Beam Corp. and Ubique Ltd in May, Lotus moved toward providing chat, instant messaging, and real-time communications capabilities to its software. These and other developments, including a new web streaming technology, continued to strengthen Lotus's leading position in the networking and communications industry.

Principal Subsidiaries

cc:Mail, Inc.; Iris Associates, Inc.; Soft Switch, Inc.; Samna Corp.

302   **Lotus Development Corporation**

Further Reading

Berst, Jesse, "Can Lotus Stay Hot as It Faces Future Heat?," *PC Week,* December 20, 1993, p. 102.

Bicknell, David, "Lotus Looks to a Brighter Future," *Computer Weekly,* October 7, 1993, p. 18.

Cole, Barb, "Groupware vs. The Web," *Network World,* December 30, 1996, p. 62.

Cortese, Amy, "Lotus: One Step Forward, Two Back," *Business Week,* October 24, 1994, p. 92K.

Doler, Kathleen, "Executive Update," *Investor's Business Daily,* December 29, 1993, p. 4.

Fisher, Lawrence M., "With a New Smart Suite, Lotus Chases Its Rivals' Success," *New York Times,* June 15, 1998, p. D6.

Green-Armytage, Jonathan, "Can Lotus Still Go It Alone?," *Computer Weekly,* October 27, 1994, p. 18.

Hammonds, Keith H., "Software, It's a New Game," *Business Week,* June 4, 1990.

Hayes, Mary, and Stahl, Stephanie, "Lotus in a Desktop Dive," *Information Week,* October 31, 1994, p. 14.

Ichbiah, Daniel, and Knepper, Susan L., *The Making of Microsoft,* Rocklin, Calif.: Prima Publishing, 1991.

Knell, Michael E., "Challenges Ahead for Lotus, IBM," *Boston Herald,* August 11, 1995, p. 025.

Levering, Robert, Katz, Michael, and Moskowitz, Milton, *The Computer Entrepreneurs,* New York: New American Library, 1984.

Lorant, Richard, "Lotus Strong 2 ½ Years After IBM Takeover," *Austin American-Statesman,* February 2, 1998, p. D1.

"Lotus Acquisition May Start Trend," *CTI News,* June 16, 1998.

"Lotus All Stars," http://www.lotus.com/lotus/about.nsf

"Lotus cc:Mail and Notes Installations Exceed 10 Million Seats," *PR Newswire,* August 29, 1995.

Morrissey, Jane, "Shift to Suites Risky for Vendors," *PC Week,* October 18, 1993, p. 147.

Musich, Paula, and LaPolla, Stephanie, "A Tale of Two Mergers," *PC Week,* September 22, 1997, p. 20.

"The Network Connection, Inc. Set To Deliver Higher Quality Training over the Internet," *PR Newswire,* June 22, 1998.

Rifkin, Glenn, "Business Technology: From Downcast to Upbeat at Lotus," *New York Times,* October 13, 1993, p. D1.

Sager, Ira, "The View from IBM," *Business Week,* October 30, 1995, p. 142.

Teresko, John, "Electronic 'Keiretsu,' " *Industry Week,* December 19, 1994, p. 17.

"The Three Eras of Lotus History," http://www.lotus.com/lotus/about.nsf

Wilke, John R., "Lotus Development Relies on Notes To Write Success," *Wall Street Journal,* February 11, 1992.

—updated by Ellen D. Wernick

The MacNeal-Schwendler Corporation

815 Colorado Boulevard
Los Angeles, California 90041
U.S.A.
(213) 258-9111
Fax: (213) 258-3838
Web site: http://www.macsch.com

Public Company
Incorporated: 1963 as The MacNeal-Schwendler
    Corporation
Employees: 700
Sales: $134.8 million (1998)
Stock Exchanges: New York
Ticker Symbol: MNS
SICs: 7372 Prepackaged Software

The world's largest provider of mechanical computer-aided engineering (MCAE), The MacNeal-Schwendler Corporation develops software that simulates the functionality of complex engineering designs. With the software developed by MacNeal-Schwendler, engineers gained the ability to determine design flaws before embarking on the final stages of development. The company began providing such capability to engineers in 1963, when Richard MacNeal and Robert Schwendler developed design verification solutions for the aerospace industry. MacNeal-Schwendler's signature software, MSC/NASTRAN, was introduced in 1971 and was joined in the 1990s by MSC/PATRAN, a pre- and post-processor for engineering analysis. With operations in 38 countries and 50 direct sales offices, MacNeal-Schwendler marketed its products to aerospace, automotive, industrial, computer, and electronics manufacturers. The company also offered products such as geometric modeling and automatic meshing tools, which were used by engineers during a product's development stage, and a product that solved problems involving high-speed impact.

The Early Years

MacNeal-Schwendler's most senior employee during the late 1990s was the company's founder, Richard MacNeal, whose penchant for self-deprecation masked one of the pio-neering minds in computer software development. Born in Warsaw, Indiana, MacNeal moved with his family at age three to Philadelphia, where the well-to-do MacNeals enrolled their son in Penn Charter, a 300-year-old private school run by the Quakers. A student at Penn Charter through the 12th grade, MacNeal distinguished himself in his studies, but by his own admission he was a failure in nearly every other pursuit. He characterized his social development as "retarded." He described himself as a "nerd." His hours away from the classroom were painfully frustrating. "I was the worst football player you have ever seen," MacNeal remarked to a reporter from *Forbes* magazine. "I was 17 and hadn't kissed a girl."

MacNeal's embarrassments outside the classroom did not disappear after he left Penn Charter for Harvard University. Feeling a need to distance himself from his youth, MacNeal applied to the revered Ivy League university because "Harvard was the best, and I wanted to get away from home," but the experiences in Philadelphia repeated themselves at Harvard. Intent on studying engineering, MacNeal's extracurricular foibles surfaced again, but this time in the classroom. "I had the highest glass-breaking bill in the history of the school," he remembered, referring to the glass beakers used in experiments. But as he had at Penn Charter, MacNeal excelled in the classroom, completing his studies at Harvard in three years. After graduation, he joined the Army at the height of World War II, ending up at the predecessor facility to Edwards Air Force Base, where his duties included calculating the trajectories of bombs. At the end of the war he took the $250 soldiers received to pay their way back home and used the stipend to settle in southern California, where he enrolled at California Institute of Technology (Cal Tech) to continue his studies. At Cal Tech, MacNeal earned a Ph.D. in electrical engineering and stayed at the university for a short time to teach and work for a company formed by Cal Tech students and faculty called Computer Engineering Associates.

Once MacNeal cut his ties to Cal Tech during his late 30s, he began working for Lockheed Corp., the giant aerospace company. His stint at Lockheed was brief, lasting only a year: "I was impatient," MacNeal recollected, "I just didn't fit into a big company. On my exit interview, they asked me if I wanted to know what my supervisor wrote about me. He said I was intelligent and talented and stuff like that, and then he said I was

Company Perspectives:

Simply, we enable our customers to design and build better products faster. We do this with computer aided engineering software and services. We minimize the need for costly prototypes and time-consuming tests with computer simulations of product performance and the manufacturing process.

lacking in tact.'' After he left Lockheed, MacNeal teamed up with Robert Schwendler, and the pair formed MacNeal-Schwendler. The formation of his own company marked a turning point in MacNeal's life, a signal transition that he needed to make. ''Here I was,'' he recalled, thinking back to the months prior to MacNeal-Schwendler's formation, ''39 years old and hadn't really done anything. I wasn't satisfied.''

MacNeal-Schwendler Gets Under Way in the 1960s

For MacNeal, the awkward genius unable to fit in wherever he went, a career as an entrepreneur at last provided his niche in life. The years of searching were over and personal satisfaction was at hand. Working with an initial investment of $18,000, MacNeal and his partner developed their first program in 1963, an innovation called SADSAM. SADSAM was an acronym for Structural Analysis by Digital Simulation of Analog Methods, a product they designed for the aerospace industry. As with all their programs, MacNeal and Schwendler built products that helped manufacturers build their own products faster, better, and cheaper. The concept, a revolutionary idea in the early 1960s that would become commonplace by the end of the century, centered on simulating the effectiveness of a product well before the particular product reached the final stages of its development. By gaining the ability to determine fundamental flaws related to stress, vibration, and other conditions early in the design process, manufacturers involved in complex engineering businesses could make necessary adjustments before their products reached final development stages. The result was tremendous cost savings to the manufacturer, cash that otherwise would have been earmarked for the construction of prototypes and the innumerable revisions to a product's original design. It was a method for foreseeing the problems inherent in creating sophisticated machinery that would become known as computer-aided engineering (CAE). With the introduction of SADSAM in 1963, MacNeal and Schwendler had positioned themselves as important innovators in the promising science of CAE, a field that would become an integral partner in the growth of high-technology industries during the latter half of the 20th century.

With the power of hindsight, MacNeal's and Schwendler's position in 1963 appeared poised on the brink of resounding success, but from the pair's perspective after the introduction of SADSAM, there was much to be concerned about. The partners had a product, they believed, that would serve as a valuable aid for the aerospace clientele they courted, but unless their prospective customers believed in the value of SADSAM, MacNeal and Schwendler would have little cause for celebration. Fortunately, the pivotal struggle to secure contracts received a boon when the company participated in a project

sponsored by the National Aeronautic and Space Administration (NASA) in 1965. The NASA project called for the development of a unified approach to computerized structural analysis, resulting in the creation of NASTRAN, or NASA Structural Analysis Program. NASTRAN represented one of the first efforts to consolidate structural mechanics into a single computer program. It was a signal step forward. As the leading edge of CAE development moved forward, MacNeal and Schwendler were again positioned at the forefront. Their biggest contribution to the evolution of CAE occurred in the wake of the 1965 NASA-sponsored project; its arrival secured a lasting future for The MacNeal-Schwendler Corporation.

MSC/NASTRAN Debuts in 1971

Six years after MacNeal-Schwendler participated in the NASA-sponsored NASTRAN project, the company developed its proprietary version of NASTRAN, a program dubbed MSC/NASTRAN. The 1971 introduction of MSC/NASTRAN marked a momentous leap forward for the company, giving it a powerful and consistent revenue-generating engine to propel itself in the decades ahead. (The market strength of MSC/NASTRAN was represented by its longevity as revenue producer—by 1995, MSC/NASTRAN was in its 68th release.) From the business attracted by MSC/NASTRAN, the small entrepreneurial partnership formed by MacNeal-Schwendler developed into a genuine corporation, its structure and geographic range of operations blossoming as the 1970s progressed. Two years after it began marketing MSC/NASTRAN, the company had the financial wherewithal to make its first foray into foreign markets, establishing an office in Munich, Germany in 1973. Three years after entering Europe, MacNeal-Schwendler turned its sights eastward and opened an office in Tokyo, Japan. Highlighted by these important first steps overseas and underpinned by steady and meaningful growth on the domestic front, the company matured during the 1970s, a decade that witnessed the legitimization of MacNeal-Schwendler as a recognized world leader in CAE software. The decade also brought its own significant misfortune: the death of one its founders. In 1979 Schwendler died unexpectedly, a traumatic experience for MacNeal that left him in charge of achieving the dream the two partners had envisioned. Although the loss of Schwendler represented a severe personal blow to MacNeal, the company pressed forward with little hesitation as the 1980s began, inching toward greatness in the CAE field.

In 1983 MacNeal-Schwendler made its debut as a publicly traded company, completing an initial public offering that raised proceeds for future expansion and established the company's ticker symbol on the over-the-counter exchange. A year later, the company's stock migrated to the American Stock Exchange, a move toward greater prominence that befitted the stature of a fast-growing, industry innovator. The company's MSC/NASTRAN software by this point had grown into an industry standard. In the engineering departments of many of the leading high-technology corporations—companies that involved the aerospace, automotive, heavy machinery, and shipbuilding industries—MSC/NASTRAN was relied heavily upon to provide detailed simulation and design verification data. MacNeal-Schwendler's mainstay product had become instrumental to the success achieved by those companies undertaking projects facing complex engineering challenges. As the 1980s progressed, however, the company had to contend with its own complex challenges. Its industry was evolving rapidly, changing the dynamics of its business environment.

Technological breakthroughs during the 1980s engendered tremendous advances in interactive computer graphics and lowered the cost of producing powerful engineering workstations. These advantages broadened MacNeal-Schwendler's customer base, increasing the size of the company's potential consumer community. At the same time, the technological breakthroughs also caused the general computer industry to grow explosively, which, in turn, attracted a legion of new competitors in the industry, stiffening competition. This new surge of competition coupled with defense industry cuts toward the end of the decade conspired against MacNeal-Schwendler, tarnishing the company's long record of consistent success. The problems intensified as the 1990s began, prompting one analyst to remark, "They have an excellent product and they're an extremely well-run company, but they have not anticipated the kind of competition they've gotten."

Although MacNeal-Schwendler was by no means in a precarious financial situation as the 1990s began, the superficial damage stemming from an overdependence on military spending did provoke changes at the company. Focus shifted to the commercial market, leading the company to create testing software for automobile and satellite makers, as well as for large manufacturing companies. Toward this end, the company entered into a joint marketing and development partnership with Aries Technology in 1992. The following year (its 30th year of business) the company allied itself with Aries Technology to the fullest extent by acquiring its joint venture partner and thereby widening the design engineer audience the company targeted. The company's anniversary year also marked the establishment of a subsidiary office in Moscow, where MacNeal-Schwendler hoped to take part in the massive development under way in Eastern Europe.

As the company's 30th anniversary celebrations were winding down, so too was the development work for a significant product introduction, MSC/NASTRAN for Windows. The software, introduced in 1994, made MacNeal-Schwendler's signature code—ranked as the world's most popular finite element analysis software—available to personal computer users. This achievement was followed by another encouraging development, an acquisition that swelled the company's stature to unrivaled size. In 1994 MacNeal-Schwendler acquired PDA Engineering, a producer of pre- and post-processing software. Once completed, the absorption of PDA Engineering into the company's fold made MacNeal-Schwendler the largest single provider of products to the mechanical CAE market in the world.

MacNeal-Schwendler achieved global dominance just as its pioneering leader was beginning to step aside and make room for a new generation of leadership. MacNeal, in his early 70s during the mid-1990s, vacated the presidential post in 1995, setting the stage for the appointment of Tim Curry to the office of president and chief operations officer. The following year, when the company expanded its operations in Latin America by opening a new office in Brazil, Curry was named chief executive officer, as MacNeal reduced his work schedule to three-and-a-half days a week. Under Curry's stewardship, the company moved toward the late 1990s, its position as an industry pioneer and a market leader secured by three decades of MacNeal's leadership. Hope for the future rested on the shoulders of the company's new leader and new, innovative software solutions for the engineering challenges of the 21st century.

Principal Subsidiaries

MacNeal-Schwendler GmbH.

Principal Operating Units

Aerospace; Automotive; OEM; Growth Industries.

Further Reading

"Competition, Defense Industry Cuts Hurt Price of MacNeal-Schwendler Corp. Stock," *Los Angeles Business Journal,* June 4, 1990, p. 32.
Deady, Tim, "Revenge of the Nerd," *Los Angeles Business Journal,* April 29, 1996, p. 13.
"MacNeal-Schwendler Corp.," *Machine Design,* November 26, 1992, p. 103.
Teague, Paul E., "Pioneer in Engineering Analysis: Dick MacNeal Conceived One of the Most Widely Used Finite Element Analysis Codes in the World," *Design News,* July 10, 1995, p.50.

—Jeffrey L. Covell

Manor Care, Inc.

11555 Darnestown Road
Gaithersburg, Maryland 20878-3200
U.S.A.
(301) 979-4000
Fax: (301) 979-4062
Web site: http://www.manorcare.com

Public Company
Incorporated: 1968
Employees: 38,000
Sales: $1.53 billion (1997)
Stock Exchanges: New York
Ticker Symbol: MNR
SICs: 8051 Skilled Nursing Care Facilities; 8052
    Intermediate Care Facilities; 8059 Nursing & Personal
    Care, Not Elsewhere Classified

Manor Care, Inc. is a holding company for health care businesses. It is the industry leader in Alzheimer's disease management and one of the largest providers of long-term health care in the United States. As of May 1998, it operated 171 nursing facilities containing 24,124 beds and 37 assisted living facilities with 3,875 units in 29 states. Seventeen of the assisted living facilities served individuals in the early to middle stages of Alzheimer's disease and the majority of its nursing homes had units that specialize in serving patients in the late stages of that disease. The majority of Manor Care's patients paid for the services themselves or through their insurance. The company also provided home health services in 19 markets through In Home Health, Inc. and operated an acute care hospital. Chairman and CEO Stewart Bainum, Jr. and his family owned approximately one-third of the company. In June 1998 the company announced it was merging with Health Care and Retirement Corporation, forming HCR Manor Care.

Combining Nursing Homes and Motels: The 1960s

Born in 1919, Stewart Bainum dropped out of college and got his start in business as a plumbing contractor. He then entered the construction business during the postwar building boom that took place in the Washington, DC area during the 1950s. In 1960 Bainum made his first entry into the nursing home field when he built a nursing home in Wheaton, Maryland. In 1963 Bainum went into the motel business. By 1968 he was president of Park Consolidated Motels, Inc., based in Silver Spring, Maryland, a suburb of Washington. Park operated five motels, franchised under the Quality Courts Motels name, and two apartment complexes.

Also in 1968, Bainum incorporated his nursing home business with his brother Robert, calling it Manor Care, Inc. The company began with a chain of eight nursing homes, and its stock was sold in the over-the-counter market. From the start, Bainum sought to keep profits high by positioning his company at the upscale end of the nursing home market, serving elderly patients who were affluent enough to pay for their own care, instead of relying on government programs.

In April 1968 Bainum merged his motel operation with the organization from which he had originally purchased his franchises, Quality Courts Motels, Inc. This organization had gotten its start in 1941 as Quality Courts United, Inc., a nonprofit membership corporation of independent motel owners and operators based in Daytona Beach, Florida. The group had been formed to counteract the negative public image that motels had acquired in the 1930s. As roadside tourist camps, motels had become known as places where criminals congregated and other social undesirables were to be found. FBI Director J. Edgar Hoover gave authority to this impression when he wrote in *American* magazine that "a majority of the 35,000 tourist camps in the U.S. threaten the peace and welfare of the communities upon which these camps have fastened themselves and all of us who form the motoring public. Many of them are not only hideouts and meeting places, but actual bases of operations from which gangs of desperadoes prey upon the surrounding territory."

To prevent their businesses from collapsing in the face of this public disapproval, motel owners banded together to police their industry and ensure that standards were raised and then maintained. In addition, Quality Courts acted as promoter and advertiser for its members. In January 1963 Quality Courts was incorporated under the name Quality Courts Motels, Inc. At this time the company adopted a more formal relationship with its members, changing to a franchise basis.

Three months later the company made its first stock offering, when it sold shares to member motel owners and operators and their employees. When the company merged with Bainum's operation five years later, it moved its headquarters from Florida to Maryland, and Bainum became its president and chief executive officer, as its former president became chairman.

By July 1968 Quality Courts had 422 motels, of which 12 were company-owned and the rest franchised, and plans were under way for continued expansion. With a large number of existing motels in the eastern United States, the company looked to the west and to Canada for further growth. In addition, Quality began to prospect for other cash-rich companies in fields related to the motel industry, and in October 1968 it purchased Revere Furniture and Equipment Company, which sold motel furniture and supplies.

Expanding the Two Businesses: The 1970s

By 1970 Quality Motels offered rooms in 33 states, and the company had established an International Division in Brussels, Belgium, to facilitate its movement into the European market. Its first hotel on the Continent was planned for a location near the German capital of Bonn. The company continued to broaden its focus, purchasing Contempo Associates, a motel interior design firm. In addition, Quality's construction subsidiary won a contract to build military housing. The company's auxiliary units contributed more than a third of the company's profits in the first three quarters of 1970.

With an aggressive marketing and advertising campaign, backed up by a computerized reservation system and sales offices in ten cities, Quality's profits remained strong as the motel industry on the whole enjoyed a boom. The company began work on a new seven-story headquarters building in Silver Spring, Maryland, alongside a showroom for its motel furniture branch.

During this time Bainum's nursing home business also grew, though at a less rapid rate. By 1971 the company operated ten different homes with a total of 1,441 beds. Early in the next year Manor Care purchased two 100-bed extended care facilities from Medical Development Services, Inc. of Memphis, Tennessee. Located in Columbia, North Carolina and Wilmington, South Carolina, this acquisition extended the company's operation to six states. Manor Care also began construction of an additional facility.

In late August 1972 Bainum's hospitality business, Quality Courts, changed its name to Quality Inns International, Inc. to reflect the ever-broadening scope of its business. In keeping with this new emphasis, in the following year the company announced its plans to open 20 new European hotels.

Those plans ran into a snag with the 1973–74 Arab oil embargo, which resulted in long lines at the gas pumps and significantly slowed the American economy. As a motel operator dependent upon customers taking long trips in cars, Quality Inns was particularly vulnerable, and the company "damn near went out of business," its president Joseph W. McCarthy later told the *Wall Street Journal.* In response to this crisis, Quality Inns ditched its plans to expand in Europe, stopped construction on projects under way, sold the properties it found most affected by the gas shortage, and worked to strengthen relations with its franchise operators.

In the nursing home business, which was largely unaffected by the fuel shortage, Manor Care continued its steady growth. By 1974 the company was operating 15 long-term care facilities in seven states, including Maryland, its home state, Virginia, North and South Carolina, New Jersey, and Ohio. Manor Care added to its holdings with the purchase of the Powell Nursing Home, in Texas City, Texas, which it renamed Manor Care of Texas City. The company already operated two properties in Houston, Texas.

Quality Inns had become the tenth largest American hotel chain in number of rooms by 1977. By the following year the company had expanded further, purchasing the Royale Inns of America chain, and entering into an agreement to open 40 motels in Mexico as a joint venture with a Mexican bank. By August 1978 the company ran 286 motels.

In early April 1978 Bainum's health care operation, Manor Care, began an effort to acquire the Hillhaven Corporation, a nursing home company based in Tacoma, Washington. Although Hillhaven resisted the takeover attempt vigorously, by the end of August Manor Care had acquired nearly 60 percent of the company's common stock and more than a third of its voting stock, and the two companies had managed to hammer out an agreement. Manor Care then sold its stake in Hillhaven to National Medical Enterprises, a California hospital management concern, at a significant profit one year later.

By 1979 Quality Inns had recovered from its slump earlier in the decade, and the company, now the seventh largest American motel chain, was reporting record profits and an increased dividend. Quality Inns was planning an additional 175 motels, to be added through franchising in the United States, and also looked to add 50 properties in Canada.

Restructuring the Company: 1980–82

In 1980 Bainum moved to merge his two separate businesses. This was accomplished by having Manor Care purchase essentially all of the Quality Inns company, in a transaction valued at $37 million. In September of the following year Manor Care reorganized as a holding company for three subsidiaries: Quality Inns, Inc., which owned and operated hotels; Quality Inns International, Inc., which franchised hotels under the Quality Inn name; and Manor Healthcare Corporation, which at that time operated a hospital, three alcohol rehabilitation facilities, and 23 separate nursing homes, including new facilities in Sugar Land, Texas and Clearwater, Florida.

One month after the company's restructuring, Manor Healthcare entered a bidding war with National Medical Enterprises for control of Cenco, Inc., a nursing home operator based in Illinois. By early November 1981 Manor Care had acquired more than 90 percent of Cenco, at a cost of $202 million. With Cenco's 83 nursing homes, containing 10,000 beds all together, the purchase nearly quadrupled the number of beds in long-term care facilities operated by Manor Care. One year later the company announced that it would sell five subsidiaries of Cenco, which manufactured items such as scientific glassware, research equipment, and valves, because they did not fit in with the company's primary mission of running nursing homes and hotels. The liquidation of these assets, in addition to the sale of 14 nursing homes, helped to defray the cost of the Cenco acquisition, which left Manor Care with a $167 million bank debt.

Quality Inns President Joseph W. McCarthy left the chain in June 1980, and, after six months without a leader at the helm, Bainum appointed Robert C. Hazard, Jr. to the post. Hazard brought a number of top managers with him from his previous position at Best Western hotels. The new team set out to double the size of Quality Inns in three years, adding new properties through franchising at the rate of one every other business day. In addition, the company looked to enter the overseas market once again, this time through an affiliated European chain, Crest hotels.

Quality Inns also divided its properties into three groups: top-quality motels, to be called Quality Royale; medium-priced outlets, which would keep the Quality Inn name; and low-priced motels, to be known as Comfort Inns. To ensure that all three sectors would live up to their name, the company instituted a strict quality-control system, and dropped 20 motels for failing to measure up. Quality Inns also planned to install a state-of-the-art reservation system and to launch a nationwide ad campaign, to keep its ever-burgeoning number of rooms filled.

Stop Buying, Start Building: 1983–86

In the fall of 1983 the nursing home arm of Manor Care began an attempt to expand into the southwest by taking over the Anta Corporation, a company based in Oklahoma City that operated nursing homes, as well as aluminum and energy businesses. Although its efforts were initially rebuffed, in January 1984 Anta agreed to sell Four Seasons Nursing Centers, Inc., its 47-home long-term care subsidiary, to Manor Care for $56 million. Like Manor Care, Four Seasons served private-pay patients. One month earlier the company had acquired three facilities in central Pennsylvania owned by the Barley family for $11.7 million. These purchases helped to make Manor Care the fourth largest publicly traded nursing home operator in the United States, with a total of 154 homes.

Following this period of expansion through acquisition, Manor Care reevaluated its growth policy. The company concluded that the prices of nursing home properties had begun to outstrip their value and that operations the company started from scratch were, in general, more profitable than those it bought from others. Manor Care, therefore, decided to achieve

its next phase of expansion in the health care industry through development and construction from the ground up, rather than through acquisition.

Anticipating a demographic shift that would result in a large growth in the elderly population, Manor Care turned its attention to upgrading its nursing home facilities in 1985, undertaking an extensive program of refurbishment that would allow it to attract and hold onto the most wealthy, and most profitable, nursing home patients. In addition to locating its facilities in affluent areas, the company expanded its ''Williamsburg Concept.'' Operating Williamsburg wings in eight nursing centers, Manor Care provided its patients with gourmet food, private dining areas, limousine service, and cultural outings, as well as a hostess that acted as a concierge, catering to the special needs of patients. Programs such as this were rewarded by Manor Care's profits, which were twice as high as the industry average.

In 1985 Manor Care increased its holdings in the hotel industry when it became the largest shareholder in a British chain of hotels, with nearly a third of Prince of Wales Hotels, P.L.C. This purchase provided the company with a toehold in Europe, from which to launch further expansion. In September 1985 Manor Care announced that it planned to add 40 new hotels overseas within the next year. In addition, the company franchised 82 more Quality Inn hotels.

As Manor Care moved into the late 1980s, it began a program to shed less profitable properties and use the proceeds from their sale, as well as profits generated by its hotel operations, to finance the further growth of its health care division. To that end, eight nursing centers, four hotels, and an office building were sold in 1986, and the company began construction of six new nursing homes and nine additions to previously existing facilities. Manor Care also targeted 64 sites for future development, all in demographically desirable areas, with a large number of wealthy old people. With this strategy, the company hoped to maintain its ratio of 60 percent privately paying patients, the industry's highest.

The primary arena of growth for Manor Care's hotel business during this time continued to be overseas. The company entered the New Zealand market in 1986, with ten franchised hotels, and also added properties in Canada, Mexico, the United Kingdom, Belgium, Germany, Switzerland, and Italy.

Changing Management: 1987

In 1987 Manor Care's management underwent a shift, as founder Stewart Bainum's son, Stewart Bainum, Jr., took over as chairman. Stewart Bainum, Jr. had been a Maryland state senator, and he took his place in the family business in the wake of his loss in a race for a seat in the U.S. House of Representatives. The older Bainum assumed the post of vice-chairman of the board, and under his guidance the younger Bainum continued the company's policy of emphasizing growth in the health care sector. Manor Care sold four hotels, its stake in the Prince of Wales hotel chain in England, and its alcoholic rehabilitation centers in 1987 and opened two new nursing homes, in addition to one that was acquired. The company laid ambitious plans to build 20 new nursing homes each year, to double in size in less than ten years. In the midst of this building spree, Manor Care also diversified its health care operations slightly, adding assisted living facilities for those requiring less intense medical care than nursing homes provide, and special units called "Arcadia Units" to care for people with Alzheimer's disease.

In its lodging operations, Manor Care moved more strongly into the upscale market when it formed Clarion Hotels and Resorts, a group of 37 luxury resorts operated as a joint venture with the Associated Inns and Restaurants Company of America. It also dropped 76 motels from its line that failed to meet its standards of quality and added France, India, and Ireland to its roster of locations abroad.

In late 1987 Manor Care's Quality Inn motel division became involved in a dispute with the U.S. Immigration and Naturalization Service over its alleged hiring of illegal aliens, underlining the shortage of menial workers that plagued both Manor Care's hotel and nursing homes divisions, driving costs up. Facing almost 100 percent annual turnover among some types of nursing home employees, the company implemented incentive programs, such as scholarships for outstanding workers, in an effort to keep employees on the job. Nevertheless, high labor costs in the health care field continued to eat into Manor Care's profits, leaving the company's new nursing homes in the red for longer and longer periods of time. Faced with a temporary dead end in this field, for which it had nurtured such high hopes, Manor Care turned its focus to its hotel subsidiaries in the late 1980s.

Concentrating on Lodging: 1988–91

In 1988 the company broadened the scope of its hotel offerings, hoping to induce new growth. Quality Inns introduced two lines of hotels consisting entirely of suites: Quality Suites and Comfort Suite Hotels. In all, 46 all-suite outlets came on-line. In addition, the company began marketing a chain of newly constructed budget motels it called "McSleep Inns," which soon became known as "Sleep Inns" after a dispute with McDonald's over rights to the "Mc" prefix.

In June 1990 Manor Care made an unsuccessful attempt to buy the Ramada and Howard Johnson hotel franchises. In early July it made a successful purchase when it acquired the Rodeway Inns International franchise system, with 148 budget motels, for nearly $15 million. Later that month Manor Care changed the name of its Quality Inns International division, responsible for franchising hotels around the world, to Choice Hotels International, Inc., reflecting the diversity of hotel trade names the company now controlled. By number of outlets, Choice had become the largest hotel franchise system in the world.

Manor Care's hotel buying binge continued that fall, when it completed acquisition of Econo Lodges of America, with 615 motels, along with 85 related Friendship Inns, for $60 million. With seven brand names, including Quality, Comfort, Clarion, Sleep, Econo Lodge, Friendship, and Rodeway Inns, Choice now held one quarter of the low-cost hotel room market. The company began heavy television advertising featuring celebrities popping out of suitcases. As Choice Chairman Robert C. Hazard, Jr., told *Forbes,* "Our goal is 1 million hotel rooms and 10,000 hotels worldwide by the year 2000."

The rapid pace of acquisitions left Choice with the daunting task of integrating the new chains into its old system. The main link between the disparate parts became a new $5 million computerized reservation program. Although the war in the Persian Gulf depressed travel and tourism in early 1991, by the end of the year, business had rebounded and occupancy rates were again running above industry average.

Although Manor Care's lodging division accounted for only 12 percent of its revenues in the fiscal year ended in May 1991, Choice contributed more than 20 percent of the company's profits, as the nursing home business continued to lag.

Betting on Frailty: 1991–95

In 1991 the company sold 20 percent of its institutional pharmacy subsidiary in a public offering. The proceeds from the Vitalink Pharmacy Services, Inc. sale were used to buy and develop more pharmacies and to pay down some of Manor Care's debt. Beset by continued high labor costs and limits on earnings enforced though Medicare caps, Manor Care began to search out more highly profitable niches within the health care field.

In 1994 Manor Care was the third largest nursing home operator in the United States, with 22,089 beds in 164 facilities in 28 states. The company decided to make greater investments in the assisted living business it had started seven years earlier. In addition to building new Springhouse facilities for what the company called the "frail elderly," Manor Care refurbished hotels and turned them into communal residences for the elderly. With room costs ranging from $1,400 to $2,300 a month, the residences were considerably less expensive than the $4,000 to $6,000 per patient per month costs of a nursing home. The company also began building residential assisted living homes, which they named Arden Courts, for people affected with Alzheimer's disease.

In December 1994 Manor Care reorganized its structure. It consolidated its hotel division, which operated 51 properties, with its Choice Hotels International, Inc. franchising unit and created a single business dealing with lodging. The company also split its health care operations into three units: its nursing home subsidiary, a division for its Springhouse and Arden Courts assisted living centers, and a unit exploring opportunities in home health care and rehabilitation services.

In 1995 the company expanded beyond long term care with the purchase of 64 percent of Minneapolis-based In Home Health, Inc. The acquisition moved Manor Care into a new market, supplying skilled nursing, rehabilitation, personal care, and other services to patients in their own homes. With 75 percent of the patients discharged from Manor Care nursing homes needing some level of home health care, it was a logical purchase as the company developed "a continuum of care" approach to health services.

Later that year Manor Care paid Beverly Enterprises $74.3 million for six assisted living centers and five nursing homes in California, Illinois, Ohio, and Florida. Vitalink Pharmacy Services also expanded through acquisitions that year to become the sixth largest institutional pharmacy chain in the United States. With the company's expansion, it needed more room, and in July 1995 Manor Care announced it would be moving to

Gaithersburg, Maryland, where it had bought the National Geographic Society's office building plus 100 acres and a warehouse facility.

A New Health Services Company: 1996–98

Deciding its future lay in the health care business, Manor Care consolidated all of its health care facilities under the name ManorCare Health Services and, in November 1996, spun off its $342 million Choice Hotels International subsidiary. That new publicly owned company, with some 3,145 hotels worldwide, was the second largest hotel company in the world. Manor Care shareholders received the same number of shares of the new company as they owned of Manor Care.

At the same time, Vitalink merged with the institutional pharmacy division of GranCare, another long term care company, reducing Manor Care's share to 45 percent. The move catapulted Vitalink into the number two position in that market. Manor Care bought more Vitalink shares in 1997 to restore its majority interest and in 1998 announced that it had reached an agreement with Pennsylvania-based Genesis Health Ventures, Inc. to sell Vitalink for approximately $690 million. Once the sale was completed in late 1998, Manor Care would continue to purchase its pharmacy services from Vitalink.

In September 1997 Manor Care also announced that it would split into two publicly traded companies in 1998, separating its real estate and health care operations. ManorCare Health Services Inc. would own and operate the Springhouse and Arden Courts assisted living centers and operate and pay rent on the nursing home facilities owned by the real estate operation. It would also own 18 percent of Vitalink and the controlling interest in In Home Health. Manor Care Realty Inc. would own, develop, and acquire health care properties. Expected to close by the end of 1998, the separation meant that the health care operation would no longer have to carry construction and real estate debts. The real estate company would carry the loss and then get its money back by selling the occupied and profitable assisted living facility to ManorCare Health Services.

But those plans were abruptly canceled on June 10, 1998, when Manor Care and Health Care Retirement Corporation announced that they were merging the two companies in a stock swap worth about $2.45 billion. The new company, HCR Manor Care, would be the largest in the industry, with about $4 billion in market value, and one of the biggest in number of facilities. Under the agreement, HCR head Paul Ormond became president and CEO of HCR Manor Care, which was to be based in Toledo, and Stewart Bainum, Jr. was named chairman.

Principal Subsidiaries

In Home Health, Inc. (64%); Vitalink Pharmacy Services, Inc. (51%).

Further Reading

Beckford, Tanayha, "Manor Care Boosts Stake in Vitalink," *The Washington Times,* May 23, 1997, p. B9.
Clark, Kim, "Manor Care Completes Purchase of 11 Facilities," *The Baltimore Sun,* October 3, 1995, p. 3C.
Cuff, Daniel F., "A Wake-Up Call at Quality Inns," *New York Times,* September 13, 1981.
Escobar, Louisa Shepard, "Manor Care Inc. To Go Public with Total-Care Pharmacies," *Washington Business Journal,* October 21, 1991, p. 4.
Fairhall, John, "Manor Care Takes Control of Supplier; Company Gains Entry into Home Health Area," *The Baltimore Sun,* October 25, 1995, p. 2C.
Galle, William, "Quality Motels Broadening Base Via Overseas Expansion," *Investment Dealers Digest,* October 20, 1970.
"Genesis Health Ventures To Acquire Vitalink Pharmacy Services, Inc., Establishing a $900 Million Integrated Pharmacy Services Business," Press Release, Kennett Square, Penn.: Genesis Health Ventures, Inc., April 27, 1998.
Haggerty, Maryann, "Manor Care Moving Its Headquarters," *The Washington Post,* July 13, 1995, p. D9.
Hall, Jessica, "Manor Care Annual Earnings Soar; Silver Spring Health Provider Seen Positioned for Growth," *Daily Record* (Baltimore), June 27, 1995, p. 3.
"HCR, Manor Care To Merge in $2.45 Bln Stock Swap," *Bloomberg,* June 10, 1998.
Hilzenrath, David S., "Manor Care Layoffs To Top 100; Most Cuts To Come at Headquarters," *Washington Post,* April 18, 1998, p. D1.
Hong, Peter, "Manor Care Says: Hotel Glut? What Glut?," *Business Week,* January 13, 1992.
Kopecki, Dawn, "Manor Care's Split Offers Good Choice," *Washington Times,* October 14, 1996, p. D20.
"Manor Care, Inc.," http://www.manorcare.com/corpfr.htm
"Manor Care, Inc. To Separate Health Care Services and Realty Operations," Press Release, Gaithersburg, Md.: Manor Care, Inc., September 15, 1997.
"Manor Care Preps $350M High-Yield Deal," *Corporate Financing Week,* February 16, 1998, p. 6.
"Manor Care Targets Assisted-Living Business," *Health Line,* September 4, 1996.
McCabe, Robert, "The Inn Thing; Reshaping Hotels; Former Ramada Inn in Boynton Beach Is the Prototype for Manor Care Inc.'s Venture To Build 30 Communal Residences," *Fort Lauderdale Sun-Sentinel,* April 18, 1994, p. 4.
McCollum, James D., "Merger Makes Quality Courts Motels One of Nation's Leading Chains," *Investment Dealers Digest,* July 1, 1968.
Murphy, H. Lee, "Nursing Home Drug Distribution Expands Niche Via Acquisitions," *Crain's Chicago Business,* October 30, 1995, p. 40.
——, "Rx for Vitalink's Stock; Bigger Float, Merger Drug Company's Cure," *Crain's Chicago Business,* September 30, 1996, p. 46.
Novack, Janet, "Tip O'Neill Works Here," *Forbes,* December 10, 1990.
Riley, Karen, "Manor Care Realigns for Profitable Future," *Washington Times,* December 22, 1994, p. B9.
Salganik, M. William, "Manor Care Plans Spinoff; Company To Divide into Building and Operational Firms," *Baltimore Sun,* September 17, 1997, p. 1C.
Shenot, Christine, "Leader's & Success: Manor Care Inc.," *Investors Business Daily,* August 12, 1992, p. 1.
"Spinoff of Unit Boosts Manor Care Profits," *Washington Post,* June 30, 1992, p. C3.
Williams, Elisa, "Manor Care Healthier Due to Nursing Homes," *Washington Times,* June 28, 1991, p. C3.

—updated by Ellen D. Wernick

Mattel, Inc.

Mattel, Inc.

333 Continental Boulevard
El Segundo, California 90245-5012
U.S.A.
(310) 252-3070
Fax: (310) 524-4443
Web sites: http://www.hotwheels.com
http://www.barbie.com
http://www.mattelmedia.com

Public Company
Incorporated: 1948
Employees: 25,000
Sales: $4.8 billion
Stock Exchanges: New York
Ticker Symbol: MAT
SICs: 3944 Games, Toys & Children's Vehicles; 3942
    Dolls & Stuffed Toys; 3940 Toys & Sporting Goods;
    2361 Girls' Dresses & Blouses

The world's largest toy company, Mattel, Inc. designs, manufactures, markets, and distributes a wide variety of toy products in 150 countries. The company's products comprise a number of core toy lines, including Barbie dolls, clothing, and accessories; Hot Wheels toy die-cast vehicles; Disney merchandise; the American Girl Collection of books, dolls, clothing, and accessories; Fisher-Price toys; See 'N Say talking toys; a line of large dolls, including the Cabbage Patch Kids; and games like Scrabble and UNO. Mattel's toys are produced in manufacturing facilities in the United States, the United Kingdom, China, Malaysia, Mexico, Italy, and Indonesia and have delighted generations of children throughout the world.

From Picture Frames to Toys: 1944–49

Mattel was founded in 1944 by Elliot and Ruth Handler. The youngest of ten children of Polish immigrants, Ruth was a secretary for Paramount Pictures in Los Angeles when she married Elliot Handler, an industrial engineer. Handler started out designing light fixtures but soon began making furniture to sell out of his garage. The business attracted four partners and quickly rose to become a $2 million enterprise making giftware and costume jewelry. By 1945 Elliot Handler grew restless and wanted a new business approach to remain competitive in the fast-changing postwar world. Handler's plans led to a dispute with his partners and he sold his interest in the company at a loss. Meanwhile, in 1944 Ruth hooked up with an old friend, Harold Matson, and they started Mattel Creations, with Elliott designing products. The name Mattel was formed by combining Matson's last name with Handler's first name. Ill health soon forced Matson to sell out.

Mattel first entered the picture frame business using scrap plastic and wood. With the leftover wood slats and plastic, Handler designed doll house furniture. Matson manufactured and Ruth Handler formed a simple sales organization, and the company was off to a winning start. In its first year the company pulled in $100,000, netting $30,000.

The Handlers had little business experience and even less capital, but the demographics of a baby boom plus a virtual toyless marketplace immediately after World War II gave them a unique opportunity to make their mark. Even so, it took a couple of years to see profits. In 1946 another low-cost line of molded furniture with meticulous detail put the Handlers out of the doll furniture business. Because of their introduction of a ''birdy bank'' and a ''make-believe makeup set,'' however, they managed to break even, and in the following year the Handlers introduced the first in a long string of hits in the toy industry. The ''Uke-a-Doodle,'' a miniature plastic ukelele, was an immediate success and drew large orders. In 1948 the Handlers introduced another hit—a new all-plastic piano with raised black keys. Although a winner, the company lost ten cents for each piano it sold because of quality problems relating to the die-cast sound mechanism breaking loose from the plastic.

These early business experiences taught the Handlers some poignant lessons in avoiding obsolescent products, ruinous price competition, poor cost control, and product quality problems. They realized that a successful business had to produce unique and original products of superior quality and strength that could not be copied easily by competitors.

The company incorporated in the state of California in 1948. At the same time the Handlers and an outside inventor began developing a music box employing a unique mechanism. A shortage of capital and the refusal of banks to gamble on the struggling young firm put the project on hold. With a $20,000 loan from Ruth Handler's brother-in-law, however, Mattel completed the project and produced another winner. As Elliot Handler later recalled, "our music box had a patented mechanism which had continuous play value because it operated only when the child turned the crank. It was different, it was well-made, and because we were able to mass-produce it, the price was lower than the imports." By taking an Old World idea and adapting it to modern production techniques, the Handlers beat out their Swiss competition, which up to then had dominated the domestic market for music boxes.

The success of the music box taught the Handlers a few other lessons. First, they discovered that child participation was essential for any quality toy; children should be able to interact with a toy and want to play with it often and for extended periods of time. Second, the Handlers recognized that a toy with lasting appeal is preferable to short-lived faddish products and can serve as a basis for other toys to follow.

Innovation, Diversification, and Success: 1950–69

Mattel reached several important firsts in 1955. Sales climbed to $5 million; the company introduced another hit, Burp Guns; and the Handlers decided to take a gamble that would change the toy business forever. In what seemed a risky venture, the Handlers agreed to sponsor a 15-minute segment of Walt Disney's "Mickey Mouse Club" on the ABC television network. The Handlers signed for 52 weeks at a cost of $500,000, equal to Mattel's net worth at the time. Up until this time, toy manufacturers relied primarily on retailers to show and sell their products and advertising occurred only during the holiday season; never before had a toy company spent money on advertising year-round. With television, however, toys could be marketed directly to children throughout the country. Thus with the slogan, "You can tell its Mattel, it's swell," the Handlers began a marketing revolution in the toy industry that produced an immediate payoff. The company sold many toy Burp Guns and made the Mattel brand name well known among the viewing audience.

In 1957, the company, exploiting the popularity of television westerns, introduced toy replicas of classic western guns and holsters. From the basic Burp Gun mechanism, Mattel developed the "Fanner 50" western pistol and a toy version of the Winchester rifle, complete with ejecting bullets. Mattel's sales reached $9 million and the following year hit $14 million. Then

in 1959 Mattel made toy industry history with the introduction of the Barbie Doll, the best-selling toy of all time. The idea for the doll originated with Ruth Handler, who had observed that their daughter favored adult-looking paper dolls over baby dolls. So the Handlers set to work designing a teenage fashion model doll and, despite a cool reception at the 1959 New York Toy Fair, the result was a smash hit, propelling Mattel into the national spotlight. Barbie, the famed doll named after the Handlers' own daughter, soon prompted the founding of official fan clubs across the United States, which by 1968 had a total membership of about 1.5 million. Mattel marketed Barbie as an insatiable consumer of clothes and accessories, which were sold separately. Soon the company provided her with a boyfriend, the Ken doll.

After the phenomenal success of Barbie, Mattel entered the competitive large doll market in 1960 with another winner, Chatty Cathy, the first talking doll. That year Mattel made its first public stock offering, and by 1963 its common stock was listed on the New York Stock Exchange (NYSE). Mattel's sales skyrocketed from $26 million in 1963 to more than $100 million in 1965, due in part to the expansion of the Barbie line with Ken (named after the Handlers' son), Midge, Skipper, and Christie (an African-American doll).

Throughout the 1960s the company continued to introduce popular toys: Baby First Step (the first doll to walk by itself), live action dolls with moving eyes and mouths, See 'N Say educational toys, the Vac-U-Form machine, and an entire line of Thingmaker activity toys, including Creepy Crawlers, Fun Flowers, Fright Factory, and Incredible Edibles. Another spectacular hit, Hot Wheels miniature model cars, was introduced in 1968, which proved to be a pivotal year for Mattel as a host of its products dominated the market, including its original toy music boxes, which had sold more than 50 million. The company reincorporated in Delaware, and by the end of the decade it was the world's number one toy maker.

During the 1960s the company began aggressively diversifying its operations into a worldwide enterprise with a host of acquisitions: Dee and Cee Toy Co. (1962); Standard Plastics (1963); Hong Kong Industrial Co., Ltd. and Precision Moulds, Ltd. (1966); Rosebud Dolls Ltd. (1967); Monogram Models and A & A Die Casting Company (1968); Ratti Vallensasca, Mebetoys, Ebiex S.A., H & H Plastics Co., and Metaframe Corp. (1969).

Stretched Too Thin: 1970 Through the Mid-1980s

At the dawn of the 1970s, Mattel still was gobbling up other companies, such as Ringling Bros., Barnum & Bailey Circus and others. But the good times soon soured. In 1970 Mattel's plant in Mexico was destroyed by fire, and the following year a shipyard strike in the Far East cut off their toy supplies. To maintain the appearance of corporate growth, Seymour Rosenberg, executive vice-president and chief financial officer, fixed the books by reporting orders as sales, although many of the orders had been canceled and shipments had not been made. For two years Mattel issued false and misleading financial reports, until 1973, when the company reported a $32 million loss just three weeks after stockholders had been assured that the company was in sound financial condition. Mattel's stock plummeted and the Security and Exchange Commission (SEC) stepped in to investigate. Before Judge Robert Takasugi of the federal district court in Los Angeles, Ruth Handler and Rosenberg pleaded no contest to the SEC charges.

Rosenberg was fired, the banks pressured the Handlers to resign, and the court ordered Mattel to restructure its board so that its majority would be company outsiders. In addition, the court fined Ruth Handler and Rosenberg each $57,000 and gave them 41-year sentences, which were suspended on the condition that they both performed 500 hours of charitable work annually for five years. Finally, in 1980 the Handlers cashed in most of their Mattel stock, ending their involvement in the company they had founded. Comprising approximately 12 percent of the company, the stock was worth about $18.5 million. Ruth Handler then went on to start Nearly Me, a company producing prosthetic breasts for mastectomy patients.

A new management team under Arthur S. Spear, a Mattel vice-president, replaced the Handlers in 1975 and by 1977 the company had returned to profitability. By 1980 Mattel was running a slew of other businesses, including the Ringling Bros., Barnum & Bailey Circus; Shipstad & Johnson's Ice Follies; Western Publishing, the largest publisher of children's books; and an entire line of electronic toys, most notably Intellivision video games. Yet, unfortunately, Mattel stumbled badly for much of the 1980s. Many of the company's business acquisitions turned out to be unprofitable and had to be sold. Further, a big slump in video game sales in the early 1980s drove Mattel out of the video game business with a $394 million loss, putting the company on the edge of bankruptcy. The company might have gone under if the New York venture capital firms E. M. Warburg, Pincus & Co. and Drexel Burnham Lambert had not stepped in with $231 million in 1984 to save the company from the video game debacle. Still, in 1985 the company fell behind Hasbro as the world's largest toymaker.

A New Direction: 1987–92

By 1987 Mattel suffered a $113 million loss when the market for its Masters of the Universe toy line for boys evaporated. As a result of Mattel's troubles, its stock plummeted from 1982's peak of $30 per share to just $10 per share in 1987. But the company's fortunes took a dramatic upswing when John W. Amerman, who had joined the company in 1980 as head of the international division, was named chairman. Under his direction the division's sales had quadrupled, far outpacing the profitability of Mattel's domestic operations. In his new role, Amerman moved quickly to cut Mattel's overhead by closing 40 percent of the company's manufacturing capacity, including plants in California, Taiwan, and the Philippines. He slashed the payroll by 150 at Mattel's corporate headquarters in California, saving an estimated $30 million annually. Mattel also refinanced high-cost debt and curbed advertising costs.

Amerman turned the company around by focusing on core brand names with staying power, such as Barbie and Hot Wheels, and by making selective investments in the development of new toys. One such selection was the re-emergence of Disney toys, due to a chance meeting in Tokyo, which gave Mattel licensing rights for a new line of infant and preschool plush toys. Renewing its collaboration with Disney proved more than serendipitous for

Mattel, as their union in the 1990s would prove far more advantageous than Amerman ever imagined.

Despite a lackluster economy and generally flat sales in the toy industry, Amerman's strategy paid off big for Mattel. The Barbie line was bolstered and expanded to include approximately 50 different dolls per year and about 250 accessory items, including everything from shoes and clothing to linens, backpacks, furniture, and a cosmetics line. A promotional campaign in honor of Barbie's 30th birthday in 1989 propelled her onto the cover of *Smithsonian Magazine,* confirming her status as a true American icon. In 1990 Mattel moved from the Handlers' original offices to new headquarters in El Segundo, propelled in large part by Barbie's continuing popularity. By the next year the company estimated that 95 percent of all girls in the United States aged three to 11 owned several Barbie dolls; in fact, Barbie was so good for Mattel that between 1987 and 1992 sales shot up from $430 million to nearly $1 billion, accounting for about half of the company's $1.85 billion in sales. As a result of this phenomenal growth, Mattel opened a new state-of-the-art Barbie manufacturing plant in 1992 just outside Jakarta, Indonesia.

Mattel's emphasis on other core brands, including Hot Wheels die-cast vehicles, large dolls, Disney products, and See 'N Say educational preschool toys, provided a string of continuous hits. Mattel also pushed aggressively into other areas of the toy business, including plush toys, games, boys' action figures, and activity toys, which comprised 46 percent of the total toy market. By entering these areas, Mattel increased its participation in the total industry business from 34 percent to approximately 80 percent, becoming a full-line toy company. The company made a particularly strong move into the toys for boys market, where it had been weak traditionally, with a range of new products, including the following: Bruno the Bad Dog (a monster truck that changed into a ferocious dog); action figures based on Arnold Schwarzenegger movies; and Nickelodeon's gooey Gak, a stretchy, oozing substance.

A strengthened strategic alliance with the Walt Disney Company allowed Mattel to sponsor attractions and to develop and sell toys at three Disney theme parks. The agreement gave Mattel unparalleled exposure to millions of children and adults who visited the parks each year. Mattel also negotiated the exclusive rights to sell dolls, stuffed characters, and preschool toys based on Disney movie characters, such as those from *Cinderella, Beauty and the Beast,* and *Aladdin.* The agreement was a boon for Mattel, and Amerman predicted that sales for the Disney line would top $500 million by 1995. Beyond Disney, Mattel also had reached an agreement with Hanna-Barbera to market toys based on the cartoon characters Yogi Bear, Boo-Boo, Cindy Bear, and the Flintstones; another agreement with Turner Broadcasting allowed Mattel to develop and sell Tom and Jerry products. A push into the game market led Mattel to acquire International Games, Inc. in 1992, the producer of such profitable core franchises as the UNO and Skip-Bo card games.

Mattel executives believed that the company's best growth opportunities for the mid-1990s were overseas markets, and sales for its international division exploded from $135 million in 1982 to $1.7 billion in 1992, with much of the sales through retail giants Toys 'R' Us and Wal-Mart. Overall net sales of Mattel products reached $2.6 billion, and Jill Barad, who had joined the company in 1981 as a product manager and had been most recently president of Mattel's U.S. operations, was promoted to president and COO of the company.

Bigger and Better Than Ever: 1993–97

In 1993 the company embarked on the landmark acquisition of venerable toy producer Fisher-Price. The stock-for-stock deal, valued at $1.19 billion, bought Fisher-Price from the Quaker Oats Company and further cemented Mattel's unrivaled position in the toy industry. Year-end net sales hit $3.4 billion, and although Fisher-Price products contributed $750 million to the pie, Mattel had an extraordinary year—business was up a whopping 27 percent, aided by the sturdy dollar overseas. The distribution of sales relied heavily on Mattel's old standby, Barbie, with 35 percent or $1 billion, with Hot Wheels (five percent or $150 million) and Disney (ten percent or $330 million) bringing in healthy shares, while other popular products like the Polly Pocket line, Mighty Max toys, and UNO card games brought in the rest. Mattel also doubled the capacity of its Indonesia plant; opened offices in Austria, Scandinavia, and New Zealand; and had hopes of adding others the next year in Portugal, as well as Argentina and Venezuela, in an effort to tap into Latin America's market of 120 million children. Latin America's child population was second only to Asia's at 800 million in 1993, far beyond the United States's 40 million and Europe's 70 million.

Mattel made two strategic acquisitions in 1994: those of J.W. Spear, a British company that owned the popular Scrabble games, and Kransco, whose Power Wheels and Wham-O (which included Frisbee and Hula Hoop) brands complemented its ever-growing products list. The next year Mattel became the new licensee of the Cabbage Patch Kids dolls, a top-notch addition to the company's large dolls line. Both 1994 and 1995 were record years for the company, with net sales of $4.0 billion and $4.4 billion, respectively, and net income of $225 million in 1994 and $338 million in 1995. The company also was looking to the future; it initiated a $72 million restructuring program in 1994 to consolidate manufacturing operations and slash unnecessary corporate expenses.

In 1996 sales grew to $4.5 billion, with income topping $372 million. The 38-year-old Barbie was once again the backbone of Mattel's net sales, hauling in $1.7 billion, up by 20 percent from the previous year. Hot Wheels sales also increased by nearly 20 percent, and Disney products were up eight percent, surpassing the $500 million mark. International sales, however, were relatively flat—complicated by a strengthened dollar. At the end of the year Mattel initiated the acquisition of another major player in the toy industry, Tyco, the third largest toy manufacturer in the United States. The merger of Tyco into Mattel's lineup made the latter the unparalleled leader of the industry, far beyond any of its other competitors. Tyco's successful products, such as Sesame Street brand toys and its radio-controlled and electric race cars, bolstered Mattel's infant and preschool as well as boys' toy lines.

As the decade was coming to a close, a changing of the guard was imminent. John Amerman, who had turned Mattel away from slumping sales and mismanagement, retired as Mattel's chairman of the board after 17 years, tossing the reins to Barad, who had been promoted to CEO earlier in the year. At the time of her appointment as chairman in 1997, Barad was one of only two women running a Fortune 500 company. Never one to rest on her laurels, Barad moved forward with new Barbie innovations and aggressive expansion. International sales climbed a cautious three percent (in local currency), with net sales at $1.2 billion for Canada and Europe and $2.1 billion in net sales from Asia and Latin America, representing a 35 percent jump for Latin America and the emergence of a market in Japan. Stateside, sales grew by 14 percent, with Barbie bringing in $1.9 billion, especially in the burgeoning interactive market, where Barbie-brand CD-ROMs quadrupled sales to $20 million. Even the adult-collector market in Barbies had reached $200 million, with new Oscar de la Renta and Vera Wang designs slated to debut. Infant and preschool toys, meanwhile, were close on Barbie's heels, bringing in $1.8 billion in net sales despite a slump in Fisher-Price. Winnie the Pooh and Sesame Street more than took up the slack, generating $175 million and $350 million, respectively.

Mattel in the Next Century: 1998 Onward

In early 1998 Mattel celebrated Barbie's 39th birthday. Continuing its interactive success, a new web site was introduced (Barbie.com), as well as new dolls, including one with an official WNBA uniform. The year also marked the 30th anniversary of Hot Wheels, with booming sales, as well as the 15th anniversary of Cabbage Patch Kids dolls. Barbie remained the bigger news, however, as the centerpiece of PBS's "P.O.V.," which dedicated an hour-long program to her evolution, entitled "Barbie Nation: An Unauthorized Tour." Although the program provided publicity, its content was sometimes controversial—dealing with the good, the bad, and the ugly, including some Barbie-inspired obsessions. Ruth Handler, extensively interviewed for the piece, vehemently supported her creation.

Still on the prowl for acquisitions, mid-year Mattel announced the $700 million acquisition of Pleasant Company, the Wisconsin-based maker of the popular American Girl brand comprised of books, dolls, clothing, accessories, and the *American Girl* magazine. Pleasant's founder and president, Pleasant Rowland, became Mattel's vice-chairman. The company also was gaining a reputation as an excellent employer, named one of the "100 Best Companies To Work For" by *Forbes* magazine, and similarly lauded by *Working Mother* for the fifth consecutive year. With a state-of-the-art in-house daycare center, health and fitness facility, half-day Fridays, and generous vacation days, which included shutting down operations the week between Christmas and New Year's, the toymaker seemed to provide employees with almost as much fun as consumers.

With Barbie a force to be reckoned with, earning an additional $100 million annually since 1987, and its other brands picking up speed as well, Mattel was poised not only to maintain its status as the top toy producer in the world, but to stake an even greater claim in the United States and internationally. Its brand recognition was second to none and, with the 1998 acquisition of the Pleasant Company, the sky was the limit for Mattel.

Principal Subsidiaries

Arco Toys, Limited (Hong Kong); ARCOTOYS, Inc. (U.S.); Far West Insurance Company, Ltd. (Bermuda); Fisher-Price, Inc. (U.S.); Mabamex, S.A. de C.V. (Mexico); Matchbox Collectibles (Europe) Ltd.; Matchbox Toys (USA), Inc.; Mattel Argentina S.A.; Mattel Chile S.A.; Mattel Colombia S.A.; Mattel East Asia Ltd.; Mattel Espana, S.A.; Mattel Factoring, Inc.; Mattel (HK) Limited; Mattel Holding, Inc.; Mattel Holdings Limited (Canada); Mattel I., Inc.; Mattel N.V. (Netherlands Antilles); Mattel Japan Limited; Mattel (K.L.) Sdn.Bhd. (Malaysia); Mattel (Malaysia) Sdn.Bdn.; Mattel Media, Inc.; Mattel de Mexico, S.A. de C.V.; Mattel (NZ) Limited; Mattel Operations, Inc.; Mattel Overseas, Inc.; Mattel Polska Sp. Z.O.O.; Mattel Pty., Ltd. (Australia); Mattel Realty Corporation; Mattel Servicios, S.A. de C.V.; Mattel Sales Corp.; Mattel Southeast Asia Pte. Ltd.; Mattel Specialty, Inc.; Mattel Tools Sdn.Bhd.; Mattel Taiwan Corporation; Mattel de Venezuela, C.A.; Montoi S.A. de C.V. (Mexico); Precision Moulds Ltd. (Hong Kong); Tyco Hong Kong Ltd.; Tyco Preschool Toys, Inc.; Tyco Toys (Europe) N.V.; Tyco Toys (Switzerland) AG; Tyco Toys (UK) Ltd.; Universal International Holdings Ltd. (Hong Kong).

Further Reading

"Barbie at 30," *Forbes*, November 1988.

"Barbie Does Budapest," *Forbes*, January 7, 1991.

Deutsch, Stefanie, *Barbie, The First 30 Years, 1959 Through 1989: Identification and Value Guide Collector*, Collector, 1995.

Everybody's Business (1st ed.), 1980.

Fennick, Janine, *The Collectible Barbie Doll: An Illustrated Guide to Her Dreamy World*, Running Press, 1996.

Guide to Company Profiles, New York: Doubleday, 1990.

"The Impossible Is Really Possible: The Story of Mattel," Newcomen Address, 1968.

"Jill Elikann Barad Named Chairman of the Board of Mattel," *PRNewswire*, October 8, 1997.

"Looking for a Few Good Boy Toys," *Business Week*, February 17, 1992.

"Mattel Agrees To Acquire Pleasant Company; Names Pleasant Rowland Vice Chairman of Mattel, Inc.," *PRNewswire*, June 15, 1998.

"Mattel Celebrates the Birthday of Barbie Doll with the Launch of barbie.com for Girls," *PRNewswire*, March 9, 1998.

"Mattel Has To Play Harder Than Ever," *Business Week*, May 25, 1987.

"Playing Favorites," *Marketing & Media Decisions*, March 1990.

"The Story of Mattel, Inc.: Fifty Years of Innovation," Newcomen Address, 1995.

—Bruce P. Montgomery
—updated by Taryn Benbow-Pfalzgraf

Maxicare Health Plans, Inc.

1149 South Broadway Street
Los Angeles, California 90015
U.S.A.
(213) 765-2000
Fax: (213) 765-2693
Web site: http://www.maxicare.com

Public Company
Incorporated: 1980
Employees: 540
Sales: $663.8 million (1997)
Stock Exchanges: NASDAQ
Ticker Symbol: MAXI
SICs: 6311 Life Insurance; 6321 Accident & Health
 Insurance; 6324 Hospital & Medical Service Plans

Maxicare Health Plans, Inc. provides managed health care and other employee benefits to over half a million customers. The benefits provided by the company include group benefits, Medicaid, and Medicare HMO policies, as well as PPO insurance, group life and accidental death and dismemberment policies, and organization insurance. The company also deals in administrative services, wellness plans, claims processing, and pharmacy programs. Maxicare Health Plans helped popularize the concept of national health maintenance for profit in the 1980s. By the end of that decade, however, it epitomized the problems and pitfalls of the new industry. Maxicare began its second decade struggling to emerge whole from bankruptcy, under the protection of the federal courts. The company began an innovative concept for reshaping the country's health care-delivery system, and rapidly mushroomed into a profitable chain. At one point, Maxicare stock traded at 55 times earnings.

Early History

Maxicare began as Fred W. Wasserman's dream. It was founded by Wasserman and his wife, Pamela K. Anderson. Wasserman saw his opportunity in the 1973 Federal HMO Act, which required employers who were engaged in interstate commerce to offer workers a choice between conventional insurance coverage or HMO membership. Maxicare originated as a California nonprofit HMO in 1973. In 1980 Wasserman convinced a group of Los Angeles-area physicians to convert the company into a for-profit HMO. Maxicare was supported by the charter participation of Lockheed Corporation and Northrop Corporation. Selling prepaid health care plans to employers, Wasserman rapidly built Maxicare into a national network by acquiring HMO's across the country.

Maxicare began interstate operations in 1982, by purchasing CNA Health Plans, which had operations in Illinois, Indiana, and Wisconsin. Maxicare's net income ballooned from $5.4 million in 1983 to $20.4 million in 1985. By the end of 1987, Maxicare owned or managed 33 consumer-oriented, high-quality health maintenance organization systems in 26 states, with a combined enrollment of 2.3 million members. By the mid-1980s, the husband-and-wife duo had parlayed their initial $37,000 investment into the nation's largest for-profit HMO. As the number of HMO's in the United States nearly doubled—to more than 600—between 1984 and 1986, competition stiffened and Maxicare found itself paying inflated prices for the local health-maintenance organizations it acquired as part of its growth strategy. Maxicare grew quickly, especially in the Southeast, but some of the local plans it acquired proved to be poorly managed, with sizably underestimated expenses.

Wasserman's dream began to unravel in 1986, when Maxicare acquired two HMO's, HealthCare USA and Health-America Corporation, for $446 million. The highly leveraged transaction doubled Maxicare's enrollment and boosted the company's overall revenues to $1.8 billion, from only $118 million in annual revenues six years earlier. The two new HMO subsidiaries, however, brought hidden costs and considerable debt. Maxicare's undiscriminating growth strategy had emphasized fast expansion, and the company had simply purchased almost every HMO that it could. Maxicare soon became a victim of its own centrally managed, inter-entity borrowing system, which was taxed by a handful of overextended HMO subsidiaries.

Maxicare's long-term debt soared to $464 million in 1987, at a time when competition and health care costs intensified.

Shortly after the acquisitions, the company began experiencing serious financial and operating difficulties, which resulted in Maxicare reporting net losses of $255.9 million in 1987 on $1.8 billion in revenues. In 1988 Maxicare's losses swelled to $611.8 million on revenues of $1.6 billion. The growing reservations of lenders toward the HMO industry made it difficult for Maxicare to obtain the further financing needed to turn the company around.

Management Changes in 1988

In the wake of Maxicare's inability to stem losses, the company's senior management—including Chairman Wasserman and President Anderson—and five of its seven directors resigned in August 1988. Peter J. Ratican, who had been an outside member of Maxicare's board since 1983, was named Maxicare's second chairman, chief executive officer, and president. The senior management team Ratican assembled immediately launched an in-depth review of Maxicare's operations. Wasserman remained for a time after his resignation as a consultant to the company. Ratican brought more financial, rather than health care management, experience to the job. He had worked for a time at Price Waterhouse, where Maxicare was among his audit clients. He also had served as a medic in the California National Guard. Prior to joining Maxicare in 1988, Ratican was a member of the office of the president, and chief financial officer of De Laurentiis Entertainment Group.

In mid-1988 New York-based Bankers Trust Company dealt Maxicare a particularly critical blow. Bankers Trust and five other lenders had provided Maxicare with a revolving bank loan. In mid-1988, Maxicare lost its ability to make interest payments on the $175 million loan, and Bankers Trust forced a fire sale of some of Maxicare's local HMO plans.

Initially, under pressure from Bankers Trust, Ratican abandoned Wasserman's plan for a national HMO company, focusing instead on California and select midwestern and southern states. Beginning in late 1988 Ratican began selling some of Maxicare's plans, for an estimated total of $120 million. The money was used to reduce the company's overall debt and to offset ongoing administrative and personnel costs. Ratican also hired McKinsey & Company, New York-based management consultants, to identify ways to improve management, client relations, and claim processing. McKinsey was the first of three management consultants Ratican would hire between August 1988 and March 1989.

Further dramatic change was spurred by Ratican's decision to increase Maxicare's premiums by an average 32 percent—twice the annual hike of its competitors'—combined with the company's highly publicized financial problems. The move prompted massive client defections.

After missing principal loan payments in January 1989, Maxicare's new management unsuccessfully attempted to pursue several financial restructuring alternatives, including exchange offers, new arrangements with trade creditors, new infusions of equity, securing new investors, and selling Maxicare or any of its subsidiaries outright. Discussions with outside parties concerning such alternatives, however, never moved past the preliminary stage.

Chapter 11 Bankruptcy in 1989

Ratican's goal simply became to avoid complete liquidation of Maxicare's assets while nursing the ailing company. Increases in health care costs continued to outpace increases in premiums and overall revenues by nearly two to one. On March 17, 1989—still wrestling with close to $300 million in long-term debt, mounting losses, and unavailable financing—Maxicare and 45 of its direct and indirect subsidiaries filed for protection from creditors under Chapter 11 of the Federal Bankruptcy Code. Two additional local Maxicare subsidiaries subsequently filed for Chapter 11 protection in April 1989.

Soon after filing, Maxicare found itself inundated with lawsuits filed by participating hospital and doctor groups, alleging delinquency in making payments. Even Maxicare shareholders filed a class-action suit, alleging violation of securities laws. State insurance regulators struggled with the dilemma of how to repay Maxicare's medical constituents. Federal bankruptcy laws shielded Maxicare from state regulators' attempts to seize plan assets in their respective states in order to cover enrollees' unpaid claims. In 1989 a handful of states unsuccessfully appealed to the bankruptcy court to allow their individual insurance regulators to supervise debt repayment to creditors under their authority.

Through the reorganization process, the bankruptcy court consistently dismissed claims by various states, including Illinois, Indiana, Ohio, and California, seeking jurisdiction over Maxicare's local subsidiaries. Perhaps the most difficult and influential group of constituents to appease was the nation's health care providers, many of whom unabashedly challenged Maxicare in bankruptcy court. Two dozen Philadelphia hospitals and other providers participating in Pennsylvania's Medicaid program, for instance, asked the judge to appoint a trustee to oversee Penn Health, the Maxicare subsidiary that administered the program. Settlement in some of the many disbursement cases involved transferring existing Maxicare plans to other health maintenance organizations. Many Maxicare providers had to settle for partial payment. The bankruptcy court eventually extended full protection to Maxicare from creditor interference, pressure, or cancellation during the reorganization process.

At the time of its filing, Maxicare was in the midst of an asset-disposition program. At the end of 1987 Maxicare had managed a system of 33 HMO's in 26 states with combined enrollment of about 2.3 million members. By the time it filed for bankruptcy, Maxicare had sold or closed 23 HMO's in 17 states with a combined enrollment of about 837,000 members in order to raise cash and reduce its operating losses. Between March 1989 and May 1990, Maxicare sold or closed an additional seven HMO's located in six states. Maxicare also sold nearly $5 million in real estate and property, including a California medical building and other clinic facilities located throughout the United States. During the disposition process, in early 1990, Maxicare rejected an unsolicited buyout bid from competitor PacifiCare Health Systems. In acknowledging that the two companies had been unable to reach an accord, Maxicare management reiterated its commitment to an independent reorganization.

Many other HMO companies struggled with similar problems. The concept of providing a full range of medical services for one annual fee appeared to have worked better in theory than it did in practice. Other national HMO's were also unable to hold down costs by keeping patient visits and charges to a minimum.

Wall Street also had its reservations. Maxicare stock plummeted to $2 a share just before the company filed for bankruptcy, from its all-time high of $28 a share. Maxicare's management, however, found itself facing a broader challenge: regaining the confidence of investors, consumers, financial institutions, and the medical community. Based on surveys it conducted in 1988 and 1989, Maxicare reported that at least 80 percent of its enrollees remained satisfied with the services the company provided, even though many employers had opted not to renew their Maxicare contracts. To curb defections, Maxicare moved quickly to improve its services, instituting new practices such as paying claims within 15 working days after receipt.

By 1990 Maxicare was marketing its services aggressively with the help of an advertising agency, trying to convince the public that as one of the nation's first HMO's, it remained one of the best. Maxicare signaled its revitalization with a new patriotic logo. Decked in red, white, and blue, the logo silhouettes three Maxicare members looking ahead to what was hoped to be a brighter future. The new logo was an inverted, updated version of Maxicare's old logo. Maxicare officials also began commenting publicly about assuming new HMO accounts, but declined to identify them. On July 9, 1990, Ratican told *Managed Care Report* that his personal goal was independently to build Maxicare back to a 500,000-plus-enrollee concern within five years. Refuting suggestions that Maxicare management would sell out after completing the company's financial reorganization, Ratican stated that he and his management team were determined ''to stick it out and turn it around because that's what we came to do.''

Reorganization in 1990

A reorganization plan first filed in January 1990 was adopted by Maxicare and its subsidiaries, creditors, and bondholders in May 1990 and received final approval from the bankruptcy court in July 1990. The plan provided creditors and shareholders of the multistate health maintenance organization with $129.3 million in cash payments; ten year 13.5 percent senior notes with a face amount of $67 million; and common stock and stock warrants that were to be traded publicly. Creditors were also to share in the cash proceeds of a distribution trust established to liquidate Maxicare assets that would not be used in its ongoing businesses and operations.

Maxicare's reorganization called for creditors and shareholders to receive at least as much as they would have if the company had been completely liquidated. The reorganization plan also called for an estimated $200 million in claims from general unsecured creditors of Maxicare's ongoing operations—mostly physicians and hospitals—to receive $47 million in cash, $35 million in senior notes, and 49 percent of the reorganized company's common stock. Another $110 million in claims from general unsecured creditors of Maxicare's discontinued or divested operations were to receive $17.8 million in cash and $10 million in face amount senior notes.

Members of the Bankers Trust-led bank group—who were general unsecured creditors of the parent holding company—represented about $150 million in claims, and were to receive up to $12 million in cash, $22 million in face amount of senior notes, and 15.9 percent of the common stock of the new Maxicare. The company also pledged approximately $7 million of notes to the banks as collateral. Holders of four bond issues, representing about $300 million in claims as general unsecured creditors of the parent holding company, were to receive approximately $2 million in cash and 33.1 percent of the new common stock. Maxicare's public shareholders were to receive two percent of the reorganized company's common stock and stock warrants entitling them to acquire up to an additional five percent of the common stock on a fully diluted basis.

The reorganization plan also provided Maxicare's senior management golden parachutes, including severance and benefits up to annual base compensation if Maxicare was bought out or if management control was changed. Top management was also assured of $500,000 to $1 million in collective cash bonuses if the firm had at least $60 million cash in hand at the time of the company's effective reorganization date. Top management also had an option to acquire five percent of the company's new common stock at a 20 percent discount. On the effective date, Maxicare merged into its own subsidiary, HealthCare USA. HealthCare USA, as the surviving entity, was renamed Maxicare Health Plans. On July 16, 1990, the bankruptcy court approved Maxicare's reorganization plan.

At the time the bankruptcy court approved Maxicare's reorganization plan, company officials said it had about 305,000 enrollees in seven states—Illinois, Indiana, Wisconsin, California, North Carolina, South Carolina, and Louisiana. The disposition or closing of local HMO subsidiaries resulted in a reduction of Maxicare employees from a one-time high of 8,000 to about 600. Maxicare's annual sales also had declined in 1989, to $400 million from a one-time annual high of $1.84 billion. A vastly streamlined Maxicare also had cut its losses from $611.8 million at the end of 1988 to $22.3 million in the third quarter of 1989, primarily reflecting the expense of its reorganization. Ratican told *Managed Care Report* that he remained optimistic about the company's revamped future.

Growth in the Mid-1990s

Maxicare had approximately 370,000 members nationwide by May 1996—its growth was slower than expected due to increased competition in an ever-growing arena. An expected boost to membership came later that year due to an agreement reached by Maxicare California to become a health care partner with the

Local Initiative Health Authority for Los Angeles County. The California Department of Health Services' effort was in line with its strategy to improve access to quality health care for Medi-Cal recipients by moving them into managed care.

A similar deal in North Carolina was announced a week later, which brought Maxicare's involvement with Medicaid programs to four states, including also Indiana and Wisconsin. Chairman and Chief Executive Officer Peter J. Ratican explained, ''Our partnerships with state and local governments are helping solve the challenge of how to arrange for quality health care at a reasonable cost for Medi-Cal and Medicaid eligibles around the country.''

A significant increase in operating revenues (18 percent) from the three months ended June 30, 1995, to the same period in 1996, resulted mainly from the 25 percent increase in Maxicare's membership. The doubling of membership—which occurred primarily in the company's California and Indiana Medicaid and Medicare lines of business—helped boost the numbers. Maxicare experienced a decline in net income (from $4.9 million to $500,000) between 1996 and 1997, although sales growth from year end 1996 to 1997 reflected a 17.9 percent increase.

Thus, Maxicare initiated a restructuring of management and began an evaluation of the company's operations and businesses. Focusing on those operations which had substantially generated membership growth and profits in recent years, Maxicare entertained plans which included possible dispositions and or acquisitions of already-owned or other health plans. The health plans in Illinois and the Carolinas suffered a loss from operations of over $4 million for the three months ended March 31, 1998, and slight increases in Indiana and California memberships did not compensate for the negative slide elsewhere. Higher drug prescription costs boosted health care expenses as the medical loss ratio increased to 94.2 percent for the first quarter of 1998.

1998 Shareholder Disagreement

Shareholder Paul R. Dupee launched a campaign in March 1998 to investigate the possibility of selling Maxicare by electing an expanded slate of directors. Dupee was quoted in *The Boston Globe* as saying, ''On a stand-alone basis it doesn't make any sense. They need to be consolidated with somebody else.'' After several months of hostile disagreement, Maxicare

announced a settlement it had reached with Dupee. The agreement included the election of Dupee, Robert M. Davies, and Elwood I. Kleaver, Jr. to serve as directors of the company. Dupee would additionally become a member of the Board of Directors' Executive Committee. Chairman Ratican explained the situation: ''After extensive discussions with Mr. Dupee and his representatives, and several of the company's larger shareholders, as well as the new board members, our board concluded that all parties share the same collective goal of enhancing shareholder value. The board welcomes the new members to the board and believes the company and its shareholders will benefit from these additions.''

A.M. Best's B + + rating of Maxicare in June 1998 cited ''strong earnings and good enrollment growth'' in 1997. Maxicare stock continued to struggle in August 1998, however, dipping as low as $4.25 a share, from a 52-week high of $20 a share. Even so, a membership of over 500,000 and the August 1998 cash sale of all of the stock of Maxicare Health Insurance Company in Wisconsin were both encouraging.

Principal Subsidiaries

Health America Corp. (California); Maxicare Health Plans of Southern California; Maxicare Life & Health Insurance Co. (California); Maxicare Northern California; Maxicare Pharmacies Inc. (California); Maxicare Health Plans–Midwest (Illinois); Maxicare Indiana Inc.; Maxicare Louisiana Inc.; Maxicare North Carolina Inc.; Maxicare Southeast Health Plan (South Carolina).

Further Reading

A.M. Best Company, ''A.M. Best Affirms Maxicare Rating of B + +,'' *quoteserver.com,* http://quoteserver.dogpile.com, June 15, 1998.
Andresky, Jill, ''The Mess at Maxicare,'' *Forbes,* June 27, 1988.
Bailey, Steve, and Steven Syre, ''Dupee in Fight for California HMO,'' *The Boston Globe,* April 10, 1998.
Cole, Patrick, and Jon Friedmann, ''Even Heroic Measures May Not Save Maxicare,'' *Business Week,* March 27, 1989.
''Maxicare Poised to Reorganize,'' *Managed Care Report,* July 9, 1990.
Maxicare Corporate Web site, http://www.maxicare.com.
Smith, Scott, ''Maxicare's New N.C. Chief Promises Changes at HMO,'' *The Business Journal of Charlotte,* October 20, 1997.

—Diane C. Mermigas
—updated by Allison A. Jones

The Maxim Group

210 Town Park Drive
Kennesaw, Georgia 30144
U.S.A.
(770) 590-9369
Fax: (770) 590-7709

Public Company
Incorporated: 1989
Employees: 2,660
Sales: $365.13 million (1998)
Stock Exchanges: NASDAQ New York
Ticker Symbol: MAXM MXG
SICs: 5713 Floor Covering Stores; 6794 Patent Owners
    and Lessors

Headquartered in Kennesaw, Georgia, The Maxim Group is North America's largest—and only—publicly traded retail floor covering franchise. The company offers a variety of floor covering products, merchandising programs, and human resources and administrative consultation to its franchises and outlets. Its products include carpets, hardwoods, area rugs, vinyl, and ceramic tile. A leading floor covering distributor, the Maxim Group operates two retail chains: full-service stores under the name CarpetMAX and cash-and-carry discount stores known as Georgia Carpet Outlets (GCO). The company also manufactures floor coverings through its subsidiary Image Industries, Inc., one of the larger makers of polyester carpeting in the United States.

Beginnings in 1989

The Maxim Group was founded in 1989 as a floor covering retailer, and its franchising operations began in 1991. The company's franchise service involved up-front membership fees; ongoing royalties or product brokerage fees; advertising; employee training; and fees for other services. The Maxim Group's franchise network grew quickly, establishing an integrated retail infrastructure comprised of store development, marketing, advertising, credit, sales training, and product sourcing. The

company issued its initial public offering on the NASDAQ stock exchange in 1993.

With successful franchised outlets, the Maxim Group was committed to a store acquisition strategy for its CarpetMAX Division by May 1994. The company aggressively developed its own outlets, as well as acquired other retailers. Within the year, the Maxim Group opened its first company-owned Carpet-MAX store, with additional company-owned stores in Tampa, Florida, following later in the year. By July 1995, the Maxim Group had purchased nine floor covering retailers. The company's tenth acquisition, Las Vegas-based Cloud Carpet, put 54 company-owned stores in operation. (Cloud Carpet earned about $8 million in revenues and operations from two sites.) A. J. Nassar, the Maxim Group's president and chief executive officer, explained that "the Cloud Carpet acquisition will immediately give us sizable market share in one of the fastest growing markets in the country. We will use Cloud Carpets as our springboard in Las Vegas. Cloud will serve as our hub in this quickly developing part of the country."

The following month—August 1995—the Maxim Group finalized its acquisition of Carpet Country, Inc., a Des Moines, Iowa, company with $14 million in sales for 1994. Maxim's 11th purchase in 16 months, this acquisition marked the Maxim Group as a leader in the consolidation of the floor covering industry. At this time, the Maxim Group maintained 600 franchised outlets and earned $12 million in annual sales from 63 company-owned stores. In addition to acquisitions and new stores, Maxim created a new infrastructure within the company, added to its management team, and developed its information systems. The company also built a new 100,000 square foot distribution center.

In October 1995, the Maxim Group filed a registration statement with the U.S. Securities and Exchange Commission for more than one million shares of common stock. The company then bought existing CarpetMAX franchises and opened more of its own CarpetMAX outlets throughout fiscal 1995 and 1996.

Now itself attractive as an acquisition, the Maxim Group entertained a merger offer. The Dalton, Georgia-based company Shaw Industries sought to expand its line of services to the commercial carpet market in 1996. Shaw Industries signed letters of intent in January to purchase a commercial carpet contractor—Bill-Mann, Inc., headquartered in Doraville, Georgia—and the Maxim Group. The companies could not agree on terms, however, so negotiations ended. Yet both the Maxim Group and Shaw Industries expected to continue their relationships as contractor and supplier after the deal soured.

Growth Plans for the Future

The Maxim Group also established a corporate goal of 25 percent market share in 1996. Relying on its extensive infrastructure and industry expertise, the company instituted a growth initiative centered around the development of a network of company-owned stores and the development of franchises based on a Masterpiece Store concept. To achieve this goal, James W. Inglis, formerly the executive vice-president of strategic planning at Home Depot Corporation, was hired as chief operating officer, senior executive vice-president, and president of the CarpetMAX Division. Nassar reported to *Business Wire* that the Maxim Group "recently embarked on several important growth initiatives, including the franchising of our highly successful Masterpiece Store Concept. Our two-year plan is to franchise hundreds of Masterpiece stores in existing franchise markets and continue to develop our network of company stores. Jim Inglis's unique experience makes him invaluable to us as we pursue these goals."

By now, the Maxim Group included 700 franchise locations in the United States and Canada and 70 company-owned stores generating $120 million in annual revenues. The Maxim Group continued searching for a merger partner throughout 1996, only now as a buyer. In April, Maxim purchased Manasota Carpet, Inc., a chain with four Florida locations and $10 million in annual sales. The acquisition established a business base in Florida for the Maxim Group, as well as ensured growth opportunities in the market. According to Nassar, the Maxim Group developed its "infrastructure to grow contiguous markets on an accelerated basis. Geographically and strategically, Manasota is a logical fit for Maxim."

The following month, the Maxim Group announced a planned merger with Image Industries, Inc., a residential carpet manufacturer since 1976 and a polyethylene terephthalate (PET) recycler. Image Industries became a wholly owned subsidiary of the Maxim Group, bringing the company "a captive source of high quality products styled and priced to meet the particular needs of our customers," Nassar reported to *Business Wire*. "Image Industries," Nassar said while explaining the importance of the merger, "will stabilize a fluctuating product source while we continue to aggressively grow our retail network. The merger with Image also guarantees us a low-cost

position in proprietary carpet products for our 700-store retail network. We expect Image to fill a small but important portion of our merchandising needs, allowing us to continue to grow key manufacturing alliances."

The Maxim Group went on to purchase Classic Tile and Ceramics, Inc., and Flint's Carpet Center, Inc.—both of Albuquerque, New Mexico—in June 1996. With combined annual revenues of $8 million, the added companies advanced the New Mexico market for the Maxim Group. "Classic Tile and Flint's will give us the infrastructure that we need to develop the attractive Albuquerque market," Nassar told *Business Wire* in 1996. "We expect to quickly open new Masterpiece store locations to enhance a profitable and very well-run operation."

The following September, Maxim closed a $125 million commitment from the First Union National Bank for credit facilities. The merger of the Maxim Group and Image Industries brought on the credit facility, which was utilized in refinancing the debts of both companies. In addition, the refinancing equipped Maxim with working capital.

Shortly after refinancing, the Maxim Group expanded into yet another area of opportunity with the purchase of Baily and Roberts Flooring, Inc. Headquartered in Knoxville, Tennessee, Baily and Roberts provided the Maxim Group with a presence in the specified contract sector of the floor covering industry. (Baily and Roberts earned about $14 million in annual sales.) At the time, Nassar commented through *Business Wire* that "Baily and Roberts focus has been in the specified contract area, a segment of the industry where we see significant opportunity. Under the leadership of Doug Baily and Mike Roberts, we feel confident that we will see rapid and profitable growth in this important segment of the floor covering industry."

The Maxim Group also acquired Sexton Floor Covering, Inc., in September 1996. With $5.5 million in sales annually, this profitable and well-managed firm represented yet another opportunity in the Knoxville, Tennessee, market.

In November 1996, the Maxim Group began converting its CarpetMAX stores to a Gallery store concept. According to the company's 1997 annual report, "Historically, shopping for floor covering has been confined to warehouse-type environments or to small retailers with limited selection, pricing, and customer service options. Neither scenario particularly appeals to today's consumer, who values quality, convenience, and superior selection. The CarpetMAX Flooring Idea Gallery was designed to exceed customer expectations in these important areas." This "category killer" featured a full line of floor coverings: carpets, area rugs, hardwood flooring, ceramic tile, vinyl flooring, laminates, and stone. Located in prime retail areas, Gallery stores relied on high consumer visibility and specialized sales staff, including interior design consultants and delivery and installation personnel.

In order to decrease outstanding amounts under Maxim's credit facilities, the company initiated another public offering of more than three million shares of common stock at $16 per share in February 1997. With finances secure, the Maxim Group sought to expand the Flooring Idea Gallery Store concept to additional stores. In March, the company acquired McSwain Carpets, a Cincinnati, Ohio-based company, and the Flooring

Center, Inc., of Orlando, Florida. The purchases solidified the Maxim Group's presence in five major markets—four in Ohio (Cincinnati, Toledo, Columbus, and Dayton) and one in Florida. As Nassar revealed: "Both McSwain and the Flooring Center give us the basic infrastructure to support a full-scale rollout of our Flooring Idea Gallery stores in most of Ohio and Orlando east to the Atlantic coast. Both strategic markets are contiguous to existing company-owned territories. McSwain and the Flooring Center will give us the required infrastructure and distribution resources to open up 25 to 30 new gallery stores."

In June 1997, the Maxim Group listed its stock on the New York Stock Exchange under the MXG symbol. Nassar stated at the time, "Our New York Stock Exchange listing is an important milestone for the company and highlights the success of our growth plans since an initial public offering in 1993. We believe that a New York Stock Exchange listing will maximize shareholder interest and enhance our trading visibility and efficiency."

At the end of the year, Maxim began offering Color Tile brand products in its GCO Carpet Outlet stores. The company negotiated with Color Tile to establish departments in GCO Carpet Outlet stores for hard-surface products such as ceramic tile, hardwood flooring, and vinyl surfaces. Since hard-surface products were the fastest growing industry segment at the time, the Maxim Group hoped to capitalize on Color Tiles's widely recognize brand name and its ability to obtain and distribute hard-surface products, thus giving GCO Carpet Outlets a commanding position in the hard-surfaces market. As Nassar explained in a press release: "Maxim's retail divisions including CarpetMAX and GCO Carpet Outlet have achieved product dominance in carpet and seek similar success with its hard-surface products."

In January 1998, the Maxim Group entered into an alliance with Home Steps, part of the Federal Home Loan Mortgage Company. One of the larger home sellers in the United States, Home Steps sold nearly 20,000 homes annually. According to Nassar, the Maxim Group had "the floor covering products and the national infrastructure to add significant value to Home Steps' selling process." Maxim agreed to stock floor covering for Home Steps—about nine million square feet annually. This arrangement allowed the Maxim Group to offer services and to distribute products on a national scale, and Home Steps gained better quality floor coverings for its properties at a reduced cost.

By mid-1998, the Maxim Group grew to 380 franchised territories in 49 states. It maintained 463 CarpetMAX stores—71 of which the company owned and 31 of which were Gallery stores—and 101 GCO Carpet Outlet stores. The company's future goals included combining proven retailing resources such as marketing, sales training, and strong manufacturing alliances to achieve a dominant share of the floor covering industry's market and to develop a national retail brand. The Maxim Group intended to rely on Gallery stores as the company's vehicle for growth. In his 1997 Letter to Shareholders, Nassar revealed: "With a solid retail base in place, the cornerstone of our growth strategy is the CarpetMAX Flooring Idea Gallery, developed as a 'category killer' for the floor covering industry. Our Gallery stores are engineered to operate with strong fundamentals, including sales per square foot roughly double the industry standard and operating margins two to three times the industry norm." Maxim intended to open about 70 Gallery concept stores through fiscal 1999 in its existing markets or in markets contiguous to those in which the company maintained a presence.

Principal Subsidiaries

Image Industries, Inc.

Principal Divisions

CarpetMAX; GCO (Georgia Carpet Outlets).

Further Reading

"Maxim Acquires Manasota Carpet," *Business Wire*, April 3, 1996, p. 4031043.

"Maxim Closes $125 Million Credit Facility," *Business Wire*, September 4, 1996, p. 9041335.

"Maxim Completes Merger with Image Industries," *Business Wire*, August 30, 1996, p. 8301117.

"Maxim Completes Purchase of Iowa Retailer," *Business Wire*, August 21, 1995, p. 8211210.

"Maxim Group, Image Industries Announce Definitive Agreement," *Business Wire*, May 31, 1996, p. 5311325.

"The Maxim Group, Inc., Announces Public Offering of 3.6 Million Shares of Common Stock," *Business Wire*, February 19, 1997, p. 2191261.

"Maxim Names New Chief Operating Officer," *Business Wire*, May 15, 1996, p. 5151467.

"Maxim to Acquire Bailey & Roberts," *Business Wire*, September 5, 1996, p. 9051253.

"Maxim to Acquire Las Vegas-Based Cloud Carpet, Inc.," *Business Wire*, July 18, 1995, p. 7181071.

"Maxim to Acquire New Mexico Retailer," *Business Wire*, June 27, 1996, p. 6271194.

"Maxim to Acquire Sexton's Floor Covering," *Business Wire*, September 23, 1996, p. 9230234.

"Maxim to Enter Five Major Markets for Gallery Expansion," *Business Wire*, March 20, 1997, p. 3201054.

"Shaw Industries, Inc.," *Textile World*, January 1996, p. 10.

"Shaw, Maxim End Merger Negotiations," *Textile World*, February 1996, p. 25.

—Charity Anne Dorgan

Mercury General Corporation

4484 Wilshire Boulevard
Los Angeles, California 90010
U.S.A.
(213) 937-1060
Fax: (213) 857-7116
(800) 956-3728
Web site: http://www.mercuryinsurance.com

Public Company
Incorporated: 1962
Employees: 2,100
Sales: $1.12 billion (1997)
Stock Exchanges: New York
Ticker Symbol: MCY
SICs: 6331 Fire, Marine & Casualty Insurance

The largest agency writer of private passenger automobile insurance in California, Mercury General Corporation sells various types of insurance in selected regions stretching from Florida to California. From its inception in 1961 until 1990, Mercury operated exclusively in California, building a prodigious business from selling automobile insurance. During this formative period, the company stood out as an industry innovator, developing a complex system of rate levels for California customers that often offered considerable discounts to drivers. Known for shrewdly keeping overhead costs to a minimum and for its attention to detail in the screening process of potential customers, Mercury began expanding geographically in 1990, nearly doubling its revenue during a three-year period during the mid-1990s. During the late 1990s, the company sold insurance in Georgia, Illinois, Texas, Kansas, Oklahoma, and Florida, yet continued to depend heavily on its California business, which accounted for 90 percent of the direct premiums written in 1997. In addition to writing private passenger and commercial automobile insurance, Mercury sold homeowner, commercial and residential fire, and commercial property insurance. The company was founded by George Joseph, who continued to preside over operations during the late 1990s.

Origins

Like many other entrepreneurs before him, George Joseph started his own business because he believed he could do a better job than those who ran the company he worked for. He was born in 1921, the eldest son of a Lebanese-born storekeeper. Joseph spent his youth in Beckley, West Virginia, a small town in Appalachia where he stayed until World War II. During the war Joseph served as navigator aboard a B-17 airplane, and afterward he used his GI Bill tuition to attend Harvard. At Harvard, Joseph majored in mathematics and physics; upon graduating he settled in Los Angeles.

Joseph spent the 1950s working two jobs. During the day, he worked in the actuarial department of Trans-America's Occidental Life Insurance Co. At night, he sold insurance door-to-door. Working in insurance day and night, Joseph became intimately familiar with the way the business operated and the inadequacies in its execution, particularly in regard to automobile insurance. At that time, large insurance companies divided the driving population into two broadly defined categories: bad drivers and good drivers. The problem, as Joseph perceived it, was that the driving habits and histories of Los Angeles drivers did not neatly fall neatly into these two categories. Many drivers who fell somewhere between those with spotless driving records and those with a history of repeated accidents were categorized as high-risk drivers, and were forced to pay the resulting high premiums. It was this category of drivers that Joseph believed he could better serve, reasoning that he could offer lower premiums than his much larger competitors and gain legions of happy customers. In 1961 Joseph founded Mercury to test his theory.

What was needed, Joseph realized, was greater scrutiny of automobile insurance applicants. By delving deeper into the screening process than his larger counterparts, Joseph could more accurately define his customers, create more complex driver classifications, and grant discounts where appropriate. He took the time, for instance, to check a map to verify if an applicant's commuting distance really was five miles. He studied an applicant's credit history, took into account the type of car an applicant drove, and factored in these details into a premium formula that generated numerous rate levels—far

Company Perspectives:

Today, as many other insurers are exploring alternative means of distribution, becoming in part direct writers and, in some cases, placing themselves in direct competition with their own appointed agents, Mercury has reemphasized its commitment to the agency system by adopting strategies which involve the agent ever more closely in both the underwriting and claims management process. It is this integration, supported by continuous improvement in systems and communications, which is producing the savings and loss controls which make Mercury's competitive pricing possible. While other companies are attempting to reduce costs by cutting agents' commissions and by marginalizing the role of the agent, Mercury is holding the line on agents' compensation. We have to realize savings from the greater efficiencies achieved within our agents' offices as they build and improve their systems to handle tasks traditionally done at the home office. The professional insurance agent, our front-line underwriter, lies at the heart of the Mercury system, and the Company intends to continue to grow its business on the foundation of the independent agent.

more than his competitors relied on. Consequently, a driver looking to be insured could either be grouped into one of two large risk pools defined by one of the large insurance corporations, or the driver could approach Joseph and, for example, receive a ''good student'' discount. As he soon discovered, insurance applicants were often eager to opt for the latter.

Joseph was able to turn his insurance venture into a going enterprise by concentrating on what he determined were the ''good,'' or lower, risks relegated to the high-risk pool, and he focused on these drivers exclusively for more than a decade. After building a foundation on such clientele, he began expanding his business to embrace other classifications of drivers.

1970s Expansion

Joseph formed a subsidiary in 1973 to undertake the underwriting of preferred-risk policies. Emphasis was placed on examining applications thoroughly, a responsibility that fell to a network of independent insurance agents. From its outset the company had relied on independent insurance agents paying its representatives a commission based on losses in relation to premiums rather than standard commissions derived from premiums alone. For Joseph's strategy to work, everything hinged on the assiduous work of the agents, the individuals those at company headquarters referred to as Mercury's ''front-line underwriters.'' It was at this level that Joseph's underwriting strategy was won or lost, and he spent considerable effort instructing the company's front-line officers about the importance of thoroughly vetting potential customers. Eventually, Mercury's independent insurance agents were governed by an underwriting manual stretching to 34 pages, made up of rules written by Joseph himself. The independent insurance agents were told to meet personally with applicants, to fill out detailed policy applications, complete with photographs taken at different angles of

the applicant's vehicle, and to verify that the applicant did indeed live where he or she claimed to reside. Through their dedication to the philosophy espoused by Joseph and his senior executives, Mercury eclipsed much of its competition, steadily increasing its share of the nation's largest automobile insurance market.

Rapid Financial Growth in the 1990s

In 1985 Mercury converted to public ownership in an initial public offering on the NASDAQ exchange. Five years later the company took its first steps outside its home state of California, opening operations in Georgia and Illinois.

Mercury continued to prosper. In 1993 the company's underwriting losses were 61 percent of premiums earned, a figure that compared favorably to the higher (and less profitable) average of 73 percent registered by Mercury's eight largest California competitors. Furthermore, Mercury's underwriting expenses, tabulated before commissions and taxes, were 5.8 percent of premiums, which bettered the industry average of 12.1 percent. All told, the company enjoyed a premium volume that stood at $467 million, a total achieved after 32 years of hard work—but the 73-year-old Joseph was not content to rest on his laurels. At Mercury's annual shareholder meeting in May 1994, he made a startling announcement. He maintained that he intended to lift Mercury's premium volume past the $1 billion mark by the end of 1997, a feat that would more than double the size of the company in the space of three years.

Mercury executives began trying to meet this formidable challenge. A print media advertising program was introduced, featuring a toll-free number supported by the company's independent agents, that provided specific rate comparisons against Mercury's major competitors. In December 1996, the company purchased American Fidelity Insurance Group for $35 million. Based in Oklahoma City, American Fidelity operated as a writer of automobile insurance (which made up 57 percent of its total business) and other casualty lines of insurance, underwriting more than $90 million of direct premiums in the year leading up to its acquisition by Mercury. The acquisition was reorganized as American Mercury Insurance Group, giving Mercury operations in Oklahoma, Texas, and Kansas. Despite the geographic expansion of the 1990s, 90 percent of the company's direct premiums in 1997 were written in California.

When the financial totals were tallied at the end of 1997, the ambitious goal set out by Joseph in 1994 was fully achieved. For the year, written premiums increased 28 percent, swelling to $1.08 billion. In addition to meeting Joseph's goal, Mercury's executives and vast cast of independent insurance agents could take pride in several other heartening achievements. Operating as one of the fastest-growing automobile insurers in the nation, Mercury ranked as the largest independent agency writer of automobile insurance in California and the sixth-largest of all automobile insurers in California, up from the seventh position it had occupied in 1996. With an estimated 7.2 percent market share of the California market, Mercury was the insurer of more than one million vehicles in California. Additionally, the company's net income amounted to $156.3 million in 1997, more than three times the total recorded in 1994, when the concerted effort to dramatically increase revenues began. After establishing operations in Florida in January 1998, Mercury, with Joseph in charge, prepared for the new century ahead, its business thriving under the operating strategy created by its septuagenarian founder.

Principal Subsidiaries

Mercury Casualty Company; Mercury Insurance Company; Mercury Insurance Company of Illinois; Mercury Indemnity Company of Illinois; Mercury Insurance Company of Georgia; Mercury Indemnity Company of Georgia; California Automo-bile Insurance Company; California General Underwriters Insurance Company, Inc.; American Mercury Insurance Company; Cimarron Insurance Company; AFI Management Company, Inc.

Further Reading

Fondiller, David S., "Secret's Out," *Forbes,* March 25, 1996, p. 14.
Munk, Nina, "'George Knows Whom to Call,'" *Forbes,* November 7, 1994, p. 113.

—Jeffrey L. Covell

Metro-Goldwyn-Mayer Inc.

2500 Broadway Street
Santa Monica, California 90404-3061
U.S.A.
(310) 449-3000
Fax: (310) 449-3100
Web site: http://www.mgm.com

Incorporated: 1986
Employees: 1,020
Sales: $831.3 million
Stock Exchanges: New York
Ticker Symbol: MGM
SICs: 7929 Entertainment & Entertainers

Though it has undergone several name changes and owners, Metro-Goldwyn-Mayer Inc.'s legacy is as classic as one of its movies. Formed by the merger of Metro Pictures Corp., Goldwyn Pictures, and Louis B. Mayer Productions, the original MGM was responsible for.some of the world's most beloved films. In 1981 MGM merged with United Artists Corporation and then 16 years later bought Orion Pictures, Goldwyn Films, and the Motion Picture Corporation of America. Rechristened Metro-Goldwyn-Mayer Inc., the new MGM went public in 1997 and once again has become a force to be reckoned with in the entertainment industry. Headquartered in Santa Monica and with offices in New York, London, Santiago, and Sydney, MGM's reach extends from hit films like *Tomorrow Never Dies, The Birdcage, Get Shorty, Ulee's Gold,* and others, to television series and original films, branded entertainment channels in Asia and Latin America, interactive CD-ROMS, and its one-of-a-kind film library with 4,000 titles, 186 of which are Academy Award-winning films, including 15 Best Picture Oscars.

The Early Days of MGM and United Artists: 1919–29

United Artists Corporation (UA) began in 1919 as a partnership between Mary Pickford, Charlie Chaplin, Douglas Fair-banks, and D.W. Griffith, four of the biggest names in motion pictures at the time. With the widespread disillusionment that followed World War I, motion pictures became a welcome source of escapist entertainment. America's fascination with movie stars had begun, movie houses sprouted up all over the country, and movies became big business. United Artists was created by these artists to wrest creative control of their own projects from the powerful Hollywood magnates. The new company could hardly keep up with America's voracious appetite for movies. UA was essentially a cooperative distributor of individual productions; there was no company studio, no stars or directors under contract, and each producer was required to finance his/her own project, giving United Artists a percentage of each film's revenues as the distributor.

Despite the resounding success of UA's first picture, *His Majesty, the American,* starring Douglas Fairbanks, financing new productions was difficult at times during the early years. Conventional bank loans were almost unheard of for such a risky investment as films. Whereas other motion picture companies offered stock to the public to finance expansion, UA remained private to retain control. Some assistance came in the form of advances from theater owners, who prepaid for upcoming features in weekly installments. In its first five years, United Artists scored a number of hits, but the studio's schedule was slow, producing an average of only eight films a year until 1924.

Unlike United Artists, MGM was a complete production studio from the start, with actors, writers, directors, and production coordinators all under long-term contract. MGM rarely had trouble finding financing, producing enough movies, or attracting audiences. MGM, symbolized by Leo the Lion's roar, was for years the king of the Hollywood jungle. It all began with Marcus Loew of Loew's, Inc., one of the nation's largest theater chains, and his 1919 purchase of Metro Pictures to help fill his theaters with a steady flow of quality motion pictures. By 1924 Loew was disappointed in both the quality and quantity of Metro's films. When approached by Lee Shubert, of Shubert Theater fame, to merge Goldwyn Pictures with Metro, it sounded like an excellent idea. Goldwyn Pictures had been plagued by personality conflicts, resulting in the departure of Sam Goldwyn in 1922. Meanwhile, filmmaker Louis B. Mayer, who had a successful production company of his own, heard of the pending merger and flew to New York to negotiate with Loew. When all was said and done, Metro, Goldwyn, and Louis B. Mayer studios became a subsidiary of Loew's, and Mayer was chosen to head the new studio.

Mayer had brought along the 24-year-old Irving Thalberg, the prodigiously talented "boy wonder" of Hollywood. Under the leadership of Mayer and Thalberg, the new company produced more than 100 feature films in its first two years. In 1925 MGM released the extravagant *Ben Hur,* which was a huge success, and MGM-Loew's recorded a $4.7 million profit in its first full year.

While Mayer was heading up the new MGM, Joseph Schenck became president of UA and reorganized the company. He brought in stars like Buster Keaton, Norma Talmadge, and Gloria Swanson, as well as producer Sam Goldwyn. By the late 1920s Schenck had added a number of producers to the company's roster, and UA's production schedule had improved considerably. In 1927 a Howard Hughes film, *Two Arabian Knights,* garnered UA its first Academy Award. That same year, with the release of Warner Brothers' *The Jazz Singer,* sound came to motion pictures.

The Emergence of Sound and Change in the Industry: The 1930s and 1940s

The introduction of sound revolutionized the motion picture industry and brought the downfall of silent-screen stars who were unwilling or unable to adjust to the new technology. Millions were spent to upgrade film production facilities and buy new equipment for movie houses, many of which were affiliated with major studios. The sound revolution took place over a very brief span of time—by 1930 almost no silent films were being produced. UA's performance had been inconsistent in its first decade, showing a loss six out of ten years between 1920 and 1930, and the early 1930s were no better. The Depression took its toll on movie attendance in 1931 and 1932, and the five big Hollywood studios—MGM, Warner Brothers, Fox, Paramount, and RKO—dominated what market remained. UA struggled to survive, and did so in large part because of the talents of Schenck, who also formed an independent production company, Twentieth Century Pictures, with former Warner Brothers production head Darryl Zanuck. This company's success contributed greatly to UA's profits. Despite the fact that Twentieth

Century Pictures accounted for almost half of UA's films, Fairbanks, Pickford, and Chaplin (Griffith sold his shares in 1933) would not give the production company a slice of their pie. In 1935 Schenck and Zanuck left and merged Twentieth Century Pictures with the Fox Film Corporation. Al Lichtman replaced Schenck as president of United Artists.

Throughout the 1930s many of Hollywood's greatest independent producers worked through UA, among them Walt Disney, Alexander Korda, Sam Goldwyn, Hal Roach, Walter Wanger, and David O. Selznick. The company, however, was plagued by low production, resulting in continued financial difficulties. MGM, on the other hand, was the most successful studio in Hollywood. MGM's long list of stars under contract and its reputation for excellence helped it survive the Depression, when theater attendance dropped to half of what it had been between 1927 and 1930. The guaranteed purchase of productions by Loew's theater chain also gave the studio much needed stability. By 1933 attendance began to rise again, and as MGM produced fine films, UA's mere existence was an uphill battle. Although UA managed to earn a profit in the latter part of the decade, one of its best and brightest, Sam Goldwyn, who had produced almost half of UA's pictures in the late 1930s, felt that he was not adequately compensated for his efforts. Disputes between Goldwyn and Pickford, Fairbanks, and Chaplin led to a number of lawsuits, and eventually Goldwyn left UA (just as he had left the company bearing his name, Goldwyn Pictures, years earlier).

As UA dealt with the departure of Goldwyn, MGM suffered the untimely death of Irving Thalberg in 1936. With his death, MGM productions turned away from the literary toward purely escapist entertainment, but it continued to pursue excellence, including such hits as *The Wizard of Oz* and *Boys Town.* While UA continued to struggle, MGM thrived with huge hits in 1939—including *Gone With the Wind.* Starring Clark Gable and Vivien Leigh, the film became one of the top moneymakers of all time. Interestingly, the movie was actually a David Selznick production and should have been released through UA, as were his other films. Yet Selznick had wanted Clark Gable to play Rhett Butler, who was under contract to MGM, and to use him (and acquire a $1.5 million loan from his father-in-law Louis B. Mayer), Selznick had to release the picture through MGM and give the studio half the profits. The film set attendance records worldwide and snatched up ten Academy Awards.

As MGM reveled in its triumph, UA became embroiled in lawsuits, when Chaplin and Pickford (Fairbanks had died in 1939) accused Selznick of breaching his UA contract by distributing a number of films through RKO and Selznick fired back that UA did a sloppy job of distribution. The producer went on to form his own distribution company, and UA lost another key contributor. By the end of the 1940s, plagued by poor-quality pictures and shrinking cinema audiences because of the emergence of television, United Artists was bleeding red ink. MGM, too, began to feel the sting, as its high overhead weighed heavily on the company. Loew's president Nicholas Schenck (brother of UA's Joseph Schenck) told Mayer to find a new "boy wonder" to snap the company's production back into shape. Mayer hired Dore Schary, formerly of RKO, as the new production head. Schary pointed MGM in the direction of spectacular musicals to give audiences what they could not get anywhere else and the release of such hits as *Easter Parade, Annie Get Your Gun, Show Boat, Singin' in the Rain, An American in Paris,* and *Seven Brides for Seven Brothers* gave MGM the necessary boost.

A Change of Fortune: 1950–79

With a drastic reorganization needed for UA, Pickford and Chaplin finally brought in Paul V. McNutt, former governor of Indiana, as chairman and Frank L. McNamee as president. McNutt, however, did not have the expertise to solve UA's financial woes. Within a few months he turned over the reins to a group headed by Arthur Krim and Robert Benjamin. Krim had been president of Eagle-Lion Films, and Benjamin had headed the American operations of the Arthur Rank Organisation, a British filmmaker. The two made a deal with Pickford and Chaplin to give them control of the company for ten years with a guarantee of half the company if they could turn the debt-ridden distributor around. Krim and Benjamin secured a $3 million loan from Fox Film Corporation president Spyros Skouras. UA then scored two big box office hits with *High Noon* and *The African Queen.* Within a year the company was showing a profit, and Krim and Benjamin had begun a 20-year reign.

In 1952 the major studios were ordered to divest themselves of their theater holdings. Loew's held out for some time, but finally was forced to split from MGM. Without a guaranteed market for its pictures, filmmaking suddenly became a risky business. MGM faced the kind of pressures UA had known since its creation, and in 1955 theater attendance dropped to its lowest since 1923. During this crisis, Chaplin sold his UA shares, which amounted to 25 percent of the company, to Krim and Benjamin for $1.1 million. A year later Mary Pickford sold her shares for $3 million, giving full ownership to the Krim and Benjamin group, and the next year, 1957, UA went public with a $17 million stock and debenture offering. The company that had struggled so long and once had been chronically short of movies was now turning out 50 pictures a year. As UA prospered, MGM lost money for the first time in 1957; although it bounced back with a profit in 1958, MGM's profits were on-again-off-again for the 1960s and beyond.

By the middle of the 1960s major studios began catering to younger patrons; movies began to explore controversial topics and sex and violence became more acceptable. By the end of the decade MGM was no longer at the top and the industry was rife with takeovers and mergers. Paramount was bought by Gulf and Western, MGM diversified into real estate, and Warner Brothers merged with a television company, Seven Arts Limited. UA, meanwhile, was having one of its most successful decades, winning 11 Academy Awards, five of them for best picture. In 1963 Eon Productions released *Dr. No,* the first James Bond movie through UA, beginning what proved to be the longest-running series in cinema history.

In 1967 the Transamerica Corporation bought 98 percent of UA's stock and in 1969 brought in the Picker brothers, David and Arnold, to run the company. This was the same year Las Vegas investor Kirk Kerkorian began his reign at MGM. Kerkorian appointed James Aubrey, a former television executive, as president of MGM and then sold many of the company's assets, including a number of theaters owned overseas, the MGM record company, and parts of the company's Culver City lot. When UA lost $35 million in 1970, Arthur Krim and Robert Benjamin were brought back, and in 1973 the company purchased the domestic distribution rights to all of MGM's pictures for ten years, after Kerkorian decided to cut back on production and invest in the $120 million MGM Grand Hotel in Las Vegas. High budgets and unpredictable audiences combined to make film production more risky than ever.

In 1975 UA released *One Flew Over the Cuckoo's Nest.* The film was a smash, cleaning up at the Oscars, and earning more than $56 million. A year later UA's *Rocky* won the Oscar for Best Picture, and in 1977 Woody Allen's *Annie Hall* captured the same honor for UA for the third year in a row. In 1978 Krim split from UA after a dispute with Transamerica chief John Beckett and Krim, Benjamin, Eric Pleskow (then UA's president), and a number of other key executives formed Orion Pictures. One era had ended at both UA and MGM, but another was about to begin.

Before and After the Merger: 1980–88

MGM, once a major player in the production and distribution of motion pictures, was involved only peripherally in films during the 1970s. Kerkorian and his crew focused on other activities; by the end of the 1970s the MGM Grand Hotels in Las Vegas and Reno were bringing in more money than the film production unit. Over at UA, after the departure of Krim and Benjamin, a former vice-president and assistant of Krim's, Andy Albeck, was installed as president. In 1979 *Rocky II, Manhattan, Moonraker,* and *The Black Stallion* gave UA its most successful season ever. A year later the studio released *Heaven's Gate,* by Michael Cimino, known for such hits as *Thunderbolt and Lightfoot* and *The Deer Hunter.* But *Heaven's Gate* had grossly exceeded its budget, finally tallying $44 million, and the film was a debacle for UA. In the wake of *Heaven's Gate,* Albeck resigned and Norbert Auerbach took his place. In a surprising move in May 1981 at the Cannes Film Festival, Auerbach announced that UA had been purchased by MGM and the new company would be called MGM/UA Entertainment Corporation.

The new MGM/UA Entertainment Company was established at a time when the entertainment industry was going through many changes. Pay television and video offered new avenues for marketing old movies. Suddenly, MGM/UA's movie library was a vital asset; at the same time, theater audiences were growing. In 1983 the company launched a number of subsidiaries: the MGM/UA Home Entertainment Group, MGM/UA Classics, and the MGM/UA Television Group. Also in 1983, majority stockholder Kirk Kerkorian bid $665 million for the MGM/UA shares he did not hold already. The bid caused an uproar (and a lawsuit), which convinced Kerkorian to drop the idea of taking the company private, at least for the time being. MGM/UA scored a number of hits at the box office in the early 1980s, including *War Games* and *Octopussy,* but profits did not keep up with Kerkorian's expectations. In the mid-1980s the Las Vegas financier instigated a number of deals that eventually led to the formation of a different company with some of the same assets, and nearly the same name. The MGM/UA Communications Company was incorporated in 1986, but the complicated story of its formation began a year earlier.

In 1985 the MGM and UA production units of MGM/UA Entertainment were separated under a general corporate restructuring. Alan Ladd Jr. and Frank Yablans, who until then had run the combined studios together, each were put in charge of one unit. Analysts speculated Kerkorian was preparing to sell one of the studios, probably UA, to raise cash to take MGM private. That theory went out the window, however, when Yablans was fired shortly after the restructuring and Ladd was put in charge of both studios' production units. In August 1985 cable television magnate Ted Turner began negotiations with Kerkorian to buy MGM/UA Entertainment for $1.5 billion. Turner's key interest in the company was its 3,000-title MGM film library, which would provide an excellent source of programming for Turner's WTBS television station. By January 1986 Turner's buyout, at $20 per share and one new preferred share of Turner Broadcasting System stock, went through. At the same time, Turner sold the United Artists assets back to Kerkorian for $480 million. The MGM/UA Entertainment Company was now a subsidiary of the Turner Broadcasting System, but United Artists was a separate company.

In June 1986 UA, under Kerkorian's control, bought back many of the original MGM assets for $300 million, including the production and distribution units, the Home Entertainment Group, and the UA film library. Turner kept the MGM library and sold the original MGM Studios real estate in Culver City to Lorimar Telepictures for $190 million. United Artists changed its name to MGM/UA Communications Company and again restructured its operations. The "new" company grouped the two television production units together, but kept the film units separate. Alan Ladd headed the MGM group, while Anthony Thomopoulous took over at UA, and David Gerber presided over the combined TV unit. The company began a comeback during the next year. In 1987 *Spaceballs, The Living Daylights,* and *Moonstruck* were big hits for the studio; yet despite these successes MGM/UA recorded an $88 million loss for 1987.

In April 1988, frustrated by the company's performance, Kerkorian began shopping for potential buyers for his 82 percent holding in MGM/UA. By July he was planning to split the two companies again. Kerkorian struck a deal with investor Burt Sugarman and producers Jon Peters and Peter Guber to sell a quarter interest in MGM; the agreement fell through, however, and top MGM/UA executives, confounded by Kerkorian's unpredictable maneuvers, began to abandon ship. Chairman Lee Rich was the first to go, followed shortly by Ladd and Thomopoulous. At the zenith of this corporate crisis during the summer of 1988, production on many of the company's film projects was canceled.

Stephen Silbert briefly took Lee Rich's place as chief executive in July 1988. By October he had stepped aside to let former Merrill Lynch executive Jeffrey Barbakow take the reins. Barbakow was experienced in packaging limited partnerships to finance film ventures. He set out to nurse the ailing studio back to health. In fiscal 1988 MGM/UA lost $48.7 million, considerably less than in 1987. The success of *Rain Man* (winning the 1988 Oscar for best picture as well as three others) promised improvement, but MGM/UA was debt-ridden and had only a handful of films in production.

More Troubles, New Leaders: 1989–94

In 1989 the media company Qintex Australia Limited agreed to acquire MGM/UA, but the questionable deal collapsed in October of that year and Quintex's owner, Christopher Skase, later disappeared amid a flurry of charges concerning financial misdeeds. While Kerkorian continued to look for a buyer, many wondered how MGM/UA would continue to fund the production of movies and TV shows—and the answer was "not easily." Kerkorian found another buyer for MGM/UA in 1990 with financier Giancarlo Parretti's Pathe Communications Corp. for $1.3 billion. The ink was barely dry when rumors swirled: Parretti was charged by the SEC for "materially false and misleading disclosures" during the acquisition, and Pathe had soon defaulted on loans and was in bankruptcy court. France's Credit Lyonnais assumed control of MGM/UA in 1992 and initiated two lawsuits against Kirk Kerkorian for stripping the company of its cash before selling it to Parretti and Pathe Communications Corp. Kerkorian, ever the mover-and-shaker, settled the lawsuits in 1995 for an undisclosed sum and turned his attention to a hostile takeover attempt of Chrysler Corp. But this was not the last of Kerkorian's maneuvering with MGM/UA.

MGM/UA and its many incarnations had been carved up, sold, repurchased, sold again, and involved in numerous legal imbroglios. Yet the venerable institution was given new life in 1993 when Credit Lyonnais brought in a crack management team, headed by Frank Mancuso, the former head of Paramount Pictures, to revive the slumbering company. Within months a resurgence was under way, including an agreement with Showtime to co-produce original programming, the establishment of MGM Animation, and a host of other innovations to bring the once golden company back to full tilt.

A Look to the Future: 1995 and Beyond

The dawn of 1995 brought much good news for MGM, as Consortium de Realisation (CDR) took control of the company from Credit Lyonnais. Throughout the year UA and MGM premiered several critical and box office successes, including *Rob Roy, Species, Stargate, The Birdcage, Get Shorty, Leaving Las Vegas,* and *GoldenEye.* The latter film, the 17th installment in the languishing James Bond series, became the highest-grossing Bond movie in history, and several of the year's films were nominated in various categories for Academy Awards. On the small screen, MGM Worldwide Television debuted "The Outer Limits," which soon earned its first Cable Ace award for Best Dramatic Series and would go on to win another the following year. MGM Online and MGM Interactive were launched, and the company entered into lucrative co-production agreements with Rysher Entertainment and Largo Entertainment.

In the first quarter of 1996 MGM was again on the selling block, this time put up for sale by CDR to the company's top management with the backing of Australia's Seven Network Limited and Kerkorian's Tracinda Corporation. The deal became official in October, and the new company made its first major acquisition in July 1997 for Orion Pictures Corp., Goldwyn Entertainment, and the Motion Picture Corporation of America, establishing the largest post-1948 film library in the world with more than 4,000 titles, 186 of them Academy

Award-winners, including 15 for Best Picture, and television and animated classics as well.

MGM went public in November 1997 with an offering of nine million shares of common stock on the NYSE under the ticker symbol "MGM." The initial public offering (IPO) raised $235 million, and Tracinda Corporation went on to purchase another four million shares as well, placing Kerkorian once again in a well-powered position within the company. Meanwhile, MGM had continued to venture into unknown territory—first, in live entertainment, with the debut of *The Magic of MGM,* a touring ice show, and second, with the creation of MGM Gold, a branded entertainment channel in Asia, through its MGM Worldwide Television Group division. Next came another MGM Gold channel, this one in Brazil, followed by two subsequent channels and a joint venture called MGM Networks Latin America. Then the TV group signed licensing agreements for its library titles to North Africa and the Middle East and in the United States debuted its remake of 1957's *12 Angry Men,* as an original made-for-television movie on Showtime. The film not only scored rave reviews, but was Showtime's highest-rated original movie and earned both a Cable Ace award and a Golden Globe.

In keeping with the continued popularity of art-house films, MGM contributed to the field with the establishment of Goldwyn Films, which was backed by the marketing and distribution team shared by its siblings MGM Pictures and United Artists Pictures. The latter, United Artists, had a triumph of its own at the end of 1997, with the release of *Tomorrow Never Dies,* the 18th film in the enduring Bond series, with Pierce Brosnan reprising his role as Bond and Asian action star Michelle Yeoh as his partner rather than a standard "Bond girl." The movie broke all previous Bond records.

In the first quarter of 1998 MGM was riding high from the success of Bond film *Tomorrow Never Dies* and Peter Fonda's award-winning performance in MGM/Orion's *Ulee's Gold.* Next came the release of *The Man in the Iron Mask,* with an all-star lineup including Gerard Depardieu, Gabriel Byrne, and the immensely popular Leonardo DiCaprio (fresh from his *Titanic* triumph), which grossed $150 million by mid-year. MGM's television arm also continued its success, with several new series, including "LAPD: Life on the Beat," "Stargate SG-1," "Poltergeist: The Legacy," and animated children's shows "All Dogs Go to Heaven: The Series," "The Lionhearts," and "RoboCop: Alpha Commando." Another series, "The Magnificent Seven," debuted on CBS, and MGM scored longer-term programming agreements with both Showtime and USA Networks.

MGM's interactive division was picking up speed with *The Ultimate James Bond: An Interactive Dossier* and a fleet of children's CD-ROMs, including *Babes in Toyland, Chitty Chitty Bang Bang's Adventure in Tinker Town, All Dogs Go to Heaven Activity Center,* and others, with CD games of *Wargames* and Bond's *Tomorrow Never Dies* also slated for distribution. Although the MGM name was most associated with classic films and the biggest stars of a bygone era, the new MGM was carving a comfortable niche in the film, television, interactive, and even music industries. Major movie figures of the 1990s had graced MGM's and UA's pictures, just as many more were in production in late 1998, including Robert De Niro and Jean Reno in *Ronin,* Elisabeth Shue in *Rescue Me,* a theatrical original movie based on the hit TV series "The Mod Squad," and Val Kilmer, Nathan Lane, and Mira Sorvino in *At First Sight.*

Principal Operating Units

MGM Animation; MGM Distribution Co.; MGM Home Entertainment and Consumer Products Group; MGM Interactive; MGM Music; MGM Pictures Inc.; MGM Worldwide Television Group; Goldwyn Films; Orion Pictures Corp.; United Artists Pictures Inc.

Further Reading

Balio, T., *United Artists: The Company Built by the Stars,* Madison: University of Wisconsin Press, 1976.

Berg, Scott, *Goldwyn: A Biography,* New York: Knopf, 1989.

Bergan, Ronald, *The United Artists Story,* New York: Crown, 1986.

Browning, E.S., and Bruce Orwall, "Heard on the Street: Kerkorian's Deals Have Often Drawn Fire," *Wall Street Journal,* October 26, 1995, p. C1.

Eames, John D., *The MGM Story: The Complete History of Fifty Roaring Years,* New York: Crown, 1975.

Easton, Carol, *The Search for Sam Goldwyn: A Biography,* New York: William Morrow, 1976.

Hay, P., *MGM: When the Lion Roars,* Turner Publishing Inc., 1994.

Marx, Arthur, *Goldwyn: A Biography of the Man Behind the Myth,* New York: Norton, 1976.

Orwall, Bruce, "Tracinda Settles a Pair of Lawsuits with Credit Lyonnais Over MGM," *Wall Street Journal,* October 9, 1995, p. B2.

Rundle, Rhonda L., "Marketing & Media: Pathe's Ex-Chief, Two Others Settle Fraud Complaint," *Wall Street Journal,* January 4, 1996, p. B2.

Yemenidjian, Alex, "Letters to the Editor: Kirk Kerkorian Nursed MGM Back to Health," *Wall Street Journal,* April 19, 1996, p. A23.

—updated by Taryn Benbow-Pfalzgraf

MICHAEL FOODS

Michael Foods, Inc.

Suite 324, Park National Bank Building
5353 Wayzata Boulevard
Minneapolis, Minnesota 55416
U.S.A.
(612) 546-1500
Fax: (612) 546-3711
Web site: http://www.michaelfoods.com

Public Company
Incorporated: 1987
Employees: 3,900
Sales: $956 million
Stock Exchanges: OTH
Ticker Symbol: D.MDW
SICs: 5143 Dairy Products, Except Dried or Canned;
2037 Frozen Fruits & Vegetables; 2099 Food
Preparations, Not Elsewhere Classified; 0252 Chicken
Eggs; 2020 Dairy Products; 6719 Holding Companies,
Not Elsewhere Classified

Michael Foods, Inc., through its Egg Products Division, is the largest producer, processor, and distributor of extended shelf-life liquid eggs and dried, hard-cooked, and frozen egg products in the United States. In addition to its domestic market, the Egg Products Division distributes its products to the Far East, Europe, and South America. The company is also a diversified producer and/or distributor of food products in three other areas: dairy products, potato products, and refrigerated distribution. The Dairy Products Division processes and distributes soft serve mix, ice cream mix, and extended shelf-life ultrapasteurized milk and specialty dairy products to domestic fast food businesses and other foodservice markets, independent retailers, ice cream manufacturers, and others. The Potato Products Division processes and distributes refrigerated potato products sold to the foodservice and retail grocery markets in the United States. The Refrigerated Distribution Division distributes a variety of refrigerated grocery products directly to supermarkets, including cheese, shell eggs, bagels, butter, margarine, muffins, potato products, juice, and ethnic foods.

1987 Spin-Off

Michael Foods, Inc. was formed out of a 1987 spin-off from North Star Universal, Inc., a St. Louis Park, Minnesota conglomerate that funds itself with the direct marketing of unrated subordinated notes. North Star was created in 1980 when James H. Michael merged Universal Marking Systems, a public company he controlled, with a St. Paul, Minnesota company called North Star Acceptance and Investment Corporation. Michael owned about 70 percent of the stock, and he frequently guaranteed the company's debt as it went about making acquisitions, according to *Corporate Report Minnesota*. Since the spin-off of Michael Foods, that stock remained North Star's most valuable asset.

James Michael received his undergraduate and law degrees from the University of Minnesota. Rather than entering into the practice of law, he managed the Metropolitan Building in downtown Minneapolis, one of many real estate properties held by Michael's parents. Other of his assets include real estate, a foreign trade company, and Michael/Curry Companies, Inc., which owns Knutson Construction.

At the time of the Michael Foods spin-off from North Star, the company made its initial public offering at $7.11 per share, netting $170 million. Committed to producing extended-life, value-added food products, the company offered their "ultrapasteurized" liquid whole-eggs for approval by the U.S. Food and Drug Administration and the U.S. Department of Agriculture. Called "Easy Eggs," researchers came up with a process that killed bacteria, making the eggs salmonella and listeria negative, while allowing for a shelf life of 45 days. The longer shelf life promised to provide a savings in storage and labor costs. The company gained licensing approval, which immediately precipitated a 25-cent rise in share price. Initial shipments were made from Michael Foods' pilot plant in North Carolina, a plant capable of producing 25 million pounds of product annually. They began construction on a second plant at Michael Foods' Crystal Food facility in Gaylord, Minnesota, providing an additional capacity of 150 million to 200 million pounds annually. Easy Eggs were targeted for major restaurants and food service operators and were produced by the company's Morning Glory Eggs Division.

By April of 1989 the company was reporting flat profits, sending Michael Foods' shares plummeting. The decline was

Company Perspectives:

Our strategic thrust is to further transition Michael Foods into a value-added food products company by being a leader in the food industry in introducing innovative food technology and customer solutions. The key to this strategy is "value-added," whether that is in the product, the distribution channel or in the service we provide to our customers.

balanced, however, by record gains earlier in the year. Some analysts began expressing the concern that most of the company's business was dependent upon highly competitive commodity food products, rather than on consumer brands that could bring brand loyalty and more consistent margins. Others had more faith in the novelty of Michael Foods' concept of "value-added eggs," liquid eggs that could become substitutes for eggs in omelets, scrambled eggs, and as an ingredient in baked goods. After allowing for savings on labor costs, egg breakage, storage and refrigeration savings, the company claimed that their pricing was competitive.

Following the company's announcement that 1989 earnings would be lower than expected, stocks took a major dive. In October of 1989 two disgruntled shareholders filed a lawsuit against Michael Foods, alleging that the company violated securities laws by giving investors false and misleading information concerning expected demand for its Easy Eggs product. One of the complaints stated, "The statements to the effect that there was almost unlimited demand for Easy Eggs were materially misleading in that defendants did not have a reasonable basis for their statements about existing or projected demand." Michael Foods attributed the lower earnings to slower-than-anticipated sales of their new product. Legally, the company could not be held accountable since it could not be proved that Michael Foods had misled investors intentionally.

Michael Foods acquired four companies, including the first half of M.G. Waldbaum Company, a producer of egg products. The company also bought Drallos Potato Company of Detroit and Farm Fresh Foods of Los Angeles—two companies that produced and sold fresh refrigerated potato products, which were important products for Michael Foods' potato processing subsidiary, Northern Star Co. Michael Foods was hoping to strengthen its position in the potato product category by increasing its market share in Eastern markets and extending its coverage to the West Coast.

Reduced Cholesterol Liquid Whole Eggs Introduced in 1992

Michael Foods began investing heavily in the research of the "decholesterolization" of eggs, in response to public concern about heart disease and a trend toward decreasing the level of artery-clogging dietary cholesterol. During this period, it was reported that a small Pennsylvania company called C.R. Eggs, Inc. would introduce to the United States eggs laid by kelp-fed chickens. Already marketed in Japan, the kelp-fed chickens supposedly produced eggs capable of lowering human blood

cholesterol levels. Some worried that the C.R. Eggs product would seriously threaten sales of Michael Foods' low-cholesterol egg alternative, a product still being tested. By 1991 the government had ordered C.R. Eggs to stop selling their eggs because the iodine levels in their product were considered prohibitively high. Several other egg-substitute products were already on the market, but they did not contain yolk, which is where most of the egg's cholesterol resides. A New Jersey company, Papetti Hy-Grade Egg Products, Inc., another rival in the egg business, also announced that it had plans to introduce a cholesterol-stripped egg.

The process that Michael Foods was proposing removed about 80 percent of an egg's cholesterol, which was extracted from the yolks, then recombined with whites in a liquefied, pasteurized product. Their process was developed by a German company, SKW Nature's Products, Inc., a unit of Viag AG, which had formed a $30 million joint venture with Michael Foods. Their process involved encapsulating cholesterol molecules with a starch substance known as beta-cyclodextrin. The yolk then would be centrifuged and the enrobed cholesterol removed. Michael Foods planned to call their product "Simply Eggs." The eggs still contained fat, another concern for potential consumers, many of whom had felt the need to eliminate eggs from their diets altogether. The company intended to sell "Simply Eggs" to food manufacturers, restaurants, and other food-service customers and the retail market. According to Richard Gibson of the *Wall Street Journal,* "The company intends to market the product even if it hasn't received Food and Drug Administration approval of the process by which cholesterol is removed from yolks. If the FDA later decides the processing substance, beta-cyclodextrin, isn't safe, it could order the product recalled." Whether or not Simply Eggs contributed to better nutrition was the question considered critical—by many outsiders—to the success or failure of the product.

In July of 1992 Cargill, Inc. challenged the validity of four patents underlying the processing of egg products made by Michael Foods. Cargill contended that Michael Foods and North Carolina State University, which licensed the processes to the food company, knew that the invention (the pasteurization process that kills salmonella and other bacteria) was not original but withheld that information from the U.S. Patent and Trademark Office. By this time Simply Eggs was in retail tests in several Midwestern markets. The *Wall Street Journal* reported, "Cargill's lawsuit may have been preemptory. Its complaint says the defendants 'have engaged in a course of conduct' that suggests Cargill would be sued over the egg-processing patents. Sunny Fresh Foods, a Cargill unit, is a relative newcomer in the production of extended shelf-life egg products," although Cargill stated in their complaint that they had abandoned the patented processes and used another procedure.

Michael Foods filed patent infringement suits against two other rivals, Papetti Hy-Grade Egg Products, Inc. and Bartow Food Company. News of the flurry of lawsuits caused Michael Foods' stock to fall. Federal Court rulings favored Michael Foods in both of the patent-infringement suits. In 1994 the U.S. Federal Court of Appeals upheld the validity of the patents subject to the license agreement. Subsequently, a patent examiner at the U.S. Patent and Trademark Office rejected the patents. The company appealed the decision; during the appeal process, the patents remained valid.

1993 Restructuring

At the end of 1993 the company announced that it would be abandoning its reduced-cholesterol egg product and that it would be taking a restructuring charge of $23 million, against then-current quarter earnings. Higher-than-expected production costs and lower than expected sales prompted the decision. In conjunction with that news, the company's president and chief executive officer, Richard G. Olson, announced that he would retire at year's end. His designated successor was Gregg A. Ostrander.

Michael Foods continued to increase resources devoted to the research and development of new food products, through internal food scientists, and externally, through the sponsorship of research projects at American universities. The Potato Products Division introduced special recipe mashed potatoes marketed to the food service industry. For the retail market they introduced Country Mashed Potatoes, made with skins and butter, under their Simply Potatoes brand, which was well received. In early 1994 Simply Eggs was re-introduced into the retail and food service markets as a cholesterol and fat-reduced scrambled egg mix. *Consumer Reports* rated Simply Eggs, "the best tasting egg substitute of the 13 tested," but by 1995 Simply Eggs and Brand Scrambled Egg Mix were discontinued in the retail market. Management concluded that the consumer support costs to grow the sales would be too high relative to the product's longer-term profit margin potential—although the products remained available in the foodservice market.

In late 1995 Michael Foods entered into an agreement with North Star Universal, Inc. to enter into a tax-free business combination of the two companies, in which Michael Foods would be the surviving company. The company repurchased and retired a portion of North Star's Michael Foods stock holdings (approximately 38 percent of Michael Foods' common stock), at a discount to the market price of Michael Foods' stock prior to closing, by assuming North Star's debt. Michael Foods assumed debt of $25-$38 million, and North Star's other assets and liabilities were transferred to a new company and distributed to its stockholders.

The company's Crystal Farms Division introduced 26 new products in 1995, including a line of bagel spreads, "cracker toppers" spreadable cheese, and two new flavors of cheese sauce. The company's retail sales and broker network was combined with the sales group of the Crystal Farms Division, providing a more unified sales presence and better access to other geographic areas. In the Dairy Products Division, a similar consolidation of sales groups occurred, adding to the presence of Kohler's specialty dairy products, including "no chill" creamers, targeted to the foodservice market.

The company reported sales growth of 15 percent for 1996, with the Refrigerated Distribution and Dairy Products divisions leading in profits. The Egg Products and Potato Products divisions were buffeted by raw material cost pressures and other operating difficulties, according to company reports. Excepting

the refrigerated potato products wholesale and retail markets, Michael Foods found it increasingly difficult to operate the frozen line profitably and announced that they would exit that business. The value-added line of egg products performed satisfactorily, although below-average corn and soybean crops from the fall of 1995 caused a rise in chicken feed prices—pushing feed prices up 50 percent from the previous year.

Convenience into the Next Millennium

Michael Foods acquired Papetti's Hy-Grade Egg Products, Inc., the world's largest preeminent egg products company, and added it to the second largest, M.G. Waldbaum Company, of which the company had completed the purchase in 1990. Papetti's began as a business in 1908, when the Papetti family started a store-front fresh poultry business. By the 1950s that company switched entirely to the egg products business, and operations grew to include facilities in New Jersey, Pennsylvania, and Iowa. Third- and fourth-generation Papetti family members remain active in management. Products included whole eggs, scramble mixes, reduced-cholesterol products, bakery blends, hard-cooked eggs, and precooked omelets and patties—products that Michael Foods considered complementary to those produced by Waldbaum. The substantial combined volumes of the two companies would allow cost savings in the areas of plant operations, distribution/freight, egg and ingredient souring, sales force optimization, and supplies and packaging purchases. Several capital spending projects related to the egg segment were initiated in 1996, including egg laying barn renovations and capacity expansions.

In 1997 Michael Foods stocks hit an all-time high of $28.375, in part a result of the earlier North Star merger, whereby Michael Foods emerged with a reduced share base, enhancing earnings per share—and record net earnings. The egg business had grown to comprise nearly two-thirds of Michael Foods' revenue. The company introduced "Simply Omelet" in 1998, a precooked meal that can be heated in a microwave oven. Approximately 22 percent of Michael Foods' yearly sales came from refrigerated distribution services. The company started shipping several new types of packaged cheese and refrigerated bread sticks with the Crystal Farms brand name. The dairy products segment made up 11 percent of sales, while the refrigerated potato products accounted for the remaining seven percent of Michael Foods' revenue.

A fresh ad campaign was begun in 1998 and aimed at increasing awareness that Michael Foods is the umbrella company for the brand-name products offered by each of the company's divisions. The ads promoted the company's food innovations and how those products could be used at foodservice companies. In one of the ads for M.G. Waldbaum, an egg is pictured with a zipper, with a headline reading, "Excuse me while we slip eggs into something more practical."

According to Pachuta in *Investor's Business Daily,* "Three years ago, Michael Foods set three goals to be achieved by 2000: $1 billion in yearly sales; earnings growth of 12 to 15 percent a year; and return on equity of 13 to 15 percent. The company's sales should easily surpass $1 billion this year, analysts say."

Principal Subsidiaries

Crystal Farms Refrigerated Distribution Company; Farm Fresh Foods, Inc.; Kohler Mix Specialties, Inc.; M.G. Waldbaum Company; Northern Star Co.; Papetti's Hy-Grade Egg Products, Inc.; Wisco Farm Cooperative.

Principal Divisions

Refrigerated Distribution Division; Dairy Products Division; Egg Products Division; Potato Products Division.

Further Reading

"Cargill Challenges Michael Foods Patents on Egg Processing," *Wall Street Journal,* July 10, 1992, p. B–6.

"Ex-Chief at Pillsbury Named Head of Unit at Michael Foods, Inc.," *Wall Street Journal,* August 1, 1989, p. B–6.

Gibson, Richard, "Michael Foods Draws Analysts' Long-Term Bet," *Wall Street Journal,* March 2, 1992, B–6H.

——, "Strip Cholesterol from Whole Eggs," *Wall Street Journal,* February 19, 1992.

Johnson, Tim, "Michael Foods Hatches First Branding Eggs," *City Business,* May 29, 1998, p. 3.

Marcotty, Josephine, "Disappointed Shareholders Sue Michael Foods," *Minneapolis Star Tribune,* October 13, 1989, p. 02D.

"Michael Foods Buys Potato Firm," *Minneapolis Star Tribune,* October 6, 1989, p. 02D.

"Michael Foods, Inc.," *Wall Street Journal,* November 16, 1992, p. B-4.

Norris, Floyd, "Behind Interest in Michael Foods," *New York Times,* April 25, 1989, p. IV, 10:3.

Pachuta, Michael, "Michael Foods Cracks Open New Processed-Food Markets," *Investor's Business Daily,* May 27, 1998, p. A3.

"Stoppage of Egg Product Leads to $23 Million Charge," *Wall Street Journal,* December 16, 1993, p. B–4.

"The Wealthiest Minnesotans," *Corporate Report of Minnesota,* May, 1991, p. 56.

—Terri Mozzone

Midway Games, Inc.

3401 North California Avenue
Chicago, Illinois 60618
U.S.A.
(773) 961-2222
Fax: (773) 961-1099
Web site: http://www.midway.com

Public Company
Incorporated: 1988
Employees: 553
Sales: $388.2 million (1996)
Stock Exchanges: NYSE
Ticker Symbol: MWY
SICs: 3651 Household Audio & Video; 3999
Manufacturing Industries, Not Elsewhere Classified;
7372 Prepackaged Software; 7993 Coin-Operated
Amusement Devices; 7999 Amusement & Recreation,
Not Elsewhere Classified

Midway Games, Inc., is one of the world's leading producers of video games. The company designs, publishes, and markets games for coin-operated arcade machines as well as for home video game consoles and personal computers. Midway has published or distributed some of the most popular games in the industry, including the "Mortal Kombat" series, "Cruisin' USA," "NBA Jam," "Defender," and "PacMan." The "Mortal Kombat" line alone has sold more than 14 million units. It has brought Midway over $1 billion and at the beginning of 1998 accounted for more than 20 percent of the company's annual revenue. In the early years of its development Midway produced games exclusively for arcades and was the number one company in the coin-op market. Through its subsidiary Midway Home Entertainment, however, it has moved aggressively into the home market. Midway makes its home games in formats compatible for all the leading game models, including the popular Nintendo 64, Sony PlayStation, and personal computers.

Company Roots: 1969–1988

In 1969 the Midway Manufacturing Company, a maker of amusement machines, was acquired by Bally, one of the nation's leading manufacturers of gaming pinball machines. In 1988 Bally's amusement game divisions were purchased for $8 million by its main competitor in the arcade game industry, WMS Industries of Chicago. That same year Midway Manufacturing Company was incorporated as a wholly owned subsidiary of WMS. Midway worked on some WMS pinball games, but the company primarily designed and produced video games for arcades.

"Mortal Kombat" Revives Industry: 1992

Video games were going through a slump as the 1980s turned to the 1990s, but the entire industry revived abruptly when Midway introduced "Mortal Kombat" in 1992. The game achieved notoriety inside and outside the gamer community when it became known that secret codes had been programmed into the game: when activated, the codes changed "Mortal Kombat" from a run-of-the-mill kick-and-punch match between mutants into a bloody battle to the death at whose conclusion the victor would rip the still-beating heart from his vanquished opponent's chest, or tear his hapless opponent's spine out and hold it triumphantly aloft, or blast his prostrate opponent to ashes.

The game unleashed a debate over the effect of violent video games on children, which continued throughout the 1990s. But the immense popularity of "Mortal Kombat" guaranteed that other games would compete to outdo it in both violence and realism. The game established Midway as a major force in the video game field and provided the company with the financial resources to develop new games and eventually expand beyond the arcade market.

In March 1994 Midway and Nintendo formed a 50-50 joint venture. Under its terms, Midway was to develop video games for new game machines being developed by Nintendo, among them the Nintendo 64, a home game console for which Midway agreed to develop a version of "Cruis'n USA." The agreement gave the joint venture the distribution rights for home versions of any "Cruis'n" sequels developed for coin-op machines. It also had first rights for negotiating distribution of the games Midway designed for Nintendo's next coin-operated system. As of early 1997 the joint venture had not yet released any home video games, but the deal was an early step for Midway into the blossoming home video game market.

Expansion in the Mid-1990s

Midway moved more decisively into the home market in April 1994 when it acquired three companies, Tradewest Inc., Tradewest International Inc., and the Leland Corporation, known collectively as Tradewest. Tradewest, located in Corsicana, Texas, designed and manufactured home video games. The initial price was $15 million with the remainder calculated as a percentage of future annual revenues. In June 1998 when Midway made the final payment, those additional costs had totaled $37 million. Tradewest retained its autonomy within Midway. Its fifty-person staff formed the core of a new Midway subsidiary which, like Tradewest, developed home video games. Midway's most profitable unit, Tradewest was eventually renamed Midway Home Entertainment.

Midway's decision to begin producing its own home games followed the incredible success of the first two "Mortal Kombat" games. Those games, like all Midway's games at the time, were originally developed as arcade games. The home rights to Midway games were licensed to another game developer, Acclaim Entertainment, in 1989, a time of uncertainty in the home video game market. Acclaim sold five million copies of "Mortal Kombat" at a retail price of about $65 each.

Midway ended its licensing relationship with Acclaim in 1993. The marketing strategy it adopted when it began producing home video games was one Acclaim had pioneered with a great deal of success. Home games were released simultaneously in versions for all the popular home game systems. Midway Home Entertainment's staff was ideally suited for the strategy, because Tradewest had specialized in developing games for multiple platforms. The cross-platform strategy was extremely effective: it enabled the company to hit every potential market while a game was still popular; development, advertising, and promotional expenses could be spread out over more

game units, lowering costs; and a successful arcade version operated as advertising for all home versions.

Midway's leadership in the arcade field gave it an additional advantage. Acclaim established earlier that successful arcade games almost invariably went on to be successful home games. Its arcade sales thus functioned as market research, reducing the likelihood that a home game would not pay back its development costs. In September 1995, Midway released "Mortal Kombat 3," the first home video game that it had developed in house. Despite its release so late in the year, the game went on to be the nation's best-selling home video game in 1995, according to *TRSTS Reports,* an industry magazine.

In March 1996, Midway purchased Atari Games from Time-Warner. Midway paid $2 million up front for Atari, which had been experiencing problems since the early 1980s, and additional costs linked to the division's performance through the year 2000, with the total price paid estimated to have been $24 million in all. Midway obtained Atari's game development capability and its full library of classic video games like "Pac-Man" and "Centipede," as well as the right to use the Atari name on its coin-operated games. After the acquisition, the Atari division in Milpitas, California, remained an autonomous operation within Midway Games.

1996 IPO

On September 13, 1996, Midway filed its intention with the Securities and Exchange Commission to make an initial public offering of 5.1 million shares of common stock. Less than 15 percent of Midway common stock was being offered, with WMS Industries, Midway's parent company, continuing to hold approximately 33.4 million shares. The offering was greeted favorably by investors, because Midway seemed to be a strong presence in the video game market. Sales had increased to $245.4 million annually by June 1996, which represented five-fold growth since 1992. An important reason was the "Mortal Kombat" series, which accounted for 17 percent of Midway's sales in 1995 and 35 percent in 1996.

Midway's increasing involvement in home games was also a positive factor for investors. Midway Chairman Neil Nicastro told *Crain's Chicago Business,* "The home business provides superior earnings potential. It's so much bigger a market." Indeed, in 1996 there were 15,000 arcades in the United States, but 35 million homes with video games. Furthermore, the coin-op business had begun to erode at a rate of 10 to 15 percent a year. By contrast, in 1994 home video games had accounted for 20 percent of Midway's total revenues, and by 1996 they made up 63 percent. In addition, Midway was the only American Video game manufacturer that was strongly established in the arcade market, the testing grounds for home games.

Investors had questions about Midway as well. Would the untested company be able to get home products out on schedule? How would the added administrative, R&D, and marketing costs associated with the shift in focus to home video games affect Midway's financial performance? Those costs had already grown significantly. Between June 1995 and June 1996, the company's annual R&D outlays increased from $8.4 million to $32.5 million, while marketing costs jumped from $1.6 million to $22.8 million.

The offering was completed on October 29, 1996. The stock went for $20 a share and raised $108 million. According to *Crain's Chicago Business,* investor confidence in Midway was high, as indicated by the level of trading in the weeks immediately after the spin-off, and within two months the value of Midway stock was 15 percent higher. The company changed its name at the same time from Midway Manufacturing Company to Midway Games. All pinball operations handled by Midway for WMS were transferred to another subsidiary just prior to the public offering.

Midway's fall 1996 home video line was marketed exclusively under its own trademark. Prior to that, its products had carried the Williams, Tradewest, Tengen, and Time Warner Interactive trademarks. Midway Games had a number of achievements during its 1996 fiscal year. It released five coin-operated games under its own name; it published eight new home games, including one of its most popular, "Mortal Kombat 3"; it released the Touchmaster, a coin-op game platform with a touchscreen; and "Cruis'n USA" won awards for innovation from various industry groups.

Three months after Midway's public offering, investors noted a strange discrepancy in the stock prices of Midway and its parent company, WMS. When Midway went public, WMS retained just over 86 percent of the total shares. Based on that figure, analysts calculated, each WMS share effectively owned 1.38 shares in Midway. At the mid-January 1997 price of $20 for a Midway share, every WMS share owned about $27.95 worth of Midway stock. WMS, however, was selling for only $23. The primary factor holding down the price of WMS shares, analysts reasoned, was the large percentage of Midway shares it held. That was Midway stock that was inaccessible to the market and investors could not arbitrage the difference in prices.

WMS Industries was itself uncertain how to deal the problem. Keeping its Midway holdings would continue to depress its own value, but if WMS sold its Midway holdings it could end up paying 40 percent of the proceeds in taxes, and if it distributed the stock among its shareholders they could be liable for taxes. On August 11, 1997, WMS announced that it had decided on the latter course. It stockholders would receive the company's Midway stock on a pro-rata basis. The proposed spin-off hinged upon an Internal Revenue Service ruling over whether the deal would be tax free to WMS and its stockholders. The company hoped everything would be completed by early 1998. Thereafter Midway would be listed as a "discontinued operation" on WMS's financial records.

Midway Games has developed or licensed a broad line of games, including sports games, like "Wayne Gretzky's 3D Hockey," racing games like "San Francisco Rush," and fighting games like "War Games," and "Mace." But the most successful of all Midway's game titles has been the "Mortal Kombat" line. "Mortal Kombat" ushered in boom times in the video game market, in particular for Midway Games. More than 15 million "Mortal Kombat" home games were sold. The game spawned a series of sequels, including versions 2, 3, and 4,

"Ultimate Mortal Kombat," "Mortal Kombat Trilogy," and "Mortal Kombat Mythologies: Sub Zero." By the beginning of 1998 Midway had earned a net $1 billion from all the "Mortal Kombat" arcade games. "Mortal Kombat" 3 sold 250,000 units and brought in $15 million during its first weekend on the market. In 1997, after other popular games appeared, the percentage was still 22 percent.

Debate over Violence in the Late 1990s

The debate about violent games was resumed after a series of schoolyard shootings in 1997 and 1998, after it was discovered that some of the boys involved in the shootings had played "Mortal Kombat." Experts, however, were divided on the degree to which such games actually influenced violent behavior. What was important for game makers was the enthusiasm of video game players for carnage, and they began incorporating it into other games. Midway Games was no exception, producing "Blitz," a no-holds-barred contest in which players maim and dismember opponents, and "Bio Freaks," in which players can decapitate opponents.

In 1994 Midway licensed multimedia rights to "Mortal Kombat" to Threshold Entertainment, which turned the license into a property worth $3 billion. According to Threshold CEO Larry Kasanoff, "Mortal Kombat" has become the fifth-largest entertainment franchise in the world, ranking just after "Batman" and "Star Trek." In all there are over 100 licensed "Mortal Kombat" products on the market. Threshold released two "Mortal Kombat" movies, the first of which made $100 million worldwide in 1995, the second of which was the country's number one movie the weekend it opened in November 1997. Besides the movies, Threshold produced an animated TV series, a "Mortal Kombat" stage show at Radio city Music Hall, a "Mortal Kombat" CD-ROM, a "Home Mortal Kombat Special" on DIRECT TV, three soundtrack albums, one of which went platinum (one million copies sold), a live action TV show, and one of the Internet's most popular websites, mortal-kombat.com.

In October 1997 the arcade version of "Mortal Kombat 4" was released. The game, which the company dubbed "the final version" in press releases, was the first to utilize Midway's new Zeus Chip. The chip was the key to a powerful new graphic system that enabled the game to process visual data about ten times faster than other systems, increasing the levels of realism proportionately. In 1998 Midway began pushing the Nintendo 64 version of "Mortal Kombat 4" more aggressively than ever, weeks before the game was due to be released. A multi-million dollar, music video-style television ad campaign coincided with the airing of the first "Mortal Kombat" movie on TBS, a film shown five times during May 1998. Midway also lowered the suggested retail price of "Mortal Kombat" 4 from $59.95 to $49.95. The game itself was scheduled to be released on June 29.

At the end of 1997, Midway announced that revenues had risen 13 percent to $73.7 million during its July–September 1997 quarter. During the same period, however, home game revenues fell from $47.6 million to $40.1 million, largely because the company had postponed the release of "Top Gear Rally" and "Mace: The Dark Age" until the end of September. Nonetheless, *TRSTS Reports* ranked Midway Games fourth among 62 video game companies in sales of 32- and 64-bit home video games for fiscal 1997, up from seventh place the previous year. The company released seven new arcade games and fifteen new home games. In 1997 Midway released more games for the new Nintendo 64 system than any company except Nintendo itself.

In February 1998, Midway broke with its previous marketing strategy and announced that the following summer it would release home versions of the game "Bio Freaks" before an arcade version had appeared. According to a company spokesperson, Midway had made the decision in response to high consumer demand for a new fighting game that took advantage of the graphic possibilities of the next generation game systems like the Sony PlayStation and Nintendo 64. The company described the release as additional evidence of its commitment to the home market it was courting.

In March 1998 Midway expanded its product line into the market for personal computer games. It purchased back North American and Japanese distribution rights to Midway personal computer games that the company had granted to GT Interactive Software in 1995, a time when it was focusing its attention on the home console market. GT retained rights to distribute Midway personal computer games outside North America and Japan.

The Internal Revenue Service finally issued its ruling that the company's proposed spin-off would be tax free. On April 6, 1998, all Midway shares held by WMS were distributed among its shareholders. Each WMS share received 1.19773 Midway shares, and fractional shares were paid out in cash. Upon completion of the spin-off, Neil NiCastro resigned his positions as president, CEO, and chief operating officer of WMS to take over the chairmanship of Midway Games.

Focus on R&D in the Late 1990s

Midway significantly boosted its outlay for R&D from $32.5 million in fiscal 1996 to $55.9 million in 1997. Part of that was for advanced technologies whose ultimate marketability would only be proved in the indeterminate future. One example was WaveNet, a system for interactive video gaming. Once in place,

WaveNet would comprise a private network of arcades linked electronically. Gamers would be able to play video games against opponents in different arcades, and even in different cities. Test arcades were set up in San Francisco and Los Angeles, but as of mid-1998 Midway was still evaluating the feasibility of the system and the company had no plans for national deployment.

The trends evident at Midway Games over the previous two years showed no sign of abating in summer 1998. Total revenues grew by about ten percent and the company expected its home video game revenues to double from the same quarter a year earlier, thanks to sales of games for the so-called "new generation" video consoles manufactured by Nintendo and Sony. Midway's arcade business continued to shrink, dropping by 25 percent compared to the previous year.

Midway planned, in fiscal 1999, to continue its strong presence in the Nintendo 64 and Sony PlayStation markets by releasing 28 new home video games, while planning 11 new arcade games. Midway was looking to become more active in other markets it had neglected. For example, the company planned to release twelve personal computer home games, in comparison to the previous year's total of two. Midway was also developing four games for the Game Boy system.

Further Reading

"Bally Zaps Its Video Games," *Time,* July 25, 1988.

Borden, Jeff, "Zapping Bad Guys Is Good Biz for Videogames Maker but Look Out! Rising Costs Could Whack Midway," *Crain's Chicago Business,* December 9, 1996.

Chronis, George T., "Williams Buys Time Warner Interactive and Brings Back the Atari Brand Name," *Video Store Magazine,* April 7, 1996.

"Game Companies Post Upbeat Quarter," *Television Digest,* October 27, 1997.

Henry, David, "WMS Stock Offers Bargain—For Brave," *USA Today,* January 1, 1997.

McGarry, Mark J., "Short Cuts," *Newsday,* April 6, 1994.

Van De Mark, Donald, "Mortal Kombat: Interview with Larry Kasanoff, Threshold Entertainment," *Biz Buzz CNN,* November 20, 1997.

—Gerald Brennan

MILLIPORE

Millipore Corporation

80 Ashby Road
Bedford, Massachusetts 01730-2271
U.S.A.
(781) 533-6000
(800) 645-5439
Fax: (781) 533-3110
Web site: http://www.millipore.com

Public Company
Incorporated: 1954 as Millipore Filter Corporation
Employees: 4,800
Sales: $758.92 million (1997)
Stock Exchanges: New York
Ticker Symbol: MIL
SICs: 3826 Analytical Instruments

Millipore Corporation, a multinational high-technology company, is a world leader in membrane separations technology and has pioneered the use of membrane technology in hundreds of diverse applications. The company applies its purification technology to critical research and manufacturing problems in the microelectronics, biopharmaceutical, and analytical laboratory markets. Millipore has manufacturing plants in the United States, Europe, South America, and Asia; it offers more than 10,000 products. Within the United States, the company sells its products through its own direct sales force, while in international markets the company sells primarily through wholly owned subsidiaries and branches located in more than 31 major industrialized and developing countries, including Canada, Central and South America, Europe, and the Asia/Pacific region. The company's customers in the microelectronics, bio-pharmaceutical, and food and beverage companies use Millipore products in their manufacturing processes. Millipore also sells its analytical products, filter cartridges, and laboratory water-purification systems to chemical manufacturers and processors. Universities, governments, and private and corporate research laboratories, environmental science laboratories, and regulatory agencies purchase a wide range of Millipore products. Approximately 57 percent of Millipore's net sales were made to customers outside the United States in 1997.

Early Years: 1954–69

During World War II, European drinking-water supplies and testing laboratories were destroyed. As a result, there was a massive increase of water-pollution problems and the threat of water-borne diseases. Concerned about this situation, scientists developed a crude microporous membrane filter to detect bacteria in drinking water. When information about this purification technology became available after the war, the California Institute of Technology perfected the membrane, and the U.S. government contracted the Lovell Chemical Company of Watertown, Massachusetts, to begin pilot production of the membrane. John H. Bush, a Lovell engineer, recognized the potential for applications beyond the analysis of drinking water; he purchased the rights to the membrane-production process of his employer. Using the word *millipore* to refer to the large number of small openings in the microporous membrane, Bush founded the Millipore Filter Corporation in 1954

In the mid-1960s Bush changed the company's name to Millipore Corporation, reflecting that the company had gone beyond manufacturing filter membranes for water analysis to making a wide range of products for the analysis and purification of many other fluids. By year-end 1967 Millipore was circulating its General Catalog in five different editions and was distributing its products throughout the world. Through significant investments in research and development, as well as acquisitions, the company operated nationwide and in wholly owned subsidiaries in Canada, England, France, Germany, and Italy. Revenue for 1963 reached $3.43 million. Equipping the brewing industry for the production of draft beer resulted in 30 percent of 1966 sales, which peaked at $9.96 million, allowing for a three-for-one stock split in that year.

Among new products introduced in 1967 were the Super-Q water purification system and the PhoroSlide electrophoresis system, examples of how the company applied its integrated-systems approach and gave customers a total solution to processing and analytical problems. The Millitube expendable-cartridge filter for high-volume processing reduced customers' operating and handling costs for many process applications. In 1968 Millipore introduced a fully automated, high-volume filtration system.

An Industry Leader: 1970–79

During the 1970s Millipore built on the technological base of the preceding 16 years to establish its leadership in markets related to membrane technology. The company was the leader in the manufacture of products and systems embodying "microstate technology" (words used to describe Millipore's expertise in treating the microscopic and submicroscopic organic and inorganic components of fluids). Continuous development and production of the company's original microporous-membrane filter and membrane-based systems led to a wide range of applications in laboratories, hospitals, and various industries. The Milli-R/Q water system combined the technologies of reverse osmosis, de-ionization, and membrane filtration to replace the expensive stills laboratories used to obtain the high quality water they needed.

The 1975 purchase of Worthington Biochemical Corporation (integrated into Millipore as the Worthington Diagnostics Division) expanded Millipore's expertise in enzymology and immuno-chemistry and gave it a segment of the diagnostics market. The acquisition of Texas-based Continental Water Conditioning Corporation allowed Millipore to establish a service base for the Water Systems Division; Continental had a nationwide network of 67 sales and service locations. During the last half of 1979, Millipore's Water Systems Division was consolidated with Continental's operations in El Paso. Acquiring California-based Chemetrics Corporation filled Millipore's need to protect its market position in diagnostic reagents by making available complete diagnostic systems, such as the Chemetrics' Analyzer II. This preprogrammed and user-reprogrammable instrument performed all routine blood chemistries and even printed out test results. Less expensive than most other comparably priced instruments, the Analyzer II was especially suited for small laboratories and hospitals not able to afford large automatic systems.

The Worthington Diagnostics Division produced purified enzymes for use in clinical assay applications, as well as enzymatic tools for protein chemistry, nucleic acid research, genetic engineering, and tissue culture. This division also developed a full line of lipid tests that could check for predisposition toward coronary artery disease. Another new product was Ultrafree, used to detect the levels of free and bound drug in a patient's blood, thereby enabling a physician to determine the appropriate level of total drug to be administered to a patient. Other Millipore products for hospitals included the Ivex-2, a final

sterilizing filter for intravenous solutions; and reverse osmosis systems engineered to process water for hermodialysis.

Millipore offered products to provide clean, sterile fluids for use in manufacturing, to clean or sterilize final products, and to concentrate or reclaim materials from industrial waste water. The food and beverage industry, the pharmaceutical industry, and the electronics industry were the primary industrial users of Millipore products. Millipore products prevented contamination of foods and beverages during their preparation and packaging; a quality-assurance program introduced to bottlers specified how monitoring micro-organisms during the bottling operation could detect contamination before it caused product spoilage. Millipore offered the pharmaceutical industry the means of assuring pure water for the production of pharmaceuticals and provided for the sterile air and liquids necessary in the fermentation process that produced antibiotics. Furthermore, the 1979 introduction of the Durapore membrane stood out as a highlight of the company's technological achievement. This membrane, made from a fluorocarbon polymer, had a temperature resistance of greater than 135 degrees centigrade and could be in-line sterilized. It was used principally for sterilizing injectable pharmaceutical products, such as antibiotics, blood fractions, and vaccines.

In the electronics industry, all fluids used in manufacturing integrated circuits (ICs) had to be free of bacteria and particles in order to prevent contaminants from bridging the microscopic gaps between circuit components. Large quantities of water de-ionized by Millipore water systems were used to rinse the wafers on which the circuits were printed. Millipore introduced MilliChem, a filtration system for acids. This was a small self-contained unit used at the etch station to continually recirculate the acid used in the process of etching the printed circuit pattern into the wafer. MilliChem increased the production yields for integrated circuits by five to ten percent; it also extended the life of the acid bath, thereby saving on both the original cost of the acid and on the expense of safely disposing of the depleted acid.

During the 1970s, Millipore's fundamental separations technology gained acceptance in many new markets. As a whole, the company grew tenfold. Consolidated net sales reached $153.39 million and net income was $16.84 million.

Rising and Slipping: 1980–89

Millipore entered the 1980s well positioned to compete in the multi-billion-dollar separations industry. The company opened two new subsidiaries, built two new overseas manufacturing plants, acquired two additional plants, tripled the capacity of its French plant, and initiated limited manufacturing in Brazil and India. In Japan, Millipore maintained local manufacturing and product development operations; the Japanese government and industry invested heavily in electronics and pharmaceutical processing—two of Millipore's strengths. The United States remained the company's largest market.

Millipore founder John Bush retired from Millipore management in 1980, remaining on the board of directors. He was succeeded as chairman and CEO by D.V. d'Arbeloff, who had served as president for the prior 15 years. D'Arbeloff died in 1985. His successor, Jack Mulvany, served as chairman, president, and CEO for one year before he was killed in a tragic helicopter accident. Mulvany was succeeded by John A. Gilmartin, who had been Millipore's chief financial officer and had just been put in charge of Millipore's largest operating division.

Millipore introduced new products to its various clients. The industrial customer base included pharmaceutical, biotechnology, semiconductor, chemical, environmental testing, and food and beverage companies. Separations technology was particularly important for the new generation of biotechnology-derived pharmaceuticals. Millipore's technologies played a major role in eliminating and reducing particulate and chemical contamination in the growing manufacture of semiconductors. As environmental concerns drew increased attention, Millipore's analytical devices and instrumentation helped monitor and control environmental contamination. The company made products for university, government, private analytical, and research laboratories, as well as defense and regulatory agencies. Healthcare and medical research companies were also served by Millipore.

During the first half of the 1980s, Millipore earned more than 13 percent on capital and grew per-share earnings by 20 percent annually. Around 1985, however, problems began to surface in the company's Waters Chromatography Division, Millipore's first attempt at diversification. Waters, which made equipment for separating liquids, was a highly profitable company when it was acquired in 1980, but it soon adversely affected Millipore's profitability. While Millipore's business depended on products made to customer specifications, Waters' focus was the launching of new instruments for a very different market from that of Millipore's membrane business. In 1985, Jack Mulvany had started up the MilliGen/Biosearch Division, focused on the emerging market for automated DNA synthesis and sequencing, and on protein and peptide synthesis and sequencing. Part of the impetus for this step was the Human Genome project and the dynamics of the life-science research market of the mid-eighties. The new division incorporated the instrumentation skills of Waters Chromatography as well as the membrane and chemistry skills of Millipore's filter business. MilliGen/Biosearch, however, never turned a profit.

Sales of chromatography products slowed down in both the United States and Europe. At the end of the 1980s, a stronger U.S. dollar on the worldwide market depressed growth by three percentage points; the sale of the Process Water Division in November 1989 depressed growth by an additional percentage point. In Europe, however, membrane product lines—especially those sold for analytical purposes—sold particularly well. Millipore benefitted from strong sales of electronics in the Pacific region and from increased sales to its pharmaceutical customers. In 1989 consolidated net sales increased six percent to $365.83, but net income declined three percent to $52.5 million.

Refocusing Strategies: 1989 and Beyond

By 1989 the $3.5-billion separations industry in which Millipore competed had slowed from a ten to 12 percent growth rate to a five to six percent rate. Competition was on the increase: more and smarter competitors were investing heavily in Millipore's market segments. On the other hand, there was a broader, deeper appreciation of discoveries in biochemistry and their potential applications in human therapeutics, agriculture,

and clinical diagnostics. These discoveries occurred in the micro-chemical research laboratories utilizing membrane technologies and bioinstrumentation systems. Millipore benefitted from the electronics industry's growing need for ultra-clean manufacturing environments to produce ever more complex semiconductor chips. The pharmaceutical and biotechnology industries showed increased interest in purifying the manufacturing processes of viruses and bacteria. Moreover, the environmental industry needed products for the precise monitoring of very low levels of pollutants. Millipore entered the 1990s determined to refocus its strategic vision and capitalize on the opportunities created by these emerging global trends.

In August 1994 the company sold its Waters Chromatography and Bioscience Divisions, used the proceeds to buy back 12 percent of Millipore's stock, and focused more intensely on developing internally and through selected acquisitions. The 1996 acquisition of the Amicon Separation Science Business added molecular separation and purification products for the life-science research laboratory as well as for biopharmaceutical and manufacturing applications. In January 1997, the company's purchase of Tylan General, Inc. expanded Millipore's role as a supplier of liquid and process gas purification products to the semiconductor industry, thereby including the manufacture, marketing and sale of a broad range of precision processes and instruments for manufacturing ICs.

Millipore had begun to implement the priorities and goals defined in 1995 when, in 1996, John Gilmartin tendered his resignation after 17 years with the company, for ten of which he had served as chairman, president, and CEO. He was succeeded in those responsibilities by C. William Zadel, president, and chief executive officer of CIBA-Corning Diagnostics Corp., a leading supplier of diagnostic instruments, reagents and data management systems to the global clinical laboratory market.

Millipore continued to emphasize technical expertise, product quality, and responsiveness to customer needs. The company developed more effective customer-feedback techniques and expanded its use of customer surveys. New market-assessment techniques were implemented to define and segment major markets, and a process called "Future Mapping" was initiated to conduct five- to seven-year assessments of all the company's market segments and businesses. For better clarity, accountability, and alignment with customer-focused divisions, in 1995 Millipore identified its three major markets for purification technologies as being microelectronics manufacturing, the analytical laboratory, and biopharmaceutical manufacturing.

The following products were some of the new contributions that Millipore offered to these markets. The company provided the microelectronics industry with cost-cutting and technology-enabling "smart purifiers," consisting of chemical purifiers that selectively removed ions from acid solutions; an in-line monitor gave ongoing feedback on the level of molecular contaminants in process gases. The IntelliGen Photochemical Dispense System with Impact LHVD Filter was an integrated filter and pump designed for easy, rapid and safe filter changeouts. Pre-wetted filters and a new gas process control system were also launched.

The company's products were sold to hospitals, dialysis centers, and healthcare providers, among other customers. Millipore sold disposable filters/devices and water purification systems to more than 200,000 laboratories. Millipore products were used to provide the ultrapure water needed for research, and to purify, sterilize, concentrate, and isolate various biologicals, chemicals and particulates. The company's membrane and device expertise was used to develop home diagnostic kits, and clinical-laboratory and infection-control devices. Laboratory customers were very receptive to a new family of Milli-Q water purification systems.

The company capitalized on the fact that the biopharmaceutical industry was rapidly changing through mergers and acquisitions, globalization, worldwide regulations, biotechnology, genetics, and new approaches to healthcare for an aging population. In 1995 there were 226 biotech drugs in Phase III clinical trials. Millipore, particularly well suited for the isolation of cells and the purification of protein solutions, worked closely with biotechnology companies to design purification systems and protocols at each stage of scale-up, manufacturing, and final formulation of new drugs. New products included Pellicon XL, a laboratory bench-size filtration device; Integritest Exacta, a new on-site integrity tester for filters in the pharmaceutical environment; and a new Millipak sterility filter family. Furthermore, through its global infrastructure, Millipore helped multinational biopharmaceutical companies set up new manufacturing facilities in China, Southeast Asia, and Latin America.

Over the years, Millipore products effectively enabled many countries to safeguard the environment—and Millipore played its part well. Millipore's worldwide manufacturing operations continually improved their efficiencies and exceeded environmental milestones while increasing their volumes of manufactured products. From 1990 through 1997, the company's plants reduced the total amount of chemical emissions by 68 percent. In December 1997 Millipore began constructing new headquarters in Allen, Texas, for its microelectronics gas business. The cost-cutting purpose of the new plant was to consolidate into one unit three Tylan manufacturing sites. Millipore expected to have pilot manufacturing operations certified by August 1998 and full-scale operations running by October 1998. Products to be manufactured at this facility included components to control flow and pressure of gases used in semiconductor manufacturing.

Much time and energy went into incorporating Amicon and Tylan as part of Millipore. Amicon was smoothly integrated into Millipore and actually added to Millipore's total profitability. The accretion of Tylan was more challenging not only because of a downturn in the microelectronics industry but also because Tylan was a composite of three small companies: Vacuum General, Tylan, and Span! The slow accretion of Tylan affected Millipore's 1997 results. Nevertheless, 1997 sales grew more than 15 percent to $758.92 million (due in part to sales from the acquired companies), despite the negative impact of currency fluctuations during the year. Among external events affecting the company were the economic turmoil in Asia and the shift in business mix resulting from the acquisition of Amicon and Tylan. While the Japanese yen had weakened against the dollar by more than 30 percent, the severest negative impact

was from the Korean business: the Korean won had dropped 50 percent in value—and Korea was a major microelectronics center.

China was less affected by the economic crisis than many of the other Asian countries in which Millipore did business. In 1969 the company had established a presence in China with limited chromatography sales, mostly to research institutions and universities. During the early 1970s and 1980s, the company had participated in technical seminars, conferences, and trade shows. Millipore had opened a sales office in Beijing as early as 1981, a sales office in Shanghai in 1985, and two other offices in 1990: one in Guangshou, one in Shenyang, and two in Hong Kong, which became part of China in July 1997.

March 1998 marked a milestone for Millipore's business in The People's Republic of China: the official opening of The Millipore Suzhou Filter Company, the company's first manufacturing operation in that country. The dominant markets for Millipore products in China were the pharmaceutical and food-and-beverage markets. In 1998, throughout China, there were more than 2,000 factories making drugs and more than three factories making bottled water, beer, and soft drinks. Demand for Millipore products were increasing because of their numerous critical applications in Chinese pharmaceutical and food-and-beverage production.

Revenues grew during the first quarter of 1998, but there was a loss in gross margin for the quarter. Millipore dealt with slower sales growth by reducing expenses throughout the company but protected future-oriented programs. For the first six months of 1998, revenues were down three percent. Chairman and CEO Zadel commented that the revenue shortfall and the poor earnings performance were due to the continuing worldwide slowdown in the microelectronics industry, a slowdown that showed no sign of a near-term rebound. The second quarter brought no overall growth in the biopharmaceutical business, due primarily to the food and beverage part of that business. However, the drug-approval pipeline and ordering trends boded well for growth in the next six months. Millipore's strategic direction and investments in research and development, new products, and new sales channels paid off in the analytical business, which reported ten percent growth in the second quarter.

As the 21st century drew near, although Millipore remained subject to the volatility of its ultrafiltration and microelectronics segments, the downsized company's new products, established reputation for customer satisfaction, and strong worldwide infrastructure in the analytical laboratory and biopharmaceutical markets, over the long term seemed able to mitigate cyclical declines in the microelectronics business.

Principal Subsidiaries

Millipore Asia Ltd.; Millipore Cidra, Inc. (Puerto Rico); Millipore Intertech, (V.I.), Inc.; Millipore (Canada) Ltd.; Millipore S.A. de C.V. (Mexico); Millipore GesmbH (Austria); Millipore International Holding Company B.V., (Netherlands); Millipore (Suzhou) Filter Company Limited (Peoples Republic of China).

Further Reading

Beard, J., and A. Coghlan, ''Filters Provide Traps for Catching Viruses,'' *New Scientist,* July 20, 1991, p. 20.

''Going Beyond Green,'' *Modern Materials Handling,* September 1995, pp. 12–14.

McGrath, Dylan, and Chad Fasca, ''The Fab Line,'' *Electronic News,* June 15, 1998, pp. 40–41.

''Portable Environmental Tools Make Field Testing a Breeze,'' *R&D Magazine,* July 1994, pp. 31–32.

Powitz, Robert W., and James J. Balsamo, ''The Millipore Sanitarian's Kit,'' *Journal of Environmental Health,* April 1998, p. 34.

''Pure Water Tap,'' *Soap, Perfumery & Cosmetics,* May 1996, p. 55.

''Products and Materials: Scientific Apparatus and Instruments,'' *Science,* March 21, 1997, pp. 1811–13.

''Show Products Quality Control,'' *Beverage World,* October 1996, pp. 190–98.

Ward, Amanda E., and Michael K. Ozanian, ''Out to Pasture: Badgered by Big Shareholders, Millipore Is Finally Selling Its Losers. Now What?,'' *Financial World,* September 27, 1994, pp. 28–29.

—Gloria A. Lemieux

Mizuno Corporation

12-35, 1-chome, Nanko-kita
Suminoe-ku, Osaka 559
Japan
81-6-614-8315
Fax: 81-6-614-8389
Web site: http://www.mizuno.co.jp

Public Company
Incorporated: 1906
Employees: 3,911
Sales: $1.59 billion (1996)
Stock Exchanges: Tokyo Osaka Nagoya
SICs: 2329 Men's and Boys' Clothing, Not Elsewhere
Classified; 3949 Sporting and Athletic Goods, Not
Elsewhere Classified; 7999 Amusement and
Recreation, Not Elsewhere Classified

Mizuno Corporation is a world leader in sports equipment manufacturing. In particular, Mizuno's baseball equipment is considered one of the foremost brands, and the manufacturer's irons are the leading clubs used on the Professional Golf Association tour. As of 1997, six of the past ten Masters winners had played with Mizuno irons. The company produces its products in-house and maintains offices and dealers across the globe, including in Japan, France, Canada, Germany, England, Taiwan, and the United States.

The Early Years

In 1906, a devoted fan of baseball—Rihachi Mizuno—started a sporting goods store that would grow into the international corporation of the 1990s. Rihachi Mizuno, a kimono shop worker, saw his first baseball game in Kyoto when he was 18 years old. He loved the game, which dated back to 1867 in Japan, and soon opened his own baseball equipment store, offering custom uniforms as well as sports clothing. Eventually, Rihachi Mizuno expanded into manufacturing sports equipment. His baseballs became the standard of excellence for the

product in Japan; Rihachi Mizuno rejected any baseballs that did not bounce to his eye level—4 feet and 5 inches—when dropped 16.5 feet.

During the 1920s, Mizuno supported the Olympic games and began to expand the operations of his company. In 1927, the company started manufacturing ski equipment; by 1933, Mizuno engaged in the manufacture of golf equipment. Mizuno opened a small factory based near Osaka, Japan, in 1934 for making baseball bats, balls, and uniforms, as well as for manufacturing golf clubs and skis. The company continued to expand into other areas of sports and began manufacturing tennis equipment in 1943.

The purpose of the Osaka factory changed drastically during World War II. At the request of the Japanese government, Mizuno fitted its manufacturing facility for making military ordnance building gliders instead of bats and balls. After the war, Mizuno manufactured housewares such as furniture and kitchenware. Eventually, the company returned to producing baseball equipment, in particular sailcloth for gloves and wooden bats with resin added for longevity.

By the mid-1900s, Mizuno was once again at the forefront of the sporting goods industry, supporting the 1964 Olympics and the Sapporo Winter Olympics in 1972. The company became known as an innovator in its field in 1977, creating customized gloves for major league baseball players. Nubuyoshi (Yoshi) Tsubota, a master craftsmen for Mizuno, began holding glove making workshops at the spring training camps of major league teams. On the spot, he would customize gloves and other equipment for the teams' players. Owing to his efforts, the number of professional baseball players using Mizuno equipment grew, with 29 percent opting for the company's merchandise.

The Need to Rejuvenate in the 1980s

Despite the company's many past successes, the need to revitalize Mizuno became clear during the 1980s. The company suffered from a lagging corporate image, not to mention a sluggish Japanese economy, so in 1982 Mizuno launched an American division under the direction of Jack Curran. A sports equipment veteran, Curran worked at bowling's Brunswick

Corporation for 18 years and headed golf's MacGregor Corporation until 1982. At the Masters golf tournament that year, Curran asked Mizuno executives to consider starting a U.S. operation. The company had been contemplating the idea for some time and decided Curran's timing was right. He began Mizuno Corporation of America from his home, with one other employee for support. "From the Japanese side," Curran explained to *Industry Week,* "we had strong R&D, a strong product line, and, initially, a strong sourcing base overseas. Within a relatively short time, Mizuno had catapulted into the American sporting-goods scene with several technologically advanced products and nationally known endorsers."

The following year, the U.S. division launched the Black Turbo, a golf club with a graphite head. The company also offered its first mobile golf workshop to the pros on the Professional Golf Association's (PGA) tour in 1983. Within two years, Mizuno Corporation of America's golf division established a manufacturing plant in Norcross, Georgia.

In 1987, Masato Mizuno, grandson of the firm's founder, gained control of all the company's operations, assuming the presidency from his father. Though considered an "untraditional" leader, Masato Mizuno nevertheless helped the company prosper. According to one company advisor, commenting in *Sports Illustrated,* Masato Mizuno is "not the regular Japanese president of a billion-dollar company." This Mizuno had studied at Carthage College in Wisconsin during the 1960s. He utilized technology to enhance the company's operations, added a computerized inventory system, and increased automation in manufacturing; for example, Mizuno installed robots able to wind 4,000 baseball cords daily in company plants. He was also an aggressive marketer. By 1989, Mizuno controlled 30 percent of the Japanese golf club and baseball markets. Mizuno's goal became global dominance of the markets. He espoused "full-service sports marketing," including computerized golf lessons, acupuncture treatments, and massages for Mizuno customers. "We want to be able to meet every sports need," he explained to *Sports Illustrated,* "and we want true internationalization. Those are our goals."

By the end of the decade, the company secured the endorsements of numerous star U.S. athletes, including football's Joe Montana and John Elway and Olympians such as Carl Lewis. Two hundred and forty major league baseball players in the United States utilized Mizuno equipment during 1989, notably gloves and shoes. "You see the name so much," San Francisco Giants manager Roger Craig told *Sports Illustrated,* "you hardly think it's Japanese." The company also launched new products. Prior to the Seoul Olympics in 1988, track-and-field star Florence Griffith Joyner signed a million dollar shoe contract with Mizuno, then in 1989 the company introduced her line of Flo-Jo sportswear. Mizuno also made golf history that year, debuting the first all-titanium iron—the MGC-35. By the end of the year, Mizuno achieved $1 billion in sales.

Dominance in the 1990s

In 1990, Japan's Ministry of International Trade and Industry (MIDI) hoped to make sports and recreation a formidable industry for the country, projecting an $821 billion market by the year 1999. Masato Mizuno committed to this vision as well. He told *Time:* "Grandfather founded the company, and father introduced technological innovations. Now it's my turn to expand and truly internationalize it."

Capitalizing on the cost-effective labor market and its close proximity to the U.S. border, in February 1990 Mizuno established a $3 million production facility in Juarez, Mexico, for the manufacture of golf bags. This brought the company a product total of 35,000 and dominance in the United States. Hundreds of baseball players in both U.S. professional leagues wore Mizuno shoes and gloves, and one million of the company's golf clubs sold in the United States in 1990, including the first all-titanium wood—the Ti-110.

Mizuno gained further notoriety at the summer Olympics held in Barcelona, Spain, during 1992. Twelve of the gold medalists at the games wore Mizuno shoes, as did 30 of the silver and bronze medalists. In fact, more winning track-and-field athletes wore Mizuno footwear than that of any other manufacturer. The company improved its manufacturing processes in 1992. It began sheet rolling golf shafts and utilizing structural reaction injection molding (SRIM)—a completely automated, nonsolvent process—for tennis racket production. Mizuno also started production of graphite skis, tennis rackets, baseball bats, and sports shoes. Employing composites stronger and wood or steel, the company incorporated 20 types of carbon fiber into its production operations.

By 1993, Mizuno achieved $1.6 billion in sales and controlled a 7 percent market share of the $750 million golf-club industry, making it the world's number one sporting goods manufacturer. With products built around technology and innovation, Mizuno launched new items such as the Reactor tennis racquet, which claimed a 200 percent increase in accuracy owing to its symmetrical head and patented string system.

In America, Jack Curran became president of Mizuno Corporation of America, based in Atlanta, Georgia. This branch of the company grew to include 320 employees, five divisions (one in Canada), and manufacturing operations in Georgia, Texas, and Mexico. Mizuno Corporation of America earned $100 million in sales in 1993.

A division of Mizuno's U.S. arm, Mizuno Golf, began an aggressive marketing campaign to promote the TC29 irons in 1994. The company named Doug Woods as marketing director and developed trade and consumer print ads for publication in the fall, as well as television ads for 1995. Similarly, Mizuno Corporation of America's baseball division earned notoriety in 1996 as the only manufacturer of handcrafted professional catchers' mitts.

Company Perspectives:

Mizuno's mission is to contribute to society through the advancement of sports and the promotion of better sporting life.

Once again, Mizuno played an active role in the 1996 Olympics, which were held in Atlanta, Georgia—home of Mizuno Corporation of America. Athletes wearing Mizuno products performed well in the games. In fact, five of every six medal winners in baseball and softball used Mizuno equipment. Mizuno opened an exclusive chain of retail stores that year to market its baseball equipment. Known as K-KLUB, the shops offered high-quality baseball and softball products with the intention of promoting and developing both sports.

Beginning in October 1996, Mizuno became involved with the Golf Network. The network's digital satellite broadcasts provided a base for the company's public activities. Mizuno averaged 15 to 20 commercials each day on the Golf Network.

Mizuno also renewed it commitment to the environment in 1996. The company began preparations for ISO 14001 qualification that year. Mizuno hoped its main Yoro factory would qualify for the International Standards Organization's benchmark for management control systems that protect the environment. Indeed, the company achieved its certification on June 30, 1997, prompting Masato Mizuno to comment: "Every possible effort will now be exerted to publicly show our corporate attitude, that Mizuno has much interest in and is actively tackling global environment problems."

A Tightening Market in the Late 1990s

By 1997, the market for sporting goods had become a "confining situation," according to Mizuno's Letter to Shareholders in the company's 1997 annual report. Masato Mizuno explained: "All of us at Mizuno will promote management renovation to get us out of such a stringent situation. At the same time, the organization will continue to improve, so that we can cope with any changes in the form of physical distribution. In this way, business forces as well as the strength of product development will be enhanced to further improve business performance and strengthen our corporate structure." Mizuno pledged to execute management reforms, to institute a merchandising policy, to establish a personnel management system, and to develop overseas marketing and diversified distribution channel strategies. The company's long-term plans included global marketing strategies, as well as using state-of-the-art technology and precision craftsmanship in production. Mizuno established a production base in Shanghai, China, and began developing global sales and production tactics.

During this time, Mizuno liquidated the Mizuno Corporation of America and closed the golf equipment and apparel distribution company located in Georgia, owing to unprecedented losses. Instead, the company established Mizuno USA Corporation as its presence in the United States, consolidating its golf brands into T-ZOID and cutting its shoe line by 40 percent. Mizuno also decreased staffing and marketing costs at the U.S. subsidiary, but continued developing its golf products. In order to achieve larger and lighter club heads, for example, Mizuno adapted 7J55—a super Duralumin alloy manufactured by Kobe Steel—for its golf clubs. Lighter than titanium, this strongest type of Duralumin was typically used in aircraft and defense equipment.

Mizuno acted as a gold sponsor of the winter Olympic games held in Nagano, Japan, in 1998. To encourage the spirit of the games, the company offered prizes on 200 Japanese media stations. Mizuno also auctioned Olympic t-shirts over the Internet.

Mizuno's long-term plans after 1998 included global development of the markets for its merchandise. In particular, the company hoped to advance the positions of it golf, baseball, running, and soccer products in the worldwide marketplace.

Principal Subsidiaries

Mizuno Canada; Mizuno Corporation Niederlassung (Germany); Mizuno Corporation (United Kingdom); Mizuno France; Mizuno Taiwan Corporation; Mizuno USA Corporation.

Further Reading

"Alloy for Golf Clubs," *New Materials Japan,* October 1, 1997.

"Japanese Companies in the United States: Miscellaneous," *Japanese-U.S. Business Report,* September 1, 1997.

Kenise, Seiichi, "Master of the Games: Japan's Leading Sporting-Goods Maker Takes Aim at the U.S.," *Time,* July 16, 1990, p. 49.

Lord, Mary, "Japan's Sports Machine: Looking Greensward, Tokyo Is Taking Aim at the Leisure Industry," *U.S. News & World Report,* October 15, 1990, p. 84.

McKenna, James F., "Jack Curran: Up against an All-Star Lineup," *Industry Week,* September 6, 1993, p. 22.

"Mizuno Golf Looks for Creative," *ADWEEK* (Eastern edition), July 4, 1994, p. 28.

Smith, Shelley, "Grandpa Would Be Pleased," *Sports Illustrated,* August 21, 1989, p. 62.

—Charity Anne Dorgan

Network Associates, Inc.

2805 Bowers Avenue
Santa Clara, California 95051-0963
U.S.A.
(408) 988-3832
Fax: (408) 970-9727
Web site: http://www.nai.com

Public Company
Incorporated: 1989 as McAfee Associates, Inc.
Employees: 1,600
Sales: $612 million (1997)
Stock Exchanges: NASDAQ
Ticker Symbol: MCAF
SICs: 7372 Prepackaged Software

Network Associates, Inc. (NAI) is the world's largest provider of computer network security and management software. It is also the tenth largest independent software company overall, with more than 1,600 employees worldwide and operations on six continents. The company was formed through the 1997 acquisition of Network General, Inc. by McAfee Associates. NAI's flagship product is an integrated network security and management solution called Net Tools. Net Tools is built around two software suites: Net Tools Secure, which includes the antivirus applications that first brought McAfee to prominence; and Net Tools Manager, which includes Sniffer, the network management tool created by Network General. NAI currently maintains a presence in about 65 countries. It is estimated that 80 percent of the companies on the Fortune 100 list rely on NAI products to keep their computer networks running smoothly.

The Beginnings of NAI

The business that would eventually evolve into NAI began to take root in the mid-1980s. At the time, John McAfee was working as a senior engineer for Lockheed Corporation. As a spare time hobby, McAfee began operating his own computer bulletin board in 1986. Through his bulletin board, McAfee quickly became aware that computer viruses were one of the

hottest topics among the electronically inclined. McAfee began working on a software product that could scan for viruses. In 1987 he began distributing his first antivirus product as shareware through his bulletin board.

The antivirus software was instantly popular. From the start, McAfee's strategy was to hook individual users on the software. The individuals would then take it to work, and those corporations would like it so much that they would happily pay the licensing fee. By 1989 the product had begun to penetrate the corporate market significantly. McAfee decided to turn the operation into a real company, dubbed McAfee Associates, that year. McAfee's company lost $95,000 on revenue of $48,000 during its first year of operation. By 1990 money from corporate purchases began to pour in. Sales reached $1.6 million that year, and McAfee earned a cool million in profit. In January of 1990, McAfee quit his job at Lockheed to concentrate on the new venture full-time.

By 1991 McAfee's profit zoomed to $4.3 million on revenue of $6.9 million. A study by the San Jose, California research firm Dataquest Inc. indicated that as of November of 1991, 62 percent of antivirus software users bought licenses from McAfee. In spite of the product's popularity, the company continued to give its software away to anybody who wanted it. All they had to do was download it from one of thousands of electronic bulletin boards. As risky as this system seemed, by 1992 McAfee had 10,000 paying licensees at corporations, government agencies, and other institutions, including 66 Fortune 100 companies. A big factor in McAfee's spectacular surge during 1992 was the widespread panic about a computer virus called Michelangelo, which destroyed all of the data on a computer's hard drive. By coming up with a cure for Michelangelo, McAfee not only sold lots of antivirus software, but also became the focus of a great deal of media attention. During the Michelangelo scare, McAfee was quoted widely as predicting that the virus could affect as many as five million PCs worldwide. As it turned out, the impact was far smaller.

An IPO in 1992

McAfee went public in October of 1992, raising $42 million in an initial public stock offering. By 1993 the company had licensed its antivirus software to more than 15,000 corporations.

347

One of the most amazing aspects of McAfee's phenomenal success in its early years was its stunning after-tax profit margin of about 45 percent, a figure substantially higher than the industry average. The key was in the company's minimal overhead costs. As late as 1993, McAfee still had only 36 employees. This was made possible by the fact that McAfee software was distributed electronically. There was no need for the labor, equipment, or space a company would normally need for manufacturing, packaging, distributing, and marketing operations. All the company needed were programmers, support personnel, and some computers, all of which fit neatly into 6,400 square feet of space in Santa Clara, California.

In spite of McAfee's success, however, the stock market was not always kind. In 1993 stories began spreading that the company's Michelangelo cure, known as Clean-Up, was causing damage of its own to the computers on which it was installed. Although these claims were apparently exaggerated, McAfee saw the value of its stock plummet from the mid-20s to below ten during the early part of the year. Further bad press resulted from a lawsuit that forced McAfee to stop distributing two of its applications because they were incorrectly identifying Imageline Inc.'s PicturePak software as a virus carrier.

After suffering a mild heart attack later in 1993, McAfee handed over the day-to-day operation of the company to Bill Larson, who had been recruited from his position as vice-president of sales and marketing at Sun Microsystems. Larson, who had also spent time at Apple Computer, was given the title of chief executive officer, and McAfee dubbed himself chief technology officer. From that post, McAfee's chief role was to get back to his first love—namely, developing new technologies—while also seeking out acquisition candidates. With Larson at the reins, the company sought to broaden its offerings beyond virus battle gear. His goal was to make McAfee a software company that happened to distribute its wares electronically, rather than just an antivirus company. Distributing software without having to ship boxes around remained central to the company's approach. Electronic distribution not only saved money, but it also made it possible to provide upgrades almost every month—a necessity to keep up with new viruses popping up every day—rather than every 18 months like most software companies.

Despite its high-profile role in the Michelangelo affair, McAfee was still stuck in the minor leagues of software companies as long as it was relying strictly on antivirus packages. In Larson, the company found a leader who could take the company to the next level. Expanding into areas outside of virus detection, McAfee bought two network-management software companies in 1994. By the middle of the year the company was offering about a dozen new software tools designed to help automate network management. Although Larson managed to convince a reluctant McAfee that they should sell their products in stores, the new network software also would be offered as shareware on a free-trial basis.

Focus on Networks in the Mid-1990s

With success inevitably comes competition. Even with the presence of bigger companies such as Symantec, however, McAfee still commanded about two-thirds of the market for antivirus software. Meanwhile, the company sought to attain a position in network management software as dominant as the one it held in virus combat. Larson pulled this off mainly through acquisitions, using McAfee's slow but steady trickle of reliable cash flow. In 1994 McAfee purchased Brightwork Development Inc., the New Jersey-based maker of the BrightWorks network management software suite, and the network application company Automated Design Systems, based in Atlanta. The following year McAfee bought Saber Software Corp. for $40 million. The acquisition of Saber, combined with the earlier purchase of Brightwork, gave McAfee control of 41 percent of the U.S. market for LAN management software.

For fiscal 1995, McAfee earned $15 million on sales of $90 million. By 1996 antivirus programs were generating only 60 percent of the company's revenue, although it still dominated the market. The rest came primarily from network security and management software products, which McAfee was able to sell at prices not much more than half of what its competitors were charging, since McAfee distributed its products over the Internet and the others had to shrinkwrap theirs and ship them to retail outlets. In come circles, Larson's work was seen as nothing short of a miracle. In a 1996 article, *PC Week* trumpeted, "What's happened to McAfee since Michelangelo . . . is a classic software industry turnaround story. Actually, since the company was never really going anywhere to begin with, blast-off might be a better word."

McAfee's string of successful acquisitions was interrupted briefly by its failed attempt to buy Cheyenne Software, Inc. for $1 billion. It turned out that Cheyenne, a developer of storage software for computer networks, was not keen on the idea of being taken over by McAfee. Cheyenne mounted a takeover defense strategy that included a media blitz publicizing the bid and disparaging Larson both personally and professionally. A war of words ensued, with both sides working the media furiously. Larson eventually withdrew the offer, but not before cementing his reputation as a brutal fighter in the corporate arena.

Nasty as it was, Larson's scuffle with Cheyenne CEO ReiJane Huai was a mere tune-up bout for his conflict with Gordon Eubanks, chief executive of McAfee's archrival Symantec. In the spring of 1997 Symantec filed a suit alleging that McAfee had stolen some of its proprietary code from a product called CrashGuard for use in one of its own software products, PCMedic. In response, McAfee countered with a $1 billion dollar defamation suit. As the verbal sparring heated up, Larson sent out a press release in which Eubanks was described as ''once himself an accused felon for trade-secret violations,'' in reference to a criminal case involving an employee Symantec had lured away from another rival, Borland International. Since Symantec had been cleared in the case, many observers saw Larson's comment as a bit of a cheap shot. The two companies also exchanged accusations about misleading advertising claims on a regular basis. The rivalry between Larson and Eubanks, epic in the eyes of the software industry, accomplished something else—it kept the company's name in the headlines of newspapers and trade journals. Larson has been known to play hardball with other industry executives as well, notably Alan Solomon of British competitor Dr. Solomon's Software Ltd., whose name McAfee plastered over with the word ''retired'' in a 1996 ad, accompanied by the slogan ''no wonder the doctor left town.''

Meanwhile, McAfee's acquisition binge continued, notwithstanding the aborted takeover bid for Cheyenne. The year 1996 brought two significant annexations. Vycor Corporation of College Park, Maryland was purchased for $9 million and FSA Corporation, a Canadian security software manufacturer, was bought for $14.8 million. This expansion helped the company double its revenue in fiscal 1996 to $181 million, with net income soaring to $39 million.

1997 Merger Created Industry Giant

These acquisitions were followed by the 1997 purchase of Japanese antivirus software manufacturer Jade KK for $21 million. The climax of McAfee's expansion drive came later that year, when the company acquired Network General, a California-based network management software company, for $1.3 billion. Network General, which was actually larger than McAfee, was merged into the company to create Network Associates, Inc. (NAI), which instantly became the undisputed leader in the field of network management and security and the tenth largest independent software company of any kind. In Network General, the company obtained the well-regarded diagnostic tool Sniffer, one of the industry's leading products for troubleshooting and monitoring the performance of computer networks. Larson was named chairman and chief executive of NAI, and Network General CEO Leslie Denend took the title of president.

Even the absorption of Network General was not enough to satisfy Larson's appetite. Rather than rest, NAI plunged on with its master plan of industry domination. In December of 1997 NAI paid $35 million in cash for Pretty Good Privacy, Inc., a California maker of encryption software. Pretty Good Privacy's encryption products then were bundled with McAfee's antivirus software to create the Net Tools Secure portion of NAI's Net

Tools package. Further acquisitions followed in 1998, including Trusted Information Systems, Inc. and Secure Networks, Inc. These additions further enhanced NAI's reputation as the dominant force in network security and management.

July 1998 marked another important merger agreement for Network Associates, this time with Cybermedia, Inc., the producer of computer fix-it software products such as First Aid, Oil Change, and Guard Dog. Cybermedia benefitted from the deal by gaining access to NAI's well-established marketing, distribution, and sales services, giving Cybermedia products increased access to the computer software marketplace. The merger gave NAI an even larger array of product offerings, adding Cybermedia's diagnostic and problem-prevention software solutions to its already huge line of computer safeguarding applications.

Principal Subsidiaries

Cybermedia, Inc.

Principal Divisions

Net Tools Secure Division; Total Service Desk Division; World Wide Sales.

Further Reading

Carlton, Jim, ''Network Associates Agrees To Acquire Encryption Firm,'' *Wall Street Journal,* December 2, 1997, p. 1A.

Clark, Don, ''Antivirus Marketer Finds Tough Treatment Pays,'' *Wall Street Journal,* July 29, 1997, p. B1.

——, ''McAfee Associates Agrees To Acquire Network General for $1.3 Billion in Stock,'' *Wall Street Journal,* October 14, 1997, p. A3.

Daly, James, ''McAfee Pushes Beyond Virus Market,'' *Computerworld,* September 13, 1993, p. 131.

Gomes, Lee, ''McAfee's Anti-Viral Outbreak,'' *PC Week,* June 3, 1996, p. A1.

Helft, Miguel, ''McAfee's Pretty Good Deal,'' *San Jose Mercury News,* December 2, 1997, p. 1C.

——, ''Samurai Executive,'' *San Jose Mercury News,* March 29, 1998.

''McAfee Associates,'' *Fortune,* July 11, 1994, p. 124.

''$1.3 Billion McAfee Deal To Flesh Out Software Line,'' *New York Times,* October 14, 1997, p. D6.

Power, William, ''An Anti-Virus Crusader Gets Infected,'' *Wall Street Journal,* March 1, 1993, p. C1.

Weeks, Laurie Delater, ''McAfee, Maker of Antiviral Software, Plans Offering To Build on Its Success,'' *Wall Street Journal,* September 21, 1992, p. A4D.

Wilson, David L., ''California Software Firm McAfee To Acquire Network General,'' *San Jose Mercury News,* October 14, 1997, p. 101.

Woolly, Scott, ''The New Distribution,'' *Forbes,* November 4, 1996, p. 164.

—Robert R. Jacobson

New Balance Athletic Shoe, Inc.

61 North Beacon Street
Boston, Massachusetts 02134
U.S.A.
(617) 783-4000
Fax: (617) 787-9355

Private Company
Incorporated: 1906 as The New Balance Arch Company
Employees: 1,600
Sales: $555 million (1997)
SICs: 3149 Footwear Except Rubber, Not Elsewhere Classified; 3021 Rubber & Plastics Footwear

A leading second-tier athletic footwear company, New Balance Athletic Shoe, Inc. manufactures running, hiking, tennis, basketball, and cross-training shoes, offering its footwear in a broad range of width sizes. New Balance, in contrast to its larger competitors, manufactured nearly all of its footwear in the United States, as opposed to manufacturing its merchandise overseas. The company's five, company-owned manufacturing facilities during the late 1990s were all located in Massachusetts and Maine. In addition to its lines of footwear, New Balance also produced a variety of athletic apparel.

Early 20th Century Origins

New Balance was founded in 1906 in Belmont, Massachusetts, where the company began operations as The New Balance Arch Company. Initially, the company manufactured arch supports and orthopedic shoes and, in fact, for much of the 20th century it continued to focus on this narrow, niche-oriented business line, rarely expanding and never moving beyond the boundaries of its native state. Like its physical growth, The New Balance Arch Company's financial growth occurred at a crawling pace as well, inching nearly imperceptibly forward as the decades passed. About the only notable achievement during the company's first half-century of existence was the establishment of a solid reputation, a renown forged by the quality of its specialty shoes and buttressed by decades of consistent high-quality craftsmanship. Though the work of the company was held in high regard, there was only a small circle of customers who could profess to the quality of New Balance's footwear. Beyond this tight circle, the company was unknown; it was a small, Northeastern enterprise blanketed in anonymity.

Widespread notoriety and a worldwide customer base eventually would come New Balance's way, but it would take roughly 70 years before the New Balance brand name stormed onto the national stage. One important step in this direction was taken sometime before the 1950s, when New Balance began manufacturing specially designed orthopedic footwear for baseball players and track and field athletes. The foray into the athletic market was a pivotal one, moving the company into a business area that years later would provide plenty of fuel to drive its financial growth upwards. It also was an entry most likely forced upon the company by special requests from the athletes themselves, rather than arising from management's own initiative, but however the diversification originated, its occurrence planted the seed for further involvement. In 1955 the seed flowered, this time under management's directive, when New Balance applied its experience in producing specially designed athletic footwear to a new shoe dubbed "Trackster," a ripple-soled running shoe for men. The Trackster was unique, manufactured in a range of widths ranging from AA to EEEE, which set it apart from all other competing brands. Like its predecessor New Balance models, the Trackster gained a loyal following, winning over wearers who admired the workmanship and tailored fit of the shoes. But, like all New Balance models before it, the Trackster enjoyed only a limited customer base. The majority of Trackster sales were made through mail order purchases from local high schools and colleges. No other attempt was made to market the shoe. Although New Balance had moved into a promising market, one that offered a greater potential for growth than the market for orthopedic shoes and arch supports, the personality of the company had not changed. New Balance remained tied to its demure roots, preferring a corporate existence in the shadows rather than a more ambitious life as an innovative trendsetter with mass-market appeal. New Balance's mellow and staid existence persevered for years after the introduction of the Trackster, but in the early 1970s an abrupt change took place, sparked by the arrival of a new owner, James S. Davis.

New Ownership in the 1970s

A 1964 graduate of Middlebury College, Davis was 28 years old when he acquired New Balance in 1972. Academically, Davis's interests were in biology and chemistry, but he only pursued these disciplines tangentially as a professional. His chief interests were in marketing and sales, and he learned these skills while working as a sales representative for a high-technology medical electronics company. After two successful years in sales, Davis was promoted to sales manager, but he did not linger long in his new position. By the beginning of the 1970s Davis was ready to fulfill his next dream: owning and managing his own business. A friend of Davis's suggested that he talk to Paul Kidd, who wanted to retire and sell his company, New Balance Shoes. Davis talked with Kidd and spent some time investigating the company by canvassing New Balance's small band of customers. His findings piqued his interest. "I felt that leisure-time products would be a high-growth market," Davis remembered, recalling his thoughts prior to purchasing the company, "and I found that New Balance had a good product. After running in them myself, I was very impressed with the shoe. I got the same reaction from other runners. The company had relied entirely on word-of-mouth advertising and I was confident that with some marketing, sales could be expanded substantially." Using his savings and money obtained from a long-term bank loan, Davis bought New Balance in 1972 for $100,000, the same amount the company was collecting in sales per year.

When Davis acquired New Balance, the company employed five workers who worked in a Watertown, Massachusetts garage producing approximately 30 pairs of Tracksters per day. Davis was intent on dramatically magnifying the scale of the company's operations, but first he needed to establish a nationwide sales distribution system to support such growth, and he spent much of his first year establishing a network of geographically based sales representatives. After doing this, forces beyond Davis's control swept the company toward prolific growth, making his tenure of ownership overwhelmingly successful soon after he took control. The era of recreational jogging exploded with widespread excitement in 1973 and 1974, as vast multitudes took to the streets and parks and began logging miles in earnest. In a matter of months, running transformed from an activity that attracted only serious racers and physical fitness enthusiasts into major leisure-time activity. The timing of Davis's acquisition had proved superb. Amid the sweeping passion for running appeared a collection of new magazines that catered to the jogging enthusiast, one of which was *Runner's World,* which in 1975 published its first annual supplement that rated the leading running shoes. In the first issue, New Balance placed third, an encouraging result in itself, but the following year, in October 1976, the New Balance 320 was judged to be the best running shoe in the world, with two other New Balance entries placing third and seventh. The notoriety received from being billed as the best tied New Balance to a rocket; at company headquarters in Watertown the telephone did not stop ringing with urgent requests for the New Balance 320. "Our biggest problem," Davis noted, "was getting enough of them out the door."

Energetic Growth Begins in the Mid-1970s

Quickly, Davis found himself marketing a highly popular product, the success of which forever altered the face of the once sleepy New Balance. As the company struggled to meet demand by increasing production, an order backlog swelled with each passing month. Annual sales leaped upward, jumping from $221,583 in 1973 to more than $1 million by 1976 and eclipsing $4.5 million in 1977. Everything was changing at the company that labored 70 years to achieve a sales volume of $100,000, but there were aspects of the company that did not change and, in the years ahead, would stand as hallmarks of New Balance. Chief among these qualities that tied the company to its 1906 origins were its attention to craftsmanship (something Davis continued to preach as his staff frenetically endeavored to meet demand) and to making shoes for a wide range of width and length sizes. Marketing shoes with widths stretching from AA to EEEE and lengths up to size 20 was something no other athletic footwear manufacturer did, not in the 1970s and not 20 years later when the athletic footwear industry represented a nearly $10 billion business. Another thread of continuity was the company's long-time presence in New England. As the athletic footwear industry grew by leaps and bounds from the early 1970s forward, registering robust growth through the 1980s and into the 1990s, nearly all of the manufacturers moved their production overseas where labor costs were an infinitesimal fraction of labor costs in the United States. New Balance did not make such a move. Davis, through the years, was steadfast about his refusal to establish manufacturing operations in Asia, preferring to keep his production operations close to home where he believed he could exert greater control over manufacturing quality. As New Balance moved forward from the early 1970s on, its domestic production operations and width-sizing choices would stand as two of the most distinctive qualities describing the company.

The massive surge in the popularity of running that began in the early 1970s and swept up New Balance in late 1976 pressed forward into the 1980s, never losing much of its energy. Though the intensity of the running craze suggested it might be a fleeting fad, the athletic footwear industry recorded numbing growth throughout the 1980s, distinguishing itself as a legitimate multibillion-dollar business. As the industry expanded at an annual pace of roughly 20 percent, New Balance shared in the riches, registering great gains in its revenue volume. By 1982, a decade after Davis acquired a $100,000-a-year-in-sales company, New Balance was collecting $60 million a year in sales, with its future prospects as bright as they had been during the previous six years. Three years later the company was generating $85 million a year in sales, but it was at this point that the perpetually growing athletic footwear industry and New Balance parted company. Though the industry continued to expand at an exhausting rate, New Balance no longer was sharing in the riches. The company faltered, and Davis blamed himself. "We lost our focus," he later mused, recalling the years when industrywide growth pushed the company forward. "Growing that dramatically, you're behind the eight ball all the way. It was out of control. We didn't execute well . . . we tried to chase Nike and Reebok in terms of design, which we never should have done. The result was a lot of closeouts, a lot of selling below the recommended wholesale price." Between 1986 and 1989, New Balance's prolific financial growth all but vanished, leaving Davis searching for answers.

New Balance Falters During the Late 1980s

The bleakest point during the anemic late 1980s occurred in 1989 when Davis's leading executives urged him to shutter the company's domestic manufacturing operations and move production overseas. The benefits of such a move were easily identifiable. Instead of paying $10 an hour plus benefits to its U.S. workers, New Balance could conduct its manufacturing in Asia and pay manufacturing workers $1 dollar a day or less. Moreover, all of New Balance's biggest competitors had made the move overseas years before and were realizing startling financial growth—companies such as Nike, which was hurtling past the $1 billion sales mark while New Balance was beginning to flounder below the $100 million sales mark. Despite the overwhelming evidence, Davis could not be swayed. He insisted on keeping his production facilities close to the company's headquarters and, in fact, did the opposite of what his management team was prodding him to do. Davis began pouring money into his U.S. manufacturing facilities, entrenching his position as others persuaded him to move abroad. "The sizzle of the 1980s is gone," Davis proclaimed, "and the steak of the 1990s is here. We've never made sizzle. We've always made steak."

Davis reasoned that New Balance's strength was its attention to quality and the company's ability to respond quickly to retailers' needs, both of which would diminish if the company began subcontracting manufacturing thousands of miles away across the Pacific Ocean. His goal, as the 1990s began, was to shorten significantly the time required to roll out a new shoe model, slashing development time from one year to four months. Toward this objective Davis began investing heavily in capital improvements to increase efficiency and lift capacity. "What always sold," he remarked, "were our core running products and our tennis shoes. But we never had enough of them because we had spread ourselves too thin in all these peripheral areas." Accordingly, Davis narrowed the company's focus and

began funneling money into its manufacturing facilities in Massachusetts and Maine. In 1991, as sales approached $100 million and profitability returned, Davis set aside $2 million for new equipment, spreading the investment over two years. In 1993 $3 million was earmarked for high-technology equipment such as automated cutting and vision-stitching machines. By the end of 1994 $6 million had been spent during the previous three years on new equipment, including a new computer-assisted design system that, along with other new machinery, enabled New Balance's research-and-development team to cut the required time for new product introduction from one year to four months. In addition, the investment in new equipment helped boost New Balance's gross profit margins from the mid-20 percent range averaged in the 1980s to the mid-30 percent range by 1993, a figure that compared favorably to the 38 percent reported by Nike, whose labor costs were much lower.

Flourishing in the 1990s

By the mid-1990s New Balance was again a thriving enterprise recording encouraging financial gains. Revenues in 1995 were up to $380 million and successful forays into apparel and a variety of athletic footwear niches had been completed. At the company's five, company-owned manufacturing facilities—all in Massachusetts and Maine—running, walking, cross-training, tennis, basketball, and hiking shoes were assembled, giving the company wide exposure to a variety of popular recreational activities during the 1990s. When annual sales jumped to $474 million in 1996 and New Balance ranked as one of the top six best-selling footwear brands in the world and one of the top five domestically, Davis set his sights on reaching the $1 billion sales mark by 2000. Toward this end, the company made encouraging progress in 1997, when sales increased to more than $550 million. During the year, as many of the company's competitors recorded lackluster growth, New Balance exuded confidence that years ahead would bring continued success. The company established a new factory in Norway, Maine and opened a $15 million distribution center in Lawrence, Massachusetts. To reach its goal of $1 billion in sales by the beginning of the new century, the company intensified its advertising efforts, setting aside $13 million for advertising in 1998 compared with the $4 million spent in 1997. On this ambitious note, the company prepared its plans for the future, confident that the awareness of the New Balance brand name would increase as sales climbed toward the $1 billion goal.

Further Reading

Finegan, Jay, "Surviving in the Nike/Reebok Jungle," *Inc.,* May 1993, p. 98.

Melville, Greg, "Balancing Act; Bolstered This Year by Innovative New Products New Balance Continues To Buck the Odds in the Flagging Athletic Industry, *Footwear News,* December 15, 1997, p. 9.

Tedeschi, Mark, "New Balance Looks To Double Sales," *Footwear News,* January 28, 1991, p. 73.

——, "New Balance Targets $200 Mil. Sales," *Footwear News,* June 29, 1992, p. 15.

——, "The SGB Interview," *Sporting Goods Business,* February 4, 1998, p. 38.

—Jeffrey L. Covell

99¢ Only Stores

4000 Union Pacific Avenue
City of Commerce, California 90023
U.S.A.
(213) 980-8145
Fax: (213) 980-8160

Public Company
Incorporated: 1982
Employees: 2,189
Sales: $230.9 million (1997)
Stock Exchanges: New York
Ticker Symbol: NDN
SICs: 5331 Variety Stores

Operator of a fast-growing chain of stores, 99¢ Only Stores buys merchandise from suppliers getting rid of excess, discontinued, or expiration-dated inventory and sells the products in a chain of retail outlets, pricing every item at $.99. Most of 99¢ Only's merchandise consists of name brand products and nearly half is consumable goods. The company's stores—numbering more than 60 units during the late 1990s—were large, brightly-lit, and filled with shelves displaying household, staple merchandise, attracting largely middle-class customers who patronize the stores on a weekly basis. All of the company's stores during the late 1990s were located within 50 miles of downtown Los Angeles, but as the decade drew to a close there were signs of much broader geographic expansion. In November 1997, the company acquired 48 percent of Universal International, Inc., owner of a Minnesota-based deep discount chain with 49 stores in the upper midwestern United States and in Texas and part owner of a closeout retail chain with 22 stores in upstate New York. In February 1998, 99¢ Only announced a proposal to acquire the balance of Universal International, which was expected to be concluded by mid-1998. In addition to its chain of retail outlets, 99¢ Only also operated a wholesale business named Bargain Wholesale, which distributed discounted merchandise to retailers, other distributors, and exporters.

Store Origins

The founder of 99¢ Only, David Gold, most likely drew his inspiration for the deep-discount chain he created from an epiphany decades before he opened his first store. While Gold was working at a liquor store he co-owned with his brother-in-law, he reportedly noticed that bottles of wine priced at $.99 sold better than bottles priced just a few pennies more. The allure, he knew, was more psychological than financial, a ploy on the minds' of consumers that was universally effective. He vowed to open his own store one day that offered a full gamut of merchandise all priced under one dollar, but for years his entrepreneurial plan remained on the drawing board. Before putting his plan into action, Gold, the son of Russian immigrants, established himself in a business that required many of the same talents he would need to make his dream a reality. Gold began as a wholesaler, starting his own operation in 1976 that purchased and sold name brand, closeout merchandise. It was Gold's responsibility to locate the best bargains and then find retailers willing to purchase the merchandise, a task that he executed with skill. One of Gold's competitors would later note as much, remarking that Gold was "the best merchant I've ever seen." Other observers directed more praise Gold's way, with one of his retail customers describing a particular talent that was indispensable in the discount business arena. "He has a retentive, calculator mind," the candy retailer explained, referring to Gold. "He will remember the price of something you showed him a year or two earlier, even if he didn't buy it." His native inclinations served him well in the wholesale business, but always in the back of Gold's mind was the desire to open his own "dollar store." It took until Gold was in his 50s to finally put his liquor-store observations to the test, but when he did take that first fateful step, his seasoned experience as a bargain hunter bred instant success.

"I talked about opening a store that would sell only name brands and everything for a dollar for 20 years before I did it," Gold said, explaining his latent foray into the retail world. "Finally my wife said, 'Why don't you just do it'." Gold made his move in August 1982, when he opened his first 99¢ Only store in the Los Angeles area. Opening day was an unqualified

Company Perspectives:

99¢ Only Stores is dedicated to providing exceptional value. The Company's strategy is to consistently offer a wide selection of name brand value priced, consumable merchandise. The Company strives to provide its customers with a wide variety of first quality merchandise that exceeds the customers' expectations of the selections available and the quality of name-brand consumable products available that can be purchased for only 99¢. The Company believes that its name-brand focus on food and other everyday household items increases the frequency of consumer visits.

success, with long lines of eager customers waiting to see what they could purchase for $.99. News cameras appeared as well, arriving to record the event and feed the public's curiosity, which added to the panoply of the grand opening.

The excitement generated by the first store opening set a precedent, demonstrating to Gold the importance of starting out with strong publicity. As other 99¢ Only stores opened in the wake of the first store's success, grand opening promotions served as an effective tactic to draw attention to a new location. One favorite grand opening gimmick used by Gold repeatedly was offering a 19-inch television for $.99 to the first nine patrons at a new location. When news of the offer spread, it was not uncommon for people to stand outside the doors of a new 99¢ Only for as long as two days to secure one of the coveted first nine places in line.

The fascination surrounding Gold's dollar store concept, particularly as introduced into the sophisticated Los Angeles area, was difficult for some industry observers to comprehend. In fact, the concept had existed for years and had reached its peak in popularity decades before Gold opened his first 99¢ Only store. However, there were several unique characteristics of Gold's retail business that partly explained the attention it attracted. Perhaps most important, Gold filled his stores with name brand merchandise, such as housewares and household staple items, rather than an eclectic assortment of odds and ends from obscure, or anonymous, manufacturers. Moreover, the stores themselves were different from the typical deep discount store. They were large—and would increase substantially in size as the concept flowered into a full-fledged chain—and brightly lit, with attractive interiors that belied the fact that every item was available for 99¢. The manner in which the merchandise was displayed was different as well. Instead of lumping merchandise in bins, the store's inventory was displayed on color-coordinated shelving, with each color denoting a particular product category. The store's product mix was different too; instead of the trinkets that filled most dollar stores, 99¢ Only stores carried a substantial percentage (40 percent of product mix) of consumable items, such as packaged foods and beverages. Further, company executives and store managers established a policy of carrying at least one item from each product category, striving to maintain a consistency of product availability. "They (99¢ Only customers) can't walk in and think 'maybe they've got toothpaste and maybe they don't,'" explained the company's chief financial officer, "because if that's the case then they're going to shop you like a treasure hunt."

Thus, 99¢ Only Stores presented themselves as the equivalent of supermarkets, minus fresh produce, meats, and dairy goods, but with one enormous advantage: everything inside the store was priced 20 to 80 percent lower than similar items at conventional stores. The trick to filling stores with name brand, staple items at dramatically lower prices was locating the wholesale bargains in the first place (a duty that fell to Gold as the company's chief buyer) and then possessing the purchasing power to acquire merchandise in large volumes, thereby reducing the price of the wholesale merchandise. Gold was a proven bargain-hunter, and his purchasing power was augmented by keeping his wholesale business, Bargain Wholesale, running, which gave him the purchasing might to buy in great quantities. As the chain of retail stores grew larger, it developed its own ability to acquire in bulk, but with the wholesale operation always in support, the two entities formed a wonderful synergy that greatly enhanced Gold's ability to purchase in volume.

With a sound business strategy underpinning the success of the first 99¢ Only store, Gold moved methodically forward with his expansion plans. He gradually opened additional units, locating each within a 50-mile radius of downtown Los Angeles and selecting locations whose demographics conformed to his criteria. "We like to be where families are largest, because they buy the most consumables," Gold noted, explaining part of the company's site-selection process.

As expansion moved forward, Gold was careful not to accumulate any debt, and never did—even when the chain numbered more than two dozens units. As the chain grew, it developed a particular clientele, attracting middle class patrons who frequented a 99¢ Only store more than once a week. This was another characteristic of the company's stores that strayed from convention, which dictated that dollar stores generally attracted poorer clientele who visited the stores once a month and purchased decorative or nonessential items. Gold's customers used his stores as they used drug stores or supermarkets. Everyday, staple merchandise attracted a regular and loyal customer base, and it was this strength that spurred Gold forward with his expansion plans. By the mid-1990s, he was ready to significantly increase his pace of expansion.

1996 Public Offering Fuels Expansion

By 1996, there were more than 30 99¢ Only stores scattered throughout the Los Angeles area, with annual sales topping $150 million. The company was debt-free, and Gold intended to keep it that way, but he also wanted to accelerate expansion, so in May 1996 he offered a piece of ownership in the company through an initial public offering (IPO) of stock. He sold one-third of the company to the public in the IPO, with Gold family members, who occupied most of the company's top executive posts, retaining ownership of the balance. With the proceeds raised through the IPO, Gold opened a number of new stores before the end of the year, giving the company a total of more than 40 stores as it entered 1997.

The growing chain was supported by the addition of a new 840,000-square-foot warehouse in the City of Commerce, near downtown Los Angeles, that served as the nerve center for the company's operation. From this warehouse, merchandise could be quickly shipped to each of the company's stores, all clustered around downtown Los Angeles. The logistical abilities of the warehouse would be taxed in 1997, as Gold established ten additional 99¢ Only stores during the year, giving him a total store count of 52 by year's end.

Future Growth

Aside from opening ten new units in 1997, company executives busied themselves during the year by completing an acquisition. In November 1997, 99¢ Only acquired 48 percent of Minnesota-based Universal International, Inc. for $4 million in cash and merchandise. Universal, for years a wholesaler, operated a chain of discount stores named Only Deals, 49 of which were scattered throughout eight upper Midwest states, with another eight stores in Texas. Three months later, in February 1998, 99¢ Only announced a proposal to acquire the remainder of Universal International, a deal that would also give the company control over the 40 percent stake Universal held in Odd's-N-End's, a 22-store closeout retailer operating in upstate New York. The transaction was expected to be concluded by mid-1998 for approximately $17 million.

As details of the Universal International acquisition were being released, 99¢ Only was posting record financial totals and attracting the attention of investors, who had nothing but praise to heap on the company. "Forget everything you know about 99 cent stores," one analyst remarked, adding that 99¢ Only Stores "has some of the characteristics of a drug store with the price point of a dollar store. It's big and clean and merchandised like a full-priced drug store . . . and the lighting is good and people walk around the store to help you." Another analyst envisioned the proliferation of Gold's concept throughout the country, projecting that if 99¢ Only extended its presence into other major markets, there was room for 4,000 or more stores. Gold distanced himself from that claim, stating, "I don't think that far ahead. If you do," he warned, "you just get into dreaming."

With his mind focused on the near future, Gold set the pace for 99¢ Only's expansion during the late 1990s. The company was gearing towards a 20 percent annual growth rate in terms of its physical expansion, with 12 new stores slated to open in 1998. One of the new stores in 1998 was scheduled to open in the San Diego area at roughly the same time the Universal International acquisition was consummated. While some industry observers regarded the new San Diego store as the beginning of a nationwide expansion program, Gold was unwilling to entertain speculation about his company's ultimate expansion plans. What was known as the 1990s drew to a close was the encouraging success the company had recorded in the Los Angeles area, and that, should expansion into other major markets occur, results were likely to be as profitable as the company's past achievements.

Principal Subsidiaries

Bargain Wholesale; Universal International Inc. (48%).

Further Reading

Daniels, Wade, "99¢ Flush with Cash, Poised for Slow Expansion," *Los Angeles Business Journal,* December 8, 1997, p. 28.
"David Gold," *Chain Store Age Executive,* December 1997, p. 128.
Ferguson, Tim W., "Frozen Peas, Half Off," *Forbes,* August 12, 1996, p. 88.
Porter, Thyra, "99¢ Only Stores Broadening in Kitchen," *HFN—The Weekly Newspaper for the Home Furnishing Network,* March 23, 1998, p. 44.
Scally, Robert, "99¢ Only Prepares for Continued Growth," *Discount Store News,* May 25, 1998, p. 3.
——, "99¢ Only to Venture Out of LA to Eastern, Midwestern Markets," *Discount Store News,* March 9, 1998, p. 10.
——, "Brand Names Make Dollars and Sense for 99¢ Only," *Discount Store News,* March 17, 1997, p. 3.

—Jeffrey L. Covell

Norrell

Norrell Corporation

3535 Piedmont Road Northeast
Atlanta, Georgia 30305
U.S.A.
(404) 240-3000
Fax: (404) 240-3312
(800) 765-6342
Web site: http://www.norrell.com

Public Company
Incorporated: 1961 as Southeastern Personnel
Employees: 8,000
Sales: $1.3 billion (1997)
Stock Exchanges: NYSE
Ticker Symbol: NRL
SICs: 7363 Help Supply Services; 6794 Patent Owners &
    Lessors

Though it is best known as a temporary agency, Norrell
Corporation offers a wide variety of services. In 1996, the
company began using the term "Strategic Workforce Management" to describe the range of resources available under its
corporate umbrella, including staffing, outsourcing, and professional services. Working with more than 19,000 clients in the
United States, Canada, and Puerto Rico, Norrell staffs offices,
provides outsourcing for functions ranging from accounting to
shipping, and—through various corporate divisions—
addresses areas such as home health care and call center management. Thus the company is able to offer its clientele—which
includes both individuals and large corporations such as IBM
and UPS—a large and varied package of services. For its
temporary workers, who numbered 236,000 in 1997, Norrell
offers competitive benefits and an array of job assignments that
can last for one day or many years.

The Early Years as Southeastern Personnel

Born February 16, 1936, Guy Millner came from an entrepreneurial line. His father, Jack, operated a used furniture store

and a service station north of Daytona Beach, Florida, and
Millner worked at the station pumping gas during his high
school years. Yet it was his mother, Nell, who truly inspired his
business ambitions with her success selling magazine subscriptions over the telephone.

Millner later described himself as a "skinny, gawky kid,"
and in 1996 told a group of minority business people, "I was, in
my context, the underdog. I was the skinny kid, never in the
clique. Probably that did more to develop me than any influence
in my life. I developed an ambitious hunger to succeed because
success didn't come easy to me." Millner paid his way through
Florida State University with a pair of business operations. He
sold birthday cakes to classmates' parents, contacting the parent
just prior to their son's or daughter's birthday and arranging to
deliver the cakes. He also sold cookware door-to-door, using
skills he learned from motivational speaker Zig Ziglar. Working
thirty hours a week, he still managed to maintain a 2.75 grade
point average, and graduated in 1958 with a degree in political
science.

After college, Millner attended Navy basic training, and
served eight years in the Naval Reserve. In November 1961,
having moved to Atlanta, he founded a company called Southeastern Personnel to help college graduates find jobs. His was
the first company of its kind in the southeastern United States,
and indeed the temporary services industry itself was a new
phenomenon. The latter had its roots in World War II, when
women went to work filling jobs vacated by men who had gone
to war, a phenomenon symbolized by illustrator Norman Rockwell's character "Rosie the Riveter." The first major temporary
agency was Kelly Services, founded in Detroit, Michigan, in
1946; for many years thereafter, temporary services constituted
a small-scale industry devoted to placing clerical workers in
short-term jobs such as that of a typist or file clerk.

In time, the industry grew by leaps and bounds, and Millner's company grew with it. From the beginning, he had a
vision for that growth, and developed a number of unusual work
habits. He began clipping articles from business magazines,
creating an extensive resource library on various companies in
order to track their growth and methods. He also began eating
two lunches a day—soup at one, salad at the other—because he

believed that mealtimes provided one of the best opportunities for meetings. "I've sat with him on a couple of Thursday afternoons when he didn't know whether he'd be able to make the payroll on Friday," a friend told the *Atlanta Journal and Constitution* in 1996. "But he didn't know he was in a start-up business. He was sure he was in the process of building a major corporation."

Southeastern Becomes Norrell in 1963

In 1963, Millner purchased Norrell Personnel Services, a tiny Atlanta-based clerical employment agency which had only one full-time employee. Soon afterward, he renamed his own company Norrell Southeastern Corporation. At that point, the company had expanded its services to include placement of light industrial workers as well as clerical workers. In 1965, sales reached $1 million.

Norrell Southeastern became the first company in the temporary services industry to franchise its operations, which it did in 1966. Thus it was able to reach new markets, and it began to grow beyond its Atlanta base with eleven company-owned locations and one franchise. Due to its increasing geographic expansion, Millner decided to drop the "Southeastern" from his company's name, and in 1972 the company became Norrell Corporation.

Sales reached the $10 million mark in 1973, and by 1976—when they hit $15 million—Norrell had thirty-two company-owned locations and ten franchises. Three years later, in 1979, the company created a special franchise division to focus on expansion, and to serve the needs of franchisees.

Growth in the 1980s

In 1980, Norrell opened fourteen offices, bringing its total number of locations to 114. The following year, it created a subsidiary and another line of services through the establishment of Norrell Health Care, Inc. Also in 1981, having expanded throughout the United States, Norrell began operating in Canada, and in 1987 would open its first Canadian franchise, in Vancouver, British Columbia.

The 1980s held much more in store for Norrell, which experienced tremendous growth during the decade. In 1981, Norrell undertook the first in a series of acquisitions that would continue into the 1990s. In that year, it acquired three different health care staffing companies: Medical Team, East Coast Healthcare, and Adana, the last of which was a California-based corporation. Two years later, in 1983, it purchased Accurate Temporary Services.

Norrell was growing rapidly—in part through acquisitions, and in part through expansion from within. By 1983, revenues had reached $100 million, and in 1986 they were close to $230 million. In that year, Norrell purchased Workforce, bringing its total to number of company-owned locations to 293, with an additional 90 plus franchises. Also in 1986, the company celebrated twenty-five years of operations since its foundation as Southeastern Personnel.

The *Atlanta Business Chronicle* noted the milestone with an article bearing the headline "A Few Clouds on Norrell's Silver Anniversary." But the clouds turned out to be small; one of these minor worries was what Millner called a "flat" growth rate of 15 percent. "Flat?" asked Michael Pousner of the *Atlanta Business Chronicle*. "Most companies brag about 15 percent growth." Pousner went on to say of Millner, "indeed, if the tall, slim physical fitness buff is worried he doesn't show it. He feels that his company has kept abreast of some important trends that are going to lead it to renewed success in its next 25 years." Among those trends were the growth of temporary healthcare services; the use of "facility staffing," by which a company might replace an entire department with temporary employees; and the increasing numbers of mothers taking temporary jobs rather than incur the difficulties of putting their children in day care while they worked full-time.

By the late 1980s, business was booming at Norrell Corporation. "You can't miss the bright blue billboard on Peachtree Road," wrote Judith Schonbak in *Business Atlanta*. "... The words 'fast temporary relief' accompany a picture of two white marble tablets fizzing in a glass of water. [But] In this case, relief is not an antacid"; rather, the billboard campaign was just one example of Norrell's advertising. In all, the company spent $2 million on ads in 1986, including a radio spot with former talk show host and announcer Dick Cavett.

In 1987, the year it opened its first Canadian franchise, Norrell acquired London Temporary Services and American Temporaries. The next year it introduced BOSS—its Branch Office Support System—which provided a computerized database for matching up clients with temporary personnel. Also in 1988, Norrell acquired Cosmopolitan Care, and in 1990 it began a new decade by signing an agreement with Sears to provide outsourcing services.

An Expanding Vision in the Early 1990s

According to research by The Omnicorp Group, in the decade between 1986 and 1996 the staffing industry—as the temporary services industry was increasingly called—tripled in size, from annual revenues of $10.4 billion to $36.9 billion. By the year 2005, this research indicated, it would grow to a $75 billion-a-year industry. Therefore, the local, regional, and national staffing companies would have to tailor their services to a changing market. For this reason, Norrell began to broaden the range of services it offered in the 1990s.

At the core of the company's business was traditional staffing. The early 1990s, however, saw an economic recession which forced U.S. companies to cut their payroll, and Norrell responded to this by expanding into outsourcing. Under its 1990 agreement with Sears, Norrell took over management of office operations at the retail giant's Chicago headquarters. The functions covered were non revenue-producing, and included mailroom, photocopying, switchboard, shipping and receiving, and secretarial operations. The result for Sears, Norrell reported, was an annual savings of 30 percent over the cost of those operations under the traditional in-house situation.

In 1991, Norrell introduced a second component (after BOSS) to its quality system for matching clients and temporary employees. This was "Exact Match", which matched employees and clients just as BOSS did, but also screened temporary employment candidates. In the following year, Norrell established Tascor as a joint venture with IBM Corporation. Tascor, which later became a wholly owned Norrell subsidiary, assumed responsibility for administrative support functions ranging from telephone coverage to desktop publishing.

Also in 1992, Norrell added vendor consolidation to its range of services with the establishment of MVP, or Master Vendor Partnering. MVP helps corporations such as MCI and Equifax—some of the first customers for this service—to consolidate the number of vendors they deal with on a regular basis. Near the end of the 1990s, Norrell had over 100 MVP clients.

Strategic Workforce Management and the Turn of the Century

In 1993, as part of an effort to tighten its bottom line, Norrell divested most of its 55-location Health Care Division, though it retained Norrell Health Care, Inc. The latter provided home health care services ranging from cooking to the monitoring of nursing homes' compliance with insurance company regulations. Also in that year, the company introduced another component to its employee training and skills-matching system—"Matchware"—a skills assessment and office automation training software system.

Norrell's revenues reached the $500 million mark in 1993, and in the following year the company announced an initial public offering of its stock at $7 per share. It began listing on NASDAQ under the symbol NORL, and in 1995 switched to the New York Stock Exchange, where it traded under the symbol NRL. The company received the Ford Q1 Quality Supplier Award in 1994, and in 1995 earned the Arthur Andersen Enterprise Award for best business practices.

The mid-1990s saw a number of acquisitions and joint ventures, as well as the formation of new divisions. In 1994, Norrell entered a joint venture with Ernst & Young, and in 1995 it bought The Executive Speaker, an Atlanta firm which taught public speaking skills to corporate clients. Also purchased was Liken Temporary Services. Norrell Financial Staffing, specializing in placement of accountants and other financial personnel, was formed. In 1996, Norrell formed NorCross, a call-center management service, as a joint venture with The Cross Country Group, a Boston-based company. It also entered into a joint venture with Harvard Ventures called CallTask, and acquired Valley Staffing and Accounting Resources.

The year 1996 was a big one for Atlanta, which hosted the Centennial Olympic Games, and it was big for Norrell as well. The company's stock split, and by the end of the year, it

had revenues of $1 billion, with 268 company-owned locations and 133 franchises. That year, Norrell became involved in information technology services, offering technology consulting, project management, software development, documentation services, systems planning, and other services. With such a wide array of packages available to the customer, the company sought to offer bundles of services tied to the clients' needs, and the result was Strategic Workforce Management. Under this system, Norrell diagnosed problems in a company's workforce, joined company management in planning and/or implementation of services, and took responsibility for results.

For Millner himself, however, 1996 was not a year of triumph, as it marked his second failed bid for elective office. He had long had political aspirations, and to many observers possessed the skills of a politician. Despite these skills, Millner failed to win election to the state governor's seat in a 1994 race against Democratic incumbent Zell Miller. Had Millner won—it was a very close race—he would have been Georgia's first Republican governor since Reconstruction. In 1993, he had stepped down as Norrell CEO to campaign full time, but retained the title of chairman.

In 1996, during his campaign to fill the seat vacated by retiring Senator Sam Nunn, Kathey Alexander of the *Atlanta Journal and Constitution* observed that "underestimating the need to appeal personally to voters" had cost him the earlier election. Therefore Millner began getting out of the office more, in order to meet more voters. Still, he failed to win an election over Democrat Max Cleland, who had been a member of President Jimmy Carter's administration.

"This man is portrayed as a high-powered businessperson who doesn't have a heart," Mary Ann Schrecengost told the Atlanta paper. Former principal of Cedar Grove High School in financially depressed south DeKalb County, Schrecengost had personally observed Millner's generosity: he had provided funding for college scholarships, and worked with troubled youth. To ensure that word got out about himself, in October 1997 Millner stepped down as chairman to campaign again for the state governor's seat in 1998, when Governor Miller would leave office. Nonetheless, Millner retained ownership of about 35 percent of the shares of Norrell.

Just as the 1994 governor's race had featured a confusing set of names—Millner vs. Miller—the top leadership of Norrell had also included the same tongue-twisting mixture until Millner's departure in 1997. Norrell's Miller was C. Douglas Miller, who became CEO and chairman upon Millner's departure from those two offices. Miller was considering the possibility of expanding Norrell's operations overseas; but ultimately he would not make significant alterations to the formula that had established Norrell as a company with 50,000 temporary employees on assignment throughout North America on any given workday.

In 1997, Norrell made two more acquisitions, Comtex Information Systems and Houston-based M. David Lowe Staffing Services. *Fortune* magazine named the Norrell Staffing Services business group as one of the nation's top ten temporary help companies, to its "Most Admired Companies" list in 1998.

Principal Subsidiaries

Norrell Health Care, Inc.; Norrell Information Services, Inc.; Norrell Services, Inc.; Norrell Franchised Operations; Tascor, Inc.

Further Reading

Alexander, Kathey, ''Campaign '96: Millner: Selling Himself as Candidate,'' *Atlanta Journal and Constitution,* October 27, 1996, p. G5.

Brown, Carolyn M., ''Four Great Franchise Opportunities,'' *Black Enterprise,* June 30, 1995.

Fierman, Jaclyn, ''The Contingency Work Force: Just-in-Time Employees, Throwaway Execs,'' *Fortune,* January 24, 1994, p. 30.

Levin, Rob, ''Guy Millner: Entrepreneur of the Year,'' *Business Atlanta,* October 1988, p. 52.

Norrell Corporation, ''Background Information,'' Atlanta, GA: Norrell Corporation, 1998.

Pousner, Michael, ''A Few Clouds on Norrell's Silver Anniversary,'' *Atlanta Business Chronicle,* September 8, 1986, p. 3A.

Schonbak, Judith, ''Can Norrell Really Give You Fast 'Temporary' Relief?'', *Business Atlanta,* November 1986, p. 76.

Smith, Faye McDonald, ''Executive Temps: A New Breed,'' *Business Atlanta,* June 1988, p. 108.

Walker, Tom, ''The Georgia 100: Corporations Creating Space for Norrell,'' *Atlanta Journal and Constitution,* p. E16.

—Judson Knight

Occidental Petroleum Corporation

10889 Wilshire Boulevard
Los Angeles, California 90024
U.S.A.
(310) 208-8800
Fax: (310) 208-5701
Web site: http://www.oxy.com

Public Company
Incorporated: 1920
Employees: 14,270
Sales: $8 billion (1997)
Stock Exchanges: New York Pacific Amsterdam Antwerp
    Brussels Düsseldorf Frankfurt Hamburg London
Ticker Symbol: OXY
SICs: 1311 Crude Petroleum and Natural Gas; 4613
    Refined Petroleum Pipelines; 4923 Gas Transmission
    and Distribution; 2865 Cyclic Crudes and
    Intermediates; 2819 Industrial Inorganic Chemicals,
    Not Elsewhere Classified; 2812 Alkalies and Chlorine

Occidental Petroleum Corporation is a giant U.S.-based oil, gas, and chemical firm. The largest public company in Los Angeles County, Occidental pumps oil from fields in the United States and abroad; transmits oil and gas through pipelines; conducts oil and gas exploration and marketing, and manufactures chemicals, principally petrochemicals and chlorovinyls. About two-thirds of the company's business involves oil and gas, and the remaining third is dedicated to chemicals.

Early History

Occidental Petroleum was founded in 1920 in California. Its early years as an oil-finding entity were largely undistinguished, with the company almost bankrupt by the mid-1950s. It was Occidental Petroleum's early difficulties, however, that laid the groundwork for its later success. In 1956 Occidental Petroleum came to the attention of Armand Hammer, a millionaire well-known for his savvy and success in business dealings with the Soviet Union in the 1920s. In 1921 Hammer had met Vladimir Lenin, the leader of the Russian Revolution, and had become the first U.S. businessman to establish ties with the Soviet Union. Among other enterprises, Hammer had operated an asbestos mine, imported grain, and manufactured pencils. While in Moscow, he had purchased Russian art treasures at bargain prices, later reselling many art objects in the United States at considerable profit. (Later it was revealed that many of Hammer's treasures were fakes, and he was well aware of it.)

In 1956 Hammer and his wife Frances each invested $50,000 in two oil wells that Occidental planned to drill in California. When both wells struck oil, Hammer, nearly 60, took an active interest in further Occidental oil exploration.

At Hammer's first association with Occidental, the company was run by Dave Harris, Roy Roberts, and John Sullivan. Hammer's increased involvement, his strong personality, and his ability to raise money for oil drilling propelled him more and more into the limelight. By July 1957 Hammer had become company president.

Growth Under Hammer in the 1960s

Hammer's influence played a key role in the development of Occidental. As Steve Weinberg wrote in *Armand Hammer: The Untold Story*, "Few Fortune 500 corporations have come so totally under the sway of one person, especially one who owned such a tiny percentage of stock."

From his earliest days as president of Occidental, one of Hammer's overriding drives was for Oxy to diversify. In his autobiography, Hammer reported that a prime rationale for diversifying was to make Oxy too big for the other major oil companies to take over. Acquisitions included energy and chemical companies, as well as meat-producing operations.

At the time Hammer became involved with Occidental, the company was listed on very small stock exchanges on the West Coast; within several years, however, Oxy was on the American Stock Exchange, boosted by the 1959 Hammer-led acquisition of Gene Reid Drilling Company of Bakersfield, California. This acquisition was to prove fortuitous for the growth of Occidental.

Hammer attracted Reid, an engineer, and his son Bud, a geologist, to the cash-poor Occidental by offering them shares of the company. Hammer was to use the stock strategy to attract talent in other acquisitions as well.

In 1961 while working with Occidental employees Richard Vaughn, Robert Teitsworth, and the Reids, Hammer took a chance on drilling the Lathrop field, near San Francisco. It had been drilled previously for natural gas by Texaco and other companies, but only to a depth of about 5,600 feet. Reid and the others suggested that there was gas farther down, and at 6,900 feet they were proven correct. Occidental made one of the largest gas finds in California. Over the course of one night, the company found gas worth hundreds of millions of dollars.

By the end of 1961, Occidental was reporting a $1 million profit on revenues of over $4 million. The company's reputation and fortune were bolstered by continued success in natural gas, as well as through more oil finds. By March 1964 Oxy's shares were trading on the New York Stock Exchange.

Through the mid-1960s, Hammer pushed Oxy more and more to occupy an international position. The company built, for example, a superphosphoric-acid plant in England and helped build a $33 million ammonia and urea plant in Saudi Arabia. Oxy also had dealings with other countries, among them Nicaragua, Venezuela, Morocco, and Turkey.

Throughout the 1960s, Hammer kept up negotiations with Libya's King Idris for the use of Libya's natural resources. This persistence was to pay off handsomely. In 1966 Oxy's potential skyrocketed, with a billion-barrel oil field find in Libya. The find was vintage Hammer, as he wined and dined important Libyan officials and then took a risk on land previously drilled by others. The Libyan oil finds established Oxy as one of the largest petroleum companies in the world. From early 1967 until November of that same year, Oxy's stock doubled in value to more than $100 a share.

Hammer's skills as a negotiator were put to the test when the Libyan king was overthrown in a bloodless coup in 1969 and replaced by the Revolutionary Command Council, soon to be headed by Moammar Khadafi. Many analysts feared the new government would nationalize the oil fields; however, Hammer negotiated in late 1970 an agreement by which Libya received an immediate increase of 30 cents per barrel of oil, with another ten-cent increase spread over five years. Some industry observers viewed this agreement as the beginning of the end of cheap energy, as other multinational oil companies quickly signed similar agreements with their host countries. Most petroleum-producing countries called for matching increases, and oil prices headed upward.

Wheeling and Dealing in the 1970s–80s

In the early 1970s, Hammer caused a sensation with a $20 billion long-term deal with the Soviets that featured a barter agreement by which Oxy would supply phosphate fertilizer to the USSR in exchange for Soviet ammonia and urea. Many in the U.S. government criticized the deal, saying the agreement helped a communist country, despite the fact that the deal was consummated during a period of *détente* between the United States and the Soviet Union. Hammer, in fact, considered his dealings as *détente* through trade, and he continued this notion through trade with the Chinese, with whom he began negotiating in 1979. Oxy ended up with two offshore oil exploration and development contracts and a joint agreement to develop a Chinese coal mine.

In 1981 Oxy moved beyond the energy and chemical fields to acquire Iowa Beef Packers (IBP), the largest meatpacker in the United States. IBP cost Oxy $750 million in stock and proved a sound investment; in 1987 Oxy sold 49.5 percent of IBP to the public for $960 million. The astute business deal would be somewhat overshadowed, however, by numerous union strikes over pay and working conditions, as the United Food and Commercial Workers Union maintained Oxy management was unconcerned with workers at the packing plants.

In 1982 Hammer engineered Oxy's $4 billion acquisition of Cities Service Company, a huge domestic oil company headquartered in Oklahoma. The deal was viewed with skepticism by many investment bankers who, as reported in Hammer's autobiography, *Hammer,* regarded it as "Jonah trying to swallow the whale." Nevertheless, the deal made Occidental the eighth-largest oil company in the United States and the country's 12th-largest industrial concern. One of Hammer's first steps after the acquisition was to sell off those Cities Service units he felt Occidental did not need, resulting in about $1 billion in revenue for Oxy. Some 16,000 jobs were lost as the Cities Service work force dropped 80 percent.

In late 1985 Hammer made another multi-billion dollar transaction, acquiring Midcon, the huge domestic natural-gas pipeline company, for $3 billion. Shortly after the acquisition, the natural-gas industry was deregulated. The industry, as a whole, suffered from strong competition because of deregulation, and Occidental was no exception.

In a reorganization move in May 1986, Occidental Petroleum Corporation of California became a wholly owned subsidiary of the parent company. Corporate headquarters remained in Los Angeles.

The most successful of Oxy's operations during the mid- to late 1980s was its chemical branch, Occidental Chemical (Oxychem). The chemical operations were built largely through the acquisitions of other companies. Occidental purchased holdings from Diamond Shamrock Chemicals in 1986 and from Du Pont and Shell Chemical in 1987, among others. In the five year period from 1983 through 1987, Oxychem almost doubled its sales to nearly $3 billion. According to J. Roger Hirl, president and chief operating officer of Oxychem, as reported in *Chemical & Engineering News*, Oxy moved into the chemical industry as a balance to its petroleum business. While noting the cyclical nature of both the petroleum and chemical industries, Hirl said they normally were not in parallel cycles.

In 1988 Occidental, spending $2.2 billion to purchase Cain Chemical, moved up to become the nation's sixth-largest chemical producer, with sales accounting for almost 25 percent of Oxy's total. Cain Chemical then became known as Oxy Petrochemicals Inc.

The late 1980s brought challenges in the form of environmental litigations. In February 1988 Oxy was found liable for cleaning up the toxic wastes at the country's most infamous landfill, Love Canal in Niagara Falls, New York. After eight years of deliberations, a Federal judge ruled that Occidental was responsible for the improper disposal by Hooker Chemical of more than 21,000 tons of chemicals on the site, during the 1940s and 1950s. Occidental had purchased Hooker Chemical in 1968, unaware of the problems that began to surface in 1978. Before the ruling, Oxy had paid $20 million in damages to 1,300 former Love Canal residents, but nothing toward the cleanup of the site. Total cleanup costs were expected to exceed $100 million.

Also during this time, Oxy was hit by a disaster unequaled in oil production history. In July 1988, the company's Piper Alpha offshore oil platform exploded in Britain's North Sea, killing 167 people. The accident panicked the oil market, already made nervous by the continuing Iran-Iraq War. Oil prices were driven up immediately after the accident by as much as $1 a barrel. The accident was thought to be caused by a leak in a pressurized natural-gas line that triggered the massive explosion. Occidental immediately shut down the pipeline that served the platform and five others. In August 1989 Oxy resumed North Sea production. The accident was estimated to have cost over $1 billion, including an approximately $183 million settlement with families of the victims and surviving workers.

During 1989 Oxy restructured its domestic oil and gas operations, which resulted in the loss of 900 jobs, the majority from the Oxy Oil and Gas subsidiary's headquarters in Tulsa, Oklahoma. For the year 1989, however, Oxy reported an overall increase of about 1,000 workers, due primarily to expansion at IBP and Oxychem.

Hammer's Last Years

Hammer's decisions did not always please stockholders. One such circumstance centered around Occidental's funding of a $95 million museum to house Hammer's valuable painting collection. The collection was worth an estimated $250 million. Many shareholders did not see the expense of building and operating a museum as serving the best financial interest of the company. The disagreement ended in the courts, in 1990, and although the Armand Hammer Museum of Art and Cultural Center would be built as planned alongside Occidental's corporate headquarters in Los Angles, the proposed settlement called for limits on the amount of future contributions by Occidental to the museum and to other charities associated with Hammer.

Throughout his career Hammer had been able to attract talented people to Occidental. Nowhere was this more evident than with Ray Irani, the president and chief operating officer during Hammer's last years at Occidental. In 1983 Hammer had con-

vinced Irani, the president of Olin Corporation, to run Oxychem. When Irani took over, Oxychem had an operating loss of $23 million and supplied about nine percent of Occidental's total sales. In 1989 Oxychem had an operating profit of $1.2 billion and supplied about one-quarter of Oxy's total sales. In February 1990, the board of directors of Occidental proposed Irani as the successor to Armand Hammer as chairman and chief executive officer whenever Hammer should vacate those offices.

In 1989, Occidental reported that 94 percent of its revenues came from domestic operations compared to 55 percent from the same source in 1980. Still, Oxy continued to be involved in large foreign operations. In June 1990, for example, Oxy was the only U.S. company in a four-country agreement to build a $7 billion petrochemical plant in the Soviet Union, the largest-ever joint Soviet-Western project.

Restructuring in the 1990s

When Armand Hammer died at the age of 92 on December 10, 1990, the changeover in command at the top was expected: Ray Irani, president and chief executive officer under Hammer for six years, took over as chairman of the board. Irani worked quickly to get Oxy out from under Hammer's slew of pet projects, many of which had no place in an oil company's portfolio. He sold the meat packing business, shed Oxy's investments in Arabian horses, got rid of its 5.4 percent stake in the makers of Arm & Hammer baking soda, and cancelled a $485,000 contract for a fourth authorized Hammer biography. The University of California agreed to take over the Armand Hammer Museum, which became known as the UCLA Arts Center. Occidental even sold off the "Codex Hammer," a Leonardo Da Vinci manuscript Hammer had bought with $5.6 million of the company's money and renamed for himself. Irani also announced he was cancelling the company's billion-dollar petrochemical deal with the Soviet Union. Perhaps most importantly, Irani outlined a strategy to reduce the company's debt load by 40 percent by 1992. Upon Hammer's death, the company's debt stood at a staggering $8.5 billion, and dealing with this was paramount. Irani's strategy called for selling unneeded assets, and also included slashing stockholder dividends to $1 a share from $2.50.

Occidental's restructuring went on in several stages throughout the early 1990s. By the end of 1992, the company had met its first set of goals, reducing its debt by $3 billion. However, Occidental announced that it still intended to cut its costs by $300 million by cutting capital spending, eliminating jobs, and instituting a salary freeze. At the same time, the company dedicated more money to international oil and gas exploration, increasing its production of oil from abroad, with operations in Yemen, Oman, and Ecuador. At that time, about half of the company's revenues came from its chemical business. In 1995, Oxy announced it was simplifying the management of its oil and gas operations in an attempt to grow that business and get away from its dependence on chemicals. Occidental formed a single operating company to take on all its oil and gas business, and then split this into four divisions: exploration, production, enhanced oil recovery, and finance and administration. The company hoped that by focusing its resources, it could both cut costs and improve future earnings.

Occidental's next big move came in 1997. The company spent $3.65 billion to buy a huge oil field, the Naval Petroleum Reserve, from the U.S. government. The naval reserve, called Elk Hills, produced both oil and natural gas. The field, near Bakersfield, California, had been owned by the government since 1900, as a secure source of domestic oil. Deciding it no longer needed the source, the government auctioned the reserve in a deal that was the largest privatization in U.S. history. Occidental bought 78 percent of Elk Hills; the remainder was already owned by Chevron Corporation. To finance this purchase, Oxy decided to sell its MidCon unit, a huge natural gas pipeline the company operated between the Gulf and western states and Chicago. Oxy soon sold MidCon to KN Energy Inc. for almost $4 billion. The company also sold off various oil production units it judged unnecessary, including properties in Louisiana, Mississippi, and Wyoming. By mid-1998, Occidental had transformed itself into a much more focused company than it had been during Hammer's reign. It had five major oil and gas operations in the United States, including Elk Hills, which was thought to have huge growth potential. For international growth, the company counted on a blossoming oil field it ran in Qatar. Only about one-third of Occidental was still invested in chemicals, freeing the company somewhat from the volatility of the chemical business cycle. Occidental was not nearly as complicated as it had been in 1990. It had reshaped itself into a genuine oil company, instead of a sprawling conglomerate, and though its growth in the 1990s still underperformed the stock market in general, Occidental had by 1998 put itself in a position to do much better.

Principal Subsidiaries

Occidental International Corporation; Occidental Oil and Gas Corporation; Occidental Chemical Corporation.

Further Reading

Brown, Christie, "The Master Cynic," *Forbes,* October 17, 1994, pp. 364–68.
Bryant, Adam, "At Occidental, So-So Results But Big Pay for the Boss," *New York Times,* March 19, 1998, pp. D1, D8.
Fan, Aliza, "Occidental Plans Broad Restructuring to Save Firm $100 Million per Year," *Oil Daily,* October 26, 1995, p. 1.
Fritsch, Peter, "Occidental Plans $3.65 Billion Purchase," *Wall Street Journal,* October 7, 1997, pp. A3, A6.
Glover, Kara, "Ray Irani Brings New Ways to Occidental," *Los Angeles Business Journal,* March 23, 1992, p. 12.
Hammer, Armand, and Neil Lyndon, *Hammer,* New York: G.P. Putnam's Sons, 1987.
Rundle, Rhonda, "Occidental Acts to Pare Further Its 1993 Costs," *Wall Street Journal,* November 20, 1992, p. A3.
Shook, Barbara, "Oxy Nears Emergence from Restructuring as Simpler Company with New Profile," *Oil Daily,* April 1, 1998, p. 62.
Weinberg, Steve, *Armand Hammer: The Untold Story,* Boston: Little, Brown and Company, 1989.

—Mark Uri Toch
—updated by A. Woodward

Ocean Spray Cranberries, Inc.

One Ocean Spray Drive
Lakeville-Middleboro, Massachusetts 02349-0001
U.S.A.
(508) 946-1000
Fax: (508) 946-7704
Web site: http://www.oceanspray.com

Cooperative
Incorporated: 1930 as Cranberry Canners, Inc.
Employees: 2,500
Sales: $1.44 billion (Fiscal 1997)
SICs: 0171 Berry Crops; 2033 Canned Fruits and
Vegetables; 2034 Dried & Dehydrated Fruits,
Vegetables & Soup Mixes; 2037 Frozen Fruits, Fruit
Juices & Vegetables; 2099 Food Preparations Not
Elsewhere Classified

Ocean Spray Cranberries, Inc. is a marketing cooperative owned by almost 1,000 cranberry and grapefruit growers in the United States and Canada. A leader in the marketing of shelf-stable juice drinks, Ocean Spray Cranberries, Inc. is responsible for 75 percent of the cranberries sold worldwide. Since its beginning, the company has functioned as a grower-owned agricultural cooperative; however, its strong emphasis on new product introduction, advertising, and packaging places it in direct competition with many publicly owned companies. Once known only as a seasonal cranberry sauce business, Ocean Spray now markets blended juice drinks, bottled juices, juice concentrate, fresh fruits, and several other items to both retail and food service outlets year-round. Ocean Spray's Cranberry Division still accounts for the bulk of the company's operations. However, since the addition of grapefruit growers to the cooperative in 1976, the company has displayed an increasing tendency to develop a broad fruit-oriented product line to fortify its presence in the consumer market. Preserving a strong brand image, perfecting production forecasting techniques, and promoting operational efficiency have all led the cooperative to its position as the leader producer of canned and bottled juices and juice drinks in North America. Ocean Spray's stock is held by some 250 grapefruit growers in Florida and nearly 700 cranberry growers in Massachusetts, New Jersey, Wisconsin, Oregon, Washington, and Canada.

Early History

The history of Ocean Spray is naturally tied to the history and lore of the cranberry, an unusual Native American wetland fruit. Small, reddish, and distinguished by a strong, bitter flavor, the cranberry was first used by various Native American tribes in the New England area to make dyes as well as a high-energy food called pemmican: a concentrated mixture of dried venison, fat, and cranberries shaped into cakes. Cranberries were believed to have been present at the first Thanksgiving feast in 1621. The first cranberry juice recipe dates back to 1683. Throughout colonial times, cranberries also became widely used in tarts, preserves, and sauces.

Exports to Europe also began during this era. However, commercial cultivation of cranberries did not commence until the early 19th century, when Captain Henry Hall began experimenting with cranberry vines in East Dennis, Massachusetts. As many already knew, the Cape Cod marshland, with its high concentration of peat, was particularly conducive to cranberry growing. Hall, however, made the singularly important observation that when sand from the nearby dunes blew into the marshes, or bogs, the cranberries thrived. He began applying sand manually and found he could grow cranberries that were larger and juicier than those found elsewhere. Growers from another state in which the cranberry was native, New Jersey, soon followed Hall's lead. Among such pioneers were Benjamin Thomas and John Webb.

During the 1850s, cranberry cultivation spread to Wisconsin; three decades later, farmers in both Washington and Oregon began establishing cranberry bogs of their own. By the mid-twentieth century, mechanical pickers were invented to replace manual procedures, and soon wet-harvesting techniques were developed to take advantage of the cranberry's natural buoyancy.

The Ocean Spray name was conceived by a Boston lawyer named Marcus L. Urann, who gained a reputation as the "Cranberry King'' for a cranberry sauce he packaged in tins and marketed under the brand as early as 1912, as well as for his later promotions. Urann headed the Ocean Spray Preserving Co. of South Hanson, Massachusetts, and was one of the principal proponents behind a merger of similar companies to form a large, powerful cooperative. Urann reasoned that a merger would erase the stiff competition he faced from the Makepeace Preserving Co. of Wareham, Massachusetts, and The Enoch F. Bills Co. of New Egypt, New Jersey. The merger would also allow for greater marketing clout. John C. Makepeace and Elizabeth F. Lee, the other two owners involved in Urann's proposed merger, joined Urann in signing a certificate of incorporation in June 1930. A delay by Urann in transferring the Ocean Spray trademark jeopardized the merger for a short time; however, by August, Cranberry Canners, Inc. had been formed and Ocean Spray's survival was thus ensured.

Urann, as president and general manager, assumed responsibility for advancing the cooperative by meeting with and encouraging growers and by enlarging the demand for cranberries. Among the products introduced by Cranberry Canners during the 1930s were Cranberry Juice Cocktail and Ocean Spray Cran, both tart-tasting forerunners of later, sweetened juice and juice concentrate products. With the 1940s and the addition of Wisconsin, Oregon, and Washington growers to the cooperative, the product line expanded to include dehydrated cranberries (for U.S. troops) and cranberry-orange marmalade. By 1943 the co-op controlled 15 facilities for production, storage, and distribution. Because of the rising prominence of the cranberry and the Ocean Spray label, the cooperative renamed itself the National Cranberry Association (NCA) in 1946. During that same year, the company also began marketing fresh cranberries, in cellophane packaging, for the first time.

Facing a Serious Crisis That Began in Late 1959

The NCA, with a membership nearly double that of its modern-day variant, continued to sustain itself throughout the 1950s principally as a seasonal business that revolved around the Thanksgiving and Christmas holidays. Highlights of this decade were numerous, and included the incorporation—and then formal assimilation—of Canadian growers; the first Ocean Spray television commercials; the retirements of Urann in 1955, and Makepeace (who had served as secretary-treasurer) in 1957; the introduction of frozen cranberry-orange relish and frozen cranberries; and the final renaming of the cooperative in 1959 to reflect the central importance of the Ocean Spray brand.

On November 9, 1959, the newly-named Ocean Spray Cranberries, Inc. was faced with its first major crisis. On that day, the

Secretary of the Department of Health, Education and Welfare announced that residue from the potentially cancer-causing weed killer aminotriazole had been found in cranberries produced in Washington and Oregon. Because of the ill-timed announcement—just prior to Thanksgiving—Ocean Spray's entire cranberry business was in jeopardy. Cranberries quickly became known as ''cancer berries'' and hopes for any profits from that year's holiday sales were dashed.

Although the co-op's new president, George C. P. Olsson, rightly asserted that the purported danger was nonexistent, it was too late to avert the widespread fear that had arisen. Grocers were forced to take all suspect products off their shelves. Ironically, ''The History of Ocean Spray Cranberries'' records that a membership newsletter dated December 1957 had actually alerted growers to the dangers of aminotriazole—then an unapproved weed killer—which, if used, could ''cause needless expense to your cooperative and result in the condemnation of your crop.'' The Department of Agriculture had actually approved the compound in 1958 for use after harvests, but the linkage to cancer and the tests for detecting residues were not established until the following year.

The Debut of Juice Drinks in the 1960s

For a time, the co-op was in danger of folding, but a partial comeback in sales for 1960, as well as a government subsidy for unsold cranberries found to be free of residue, kept the business going. However, Ocean Spray's earlier successes had now created the problem of overproduction. New marketing avenues needed to be explored if the high demand for cranberries were to be revived. Edward Gelsthorpe, an executive with experience at both Colgate-Palmolive and Bristol-Myers, was brought in to develop a new, long-term marketing plan for the company.

Gelsthorpe's answer, unpopular at the time, was to emphasize juice drinks under the Ocean Spray brand. Between 1963 and 1968 the company committed itself to the consumer drinks market with Cranberry Juice Cocktail, Cranapple, and Grapeberry (later changed to Crangrape). The guiding philosophy was to compete against both the large soft drink and orange juice markets not through product imitation but through product diversity. As consumers became more health conscious during the 1960s and 1970s, the Ocean Spray formula for success struck a responsive chord. By the mid-1970s the cooperative was on the fast track to achieving Fortune 500 status and appeared all the more healthy after its bold expansion into grapefruit growing. A minor setback occurred in 1979 when the Federal Trade Commission, as part of an investigation of all agricultural cooperatives, threatened an antitrust action against Ocean Spray. No suit was launched, however, and so the company began the 1980s with its $235 million in annual revenues intact.

In 1981 the company made packaging history with its introduction of the ''juice box,'' a block-shaped juice container with attached drinking straw. The innovation captured a new segment of the juice-drinking public, children, and has since become a staple of the Ocean Spray product line. That same year Ocean Spray achieved its ranking as the largest domestic seller of canned and bottled juice drinks. The co-op fought vigorously to retain the title during the decade, as new competitors entered the fray, with a growing number of product introductions, including Mauna-La'i, a guava-lemon drink; Firehouse Jubilee, a tomato drink; Ocean Spray Liquid Concentrates; and Cranberry Fruit Sauces. By the mid-1980s, the company had reached annual revenues in excess of $500 million. The company also improved its distribution system, expanded its marketing to food services, and capitalized on the Cape Cod tourist industry by attracting millions of visitors each year to its headquarters and museum near Plymouth Rock.

Acquired Milne Fruit Products in 1985

One of the most important developments for Ocean Spray came in 1985 with its acquisition of Milne Fruit Products, Inc. of Prosser, Washington. A manufacturer of fruit concentrates and purees, Milne was once primarily a grape business but grew under Ocean Spray to process cherries, blueberries, blackberries, plums, raspberries, strawberries, and cranberries. Milne's largest customer was Ocean Spray, but the subsidiary also served such major food companies as Kraft General Foods, Gerber Products, Nestlé, Sunkist, Welch's, and Baskin-Robbins. Most importantly for its parent company, Milne tripled in size from the acquisition through the early 1990s and became a significant generator of non-patronage revenue, which was reinvested in the cooperative for future expansion.

The only blight on the company during the eventful 1980s occurred in 1988, when it was charged under the Clean Water Act with illegally dumping insufficiently treated effluent from its Middleboro plant into the town's sewer system. Ultimately, Ocean Spray was fined $400,000; the company also donated $100,000 in water-treatment equipment to the town of Middleboro. Since that event, Ocean Spray has become an industry leader in promoting environmentally sound operations, and has spent more than $26 million upgrading waste-treatment facilities.

While the cooperative reformed itself environmentally, it was also in the process of analyzing all of its internal operations. A program called Right Turn Only (RTO), dedicated to quality improvement, problem-solving, and teamwork, was adopted to aid Ocean Spray in remaining competitive while fostering an open working environment. In the area of market research, crucial in a brand-driven industry, Ocean Spray decided to take advantage of new database technologies by entering into a joint venture with Information Resources of Chicago. The result was a state-of-the-art software program called CoverStory that offered market information from universal product code (UPC) figures and trends. Other innovations included techniques to boost crop yields and forecast harvest results.

Billion-Dollar Company in the 1990s

Under John S. Llewellyn Jr. (who took over as president and CEO in 1987 from Harold Thorkilsen), Ocean Spray became a billion-dollar company by 1992 and continued to build on its strong brand image. A very important development in 1992 involved a joint arrangement with PepsiCo, Inc. to distribute individual cans and bottles of Ocean Spray juices and drinks. This agreement offered Ocean Spray a relatively inexpensive opportunity to increase its individual serving segment, which at the time of the agreement accounted for roughly $100 million in sales, through vending machine, convenience store, and related outlets. According to reporter Jon Berry, "The logic behind the

New Age partnership is forceful. During the past decade, Ocean Spray has burst from obscurity to become one of the acknowledged innovators in the beverage industry. But its strength has been notable only in supermarket aisles. To become an equal power in single-serve sales, Ocean Spray would have to spend millions building a distribution system."

Throughout the 1990s Ocean Spray rolled out a steady stream of new products. In 1991, Refreshers Fruit Juice Drinks and Ruby Red Grapefruit Juice Drink came on line. The following year Cran-Cherry Juice Drink joined the lineup, while Ruby Red & Tangerine Grapefruit Juice Drink was added in 1993. Craisins sweetened dried cranberries—a direct competitor to raisins in the dried fruit category—had their national launch in 1995, with Cran-Currant Black Currant Cranberry Juice Drink made available for purchase in 1997.

Ocean Spray also increasingly sought out joint ventures to extend its product line. The co-op joined with Nabisco in 1993 to market a cookie called Cranberry Newtons. Ocean Spray and Warner-Lambert joined forces to debut Fruit Waves hard candy in 1994. With PepsiCo, Ocean Spray that same year launched Breakers, a soft drink with 2 percent juice and available in three flavors. The following year saw the introduction of Cranberry English Muffins, a venture with Thomas' English Muffins. And Craisins were included in the 1996-introduced Post Cranberry Almond Crunch Cereal.

Ocean Spray also placed a high premium on effective advertising, signing Sarah Ferguson, the Duchess of York, in 1996 for the "It's Your Zing!" campaign. In March 1998 the co-op announced that it had signed tennis star Martina Hingis to a three-year spokesperson contract. Hingis' first promotion for Ocean Spray involved the 1998 debut of Ruby Red & Tango Grapefruit Juice Drink, the third member of the Ruby Red line.

Meanwhile, Ocean Spray continued to upgrade its manufacturing facilities, combining just-in-time inventory systems and computer integrated manufacturing in a 1995-opened facility in Henderson, Nevada, that increased output without increasing costs. In January 1997, Llewellyn retired as president and CEO of the co-op and was replaced by Thomas E. Bullock after a 16-month transition period. Bullock had to contend with the after effects of poor cranberry harvests in two of the previous three seasons, which forced Ocean Spray to delay some product introductions. He also soon faced the end of Ocean Spray's five-year relationship with PepsiCo after the soft drink giant announced that it planned to abandon the distribution agreement in May 1998. By the end of the 1997 fiscal year, the Ocean Spray-PepsiCo arrangement had helped Ocean Spray achieve $225 million in sales for its single-serving products (out of total revenue of $1.44 billion, or almost 16 percent). It had grown from number six to number two among makers of single-serve juices and drinks.

Surprisingly, Ocean Spray and PepsiCo announced in March 1998 that a three-year extension had been reached on the distribution agreement. In August of that same year, however, the partnership once again appeared threatened when Ocean Spray said that it might attempt to block PepsiCo's proposed $3.3 billion acquisition of juice maker Tropicana Products from the Seagram Company Ltd. The co-op believed that the purchase violated its agreement with PepsiCo. It was speculated that PepsiCo planned to distribute single-serving packages of Tropicana juices and drinks, which would directly compete with Ocean Spray products.

In December 1997 Ocean Spray acquired a major interest in Nantucket Allserve Inc., a juice drink company based in Cambridge, Massachusetts, and famous for its offbeat "Nantucket Nectars" line of single-serve drinks, including Orange Mango and Protein Smoothie flavors. Nantucket, whose younger clientele complemented the typical consumers of Ocean Spray products, would continue to operate independently. In July 1998 Ocean Spray acquired Sydney, Australia-based Processing Technologies International, a leading food technology research company and holder of the patents to the technologies used to create Craisins. The co-op, which renamed the acquired company Food Ingredients Technologies (Australia), planned to take the process used to create Craisins and apply it to numerous other fruits and vegetables, mainly to create ingredients for sale to other food companies. The potential for success of this venture appeared large as Craisins had proved to be a smash hit, becoming the fastest-growing product and the number-three brand in the dried fruit market. These deals proved that Ocean Spray was not going to rest on its cranberry laurels.

Principal Subsidiaries

Milne Food Products, Inc.; Nantucket Allserve Inc.; Food Ingredients Technologies (Australia).

Further Reading

Appelbaum, Cara, "Ocean Spray, Pepsi Ink Vending Machine Deal," *Adweek's Marketing Week,* November 25, 1991, p. 6.

Berry, Jon, "Ocean Spray Joins the Pepsi Generation," *Adweek's Marketing Week,* March 9, 1992.

Buell, Barbara, "How Ocean Spray Keeps Reinventing the Cranberry," *Business Week,* December 2, 1985.

Carton, Barbara, "Bog Heaven: Forget Cows and Corn; Let's Bet the Farm on Cranberry Crops," *Wall Street Journal,* July 23, 1997, p. A1.

"Cranberry Growers Reel under Pre-Holiday Blow," *Business Week,* November 14, 1959.

"Crushed Cranberries," *Time,* February 8, 1988.

Daly, Christopher B., "Squeezing the Humble Cranberry into a Success Story," *Washington Post,* November 21, 1990.

Deogun, Nikhil, "Ocean Spray May Try to Block PepsiCo from Acquiring Seagram's Tropicana," *Wall Street Journal,* August 6, 1998.

Donahue, Christine, "Can Ocean Spray Sell Cranberry Sauce Off-Season?," *Adweek's Marketing Week,* June 26, 1989.

Eichinger, Mark S., "Empowerment: A Blue-Collar Perspective," *Personnel Journal,* October 1991.

Elliott, Stuart, "Ocean Spray and Napier Try to Tinker with Success," *New York Times,* September 11, 1991, p. D16.

Hanson, Peter D., "How Ocean Spray Trims the Risks of Seasonal Borrowing," *Corporate Cashflow,* May 1990.

The History of Ocean Spray Cranberries, Inc., Lakeville-Middleboro, Massachusetts, 1981.

"How Ocean Spray Gave Cranberries Some Sparkle," *New York Times,* November 26, 1992, p. D1.

Ling, Flora S. H., "The Little Man's Monopoly," *Forbes,* December 8, 1980.

Pace, Eric, "George Olsson, 88, Head of Cooperative Built on Cranberries," *New York Times,* November 16, 1991.

Prince, Greg W., "The Urge to Surge," *Beverage World,* December 1995, p. 41.

Schmitz, John D., Gordon D. Armstrong, and John D. C. Little, "Cover Story—Automated News Finding in Marketing," *Interfaces,* November/December 1990.

Skilnik, Rayna, "Ocean Spray's Canny Marketing," *Sales & Marketing Management,* August 18, 1980.

Stevens, Tim, "Making Waves: Product Innovation, Widespread Distribution, and Global Expansion Set the Table for Growth at Ocean Spray," *Industry Week,* November 18, 1996, p. 28.

Swientek, Bob, "Ahead of the Pack," *Prepared Foods,* March 1995, p. 96.

Theodore, Sarah, "Ocean Spray's New Zing," *Beverage Industry,* March 1997, p. 20.

Willman, Michelle L., "Crantastic!: Ocean Spray Makes a Splash with Partnering, New Products, Fresh Flavors and Expanded Distribution," *Beverage Industry,* November 1993, p. 34.

—Jay P. Pederson
—updated by David E. Salamie

OTR Express, Inc.

804 North Meadowbrook Drive
P.O. Box 2819
Olathe, Kansas 66063-0819
U.S.A.
(913) 829-1616
Fax: (913) 829-0622
Web site: http://www.otrx.com

Public Company
Incorporated: 1985
Employees: 651
Sales: $63.8 million (1997)
Stock Exchanges: NASDAQ
Ticker Symbol: OTRX
SICs: 4213 Trucking, Except Local

OTR Express, Inc. (OTR) is a long-haul, dry-van truckload carrier which operates in the 48 continental states and generates operating margins which rank the company in the top 10 percent of all U.S. trucking companies for operating profitability. The company owns and operates more than 520 tractors and 765 trailers, which ship commodities including furniture, hardware, food products, paper products and various retail goods throughout the United States. Customers include Michaels Stores, Anheuser-Busch, Rheem Manufacturing, and J.C. Penney.

1985 Beginnings With One Truck

Beginning with a single truck, OTR Express was founded in 1985 by William P. Ward, along with co-founders Richard Walpole and Ward's wife, Kathy Ward. Prior to OTR's inception, Ward had earned his Bachelor of Science Degree in geological engineering from the University of Kansas in 1961, and a Masters of Business Administration Degree in 1963. From 1964–1966, he was an operations research analyst for Hallmark Cards, before leaving to work as an executive vice-president at the Paul Hamilton company—selling and syndicating commercial real estate—until 1973.

Following that period, Ward became chairman and president of ACA Corporation, a real estate management and syndication firm he founded in 1973 for office, multi-family and farm leasing investments. In collaboration with Richard Walpole, the two developed, sold and managed over 35 limited partnerships between the years 1973 to 1985.

By the early 1980s, the languishing real estate market surrounding Kansas City prompted Ward and his wife (a former schoolteacher), along with Walpole, to use the earnings accumulated while at ACA to supply start-up capital for the formation of OTR. The partners decided to apply the same investment concept to their trucking company that had worked for them in the real estate business, feeling that they could just as easily have partners buy shares in an individual truck as in an apartment building. Within a year, however, OTR management decided that operating their own freight line rather than leasing trucks to other carriers was a better way to go, as it would give them greater control over the performance of the drivers (equipment managers) and their vehicles.

Expansion of Assets in the Late 1980s

With little knowledge of the trucking industry, OTR's management team came into the business without a preconceived idea of how to run it most profitably. The company's unusual strategy initially targeted the long-haul, low-volume segment of the truckload market in the belief that optimization of available freight rates and trip lengths—coupled with minimization of fixed-cost per road unit—would produce higher operating margins than were considered typical in the industry. The requirements necessary for the success of this strategy included the availability of a large, geographically diverse customer base, along with frequent updates to and reprioritizations of the customers database.

Ward combined his high-tech data processing expertise with the relatively low-tech trucking business in order to compete with efficiencies of scale offered by competitors. His level of technological sophistication was relatively new to the freight industry, and so when Ward instituted the OTR system—using elaborate proprietary software that he and two OTR program-

Company Perspectives:

Our company excels in the areas of technology and customer service. We have the ability and intent to take advantage of our strengths in both of these areas. OTR has always been a cost-conscious company, maintaining a low cost per mile due to our experienced fleet of drivers, dedicated staff and high level of computer automation. We have significant potential to increase our revenue rates by adding new transportation service, modifying our customer data base and optimizing profitability on loads offered to us by customers.

mers had developed—it gave OTR an edge. The company now had increased operating flexibility. Its system could function with as much computing power as the mainframe computers utilized by other companies, but at one-tenth the cost. The new OTR software charted, tracked, and measured various facets of the company's operation, including fuel consumption and comparative automotive-parts costs. Most importantly, the computer could now position and deploy the company's fleet and freight in the most efficient way possible, saving valuable time and money.

Despite the capital-intensive nature of the trucking business, by November of 1991 OTR had acquired and begun operating a fleet of 150 tractors and 165 trailers (each rig, consisting of both tractor and trailer, costs around $100,000). With 205 employees on the payroll, and operating revenues of $12.3 million, the following year the company made their Initial Public Offering (IPO) of 1.1 million shares of common stock, raising $5 million. Proceeds were used to reduce debt that had accumulated due to the capital expansion, and also to further expand working capital in order to acquire additional equipment and to establish remote fuel facilities.

A Shift in Strategy in the Early 1990s

In 1992, OTR's trucks consumed more than $3.3 million worth of diesel fuel, accounting for about 15 percent of revenues. To economize, the company built five unmanned fuel depots, each costing around $80,000 and served directly by pipelines. The depots were strategically located in various regions across the country so that drivers could go from coast to coast without having to purchase retail fuel. Drivers used special access cards and paid wholesale prices instead of retail prices, saving as much as 15 cents per gallon. Each of the depots paid for itself within two years of installment, in the form of savings on the cost of fuel.

In 1992, Ward hired Gary Klusman as chief financial officer to help develop a strategy that would redirect the company. By that time, the trucking industry was experiencing problems related to excess capacity, causing freight rates to plummet. Competition was intense, with 40,000 trucking companies operating in the United States. Many companies were failing—as many as 10 percent of the total—and OTR executives worried that being a ''spot'' carrier that offered efficient and cheap service to freight brokers would no longer sustain them.

Klusman determined that the company needed more intensive management, and that OTR was growing too large to continue as a spot carrier—they owned too many trucks in proportion to the amount of available freight. Klusman steered the company toward becoming a ''core'' carrier that sought national accounts where they dealt directly with companies, rather than operating through brokers. That meant that OTR could command higher rates, but would need to offer greater services. At that point, the company added a $1.6 million satellite communications systems to each of its trucks. Prior to the system's installation, drivers had to contact headquarters from pay phones, and the company could not easily contact drivers concerning freight re-routing decisions. Another change brought about by the restructuring was the fact that OTR decided to create a customer service department, and hired sixteen employees to handle customer service calls.

OTR altered its fleet in order to provide better service to customers. Trailer dimensions were lengthened to 53 feet, rather than the 48 foot-length of the previous fleet. The company was equipped with 1.2 trailers for every tractor so that they could use ''drop trailers'' which could remain situated on a customers' lot for convenient loading. This made the company more responsive to the timing of their customers' production and distribution needs.

In 1992, OTR's trucks ran empty 6.05 percent of the total miles they traveled, compared to the industry average of 10 percent, which gave OTR a revenue-producing advantage. Also, at an average freight rate of $1 per mile, the company gained a 4-cent edge over the average competitor, allowing them to quote lower rates to customers. The company's average haul was 1,451 miles long, versus an industry average of 700. Despite the higher rates paid for shorter hauls, OTR management believed that the less-frequent loadings and unloadings, and decreased paperwork, were among the time/cost savings advantages that made up for the lower long-haul rates.

Technology-Driven Business in the Mid-1990s

Ward's technology-driven business stemmed from his belief that the trucking industry experienced daily shifts and turbulence. Factors such as a storm affecting crops on the west coast, for example, could hamper the normal movement of produce; similarly, a midwestern auto strike might eliminate a season of auto shipments across country. Unexpected bad weather might make truck travel impossible for days or weeks—or, possibly create the need for shipping emergency supplies into an area, as was the case when Hurricane Andrew hit Florida.

In designing his computer software, Ward decided not only concentrate on where each truck was headed, as all the carriers tended to do, but also on where that truck's next move should be, since daily fluctuations affected efficient routing. Additionally, his system scanned and evaluated which customers had paid the highest rates, and then ranked which of the possible loads are most desirable to accommodate. OTR's Dispatch Department came to consist of a room full of ''load planners,'' who received hourly updates on their video terminals, showing where all their trucks were and when they were due to arrive at their next destination. The planners' job was to find a new and profitable load for each of those soon-to-be-empty trucks.

The company placed an emphasis on the quality of drivers it hired. The average age of an OTR driver was 43, with 14 years of experience. The company did not hire anyone under the age of 25, or anyone who had a traffic accident within the previous two years—measures which management believed accounted for their lower accident rates and corresponding lower insurance premiums. OTR also offered an incentive-based program, which attracted quality drivers to the company's policy of providing exceptional equipment and maintaining it well. The company's Driver Incentive Management System rewarded their equipment managers with mileage pay based on fuel efficiency—which is effected by running equipment at efficient speeds, the reduction of out of route miles, idling less, and maintaining equipment in peak operating condition.

Despite the technological advancements and measures taken to increase customer and employee satisfaction, 1995 was a year of disappointment for OTR. The trucking industry experienced a severe slump in the freight market, and OTR reported a net loss of $157,000 for the year, compared to a net income of $1,278,000 in 1994. Thus, the company was encouraged to modify its marketing approach again in 1996, following a challenging year. The marketing department grew to three times its former size, and implemented a strategy that would market their services to larger national accounts. In order to attract new business, the company guaranteed equipment availability and set rates. It acquired additional drop trailers, and expanded its brokerage department, which was responsible for finding carriers for loads that OTR could not accommodate efficiently. The company also started providing warehouse solutions for customers.

The End of the Century and Beyond

By 1997 the company had returned to profitability, with especially strong third and fourth quarter results. OTR grew to include several new, large, national account customers—and they continued to improve in areas of customer service and improved technological systems. Credited with developing and implementing the restructuring plan, Gary Klusman was promoted to president and chief executive officer. Commenting on Klusman's promotion,

Ward stated in a press release that "Since joining the company, Gary has led many strategic initiatives that have resulted in substantial operating improvements. I am confident that Gary will successfully lead the implementation of our plans to become a more dynamic transportation services company. This change will provide the framework to take advantage of capital formation opportunities as well as acquisition opportunities." Ward remained with the company as chairman of the board.

Soon thereafter, OTR increased the percentage of direct shipper freight to 77 percent from 61 percent in 1996, which reduced the company's reliance on less consistent and lower paying broker freight. To complement its national fleet, a regional short haul division was created at the Olathe terminal facility, and a second short haul division was later created in Chicago. The two short haul divisions accounted for 6 percent of OTR's fleet.

In July of 1998, OTR's stockholders voted to increase the number of authorized shares of common stock from 5 million to 20 million shares. The purpose of the share increase was intended to provide the company with the flexibility to meet current and future capital needs through a variety of measures, including possible future stock offerings. It was decided that the filing of the SEC registration would await a favorable pricing climate. In a show of confidence, several OTR executives purchased substantial shares during the first half of the year.

Principal Divisions

OTR Services; Short Haul Division.

Further Reading

"CEO Interviews: OTR Express, Inc." *The Wall Street Transcript,* January 2, 1995, pp. 1–4.
Heaster, Randolph, "OTR is Riding High Again," *The Kansas City Star,* July 1, 1997, p. B3.
Welles, Edward O., "Tech Highway, *Inc.,* March, 1993, pp. 73–84.

—Terri Mozzone

Outdoor Systems, Inc.

2502 N. Black Canyon Highway
Phoenix, Arizona 85009
U.S.A.
(602) 246-9569
Fax: (602) 433-2482

Public Company
Incorporated: 1980
Employees: 1,490
Sales: $471 million (1997)
Stock Exchanges: New York
Ticker Symbol: OSI
SICs: 7312 Outdoor Advertising Services

The largest outdoor advertiser in North America, Outdoor Systems, Inc. owns roughly 250,000 display properties in the United States, Canada, and Mexico. The display properties are of various types, including billboards, transit shelter displays, subway displays, and mall displays. The company was founded in 1980, but did not begin to grow robustly until it converted to public ownership in April 1996. A flurry of acquisitions followed in the next several years, including the $690 million purchase of Gannett Inc.'s outdoor advertising business and the $1 billion purchase of Minnesota Mining & Manufacturing Co.'s outdoor advertising business. In the process, Outdoor Systems leaped from ranking as the sixth-largest billboard operator in the country to the champion of the North American industry. In 1998 the company owned advertising displays in 96 of the top 100 U.S. advertising markets and in seven of the top ten markets in Canada. As the company prepared for the 21st century, it was beginning a concerted push into Mexico, where a July 1998 acquisition made it the largest outdoor advertiser in the country.

Moreno's Arrival in 1984

Outdoor Systems entered the billboard business in 1980, starting out in Phoenix, Arizona. By 1984, three years of operation had produced a respectably-sized, local outdoor advertiser,

a company with 80 billboards to its name in the Phoenix area. From this juncture forward, however, the small Phoenix advertiser began to expand. Although Outdoor Systems' portfolio of outdoor displays did not dramatically increase immediately after 1984, the year did mark the arrival of the company's greatest promoter, Arturo "Arte" Moreno, a fourth-generation Arizonan who would lift Outdoor Systems to eye-catching heights.

Moreno was born and raised in Tucson, Arizona, where his parents ran a print shop and published a Spanish newspaper. During his teenage years, Moreno helped with the family business, often working late into the night on the newspaper. The long hours reportedly led him to pursue a different career path, and in 1973, he was graduated from the University of Arizona with a degree in marketing. Moreno then began accumulating experience in the billboard business, allying himself to the profession that eventually would make him a multi-millionaire. He worked for Gannett Outdoor, the outdoor advertising subsidiary belonging to Gannett Inc., for a number of years, representing the company's interests in Arizona, Missouri, and New Jersey. It was while Moreno was working for Gannett that he first came in direct contact with Outdoor Systems. Moreno, at the time, was employed by an established veteran in the billboard business, and in Outdoor Systems he saw a small, young billboard operator that offered a wealth of opportunities to a shrewd operator. Moreno was intrigued.

In 1984, Moreno and a friend, Wally Kelly, approached the owner and founder of Outdoor Systems, William S. Levine, and inquired about purchasing the company. When he made his proposal, Moreno was in charge of Gannett's billboard operation in New Jersey; Kelly was employed as the vice-president of national sales for WhitecoMetrocom Inc., an outdoor advertising company. Levine, a Phoenix businessman involved in real estate and other business endeavors, was unwilling to sell his billboard assets. He was, however, impressed with the presentation pitched by Moreno and Kelly, enough to offer the pair the opportunity to come work for him in a partnership. Moreno and Kelly agreed, and a union was formed.

"We tried to position ourselves," Moreno later recalled, "saying, 'Obviously we can't be the largest. There's just no chance—but we can position ourselves to be the Cadillac of billboard companies'.'' Standing out as a cut above the rest meant an emphasis on service. Moreno and Kelly brought a commitment to service when they joined Outdoor Systems and immediately began setting up an organization to support an intensified sales effort. Their emphasis on service was simple in its nature, but the basic changes worked. Under the direction of the ambitious pair, telephone calls were returned as quickly as possible. Potential clients received information immediately. When a client's billboard advertisement appeared for the first time, a confirmation telephone call was quick to follow, along with a photograph showing the billboard in question. Because of the attention to these fundamental services, Outdoor Systems' business blossomed, energized by the new spirit instilled by the new arrivals.

Moreno worked to fashion Outdoor Systems into the premier billboard operator in the Phoenix area, and then set his sights beyond the city, acquiring display properties that gradually broadened the company's geographic presence and turned Outdoor Systems into a regional operator rather than a local operator. Progress during the 1980s was slow, checked by the limited financial resources available to expand through acquisition, but the decade did bring the company forward. Within a decade, Moreno lifted Outdoor Systems' revenue volume past the $50 million mark. Moreno did not begin to demonstrate his most striking talent until he took Outdoor Systems public in 1996, 12 years after Levine named him a director of the company. From 1996 forward, progress occurred at a lightening pace, enabling Moreno to by far exceed the expectations he held a decade earlier.

1996 IPO Ignites Growth

At the time of Outdoor Systems' initial public offering (IPO) of stock, the outdoor advertising industry was undergoing dynamic changes. There was a movement toward consolidation, sparked, in part, by the potential ban on outdoor advertising by tobacco companies. In the general trend toward consolidation, no company would stand out more than Outdoor Systems, which embarked on an exhaustive acquisition campaign that quickly vaulted the company toward the number one position in its industry. Within a year, all of Outdoor Systems' competitors would be dwarfed by the acquisition spree directed by Moreno.

The last annual sales total recorded by Outdoor Systems as a private company stood at $64.8 million. The IPO was completed in April 1996, raising $37 million to use to acquire other billboard companies throughout the country. At the time, Outdoor Systems ranked as the sixth-largest outdoor advertiser in the country, but within four months after the IPO the company leapt past all competitors to rank as the number one company of its kind in North America. The acquisition that pushed Outdoor Systems to the industry's top spot was the August 1996 purchase of Gannett's billboard business, the same company Moreno had worked for prior to joining Outdoor Systems. It was a transaction that could rightly be defined as a megadeal, a $690 million purchase that was the largest of the 11 acquisitions completed within a year after the IPO. With the 160,000 display faces gained in the Gannett deal, Outdoor Systems stood as the industry leader, its display properties clustered in major markets. Except for the purchase of Dallas-based Reynold Media,

all of the display properties acquired between the spring of 1996 and the spring of 1997 were located in markets where Outdoor Systems already owned billboards.

Gannett and the other acquisitions of 1996 proved to be just a foretaste of Moreno's acquisitive bent. In 1997, the company acquired 20 outdoor advertising companies, widening the gap separating it and those companies struggling to keep pace. "We have a big appetite," Moreno noted, understating the extent of his company's activity on the acquisition front. Among the acquisitions completed during the year, none was bigger than the company's purchase of the outdoor advertising business belonging to Minnesota Mining & Manufacturing Co. (3M), which outstripped the magnitude of the Gannett acquisition. In May 1997, one month after paying $170 million for roughly 45 "Spectacular" signs in New York City's Times Square, Outdoor Systems shelled out $1 billion to acquire 3M's outdoor advertising subsidiary, 3M Media, which ranked as the third-largest billboard company in the United States. Based in Bedford Park, Illinois, 3M Media collected approximately $220 million in sales from its billboards, poster panels, and advertising displays. "This acquisition," Moreno remarked at the time of the 3M deal, "gives us the opportunity to offer broader national, regional, and local advertising coverage, as well as maintain our leadership of the outdoor advertising industry." Specifically, the acquisition strengthened Outdoor Systems' presence in several lucrative states, including California and Texas, and provided an entry into numerous Florida markets.

When the 3M deal was concluded, Outdoor Systems gained nearly 100,000 billboards in 40 states, including display properties in 20 of the top 25 U.S. markets and seven of the top ten Canadian markets. The addition of these display properties lifted the company's total number of display faces above 200,000, but Moreno did not stop there. He pressed forward, completing a dozen more acquisitions before the end of the year, including the December purchase of Outdoor Media Group Inc. which provided the company with its first foray into the greater Las Vegas area, one of the fastest-growing markets in the United States. "He's a billboard genius," one industry analyst said of Moreno at the end of 1997, adding "He saw value where a lot of others didn't. In so doing, he's created a very substantial return for shareholders." The company's shareholders, who watched the price of their stock soar 322 percent during Outdoor Systems' first year as a public company, expectantly awaited Moreno's moves in 1998, confident that further acquisitions were imminent. The billboard genius did not disappoint.

Late 1990s Acquisitions in Mexico

Entering 1998, Outdoor Systems was poised atop a broad and firmly-built geographic foundation. The company held sway as the largest outdoor advertiser in the United States, and its wholly-owned Canadian subsidiary, Mediacom Inc., ranked as the largest outdoor advertiser in Canada. The next logical region to establish a third leg of operations was in Mexico, where Moreno turned his sights in 1998. In July, Moreno acquired Vendor, S.A. de C.V. for $215 million, gaining the largest outdoor advertising company in Mexico. Concurrently, Outdoor Systems purchased the outdoor advertising assets of Multimedios Estrellas de Oro, S.A. de C.V. for $22.5 million.

Together, the two acquisitions included more than 6,600 advertising displays in more than 20 of Mexico's largest markets, including Mexico City, Monterrey, and Guadalajara.

Ranking as the largest billboard operator in the United States, Canada, and in Mexico, Outdoor Systems occupied an enviable position as it prepared for the 21st century. Its formidable grip on the major markets in each of the three countries where it operated, provided more than a foundation for future growth: it positioned the company as the industry giant and the target for every other billboard operator to shoot for. Whether Outdoor Systems would be able to withstand challenges to its position remained to be seen, but with Moreno guiding the company its future pointed to further acquisitions and a deeper market presence throughout North America.

Principal Subsidiaries

Mediacom Inc. (Canada).

Further Reading

Brodesser, Claude, "A Billion for Billboards: Giant Outdoor Systems Gets Even Bigger with Deal for 3M Unit," *MEDIAWEEK,* May 5, 1997, p. 5.

Davis, Riccardo A., "3M Expected to Sell Billboard Subsidiary," *Knight-Ridder/Tribune Business News,* April 30, 1997, p. 43.

"Ford Motor Company and Outdoor Systems, Inc. Announce Historic Advertising Package," *PR Newswire,* June 29, 1998, p. 6.

Halliday, Jean, "Ford Secures $50 Mil-Plus in Outdoor Space: Huge Pact with Outdoor Systems Solves Short-Term Buying Dilemma," *Advertising Age,* June 29, 1998, p. 3.

Hudis, Mark, "Way Beyond a Great Gorge: Despite Antitrust Concerns, Outdoor Systems Continues to Feast," *MEDIAWEEK,* May 19, 1997, p. 12.

Mull, Angela, "Outdoor Aims to Be One-Stop Shop," *The Business Journal-Serving Phoenix & the Valley of the Sun,* June 12, 1998, p. 10.

"Outdoor Systems Completes Purchase of Largest Outdoor Advertising Company in Mexico," *Business Wire,* July 6, 1998, p. 1.

"Phoenix-Based Outdoor Systems Inc. Buys 3M's Billboard Ad Division," *Knight-Ridder/Tribune Business News,* May 2, 1997, p. 5.

Western, Ken, "Phoenix-Based Outdoor Systems Goes on a Buying Binge," *Knight-Ridder/Tribune Business News,* December 8, 1997, p. 12.

Wilke, Michael, "Outdoor Woes: Gannett Could Suffer Layoffs," *Advertising Age,* August 19, 1996, p. 3.

—Jeffrey L. Covell

Pharmacia & Upjohn Inc.

95 Corporate Drive
Bridgewater, New Jersey 08807
U.S.A.
(908) 306-4400
(888) 768-5501
Web site: http://www.pnu.com

Public Company
Incorporated: 1995
Employees: 30,000
Sales: $6.71 billion (1997)
Stock Exchanges: New York
Ticker Symbol: PNU
SICs: 2834 Pharmaceutical Preparations; 2836 Biological
   Products, Excluding Diagnostics; 2833 Medicinal
   Chemicals, Botanical Products; 2835 In Vitro, In Vivo
   Diagnostics; 8731 Commercial Physical, Biological
   Research

An international manufacturer of pharmaceuticals formed through the 1995 merger of the Pharmacia A.B. and the Upjohn Company, Pharmacia & Upjohn Inc. researches, develops, manufactures, and markets a variety of pharmaceutical and health-related products, including those for infectious and metabolic diseases, central nervous system disorders, cancer, and women's health concerns. The company also develops and sells vaccines and pharmaceuticals for pets, livestock, and other food animals. Pharmacia & Upjohn manufactures pharmaceutical chemicals and intermediates, as well as selling specialty products for hospitals, as diagnostics, and as nutritional supplements.

The Origins of Upjohn

It is not inaccurate to describe Upjohn's Victorian beginnings as marking the origin of modern pharmaceuticals in general. In 1885 Dr. William Upjohn revolutionized the drug industry when he patented a tedious process for the making of a "friable" pill capable of crumbling under the pressure of an individual's thumb. The image of Dr. Upjohn's thumb crushing a pill eventually

became a trademark of the Upjohn Pill and Granule Co., founded in Kalamazoo in 1886 by Upjohn and his brother Henry. A talent for promoting its products ensured the company's steady growth through the turn of the century. By 1893 Upjohn could be seen at the Chicago World's Fair distributing souvenirs of its exhibit—an enormous bottle filled with colored pills. In 1903 the company shortened its name to The Upjohn Company. Quinine pills and "Phenolax Wafers" (the first candy laxative) were two of the early and successful products made by Upjohn. By 1924 the extremely popular wafers were bringing in $795,000 a year or 21 percent of Upjohn's sales revenue.

From the very beginning, however, Upjohn not only emphasized the marketing of drugs, but also the research and development of new compounds. In 1913 the company hired its first research scientist, a chemistry professor named Dr. Frederick W. Heyl. The doctor proved to be a sound investment for Upjohn. One of his developments, Citro-carbonate, an effervescent antacid, reached sales of one million dollars in 1926. Heyl was also responsible for patenting a digitalis tablet called Digitora, used in the treatment of heart disease and still sold by Upjohn into the 1990s.

William Upjohn was largely responsible for the firm's early research orientation as well as its entrepreneurial spirit. When William Upjohn died in 1932, the job of running the company fell to his nephew, Dr. Lawrence N. Upjohn, who served in that post for 12 years. In 1944 Lawrence Upjohn retired and Donald S. Gilmore became president. Gilmore brought to the company valuable experience as a corporate executive from the business world, but even he was by no means an outsider. In fact, he was both the stepson and the son-in-law of William Upjohn. Ray T. Parfet, president of the company beginning in 1961, also married into the family. The company had been so tightly held that until 1968 no one who was not a family member or employee of Upjohn was permitted to sit on its board of directors.

Major Developments at Upjohn
Through the 1980s

During the 1930s and 1940s, under the guidance of Lawrence Upjohn and later under Gilmore, the company expanded its research and manufacturing facilities and added 12 more research scientists. This expansion paid off when Upjohn became the first to market an adreno-cortical hormone product in 1935. The actual impetus for the company's success occurred during World War II when Upjohn, like many other drug companies, developed a broad line of antibiotics, including penicillin and streptomycin. Upjohn was fortunate enough to be selected by the armed forces to process human serum albumin and penicillin. By 1958 Upjohn was the sixth largest manufacturer of antibiotics.

In addition to antibiotics, Upjohn also developed a product called Gelfoam during World War II. A substance made from beef bone gelatin, Gelfoam was a porous, sponge-like material which, when used during surgery, absorbed many times its volume in fluid and was itself absorbed by body tissues. Gelfoam was also useful in the treatment of hemophiliacs, and when manufactured in a powder form that could be swallowed, Gelfoam was used to stop internal hemorrhaging that occurring in the digestive tract. Another successful product for the Upjohn Company during the postwar period was the injectable contraceptive Depo-Provera. This drug provided protection against pregnancy for about 90 days. Though the drug would not gain FDA approval in the United States until the 1990s, it was marketed in more than 80 foreign countries through subsidiaries located abroad.

Upjohn's international expansion during the 1950s was critical not only in allowing it to compete with other large drug manufacturers in foreign markets, but also in enabling it to make genuine advances in the area of research. Challenged by Merck, which introduced cortisone into the market, Upjohn joined forces with S.B. Penick & Company on an expedition to Africa in 1949 and 1950 in search of a plant that could provide a cheaper source of the drug. This venture ended in failure, but the company was fortunate enough to discover accidently—growing on a petri dish—a mold capable of fermenting progesterone, the basic building block for cortisone, out of diosgenin. Upjohn was able to capitalize on its discovery by forming a partnership with a Mexican firm, Syntex, which isolated diosgenin from yams.

In 1957 the Upjohn Company introduced the first oral anti-diabetes agent called Orinase. Many physicians and patients considered Orinase to be the greatest advancement in the treatment of adult-onset diabetes since insulin. Studies conducted in the 1970s, however, linked the drug with heart disease, and its use was subsequently discouraged by the National Institutes of Health. Yet Upjohn continued to produce a line of oral anti-diabetes agents, including Tolinase and the more potent Micronase.

One of the more significant developments for the company during this time was its 1974 development of Motrin, an anti-inflammatory agent widely prescribed in the treatment of arthritis and menstrual cramps. Boots Company of Britain licensed Upjohn to sell ibuprofen (Motrin's active ingredient), but in 1977 Boots entered the U.S. market itself, even while continuing to license Upjohn. A price war ensued in 1981 when Boots sold its version of the drug at 20 to 30 percent less than Upjohn. By 1984 both companies had extended the battle by producing over-the-counter ibuprofen pills Nuprin and Advil. As a result of this competition, Upjohn's dominant market position was eroded; by mid-1984 Boots gained 25 percent of the market share of prescriptions for ibuprofen.

During the mid-1980s, Upjohn produced two prostaglandin products, one for cardiovascular disorders and the other a pregnancy termination product. The company also introduced its Monoxidil, a treatment for baldness. Originally intended as a drug for heart disease, Monoxidil produced unwanted hair growth in patients. When rumors of the drug's restorative powers spread, Monoxidil's sales doubled. Upjohn marketed Monoxidil as a baldness treatment under the name Rogaine.

In 1987, the grandson of Upjohn's founder—Ray ("Ted") Parfet—left the company's presidency, and Theodore Cooper assumed control of Upjohn. Remarkably, at the time Cooper was one of the few medical doctors responsible for a U.S. pharmaceuticals firm. Cooper had joined Upjohn in 1980 and became renowned for improving the company's quality control and regulatory areas.

Challenges and Controversy in the Early 1990s

By 1989, the patents on many of Upjohn's major products began to expire, and development of it most advantageous new products was far from immediate. Other products simply were not performing as expected. Rogaine, for example, did not achieve anticipated sales levels, despite the fact that it earned in excess of $100 million in worldwide sales. Some patients complained that the drug did not produce the results that they desired, while Rogaine's position in general was compromised by a glut of inferior over-the-counter hair growth drugs that were eventually prohibited by the U.S. Food and Drug Administration.

Nevertheless, Upjohn remained competitive throughout the world. Much of its sales forced worked in non-U.S. markets, and the company established research centers abroad—in Japan and the United Kingdom, in particular. Upjohn also built a large lab near its Kalamazoo, Michigan, headquarters, increasing its research power by 50 percent.

Upjohn also emphasized growth and diversity at this time. William Parfet, great-grandson of Upjohn's founder, hoped to develop the sales of the company's over-the-counter drugs such as Motrin IB. He also looked to revitalize areas of the company that had stagnated over time. He sought to enhance the health service and animal health segments of the business; for example, the development of a pseudo-rabies vaccine for swine.

Introduced in 1983, the benzodiazepine Halcion achieved the level of the most widely prescribed sleep medication with 17 million prescriptions written annually in the United States by 1992. The drug, however, drew some negative attention towards

Upjohn, since a controversy arose owing to patients experiencing psychiatric side effects such as memory loss or depression from Halcion. In fact, Halcion supposedly caused 8 to 45 times the adverse side effects as other frequently prescribed sleep aids. Some European countries, notably Great Britain, even barred the drug's sale around 1991. Yet psychiatrists such as Stuart Yudofsky, chief of psychiatry at Methodist Hospital in Houston, Texas, found value in the drug. "I don't believe that medications such as Halcion, which have such potential to help people, should be removed from the market without clear, specific scientific data," he told *People Weekly*. "So far, the evidence against Halcion is not sufficiently convincing to justify denying it to the many people who benefit from it now. We should not blame medication that has value because it has been misapplied."

Like Halcion, Xanax had been well received then met with controversy during the early 1990s. Introduced in 1981, Upjohn's Xanax became more widely prescribed than Valium as a tranquilizer by 1987. Also called Alprazolam, Xanax became the only FDA-approved drug for treating panic attacks in 1991. A minor tranquilizer classified as a benzodiazepine, Xanax worked quickly for patients and resulted in few side effects—except for one: drug dependence. Still, many—such as the Medical University of South Carolina's Dr. James Ballenger—felt that the benefits of Xanax were more worthwhile than any risk of drug dependency, which he attributed more to a media-created furor than to scientific data. As Ballenger told *The Nation:* "Patients hear things that unnecessarily scare them, and they feel guilty about becoming dependent. But dependence is not a weakness. It's a physiological condition."

The year 1992 proved difficult for Upjohn as well. Halcion, one of its product mainstays, lost 45 percent of its sales due to concerns about its side effects. Patent expirations on other important products, including Xanax, loomed—paving the way for competition among lower-priced generic brands. The company's new products—Vantin, for example, a treatment for skin and respiratory infections—were not expected to offset the revenue losses of the patent expirations in the long term. By November 1992, Upjohn showed the lowest multiple of all pharmaceutical stocks. Rumors of a merger with German company Hoechst AG to increase the value of Upjohn's stock circulated again as they had in 1991.

The Origins of Pharmacia

Pharmacia began in 1911 in Stockholm with one product, the phospho-energon energy pills made from animal products. The recipe for the energy pills was created by C. Më Kunwald and was patented in 1910. Phospho-energon sold so well that the turnover during Pharmacia's first year was above SKr 20,000. From 1912 to 1962 phospho-energon, in various forms, was sold in Finland, Russia, the United States, Denmark, Norway, and England, and remained throughout that time a strong 30 percent of Pharmacia's total production.

While Pharmacia began with one product, it had never been the intention of the company to rely on a single item. From the outset, the 21 people who invested SKr 32,100 in initial shares were told that the new company would produce medicines on a commercial scale. In 1912 Pharmacia took on the production of

cedar oil, from cedar wood from Lebanon, to produce Cedrolinol, an ointment used for rheumatic complaints. In 1913 another product, Sodamint, to be used against "throatache" and stomach complaints, was launched. Paraform, which contained formaldehyde, was another product Pharmacia made to fight throat infections.

Major Developments at Pharmacia Through the 1980s

By 1922 Pharmacia was still expanding, with ever larger orders, but the profits were so low that all employees had to take a cut in wages. The next year the company began producing laxatives, a product with a proven market. Then came the 1926 launch of Kreosan Simplex, used in the treatment of bronchitis and tuberculosis, and in 1927 Pharmacia started to produce vitamins.

Prior to World War II the research department of Pharmacia received the increased resources that came in from the dramatic new product created by Nanna Svartz of the Karolinska Institutet. Her interest in the treatment of rheumatic diseases and her brilliant research with sulpha led to the launch of Salazopyrin, a product which is still used, now in the treatment of ulcerative colitis. With the proceeds from this and other sulpha products, Pharmacia could afford to launch, with Uppsala University, another major product. Professor T. Svedberg and Arne Tiselius, both Nobel Prize-winners, had been asked by sugar manufacturers to do research on the sugar beet. Björn Ingelmann, a student working with them on the project in 1941, identified and separated dextrose. During World War II the team developed from this Dextran, a plasma substitute, which was in use by 1943.

Ingelmann began working on pectin as well as dextrin. In the 1950s he had developed a separation process, using a centrifuge, that had been unsatisfactory. Later, Jerker Porath and Per Flodin developed a new separation method using a cellulose powder which eventually was marketed as Sephardex. A success, this took Pharmacia into the new production area of research aids. In 1955, in conjunction with the Danish AS Pharmacia and the Dutch Organon, Pharmacia launched and marketed a line in hormones.

As Pharmacia expanded, it licensed the manufacture of its products in foreign countries, allowing for foreign expansion through subsidiaries. Pharmacia GB Ltd. was formed in Great Britain to produce Dextran, Macrodex, and Rheomacrodex, and for the sale of Sepharon. In 1960, Pharmacia cooperated with Green Cross KK in Japan, with Pharmacia KK forming in 1971 so that the Swedish company could work on its own. To control these and other licensing requirements, a separate company, Pharmacia International, was formed in 1967.

1980s Turnaround of Pharmacia

Part of the state-owned Kabi-Vitrum, Pharmacia performed poorly despite the Scandinavian company's position as a leader in separation and purification technology, an integral component in biotechnology. The company was in such sorry financial straights in 1985 that it borrowed funds just to pay the staff. Pharmacia was privatized the following year, and its new chairman Jan Ekberg introduced the company to profitability. "When I look at Ekberg's accomplishments, he is above average in this industry as a CEO," remarked Arvind Desai, an analyst at New York City's drug research Mehta & Isaly, remarked in *Financial World.* "Among pharmaceuticals CEOs you find two kinds of individuals. There is the kind with all the strategic vision and all the lofty ideas and dreams. He has that. But not everyone has that and also has their operating hat on at the same time. That is what distinguishes him."

Foreign enterprises aggressively increased their shares of the biotechnology and pharmaceuticals markets in the United States in 1986, and Pharmacia was no different. In fact, Pharmacia considered the United States to be its primary market. Indeed the company captured 40 percent of its 1985 sales in the United States. The Swedish company also participated in joint ventures with American firms, some that it went on to acquire. Deltec Inc., of St. Paul, Minnesota, was one such medical device company in 1986—as was Pasadena, California-based Intermedics Interocular Inc.

Under Ekberg's direction, the company also reconfigured as a pan-European enterprise. By 1988, it acquired companies in Germany, Scandinavia, and Italy. Then in 1990 Pharmacia entered into a major merger with Procordia, a Swedish food-and-drug company, and Provenda, also a food company. The new enterprise formed through the merger—Procordia by name—also had Volvo as a major shareholder, yet Pharmacia, the smallest company involved in the deal, took control of the new company's pharmaceuticals business. Ekberg continued seeking out acquisition properties for Pharmacia, including Italy's Farmitalia Carlo Erba in 1993, until the company ranked third among pharmaceutical companies worldwide.

Pharmacia sales in 1993 totaled more than $3 billion. Capitalizing on its niche sales, Pharmacia sold mostly to hospitals, thereby decreasing its marketing costs compared to other companies relying on large sales staffs to conduct visits at doctor's offices. Also, after privatizing years earlier, the Swedish company lessened its staffing, closed some factories, and prepared to increase operating margins to 20 percent within two years.

Industry Consolidation: Pharmacia Joins Upjohn

Mergers of large operators in the pharmaceutical business throughout the 1990s changed the industry. The larger companies captured more resources than smaller ones. They engaged in global activities and were capable of greater research and development efforts. By 1995, Pharmacia's position dropped to the ninth largest pharmaceutical company in the world.

Pharmacia prepared to introduce a new drug for the treatment of glaucoma at this time, but the company realized that it needed a partner with the capabilities for mass marketing in the United States. Since Upjohn maintained a notable distribution network with the United States, Ekberg contacted Upjohn's chief executive officer John Zabriskie. At their meeting in Washington, D.C., Zabriskie suggested a merger. Viewing the companies as complementary—Upjohn the generalist and Pharmacia in specialized niches—Ekberg considered the idea seriously. He sent a team from Pharmacia to ascertain the state of Upjohn's research and development activities, and—finding

them viable—agreed to the merger. The new company—Pharmacia & Upjohn—established its headquarters in Kalamazoo, Michigan.

The merger of Pharmacia & Upjohn created a "truly global" enterprise, with business activities in Europe, the United States, and Asia. Yet, the combined company reported poor earnings.

In 1996, the company issued the first public stock offering for one of its subsidiaries, Biacore International AB. In the transaction, Pharmacia & Upjohn sold nearly 60 percent of its share of the company. During 1997 the company's biotechnology supply subsidiary Pharmacia Biotech merged with Amersham Life Science. A new company, Amersham Pharmacia, was born from the agreement.

Despite the power of the combined companies, Pharmacia & Upjohn's stock value fell owing to poor earnings and management confusion after the merger. Sales growth slowed, which accounted for some of the disappointing earnings. Moreover, British, Italian, American, and Swedish executives now shared management of the company, and many literally did not speak the same language. The chief executive officer contributed to the confusion by resigning.

In response to these challenges, Pharmacia & Upjohn appointed Fred Hassan as the new chief executive in 1997. A native of Pakistan but a citizen of the United States, Hassan worked for many years in Switzerland, so he was well acquainted with cultural differences. In fact, Hassan earned a reputation for pulling together separate businesses in his previous work at American Home Products. The company counted on him to amalgamate and resolve the many differences that emerged after the merger.

New Products and Markets for the Future

The merger of Pharmacia & Upjohn did not bring the expected results immediately. Nevertheless, the new chief officer showed potential for executing a turnaround at the company, and the company's new products in development or awaiting approval looked encouraging. In 1996, the company launched the glaucoma drug Xalatan in the United States. After achieving the status as a leader among branded ophthalmic medications there, Xalatan was scheduled to be available in Europe by 1998. Detrusitol, another new product, offered treatment for patients with overactive bladders. Approved in 14 European markets, the therapy was expected to be available in the United States as Detrol. Pharmacia & Upjohn introduced Edronax, an antidepressant, in the United Kingdom before marketing the drug to a dozen European countries.

In addition to new products, the company expanded its markets for existing medications. For example, Pharmacia & Upjohn retrieved the sales and marketing rights in Japan for one of its more prominent drugs, the growth hormone therapy Genotropin, beginning in January 1997. Sales of Camptosar, a therapy for colorectal cancer, and the anithrombotic Fragmin each increased throughout 1997, and the company's drug for Parkinson's disease performed well enough in the United States to introduce the product in Europe during 1998. Over-the-counter medications—including Nicorette nicotine-replacement therapy for the cessation of smoking and Rogaine hair replacement products—continued to gain thrive in the marketplace as well.

To add slightly to the minor chaos that had come with the merger, in early 1998 Pharmacia & Upjohn announced that the company was considering moving its headquarters out of Kalamazoo, Michigan. Employees and residents of the city, alike, did everything they could to persuade the company to stay put. Employees wanted some continuity, which had been somewhat absent since the merger, with employees traveling back and forth a lot between the Kalamazoo offices and the Pharmacia & Upjohn offices that were located in London, England—serving as a gateway to the European side of the operation. Furthermore, the Kalamazoo community wanted the company to stay put, due in large part to the high level of involvement that Pharmacia & Upjohn had in local business, education, and community life. Ultimately, however, the company announced that it would be moving to New Jersey later that year.

In the company's 1997 annual report, Fred Hassan explained that the future would hold more changes for Pharmacia & Upjohn. "We believe the changes we are making will help us become a stronger company that is more fit to compete in the global arena," he wrote. "We acknowledge that some of these changes have been difficult for our employees, who have undergone a challenging transition . . . . We are indebted to them for their patience, understanding and resilience." Soren Gyll concurred in his 1997 Message from the Chairman of the Board: "Our company is continuing to undergo a transition from two mid-sized multinational companies to a large, global competitor. We are taking decisive action to stabilize the company, maximize our most important products and improve our financial performance. The board of directors is confident that Fred Hassan is on the right course, and we are pleased with the progress he has made. The directors are fully united behind the chief executive, and we are confident about the future."

Principal Subsidiaries

Pharmacia AB (Sweden); Pharmacia Hepar Inc.; Upjohn Company (United States).

Principal Divisions

Allergon.

Further Reading

Abelson, Reed, "Regulating the Regulators," *Forbes,* March 4, 1991, p. 126.

Benoit, Ellen, "Rip Tide; Can Upjohn Manage its Way out of a Product Gap?," *Financial World,* September 5, 1989, p. 26.

Cotts, Cynthia, "The Pushers in the Suites; Xanax Panic," *The Nation,* August 31, 1992, p. 208.

Gold, Jacqueline S., "Upjohn: Down in the Dumps," *Financial World,* November 24, 1992, p. 16.

Jaffe, Thomas, "Is There Fire as Well as Smoke?," *Forbes,* November 11, 1991, p. 418.

Lawler, Andrew, "Doe to Industry: So Long, Partner," *Science,* October 4, 1996, p. 24.

Ligos, Melinda, "Pharmaceutical Reps Go Head-to-Head," *Sales & Marketing Management,* March 1998, p. 16.

McClenahen, John S., "The Nordic Invasion; Scandinavia Has Designs on the U.S. Market," *Industry Week,* November 24, 1986, p. 36.

McNeil, Liz, "Under a Cloud," *People Weekly,* May 11, 1992, p. 125.

Moser, Penny Ward, "The Bald Truth about Growing Hair," *Discover,* June 1986, p. 72.

Rapoport, Carla, "A Different Kind of Healthy Deal," *Fortune,* July 25, 1994, p. 34.

Reier, Sharon, "Dark Horse," *Financial World,* November 21, 1995, p. 48.

Salomon, R. S., Jr., "Three Bombed-Out Stocks to Buy Now," *Forbes,* December 16, 1996, p. 393.

——, "Three to Sell Now," *Forbes,* August 11, 1997, p. 142.

Scherreik, Susan, "Take These Three Stocks and Wake up Richer in the Morning," *Money,* November 1996, p. 74.

Schiffres, Manuel, "Four Ominous Events That Could Gore the Bull for Sure," *Kiplinger's Personal Finance Magazine,* October 1997, p. 23.

Schwartz, Nelson D., "A Tempting Drug Deal: Has Wall Street Overdosed on the Bad News at Pharmacia & Upjohn?," *Fortune,* June 9, 1997, p. 199.

"Study on Minorities with Parkinson's Disease Gets Endorsement from Muhammad Ali," *Jet,* October 14, 1996, p. 34.

"What's in a Name?," *Forbes,* November 20, 1995, p. 18.

—updated by Charity Anne Dorgan

Playskool, Inc.

1027 Newport Avenue
Pawtucket, Rhode Island 02862
U.S.A.
(401) 431-8697
Fax: (401) 727-5047

Division of Hasbro, Inc.
Incorporated: 1928 as Playskool Institute
Employees: 795
SICs: 3944 Games, Toys & Children's Vehicles; 3751
 Motorcycles, Bicycles & Parts; 3940 Toys & Sporting
 Goods; 3942 Dolls & Stuffed Toys

Playskool, Inc. is a leading manufacturer of children's and infants toys. Its core line consisted through much of the company's history of wooden toys such as blocks and peg boards, which were considered by the public and by child experts as educational. The company also owns some of the best known American toy brands, such as Mr. Potato Head and Play Doh. The Playskool brand name is found on diverse items such as clothing, stuffed animals, and ride-on vehicles. Playskool is the largest manufacturer of wooden blocks in the United States. The company licenses its name to a line of preschool books published by Dutton and has entered the interactive computer game market with software based on the Mr. Potato Head character.

Early History

Playskool was founded by a former Milwaukee schoolteacher, Lucille King, in the 1920s. King apparently had abandoned her teaching career and was working at the John Schroeder Lumber Company in Milwaukee when she came up with the idea for Playskool toys. She and another teacher had developed plans earlier for wooden toys for use in the classroom. King took her plans to the lumber company's management and launched the Playskool Institute in 1928. King's line of toys consisted of basic, durable wooden items that aimed to develop coordination and stimulate the minds of children. By 1930 Playskool produced more than 40 different toys, including a pound-

ing bench, wooden beads and blocks, a table-mounted sandbox, a pegboard, and others. Playskool Institute's slogan was "Learning While Playing," and some items were billed as "Home Kindergarten." Another slogan the company used was "Playthings with a Purpose." As early as 1930 Playskool's toys were endorsed by child guidance experts, and the aura of educational enrichment clung to the brand.

Playskool Institute first operated as a division of the John Schroeder Lumber Company. In 1935 the lumber company sold the division to a Chicago manufacturer, Thorncraft Inc. Thorncraft next sold Playskool to Chicago's Joseph Lumber Company in 1938. Harry Joseph, the lumber company's head, then hired Manuel Fink, a buyer for a leading Chicago department store, to head the Playskool unit. Fink brought in Robert J. Meythaler to assist him. Meythaler was trained as an accountant and also was an amateur woodworker. He quickly sensed the possibilities in the Playskool line, and within a few years of being hired by Joseph Lumber, he and Manuel Fink bought the Playskool division themselves. They named the new company Playskool Manufacturing Company.

Meythaler built on the educational cachet with which the brand already was invested by advertising in magazines for sophisticated consumers such as *Parents, Redbook,* and *Psychology Today.* Some of the early Playskool toys were deemed to boost a child's intelligence or, at least, to prepare children for intelligence tests. For example, a wooden mailbox introduced in the 1940s had differently shaped holes and pegs. Learning to push the round peg into the round hole and the square peg into the square hole prepared children for a standard test of development. Playskool also extended its line of educational toys by acquiring other manufacturers. In 1943 the company bought the J.L. Wright Company, manufacturer of Lincoln Logs. J.L. Wright was the son of famed American architect Frank Lloyd Wright. While with his father during the building of the landmark Imperial Hotel in Tokyo, J.L. Wright came up with the idea for interlocking logs as a construction toy for children. Lincoln Logs was a leading brand in the American toy market and is still manufactured.

Another essential purchase Playskool made was that of Holgate Toys in 1958. Holgate was a Philadelphia woodworking company dating back to 1789. The company specialized in utilitarian products such as broom handles and brushes until some time in the 1930s, when a daughter of the firm's treasurer married a notable child psychologist, Lawrence Frank. Frank had been a leader of a movement in the 1920s to establish child study institutes in the United States. He persuaded his father-in-law's company to begin producing wooden toys, which, like Playskool's, would be good for children. Holgate's toys were designed by Jerry Rockwell, brother of the artist Norman Rockwell. Jerry Rockwell is credited with designing some of the most enduring toys in the Holgate and, later, Playskool line, including a cobbler's bench, stacking rings, nesting blocks, pegboards, and lacing shoes. When Playskool bought Holgate in 1958, Rockwell went to work for the new company. There he created Playskool's Tyke bike, another enduring favorite toy that is still part of the Playskool line.

Growth in the 1960s

Another important acquisition was that of the South Bend Toy Manufacturing Company, which Playskool bought in 1960. South Bend had an established line of doll carriages and also made equipment for wooden outdoor games such as croquet and horse shoes. Playskool built its product line up carefully, buying companies that meshed well with its own existing lines. In 1962 it acquired the Halsam Company, an established manufacturer of wooden blocks. Halsam also owned the Embossing Company, which was the only American manufacturer of embossed wooden blocks—the common alphabet blocks. The Embossing Company also was also a major manufacturer of checkers and dominoes. Playskool got the block, embossed block, and checkers and dominoes lines when in it bought Halsam in 1962.

In 1960 Playskool's sales stood at about $12 million, which was considered respectable in the notoriously difficult and unstable toy business. Robert Meythaler continued to direct the company's marketing efforts toward magazines for educated parents, and the theme ''Learning While Playing'' was still in use. By 1966 sales had almost doubled, to $23 million. Meythaler attributed this big jump to the introduction of the federal Operation Headstart program. Headstart emphasized just the type of play-learning that had long been associated with Playskool's products, and the popularity of the program expanded the market for educational toys.

The Milton Bradley Years: 1968–84

Playskool had to start up new factories in the mid-1960s to keep up with demand. Though the sales outlook for the company was good, costs associated with plant construction led to steep declines in earnings. In 1968 Playskool was bought out by the Milton Bradley Company. Milton Bradley, located in Springfield, Massachusetts, was famous for its board games, including Monopoly. As a subsidiary of Milton Bradley, Playskool retained its focus on preschool and infant toys. The company did begin advertising on television, which it had previously shunned, and in 1970 spent $1.5 million on print and TV ads. Playskool advertised during the popular children's show ''Captain Kangaroo,'' while still reaching out to parents and teachers through magazines such as *Good Housekeeping, McCall's,* and *Instructor.*

Playskool retained its own headquarters, separate from Milton Bradley's Massachusetts establishment. In 1973 Playskool consolidated its various offices and plants into a giant million-square-foot complex on Chicago's northwest side. The company operated there throughout the 1970s. By 1980 Playskool's factory employed approximately 1,200 people. In that year the city of Chicago issued $1 million in industrial revenue bonds to help Playskool modernize its production facility. Though the bonds were issued as an incentive for the factory to stay in the city and add jobs, Playskool soon announced that it was laying off almost half its work force. Then in 1984 the largest toy company in the United States, giant Hasbro, Inc., bought Milton Bradley, Playskool's owner. Hasbro was known for its G.I. Joe doll, one of the best-selling toys on the American market. Shortly after Hasbro purchased Playskool, the company announced it would close the old Playskool plant in Chicago. The factory employed approximately 700 workers, and Hasbro announced that most of them would be dismissed. Manufacturing was to be consolidated with other Hasbro plants on the East Coast. This action prompted a lawsuit by the city of Chicago, which was incensed at the factory closing coming on the heels of the renovation the city had subsidized. The case made national news, as it was one of the more prominent of a series of similar apparent abuses of industrial revenue bonds. Outraged civic groups in Chicago organized a boycott of Hasbro. Eventually, Hasbro agreed to keep the factory operating for a short time while it retrained and found jobs for the dismissed workers.

Under Hasbro in the 1980s and 1990s

In 1985, the year after Hasbro bought the company, Playskool unveiled an updated line of infant products, such as bibs and bottles, under its Tommee Tippee brand name. Hoping to snare a wider share of the infant market, which was swelling because of a mini baby boom, Playskool spent an estimated $5 million on advertising, using Hasbro's ad agency. Like other Playskool products, the Tommee Tippee line had been researched extensively and was advertised in magazines catering to sophisticated and educated parents. Playskool also used television spots, with the theme ''Feeling good about the Playskool years.'' Under Hasbro's ownership, Playskool's management worked out of Pawtucket, Rhode Island, operating Playskool as a division of the parent company. Most of Hasbro's toys were for older children, and Playskool toys were made almost exclusively for children under six. Hasbro let the Playskool division concentrate on toys for preschoolers, even putting the Playskool brand name on existing Hasbro preschool toys. For instance, Playskool put its brand name on Play Doh, a favorite children's modeling clay. Play Doh had been acquired by Hasbro in 1987 when it bought Tonka Corp., which owned Play Doh's maker. So this well-known product became Playskool Play Doh, and its line was revitalized with tie-ins to other Playskool and Hasbro toys.

Playskool also extended its product line by offering lower-priced toys that were in direct competition with toys sold by Fisher-Price, the long-time leader in the infant and preschool market. Playskool's rattles, shape sorters, stacking toys, and musical mobiles gained market share for the company, as these were all priced under Fisher-Price's similar models. Playskool licensed toys from other designers as well, lending its name to items that were perhaps not as educational in focus as its original line. In

1991 Playskool bought the rights to Teddy Ruxpin, a talking teddy bear made by Worlds of Wonder. Teddy Ruxpin, selling for about $60 retail, had been one of the most popular toys of the mid-1980s, bringing in about $200 million annually at its peak. When the bear lost its fad appeal, its manufacturer went bankrupt. But Playskool bought the rights to produce and market not only the Teddy Ruxpin bear itself, but peripheral products such as software associated with it. In a similar move, Playskool signed a licensing agreement in 1993 with the creators of the Barney dinosaur. Barney's television show fixated children worldwide in the early 1990s. Playskool produced a talking Barney doll, a Barney phone, Barney's Animal Keyboard, and Barney Play Doh, among other Barney items.

Playskool products proliferated in the mid-1990s. Some toys remained close to the company's early theme of "Learning While Playing," such as a preschool baseball game that developed coordination and a toddler tricycle. Other new Playskool toys were extensions of other brands, such as Play Doh play sets and Mr. Potato Head products. Playskool also marketed a variety of general preschool toys such as its Magic Glamour Party makeup and jewelry and the Cool Tools toddler tool set. Infant items included a swing, walker, and musical crib toy. And as Playskool had licensed Barney and Teddy Ruxpin, the company also licensed its name to other vendors. In 1995 the Dutton publishing company signed an agreement with Playskool to use the toy maker's name on a series of children's books. The books were to be color coded to match Playskool's Ages and Stages program. Playskool used four different colors on a line of infant and toddler toys called Ages and Stages, to indicate four levels of child development. The book publisher wanted to build on the visibility of the Ages and Stages theme to market books for young children. Also in 1995 Playskool entered an agreement with Nickelodeon, the children's cable television network, to develop products based on its popular shows.

Despite all the new products, Playskool apparently was not producing profits. In 1996 Hasbro switched the Playskool division advertising account, worth $30 million, from Griffin Bacal to Arnold Communications in Boston. A year later Hasbro switched the account again, moving it from Arnold to Grey Advertising in New York. In 1997 Hasbro attempted to scale back the Playskool organization, dropping unprofitable toys. More difficulty for the company followed, as it launched a new series of toys that became controversial. In January 1997 Playskool began marketing a line of toys and infant's products made with a special antibacterial plastic. The antibacterial agent, Microban, was infused in the plastic and was supposed to reduce the spread of bacteria from children sharing toys. Microban received a lot of publicity, both good and bad. But by the end of 1997 Hasbro was forced to pay a fine and retract claims it had made regarding Playskool's Microban-treated toys. By 1998 Playskool had scaled down its toy line considerably, dropping from 80 to 100 items. The brand was sustained by licensed products such as those associated with Barney and another children's television character, Arthur. The company also placed its hopes in Teletubbies, a British television sensation. Hasbro licensed Teletubbies for Playskool, and manufactured Teletubbies dolls to hit the market when the show began airing on American television in April 1998.

Hasbro admitted that its preschool division was not performing well in the late 1990s and attempted to bring it back to profitability by cutting some items and bringing in more licensed products. The toy market had changed considerably since Playskool was invented in the 1920s. At the end of the 1990s the toy industry was dominated by two major players, Playskool's parent Hasbro and its rival Mattel. Many of the best-selling toys of the 1990s were tied to movies, such as *Star Wars, Jurassic Park,* and *Batman.* Playskool's original educational mission seemed somewhat at odds with the intense competition and faddishness of the 1990s toy marketplace. Yet Playskool was part of a huge company with expanding international markets and extensive marketing ability. It seemed possible that Playskool as a brand would evolve into new toy areas. Hasbro had great success with a new division of Interactive Games, computer-based games for children. Playskool's Mr. Potato Head was the star of one such game, for children aged three to seven years. Hasbro's ability to turn the Playskool brand to many different uses seemed indicative of Playskool's strength and renown and, no doubt, its continued prevalence.

Further Reading

Bayer, Tom, "Playskool Relaunches Tommee Tippee," *Advertising Age,* October 21, 1985, p. 80.
Berg, Eric N., "King of the Playroom Hath Fallen," *New York Times,* December 25, 1989, pp. 37, 39.
Byrd, Veronica, "Playskool Gives Voice to Purple Dinosaur," *New York Times,* July 9, 1993, p. D3.
"Dutton Creates Playskool Imprint," *Publisher's Weekly,* January 30, 1995, p. 40.
Furger, Roberta, "Spud Alert," *PC World,* May 1996, p. 306.
Greenhouse, Steven, "Suit on Toy Plant Ended in Midwest," *New York Times,* February 2, 1985, p. 42.
——, "Tighter Rein on Incentives for Business," *New York Times,* January 13, 1985, p. E4.
"Hasbro Battles Mattel at Toy Fair 1998," *Knight-Ridder/Tribune Business News,* February 9, 1998, p. 209B0975.
"Hasbro Picks Arnold for Playskool," *Adweek,* May 27, 1996, p. 6.
"Hasbro Shifts Playskool Account," *Adweek,* March 31, 1997, p. 6.
"Hasbro Unit in Agreement To Sell Teddy Ruxpin Toys," *Wall Street Journal,* September 9, 1991, p. B5.
Henderson, Bruce, "EPA Fines Microban $160,500 for Making Public Health Claims," *Knight-Ridder/Tribune Business News,* December 16, 1997, p. 1216B0916.
"New Playskool Toys To Have Antibacterial Protection," *Knight-Ridder/Tribune Business News,* January 28, 1997, p. 128B0949.
"Nonviolent Toymaker," *Forbes,* May 1, 1966, p. 36.
"Playskool Gears Up for '95 with Broad-Based Line Extensions," *Playthings,* February 1995, p. 82.
"Playskool Hikes Its '70 Ad Budget 50% to $1,500,000," *Advertising Age,* April 6, 1970, p. 30.
Vander Schaaf, Rachelle, "Germ-Fighting Toys," *Parents,* July 1997, p. 25.
"Viacom's Nickelodeon Sets Venture To Make Children's Products," *Wall Street Journal,* May 11, 1995, p. B2.

—A. Woodward

Primedex Health Systems, Inc.

1516 Cotner Avenue
Los Angeles, California 90025
U.S.A.
(310) 478-7808
Fax: (310) 445-2980
Web Site: http://www.pmdx.com

Public Company
Incorporated: 1985 as CCC Franchising Corporation
Employees: 505
Sales: $67.0 million (1997)
Stock Exchanges: NASDAQ
Ticker Symbol: PMDX
SICs: 8093 Specialty Outpatient Clinics; 8741
    Management Services; 6719 Holding Companies

Primedex Health Systems, Inc., headquartered in Los Angeles, is engaged in the delivery and administration of managed health care. Through its RadNet subsidiary, the company owns and operates 19 imaging centers that provide high-quality, cost-effective diagnostic radiology services throughout California. The company also engages in administrative and managerial activities through subsidiaries such as RadNet Management, Inc.

Primedex Beginnings: The 1980s to Early-1990s

Primedex's beginnings can be traced to 1985, when a group of associates joined together to form a holding company called CCC Franchising Corporation. At that time, they had no way of knowing about the long, rocky journey the future held in store for their new enterprise. Controlled by financier Robert E. Brennan, the company went public just a year after inception, in 1986. CCC Franchising Corp. later made its entry into the medical services field in November 1990, when the company acquired 51 percent of an organization called Viromedics for the sum of $700,000. Viromedics was a company based in Hauppage, New York, and was a world leader in AIDS research; the company worked in cooperation with New York's Albert Einstein College of Medicine to develop a treatment for AIDS.

Soon thereafter, in 1992, the company purchased approximately 90 percent of common stock of the Moorhead, Minnesota-based Immuno Therapeutics, Inc. Like Viromedics, Immuno Therapeutics was a disease researcher; its work involved the research and development of treatments for cancer, as well as other diseases.

At that time, Robert E. Brennan held 60 percent of the shares for CCC Franchising, but did not serve as an officer or director for the company. In partnership with Los Angeles-area doctors, Brennan and the CCC Franchising associates announced plans to buy Primedex Corporation, a southern California workers' compensation medical enterprise which supplied management, administrative and financial services to six Los Angeles clinics. Shortly thereafter, in March of 1992, an agreement was also reached with RadNet Management, Inc. This $66 million deal would make RadNet, a service provider to 11 imaging centers in California, an important part of the ever-evolving CCC Franchising. Later in January, 1992, the company's wholly owned subsidiary, CCC Franchising Acquisition Corporation I, entered into an asset purchase agreement with Primedex Corp. for approximately $46 million. CCC Franchising Acquisition Corporation II, another wholly owned subsidiary, made a similar purchase agreement with RadNet Management, Inc.

Due to their ever-growing presence in the medical service industry, shareholders approved a corporate name change to Primedex Health Systems, Inc., in November, 1992. Now with a name that better reflected the company's role in the health care services market—as well as the acquisitions of Primedex Corp. and RadNet—the company began to focus on its medical field services. A concentration on management, financial and administrative support in workers' compensation, and diagnostic radiology and imaging was underway.

The company's subsidiaries remained intact, and their business operations were not changed much. RadNet managed and provided related services to a group with two imaging centers in the Los Angeles area, owned three imaging centers elsewhere in the state, and was a joint partner in seven others California

382

Company Perspectives:

If the concept of managed care is accepted as central to health-care reform—and we strongly believe it will be—then building a competitive capability will be the determinant of survival for medical services companies. Managed care will become a lower-margin, volume-driven business where the ability to compete on price and quality will be essential. Also, crucial to the success of managed care companies will be extensive provider networks, sophisticated administrative systems, and vertical integration of businesses within defined geographic areas. Our emphasis will be on aggressively expanding our Company in a manner compatible with the many opportunities we believe will be available in a managed care environment.

centers, while developing plans for regional expansion. Primedex Corp. managed medical practices serving those with work-related injuries. To get an edge over competitors in the workers' compensation market, the company used the best available technology for x-ray capabilities, brain-mapping and computerized back-testing equipment. Workers' compensation attorneys sought providers who could expedite claims with fast, accurate evaluations, and Primedex filled that niche.

Late in fiscal 1993, the company acquired Advantage Health Systems, Inc. This addition brought what Primedex's president and CEO at the time, John H. Petillo, Ph.D., called "advanced medical management procedures which draw heavily on expert medical and technical systems to achieve efficient, high-quality and cost-effective health care delivery." Products offered by Advantage included Physician Directed Care Management—a medical/surgical management program—and Network Management Services, which was a network modification and management service used to lead traditional indemnity-type insurance into managed care.

Legal Entanglements in the Mid-1990s

The company's acquisitions had been made in hopes of accommodating the expected growth in managed care due to 1990s health care reforms. With the additions of RadNet and Advantage, Primedex owned and provided management services and/or had interests in 17 different California diagnostic imaging centers. This enlargement of the company came with a price, however. In 1993, Primedex experienced a net loss of $47.8 million, or $1.25 per share; RadNet suffered operating losses of $13.5 million. These figures were due, at least in part, to the negative impact on the company's business that came from California legislation that cracked down on workers' compensation fraud. These reductions in collection percentages of the company's workers' compensation-related accounts receivable, resulted in a poor financial performance.

As a result of this negative financial impact, all offices of Primedex Corp. were closed. While this was a difficult decision for the company to make, Primedex Health System management determined that it was in the best interests of the

company and its stockholders to phase out the workers' compensation business and to concentrate instead its other areas of business.

According to a June, 1994 *New York Times* article by Diana B. Henriques, the Los Angeles District Attorney's office issued search warrants to Primedex controlling shareholder, Robert E. Brennan, whom she described as an "embattled Wall Street financier." This investigation was to determine if the company committed fraud, as they allegedly submitted inflated bills to workers' compensation insurers. Additionally, the Los Angeles D.A.'s office searched executive Primedex offices in Newark, New Jersey, and other company facilities in California.

This investigation of the Primedex Corp. unit and its association with worker's compensation plan treatment and evaluation went on for about two years. Having first performed a raid of the Primedex Health Systems' California offices in late 1992, fraud squad investigators again raided offices in 1994 in Los Angeles, New Jersey and New York for evidence of wrongdoing. Specifically, the warrants pertained to activities including alleged criminal conspiracy, tax and securities fraud, and grand theft. A Los Angeles grand jury sought additional related documents, and Robert Brennan was charged with securities fraud and ordered to repay $71 million in illegal profits made from the manipulation of stock trading in the early 1980s. He and his new company—First Jersey Securities—filed for bankruptcy less than one week before they were due to pay the judgment against them.

Brennan also managed to sell 10 million shares of Primedex, which accounted for 26 percent of the company, in August of 1994 for a sum of approximately $1.4 million. These shares, bought by Dr. Howard G. Berger—the company secretary, as well as a director and chairman of RadNet—made him Primedex's principal shareholder, with about 32 percent ownership. The same shares that added to Brennan's wealth in August, soon dropped in value and were worth only about $.50 per share six months later.

The company decided to spin off its Care Advantage, Inc. subsidiary, and place former Primedex CEO John J. Petillo as its leader. This unit, which handled Advantage Health Systems, Inc., advised insurance companies on how to reduce medical claim costs. Declared effective as of June 12, 1995, over 40 million shares were distributed to company shareholders, one share per each Primedex share owned prior to market close on June 28, 1995.

Robert Caruso, who had served as vice-president and chief financial officer under Petillo, succeeded him as chairman. In June, 1995, authorities charged Caruso with 18 counts of alleged tax evasion, money laundering and fraud. These accusations stemmed from charitable donations he had made to his college alma mater. As Caruso donated money to the school, the company for which he had worked—the accounting firm of Coopers & Lybrand—reimbursed him. Then, Caruso had his donations refunded to him by the university on the premise that he would return the money. This meant that he was getting tax breaks and reimbursement dollars for donations that allegedly never existed. He claimed to have made more than $176,000 in contributions between 1987 and 1993; however, after reimbursements and refunds, the actual amount was stated to be roughly $2,000.

Less than a year later, the Los Angeles District Attorney's office announced that it was not investigating the current management or present business activities of Primedex Health Systems or its subsidiaries. The probe continued, however, with the investigation of activities of individuals who were part of Primedex Corp. One of the founders of Primedex Corp., Dr. David G. Gardner, surrendered to police in June of 1996 after being charged in a $4.2 million tax fraud and money-laundering scam relating to the said organization.

The Late 1990s and Beyond

Meanwhile, Primedex Health Systems continued to amass a wealth of medical service provider subsidiaries. November 1995, saw the acquisition of a California preferred provider organization network business, Future Diagnostics, Inc., for terms totaling approximately $3.2 million. The addition of this company formed the foundation of the new Primedex subsidiary, RadNet Managed Imaging Services. In addition to providing quality assurance and comprehensive utilization management, this new unit was now one of the largest diagnostic radiology networks in the state of California.

Diagnostic Imaging Services, Inc. (Diagnostic) became the next business associate of the company when a series of agreements were entered into in March 1996. Although the two companies intended to remain separate, the purchase of almost three million shares of Diagnostic stock—with arrangements to acquire about 1.5 million more shares over the next five years—made Primedex the single largest Diagnostic stockholder, owning roughly 31 percent of outstanding shares. In addition, the companies executed two management agreements. The first arranged for the company to assume the management of Diagnostic's corporate responsibilities. The second was in regard to the company assuming management responsibilities for various patient services, and billing and collection activities at all Diagnostic facilities. Primedex owned and operated 19 diagnostic imaging centers, and with this arrangement added the 10 imaging centers, 15 ultrasound laboratories located in hospitals, 13 mobile ultrasound units which served hospitals and office buildings, and one mobile magnetic resonance imaging unit owned and operated by Diagnostic. Diagnostic also operated a cancer care therapy center in California.

By May 1996, the two companies had begun to talk about merging. Together, Primedex and Diagnostic had a gross revenue of about $135 million. Upon completion of the merger, shareholders of Primedex were to receive one share of Diagnostic for every 1.33 shares of Primedex. Furthermore, Primedex still owned the warrant to acquire more than 1.5 million additional shares of Diagnostic common stock.

The Los Angeles District Attorney filed additional charges regarding the indictment of David Gardner on June 1, 1996. Other company executives were added to the now expanded fraud case. Stanley Goldblum, controller of Primedex Corp., and Vincent Punterere, medical staff director of Primedex Corp. were both charged as well. No current management or present business operations of Primedex Health Systems were included in the indictment. The defendants were charged with insurance fraud, providing illegal kickbacks to doctors, charging for medical services that were never performed, and ghostwriting medical reports. Gardner, who had previously turned himself in to authorities, was free on bail of $3.2 million.

Soon thereafter, merger negotiations were suspended indefinitely between Primedex and Diagnostic, for reasons which were not disclosed. All previously arranged management contracts, however, remained in place. Primedex continued to increase its ownership of Diagnostic with a purchase of approximately 2.5 million shares of Diagnostic Health common stock that had been owned by Norman Hames, president of Diagnostic. Primedex now held a controlling 53 percent interest in the company. Primedex was also to acquire Hames' options to buy up to 507,737 more various-priced shares of Diagnostic Imaging Systems. More Diagnostic stock acquired in August of 1996 raised the company's equity interest up to approximately 60 percent.

Dr. Howard Berger, the company's largest shareholder, filled the post of presidency after Herm Rosenman resigned from the position in September, 1996. Already chairman of Primedex, Berger added the duties of president and chief executive officer.

By late 1996, Primedex and its subsidiaries owned and operated 32 imaging centers for radiologic services. Diagnostic operated 15 ultrasound laboratories and 13 mobile ultrasound units. Through its Future Diagnostics subsidiary, Primedex arranged imaging services through a network of 180 contracted imaging centers in California which provide diagnostic services to health plans, insurance companies, and others. Future Diagnostics provided a variety of healthcare management services to contracted centers, as well as physician credentialing and financial information systems services.

In March of the following year, the first phase of a sales transaction between Diagnostic Services, Inc. and Diagnostic Health Services was arranged by Primedex. Through this agreement, Diagnostic was to sell Diagnostic Health 13 mobile ultrasound units and 15 ultrasound laboratories for approximately $7.5 million cash and assumption of about $1.5 million in debt. Intended to assist Diagnostic in reducing its debt, the sale would also allow the company to focus on the operations of its eight mostly multi-modality free-standing diagnostic imaging centers. As part of the agreement, Primedex was to provide information management and business services to Diagnostic Health for the operation of their four magnetic resonance imagining centers. By late 1997, Future Diagnostics was sold to Preferred Health Management, Inc.

Principal Subsidiaries

RadNet Management, Inc.; Diagnostic Imaging Services, Inc.; Primedex Corporation; RadNet Managed Imaging Services, Inc.; Beverly Radiology Medical Group III; Radnet Sub, Inc.; Woodward Park Imaging Center; Imaging Center of La Habra; Westchester Imaging Group; Wilshire Imaging Group; Scripps Chula Vista Imaging Center, L.P.

Further Reading

Darlin, Damon, "Like a Fly to Honey," *Forbes*, March 13, 1995, p. 132.

Henriques, Diana B., "New Brennan Inquiry Reported in California," *New York Times,* June 23, 1994, p. D2.

"Primedex's Berger Buys," *Dow Jones News Service,* June 5, 1995.

Quinn, William T., "Executive Reconnects with the Blues," *The Star-Ledger,* July 20, 1995.

——, "Besieged Brennan File for Chapter 11," *The Star-Ledger,* August 9, 1995.

——, " 'Movers and Shakers' End Up Brennan's Strange Bedfellows," *The Star-Ledger,* September 30, 1995.

Rudolph, Robert, "Executive Accused of Bogus Seton Hall Donations—U.S. Indicts 'Distinguished Alum' in charity Refund-Check-off Scheme," *The Star-Ledger,* June 28, 1995.

Silverstein, Stuart, "New Charges Added in Workers' Compensation Case," *Los Angeles Times,* June 1, 1996, p. D7.

—Melissa West

Rainforest Cafe, Inc.

720 South Fifth Street
Hopkins, Minnesota 55434
U.S.A.
(612) 945-5400
Fax: (612) 945-5492
Web site: http://www.rainforestcafe.com

Public Company
Incorporated: 1994
Employees: 5,000
Sales: $108.1 million (1997)
Stock Exchanges: NASDAQ
Ticker Symbol: RAIN
SICs: 5812 Eating Places

Rainforest Cafe, Inc. owns, operates, and licenses large, high-volume, themed restaurants/retail shops under the name ''Rainforest Cafe—A Wild Place To Shop and Eat.'' The company has received industry recognition for its family-oriented restaurant and themed entertainment achievements. The retail area included in each unit offers items ranging from cooking sauces and personal accessories to children's toys and clothing. A majority of the merchandise carries the Rainforest Cafe brand name. The restaurants are located in the United States and abroad.

Creative Urge Drives Founding in 1994

Steven Schussler demonstrated his marketing flare in a number of undertakings prior to the creation of the Rainforest Cafe. Boxed in a crate, he had himself delivered to the general manager of a Miami radio station in a successful ploy for a sales job. After a stint in electronic media marketing in his hometown of New York City, he established a vintage jukebox retail shop. The venture led to the development of JukeBox Saturday Night, a chain of eight restaurant/nightclubs, including one in Minneapolis. But when interest in the 50s-style concept faded in the late 1980s, business fell off. He was forced into bankruptcy in 1991.

But the idea man already had another plan in the works. In 1989 Schussler transformed his suburban Minneapolis home into a prototype for a rainforest motif restaurant. Erick Schonfeld wrote in a 1996 *Fortune* magazine article, ''Three years ago, Steven Schussler was headed for either restaurant heaven or the psychiatric ward.''

Parrots, 150-pound tortoises, and a baboon were among the animals that at one time or another lived among the artificial waterfalls, greenery, and huge fish tanks that filled his home. But that was not the half of it—he spent more than half a million dollars in developing a simulation of the sensory experience of the rainforest.

Schussler pitched the concept to stream of potential investors, including Lyle Berman, a successful casino developer and former leather retailer. Although he repeatedly declined to invest, Berman eventually hired Schussler to develop a restaurant for Grand Casinos, Inc. Backers gained during his work with Grand Casinos plus a favorable lease with the Mall of America in Bloomington, Minnesota, finally brought Berman aboard.

The Rainforest Cafe was incorporated in February 1994; Berman led the private stock placement that allowed Schussler to bring his dream into reality. The doors opened for business in October 1994. Within a week the wait for a table was as much as three hours.

Going Public: 1995

Just six months later the Rainforest Cafe made its initial public offering (IPO). The IPO consisted of one share of common stock with a warrant to purchase one additional share. The company raised $9.5 million from the IPO and an additional $14.2 million from the warrants. The newly issued stock climbed from its asking price of $6 to the mid-teens by October, when a second, larger restaurant opened in the Woodfield Mall in suburban Chicago.

Martin O'Dowd came on board in May 1995 to guide the store expansion. The new president and chief operation officer was a veteran of the industry, having served as director of food and beverage services with Holiday Inn Worldwide and as store manager for the Hard Rock Cafe. Berman continued in his capacity as chairman and CEO. Schussler held a position as executive vice-president.

The Mall of America unit earned $10 million in 1995; operating margins were 23 percent for the second half of the year. The restaurant, expanded three times since opening, seated 295 customers. "The appeal is really in the space, which was designed to wow children and those adults with a child-like worldview. It has live birds, bright fish tanks, and mechanical animals. Every 25 minutes, the lights dim, and a rain storm sweeps through the place. Nothing on the menu is particularly noteworthy (the most popular dish is called Rasta Pasta, a white-sauce dish with chicken and spinach), but the plates are full and the service is brisk," wrote Lee Schafer in an October 1995 *Corporate Report Minnesota* article.

A secondary common stock offering brought in $73.7 million in January 1996 to fuel expansion. Rainforest stock was trading in the $45 to $50 range in June of 1996, about the time a third store, again in suburban Chicago, began operation. Jennifer Waters, in June 1996 *Minneapolis/St. Paul CityBusiness* wrote, "To be sure, the pricey stock is based on some pretty high expectations, many analysts said."

Expansion Accelerates: 1996

Expectations for Rainforest Cafe were elevated by the sites for new restaurants. A new unit was set to open at Walt Disney World Resort in Orlando, Florida, and a second 500-seat unit was being planned for the new Animal Kingdom opening in Epcot Center in 1998. Both were expected to do well in the high-profile areas. Other heavy-traffic sites on tap included the Trump Taj Mahal Casino and Hotel in Atlantic City and the Stratosphere in Las Vegas. More regional mall sites also were staged to open.

Some analysts thought an even greater earnings potential lay on the retail side of the store. About a quarter of sales already came from the cafes' adjacent retail areas. A line of proprietary animal characters was in the works to help heighten brand identification. Analyst Rob Nicoski said in the Waters article, "The Rainforest theme is a good one for kids, and once they start developing Disney-like characters for that side of the business, there will be opportunity."

The family-oriented Rainforest Cafe operated in a restaurant industry segment dominated by businesses catering to adults, such as the Hard Rock Cafe, which reached the quarter century mark in 1996. Rainforest Cafe liquor sales, for example, were comparatively low. Passersby in the malls could watch the daily on-site educational presentations, which included resident parrots, and an outreach program conducted in schools and for other community groups focused on vanishing habitats and wildlife.

Rainforest Cafe, like the other theme restaurants, drew a horde of customers with the promise of entertainment. Planet Hollywood's Disney store was pulling in more than $40 million a year. Altogether, the restaurant niche reported an estimated half billion dollars a year in sales and was expected to climb to $5 billion by the year 2000, according to a 1996 *Star Tribune* article by Ann Merrill.

Capitalizing on the strength of the market, the Rainforest Cafe made another secondary stock offering, in September 1996, and raised an additional $96 million. Four new restaurants opened during the year, including the Disney unit. But two sites were scratched. One of them was in the struggling Stratosphere Tower—Berman held a 42 percent interest in the Las Vegas casino-hotel complex.

The first stand-alone site was planned for downtown Chicago in an entertainment district already home to Planet Hollywood, the Hard Rock Cafe, and Rock 'n' Roll McDonald's. But the locale presented the company with some new problems. The Rainforest Cafe had relied on a "tag-and-release" system that allowed customers to shop or sightsee to ameliorate long waits for a table. The system was less conducive for the downtown location.

Revenue for 1996 was $48.7 million, more than triple the previous year. Net income was $5.9 million. In addition to racking up earnings and profits the company brought in awards from various industry groups: Retailer of the Year Award from the National Retailer Federation, an Outstanding Achievement award from the Themed Entertainment Association, and a winner of *Nation's Restaurant News* 1997 Hot Concepts.

Growing Pains: 1997

Although the Rainforest Cafe began the year with strong sales and operating margins, some glitches had appeared on the screen. Another large project stalled, this time the Trump Taj Mahal. A $1.9 million write-off was taken to cover that development and the previously scratched Stratosphere unit. In May, President and Chief Operating Officer Martin O'Dowd resigned, citing personal reasons. When he came on board analysts had touted his arrival as crucial to the future growth of the business. Two months later the company's largest institutional investor, Putnam Investments Inc. of Boston, dropped its holdings from nearly 13 percent to just less than two percent.

In spite of the difficulties, expansion continued. By the end of the year 13 domestic restaurants were in operation. The company opened seven during the year, including one at the MGM Grand Hotel in Las Vegas. The first international sites also opened, one each in London, Cancun, and Mexico City.

Rainforest stock dropped 40 percent when the company announced in early 1998 that fourth quarter earnings would fall short of expectations. The three units that had been open more than 18 months were down by 11 percent compared with the previous year's fourth quarter earnings. A number of class action lawsuits were filed against the company, claiming management had known of but not reported in a timely manner a declining trend in sales figures while selling their own stock at the higher price. The company withdrew plans for a proposed public offering of convertible subordinated stock.

But overall net income and revenue doubled for the year. Revenues were $108 million and net income amounted to $12 million. The original Mall of America store increased sales by three percent on the year. And the Disney World unit was among one of the nation's busiest restaurants, with sales of $33 million, according to a January 1998 *Twin Cities Business Monthly* article. The company expected to proceed with its plans for 13 to 15 new restaurants in 1998. Costs ranged from $7 million for a mall-based unit to $16.5 million for a major tourist site.

Rainforest Cafe was not alone in its earnings woes in 1997. Publicly traded Planet Hollywood stock nose-dived when they reported fourth quarter losses of $44 million. The company had opened more than 30 outlets during the year. "Fueled by the faddish success of just a handful of outlets, theme restaurant chains have a history of pursuing breakneck expansion plans. For a while, all the new openings create strong earnings momentum. In most cases, though, customer fascination wears off, repeat business disappears, and market saturation dooms further growth," wrote Nelson D. Schwartz in a March 1998 *Fortune* magazine article. Unlike Planet Hollywood, with only 16 outlets, the Rainforest Cafe still had room to grow.

In May 1998, Kenneth Brimmer, involved in the financial aspects of the business since the development stage, was named president. He had served in that capacity on an interim basis since O'Dowd's departure. Stock price continued to remain well off its peak. "It has yet to rebound much, despite a generally strong financial performance. Rainforest's stock price likely is being influenced by negative news from others in the segment, too," Ann Merrill wrote in a June 1998 *Star Tribune* article.

Prospects for the Future

The Rainforest Cafe competed on an increasingly crowded field. Although "eatertainment" ventures held only a single-digit percent of the overall restaurant market, the segment was growing 20 percent per year or more, twice the pace of the industry in general. Established theme restaurants were trying to pull in crucial repeat business by revising menus, accepting reservations, and promoting group sales. With nearly 90 outlets in the marketplace, Planet Hollywood began experimenting with other concepts and joint ventures.

The Rainforest Cafe hoped to build future revenue from its growing children's retail line as well as from added restaurants. Small units outside major tourist areas were being considered for the domestic front, while the company continued to search for high traffic locations overseas. Five exclusive international licensing agreements allowing a total of 24 units were already in place in the United Kingdom and Ireland, Mexico, Canada, and Asia.

Further Reading

Barshay, Jill J., "Rainforest Cafe Says Growth Plans Are on Schedule," *Star Tribune* (Minneapolis), February 5, 1998, p. 8D.

"Corporate Capsule: Rainforest Cafe Inc.," *Minneapolis/St. Paul CityBusiness,* May 23, 1997, p. 26.

Elmstrom, Dave, "Will Rainforest Reign?," *Twin Cities Business Monthly,* January 1998, pp. 32–36.

Fiedler, Terry, "Rainforest Suits Cite Sales Drop," *Star Tribune* (Minneapolis), January 15, 1998, p. 1D.

Forster, Julie, "Rainforest Investors Learn It's a Jungle Out There," *Corporate Report Minnesota,* March 1998, pp. 11–15.

Johnson, Greg (Los Angeles Times), "Themed Restaurant Competition Grows," *Star Tribune* (Minneapolis), March 11, 1998, p. 1D.

Kennedy, Tony, "Rainforest Cafe Gets President-COO," *Star Tribune* (Minneapolis), May 19, 1995, p. 3D.

Merrill, Ann, "The Adventure Is About To Begin, Rainforest Cafe's Flying High and Ready To Expand," *Star Tribune* (Minneapolis), October 14, 1996, p. 1D.

——, "It's a Jungle out There: Rainforest Cafe, Amazon in Legal Battle," *Star Tribune* (Minneapolis), June 7, 1997, p. 1D.

——, "Making Eating an Adventure," *Star Tribune* (Minneapolis), June 8, 1998, pp. 1D, 6D.

——, "Rainforest Drops Interim from Brimmer's Title," *Star Tribune* (Minneapolis), May 5, 1998, p. 3D.

——, "Rainforest Plans Offering To Raise Expansion Capital," *Star Tribune* (Minneapolis), December 4, 1997, p. 1D.

——, "Stormy Day: Rainforest Stock Drops 40 Percent," *Star Tribune* (Minneapolis), January 8, 1998, p. 1D.

"Rainforest Cafe Going Downtown in Chicago," *Star Tribune* (Minneapolis), December 5, 1996, p. 1D.

"Rainforest Cafe Inc." *Corporate Report Fact Book 1998,* p. 433.

Schafer, Lee, "Corporate Report Restaurant Review: Rainforest Cafe Inc.," *Corporate Report Minnesota,* October 1995, pp. 47–48.

Schwartz, Nelson D., "How Investors Got 86ed by Theme Restaurants," *Fortune,* March 2, 1998, pp. 234, 236.

Schonfeld, Erick, "Meanwhile in Money-apolis," *Fortune,* May 27, 1996, pp. 95–96, 102.

Shiber, Susan I., "Forest of Dreams," *Entrepreneurial Edge,* Volume 4, 1997, pp. 55–59.

Walkup, Carolyn, "Rainforest Cafe: It's a Jungle in There," *Nation's Restaurant News,* May 12, 1997, pp. 129–30.

Waters, Jennifer, "Rainforest Serves up Exotics," *Minneapolis/St. Paul CityBusiness,* April 22–28, 1994, pp. 1, 30.

——, "Rainforest's New Branches Spread," *Minneapolis/St. Paul CityBusiness,* June 21, 1996, pp. 1, 36.

—Kathleen Peippo

Rally's Hamburgers, Inc.

14255 49th Street North
Clearwater, Florida 33762
U.S.A.
(727) 519-2000
Fax: (727) 519-2001
Web site: http://www.rallys.com

Public Company
Incorporated: 1984
Employees: 5,500
Sales: $144.9 million (1997)
Stock Exchanges: NASDAQ
Ticker Symbol: RLLY
SICs: 5812 Eating Places; 6794 Patent Owners & Lessors

Rally's Hamburgers, Inc. operates a chain of limited-menu, fast-food establishments featuring double drive-thru order and pickup service but no indoor seating except at five experimental locations. One of the largest chains using this arrangement, Rally's has always placed its emphasis on delivering a quality hamburger more cheaply and quickly than its competitors. It features the original signature Rallyburger and Big Buford (a double-patty cheeseburger), two other, newer signature burgers, and a chicken breast sandwich, plus uniquely seasoned fries and onion rings, and soft drinks and milkshakes to complement its entrees. Its menu has remained simple, originally consisting of 11 basic items, all of which are readied within 45 seconds after a customer places an order.

By the close of 1997, the Rally system operated 477 restaurants in 18 states, predominantly in the Midwest and the South. Of these, the company owned 229 units. Another 221 were private or group-owned franchises, and an additional 27, operating under Rally's name, were owned by CKE Restaurants, Inc., one of the principal shareholders of Rally's Hamburgers. CKE, which is the parent company of the Hardee's and Carl's hamburger chains, operates its units as Rally's Hamburgers in California and Arizona and has an affiliate relationship with Rally's.

Rally's is a franchiser and, under the names Rally's Management, Inc. and Rally's Finance, Inc., both a corporate manager and lending agency for franchisees needing loans to finance the purchase of equipment and construction of Rally's modular restaurant units. Within the Rally's system, its subsidiaries—Rally's Hamburgers, Inc., Rally's of Ohio, Inc., Self-Service Drive Thru, Inc., and Hampton Roads Food, Inc.—own and operate Rally's drive-thru restaurants in diverse locales. The company also owns Zipps Drive-Thru, Inc. (ZDT), a subsidiary created to procure and manage the Zipps company and its franchise system.

A Recent Company

Rally's Hamburgers, Inc. is a recent addition to the fast-food business. It was founded and incorporated in Tennessee in 1984 and opened its first restaurant in January 1985, but did not offer franchises until November 1986. It waited an additional three years, until 1989, to go public, the same year in which it created its first subsidiary, Rally's of Ohio, Inc.

At the outset, Rally's adopted its double drive-thru system, basing it on the fact that about half of all fast-food hamburger service is takeout or drive-thru. Rally's restaurants do provide outside patio benches and tables, but, except for the five experimental units, no interior seating, hence the emphasis has always been on quick takeout service and quality food. The arrangement has a 1950s drive-in ambiance, providing a bit of nostalgia that sets it apart from giant chains like McDonald's, Burger King, and Wendy's and giving it a distinct identity.

In 1990, one year after Rally's went public, the company's management reins passed to Burt Sugarman, a film and television producer and major investor in the business. To attract new owner-managers, Sugarman began reducing royalty costs for franchise holders, and, in 1992, after two very promising and profitable years, Rally's even rebated $700,000 to franchisees. These moves and the company's quick expansion prompted analysts to note that Rally's had become a serious contender in the fast-food chain market.

Sugarman oversaw the expansion. It included the buyout of Maxie's of America and Snapps Drive-Thru in 1991 and Zipps

Company Perspectives:

As we work on delivering great food served consistently, our marketing group is working to ensure that a consistent brand positioning gives the consumer a reason to stop in at Rally's. An overall brand positioning focused on serving the BEST hamburger in the industry is being established. A new creative positioning was introduced in April 1998 to support the new brand positioning. "Make me a burger. Hold the hype." communicates the message that great food is the reason to visit a hamburger restaurant, and that toys, movie tie-ins or massive playlands are not a substitute for a great burger.

Drive-Thru in 1992, purchases which added an additional 100 units to Rally's chain. In that same year, Rally's organized MAC 1 to purchase Beaman Corporation, after that company became insolvent and was forced into bankruptcy. Rally's bought all of Beaman's common stock for about $200,000. Beaman, located in Greensboro, North Carolina, had been the contracted fabricator of Rally's modular restaurant units.

1993–96: Difficult Years

The expansion continued in 1993, when Rally's bought West Coast Restaurant Enterprises in a stock exchange agreement and acquired three franchised Rally's restaurants in Bakersfield, California. However, the expansion was becoming too rapid, and in that same year the company lost money, primarily from a $12 million outlay to cover the cost of closing 26 units. It also opened only half the number of its projected 100 new units. Rally's management responded to the losses with attempts to improve efficiency through streamlining its operations. Among other things, it installed computers in each of the company-owned units. Networked to the main office, these point-of-sale computers gave the company logistical control of the day-by-day operation of its restaurants. They also provided a means of monitoring the progress of the various units and making better-informed decisions about market strategies. Still, losses worsened, increasing by 100 percent between 1993 and 1994.

A managerial shake-up followed. Sugarman, who had earlier stepped down, returned as chairman. Losses continued, however, largely because the company's overexpansion and discount-pricing strategy was not advancing Rally's share of the fast-hamburger market. It was reeling under the impact of the "margin-eroding 99-cent sandwich wars" being conducted by giant competitors. Thus, in 1994, the company was forced to abandon some planned expansion projects, including additional real estate purchases and infrastructure investments. It made alternative plans to dispose of up to 60 company-owned units. However, the drastic reduction was modified the following year, despite the fact that the company suffered a net loss of $47 million. Alternative financial strategies helped planners limit downsizing to the closure of 16 of the 60 selected units and an additional nine units that had been performing poorly at core market sites.

In 1995, Rally's introduced some new sandwiches and price points in an effort to outflank the value-meal strategy adopted by Wendy's and McDonald's that was deeply undercutting the 99-cent signature hamburger market of the double drive-thru chains. It also bought out Hampton Roads Food, Inc. and divested itself of the Beaman Corporation, selling all common stock in the module-fabricating company for about $3.1 million. However, it still lost ground. Its stock, once valued at $20 a share, dropped to about $2.50 in the last quarter of 1995, and the company was suffering losses at 55 underperforming units outside its core market. In addition to a frustrating failure to make gains in its tough market, mostly out of its control, in its worst years the company also faced problems of its own devising. For example, its 1996 advertisements were found by industry analysts to be extraordinarily inept, "adolescent, brainless, and offensive," full of appetite-suppressing sexual suggestiveness. Nevertheless, Don Doyle, the new president and CEO of Rally's remained convinced that value and convenience were the keys to a financial turnaround, and despite repeated losses, Rally's was not ready to abandon its basic double drive-thru scheme. What it needed was some new marketing strategies and restructuring.

1997: Checkers Attempt to Purchase Rally's and Alternative Arrangements

At the end of 1966, Rally's shifted its brand positioning strategy partly away from price towards even better quality. The changes resulted in an increase in the size of its basic hamburger patty from 2.8 to 3.2 ounces and the addition of two new signature hamburgers to its core product line—the Barbecue Bacon Cheeseburger and the Super Double.

Other, more essential changes began in 1997. In response to its financial reversals, Rally's began negotiations with a projected buyout of its chain by Checkers Drive-In Restaurants, partly owned by CKE Restaurants, but financial obstacles imposed by the Securities and Exchange Commission prompted the two companies to withdraw from a full merger.

However, both companies saw potential benefits in a close affiliation. In fact, they had actually entered agreements as early as November 1994, when Rally's, through an exchange of property and a waiver arrangement, acquired some leases for Checkers restaurants and converted five existing units into Rally's restaurants. New negotiations were started in November 1997, when Rally's entered a management agreement with Checkers. Under its terms, Checkers began providing various administrative services for Rally's. That move was followed by a stock exchange agreement in December. Rally's purchased over 19 million shares of Checkers common stock, including 14.4 million shares owned by CKE and Fidelity National Financial (FNF), a California-based title insurance underwriting firm headed by William P. Foley, II, who was then chairman of both CKE and Checkers. Also involved in the arrangement was the Giant Group, a masonry and portland cement company headed by Sugarman and holder of a large block of Rally's stock. In the exchange, Rally's issued shares of its common stock and a new series of preferred stock. The purchase made Rally's, with 27 percent of the outstanding shares, the largest holder of Checker's common stock. When converted, the two major investors, CKE and FNF, would own about 44 percent of the outstanding shares of Rally's common stock.

Although it was not an official merger, the stock-exchange plan allowed Rally's and Checkers to restructure and consolidate their managerial staffs. Foley replaced Sugarman as Rally's chairman. Corporate headquarters also moved from Louisville, Kentucky, to Clearwater, Florida, into the same building housing the headquarters of Checkers. This was a cost-saving move that combined the operational and administrative functions of the two companies. It thereby allowed for the benefits of a merger without obligating either company to undertake the costly accounting procedures required by the Securities and Exchange Commission. Among the benefits was a reduction in food costs made possible by the fact that the 5,000 restaurants in the CKE family were in a better position to leverage prices than was possible for the individual companies comprising the cooperative group.

New Strategies for 1998 and After

The cooperative managerial team also sought to develop a new "positioning" strategy designed to counter the low-price promotional strategy employed by other major chains like McDonald's and Burger King in their special "value" packages and low-price promotions. As part of the new strategy, Rally's began experimenting with indoor seating, responding to the fact that about 50 percent of fast-food customers want to dine in. Beginning in 1997, as a test, it remodeled five double drive-thru units into restaurants with indoor dining, with encouraging but inconclusive results. In addition, it has permitted a few franchisees to open Rally's restaurants in some empty buildings that had formerly housed restaurants using concepts incompatible with a double drive-thru arrangement. In 1998, Rally's also sought to enhance its public face by negotiating a $12 million ad campaign with M&C Saatchi, replacing the agency that prompted the harsh criticism of its earlier Rally's ads. The new spots with the keynote motto—"Make me a Burger. Hold the hype."—began airing on national television in March. The company also entered into an agreement with the North Carolina-based Fresh Foods, Inc. (formerly named WSMP, Inc.) that resulted in the placing of Rally's brand products in retail stores and clubs. Fresh Foods, comprised of wholly owned subsidiaries, packages and markets branded sandwiches in its prepared food division. Its tie-in with Rally's as well as CKE and Checkers was strengthened with the addition of Foley and Andrew F. Puzder, executive vice-president of both CKE and FNF, to its board of directors in May 1998.

Nonetheless, Rally's continued to face problems. In 1997, its revenues dropped to $144.9 million, off about 11 percent from the previous year. Its slide in a very difficult market needed to be reversed, but as of mid-summer 1998 there had been no indication of an imminent turnaround. Its original strategy of offering a good hamburger at a low price was still being hurt by the marketing strategies of much larger competitors. In addition, it remained a defendant in putative class-action lawsuits originating in 1994 which were yet to be resolved and could prove costly, although Rally's management assured investors that the litigation should not have a negative impact on either its operations or financial condition.

Rally's management believed the company would survive and prosper, though perhaps in modified form. In the playing out of the financial arrangements, CKE would have effective control of Rally's, Checkers, Hardee's, Carl's, and Carl's, Jr., and appeared in a position to further streamline operations in cost-cutting maneuvers that should promote a greater profit margin for each of the associated companies. That and Rally's flexible marketing strategies kept the company's officers upbeat about the future.

Principal Subsidiaries

MAC 1, Inc.; RAR, Inc.; Rally's Finance, Inc.; Rally's Management, Inc.; Rally's of Ohio, Inc.; Self-Service Drive Thru, Inc.; Zipps Drive Thru, Inc. (ZDT); Rapid, Inc.; Hampton Roads Food, Inc.

Further Reading

Carlino, Bill, "Doyle Sets Course to Steer Rally's into Less 'Troubled' Seas," *Nation's Restaurant News*, April 8, 1996.

Garfield, Bob, "Rally's Touts Taste, Though It Has None," *Advertising Age*, March 4, 1996, p. 37.

Hamstra, Mark, "CKE Crafts Merger of Checkers, Rally's," *Nation's Restaurant News*, April 7, 1997, pp. 1, 6.

Hayes, Jack, "Drive-Thru Players Rev up for Test of Indoor Seating," *Nation's Restaurant News*, September 1, 1997, pp. 3, 79.

——, "Seeking New Weapons to Defuse the Price Wars," *Nation's Restaurant News*, May 2, 1994, p. 11.

Howard, Theresa, "Double-Drive-Throughs Tuning Engines: Big 3 Shift Gears to Stay on Course," *Nation's Restaurant News*, April 11, 1994, pp. 1, 37.

——, "Rally's Shifts Gears with New Chief Exec Laney Howard," *Nation's Restaurant News*, February 14, 1994, pp. 1, 80.

Kim, Hank, "Rally's Makes Its Pick," *Adweek*, 38, November 24, 1997, p. 4.

Martin, Richard, "CKE Adds Checkers to Rally's Effort Fix," *Nation's Restaurant News*, 30, November 25, 1996, pp. 1, 56.

Papiernik, Richard L., "Goliath Slams David: Rally's Takes a Tumble in QSR Value Wars," *Nation's Restaurant News*, September 25, 1995, pp. 9, 22.

——, "Rally's Clears Nasdaq Hurdle with $10.8m, Posts 2q Profit," *Nation's Restaurant News*, October 14, 1996, p. 12.

Pollack, Judann, "Rally's Big Buford Ads Stir Small Controversy," *Advertising Age*, March 4, 1996, p. 12.

"Rally's Hamburgers Agrees to Acquire 16.8 Million Shares of Checkers," *Meat Industry Insights Newsletter*, http://www.pb.net/spc/mii/970926.htm.

"Rally's into Major Change As Losses Mount in 3rd Q," *Nation's Restaurant News*, November 27, 1995, p. 12.

Welling, Kathryn M., "1994 Roundtable (Part 2): Pick of the Portfolio," *Barron's*, January 24, 1994, pp. 12–37.

—John W. Fiero

Recovery Engineering, Inc.

9300 North 75th Avenue
Minneapolis, Minnesota 55428
U.S.A.
(612) 315-5500
Fax: (612) 315-5505
(800) 787-5463

Public Company
Incorporated: 1986
Employees: 345
Sales: $71.2 Million (1997)
Stock Exchanges: NASDAQ
Ticker Symbol: REIN
SICs: 3589 Service Industry Machinery; 2899 Chemical
    Preparations, Not Elsewhere Classified; 3569 General
    Industrial Machinery, Not Elsewhere Classified; 3400
    Fabricated Metal Products

Recovery Engineering, Inc. (Recovery) is an industry leader in the design, manufacture, and marketing of small-scale drinking water treatment systems, which are sold under the PUR brand name. It is the fastest-growing company in the household water filter industry, claiming the number one brand of in-line water filters and the second leading brand of all household water filters sold in the United States. Recovery's products include a line of self-monitoring water filters for household use, portable drinking water systems for outdoor enthusiasts, and the world's most energy efficient line of desalinators for sailors and military personnel. PUR household water filters are offered in a variety of configurations, including pour-through pitchers and dispensers and in-line faucet-mounted, countertop, and under-sink filter systems. The company competes with brands such as Rubbermaid, Culligan, Mr. Coffee, and Honeywell. Its 1997 market share was greater than the combined market shares of all other competitors, excluding Brita, a division of Clorox. Recovery Engineering's products are distributed through approximately 26,000 retail outlets in the United States and Canada, including Wal-Mart, Sears, Target, Costco, Kmart, Macy's, and Walgreens. In 1994 *Business Week* named Recovery Engineering one of the 100 best small companies in America.

Channeling Resources in the 1980s

Brian Sullivan founded the Minneapolis-based company in 1986 after raising $400,000 from private investors. The 24-year-old Harvard economics graduate grew up in Baltimore learning business from his father, Richard Sullivan, who ran the *Fortune* 500 Easco Corporation, a $600-million-per-year company. In a *Twin Cities Business Monthly* interview with Laura Silver, Brian Sullivan said that his father "... provided an example of what you could do—that the only limitation really was yourself." He further explained that following the example of his father and his father's friends, Sullivan assumed that "he would one day run his own company too." After graduating from Harvard, Brian Sullivan moved to London to work for Smith Barney, followed by a move back to the United States and a stint with a New York investment bank. While employed there, he was responsible for the successful turnaround of a manufacturing firm previously overwhelmed by debt. During this period he met Bill Wanner, a Minnesotan whose father had invented a prototype of a manual water desalinator. It was a small, hand-operated device that could make potable water from salt water. Earlier desalinating devices had been cumbersome motorized contraptions, and although a Canadian company had been working on a similar desalination invention, their technology had not yet reached the level of development that Wanner's work had produced. Wanner recognized an opportunity and was looking for someone to develop his fathers' invention—someone who could effectively organize a company to manufacture and market the devices. "When this [desalination] became known, [Paul Wanner] was looking at hiring some other, much older, individual who had a strong background and a lot of business experience," reported investment banker Robert Fullerton, according to Silver. One of Sullivan's professors from Harvard, who knew all the parties involved, intervened and recommended Sullivan over the other individual who had been considered. Sullivan seized upon the opportunity to run a company and hastened to form Recovery Engineering, Inc., recruiting a young Canadian engineer, Dick Hembree, to help him. Hembree became vice-president of engineering for the company. Sullivan and Hembree succeeded in buying Wanner's ideas in exchange for a 40 percent stake in the firm. Offices and manufacturing facilities were established in a 30,000-square-foot Minneapolis plant.

Company Perspectives:

Our mission is to establish PUR as the leading brand of consumer water filters in the world. To accomplish this mission, we will execute the following strategies: We will determine where consumers' needs are unmet and create proprietary technology based on solutions to address these needs; we will offer consumers "good, better, best" models that provide the highest performance and highest quality of any products in the category at prices sufficient to generate above average gross margins; we will distribute products through relevant retail channels and offer derivative products to minimize channel conflict; we will build awareness of the PUR brand and drive sales through aggressive consumer advertising, promotions, and in-store merchandising; we plan to become the low cost manufacturer of products in our categories by designing products for manufacturing and investing aggressively in appropriate capital equipment; and we will initiate product development in other areas where related consumer needs are unmet.

A defining moment occurred for the company when in 1986 it won a $500 million contract with the U.S. Navy to develop a portable hand-pumped saltwater desalinator for use on its life rafts. It had taken two-and-a-half years to prepare the request for the proposal, followed by an eight-month bidding process. While working in Canada, Hembree had been experimenting with high-pressure seawater pumps and the processes involved in desalination. Having moved to Minneapolis in order to provide technical and design expertise for the company, and having developed a purification method comparable to Wanner's, Hembree began work to produce a model to fit the Navy's difficult specifications. Company officials and engineers recognized the enormous engineering and financial risks involved, especially following the explosions of several of their early models, but the modified designs proved successful. They delivered the Navy's desalinator in 1988. Their model was capable of producing up to 35 gallons of water a day, and reduced the energy needed to purify seawater by 90 percent.

That eventual triumph allowed Sullivan to quickly raise another $1.5 million privately, in order to develop the product for the commercial marketplace. Sullivan intended to extend the application of its unique desalinators by making them available to military and civilian sailors, as well as to aviators. Early models had been impractical for lifeboat use, with enormous motorized units pumping at pressures of up to 1,000 pounds per square inch. Recovery's version was a lightweight portable desalinating pump that could be hand-operated by a single person. The pumps operate using a process of reverse osmosis, by forcing water through a semipermeable membrane with a lever driven piston that blocks the salt but allows the liquid to pass through. Water is circulated behind the piston as well, balancing the pressure on the piston's face, requiring little exertion to operate.

Fifteen Minutes of Fame in 1989

Recovery made *People Magazine* in 1989 and was covered by Charles Kuralt for CBS News when one of its products was

responsible for saving the lives of two people sailing around the world. A Florida couple, William and Simone Butler, endured 66 days adrift in the Pacific Ocean, 1,200 miles off the Costa Rican mainland, following an attack on their 40-foot yacht by whales. The yacht sank and survival under such conditions for the couple, without potable water, would usually amount to a time frame of 10 to 12 days. Fortunately for the Butlers they were able to grab their Recovery Survivor-35, a manually operated seven-pound pump for converting saltwater to fresh water, along with a small amount of food and some fishing gear. They subsisted for more than two months on raw fish and the three liters of potable water that William Butler extracted from the Survivor each day. Sullivan contacted the family after hearing the CBS News report, congratulated them on surviving their ordeal, and told Silver in an interview that they [the company engineers] wanted to "look the desalinator over," adding "We were looking for scientific data: what was its condition after usage." The device was proven reliable, and Recovery's reputation was given a substantial boost.

A second product line was introduced in 1990. Geared to campers, backpackers, international travelers, military personnel, and others accessing fresh though potentially contaminated water, the company offered portable water purifiers. Recovery developed its proprietary Tritek disinfection technology, sold under the PUR label as the Traveler, Explorer, and Hiker, which allowed for instant portable disinfection of drinking water, making it microbiologically safe for consumption. In 1993 Recovery raised $4 million through an initial public offering in preparation for expanding into the household filtration products market. Just prior to 1993 Recovery redefined its mission, deciding to focus on becoming "the dominant manufacturers of consumer drinking water products in the world," Sullivan told Silver. In that year the U.S. Environmental Protection Agency had identified microbiological cysts, especially cryptosporidium, as contaminants likely to occur in 55 percent of the nation's surface waters and in 17 percent of the nation's municipal water supplies—as evidenced by the 1993 outbreak of cryptosporidia in Milwaukee, Wisconsin's water supply, which caused 400,000 people to become ill with symptoms of diarrhea, vomiting, fever, and stomach cramps. Since that time sales of residential filtration and purification systems have soared. By 1993 Recovery was earning $5.3 million on sales of $10 million, having increased sales 86 percent over the previous year, and growing to $16.7 million in 1994 following the EPA reports on the hazards of potential cancer-causing chlorine byproducts in addition to high levels of lead, pesticides, and herbicides entering sources of drinking water. Consumers were becoming increasingly aware that even after municipal treatment, water treated with chlorine to kill waterborne microorganisms could be causing certain cancers and other health problems. The type of fluoride used in treating water was also disputed by some—sodium fluoride, with possible deleterious effects was being used in municipal supplies instead of calcium fluoride, which is the form natural to the human body for healthier teeth and bones. Outdated household plumbing could also contribute to lead-tainted tap water. The EPA reported that up to 25 percent of American household water supplies contained unsafe lead levels, making a huge potential market for purification and filtration systems.

Entering the Household Market in the 1990s

Surveying the industry, Sullivan determined that the bottled water business had boomed, while competing companies had tried and failed, for some reason, to provide filters for residential drinking water. In 1994, Recovery offered a faucet-mounted water filter. Consumers had indicated that they were concerned about whether filters prior to PUR's filtration system really worked, and how to know for certain if they did not. Responding to these fears, Recovery added an automatic-safety-monitor technology to show the consumer exactly how much life the filter had remaining. The device worked by automatically shutting off the cartridge when used up, keeping maintenance to a minimum. The company then targeted customers in the United States and Europe and those in developing countries in order to address separate sets of concerns. Products to be sold in America and in Europe were developed to accommodate taste, odor, color, and such chemical contaminants as lead. In Mexico, Brazil, Indonesia, Korea, and other countries where infrastructure lags behind need, the water quality is often unsafe to drink unless boiled, at best. Consumers in those areas frequently have to buy water or wait long periods for water to be purified. Recovery utilized its Tritek technology to offer developing countries a safe in-house alternative. Increasingly, public concern over potentially dangerous contaminants in both private and municipal water supplies was addressed, making the option of home point-of-use water treatment desirable. In 1996 PUR introduced a countertop water filter system and its PUR under-sink water filter system in 1997, with filter cartridges having a useful life of four to six months. The under-sink systems measured approximately nine inches high and offered greater contaminant reduction and longer filter life than the faucet-mounted units. Both types of units employed carbon block technology. Also in 1996, Recovery began marketing its initial pour-through water pitcher which held approximately a half-gallon of water. Further developments resulted in the production of the PUR PLUS pitcher and PUR PLUS dispenser, the only gravity-fed water filters capable of filtering microorganisms as small as cryptosporidium and giardia lamblia. These products incorporated a three-stage filtration cartridge which used activated carbon, ion exchange resin, and a microfilter, and had a useful life of one to two months. In 1997 the company claimed a 28 percent market share, while Brita claimed 57 percent, and Recovery's stock price shot from $6.25 to $31.50 per share, after the company spent $20 million on a marketing campaign to promote the PUR brand name. In February 1998 the company began airing a 30-minute infomercial featuring the PUR PLUS pitcher, designed to generate direct and retail sales by educating consumers about the advantages of its products over those of competitors.

Recovery established an international distribution agreement in 1996 with Groupe-SEB, one of the world's leading suppliers of small household appliances. Groupe-SEB distributed products to over 80 countries under the brand names Rowenta and T-Fal, and was under agreement with Recovery to distribute PUR household water filters in all countries outside North America and Japan. The company also distributed to outdoor enthusiasts and international travelers through a network of outdoor and travel stores, and through mail-order catalogues. Sales to foreign military forces and others were made through approximately 30 distributors located in Europe, Asia, and the Middle East. Other avenues of distribution included advertisements in consumer and trade publications, participation in consumer and trade shows, a periodic newsletter, and promotions through retailers.

The company made large investments in product development, capital equipment, and advertising and promotional expenses. Sales increased 114 percent in 1997 from the previous years revenues, but the company reported a loss of $3.5 million, down from a loss of $12.5 million in 1996. Gross margins had been adversely affected by costs related to entering the household water filter market, including investments made in designing and implementing automated manufacturing and assembly processes, together with the cost of conducting manual assembly operations pending the installation of such automated processes. The enhanced manufacturing capabilities due to these expenditures were expected to be offset by future efficiencies in production.

A second public stock offering was completed in April 1998, netting approximately $33.2 million. Proceeds from the sale were intended to provide additional capital resources for covering the expansion of operations and the introduction of new products. The company launched an innovative pour-through water filter offering a higher level of protection against contaminants. The new products were certified to remove dangerous microorganisms previously available only from in-line systems relying on water pressure, and were affordably priced at less than $40. The pour-through segment accounted for 65 percent of all consumer water filters sold, or roughly five million units annually, according to company reports.

Recovery also introduced a new faucet-mounted water filter that incorporated further advancements in its carbon matrix filtration technology, which filter volatile organic compounds (VOCs) such as trihalomethanes, a byproduct of chlorine and organic matter. The EPA had determined that VOCs can lead to cancer, as well as cause damage to the liver, kidney, nervous, reproductive, or circulatory systems. Recovery expected that the increased sales of its units would result in very significant increased sales of replacement filters as the base of owners of PUR brand products continued to grow. The company also expected that as penetration increased and old systems were replaced, the market for systems could grow to eight to ten million units.

According to John D. Fisher of *Minnesota Technology,* Recovery reportedly employed 36 people in its research and development department—which, Hembree reported, "represents more research and development than all of our other competitors combined." Reasonably assured of the company's dominance in the industry, Hembree added that "It's because we figured out what consumers really wanted and designed a good product to meet the demand."

Further Reading

Finnerty, Brian, "Portable Water Purifiers Make Recovery Engineering a Splash," *Investor's Business Daily,* August 2, 1994.
Fisher, John D., "Water, Water," *Minnesota Technology,* March–April 1998, pp. 8–10.
Silver, Laura, "Prepared for the Worst," *Twin Cities Business Monthly,* August 1994, pp. 1–3.

—Terri Mozzone

Roadway Express, Inc.

1077 Gorge Boulevard
Akron, Ohio 44039
U.S.A.
(330) 384-8184
Fax: (330) 258-6042
Web site: http://www.roadway.com

Public Company
Incorporated: 1930 as Roadway Express, Inc.
Employees: 26,100
Sales: $2.67 billion (1997)
Stock Exchanges: NASDAQ
Ticker Symbol: ROAD
SICs: 4213 Trucking Except Local

Roadway Express, Inc. is the second-largest motor freight carrier company in the United States. It specializes in less-than-truckload (LTL) hauling, principally on two-day or longer trips. The company operates more than 400 shipping terminals in the United States. It also manages shipping facilities in Mexico, and operates a Canadian subsidiary. Roadway ships internationally to more than 60 countries worldwide. Its Asian Roadway Express joint venture offers transportation services between North America and Singapore, Indonesia, Malaysia, and Thailand, with further links to other countries in Asia. Roadway also serves customers in Africa, Australia, Europe, and the Middle East. Roadway Express was formerly a subsidiary of Roadway Services, Inc., but since 1995 it has operated as an independent, publicly owned company. Roadway Services, its former holding company, now operates as Caliber System, Inc.

Early History

Roadway Express was founded in 1930 by brothers Galen and Carroll Roush in Akron, Ohio. Although trucking had made great strides during the 1920s, the motor carrier industry was still in its infancy. Railroads provided the primary transportation for goods from point of manufacture to point of sale. Trucks were used for less than full-load shipments, which was still Roadway's primary market. In 1930 Roadway entered the business it would come to lead with a load of tires shipped from Akron to St. Louis, Missouri.

Roadway Express started with ten owner-operators, and moved shipments to Chicago; Houston, Texas; and Kansas City. Within several months terminals were opened in Atlanta, Georgia; Baltimore, Maryland; Birmingham, Alabama; Charlotte, North Carolina; Indianapolis, Indiana; Knoxville, Memphis, and Nashville, Tennessee; New York; and Philadelphia, Pennsylvania. Roadway's rapid expansion reflected the growth of interstate trucking in general.

Before long, railroaders, fearful of unrestrained competition, began to clamor for regulation. In 1935 Congress passed the Motor Carrier Act, limiting the right to operate in interstate commerce to those carriers already in operation and to new ones that could prove "necessity and convenience." The Interstate Commerce Commission would oversee standard rates, preventing particular customers from receiving preferential rates.

While regulation had its disadvantages, founder Galen Roush, originally trained as a lawyer, saw great potential in the new regulated business climate. Roadway had kept detailed records of its shipments over the years. These records became the basis of Roush's claim to some of the busiest freight routes in the country. Regulation helped limit competition, and at the same time elevated the status of the trucking industry to the equivalent of a public utility. Although it took 16 years of court battles before Roadway's routes were finally secured, the company held exclusive rights to its most lucrative routes.

The Roush brothers recognized the significance of hiring good managers, and instituted tight financial controls early on. Roadway was conservatively run, and kept a very low profile. It maintained this approach for decades.

World War II and Postwar Expansion

In the 1940s demand for truck transportation increased as the defense economy of World War II eliminated the last effects of the Great Depression. At the same time, new trucks were not being built as the necessary materials were being diverted for

Company Perspectives:

Roadway's mission is to contribute to customer success and satisfaction by providing reliable, responsive, and efficient service. Its principal product is LTL (less-than-truckload) transportation on two-day and longer lanes within North America, and on international lanes to and from North America.

war goods. In 1945 Roadway Express began replacing owner-operators with hired drivers to run its own fleet. After the war, trucking gained significant ground from the railroad industry. By 1950 the ratio of truck to train ton-miles was 20 percent, twice that of two years earlier. Roadway began to stress its less-than-truckload service in the early 1950s. The price charged per pound shipped was sometimes three or more times the cost of a full load, and the flexibility of the service improved the chances of a return load.

Business boomed, and Roadway needed to establish a broader terminal network. The company's excellent financial record helped Galen Roush convince Chase Manhattan Bank to loan Roadway millions of dollars for expansion. Trucking companies were previously poorly regarded by most financiers. By 1956 Roadway's fleet and terminal expansion program had progressed to the point where Roadway no longer used owner-operators at all.

In 1956 Carroll Roush, the younger of the two founding brothers, decided to sell his interest in Roadway. He was barely speaking with his brother, Galen, and in a move designed at least in part to annoy him, Carroll sold his shares to the public for about $5 million. Traveling west, he bought ONC Fast Freight, which later became a part of ROCOR International.

In the late 1950s and 1960s, Galen Roush set out to expand the terminal network. Population centers were spreading out, and trucking needed to be less centered around big cities. The greater number of terminals allowed decentralized service. Roadway Express expanded its network from 60 terminals in 1958 to 135 in 1968.

At the same time, Roadway instituted the most sophisticated accounting procedures in the industry, which were the brainchild of cost accountant John L. Tormey. The company could identify profit and loss by route, commodity, weight bracket, and individual customer. As the company expanded rapidly, it was able to focus on profitable business and easily control costs. Roadway truckers continued to haul less-than-truckload shipments and produce higher profit margins. Each terminal was a profit-and-loss center, and aggressive managers were enriched with hefty bonuses.

New Horizons in the 1970s and 1980s

Roadway's expansion during the 1960s required heavy borrowing, but the decision to risk the debt paid off later. The loans were paid off by the 1970s, and cash flow was high. Meanwhile Roadway's competitors were still heavily burdened. When the

recession hit in 1974–75, this financial strength kept Roadway in the leading position in the industry despite the economic hard times. Roadway's return on investment averaged 20 percent a year in the early 1970s. Direct coverage grew to 40 states in the mid-1970s, and the company became a transcontinental carrier in 1977.

In 1980 deregulation of rates and services opened new avenues for motor carriers. This gave Roadway Express the opportunity to expand into new areas of business, but at the same time, the company faced new challenges from competitors. While other trucking companies slashed prices to attract customers, Roadway marketed itself as the high-quality carrier with the widest geographic coverage, and clung to its high margins. By 1982, however, with revenues slipping, Roadway chose to discount its prices. The company had fallen to third in market share, surpassed by Yellow Freight and Consolidated Freightways. Realizing the need to step out of the shadows and reassert its position, Roadway launched its first advertising campaign in history.

After the initial shock of deregulation settled, Roadway embarked on a campaign of acquisition and new services. In 1982 a holding company, Roadway Services, Inc., was set up with Roadway Express as its chief operating subsidiary. In 1984 Roadway Services acquired Spartan Express, Inc.; Nationwide Carriers, Inc.; and Roberts Express, Inc. Spartan Express, Roadway's first acquisition, operated as a short-haul carrier in the South. Unlike Roadway Express, Spartan handled shipments with 24- and 48-hour service requirements. Nationwide Carriers specialized in irregular route truckload shipments throughout the continental United States. Nationwide hauled dry freight, temperature-controlled freight, and freight requiring flatbed transport. Roberts Express specialized in critical or fragile shipments needing special handling or speedy delivery.

In 1985 Roadway's earnings dipped for the first time in 32 years. Conversion of Roadway's truck fleet to twin trailers and start-up costs of a new unit were the chief reasons. The new subsidiary, Roadway Package System (RPS), got a slow start, but became a transportation success story in the 1980s.

RPS set out to take a piece of the $12 billion small-package surface delivery business, then dominated by United Parcel Service (UPS). RPS concentrated on business-to-business delivery of packages of up to 100 pounds, and implemented some innovative procedures to keep costs down. By selling or leasing RPS trucks to independent owner-operators, the company cut labor costs to 60 percent of UPS's while giving each driver a personal stake in efficient service.

It took three years and $103 million in investments before RPS showed a profit, but considering the scale of the start-up, it was an impressive accomplishment. By 1988 the subsidiary boasted 130 terminals, and geographic coverage of 70 percent of the United States. By 1990, 147 terminal facilities served 42 states. While UPS had 20 times the revenue of RPS, Roadway's subsidiary had carved a healthy niche out of a growing segment. RPS contributed one-fourth of Roadway Services's profits in 1989. Growth prospects looked excellent.

Roadway Services, meanwhile, continued to seek less-than-truckload carriers that would complement its existing geographic coverage. In 1988 Roadway acquired Viking Freight, the largest regional carrier in the western United States. Viking had two operating subsidiaries: Viking Freight System, a regional LTL carrier, and VFS Transportation, an irregular-route truckload carrier. Viking was almost alone among carriers in being nonunion.

In 1989 Roadway closed its Nationwide Carriers subsidiary. Nationwide had been unprofitable despite reorganization. The Roadway Express unit struggled with discounted rates in the later 1980s, but successfully held its position against smaller carriers. In 1987 a New York City trucking firm, Lifschutz Fast Freight Inc., filed suit against trucking's big three—Yellow Freight, Roadway Services, and Consolidated Freightways—charging predatory pricing and conspiracy to restrain trade and free competition in certain segments of the industry. The suit sought $598 million in damages. Lifshutz lost his case, but appealed it all the way to the Supreme Court. When the Supreme Court finally declined to hear the case in 1993, the big three trucking firms had spent more than $6 million in refuting the charges made by Lifshutz.

Competition from the railroad industry also grew fierce as the 1980s closed. Threatened by the prospect of bigger double and triple trailers hauling freight on highways, railroad lobbyists launched campaigns painting a grim picture of motor carriers' safety standards. When one such group, the Coalition for Reliable and Safer Highways (CRASH), used a photo of a Roadway Express truck accident at government hearings in California, Roadway's chairman Joseph Clapp objected, citing Roadway's top safety record. Competition between railroaders and truckers promised to become increasingly heated in the 1990s.

Changes in the 1990s

In March 1990 Roadway's Roberts Express unit launched a European subsidiary, Roberts Express, B.V., headquartered in Maastricht, the Netherlands. The subsidiary offered Roberts's traditional services in Belgium, France, Luxembourg, the Netherlands, and Germany. Roadway Express in 1990 set up a Mexican subsidiary, Roadway Bodegas y Consolidación, and expanded operations in Canada.

As Roadway Services entered the 1990s, its various units showed mixed results, although as a whole the company continued to expand. Roadway Express increased revenues and profits. Spartan Express was divided into two geographic divisions in 1988 but remained unprofitable; in 1990 it became a subsidiary of Viking Freight. Roberts Express's growth was good, but less than expected. RPS and Viking Freight both performed well, but the latter's VFS Transportation subsidiary did not, and was closed down in 1990. The surface transportation industry was in for some turmoil, as railroads promised to fight for their space, and as air transport became more competitive. Roadway had dropped its image as a stodgy company, and no longer hesitated to step into the public eye as had been characteristic of the company from its founding through the 1970s. The change at Roadway Services was characteristic of the industry as a whole, illustrated by the fact that in 1991 the Dow Jones transportation averages added Roadway Services as one of the key indicators of the industry's overall performance.

A depressed economy and the pressure of low-cost competitors kept prices down for Roadway in 1991. Its two major competitors, Yellow and Consolidated Freightways, both announced price increases that year. But when Roadway declared that it would not hike its rates, the other two companies backed down. The whole LTL industry was operating with very narrow profit margins. In this environment, Roadway Express found that it was competing with its sibling companies for resources from parent Roadway Services.

Nevertheless, Roadway pressed for expansion. It began offering services to 20 countries in Europe in 1991, and opened export services to the Middle East two years later. It also extended its reach to 24 ports in the Pacific Rim. Much of its international business was shipped from North American origins to port cities, and then to England. From the English distribution site, cargo went on to further ports. Roadway developed an advanced internet tracking system to handle its international shipping.

Roadway Express differed from the newer companies that had come under the wing of Roadway Systems in that it was unionized. The Teamsters Union had negotiated salaries and benefits for their workers that were up to 30 percent more than non-union companies were paying. In 1994 the Teamsters called a strike at Roadway Express that lasted for 24 days. The union was trying to resolve issues of job security and the use of part-time labor. The strike put the Roadway Express in the red for $68 million for that quarter, and the company felt the effects for at least the next year.

So when Roadway Systems announced in August, 1995, that it was spinning off its principal subsidiary, analysts suspected that the company was trying to ditch its unprofitable unionized member. Roadway Systems changed its name to Caliber System, Inc., and moved out of the old Akron headquarters. Its components were then Roadway Package System, its small-package carrier; Roadway Global Air, its air and freight package carrier; and a group of small, non-union regional carriers including Roberts Express and Viking Freight. Roadway Express spun off as a debt-free company, with its own stock, listed on NASDAQ. Its revenues at the time of the spin-off were approximately $2.2 billion, and it served around 500,000 customers worldwide.

The expectation among trucking analysts seemed to be that Caliber would prosper, and Roadway Express might well go under. Its unionized workforce was seen as a huge disadvantage, and Caliber's newer companies were expected to prevail. Instead the opposite happened. A year after the spin-off, Roadway announced profits of $21.8 million. Under its new organization, the company had taken measures to cut costs considerably, closing more than a hundred of its shipping terminals and saving on administrative costs by dividing its operations into four regional units instead of five. Roadway's CEO, Michael Wickham, went to Teamsters headquarters and outlined a plan for cooperation between workers and management that would keep the company competitive. Wickham kept costs down without asking for monetary concessions from the union, and, as a result, got an extremely loyal workforce. Turnover at Roadway was less than three percent annually, while it was not unusual for similar firms to have turnover of close to 100 percent. Roadway did not need to expend resources recruiting and training, and that in itself translated into untold savings for the company.

Roadway seemed poised for greater success free of its holding company. In 1997 Roadway spent $15 million to acquire a Canadian trucking firm, Reimer Express Lines. It expanded its access to Asia by launching Asian Roadway Express, and it released a new computerized tracking system that allowed its agents worldwide quicker access to shipping information. In April 1998 Roadway reached agreement with the Teamsters on a new five-year contract. The contract offered a slight wage and benefit increase, but its longevity was considered its best feature. The five-year span promised a period of stability for both company and workers.

Principal Subsidiaries

Reimer Express Lines, Ltd. (Canada); Roadway Express BV (The Netherlands); Roadway Express Inc. (Canada); Roadway Express International, Inc.; Roadway Express Special Services, Inc.; TNL-Roadway SA de CV (Mexico); Transcontinental Lease SA de CV (Mexico).

Further Reading

Adams, David, "Non-Union Employees Suffer Brunt of Teamsters Strike as Layoffs Mount," *Knight-Ridder/Tribune Business News,* April 24, 1994, p. 04240085.

Briggs, Jean A., "Easing into High Gear," *Forbes,* August 31, 1981.

"Doing It the Hard Way," *Forbes,* December 1, 1975.

Hannon, Kerry, "Shifting Gears," *Forbes,* December 11, 1989.

Hoffman, Kurt, "Spinning Off and Cutting Loose," *Distribution,* November 1995, p. 85.

James, Robert P., "Supreme Court Ends Lifschutz's Six-Year Crusade Against Big Three," *Knight-Ridder/Tribune Business News,* December 5, 1993, p. 12050061.

Lazo, Shirley, "Trucker Declares Its First Payout," *Barron's,* April 15, 1996, p. 41.

Mathew, Anna Wilde, and Glenn Burkins, "Teamsters Reach Tentative Agreement with Truckers on a Five-Year Contract," *Wall Street Journal,* February 10, 1998, p. A2.

Moore, Janet, "Akron-Based Roadway Express Completes Phase-In Export Service to Middle East," *Knight-Ridder/Tribune Business News,* December 28, 1993, p. 12280112.

"Nation's LTL Carriers Back Down on July Rate Increases," *Traffic Management,* July 1991, p. 16.

"The No. 1 Trucker Joins a Price-Cutting Convoy," *Business Week,* February 8, 1982.

Russell, John, "A Year Later, Spinoff Roadway Express Surpasses Parent Caliber Systems," *Knight-Ridder/Tribune Business News,* February 23, 1997, p. 223B0942.

——, "Roadway Earnings Get Boost from Economy, UPS Strike," *Knight-Ridder/Tribune Business News,* October 1, 1997, p. 1001B1080.

Salpukas, Agis, "A Whole Lot of Shaking Going On," *New York Times,* May 5, 1991, p. F5.

—Thomas M. Tucker
—updated by A. Woodward

Rock Bottom Restaurants, Inc.

248 Centennial Parkway
Louisville, Colorado 80027
U.S.A.
(303) 664-4000
Fax: (303) 417-4199
Web site: http://www.rockbottom.com

Public Company
Incorporated: 1994 as Rock Bottom Restaurants, Inc.
Employees: 5,295
Sales: $150.2 million (1997)
Stock Exchanges: NASDAQ
Ticker Symbol: BREW
SICs: 5812 Eating Places; 5813 Drinking Places; 6719
   Holding Companies, Not Elsewhere Classified

The first publicly traded restaurant-brewery company in the United States, Rock Bottom Restaurants, Inc. operates more than 60 casual restaurants underpinned by either an extensive collection of domestic and imported bottled beers or on-site breweries. Predominately located in Colorado, Rock Bottom's restaurants are operated under three banners: Old Chicago, Rock Bottom Brewery, and ChopHouse & Brewery. The company's 42 Old Chicago restaurants feature deep-dish pizza and a trademark 110-brand beer list. The more than 20 Rock Bottom Brewery units feature an eclectic menu and microbeers brewed on the premises. The company's upscale dining and beverage concept is its ChopHouse & Brewery formula, comprising two restaurant-breweries located in Denver and Washington, D.C.

Origins

The central personalities responsible for Rock Bottom's rapid expansion during the 1990s first met in 1973, roughly 20 years before they joined forces to create a chain of combination restaurant-breweries. One of the pair, and the junior of the two, was Thomas A. Moxcey, who was working in Boulder, Colorado as a waiter at a restaurant named Cork & Keg during the

early 1970s. Moxcey proved to be in the right place at the right time because in 1973 he was recruited by a restaurateur named Frank Day, who was putting his academic training as a Harvard M.B.A. to the test. Day was opening his first restaurant, an establishment called The Walrus, and hired Moxcey to help him run the Boulder-based business. Day and Moxcey spent two years working together, then went their separate ways, beginning a 15-year period that saw Day continue as an entrepreneur and Moxcey embark on a career in restaurant management. Day opened a restaurant named Old Chicago in 1976 and developed it into a small chain, while Moxcey climbed the managerial ranks at two restaurant chains, Cork & Cleaver and Village Inn. When Day and Moxcey reunited in 1990, they brought together their experience to launch a new concept in the food service industry, one designed to appeal to the interest in microbrewed beer. The result of their efforts would become known as Rock Bottom Restaurants, Inc.

The idea behind the new establishment was a restaurant that featured an open kitchen and a prominently displayed brewing operation, complete with shining steel vats in which premium beers were produced. Specialty beers as an instrument to lure dining patrons was not a new idea for Day. His Old Chicago restaurants featured more than 100 different types of imported beers and used bottled beers and keg taps as an integral part of their décor. What Day and Moxcey had in mind with the new concept, however, was distinctly different from Day's Old Chicago units. The brewery-restaurant they opened in 1990, named Walnut Brewery, was slightly more upscale than Old Chicago, and the new concept was underpinned by the on-site brewing facilities. The ability to brew their own beer enabled them to realize hefty profit margins, as much as 94 percent of the $3 per pint price they charged, giving the two entrepreneurs much to hope for with their new concept.

When Moxcey and Day opened their second brewery, they struck upon the name for the holding company that would be created to superintend the operation of the restaurant-breweries and Day's chain of Old Chicago restaurants. The second restaurant-brewery was opened in Denver in the Prudential Plaza, which was owned by the giant insurance company of the same name. Day and Moxcey came up with a twist on Prudential's long-standing advertising theme of "A Piece of the Rock" and dubbed their new restaurant-brewery "Rock Bottom Brewery," thereby lending a permanent name to their enterprise. After the opening of the second restaurant-brewery, Day and Moxcey opened another, with the idea of expanding the concept into other regions set in their minds. At the time it was an unusual strategic objective to pursue: There were many independently owned brewery restaurants scattered throughout the country, but there were only a limited few companies operating multiple, full-service restaurant-breweries. The number of companies operating multiple, full-service restaurants in multiple states—as Day and Moxcey would do—was lower still. Day and Moxcey's limited number of compatriots would be wiped away completely once they executed their next strategic move. They were going to take their business public, something no other restaurant-brewery operator had ever done before.

1994 Initial Public Offering

Before converting to public ownership, Day and Moxcey needed a single corporate entity to offer to Wall Street. Rock Bottom Restaurants, Inc. was formed in April 1994 to serve such a purpose, combining what previously had been a number of "S" corporations under the umbrella of a holding company. From its first day of existence, Rock Bottom comprised the three restaurant-breweries operating under the names Rock Bottom Brewery and Walnut Brewery and eight Old Chicago restaurants. A majority of the restaurants were located in Colorado, but the geographic scope of the company was expected to broaden after its initial public offering (IPO), which was completed in July 1994. The IPO netted Day and Moxcey nearly $16 million, a total drawn from the two million shares of stock that debuted at $8 per share, giving them the financial wherewithal to move forward with their expansion plans. Rock Bottom's development program, funded by the slightly more than $10 million set aside from the IPO, called for the establishment of five Rock Bottom Brewery units and 14 Old Chicago restaurants by the end of 1994. Expansion plans for 1995 projected the establishment of three or four Rock Bottom Breweries and eight Old Chicago restaurants.

By February 1995 Day and Moxcey had opened eight new restaurants during the previous 12 months, giving them a total of five Rock Bottom Breweries and 16 Old Chicago restaurants. On the heels of this ambitious effort, they continued to stick to their plans for opening four Rock Bottom Breweries and eight Old Chicago restaurants in the coming year. To finance the expansion, the company needed additional capital, having essentially exhausted the funds gained from the July 1994 IPO. Once again, Day and Moxcey turned to Wall Street for financial help, announcing a second public offering in February 1995 that found a receptive audience more than willing to invest its cash in the fortunes of an aggressive restaurant-brewery operator.

Investors' interest was piqued by Rock Bottom's sound management, its attention to food quality and service, and by the profit margins the company was realizing from the sale of its microbrewed beers. When the second public offering was completed in March 1995, 2.1 million shares had been purchased at $18 per share, grossing $37.8 million for Rock Bottom's future expansion efforts. With this cash, Rock Bottom pushed ahead into new geographic areas, building on its presence in Colorado, Minnesota, Texas, and Oregon.

The second public offering resolved the financing problems for Rock Bottom's immediate expansion, but there was another nagging issue with which Day and Moxcey had to contend in the early months of 1995. Both of the executives knew there was a finite number of urban markets capable of supporting a Rock Bottom Brewery and that they could not expect to rely heavily on the Rock Bottom Brewery concept as a vehicle for expansion. More Rock Bottom Breweries could be established in new markets, to be sure, but for greater market penetration the pair felt a need for a third concept to drive future sales and earnings growth. In March 1995, the same month the second public offering was completed, they celebrated the debut of their new, third concept, the Denver ChopHouse & Brewery. Expected to generate $4 million a year in sales, the Denver ChopHouse provided Rock Bottom with an entry into the top tier of the restaurant-brewery industry, giving Day and Moxcey a more upscale concept to flesh out their restaurant business. As the company moved forward from this point it could wage a three-pronged attack, with Old Chicago units competing for business in the low-end segment of what insiders referred to as the "brew and chew" market, while Rock Bottom Breweries competed in the middle tier and the new ChopHouse formula competed in the upper tier.

Troubles Arise in 1996

By the beginning of 1996 Rock Bottom was a $70-million-in-sales company deriving nearly half of its revenue volume from the sale of its high-profit-margin beverages. Scattered throughout the country were 28 Old Chicago restaurants, ten Rock Bottom Breweries, and the company's lone ChopHouse & Brewery in Denver, with more restaurant openings in the offing. Much had been achieved since Day and Moxcey began developing new restaurant-breweries in earnest in 1994, but by the beginning of 1996 problems began to surface that were related directly to the ambitious efforts of the two long-time partners. The aggressive expansion undertaken by Day and Moxcey had produced prodigious leaps in sales, driving the company's revenue volume upward as more and more restaurant-breweries joined Rock Bottom's operational fold. Consistently rising sales, however, did not represent the only ingredient for a company's success. Profitability, important to any company's vitality, was particularly important for a publicly traded company such as Rock Bottom, which had made a tacit agreement with investors to give them a meaningful return on their investments. In this area, Rock Bottom was suffering. Sales for the first fiscal quarter of 1996 jumped more than 60 percent, but the increasing cost of opening new restaurants began to hobble earnings growth, engendering a nearly six percent decline in profits for the quarter. Although the decline in earnings did not represent a staggering loss, it was sufficient to set off alarms both inside the company and in the minds of industry observers. An analyst from the underwriting firm for Rock Bottom's public offerings offered his riposte to the company's anemic earnings growth, remarking, ''The company committed one of those rookie mistakes—they got a little ahead of themselves.'' Moxcey admitted as much, saying, ''The development side became distracting.'' The ensuing months were spent trying to lessen the sting delivered by Rock Bottom's growing pains.

Despite the financial ills stemming from the company's rapid expansion, Rock Bottom officials reiterated their intention to move forward with the expansion of the ChopHouse concept, although no particulars were offered. Moxcey, whose promotion to chief executive officer in 1995 conferred upon him the responsibilities of curing the problems Rock Bottom faced, handled the more pressing concerns regarding slipping earnings. As president of the company, Moxcey had earned the reputation of a ''hands-on'' leader, devoting considerable time to visiting each restaurant-brewery, meeting with employees and managers, and overseeing day-to-day issues. In 1996, as Rock Bottom began to reel from fundamental problems, Moxcey had to check his desire to know everyone and everything on an operational level and blossom into a genuine chief executive officer, that is, less of an in-the-field leader and more of a tactician in the realm of strategic planning. Along these lines, Moxcey realigned Rock Bottom's businesses into two divisions in late 1996, organizing a Brewery Restaurant Division and an Old Chicago Restaurant Division.

Despite the menacing cloud that loomed in Rock Bottom's future, the company opened 16 new restaurants in nine new markets in 1996, exceeding its own projections for the year by two units. In 1997 the company opened its second ChopHouse in Washington, D.C., at last moving forward with its expansion plans for its third dining concept, but optimism at Rock Bottom's headquarters did not eliminate the problems that arose in early 1996. Financial losses continued to pile up, particularly in the company's fourth fiscal quarter when it registered a numbing $4.25 million loss as it shuttered unprofitable units. For the year, sales were up because of continued expansion, swelling from $109 million to $150 million, but $4.7 million in losses were racked up, intensifying the need for righting the floundering company. Rock Bottom's precarious but not fatal financial position was compounded in December 1997 when the company lost its primary caretaker. Moxcey resigned from the company in December 1997, leaving to pursue other business interests. His departure left Day in charge and as the holder of

Rock Bottom's three top executive positions of president, chief executive officer, and chairman.

By 1998 several strategic options had been explored, including the possible sale of Rock Bottom in its entirety or in parts, but as the company looked to its future from the vantage point of early 1998 it was pressing ahead with the pace of expansion that had characterized its growth throughout the mid-1990s. With Day at the helm, Rock Bottom planned to open five Rock Bottom Brewery units, a third ChopHouse, and three restaurants through Trolley Barn Brewery Inc., a joint venture partner. Whether the financial troubles resulting from the company's mid-1990s expansion were temporary or indicative of a more serious flaw was a question to be answered by the future progress of Rock Bottom. To Day fell the responsibility for making his creation an unequivocal success.

Principal Subsidiaries

Trolley Barn Brewery Inc. (50%).

Principal Divisions

Brewing Restaurant Division; Old Chicago Restaurant Division.

Further Reading

Howard, Theresa, ''Rock Bottom Brewery,'' *Nation's Restaurant News,* May 22, 1995, p. 136.
Liddle, Alan, ''Rock Bottom Accelerates 'Brew-n-Chew' Growth,'' *Nation's Restaurant News,* October 3, 1994, p. 4.
Papiernik, Richard L., ''Rock Bottom Hits Rocky Road; Day Back as Chief,'' *Nation's Restaurant News,* March 9, 1998, p. 3.
''Rock Bottom Names Day Prexy, Chief Executive,'' *Nation's Restaurant News,* December 22, 1997, p. 4.
''Rock Bottom Profits Rise 23% in Fiscal Year 1996,'' *Nation's Restaurant News,* February 17, 1997, p. 12.
''Rock Bottom Raises $38M in 2nd Offering,'' *Nation's Restaurant News,* March 13, 1995, p. 14.
''Rock Bottom Rests. Forms into Two Operating Divisions,'' *Nation's Restaurant News,* December 9, 1996, p. 2.
Ruggless, Ron, ''Rock Bottom Fuels Growth with Second Stock Offering,'' *Nation's Restaurant News,* February 27, 1995, p. 14.
Smith, Brad, ''Rock Bottom Serves Up ChopHouse Concept; Popular LoDo Eatery Considering Expansion Sites in Chicago, D.C.,'' *Denver Business Journal,* May 31, 1996, p. 15A.
Walkup, Carolyn, ''Rock Bottom Expansion Takes Its Toll,'' *Nation's Restaurant News,* May 20, 1996, p. 11.

—Jeffrey L. Covell

Rooney Brothers Co.

111 West 5th Avenue
Suite 1000
Tulsa, Oklahoma 74103-4235
U.S.A.
(918) 583-6900
Fax: (918) 592-6900
Web Site: http://www.mccbuilds.com

Private Company
Incorporated: 1896 as Manhattan Construction Company
Employees: 1,800
Sales: $611.0 million (1997)
SICs: 1541 General Contractors, Industrial Buildings & Warehouses; 1542 General Contractors, Nonresidential Construction, Not Elsewhere Classified; 6719 Holding Companies, Not Elsewhere Classified

A privately held company, Rooney Brothers Co. was founded in 1984 in order to acquire and operate the Manhattan Construction Company, a nearly 100-year-old general contractor for industrial and commercial buildings. Manhattan has been responsible for constructing many prominent buildings in Houston, Texas, including The Amoco Center Office Building, The Harris County Jail, The Spires Condominiums, Hermann Hospital, The Bayou Bend Tower Condominiums, The Methodist Hospital, The M. D. Anderson Cancer Center, St. Luke's Medical Tower, and The Forum at Memorial Woods, in addition to The George Bush Presidential Library Center in College Station, Texas. Other major projects have included buildings in many other Texas cities; Tulsa and Oklahoma City, Oklahoma; Mobile, Alabama; and Washington, D.C. The company's main operations are in the United States, with the Rooney Bros. corporate headquarters located in Tulsa, Oklahoma and Manhattan Construction operating out of Dallas, Texas. Rooney Bros. has expanded its operations to include the electronics, lumber, and building materials industries. Some of the company's top competitors include Austin Industries, Bechtel, and The Turner Corporation.

The First Century as Manhattan Construction Company

Manhattan Construction Company was established by Laurence H. Rooney in 1896 when a small company opened its doors in what was then known as the Oklahoma Territory—now known as Oklahoma City, Oklahoma. Majority ownership of the company has remained in the Rooney family throughout four generations, and in its century of existence, the company has served a wide variety of customers who have remained loyal over the decades.

In 1907, Manhattan Construction won the contract on Oklahoma's first State Capitol Building in Guthrie, because it was the lowest bidder. The company completed the monumental structure in a mere eight months, and ended up under budget by $317. Thus, the building was ready in time for the first session of the legislature. A company legend has it that "several legislators, however, did manage to make contact with the still-drying paint."

The early days saw the company constructing court houses, offices, corporate headquarters, industrial plants, schools and university buildings, hospitals, and a bridge, all within the growing economy of Oklahoma, Arkansas, and Texas. With such growth, the company was able to open up a full-service office in Tulsa, Oklahoma in 1910, followed by an accounting and data processing office in Muskogee, Oklahoma in 1923.

New Business Ventures In and After World War II

During the years surrounding World War II, Manhattan Construction was called upon to construct more than a billion dollars worth of military facilities, manufacturing plants, hangars, barracks, and the like for the United States under the direction of the U.S. Department of Defense. Included in these contracts were the four month, $29.4 million project of Camp Gruber near Muskogee; the Tulsa Aircraft Plant (the country's largest enclosed structure); and the four month project of Fort Chaffee near Fort Smith, Arkansas, for which the company received The Army-Navy "E" Award for excellence. It was one of the few companies to be so honored. By this time, the company employed nearly 80,000 people.

In 1945, Manhattan began what has grown into more than a half-century partnership with American Airlines, constructing the first maintenance facility for the major air carrier in Tulsa. The company later went on to build another maintenance building at the Dallas-Fort Worth Airport and the Centerport complex in 1963. More offices followed throughout the years, as the company expanded to Houston (1946); Mobile, Alabama (1952); Dallas-Fort Worth (1965); and Fairfax, Virginia (1983).

The 1980s marked the company's chance to complete the country's first design/build/finance projects in South Texas at the beginning of the decade. The company had always tried to be an industry leader in seeking solutions to the most complex facility development challenges, and thus was able to champion the use of alternative project delivery systems to complete the task.

Rooney Brothers Emerges: 1984

In 1984, Rooney Brothers Co. was founded by L. Francis Rooney III and Timothy P. Rooney in order to purchase the Dallas-based Manhattan Construction Co. that had been founded by the two men's ancestors almost a century earlier. Francis, who earned his juris doctorate from Georgetown University Law Center, gave up on his planned career as a legal eagle in order to join the family business, becoming the president of Rooney Brothers Co., while Timothy would hold the same position at Manhattan Construction Co.

The "new" company worked to maintain a solid customer base and track record for the rest of the decade. Then in the 1990s, it began to focus on the general building markets of corporate and commercial offices, healthcare and bio-medical research, aviation, corrections, sports facilities, institutional and academic, hospitality, and leisure and entertainment facilities. The company tried to specialize in highly complex, multi-phased, renovation and/or addition-type construction with demanding schedules and strict budget constraints.

An Abundance of Work in the 1990s

In April 1992, Manhattan completed the $90 million Fiesta Texas project, a multi-activity theme park built on a 150-acre site which was formerly a working quarry. The project was complete three weeks before the 21-month deadline, and utilized more than one million board feet of lumber in the framing for the project. USAA/Opryland USA, the operator of Fiesta Texas, rewarded the workers and their families with a special day at the park before it was opened to the public.

In October 1993, Manhattan Construction, recognized for nearly a century by the building industry as a "can-do" operation, proved it had earned its moniker when the company was contracted to rebuild Texas Stadium's luxury boxes, called "The Crown Suites," which were destroyed by fire three days before the Dallas Cowboys-San Francisco 49ers football game on October 17th. The company put 100 employees on the site for three days and nights, and worked around the clock to complete the $2 million job in time for kickoff. Francis Rooney and Cowboys owner Jerry Jones treated the crew to the game, which Dallas won, 26–17.

Also in 1993, the $62 million Harris County Detention Center in Houston was completed, as was the $80 million Delta Air Lines expansion and renovation at DFW Airport, and the $30 million John Zink International Headquarters in Tulsa.

In April 1994, Manhattan finished construction on the highly publicized "Ballpark at Arlington," home of The Texas Rangers professional baseball team. As was typical of the company, the job was completed on schedule, and just in time for the team's season opener game. The 48,000-seat, $90 million stadium project included 180,000 square feet of below-grade, back-of-house facility development; an incorporated four-level office building; two levels of suites; an adjacent 115-space parking garage; and vehicular tunnels and media bays, made up of 70,000 cubic yards of concrete and 7,200 tons of structural steel. Also in 1994, the company completed the $75 million Sisters of Charity Hospital in Texarkana.

In July 1995, Manhattan Construction and Bethesda, Maryland-based George Hyman Construction Co. completed work on The Brooke Army Medical Center in San Antonio, Texas. The $230 million hospital facility, with 1.5 million square feet of space to serve 1 million outpatients a year, featured a state-of-the-art burn care institute. The facility was finished nearly eight months before the projected date, by more than 100 subcontractors and 1,200 workers. The U.S. Department of Labor awarded Hyman and Manhattan with its Exemplary Volunteer Efforts Award for the project. Additionally, the project was nominated for a national safety award from The Army Corps of Engineers, and was commended for safety compliance from The Occupational Safety and Health Administration (OSHA).

By 1996, annual sales for the company had reached $500 million. The company then started 1997 with a bang, being awarded numerous projects in January of that year. The first project the company received was a $12 million deal with American Airlines on the campus south of the Dallas-Fort Worth Airport. The project—named the American Airlines STIN (Sabre Travel Information Network) Remodeling Project—began that month and was completed early in 1998. The project was a continuation of the long and successful relationship between American Airlines and Manhattan that had been established in 1945, including the construction of the original high security Sabre Underground Reservations Center. The STIN Project consisted of site landscaping; weir, roof, terrace, window and wall refurbishment and repair; interior finish; audio visual; life safety; electrical power and lighting refurbishment; and mechanical upgrades.

The second project of 1996 saw the Houston division of the company joining designer PGAL (Pierce Goodwin Alexander & Linville) Architects of Houston in being awarded the construction of the new $70 million Harris County Criminal Justice

Center. The project, which encompassed 800,000 square feet over 21 floors, began that month and was scheduled for completion in July 1999. The project included a basement with a 47-car parking area and a tunnel tying into the existing tunnel system, and 41 new courtrooms to be added to the existing facility.

A third project was negotiated in early 1996 with Methodist Retirement Communities of The Woodlands, Texas, to construct a new $9 million Moody House Independent Living Center in Galveston. The 110,000 square foot structure would provide 92 living units in a six story building. The project began construction in March 1996 and was completed in May 1998.

Yet another project during the same time frame found the company teamed with local joint-venture partner Gibbs Construction and architect Arthur Q. Davis and Partners of New Orleans (lead designer of The Louisiana Superdome). The company was awarded a $72 million contract for The New Orleans Sports Arena. The arena was scheduled to be used for basketball, hockey, and various other multi-purpose civic and cultural events, and would encompass approximately 665,000 square feet with a seating capacity of 20,000.

The Turn of the Century and Beyond

In January 1997 the company negotiated with Southwest Airlines for the fourth time in its history. Previously, the company had produced a six-bay flight simulator building, and the addition of an AFFF Fire Suppression System to the fleet maintenance hangars for Southwest. This time, the airline wanted Manhattan to construct the air carrier's General Office Expansion to the existing headquarters. The $30 million expansion program was completed quickly, by December 1997. With total revenue for 1997 topping off at $611.0 million, the company was named to the *Forbes* "Private 500" list for the year.

In January 1998, the company was honored by Associated Builders and Contractors (ABC)—a national construction association representing 19,500 construction and construction-related firms in 80 chapters across the United States—at ABC's annual convention held in Phoenix. The honor was given based on Manhattan's work in building the George Bush Presidential Library Complex, and equated to a first place award in the "Institutional, Over $25 Million" category in ABC's Excellence in Construction Awards program. The award program was designed to publicly recognize the quality and innovation of merit (open) shop construction, and to honor all the members of the construction team responsible for the project, including the contractor, the owner, and the design team. Judges included members of The American Institute of Architects, The Business Roundtable, and The American Institute of Constructors.

Manhattan Construction had helped to immortalize former President George Bush when it took on the role of project manager, overseeing the construction of three buildings located at Texas A&M University. The company also hired A&M students to help install memorabilia from The Gulf War, a World War II aircraft, and pieces of the Berlin Wall. The George Bush Presidential Library, School of Government & Public Services, and Presidential Conference Center were inducted by Bush, along with Presidents Ronald Reagan, Jimmy Carter, and Bill Clinton, in 1997.

As the company entered the last few years of the twentieth century, it had multiple projects in the works. With enough work to keep it busy for a long while, and to also maintain the level of income that the company had become accustomed to, the company was positioned to enter the upcoming century as a continued powerhouse in the construction industry.

Principal Subsidiaries

Manhattan Construction Co.

Further Reading

"California, Oct. 9," *ENR*, September 16, 1991, p. 118.
"Corgan Architects," *Building Design & Construction*, April 1997, p. 10.
Hartnett, Dwayne. "Tulsa, Okla., Construction Firm Builds a Solid Reputation," *Knight-Ridder/Tribune Business News*, November 7, 1993.
"The *Tulsa World*, Okla., F.Y.I. Business Briefs Column," *Knight-Ridder/Tribune Business News*, July 12, 1995.

—Daryl F. Mallett

SBS Technologies, Inc.

2400 Louisiana Boulevard Northeast
Albuquerque, New Mexico 87110
U.S.A.
(505) 875-0600
Fax: (505) 875-0400
Web site: http://www.sbs.com

Public Company
Incorporated: 1986 as SBS Engineering, Inc.
Employees: 280
Sales: $52.8 million (1997)
Stock Exchanges: NASDAQ
Ticker Symbol: SBSE
SICs: 3571 Electronic Computers; 3663 Radio and TV
     Communications Equipment; 3812 Search and
     Navigation Equipment

SBS Technologies, Inc. is a leading designer and manufacturer of embedded computer components. The company's original focus, upon its founding in 1986, was on products and services for the aerospace and defense industries, such as flight simulators. However, SBS quickly expanded into the embedded computer market, first offering an avionics interface board used in aircraft and missiles. In this highly competitive market, SBS became extremely successful, largely through a rapid series of acquisitions of other companies in the market. By the mid-1990s, the embedded computer market was growing so enormously that SBS decided to discontinue its engineering and flight simulation operations, allowing it to focus completely on embedded computers. The market for these computers in the late 1990s was estimated by SBS to be $3.2 billion. The company's 1997 sales reached $52.8 million, a 68.7 percent increase over those of the previous year; the number of SBS employees also doubled. In the same year, Andrew C. Cruce, SBS's founder and former chairman, announced his retirement.

SBS Finds Early Niche in Embedded Computers

In November 1986 Andrew C. Cruce founded SBS Engineering, Inc. in Albuquerque, New Mexico. His company won its first contract the following year, when the U.S. Navy se-

lected it to support development of the V-22 Tilt-Rotor ("Osprey") flight simulator. Aided by this contract, SBS developed products and services in three areas: flight simulators, avionics computer products, and engineering services. In 1988, the young company made what turned out to be an excellent business decision; it developed its first embedded computer product, an avionics interface board. According to company literature, embedded computers are "small, highly specialized computing modules that perform specific tasks . . . the 'invisible' components of larger systems that do everything from testing car brake systems to communicating with satellites."

SBS was already experiencing steady growth. Between 1991 and 1993 the company began to acquire other small companies, the first being Simaltech, Inc., which produced flight simulator visual display systems. In 1992 it acquired Berg Systems International, a manufacturer of telemetry-related computer products for the aerospace industry, giving SBS a second embedded computer product. The Sensor Systems Division of Merit Technology, Inc. (a developer of radar and flight simulation systems) and rights to a use-of-force trainer system were added in 1993.

Based on its obvious success at this point, SBS decided to offer its stock publicly in 1992. Along with becoming a publicly held corporation, SBS also announced that its name was changing from SBS Engineering, Inc. to SBS Technologies, Inc., to emphasize its new direction. Revenues were $19.1 million in 1993, and rose to $28.8 million in 1994.

A Change of Strategy in 1995

By 1995 it had become clear to SBS management that, while the embedded computer component market was booming, the flight simulation products and basic engineering services it offered were lagging. A decline in the defense industry was a significant contributor to the drop in this part of the business. SBS thus made the decision to discontinue these operations, selling the flight simulator business to Camber Corporation in April 1995 and focusing completely on the embedded computer market. As a result, SBS revenues dipped sharply that year, to about $16.2 million.

The company also made a key acquisition in April 1995: GreenSpring Computers, a California manufacturer of computer input/output (I/O) products used in commercial and industrial embedded computers. At the time GreenSpring was the owner of a pioneering product, IndustryPack, which it had developed in the late 1980s. IndustryPack was a modular I/O device that had been incorporated into almost 100 computer mezzanine boards. One of its greatest early successes was being selected for use by the Motorola Computer Group in the early 1990s. Within a year after SBS bought GreenSpring, this decision proved sound; IndustryPack was chosen as an industry standard, which carried a coveted "ANSI" accreditation.

In 1996, SBS continued its acquisition strategy with the purchase of two more embedded computer companies: Logical Design Group (LDG) of Raleigh, North Carolina, a manufacturer of Intel processor-based CPU boards (acquired in August 1996); and Bit 3 Computer Corporation, a Minneapolis manufacturer of hardware and software used in computer networking and interconnection (acquired in November 1996). The LDG acquisition was carried out so that SBS could share in the growing use of Microsoft software in embedded computers. With the addition of Bit 3, SBS also could become involved in new embedded computer standards, such as "PCI" and "CompactPCI" and enter the networking and interconnection market. The acquisitions had an immediate positive impact on SBS' revenues and income. Revenues almost doubled in 1996, from $16.2 million to $31.3 million; income rose about 78 percent, from $7.4 million to $9.5 million.

No single customer, domestic or foreign, accounted for more than ten percent of the company's sales during this time. Although SBS conducted all of its manufacturing in the United States, it maintained foreign sales offices in Reading, England, and Glasgow, Scotland. Its international sales in 1995, 1996, and 1997 were $1.6 million, $5.1 million, and $8.6 million respectively. In 1995 three-quarters of the foreign sales were made in Canada and France. The opening of the Glasgow office in 1996 boosted foreign sales significantly. In 1997 Canada was the largest foreign market ($1.4 million), followed by Japan ($1.3 million), the United Kingdom ($1.1 million), Korea ($1 million), Germany ($800,000), and France ($700,000). The remaining SBS foreign sales were divided among other countries.

Reorganization for New Markets in 1997

Largely due to these shrewd acquisitions, SBS had a stellar year in 1997. Revenues increased another 68.7 percent, from $31.3 million to $52.8 million, and income almost doubled, rising from $3.6 million to $7.1 million. SBS once again decided to discontinue one of its existing operations. In June 1997 it sold its "ICAT" judgmental use-of-force training program to Firearms Training Systems, Inc. of Georgia. The "ICAT"

program was used to teach military and police personnel what force would be appropriate in a given situation. In the 1997 SBS annual report, CEO and Chairman Christopher J. Amenson, and President and COO Steve Cooper, also announced that the founder and former chairman of SBS, Andrew C. Cruce, was retiring.

SBS next set its sights on a California-based supplier of embedded computer modules and, in December 1997, announced that it had a new operating unit, renamed SBS Micro Alliance. This five-year-old company manufactured a variety of rack mount computers, work stations, and similar products to customers throughout the United States, Europe, and Asia.

The year 1997 marked the beginning of another refocusing within the company. The rapid series of acquisitions had led to five separate subsidiaries with individual sales forces within the company. To achieve a more cohesive operation and public image, SBS regrouped its subsidiaries and units into two new operating groups, the SBS Computer Group and the SBS Aerospace Group. The SBS Computer Group would comprise SBS GreenSpring Modular I/O, Inc., SBS Bit 3 Operations, Inc., SBS Embedded Computers, Inc., and SBS Micro Alliance, Inc. The SBS Aerospace Group would encompass SBS Berg Telemetry Systems, Inc., SBS Avionics Technologies, Inc., and DataExpress (TM) software operations.

This consolidation was an outgrowth of the "One SBS" program that began in mid-1997 and resulted in the renaming of all subsidiaries to include "SBS" at the head of their names. As explained by CEO and Chairman Amenson in a February 1998 *PR Newswire* release, "The step we are now taking is targeted at developing the technical, marketing, and sales synergies that are inherent in our company. . . . This alignment provides a structure within which we can readily integrate our future business acquisitions, and will position SBS to continue to meet our goal of continued growth in profitability and shareholder value."

Along with this realignment of operations, SBS reorganized its strategy to address important market trends. It planned to develop open, standard systems rather than proprietary systems. Military system developers, for example, were increasingly turning to open systems as a way of allowing easier, faster, and more economical adaptation to technology changes, and SBS saw others in the industry following this trend. Additional market trends that SBS hoped to address were the growing markets for standard board-level products and for "WINTEL" embedded computer platforms. SBS saw four rapidly growing market segments for itself in the coming years: (1) military and commercial aviation (claiming military technology was "several generations" behind industry standards); (2) the communications industry, including telecommunications, data communications, networking, and cellular phone service; (3) factory automation and process control; and, (4) medical equipment, encompassing applications from complex CAT scanners to portable diagnostic equipment.

Outlook in the Late 1990s

Given its rapid growth and financial success during its short history, it was likely that SBS would continue to flourish through the late 1990s. The year 1998 brought several promising new projects and, along with them, expert recognition for SBS' performance.

First, SBS formed a partnership with Micro Elektronic Nuremburg GmbH, of Nuremburg, Germany. Together they developed a compact mezzanine card (known as PC-MIP) that would be used to add capabilities or interfaces onto a computer's motherboard. A standard for add-on cards had been sought after by the computer board industry for years, and SBS hoped that the development of a compact card would ''become the worldwide standard mezzanine for industrial, embedded and OEM applications,'' as Kim Rubin, SBS Computer Group's chief technical officer, told *EE Times*. In March 1998 SBS formed another partnership, this one with Massachusetts based Digital Equipment Corporation (DEC), to develop an aircraft simulation product using the DEC platform. Shortly afterward, however, DEC was acquired by Compaq Computers and numerous staff cutbacks and reorganizations were in the works, and so the future of this project was unclear.

SBS launched another pair of acquisitions in July 1998. It announced that it had purchased a controlling interest (50.1 percent) of the shares of or Industrial Computers GmbH, a German designer and manufacturer of CPU boards used in embedded computers. Most of or's customers were located in Europe. However, the acquisition also included purchase of all of the shares of Computers, Inc., a Virginia-based marketing arm of or. Simultaneously SBS announced that it planned to purchase V-1 Computer in its entirety. This California company designed, manufactured, and marketed CPU boards using Motorola processors in telecommunications, industrial automation, and defense applications. With these two purchases, SBS now could target products at customers using almost all types of embedded computers.

SBS also cleverly began to utilize the World Wide Web as a way of providing very up-to-date product information to engineers making purchases, as well as to customers seeking technical assistance. Knowing that its product catalog included several hundred items, scattered among its subsidiaries, SBS set up a Web site with a database of product information. When a user went to the site, he or she could pull a current product descrip-

tion from the database, so that the Web pages did not need to be constantly updated. SBS's main site also served as a portal to individual Web sites for each of its subsidiaries.

It also appeared that fiscal 1998 would be another record-setting year for SBS, based on its performance through the first three quarters. Its sales of $18.9 million for the third quarter set an all-time quarterly record for the company. For the entire three quarters, sales of $53.6 million represented an increase of 42 percent over the same quarters in the previous year, and income of $7.2 million represented an increase of 47 percent. Recognizing SBS as a top performer in its segment of the embedded computer industry, *The Red Chip Review* (which analyzes top-performing publicly traded companies for investors) selected SBS as one of 20 companies to be invited to its June 1998 investor conference. It noted that SBS stood out for its ''history of earning reliability, and for making accretive, complementary acquisitions,'' as well as for its 46 percent compound annual growth and history of meeting customer expectations.

Principal Subsidiaries

SBS Avionics Technologies, Inc.; SBS Berg Telemetry Systems, Inc.; SBS Bit 3 Operations, Inc.; SBS Embedded Computers, Inc.; SBS GreenSpring Modular I/O, Inc.

Principal Operating Units

SBS Computer Group; SBS Aerospace Group.

Further Reading

''Digital and SBS Technologies, Inc. to Deliver Powerful Alpha-Based Avionics Solutions,'' *PR Newswire*, March 31, 1998.
''Firearms Training Buys Division of SBS,'' *Atlanta Business Chronicle*, July 7, 1997.
''The Red Chip Review Investor Conference Showcases Investment Opportunities in High-Performance Small-Cap Area,'' *PR Newswire*, June 2, 1998.

—Gerry Azzata

The Seagram Company Ltd.

1430 Peel Street
Montreal, Quebec H3A 1S9
Canada
(514) 849-5271
Fax: (514) 987-5201
Web site: http://www.seagram.com

Public Company
Incorporated: 1928 as Distillers Corporation Limited
Employees: 30,000
Sales: $12.56 billion (1997)
Stock Exchanges: Montreal Toronto Vancouver New
   York London
Ticker Symbol: VO
SICs: 2084 Wines, Brandy & Brandy Spirits; 2085
   Distilled & Blended Liquors; 2741 Miscellaneous
   Publishing; 3652 Phonograph Records & Pre-
   Recorded Audio Tapes & Discs; 5182 Wines &
   Distilled Alcoholic Beverages; 5947 Gift, Novelty &
   Souvenir Shops; 6719 Offices of Holding Companies,
   Not Elsewhere Classified; 7812 Motion Pictures &
   Video Tape Production; 7822 Motion Picture & Video
   Tape Distribution; 7996 Amusement Parks

The Seagram Company Ltd., which is 32-percent owned by the Bronfman family, is a major international liquor giant (trailing only Diageo PLC), selling such brands as Seagram's, Chivas Regal, Crown Royal, Martell, Absolut, Captain Morgan, and Mumm in more than 150 countries. The company has also quickly gained significant holdings in the world of entertainment, most notably the mid-1990s purchase of an 84-percent interest in MCA Inc., which was renamed Universal Studios, Inc. (films, television programs, theme parks, music labels), and the 1998-announced acquisition of PolyGram, the world's number one music company (the music labels of Universal and PolyGram would be combined as the Universal Music Group). The addition of PolyGram and the proposed sale of the Tropicana Products juice business to PepsiCo would mean that

Seagram would derive more of its revenue from entertainment than from distilling. The Bronfman family operates one of the largest family-controlled capital pools in the non-Arab world.

Early History

In 1889 the Bronfman family fled Czarist anti-Semitic pogroms in Bessarabia to make their home in Canada. A wealthy family, they were accompanied by their rabbi and two servants. In the century since, the Bronfmans (whose name, ironically, means "liquor man" in Yiddish) experienced a brief period of poverty but then went on to build one of the world's largest distilling businesses.

Soon after the family's arrival in Canada, patriarch Yechiel Bronfman learned that tobacco farming, which had made him a wealthy man in his homeland, was incompatible with the cold Canadian climate. The Bronfmans found themselves without a livelihood, and Yechiel was forced to leave his family to work as a laborer clearing the right-of-way for a line of the Canadian Northern Railway. He bought a shed for $12 for his family and after a short time moved to a better job in a sawmill. Yechiel Bronfman and his sons then started selling firewood, making a fairly good living, and began a trade in frozen whitefish to earn a winter income. Eventually they turned to trading horses, a venture through which they became involved in the hotel and bar business. On reaching adulthood, two of Yechiel Bronfman's sons, Harry and Sam, took charge of the family's business interests. Harry Bronfman owned his first hotel in 1903 when he was 17 years old.

When Prohibition came to Canada in 1916, the Bronfmans decided to leave the hotel business and enter the whiskey trade. Canada had implemented Prohibition only to appease foes of drinking; in reality, alcohol consumption remained high in Canada. The Bronfmans took advantage of the imprecise Canadian Prohibition laws to maximize their bootlegging profits. Sam Bronfman bought the Bonaventure Liquor Store Company, conveniently located near the downtown railway in Montreal, in 1916. People traveling to the "dry" west could stock up on liquor before boarding the train. Business was brisk until March

1918, when a law was passed that prohibited the manufacture or importation of alcohol containing more than 2.5 percent spirits.

The prohibition excluded alcohol intended for medicinal purposes, so Harry Bronfman promptly went into the drug business. He bought a Dewar's whiskey sales contract from the Hudson's Bay Company and began selling straight liquor through drugstores and to processors who made "medicinal" mixtures. One such concoction was known as a Dandy Bracer—Liver and Kidney Cure; it contained sugar, molasses, bluestone, 36 percent alcohol, and tobacco.

When the Volstead Act instituted Prohibition in the United States in 1919, the Bronfmans imported 300,000 gallons of alcohol from the United States, enough to make 800,000 gallons of whiskey. They reduced 65-overproof white alcohol to the required bottling strength by mixing it with water, some real whiskey and a bit of burnt sugar to provide color. A shot of sulfuric acid brought on a quick simulated aging process. The Bronfmans' mixing equipment could fill and label 1,000 bottles an hour. All the whiskey came out of the same vats, but it was bottled under several different labels to raise the liquor's value. Materials cost of the whiskey mixture was no more than $5.25 per gallon. Bottled, the whiskey sold for the equivalent of $25 a gallon.

Incorporating and Going Public in the 1920s

In 1924 the Bronfmans opened their first distillery in La Salle, across the St. Lawrence River from Montreal. In the same year they incorporated under the name Distillers Corporation Limited.

Two years later the family sold a 50-percent interest to Distillers Company, an amalgamation of British distillers that controlled more than half the world's scotch market and from which the Bronfmans had been importing scotch in bulk. In exchange for a half share in Distillers Corp., the British Enterprise gave the Bronfmans Canadian distribution rights for its brands, which included Haig, Black & White, Dewar's, and Vat 69.

At about the same time the Seagram family's distilling business became a public company. The enterprise had begun in 1883 when Joseph Emm Seagram became sole proprietor of a distillery in Waterloo, Ontario, where he had worked since the 1860s. Seagram later turned to politics (he was a Conservative member of Parliament from 1896 to 1908), and also devoted much of his time to horse racing. His company was a leading Canadian rye producer with two popular brands, Seagram's '83

and V.O., which was introduced in 1909. (Joseph Seagram's racing colors, black and gold, still appear on the labels of V.O. bottles.)

In 1928, two years after Seagram went public, the Bronfmans' Distillers Corp. acquired all stock in the distillery and itself became a public company. The merged company took the name Distillers Corp-Seagram Limited. W. H. Ross was president, and Sam Bronfman was vice-president. In its first year the company netted $2.2 million in profits, most of it from the Bronfmans' busy bootlegging work. In 1929 Sam Bronfman prepared a $4.2 share offering to finance expansion in the highly successful export business. By 1930, however, company profits were declining, and the share offering had to be postponed.

By that time the border between Canada and the United States was extremely dangerous for illegal alcohol transport, so most trading was done by sea. The Bronfmans had established warehouses on the coast and subsidiaries called Atlantic Import and Atlas Shipping. Schooners shipped the contraband goods into the United States in the dead of night.

Post-Prohibition Expansion

Prohibition ended in the United States in 1933. The next year a conservative lawyer, Richard Bedford Bennett, was chosen to head the Canadian Conservative Party and immediately launched an investigation into the liquor smuggling industry. The Bronfmans were arrested, and a year later they were tried. The judge threw the case out of court.

In 1928 Sam Bronfman had anticipated the end of Prohibition and begun to stockpile and age whiskey. Now the company owned the largest private stock of properly mellowed whiskey. This lucrative position enabled it in 1933 to acquire 20 percent of Schenley, whose product line included the well-known Golden Wedding brand of rye whiskey. When Sam Bronfman informed the Distillers Company board in Scotland of the move and requested an increase in whiskey prices, he was told at an acrimonious board meeting that Distillers would not agree to either proposal. In response, the Bronfman brothers raised $4 million and bought out the Distillers Company's holding in Distillers Corporation-Seagrams Limited. W. H. Ross resigned after the split, and Sam Bronfman became president.

The company then purchased the Rossville Union Distillery in Lawrenceburg, Indiana, and set up Joseph E. Seagram & Sons Inc. to operate the U.S. venture. Schenley's board of directors suggested an equal partnership in the American operation, but when Sam Bronfman found out that Golden Wedding was not aged before it was sold, he immediately rejected the plan. Soon afterward, Seagram and Schenley parted company. Schenley held the top position in the whiskey market until 1937, lost it to Seagram until 1944, regained it until 1947, then lost it to Seagram for good.

Blending and aging became Seagram's hallmark. Sam Bronfman wanted to quash the somewhat dubious image of drinking whiskey that had developed in the bootlegging era and replace it with a more respectable and refined one. In promoting his products he would use one of three descriptions of the blending process: a formal outline of the details of the process; a short definition ("Distilling is a science; blending is an art");

and an informal explanation ("Look, when a man goes into a store for a bottle of Coca-Cola, he expects it to be the same today as it will be tomorrow.... The great products don't change. Well, our product's not going to change either"). Seagram would maintain "blending libraries" at its offices in New York, Montreal, and Paisley, near Glasgow, where samples of the company's different types of straight whiskies were continually catalogued and tested into the 1990s.

The company purchased Maryland Distillers, Inc. and its Calvert affiliate in Relay, Maryland, in 1934 and imported its own aged Canadian stock to blend with its new American distillates. The resulting product came out under the Five Crown and Seven Crown labels. A few years later the company built a new distillery in Louisville, Kentucky. By 1938 Distillers-Seagram had approximately 60 million gallons of whiskey aging in its three American plants.

The Bronfman brothers revolutionized liquor marketing by selling their products to distributors already bottled. Other distillers sold liquor to local rectifiers in barrel consignments, thereby losing control over the final product. The Bronfmans' method allowed Seagram to maintain the kind of quality control that builds brand loyalty. The practice became industry standard. By the end of 1936 Seagram sales were up to $60 million in the United States, with another $10 million in Canada. By 1948 total sales exceeded $438 million, and the company posted an aftertax profit of $53.7 million.

Sam Bronfman had always been impressed with British aristocracy. When George VI and Queen Elizabeth visited Canada in 1939, Bronfman blended 600 samples of whiskey before creating the prestigious Crown Royal brand in their honor. He also purchased the Chivas distillery in Aberdeen, Scotland, because its operators owned a grocery store that served the royal family when they were in Scotland. Chivas Regal developed into the best-selling deluxe scotch whiskey in the world.

Expanding Beyond Whiskey in the 1940s

In the 1940s Seagram expanded from the whiskey business into the larger liquor industry. Its entry into the wine markets began with a 1942 partnership with German vintners Fromm & Sichel to purchase the Paul Masson vineyards in California. (Seagram would not sell its 96-percent interest in Paul Masson until the mid-1980s.) Eight years later the company bought a majority interest in Fromm & Sichel. During World War II Seagram imported rum from Puerto Rico and Jamaica and acquired several West Indies distilleries which would later introduce the Captain Morgan, Myers's, Woods, and Trelawny labels. Seagram also purchased Mumm's Champagne, Perrior-Jouet Champagne, Barton & Guestier, and Augier Frères.

Sam Bronfman took the company in a dramatically new direction in 1950 when he invested in the Alberta oil company Royalite. He later sold his interest in Gulf and purchased the Frankfort Oil Company. In 1963 Seagram acquired the Texas Pacific Coal and Oil Company for $276 million. Frankfort and Texas Pacific were then merged to form Texas Pacific Oil Company, Inc.

In 1957 Edgar Bronfman, Sam Bronfman's son, became the company's president. He resurrected Calvert Reserve by re-

marketing it as Calvert Extra and promoting it with a personal tour. He also expanded Seagram's brands of rum, scotch, and bottled cocktails (manhattans, daiquiris, whiskey sours, and martinis), and began to import wine on a large scale. By the end of 1965 the company was operating in 119 countries and had surpassed $1 billion in sales.

Between 1961 and 1971, sales of blended whiskey by all makers dropped from 60 to 20 percent of the total hard liquor market, but 7 Crown, V.O., Chivas, and Crown Royal continued to capture an increasing share of their shrinking markets and Seagram revenues and profits maintained their growth. In 1975, however—the same year the company name was changed to The Seagram Company Ltd.—Seagram's earnings slipped 9 percent to $74 million. 7 Crown sales dropped by 600,000 cases, and V.O. was down 300,000 cases. Edgar Bronfman decided to reorganize the company's board of directors and management. A new executive committee was formed with another Bronfman brother, Charles, at its head. In 1977 Seagram recorded a net income of $84 million on sales of $2.2 billion.

In the late 1960s Edgar Bronfman decided to get involved in the film industry. He bought $40 million of MGM stock, and in 1969 replaced Robert O'Brien as the studio's chairman. MGM lost $25 million in the next year, and Bronfman resigned from the studio. Seagram lost about $10 million in the short-lived venture. He found some success in the entertainment industry later when his Sagittarius Productions Inc. staged several Broadway successes (including *1776* and *The Me Nobody Knows*).

The fabulously wealthy Bronfman family received extensive media attention in the 1970s. Details of Edgar's private life, exposed in divorce proceedings, were eagerly reported in the tabloids; and in 1975, the family had to contend with the alleged kidnapping of Edgar's 23-year-old son, Samuel II. The incident and subsequent trial became headline news in many countries. Mel Patrick Lynch, the defendant (a fireman from Brooklyn, New York) was acquitted of kidnapping charges but convicted of extortion. Throughout the trial, Lynch maintained that Sam II was his lover and that the kidnapping was a hoax cooked up by Bronfman in order to lay his hands on some of the family cash. Sam II was reunited with his father; both of them hotly denied Lynch's version of events.

Continued Diversification in the 1980s

In 1980 Seagram sold Texas Pacific to the Sun Company for $2.3 billion, but when Edgar wanted to reinvest the money in St. Joe Minerals, he was turned down even though he offered $45 a share for stock that had been selling at $28 a share. Conoco also rejected Seagram's advances. Du Pont, Seagram's third choice, accepted a bid on 20.2 percent of the company's stock.

Seagram made several other diversification moves in the 1980s. In 1981 the company formed Westmount Enterprises to finance its beverage ventures and market its new gourmet frozen dinners. Seagram also began manufacturing and marketing premium mixers jointly with the Coca-Cola Bottling Company of New York, and purchased 11.6 percent of Biotechnica International. Seagram ventured increasingly into the wine industry through its Seagram's Vinters division. In 1984 Sterling Vineyards of Calistoga, California, was acquired. Three years later, Mumm Napa Valley was founded in Rutherford, California, as a California sparkling winery. Seagram further expanded its beverage offerings in 1988 when it acquired fruit juice and fruit beverage maker Tropicana Products, Inc.—the second-largest U.S. orange juice producer—from Beatrice Co. for $1.2 billion. Seagram, meantime, had also acquired in 1984 the Oddbins Limited retail outlet chain in the United Kingdom.

In 1985 Seagram underwent a thorough reorganization of its companies, brands, and personnel. The company spent $924 million for Martell S.A. of France, adding the Martell brand of cognac to its product line. Seagram also launched a new advertising campaign aimed at upgrading the image of liquor consumption, and Edgar Bronfman asked the television networks to suspend their ban on advertising for distilled spirits. However, the three major broadcasters all refused to air a commercial comparing the alcohol content of whiskey, wine, and beer.

Entertainment over Distillation in the 1990s

By the late 1980s Edgar Bronfman had settled upon his successor, surprising many observers with his choice of his maverick younger son, Edgar Jr., over the college-educated Samuel II. This choice would quickly have a profound impact on the direction of Seagram. Before joining the family firm in 1982, Edgar Jr. spent much of his time in Hollywood, where he coproduced the 1980 box-office failure *The Border* (which starred Jack Nicholson). It was in the direction of entertainment that Edgar Jr. eventually—and dramatically—moved Seagram.

His first moves of the 1990s, however, came in the company's core distilled spirits business. In 1991 Seagram sold seven brands to the Jim Beam subsidiary of American Brands Inc. for $372.5 million. Those divested—which included Lord Calvert Canadian Whiskey, Wolfschmidt Vodka, and Ronrico Rum—were mid-range brands, and Seagram wished to concentrate on higher-margin premium brands, such as Crown Regal. Two years later, Seagram added another premium brand to its stable when it acquired the worldwide distribution rights to Absolut vodka for about $1.25 billion. Seagram also expanded its Tropicana Products unit through the early 1995 purchase of the beverage operations of Dole Food Co. for $285 million.

The expansion into entertainment began in 1993 with the purchase of a 15 percent interest in Time Warner Inc. for $2.2 billion. After Edgar Jr. added the CEO title in 1994 to his position as president (with Edgar Sr. remaining chairman), Seagram in April 1995 sold its holdings in Du Pont, receiving about $11 billion in the process. (This sale was widely criticized in the next few years as Du Pont's stock ran ahead of even the extraordinary bull market.) The proceeds were almost immediately reinvested when Seagram later that month acquired 80 percent (later increased to 84 percent) of MCA, Inc. from Matsushita Electric Industrial Company, Ltd. for $5.7 billion. MCA—whose name Seagram changed to Universal Studios, Inc.—included Universal Pictures film studios, MCA Television Group (renamed Universal Television Group), Putnam Berkley Group publishing unit (which Seagram sold in December 1996 for $330 million), MCA Music Entertainment Group

(later known as Universal Music Group), Universal theme parks, and Spencer Gifts, a chain of specialty gift shops.

In June 1996 Seagram, prompted by declining liquor sales in the United States, began advertising its brands via television and radio, breaking the voluntary U.S. ban. The company fell from its position as the world's number one distiller when Guinness PLC and Grand Metropolitan PLC merged in December 1997 to form Diageo PLC. Seagram in 1997 and 1998 divested its holdings in Time Warner, ending up with a pretax profit of $2.13 billion on its short-term investment. Seagram then in late 1997 purchased the 50 percent of USA Networks that it didn't already own for $1.7 billion. The following February Seagram spun off USA Networks (which owned three cable services: USA Network, the Sci-Fi Channel, and Sci-Fi Europe) and most of its Universal Television Group to HSN Inc. in return for $1.2 billion in cash and 45 percent of the stock of HSN, which was controlled by media titan Barry Diller and soon changed its name to USA Networks Inc.

With the proceeds from these deals in hand, Seagram announced in May 1998 that it would acquire PolyGram N.V., the world's largest music company, for $10.4 billion. It planned to merge PolyGram's music labels into those of Universal Music Group, which would then be the world leader in music. Seagram planned to sell PolyGram's nascent film unit, PolyGram Filmed Entertainment, and was also considering other sales of noncore operations and real-estate holdings. Further funds were to be raised through the divestment of Tropicana Products. Originally, Seagram announced that it would sell the unit to the public through an initial public offering. However, with the IPO market not as attractive as it was earlier in the decade, Seagram struck a deal with PepsiCo, Inc., announced in July 1998, whereby the juice business would be sold to the beverage giant for $3.3 billion in cash. The following month Ocean Spray Cranberries Inc., a juice maker with a distribution deal with PepsiCo, planned to attempt to block this sale. Also up for speculation was the future of Seagram's liquor business, which was suffering from the collapse of several lucrative markets in Asia because of the Asian financial crisis. The addition of PolyGram and the subtraction of Tropicana would create a Seagram where entertainment had the lead role, while liquor played second banana—an amazing turn of events in an even more amazingly brief span of time.

Principal Operating Units

The Seagram Spirits and Wine Group; Seagram Chateau & Estate Wines Company; Universal Pictures; Universal Studios Home Video; Universal Television Group; Universal Music Group; Universal Studios Recreation Group; Universal Studios Consumer Products Group; Spencer Gifts; Universal Studios New Media Group.

Further Reading

Bronfman, Edgar M., *Good Spirits: The Making of a Businessman,* New York: Putnam, 1998, 248 p.
Dalglish, Brenda, ''The Bronfman Gamble: Seagram's $8-Billion Purchase of MCA Shows That Show Biz Is Hot,'' *Maclean's,* April 24, 1995, pp. 40+.

Deogun, Nikhil, "Ocean Spray May Try to Block PepsiCo from Acquiring Seagram's Tropicana," *Wall Street Journal,* August 6, 1998, p. A7.

Deogun, Nikhil, and Vanessa O'Connell, "Storming the OJ Wars, Pepsi to Buy Tropicana," *Wall Street Journal,* July 21, 1998, pp. B1, B6.

Egan, Jack, "Jr.'s Got Show Biz; What About Booze?," *U.S. News & World Report,* June 22, 1998, pp. 50+.

Fabrikant, Geraldine, "At Seagram, Waiting for the Glitz to Pay Off," *New York Times,* September 18, 1997, pp. D1, D8.

Flynn, Julia, and Laura Zinn, "Absolut Pandemonium," *Business Week,* November 8, 1993, pp. 58, 62.

Freedman, Alix M., "Seagram Scion: He Has Style Galore, but Can the Boss's Son Run a Liquor Empire?," *Wall Street Journal,* December 3, 1987, pp. 1, 20.

Freedman, Alix M., and Ed Bean, "Seagram to Buy Beatrice Unit for $1.2 Billion," *Wall Street Journal,* March 11, 1998, pp. 2, 12.

Harris, Kathryn, "Edgar in Hollywood," *Fortune,* April 15, 1996, pp. 102+.

Kelley, Kristine Portnoy, "Looking Outside the Box: The Seagram Beverage Co. Studies Alternatives in Its Search for Success," *Beverage Industry,* May 1994, pp. 30+.

Koselka, Rita, and Randall Lane, "What Matsushita Left on the Table," *Forbes,* July 3, 1995, pp. 46+.

La Franco, Robert, "The High Cost of Hollywood," *Forbes,* April 7, 1997, pp. 44+.

Laing, Jonathan R., "Lights! Camera!: After Years of Preparation, the Action Is About to Start at Seagram," *Barron's,* April 27, 1998, pp. 35–36, 38–39.

Leinster, Colin, "The Second Son Is Heir at Seagram," *Fortune,* March 17, 1986, pp. 28+.

Newman, Peter C., *King of the Castle: The Making of a Dynasty: Seagrams and the Bronfman Empire,* New York: Atheneum, 1979.

Norman, James R., "Turning Up the Heat at Du Pont," *Forbes,* August 5, 1991, pp. 45+.

O'Connell, Vanessa, "Seagram May Be About to Seek a Buyer for Tropicana," *Wall Street Journal,* May 18, 1998, p. B10.

Orwall, Bruce, "Seagram Considers Sale of Film Unit of Polygram and Real-Estate Assets," *Wall Street Journal,* August 3, 1998, p. B4.

Orwall, Bruce, and Eben Shapiro, "Seagram to Sell Tropicana Unit to Public," *Wall Street Journal,* May 22, 1998, pp. A3, A12.

Reilly, Patrick M., "Slipped Disks: PolyGram, EMI Await Dance Partner," *Wall Street Journal,* May 7, 1998, p. B18.

Rothman, Andrea, and Mark Maremont, "The Maverick Boss at Seagram," *Business Week,* December 18, 1989, pp. 90–93, 96, 98.

Shapiro, Eben, "Seagram Completes Spinoff to HSN of TV Businesses," *Wall Street Journal,* February 13, 1998, p. A5.

——, "Seagram Sells Last Time Warner Block for $911 Million," *Wall Street Journal,* May 28, 1998, p. B8.

Sherrid, Pamela, "Give Me a Chivas and Natural Soda," *U.S. News & World Report,* July 17, 1989, pp. 42+.

Stevenson, Mark, "Indomitable Showman," *Canadian Business,* October 1994, pp. 22+.

Zinn, Laura, and Julia Flynn, "Edgar Jr.'s Not So Excellent Ventures," *Business Week,* January 16, 1995, pp. 78–79.

—updated by David E. Salamie

Sempra Energy

101 Ash Street
San Diego, California 92101-3017
U.S.A.
(619) 696-2034
Fax: (619) 696-1814
Web site: http//www.sempra.com

Public Company
Incorporated: 1998
Employees: 12,000
Sales: $5.0 billion (1997 est.)
Stock Exchanges: New York
Ticker Symbol: SRE
SICs: 4911 Electric Services; 4922 Natural Gas
    Transmission; 4924 Natural Gas Distribution; 4931
    Electric & Other Services Combined

Sempra Energy is a Fortune 500 energy services holding company which was formed by the 1998 merger of Pacific Enterprises and Enova Corporation. Sempra Energy's eight subsidiaries provide electricity, natural gas, and value-added products and services. After the merger was completed. Sempra possessed the largest regulated utility customer base in the United States. The Sempra name is derived from the Latin word for ''always.''

Early History

Pacific Enterprises was formed in 1988, two years after Pacific Lighting Corporation bought Thrifty Corporation, which owned drug, discount, and sporting-goods stores. Pacific Lighting's main business had been through Southern California Gas Company—the largest gas utility in the United States—which supplied about 15 million people in a 23,000-square-mile territory that included the Los Angeles area. Pacific Enterprises also engaged in oil and gas exploration and drilling.

Pacific Lighting Corporation's roots, however, ran much deeper. The company was founded in San Francisco in 1886 as Pacific Lighting Company by C.O.G. Miller and Walter B. Cline. Both men, who had worked for Pacific Gas Improvement Company—a company owned by Miller's father—saw an opportunity to start their own business when their employer decided not to use the newly invented Siemens gas lamp. Miller and Cline began buying Siemens lamps in San Francisco and soon expanded into the southern California utility business, buying a one-half interest in a gas manufacturing plant in San Bernardino, California. Their business flourished, and in 1889 Pacific Lighting Company bought three Los Angeles-area gas and electric firms with combined assets of more than $1 million. Miller and Cline created a subsidiary, called the Los Angeles Lighting Company, to consolidate the three formerly competing firms. Pacific Lighting's attention remained focused on the Los Angeles area for most of the next century.

Pacific Lighting supplied the gas and lighting for the small but rapidly growing city of Los Angeles. Los Angeles Lighting immediately began to make needed improvements in the Los Angeles gas system, which subsequently led to a decrease in prices. The company faced stiff competition from numerous small utilities during the 1890s, however, that retarded its growth. To help increase profits, Los Angeles Lighting began importing and selling coal and gas-powered appliances, hoping to stimulate the demand for gas. Pacific Lighting then bought a controlling interest in Los Angeles Electric Company in 1890, and in 1904 it combined all of its Los Angeles lighting and electric operations to form Los Angeles Gas and Electric Company (LAG&E). In 1907 Pacific Lighting Company was incorporated and changed its name to Pacific Lighting Corporation.

Pacific Lighting's gas sales increased tenfold between 1896 and 1906 as Los Angeles expanded. Sales grew further, after the San Francisco earthquake of 1906 caused many to move from northern California to Los Angeles. The city grew so fast that Pacific Lighting could not meet demand, and some parts of the city went without gas for days during cold spells in the winter of 1906 to 1907. Seeing an opportunity, a group of Los Angeles businessmen created the City Gas Company in an effort to win Pacific Lighting's dissatisfied customers. The City Gas Company could not match the resources of the older Pacific Lighting, however, and in 1910 it sold out to Pacific Light and Power, which owned Southern California Gas Company, one of Pacific Lighting's largest competitors. A conservatively run company, Pacific Lighting concentrated on supplying its service area and collecting its rates while rivals Southern Gas and Southern Counties Gas Company of California worked on new gas technology.

By 1915, the Los Angeles utility industry was dominated by Pacific Lighting Corporation and three other firms. These utilities were extremely unpopular with the public and had to continually fight off the threat of municipal ownership and government regulation. Pacific Lighting and the other utilities fought Los Angeles's attempts to build a municipal electric system by trying to block the financing and by launching time-consuming lawsuits. In 1917, the utilities came under the jurisdiction of the newly-formed California Public Utilities Commission (CPUC).

Because Pacific Lighting supplied its services to Los Angeles's densely populated downtown area, where operating costs were low, another municipal utility would not be able to match its rates. This situation slowed the momentum of the municipal ownership movement, and the battle remained stalemated throughout the 1920s. Meanwhile, southern California continued to grow rapidly, and Pacific Lighting put its resources into expanding its services, spending $10 million to build a new electric plant and to enlarge its substations. To fight off municipal ownership, Pacific Lighting began a public relations campaign and sold stock.

The Depression and the Years That Followed

After the Great Depression began in 1929, the tide shifted toward municipal ownership of utilities, partly because cash-starved citizens hoped municipal ownership would lower their bills, and partly due to the anti-corporation political climate. In 1929 the city of Los Angeles announced it was going to buy Pacific Lighting's electrical properties. The city had contracted to buy a share of the hydroelectric power produced by the new Hoover Dam and wanted to use Pacific Lighting's power grid to deliver it. The company's electric properties provided one-sixth of its revenue, so it fought the move as long as it could. Pacific Lighting, however, needed to renew its gas franchise, and the city would do that only if the company agreed to sell its electric properties. The properties were sold to the city in 1937 for $46 million.

Though stung by the loss of its electric operations, Pacific Lighting continued to grow as a gas utility. It ran its operations

conservatively, initially expanding its services only to regions that could be served by existing gas generating plants. As natural gas became more widely available in California, Pacific Lighting's gas operations expanded.

Pacific Lighting had acquired control of the gas distribution systems of Southern Counties Gas in 1925, Santa Maria Gas Company in 1928, and Southern California Gas in 1929. These companies had expanded more aggressively than Pacific Lighting—particularly around Los Angeles—in some cases quadrupling output during the 1920s. Part of this expansion came from the rapid growth of Los Angeles, and part from new uses for gas, such as space heating and water heating. By 1930, Los Angeles led the United States in natural gas consumption, and Pacific provided gas to half the population of California. It was the largest gas utility in the United States, serving nearly two million people. Pacific Lighting made broad policy decisions for its new subsidiaries, but left the day-to-day operating decisions to the management of the individual firms.

Natural gas was a more efficient and less expensive fuel than manufactured gas. Because Pacific Lighting and its subsidiaries had switched to natural gas during the 1920s, both gas rates and gas consumption had dropped. To compensate for the loss in volume, Pacific Lighting successfully promoted gas for industrial use. Industrial customers were attracted to the low rates and ease of handling associated with natural gas, as well as to the fact that natural gas did not require storage facilities. Industries used natural gas primarily during the summer to absorb Pacific Lighting's excess capacity, while during the winter Pacific Lighting required industries to use more energy from other sources. To maintain natural gas sources as the fuel became more scarce in the Los Angeles area, Pacific Lighting built longer pipelines, aided by improvements in technology.

Pacific Lighting worked on advertising campaigns with other gas utilities during the Great Depression to counter the belief that gas supplies would soon run out, and to promote the sales of gas-fueled appliances. This successful campaign helped the company weather the Depression, despite decreased use of its gas by industry.

In 1933 an earthquake caused extensive damage to Pacific Lighting's gas pipeline system, as did torrential rains in 1938. In an attempt to help recoup some of the losses suffered during the 1930s, Pacific attempted to combine Southern Counties Gas and Southern California Gas. The request was denied by California regulators, however, on the grounds that two companies, even if owned by the same holding company, would produce more competition than would one company.

A Changing Industry Environment After World War II

During World War II Pacific Lighting diverted energy to defense manufacturers and converted an old gas plant to the manufacture of war-related chemicals. The demand for natural gas increased dramatically during and after the war, and Pacific Lighting sought new means of keeping pace. Because new defense industries drew even more people to southern California, conditions for the company during the late 1940s and 1950s were similar to those during the 1920s, requiring large capital outlays for new construction.

In 1947 Pacific Lighting spent $25 million to build the Biggest Inch pipeline, which brought large amounts of natural gas to California from southern Texas. Demand grew so quickly that an extension to the large gas fields of the Texas panhandle was built in 1949. The company also built vast underground storage areas in southern California. Over the next ten years, Pacific Lighting greatly increased the volume of its interstate delivery system, and out-of-state gas made up 90 percent of the company's supply. In addition, the company had promoted gas-powered appliances so effectively that 90 percent of all cooking ranges and 98 percent of water heaters and home heating systems in southern California used natural gas. To meet demand, Pacific Lighting offered industries low rates in exchange for using other energy sources when demand peaked on cold winter days.

By 1950 the cost of bringing gas to customers had doubled since the years before World War II, but rates had risen only 15 percent. Pacific Lighting repeatedly sought unpopular rate hikes during the 1950s, and it increased its public relations efforts to help improve its image. Prices stabilized in the early 1960s as a result of regulatory changes that gave Pacific Lighting and its suppliers greater pricing flexibility. By the mid-1960s Pacific Lighting had become the largest gas supplier in the world, and its prices were among the lowest in the United States. Company head Miller died in 1952, and his son Robert Miller became chairman.

Restructuring in the 1960s and 1970s

In 1965 Pacific Lighting restructured its pipeline subsidiary—Pacific Lighting Gas Supply Company—and changed its name to Pacific Lighting Service and Supply. In 1967 the firm moved its headquarters from San Francisco to Los Angeles. Three years later, Pacific Lighting received regulatory permission to merge Southern California and Southern Gas into one company, called Southern California Gas Company. Pacific Lighting created another subsidiary in 1972—Pacific Lighting Coal Gasification Company—to build a coal gasification plant.

Meanwhile, despite the new pipelines, by the late 1960s gas supplies were dwindling again. Paul Miller, who became president of Pacific Lighting in 1968, sought additional supplies across an increasingly wider area, including Alaska, the Canadian Arctic, and the Rocky Mountains. In 1970 the company created another subsidiary called Pacific Lighting Gas Development Company, to find new gas sources. It soon signed a contract with Gulf Oil Canada to purchase large amounts of gas from a new pipeline that the company was building in Canada's Northwest Territories. Pacific Lighting also got involved in the Alaska Natural Gas Transportation System approved by the U.S. government in 1976, although more than a decade passed before any gas from the project was transported to southern California.

Energy Crisis of the 1970s

The energy crisis in the 1970s presented grave problems. Energy needs were increasing while Pacific Lighting's gas suppliers began cutting back the company's supplies. Pacific

Lighting considered bringing in liquid gas from overseas, while working with Pacific Gas & Electric, another California utility. The two firms began construction of a liquid natural gas plant at Little Cojo Bay, California, in 1979, although construction was halted in 1984 because the natural gas shortage had eased. The shortage ended because of conservation efforts and a federal law passed in 1978 that partially deregulated prices for new gas finds. The deregulation led to higher prices, which in turn caused widespread complaints. The company launched another public relations campaign on radio and television to explain why prices were rising.

The price increases, fuel shortages, and slowing population growth in southern California convinced Pacific Lighting executives to begin diversifying. At first Pacific Lighting's new affiliates were gas-related, but soon the company branched into real estate, air conditioning, agriculture, alternative energy, and retailing. In the early 1970s, Southern California Gas began two major solar energy research projects. More importantly, the company moved into gas and oil exploration and development. In 1975 Pacific Lighting Exploration Company invested in drilling in the Dutch sector of the North Sea. The ventures into agriculture and air conditioning were sold off in the late 1970s and early 1980s. In 1987 the firm sold its real estate operations for $325 million, believing the money could be more profitably invested elsewhere.

Expansion in the 1980s

In 1983 Pacific Lighting bought Terra Resources, which owned oil and gas property in 18 states. Five years later it bought Sabine Corporation, a Dallas, Texas-based exploration firm. By the late 1980s, oil and gas exploration provided 11 percent of Pacific Lighting's revenue. Pacific Lighting still wanted to move into areas unrelated to the utility business, however, and in 1986 it bought Thrifty Corporation, a chain of Los Angeles-based retail stores. The purchase gave Pacific Lighting ownership of 500 Thrifty Drug Stores, 27 Thrifty Jr. Drug Stores, and 89 Big 5 sporting goods stores. Pacific acquired Thrifty in a stock swap valued at $886 million, or 25 times Thrifty's annual earnings.

Thrifty had been founded in 1919 by two brothers, Harry and Robert Borun, and their brother-in-law, Norman Levin. Initially the firm sold drugs and sundries wholesale. After the stock market crash in 1929, the firm opened its own cut-rate drugstores. By World War II the firm operated 17 stores in the Los Angeles area. In the 1950s, with strip malls appearing and Thrifty's sales dropping, the firm switched to larger stores with a broader selection. In the 1970s, with competition increasing, Thrifty adopted a more aggressive marketing strategy, switching from low-end promotions to a policy of total discounts. By the mid-1980s the firm feared a hostile takeover. When Pacific Lighting offered to buy Thrifty, the company reluctantly accepted, partly because Pacific Lighting had a reputation for allowing its subsidiaries great freedom.

Pacific Lighting moved further into retailing in the next two years, buying more sporting-goods retailers in the Midwest and in Colorado, more than 100 Pay'n Save drugstores, and 37 Bi-Mart general merchandise stores. These purchases made Pacific Lighting the second-largest sporting-goods retailer in the United States and the largest drugstore chain in the western United States. To reflect its increasing diversity, Pacific Lighting changed its name to Pacific Enterprises in 1988. Paul Miller retired in 1989, and James R. Ukropina became chairman and CEO, ending 103 years of leadership by the Miller family.

In buying Thrifty, Pacific Enterprises had decided to trade short-term profits for long-term growth. The purchase left Pacific Enterprises short of funds, while its retail operations suffered from price wars, shoplifting, increased competition from supermarkets, and changing economics. The company also failed to find any large oil or gas deposits, and its core business suffered. To pay its stock dividends, Pacific Enterprises borrowed money and raised it by issuing stock—a move which worried some Wall Street analysts. To deal with the situation, Ukropina restructured management and temporarily cut back on oil and gas drilling. Revenue for 1990 was $6.92 billion, though the firm suffered a net loss of $43 million due to write-offs incurred by both its retail and gas and oil exploring operations.

The 1990s and the Birth of Sempra Energy

Willis B. Wood Jr. was named CEO in 1991 and led the company through restructuring that refocused on the core utility business and restored the parent company to a sound financial footing. Wood was succeeded by Richard D. Farman near the end of the decade, shortly before Pacific Enterprises' announced a merger with Enova Corporation.

Having announced the merger plans in October 1996, Pacific Enterprises and Enova Corporation awaited approvals by the California Public Utilities Commission, the Federal Energy Regulatory Commission, and the Securities and Exchange Commission. The merger was completed in June 1998, and the entity that resulted from the combined operations of both companies was named Sempra Energy. The new board of directors was comprised of 16 members, with eight representatives from each of the merging companies.

Enova Corporation, a leading energy management company providing electricity, gas, and value-added products and services in the United States and Mexico, joined Pacific Enterprises to form the largest public company headquartered in San Diego. Prior to the merger, Enova boasted the ownership of San Diego Gas & Electric Company, which had 1.2 million electric meters and 715,000 natural gas meters, serving 3 million consumers. Pacific Enterprises' contribution to the deal included its

interstate and offshore natural gas pipelines, centralized heating and cooling facilities, and natural gas distribution operations in Latin America. Thus, at its inception, Sempra Energy had the largest regulated gas and electric utility customer base in the United States, serving 21 million customers.

After reorganizations, the new corporation was the parent company of eight subsidiaries based in the United States, including Sempra Energy Solutions. That subsidiary's vice-president, Amy Reece, was elected by the National Energy Marketers Association (NEMA) to serve as chairperson. NEMA is a non-profit trade association which works with government entities, consumer representatives, and utilities to devise impartial ways to realize deregulation for natural gas and electricity markets.

Former Pacific Enterprises shareholders received 1.5038 shares of Sempra Energy common stock for each share of Pacific that they had owned prior to the merger deal. The new company's annual dividend rate was set initially at $1.56 per share. Sempra Energy's market value was deemed to be $6.2 billion on the day of its founding. Its stock remained in the mid-$20 range throughout its first three months. Given this solid financial base, and the combined assets of two of the largest regulated utility providers in the United States, Sempra's future potential looked to be strong.

Principal Subsidiaries

Southern California Gas Company; San Diego Gas & Electric; Sempra Energy Solutions (Los Angeles); Sempra Energy Trading (Greenwich, Connecticut); Sempra Energy International (San Diego); Sempra Energy Resources (San Diego); Sempra Energy Utility Ventures (Los Angeles); Sempra Energy Financial (San Diego).

Further Reading

Littlefield, Douglas R., and Thanis C. Thorne, *The Spirit of Enterprise,* Los Angeles: Pacific Enterprises, 1990.
''National Energy Marketers Tap Top Power Companies for New Leadership,'' *Business Wire,* August 7, 1998.
Pechdimaldji, Stephan, ''Amex to Trade Options on Sempra Energy,'' *PR Newswire,* June 29, 1998.
Sempra Corporate Web site, http://www.sempra.com

—Scott M. Lewis
—updated by Allison A. Jones

Sinclair Broadcast Group, Inc.

2000 W. 41st Street
Baltimore, Maryland 21211
U.S.A.
(410) 467-5005
Fax: (410) 467-5090

Public Company
Incorporated: 1965
Employees: 613
Sales: $46.4 million (1997)
Stock Exchanges: NASDAQ
Ticker Symbol: SBGI
SICs: 4832 Radio Broadcasting Stations, 4833 Television
    Broadcasting Stations, 6719 Holding Companies, Not
    Elsewhere Classified, 7812 Motion Picture & Video
    Production

Headquartered in Baltimore, Maryland, Sinclair Broadcast Group, Inc. owns and/or provides programming services to television stations in 20 different markets and to radio stations in eight different markets around the country. The company is one of the largest broadcasting groups in the nation, with the television portion of the company's business reaching approximately 15 percent of all U.S. households, and the radio portion ranked as one of the United States' top-20 groups.

Sinclair's Beginnings in the 1960s

What is now Sinclair Broadcasting started out as one man, Julian Smith, and an idea he had for a television station in Baltimore, Maryland. Smith, a Johns Hopkins-educated engineer, had worked for twenty years as an aerospace engineer. But in 1965, at the age of 45, he filed for an FCC license for a UHF television station in Baltimore. Although it was difficult at that time to receive anything other than local affiliates of the three major networks, Smith was not dissuaded. It took five years for him to receive his license from the FCC, and at that point he left his career in engineering to work in the television industry full-

time. The company's first television station, WBFF-TV Channel 45, finally went on the air in 1971.

Smith's first son, Frederick, followed in his father's footsteps by attending Johns Hopkins, but instead earned his degree in dentistry. Smith's second son, David, dropped out of electronics school after only a few years. "I didn't want to be a digit head; I wanted to be an entrepreneur," he later claimed in a 1996 interview with *Forbes* magazine. Thus, at the age of 23, David Smith joined his father's company. While his father was the visionary of the family, David became the money maker. Along with an engineer who had done work for their company, David became co-owner of Comark, a maker of television transmitters. The project's smash success would later allow them to sell the enterprise for almost $5 million in 1986. Prior to that, in 1981, David left Comark to return to the family business when his father's health began to fail. By then the company owned stations in Pittsburgh, Baltimore and Columbus.

Due to Julian Smith's health problems, six outside investors—who owned nearly 50 percent of the company's stock—decided they wanted him to end his involvement with the company. Julian Smith owned just 40 percent of the company's shares. In 1986, however, David Smith was able to persuade one of the outsiders, who happened to hold a 10.2 percent share, to take the Smith's side of the issue. The Smith family and their ally were now 50.2 percent owners, and were soon able to buy the other stock holders out with $20 million in cash and notes.

It was at this time, in 1986, that the name Sinclair Broadcast Group name was coined, and the company began its affiliation with the Fox Broadcasting Co. David Smith borrowed $15 million against the company so that he was able to buy his father's interest in Sinclair. He first turned his attention to one of the company's stations in Pittsburgh—WPTT—that had been losing money for years. Smith realized that he would either have to sell the station or buy up the competitors; he chose to buy. It was a risky move, but the decisions paid dividends in the long-run. Within a decade, his purchase was worth around $300 million.

Soon thereafter, Sinclair began acquiring more and more non-affiliate television stations from ABRY Communications

LP. These five additional stations in Baltimore, MD; Milwaukee, WI; and Birmingham, AL helped make the Company an influential television station owner that, conversely, did not own a property in the top 10 market.

1990s Growth of the Market

Warner Brothers and Paramount began a mad scramble after Warner Brothers' November, 1993 announcement that it would introduce its own WB Network the following summer. Independent stations were key to secure a fledgling network. The owners of these important independent stations included Sinclair, as well as Clear Channel TV, and Cannell Communications. The following year, in October 1994, Sinclair turned its own deal and bought WLFL-TV in Raleigh/Durham, North Carolina from Paramount Stations Group for an undisclosed amount. The station was then aligned with Paramount's new broadcast network, which was scheduled to start in 1995. The Federal Communications Commission (FCC) was requested to investigate Sinclair's purchase of the Raleigh/Durham television station, however, due to the fact that Sinclair already owned local station WRDC and the FCC regulations ban the ownership of more than one station in a given market. According to Sinclair, another entity—Communications Corp. of America—would retain control of WRDC, which it had reportedly purchased just two months earlier using a 98 percent equity investment from Sinclair.

In early 1995, Sinclair purchased non-license assets for television station WTVZ from Max Television Co. for $47 million. The company was operating under a lease management agreement, until the station's federal license transfer was approved by the FCC license. At that point, Sinclair owned 11 television stations. Thus, in March of 1995, the company filed for clearance for an initial public stock offering of 3.75 million shares for $19-$21 a share. The proceeds of a possible $78.75 million were going be used to repay bank debt.

Instead of the 3.75 million shares planned for Sinclair's initial public offering on June 8, 1995, five million shares sold for $21 each, with stock prices closing up at $24.125. The larger-than-expected proceeds were slated to pay off the company's significant interest expenses from the previous year, which totaled $25.4 million.

Nearly a year later, in the spring of 1996 Sinclair became the owner of WYZZ-TV in Bloomington/Peoria, Illinois. This acquisition was particularly noteworthy in that it gave Sinclair the

distinction of becoming the second TV group to pass the former limit of national ownership of 12 stations. One month later, plans for a joint bid on Palmer Communications were announced by Sinclair and River City Television.

In just a matter of days after the joint bid announcement was made, Sinclair indicated that it had acquired privately-held River City Broadcasting of St. Louis for approximately $1.2 billion. This purchase, which included River City's Sacramento Channel 13 (KOVR), made the company the country's seventh-largest television owner, with a total of 29 stations and the capability to reach 14.82 percent of all U.S. households. Its stock soared 18 percent—to $32.25—in reaction to these developments. Also part of the agreement were River City's 19 radio stations, which positioned Sinclair among the United States' top 10 station owner/operators, with 34 stations in 27 different markets. Its affiliates included ABC, CBS, Fox and UPN. Financial information released after the announcement revealed that River City showed an operating loss for 1995 and had $525 million in liabilities.

The broadcasting assets of the two companies were combined, forming a new subsidiary known as Sinclair Communications Inc.. This newly-formed public company had a market value of approximately $2.3 billion, and was set to control multiple television and radio stations in approximately 15 cities around the country. After the completion of the merger, the new company was expected to aggressively pursue acquisition of multiple additional stations in other markets.

In July of 1997, Sinclair completed the acquisition of the Heritage Media Group, which included both television and radio properties. This arrangement increased Sinclair's total holdings to 56 radio stations and 27 television stations. During the same time period, Sinclair worked with Glencairn Ltd. to develop more duopolies. A $1.2 billion deal was announced that year, and was slowly being realized as Sinclair exercised its option to buy one of Glencairn's stations at a time to spread out the cost of the deal.

The Late-1990s: Legal Entanglements and Technology Advancements

As always, David Smith continued looking for new venues for his business. The latter half of 1996 brought about the concept of Supercast, which would provide what Sinclair calls "internet and internet-type information" to computers, but without a wired connection to the internet. Reportedly able to transmit data at seven times the conventional 14.4 kilobit computer modem, Supercast would receive the television signal with modem and antenna plugged directly into a PC expansion slot on a standard computer. Although Intel had already created a similar product, and other companies continually testing their versions, Sinclair still forged ahead.

Sinclair Broadcast Group and Comark Digital Services sponsored a DiviCom demonstration of live multi-channel DTB broadcast from the show floor at NAB '98. Unfortunately, however, it had become apparent that while the technology existed, implementation would not be practical as early as had been expected. Digital television would pose high costs to both broadcasters and consumers—high enough to make the project appear to be not worth it, for the time being. Furthermore, a shortage of trained individuals to build the digital transmitter towers existed, and more problems were posed by the hefty $3000-$5000 price tags that early HDTVs would carry.

Meanwhile, an enticing offer was made to Sinclair by Warner Brothers near the end of the decade which caused a major clamor due to the huge blow to United Paramount Network (UPN) that resulted. UPN was informed of the termination of their contract with Sinclair, when the company was offered an $84 million, 10-year deal to switch the affiliation of five major markets over to the Warner Brothers network. A dazed UPN had no comment on the subject until it filed a law suit against Sinclair for breaking a contract that bound the two companies until January of 2001. Sinclair replied by filing against UPN in return, stating that proper notification regarding the contract had been given to UPN.

A December 9, 1997 Maryland Court judgment was made in favor of Sinclair, stating that they had given "timely and proper notice" of UPN's contract termination. Sinclair issued a press release of its plans to begin broadcasting WB Network programming effective January 16, 1998. A similar law suit was again filed by UPN. Sinclair announced, in reply, that the Los Angeles Superior Court had issued an Order staying UPN's action against Sinclair, based on the previous Maryland Court judgment in Sinclair's favor. With all legal obstacles cleared, Sinclair decided to cease its affiliation with UPN for four of its stations, and was prepared to turn at least six stations over to WB outlets in January, 1998.

In an effort to repay a debt to an outstanding revolving credit facility, 5.3 million common shares of Sinclair was made available for sale in September of 1997. With shares priced at $36.50 each, the offering was financed through underwriters led by Smith Barney Inc. Shortly after this offering, the company announced that it had completed the public offerings of approximately $150 million of Class A Common Stock and $150 million aggregate liquidation amount of Convertible Exchangeable Preferred Stock. Net proceeds to the company from these offerings were roughly $285.7 million.

Three more deals were completed in July of 1998, allowing Sinclair to announce that it had become one of the largest owners of radio and television stations in the United States. The largest of these purchases was Max Media Properties LLC of Virginia Beach—the owner of nine television stations and eight radio stations—and was acquired by Sinclair for a $252 million cash agreement. As the end of the decade approached, Sinclair's goal was set at obtaining 100 TV stations and over 100 radio stations.

Principal Subsidiaries

Chesapeake Television, Inc. (MD); Chesapeake Television Licensee, Inc. (DE); FSF-TV, Inc. (NC); KABB, Inc. (DE); KABB Licensee, Inc. (DE); KDNL, INC.(DE); KDNL Licensee, Inc. (DE); KSMO, Inc. (MD); KSMO Licensee, Inc. (DE); KUPN, Inc. (MD); KUPN Licensee, Inc. (DE); SCI - Indiana, Inc. (DE); SCI - Indiana Licensee, Inc. (DE); SCI - Sacramento, Inc. (DE); SCI - Sacramento, Inc. (DE); Sinclair Communications, Inc. (MD); Sinclair Radio of Albuquerque, Inc. (MD); Sinclair Radio of Albuquerque Licensee, Inc. (DE); Sinclair Radio of Buffalo, Inc. (MD); Sinclair Radio of Buffalo Licensee, Inc. (DE); Sinclair Radio of Greenville, Inc. (MD); Sinclair Radio of Greenville Licensee, Inc. (DE); Sinclair Radio of Los Angeles, Inc. (MD); Sinclair Radio of Los Angeles Licensee, Inc. (DE); Sinclair Radio of Memphis (MD); Sinclair Radio of Memphis Licensee, Inc. (DE); Sinclair Radio of Nashville, Inc. (MD); Sinclair Radio of Nashville Licensee, Inc. (DE); Sinclair Radio of New Orleans, Inc. (MD); Sinclair Radio of New Orleans Licensee, Inc. (DE); Sinclair Radio of St. Louis, Inc. (MD); Sinclair Radio of St. Louis Licensee, Inc. (DE); Sinclair Radio of Wilkes Barre, Inc. (MD); Sinclair Radio of Wilkes Barre Licensee, Inc. (DE); Superior Communications of Kentucky, Inc. (DE); Superior Communications of KY License, Inc. (DE); Superior Communications of Oklahoma, Inc. (OK); Superior Communications of OK License, Inc. (DE); Tuscaloosa Broadcasting, Inc. (MD); WCGV, Inc. (MD); WCGV Licensee, Inc. (DE); WDBB, Inc. (MD); WLFL, Inc. (MD); WLFL Licensee, Inc. (DE); WLOS, Inc. (MD); WLOS Licensee, Inc. (DE); WPGH, Inc. (MD); WPGH Licensee, Inc. (MD); WSMH, Inc. (MD); WSMH Licensee, Inc. (DE); WSTR, Inc. (MD); WSTR, Inc. Licensee (MD); WSYX, Inc. (MD); WTTE, Channel 28, Inc. (MD); WTTE, Channel 28 Licensee, Inc. (MD); WTTO, Inc. (MD); WTTO, Licensee, Inc. (DE); WTVZ, Inc. (MD); WTVZ, Licensee, Inc. (MD); WYZZ, Inc. (MD); WYZZ, Licensee, Inc. (DE).

Further Reading

Brodesser, Claude, et al., "Sinclair Broadcast Group, Inc. Switches Affiliation of Five Television Stations From the United Paramount Network to the Warner Brothers Network, Erasing UPN's Former Distribution Advantage," *Media Week,* July 21, 1997, p.2.

Foisie, Geoffrey, "Sinclair, Edwards Buy LMAs From ABRY," *Broadcasting and Cable,* August 30, 1993, p. 31.

Gubernick, Lisa, "I Didn't Want to be a Digit Head," *Forbes,* September 9, 1996, pp. 80–84.

Lafayette, Jon, "Sinclair Plans Side-by-Side Digital Demonstration: Baltimore Will See 1080I, 480P," *Electronic Media,* June 8, 1998, p.39.

Leffall, J., "HDTV Demonstration Gets Imperfect Reception: Live Digital Screening Brings Mixed Reviews," *Baltimore Sun,* June 11, 1998, p1C.

LeFranco, Robert, "Tough Customers," *Forbes,* June 1, 1998, p.78.

Peck, Jeanne, "Baltimore's Sinclair Broadcast Group Seeks Approval to go Public," *Daily Press (Newport News),* March 30, 1995.

—Melissa West

SkyWest

SkyWest, Inc.

444 South River Road
St. George, Utah 84790
U.S.A.
(435) 634-3000
Fax: (435) 634-3505
Web site: http://www.skywest.com

Public Company
Incorporated: 1972 as Inter American Aviation, Inc.
Employees: 2,123
Sales: $297.1 million (1998)
Stock Exchanges: NASDAQ
Ticker Symbol: SKYW
SICs: 4512 Air Transportation-Scheduled; 6719 Holding
Companies, Not Elsewhere Classified

SkyWest, Inc. is the holding company for three related companies. First is SkyWest Airlines, which after its 1998 expansion became the nation's fifth largest regional airline, with scheduled flights for passengers and freight to 12 western states and Canada. It serves both business travelers who use SkyWest as a commuter airline and tourists vacationing at ski resorts or California's beaches. SkyWest Airlines' close ties to both Delta and Continental airlines have been a key to its success. Second, Scenic Airlines offers air tours, general aviation, and scheduled flights to the Grand Canyon and other areas of Arizona, Utah, and Nevada. Third, National Parks Transportation maintains a fleet of Avis rental cars to assist sightseers and others who have flown to selected locations.

Origins in the Early 1970s

Skywest was built on the ruins of another airline. In the small southern Utah city of St. George, Dixie Airline finally called it quits in 1972. Local attorney J. Ralph Atkin and four other men acquired Dixie's airport lease and the intrastate rights for a commuter airline. Atkin also began a fixed base operation (FOB) consisting of air charters, a flight school, aircraft maintenance, and air ambulance service.

The descendent of Mormon pioneers, Atkin had graduated from Brigham Young University and then earned a law degree from the University of Utah. Atkin and his wife returned to St. George, where he worked in a law partnership and in 1970 was elected county attorney. In 1971 one of his law clients happened to be a flight instructor, so soon Atkin took flying lessons. On March 2, 1972 he started a company called Inter American Aviation, Inc., so that he and four friends could own a plane just for fun. Then Atkin decided to offer commercial flights, and the firm's name was changed to SkyWest Airlines, a division of SkyWest Aviation Inc.

By June 1972 the young company had four planes and three part-time pilots. Jerry Fackrell piloted a twin-engine, six-seat Piper Seneca N1021U on the company's first scheduled flight on June 19, 1972, from St. George to Cedar City and on to Salt Lake City. In the early days SkyWest pilots also served as ticket agents and baggage handlers. They were paid only $5 per flight hour and $10 for extended layovers in Salt Lake City.

By 1973 and 1974 SkyWest had acquired a few more small passenger planes and expanded with a route to Las Vegas, the closest big city. In these early years, however, it did just about anything to make money. It flew oil exploration crews in and out of Moab, Utah, and even conducted some cloud seeding operations.

Probably the most unusual early venture was providing charters for the federal Immigration and Naturalization Service. It used its Cessna 206s and Piper Cherokee Sixes to pick up illegal immigrants in different locations in the West and fly them to just north of the Mexican border, where they were deported. Since some deportees returned to the United States, SkyWest pilots occasionally flew the same individuals repeatedly back to the Mexican border.

By 1974 the company had large debts and considered declaring bankruptcy. Jerry C. Atkin, Ralph Atkin's nephew who joined the firm in 1974, recalled that they tried to sell the company for $25,000, but nobody wanted it at that price. They even offered to give SkyWest away, but nobody would take it.

Sidney J. Atkin, Ralph Atkin's brother and the majority whip in the Utah legislature, helped the firm gain a state grant in 1975. That grant for $15,000 helped save the company.

In October 1975 the company was reorganized with Jerry Atkin named president, Ralph Atkin as board chairman and vice-president of corporate development, Sid Atkin as vice-president of finance, and Lee C. Atkin (Ralph and Sid's older brother) as secretary. By selling three aircraft, route reductions, and personnel cutbacks, SkyWest barely survived this crisis. It paid its creditors just $50 per month for one year, but eventually all were paid in full.

Expansion in the Late 1970s

In 1976 the firm made a modest profit—its first. That was helped by Hughes Air West dropping its Cedar City-Salt Lake City route. At that point SkyWest expanded its fleet by purchasing two more Navajo Chieftans, making a total of five. SkyWest Aviation Inc. also expanded its car rental business. It formed National Parks Transportation Company to manage two Avis franchises at Cedar City and St. George.

In 1977 the company signed its first interline agreement with American Airlines, which allowed passengers to be ticketed to their final destination in just one check-in procedure. Later several other airlines would also sign interline contracts with SkyWest.

Three major events marked the company's history in 1978. First, SkyWest became the third commuter airline in the nation's history to become a certified air carrier subject to federal government regulations just like major airlines.

Second, the Civil Aeronautics Board (CAB) granted SkyWest its first federal subsidy, a three-year agreement for annual amounts of $160,000 for flights to Page, Arizona. The CAB also granted SkyWest authority for routes to Yuma, Kingman, Prescott, Grand Canyon, Tucson, Winslow, and Phoenix, Arizona, as well as Blythe, Los Angeles, and El Centro, California.

Third, and maybe most important, SkyWest in 1978 acquired its first Fairchild Metroliner II, worth $1.4 million, far more than its earlier planes, which cost about $150,000 apiece. A twin-propeller, 19-seat aircraft, the Metro became the company's main plane as it entered the era of federal deregulation.

Growth from Deregulation, Acquisition, and Affiliations in the 1980s

After the federal government passed the Airline Deregulation Act in 1978, major airlines no longer were required to service small markets. Thus airlines such as United, Western, and American left less profitable communities, which in turn opened the door to regional airlines like SkyWest.

For example, in 1980 SkyWest began flying three daily flights into Pocatello, Idaho, after Western Airlines left that city. Pocatello became SkyWest's main market in the early 1980s. And in 1982 SkyWest received government permission to fly into Ely, Elko, and Reno, Nevada after United and Frontier departed and Golden Gate, another commuter, declared bankruptcy. The same year SkyWest replaced Frontier Airlines at Vernal, Utah, and Rock Springs, Wyoming, and in September 1982 took over the route to Idaho Falls from departing Republic Airlines.

Adding such cities was expensive for the still modest regional airline. Without adding new planes, SkyWest invested between $50,000 and $100,000 for a new destination, which covered ground equipment, counter space, and passenger lounges. If a new plane was needed, more than $2 million could be spent.

By 1983 the company had purchased a total of seven Metros, and it still had five smaller Navajo Chieftans and even smaller Cessna 207s for charters. This fleet expansion indicated that SkyWest was prospering in spite of the recession early in the Reagan Administration.

Like other airlines, SkyWest also had been hurt by President Reagan's 1981 firing of the air traffic controllers after the illegal strike by the Professional Air Traffic Controllers Association. The 1981 controllers strike contributed to SkyWest's first accident. On September 24, when the Flagstaff, Arizona control tower was closed because of the strike, a SkyWest Metro collided on the ground with an inbound corporate jet. The corporate pilot was blamed for this accident, which caused no deaths.

During SkyWest's tenth year anniversary in 1982, it adopted its first computerized reservation system. It replaced its card files with Republic's Escort computer system, a necessary step because SkyWest was flying 550 flight segments every week.

In the early 1980s SkyWest expanded its freight deliveries so that about ten percent of its revenues were from mail, small packages, and bank documents. This helped small communities that lost bus and rail services after those industries were deregulated.

SkyWest enjoyed eight straight years of profitability by the end of 1983, when it was ranked 42nd among the nation's top 100 regional airlines. From its base in St. George, it served 17 locations in six states. It employed about 250 individuals, so the intimate family atmosphere of the early days was dissipating. This growth also resulted in President Jerry Atkin delegating fiscal responsibilities to a new financial vice-president position. At the same time separate marketing and customer service departments were created.

That set the stage for SkyWest's major acquisition. In August 1984 SkyWest began flying from Las Vegas into Palm Springs, California, its first ventures into the highly competitive Southern California market. That led to SkyWest acquiring Palm Springs-based Sun Aire, from its owner, the DiGiorgio Corporation. Sun Aire had been founded in 1968 in Borrego

Springs, California by H. L. Van Sickle to shuttle travelers to and from San Diego, just 90 miles to the south. In 1983 Sun Aire carried 330,000 passengers, about twice as many as SkyWest. SkyWest operated the two firms separately until the merger was completed in 1985. The acquisition boosted SkyWest to the nation's 11th largest regional carrier.

The Sun Aire acquisition resulted in major changes for SkyWest. First, its fleet expanded. With SkyWest's 12 Metros and Sun Aire's 14 Metros, the merged company had the world's largest fleet of Fairchild Metros. The combined company flew to 28 sites. Sun Aire had opened a new facility within American Airlines's Los Angeles terminal three months before the merger, so the renamed firm SkyWest/Sun Aire Lines gained access to that major market.

The merger also resulted in forming the holding company SkyWest, Inc., with its three subsidiaries: SkyWest Airlines Inc. (changed from the earlier SkyWest Aviation Inc.), National Parks Transportation Company for the Avis rental car business, and Aviation Services West, Inc. for the fixed base operations. In addition, SkyWest as a result of the merger replaced its Escort CRS (computer reservation system) with the more advanced Sabre CRS, an American Airlines system used by Sun Aire.

In *Time Flies,* the SkyWest corporate history, Sid Atkin said the merger with Sun Aire "really did make us a professional airline when the resources and talents of both organizations came together." The complete merger took several years, however. Long-time employee Jan Nelson described the transition in *Time Flies,* as follows: "We ran a northern operation and a southern operation. This was like running two different airlines even after we merged. We had different things to worry about in each section. They didn't have to worry about the extreme temperatures, altitudes or the long hauls we had. They were strictly operating in Southern California. . . . They [Sun Aire employees] viewed us as a Mormon company. They had different management methods and attitudes. California people were just entirely different."

Meanwhile, another major change occurred. In 1985 SkyWest became affiliated with Western Airlines through a code-sharing agreement in which SkyWest adopted Western's two-letter code in computer reservation systems. Western had 70 percent of Salt Lake City's market at the time, so this joint venture increased SkyWest's flights. Code sharing was a very controversial decision, however, for regional airlines tended to lose their identity.

In any case, later in 1985 Delta Airlines announced its purchase of Western, which led to SkyWest becoming one of the regional airlines that flew as the Delta Connection using the Delta code DL in computer reservation systems. The Delta Connection became effective April 1, 1987, when the Delta/Western merger was completed. Thus in the mid-1980s some SkyWest personnel daily wondered what the company logo was, since the company had planes with different paint designs as it evolved rapidly from SkyWest to SkyWest/Sun Aire and then to affiliations as Western Express and Delta Connection.

These code-sharing affiliations were a major trend in the evolving relationships between major and regional airlines in the 1980s. United Airlines signed agreements with regionals to become United Express carriers, and American Airlines established its American Eagle network. The major airlines needed commuter connections, yet some of their executives worried about increased liability for their smaller partners who now carried their name.

Larraine Segil, a leading consultant for airline alliances, wrote about such issues in her book *Intelligent Business Alliances* (Random House, 1996). In the January 1998 issue of *Business & Commercial Aviation,* Segil pointed out that about 55 percent of all business alliances fail after three years of trying. She explained some of the difficulties when two corporate cultures collide: "You take a look at the airline industry and you suddenly find local regional airlines that are very much either in start-up or in high-growth mode. The larger national and international airlines are mature and even some of them are in a declining mode. When you partner a declining or a mature company with a start-up or a high-growth company, you have inherent potential incompatibilities. Those . . . are unavoidable, but they can be managed."

Segil praised Delta Airlines for its efforts to integrate with its junior partners like SkyWest. She said Delta had a "real commitment to make the relationship work. I think that is a distinguishing factor." The Delta Connection with SkyWest, begun in 1985, still functioned in 1998, backing up Segil's assessment.

In the mid-1980s SkyWest faced expanded opportunities, so it purchased new planes, namely the Brasilia EMB-120 turboprop, manufactured in Brazil by Embraer. This was SkyWest's first plane designed specifically for regional airlines. The smaller Metros were corporate planes modified for regional use and thus required increased maintenance to fly many more miles than originally intended. Brasilia service was started on February 1, 1986 in Palm Springs. Even into the 1990s SkyWest used most of its Brasilias in the highly competitive California market.

To pay off the Sun Aire acquisition and to raise capital for its expansion, SkyWest became a public corporation in 1986. After its initial public offering under the symbol SKYW on the NASDAQ market, Jerry and Ralph Atkin flew to New York City to get a check for almost $12 million, far more than the less than $1 million raised in private offerings since the company had been founded.

In 1987 SkyWest received *Air Transport World's* Commuter/Regional Airline of the Year award, after being chosen from some 500 regional airlines in the world. In fiscal year 1988, however, SkyWest lost $2.3 million, its first loss in several years. Company leaders had expanded too fast into California, the graveyard of at least 28 airlines, so they canceled some routes and concentrated on core markets. In 1989, for the first time, SkyWest flew more than one million passengers, a far cry from the 256 it had flown in 1972, its first year in business.

Events in the 1990s

SkyWest founder Ralph Atkin retired in 1991 as board chairman and CEO; Jerry Atkin replaced his uncle in those positions. In 1992 the firm broke ground for a new corporate office in St. George. The $3.6 million facility on a 15-acre site provided offices for more than 250 employees.

Some stock analysts in 1993 encouraged investors to consider the rising stocks of regional airlines, such as SkyWest, since the major airlines were losing a lot of money. Since 1990 the airline industry had lost nearly $10 billion, so investors naturally were skeptical. Yet most regionals remained profitable. And SkyWest's nonunion work force helped it keep down labor costs.

In June 1993 SkyWest's subsidiary Aviation Services West, Inc. acquired the flight tour operations of Scenic Airlines, Inc., a company formed in 1967 to provide tours to the Grand Canyon from Las Vegas and other sites. Following the acquisition, Aviation Services West changed its name to Scenic Airlines, Inc.

In 1994 SkyWest replaced Delta after the major airline canceled its jet flights from Salt Lake City to five low-volume cities: Casper, Wyoming; Butte, Montana; Burbank, California; and Rapid City and Sioux Falls, South Dakota. To service those routes, SkyWest ordered ten Canadair Regional Jets (CRJs) from Bombardier, Inc. These jets cost far more to purchase ($17 million each) and operate than the earlier Brasilias. CRJ advantages included greater range, up to about 1,200 miles. Powered by two General Electric turbofan engines, the CRJs cruised at about 540 miles per hour (Mach 0.8). This increased speed allowed SkyWest to offer additional flights in some markets. The CRJs featured seats for 50 passengers and the ability to fly up to 41,000 feet, above most turbulent weather.

SkyWest leaders struggled with the transition to jets. President Jerry Atkin in the September 1994 *Business & Commercial Aviation* admitted, "It is a good thing I did not know how big a task it was." And Ron Reber, senior vice-president of marketing and sales, said, "I did not think the [regional airline] industry would ever accommodate a . . . 50-passenger jet." Reber changed his mind, especially after SkyWest worked through the protests of city leaders in Butte, Montana. For years Butte had enjoyed Western and then Delta flights. Montana's congressional delegation even visited Delta's Atlanta headquarters to request continued flights, but in the end the city rejoiced at the nonstop and more frequent flights provided by SkyWest.

SkyWest pilots faced challenges from the new cockpits in the Canadair jets. None had any experience with the more sophisticated video screens in the CRJ's glass cockpit, which provided an overwhelming amount of information. After new training manuals were written, the pilots spent hours on flight-training devices and simulators to make the transition.

In October 1995 Skywest and Continental Airlines signed a marketing and code-sharing agreement whereby SkyWest became a Continental Connection in markets operating in and out of Los Angeles. Only about three percent of SkyWest passengers connected with Continental flights in 1996, however, far less than the approximately 48 percent interline passengers who connected with Delta flights the same year.

In 1996 the firm flew more than 2.5 million passengers and bought its sixtieth plane as it continued to expand in the western United States. The fleet then consisted of 50 Brasilias and ten Canadair Regional Jets. That same year it retired its last Metroliner, the company's mainstay for many years.

SkyWest announced a marketing agreement with United Airlines effective October 1, 1997, in which SkyWest began operating as United Express. This code-sharing agreement, which replaced WestAir, gave SkyWest more connecting opportunities at the Los Angeles International Airport, where United was the largest major carrier. At the same time SkyWest reaffirmed its Delta Connection contract for flights between Los Angeles and Salt Lake City.

In 1997 SkyWest celebrated its 25th anniversary. As of October 1, 1997, it operated 585 daily departures to 45 cities in 12 western states and Canada. Its longest and only international flight was between Salt Lake City and Vancouver, Canada, using the Canadair Regional Jets.

SkyWest and United on January 19, 1998 signed an agreement that SkyWest would begin operating as the United Express carrier at United's San Francisco hub on June 1, 1998. At that time it began offering some 90 departures daily to 12 California communities. In 1998 SkyWest expanded its United Express flights to include shuttles between outlying communities and the airports in Portland and Seattle. Thus in 1998 SkyWest operated as a connecting carrier to three major airlines: Delta, United, and Continental. Company executives planned to add 30 more Embraer Brasilias by October 1, 1998 to handle its new West Coast lines. These purchases would use some of the $40 million raised in a secondary stock offering completed February 12, 1998.

The firm's financial performance for fiscal year 1998, ending on March 31, showed that its annual revenues increased to $297.1 million from $278.1 for fiscal year 1997. SkyWest's fiscal year 1997 net income was $10.1 million or 50 cents per share. In fiscal year 1998 those figures more than doubled, with net income rising to $21.4 million or $1.06 per share. Not bad for a company that its owners once wanted to give away!

Principal Subsidiaries

SkyWest Airlines, Inc.; National Parks Transportation Co.; Scenic Airlines, Inc.

Further Reading

Creedy, Kathryn B., *Time Flies . . . The History of SkyWest Airlines,* San Antonio, Texas: Loflin & Associates, 1992.
Douglas, Diane, "How Time Flies," *OutPosts* (SkyWest's inflight magazine), anniversary issue, 1997.
Henderson, Danna, "SkyWest Has Found Both Prosperity and Problems in the Golden State," *Air Transport World,* February 1988, p. 88.
"High-Flying Skywest Inc. Doubles Its Net Income," *Salt Lake Tribune,* May 22, 1996, p. D15.
Hughes, David, "SkyWest Buys Regional Jets To Fly Former Delta Routes," *Aviation Week & Space Technology,* August 23, 1993, p. 34.
Knudson, Max B., "SkyWest Escapes from 'The Hangar of Doom,'" *Deseret News* (Web Edition), March 27, 1994.
Labate, John, "SkyWest," *Fortune,* July 25, 1994, p. 233.
Lewin, Rebecca, "Airline Stocks: Upstarts Leave the Majors Behind," *Medical Economics,* October 25, 1993, p. 120.

Lewis, Arnold, "Corporate Alliances," *Business & Commercial Aviation,* January 1998, pp. 82–89.

——, "SkyWest Airlines: Making the Jet Transition," *Business & Commercial Aviation,* September 1994, pp. C2–C6.

Moorman, Robert W., "Survivor of the West," *Air Transport World,* August 1992, p. 38.

Oberbeck, Steven, "SkyWest Continues Expansion with United Routes in Northwest," *Salt Lake Tribune,* February 18, 1998, p. D6.

Proctor, Paul, "SkyWest Balances Turboprop-Turbofan Fleet," *Aviation Week & Space Technology,* March 2, 1998, pp. 49, 51–52.

Segil, Larraine, *Intelligent Business Alliances,* New York: Random House, 1996.

"SkyWest Relocates Headquarters," *Deseret News* (Web Edition), February 9, 1993.

"SkyWest To Add 12 California Cities," *Deseret News* (Web Edition), January 23, 1998.

—David M. Walden

SallieMae

SLM Holding Corp.

11600 Sallie Mae Drive
Reston, Virginia 20193
U.S.A.
(703) 333-8000
Fax: (703) 810-7053
Web site: http://www.salliemae.com

Public Company
Incorporated: 1972
Employees: 4,608
Assets: $47 billion
Stock Exchanges: New York
Ticker Symbol: SLM
SICs: 6111 Federal & Federally-Sponsored Credit

SLM Holding Corp. is the publicly-traded umbrella organization over the Student Loan Marketing Association, better
known as Sallie Mae. It is the largest provider of student loan
funding in the United States. The company buys student loans
from originators under the Federal Family Education Loan
(FFEL) program, helping to keep student loan money liquid.
Sallie Mae also offers tools to college financial aid offices for
dealing with loan disbursement and debt counseling, and offers
privately-insured loans to borrowers. Sallie Mae is a leader in
loan tracking and management technology as well. It services
loans through nine regional offices in the United States. Though
the company began as a quasi-public entity, with an implicit
government guarantee of its loans its status changed in 1997.
Sallie Mae's current debt is backed by the federal government
only until 2008, when the company's government-sponsored
enterprise charter expires.

Early History

Sallie Mae was created by Congress in 1972 as a publicly-
owned, for-profit company. Its mission was to provide a secondary market for the exchange of federally-insured, guaranteed
student loans. Congress created Sallie Mae to make student loans
more liquid, and therefore give lenders a greater incentive to

participate in the Guaranteed Student Loan Program (GSLP).
Sallie Mae began by offering two basic services: loan purchases
and warehousing advances (secured loans and lines of credit). By
purchasing student loans, Sallie Mae offered lenders liquidity; the
knowledge that they could sell the loans and were not required to
use the money to make new student loans made lenders less
nervous about tying up money in student loans in the first place.
Under its warehousing program Sallie Mae lent financial institutions money to make new student loans by accepting existing
loans or other government securities as collateral.

Guaranteed student loans were a special market for several
reasons. The Guaranteed Student Loan Program (GSLP), created in 1965 by the Higher Education Act, was established to
supplement the government's grant and work-study programs,
which helped students finance higher education. Under the
GSLP, the federal government assumed the risk for defaulted
student loans. Originally, the government guaranteed the loans
directly, but state and nonprofit agencies later directly insured
the loans, backed up by federal reinsurance.

The GSLP allowed qualified students to borrow a certain
amount at a special fixed interest rate each year they were in
school. While students were in school and for a short grace period
after they left, the federal government paid the interest on their
loans, so that a student had to pay back only the principal plus the
interest accrued after graduation. In addition, the government
paid a special allowance to lenders to make up the difference
between the low rate of interest students paid and the market rate
of return. It was typically set a few percentage points above the
90-day treasury bill rate. Thus, if the borrowing rate for students
was 8 percent, and the treasury bill rate was 10 percent, lenders
got the 2 percent difference between that rate and the 8 percent
students paid, plus 3.25 percent on top of that—adjusted quarterly according to the treasury bill rate.

Since collection procedures made carrying student loans
costly once they reached the repayment phase, many lenders
sold student loans to Sallie Mae when the student graduated.
Student loans were costly not because student default rates were
high (defaults were guaranteed by the government anyway), but
because they were relatively small loans that required a lot of
work. In addition to the federal collection and reporting require-

ments that had to be followed to qualify for the government guarantee in the case of default, student loans were often complicated to keep track of. For example, students had to be granted deferments for unemployment, a return to school, or any of a host of other reasons.

Sallie Mae's high volume meant that the company could administer the collection of loans with greater cost effectiveness—by 1988, Sallie Mae held 24 percent of all outstanding student loans. Thus, Sallie Mae insured an adequate supply of credit for educational needs by enabling lenders to hold onto their loans during the lucrative in-school phase, sell the loans when they began to require more attention, and use the money to make new loans.

As a federally-chartered corporation, Sallie Mae's history was shaped by legislation. After adjusting the interest rates and special allowances for GSLP borrowers and lenders for several years, in its efforts to make enough educational credit available, Congress chartered Sallie Mae in 1972 to create a secondary market for student loans. The company opened for business in 1973 with financing from Washington, D.C. banks, repaying these loans through the sale of federally-guaranteed securities the same year. After that, Sallie Mae depended on financing from the Federal Financing Bank—an arm of the Treasury Department—from which it could borrow money at very attractive rates. But Congress never intended for Sallie Mae to be government-supported, and in 1981 Sallie Mae started raising the money it needed on public capital markets. After that, it became known for its inventive financing schemes, which were designed to lock in floating-rate liabilities to match its floating-rate assets.

In 1974, Sallie Mae made its first issue of common stock, raising $24 million in capital. The sale of this stock was restricted to banks or educational institutions, who were required to buy 100 shares in order to participate in Sallie Mae's programs. This requirement was later lowered to 50 shares, and small institutions were exempt.

In 1976, the lender allowance was tied to the 90-day treasury bill rate, and its ceiling was raised from 3 percent to 5 percent. That year, in an effort to reduce the red tape and inefficiencies that often accompany federal programs, the government transferred responsibility for the GSLP to the states and encouraged them to set up their own guaranteeing agencies. It also authorized Sallie Mae to buy loans originated under a newly-created Health Education Assistance Loan Program (HEAL) to help graduate students in the health professions finance their educations.

By 1977, Sallie Mae was able to issue its first dividend. The next year, the Middle Income Assistance Act removed all income restrictions for student borrowers in response to complaints from middle-income families that they were too rich to get assistance but too poor to pay rising education costs—especially if they had more than one child in college at a time. Since students were no longer required to demonstrate financial need to qualify for loans, the program expanded rapidly—from $2 billion in new loans in 1978, to $3 billion in 1979, to $8 billion in 1980.

In 1978 Congress also removed the ceiling on the special allowance to lenders, setting the allowance simply at 3.5 percent above the 90-day treasury bill rate, so that lenders were guaranteed a market rate of return. That, and the elimination of the paperwork involved in determining eligibility, made student loans more attractive to lenders. Sallie Mae grew accordingly, from assets of $1.6 billion in 1979 to $7.5 billion in 1982.

Making Money in the 1980s

In 1980, as a prime rate near 20 percent pushed the cost of the GSLP sky-high, Congress made further amendments to the Higher Education Act. For the first time since 1968, the interest rate charged to student borrowers was raised, from 7 percent to 9 percent. It was determined that the higher rate would stay in effect as long as treasury bill rates remained at a higher level.

The rate stayed at 9 percent until 1983, when treasury bill rates fell enough to lower the rate to 8 percent. The amendments of 1980 also established a new educational lending program called PLUS, for parents of dependent students.

More important to Sallie Mae, however, were changes that increased the company's range of operations and gave it new ways of raising capital, to begin weaning it from federal support. Congress set the expiration of Sallie Mae's authority to issue federally-guaranteed obligations at 1984, but gave the secretary of the treasury power to buy as much as $1 billion of nonguaranteed Sallie Mae securities and authorized Sallie Mae to issue nonvoting common stock.

Congress also broadened the services Sallie Mae could offer, giving the company much greater flexibility in making warehousing advances by loosening the restrictions on what Sallie Mae could accept as collateral for them and by liberalizing the requirement that warehousing advances go directly back into student loans. Sallie Mae was also permitted to consolidate or refinance loans for highly indebted students; to make advances to state and other nonprofit agencies for their student loan operations; and to make loans directly to students in areas of the country where there was insufficient credit available.

In 1981, under the new Reagan administration, Congress reinstated a needs test for borrowers with a family income above $30,000. Congress also pushed Sallie Mae to lessen its reliance on federal funds more quickly. Accordingly, expiration of Sallie Mae's authority to issue federally-guaranteed obligations was moved up to 1982, and in mid-1981 Sallie Mae made its first public offering, of short-term discount notes.

Congress also continued to broaden Sallie Mae's activities, authorizing the company to deal with educational loans not insured by the GSLP and to buy and sell the obligations of state and nonprofit educational-loan agencies.

During the remainder of the 1980s, Sallie Mae experimented with ways of raising funds at as low a cost as possible. Since all of its assets—the student loans it had bought and the warehousing advances it had made—earned a floating rate of interest tied to the 90-day treasury bill rate, Sallie Mae preferred to borrow money at a floating rate tied to the same indicator. The company was very successful at doing this. With both assets and liabilities tied to the treasury bill rate, Sallie Mae was insensitive to changes in the interest rate; as a quasi-governmental agency whose assets (those same student loans) were guaranteed by the federal government, Sallie Mae was able to raise money easily, and fairly cheaply.

As the cost of education continued to outdistance inflation, student loans continued to be in heavy demand. Thus, Sallie Mae's assets grew at a breakneck pace in the 1980s: from $1.6 billion in 1979 to $28.63 billion in 1988, an increase of nearly 1,700 percent. And to Sallie Mae, which made its money on the fixed spread between its floating-rate assets and floating-rate liabilities, increased assets meant increased profits.

In April 1983, Sallie Mae made its first offering of preferred stock, and in September of that year it made its initial offering of nonvoting common stock, thus becoming a publicly-owned company.

In 1986, when Congress reauthorized the Higher Education Act of 1965, it again broadened Sallie Mae's range of operations. It also required a needs test for all loan applicants—even those with family incomes of less than $30,000—and lowered the allowance to lenders to 3.25 percent above the treasury bill rate. Sallie Mae was given the latitude to deal loans to educational institutions for physical improvements. Congress also authorized the establishment of the College Construction Loan Insurance Association (Connie Lee) to provide insurance for loans to academic institutions for facilities. Sallie Mae helped set up Connie Lee, which opened for business in 1988.

Changes in the 1990s

By the early 1990s, Sallie Mae was known as one of the most innovative borrowers around. It experimented with exotic deals such as New Zealand-dollar-denominated notes, and securities tied to the dollar-yen exchange rate. It was a consistent money-maker, and its stock flew high on Wall Street. Institutions owned three-quarters of its shares by 1991. Sallie Mae was perceived as a champion money-maker because it was the Department of Education—not Sallie Mae—that would be responsible for defaulted loans. The only way Sallie Mae could falter was if it bought loans that did not comply with federal regulations.

To avert this, the company kept very close tabs on the banks it bought loans from. It also began servicing more of its own loans. In 1990 it serviced about 40 percent of its loans in-house, and by the next year this figure had grown to almost 50 percent. This kept operational costs down, while assets continued to rise. By 1991 Sallie Mae owned a third of the $49 billion market in outstanding guaranteed student loans. And the market was ex-

pected to expand further, as tuition costs rose and more lower-income students became eligible for loans.

In spite of Sallie Mae's evident health and vitality, various government figures began to posit ways of changing the company. In April 1991 the Congressional Budget Office recommended closer government scrutiny of Sallie Mae and her government-sponsored siblings Fannie Mae (Federal National Mortgage Association) and Freddie Mac (Federal Home Loan Mortgage Corporation). Though all three of these companies were not only financially sound but actually quite profitable, the costly federal bail-out of the Savings and Loan Association made the government more cautious about entities it guaranteed. President George Bush suggested that the government might make loans directly to students, as a cost-saving measure. Sallie Mae's chief executive, Lawrence Hough, had been given a salary package worth over $2 million, and this apparently seemed wasteful to the Bush administration. However, quick criticism from many quarters brought an end to Bush's plan, and Sallie Mae seemed destined to go along its way as merrily as ever.

But Sallie Mae's bubble burst soon after. In 1993, its stock was selling at a high of $74.50, but then began a slide, landing at almost half that price two years later. Profits fell as well, as President Bill Clinton revived Bush's idea to have the government lend directly to students. The government program started up in 1994, landing about 5 percent of student loans. By the 1995–96 school year, however, the government handled about 40 percent. Clinton also asked Sallie Mae to pay new fees on loans it handled, eroding profits. The company was divided on how to proceed, precipitating a shareholder revolt.

Sallie Mae's chief operating officer, Albert Lord, resigned from his post in January 1994 over differences with CEO Hough. But in 1995 Lord organized a slate of dissidents to run for seats on Sallie Mae's board. Though both sides favored the inevitable privatization of the company, Lord's faction wanted to move faster and more aggressively, and to expand into new business areas. Hough and Lord had once been friends, but the proxy fight became bitter. Finally Hough announced that he would resign his post if his side won the board elections, hoping to appease shareholders who were critical of him personally. But Lord's side won the crucial board seats, and his Committee to Restore Value at Sallie Mae had their way.

Lord and his new management quickly implemented a reorganization plan. They set up a Delaware-chartered holding company—SLM Holding Corp.—a publicly-traded company that held Student Loan Marketing Association. Lord also moved to cut costs, both in loan acquisition and in overhead. His plan was to cut the cost of buying student loans by 50 percent over the next five years. Lord's new management also raised cash by "securitizing" a large portion of its loans. This means loans were sold to trusts, which then issued securities to back the loans.

The new corporation wanted to be able to invest in new products and services, and get out from under the instability caused by government oversight. For example, the Higher Education Act of July 1998 asked for changes in the way student loan rates were set, but it was not clear how the changes would be implemented and what the effect on Sallie Mae would be. The uncertainty of this legislation, and other legislation that might follow, made it difficult for Sallie Mae to predict its finances. Sallie Mae's new management emphasized working with congress and the president to find ways to hold costs down for students, without making student loans completely unprofitable for financial institutions. The new company hoped to have more flexibility to respond to changes, and to pursue new business as opportunities presented themselves.

Principal Subsidiaries

Student Loan Marketing Association; Sallie Mae, Inc.; Sallie Mae Servicing Corporation.

Further Reading

Barrett, Amy, "The Bees in Sallie Mae's Bonnet," *Business Week,* May 8, 1995, p. 86.
Beckett, Paul, and Scott Ritter, "Dissidents Win Sallie Mae Board Vote," *Wall Street Journal,* August 11, 1997, pp. A3–A4.
de Senerpont Domis, Olaf, "Sallie Mae and Dissidents Agree on a Divided Ballot," *American Banker,* May 2, 1997, p. 2.
Eaton, Leslie, "Sallie Mae Does It Again," *Barron's,* February 26, 1990, p. 13.
Felsenthal, Edward, "Sallie Mae Appeal on Fees Is Rejected by Supreme Court," *Wall Street Journal,* October 15, 1997, p. B8.
Foust, Dean, "Off with Sallie Mae's Head?" *Business Week,* August 4, 1997, p. 4.
——, "Student Loans Ain't Broke. Don't Fix 'em," *Business Week,* April 5, 1993, p. 74.
Kleege, Stephen, "Sallie Mae Withdraws Suit Disputing Election," *American Banker,* June 29, 1995, p. 24.
Kraus, James R., "Chase, Sallie Mae Pooling their Efforts to Market and Service Student Loans," *American Banker,* September 10, 1996, p. 5.
McTague, Jim, "Sallie Mae and the Administration Near a Showdown over Her Role If Banks Boycott Student Loan Program," *Barron's,* March 23, 1998, p. 28.
Yang, Catherine, "Fannie, Freddie, and Sallie: Regulate with Care," *Business Week,* May 13, 1991, p. 89.
Zipser, Andy, "Waltzing with Sallie Mae," *Barron's,* July 29, 1991, pp. 32–33.

—updated by A. Woodward

SMITHS INDUSTRIES
Aerospace · Medical Systems · Industrial

Smiths Industries PLC

765 Finchley Road
Childs Hill
London NW11 8DS
England
011 44 181 458 3232
Fax: 011 44 181 458 4380
Web site: http://www.smiths-industries.com

Public Company
Incorporated: 1914 as S. Smith & Sons (Motor
    Accessories) Ltd.
Employees: 14,000
Sales: £1.076 billion (1997)
Stock Exchanges: London
Ticker Symbol: SMIN
SICs: 3728 Aircraft Parts & Equipment; 3643 Current-
    carrying Wiring Devices; 3841 Surgical & Medical
    Instruments; 3842 Surgical Appliances & Supplies;
    3822 Environmental Controls; 3670 Electronic
    Components & Accessories; 3823 Industrial
    Measuring Instruments

Smiths Industries PLC is a diversified multinational corpora-tion with core businesses in aerospace electronics; medical instruments, appliances, and supplies; and specialized industrial products. The company has garnered a reputation for its design and production of high-technology avionic systems, especially for the commercial aircraft market, and for military and marine fighting aircraft and vehicles. Smiths Industries also provides an extensive array of single use disposable medical products for critical care applications, and a host of other medical equipment and supplies. With its corporate headquarters located on the north side of London, the company has gradually expanded its manufacturing and sales offices around the world and presently operates facilities and offices in 51 countries.

Early History

The roots of Smiths Industries PLC date back to 1851, when Samuel Smith established his own clock and watch business in London, not far from the landmark Elephant & Castle Pub. Because of his attention to detail and his friendly manner, gen-tlemen throughout London flocked to Smith's small shop, and by 1871 the proprietor had opened his second location. Smith's death in 1875 did not interrupt the prosperity of his enterprise, which was taken over by his son, Samuel Smith, Jr. In fact, the company was growing so rapidly that Samuel Smith, Jr. decided not only to move to a larger space in London, but to open three new shops in different parts of the city.

By the turn of the century, the Smith family clock and watch business had become one of the notably successful enterprises in the imperial city of London. It was not surprising then when the company turned its attention to the needs of the nascent automobile industry. Employing the skills of watchmaking from his father, Allan Gordon Smith diversified into the design and manufacture of automobile instruments and was one of the driving forces behind the creation of the odometer. In just a few short years Smith had garnered a reputation as one of the most innovative designers of instrumentation for the automobile in-dustry. As a result, at the request of King Edward VII, Smith invented the speedometer and had the first one inserted in the monarch's Mercedes. By 1908 the family business was selling more than 100 speedometers each week.

With the company taking advantage of the increasing popu-larity of the automobile, Smith decided to incorporate the family enterprise as S. Smith & Sons (Motor Accessories) Ltd. in July of 1914. Business was booming, and the firm employed more than 300 people. More than 50,000 Smith speedometers were being used in cars of various design and manufacture throughout the United Kingdom, while more and more orders were received at company headquarters every day. Yet it was the advent of World War I that not only increased the firm's productivity, but made it a reputation throughout Europe.

When the conflict began in August of 1914, the British government immediately contracted Smith & Sons to design and manufacture a wide range of products for the war effort, including such items as wristwatches, kite balloon wind indica-tors, and tachymeters. As the war progressed and the British Isles were drained of manpower and material goods, the govern-ment called upon Smith & Sons to expand its product line to include wire rope, signal lamps, spark plugs for airplane engines, and shell fuses. In 1917 the company originated the standard Clift airspeed indicator, which soon became the most widely used airspeed indicator within the aviation industry.

The 1920s, 1930s, and War Years

When World War I ended in 1919, Smith & Sons continued the diversification program that it started during the conflict. Soon the company was selling ebonite batteries and spark plugs and manufacturing jacks for automobiles. Throughout the decade of the 1920s Smith & Sons continued its emphasis on manufacturing automotive accessories, such as speedometers. Allan Gordon Smith was well aware of the burgeoning demands of the aviation industry, however, and this led him to form Smiths Aircraft Instruments Division during the late 1920s. At approximately the same time, Smith established the All British Escarpment Company LTD to manufacture platform lever escarpments for clocks.

Although the company maintained its strong presence in the automotive accessories market, including the manufacture of ignitions, starters, and automotive lights, it was the Aircraft Instruments Division that came up with innovative designs throughout the decade of the 1930s. In 1932 the company produced the first electrical aviation fuel gauge, and not long afterwards the Aircraft Instruments Division established and opened its own aircraft manufacturing factory. Within this facility during the middle and late 1930s company engineers were at the forefront of experimenting with and developing oil pressure gauges for aircraft and electrical thermometers. By 1936 the company's system of remote indication has been installed on almost all aircraft built in Britain and soon would become the standard within the industry.

As the clouds of war once again began to hover over the European continent and the aggressive expansionist policy and theories of racial superiority promulgated by the Nazi Regime in Germany started to concern many governments around the world, in 1937 Allan Gordon Smith was invited to the United States to discuss developments in the aviation industry. Along with seven of his best engineers, Smith conducted a comprehensive analysis of U.S. aviation technology and manufacturing methods and also discussed how Britain and the United States could best share this technology in the event of another world war. Gathering as much information from the United States as he could, upon returning to London Smith and his management team decided to decentralize the company's operations in anticipation of Nazi aircraft raids on Britain. Management's first move was to relocate many of the company's manufacturing facilities to rural areas outside London.

When World War II started on September 1, 1939, as the Nazi war machine invaded Poland, S. Smith & Sons (Motor Accessories) Ltd. was well prepared for the conflict. Almost immediately, the company's manufacturing facilities were retooled to produce war material and supplies, including large quantities of aircraft spark plugs, gauges, clocks, watches, speedometers, and a wide variety of aviation instruments. In May of 1940, with the fall of France to the Nazi Regime imminent, the British government helped the company to open a new manufacturing facility for highly sophisticated aviation clocks in Cheltenham, England.

With high-volume production methods learned from the United States a short time earlier, Smith & Sons significantly contributed to the Royal Air Force's ability to prevent Nazi Germany from invading the British Isles. Pilots from Britain's famous Spitfire fighter aircraft relied heavily on the aviation instrumentation and accessories provided by Smith & Sons. As the tide of war turned in favor of Britain and its Allies, especially after the invasion of Nazi-occupied Europe on June 6, 1944, the company began to focus its attentions on the opportunities that would present themselves in the postwar period. Approving a comprehensive strategic plan near the end of 1944, management reorganized the entire firm, first by changing the name to S. Smith & Sons, Ltd., and then by dividing its commercial operations into four subsidiaries: Smiths Motor Accessories, Ltd., Smiths Aircraft Instruments Ltd., Smiths English Clocks, Ltd., and Smiths Industrial Instruments, Ltd. In addition, the company formed a joint venture to manufacture car radios, as well as another joint venture, the Anglo-Celtic Watch Company.

The Postwar Era

The late 1940s and the entire decade of the 1950s were years of rapid expansion and growth for the company. In 1947 management at the firm implemented a strategic plan that led to the establishment of the company's first subsidiaries outside the United Kingdom. A factory in Witney, Oxfordshire was purchased in 1949 to enhance the company's automotive product line, while at the same time management decided to diversify product lines in its other operating divisions. One of the most important acquisitions during this time involved the purchase of Portland Plastics and its subsidiary, Surgical Plastics, two companies well positioned for growth in the burgeoning medical equipment business. As the company grew, it did not ignore the welfare of its workers. Sympathetic to the ideals and vision of the postwar socialist-leaning governments of Britain, the company joined with housing authorities near Smith & Sons factories to build a total of 192 employee dwellings.

By the early 1960s Smith & Sons had grown so large that management initiated a comprehensive reorganization strategy, including the decentralization of its operations, greater diversification of its product lines, and a broader delegation of authority. Although the primary source of revenue continued to be the automotive accessories division, nonetheless, the company was making a strong move to capture more of the aviation instruments market. This aggressiveness paid off handsomely in 1961 when the company won a large contract to make aviation instruments for the Boeing Company, one of the largest aircraft manufacturers in the United States. During the middle of the decade the company expanded its capacity to produce automotive spark plugs through the acquisition of Lodge Plus, Ltd. and established a technical service center at Heathrow Airport, one of the first of its kind. The one engineering feat that brought the company international recognition was the design of an innovative autopilot equipment system that enabled a civil airliner to land in foggy weather with no more than 50 feet of visibility. From this time forward, the company's reputation in the civil aircraft instrumentation market was assured. To reflect the growing diversity of its product line, management changed the company name from Smith & Sons to Smiths Industries PLC.

Decline in the 1970s and Resurgence in the 1980s

Yet trouble was just over the horizon. During the late 1960s the company's clock business suffered from the glut of Eastern

European imports and low-cost components manufactured in Asia. Smiths Industries attempted to counterbalance these trends with a network of its own low-cost suppliers from foreign countries, but sales for the firm's clock business continued to decline throughout the 1970s. In 1979 management decided finally to discontinue the firm's clock business and permanently closed all related manufacturing facilities. Simultaneously, the automotive industry across Britain entered into a lengthy period of sluggish sales, and the firm's motor accessories production output dropped dramatically.

Traditionally, Smiths Industries has revealed the talent and resourcefulness of its management at times when the company has been confronted with major problems. Acting quickly and decisively, management implemented a new strategic policy that involved divesting all of the less profitable operations, while expanding the more lucrative and promising businesses. During the early 1980s the company sold its automotive instrumentation business and ceased operations in the automotive radio business. These two divestitures were followed by an announcement that Smiths Industries no longer would manufacture or supply original equipment to the automotive industry in Europe.

Building upon the foundation already established in the 1950s and 1960s, management focused on developing the company's medical and aerospace businesses. Portex, formed from the firm's Portland Plastics and Surgical Plastics subsidiaries, quickly grew into the most lucrative operation within the company. An ever-increasing line of new products and an aggressive acquisitions strategy catapulted Portex into a leadership position within the medical supplies market. The company's newly created Smiths Industries Aerospace and Defense Systems division also grew rapidly. Adhering to a similar aggressive acquisitions policy in the aerospace business, the company purchased Lear Siegler Holdings Corporation in 1987 and immediately skyrocketed to a leadership role within the American aerospace industry. By the end of the 1980s Smiths Industries had reorganized its operations into three divisions, including Aerospace and Defense, Medical Systems, and Industrial. In 1988 the company reported a rise in pre-tax profits of nearly 50 percent.

The 1990s and Beyond

During the early 1990s Smiths Industries not only consolidated its share in the aerospace, medical systems, and industrial components markets, but continued an aggressive and unabated campaign to grow through strategic acquisitions, research and development, and new manufacturing technologies. The company placed particular emphasis on increasing its presence in the United Kingdom, Germany, Japan, and the United States. Two of the major achievements by the company at this time involved the acquisition of Japan Medico, a large medical equipment manufacturer that provided Smiths Industries with access to a burgeoning Asian market, and a contract with

Boeing to supply electrical load management systems for the newly designed Boeing 777 commercial jumbo-jet.

In the mid-1990s the company's Aerospace business had become known as one of the most innovative manufacturers within the industry. The company's Flight Management System, autothrottles, standby instruments, and fully integrated sattelite-based navigation system were purchased by commercial airlines around the world. Smiths Industries' Medical Systems, manufacturing a wide array of products such as disposable colostomy pouches, speaking aids for tracheostomy patients, and single use devices for administering anaesthesia, also became known for its innovative approach to health care products. And the Industrial components business, focusing on international ducting and hosing manufacturing, and airmoving products for consumer, industrial, and commercial applications, such as heating elements for clothes dryers, had developed into one of the most lucrative operations in the company's recent history, with an annual increase in sales of more than 20 percent from 1994 to 1997.

Smiths Industries PLC is not only well positioned for future growth, but has one of the best management teams in the corporate sector. When these two facts are added to the creativity and innovation of the company's engineers, the success of Smiths Industries seems assured for many years to come.

Principal Subsidiaries

Smiths Industries Aerospace & Defense Systems Ltd.; SIMS Portex Ltd.; Eschmann Bros. & Walsh Ltd.; Smiths Industries Industrial Group Ltd.; Air Movement (Holdings) Ltd.; Lighthome Ltd.; SI Properties Ltd.; Smiths Industries, Inc.; Smiths Industries Aerospace & Defense Systems, Inc.; SIMS Portex, Inc.; SIMS Deltec, Inc.; SIMS Level 1, Inc.; Tutco, Inc.; Flexible Technologies, Inc.; Japan Medico Co., Ltd.

Further Reading

Deveney, Paul J., "Smiths Industries PLC," *Wall Street Journal,* October 16, 1997, p. A15(E).

Endres, Gunter, "Toward The 'Intelligent' Aircraft," *Interavia Aerospace Review,* April 1991, p. 57.

"Hi-Tech Engine Monitoring Systems," *Interavia Business & Technology,* June 1994, p. 51.

Nordwall, Bruce D., "Glareshield Displays, Voice Control To Aid Pilots," *Aviation Week & Space Technology,* July 17, 1995, p. 59.

——, "New FMS To Offer 737 Fuel Savings," *Aviation Week & Space Technology,* March 27, 1995, p. 48.

——, "Smiths Industries Will Supply," *Aviation Week & Space Technology,* August 1, 1994, p. 64.

Proctor, Paul, "Sonic Fuel Measuring," *Aviation Week & Space Technology,* August 8, 1994, p. 13.

The History of Smiths Industries Plc., London: Smiths Industries, Plc., 1994.

Young, Jonathan, "Young Gun To Industry Bigshot," *Management Today,* June 1996, p. 96.

—Thomas Derdak

SOS Staffing Services

1415 South Main Street
Salt Lake City, Utah 84115
U.S.A.
(801) 484-4400
Fax: (801) 486-3131
Web site: http://www.sosstaffing.com

Public Company
Incorporated: 1973
Employees: 800
Sales: $209.3 million (1997)
Stock Exchanges: NASDAQ
Ticker Symbol: SOSS
SICs: 7363 Help Supply Services

SOS Staffing Services is one of the nation's largest firms providing temporary employees for clerical, light industrial, technical, and information technology positions. It also provides its customers with consulting services and outsourcing for payroll and drug testing. Most of its more than 140 offices are located in the western United States, although recently it has expanded into other areas. Its rapid growth in the 1990s reflects internal expansion, numerous acquisitions in several new markets, and the trend to rely on more part-time and temporary workers in both business and government.

The Early Years of SOS

SOS followed in the footsteps of national temporary staffing companies which had been started in the 1940s. Kelly Services was started in 1947 and the next year Manpower was created to help alleviate the post-World War II labor shortage. By the 1970s the labor market was shifting from industrial workers to clerical and other office workers. Advanced technology, including computers and solid-state electronics, was replacing many of America's blue-collar workers.

Meanwhile, Richard D. Reinhold, SOS' future founder, planned even in high school to run his own business. After

graduating in 1960 from the University of Kansas with a B.S. in marketing, Reinhold worked for International Telephone and Telegraph and the Bank of America. During that time, he learned about the exciting possibilities in the new field of temporary staffing. He began working for Employer's Overload, which in the 1960s was the nation's third largest temp agency with about 100 offices. Then he helped Century Finance start a new temporary staffing company called Cencor. Reinhold traveled extensively supervising the Cencor offices, an experience which motivated him to start his own business so he could spend more time with his wife Sunny and his young family. He then served as vice-president of Greyhound Temporary Services from 1971 to 1973, in order to gain experience. Soon he decided he had enough experience to start his own firm, and he began forming what would become SOS Staffing Services.

Using market research, Reinhold concluded that seven cities were prime targets for a new temporary labor firm. San Jose, California had the most potential, while Salt Lake City, Utah was ranked seventh. However, his savings of just $12,000 was inadequate to start a firm in the larger market of San Jose, so he narrowed it down to three smaller cities: Grand Rapids, Michigan; Salt Lake City; and Indianapolis, Indiana. In the fall of 1972, he received a call from Russ Christen—a former Cencor manager—who asked Reinhold if any temp firms in Salt Lake City needed a manager. Surprised by the timing of this call, Reinhold decided to make Salt Lake City his new firm's headquarters, and hire Christen to help get the project onto its feet.

On January 15, 1973 Reinhold started his own company, naming it SOS Staffing Services, with the help of Russ Christen. Reinhold was the founding chairman, president, and CEO. Reinhold and Christen both sold accounts in Salt Lake City and did the office paperwork by hand. Soon they hired Richard Tripp, a Brigham Young University graduate, to run their small office.

Early Challenges in the 1970s

The first year of business proved successful, with SOS providing just under 2,000 hours of temporary help per week. The firm's original industrial office was leased space at 152 East

700 South; later in 1973, SOS opened its clerical office in a nearby building. The firm enjoyed an 80 percent increase in 1974, with some weeks peaking at over 4,000 hours. However, 1975 was so slow that Reinhold had to use all his reserves just to survive. At one point, he took a two-week vacation and thought about other career options.

In 1976, SOS recovered enough to keep going, but the company suffered from a severe cash flow problem and struggled to pay its temporary employees. In spite of a 20 percent increase in rates, SOS sales in 1977 increased 40 percent; unfortunately, it still looked as though SOS might have to close its doors. Russ Christen saved the day by loaning SOS $25,000 from mortgaging his home. Almost 20 years later, Richard Reinhold wrote that without that loan, "We would just be another company which failed, because it was undercapitalized and the founders were probably *too* good in sales."

Growth in the 1980s

By about 1980, SOS was standing on more solid ground and was prepared for a modest expansion. It finally had enough cash flow so Richard Reinhold and his officers did not have to anxiously wait every day for the mailman to bring another check. With the support of a bank, SOS opened new Utah offices in Ogden, Murray, and Orem. Also, the company finally owned its own building at 26 East 800 South in Salt Lake City.

SOS enjoyed the fact that the temporary staffing industry grew rapidly in the 1980s. The annual temporary workers' payroll jumped from $3.5 billion in 1981 to $14 billion in 1991, according to the National Association of Temporary Services.

This boom was reflected in SOS' growing business in the 1980s. In 1983, for example, the firm's sales increased 83 percent. Reinhold later wrote: "Totally unprepared for this increase, we had to have a computer conversion in August and September—at our busiest time of the year. All of us . . . worked at least 14 hours per day. We were not proud of the service we provided, as every day we had to go to 'the bottom of the barrel' to find people to work . . . As for others, and myself, it took many weeks to recover mentally and physically after that ordeal."

Russ Christen retired in the late 1980s. Richard Reinhold served as the president of the National Association of Temporary and Staffing Services (NATSS) in 1989 and 1990. When he returned to SOS, he set some major goals for the new decade.

1990s Acquisitions and Expansion

SOS started the decade with just eight offices. It provided clerical and light industrial workers, which were typical of the temps of that time. But the 1990s would see SOS acquire many firms and diversify to work with new kinds of workers, especially those skilled with computers, to meet the demands of a changing American economy.

In 1995 SOS acquired the following firms: Add-a-Temp, Inc. of Las Vegas; Active Personnel Services, Inc. of Phoenix, Arizona; Patient Accounting Management Services of Phoenix, Arizona; and Geomine Personnel, Inc. of Sparks, Nevada. To finance this growth, SOS became a public firm in 1995. It completed its initial public offering in July 1995.

Because there were over 3,500 temporary agencies in 1995, and 10,000 offices in the USA, SOS took the opportunity to acquire the following smaller firms in 1996: Snake River T.E.M.P.S., Inc. of Burley, Idaho; A.C.E. Personnel Services of Yuma, Arizona; VIP Employment Services Limited, LLC of Lakewood, Colorado; Allyn Colorado Enterprises, Inc. of Aspen, Colorado; The Performance Group of Denver, Colorado—the first significant SOS acquisition in the fast-growing information technology field; Impact Staffing, a division of Pacific Design Engineering, Inc. of Portland, Oregon and San Diego, California; Key Personnel Service of Amarillo, Texas; a USA Temps of Prescott, Arizona; Executive Personnel Associates, Inc. of Fort Collins, Colorado; Steamboat Temps, Inc. of Steamboat Springs, Colorado; R.H.W., Inc.—doing business as The Temporary Connection and The Employment Connection out of Billings, Montana; Wolfe & Associates, Inc. of Albuquerque, New Mexico; Workstyle 2000, Inc. of Dallas, Texas; and Human Resources, Inc. of St. George, Utah.

To finance this expansion program, in December 1996 SOS offered 2.2 million shares of its common stock for sale at $9.75 per share. The firm itself offered 2 million of those shares, while the rest were offered by a shareholding charitable foundation founded by Richard Reinhold and a church. This offering was underwritten by Unterberg Harris, PaineWebber, and George K. Baum & Company.

Following this successful offering, Chairman/CEO Richard Reinhold said he was "very pleased with our performance for 1996." SOS revenues reached $136.2 million, up 56 percent from $87.5 million in 1995. The firm's net income increased 51 percent from $2.677 million in 1995 to $4.029 million in 1996. SOS added 39 offices in 1996, including those from acquisitions, to reach a total of 87 offices.

SOS continued its expansion in 1997 by purchasing 14 more firms: Computer Group, Inc. of Bellevue, Washington; The Agency of Albuquerque, New Mexico; The Solution Team, Inc. of Oklahoma City, Oklahoma; Toma Employment Service of Las Vegas, Nevada; Bedford Consultants, Inc. of San Francisco, California; Telecom Project Assistance, Inc. of Mountain View, California; Execusoft, Inc. of Orange, California; VIP Plus, Ltd. of Lubbock, Texas (also known as VIP Employment and VIP Workforce); JesCo Technical Services, Inc. of Bellevue, Washington; TempWorks, Inc. of Denver, Colorado; Century Personnel, Inc. of Overland Park, Kansas; TSI of Utah, Inc. of Salt Lake City; Von Stroheim-Seay, Inc.—doing business as Staffing Partners Employment Solutions in Honolulu, Hawaii; and Prestige Consulting Corporation of Salt Lake City, Utah.

The Late-1990s and Beyond

On October 16, 1997 SOS offered 4 million additional shares of its common stock at $16.75 per share. In November the company announced the addition of two new members to its Board of Directors: Samuel C. Frietag, senior managing director for George K. Baum Merchant Bank, and Annette Strauss, the former mayor of Dallas, Texas who was an officer and/or director of several other organizations. Also in November 1997,

SOS received ISO-9002 registration as part of its efforts to maintain high standards.

More than once, *Forbes* included SOS Staffing Services in its list of the nation's 200 best small companies in the late-1990s, ranking it number 88 in 1996 and number 139 in 1997. SOS enjoyed another great year in 1997, with revenues increasing to $209.3 million from $136.2 million in 1996. And its net income rose from $4 million in 1996 to $7.5 million in 1997. In 1997, SOS supplied over 80,000 temporary workers to about 8,000 businesses, government agencies, and service organizations.

With no total debt in 1997, and a $30 million line of credit available, in 1998 the company was able to continue its acquisitions as follows: Hutton, Graber & Associates of Venice, California; Purchases Mortgage Staffing, Inc.; Computer Professional Resources, Inc. of Prairie Village, Kansas; the temporary and professional employment divisions of TOPS Staffing Services, Inc. of San Diego, California; the information technology staffing division of Aquas, Inc. of Sunnyvale, California; Abacab Software, Inc. of Cupertino, California; and Neosoft Inc. of Cambridge, Massachusetts.

On March 2, 1998 SOS directors elected JoAnn W. Wagner as the new chair of the Board of Directors, to succeed Richard D. Reinhold, the founding chair who resigned to serve his church for two years. Between November 1987 and January 1991, Wagner had served as the president and director of INTERIM Services, Inc., a temporary staffing company. After Interim was acquired by H & R Block in 1991, she worked as Interim's vice-president of market development until January 1994. She then worked as a consultant for Interim until July 1995. At that time, she joined SOS as a director and consultant and in 1997 became the vice-chair and executive vice-president of corporate development.

Also on March 2, 1998, Peter R. Sollenne was chosen to replace the departing Richard Reinhold on the board of directors. He had joined SOS in August 1997 as its president and chief operating officer. Previously he held management positions with financial and insurance firms and had worked in the staffing industry since 1995, when he became president of San Francisco's Abar Staffing.

In 1998, Howard W. Scott, Jr. remained as a SOS director and its chief executive officer. A 1957 graduate of Northwestern University, Scott was a 30-year veteran of the staffing industry, including terms as president of CDI Temporary Services from 1978 to 1991 and president of Dunhill Personnel System from 1991 to 1994. In February 1994, he became SOS' vice-president, and in April 1995 was appointed president and chief operating officer. Beginning in August 1997, he served as the firm's chief executive officer.

Under the leadership of these various officers and directors, SOS made some major changes near the end of the decade. One development was that the company began supplying its clients with more information technology (IT) personnel, including men and women skilled in IT management and planning for desktop systems, computer networking, and a variety of voice, data, and video applications. The SOS acquisitions of Wolfe & Associates, Hutton, Graber & Associates, and Telecom Project

Assistance provided much of the leadership needed in the fast changing field. Those three acquired firms served an impressive list of clients in diverse fields, ranging from health care and biotechnology to financial services and higher education. Representative clients included UCLA, Wells Fargo Bank, and Kaiser Permanente.

According to Gary Crook, SOS chief financial officer, the company usually paid only 25 percent of a traditional staffing firm's annual revenues to acquire it. To buy a specialty or IT staffing firm, SOS paid an amount equal to that firm's annual revenues. The advantage of IT acquisitions was that they enjoyed operating margins of 15 percent or more, while traditional firms had operating margins ranging from 5 to 10 percent.

Curtis L. Wolfe of Wolfe & Associates served as president of the SOS Information Technology Division. ''The rapid evolution of information technologies has forced businesses to 'get smart' fast or risk competing at a disadvantage,'' said Wolfe. ''That's where SOS comes in.'' SOS' IT revenue as a percentage of the firm's total revenues increased from just 5 percent in 1996 to about 22 percent at the end of 1997. In early 1998 the company added a more attractive benefits package to attract the best IT personnel, and it also was working to integrate its IT Division by setting up a computer system to scan in and retrieve resumes.

Although the Information Technology Division was rapidly expanding, at the end of 1997 the firm's Commercial Division remained its largest. It included AccountStaff temporaries, such as auditors, accountants, financial managers, tax analysts, and collections personnel. The Commercial Division's Skill Staff provided carpenters and related workers. Also included was PAMS (Patient Accounting Management Services), which supplied specialized clerical help—such as medical insurance coders and claims processors—for hospitals, clinics, and insurance companies.

SOS provided a variety of temporary technical specialists. For example, its 1996 acquisition of CGS Personnel allowed SOS to supply clients with geologists, hydrologists, and environmental engineers and technicians. CGS Personnel had been founded in 1985 as part of the growing trend for temporaries in all fields.

With increasing government regulations, some firms have looked to SOS for consultation on several matters, such as how to administer workers' compensation and unemployment programs. SOS has also helped companies start drug testing programs, design benefits programs, conduct job risk analysis, and make sure they comply with laws like the 1990 Americans with Disabilities Act. SOS' experience with its own temporary employees has given it the expertise to advise other firms on such complicated issues.

After first quarter 1998 results showed increased financial performance compared to first quarter 1997, two stock analysts gave SOS good marks. C. E. Unterberg, Towbin, which rated SOS stock as a ''good buy,'' said, ''SOS has demonstrated its ability to grow steadily, both organically and through acquisitions, and we expect this strong performance to continue . . . Its continuing growth, steadily improving margins, strong balance sheet and management team make SOS shares an outstanding investment.'' *The Red Chip Review* concluded that ''SOS continues to outpace our projections . . . We are maintaining our 'A' rating.''

The strong U.S. economy helped SOS expand; however, the long-term economic changes showed the potential to be even more beneficial. In reality, the pattern of workers maintaining one job with one company for many years had pretty much disappeared near the end of the 20th century. That tradition began around 1800 with mass production and centralization resulting in facilities like factories, hospitals, and libraries. With the post World War II development of computers—especially personal computers—and advanced telecommunications, the United States and other advanced nations entered the postindustrial era or Information Age, based on the principles of decentralization, empowerment of the individual, and especially rapid economic change. Frequent retraining became imperative as people frequently changed jobs. Thus, as SOS celebrated its

25th anniversary in 1998, the company was in a good position to reap the rewards of a restless and ever-changing workforce.

Further Reading

Fernberg, Patricia M., ''The Skills Shortage: Who Can Fill These Shoes? [Sacco interview]'' *Managing Office Technology,* June 1995, p. 16.
Grugal, Robin M., ''Westward Ho: SOS Staffing Finding Work Outside Core Mountain Region,'' *Investor's Business Daily,* March 5, 1997.
McClure, Laura, ''Working the Risk Shift,'' *The Progressive,* February 1994, p. 23.
Reinhold, Richard D., ''Continuing to Deliver the Shareholder Value,'' *Wall Street Corporate Reporter,* March 24–30, 1997.
''SOS Staffing Services,'' *The Red Chip Review,* March 17, 1998.
''SOS Staffing Services,'' *C. E. Unterberg, Towbin,* April 24, 1998.
Thomson, Allison, ''The Contingent Workforce,'' *Occupational Outlook Quarterly,* spring 1995, p. 45.

—David M. Walden

Spaghetti Warehouse, Inc.

402 West I-30
Garland, Texas 75043
U.S.A.
(972) 226-6000
Fax: (972) 203-9594
Web site: http://www.meatballs.com

Public Company
Incorporated: 1972
Employees: 750
Sales: $64.9 million (1997)
Stock Exchanges: New York
Ticker Symbol: SWH
SICs: 5812 Eating Places; 6794 Patent Owners and
Lessors; 6719 Offices—Holding Companies, Not
Elsewhere Classified

Spaghetti Warehouse, Inc., owns, operates, and franchises full-service, family-style Italian restaurants. Each restaurant is decorated nostalgically, with antiques, stained glass, Tiffany lamps, and mismatched tables and chairs. Many even feature a retired trolley car in their dining rooms. Based in Garland, Texas, the company typically establishes outlets in abandoned factories and warehouses in the downtowns of large metropolitan areas, using any tax assistance for developing an urban downtown property to pay for the facility's conversion to a restaurant. Spaghetti Warehouse menus feature basic pasta dishes, including 11 pasta sauces, 15-layer lasagna, manicotti, cannelloni, and chicken parmigiana. The restaurants are known for their reasonable pricing; a dinner bill—with tip and beverage—typically totals about $8.00. The company operates restaurants under the names of Spaghetti Warehouse and Spaghetti Warehouse Italian Grill in the United States and as the Old Spaghetti Warehouse in Canada.

Robert Hawk Founds a Restaurant Chain

The Spaghetti Warehouse was founded by Robert Hawk, a vice-president at Pier 1 Imports in the mid-1960s. In 1966, that company was purchased by Tandy Corporation, and after Pier 1's initial public offering in 1970, Hawk found that his stock shares made him a millionaire. On the advice of his mentor Charles Tandy, the 43-year-old Hawk established his first Spaghetti Warehouse restaurant in Dallas, Texas, in 1972. Six months later, Hawk resigned from Pier 1 to build a restaurant chain.

Hawk built his first restaurant in a former pillow factory in Dallas's warehouse district. The menu offered the family recipes of chef Victor Petta, Jr., who specialized in authentic Italian cooking. It was Petta who invented the restaurant's patented system of spaghetti preparation. Attracted by the novel atmosphere and the genuine Italian fares, customers began frequenting the restaurant regularly. "The concept brings them in," Hawk explained to *Forbes,* adding that "the food brings them back."

In 1985, Spaghetti Warehouse issued its initial public offering of stock, and expansion of the chain ensued. The restaurants' fare was relatively inexpensive to reproduce, and decor for each outlet came from such money-saving sources as the semi-annual Red Baron's Antiques auction in Atlanta, Georgia. Here Spaghetti Warehouse purchased its antique tables, old gasoline pumps, and other outlet focal points such as a large bronze elephant. "You'll find amazing things at auctions that you won't find anywhere else," James Aitkin, Spaghetti Warehouse's vice-president of development, shared with *Restaurant Hospitality.* "They can be very tiring, but a lot of fun, and if you use a little common sense, you can walk away a winner," he noted.

The company also sought sites with low acquisition costs. Warehouses and factories in inner cities represented inexpensive real estate, while development in historic areas brought tax breaks or tax credits for renovating the buildings. Spaghetti Warehouse then refurbished the buildings, using the savings from the low purchase costs of the properties. In 1989, for instance, Spaghetti Warehouse purchased a facility for $189,000 in an historic area in Oklahoma. That site generated $3.8 million dollars in sales in its first year. In all, the 1989 fiscal year ended with $28 million in sales and $1.9 million in profits.

By 1990, there were 15 Spaghetti Warehouse restaurants in operation, generating $43 million in revenues. The company ranked 140th on *Forbes* magazine's list of the 200 Best Small Companies, rising to number 135 the following year.

Company Perspectives:

Every day at Spaghetti Warehouse we roll hundreds of meatballs by hand. Sauces are prepared fresh from scratch following authentic Old World recipes. We use real domestic and imported cheeses in our recipes. Fresh vegetables and meats are purchased from local suppliers. Our lasagna is layer after layer of fresh meats, cheeses, noodles, spices, and sauce. We slice fresh eggplants, use whole boneless and skinless chicken breasts and veal for our parmigiana entrees. We serve authentic San Francisco sourdough bread hot out of the oven. . . . We are proud of our restaurants, our employees, and our food. Our goal is to provide the best overall dining value in the market.

Franchising in the 1990s

The chain negotiated its first franchise agreements for Spaghetti Warehouses in Kansas, Tennessee, and California in 1991. It established new outlets in Rochester, New York; Charlotte, North Carolina; and Tampa, Florida—in addition to planning for five new restaurants in San Antonio, Texas; Cleveland, Ohio; and Columbia, South Carolina. Spaghetti Warehouse based these expansion plans on cash raised in the company's second stock offering of May 1991. The company raised $20 million through this effort, using the capital to pay off debts and to refurbish the first Spaghetti Warehouse restaurant.

Hawk retired as president and chief executive officer of Spaghetti Warehouse in July 1991, although he remained active in the company as chairman. Louis Neeb then assumed control of the company. Neeb joined the Spaghetti Warehouse as a director in 1989. He came to the position with considerable restaurant experience, having developed the Bennigan's concept with Norman Brinker during the 1970s, as well as having held executive-level positions throughout the industry. Before coming to Spaghetti Warehouse, Neeb had served as president and chief executive officer of Del Taco, president and chief operating officer of Steak and Ale, and chairman and chief executive officer of Burger King.

Under Neeb's leadership, the restaurant chain continued to grow. Seven new outlets opened in 1992, and an additional location was purchased in Austin, Texas. Nine new units debuted in 1993, with another planned to open in Houston, Texas, the following year. Much of the expansion during this time occurred in suburban areas. Within two years, Spaghetti Warehouse grew to include 31 restaurants in 15 states, six franchised restaurants, and five Old Spaghetti Warehouse units in Canada.

Then Spaghetti Warehouse embarked upon a joint venture of international scope in September 1993. Under an agreement with two Australian companies—Competitive Foods PTY Ltd. and Tarlina PTY Ltd.—Spaghetti Warehouse gained the worldwide rights to operate and franchise Fasta Pasta outlets outside of South Australia. Headquartered in Adelaide, South Australia, Fasta Pasta operated nine limited-service Italian restaurants. The chain had been active for nine years prior to the agreement.

New Leadership in the Mid-1990s

Despite Spaghetti Warehouse's successful expansion plans, the company's stock decreased in value by half during 1993, as its new units were unable to compete effectively, and the older units experienced slow sales. Financially compromised units proved incapable of executing a turn-around.

Hawk resigned as chairman that year, recommending Neeb for the position. Hawk continued to serve as a consultant and as a member of the board of directors. Neeb remained as chairman for only 90 days before being dismissed by the board owing to "philosophical differences" over Neeb's strategies, which came as a surprise to the executive. According to Hawk in *Nation's Restaurant News,* Neeb "felt strongly that the company was headed in the right direction. However, from the board's viewpoint, the results just weren't there, and after two and one-half years, the board felt it was obliged to take some action." Hawk resumed the duties of president and chief executive officer until a replacement for Neeb was hired.

Hawk agreed that expansion was in order, although not at the level Neeb espoused. He chose to slow the expansion started by Neeb, finding the new suburban stores too costly to build. Hawk thus postponed their development until a method of reducing start-up costs was determined. The executive told the *Nation's Restaurant News* that "we are going ahead and closing on several sites for future stores, but we are just going to put those in inventory so that when we develop the new plan for the suburban store, we will be able to go forward immediately without having to wait six months to find a location."

Hawk's priorities at the time included improving sales at Spaghetti Warehouse's older units, especially those faced with potential patrons anxious about venturing to old factories in urban downtowns. He established task forces to reconsider the viability of these underperforming units and decreased prices at Spaghetti Warehouse restaurants, while expanding their wine lists and adding imported beers to their offerings. Finally, he eliminated some corporate staff and added personnel to key areas. For example, he hired Ray Petta, nephew of founding chef Victor Petta, in 1994 as the food and beverage director to reestablish the original recipes featured by Spaghetti Warehouse.

In July 1994, Phil Ratner, former president and chief executive officer of Acapulco Restaurants, Inc., joined Spaghetti Warehouse as president and chief executive officer. Ratner revealed to the *Nation's Restaurant News:* "I've been in Mexican food for 15 years, and obviously Spaghetti Warehouse is in the ethnic category. But it's all new for me. It gives me a chance to learn a whole new business, and that's exciting." Known as an effective leader with solid experience in the industry, Ratner expected to make a positive impact on Spaghetti Warehouse.

Repositioning the Company for the Future

Within a year of Ratner's appointment, the company began reporting losses. Rumors of a takeover circulated in 1995 as the company endeavored to command attention in the highly competitive casual dining market and among suburbs often unfriendly to the Spaghetti Warehouse concept. According to one analyst commenting in *Restaurant Business:* "Clearly, Spaghetti Warehouse needs to act, since their traditional concept sales have been stagnant for several years."

In September 1995, Spaghetti Warehouse issued a stock offering for growth opportunities. The company then launched Cappellini's, a family restaurant in Addison, Texas, in December. Located in a former Spaghetti Warehouse restaurant site, Cappellini's resembled an Italian vineyard and offered family-style meals in shared serving bowls and platters. The company also developed the Italian Grill concept for its restaurants. Much like Spaghetti Warehouse, the Italian Grill served an expanded menu with steaks and pork chops, as well as featuring updated decor.

These moves helped to reposition the company in the marketplace in 1996. Spaghetti Warehouse closed seven underperforming units in February 1996—in Hartford, Connecticut; Buffalo, New York; Rochester, New York; Providence, Rhode Island; Columbia, Georgia; Greenville, South Carolina; and Little Rock, Arkansas—leaving 30 restaurants in operation. As H. G. Carrington, Jr., senior vice-president of finance at Spaghetti Warehouse, told the *Nation's Restaurant News:* "We had to make the decision to close poorly performing stores to focus energy on the further development."

By the third quarter of 1996, Spaghetti Warehouse put in place a restructuring plan to strengthen its competitive position, improve cash flow, and increase profitability. Based on its continued success in Canada, Spaghetti Warehouse opened its seventh Old Spaghetti Factory there, while determining to re-evaluate its properties elsewhere. The company sold an alternative location in Austin, Texas, that it had purchased earlier and sold its Richmond, Virginia, operation to a franchise. Spaghetti Warehouse also wrote off its investment in the Australian chain Fasta Pasta at this time and closed Cappellini's in December 1996.

In 1997 Spaghetti Warehouse converted five of its traditional restaurants to Italian Grills, and the company instituted improvements at its other outlets. "We've added greater variety and brightened the restaurants," Robert Bodnar, treasurer and controller at Spaghetti Warehouse, reported in the *Nation's Restaurant News,* adding "We've improved portion sizes and products, and the response from consumers has been very favorable." The results of the changes were seen quickly, with financials for the quarter ending March 30, 1997 showing improvement.

In April 1998, the Dallas firm Conquest Partners attempted to acquire Spaghetti Warehouse for $47 million, plus debt refinancing and transaction costs—about $58 million total. This offer—just as another that followed it—was rejected by the company, as both offers undervalued Spaghetti Warehouse's stock in light of its now-favorable sales results from the Italian Grill restaurants. With the conversions, Spaghetti Warehouse sales increased 6.4 percent over the previous year in fiscal 1997, and the company planned to turn six to eight additional units

into Italian Grills in 1998. The first traditional Spaghetti Warehouse was converted during the first quarter. The Pittsburgh, Pennsylvania, location followed in May, with the transformation of 50 percent of all units completed by the end of the year.

Spaghetti Warehouse expected to convert the remainder of its restaurants to Italian Grills in 1999. The company also anticipated opening three or four Italian Grill units during the year. The restaurant chain expected modest expansion in the future, perhaps a 20 percent increase in earnings for 1999.

Principal Subsidiaries

Old Spaghetti Warehouse; Spaghetti Warehouse Italian Grills.

Further Reading

Autry, Ret, "Old Spaghetti Warehouse," *Fortune,* September 24, 1990, p. 126.

"Buy Side Activity," *CDA-Investment Insiders' Chronicle,* March 21, 1994, p. 1.

"Carrington Names CFO of Spaghetti Warehouse Inc.," *Nation's Restaurant News,* August 16, 1993, p. 2.

Coeyman, Marjorie, "Praise the Decor and Pass the Pasta Bowl," *Restaurant Business,* December 10, 1995, p. 21.

Keegan, Peter O., "Spaghetti Warehouse Ousts Chief Exec Neeb," *Nation's Restaurant News,* February 7, 1994, p. 3.

"Mergers and Acquisitions," *The Food Institute Report,* May 4, 1998.

Poole, Claire, "Crazy Like a Hawk," *Forbes,* November 11, 1991, p. 248.

Ruggless, Ron, "Acapulco Prexy Moves to Spaghetti Warehouse," *Nation's Restaurant News,* July 11, 1994, p. 3.

——, "Spaghetti Warehouse Cuts Prices, Costs," *Nation's Restaurant News,* February 14, 1994, p. 7.

——, "Spaghetti Warehouse Debuts New Formats, Closes Seven Units: Declining Sales Spark Changes," *Nation's Restaurant News,* February 12, 1996, p. 3.

——, "Spaghetti Warehouse Founder to Exit as Chairman of the Board; Supports Company Prexy Neeb as Successor," *Nation's Restaurant News,* July 5, 1993, p. 7.

——, "Spaghetti Warehouse on Road to Recovery after Unit Shutdowns," *Nation's Restaurant News,* May 19, 1997, p. 12.

Sanson, Michael, "Everything Old Is New Again," *Restaurant Hospitality,* December 1993, p. 114.

"Spaghetti Prepares for Saucier Deal," *Mergers & Acquisitions Report,* May 11, 1998.

"Spaghetti Warehouse in Pact to Acquire Nine-Unit Italian Concept," *Nation's Restaurant News,* September 20, 1993, p. 2.

"Spaghetti Warehouse Inc. of Garland, Texas, and El Chico Restaurants Inc. of Dallas," *Nation's Restaurant News,* March 27, 1995, p. 14.

"Spaghetti Warehouse Mulls Acquisition Bid," *Nation's Restaurant News,* May 4, 1998, p. 6.

—Charity Anne Dorgan

Specialty Equipment Companies, Inc.

<table>
<tr><td>

1245 Corporate Boulevard, Suite 401
Aurora, Illinois 60504
U.S.A.
(630) 585-5111
Fax: (630) 585-9450
Web site: http://www.specialty-equipment.com

Public Company
Incorporated: 1984
Employees: 2,565
Sales: $433.1 million (1998)
Stock Exchanges: NASDAQ
Ticker Symbol: SPEQ
SICs: 3556 Food Products Machinery; 3589 Service
Industry Machinery, Not Elsewhere Classified; 3999
Manufacturing Industries, Not Elsewhere Classified

</td></tr>
</table>

Specialty Equipment Companies, Inc., is a leading designer and manufacturer of cooking, refrigeration, and sanitation equipment for the foodservice industry, and the world's top manufacturer of softserve ice cream, shake, and frozen yogurt machines. Its products include espresso/cappuccino coffee machines, warm-air hand dryers, freezers and refrigerated cabinets, electric grills, and roll warmers. Its customers include quick service restaurant chains, convenience stores, supermarkets, specialty stores, soft drink bottlers, international breweries, and institutional foodservice operations. The company operates its business through Specialty Equipment Manufacturing Corporation, a wholly owned subsidiary, its four operating divisions (Beverage-Air, Taylor Company, Wells Manufacturing/Bloomfield Industries, and World Dryer) and Gamko Holding N.V., another wholly owned subsidiary. In fiscal year 1998, international sales accounted for over 32 percent of the company's $433.1 million in revenues. Malcom Glazer, owner of the Tampa Bay Buccaneers football team, owns about 42 percent of the company.

Early History, 1920s–50s

Specialty Equipment Companies can trace its history back to the 1920s, when Wells Manufacturing in South San Francisco

started producing its first waffle bakers. A few years later, in 1926, Taylor Freezer was founded in Rockton, Illinois, and that same year sold its first ice cream freezer to a restaurant. In the 1950s, Taylor began supplying shake machines to McDonald's. Beverage-Air first started making refrigerated cabinets in 1944. World Dryer was established in 1950 in Illinois, and introduced its first warm-air hand dryer in 1951. During that decade, Bloomfield Industries of Chicago introduced its coffee service products. Market Forge Industries, Inc., of Everett, Massachusetts, was founded as a metal forging company in 1896, and after World War I began making bicycle carriers, bicycle stands, baby hammocks, and florist racks. During World War II, the company shifted to making steam cooking systems and stainless steel hospital equipment.

The Beatrice Years, 1960s–83

Over the years, Beatrice Foods company acquired Taylor, Wells, Bloomfield, World Dryer, and Market Forge as part of its strategy of accelerated growth and diversification under president William Karnes. Beatrice bought small companies, expanded their markets, and, in keeping with its long-standing policy, left them alone to be managed by their own, local executives, whose intimate knowledge of their own conditions, Beatrice believed, produced the best business decisions. During the 1970s, for example, Market Forge emerged as one of the leading suppliers of steamers and ovens, and later introduced sterilizers for hospitals.

After spending twenty years building its profitability on acquisitions, in 1983, Beatrice Foods announced it was getting out of the industrial field and would be selling more than fifty of its three hundred companies in the next several years. That move was accelerated in 1984, when Beatrice assumed $3.5 billion in debt in its acquisition of Esmark Inc., and had to sell off assets to pay down some of that liability. The list included chemical, specialty apparel, agri-products, and cookie and bakery operations, as well as those companies that manufactured commercial cooking and food handling equipment.

Management Buyout I, 1984–87

In November 1984, Beatrice announced it was selling its five foodservice equipment businesses for $116 million to Gibbons Green van Amerongen, a New York investment banking firm

---

Company Perspectives:

Specialty Equipment has built its position with our customers by striving to provide Total Customer Satisfaction Through Integrated Engineering and World Wide Service, supported by an experienced hands-on management team.

---

that specialized in buyouts. The firm incorporated Specialty Equipment Companies before the end of the year, and in January 1985, acquired Wells, Taylor, Bloomfield, World Dryer, and Market Forge from Beatrice. Current management continued to operate the business, and Daniel Greenwood, president of Taylor Industries with a 30-year history at that company, was named chairman and chief executive officer. William Dotterweich, group president of Beatrice's commercial equipment division, was elected president.

In November 1986, Specialty purchased Beverage-Air from Gerlach Industries, Inc., in order to expand its offerings. The acquisition moved Specialty Equipment into beverage refrigeration, and the company planned to develop customized refrigeration products for the major chains. The new division's products, sold under the Beverage-Air® and Marketeer® brand names, included vertical and horizontal reach-in beverage coolers, freezers, refrigerators, pizza and food preparation units, school milk coolers, self-contained beer dispensing units, and delicatessen and floral display cases. For the fiscal year ending January 31, 1987, Specialty had sales of $225.1 million, with net income of $5.3 million.

In July 1987, the company went public, offering $44 million in new and existing shares. According to *Crain's Chicago Business,* Specialty Equipment was one of the best-performing initial public offerings in 1987, and revenues that year increased to $287.9 million, with net income jumping more than 17 percent to $14.2 million.

Management Buyout II, 1988–91

The company was doing so well that its two biggest shareholders, Prudential Insurance, with 36 percent, and a limited partnership controlled by Gibbons Green van Amerongen, with 29 percent, decided to get their money out. ''The environment is right to take a look at our options,'' president Dotterweich told *Crain's Chicago Business* in March 1988.

Later that year, company executives led by James Knoll formed SPE Acquisition, Inc., and bought Specialty for $500 million in a leveraged buyout. In completing the transition, SPE Acquisition Sub, a wholly owned subsidiary of SPE Acquisition, merged with Specialty. The buyout left the company with a debt of some $400 million, as the new owners invested just $8.3 million of their own money.

The company enjoyed strong annual growth initially, but by the end of the fiscal year in January 1990, Specialty had a net loss of $6.5 million. That amount ballooned to $37.6 million in fiscal 1991.

Specialty's losses could be traced to three problems. First, the foodservice industry was feeling the effects of the recession as stores and restaurants began failing. Second, the industry was experiencing a general maturation. As the yogurt craze waned, for example, sales of Taylor's yogurt machines fell by more than 16 percent. These conditions resulted in greatly increased price competition, and when combined with the third factor, Specialty's heavy debt from the 1988 leveraged buyout, caused the company to default on its obligations. Both Specialty and SPE Acquisition had to seek Chapter 11 bankruptcy protection in 1991.

Reorganization, 1992–93

The company emerged from Chapter 11 in March 1992, with SPE Acquisition merged into Specialty Equipment. The company paid all its trade creditors in full, but holders of prebankruptcy stock in Specialty Equipment and SPE Acquisition received no distribution in the bankruptcy cases. The original executives re-took control of the company. In November Daniel Greenwood resumed his position as CEO, and in December William Dotterweich was elected president again and also assumed the duties of chief operating officer.

The company came out of bankruptcy just as the market for foodservice equipment began a gradual recovery, led by quick service restaurant chains. The chains were not only opening new sites in the United States and overseas, but were also modernizing their equipment and remodeling existing locations as they added new items to their menus and changed their layouts to be more competitive.

The company underwent several major changes during 1993, including being listed on the NASDAQ exchange. Specialty combined the operations of Wells Manufacturing (electrical cooking equipment) and those of Bloomfield Industries (coffee and tea beverage products) at the Wells facility in Verdi, Nevada, creating the Wells/Bloomfield division. The company also announced it was closing its Market Forge division, after having had it on the market for eight years. But instead of that occurring, the 150 employees of Market Forge bought the division, saving their jobs. In selling the division, Specialty kept FM Manufacturing, Inc., its wholly owned subsidiary, although operations obviously ceased.

At the end of the year, Specialty completed a refinancing plan, consisting of a $50 million line of credit, a $15 million term loan, and a $185 million public offering of senior notes. The company owned about $215 million in long-term debt, a heavy burden for an organization with sales of $320 million.

Growth and Innovation, 1994–97

Specialty aimed at strengthening its financial picture with a four-step business strategy: focus on major national chains, expand international opportunities, leverage long-term relationships with major customers, and enhance the core product lines by adapting customized equipment innovations. Within the company, each division operated separately, with its own management, marketing, manufacturing, and product development teams. Specialty's business and growth can best be understood by examining each division.

Taylor Company

When Specialty Equipment acquired Taylor from Beatrice, the division was producing "cold" equipment, such as ice cream freezers and dispensers for frozen yogurts and frozen cocktails. Within a year, Taylor expanded into "hot" equipment and began designing and manufacturing cooking equipment such as flat grills and customized hot and cold food preparation and holding cabinets. In cooperation with McDonald's, Taylor developed the automated "clam shell" grill, incorporating upper and lower grill plates that grilled both sides of a hamburger patty (or other food) simultaneously. Although Taylor held a joint patent for this grill with McDonald's, the company was able to develop a similar grill that it marketed to other quick service restaurants.

Taylor also held a patent on its Softech® technology. This was an integrated memory system that automatically controlled the hardness or softness of a frozen product. With its Labor Saver™ heat treatment equipment, developed during the early 1990s, the division produced softserve and shake freezers that only needed to be taken apart and cleaned every other week, not daily as was the case with standard machines. Taylor also developed two specialized ovens for baking and holding applications, and frozen, non-carbonated beverage equipment.

Taylor sold and serviced its machines through a worldwide network of more than 140 independent distributors, whose sales and service staffs doubled from 300 in 1995 to 600 in 1997. In 1995 Taylor initiated a long-range service plan, called Service 2000, to achieve service excellence. The first step was a communication network to track service performance and provide a benchmark for measuring improvement. That was followed, in February 1997, with the opening of the Taylor Technical/Development Center at the division's manufacturing plant in Illinois. In addition to providing training for its sales and service personnel, the facility served as a technical resource center. That same year, Taylor embarked on its Freezer and Grill of the Future development program, to produce a new generation of equipment.

Beverage-Air

The Beverage-Air division manufactured refrigeration equipment for the soft drink bottling and foodservice markets. When Specialty Equipment bought Beverage-Air in 1986, the division sold its equipment primarily to soft drink bottlers, which bought coolers to put in supermarkets and convenience stores. Over the years, the division worked with the bottlers to customize these coolers to meet special marketing needs, such as Coca-Cola's Fast Lane™, used in the express checkout lines at supermarkets. Other innovations included the Maxi-Marketeers®, a line of curved-front vertical merchandisers introduced in 1995, and the Contour Cooler™, an eight-foot cooler in the shape of the traditional Coca-Cola bottle, for the international bottler market.

As part of Specialty, Beverage-Air's sales to foodservice companies grew substantially. Products for that market included stainless steel refrigerators and freezers, deli display cases, pizza and food production tables, refrigerated display cases, and beer dispensing equipment. In addition to restaurants, customers included hotel kitchens, university cafeterias, supermarkets, convenience stores, and florists.

In 1996 Beverage-Air opened a 60,000 square foot manufacturing facility in Honea Path, South Carolina. In 1997, when the federal Food and Drug Administration changed its unified food codes, Beverage-Air completely redesigned its existing core product line, generating replacement equipment sales, especially to quick service restaurant chains. During fiscal 1998, Beverage-Air became the company's top-selling division, moving ahead of Taylor with 43.4 percent of net revenue.

Wells/Bloomfield

Under the Wells name, the Wells/Bloomfield division produced a line of electric countertop and built-in cooking appliances, including fryers, griddles, food warmers, broilers, and waffle bakers, which it sold to restaurants, hotels, schools, and hospitals. Wells also developed larger, specialized products, such as Crispy Lite™, a unit combining a pressure fryer, rotisserie oven, and storage, that enabled grocery and convenience stores to offer fried and roasted chickens to customers who didn't have the time to cook.

The Bloomfield part of the division specialized in equipment for making and serving coffee and tea. Working with major chains, Bloomfield designed specialized coffee and tea brewing systems, which were purchased by 7-Eleven, Boston Market, Wendy's, and Hardee's. In the mid-1990s, in the face of a national coffee craze, the division introduced its Cafe Elite™ line, a powder cappuccino dispenser and fully automatic espresso machine. That was followed, in 1997, with the Electronic Brew Control™ coffee equipment, and satellite brewing systems, multi-brewers, and docking stations to meet the growing demand for high-quality coffee in specialty coffee shops and convenience stores. As the market for fresh brewed tea increased, Bloomfield developed a new flavored tea system to attach to its tea brewers.

World Dryer

The World Dryer division's wall-mounted, warm-air hand dryers can be found in public restrooms throughout the world. In 1994 World Dryer acquired Electric Aire™, a line of less expensive, plastic encased hand dryers, to augment its stainless steel and cast iron hand and hair dryers. The division developed the No-Touch™ dryer, which it incorporated into a hand wash station for use in kitchens and health care settings that enabled workers to wash their hands without having to touch the soap dispenser, faucet, or dryer. The station even had a built-in counting feature that recorded each hand washing, making it possible to monitor under federal and health codes.

Gamko

In August 1997, Specialty announced it would purchase Gamko Holdings B.V., a Dutch manufacturer of refrigeration equipment for the beverage/beer markets. Gamko had been making coolers since 1965, and its brand names included Euro-Line™, Eco-Line™, Party-Cooler™, and Maxi Glass™. Its product lines included beverage and bottle display coolers, dispensing and keg coolers, and food display and waste disposal coolers.

Included in the $21 million cash purchase was CoolPart B.V., a separate refrigeration company operating in Eastern

Europe, with business in Slovakia, the Czech Republic, and Poland. The purchase of Gamko, which had annual sales of about $25 million, gave Specialty its first manufacturing facility outside North America, positioned the company for both the West and East European markets, and added global breweries to its customer base.

In 1995 Greenwood resigned as CEO while William Dotterweich assumed that responsibility along with his duties as president and chief operating officer. That same year, Malcolm Glazer used his shares in Specialty and Houlihan Restaurants as collateral to raise $66 million, part of the $172 million Glazer paid for the Tampa Bay Buccaneers football team. In 1996 Jeffrey Rhodenbaugh, president of Beverage-Air, was named president and chief operating officer. Dotterweich continued as CEO until his retirement in May 1997, at which time Rhodenbaugh assumed the CEO responsibilities as well.

In September 1997, the company decided it would buy back $10 million of its own stock. In a press release announcing the plan, president and CEO Rhodenbaugh explained, "With our stock trading at a deep discount to both the S&P 500 multiple and that of our peer group, we believe that the current price undervalues our company and presents an attractive investment opportunity to increase shareholder value. Our strong cash flow and our confidence in our long-term outlook are the driving factors behind this move."

1998 to the Present

On January 31, 1998, Specialty organized Specialty Equipment Manufacturing Corporation as a wholly owned subsidiary to conduct the U.S. operation of its divisions. For the fiscal year, Specialty reported sales of $433.1 million, net earnings of $38.5 million, and debt reduction of $135 million. Its divisions continued to innovate, with Taylor introducing the Razzle®, a frozen dessert program that mixed hard candies or cookies into softserve ice cream or frozen yogurt, and Beverage-Air marketing the Breeze™, a new soft drink merchandiser. People were drinking more coffee and tea, soft drinks, juices, and other beverages, and they wanted to be able to buy them quickly and conveniently. Specialty also began moving into the recreation market, to help supply the numerous new stadiums being built throughout the United States. By adapting its traditional products to meet its customers' needs as well as changing eating and drinking habits, Specialty now dominated its niches.

Principal Subsidiaries

FM Manufacturing, Inc.; Bloomfield Industries Canada Ltd.; Taylor Freezer International, S.r.l., (Italy); Taylor Freezer (Cyprus) Ltd.; Specialty Equipment Foreign Sales Corp.; Taylor-Chicago Corp.; CoolPart B.V.; Specialty Equipment Manufacturing Corp.; Gamko N.V. [principal—operating—divisions] Beverage-Air, Taylor Company, Wells Manufacturing / Bloomfield Industries, World Dryer.

Further Reading

"Beatrice Changes Course," *Dun's Business Month*, April 1983, p. 34.

Bordon, Jeff, "Bankrupt Machine Firm Hungers for Reorganization," *Crain's Chicago Business*, January 6, 1992, p. 29.

Dean, Suellen E., "Beverage-Air Product Goes Worldwide," *Spartanburg Herald-Journal*, June 19, 1996, p. B3.

"Former Beatrice Firms Planning Stock Offering," *Crain's Chicago Business*, May 11, 1987, p. 1.

Greenhouse, Steven, "Beatrice to Sell Food Service Unit," *New York Times*, November 29, 1984, p. D2.

Henderson, Rex, "Glazer Used 2 Firms as Bucs Collateral," *Tampa Tribune*, August 5, 1995, p. Business 1.

"Ice Machine Maker to Locate in South Beloit," *United Press International*, November 15, 1989.

Mishra, Upendra, "Employee-Owners Forge New Life for Market Forge," *Boston Business Journal*, December 16, 1994, p. 1.

Snyder, David, and Steven R. Strahler, "Sellout Talks Spurs Specialty Equipment," *Crain's Chicago Business*, March 28, 1988, p. 2.

"Specialty Equipment Cos Reports Earnings," *New York Times*, March 9, 1988, p. D11.

"Specialty Equipment Expands Asian Plan," *Nation's Restaurant News*, December 7, 1992, p. 40.

"Specialty Equipment Mulls Sale," *Chicago Tribune*, March 25, 1998, p. Business 3.

"Specialty Equipment Names Chief Executive," *Reuters Financial Service*, March 4, 1997.

"Specialty Equipment Names President," *Reuters Financial Service*, September 3, 1996.

"Specialty Makes Dutch Purchase," *Chicago Daily Herald*, August 6, 1997, p. Business 1.

Thornton, Jack, "Beatrice Foods Considering Departure From Ind'l Field," *American Metal Market*, February 28, 1983, p. 13.

Vise, David A. "Beatrice Cos. Tries to Sell Itself to Consumers, Investors," *Washington Post*, September 9, 1994, p. F9.

—Ellen D. Wernick

SpeeDee Oil Change and Tune-Up

P.O. Box 1350
159 Highway 22 East
Madisonville, Louisiana 70447
U.S.A.
(504) 845-1919
Fax: (504) 845-1936
(800) 451-7461

Private Company
Incorporated: 1980 as SpeeDee Oil Change
Employees: 85
Sales: $60 million (1995 est.)
SICs: 7538 General Automotive Repair Shops; 6794
Patent Owners & Lessors

SpeeDee Oil Change and Tune-Up started out as a single quick-oil-change shop in the New Orleans, Louisiana, metropolitan area in 1980. It began offering franchises in 1982 and grew rapidly during the 1980s. The 1980s was a good decade in general for the quick-lube industry, with several factors propelling industry growth. After several years of unchecked growth, however, the industry experienced problems at the end of the decade, and SpeeDee was unable to grow as fast as it wanted to. By the early 1990s SpeeDee had about 130 locations and was the seventh largest quick-lube company in the United States. By comparison, industry leader Jiffy Lube International Inc., which was taken over by Pennzoil Co. in 1989, had approximately 1,100 locations. Although it tried several times, SpeeDee was unable to negotiate a successful joint venture agreement with a major corporation to raise the capital it needed for the kind of dramatic expansion that it wanted, and the company's growth leveled off in the 1990s.

Founded by Two High School Buddies in 1980

SpeeDee Oil Change and Tune-Up was founded in 1980 by two high school buddies, Gary Copp and Kevin Bennett. Copp became president and Bennett director of franchising. Copp and Bennett went to high school together in New Orleans at Arch-bishop Rummel High School. Copp admitted that he was not a mechanic, but he did not consider that a drawback. "The people who were in it before, they were mechanically-oriented, 'grease monkeys.' They didn't know anything about marketing the business. We changed that," he said in *New Orleans Business*.

Copp and Bennett were 26 years old when they started. Copp had studied marketing and transportation at the University of Tennessee, expecting to go into airline management. When Gulf Oil offered Bennett, who owned several car washes, a small piece of land next to a service station on Veterans Boulevard in Metairie in the New Orleans metropolitan area, Copp suggested they set up a quick-change oil shop similar to ones he had seen in California.

Their first office, set up with a loan from a friend, was in the Odd Fellows Rest Cemetery on Canal Street in New Orleans. Neither Copp nor Bennett had much money to work with, so they borrowed whatever they could. They added a third partner, Conrad Kuebel, because he was a local contractor and friend of Bennett who had enough assets and business experience to make the young company more appealing to bankers.

When it first opened, SpeeDee Oil Change avoided using the word "lube," because everyone else had it in their name. The company also promised a nine-minute oil change when everyone else was advertising ten-minute oil changes. Three months after signing their initial agreement, Kuebel died from cancer. Copp and Bennett had to hustle to obtain the necessary financing, going to manufacturers. Not having much management experience, they found they had too many employees on their opening day in 1980. As Copp said, "Our most expensive payroll was the first day we opened. I think we had 89 people standing around, expecting all these vehicles to come rolling in. It didn't happen."

However, direct-mail coupons helped SpeeDee turn the corner. By March 1981 Copp and Bennett knew they had a winner. That was when they started opening more shops and reincorporated as SpeeDee Oil Change and Tune-Up. Their goal initially was to own the New Orleans market, and by 1986 they had 11 shops there and were the dominant quick-lube chain. Sales for 1980, the company's first full year in business, were just over

$100,000. By 1984 the company was doing $2.5 million worth of business, and sales doubled in 1985 to around $5 million.

Offered First Franchises in 1982

In 1982 the first franchises were offered. The partners had not originally intended to franchise their business, but it seemed the logical way to grow. The first franchisee was Ed Mikkelson, who opened a SpeeDee shop in nearby Baton Rouge, Louisiana. By 1989 Mikkelson had opened eight stores, sold two, and reduced his debt to $80,000 by paying off his construction loans with cash flow. According to *New Orleans City Business,* Mikkelson's net worth soared above $1 million and his income tripled to six figures by the end of the decade.

Mikkelson was the subject of an article in *Success* magazine in March 1993. He built an 11-unit franchise in New Orleans and became SpeeDee's master franchiser in New England. *Success* reported his franchises were generating $16 million a year by 1993. One of the keys to his success was called "big fish marketing," which meant going after fleet accounts and corporate clients. When his franchise opened in 1982, he was pulling in $4,000 to $5,000 per week from drive-in trade. Then he signed up a local police department for his first account and added $600 a week to his cash flow. Other corporate accounts followed, eventually accounting for 20 percent of Mikkelson's revenue. He offered them volume discounts, central billing, and convenience. Explaining the key to obtaining corporate accounts, he told *Success,* "You've got to network and you've got to have more than one store to succeed." His biggest account was Louisiana Power and Light, with a fleet of more than 300 vehicles.

Offered Time-Savings and Other Benefits to Customers

The company's main selling point to customers was the time-saving offered by a quick oil change. Price was less of an issue, with SpeeDee Oil Change charging around $20, which was, according to Copp, "probably less than a service station, less than a dealership, but more than a Goodyear or a Firestone." However, at Goodyear or Firestone, customers would have to leave their car all day for a $10 oil change. At SpeeDee, they could be in and out in less than 10 minutes.

SpeeDee shops offered oil changes, tune-ups, and diagnostic services. Each shop featured a clean waiting area, hot coffee, friendly non-grease-stained employees, and a rack of take-home reading material. Customers could see the service bays through a window in the waiting room. The company felt that letting the customers see the work being done helped reduce paranoia and make the company seem upfront with its customers. Repeat business was very important. Copp explained, "The name of the game is to get people in again and again and again. We want a lifetime customer because it's very expensive to get them in the first time."

Explaining how SpeeDee Oil Change marketed itself, Copp said, "Our market research was mainly in my head, from growing up here and knowing where the action was and where the growth was. The whole name of the game is market penetration, with the best locations you can pay for." The company used direct mail, then aired some radio spots. However, it found that television advertising worked best. The company's advertising budget came from a five percent advertising fee paid by franchisees, which was later increased to six percent.

The company's advertising also targeted women, and its television spots in 1986 featured a female customer. Copp reasoned that men already knew what was going on, but women had to be educated somewhat, and the negative image associated with service stations had to be overcome.

One of the Fastest-Growing Private Companies, 1984

In 1984 SpeeDee ranked 84th on *Inc.* magazine's list of "America's 500 fastest-growing private companies," based on a phenomenal increase of 2,158 percent in sales between 1980 and 1984. The same year the company was also listed in *Entrepreneur* magazine's "Franchise 500." Sales for 1984 were $2.5 million and around $5 million in 1985.

By 1986 the company had 16 franchised shops located in Florida, Mississippi, and Louisiana, and it was working on an 18-region franchising plan. Copp told *New Orleans Business* that as many as 1,800 SpeeDee shops may open by the end of the 1980s, but several factors would prevent SpeeDee from reaching that goal. Prospective franchisees could expect to invest anywhere from $75,000 to $350,000 per shop in start-up expenses, depending on the cost of real estate and whether the equipment was purchased or leased. Those costs would be in addition to a $20,000 franchise fee. As Copp said, "The franchise fee gets them started. They're buying all of our mistakes so that they don't make them."

SpeeDee's expansion had been financed internally up to this point, but it was beginning to receive buyout offers. A takeover offer from Jiffy Lube International, Inc. was rejected. Then a proposed joint venture with Gulf Oil was sidelined when Gulf was taken over by Chevron Corporation. "That set us back years," Copp later said. When the deal with Gulf fell apart, Copp and Bennett settled on a franchise plan in order to obtain capital needed for expansion. They modeled their plan after real estate company Century 21, which would sell regional master franchises to investors who would then sell individual franchises.

SpeeDee's franchise plan was set up to offer regional, or master franchisers, who would in turn sub-franchise about 150 franchises in their region. A regional franchiser would be responsible for handling the franchisee relationship and services as well as any necessary financing. Requirements to obtain a master franchise included payment of a $150,000 franchise fee (later increased to $200,000) and a net worth of about $600,000. The master franchiser could then sell up to 150 franchises in the region for about $25,000 each.

To market their franchising plan, the partners retained an advertising agency in New Orleans and Networks Unlimited of Newport Beach, California, to really begin pushing franchises in 1986. Around this time a third partner was added, Frances K. Thomas, who handled financial matters.

Between 1986 and 1989 SpeeDee sold 11 master franchises for $150,000 or $200,000. Nine of the 11 survived, and by mid-1989 SpeeDee's regional franchisers had sold a total of 256 franchises. The company's 100th store was set to open in the fall of 1989.

Problems Plagued Quick-Lube Industry, 1989

After several years of unchecked growth, the quick oil change business began to run into some problems in 1989. Industry leader Jiffy Lube announced a $39 million loss in the spring of 1989 and was quickly taken over by Pennzoil Co. It closed 100 of its 1,040 shops in an effort to trim costs. Other smaller chains, such as Autospa and Eaglespeed, filed for bankruptcy.

In 1989 SpeeDee was in joint venture negotiations with Mobil Oil. By 1989 SpeeDee was the sixth largest quick-lube chain in the United States with 80 stores and systemwide revenues of $18 million expected in 1989. A joint venture with Mobil Oil would enable SpeeDee to build as many as 400 stores in five years and to purchase other smaller quick-lube operations. Under the proposed agreement with Mobil, SpeeDee would be obligated to buy oil, filters, and other supplies exclusively from Mobil for at least 10 years. However, the failure of Jiffy Lube cast a pall over negotiations, and SpeeDee remained an independent chain.

Other Factors Also Slowed Growth for SpeeDee

SpeeDee was fairly selective about selling its franchises. One analyst noted that "they have not been eager to sell a franchise to just anyone." As a result, SpeeDee did not expand as fast as it could, but it enjoyed a low rate of failure among its franchisees. Also slowing growth was a lack of capital. Even though some $3.5 million in franchise fees was ploughed back into the company, SpeeDee did not have the "deep pockets" of its competitors. The top three quick-lube chains in the industry were all owned by major corporations who had the capital to invest in new buildings and new locations. SpeeDee, on the other hand, placed the burden of developing new locations and financing new buildings on its regional franchisers. In some cases, the regional franchiser had to turn away potential franchisees because they ran out of money. Although its franchisers tended to remain loyal, many wished that SpeeDee would become more involved in underwriting the construction costs of new locations, or offer a loan program. To do that, SpeeDee needed a source of capital, such as a joint venture partner.

One example of how SpeeDee's lack of a loan program for new construction slowed the company's growth was in Atlanta, Georgia. Even though Atlanta was a hot market for quick-lube shops, growing from 91 to 227 stores in just one year, SpeeDee's master franchiser in Atlanta, Tom Slimp, was only able to sell 10 franchises in two years. He had to turn away as many as 200 people, simply because he did not have the capital to build new locations on speculation. Slimp told *New Orleans City Business,* "My typical customer [for a new franchise] is some middle manager who is about to be transferred out of town and has 90 days to find something else to do. If you don't have something ready for them, they'll go buy a pizza shop." Slimp called it quits in 1991.

SpeeDee Anticipated Growth in the Early 1990s

In 1990 SpeeDee explored a major acquisition, Sparks Computerized Car Care Centers based in Illinois. Sparks had 130 automotive service centers. However, once Copp and Bennett looked into merging the two companies, they realized they would have had to build pits for the automotive technicians in order for them to perform a nine-minute oil change. The partners decided it was not worth the expense. According to Copp, "It just didn't fit. It's a lot easier to buy an oil change business and add tune-ups than it is to buy a tune-up shop and add oil changes."

New store openings for SpeeDee averaged 13.5 a year for the past two years. However, in 1991 SpeeDee announced it would roll out another 43 units for a systemwide total of 150 shops. That would have made SpeeDee the fastest-growing quick-lube chain, since none of the other top ten companies surveyed planned to open more than 30 facilities in 1991. As it turned out, SpeeDee opened about 30 shops in 1991 and, according to information in *Entrepreneur* magazine's annual "Franchise 500" issue, SpeeDee had 139 franchises operating in 1992, none of which were company-owned. That number declined to 131 operating franchises in 1993, and the company had taken over ownership of two of the franchises. For 1994 the company had 134 operating franchises, three of which were company-owned.

SpeeDee brought in new managers and executives to run the business, which the partners expected to expand dramatically. Bruce German was hired as the new chief operating officer (COO), and Peter Stewart was brought in as executive vice-president of marketing. German had previously been in charge of operations of a 515-unit Hardee's franchise in the Southeast. Stewart was marketing vice-president at both Godfather's Pizza and the Straw Hat restaurant division of SAGA Corp. Maurice Gaudet was named the new chief financial officer.

In 1991 the company stopped selling master franchises in the United States. Looking overseas, it began to expand internationally. In December 1991 it sold half of the Brazil territory, and it was looking to make deals in Taiwan and Mexico. However, with 18 locations in the New Orleans area by 1992, SpeeDee was the dominant quick-lube shop there. The company decided to go after new car owners by validating new car warranties. With the cost of new cars rising, new car loans sometimes went for five years or more, and that helped bring in business with people taking care of their cars for longer periods of time. Environmental issues, especially the safe disposal of used oil, also served to bring in more of the do-it-yourself owners.

Some SpeeDee Franchisers Had Major Problems in the 1990s

In 1992 SpeeDee was the seventh largest quick-lube company in the United States. However, the company was experiencing some discontent among its franchisers. Some investors began demanding their money back, while others sold out for a loss. In Florida, the master franchiser filed for personal bankruptcy, causing some individual Florida franchisees to sue the company for not doing a better job of selecting its master franchisers. One New Orleans franchisee claimed that SpeeDee's pre-opening projections were off by 40 percent. Bennett and Copp claimed that about 10 percent of the company's stores were unsuccessful.

However, not all franchisees were disgruntled. Ed Mikkelson of Baton Rouge now owned 10 SpeeDee locations in Louisiana. SpeeDee had 36 units under construction and projected its store count would be in the 175 to 200 range by the end of 1992. It had 130 locations in early 1992, and nearly 300 franchises had been sold. The company's hottest region was southern California, where 79 franchises were sold in three years. Other markets were slower. In New England, only one-third of the 63 franchises there opened a store over the previous six years.

Owners of one or two SpeeDee shops could be successful, however. One couple, Mike and Karen Klaubert, opened their first SpeeDee franchise in 1987 in Concord, New Hampshire. A year later they opened a second one in nearby Laconia. According to *Nation's Business,* they broke even in their first year, then saw gross sales for both locations increase by 32 percent from 1988 to 1990.

Of the nine regional franchises sold since 1986, only five remained at the beginning of 1992. The other four were taken back by the company after the master franchiser either gave up or went broke trying to make it work. In St. Louis, Missouri, the master franchiser originally sold 15 franchises. By 1992 only two remained in the SpeeDee chain. Of the rest, five never opened, two closed, and the remaining owners sought new affiliations. Other regions experiencing failure included Atlanta, Georgia, and southern Florida.

The toll on individual franchisees was enormous. One franchisee in St. Louis lost his entire $200,000 investment. He told *New Orleans City Business,* "The biggest problem we had was that we literally received no support whatsoever. The promised training never materialized, the merchandising support never materialized, calls were never returned. I was on the verge of closing and they didn't have time to visit with me."

Bennett and Copp claimed that lack of working capital was not the cause for all of the failure. They tended to blame the franchisees for running a poor shop. According to the SpeeDee system, it was the regional master franchiser who was responsible for providing support to the individual franchises in the region, with SpeeDee providing support to the master franchiser if necessary.

Individual failures proved to be a contentious point with the company. While the franchisees saw the company as being at fault, SpeeDee officials described a different pattern of failure. They said that such franchisees either do not follow the system, do not operate the stores themselves, or they put their personal expenses on the company's tab, according to *New Orleans City Business.* SpeeDee hoped that its new managers and executives would help improve franchisee relations.

The cost of opening a SpeeDee franchise and the lack of a financing program from SpeeDee may have contributed to a slowdown in the company's growth. One franchisee in Davie, Florida, obtained a Small Business Administration loan for $635,000 and put in an additional $200,000 of his own money to cover the cost of the franchise, land, buildings, and equipment. Franchisees had the option of purchasing or leasing the necessary equipment. In 1995 *Entrepreneur* magazine estimated the start-up costs to be between $39,000 and $333,000.

An article on a new SpeeDee franchise opening in Rock Hill, North Carolina, reported that it cost $700,000 to build a 3,100-square-foot facility with four service bays that could hold two cars each.

Launched National Promotional Campaigns in 1994

In 1994 SpeeDee became an associate sponsor of NASCAR driver Ricky Craven for the 1994 Busch Grand National racing season. The SpeeDee logo would appear on Craven's car and uniform, and Craven would be available for special promotional events. SpeeDee hoped the campaign would enhance its national marketing efforts. SpeeDee had sponsored Craven in the 1989 season and was his first major sponsor. SpeeDee was creating several promotional campaigns around Craven, including in-store promotions featuring Craven's likeness and a "Buckle-Up for Safety" public service campaign.

In 1994 SpeeDee also launched a national promotion, "The SpeeDee Weekend Getaway," which ran from June through November. The campaign rewarded customers for their loyalty to SpeeDee. Several "Getaway" weekends were offered at 35 destinations, including Hilton Head Island, South Carolina; Palm Springs, California; Orlando, Florida; and Puerto Vallarta, Mexico. Customers had to spend at least $200 at SpeeDee's, for which they would receive a certificate good for two free nights at participating hotels.

Number of Franchises Peaked in 1996

In 1995 revenues reached $60 million, and the company had 140 locations in operation, eight of which were company-owned. The number of operating franchises increased to 147 in 1996, but the number fell to 128 in 1997. During this period the initial franchise fee was $30,000 to $40,000, the royalty rate was still six percent, and SpeeDee was continuing its policy of not providing any type of financing for start-up costs or the initial franchise fee.

After riding the wave of growth in the quick-lube and automotive service industry of the 1980s, SpeeDee had to cut back on its plans for expansion in the 1990s. It has remained a privately owned company in an industry dominated by subsidiaries of major corporations. Although patterns of automobile ownership, environmental concerns, and busy lifestyles continue to favor growth in the quick-lube industry, SpeeDee will need sources of outside capital if it intends to meet its earlier growth projections.

Further Reading

Cheramie, Paul, "Car Maintenance Business Draws Dealers and Aftermarket Shops," *New Orleans Business,* June 15, 1992, p. 21.

Elkins, Ken, "SpeeDee Oil Change Inches Toward Rock Hill, N.C., Shop," *Knight-Ridder/Tribune Business News,* December 13, 1996.

Garrett, Echo Montgomery, "Finessing the Finance," *Inc.,* September 1993, p. 126.

Meitrodt, Jeffrey, "Revving up for Growth: Quick Lube Business Pans Out for SpeeDee Entrepreneurs," *New Orleans Business,* October 9, 1989, p. 1.

——, "SpeeDee Brings in a New Team to Help Tune up the Company," *New Orleans Business,* July 29, 1991, p. 9.

——, "SpeeDee's Growth Is Not Without Friction," *New Orleans Business,* February 10, 1992, p. 1.

"A New Hampshire Oil Baron," *New Hampshire Business Review,* April 22, 1988, p. 12.

"19th Annual Franchise 500," *Entrepreneur,* January 1998, p. 218.

Price, Scott, "Race for Fastest Oil Change Heats up Quick-Lube War," *Business Journal-Charlotte,* October 23, 1989, p. 1.

"16th Annual Franchise 500," *Entrepreneur,* January 1995, p. 144.

"SpeeDee Oil Change and Tune-Up's New 'The SpeeDee Weekend Getaway' Promotion Is Detailed," *Aftermarket Business,* June 1, 1994, p. 10.

"SpeeDee Oil Change Sponsors NASCAR's Ricky Craven," *Aftermarket Business,* May 1, 1994, p. 21.

Stanton, Arlene, "SpeeDee Oil Revs up for Even Faster Growth," *New Orleans Business,* January 6, 1986, p. 1A.

Warshow, Michael, "Big-Fish Marketing: How Retailers Hook Huge Corporate Accounts," *Success,* March 1993, p. 61.

Whittemore, Meg, "Bumper-to-Bumper Auto Care," *Nation's Business,* October 1991, p. 70.

—David Bianco

The Sports Club Company

11100 Santa Monica Boulevard
Suite 300
Los Angeles, California 90025
U.S.A.
(310) 479-5200
Fax: (310) 479-8350

Public Company
Incorporated: 1979 as The Sports Connection
Employees: 2,100
Sales: $61.2 million (1997)
Stock Exchanges: AMS
Ticker Symbol: SCY
SICs: 7991 Physical Fitness Facilities

Based in Los Angeles, The Sports Club Company owns and operates fitness and health clubs across the United States. Sports Club operations are marked by their "urban country club" feel, combining multiple fitness options with every imaginable service and luxury. The rise of The Sports Club Company parallels the 1980s era of consciousness about physical fitness; the company was actually born in the region most associated with that craze: Southern California.

A Lasting Partnership Launches Urban Country Clubs

The story of the business partnership that formed The Sports Club Company began in Mexico in 1969, when Michael Talla met Nanette Pattee Francini in a hotel in Mazatlan. Talla and Francini first became romantically involved, and later—after their relationship ended—stayed together as business partners. Their first joint venture was a bikini manufacturing company that sold split sizes for tops and bottoms in 1969. In 1972, they sold their business for $125,000. Talla moved to Milwaukie, Oregon to build a racquetball club, and Francini moved to Colorado. In 1973, she was named Miss Aspen, and she went on to work in beer sales as The Budweiser Girl. By 1975, she was fed up with this line of work, and contacted Talla about rejuvenating their business partnership. Talla sold his racquetball club for $285,000 and moved to Los Angeles.

In 1979, Talla and Francini borrowed money from a friend and leased a 40,000 square foot piece of land in a Santa Monica industrial park. With some friends selling memberships out of a trailer, Talla and Francini opened their first sports club: The Sports Connection. Here, they pioneered their "urban country club" concept, with private trainers, a pro shop, a cafe, and multiple fitness options under a single roof. In addition, The Sports Connection was one of the first coeducational health clubs (previous fitness centers were segregated by sex). Soon, a second club was opened in the exclusive city of Beverly Hills. Medium-sized health clubs in Long Beach, the South Bay, Costa Mesa, and Century City followed.

Talla and Francini's success was augmented by the membership of celebrities and sports stars—working out at sports clubs meant an opportunity to "star-gaze" as well as slim down. With a star-studded membership list, the Sports Connection began to receive attention in media stories covering the fitness boom of the 1980s. In 1985, the Sports Connection chain inspired a major motion picture about the fitness lifestyle, "Perfect," starring John Travolta as a journalist and Jaime Lee Curtis as an aerobics instructor. Jane Fonda's aerobics videos of the early 1980s also helped popularize the idea of working out to achieve supreme physical fitness. By 1985, the company owned six workout centers, which grossed $12 million annually.

From Health Clubs to Megaclubs: The Late 1980s

Positive response to the Sports Connection clubs led Talla and Francini to take the luxury concept a step further. In 1987, they opened the first Spectrum Club in Manhattan Beach. The new megaclub, a 65,000 square foot complex, was designed to emulate a beach resort, with an Olympic sized swimming pool, a full health spa and complete food and beverage service. New Spectrum Club locations were added in Santa Monica's Water Garden, Howard Hughes Center, AgouraHills and Valencia.

Company Perspectives:

The Company believes that it has developed a nationwide reputation for its ability to acquire, develop and operate first-class sports and fitness facilities, and that such facilities are increasingly sought after by developers of premiere, multi-use projects. Consequently, there exist numerous opportunities to develop the Sports Club name and concept throughout the country and internationally and to develop the Spectrum Club name throughout Southern California. The Company intends to continue to pursue those opportunities which maximize its earning potential.

Having moved on to the highest end of the sports and fitness market, the company sold its original Sports Connection clubs to focus solely on the new megaclub idea.

That same year, the company opened The Sports Club/LA, a new $30 million sports and fitness complex in an old wheelchair factory in West Los Angeles. The Sports Club/LA was a 100,000 square foot structure with marble lobbies, and housed state-of-the-art equipment, exercise classes, private trainers, valet parking, car detailing, a sundeck, shoe shine, hair salon, and an executive business center. Conceptually, the club combined an exclusive workout facility with a 5-star hotel. The club opened with a star-studded gala, and in a very short time it reached membership capacity (5,000 members), with a $2,500 initiation fee plus $160 a month for executive membership dues. Celebrities including Magic Johnson, Madonna, Bruce Springsteen, Princess Stephanie of Monaco, Jack Nicholson, Arnold Schwarzenegger, Dyan Cannon, Linda Rondstadt, Tyra Banks, and Brooke Shields could be spotted working out with the club's personal trainers, as were the powerful elite of Los Angeles' corporate and entertainment industries. According to the *Los Angeles Times*, the club was described by some as "the Acropolis of physical fitness centers."

In 1988, Oil and entertainment mogul Marvin Davis invested $34 million in the company to support its expansion. Davis received stakes in the various clubs, which were all separately incorporated at that time. In sum, Davis controlled about 50 percent of the sports club operations. Davis' investment, however, would later be plagued by the downturn in the southern California economy and the slowing of the health club craze, as well as a competitive race with another company in Irvine, California.

Heavy Competition in the Early 1990s

The Sports Club became involved in a protracted competition around the construction and operation of a new facility in Irvine, California. During the mid-1980s, money for new construction flowed freely. Laguna Niguel-based developer Birtcher decided to construct a super health club to entice tenants to its new Irvine office buildings. The Koll Company elected to develop a competitive health club, and both developers easily secured financing. Koll chose the Sports Club Company to build its health facility, while Birtcher opted for Sporting Clubs of America, a Sports Club rival company headquartered in La Jolla, California. As a result, two upscale, $20 million-plus sports clubs were soon under construction, just across the San Diego Freeway from each other.

Public opinion was that the rival health clubs—a Sports Club/Irvine and a Sporting Club—would cannibalize each other's business. The Irvine community just did not contain enough affluent fitness fans to support two luxury sports facilities. Early efforts to reach a merger agreement were unsuccessful, and neither company would scrap its new facility. The two clubs' plans predicted similar facilities, each at 100,000 square feet with executive dining rooms, child care centers, cocktail lounges, and hair salons, with projected initiation fees of around $1,000. Basic membership fees would run about $500 at both clubs, with slightly higher monthly dues at Sports Club/Irvine. Target membership for Sports Club/Irvine was 5,000 (with a capacity of 9,000), with 4,000 members sought by Sporting Club. Knowing that 9,000 potential members were not to be found in the 110,000 person community of Irvine, Sports Club/Irvine was forced to begin its promotional sales long before the planned timetable, to respond to early advertising by its rival Sporting Club. By May of 1990, Sports Club/Irvine had attracted 4,500 members at initiation fees between $550 and $1,500. However, with a capacity of 1,700 customers a day, the club had yet to reach 1,000 daily exercisers.

Despite falling short of its goals, Sports Club/Irvine had the edge. It opened almost two years sooner than Sporting Club—in February of 1990—due to a series of problems with Sporting Club's building permit and other issues. Koll, developer of the new Sports Club/Irvine, had already received the city of Irvine's approval to build a health spa in conjunction with its permit for a retail and office complex. Koll had merely returned to the city and was granted permission to build a much larger health facility. Birtcher, however, was slowed by the paperwork and procedures associated with acquiring an initial permit from the city of Irvine. A joint venture by San Diego developer Naiman Co. and two Japanese companies (Nissho Iwai Corp. and Hiroshima Yakult Co.), the Sporting Club did not actually open until July of 1992, seven years after the project began. The delays cost the clubs potential customers, and many originally planned features and services (a kayak run and indoor swimming pool, for example) were rejected due to the construction delays. When both clubs were finally opened, similar services were offered, with the only distinguishing features being rooftop paddle tennis and tanning salons at Sports Club/Irvine and outdoor volleyball courts and a soccer field at the Sporting Club. In 1992, when the Sporting Club opened, it had secured an initial 2,200 members, falling short of the minimum of 3,800 members that were needed in order to break even.

Expansion and Public Offering in the Mid-1990s

The economic recession exacerbated the difficulties of the competing businesses, as did the general slowdown in the popularity boom of health clubs in the 1990s. While health club memberships in the U.S. grew 10 to 15 percent annually in the 1980s, growth slowed to 5 percent in the 1990s. Growth did continue, however, with 17 million Americans belonging to health clubs in 1992 versus 12 million in 1980, according to the *Los Angeles Times*. Nonetheless, by 1990, billionaire investor Marvin Davis wanted to sell his investment and cut his losses. Talla sought underwriting, but loans were difficult to procure in California.

Finally, in 1994, NetWest Securities and Oppenheimer & Co. were enlisted to help. The Sports Club Company went public—the first company involved in the development, acquisition and operation of sports clubs ever to do so. The chain of clubs had revenues of $38 million, with debt of $33.4 million. The underwriters sold 4.5 million shares at $9 per share, valuing the company at about $100 million. Marvin Davis was paid $26.5 million for his interests in the clubs, which were effectively consolidated under a single corporate parent.

In 1995, the company expanded eastward, opening its Reebok Sports Club/NY in Manhattan. The $55 million, 140,000 square foot club was launched in partnership with Reebok International. The New York facility was the most ambitious to date, offering fitness and recreation options including a 45 foot rock climbing wall, three floors of weight training and cardiovascular equipment, private trainers and exercise classes, a full day spa, a gourmet restaurant, an Olympic swimming pool with underwater music, and a Kid's club.

The recipe for success in California was not easily transferable to New York, however. While Reebok Sports Club/NY boasted the same state-of-the-art fitness equipment and fake granite rock climbing walls as its California cousins, the celebrity factor was missing. Meanwhile, back in California, membership in Sports Club/LA dropped 9 percent since 1994, when it was closed due to the Northridge earthquake. Membership cancellations and low new memberships caused earnings to drop, along with stock prices, which decreased 30 percent since the public offering, to $6 per share.

Acquisitions, Continued Expansion, and the Turn of the Century

The fitness industry, accepting the fact that the explosive growth of the 1980s had matured and stabilized in the 1990s, began to consolidate. Sports Club had made a number of acquisitions since going public in 1994, and by 1997 its ownership list totaled 10 clubs nationwide with 47,000 members. In 1997, Sports Club Company seriously considered the acquisition of Gold's Gym Enterprises, a 34-year-old company with over 500 franchises worldwide. After two months analyzing Gold's books, the company chose to reject the agreement to acquire the company. Immediately afterward, the company signed an agreement to purchase an 88,000 square foot building in Thousand Oaks for $6.8 million, where it would open a new Spectrum Club. In August, 1997, the company acquired a facility in Las Vegas, and in July it opened its first suburban Spectrum Club in Valencia, California. The company's expansion and acquisitions resulted in higher revenues of $61.2 million in 1997. The company's stock price climbed back to $9 during the year.

In 1998, The Sports Club Company owned and operated 15 clubs, with seven more under development. The company began to expand nationally more than had been the case in the past. Two new Manhattan clubs were in progress, including one in Rockefeller Center, along with sites in Boston, San Francisco, and Washington D.C. In a $17 million acquisition from Sequoia Athletic Company, the company purchased four Racquetball World clubs in Fullerton, Santa Ana, Canoga Park, and Fountain Valley, California. Financing of the deal was assisted by $10 million from an affiliate of Millennium Entertainment Partners L.P., and the remaining $6.5 million was procured through company stock sales ($5 million purchased by Millennium Entertainment partners). After a million dollars worth of enhancements and renovations, the acquisitions were slated to join the company's Spectrum Club Collection. An additional Spectrum Club was under development and scheduled to open in Thousand Oaks, California in 1998. All new Spectrum Clubs would feature basketball, volleyball, aerobics, weight training, private training, cardiovascular centers, childcare services, and sidewalk cafes.

As a pioneer of fitness developments, the company received a myriad of group exercise awards. The Sports Club was the first to offer coeducational exercise classes, private training, yoga, step classes, group cycling, low impact aerobics, and the Private Trainer System program. In the late 1990s, Arnold Schwarzenegger presented Michael Talla with the Lifetime Achievement Award from the Governor's Council on Physical Fitness in recognition of his leadership in the health club industry and his achievements on behalf of The Sports Club Company. Talla and Francini were flown to San Francisco in Schwarzenegger's private jet for the ceremony.

Talla and Francini rode the wave of the 1980s fitness craze, and had managed to stay on. The Sports Club Company was challenged by competition, the slowing popularity of the workout lifestyle, earthquakes, and differing cultural environments outside of California. Yet the company has still been able to build a niche for itself among the famous and the wealthy, grooming and maintaining healthy bodies in a luxury atmosphere. Its stock prices and earnings have been vulnerable to change, and its future success remains to be seen in its first decade as a public company.

Principal Operating Units

The Sports Club/LA; The Sports Club/Irvine; Reebok Sports Club/NY; The Sports Club/Las Vegas; Spectrum Club-Agora Hills; Spectrum Club-Canoga Park; Spectrum Club-Fountain Valley; Spectrum Club-Fullerton; Spectrum Club-Howard Hughes; Spectrum Club-Manhattan Beach; Spectrum Club-Puente Hills; Spectrum Club-Santa Ana; Spectrum Club-Santa Monica; Spectrum Club-Thousand Oaks; Spectrum Club-Valencia; Spectrum Club-Water Garden.

Further Reading

Christian, Susan, ''Irvine Health Clubs Facing Off for Battle of the Spas Developers,'' *Los Angeles Times*, July 20, 1992, p. A1.
Flagg, Michael, ''Delay-Plagued Health Club to Open December,'' *Los Angeles Times*, January 25, 1991, p. D5.
——, ''Sports Clubs Likely to Play Tug of War With New Customers,'' *Los Angeles Times*, May 11, 1990, p. D5.
——, ''Super Spas Used to Lure Office Tenants,'' *Los Angeles Times*, December 1, 1989, p. D1.

"Fountain Valley Fitness Center to be Acquired," *Los Angeles Times,* December 12, 1997, p. D6.

Gubernick, Lisa, "Sagging," *Forbes,* June 19, 1995, pp. 70.

Metcalfe, Coll, "Building to House Fitness Center," *Los Angeles Times,* October 24, 1997, p. B3.

Oldham, Jennifer, "Sports Club is Weighing Purchase of Gold's Gym," *Los Angeles Times,* September 17, 1997, p. D2.

The Sports Club Company, "Profile: The Sports Club Company," Los Angeles: The Sports Club Company, 1998.

The Sports Club Company, "The Sports Club Company Celebrates 20 Years of Peak Performance With an Eye on the Future of Fitness for the Millennium," Los Angeles: The Sports Club Company, 1998.

"Sports Club Ends Deal to Buy Gold's Gym," *Los Angeles Times,* October 23, 1997, p. D2.

Tighe, John Charles, "Healthy Rivalry for Planned Chic Spas," *Los Angeles Times,* July 9, 1988, pp. 4–5.

—Heidi Feldman

Station Casinos Inc.

2411 West Sahara Avenue
Las Vegas, Nevada 89102
U.S.A.
(702) 367-2411
Fax: (702) 221-6521
(800) 544-2411
Web site: http://www.stationcasinos.com

Public Company
Incorporated: 1976
Employees: 10,000
Sales: $583.5 million (1997)
Stock Exchanges: New York
Ticker Symbol: STN
SICs: 7993 Coin-Operated Amusement Devices; 7999
   Amusement & Recreation, Not Elsewhere Classified;
   5812 Eating Places; 7011 Hotels & Motels

Station Casinos Inc. is a Las Vegas, Nevada-based, multi-jurisdictional gaming company which owns and/or operates numerous hotel and casino properties throughout the United States. In Las Vegas, the company's facilities include The Palace Station Hotel & Casino, The Boulder Station Hotel & Casino, The Texas Station Gambling Hall & Hotel, and The Wild Wild West Gambling Hall & Hotel. Catering primarily to the locals, most of the company's facilities in Las Vegas are located on the Strip. The company also provides slot machine route management services to numerous food and beverage establishments, commercial businesses, and major hotels and casinos, primarily in southern Nevada, as well as throughout the United States. The company also owns and operates Station Casino St. Charles, a gaming and entertainment riverboat facility in St. Charles, Missouri; Station Casino Kansas City, a gaming and entertainment facility in Kansas City, Missouri; and The Sunset Station Hotel & Casino in Henderson, Nevada, a suburb of Las Vegas. The company additionally owns Southwest Companies Inc. and 50 percent of Barley's Casino & Brewing Company (the other 50 percent is owned by Greenspun Inc.), which operates a microbrewery in the Henderson/Green Valley area of Las Vegas. The company has established itself with a proven track record of growth and profitability in the most competitive gaming environment in the world.

Let the Games Begin, 1976

Incorporated in Las Vegas, Nevada, in 1976, the company had as its first facility and foundation The Casino (now known as The Palace Station Hotel & Casino), which opened initially as a 5,000-square-foot facility with 100 slot machines, six table games (four of them Blackjack), a small bar, and a buffet next door to The Mini-Price Motel. Through incremental additions and significant expansion projects, The Palace Station, located at the intersection of Interstate 15 and Sahara Avenue, grew. The first addition came in July 1977 when a Bingo parlor was added, bringing 15,000 more square feet of space, including an 8,000-square-foot Bingo room, 300 more slot machines, an enlarged buffet, a Keno game, and the property's first full-service restaurant. The facility became The Casino and Bingo Palace.

By April 1978, the facility had tripled in size to 60,000 square feet, including more casino space, a new restaurant and buffet, another new Bingo room, and a sports facility. In 1979, Frank J. Fertitta, Jr., one of the original founders, bought out his three partners, becoming the sole owner. In 1981, a new Bingo room was built, and the facility was a full-scale casino. The name was changed to The Palace Station in 1983.

In April 1984, the property tripled in size again, adding more casino space, along with upgrades of the restaurant and buffet and the addition of banquet/meeting rooms on a second floor. Concurrently, Frank J. Fertitta III joined the company as a vice-president and director. In November 1985, the company bought The Mini-Price Hotel.

The years following brought tremendous growth and development for the facility and, by 1998, it featured 39 acres; a 1,028-room hotel; 3,700 parking spaces; an 84,000-square-foot casino; five full-service restaurants (including the 24-hour Iron Horse Cafe, featuring a Chinese menu in addition to American fare; the all-you-can-eat The Feast Gourmet Buffet; The Broiler, a steak and seafood restaurant; The Pasta Palace, an Italian restaurant; and The Guadalajara Bar & Grille, a Mexican restaurant); several fast-food outlets; a 20,000-square-foot banquet and convention center; two swimming pools; a gift shop; a non-gaming video arcade; over 2,200 slot and video poker machines; 55 gaming tables; two Keno lounges; a Bingo parlor; a poker parlor; a race and sports facility; and over 100,000 square feet of public space.

Explosive Growth in the 1990s

In May 1994, the company introduced riverboat and dockside gaming in Missouri with the opening of its Station Casino St. Charles, located on 52 acres at Interstate 70 and the Missouri River in the city of St. Charles, approximately seven miles from the St. Louis airport. The facility would quickly become the number one tourist attraction in the region. The three-deck, 387-foot riverboat and dockside facility, with over 170,000 cars passing it daily, included all the newest, exciting games, fine dining, and live entertainment, and could handle 2,000 passengers at a time. Including a 150-seat bar and lounge, fast-food outlets, a lobby and ticketing facility, and a gift shop, it was the first dockside gaming facility in Missouri to offer two casinos with fluctuating odd/even hours so that customers would not have to wait to board, revolutionizing gaming in the state and leading to duplication by other Missouri gaming operators. The facility additionally introduced a number of new games to its customers, as well as featured its standard creations such as Reversible Royals Video Poker, Million-Coin Video Poker, and the state's first Red, White and Blue Progressive Slot Machine Game.

Several months later, in August, the company opened The Boulder Station Hotel & Casino at the intersections of Interstate 515 and Boulder Highway in Nevada. The facility featured 337,000 square feet of main facility area in a low-rise complex; a 15-story hotel tower; 4,350 parking spaces; an 83,000-square-foot casino; 300 hotel rooms; five full-service restaurants with a total of over 1,400 seats (including The Iron Horse Cafe; The Feast Gourmet Buffet; The Broiler; The Pasta Palace, with an adjacent 24-seat pizza bar; and The Guadalajara Bar & Grille); a number of quick-service food outlets; a 280-seat entertainment lounge; eight additional bars; a swimming pool; a non-gaming video arcade; a gift shop; over 3,000 slot and video poker machines; 54 table games; a Keno lounge; a poker room; and a race and sports facility. Total revenue for 1994 climbed to $169.5 million, with net income of $9.4 million.

In July 1995, the company opened The Texas Station Gambling Hall & Hotel at the corner of Lake Mead Boulevard and Tonopah Highway in North Las Vegas. Offering a fully integrated, ''down-home'' Texas atmosphere throughout, the property is located on 47 acres, featuring over 198,000 square feet of public space, with 67,800 square feet of casino space; 200 hotel rooms; five full-service restaurants with over 1,400 seats (including the 24-hour Yellow Rose Cafe coffee shop; The Stockyard Steakhouse; The Laredo Cantina and Cafe Mexican restaurant; The San Lorenzo Italian restaurant; and The Feast Around the World Buffet, featuring authentic Texas-style barbecue); three bars (including The Whiskey Bar, with its seven-foot-high bronco rider which rotates on a pedestal; The Garage Bar, with its 1976 fire-engine-red Cadillac Eldorado featuring seven-foot Texas Longhorns on the hood; and The Armadillo, with its 3,000-piece cut-glass armadillo in the dance hall); several quick-food outlets; 1,840 slot and video poker machines; 35 table games; a 165-seat race and sports facility; parking for 3,000 vehicles; and a 12-screen movie complex, which opened in August, operated by Portland, Oregon-based Act III Theatres.

In November of that year, the company added to its Boulder Station facility Boulder Cinemas, an 11-theater movie complex operated by Act III, and a ''Kids Quest'' child care center, the first such facility in a gaming entertainment complex in Las Vegas, and planned a 500-room expansion of its hotel facilities in 1999. Total revenue for 1995 jumped to $290.3 million, with a net loss of $7.9 million.

In 1996, the company introduced two of its most successful Las Vegas dining concepts, The Feast ''Action'' Buffet and The Broiler Steak and Seafood Restaurant, into the Midwest at the Station St. Charles facility. The Feast, which copied the Japanese restaurant style of having food prepared right before the customers, was the largest buffet dining room in the St. Louis area with over 800 seats. Business was so successful that only three months after it opened the restaurant was expanded with an additional 140 seats. Like its Las Vegas and Kansas City counterparts, the Station St. Charles restaurant offered breakfast, lunch, and dinner, ranging in price from $3.95–$9.95, seven days a week, featuring Mexican, Chinese, Italian, barbecue, and American fare. The Broiler's gourmet dining selections quickly earned it many five-star reviews from the *St. Louis Post-Dispatch,* the *St. Louis Business Journal,* and the *Riverfront Times,* the region's leading daily and weekly newspapers. Following traditional menu guidelines beta-tested in Las Vegas at Palace Station and Boulder Station, broiler chefs at the Station St. Charles developed fare consisting of steak, seafood, and veal specialties which were soon major hits in the Midwest, complete with a gourmet wine list.

In May, the company opened a 10,000-square-foot Bingo parlor on the south side of The Texas Station complex, with space for 85 additional slot and video poker machines, and a snack bar. The following month, the company expanded its buffet into space previously used by The Galveston Bay Seafood Co. restaurant, renaming the facility The Feast. Total revenue for 1996 jumped again, this time to $466.9 million, with a net income of $25.5 million.

The company started off 1997 by opening The Station Casino Kansas City. It would become one of the nation's largest casinos and Missouri's largest gaming and entertainment complex. The facility featured 730,000 square feet of gaming and entertainment space, with twin, 70,000-square-foot floating casinos that held 3,000 slot machines and 190 gaming tables; a 200-room hotel; six full-service restaurants; six quick-serve and specialty restaurants; 11 bars and lounges; the 1,400-seat, state-of-the-art Grand Pavilion; parking for 5,000 vehicles; a "Kids Quest" child care facility; The Phoenix Piano Bar & Grill; and Arthur Bryant's Barbecue.

In June 1997, the company opened The Sunset Station Hotel & Casino in the Henderson/Grass Valley area, near Las Vegas, the first full-service gaming and entertainment facility in that area, one of the fastest-growing communities in the country. The facility featured a Spanish/Mediterranean theme, with 350,000 square feet of entertainment space, including an 80,000-square-foot casino; a 20-story hotel with 450 rooms; a 13-screen Act III movie theater complex; 12 world-class, full-service restaurants; over 2,700 slot and video machines; 41 table games; a poker parlor; a Keno lounge; a race and sports facility; and over 5,000 parking spaces all located on 100 acres at the intersection of Interstate 515 and Sunset Road.

In October 1997, the Station St. Charles introduced Silicon Gaming Inc.'s new Odyssey Interactive Slot Machine game, featuring five games in one machine, an exclusive in the state of Missouri and in the St. Louis market until the fall of 1998. Total revenue for 1997 soared to $583.5 million, with a net income of $13.8 million.

In January 1998, Crescent Real Estate Equities Company announced its plans to merge with Station Casinos Inc. in a stock swap and debt assumption transaction valued at a total of approximately $1.7 billion, which would give the former a total market capitalization of nearly $8.5 billion. Crescent Real Estate was a fully integrated real estate company owning, through its various subsidiaries, a portfolio of real estate assets consisting of 88 office and seven retail properties totaling 32 million square feet; a 38 percent interest in 94 refrigerated warehouse facilities; 89 behavioral healthcare facilities; six hotel and casino properties; seven full-service hotels totaling 2,276 rooms; two destination health and fitness resorts; and economic interests in five residential development corporations, all in 21 metropolitan submarkets in the states of Texas and Colorado.

Crescent Real Estate also announced plans to contribute substantially all of the real estate assets it would acquire from Station Casinos to a new Casino Partnership, owned initially in full by Crescent Real Estate, which would invest primarily in casinos, other gaming properties, and other real estate properties in the Las Vegas area. The hotel and casino properties were leased to an operating company, with the profits being shared equally by Crescent Operating Inc. and Station Casino's management team. Frank J. Fertitta III, president and CEO, and the over 10,000 employees of Station Casino continued to operate the properties as the tenants.

In April, expansion began at the company's Sunset Station facility. The $45 million master-plan expansion featured 11 new movie screens with THX sound and stadium-style seating to complement the existing 13-screen multiplex movie theaters operated by Act III, which resulted in the largest movie theater complex to date in the Las Vegas area; a 2,000-space covered parking garage adjacent to the theater; a 20,000-square-foot expansion of the casino; The Wayne Gretzky Roller Hockey Center and Ice Skating Arena, a dual-rink, state-of-the-art complex featuring in-line roller hockey and ice skating surfaces for a wide range of league activities, public skating, clinics, instruc-

tion, and other events; a steakhouse restaurant; a food court area; and expanded and improved conference facilities.

Phase II expansion on The Texas Station Gambling Hall & Hotel began in May of that year. The $51 million project, designed to enhance Texas Station's reputation for quality entertainment, included six additional movie screens with THX sound and stadium-style seating being added to the existing 12-screen multiplex movie theater operated by Act III; a 2,000-space covered parking garage adjacent to a new theater entrance, designed to provide maximum convenience for customers and featuring a valet; a 10,000-square-foot "Kids Quest" child care facility; a new bar and lounge similar in nature to the popular Gaudi Bar at Sunset Station, only featuring a Texas motif; a food court with several brand-name tenants; an expanded arcade; and a 21,000-square-foot expansion of the casino.

In July of that year, the company announced that it had received approval from The Nevada Gaming Control Board to lease and operate a property known as The King 8 Hotel & Gambling Hall, located on Tropicana Avenue and Industrial Road, just west of Interstate 15 in Las Vegas. Following a five-day closing from July 1–5, the property was reopened on July 6 and renamed The Wild Wild West Gambling Hall & Hotel. Also in July, the company announced that the proposed merger with Crescent Real Estate had been stalled but was still pending.

As Las Vegas continued to thrive as one of the fastest-growing communities in the United States, with the population expected to double over the course of nine years, the new ownership and management of Station Casino planned to move forward confidently into the 21st century.

Principal Subsidiaries

Barley's Casino & Brewing Company (50%); Boulder Station Hotel & Casino; Palace Station Hotel & Casino; Southwest Companies Inc.; Station Casino Kansas City; Station Casino St. Charles; Sunset Station Hotel & Casino; Texas Station Gambling Hall & Hotel.

Further Reading

"Bet on Barley's," *Beverage World*, February 1996, p. 18.
"Gamblers Spend Record Amount in January at Kansas City, Mo., Area Casinos," *Knight-Ridder/Tribune Business News*, February 26, 1998, p. 226B1166.
Goldblatt, Jennifer, "BankAmerica's Chief of Junk Trading Leaves: Unit Had Stumbled in $150 Million Debut Offering As Lead Manager," *American Banker*, April 28, 1997, p. 27.
Margolies, Dan, "Lots of People Drop Little Money," *Kansas City Business Journal*, March 28, 1997, p. 1.
O'Regan, Rob, "Station Casinos Hits Jackpot with OLAP System," *PC Week*, December 11, 1995, p. 49.
"Restructuring by Station Casino Kansas City Pleases Stockholders," *Knight-Ridder/Tribune Business News*, February 22, 1998, p. A20318641.
Sharav, Ben, et al, "Hotel/Gaming Industry," *Value Line Investment Survey (Part 3—Ratings & Reports)*, May 29, 1998, p. 1802.
"Station Casinos Inc.," *Wall Street Journal*, April 30, 1998, p. A9.
"Station Casinos Reports 36 Percent Increase in Cash Flow for First Quarter," *PR Newswire*, July 23, 1998, p. 723LATH056.

—Daryl F. Mallett

Sun Healthcare Group Inc.

101 Sun Avenue NE
Albuquerque, New Mexico 87109
U.S.A.
(505) 821-3355
Fax: (888) FAX-SUNH (329-7864)
Web site: http://www.sunh.com

Public Company
Incorporated: 1989 as Sunrise Healthcare Corp.
Employees: 68,900
Sales: $2.01 billion (1997)
Stock Exchanges: New York
Ticker Symbol: SHG
SICs: 2834 Pharmaceutical Preparations; 5122 Drugs,
Proprietaries & Sundries; 8049 Offices of Health
Practitioners, Not Elsewhere Classified; 8051 Skilled
Nursing Care Facilities; 8059 Nursing & Personal
Care, Not Elsewhere Classified; 8062 General
Medical & Surgical Hospitals; 8069 Specialty
Hospitals, Except Psychiatric; 8093 Specialty
Outpatient Clinics, Not Elsewhere Classified; 8099
Health & Allied Services, Not Elsewhere Classified;
8361 Residential Care

Headquartered in Albuquerque, New Mexico, Sun Healthcare Group Inc. is a fast-growing, diversified care provider which operates companies with long-term, subacute nursing care, postacute nursing care, and ancillary healthcare services facilities in the United States, the United Kingdom, Spain, Germany, and Australia; Sun Healthcare also has subsidiaries which provide therapy and pharmacy services, and fulfill the medical supply needs of nursing homes.

In less than a decade, Sun has grown to become one of the largest nursing home operators in the United States, with its dramatic growth built on providing quality healthcare services to nursing homes, including rehabilitation therapy (through its SunDance subsidiary), respiratory therapy (through its SunCare subsidiary), pharmaceutical services (through its SunScript subsidiary), medical supplies (through its SunChoice subsidiary), and other healthcare services for the long-term care industry. Sun companies also provide home healthcare services and hospice care.

The Inpatient Services Division consists of several groups. The company's SunRise Healthcare Corporation consists of skilled nursing and long-term residential care; postacute medical care for patients with complex medical conditions or who are recovering from accidents, strokes, or other debilitating conditions; specialized care for patients with Alzheimer's disease and other types of dementia; and 321 facilities with more than 36,000 beds in the United States. Sun Healthcare Group International Ltd. contains the second largest nursing home operator in the United Kingdom (in Ashbourne PLC) with 133 facilities with more than 8,000 beds throughout England, Scotland, Wales, and Northern Ireland; a majority interest in Germany's Heim-Plan Unternehmensgruppe, with 11 facilities and more than 900 beds; a majority interest in Spain's Eurosar S.A., with eight facilities and more than 1,300 beds; and interests in Alpha Healthcare Ltd., which operates 10 acute care facilities, and a majority interest in six acute care facilities operated by Moran Health Care Group Ltd., both in Australia. The SunBridge Assisted Living group consists of upscale residences for older adults who need help to remain independent, offering luxury living combined with quality healthcare, with residences operating in Denver, Colorado; Roswell, Georgia; Tucson and Sun City, Arizona; Las Vegas, Nevada; and San Jose, California.

The Rehabilitation Services Division consists of several groups. The SunDance Rehabilitation Corporation provides contract physical, occupational, and speech therapy and has more than 8,000 therapists serving more than 1,100 facilities in 45 states. CareerStaff Unlimited Inc. is the nation's largest temporary therapy staffing service. SunCare Respiratory Services Inc. provides certified hospital-based respiratory therapy services, with more than 2,000 therapists serving more than 700 facilities nationwide, as well as respiratory supplies, medical gases, and complex medical equipment. SunAlliance Healthcare Services provides mobile radiology, laboratory and physician services, and hospice care.

Company Perspectives:

Mission: To become the nation's premier and most innovative provider of contract rehabilitation services, leaders in clinical excellence and program development, and the company for whom therapists want to work.

The Pharmaceutical Services Division's SunScript Pharmacy Corporation provides institutional pharmacy services to more than 800 facilities. SunChoice Medical Supply Inc. provides medical supplies and inventory management to nursing homes. SunScript/SunChoice U.K. provides retail and institutional pharmacy services in England, Wales, and Scotland, and contains 19 pharmacies. SunFactors Inc. is a national provider of chronic disease state pharmaceutical care. SunPlus Home Health Services provides skilled nursing, therapy, social services, and housekeeping support for patients in their homes and is Medicare certified.

Andy Turner, 1974–89

In 1974, Andy Turner, a graduate of Ohio State University in business administration, began his career in the health services industry when the pastor of his church asked him to take over the management of the church's nursing home in Springfield, Ohio. Turner became the administrator of the 150-bed skilled nursing facility and remained for five years. Turner went from there to become manager of a regional nursing home chain, and then on to Tacoma, Washington-based Hillhaven Corporation, then a subsidiary of and later spun off from National Medical Enterprises (NME) in January 1990, where he became senior vice-president of operations.

In 1986, Turner and two partners, one of whom was Neal Elliott, president of Hillhaven, left to form Horizon Healthcare Corporation in Washington, before moving the company's headquarters to Albuquerque, New Mexico. Turner served as Horizon's chief operating officer.

In 1989, Turner purchased seven unprofitable nursing homes in Washington and Connecticut from Horizon and left the corporation to form his own company, Sunrise Healthcare Corp., leaving Elliott in charge of Horizon, and eventually becoming Sun's chairman and CEO. Turner managed to slow the fledgling corporation's fiscal losses in the first year and, by the second, Sun was showing a profit, eventually growing into what it is today. Horizon and Sun continued their friendly rivalry with each other to this day.

When the company started in 1989, it was just an average nursing home company, but gradually grew and became a little more specialized, focusing on taking sicker, or heavier acuity patients, people who might otherwise be receiving inpatient services in hospitals. By 1992, total revenues had reached $135.7 million, with net income of $4.4 million.

The following year, the company began trading on the New York Stock Exchange under the symbol "SHG," and total revenue for 1993 climbed to $230.8 million, with net income of $13.5 million.

Mediplex Group Inc., 1994

In 1994, the company merged with Massachusetts-based Mediplex Group Inc., a well-known provider of skilled nursing, rehabilitative, psychiatric, and substance abuse treatment services located primarily in the northeastern United States, which moved Sun above Public Service Co. of New Mexico as the state's largest publicly traded company and transformed Sun into the sixth largest provider of subacute services in the nation.

Mediplex was founded in the 1970s as an operator of nursing home centers by Abraham D. Gosman. The company completed its initial public offering in October 1983, and built a network of subacute facilities in two specialized divisions, Skilled Nursing/Rehabilitation Services and Psychiatric Services/Substance Abuse Treatment. In 1985, Mediplex formed a real estate investment trust called Meditrust to sell and lease back facilities to save money. Mediplex was sold to Avon Products Inc. in April 1986 for approximately $265 million.

In the late 1980s, Avon abandoned its efforts to build a healthcare franchise, selling the company back to previous management for $40 million in August 1990 Diamond Health Care Acquisition Corp., a group formed by Gosman and several former members of Mediplex's management, repurchased the company from Avon and began to restructure operations. In 1991, bad press for the two leading publicly held psychiatric hospital companies, NME and Community Psychiatric Centers, brought the entire psychiatric industry down, but, in August of that year, Mediplex managed to raise $38 million from a second public offering.

In 1992, the company built a 150-bed project in Mahwah, New Jersey; a 120-bed facility at Milford, Connecticut; and an 80-bed rehabilitation facility (Mediplex Rehabilitation of Bristol) in New Bedford, Massachusetts; as well as adding 90 beds to its Wethersfield, Connecticut facility and closing its Mountain Wood, Virginia and Spofford Hall, New Hampshire facilities. Mediplex entered the ambulatory surgical business in November of that year with the acquisition of Medical Management and Development Corporation's seven freestanding ambulatory surgery centers in Connecticut and Massachusetts, with 22 operating suites, performing over 20,000 procedures annually, ranging from ophthalmology; gynecology; orthopedic; and ear, nose, and throat.

Total revenue for Sun Healthcare in 1994 jumped to $673.4 million, with net income of $19.5 million, and the company had increased its revenues 66 percent annually since its inception.

More Consolidations in the Industry, 1995–97

In 1995, Horizon attempted to purchase Hillhaven, but it was instead acquired by Louisville, Kentucky-based Vencor Inc., a long-term acute care company, one-fourth the size of Hillhaven.

By June, the top ten long-term care providers by operating revenue were: 1) Beverly Enterprises Inc. ($3.0 billion); 2) Horizon/CMS Healthcare ($1.8 billion); 3) Vencor/Hillhaven

($1.7 billion); 4) Integrated Health Services ($1.1 billion); 6) Manor HealthCare Corp. ($1.02 billion); 7) Living Centers of America ($894 million); 8) GranCare Inc. ($774 million); 9) United Health Inc. ($728 million); and 10) Life Care Centers of America ($725 million). Total revenue for Sun Healthcare in 1995 soared to $1.1 billion, with a net loss of $24 million, catapulting the company to number six on the list.

By 1996, the company's corporate headquarters grew several more buildings, including the 12,000 square foot Glaesner Training Center, featuring state-of-the-art communications and teleconferencing facilities to enable Sun Healthcare to train and communicate with its employees worldwide.

In February of that year, Horizon acquired Medical Innovations Inc. of Houston, a $70 million company with home healthcare services in Texas, Nevada, Virginia, and Florida. Also in 1996, Horizon acquired Pennsylvania-based Continental Medical Systems (CMS), the largest single provider of rehabilitation therapy services in the country, which more than doubled Horizon's size, and the newly created Horizon/CMS Healthcare Corp. took away the "largest publicly traded" laurel from Sun.

By this time, though, smaller operators were finding it hard to compete with giants like Sun and Horizon because of the increasing complexity of medical services; growing regulatory and compliance requirements; increasingly complicated reimbursement systems; and a lack of sophisticated management information systems, operating efficiencies, and financial resources to keep them going when Medicare or Medicaid reimbursements were either delayed or curtailed. The strategy from 1996 on was growth and expansion through mergers and acquisitions, as well as diversification. Total revenue for the company in 1996 reached $1.3 billion, with a net income of $21.5 million.

In 1997, the company acquired a 38 percent interest in Alpha Healthcare Ltd. and a majority of six hospitals of Moran Health Care Group Pty Ltd., both in Australia.

Regency Health Services Inc., 1997

In August 1997, the long-term care industry further consolidated as Living Centers of America and GranCare merged, and Sun Healthcare acquired Regency Health Services Inc. in a $369 million transaction. Regency, the Tustin, California-based skilled nursing facility operator and provider of related specialty healthcare services (including rehabilitation therapy, pharmacy, and home health services) had annual sales in 1996 of $558 million, and brought some 16,170 employees under Sun Healthcare's umbrella.

1998 and Beyond

In January 1998, Medicare patients were given new choices in their care programs under The Balanced Budget Act of 1997, which has the aim of moving more elderly into managed care.

In March, Sun Healthcare continued its global expansion, acquiring Procedo Stocker GmbH, a privately held German supplier of electronic forms, organizational systems, and medical and surgical devices to nursing homes and hospitals, for $2.8 million. The Allerhausen-based company serviced approxi-

mately 2,000 nursing homes and 1,000 hospitals in Germany, as well as facilities in Holland and Austria. That month, the company also created Australian divisions of its SunScript and SunChoice subsidiaries, based in Sydney, to provide pharmacy services and medical supplies to both affiliated and nonaffiliated long-term care facilities and hospitals in Australia.

In July, the company acquired Retirement Care Associates Inc. (RCA), an operator of skilled nursing facilities and assisted living centers in seven states in the southeastern United States, in a $320.6 million transaction of stock and waivers. With the acquisition, the company also picked up Tampa Bay, Florida-based Contour Medical Inc., a national provider of medical and surgical supplies for the long-term care industry and specialty products for hospitals, of which RCA owned approximately 65 percent.

As healthcare companies continued to consolidate, many analysts speculated on the potential merger of Sun and Horizon/CMS, since Neal Elliott and Andrew Turner had worked together once before. Although both companies have demurred, saying that anti-trust laws would limit complete consolidation of the industry, it would be interesting to watch both as they continued to dominate different regions of the country.

Principal Subsidiaries

Inpatient Services Division; Sun Healthcare Group International Ltd.; Alpha Healthcare Ltd. (Australia); Ashbourne PLC (U.K.); Eurosar S.A. (Spain); Heim-Plan Unternehmensgruppe (Germany); Moran Health Care Group Ltd. (Australia); SunBridge Assisted Living; SunRise Healthcare Corporation; Mediplex Group Inc.; Medical Management and Development Corporation; Regency Health Services Inc.; Brittany Rehabilitation Center Inc.; Hallmark Health Services Inc.; Harbor View Group Home Inc.; Americare Development Corp.; Americare HomeCare Inc.; Americare HomeCare of West Virginia; Americare Midwest Inc.; Americare Nursing Center Inc.; Americare of West Virginia Inc.; Assist-A-Care Inc.; Braswell Enterprises Inc.; Brel Inc.; Care Development Corp.; Care Enterprises Inc.; Care West-Sierra Co.; Care Finance Inc.; Care Home Health Services Inc.; Circleville Health Care Corp.; Executive Pharmacy; First Class Pharmacy Inc.; Glenville Health Care Inc.; New Lexington Health Care Corp.; Hampshire Insurance Company Limited; HealthCare Network; Jackson Rehabilitation Center Inc.; Lancaster Health Care Corp.; Marion Health Care Corp.; Monroe Park Center Inc.; Pomeroy Health Care Corp.; Putnam Health Care Corp.; Regency High School Inc.; RHS Management Corporation; Rittman Health Care Corp.; Rosewood Rehabilitation Center Inc.; Salem Health Care Corp.; Stockton Rehabilitation Center Inc.; Sunset Villa Corp.; Vista Knoll Rehabilitation Center Inc.; CareerStaff Unlimited Inc.; SunAlliance Healthcare Services; SunCare Respiratory Services Inc.; SunDance Rehabilitation Corporation; SunChoice Medical Supply Inc.; SunFactors Inc.; SunPlus Home Health Services; SunScript Pharmacy Corporation; SunScript/SunChoice U.K.; SunQuest Consulting Services; SunSolution Inc.

Further Reading

"Andy Turner Wants the Government Out of Health Care," *New Mexico Business Journal*, April 1996, p. 10.

Feenan, Gerard, et al, "Medical Services Industry," *Value Line Investment Survey (Part 3—Ratings & Reports)*, July 3, 1998, p. 646.

"Fourth-Quarter Loss Grew, Including One-Time Item," *Wall Street Journal*, February 27, 1998, p. B4(W)/B4(E).

Greene, Jay, "Regency Buys and Sells Nursing Homes, Seeks Less California Business," *Knight-Ridder/Tribune Business News*, January 17, 1996, p. 1170107.

——, "Regency Health Services Acquires Facilities," *Knight-Ridder/Tribune Business News*, November 29, 1996.

——, "Regency Health Services Founder, Shareholder Unload Shares," *Knight-Ridder/Tribune Business News*, April 13, 1995, p. 4130205.

Huntley, Helen, "Change Is Fast-Paced for Tampa Bay, Florida, Area Public Companies," *Knight-Ridder/Tribune Business News*, May 27, 1997, p. 527B0902.

"Justice Department Stops Probe of Billing Practices," *Wall Street Journal*, July 14, 1998, p. A10(W)/B4(E).

Marcial, Gene G., "A Good Prognosis at Sun Healthcare," *Business Week*, May 30, 1994, p. 120.

——, "Making Hay from Insider Selling?" *Business Week*, July 14, 1997, p. 57.

Markey, Keith A., et al, "Medical Services Industry," *Value Line Investment Survey (Part 3—Ratings & Reports)*, April 3, 1998, p. 649.

Martinson, Jane, "Ashbourne Recommends 95m Pounds Sterling U.S. Bid," *Financial Times*, December 5, 1996, p. 30.

"McKesson Unit Renews Contract," *Wall Street Journal*, April 24, 1998, p. B6(W)/B10(E).

Misra, Prashanta, "Sun Healthcare Rises with Savvy Acquisitions," *Money*, January 1995, p. 68.

"Net Rises 8.9% As Growth in U.S. Operations Is Strong," *Wall Street Journal*, July 31, 1997, p. B4(W)/B4(E).

Odenwald, Arlene, "See Sun. See Horizon. Watch Them Grow. And Grow," *New Mexico Business Journal*, April 1996, p. 15.

Perez, Rob, "Nursing Homes Are No Longer the Last Stop for Patients," *Knight-Ridder/Tribune Business News*, July 27, 1993, p. 07270160.

"Regency Health Sells 24 Nursing Homes and 2 Hospitals," *New York Times*, October 9, 1997, p. C4(N)/D4(L).

"Regency Health Services," *CDA-Investnet Insiders' Chronicle*, September 5, 1994, p. 8.

Shriver, Kelly, "Sun, Union Trade Punches in Conn.," *Modern Healthcare*, October 2, 1995, p. 50.

Snow, Charlotte, "Long-Term Care Jockeying: Sun Healthcare to Buy Regency; Exec Named to Lead Merger of Grancare, Living Centers," *Modern Healthcare*, August 4, 1997, p. 17.

"Sun Healthcare Agrees to Buy Regency in $369 Million Deal," *New York Times*, July 28, 1997, p. D4(L).

"Sun Healthcare Australian Deal," *Wall Street Journal*, November 7, 1997, p. C14(E).

"Sun Healthcare Buys Company," *Wall Street Journal*, October 9, 1997, p. A8(W).

"Sun Healthcare Cuts Offer for Acquisition," *New York Times*, August 23, 1997, p. 25(N)/37(L).

"Sun Healthcare Group and Retirement Care Associates Extend Termination Date of Merger Agreement," *PR Newswire*, April 6, 1998, p. 406LAM087.

"Sun Healthcare Group Completes Acquisition of Retirement Care Associates and Contour Medical," *PR Newswire*, July 1, 1998, p. 701LAW025.

"Sun Healthcare Group, Inc. Acquires German Ancillary Service Provider; Sun Also Forms Australian Pharmacy and Medical Supply Divisions," *PR Newswire*, May 5, 1998, p. 505LATU092.

"Sun Healthcare Group Prices Two Private Placements of Securities," *PR Newswire*, April 29, 1998, p. 429LAW100.

"Sun Healthcare Makes Purchase," *Wall Street Journal*, October 1, 1997, p. A12(W)/B19(E).

"Sun Healthcare Revises Its Offer for Retirement Care," *New York Times*, November 27, 1997, p. C3(N)/D3(L).

"Sun Healthcare Stake in Alpha," *Wall Street Journal*, June 5, 1997, p. A12(W).

"Sun Healthcare to Sell Clinics and Therapy Business," *New York Times*, May 2, 1997, p. C3(N)/D3(L).

"Terms Are to Be Amended in Pact to Acquire Retirement Care," *Wall Street Journal*, May 30, 1997, p. B4(W)/C16(E).

Tomsho, Robert, "Sun Healthcare Cuts Bid for Chain of Nursing Homes," *Wall Street Journal*, August 25, 1997, p. B3(W)/B2(E).

——, "Sun Healthcare Group Faces Growing Scrutiny from U.S.," *Wall Street Journal, Europe*, October 17, 1995, p. 6.

——, "Sun Healthcare to Buy Regency for $369 Million," *Wall Street Journal*, July 28, 1997, p. A8(W). !1L

—Daryl F. Mallett

TAG Heuer International SA

14 a, Avenue des Champs-Montants
2074 Marin
Switzerland
(41-32) 755-6356
Fax: (41-32) 755-6115

Public Company
Incorporated: 1985 as Heuer Watchmaking Company
Employees: 350 (1994)
Sales: $324.5 million (1997)
Stock Exchanges: Swiss Exchange NYSE
Ticker Symbols: TAGN; THW
SICs: 3873 Watches, Clocks, Watchcases & Parts; 5094
  Jewelry & Precious Stones

TAG Heuer International SA (Heuer), through its wholly owned Swiss subsidiary, TAG Heuer S.A., is a leading designer, producer, and marketer of Swiss sports watches and chronographs (instruments for recording time with extreme accuracy). The company is distinguished as the fifth largest Swiss watch brand and the third largest manufacturer of Swiss chronometers. Since the early 1900s the TAG Heuer brand has been closely associated with the world of competitive sports, providing official timing services for major international sporting events, including automobile racing and ski competitions. Heuer watches are positioned as affordable premium accessories, adapted to today's active casual lifestyles, and are distributed through its subsidiaries in most key markets worldwide. The products are sold in more than 100 countries by 7,000 selected retailers. In 1997 Heuer sold approximately 700,000 watches.

The Paris Exhibition of 1889

The first TAG Heuer workshop was founded by Edouard Heuer in 1860 in the small St.-Imier town high in the Swiss Jura mountains. While his competitors at that time concentrated on the production of luxury pocket watches, Heuer began by making a name for himself in timing devices for sports. In 1869 he patented his first stem-winding system. Heuer displayed his wares at the 1889 Paris Exhibition—an event that unveiled the Eiffel Tower as its main exhibit, heralding the advent of modern society—and won a silver medal for his pocket chronographs. In 1908 Heuer invented and patented the Pulso-meter dial division, still in use for medical applications, and introduced the first dashboard timer for automobiles with a journey-time indicator. Then, in 1916, Heuer laid the basis for a new and modern dimension to sport with his invention of the high precision 'Micrograph,' capable of measuring time to an accuracy of 1/100th of a second. The introduction of a precise timing device was considered a turning point that marked the beginning of modern sport since athletes no longer competed against one another, but against their own time records.

Heuer chronographs were used at all three Olympic Games in the 1920s. By 1930 Heuer developed its first water-resistant case, followed by a new period of emphasis on the development of the wristwatch. Continuing in its efforts toward innovative uses for timing devices, in 1949 the company patented its invention of the Mareograph chronograph, the first watch fabricated for the purpose of measuring ocean tides.

The 1960s–70s: Timekeeping in the World of Motor Sports

In the 1960s the company developed the 'Carrera,' a stylish chronograph sporting a high-legibility dial, named after a world-renowned motor race of the 1950s, and the 'Monaco,' which featured an automatic winding mechanism. Heuer's other introductions during this time included the patented 'Microsplit,' the first solid-state pocket-timer with a digital readout; the first miniaturized, electronic sports timer with readings down to 1/100th of a second; and a new Microsplit timer with LCD (liquid-crystal display) readout. Actor Steve McQueen wore the 'Monaco' throughout the filming of *Le Mans,* reflecting the growing association between Heuer products and the motor sport industry. The company's prominence was evidenced by its performance as Official Timekeeper for the Scuderia Ferrari in training and races. As Official Timekeeper, the company was responsible for providing times and details such as information about top speeds, split times, and fastest laps. In 1970 Heuer equipped all of the competing sailing vessels in the American Cup sailing event with timing instruments.

Company Perspectives:

Like a painting by Warhol or a building by Le Corbusier, TAG Heuer is authentically Modern. Just as they signify leadership in modern art and architecture, TAG Heuer is among the companies showing the way for modern business. TAG Heuer believes a company is a collection of ideas, not just capital. It sees technology as a means not an end. And it thinks with the vigor of a small company yet sells with the reach of a global business. In the coming decade, TAG Heuer plans to establish itself not only as the undisputed leader in prestige sports watches, but also as a reference for the entire watch industry. TAG Heuer aims to become synonymous with style and excellence. These goals will be achieved through energy and enterprise, but above all because Tag Heuer can combine creative instinct with commercial rigor. So perhaps the best way to appreciate TAG Heuer as a modern business is through its core creative values of understanding, vision, energy, expertise, dedication and daring.

Heuer also was the timekeeper at the 1980 Moscow Olympic Games and at Lake Placid. During this period the watch industry was revolutionized by the introduction of the new quartz mechanisms. Heuer introduced the first analog quartz chronograph with a 12-hour, 30-minute, and second elapsed-time register.

In a far-reaching move toward technological expansion the TAG group (Techniques d'Avant-Garde) acquired a majority stake in the Heuer company in 1985, forming TAG Heuer. Under the new management team the revitalized company almost immediately began realizing a significant rate of growth. The new company designed and produced their biggest-selling watch when it launched the S/el series, an unusual design still considered a benchmark in the sports watch sector. The new management team determined to tighten control over the brand's international distribution network to manage its image better, and they began to raise the average retail price of their products, targeting an upscale market. By 1988 the company sold more than 420,000 timepieces, significantly outperforming the Swiss watch industry.

TAG Heuer in the 1980s: Form Follows Function

According to company reports, a careful philosophical criterion informs the creation of Heuer watches: "In order to create the ultimate sports watch, TAG Heuer started with the premise that all its products had to be capable of high performance and reliability in extreme conditions. The brand strategy focused on the development of a well-defined product style and the implementation of distinctive centralized marketing, advertising, sponsoring and merchandising. Heuer aimed to attract a broad cross-section of upscale consumers from around the world. It drew up a list of six design features that each of its watches would include: water resistance to 200 meters; unidirectional bezel; screw-in crown; sapphire crystal; double-security clasp; and luminous markings. Within this framework Heuer expects its designers to find different ways to add unique form. Most of

their watches take two or three years to design, during which time technical feasibility studies and design work evolve cooperatively. Watches are subjected to tension and torsion tests, as well as exposure to chemicals, ultraviolet light, and extremes of temperature. State-of-the-art computer-aided design and manufacturing techniques are utilized during product development and the machining of precise tolerances.

A large part of the company's marketing strategy involved recognition as sponsors of major sporting events (its sponsorship amounts to approximately $15 million per annum), along with official recognition as professionals implementing the use of their equipment for these events. The company primarily concentrates on three sports: sailing, Formula One racing, and skiing. In Formula One TAG Heuer has been associated with the sponsorship of many great names of the sport: Niki Lauda, Emerson Fittipaldi, Jacky Ickx, Michael Schumacher, and Ayrton Senna, with an especially close association with the McLaren team since 1986 (in 1990 the McLaren team won the world title for constructors and drivers in Formula One racing with Ayrton Senna). In 1988 Heuer launched the S/el chronographs with a $\frac{1}{10}$-second register. In the following year the company became the Official Timekeeper at the Ski World Cup events in the United States and Canada. In skiing, the company has sponsored champions such as Marc Girardelli, Harti Weirather, Helmut Hoeflehner, Pedtra Kronberger, Kristian Ghedina, and Ole K. Furuseth. Heuer created the Tag Heuer Maxi Yacht World Cup competition in tandem with the release of their 1500 and 4000 Series timepieces.

To ensure high brand recognition Heuer stresses a nontraditional form of vitality and originality in their designs as well as their advertising campaigns. Their 1995 advertising campaign, "Success. It's a Mind Game" won major advertising awards globally and emphasized the relationship between competitive sports and success. To capture the attention of buyers, the exclusive boutiques and galleries featuring TAG Heuer products tend to promote an ambiance of Modernistic minimalism that contrasts starkly with the busy cosmopolitan cityscapes. The discriminating buyer is appealed to rather than the masses. The image of museumlike showcasing presents an atmosphere of artful quality. Setting itself apart from other watch manufacturers, Heuer combined the casual image of the sports watch with the design and substance of opulence when it offered the TAG Heuer Gold Series—sports watches in 18-carat gold, featuring a sophisticated case and bezel design and a unique bracelet of more than 200 elements assembled by hand.

Initial Public Offering in 1996

The company reported that since 1988, TAG Heuer has seen its sales climb by an annual compounded growth rate of 26 percent, rising from SFr 66 million in 1988 to SFr 420 million in 1996, with gross margins rising from 42 percent to 55 percent during that same period. Free cash flow rose by 13 percent for the year. In September of 1996 TAG Heuer made its initial public offering (IPO) with simultaneous listings on the Swiss and New York Stock Exchanges, where it trades under the symbols "TAGN" and "THW," respectively. A large portion of the proceeds from the offering were used to reduce long-term debt for the purpose of decreasing significant future interest expenses. As of December of 1996 Heuer had reduced its net debt level to

$86.2 million, down from $241.0 million the previous year. The company organized a stock program providing that Heuer would purchase stock on the open market as incentive awards to key executives consisting of about 30 managers.

The company worked to strengthen its presence in geographical markets such as Japan, Southeast Asia, Europe, and North America, while increasing brand awareness in areas where its products were less well known. Early in 1997 the company announced that it agreed to acquire its U.K. distributor, Duval, a company instrumental in the successful development of the Heuer brand in the United Kingdom. The purchase had the advantage of allowing Heuer to control distribution of its products in its most important European market. In July of 1997 Heuer made another move toward controlling higher yields in the marketplace when it took over the distribution of its sports watches in Japan, after signing an agreement with World Commerce Corporation of Tokyo. At that time Japan represented 20 percent of Heuer's overall sales, making it one of the company's most important markets. Approximately three quarters of Heuer's business, represented by ten key markets, came under the direct control of the company by this time. A new wholly owned subsidiary, TAG Heuer Japan K.K., was formed, which included 100 World Commerce employees and was headed by a new management team. Chief executive office of Heuer, Christian Viros, commented on the transaction, "This development is an extremely important step in TAG Heuer's strategy to increase its downstream integration in order to improve margins and exercise better control over distribution worldwide." He added, "Following the acquisition of our UK distributor in February, this transaction further consolidates TAG Heuer's potential to obtain higher returns from our key markets." Continuing in like fashion, Heuer took over the distribution of its prestige sports watches in Australia and New Zealand after signing an agreement with Swiss Time Australia Pty Ltd, the company distributing for Heuer in both countries. A new wholly owned subsidiary named TAG Heuer Australia Pty Ltd was formed, incorporating nine employees from the previous ownership and bringing Heuer's direct control of worldwide sales up to approximately 80 percent.

Heuer phased out watch models that were unpopular and added new models in segments such as women's watches, an area with considerable growth potential. From 1991 to 1996 the average factory price of Heuer timepieces had risen by nearly 40 percent, representing a compound annual growth rate of nearly nine percent. Sales growth was fastest in the North American segment in 1996, accounting for one-third of the company's sales. European sales were up more than 15 percent during the same period, followed by strong performance in Spain, the Benelux countries, and Scandinavia. In its home market of Switzerland, the company also performed well. Sales were down slightly in Japan for the year because of the weakness of the Japanese yen, impacting sales in the region's duty-free outlets, and also because of inventory imbalances.

The company had begun cutting back on the number of retailers selling Heuer watches, with the intention of focusing on presentation solely in upscale markets. Heuer prefers to offer its watches exclusively through premium retailers in premium locations, alongside other prestigious brands. The company continued to update its product range through the design of newer models and line extensions. Most of their timepieces have been refined over the years to encompass what the company has reconsidered as core features of a sports watch, namely, unidirectional turning bezel, water resistance to a depth of at least 200 meters, screw-in crown, scratch-resistant sapphire crystal, luminous hands and dial, and bracelet with a double safety clasp. The company had relaunched its classic 1964 model Heuer Carrera chronograph in 1996 and produced limited editions of high-performance specialty timepieces designed to display their technological expertise, including a limited edition platinum watch of its 6000 series. Following a two-year developmental process and the expansion of their engineering, product development, and quality control departments, Heuer released its 1997 Kirium watch series, designed by world-renowned stylist Jorg Hysek. It features a band made of the company's patented link system that follows a uniquely rigid yet flexible bracelet design. The watch sold especially well in Germany—and especially well with women—where advertising featured German sports hero Boris Becker. The company regards Germany, a relatively new geographical area for Heuer, as a potentially lucrative market.

Sales for 1997 dipped in Japan, Hong Kong, Thailand, Indonesia, and South Korea in large part due to the financial turmoil in those regions. Sales increased by 22 percent in North America, aided in part by the appreciation of the U.S. dollar versus the Swiss franc. Revenues in South America, Canada, the Middle East, Singapore, Malaysia, Taiwan, and the Caribbean were also impressive, although overall total unit sales dropped by six percent from the previous year, which the company attributed to changes made in product mix and the move toward selling more high-end items. Lower-priced products were phased out during this time.

Heuer announced in May of 1998 that consolidated net sales for the first quarter were almost identical to those of 1997, with the most promising results in Europe and the Americas. In a press release, CEO Christian Viros stated, "We are very confident that our strong growth in Europe and in the Americas, the global success of the Kirium and the planned launch of new products will enable the company to more than offset the difficult sales environment in some parts of Asia."

Principal Subsidiaries

Tag Heuer SA; Tag Heuer Deutschland GmbH (Germany); Tag Heuer Espanola SA (Spain); Tag Heuer France SA; Tag Heuer Italia SpA (Italy); Tag Heuer Malasia SDN BHD; Tag Heuer Singapore Pte Ltd; Tag Heuer USA, Inc.; Tag Heuer Asia SA; Pro Time Service Inc. (USA); Tag Heuer Far East Limited (Hong Kong); Cortech SA (Switzerland); Polidoller Sarl (France); Miserez Sarl (France); Tag Citation Limited (Grand Cayman Islands).

Further Reading

"Tag Heuer International SA," *Wall Street Journal,* June 10, 1997, p. B11.
"Tag Heuer Net Rises 15.7 Percent for 1996 as Sales Gain 10.6 Percent," *Clock and Watch Industry,* April 3, 1997, p. 14.
"Tag Heuer Profits Climb 60 Percent," *Daily News Record,* September 12, 1997, p. 9.

—Terri Mozzone

Tarkett Sommer AG

Nachtweiderweg 1–7
D-67227 Frankenthal
Germany
(49) 6233-8100
Fax: (49) 6233-81 1640
Web site: http://www.tarkett-sommer.de

Public Company
Incorporated: 1886 as Malmö Snickerifabrik
Employees: 8,800
Sales: DM 2.93 billion (1997)
Stock Exchanges: Frankfurt
SICs: 3996 Hard Surface Floor Coverings, Not
   Elsewhere Classified

The October 1997 merger of Tarkett AG with the flooring division of France's Sommer Allibert SA has created the world's leading manufacturer and distributor of hard surface flooring products. Tarkett Sommer AG operates 28 manufacturing facilities in 13 countries with an annual production capacity of more than 350 million square meters of flooring, wall covering, and vinyl foil products. The company's combined sales for 1997 is equivalent to nearly DM 3 billion. Under terms of the merger agreement, Sommer Allibert SA has acquired 60 percent of Tarkett Sommer's shares. The company's headquarters remains in Frankenthal, Germany.

Tarkett Sommer's products are marketed under the brand names Tarkett, Pegulan, Sommer, Domco, Harris-Tarkett, and Febolit. The company's primary products are its hardwood flooring and resilient (chiefly PVC) flooring; the company also produces industrial foils, wall coverings, and, with the addition of the Sommer operations, carpetings. Resilient floor coverings remain the company's principal revenue generator. Although the company distributes its products throughout the world, Germany, Scandinavia, France, and North America remain Tarkett Sommer's primary markets, generating some two-thirds of the company's total sales.

Turn of the Century Swedish Origins

In 1885 Anders Martensson opened a small woodworking workshop in Malmö, Sweden. Within a year, however, Martensson had expanded his shop, installing steam-powered machinery, to such an extent that the workshop had now become a factory. In December 1886 Martensson incorporated his growing business as the Malmö Woodworking Factory. By 1887 Martensson's business had grown to include a foreman and 18 workers, with sales of 14,000 Swedish crowns. Yet the company's original products tended toward the exotic side, featuring, for example, Turkish divans, which found less of a demand than Martensson had hoped. In 1889, in need of capital, Martensson turned to R.F. Berg, director of a nearby cement factory. Berg became a director of the Malmö concern as well, before taking over the company's leadership in 1890.

Under Berg, the Malmö factory turned its production toward a new product: materials, chiefly from oak and beech wood, for parquet flooring. Risking his own funds, Berg expanded the company, building a second plant in Limhamn, outside of Malmö, for large-scale production of parquet floorboards. By the end of 1889 the company had more than doubled its employees, and its sales topped 65,000 Swedish crowns. The addition of flooring products proved successful for the company, as parquet flooring had become popular among Sweden's turn-of-the-century middle class. By 1898 the company's annual sales neared 360,000 Swedish crowns, of which 90,000 crowns came from the flooring materials. Berg's prior construction experience with his cement factory also enabled the company not only to produce the flooring products, but also to install them, adding to their profitability.

To ensure a supply of raw materials, the company purchased forest lands, as well as two sawmills, in the southern Swedish province of Småland in 1899. Two years later, as the company intensified its forestry activity, a sulfite factory was added in the city of Böksholm, processing the company's excess logging production. Before long, the sulfite works was producing 3,400 tons of sulfite per year. By 1904 the company's sales had reached 500,000 Swedish crowns. Flooring products, however, remained a small part of the company's sales.

Berg died in 1907 and was replaced by Ernst Wehtje, who would guide the company for nearly 20 years. In 1911 the company's Limhamn factory burned to the ground, forcing the company to build an entirely new factory on the same site. This factory's production was now turned wholly to the production of boards and frames for parquet floors. The following year, the company added two more sawmills, as well as expanded timber forests. The economic climate of the time—including a national recession in the years 1911–13—would, however, nearly force the closing of the company. The construction industry had all but collapsed; in the meantime, the company faced rising competition among raw materials suppliers. By 1914 the company was forced to sell off its sawmills and forest holdings, as well as its sulfite works, to stave off bankruptcy.

Production now was focused on the company's woodworking activities, and flooring materials became the company's chief products. Recognizing this new period in the company's existence, its name was changed to Limhamns Snickerifabrik. As the construction industry recovered, the company saw its sales take off once again, reaching, by 1922, 1.6 million Swedish crowns, of which 500,000 crowns were generated by sales of flooring materials. Yet the company was facing a new crisis. A long strike by woodworkers in 1919 had led to lockouts in the construction industry, leading to a fresh collapse in demand. At the same time the company had made a series of poor investments, enabling foreign speculators to acquire some two-thirds of the company's shares. The combination of these events forced the company into bankruptcy in 1924.

A Flooring Giant in the 20th Century

By 1925 the company had been reformed as Limhamns Golvindustri AB, now led by Hugo Wehtje. Yet, before production could resume, the company's existence was threatened once again, as a new fire destroyed its Limhamn factory. Wehtje was determined to rebuild. New taxes and fire insurance requirements imposed by the local government, however, led the company to build its new production facilities in Liljeholm, outside of Stockholm. At this time, production was turned exclusively to wood flooring products.

By 1928 the company was producing some 70,000 square meters of flooring materials per year, with revenues of some 800,000 Swedish crowns. In less than ten years production and sales would double, and Limhamns would become one of the country's top two producers of flooring products. The next decades would see the company's development soar as Limhamns proved itself an innovator in the flooring market.

In 1938 the company introduced a revolution of sorts, in the form of the Lindemann board. This was the first industrially manufactured, prefinished floorboard. Produced as long boards, rather than the short pieces used for parquet flooring, the Lindemann board was both cheaper to produce and to install. The success of the new product was immediate—by 1939 the company's revenues had topped three million Swedish crowns. Two years later the company moved to take control of its sales and distribution, founding Svensk Golvindustri in partnership with its chief competitor, Atvidabergs Industrier. The following year Limhamns took full control of the distributorship.

Rising raw material prices would lead to the company's next innovation. In 1942 Limhamns introduced the first laminated floorboards. Featuring a surface of the more expensive oak or beech woods, the patented laminated board used cheaper pine for the bottom. The new board was a huge success. To meet the demand, the company was required to expand its production capacity. In 1943 the company acquired another producer of parquet flooring, Skanska Parkettfabrik, located in Hanaskog. That factory's production was converted exclusively to laminated floorboards by the end of the same year.

In the following year the company acquired another parquet flooring producer, Ronnebyredds Trävaru, which not only expanded the company's production capacity, but also gave it ocean port access. The company next moved its Liljeholm production to Ronneby as well, ramping up to full production by 1946. By then Limhamns sales had reached some 500,000 square meters of floorboards, producing some eight million Swedish crowns.

In addition, Limhamns already was developing a new product, using a new material. The postwar reconstruction in Europe had led to a boom in demand for flooring products; yet raw wood materials were becoming more difficult to find in the depleted European forests. In 1946 Limhamns introduced a new type of floorboard, using plastic. Known as Tarkett, the floorboard was especially targeted toward public uses, such as schools, hospitals, and offices. Initial production was small, only 3,000 square meters in 1947. But demand for the Tarkett floors quickly developed. By 1948 the company produced some 50,000 square meters of Tarkett floorboard; the following year production tripled. The company was now producing around the clock to meet the demand.

In 1951 the company began construction of a new plant in Ronneby, which started production of plastic flooring products in 1953. By then, the company also had expanded its product lines, adding complementary baseboard, steps, and molding products. These featured new materials, including PVC and asbestos. By 1955 the company's annual sales had topped 20 million Swedish crowns. Total production had reached 400,000 square meters. To meet the continuously growing demand, the company moved its production entirely to Haneskog, more than doubling its production capacity.

Urban Wentje took over the company in 1961, as sales topped 33 million Swedish crowns and production passed one million square meters. By then the company also had made its first moves into the international market, with foreign sales representing ten percent of total revenues. These sales had come primarily through a Swiss distributor; in 1962, however, the company moved to take control of its foreign distribution, opening its first foreign subsidiary in Denmark. In the same year the company founded Limhamns Plastindustri, a subsidiary for sales of raw plastics materials, as the company's plastic production far exceeded its own flooring requirements.

By the mid-1960s sales exceeded 75 million Swedish crowns, of which 15 percent were provided by exports. The company would top 100 million crowns two years later. To continue the company's expansion—and to limit the Wentje family's personal financial risk—the company agreed to sell 50 percent of its shares to Företagsfinans, a subsidiary of AB Custos, in 1966. The following year the company, seeking addition capital for expansion, entered the Swedish stock exchange under a new name: Tarkett. By then the company had become Sweden's largest flooring manufacturer, with sales of 122 million crowns. Tarkett also added a new product line, carpeting. A new foreign subsidiary, in Austria, opened that year, followed in 1969 by the establishment of a German subsidiary.

Merging to World Leadership from the 1980s and 1990s

In 1970 Tarkett was acquired by the industrial conglomerate Swedish Match, which soon added the carpeting production of its Anneplas subsidiary to Tarkett's activities. Tarkett's carpeting production was boosted still further in 1972, when it took over the operations of AB Wahlbecks, then Sweden's largest carpet manufacturer.

In 1974 Tarkett introduced the first printed floorboards to the industry. The company also had anticipated the growing backlash against the use of asbestos in the construction industry, introducing fiberglass-based products to replace its asbestos materials. The company ended the use of asbestos for its Scandinavian production in 1975. In the 1970s the company added a French subsidiary, then boosted its French presence with the acquisition of that country's Synfloor SA. In 1978 Tarkett grew again as its Swedish Match parent merged another of its subsidiaries, carpet and wallcovering producer Anneplas, into Tarkett. The company also introduced a line of industrial flooring products.

By the end of the 1970s Tarkett had grown to the world's number six ranked flooring manufacturer, with sales of 745 million Swedish crowns, of which more than 40 percent came from exports. The 1980s, however, would see even greater changes for the company.

As Tarkett consolidated its position in Europe—including the acquisition of Nyland Mattor and the flooring division of Protan & Fagertun, both based in Sweden, as well as the acquisition of Denmark's Orebehoved Fanerfabrik—the company next turned to the United States market. The company's first step was the 1981 acquisition of the flooring products division of GAF, adding three U.S. plants and a fourth plant in Ireland. The purchase not only doubled the company's size, it also created Tarkett as the world's leading flooring products producer. Tarkett consolidated both its world and U.S. positions the following year, with the acquisition of Harris Manufacturing Company, the oldest wood flooring producer in the United States. By the mid-1980s Tarkett's sales had swelled to 2.6 billion Swedish crowns. Some 80 percent of the company's

sales were generated overseas; the United States alone contributed 50 percent of the company's revenues.

In 1986, however, Tarkett took on a whole new dimension. In that year the company agreed to form a new company with Germany's Pegulan, a flooring and carpeting producer founded in 1946. The new company's name became Tarkett-Pegulan, and the company's headquarters were established in the former Pegulan headquarters in Frankenthal, Germany. The merger of Pegulan into Tarkett would be completed in 1996. During the 1990s the company restructured its operations, concentrating its warehouse operations, and centering much of its activities on its Frankenthal base. The company also moved to exit certain activities, including ceramics and textile floorings, as it weathered the global recession of the 1990s. By 1995 the company's sales had reached DM 1.3 billion.

Two years later the company would double in size again. Recognizing the increasing globalization of industry and the heightening consolidation of European industry as the continent prepared for the coming monetary union, Tarkett and Sommer Allibert reached agreement to merge Tarkett and the French company's Sommer flooring division. The new company, called Tarkett Sommer AG, continued to be based in Germany, while 60 percent of its shares came under Sommer-Allibert's control. Representing a combined sales total of nearly DM 3 billion for 1997, Tarkett Sommer became the undisputed leader of the world flooring industry.

Principal Subsidiaries

F und F Bodenbelagsvertrieb GmbH (Germany); Tarkett Bodenbeläge GmbH (Germany); Tarkett Pegulan Gmbh & Co. KG (Germany); Sommer Revêtements France SA (France); Sommer Sports SA (France); Arvial SA (France); Polystyl SA (France); Tarkett SA (France); Tarkett AB (Scandinavia); Tarkett Svenska Försäljnings AB (Scandinavia); Tarkett Danmark A/S (Scandinavia); Tarkett OY (Scandinavia); Tarkett Nederland BV (Netherlands); Sommer Nederland BV (Netherlands); Sommer Allibert International BV; Sommer Revêtements Luxembourg SA; Sommer SA (Spain); Tarkett Iberica SA (Spain); Tarkett Srl (Italy); Tarkett GmbH (Switzerland); Tarkett Polska SP.Z.O.O.; Harris Tarkett Inc.; Tarkett Inc.; Domco Inc. (Canada); Domco Enterprices Inc.; Sommer Ltd. (Hong Kong); Anssom Decor (China); Anshan Sommer Dalles (China); Tarkett Australia Pty. Ltd.

Further Reading

"Tarkett 100: 1886–1986," Frankenthal, Germany: Tarkett, 1986.

—M.L. Cohen

Tati SA

4, boulevard Rochechouart
75018 Paris
France
(33) 1.42.55.13.09
Fax: (33) 1.42.55.59.42.20

Private Company
Incorporated: 1948
Employees: 1,700
Sales: FFr 1.45 billion (US $250 million) (1997)
SICs: 5632 Women's Accessory & Specialty Stores;
   5699 Miscellaneous Apparel & Accessory Stores

A Parisian legend, Tati SA is on its way to becoming a worldwide name. Since the mid-1990s the operator of 14 discount retail stores in France—including its flagship store on the boulevard Rochechouart in Paris—has engaged in an ambitious international expansion, bringing the Tati name to countries including South Africa, Lebanon, Germany, Switzerland, and Israel. The opening of a Tati store on New York's Fifth Avenue in April 1998 marked the company's first entry into the United States. Tati also plans to enter Turkey, Cameroon, the Ivory Coast, and Poland, among other markets, before the turn of the century. In addition to the clothing-oriented Tati stores, the company has begun developing a network of smaller Tati Or stores, bringing its discount concept to the jewelry shopper. While Tati's expansion within France is entirely funded by the company's own resources, its international stores are operated, typically, in local partnerships or as franchises.

Tati is credited with inventing the discount shopping concept, at least in France. Under the slogan "Les Plus Bas Prix" (the lowest prices), the company has long served the clothing and accessories needs of the economically disadvantaged. Yet, especially since the extended recession of the 1990s, the company has attracted a loyal clientele among all seeking the company's wide assortment of low-priced clothing and other items, ranging from stockings for less than FFr 2 (less than US $ .50) per piece to jeans for FFr 39 (US $7) to men's suits for less than

$100 and wedding gowns ranging from FFr 390 to FFr 2,000 (US $60 to $400). Although Tati continues to fill its bins with remaindered and discontinued items, since the rising importance of "just-in-time" manufacturing among the French and world garment industries, the company also has turned more directly to manufacturers for the company's own line of clothing and accessories. The Tati Or represents an expansion of the discount concept to the jewelry shopper; the company also has plans to expand into eyewear, handbags, and other items. A disposable camera, packaged in Tati's trademark Vichy pink, white, and blue, was introduced in 1997. The company's margins on its sales range, typically, between two and seven percent—down from nearly 20 percent before the 1990s.

Plans to bring Tati public have been pushed back to the turn of the century after crossing a difficult period in the mid-1990s. Yet the company has long prided itself on funding its domestic expansion entirely from its own resources, although the opening of its international branches usually take the form of either partnerships or franchise agreements with local businesses. Tati remains under control of the founding Ouaki family, with Fabien Ouaki, the founder's son, personally controlling some 30 percent of the company. Leadership of the company is directed by President Eléonore Ouaki, widow of the founder, and by Fabien Ouaki.

Tunisien Origins in the 1940s

Jules Ouaki had been a saddle maker in his native Tunis—his passion for horses later would establish a family tradition of raising and racing thoroughbred horses—who traveled yearly to France to purchase leftover leather stock from shoemakers around the Montpellier region on the Mediterranean coast. Ouaki's career was interrupted during the Second World War, when Ouaki joined the Free French Forces led by Charles de Gaulle. The end of the war left Ouaki with the necessity of feeding his family of eight brothers and sisters, leading to a decision to emigrate to France.

Installed in Paris, Ouaki formed a partnership with another merchant, opening a small grocery-general merchandise shop on the boulevard Rochechouart in Paris's ninth arrondissement. The partners opened a second store, further south in Paris, on the avenue du General Leclerc, in the 14th arrondissement. The partnership quickly ruptured, however. Ouaki sought to expand the Rochechouart store, while his partner preferred to remain in the General Leclerc store. Dissolving the partnership, Ouaki kept the Rochechouart store; some 50 years later the Ouaki family would regain the original 14th arrondissement store with the opening of a new Tati Or branch. Ouaki originally chose his mother's name, Tita, for his store. By the time he discovered that that name had already been taken, he had already had the store's sign made up. Instead, Ouaki switched the letters to form the new name, Tati.

Ouaki had not forgotten his Tunisien origins. Equally inspired by Paris's Saint Pierre flea market, Ouaki's store would capture much of the flair of the Arab world *souk,* or marketplace, appealing to the quarter's large and generally poor immigrant population. Ouaki would become credited with bringing the discount concept to France, scouring the city's garment district for unsold and cut out items to support his slogan: ''Les Plus Bas Prix.'' Ouaki soon introduced other innovative selling techniques. For one, he was among the first to introduce mannequins to display the store's clothing items, using the store's display windows to attract customers. A more important innovation was the introduction of bins to hold the various items, set out directly on the selling floor—at a time when the retail industry had not yet discovered the self-service concept. The bins encouraged Tati customers to inspect the products themselves. Another important innovation was Ouaki's policy of displaying prices of the items in each bin. As Fabien Ouaki would tell *Elle* magazine, Jules Ouaki ''pulverized the three commercial barriers: the display window, the salesperson, and the consumer, especially since the latter's budget was modest. My father was sensitive to the shame of the poor, who didn't dare ask for a price for fear of being humiliated.'' Tati's insistence on low prices would enable generations to clothe the entire family.

Ouaki's formula was a success; before long Tati began stretching farther along the block, as Ouaki bought up the neighboring stores and small hotels. Funds for the company's expansion came only from its own resources, to the point where Tati was able to avoid any debt throughout its continuing history. The expanded selling space enabled Ouaki to develop separate men's, women's, and children's departments in each new storefront. Tati's expansion would bring much of the Ouaki family into the company, with each new employee required to spend time working on the sales floor before earning a promotion. In later years that tradition would continue, with as much as 85 percent of the company's executive and purchasing staff coming from its retail floor. The famed Tati color scheme—a Vichy pink and white checkerboard with blue lettering—also made its appearance. The store's location also proved strategic; located near the Barbès-Rochechouart metro station, as the metro emerged from the subway into its elevated extension, the Tati sign was one of the first things passengers would see. In terms of marketing, however, Ouaki long would avoid any type of direct advertising techniques. Meanwhile, the company's purchasing activities remained a matter of instinct and experience gained by the company's closeness to its customers.

As such, many of Tati's items would become store mainstays that remained unchanged from the 1950s. For example,

in the late 1990s the company continued to sell as many as five million pairs of stockings each year, at a price of FFr 2.90 per pair. The company also became a popular source for wedding gowns, which would maintain sales in the tens of thousands each year and give the company some 11 percent of that market. Tati's flair for purchasing enabled the company to offer low prices, without sacrificing too much on quality, while maintaining margins as high as 20 percent. The prospering Ouaki soon returned to his passion for the horses, raising thoroughbreds, with the jockeys' uniforms bearing Tati's trademark color pattern.

Changing the Guard in the 1990s

Jules Ouaki died in 1982, leaving his company divided equally among his six children and designating oldest son Gregory as his successor. Gregory Ouaki died, however, the following year, launching the family—including uncles and cousins—on an internal power struggle that would last into the following decade. In the meantime, Ouaki's widow, Eléonore, took over the company's leadership, maintaining the successful formula established by her husband. By the end of the 1980s Tati's revenues were nearing FFr 2 billion per year. By then the Tati empire was growing beyond Paris. With new stores opening in other Paris neighborhoods, the company began extending throughout France, with stores in Lille, Lyon, Nancy, Rouen, Nice, Montpellier, and Le Havre. Each store would maintain the Tati formula of locating in the urban center—at a time when the hypermarket boom was taking over the suburban districts.

The pressure to find a successor continued to mount, as did the bitterness within the family. In 1992 the family regrouped its interests into a holding company, Cofitel SA, controlling Textile Diffusion, which in turn operated the Tati stores. At the same time Eléonore Ouaki designated son Fabien Ouaki as successor to the company's leadership. Known as the family's ''black sheep,'' Fabien Ouaki had been all but disinherited by his father, after leaving the family business at the age of 17 for a stint in England, a career in radio and as a drummer for a rock band, then converting from Judaism to Buddhism. Yet Fabien Ouaki would prove very much his father's son, with a strong feeling for the Tati culture—and for his father's passion for thoroughbred racing.

Throughout the 1990s Fabien Ouaki would gain control of the family company, increasing his holding to some 60 percent, including the parts ceded to him by his mother. The opening of new Tati stores and warehouses throughout France created new positions for the other members of the family, so that by the mid-1990s the company's leadership was firmly grouped under Fabien and Eléonore Ouaki. The changing economy, with a recession that would become an extended economic crisis in France through the middle of the decade, brought new opportunities to the company. Whereas its traditional customer base had been the urban poor, Tati now found new customers among higher-income populations pressured by the recession. Tati soon developed a certain fashionableness not only among Parisian youth, but among members of the jet set as well, even attracting designers such as Azzedine Alaïa to create fashions for the Tati stores.

By the beginning of the 1990s Tati's success led to a new problem—that of supplying its stores. With its sales booming, the company could no longer depend solely on cutouts and seasonal leftovers to fill its bins. At the same time Tati's traditional suppliers, chiefly the small manufacturers in the Parisian garment district, themselves pinched by the recession and growing competition from foreign manufacturers, had begun to adopt "just-in-time" manufacturing methods. Tati's supply of remainders, therefore, dwindled. In response, Tati was forced to begin developing its supply of made-to-order products, ordering directly from manufacturers, chiefly in the lower wage areas of the Far East and Northern Africa. Maintaining its commitment to its discount pricing policy, Tati was forced to cut its margins, which slipped to some seven percent and as low as three percent on some items.

Fabien Ouaki looked toward diversification for fuel for the company's continued growth. Yet these efforts proved more limited in their success. The company launched its own line of ready-to-wear clothing, "La Rue Est à Nous" (the street is ours), in the early 1990s and began opening a series of in-store boutiques in the Nouvelles Galeries department stores. By the mid-1990s disappointing sales forced the company to close these boutiques and consign its label to its own Tati stores. Equally unsuccessful was the launch of a perfume in 1994. On the bright side, however, the company's Tati Or stores, bringing the discount concept to jewelry, turned out to be more of a success. From the mid-1990s the company would begin developing the Tati Or concept into a national chain of retail stores and counters for such venues as airports.

The continued recession—and Tati's success—would give rise to a growing number of competitors on Tati's discount terrain. At the same time, with its margins slimmed, Tati was required to generate larger sales to generate the necessary economies of scale. But in the mid-1990s Tati was undergoing a crisis of its own. The outbreak of a veritable civil war in Algeria cut severely into Tati's Arab customers' confidence; that conflict would spill over into Paris, in the form of a series of terrorist bombings that traumatized the city. Then, in 1995, a train workers strike paralyzed the city's rapid transit system. For Tati, the period represented a dramatic loss in sales and profits; for the 1995/1996 period Tati would post the first loss in its history, of some FFr 35 million on sales that had dipped to FFr 1.4 billion. The company, which had expected to go public in the mid-1990s, was forced to push back its entry on the Paris stock exchange to the turn of the century.

In the meantime, Tati began developing a new direction for its expansion. With the domestic market increasingly crowded by competition and offering limited opportunities for new store openings, Tati began looking overseas. The first foreign Tati opened in early 1996 in South Africa's Cape Town, in a partnership with that country's Pep, which owned some 1,000 retail stores throughout the country. That opening, however, was to be only the first of many. Tati unveiled an ambitious international expansion plan, with stores to open in Geneva and Beirut (marking the first foreign company to open a retail store in that city since the Lebanese civil war), as well as several stores in Israel and plans to enter Spain, Portugal, Australia, New Zealand, and others. Unlike the South African venture, however, the majority of new Tati stores would be operated as a franchise concept, with Tati providing the signage, store design and concepts, and products and a local partner providing the capital.

The company opened a Tati store in the Karnstadt area of Berlin, Germany in early 1997, testing that country's market for the eventual extension of the Tati concept throughout Germany. Tati stores opened as well in the Ivory Coast and Cameroon, and the company was engaged actively in negotiating new store openings in Turkey, Senegal, Gabon, Poland, and Estonia. In April 1998 Tati took its first step into the vast United States market, opening Tati Marriage on New York's Fifth Avenue. Representing an investment of some US $1 million, Tati would maintain an 85 percent share of the New York store, with a local partner holding the remaining 15 percent. The company expected to expand deeper into the United States should the New York launch prove successful, with an initial eye on the Miami market. By 1998 roughly ten percent of the company's revenues was generated outside of France.

Tati expected international sales to reach some 50 percent of yearly revenues by the turn of the century. In the meantime, the French economy's return to health in the late 1990s led to a new upswing in Tati's sales and profits. Whereas Jules Ouaki once dreamed of owning the entire block of the boulevard Rochechouart, son Fabien Ouaki now began to dream of expanding the Tati colors throughout the world.

Further Reading

Doiseau, Isabelle, "Tati cherche ses marques," *Le Point,* April 27, 1996, p. 85.

Epinay, Bénédicte, "Interview: Fabien Ouaki," *Les Echos,* January 16, 1997, p. 46.

Leon-Dufour, Sixtine, "Tati: la ruée vers l'or," *Le Figaro Economie,* May 5, 1997.

Lepercq, Vincent, "Tati n'a pa echappé à la récession," *Journal du Textile,* February 10, 1997, p. 32.

Trétiack, Philippe, "Tati: la vie en rose," *Elle (France),* March 2, 1998, p. 178.

—M.L. Cohen

Teekay Shipping Corporation

Tradewinds Building, 5th Floor
Bay Street
P.O. Box SS-6293
Nassau
Bahamas
(242) 332-8020
Web site: http://www.teekay.com

Public Company
Founded: 1973 as the Teekay Shipping Group
Employees: 1,596
Sales: $406 million (1998)
Stock Exchanges: New York
Ticker Symbol: TK
SICs: 4412 Deep Sea Foreign Transportation of Freight

Teekay Shipping Corporation, with the world's largest and most modern fleet of midsized oil tankers, is a leading transporter of crude oil and petroleum products. As of March 1998, its fleet consisted of 46 vessels with a total cargo capacity of approximately 4.6 million tons. These ships provide transportation services to major oil companies, oil traders, and government agencies, primarily in the region from the Red Sea to the west coast of the United States, with its main operating routes in the Pacific. The company claims to hold 25 percent of the medium-sized tanker market in the Indian and Pacific oceans, with about 66 percent of its net revenue coming from spot voyages. Headquartered in the Bahamas, Teekay has chartering offices in Tokyo, London, Singapore, and Vancouver, which also is its principal operating office. Two trusts hold just more than half of Teekay's common stock.

Getting into the Shipping Business: 1973–79

Jens Torben Karlshoej's lifelong passion for the sea and ships probably began with visits to the harbor when he was a child in Denmark. Although he came from a farming family, he left the land and went to work for a small Danish shipping company. Then, in his early 20s, Karlshoej emigrated to the United States. During the 1960s and early 1970s he held a progression of increasingly responsible jobs with shipping companies in New York and Los Angeles.

In 1973 Karlshoej struck off on his own, founding the Teekay Shipping Group in New York, incorporating it in Liberia, and using his initials to give the company its name. His strategy was for the company to manage and operate a range of tankers, but to charter the vessels from independent ship owners, not to own them.

Major oil companies, whether private or state-owned, as well as independent ship owners, transported crude oil and other petroleum products under two types of contract: short-term contracts, including "spot charters," which were for a single voyage, or long-term "time charters." New York was one of the shipping centers where tanker chartering occurred, with brokers (and sometimes ship owners and charterers) working around the clock to transact business.

But when the oil market collapsed, Karlshoej closed up his New York operation and moved to the West Coast. In 1975 he established an affiliated company, Palm Shipping Inc., which concentrated on chartering medium-sized tankers for Pacific routes. Tankers came in various sizes, for certain types of trips and cargoes. A charterer usually wanted the largest possible vessel for the cargo that would meet port and canal dimension restrictions for the route. Karlshoej chartered medium-sized tankers (75,000–115,000 deadweight tonnage), referred to in the industry as "aframax." These vessels typically made medium- and short-haul trades of less than 1,500 miles and carried crude oil or petroleum products. They were smaller than the Suezmax size of approximately 115,000 to 200,000 dwt used for long- and medium-haul crude oil trades and bigger than the Panamax vessels used to transport petroleum products in short- to medium-haul trades.

The West Coast was a tough market to break into. California refiners favored smaller ships to import crude oil and were hesitant to go with an unknown company. But Karlshoej persuaded them to consider a larger tanker, and within a year he had time-chartered his first ship, White Peony, an aframax owned by Takebayashi of Japan. The ship was chartered to Palm Shipping at $1.35 dwt/month, which came to $3,800 a day. By 1977 Karlshoej was operating two Norwegian vessels as well. That year, Captain James Hood, a Scotsman who left school to go to sea at age 16, joined Karlshoej to run the operational side of the business. Palm Shipping's all-chartered fleet quickly grew from 16 to 18 ships.

In 1979 Karlshoej founded another affiliated organization, Viking Star Shipping, Inc., to buy and own tankers to provide a reliable source of high-quality vessels to support Palm's chartering activities. His timing was poor, as the market began to slide in 1980, and Viking Star made no purchases.

From Charterer to Owner: The 1980s

In 1985 Palm Shipping signed a deal with Japanese ship owner Sanko Steamship to charter 12 of Sanko's aframax vessels on a two-year timecharter. The transaction was a major coup for Karlshoej and happened because Sanko, which had been the most powerful aframax operator in the world, was shaky and Karlshoej was offering three months' hire up front. As Jim Hood remembered it in a 1996 *Seatrade Review* article, "It was not exactly a vibrant market. Taking those ships was at once an act of faith and the grasping of an opportunity." Because there was not enough business on the Pacific routes, Palm Shipping extended operations into the Atlantic. "You took what you could get and ran with it," Hood said. Later that year Karlshoej bought his first ship, paying $3.9 million for the Golden Gate Sun, a ten-year-old aframax. The purchase made Viking Star Shipping a shipowner, finally. This time Karlshoej's timing was right, as the market began to turn.

The Sanko timecharter gave the Teekay Shipping Group controlled tonnage and credibility. In an improving market, it was suddenly a big player. Shell Oil saw Teekay's power as a threat and offered Sanko more money to charter ten of the tankers when Teekay's leases expired. Without even letting Karlshoej make a counterbid, Sanko agreed to the Shell offer.

Karlshoej was amazed, to say the least. After all, his financing flexibility had allowed Sanko to keep going some five months before it went bankrupt. Suddenly left out in the cold, Teekay could have gone under. Instead, Karlshoej vowed revenge and went on a building spree, ordering some 30 vessels over the next six years at a cost of $1.4 billion. "The newbuilding run was driven by Torben's conviction that massive aframax replacement would be needed and that

newbuilding prices would not come down," Hood told *Seatrade Review*. Karlshoej bet the company on that vision, ordering ships first from Hyundai in South Korea and then from a variety of yards, including 3 Maj in Yugoslavia and Imabari and Onomichi in Japan. The Onomichi yard created a design to Karlshoej's specifications, the 100,000 dwt Onomax, which would become the backbone of Karlshoej's fleet. The first of these vessels, the Palm Star Orchid, was delivered in 1989. For the fiscal year that ended in April 1989, the Teekay group had net income of $54.7 million on revenue of $200.9 million.

On the Brink of Disaster: 1990–92

Company revenues continued to climb at the beginning of the decade, first as a result of the run up after the Gulf War and then as more ships were delivered or purchased secondhand and put into service. In 1991 Karlshoej moved his operations from Long Beach, California to Vancouver, British Columbia, in part to protect it from potential liabilities under the new U.S. oil spill legislation, but primarily to take advantage of new tax laws in Canada, where headquarters of foreign companies were not taxed on their worldwide business operations. But even as he made the move, the situation was worsening.

Overcapacity in the tanker market caused freight rates and newbuilding prices to sink. On top of that, the yen, in which the company had most of its contracts, strengthened. Although Viking Star's fleet had increased from an average of 18 vessels in 1989 to 46 in 1992, it and the Teekay group was heavily in debt, owing nearly $1 billion. During 1992 Karlshoej renegotiated the debt repayments and sold the company's 50 percent interest in Baltimar Overseas Limited. Then, in September 1992, one of Viking Star's tankers collided with a container ship, resulting in the deaths of 20 crew members. The ship, the Nagazaki Spirit, was declared a total loss. A month later, on October 3, Torben Karlshoej died in his sleep of an apparent heart attack, at age 51. In columns in trade papers and in letters to the editor, Karlshoej was honored for his integrity and vision.

Lloyd's Shipping Economist credited Karlshoej with leaving two towering legacies. "The first was a leading position in a competitive market, based upon a high standard of operations and modern vessels." The second was a towering debt.

Admid speculation about the future of the Teekay group, Jim Hood was named president and chief executive officer of Teekay Shipping Ltd., the parent company. Under a contingency plan Karlshoej set up shortly before his death, a four-member executive board took over the company's operations. The board included Karlshoej's elder brother, Axel; shipowner Thomas Hsu; shipbroker Shigeru Matsui; and Arthur Coady, Teekay's general counsel.

New Leadership: 1993–94

Hood replaced Karlshoej's flair with a more cautious, financially focused approach, but he faced severe challenges. In the fiscal year ending March 31 1993, revenues dropped to $337.4 million from $416.1 million the year before. Even after Viking Star raised more than $37 million by selling vessels, the group had a loss of $47.5 million. The global recession finally had hit the tanker freight market, depressing rates, especially those for spot chartering, on which Teekay concentrated. A timecharter equivalent rate of $19,270/day the year before dropped to $13,722/day. Added to this was the company's heavy dependence on yen-dominated debt, which resulted in a $77.9 million foreign exchange loss.

The company's structure was in keeping with Karlshoej's passion for privacy. Teekay reported its activities through Viking Star Shipping, Inc., its holding company. Teekay operated and managed the Viking Star-owned fleet, while Palm Shipping Inc. handled chartering activities. As was common in the industry, each vessel was owned by a Teekay subsidiary, having been built with commercial bank mortgages to one-ship companies. Teekay also owned 50 percent of Viking Consolidated Shipping Corp, which owned three ships on long-term charter to a big Japanese company.

Under Hood, Palm became a subsidiary of Viking Star, and the company restructured. Ultimate ownership now rested in two trusts set up by Karlshoej before he died. Cirrus Trust owned 100 percent of Viking Star[/idx]'s common stock and JTK Trust held 100 percent of the redeemable preferred stock. The company's advisory board oversaw the trusts, the ultimate beneficiaries of which were charitable organizations.

In the year after Hood become president, Viking Star sold six ships, postponed building of two others, renegotiated some of its debt, refinanced 15 of its vessels, and, in a significant move for this very private company, privately placed $175 million in notes backed by its ships. These measures more than doubled the company's liquidity by early 1994, but it still faced long-term debt of more than $900 million.

To raise money, the Teekay group announced in March that it would take its ship owning company, Viking Star, public, issuing 13.5 million shares, about 27 percent of the company. Hoping to raise $250 million, the company planned to use the proceeds to build replacements for its older vessels and to repay some of its debt. Viking Star's prospectus eased speculation about the company's liquidity. The low-profile company reported net income of $4.3 million for the nine months ending January 31, 1994, on revenues of $264.2 million. But within a month the company postponed the offering, when share prices dropped ten percent as interest rates started to rise.

A Single, Public Company: 1995–96

By July in 1995, the Teekay group was ready to go ahead with a public offering, though on different terms. To begin with, the shares were no longer for Viking Star Shipping, Inc. In March, Hood restructured the group, merging the ship owning and ship management companies into a single entity. Viking Star acquired Teekay Shipping Ltd. and then reverted to the group name, Teekay Shipping Corporation. In a July 1995 article, *Lloyd's List* speculated that the change was due to market criticism about the earlier plan to leave the management of the fleet in private hands. Teekay issued fewer shares (6.9 million) at a higher price of $21.50 a share and raised $138.7 million. The bulk of the proceeds was used to pay down debt from previous newbuilding and Hood's more recent purchases of secondhand vessels. The company also sold its older ships, including the Golden Gate Sun, the first ship Karshoej bought.

Taking the company public appeared to mark the turning point for Teekay. Within a year a study by U.S. investment bank Lazard Freres reported that Teekay "was well positioned to benefit from better conditions projected for the aframax sector over the next three years." Those conditions included the strong growth in oil imports to Asia, the potential market in China, and the firming of the oil industry cycle.

According to *Lloyd's Shipping Economist,* the Teekay group had four operational strengths: fleet age, vessel uniformity, regional targeting, and in-house servicing. Because of its remarkable ship building program, the company had a youthful fleet, with an average age of under eight years during the last half of the decade. This compared with an average age of more than 13 years for the world oil tanker fleet and more than 12 years for the world aframax tanker fleet. Teekay believed that its modern fleet gave it a significant advantage, with higher fuel efficiency and lower operating costs, important considerations in an industry with increasingly stringent operating and safety standards. The large fleet also was fairly homogeneous in size, with many vessels being indentical sister ships. That uniformity made it possible for Teekay to substitute vessels, giving it greater flexibility in accommodating changes on short notice.

The company targeted the Indo-Pacific basin when it moved to the West Coast in 1975 and developed a significant presence and long-term relationships in an area that underwent explosive and sustained economic growth. That region, with the Red Sea on one border and the west coast of the United States on the other, encompassed the Arabian Gulf, Indonesia, and Australia, three major oil exporting regions, and the company derived approximately 90 percent of total revenues from its operations there.

That regional concentration contributed to the final operational plus, Teekay's ability to meet its needs in-house. Through its wholly owned subsidiaries, the company was able to operate independently, providing all of the operations, ship maintenance, crewing, technical support, shipyard supervision, insurance, and financial management services required to support its fleet.

For example, the company recruited staff through its offices in Glasgow, Manila, Sydney, and Mumbai and used two specially configured tankers to train the 24-29 crew members needed for each of its vessels. It also operated a cadet program to develop future senior officers and provided additional training for newly hired seamen and junior officers at its training facilities in the Philippines. The company budgeted about $1 million to educate crews to Teekay's standards, two to three times as much as the competition spent. "Cost is not the only thing to consider. We need quality people. You can't compromise on ship safety," the manager of technical training told *LSM* in a 1994 article.

1997 to the Present

Aframax freight rates were historically high as the new year began, with owners averaging $25,226 per day, according to *Fairplay.* This resulted from the growing importance of short-haul crude, and Teekay's net income rose 46 percent to $42.6 million for the fiscal year. Teekay claimed its fleet utilization was almost 70 percent, due to the availability of back haul cargoes from the West Coast. But recognizing the high risk involved in its spot trades strategy, Teekay began exploring the possibility of converting some of its tankers for the floating production, storage, and off-loading (fpso) market. Chief operating officer Bjorn Moller told the company's annual meeting, "During the past year we have stepped up our efforts to develop new projects where we can lever our strengths into related business opportunities, an example being offshore marine."

At the beginning of 1998, Teekay announced an eight-year contract to provide a fpso vessel to Apache Energy Ltd. and the acquisition of Australian Tankerships Pty. Ltd., a shipping subsidiary of Australian Petroleum Pty. Ltd., which brought with it the servicing of Caltex Petroleum's oil transportation requirements. In March, Jim Hood retired as president and CEO, replaced by Bjorn Moller. Moller, who came to the company in 1985, had been chief operating officer since 1997. Shortly after that, the company announced plans to order at least two new aframax tankers and to sell seven million shares of common stock.

During the 1990s Teekay Shipping survived near disaster by its careful financial policies, reputation for safety, and quality customer service. It changed from a highly secretive, wholly private company to a popular public corporation, reorganizing from a group of affiliated companies into a single entity. Although economic problems in Asia and 94 aframax vessels under construction might cause concern in the next few years, Teekay appeared well positioned to withstand a period of reduced rates.

Principal Subsidiaries

Palm Shipping, Inc.; Teekay Shipping (Vancouver) Ltd.; Teekay Shipping (UK) Ltd.; Teekay Norbulk Ltd. (Scotland); Teekay Shipping (Singapore) Pte. Ltd.; Mayon Marine Management, Inc. (Philippines); Teekay Shipping (Japan) Ltd.; Teekay Shipping (Australia) Pty. Ltd.

Further Reading

Bate, Alison, "The Newcomers," *Westcoast Shipping,* May 1997, p. 20.
Brady, Joe, "Analyst Ranks Teekay Shipping as a Good Buy," *Tradewinds,* April 26, 1996, p. 8.
Brewer, James, "Teekay Looking To Branch Out into New Areas," *Lloyd's List,* September 4, 1997.
"Down . . . But Not Out," *Lloyd's Shipping Economist,* December 1994, p. 22.
Gray, Tony, "Teekay Orders Two Aframaxes," *Lloyd's List,* May 15, 1998.
——, "Teekay President Hood Hands Over Reins," *Lloyd's List,* February 6, 1998, p. 2.
"Lazard Freres Study Lifts Teekay Spirits," *Lloyd's List,* April 30, 1996.
Lillestolen, Trond, "Teekay Faces Challenge After Founder's Death," *Tradewinds,* October 9, 1992, p. 6
"Profile: Modest Man of the Moment," *Seatrade Review,* October 1996, p. 13.
Smith, Leigh, "It's Business as Before at Teekay," *Lloyd's List,* October 19, 1992.
"Teekay Builds on Founder's Legacy," *LSM,* December 1994, p. 63.
"Teekay Prospers Again," *Fairplay,* February 6, 1997, p. 18.
"Teekay Puts Money Where Its Mouth Is," *Tradewinds,* March 4, 1994, p. 1.
"Teekay Sets Offer Price," *Lloyd's List,* July 21, 1995.
"Teekay Share Issue Capital Tagged for New Aframaxes," *Tradewinds,* March 31, 1994, p. 7.
"Teekay Shipping Acquires Australian Tanker Operation," *Worldwide Energy,* January 1998.
"Teekay Shipping Corp Outlook Revised to Positive by S&P," *Business Wire,* April 16, 1998.
"Teekay Shipping Corporation," Form 20-F, Washington, DC: Securities and Exchange Commission, March 31, 1998.
"Teekay Shipping Corporation," Prospectus, Teekay Shipping Corporation, June 9, 1998.

—Ellen D. Wernick

Texas Utilities Company

Energy Plaza
1601 Bryan Street
Dallas, Texas 75201
U.S.A.
(214) 812-4600
Fax: (214) 812-4651
Web site: http://www.tu.com

Public Company
Incorporated: 1945
Employees: 11,451
Sales: $7.9 billion (1997)
Stock Exchanges: New York
Ticker Symbol: TXU
SICs: 4911 Electric Services; 4923 Gas Transmission and
Distribution; 6719 Holding Companies, Not
Elsewhere Classified

Texas Utilities Company is a holding company with six wholly owned subsidiaries, the largest of which is Texas Utilities Electric Company (TU Electric). TU Electric produces and distributes electricity in the eastern, north central, and western sections of Texas, including the Dallas-Forth Worth metropolitan area. This region has about one-third of Texas's population and is highly diversified economically, with such industries as aerospace manufacturing, oil and gas development, banking, insurance, and agriculture. As of the late 1990s, TU Electric had close to six million electricity customers. Other Texas Utilities subsidiaries are involved in the acquisition and transportation of fuels and in various other services for the electric utility. Texas Utilities also operates a natural gas distributor, owns stakes in several telecommunications firms, operates an electric utility in Australia, and owns an English electricity company that serves approximately three million customers in southeastern England and parts of London.

Early History

Texas Utilities was formed in 1945 as a holding company for three utilities: Dallas Power & Light Company (DP&L), Texas Electric Service Company (TESCO), and Texas Power & Light Company (TP&L). DP&L had been formed in 1917, TESCO in 1929, and TP&L in 1912, while predecessors of these companies dated back as far as the 1880s. Each company had its own electricity generation and distribution system.

Before the formation of Texas Utilities, DP&L had been a subsidiary of Electric Power & Light Company, while TESCO and TP&L had been subsidiaries of American Power & Light Company. Both parent companies, in turn, were subsidiaries of Electric Bond & Share Company, which had been set up by General Electric Company in 1905 to finance electrical power systems and form operating companies.

These holding companies were required to divest themselves of their utility operations under the Public Utility Holding Company Act of 1935. To that end, under an order of the Securities and Exchange Commission, Texas Utilities was formed in 1945 to acquire and run DP&L, TESCO, and TP&L. At the time, the utilities had combined revenues of $40.4 million, with about 427,000 electricity customers.

As Texas's population and industry grew, so did the utilities. Sales surpassed $100 million in the mid-1950s, $200 million by 1960, and $400 million by 1969. During the 1960s, the number of customers grew to more than one million.

While D&L, TESCO, and TP&L retained their own identities, they often combined their efforts for acquisition of fuel and construction of power plants. Their parent company formed other subsidiaries to meet these needs, such as Texas Utilities Fuel Company, established in 1970 to provide natural gas to the utilities. Other subsidiaries formed during the 1970s included Chaco Energy Company, focusing on the production and delivery of coal and other fuels to the utilities, and Basic Resources Inc., with the purpose of developing additional energy sources and technology.

472

Expanding Resources in the 1970s and 1980s

At the beginning of the 1970s, Texas Utilities, like other utility operators in Texas, depended almost wholly on natural gas to run its electricity generating plants. During the decade, as natural gas became increasingly scarce in Texas, the company turned to lignite, an inexpensive type of coal it already had in reserve. By 1975 Texas Utilities was meeting 25 percent of its fuel needs with lignite, and was continuing to acquire lignite reserves. Texas Utilities won praise for its foresight in turning to this fuel; its chairman and chief executive officer, T. L. Austin Jr., was named top utility executive for 1978 by *Financial World*. Even environmentalists liked Austin and his company: Howard Saxton, chairman of the Lone Star Sierra Club, told *Financial World* in June 1979 that Austin represented "the good side of an industry that has been under continuous attack."

Texas Utilities also looked to nuclear power to reduce its use of natural gas. Its Comanche Peak nuclear plant, about 35 miles southwest of Fort Worth, was originally scheduled to begin operation in 1980. As was the case with many other utilities' nuclear plants, however, Comanche Peak had numerous delays and cost escalations, which Austin blamed on design changes ordered by the Nuclear Regulatory Commission (NRC). By 1983 the plant was still not in operation, and its cost had risen from $787 million to $3.4 billion.

On the positive side, by 1983 Texas Utilities was using natural gas for only 45 percent of its fuel needs, with lignite supplying almost all of the remainder. Revenues had surpassed $3 billion, its earnings were rising steadily, and its credit rating was the highest possible. In 1984 the company reorganized, with each of the operating utilities becoming a division of a new sub-holding company, TU Electric. At that time Texas Utilities Mining Company, another subsidiary, took on the job of providing lignite to TU Electric's plants.

Nuclear Startup Problems Persist

Comanche Peak continued to encounter rising costs and extended delays. In 1985 its estimated total cost was revised to $5.46 billion. Because of studies and inspections mandated by the NRC and the Atomic Safety Licensing Board, Comanche Peak's first unit was expected to go into operation in mid-1987 and the second about six months later. These dates passed without startup of the units, however. By 1987, the NRC had identified a backlog of 20,000 problems the unit needed to correct.

In addition to regulatory hurdles, the plant was subject to continuing opposition by groups leery of the plant's safety and economic viability. One such group, Citizens Association for Sound Energy (CASE), had questioned the plant's safety numerous times during its construction. Juanita Ellis, a leader of the group, found that TU Electric employees who had made safety complaints had been fired. A total of 50 such employees sued the company.

TU Electric then took an unusual approach, deciding to negotiate with Ellis and the whistle-blowing employees. William G. Counsil, an executive vice-president of TU Electric, began meeting with Ellis in 1986 and providing her with infor-

mation she requested. The NRC had certified CASE as an intervenor, with legal authority to raise questions and introduce evidence pertaining to the licensing of Comanche Peak. Until Counsil had begun meeting with Ellis, however, it had been difficult for CASE to obtain any TU Electric documents or to be taken seriously by the utility. In 1988 Ellis agreed to end her opposition to the licensing of Comanche Peak, and the utility made her a member of the plant's independent safety review committee. TU Electric also acknowledged the plant's past safety problems, and paid $4.5 million to reimburse CASE for its expenses and $5.5 million to settle with the employees who had sued. The lavishness of the settlement was unprecedented in the history of U.S. nuclear energy.

Comanche Peak's first unit finally went into operation in August 1990, with a capability of producing 1,150 megawatts of electricity. The second unit was scheduled for startup in 1993. Overall, Texas Utilities had put more than $9 billion into the nuclear plant. TU Electric's use of lignite and nuclear energy had greatly reduced its dependence on natural gas. In 1990 TU Electric generated 44.4 percent of its power with lignite; 37.7 percent with natural gas; 3.9 percent with the nuclear unit, which was in use only part of the year; and 0.2 percent with oil. The remaining 13.8 percent was power purchased from other utilities.

In 1990 the utility had record electricity sales of 84 billion kilowatt hours, up 2.2 percent from 1989. It also had record hourly peak demand of 18 million kilowatts on August 30, 1990. This also was 2.2 percent more than the previous record, set in August 1988.

Texas Utilities Mining reached a milestone in 1990, mining its 400 millionth ton of lignite. The fifth-largest coal-mining company in the United States, it produced 30.6 million tons in 1990, a single-year record. The company won praise for its efforts to reclaim mined land, with an award from the U.S. Department of the Interior in 1990.

Struggling for Growth in the 1990s

In January 1990 TU Electric requested a 10.2 percent rate increase, its first since 1984, from the Public Utility Commission (PUC) of Texas. The PUC allowed the utility to begin collecting this amount in August of that year. But late in 1991 the PUC ordered the utility to write off $1.38 billion of its investment in Comanche Peak. PUC staff members had questioned some of the expenditures on the nuclear plant. The ordered write-off meant that, after accounting and tax adjustments, Texas Utilities would have to subtract $1 billion from a year's net income. This produced a net loss for 1991 of $410 million. The posting of such a loss rendered the company unable to raise capital through debt issues or preferred stock for at least a year.

Comanche Peak's second unit finally began commercial operation in the summer of 1993. When the unit went on line, TU imposed a 15 percent rate increase on its electric customers. This added as much as $11 a month to the average residential consumer's bill. Meanwhile TU began to look for expansion opportunities. In 1995 the company paid $65 million for Southwestern Electric Service Company. It also bought a 20 percent stake in PCS PrimeCo, a wireless telecommunications firm. This move cost the company $200 million. The next year TU bought the Lone Star Gas Co. and Lone Star Pipelines from ENSERCH Corp. for $1.7 billion. This increased TU's ability to produce and deliver natural gas. Texas Utilities also began its overseas expansion by buying an Australian electric utility, Eastern Energy Limited, for $1.5 billion.

The reason for the sudden burst of acquisition activity was that new laws deregulating the power industry threatened to bring TU more competition. Fearing that changes might mean a loss of its traditional business, the company aimed to break new ground. Not only did the company become bigger, but it got involved in telecommunications—a new line altogether—and went abroad. After buying the share in PCS PrimeCo, TU went on to purchase another telecommunications entity, a privately held firm called Lufkin-Conroe Communications Co. in 1997. Lufkin-Conroe, based in Lufkin, Texas, was one of the state's largest phone companies, with annual revenue of close to $100 million. What apparently interested TU most was that Lufkin-Conroe served about 40,000 customers of TU Electric with local telephone service. TU hoped to take advantage of the customer overlap by offering a complete package of phone and energy use. Other utility companies around the country had been arranging similar deals in joint ventures or purchases of telecommunications businesses.

In 1998 TU offered to buy a large British utility company, the Energy Group PLC, for $6.9 billion. The Energy Group was one of twelve regional electric utilities in England, serving more than three million customers. It also owned Peabody Coal, one of the world's largest coal producers. The Energy Group was one of the last remaining utilities still in British hands after the privatization of the industry began in 1990. Its assets were valued at $14 billion, with 1996 revenue at around $7.3 billion. It was considered quite a prize, and TU's offer started a bidding war with another interested U.S. utility, PacifiCorp of Portland, Oregon. After a series of offers and counter-offers, British utility regulators ordered a sealed bid, and TU won, paying $7.4 billion for the Energy Group. The enormous price was considered worthwhile, as international expansion was key to TU's business strategy. TU immediately announced that Peabody Coal was up for sale.

Principal Subsidiaries

Texas Utilities Electric Company; Texas Utilities Fuel Company; Texas Utilities Mining Company; Texas Utilities Services Inc.; Basic Resources Inc.; Chaco Energy Company.

Further Reading

Aronson, Geoffrey, ''The Co-Opting of CASE,'' *Nation,* December 4, 1989, pp. 678–82.

Kranhold, Kathryn, ''Bidding War Erupts for Energy Group,'' *Wall Street Journal,* March 3, 1998, p. A3.

Levy, Robert, ''Texas' Triple-A Utility,'' *Dun's Business Month,* June 1983.

McKanic, Patricia Ann, ''Texas Utilities Taking a Charge of $1 Billion,'' *Wall Street Journal,* August 9, 1991, p. A3.

Mason, Todd, and Corie Brown, ''Juanita Ellis: Antinuke Saint or Sellout?'' *Business Week,* October 24, 1988.

O'Brian, Bridget, ''Texas Utilities Posts Big Loss in 3rd Quarter,'' *Wall Street Journal,* October 28, 1991, p. A7.

Salpukas, Agis, ''Texas Utilities Wins Fight for Energy Group,'' *New York Times,* May 1, 1998, p. D1.

''Texas Utilities to Buy Local Phone Service in Move to Diversify,'' *Wall Street Journal,* August 26, 1997, p. A4.

—Trudy Ring and Donald R. Stabile
—updated by A. Woodward

Thermo BioAnalysis Corp.

504 Airport Road
Santa Fe, New Mexico 87504-2108
U.S.A.
(508) 471-3232
Fax: (508) 473-9221
Web Site: http://www.thermo.com/subsid/tba1.html

Public Company
Incorporated: 1995
Employees: 979 (1997)
Sales: $139.5 million (1997)
Stock Exchanges: AMS
Ticker: TBA
SICs: 3823 Industrial Measuring Instruments; 3826 Laboratory Analytical Instruments; 7373 Computer Integrated Systems Design

Thermo Bioanalysis Corp. designs, manufactures, and markets instruments, consumables, and information management systems for use in biopharmaceutical research and production, as well as in clinical diagnostics. The company focuses on three principal product areas: Instrumentation, Information Management Systems, and Health Physics.

The History of "Spin-Out" vs. "Spin-Off" at Thermo Electron

Thermo BioAnalysis is considered by its parent company, Thermo Instrument Systems Inc.—and its ultimate parent company, Thermo Electron Corp.—to be a "spin-out" company, as opposed to a "spin-off." George Hatsopoulos, chief executive officer (CEO) of Thermo Electron, differentiates between the two, since his subsidiaries are created to stand on their own, but are not cast off by the parent. Instead, of the ten or so first-generation spin-outs from Thermo Electron, all of them are still partially-owned by the parent company, which is itself a leading manufacturer of environmental monitoring equipment, biomedical, and health equipment.

Hatsopoulos, whose uncles and cousins were successful in technical fields but failures in business, vowed to succeed in both. He received degrees in both engineering and thermodynamics from Massachusetts Institute of Technology, and then founded Thermo Electron in 1956. The company made its initial public offering in October 1967.

Thermo Instrument, Thermo BioAnalysis' parent company, is merely one of ten or so first-generation spin-outs of Thermo Electron. Other first-generation spin-outs include Thermedics, Thermo Fibertek, Thermo Power, Thermo TerraTech, and Thermo Trex. Each of the first-generation spin-outs has second-generation spin-outs orbiting it, and some even have third- and fourth-generation spin-outs.

Thermo Instrument—at various incarnations known as Thermo Water Management Inc., Thermo Environmental Corp., Thermo Instrument Systems, and Thermo Instrument Systems NV—made its public offering in 1986. The company manufactures instruments to identify chemical compounds, monitor pollution and radioactivity, and control industrial processes. It also makes precision measurement equipment, spectrometers, analytical optical and biochemical instruments, and industrial process optimization systems. Furthermore, the company offers services for information management systems.

Thermo Bioanalysis operated as part of Thermo Instruments from 1992–94. Total revenue for 1992 reached $24.5 million—with a net income of $2.5 million—and climbed slowly in 1993 to a total revenue of $25.1 million. In 1994, however, it slipped back to $22.5 million.

Thermo Bioanalysis Flies Solo in 1995

The following year, the company was incorporated in the State of Delaware as a wholly owned subsidiary of parent Thermo Instrument Systems Inc., and a part of its ultimate parent—Thermo Electron Corp.

Most of Thermo Bioanalysis' history consists of acquisitions of other smaller satellite companies, and of Thermo Bioanalysis' dealings with and connections to other subsidiaries of its parent, Thermo Instruments. The company's business has remained the same throughout the short duration of time that it has stood on its own; the names and entities that have surrounded it are what has mainly changed.

In February 1996, the company acquired substantially all of the assets of DYNEX Technologies Inc.—a division of Dynatech Corporation—for approximately $43.2 million. DYNEX Technologies, founded in 1960, brought $18 million in annual sales and over 100 employees to Thermo Bioanalysis in addition to its analytical laboratory instruments expertise, and line of products. DYNEX Technologies Inc., manufactured in vitro diagnostic instrumentation and plasticware for the worldwide diagnostics marketplace. DYNEX was the original developer of microtiter technology and is the world's leading supplier of microtiter technology products for clinical, research, and industrial markets.

MALDI-TOF, a manufacturer of matrix assisted, laser desorption ionization time-of-flight (MALDI-TOF) spectrometry instruments, was acquired by Thermo Bioanalysis in 1995. MALDI-YOF was created in the 1970s to provide analytical biochemists and polymer chemists with a new power for the characterization of their samples and materials in research and quality control. It was spun-off as the MALDI-TOF Division of Finnegan MAT Ltd., which, in 1991, was the first company to introduce MALDI-TOF mass spectrometry to the analytical biochemistry industry.

The Eberline Connection

Eberline Instruments was founded by Howard C. Eberline, formerly a group leader for the development of Health Physics instrumentation at the Los Alamos Scientific Laboratory in Los Alamos, New Mexico. By 1958, Eberline Instruments was spun off as a separate corporation held by REECO. In 1963, Howard Eberline left the company to start another enterprise, called Eberline and Associates.

Eberline Instruments quickly acquired Capco (an industrial capacitor manufacturer) and Thermal Engineering Corporation (an air conditioning company), and invested in Missouri Research Laboratories Inc., Madison Research Inc., and CEP Geonuclear Corp. The company also dabbled in real estate, and created a laboratory services division, which produced radioactive sources for calibration, personnel dosimetry, consulting, radiochemistry, bio-assay, and environmental services.

Eberline Instruments remained public until its purchase in 1979 by Thermo Electron, when it was eventually divided into two separate companies: Eberline Instruments, which continued to produce radiation monitoring equipment out of Santa Fe, and TMA Eberline, which provided all of the laboratory services

now located in Albuquerque. Eberline Instruments became a subsidiary of Thermo Instruments (and an eventual sibling to Thermo Bioanalysis), and TMA Eberline became a subsidiary of Thermo Environmental. Thus, Thermo Bioanalysis, upon its creation, operated in synch with Eberline Instruments as its younger sibling.

Eberline has grown to become the world leader in the design and manufacture of radiation detection and counting instrumentation and sophisticated radiation monitoring systems. It has a diversified product line covering everything from simple hand-held Geiger counters up to complex integrated digital radiation monitoring systems installed at major nuclear facilities around the world. The company has a long history in the supply of detection instrumentation, repair and calibration services, as well as supplying radioactive sources.

Other Acquisitions and Connections

There were a few other notable companies with which Thermo Bioanalysis was connected soon after its spin-out. In March 1996, Thermo Bioanalysis' parent, Thermo Instruments, acquired a substantial portion of the businesses comprising the Scientific Instruments Division of Fisons PLC, a wholly owned subsidiary of Rhone-Poulenc Rorer Inc. That July, the company acquired the Affinity Sensors Division (a manufacturer of optical biosensors for the scientific community) and the LabSystems Division (a provider of services in laboratory information management systems, chromatography data systems, and instrument integration systems) of Fisons PLC for $9 million in cash.

Affinity Sensors manufactures optical biosensors which allow analysis of molecular interactions in real time. The company's interest in evanescent wave biosensors started in the mid-1980s. In 1987 the company joined in research collaboration with GEC-Marconi and The Institute of Biotechnology at The University of Cambridge, to investigate a new generation of evanescent wave sensors, the resonant mirror, resulting in the creation of IAsys technology. The technology enabled biomolecular interaction analysis to be performed in real-time without labels for determination of kinetic profiles, molecular recognition, analyte concentration, and affinity purification. This allowed biochemists in the pharmaceutical, biotechnology, and medical research fields to rapidly study the concentration and functional properties of biomolecules and thereby aid custom design of molecules with specific characteristics. Some of Affinity's products have included the IAsys cuvette system and the IAsys Auto+.

LabSystems was founded in 1971 with the philosophy to seek new challenges and provide answers for healthcare, research, and industrial laboratories. The company holds more than 180 original patents and specializes in the design, implementation, and support of laboratory automation solutions worldwide, providing one of the world's leading laboratory information systems and instrument integration packages. The company has also worked to provide a leading chromatography data system for use in research and development, quality assurance and quality control, and processing plants in a variety of industries including chemical, pharmaceutical, environmental, oil and gas, petrochemical, plastics, food, agricultural, and medical.

The LabSystems group of companies grew to comprise Liquid Handling, Microplate Instrumentation, Biotechnology, and Affinity Sensors. In 1997, a new complementary area, Biosensor Products, became part of the company, and UK-based Denley Instruments Inc. was merged with LabSystems.

Thermo Bioanalysis' Market in the Late 1990s

By 1997, the pharmaceutical, biotech research, and bioinstrumentation industries were increasing research efforts, with the market being estimated in the $2-2.5 million range. Analysts predicted prospects for continued annual growth of 10–20 percent, as the demand for advanced testing, test validating, data calculation, storage equipment and consumables expanded. Combinatorial chemistry was helping labs such as Thermo Bioanalysis engage in pharmaceutical product development to expand the use of microtiter plates. Thermo BioAnalysis owns the registered trademark on the pioneering brand name in the microtiter plates segment—Microtiter.

In May of that year, the company purchased Helsinki, Finland-based LabSystems OY and England-based Hybaid Ltd. from parent Thermo Instrument in a $50 million transaction. Hybaid, based in the UK, was a leading manufacturer and supplier of equipment and reagents for molecular biology laboratories worldwide. Hybaid was founded in 1986 with the goal of developing applications-oriented products to semi-automate labor-intensive molecular biology procedures. In collaboration with the research community, Hybaid developed an extensive product line encompassing many molecular biology applications. In 1995, the company introduced its own range of consumables for nucleic acid extraction procedures, under the "Hybaid Recovery" brand name. The acquisition gave Thermo Bioanalysis access to this knowledge and technology.

Also that year, the company acquired Life Sciences International PLC's Clinical Products Group, itself a different "Thermo" company, in a $66.7 million stock swap from parent Thermo Instrument. The acquisition allowed Thermo BioAnalysis to build on its core bioinstrumentation business. DNA amplification was revolutionized in the 1980s by a simple technique involving a thermophillic enzyme, which operates in hot water and shuts down in cold. Isolated from a deep-sea vent worm, this polymerase allowed DNA to be copied like an old-fashioned mimeograph machine. The mechanism is a simple rocker arm that alternately dips the sample from cold water to hot water, thereby starting and stopping the reaction. Through the Life Sciences purchase, Thermo BioAnalysis became licensed to exploit this market, which previously had been dominated by Perkin-Elmer.

With 350 employees in 1997, sales units in 11 countries (including two joint ventures in China), a well-established worldwide distributor network supporting the company, and private labels and original equipment manufacturers working with the company—Thermo Bioanalysis continued to grow.

In March 1998, Colin Maddix, previously president and CEO of Life Sciences International and also of ThermoSpectra Corporation, both subsidiaries of Thermo Instruments, succeeded Barry S. Howe as president and CEO of the company. In May, the company filed for its initial public offering of stock.

In July of that year, the company acquired Arlington, Texas-based Data Medical Associates Inc. (DMA) in a $5.2 million cash transaction, naming Bret Hendzel, president of subsidiary ALKO Diagnostic, president of the new acquisition. The acquisition of DMA further expanded Thermo BioAnalysis' influence in the clinical diagnostic market, and broadened the company's product line for the chemistry, blood gas, and electrolyte analyzer markets. It also gave the company access to the latter's independent distribution network, which marketed products through distributors and original equipment manufacturers in more than 40 countries worldwide.

Early in 1998, Millennium Pharmaceuticals Inc. and The Wyeth-Ayerst Research Division of American Home Products Corp. together discovered two previously unidentified human genes that appear to play a role in central nervous system disorders. The first gene, which is brain-specific, modulates a key nerve impulse transmission channel, and the second "may provide insights into the molecular basis of psychiatric disorders," according to Jim Barrett, Wyeth-Ayerst's Vice President of Research, in a July 1998 article in *Knight-Ridder/Tribune Business News*. Additionally in 1998, The U.S. Food and Drug Administration granted subsidiary BioTransplant Inc. clearance to begin first-phase and second-phase clinical studies to evaluate its AlloMune system as an aid to reduce organ rejection in kidney transplant patients.

In this always changing environment in a industry based on changes and discovery, the company continues to grow, following George Hatsopoulos' vision. Although it faces vigorous competition, moving into the twenty-first century as a powerhouse in the bioinstrumentation industry seemed to be an achievable goal.

Principal Subsidiaries

Alko Diagnostic; Benelux Thermo BioAnalysis GmbH (Germany); Fastighets AB Skrubba; Limited Life Sciences International; Thermo BioAnalysis (Guernsey) Ltd.; Thermo BioAnalysis Holding, Limited; Thermo BioAnalysis Ltd. (England); Thermo BioAnalysis S.A.

Principal Divisions

BioMolecular Instruments Division; DYNEX Technologies Inc. (Chantilly, VA); Dynatech Laboratories SPOL. S.R.O.; DYNEX Technologies (Asia) Inc.; DYNEX Technologies GmbH (Germany); DYNEX Technologies Limited (England); Eberline Instrument Corp. (Santa Fe, NM); Capillary Electrophoresis Division (Santa Fe, NM); MALDI-TOF; Shandon Labsystems Group; Affinity Sensors Division; Biosensor Products Division; Biotechnology Division; Liquid Handling Division; Microplate Instrumentation Division.

Further Reading

"*The Boston Globe* Business Notes Column," *Knight-Ridder/Tribune Business News*, July 15, 1998, p. OKRB98196066.
"Life Sciences Unit Agrees to $66.7 Million Stock Deal," *The Wall Street Journal*, May 14, 1998, p. A12.
Macdonald, A. L. "Thermo Bioanalysis—Company Report," Lehman Brothers, Inc., May 20, 1997.

''Thermo BioAnalysis Acquires Data Medical Associates, Inc.,'' *PR Newswire*, July 13, 1998, p. 713NEM026.

''Thermo BioAnalysis Appoints New Chief, Considers Buying Firm,'' *The Wall Street Journal*, March 13, 1998, p. B8.

''Thermo Bioanalysis Corp.,'' *The New York Times*, June 15, 1998, p. C11.

''Thermo BioAnalysis Corp.,'' *The New York Times*, May 18, 1998, p. C10.

''Thermo BioAnalysis Corp.,'' *The Wall Street Journal*, June 18, 1998, p. B13.

''Thermo Bioanalysis Corp.—History & Debt,'' Moody's Investors Service, April 23, 1998.

''Thermo BioAnalysis Gets Approval to Buy Unit of Parent Firm,'' *The Wall Street Journal*, April 22, 1998, p. A4.

''Thermo Bioanalysis to Buy Another Thermo Business,'' *The New York Times*, May 14, 1998, p. C4.

—Daryl F. Mallett

TIMEX®

Timex Corporation

P.O. Box 310
Middlebury, Connecticut 06762
U.S.A.
(203) 573-5000
Fax: (203) 573-5143
Web site: http://www.timex.com

Private Company
Incorporated: 1941 as Timex Inc.
Employees: 7,500
Sales: $850 million (1998)
SICs: 3873 Watches, Clocks, Watch Cases & Parts

Timex Corporation has manufactured the largest-selling watch brand in the United States since the 1960s. Renowned for its sturdy but inexpensive timepieces, Timex distributes its watches through 100,000 outlets in the United States, as well as throughout the world.

Noble Ancestors

Timex evolved from three notable 19th-century clockmakers: the Waterbury Clock Company, a manufacturing firm established in 1857; the Waterbury Watch Company, founded in 1880, maker and seller of pocket watches on an international scale; and Robert H. Ingersoll and Brothers, also an international manufacturer and marketer of pocket watches since 1881. During World War I, a new timepiece—the wristwatch—became popular. Easier to use than the pocket watch, wristwatches were in high demand with soldiers for their convenience in battle. Both the Waterbury Watch Company and Ingersoll and Brothers marketed wristwatches during the war and afterwards when demand for the novel timepiece remained strong.

Two Norwegian immigrants to the United States, shipbuilder Thomas Olsen and engineer Joakim Lehmkuhl—both of whom fled Norway after the German invasion of their country in 1940—founded Timex Inc. in 1941. They purchased the nearly bankrupt Waterbury Clock Company, seeking to aid the allied war effort by producing bomb and artillery fuses that utilized clockwork mechanisms.

When World War II ended in 1945, Olsen, the majority shareholder, returned to Norway, while Lehmkuhl remained in the United States to run the company. During this time, Lehmkuhl decided to convert the Timex plant to mass produce inexpensive timekeeping devices. Using the simplest and most standardized production methods available, Lehmkuhl's plant incorporated a high degree of mechanization in the manufacturing process. Furthermore, the wristwatches Timex manufactured used hard alloy bearings, producing a more rugged and less expensive alternative to watches that used jewels. Timex's product and production methods eventually won Lehmkuhl a reputation as "the Henry Ford of the watch industry."

The first Timex watches rolled off the assembly line in 1949 and soon became known for their dependability. At the time, most watches were sold by jewelers, who typically marked up prices by 50 percent. To keep its prices low, Timex insisted on only a 30 percent markup, and, consequently, most jewelers refused to sell Timex watches. Robert Mohr, head of Timex's marketing operation, opted to bypass the jewelers, instead selling the watches directly to consumer outlets including drugstores, hardware stores, and even tobacco stands. During the 1950s and 1960s Mohr built a distribution network that reached nearly 250,000 outlets. By 1961, sales were up to $71 million, with after tax profits of $2.9 million.

Becoming a Market Leader in the 1960s

Advertising heavily both to build its name and to sell the dependability of its watches, Timex relied chiefly on the visual impact of television. Commercials depicted Timex watches remaining functional and accurate after being attached to churning boat propellers and the hooves of galloping horses. The phrase "takes a licking and keeps on ticking" became widely known, and by the late 1960s Timex watches accounted for about half of U.S. watch sales.

During this time, the company deliberately underproduced, manufacturing only 85 percent of the watches it thought it could sell. This practice created a scarcity that kept prices up and dealers tractable. The company further secured its leadership

---

Company Perspectives:

Timex is a direct descendant of several important nine-teenth-century American clock and watch manufacturers. Like our company today, they all specialized in durable yet affordable timepieces. . . . Timex has maintained market superiority since that time by introducing innovative designs and technology.

---

position in the market by using new designs and technology in the years following the 1960s.

In addition to the manufacture of timepieces, Timex continued to produce the clockwork mechanisms for the military that it had begun during the war. Timex facilities were also used to assemble cameras for Polaroid.

By 1970 Timex had record profits of $27 million on sales of $200 million. Yet change lay just around the corner, as the firm was facing intense competition in a changing market. Although few companies producing watches in the same price range as Timex could challenge the company for quality or popularity, digital electronic watches were rapidly overtaking the conventional watch. Timex began producing digital watches in 1972, but it had not moved as fast as its competition. In 1974 the company's net income fell by one-third to $8.7 million on sales of $348 million. By 1976 digital watch prices had fallen into the price range of the company's mechanical watches, and Timex began losing market share. Its major competitors in the electronic watch market were Texas Instruments and Fairchild Camera and Instrument Corp., both of which had more experience with electronics. A price war ensued, and by 1977 Texas Instruments had slashed the price of one of its most popular watches to $10.

Also during this time, Timex management was in turmoil. Lehmkuhl had reportedly become increasingly eccentric and difficult to work with, and in 1973 Olsen's son Fred had the 78-year-old founder and chairperson removed from office. Furthermore, the company's three presidents were constantly at odds, and when electronics experts were brought in to help the company fight for digital watch market share, the infighting intensified and the company suffered. Timex was soon restructured to reflect Fred Olsen's belief that making electronic watches required a radically different approach than that of mechanical watches. The mechanical watch operation was thereafter isolated from the new electronic operations, a change that eventually created resentment among the employees. The restructuring also led to numerous mistakes as the isolated electronic division was unable to take advantage of the mechanical division's experience.

Consequently, Timex's electronic watches were awkwardly large and 50 percent more expensive than those offered by competing firms in the mid-1970s. Believing that sales of mechanical watches were in an irreversible decline, management planned to keep production capacity below the level of likely sales in order to make as much money from the line as possible as the market shrunk. Advertising for mechanical

watches virtually ceased, and, as spending decreased, the capital was shifted to the manufacture and sale of digital watches.

The entire watch industry had a good year in 1977, and Timex decided to slow the downsizing of mechanical watch production. However, the company failed to reinstate its advertising budget, and, as a result, its only profitable product began to decline in popularity. Timex lost $4.7 million on sales of $600 million in 1979. Sister corporation TMX Ltd., a Bermuda-based company that supplied watches and parts to Timex, also lost $5 million that year.

Diversifying in the 1980s

During this time, chief executive Robert Weltzien began diversifying the company. He bought a clock and timer operation from General Electric Co., and in early 1980 he held the company's first ever press conference, announcing that as Timex had gained experience from assembling Polaroid cameras—more than 40 million between 1952 and 1979—the company would soon begin manufacturing a new type of 35-millimeter camera. However, these moves were not enough to offset Timex's declining watch sales, and later that year Olsen flew in from Norway, fired Weltzien, and took his place as CEO. Thereafter, Olsen spent two weeks a month overseeing his businesses in Norway and the other two weeks with Timex in Connecticut.

While Olsen was a brilliant long-term strategist with immense energy, he had little experience with the day-to-day running of an organization, and some managers became frustrated as he interfered with the details of their projects. He began closing factories, cutting wages, and selling off side businesses, as he reshaped the company into a consumer electronics concern that would sell watches, clocks, computers, and electronic products geared toward home health care.

In 1980 Commodore Computers explored the possibility of a merger or other working relationship with Timex, but Olsen declined. Instead, Timex opted to attempt duplicating Commodore's success by producing its own computer. Created by British inventor Clive Sinclair, the Timex computer was brought out at the end of 1982 and quickly sold 500,000 units. However, critics noted that the Timex computer was extremely limited in its capabilities and inferior to Commodore's product. After Commodore engaged Timex in a price war, Timex made little money from the venture.

In 1983 Timex brought its first home health care products to market. The products, made by Singapore subcontractors, included a $69.95 blood-pressure cuff, a $24.95 digital thermometer, and a $49.95 digital scale. Timex relied on its widely recognized name and large distribution base to give it an advantage over companies already selling similar products. The market was very competitive, however, and Timex was also hampered by the breakup of its Silicon Valley computer engineering staff due to continuing political infighting as well as the slow start of its new lab in Connecticut.

Watches still accounted for 90 percent of Timex's business in 1983. The firm's digital watches had improved considerably, and it introduced a new quartz calendar watch at $100 that was billed as the world's thinnest. While the majority of its electronic watches were more expensive than those of its competitors, Timex had succeeded in bringing out one model that sold for only $7.95.

Also in 1983, Timex endured negative press from an employee strike at its plant in Dundee, Scotland, which strikers occupied after management fired 1,900 workers. Members of the British parliament, and finally Prime Minister Margaret Thatcher, intervened before the six-week occupation was ended.

Refocusing on the Wristwatch

Throughout the 1980s, inexpensive fashion watches rapidly gained popularity and were released by a number of companies, most notably the innovative Swatch company. Timex's sales needed bolstering as some industry analysts estimated that the company only produced half as many watches as it had five years earlier. Consequently, Timex began producing watches that were more fashionable, sporty, and colorful, and invested money and energy in advertising. In the spring of 1983 the company launched a $20 million television advertising campaign focusing on its new technological sophistication and style. The commercials, by Gray Advertising, playfully exaggerated the features of Timex watches. In one ad a group of joggers ran up and down the contours of a Timex sports watch; in another, a group of people climbed out of a boat and walked across a waterproof Timex watch that served as a dock. Timex also showed its ads in movie theaters, purchasing four weeks of ad time at Screenvision Cinema Network's 4,500 theaters in 1986.

One of the firm's greatest successes during this time was its sports watches. In 1984, an Olympic games year, the company brought out the Triathlon watch, which was water resistant to 50 meters, could recall eight laps of running times, and had a 16-hour stopwatch. In its first year, 400,000 of the watches were sold at $34.95 each. Encouraged by this success, Timex brought out a ski watch that included a thermometer as well as a racing watch that could measure speeds of up to 999 miles an hour. The company launched its Atlantis 100 water resistant sports watch in 1986 with a $1 million ad shown during football's Super Bowl. This ad featured a group of divers discovering a 65-foot replica of the watch on the bottom of the Red Sea. Five other "adventure" commercials were also produced.

In 1988 Timex brought back its "takes a licking and keeps on ticking" campaign, which had not been used in ten years. This time, however, the ads were intentionally humorous and took the premise of the old ads to extremes, one ad showing the watches being thrown to ravenous piranha. Timex also stepped up advertising for its new line of men's and women's fashion watches, influenced by those being sold by Swatch. Having formerly advertised mainly in such magazines as *Time* and *Life,* Timex began buying space in sports and fashion magazines. The ads were part of an effort to help Timex shake its staid image at a time when watchmakers like Swatch were making inroads by giving their watches a fun, quirky image. The firm spent $6 million on ads during its Christmas ad campaign, representing 60 percent of its $10 million annual ad budget.

Timex released new sport watches in 1988 that were aimed at niche markets while also being designed to appeal to a broader audience. One model, the Victory, included features

useful in sailboat racing and a design influenced by traditional nautical instruments. While the Ironman watch was geared toward triathlon participants, the watch's memory feature and rugged styling proved so popular that Timex was soon able to claim that it was the best-selling watch in the United States through 1997, if not the leader among watch sales worldwide.

At the end of the 1980s the color plastic watch business pioneered by Swatch was beginning to decline, but Timex continued producing colorful watches with classic styling and increased the distribution of its watches to upscale department stores. Timex remained at the top of the U.S. mass market watch sector with a share near 50 percent. Sales for 1988 topped $500 million, and Timex was still the largest company in the $1.5 billion U.S. watch market, despite the fact that all of its watches were priced at under $75.

In 1990, with its market share under continual pressure, Timex spent $7 million on a unique two-month print ad campaign. Again picking up on the "takes a licking" theme, the ads featured portraits of people who, along with their Timex watches, had survived serious mishaps. One woman, for example, had fallen 85 feet while rock climbing and suffered only minor injuries. The ads, by the Minneapolis-based agency Fallon McElligott, appeared in 31 magazines and included several three-page spreads.

New Technologies in the 1990s

Although the information age initiatives the company had pursued in the early 1980s had been sharply scaled back, Timex had not forgone new technologies altogether. The company announced it would develop a wristwatch that would double as a telephone pager in conjunction with Motorola Inc. Moreover, in 1992 Timex introduced a watch with a luminescent dial that glowed like a full moon at the push of a button. The watch used a dial made of zinc sulphide and copper that other companies had used on clocks, though Timex was the first to adapt it to watch size. Featuring patented electroluminescence technology, Timex's Indiglo Night-Light set the standard for watch illumination. It offered night workers, campers, sports players, and moviegoers a safe, nontoxic, bright, even blue-green light superior to other watches' shine. (Other manufacturers utilized incandescent bulbs, which resulted in faint illumination, or sunlight-storing phosphorescent substances, which faded, or potentially dangerous radioactive substances such as radium or titanium.)

These innovations were well received by the public. Sales for 1992 totaled $400 million, giving Timex one-third of the U.S. watch market. The company was now the largest watchmaker in the United States. Both *Business Week* and *Fortune* named the Indiglo Night-Light one of the best products of the year in 1993, and high demand for the Indiglo Night-Light continued after its introduction. Timex incorporated the innovation into 65 percent of its watch styles and added further technological improvements; for example, Night Mode, which provided a steady, three-second light source. The powers of the Indiglo Night-Light came to the nation's attention during the bombing of the World Trade Center in New York. Amid the smoke and darkness after the bombing, a man from Arizona used the light from his Indiglo Ironman Triathlon to lead people from the ravaged building.

More recognition came for Timex products when the "first family" of the United States donated President Bill Clinton's Ironman Triathlon—the watch he wore during the 1993 inaugural celebrations—to the National Museum of American History at the Smithsonian Institution. "Nevertheless, President Clinton is not this watch's first presidential appointment," Timex revealed through an *In the News* press release, observing that "Although the Ironman Triathlon watch was designed to accommodate the needs of hard-core triathletes, it has proven a winner inside the Beltway, most notably on the wrists of the former presidential team of George Bush and Dan Quayle."

Once again, however, a labor dispute at Timex UK sullied the company's public image in 1993. Workers in the Dundee, Scotland, plant initiated a strike against Timex when the company announced impending layoff plans, wage freezes, and benefit reductions. When Timex fired the strikers and hired 250 replacement workers, violence and ill-will between the workers and company management ensued. At the time, a company supervisor told *New Statesman & Society*: "I cannot imagine the old workforce ever coming back to the factory. The rifts are so great now. It's all too personal."

Despite its image problems in the United Kingdom, Timex remained a favorite accessory brand in the United States, according to Fairchild Publications. Placing ahead of Nike and Levis, Timex ranked second in Fairchild Publications as the overall favorite fashion brand in the country in 1995. Still, despite it favorable position with the public, Timex launched ten marketing campaigns that year to compete more effectively, in particular challenging Swatch for market share.

Timex continued to develop technological innovations for its watches throughout the 1990s. In 1995, for example, it introduced the Timex Data Link, a watch employing wireless transfer technology so that watch and personal computer could communicate. Timex Data Link watches came equipped with a Windows-based PC program allowing data to be entered or imported into the program. A lens on the watch translated the data from on-screen bar codes to the watch's memory. "This is certainly not the first watch with data-storage functions," explained Steve Morgenstern in *Home Office Computing*, "but the Timex unit makes getting your information into the watch easier than any other model I've seen." Well received, the Timex Data Link won *Popular Science*'s Best of What's New Award, as well as the 1995 Design and Engineering Award from *Popular Mechanics*.

The following year, Timex debuted the 150S, a smaller model of the Timex Data Link. This updated version, featuring a software program developed in conjunction with Microsoft, included WristApps, an application capable of downloading data. The company also created a subsidiary dedicated to the design and marketing of its Nautica watch in 1996.

In 1997, Timex introduced a notebook adapter that connected its Data Link watches with notebook, laptop, and portable PCs with liquid crystal display viewing screens—the fastest growing PC market segment. "The benefits of the Notebook Adapter are twofold," Jan Mladik, marketing manager of Timex's Wrist Instruments Group, explained in a press release. "First, it provides a whole new group of consumers access to the Timex Data Link information transfer technology. Secondly, it allows those 'road warriors' who own both desktop PCs and portables to update databases and send new functions when traveling." The Data Link Notebook Adapter and the Timex Data Link 150S both won Innovations '97 awards.

Timex also began manufacturing a watch presented as an entry in the company's Bright Idea Contest in 1997. A contestant suggested a pulse timing watch designed specifically for health-care workers. Using the Indiglo Night-Light, Timex easily designed a watch with the ability to check pulse rates in low-light conditions.

In 1998, Timex introduced another new product—the Humvee. Named after AM General's all-terrain vehicle, the Humvee watch was water resistant and exceeded government standards for shock resistance. Timex entered into a licensing agreement with AM General to market a watch sharing the Humvee name. Lee Woodward, manager of marketing communications for AM General remarked in a press release: "We are proud to align ourselves with a partner that can capture the essence and qualities of the Humvee in a product such as a sports watch. Timex has a tradition of producing durable, long lasting products that can take abuse, just like the Humvee and Hummer."

Active in more than 90 countries since 1980, Timex maintained its position as a world leader in watches in 1998. The company also retained its hold on the U.S. market in particular through the introduction of innovative products and the use of technology. More of the same was expected from Timex as it approached a new century in watchmaking.

Further Reading

Brown, Christie, "Sweat Chic," *Forbes,* September 5, 1988.

Burwell, Paul, "Can Your Watch Cut It?," *Geographical Magazine,* April 1996, p. 40.

Fahey, Alison, "Another Lickin'," *Advertising Age,* November 7, 1988.

"The Great Digital Watch Shake-Out," *Business Week,* May 2, 1977.

King, Thomas R., "Timex Hopes 'True Story' Ads Will Keep Watch Sales Ticking," *Wall Street Journal,* October 30, 1990.

Magnet, Myron, "Timex Takes the Torture Test," *Fortune,* June 27, 1983.

Milne, Kirsty, "Workers All Wound Up," *New Statesman & Society,* May 14, 1993, p. 12.

Morgenstern, Steve, "Watch Out! New High-tech Wristwatches Do Everything But Phone Home," *Home Office Computing,* December 1995, p. 42.

"Motorola Plans to Develop Pager Watch with Timex," *Wall Street Journal,* July 26, 1989.

"A Reclusive Tycoon Takes Over at Timex," *Business Week,* April 14, 1980.

White, Hooper, "Human Touch Rides New Wave," *Advertising Age,* November 7, 1983.

—Scott Lewis
—updated by Charity Anne Dorgan

Tom Doherty Associates Inc.

175 Fifth Avenue
New York, New York 10010
U.S.A.
(212) 388 0100
Fax: (212) 388 0191
Web site: http://www.tor.com

Wholly Owned Subsidiary of Verlagsgruppe Georg von Holtzbrinck GmbH
Incorporated: 1980
Employees: 50
Sales: $50 million (1997 est.)
SICs: 2731 Book Publishing & Printing

Tom Doherty Associates Inc. (TDA), better known by its imprint of Tor Books, is one of the leading publishers of science fiction (SF), fantasy, and horror. Tor Books has won virtually every major award in the SF and fantasy fields and its parent has been the winner of the *Locus* award for best publisher for the past 11 consecutive years.

Tom Doherty Associates Inc., 1980

In 1980, Tom Doherty, then the publisher of Ace Books—a venerable paperback publishing company that had more recently been bought and continued as an imprint under Grosset & Dunlap—decided to set up his own publishing company. After leaving Ace, with the help of some investors, including Pinnacle Books and Dell Distributing (who would produce and distribute TDA's early titles) and silent partner Richard Gallen (one of the most successful packagers in publishing history, with his own line, Dell Emerald Books), Doherty formed a corporation in New York with the legal name of Tom Doherty Associates Inc., whose business it was to publish books. As one of its first business ventures, TDA created a new imprint in 1980 named Tor Books.

James Patrick "Jim" Baen and Harriet McDougal were the first two employees of TDA, leaving Ace Books to go with Doherty. Baen's career had previously led him to be the editor of *Galaxy* magazine (1974–77) before he went to Ace in August 1977 as a senior editor, eventually getting promoted to vice-president in 1980. He became TDA's SF editor and continued to edit the *Destinies* series freelance. McDougal, who previously worked as editor-in-chief of Ace, served as the nonfiction editor for TDA from her home in North Carolina.

Tor (an old Anglo Saxon word meaning "summit" or "peak") designed a logo of a mountain in a circle, signed a distribution agreement, printed a group of books, sold them, and the company was launched early in 1981. Some of the early books included movie tie-ins and cartoon books for Dell and Simon & Schuster, as well as packaging books for Pocket/Wallaby (featuring such authors as Andre Norton, Roger Zelazny, and Alfred Bester).

Tor debuted in the science fiction field in the March 1981 issue of *Locus: The Newspaper of the Science Fiction Field*, with a full-page advertisement of Poul Anderson's *The Psychotechnic League*, lavishly illustrated by Vincent DiFate. By May, the publisher's ads featured the phrase: "Tor Books: We're Part of the Future." The company would quickly establish its place in SF publishing history with early titles such as Norton's *Forerunner*; Fred Saberhagen's *Water of Thought*, *The Best of Berserkers*, and *Earth Descended*; Poul Anderson's *Winners*, *New America*, *Starship*, *Explorations*, *The Psychotechnic League: Cold Victory*, *The Gods Laughed*, *Fantasy*, *Conflict*, and *Guardians of Time*; Keith Laumer's *The Breaking Earth*, *Beyond the Imperium*, *The Other Sky*, and *The House in November*; Harry Harrison's *Planet of No Return* and *Planet of the Damned*; Roger Zelazny and Fred Saberhagen's *Coils*; Steve Barnes and Larry Niven's *Belial*; Gordon R. Dickson and Ben Bova's *Gremlins Go Home!*; Philip José Farmer's *Father to the Stars*, *Greatheart Silver*, *Stations of the Nightmare*, *The Purple Book*, *The Other Log of Phineas Fogg*, and *The Cache*; and C. M. Kornbluth's *Not This August*.

In the beginning, Tor published mostly rack-sized paperback science fiction, fantasy, and supernatural horror, with some westerns, historicals, mysteries, and thrillers thrown into the mix. That year, the company picked up a Nebula Award for Best Novel for *The Claw of the Conciliator* by Gene Wolfe and his *The Shadow of the Torturer* won Best Novel World Fantasy Award.

In the mid-1980s, the company began publishing hardcovers, which were distributed by St. Martin's Press (SMP). Titles during the mid-1980s included Poul Anderson's *Dialogue with Darkness, Maurai & Kith, Past Times, Time Patrolman,* and *The Long Night*; Norton's *Forerunner: The Second Venture*; the first two volumes of Norton and Robert Adams's five *Magic in Ithkar* anthologies; and Norton and A. C. Crispin's *Gryphon's Eyrie*. Awards during that time included The Prometheus Award for *The Probability Broach* by L. Neil Smith (1982) and the Nebula Award for Best Novel for Orson Scott Card's *Ender's Game* (1985). Other products during the mid-1980s included such computer games as Fred Saberhagen's Berserker and Larry Niven and Steven Barnes's Inferno, plus a computer version of the I Ching, packaged for Apple, TRS-80, and IBM computers, developed in conjunction with Pinnacle and Warner (owner of Atari).

St. Martin's Press, 1986

Macmillan Publishers Ltd. (Macmillan U.K.) was until recently a privately held British company owned by the Macmillan family (the same family that produced a British prime minister), consisting of several British divisions, including Pan Books, Picador, Macmillan General Books, Pan Macmillan Australia, Macmillan Magazines Ltd., and *Nature* magazine, among others. Macmillan U.K. used to own American Macmillan, but that company was sold to a U.S. owner in 1950 and now has no connection to the British company. At one point, American Macmillan was part of the British-owned Maxwell Communications Group and was eventually purchased by Simon & Schuster.

Because the idea of owning an American publishing company was still attractive, in the mid-1950s Macmillan U.K. started another company in the United States called St. Martin's Press (named so because, at the time, Macmillan Publishers Ltd. was headquartered on St. Martin's Street in London).

In 1986, Doherty sold his company to SMP, and TDA/Tor Books became a division of the larger company, at that time one of the ten largest book publishers in the United States, featuring a broad range of books, from fiction and biography to mysteries and cookbooks, including bestsellers such as *Silence of the Lambs*, by Thomas Harris; *All Creatures Great and Small*, by James Herriott; and *Will*, by G. Gordon Liddy, among others. SMP also included divisions such as St. Martin's Press Scholarly and Reference Division and The Stonewall Inn imprint (a trade paperback line founded at SMP in 1987 by then-editor Michael Denneny and the only gay/lesbian imprint at a major publishing house in 1998); and distributed books by companies including Rodale Books and Rizzoli.

TDA titles which won recognition that year included the Hugo Award for Best Novel and the *Science Fiction Chronicle* (*SFC*) Reader Award for Best Novel for Card's *Ender's Game* and the Nebula Award for Best Novel for his *Speaker for the Dead*; as well as the World Fantasy Award for Best Novel for Dan Simmons's *Song of Kali*.

Titles in 1987 included Poul Anderson's *The Enemy Stars*. Awards won in 1987 included a Hugo for Best Novel and *Locus* for Best SF Novel for Card's *Speaker for the Dead*; a Nebula for Pat Murphy's *The Falling Woman*; a Locus Award for Best Fantasy Novel for Wolfe's *Soldier of the Mist*; *SFC* Award for Best Editor (David Hartwell). The following year brought a World Fantasy Award for Best Anthology for Hartwell's *The Dark Descent*; a *Locus* Award for Best Fantasy Novel for Card's *Seventh Son*; *SFC* Awards for Best Novel (Wolfe's *The Urth of the New Sun*) and Hartwell picked up Best Editor the second year in a row. That year also marked the beginning of Tor's reign as Best Publisher in the *Locus* Awards, which it held every year through at least 1997, with titles including Anderson/Greenberg/Waugh's *Space Wars* and Norton's *Moon Mirror* and *Tales of the Witch World 2*.

In 1989, *Storeys from the Old Hotel* by Gene Wolfe won the Best Collection World Fantasy Award; *Red Prophet* by Card picked up the *Locus* Best Fantasy Novel Award; and *Moon of Ice* by Brad Linaweaver picked up the Prometheus Award. Other titles included Poul Anderson's *No Truce with Kings* and *Saturn Game*; Fritz Leiber's *Ship of Shadows*; and Norton's *Dare to Go A-Hunting* and *Four from the Witch World*. In 1990, Card's *Prentice Alvin* won the Best Fantasy Novel *Locus* Award; *Subterranean Gallery* by Richard Paul Russo won The Philip K. Dick Memorial Award; *The Child Garden* by Geoff Ryman was awarded The John W. Campbell Memorial Award and The Arthur C. Clarke Award; and *SFC* bestowed the Best Editor Award on Beth Meacham. Other titles that year included Poul Anderson's *The Shield of Time*; Farmer's *Dayworld Breakup*; Norton's *Tales of the Witch World 3*; and Norton/Robert Bloch's *The Jekyll Legacy*.

By 1991, the company was publishing more than 200 hardcovers and paperbacks a year. More recognition came to TDA books as well, with *Thomas the Rhymer* by Ellen Kushner winning The Mythopoeic Fantasy Award and Best Novel in the World Fantasy Awards; Card's *Maps in a Mirror* winning Best Collection in the *Locus* Awards; Gwyneth Jones's *White Queen* winning The James Tiptree Jr. Memorial Award; *Pacific Edge* by Kim Stanley Robinson picking up The John W. Campbell Memorial Award; and *The Dark Beyond the Stars* by Frank M. Robinson winning Best SF Novel in The Lambda Literary Awards.

Baen was offered the chance by Pocket Books to start his own science fiction line to replace the canceled Timescape line. So, with the help of investors including Doherty, Baen left Tor and created Baen Books.

Orb Books, 1992

As the list of new titles increased, it became more and more difficult to keep older titles (the publisher's "backlist") in print. In 1992, TDA created the Orb Books imprint in response to persistent complaints from readers and booksellers that some of their favorite science fiction and fantasy backlist titles were no longer available. Some of the books chosen for the Orb list have included previously published Tor mass market editions such as Murphy's Nebula Award-winning *The Falling Woman*; Jones's Tiptree Award-winning *White Queen*; Kim Stanley Robinson's acclaimed "Three Californias" trilogy; Storm Constantine's

"Wraeththu" novels; Chelsea Quinn Yarbro's *A Candle for D'Artagnan*; Bruce McAllister's *Dream Baby*; and Michael Bishop's *Philip K. Dick Is Dead, Alas*. The Orb list has also included new editions of books previously issued by other publishers, such as Wolfe's "Book of the New Sun" sequence; Charles de Lint's contemporary fantasy novels *Greenmantle* and *Moonheart*; Jack Vance's "Planet of Adventure" series; Kenneth Morris's rediscovered fantasy masterpiece *The Chalchiuhite Dragon*; A. E. van Vogt's classic novel *Slan*; Jack Williamson's *The Humanoids*; and Kate Wilhelm's *Where Late the Sweet Birds Sang*. New accolades included *China Mountain Zhang* by Maureen F. McHugh winning the Tiptree Award and the IAFA/Crawford Award going to *Flying in Place* by Susan Palwick.

Forge Books, 1993

The percentage of non-SF "mainstream" titles (nonfiction, thrillers, suspense, mystery, historicals, westerns, romance, etc.) in the Tor list continued to grow. By 1993, over half the list was non-SF. Because the Tor Books name had become strongly identified with SF and fantasy, however, TDA decided to create a new imprint to better market these mainstream titles and Forge Books (replete with a logo of a flaming anvil) was born.

The first Forge title, Paul Erdman's *Zero Coupon*, a financial thriller, was published in the fall of 1993. At first the imprint was only used on hardcovers but, in 1994, it began appearing on paperbacks as well. Among the books that have appeared under the Forge imprint are Douglas Preston and Lincoln Child's *New York Times* bestselling thriller *Relic*; the mainstream historical novels of Judith Tarr; and Sharan Newman's medieval mystery *The Wandering Arm*.

In 1993, Tor featured Greg Costikyan's novel *By the Sword*, which he originally wrote as a 26-installment science fiction story released on Prodigy as a weekly serial. More TDA books picked up awards that year, with McHugh's *China Mountain Zhang* receiving a *Locus* Award for Best First Novel and a Lambda Literary Award for Best SF Novel; mathematician Vernor Vinge's *A Fire Upon the Deep* garnering the Hugo Award and an *SFC* Award for Best Novel; Jack Womack's *Elvissey* winning The Philip K. Dick Memorial Award; Meacham receiving another *SFC* Best Editor Award; and Jane Yolen's *Briar Rose* claiming The Mythopoeic Fantasy Award. The following year saw Greg Bear's *Moving Mars* winning a Nebula and an *SFC* Award for Best Novel; Meacham meriting another *SFC* Award as Best Book Editor; Jonathan Lethem's *Gun, with Occasional Music* winning The IAFA/Crawford Award; and L. Neil Smith's *Pallas* taking home The Prometheus.

Verlagsgruppe Georg von Holtzbrinck GmbH, 1995

In April 1995, Stuttgart-based media giant Verlagsgruppe Georg von Holtzbrinck GmbH (The Holtzbrinck Publishing Group), acquired a majority interest in Macmillan U.K., with the Macmillan family remaining minority shareholders. The German family-owned publishing empire, founded in 1971 by von Holtzbrinck patriarch Georg, already owned several trade, academic, and business-oriented publishing operations on both sides of the Atlantic, in addition to several German book publishing houses (including fiction, nonfiction, school books, textbooks, specialist books, professional information publica-

tions, and science publications); weekly and daily newspapers and periodicals, including *Scientific American* magazine; printers; television, radio, and multimedia companies; and the publishing houses Henry Holt & Company Inc.

Holtzbrinck split Tom Doherty Associates Inc. off from St. Martin's Press and it became an independent company within the German empire. More awards followed in 1995, with Lethem's *Gun, with Occasional Music* picking up the Best First Novel *Locus* Award; Hartwell getting *SFC*'s Best Book Editor Award; The Lambda Literary Award for Best SF Novel going to *Trouble and Her Friends* by Melissa Scott; and The Prometheus to Poul Anderson's *The Stars Are Also Fire*. Similarly, in 1996 a World Fantasy Award went to *The Prestige* by Christopher Priest for Best Novel; *Locus* Awards to *Alvin Journeyman* by Card for Best Fantasy Novel and *Expiration Date* by Tim Powers for Best Dark Fantasy Novel; an *SFC* Award to Patrick Nielsen Hayden for Best Book Editor; The IAFA/Crawford Award to Canadian author Candas Jane Dorsey's *Black Wine*; The Lambda Literary Award to *Shadow Man* by Melissa Scott for Best SF Novel; and The Compton N. Crook Memorial Award to *Celestial Matters* by Richard Garfinkle. In 1997 a Hugo for Best Novelette went to "Bicycle Repairman" by Bruce Sterling, from *Intersections*; a Nebula for Best Short Story to "Sister Emily's Lightship" by Jane Yolen, from *Starlight 1*; a World Fantasy Award to *The Wall of the Sky, the Wall of the Eye* by Lethem for Best Collection and to *Starlight 1*, edited by Patrick Nielsen Hayden, for Best Anthology; a *Locus* Award to *Whiteout* by Sage Walker as Best First Novel; The Tiptree Memorial Award to *Black Wine* by Dorsey; and The Mythopoeic Fantasy Award for *The Wood Wife* by Terri Windling.

Also that year, Tor cashed in on the popularity of The Mighty Morphin Power Rangers with three full-color illustrated tie-ins to the film (*The Movie Storybook*, a "Behind-the-Scenes-Look" Scrapbook, and *Adventure on Phaedos*).

In 1998, Random House Inc., including its many subsidiaries (The Ballantine Publishing Group—Ballantine Books, Del Rey Books, Fawcett Books, Ivy Books, One World, House of Collectibles—as well as Ballantine Doubleday Dell and others) was picked up by Bertelsmann, putting nearly half of American publishing in the hands of two German media companies.

By that time, TDA was publishing annually what was arguably the largest and most diverse line of SF and fantasy ever produced by a single English-language publisher, with 1998 titles including works by TDA's early authors Poul Anderson, Andre Norton, Fred Saberhagen, Harry Harrison, Orson Scott Card, Fritz Leiber, Gordon R. Dickson, Larry Niven, Steven Barnes, and L. Neil Smith, among others. Other notable titles included Robert Jordan's bestselling epic "Wheel of Time" series; Tim Powers's award-winning *Earthquake Weather*; and physicist Robert L. Forward's *Saturn Rukh*, as well as numerous other books by a list of authors that read like a veritable Who's Who of great SF, fantasy, and horror.

Tor and Forge titles were distributed to the trade in the United States by former parent company St. Martin's Press; in Canada by H.B. Fenn and Company Ltd. (one of the top ten trade book suppliers in Canada); to the wholesale side of the book business by Hearst ICD; and elsewhere in the English-speaking world by Pan Macmillan. Nearing its third decade of operations, Tom Doherty's visionary company continued to forge ahead to a new tor in publishing.

Principal Divisions

Forge Books; Orb Books; Tor Books.

Further Reading

"Baen Quits Ace; Allison New Editor," *Locus: The Newspaper of the Science Fiction Field*, September 1980, p. 1.

"Doherty Expands SF Publishing Line," *Locus: The Newspaper of the Science Fiction Field*, January 1983, p. 1.

"Doherty Starts New Paperback SF Line," *Locus: The Newspaper of the Science Fiction Field*, August 1980, p. 3.

Feldman, Gayle, "Picador About to Enter the American Arena; St. Martin's Launching U.S. Version of U.K. 'Literary' Imprint in January," *Publishers Weekly*, May 9, 1994, p. 26.

Milliot, Jim, "Sargent, Grisebach Rise at Von Holtzbrinck," *Publishers Weekly*, February 2, 1998, p. 16.

Nathan, Paul, "Short Subjects," *Publishers Weekly*, July 10, 1995, p. 17.

Pedersen, Martin, "Serial from Prodigy to Be Hardcover Book," *Publishers Weekly*, February 15, 1993, p. 18.

Reid, Calvin, "Tor Hires Extra Reps with Money Saved by Skipping ABA Convention," *Publishers Weekly*, April 19, 1991, p. 16.

Reilly, Patrick, "Steamy, Far-Out Tale of Publishers Who Made It Big; Romance Formula Sold by the Cover; Salesman's Savvy from Alien Sources," *Crain's New York Business*, June 23, 1986, p. 3.

"TDA Opens Offices," *Locus: The Newspaper of the Science Fiction Field*, October 1980, p. 3.

"Tor/Forge Loses Age Bias Lawsuit," *Publishers Weekly*, April 1, 1996, p. 12.

"*A Wizard in Midgard*," *Publishers Weekly*, May 11, 1998, p. 55.

—Daryl F. Mallett

Tonka

Tonka Corporation

1027 Newport Avenue
Pawtucket, Rhode Island 02862
U.S.A.
(401) 431-8697
Fax: (401) 727-5047

Division of Hasbro, Inc.
Incorporated: 1946 as Mound Metalcraft
Employees: 3,600
Sales: $870.5 million (1993)
SICs: 3942 Dolls & Stuffed Toys; 3944 Games, Toys &
   Children's Vehicles; 3949 Sporting & Athletic Goods,
   Not Elsewhere Classified

Tonka Corporation has a long history as America's premier manufacturer of toy trucks. Since 1991 the company has operated as a division of Hasbro, Inc., the largest toy company in the United States. Though its famed trucks are still its best known product, Tonka also produces dolls and soft toys for girls, as well as various games, toy guns, balls, tools, and other assorted playthings.

Early History

Tonka Corporation began as a small metal manufacturing company located in an old school house in Mound, Minnesota. Its three founders, Lynn Baker, Avery Crouse, and Alvin Tesch, started the company in 1946. Mound Metalcraft, as the company was at first called, specialized in manufacturing tie racks and garden tools. But the company manufactured toy trucks as well, apparently as a sideline, and the three founders began exhibiting them at the New York Toy Fair as early as 1947. These Tonka brand trucks quickly became its preeminent product, and the company changed its name to Tonka Toys in 1955. The name Tonka came from Lake Minnetonka, which the first manufacturing facility overlooked. The company's Tonka Trucks were made of heavy, automobile-gauge steel and were extremely realistic and durable; they caught on quickly among postwar baby boom parents. Between 1955 and 1960 sales at

Tonka tripled, and the company acquired a sterling reputation for its high quality product.

Tonka went public in 1961 and two years later began selling its toys in overseas markets. Its penetration into the American market was already stupendous. Tonka trucks were a high-end product, made of expensive and durable materials. The brand became a staple in U.S. households, the toy no boy should be without. And to encourage parents to buy more than one Tonka Truck, the company restyled its product line each year. The company introduced Mini-Tonka in 1963, a smaller and cheaper truck aimed at younger children. Then the company added a jumbo truck line, Mighty-Tonka, in 1965. By 1966 one marketing survey showed that 85 percent of households interviewed owned Tonka toys. Three years later that figure had jumped to more than 90 percent. And families were buying more Tonka trucks, too. In 1966 the surveyed families had on average 3.2 trucks per household, but the 1969 survey showed families owning on average 5.4 Tonka toys, with a significant portion of the population owning upward of nine Tonkas.

The market seemed to make itself, and the company made no effort to diversify into other products. Between 1965 and 1969 sales more than doubled, from around $22 million to more than $45 million, and profit levels were high. The company seemed to be shrewdly run. Tonka's original owners left the company in 1961, and the top management position was filled by a two-man team, Gordon Batdorf and Russell Wenkstern. Wenkstern was a former high school shop teacher and Batdorf had worked in Tonka production, so both men had a deep understanding of how the toys were made. Though new models were introduced every year, they followed basic shapes, which made retooling simple. The company also controlled its labor costs by hiring mostly area housewives, who were not unionized. Problems began for the company when it changed its management structure, to operate more like a big company.

Reorganization in the 1970s

In 1968 Tonka's management decided to concentrate on long-range planning and on breaking into foreign markets. Tonka hired two consulting firms, one from Milwaukee and one from Philadelphia, to help the company plan. As a result, the company reorganized into a more complex management structure, adding many layers to its hierarchy. Tonka built new corporate headquarters, putting distance between the manufacturing plant and the executives. Batdorf and Wenkstern, who had operated as a team, then split their responsibilities, with Batdorf becoming chief of operations and Wenkstern chief executive, solely in charge of corporate policy and plans. The results of these changes were felt quickly, as earnings dropped precipitately in 1969. With management delegating more and more responsibility, problems were not dealt with quickly. Delays in tool and die delivery led to stalled production, which had to be corrected with enormous amounts of overtime at the plant. Tonka's net earnings plunged 35 percent, and it was clear that the new structure was not working. Finally, Batdorf resigned, leaving Wenkstern in control. He moved quickly to eliminate unnecessary expenditures and to bring the management structure closer to its former pattern.

The next few years were still rocky, but by 1974 Tonka seemed to have corrected some of its problems and was working hard to gain some stability. The toy industry was notoriously cyclic, with most sales occurring in the few weeks before Christmas and certain toys swooping in and out of fashion. Tonka attempted to offset this by acquiring new product lines. In the early 1970s Tonka diversified into the hydraulic component industry, making parts for farm and construction machinery, mostly control valves, filters, motors, and pumps. The company also began making educational products under an agreement with the Smithsonian Institution and acquired Vogue Dolls in 1973. To expand its original toy truck line, Tonka added some cheaper plastic trucks, wheeled toys for infants, and some girls' toys, as well as hobby kits designed for older children. The company also acquired a maker of ceramic stains and glazes in 1973. The diversification seemed to help, and sales and earnings climbed.

The company still had difficulties, however. Its market share for toy trucks fell in the 1970s, as cheaper and flashier vehicles attracted more young consumers. And despite its acquisition of Vogue Dolls, Tonka had never managed to loft a staple line of girls' toys. In a frenzy to put out more toys, Tonka introduced 70 new products in 1978. But it was difficult to iron out the manufacturing bugs in so many new items, and production costs bogged the company down. The company ended up in the red. In 1979 Tonka got a new top management team, headed by 40-year-old Stephen Shank. Shank closed the old manufacturing plant in Mound, laying off about 500 workers. Tonka moved its production to Juarez, Mexico and El Paso, Texas and also farmed out 40 percent of its toy manufacturing to outside suppliers. Earnings rebounded after the management shakeup, but then fell drastically as problems with starting up the Mexican and Texan plants delayed production. Tonka ended up with steep losses for 1982 and 1983.

New Strategy in the 1980s

Desperate to find a solution to Tonka's dwindling market share, CEO Shank hired four executives away from the Mattel toy company in 1983. Then Tonka licensed a robot toy from Bandai, the largest Japanese toy maker. Bandai had attempted to sell the robot in the United States in 1980, but was unable to make its

product appealing to U.S. children. The Mattel executives helped conceive a story line around the robots, which were marketed under the name GoBots. The GoBots' trick was that they were actually two toys in one. The robots, who came in good and evil teams, could disguise themselves as various vehicles such as airplanes and motorcycles. When the toy plane was unfolded, it revealed its robot avatar. All of the GoBots had names and personalities attached to them. Introduced with television advertising, the GoBots soon had their own television show and comic book series. Tonka also licensed a slew of tie-in products such as GoBot lunch boxes and watches. Introduced in January 1984, by the end of the year GoBots had sales of close to $100 million, and Tonka had its first profit in three years.

Despite its great success with GoBots, Tonka still was struggling to find a long-term strategy. Fad toys such as GoBots could bring in huge sales, but they had many costs, too, such as intensive advertising. And GoBots soon were imitated by Hasbro's Transformers, similar robots licensed from another Japanese toy maker, Takara. Competition between the two robot lines split the market, and Tonka had to be ready with the next big thing to keep up its sales momentum. Tonka introduced Pound Puppies in 1985, a soft dog toy that children "adopted" when they bought it. The adoption ploy was borrowed from Cabbage Patch dolls, which had been all the rage a few years earlier. Pound Puppies sold well, and Tonka's sales and earnings seemed in good shape, more than doubling between 1984 and 1987, to $293 million. Pound Puppies accounted for more than half of the company's profits in 1986. But by 1987 Pound Puppies had lost their hold on the market, and profits skidded, dropping almost 70 percent in the first half of the year.

So Tonka decided to bolster its stock of staple, tried-and-true toys by acquiring Kenner Parker Toys. Kenner was known for its Parker Brothers brand board games, including the perennial favorites Monopoly, Clue, and Risk. Other well-known Kenner products included Play Doh, Care Bears, Nerf balls, and the Ouija board. Kenner was involved in a hostile takeover from another company, and Tonka seized the chance to buy it. Tonka spent $622 million to get Kenner, borrowing almost the entire amount. With the 1987 acquisition, Tonka became the third largest toy maker in the United States. Kenner's brands were expected to offset the volatility of Tonka's hit toys and supplement its classic Tonka truck line. But the amount of debt Tonka took on was extremely heavy—86 percent of the company's total capital. So now Tonka was under even more pressure to boost sales.

Tonka lost money again in 1988, despite a huge rise in operating income. Nevertheless, the company seemed to have some good things ahead of it. Tonka management was able to revitalize some of Kenner's failing brands, and it gained marketing and distribution networks in Europe. Play Doh, a children's modeling clay first introduced in 1956, boosted its sales from $20 million annually in the 1980s to around $50 million after Tonka took over the brand. Tonka also revamped its classic toy truck line and applied more sophisticated market research to its products. By 1988 a third of Tonka's sales and profits came from overseas markets, and this figure seemed to be growing. With marketing pitches on television and on cereal boxes, Tonka also did brisk sales of a miniature electric car. So in spite of the precarious financial position imposed on it by its debt, Tonka seemed like it would manage to regain profitability in coming years.

End of Independence in the 1990s

The optimistic picture of Tonka in the late 1980s vanished in June 1990. At its annual meeting the toy company announced it had had two bad quarters in a row and predicted it would not finish the year in the black. Sales of its toys tied to the movie *Ghostbusters* had plummeted, and the craze for Teenage Mutant Ninja Turtles—one of the most successful toy introductions of all time—depressed Tonka's market. The company had lowered its debt burden from 86 percent of capital to around 70 percent, but this was still high, and Tonka began negotiating a waiver with its bank. Tonka ended the year with a loss of $10.3 million, and its financial condition deteriorated into the next year. Rumors of a takeover were published early in 1991, and the outlines of a deal with the nation's number one toy maker, Hasbro, began to appear soon thereafter. In April 1991 the deal with Hasbro was finalized, and Tonka was bought for just less than $490 million. The price was said to be somewhat high, yet it was nevertheless lower than what Tonka had paid for Kenner Parker four years earlier.

Tonka was folded into the Hasbro stable of companies, operating out of Hasbro's Pawtucket, Rhode Island headquarters. Kenner and Parker Brothers became divisions of their own and, apparently, flourished under new ownership. The Tonka brand did not seem to fare as well. In 1993 the Tonka brand's share of the toy truck market fell out of the number one position, overtaken by SLM International's Buddy L Truck. The Buddy L had battery-operated lights and sound effects and was priced similarly to Tonka's line. It took almost 30 percent of the market in 1993. Hasbro announced that it would update Tonka's packaging, and it introduced some new products, such as military vehicles that tied into Hasbro's famous GI Joe doll. By the end of the 1990s Hasbro was marketing a line of more than 30 Tonka trucks, vehicles, and playsets. Some were close to Tonka classics, such as the Mighty line and the durable Tonka dump truck. Others were closer to the battery-operated, full-featured vehicles that had robbed Tonka of market share earlier. These models included the XRC radio-controlled vehicle series and a line of so-called Super Sonic Power vehicles. Another extension of the Tonka brand in the 1990s was computer software featur-ing Tonka trucks. Kids using the software could simulate building and painting Tonka vehicles. This was apparently very successful. The Tonka interactive game, along with several others released by Hasbro, helped bring the company into fourth place in the expanding interactive game market. This kind of creative brand extension seemed destined to keep the Tonka name alive despite the vast changes in the toy market and toy industry that had occurred over Tonka's lifetime.

Further Reading

Arrington, Carl, and Velasco, Irma, "Deck the Halls with Squads of Robots," *People Weekly,* December 3, 1984, pp. 1154–57.

Benway, Susan Duffy, "Transforming Tonka," *Barron's,* June 24, 1985, pp. 16, 18, 24.

Bulkeley, William M., "Toy Warrior Robots Seen Uprooting Cabbage Patch Dolls' Record for Sales," *Wall Street Journal,* July 23, 1984, p. 29.

Dougherty, Philip H., "Two More Toys from Tonka," *New York Times,* February 11, 1985, p. D8.

"Is Tonka Toying with Trouble?," *Business Week,* October 12, 1987, p. 165.

Maher, Tani, "Tonka's Questionable Bid for Kenner," *Financial World,* November 3, 1987, p. 11.

Merrill, Ann, "No Fun in Tonka's Future," *Minneapolis/St. Paul City-Business,* June 11, 1990, pp. 1–2.

Ozanian, Michael K., "Tonka: Don't Pass Go," *Financial World,* July 24, 1990, p. 17.

Pereira, Joseph, "Hasbro Agrees To Buy Tonka for $470 Million," *Wall Street Journal,* February 1, 1991, p. A4.

Pitzer, Mary J., "Why Tonka Needs Truckloads of Paydirt," *Business Week,* August 24, 1988, pp. 96–97.

Ramirez, Anthony, "Tonka Board Backs Deal with Hasbro," *New York Times,* April 19, 1991, p. D4.

"Report Causes Tonka Plunge," *New York Times,* June 1, 1990, p. D3.

"Tonka Corp. Plays To Win," *Financial World,* April 3, 1974, p. 16.

"Tonka Helps Hasbro Net," *New York Times,* February 11, 1992, p. D4.

"Tonka Learns Not To Toy with Success," *Business Week,* August 1, 1970, pp. 38–40.

"Trouble in Toyland," *Forbes,* January 21, 1991, p. 10.

Vartan, Vartanig G., "Tonka's Role in Toy Industry," *New York Times,* August 24, 1984, p. D4.

Weiner, Steve, "Keep on Truckin'," *Forbes,* October 16, 1989, pp. 220–21.

—A. Woodward

Twentieth Century Fox Film Corporation

10201 West Pico Boulevard
Los Angeles, California 90064
U.S.A.
(310) 369-1000
Fax: (310) 203-2979
Web site: http://www.fox.com

Wholly Owned Subsidiary of Fox Inc.
Incorporated: 1915
Employees: 360
Sales: $1.2 billion (1996 est.)
SICs: 7812 Motion Picture, Video Tape Production; 7819
    Services Allied to Motion Pictures

Twentieth Century Fox Film Corporation is a subsidiary of Fox Inc., which is owned by media mogul Rupert Murdoch's News Corporation Ltd. Throughout its long history, the company has enjoyed a reputation as a major Hollywood motion picture studio. It produced some of the more prominent box-office hits—such as *The Sound of Music* and *Star Wars*—and has expanded into related areas of the entertainment industry through the development of subsidiaries such as Fox Animation Inc. and Twentieth Century Fox Home Entertainment.

William Fox and his Nickelodeons

In 1904 William Fox, a 25-year-old Hungarian immigrant, bought his first nickelodeon, an early form of movie theater, in New York City. Within a few years Fox and two partners, B.S. Moss and Sol Brill, had parlayed their success into a chain of 25 nickelodeons.

The partners soon opened the Greater New York Film Rental Company, and then in 1913, concerned that the demand for movies had begun to outstrip supply, they organized the Box Office Attraction Company to begin producing their own movies. In 1915 Fox founded the Fox Film Corporation to produce, distribute, and exhibit movies and moved his operation to California, where he believed the temperate climate would be better suited to film production.

In 1925 Fox Films relocated to its fourth California location when Fox purchased the 250 acres of land in Hollywood which was to become the company's permanent home. In 1929 Fox Films bought 55 percent of Loew's Inc., then the parent company of MGM, but was later forced by the government to sell that interest.

After several years of steady growth, the company experienced a series of shake-ups beginning in 1927, and in 1930 a group of stockholders ousted William Fox. Fox was replaced by Sidney R. Kent in 1932, and two years later Fox Film Corporation merged with Twentieth Century Pictures.

The Rise of the Twentieth Century Company

In 1933 Darryl F. Zanuck, head of production at Warner Brothers, had joined Joseph M. Schenck, head of United Artists, in forming the Twentieth Century Company. With Schenck as the administrator and Zanuck head of production, the Twentieth Century Company made 18 films in 18 months, including *The House of Rothschild, The Affairs of Cellini,* and *Les Miserables.* During this time, Twentieth Century began tapping into current news events for subject matter, with releases like the gangster films *Little Caesar* and *Public Enemy.* When the company merged with Fox Film Corporation in 1935, Zanuck became vice-president in charge of production of the new Twentieth Century Fox Film Corporation.

The company distinguished itself by producing two Academy Award-winning films during this time, *The Grapes of Wrath* in 1940 and *How Green Was My Valley* in 1941. Zanuck served as a lieutenant colonel during World War II, making training and combat documentary films. He was awarded the Legion of Merit for his wartime services.

After the war, Twentieth Century Fox produced such hits as *The Snows of Kilimanjaro, Winged Victory, Twelve O'Clock High, The Razor's Edge,* and *All About Eve.* Zanuck also attacked controversial issues in several financially successful movies, proving that audiences would not shy away from such topics as mental illness, race relations, and anti-Semitism with *The Snake Pit, Pinky,* and *Gentleman's Agreement.*

Challenges of the 1950s

By the early 1950s Hollywood's heyday was being eclipsed by the advent of television; attendance at movie theaters declined sharply, and film production declined along with it. Studios like Twentieth Century Fox could no longer afford to maintain exclusive contracts with directors and film stars. In 1953 Zanuck began producing all the studio's films in widescreen CinemaScope, but the attraction of this technology did not compensate for the lack of box office hits. Frustrated, Zanuck left the company in 1956 to become an independent film producer in Paris.

The company replaced Zanuck with Spyros Skouras, a well-known theater owner. Skouras took over the company during a very bleak period. Between 1959 and 1961, Twentieth Century Fox lost $48.5 million; in 1962 it lost $39.8 million on revenues of $96.4 million. One immediate source of trouble was the production of *Cleopatra*. From an estimated cost of approximately $7 million in 1961, the film's total expenditures ballooned to $41.5 million. The company poured money into the production, even selling 334 acres of land in Los Angeles's Fox Hills section to help finance it, but this still wasn't enough.

In 1962 Zanuck, still one of the company's largest stockholders, persuaded his fellow-stockholders not to liquidate the business and returned to replace Skouras as president. Zanuck's stability and professionalism soon bolstered the company's waning image. More importantly, however, Zanuck brought in quick cash. *The Longest Day,* an epic film about the D-Day landings at Normandy Beach, made by Zanuck's own production company in Europe, was released through Twentieth Century Fox. A smash hit nominated for an Academy Award, the film brought in enough revenue to allow the company to begin making movies again in 1963.

Blockbusters of the 1960s

That same year Zanuck made his son Richard vice-president in charge of production. Only 28 years old, the younger Zanuck began making pictures with modest budgets, producing 20 movies in 14 months, and once revenues from these films began to accumulate, the company started more expensive productions. Unlike other movie makers at the time, the Zanucks continued to favor big, expensive production extravaganzas. Forgetting the failure of *Cleopatra,* the two men planned to release as many big pictures in as short a time as they could, hoping for a hit to keep the company solvent. This "blockbuster" strategy was one most other studios had abandoned because of the risk involved.

The release of *The Sound of Music* in 1964 appeared to vindicate the Zanucks' strategy. The film became one of the top ten box office hits ever, bringing Twentieth Century Fox more than $79 million in revenues. Only a year and a half after its release, the movie had already outgrossed *Gone With the Wind,* the box office champion for nearly 27 years.

By the mid-1960s, Twentieth Century Fox had also grown into one of the largest television producers. During the 1966–1967 season, Twentieth Century Fox Television placed 12 shows on network TV. The firm also began to distribute its feature films to television. In one of the largest deals of the time, Fox leased 17 pictures to ABC for $19 million, including

Cleopatra, The Longest Day, The Agony and the Ecstasy, and *Those Magnificent Men in Their Flying Machines.*

With revenues garnered from television and *The Sound of Music,* the Zanucks went on to produce more lavish, big-budget movies such as *Hello, Dolly!, Dr. Dolittle,* and *Tora! Tora! Tora!* The success of *The Sound of Music* had fueled the Zanucks belief that expensive spectaculars were the best way to make money in the industry. In 1969 Darryl Zanuck appointed his son president of Twentieth Century Fox while he remained CEO.

However, *Dr. Dolittle* and *Tora! Tora! Tora!* turned out to be two of the biggest box office losers in the history of Hollywood; in 1969 Twentieth Century Fox's operating losses amounted to $36 million, and for the first nine months of the following year losses came to nearly $21 million.

Diversification in the 1970s

The financial strain, as well as creative differences, sparked a proxy fight for control of the company in 1970. Following a family feud, with Richard Zanuck and his mother opposing Darryl Zanuck, Richard was forced to resign. Four months later, Darryl Zanuck himself stepped down as chairman. William T. Gossett, an active boardmember and Detroit lawyer, became chairman. Richard Zanuck went on to produce several blockbuster movies, including *Jaws* and *The Sting,* for MCA's Universal Studios.

In 1971 Dennis C. Stanfill, a Twentieth Century Fox vice-president and a former Rhodes scholar, was named chairman and CEO, and later assumed the position of president. With a hands-on approach, Stanfill began a wide-ranging diversification program into the record business, broadcasting, film processing, and theme parks. Twentieth Century Fox's most important acquisitions during this time included a string of theaters in Australia and New Zealand, along with the addition of one NBC and two ABC affiliates to its chain of television stations across the United States.

In 1973 Stanfill hired Alan Ladd, Jr. to head the company's film division. Under Ladd's direction. Twentieth Century Fox produced a number of very successful movies, including *The Poseidon Adventure, Young Frankenstein,* and *The Towering Inferno,* a joint release with Warner.

More importantly, however, Ladd also invested $10 million to produce a script that other large studios had turned down. In 1977, *Star Wars* became the biggest box office hit in film history and made over $200 million by the end of its first year. During the next five years, company profits quadrupled and its movies were nominated for 33 Academy Awards.

With profits from *Star Wars,* Stanfill accelerated his diversification program, buying Coca-Cola Bottling Midwest for $27 million; Aspen Skiing, the largest ski-resort operator in the United States, for $48 million; and Pebble Beach Corporation, the owner of a resort on the Monterey Peninsula in California, for $72 million. These acquisitions were meant to allow the company to reduce its reliance on film revenues.

Citing differences with Stanfill, Ladd left Twentieth Century Fox in 1979. In January 1980 Sherry Lansing was hired to replace him, becoming the first female to head the production office of a major motion picture studio. She had previously supervised the production of both *The China Syndrome* and *Kramer vs. Kramer* at Columbia Pictures. Two weeks before her appointment, Darryl Zanuck died in Palm Springs, California.

The Troubled 1980s

The release of movies like *Norma Rae, Breaking Away, Alien,* and *The Empire Strikes Back* made money for the company. However, the company also experienced disappointing box office sales from several films, including *The Rose* and *I Ought To Be in Pictures*. In 1980 operating income dropped ten percent and entertainment profits (which accounted for 56 percent of operating income) declined by 18 percent. In late 1980, when outside groups began to purchase large amounts of company stock, Stanfill initiated a management-led leveraged buy-out to prevent a hostile takeover attempt.

In early 1981 Stanfill's plan collapsed. In a move that took the film industry by surprise, oil magnate Marvin Davis and silent partner Marc Rich hastily formed a company called TCF Holdings, Inc., which bid $722 million for Twentieth Century Fox. Borrowing heavily, Davis put up only $55 million of his own money. The purchase was completed in June of the same year. Complaining of interference, Stanfill retired in July and sued Twentieth Century Fox for breach of contract. The $22 million suit was settled for $4 million. Vice-chairman Alan Hirschfield replaced Stanfill as chairman.

In the early 1980s Twentieth Century Fox's financial position deteriorated rapidly. Several movies, including *Modern Problems, Six Pack,* and *Quest for Fire,* never recouped their production costs. Moreover, Davis burdened the company with $650 million in debt to help pay back the loans TCI had secured to buy Twentieth Century Fox. To reduce this debt. Davis sold the soft drink-bottling subsidiary and the Australian theater chain. He also arranged a joint venture with Aetna Life & Casualty to develop Twentieth Century Fox's real estate properties.

In 1982, the situation went from bad to worse. Sherry Lansing and a number of other top-level officials left the company, reportedly due to Davis's interference in the creative process and his abrupt management style. Disagreements between Davis and Hirschfield also began to increase in intensity. Moreover, Aetna terminated its interest in the joint venture and sued Davis after a deal between Davis and Aetna (unrelated to Twentieth Century Fox) soured.

In October 1984, Davis bought the other 50 percent of TCF from Marc Rich, who had fled to Switzerland following his indictment for tax evasion and fraud. Davis paid $116 million for Rich's share of the company.

During this time, Davis hired Barry Diller from Paramount to replace Hirschfield as chairman, guaranteeing him $3 million salary and a 25 percent interest in the company. Diller inherited a beleaguered company, so bad, in fact, that Diller later threatened to sue Davis, claiming that he misrepresented the studio's difficulties when he was hired. Still, Diller's expertise quickly began to turn the company around, as he mounted a program to increase film production and sought financing from a variety of different sources.

Enter Rupert Murdoch

Then, in March 1985, Australian media mogul Rupert Murdoch advanced Twentieth Century Fox $88 million after buying a half interest in the company for $132 million. Murdoch assumed an active role at the company from the beginning. He acquired seven television stations from Metromedia, Inc. for $2 billion with the intention of drawing on Twentieth Century Fox's extensive library of films and TV shows. When Davis expressed concerns about the company's film operation being tied too closely to a television network, Murdoch offered to buy him out. And so, in September 1985, Davis agreed to sell his interest for $325 million, keeping some of Twentieth Century Fox's valuable real estate.

Twentieth Century Fox Film finally enjoyed some success during the late 1980s. In late 1987 Diller oversaw the release of two big hits—*Broadcast News* and *Wall Street*—and his involvement with the studio lured back top talent that had defected elsewhere during the Davis years. A continuing string of successful films like *Big* and *Working Girl* boosted the company's earnings by 35 percent. *Die Hard,* starring Bruce Willis, grossed more than $80 million in 1989, and the film *War of the Roses,* starring Michael Douglas, Kathleen Turner, and Danny DeVito, was also a big box-office success that year.

Yet, Twentieth Century Fox Film's movie profits were eroded when Diller demonstrated more interest in the television side of the business than in film making. Specifically, Diller concentrated on bolstering the Fox Broadcasting Company to the detriment of film production. As one theatrical agent explained to *Forbes,* "Barry's been distracted."

The company then hired Joe Roth, a film director, as the studio's head, charging him with making Twentieth Century Fox Film more productive. Roth was indeed successful, producing multimillion-dollar blockbusters such as *Home Alone* and *Edward Scissorhands.* Soon Twentieth Century Fox Film placed first among the studios, controlling more than 18 percent of the box-office share in 1991. Roth's hallmark was his ability to produce entertaining films at a low cost. He frequently chose to produce movies rejected by other studios and encouraged overseas sales to conserve costs. The film remained all important to Roth, who told *Forbes,* "You have to start from the story. Then you manage the math."

Management Shake-Ups in the 1990s

Roth left Twentieth Century Fox in 1992 to become an independent producer for Walt Disney studios. The former president of the Fox Entertainment Group, Peter Chernin, replaced Roth as president. As management changed, confusion resulted regarding the responsibility for making key decisions at the Twentieth Century Fox Film studios. Rupert Murdoch himself suspended production of Steven Seagal's *Man of Honor,* the actor's directorial debut. Actor Macaulay Culkin's father appeared to be making production decisions on his son's thriller *The Good Son.* Even new president Chernin stepped in to decline the Madonna film *Angie, I Says* when its producers would not comply with a re-write request.

More management changes followed when Strauss Zelnick, president and chief operating officer since 1989, resigned after accepting a position as president and chief executive of an entertainment software company in 1993. Bill Mechanic then moved from the Disney studios, where he served as president of the home video division, to assume the presidency of Twentieth Century Fox Film Corporation. As Zelnick's successor, Mechanic came to the studio with an extensive video background. In his new position, Mechanic was responsible not only for Fox's home video activities, but for production, marketing, distribution, international theatrical activities, and pay TV as well.

Exploring New Products and Positions

Unlike some major studios, Twentieth Century Fox Film supported the development of pay-per-view (PPV) television in 1993, a service through which customers could order new movies over the telephone for in-home viewing on their televisions. Although the company was not considering pay-per-view as a venue for new movie releases, the studio developed promotional and marketing strategies for its pay-per-view releases. For example, the company engineered retail tie-ins with the Improv, a comedy club, for the pay-per-view showings of such comedies as *Hot Shots! Part Deaux!* and *Robin Hood: Men in Tights.* In 1994, Twentieth Century-Fox Film negotiated a pay-per-view distribution agreement with DirecTV.

Twentieth Century Fox Film also established an "interactive division" that year. Fox's prior experience with video games had met with mixed results, as earlier forays in the pre-Nintendo days fell victim to the video game "crash" of the mid-1980s. Since then, Fox had typically licensed its film properties to video developers. This practice slowed, however, as the announcement of the new interactive division grew closer. One of Twentieth Century Fox Film's first products in this arena was based on its movie *The Pagemaster,* an animated adventure set in a library. *The Pagemaster* game product was made available for a variety of platforms, including Sega Genesis, Nintendo Super Entertainment Systems, and Nintendo Game Boy. The company selected Al Ovadia, president of licensing and merchandising for the studio, to lead the new division.

Twentieth Century Fox Film launched another new enterprise in 1994—an animation unit headquartered in Phoenix, Arizona. Called Fox Animation Inc., the new unit expected to issue one animated feature every 18 months or so. The studio recruited exceptional talent to lead its animation division, in particular Don Bluth and Gary Goldman, creators of such animated hits as *An American Tail* and *Land before Time.*

A year later, Twentieth Century Fox Film created yet another new division, Twentieth Century Fox Home Entertainment, to distribute its video and interactive programming products. Bob DeLellis assumed the presidency of Twentieth Century Fox Home Entertainment North America, and Jeff Yapp served as president of the division's international operations.

In 1996 Twentieth Century Fox Film received the largest film financing in history through Citicorp, a bank holding company. The studio intended to use the capital for film production and acquisitions. "With the help of Citicorp," explained Simon Bax, chief financial officer of Fox Filmed Entertainment, "we were able to put together an innovative film financing structure on attractive terms. As a major studio and as a part of the News

Corporation, we were able to put in place a mechanism for funding our full production slate over the next three years, while providing investors with an attractive return on their investment.''

In 1997 Twentieth Century Fox Film's animation unit released its first feature-length production, providing Disney studios with stiff competition. *Anastasia,* the story of the Russian tsarina thought to have survived the massacre of the Romanovs, received promotion valued at about $200 million from a variety of sponsors. Pictures of characters from *Anastasia* appeared on the packages of products from Dole Foods, while Hershey manufactured *Anastasia*-themed chocolate bars. Other products offered toy coupons or movie ticket orders. *Anastasia* even had a float in the Macy's Thanksgiving Parade that year. Mechanic had great faith in the success of the unit's first feature. "If you said to me I had to put my job on the line for any movie, I would put it on this one," the executive told *Fortune.* Anastasia made in excess of $58 million at the box office.

Twentieth Century Fox Film distributed *Anastasia* through pay-per-view television during the summer of 1998. Service providers were pleased with the decision, since it attracted a new audience for them. "*Anastasia* could be the building block for the distribution of more nontraditional PPV programming in the future," Jamie McCabe, a vice-president of worldwide PPV, told *Multichannel News.*

In 1998 Twentieth Century Fox Film experienced one of its greatest successes to date, producing the Oscar-winning disaster picture *Titanic.* Breaking all box-office attendance records, the movie opened a merchandising treasure chest for the studio, which licensed merchandise, such as costumes and life jackets, to be sold through the catalog firm of J. Peterman. Other licensing agreements for t-shirts and collectibles followed, as did some unauthorized material. In fact, Twentieth Century Fox Film initiated litigation against Suarez Corporation Industries, located in Ohio and doing business as Lindenwold Fine Jewelers, for marketing a copy of a necklace featured in the movie.

A Hollywood institution, Twentieth Century Fox Film was likely to produce its share of blockbusters in the future. As technologies progressed, the company also planned to make its mark on other related areas of the entertainment industry, including interactive video games and animation.

Principal Subsidiaries

CBS/Fox Video; Twentieth Century-Fox Film Corp.

Further Reading

Benezra, Karen, and T. L. Stanley, "Fox Fire: "Anastasia" Scores Fox $200 Million in Promo Support," *Brandweek,* July 7, 1997, p. 1.

Carvell, Tim, "The Fox Vs. the Mouse," *Fortune,* November 24, 1997, p. 119.

"Citicorp Arranges Largest Film Financing Ever for Twentieth Century Fox Corporation," *Business Wire,* August 8, 1996, p. 8081294.

"DirecTV Announced DBS Distribution Deal with Twentieth Century Fox," *Communications Daily,* December 28, 1994, p. 6.

"DirecTV Signed Pay-Per-View Distribution Agreement with Twentieth Century Fox," *Communications Daily,* December 22, 1994, p. 6.

Dunne, John Gregory. *The Studio,* New York: Straus & Giroux, 1969.

Fitzpatrick, Eileen, "Fox Interactive Leaps Quickly into Game Software Fray," *Billboard,* June 4, 1994, p. 9.

Goldstein, Seth, "Twentieth Century Fox Forms Distrib Arm for Growing Biz," *Billboard,* May 6, 1995 , p. 7.

Greenstein, Jane, "Fox to Form Game Division Within Months," *Video Business,* March 18, 1994, p. 1.

Gubernick, Lisa, " 'Barry's Been Distracted'," *Forbes,* January 8, 1990, p. 42.

——, "The Greats of Roth," *Forbes,* June 24, 1991, p. 132.

Hettrick, Scott, "Mechanic Moving from Disney to Lead Fox Studio," *Video Business,* October 8, 1993, p. 1.

Kilday, Gregg, "Hollywood Shuffle," *Entertainment Weekly,* November 20, 1992, p. 10.

——, "Who's the Boss at Fox?," *Entertainment Weekly,* December 4, 1992, p. 7.

Madden, John, "Keeping 'Titanic' Afloat; Digital Images, Intranet Database Help Movie Crew Track Assets, " *PC Week,* April 6, 1998, p. 27.

McCullaugh, Jim, "Mechanic Jumps from Disney VID to Rival Fox," *Billboard,* October 9, 1993, p. 6.

Ryan, Thomas J., "Studio Sues Suarez over 'Titanic' Necklace Knockoff," *WWD,* March 13, 1998, p. 5.

Spring, Greg, "Fox Animation Unit Picks Phoenix for Headquarters; Site Location Was Personal Choice of Unit's Head Men," *Los Angeles Business Journal,* August 8, 1994, p. 12.

"Strauss Zelnick," *CD-ROM News Extra,* August 1993, p. 22.

Thomas, Tony, and Aubrey Solomon, *The Films of 20th Century-Fox: A Pictorial History,* Secaucus, N.J.: Citadel Press, 1985.

Umstead, R. Thomas, " 'Anastasia' Set for PPV Distribution," *Multichannel News,* May 25, 1998, p. 24.

——, "Universal, Fox to Back PPV with Marketing Campaign," *Multichannel News,* November 29, 1993, p. 88.

—updated by Charity Anne Dorgan

life's better here @

U S West, Inc.

1801 California Street
Suite 5200
Denver, Colorado 80202
U.S.A.
(800) 879-4357
Fax: (303) 793-6654
Web site: http://www.uswest.com

Public Company
Incorporated: 1995 as U S West, Inc.
Employees: 47,568
Sales: $10.3 billion
Stock Exchanges: New York Pacific
Ticker Symbol: USW
SICs: 4812 Radiotelephone Communications; 4813
    Telephone Communications, except Radio; 2741
    Miscellaneous Publishing

The "new" U S West, Inc. was formed in 1995 after the split of its former parent company (also named U S West, Inc.) into two separate companies—one which retained the U S West, Inc. name, and the other which was called MediaOne Group Inc. Prior to the restructuring, both the new U S West and MediaOne had been operating units with increasingly competitive businesses in the telecommunications and data delivery services industry. Though the original U S West was the largest of the Baby Bells resulting from the breakup of AT&T in 1984, after its own split it became the smallest of the Baby Bells or regional holding companies (RHCs) providing local telephone service in the United States. In the late 1990s, U S West concentrated on providing customers in its 14-state western-United States territory, as well outside this area through varied partnerships, with high-speed integrated products and services over copper and fiber-optic networks. These products included a wide range of personal and professional telephone and data delivery services, as well as electronic and traditional Yellow Pages directories.

Birth of the Regional Holding Companies in 1983 and 1984

U S West, Inc. was originally formed in 1983 as part of a consent decree between the U.S. Department of Justice (DOJ) and American Telephone and Telegraph Company (AT&T), which was at that time the world's largest corporation. AT&T had built most of the U.S. phone system, but suffered frequent criticism for allegedly suppressing competition through unfair trade practices. The decree followed a lengthy court battle with the DOJ. AT&T had led the operation of local telephone service in the United States through 22 companies, all of which existed under AT&T's umbrella. The breakup divided the 22 local companies among seven regional holding companies.

U S West was formed from the combination of Mountain States Telephone & Telegraph Co., Northwestern Bell Telephone Co., and Pacific Northwest Bell Telephone Co. Its territory comprised Arizona, Colorado, Idaho, Iowa, Minnesota, Montana, New Mexico, Nebraska, North and South Dakota, Oregon, Utah, Washington, and Wyoming. U S West and the other RHCs were not free to enter any business they chose; the consent decree forbade them to use their monopoly power to their advantage by entering certain businesses, including long-distance telephone service and telephone equipment design and manufacture. Incorporated in 1983, U S West officially began operation January 1, 1984.

From the day of its formation, U S West had built-in disadvantages compared to its sibling RHCs. It was responsible for the largest geographical territory, which covered about 45 percent of the lower 48 states' area. Unfortunately, however, much of its territory was sparsely populated and growing slowly, which limited the return on equipment and services. Furthermore, many miles of wire were needed to reach fewer people than in the other RHCs, although U S West managed to earn a higher income per line than other RHCs at a lower than average cost. Only 4 percent of AT&T's pre-breakup stock was owned by people who lived in U S West's territory, and the company feared investment might dry up. These disadvantages led the new company to react swiftly and aggressively to the AT&T breakup. It chose a name faster than any of the other Bell

Company Perspectives:

One company, one vision, one focus, makes life better here. Our vision is to provide telecommunications solutions that make the lives of our customers better, easier, hassle-free, and to deliver applications that communicate, educate, entertain, and inform.

operating companies, dropping the "Bell" name to remove associations with the past, and calling itself U S West to symbolize its desire to take on new frontiers. To get its name recognized by the public and investors, the company spent $2.5 million on a showy advertising campaign featuring cowboys and the company slogan, "If you don't make dust, you eat dust." U S West appointed Jack A. MacAllister as its president, and CEO and he gave the company a decentralized structure. Its three local phone companies and new subsidiaries were run as separate companies, and the number of employees at U S West headquarters was kept below 200.

Forging a New Frontier, 1985 to 1987

MacAllister quickly moved the company into new business ventures and pushed for relaxed regulation from the states in U S West's territory and from the consent decree governing the AT&T breakup. U S West began investing millions of dollars in commercial real estate, owning a $70-million portfolio by the end of 1985. U S West also moved into financial services, buying a commercial funding company for $10 million and the Kansas City operations of Control Data Corporation's Commercial Credit Company for $65 million.

Like most of the other regional holding companies, U S West began investing in cellular telephone services and directory publishing, two businesses in which they were not restricted to their own territories. U S West bought directory publisher Trans Western Publishing, with operations in Florida and California. The company formed U S West New Vector Group Inc. to manage its cellular operations, and U S West Financial Services to offer leasing and sales financing to its customers. In 1984, profits amounted to $887 million.

By late 1985, U S West had won pricing flexibility for some services from regulators in eight states. The company formed a subsidiary—U S West Information Systems—to direct its computer operations, and the company's New Vector Communications bought the San Diego cellular operations of Communications Industries Inc. Meanwhile, Justice Harold Greene, overseeing the AT&T breakup, turned down the RHC's first request to ease restrictions on diversification into nonregulated areas. Even so, in 1985 U S West posted profits of $925.6 million.

In 1986, U S West bought Applied Communications Inc. for nearly $120 million. That same year, the company formed a commercial real estate subsidiary, called Beta West Properties. Its first move was to buy the 54-story office building in Denver

in which Mountain States headquarters was located, for $235 million. A strike by 18,000 members of the Communications Workers of America at Mountain States ended after one day.

Decentralization led to the formation of two U S West equipment-marketing subsidiaries, FirstTel Information Systems and Interline Communication Services. The two subsidiaries soon competed with each other, however, and with the sales forces of U S West's three local phone companies. Thus, in late 1986 both companies were merged into a single new subsidiary, U S West Information Systems. U S West took a $52 million loan to pay for the restructuring and dismissed more than 1,000 employees. Though the former two subsidiaries had marketed telecommunications equipment nationwide, the restructuring narrowed the focus to selling equipment within U S West's territory, where the company was best known. U S West's profits for 1986 dropped slightly to $924 million, on revenue of $8.31 billion.

Acknowledged as the most aggressive of the RHCs, in 1986 U S West told Bell Communications Research (Bellcore)—the research consortium jointly owned by the seven RHCs—that it was going to sell its share when its funding commitment ran out in 1990. U S West wanted greater control of the kind of research that the lab did, as well as over who was aware of it. As a result of this U S West pressure, Bellcore changed the rules governing its research, allowing it to do research for a single RHC and keep it secret from the others for up to two years. The changes satisfied U S West, and it decided to stay in Bellcore.

U S West established its own 400-engineer laboratory in Colorado, however, to focus on its own research and development. The decree governing the AT&T breakup forbade any regional Bell from designing or manufacturing its own equipment, but U S West worked on artificial intelligence and voice recognition and response systems with the goal of creating a system to give repair people instructions from a talking computer via telephone.

U S West pushed for deregulation harder than any of the other regionals, often angering state regulators in the process. By the end of 1987, 11 of the 14 states the company served had loosened regulation, allowing the company to freely price new services such as central phone switching, cellular phones, and private lines. Idaho, Nebraska, and North Dakota actually had the least restrictive telecommunications policies in the United States. The moves taken by U S West soon paid off: telephone profits for 1987 fell 1 percent, although total profits rose to $1 billion.

Further Expansion & Diversification, 1988 to 1991

By mid-1988 U S West had invested $192 million in New Vector. New Vector had entered 22 cellular markets and had 51,000 subscribers, but it was losing money. Thus, U S West sold 17 percent of New Vector that year on the stock market, in order to recoup its initial investment. The stock promptly began falling, losing 28 percent of its value in just two months. U S West's growth was falling behind that of the other RHCs, largely because the population and economy of its region was stagnant, while that of most other RHCs was growing.

U S West, along with the other regionals, finally won court permission in 1988 to enter new information services like voice mail and database transmission as long as they did not create or manipulate data themselves. The relaxed restrictions meant more local telephone traffic and increased profits. U S West promptly announced a deal to test-market "Minitel", a French videotex system, in its region. The company also bought 10 percent of French cable company Lyonnaise Communications and announced plans to offer an information-gateway service in Omaha, Nebraska.

Around the same time, U S West also decided to entirely do away with the Bell name, announcing plans to restructure its three local phone companies into one subsidiary, U S West Communications. The company hoped the restructuring would accomplish several goals. First, the company wanted to cut costs by centralizing marketing and distribution. Second, U S West strived to replace a geographic approach to sales with one organized around market segments. Finally, the restructuring sought to put new emphasis on customer service. U S West hoped the name change would increase customer awareness as well, although some analysts feared the move could create resentment among customers already frustrated by the chaos following the AT&T breakup.

Meanwhile, U S West Financial Services, which bought and then leased out expensive items like airplanes and medical equipment, and engaged in mortgage banking and leveraged buyouts, had grown to nearly $105 million in annual revenue and nearly $2 billion in assets. In May 1988, it bought two reinsurance companies for $50 million. Profits for 1988 topped off at $1.13 billion.

The following year, U S West introduced miniature Yellow Pages, which was less than two inches thick and about seven inches long. The company hoped to find a niche among car-phone users and people with limited shelf space. The company's cable division invested in two British cable companies, London South Partnership and Cable London. It then joined British telephone giant STC PLC in bidding on a British cellular-communications license. The company bought Financial Security Assurance Inc. for $345 million to strengthen U S West Financial Services. Profits for 1989 were $1.1 billion.

A New Era, the Early 1990s

In 1990, U S West announced it would sell $1.4-billion in commercial real estate owned by BetaWest Properties and instead focus on real estate financing. The company planned to sell the properties over the next five-to-seven years as market conditions permitted and hoped real estate financing would bring sustained profits rather than incur the debt the company had taken on to buy property.

Around that time, U S West and its sibling RHCs launched a major push to escape from federal restrictions dating back to the AT&T breakup. They pooled nearly $21 million for a lobbying effort designed to shift regulation of their activities from Justice Greene to Congress and the Federal Communications Commission (FCC), where they expected a more sympathetic ear. The RHCs warned the decision-makers of the dire consequences of

letting the U.S. telecommunications system fall behind that of other countries—a message that found a receptive audience among those fearing a decline in U.S. economic strength. Opponents, including long-distance telephone companies, cable television companies, and newspaper publishers, said the RHCs would use regulatory freedom to raise local rates and use the increased profits to subsidize their entry into new businesses.

The telecommunications market was growing faster in most of the rest of the world than it was in the United States. Partly due to this fact, and partly due to the limits put on its U.S. activities, U S West invested $1.05 billion overseas by 1990—the second highest amount among the RHCs. U S West was the first "RHC" in Eastern Europe, with a 49 percent stake in a Hungarian cellular telephone project. U S West had also become one of the largest cable-television competitors in the world, with franchises in Hong Kong, Britain, and France. U S West's 25 percent stake in the Hong Kong franchise, the world's largest, required it to pay $125 million of the cost of building the cable network. In return, the consortium was to get six years of exclusive access to the market. The deal soured, however, when a Hong Kong company announced plans to beam programming into the country via satellite. In 1990, U S West pulled out of the consortium after the Hong Kong government refused to stop the satellite system.

U S West had also planned on being involved in a $500 million plan to lay fiber-optic cable across the former Soviet Union, although the U.S. government rejected the plan, citing national security concerns. A few months later U S West announced plans to build the first cellular telephone networks in the Soviet Union in Moscow and Leningrad. It also revealed plans to build Czechoslovakia's first cellular network in a joint venture with Bell Atlantic Corporation. Even if successful, the financial rewards from the company's ambitious foreign projects were expected to be years away because of the huge capital outlays needed to build them.

U S West announced it was investing $35 million to develop self-healing telephone networks in five cities. The networks used loops of fiber-optic cable to prevent disruption of service by earthquakes, fires, or other disasters. If a section of the loop broke, signals could be sent the other way around the loop to the telephone switching station. The service was aimed at large businesses, government offices, long-distance carriers, and others that needed to move large amounts of information without interruption. The loops were to serve about 200 large office buildings in Denver, Minneapolis-St. Paul, Phoenix, Portland, Oregon, and Seattle.

After 40 years in the telephone business, MacAllister retired in 1990, and Richard D. McCormick took his place as president and CEO. Business continued as usual, and U S West's directory publishing group established an international headquarters in Brussels, Belgium. The company also bought Cable Management Advertising Control System, a personal-computer-based system that tracked local cable television advertising. It spent a record $2 billion in 1990 to modernize its telephone system. As part of a drive to develop new telephone services, U S West set up an experimental telephone system in Bellingham, Washington, allowing customers to use touch-tone telephones to turn on, turn off, and change various telephone services themselves. New product revenues almost doubled from 1989, jumping to $54 million. The number of cellular subscribers rose 56 percent to 210,000, while paging subscribers hit 161,000. Income for 1990 was $1.2 billion on sales of $9.96 billion.

Over the next few years, U S West struggled to remain at the forefront of the telecommunications revolution, picking winners and occasionally backing operations with unforeseen costs. One of the latter was ISDN (Integrated Services Digital Network) technology, which proved more difficult to market and install than anticipated. But the company's major problems came from within, as its advances in telecommunications became increasingly linked with cable operations. In a related move—one which would later bring about repercussions—U S West paid $2.55 billion for a 25.5 percent stake of Time Warner Entertainment in 1993, as an inroad to provide data, entertainment, and telephone services over Time Warner's vast cable systems, as well as some access to HBO, and Warner Bros. Studios.

Another Break-Up, 1994 and 1995

The Time Warner venture soured when the conglomerate announced its intention to acquire Turner Broadcasting System Inc., which U S West considered a violation of their partnership pact. To stop the acquisition, U S West went to court, initiating a long, dirty fight that Time Warner counterattacked, stating that U S West had engaged in "anticompetitive practices, deception," and the squelching of several deals with other telecommunications companies.

The Time Warner legal mess intensified in 1995, as what one executive dubbed in the *Wall Street Journal* as "the world's most expensive divorce." Time Warner's latest salvo alleged that U S West was secretly dealing with rival and former parent AT&T, but industry analysts were already predicting that Time Warner would have to give U S West what it wanted—control of its cable systems—rather than risk the consequences.

U S West triumphed in one legal skirmish, when the Justice Dept. decided to allow the company to provide long-distance services outside its Northwest territory as long as any new services were offered over their own lines and in conjunction with local services. The ruling, the Telecommunications Act of 1996, was a victory—though a small one—and was immediately blasted by SBC Communications Inc., a regional phone company based in San Antonio, Texas. SBC Communications filed suit stating that the restrictions were so tight that the victory was hollow, and the ruling was in essence "anticompetitive and unlawful" against U S West, giving AT&T blanket protection from RHC competitors. Parts of the agreement were later struck down.

On the U S West homefront, its own telecommunications and cable divisions were continually at odds, competing against each other for both customers and technology. Caught in the middle and unable to side one way or the other, it became clear that the embattled parent company could not continue along its current path. The warranted action seemed to be the permanent separation of the contentious siblings, and the talk turned from "what if" to "when." The two companies' expansion came back to haunt U S West in the worst way, for both companies were not only leaders in their industries but found themselves on the very same track for the future of integrated communications and programming.

When U S West Inc. shareholders approved a plan to create two separate classes of common stock—one for the telecom company (U S West Communications) and one for the cable/media division (U S Media Group), each operating unit set out to make its mark before the eventual split of the company itself. U S West's CEO and president, Sol Trujillo, began an aggressive campaign to make the breakup as painless as possible and to bulk up the Communications division. He moved quickly to bring in an "all-star team" and immediately began a turnaround. The U S West Media Group, meanwhile, went on a purchasing spree, spending some $13 billion over the next two years to acquire additional cable systems. Chairman McCormick prepared himself to be out of a job, although he and three other top-level executives eventually received hefty severance packages and McCormick remained a board member.

Differentiation Through Integration: 1996 and Beyond

Trujillo's mission, to "differentiate through integration," was vital to the reemergence of U S West Communications as a "one-stop shop" for telecommunications. The goal was to offer customers a myriad of services all woven together with one number, one bill, and from one company—U S West Communications. One such innovation was Access2 Advanced PCS, a new wireless phone service that made home, business, and mobile phones all work together, with all calls ringing to the same voice mailbox and able to ring on any or all of the phones. The Access2 rollout was a success, and within six months was beating out its nearest competitor by a two-to-one margin. Within two years of the U S West breakup announcement, Trujillo had brought total shareholder return to 48.5 percent for U S West Communications, while cost dropped by about 20 percent to make the company the lowest of the Baby Bells. Service improved by 65 percent (the company had been known to be lax in this area), new products revenue jumped to $1.1 billion, and an addition of 683,000 access lines brought the company's total number of lines to approximately 17 million.

As U S West continued to bet on the future, one of its most recent endeavors was the rollout of DSL (digital subscriber line) technology in mid-1998, to as many as 10 million customers in 46 cities. In a heated battle, cable and telecom companies were vying for the same market, to offer customers super-fast data delivery on the Internet—from either cable modems or supercharged copper phone wires. With a potential market of some 55 million expanding by over 20 percent annually, the race for customers was broad, with heavy-hitters like Microsoft, Intel, and Compaq working with Baby Bells to further the technology. The good news was that everyone wanted to make World Wide Web access quicker, but the bad news was DSL's cost was still too expensive for anyone but big business, and available only in limited areas nationwide. For DSL to be the next widespread technological wonder, the costs for both implementation and access had to be slashed—which put installers like U S West at risk. With high initial outputs and a waiting period for markets to mature and repay original costs, lowering initial prices was not a good option.

U S West Communications also made slippery moves into widespread long-distance data and phone services through agreements with Williams Communications and Qwest, who together provided over 34,000 miles of fiber-optic networking outside U S West's territory. The latter deal paid U S West an undisclosed sum for steering customers to Qwest for long-distance phone services—a practice which ran around the perimeter of the Telecommunications Act of 1996. Using a little-known loophole that stated Baby Bells could not offer long-distance services in their own territories unless they opened up their local monopolies to rivals, but could sell the services of an unaffiliated party, U S West Communications boldly went where no other Baby Bell had tread.

While its recent pacts rankled AT&T and others, U S West kept on going, finally settling its grievances with Time Warner by merging with its Road Runner Group. Yet the biggest news of 1998 was the actual split of U S West Inc. into two separate companies—U S West Media Group was renamed MediaOne Group Inc. ("UMG" on the NYSE), and U S West Communications Group became known simply as the "new" U S West, Inc. The split also brought U S West Dex, the company's Yellow Pages and electronic directory business, which had been part of the Media Group, over to the new U S West. This brought $4.75 billion in assets and $3.9 billion in debt.

The breakup further heralded an unusual stance in the merger-mania and consolidation of the industry, with many of its rivals having gone in the opposite direction—like SBC Communications' acquisition of Pacific Telesis and its proposed purchase of Ameritech. After building itself up into a major power, the former U S West was now two smaller and valuable—yet vulnerable—companies. Though terms of the separation made a takeover prohibitively expensive over the next two years for tax reasons, it would then be open season if Trujillo and Chuck Lillis (CEO at MediaOne) failed to pump up their respective companies.

As the century came to a close, the new U S West was making technological leaps at nearly the speed of its highly-charged DSLs, announcing variations such as ADSL (asymmetrical digital subscriber line) and VDSL (very-high-speed digital subscriber line) and offering its own Internet service and enhanced capabilities to customers both within its 14-state territory and beyond. With additional pacts with Cisco Systems, Intermedia, Digital, HP, Microsoft, Novell, Oracle, and Sun Microsystems, U S West was engaged to create a "Next-Generation National Data Network" to bring the latest technology to widespread use. It appeared that time and technology would tell whether the nation's

smallest Baby Bell could keep its stance in an ever-consolidating telecommunications industry.

Principal Subsidiaries

U S West Business Resources, Inc.; U S West Communication Services Inc.; U S West Federal Services Inc.; U S West Advanced Technologies Inc.; U S West Long Distance Inc.; U S West !NTERPRISE Networking; U S West Information Technologies.

Further Reading

Arenson, Karen W., "U S West: Building an Image," *New York Times,* November 11, 1983.
Burrows, Peter, and Ron Grover, "U S West Scouts a New Frontier," *Business Week,* May 18, 1998.
Cauley, Leslie, "Technology & Telecommunications: Baby Bells Square Off Against AT&T on Callings Cards, U S West Agreement," *Wall Street Journal,* October 27, 1995, p. B3.
Cauley, Leslie and Albert R. Karr, "U S West Clears Hurdle to Long-Distance Market . . ." *Wall Street Journal,* October 12, 1995, p. A3.
Crockett, Roger O., et al, "Warp Speed Ahead," *Business Week,* February 16, 1998, pp. 80–83.
du Bois, Martin, "U S West's Belgian Multimedia Venture Irritates Tense Dutch, French Relations," *Wall Street Journal,* October 13, 1995.
Ewing, Terzah and Stephanie N. Mehta, "Williams Re-Enters Wholesale Market for Long-Distance with U S West Pact," *Wall Street Journal,* January 6, 1998.
Gonzalez, Erika, "A Faster Internet Access," *Rocky Mountain News,* May 5, 1998, p. 1B.
Ivey, Mark, "U S West: A Trailblazer That's Getting Left Behind," *Business Week,* June 6, 1988.
Keller, John and Stephanie Mehta, "U S West Strikes Marketing Alliance with Qwest in Bold Move Skirting Rules," *Wall Street Journal,* May 7, 1998.
Mehta, Stephanie, "U S West is Set to Offer TV Programming and Internet Access Over Phone Lines," *Wall Street Journal,* April 20, 1998, p. B5.
Rosenbush, Steve, "For U S West, Size Isn't Everything," *USA Today,* June 5, 1998.
Shapiro, Eben, and Leslie Cauley, "Time Warner Faces Expensive Terms to End Media Venture with U S West," *Wall Street Journal,* October 13, 1995, p. A4.
"Time Warner Allegations are Denied by U S West," *Wall Street Journal,* November 1, 1995, p. A6.
"U S West Earnings Rise 5.8%," *Rocky Mountain News,* April 25, 1998.

—Scott M. Lewis
—updated by Taryn Benbow-Pfalzgraf

U.S. Office Products Company

1025 Thomas Jefferson Street, N.W.
Suite 600 East
Washington, D.C. 20007
U.S.A.
(202) 339-6700
Fax: (202) 339-6755
Web site: http://www.usop.com

Public Company
Incorporated: 1994
Employees: 17,000
Sales: $2.61 billion (fiscal 1998)
Stock Exchanges: NASDAQ
Ticker Symbol: OFIS
SICs: 5021 Furniture; 5112 Stationery & Office Supplies;
  5149 Groceries & Related Products, Not Elsewhere
  Classified; 7334 Photocopying & Duplicating
  Services; 7389 Business Services, Not Elsewhere
  Classified

Starting from scratch in 1994, U.S. Office Products Company grew, by purchasing companies, to command annual revenues of more than $2.5 billion within three years. Unlike the five other major office products consolidators in the late 1990s, U.S. Office Products allowed the acquired companies to preserve their names and identities. In essence it planned to be a one-stop enterprise capable of meeting all the product and service needs of a small business. In early 1998 the company reversed course by spinning off four divisions into independent companies. Nevertheless, U.S. Office Products remained a giant enterprise, offering more than 33,000 brand-name products in the fields of office supplies, office furniture, and other office products (including coffee, beverage, and vending products and services). It also owned Mail Boxes Etc., the world's biggest franchiser of business communications and postal service centers.

Merging Six Companies into One, 1994–95

U.S. Office Products was founded in October 1994 by Jonathan Ledecky. Ledecky had been a manager/consultant for Steelcase Inc., a large manufacturer of office furniture, until one month earlier, when he bought General Office Products Co., a Minnesota-based company owned by Steelcase, for $4.5 million. By the time U.S. Office Products went public in February 1995, Ledecky had acquired five more contract stationers: companies that sell office supplies under contract to corporate and commercial clients. The new company thereby started public life as the sixth largest in its field.

The other five companies, all privately owned, were chosen to give U.S. Office Products immediate coverage in different areas of the United States east of the Mississippi River. They were Andrews Office Supply and Equipment Co. of Washington, D.C. (founded 1896); Burgess, Anderson & Tate Inc. of Zion, Illinois (founded 1903); Dameron-Pierson Co. of New Orleans (founded 1904); DeKalb Office Supply of Atlanta (founded 1952); and The Office Works Inc. of Lancaster, Pennsylvania (founded 1977). These companies, plus General Office Products, had combined revenues of $76.5 million in fiscal 1994 (the year ended April 30, 1994) and net income of $1.1 million.

Although the acquisitions and consolidation were simple in concept, Ledecky said the execution of the plan was "like herding cats" because he had to get the executives of the acquired companies to agree on the compensation to be received once shares of U.S. Office Products were sold to the public. The valuation agreement eventually called for half-payment to the owners in U.S. Office Products stock and the rest in the form of half the offering proceeds, amounting to cash equal to about seven times the combined earnings of the acquired companies. Another quarter of the proceeds was earmarked to pay the debts of these companies. Then Ledecky had to sell his plan to Wall Street. He was turned down by 42 investment houses before gaining an underwriter for the stock offering in Mabon Securities, a firm which needed business badly and was defunct within a year.

All six companies kept their names, management, and operational independence in what was billed as U.S. Office Products' "decentralized management strategy." In this way the companies retained their identities in their local markets while cutting costs by pooling their buying power to get better prices from suppliers. The public offering of 3.25 million shares of common stock raised slightly more than $30 million, after expenses, for some 40 percent of the company at $10 a share. Management retained about 40 percent of the rest of the shares, with Ledecky the largest single shareholder.

Acquiring Over 200 More Companies, 1995–97

A month after the merger was complete, U.S. Office Products purchased Milwaukee-based H.H. West Co. for $17.5 million in cash and stock. By the end of the year the firm had made 31 more acquisitions, including a controlling interest in New Zealand's second largest office products company. These companies, which had combined annual sales of about $800 million, consisted of two kinds: relatively large regional office-supply firms, called "hubs," and much smaller companies, called "spokes," purchased purely for their client contacts. By April 1996 the number of acquired companies had reached 52 and included businesses that sold coffee and other "break room" supplies, office furniture, and business machines as well as stationery.

Ledecky said he was moving rapidly because the office products industry was consolidating so quickly that there was only a "brief window of opportunity" to acquire remaining independent dealers. During the fiscal year ended April 30, 1996, U.S. Office Products had revenues of $701.9 million and net income of $8.7 million. But Ledecky envisioned U.S. Office Products as an $8 billion company by the year 2000. On June 6, 1996, he announced the purchase of 48 more companies, including four Starbucks Coffee suppliers, for a total of $348 million, almost all in stock. The newly acquired companies had total annual revenue of $775 million.

The announcement was enthusiastically backed by investors, who bid U.S. Office Products stock to $41.62 per share, more than four times the original offering price. In July 1995 the company had made its second offering, raising about $50 million by selling 3.5 million shares at $14.25, and in February 1996 it had brought in another $140 million by selling six million shares at $23.25 a share. About the same time it also issued $125 million worth of bonds convertible to stock. In addition, it registered 10 million shares in the fall of 1995 and another 19 million in May 1996, and it announced in October 1996 that it planned to issue 30 million more. This stock was not sold to the public; it was reserved for the purchase of companies.

Ledecky said his goal was to sell as many office products as possible through a single distribution channel, but he split his acquisitions into five divisions for different product lines. The coffee and beverage division included 15 coffee companies and was providing coffee service to about 1.6 million people in offices across the country when, on October 1, 1996, U.S. Office Products announced it had signed an agreement to become the only full-service supplier of Starbucks coffee to offices in the United States and Canada. This deal was described as "a smash success" in an April 1997 *Washington Post* story.

The pace and scope of acquisition also was rapid in other areas. U.S. Office Products entered Australia in August 1996 and Great Britain three months later, when it took a 49 percent interest in Dudley Stationery Ltd., the second largest contract stationer in the United Kingdom. It entered the print management and technology solutions fields in October 1996 and the corporate travel business in January 1997.

In February 1997 U.S. Office Products sold 10 million more shares of stock to the public at $33 a share. Shortly thereafter, however, investors looked at declining profits for the third quarter of the fiscal year and decided the company—whose roster of acquisitions reached 165 by the end of fiscal 1997—had come too far, too fast. On April 9 trading volume in the stock reached a staggering 8.6 million shares, and the price fell to half the peak six months earlier.

Despite this investor disquiet, Ledecky stayed on track, agreeing, in May 1997, to purchase Mail Boxes Etc. [see *IDCH* 18], franchiser of 3,300 stores in the United States providing mailing, packing, shipping, and copying services. The price was estimated at $267 million in stock. Although Mail Boxes had 1996 revenue of only $59 million, it was the fastest-growing nonfood franchiser in the nation, and its acquisition provided U.S. Office Products the opportunity to offer its products to a new customer base—the small-office and home-office markets. Ledecky said U.S. Office Products planned to use its central purchasing system, which was supplying its office-product dealerships, to distribute packing and mailing supplies to Mail Boxes branches at lower prices.

U.S. Office Products reported revenues of $2.84 billion and net income of $58.7 million for the fiscal year ended April 26, 1997. The company's long-term debt was $387.3 million at the end of July. In September the company announced the acquisition of 12 companies in the United States, Canada, and New Zealand with combined annual revenues of $70 million. Two months later U.S. Office said it had completed the acquisition of 17 companies in the United States, Canada, Australia, and New Zealand with combined annual revenues of about $169 million. At the same time Ledecky resigned as president and chief executive officer of the company to devote more time to other entrepreneurial activities. His successor was Thomas I. Morgan, previously the company's chief operating officer.

Shedding Four Divisions in 1998

U.S. Office Products had nine divisions at the end of 1997: office supplies, office furniture, coffee and beverage service, Mail Boxes Etc., Blue Star (the New Zealand office-supplies operation), school supplies, corporate travel, print management, and technology solutions. But in January 1998 the company announced it would spin off the latter four divisions into separate public companies and focus on its core office-supply and services businesses. The divisions that were shed accounted for about 40 percent of U.S. Office Products' revenues, and stock in them was to be distributed to shareholders of the parent company in the form of a tax-free dividend. Morgan said written agreements would be developed with the new companies to promote continued cross-selling.

Simultaneously, U.S. Office Products announced that a New York investment firm, Clayton Dubilier & Rice Inc., had agreed to pay $270 million at $8 a share for a quarter-interest in the company, with the proceeds, plus bank loans, and high-yield debt, to be used by U.S. Office Products to repurchase about 28 percent of its 133 million outstanding shares of common stock at $27 a share, payable in cash and stock in the spun-off companies. (The value of U.S. Office Products stock had been affected by a 3-for-2 stock split in November 1997.) Ledecky said he would step down as chairman of the company on the completion of the restructuring, which was accomplished in June 1998.

Since buying back more than one-quarter of its stock would cost $1 billion, U.S. Office Products was planning to take on an additional $800 million in debt. The company announced in March 1998 that it was meeting with potential lenders and investment banks to support both this effort and the refinancing of its existing $500 million credit facility.

For fiscal 1998 (the year ended April 25, 1998), U.S. Office Products reported revenues of $2.61 billion and net income of $67.2 million, including income of $27.3 million from discontinued operations.

Principal Subsidiaries

Andrews Office Supply and Equipment Co.; Blue Star Group Limited (New Zealand); Burgess, Anderson & Tate, Inc.; CK Coffee, Inc.; Coffee Butler Acquisition Corp.; Dameron-Pierson Company, Ltd.; Dudley Stationery (U.K.; 49%); General Office Products Company; The H.H. West Company; Mail Boxes Etc.; New World Vending, Inc.; The Office Works, Inc. Sharp Pencil Holdings, Inc.

Further Reading

Day, Kathleen, ''Keeping Its Nose to the Grind,'' *Washington Post,* October 2, 1996, p. C3.
Knight, Jerry, ''The Curious Case of the Missing Stock Surge,'' *Washington Post,* April 21, 1997, Washington Business section, p. 29.
——, ''New Offering Has U.S. Office Products Thinking Bigger,'' *Washington Post,* October 14, 1996, Washington Business section, p. 31.
——, ''Reversing a Strategy,'' *Washington Post,* January 14, 1998, pp. D9, D12.
——, ''U.S. Office to Buy Mail Boxes Etc.,'' *Washington Post,* May 23, 1997, pp. G1–G2.
Pressler, Margaret Webb, ''Billion-Dollar Baby,'' *Washington Post,* April 8, 1996, Washington Business section, pp. 12–14.
——, ''Ledecky's U.S. Office Products to Split in 5,'' *Washington Post,* January 14, 1998, pp. D9, D12.
——, ''Lessons for Leadership,'' *Washington Post,* January 19, 1998, Washington Business section, pp. 12–14.
——, ''U.S. Office CEO Cedes Two Titles,'' *Washington Post,* November 6, 1997, p. D2.
——, ''U.S. Office Products Buys 48 More Firms,'' *Washington Post,* June 7, 1996, pp. F1, F5.
——, ''U.S. Office Products Buys More Stationers,'' *Washington Post,* December 13, 1995, p. F3.
Troy, Mike, ''USOP to Spin Off Four Divisions,'' *Discount Store News,* January 26, 1998, p. 6.
Welsh, Jonathan, ''U.S. Office Products Plans to Spin Off Four Operations,'' *Wall Street Journal,* January 14, 1998, p. B6.

—Robert Halasz

Unison HealthCare Corporation

15300 North 90th Street
Suite 100
Scottsdale, Arizona 85260
U.S.A.
(602) 423-1954
Fax: (602) 607-4113
Web Site: http://www.unhc.com

Public Company
Established: 1992
Employees: 4,600
Sales: $148.7 million (1996)
Stock Exchanges: NASDAQ
Ticker: UNHC
SICs: 8051 Skilled Nursing Care Facilities; 8052
Intermediate Care Facilities; 8059 Nursing and
Personal Care, Not Elsewhere Classified; 8093
Specialty Outpatient Clinics, Not Elsewhere
Classified; 8099 Health and Allied Services, Not
Elsewhere Classified

Since its inception in 1992, Unison HealthCare Corporation has been among the leading providers of comprehensive long-term and specialty healthcare services in the United States. The company provides a broad range of comprehensive long-term and specialty healthcare services (such as nursing care, rehabilitation, infusion, and respiratory therapy). The company provides, either directly or through third-party providers, certain other ancillary services (such as pharmaceutical services; physical, speech, and occupational therapy; and medical supplies and laboratory testing). The company maintains facilities in 12 states.

Pre-Unison: 1989–1992

In 1989, Jerry M. Walker, Phillip Rollins, and Paul Contris were hired as troubleshooters by Samaritan Senior Services Inc., which formerly operated the subacute and long-term healthcare divisions of Samaritan Health System. Their job was to rescue the financially ailing nursing homes of that company. After they brought Samaritan back into profitability, those nursing homes were sold to competitor GranCare, another leading publicly-traded, long-term-care company.

Three years later, in July 1992, Rollins and Contris convinced Walker, a former certified public accountant who was working as the Chief Executive Officer (CEO) of Samaritan Senior Services, to leave Samaritan in order to found SunQuest HealthCare Corp. SunQuest's goal was to be the operation of long-term and specialty healthcare centers.

SunQuest HealthCare Corp.: 1992–1995

Also joining the group as Director of Professional Services at the company's inception was Samaritan's Director of Professional Services, Terry Troxnell. Troxnell was formerly a program manager of health care facility licensure and enforcement for The Arizona Department of Health, where she oversaw the licensing certification of all healthcare facilities in the state.

SunQuest HealthCare Corp. started when the three founders donated $100 each to the cause, in order to get the company off the ground. They incorporated the company in the State of Delaware as SunQuest HealthCare Corporation in July of 1992, and immediately began acquiring financially-strapped healthcare facilities. One of their first acquisitions was a one-year management contract charging them to oversee the operations of two profitable nursing homes on the campuses of the Good Samaritan Regional Medical Center in Phoenix, Arizona and the Desert Samaritan Medical Center in Mesa, Arizona.

It was a wide-eyed group that led the new company to achieve total revenue for the first year of $4.5 million, with a net income of $238,000. Total revenue growth skyrocketed from there, although profits were low the following year; total revenue for 1993 nearly doubled to $8 million, but the net income was a mere $109,000. By the end of 1994, SunQuest Health-Care owned and/or operated some 20 facilities located throughout 11 states, with total revenue on that year reaching $12.4 million, with a net income of $340,000. Troxell was promoted to vice-president of Clinical Operations in November 1994, and senior vice-president of Clinical Operations in September 1996.

503

Company Perspectives:

Unison HealthCare Corporation seeks to operate its businesses as an interrelated network of services to provide a full continuum of cost-effective long-term and specialty healthcare.

Needing access to a fresh influx of capital if it was going to continue to grow, the company began searching for private investors and venture capital firms in Spring 1995. In March 1995, the company organized its Quest Pharmacies Inc. subsidiary, bringing pharmaceutical services to the company's portfolio and facilities in Longview, Texas and Bloomington, Indiana. L. Robert Oberfield, formerly President of Sunscript Pharmacy Corp., a subsidiary of Sun Healthcare Company, was brought in as President of the subsidiary.

In August of that year, shortly before its initial public offering (IPO), the company acquired Dallas, Texas-based BritWill Healthcare Corp. for a total fixed purchase price of $26 million, plus contingent amounts of approximately $9.8 million. At the time, the company had grown to own and/or operate 24 facilities located in 11 states, and added to its repertoire BritWill's 28 facilities located in two states. The acquisition doubled the number of facilities and employees under the SunQuest umbrella, and made the company big enough to go public. BritWill Healthcare chairman Bruce Whitehead was named the new chairman of the combined company, which retained the name SunQuest Healthcare.

Unison HealthCare Corporation Is Born

In October 1995, the company filed a registration statement with the Securities and Exchange Commission to become a publicly-held company. The following month, the company changed its name to Unison HealthCare Corporation. It had grown to own and/or operate 53 facilities, including 47 long-term and specialty-care facilities and six independent-living and assisted-living facilities. By that December, the company was trading under the symbol UNHC on the NASDAQ Stock Market at $9 a share. The IPO raised $18 million for the company. Total revenue for 1995 jumped to $68.5 million, but the company's net income remained low, at only $117,000.

In February 1996, the company purchased the remaining 10 percent minority ownership in the Sunbelt Therapy Management Services Inc. group of companies. The acquisition gave the company a full therapy services stronghold, providing pharmacy services and physical, occupational, and speech therapy. The acquisition also brought the company Paul G. Henderson as President of the subsidiary.

In a June 1996 article in *The Business Journal—Serving Phoenix & the Valley of the Sun,* CEO Walker was quoted as saying, "The single greatest risk is controlling the growth. We are a growing company and will continue to grow. With growth comes the benefits we're seeking. Rapid growth is one of the frequent reasons why businesses fail." Unfortunately, the arti-

cle and Walker's words seemed to foreshadow a pitfall for the company, as it headed down the very path its CEO had hoped to avoid: too many acquisitions in too short a period of time.

In July 1996, the company acquired—for a combination of common shares, cash, and promissory notes totaling approximately $38.2 million—privately-owned Signature Health Care Corp. Also included in the deal were four of the Signature's affiliated companies, which operated 13 long-term care facilities located in Colorado and Arizona, including 11 skilled-nursing facilities and two assisted-living facilities. Former owner David Kremser joined Unison's board at the time of the acquisition.

About the same time, the company also acquired RehabWest for approximately $5.4 million in cash, giving the company rehabilitation therapy services to the Signature centers and other facilities in Colorado. Additionally in October of that year, the company acquired American Professional Holding Inc. and Memphis Clinical Laboratory Inc. in a pooling of interests cash, stock, and promissory note transaction valued at approximately $487,000. The latter acquisition was combined and renamed Ampro, and began operating as a Unison subsidiary.

The acquisitions helped occupancy levels in the company's beds in 1996 climb from 77 percent to 81 percent, and total revenue for the year soared to $148.7 million. But the company lost a staggering $23.4 million that year, having spent more than the heightened earnings could cover. Thus began a decline into debt.

By March 1997, the company ranked among the 25 largest long-term care operators in the United States, owning and/or operating facilities located in 12 states clustered in the Midwest, Southwest, and Southeast. Nonetheless, the company was having operational problems.

An early indication of trouble came when the company released a restatement of the results for the nine months ending September 30, 1996, which showed the company posting a huge loss. Quickly on the heels of the restatement came the resignations of Chief Financial Officer Craig Clark and co-founder and Executive Vice-President of Acquisitions, Paul Contris. A class-action lawsuit was filed against Unison, alleging that the company had misled investors about its financial results. The following month, Kremser's Elk Meadows Investments LLC (with 23.8 percent of the company) and Whitehead's BritWill Investments Co. Ltd. (with 7.8 percent of the company) jointly loaned Unison $2.95 million for general working capital purposes, according to Securities and Exchange Commission records.

Executive changes commenced when Clayton Kloehr—former Manager of Treasurer Operations for Placid Oil Company (a privately held oil exploration and production company based in Dallas Texas), and Treasurer for BritWill Healthcare—joined the company in July 1997 as senior vice-president and treasurer. He later added director to his title in February 1998.

Problems continued to beset Unison through late 1998, as the company, plagued by heavy debt, missed the deadline to file its quarterly report. This resulted in the company's stock being bumped down from trading on the NASDAQ Stock Market to the NASDAQ small caps market, and the company's board of directors stepped in, putting co-founder and President/CEO Jerry Walker on administrative leave, and eventually terminating him. Kremser was named interim president/CEO. The following month, Kremser brought in Michael A. Jefferies—who had extensive management experience in the healthcare field—aboard as President and CEO of the struggling company.

Further administration changes brought Nir E. Margalit in as an executive vice-president, general counsel, secretary, and director. Jimmy L. Fields also came aboard as executive vice-president and chief financial officer in April 1998.

Also in 1998, three units of the company—Britwill Investments I Inc., Britwill Investments II Inc., and Britwill Indiana Partnership L.P.—filed for Chapter 11 Bankruptcy protection. At that time, Unison was still ranked as one of the 30 largest long-term care operators in the United States. But the company was struggling financially, and moved from its posh North Gainey Center Drive location in Scottsdale, Arizona, to a smaller, nondescript office space. Finally, Unison filed for Chapter 11 Bankruptcy protection and tried to reorganize as an attempt at continuing to stay in business. Heading into the end of the century, Unison undoubtedly faced many challenges and uncertainties; most notably, whether or not it would successfully weather the hard times and emerge to reclaim its standing as one of the largest companies in the industry.

Principal Subsidiaries

Ampro; Quest Pharmacies Inc.; Sunbelt Therapy Management Services Inc.

Further Reading

"*The Arizona Republic* Earnings Arizona Column," *Knight-Ridder/Tribune Business News*, May 19, 1998, p. OKRB9813901E.

Gilbertson, Dawn, "Unison Healthcare Corp. Takes Account of Damage from Accounting Problems," *Knight-Ridder/Tribune Business News*, May 28, 1997, p. 528B0941.

Gonzales, Angela, "Men's Room Meetings Lead on to Success," *The Business Journal—Serving Phoenix & the Valley of the Sun*, June 7, 1996, p. 31.

——, "Unison Healthcare Misses Filing Deadline," *The Business Journal—Serving Phoenix & the Valley of the Sun*, August 29, 1997, p. 8.

——, "Awash in Debt, Unison Healthcare Owes Chairman: Millions Owed on Loans, Acquisition," *The Business Journal—Serving Phoenix & the Valley of the Sun*, July 11, 1997, p. 1.

"Interest Payment is Missed; Financing Plan is Weighed," *The Wall Street Journal*, November 12, 1997, p. B5.

"Investors Sue Unison HealthCare Corp. of Scottsdale, Ariz.," *Knight-Ridder/Tribune Business News*, March 26, 1997, p. 326B0987.

"Tentative Agreement is Set for Restructuring of Debt," *The Wall Street Journal*, June 16, 1998, p. B4.

"Three Units Seek Protection with Chapter 11 Filings," *The Wall Street Journal*, January 9, 1998, p. B4.

"Unison Healthcare Corp.," *The Business Journal—Serving Phoenix & the Valley of the Sun*, June 28, 1996, p. 100B.

"Unison Healthcare Corp.," *The New York Times*, January 9, 1998, p. C5.

"Unison Healthcare Corp.," *The Wall Street Journal*, May 29, 1998, p. B4.

"Unison Healthcare Corp.," *The Wall Street Journal*, October 7, 1997, p. B8.

"Unison Healthcare Corp. Agrees to Acquire Signature Health," *Knight-Ridder/Tribune Business News*, July 29, 1996, p. 7290225.

"Unison Healthcare Taps Michael Jefferies as President and CEO," *The Wall Street Journal*, September 10, 1997, p. B2.

—Daryl F. Mallett

United Press International, Inc.

1400 I Street, Northwest
Washington, DC 20005
U.S.A.
(202) 898-8000
Fax: (202) 898-1234
Web site: http://www.upi.com

Private Company
Incorporated: 1907 as United Press
Employees: 250
Sales: $85 million (1995)
SICs: 7383 News Syndicates

United Press International, Inc. (UPI) is a leading global information service and the largest privately owned news service. Its offices around the world gather news that is turned into headlines, summaries, articles, and broadcast feeds and disseminated via wire and satellite for broadcast, print, online, and other subscribers. UPI is owned by Middle East Broadcasting Centre, Ltd., a private communications company owned by a group of investors from Saudi Arabia and based in London.

The First 50 Years: 1907–57

On June 21, 1907, newspaper publisher Edward "E.W." Scripps founded the United Press (UP) to make adequate national and international news coverage available for any existing newspaper or anyone starting up a newspaper. In a dig at the older Associated Press wire service, Scripps said, "I do not believe it would be good for journalism in this country if there should be one big news trust." [Quigg]

UP was created by a merger of Publisher's Press with Scripps-McRae Press Association and Scripps News Associations. There were several organizations then using the name "United Press," and it took Scripps two years of legal battles to gain ownership of that name.

On its first day of business the new service used leased telegraph lines to send 12,000 words of Morse code to 369 afternoon newspapers, including those belonging to the Scripps chain. Early "Unipressers," as the correspondents were called, were the first wire service reporters to conduct interviews and the first to put bylines on stories. They were also the first to send feature stories over the wire and to include labor's side in coverage of industrial disputes.

In 1935 UP expanded its services and became the first wire service to tailor news for radio broadcasters. Radio announcer Ronald Reagan at WHO in Des Moines, Iowa, used the newly launched UP radio wire in 1936.

Robert Manning, a Unipresser in the 1940s, wrote in a 1982 article in the *New York Times,* "You could easily tell a U.P. man from an A.P. man, because a Unipresser worked alone and A.P. men traveled in packs to blanket a story. While suffering under it, we took an almost demented delight in our thralldom to the U.P.'s legendary parsimony. The loose organization of U.P. alumni, which includes such luminaries as Walter Cronkite, Harrison E. Salibury, William L. Shirer and Howard K. Smith, to name a few, is called The Downhold Club, in celebration of the almost constant stream of Teletyped orders to bureaus to 'downhold expenses.' "

Unipressers took great pride in their expense account stories. In his silver anniversary piece, H.D. Quigg recounted two. "Harold Jacobs, covering a Mexican revolution, listed 'one mule shot out from under me.' Edward Beattie, covering the 1935 Ethiopian war on a remote and nearly inaccessible frontier with an army of tribesmen bearing spears and shields, sent an expense account (at 35 cents a thaler) that went: 'Canvas bag for camping, 48 thalers; provisions in field, 201 thalers; mule, 240 thalers; boy's wages, 60 thalers; feed for mule, 9 thalers; Mauser rifle and ammunition, 280 thalers; high boots, 45 thalers.' "

In putting reporters' stories on the wire, UP emphasized speed and brevity. Opinions were not welcome, just the facts. One of Manning's favorite examples was a dispatch from Palestine, which read in total: "The visit of the United Nations

Company Perspectives:

We continue to provide the products and services that have defined UPI's reputation for world-class editorial excellence: instant access to fast-breaking state, national, and international news. But, with innovative technology, major infrastructure investments, and a bold vision of what this company will be, we're bringing something entirely new to the news industry. We are building comprehensive, integrated packages of audio, video, print, photographic, multimedia and online information.

Palestine Commission was marred today when the delegate of the Netherlands fell into the tomb of Nicodemus.''

To beat their competitors, Unipressers resorted to both creative and common sense methods. A UP reporter in Madrid in 1936 tricked the censors to get the first story out announcing the beginning of the Spanish Civil War. His message to London was a mishmash of words, with the first letter of each word spelling out ''foreign legion revolted martial law declared.'' Decades later, during President Nixon's first visit to China in 1972, UPI White House reporter Helen Thomas filed her story from the tunnels of the ancient, underground Ming tombs simply by asking a Chinese attendant if there were a telephone anywhere around. He led her to one nearby. In 1981 the ''mystery man'' sought by police for running from the scene of the assassination attempt on President Reagan turned out to be a UPI reporter trying to get to a telephone to call in the story.

In the early 1950s the E.W. Scripps Co. (then known as Scripps Howard) sold its Acme Newspictures photo agency to United Press, beginning a relationship that would result in eight Pulitzer Prizes for news photography.

Putting the "I" in UPI: 1958

In May 1958 United Press merged with International News Service (INS), owned by William Randolph Hearst, and was renamed United Press International. Early discussions between UP and INS had focused on merging their newsphoto services. But in 1955 the negotiations began examining consolidation of the two parent organizations. After three years of secret talks the two companies reached an agreement. United Press Associations absorbed International News Service, buying the Hearst assets and assuming responsibility for fulfilling all of INS's news and picture contracts. Frank Bartholomew, president of UP, remembered that the eight sets of the final agreement weighed 17 pounds, as measured on a bathroom scale.

UP and INS jointly announced UPI's birth at noon on Saturday, May 24, 1958. The announcement read: ''This is the first dispatch of the news service which will embrace the largest number of newspaper and radio clients ever served simultaneously by an independently operated news and picture agency.'' [p. 52, *Editor & Publisher*, Sept. 25, 1982] UPI had 6,000 employees and served 5,000 newspapers and broadcast clients.

Later that year UPI introduced the first wire service radio network, with correspondents reading their reports from around the globe. Among the voices with which radio listeners became familiar were those of Eric Sevareid, David Brinkley, and Walter Cronkite.

But reporting news internationally, as well as nationally, was an expensive business. UPI operated at a loss for years, with the parent company carrying it. Those losses increased as afternoon newspapers, the service's primary market, began to close. In 1978 E.W. Scripps Co. proposed an arrangement whereby its clients would invest in the news service, becoming co-owners. When that effort failed, the company began looking for a buyer.

New Owners: Media News Corporation, 1982–86

E.W. Scripps Co. celebrated UPI's diamond anniversary in 1982 by selling the news service to Media News Corporation, a new company formed by four investors, owners of U.S. newspaper, cable, and television stations. Scripps received $1 from the new owners and agreed to spend a further $5 million to support the service during the transition.

At the time of its sale UPI was serving more than 7,500 newspapers, radio and television stations, and cable systems in more than 100 countries. Its 2,000 full-time employees in 224 news and picture bureaus sent some 13 million words of news and other information out each day. More than 550 cable systems subscribed to UPI Cable Newswire, making UPI the largest provider of written news for cable television screens.

UPI's revenues in 1982 reached $110 million, but it was operating with a $4 million loss. Much of that was caused by huge telephone bills: $14 million a year in the United States and $30 million worldwide. Media News determined it could save as much as $7 million by using satellites rather than telephone lines to send its articles and pictures. The new owners announced that they would spend $20 million to improve communications and to beef up state and regional news coverage. They also planned to study the pricing of the news service.

But their efforts failed. In April 1985, UPI declared bankruptcy and filed for Chapter 11 protection from its creditors. Employee layoffs began. The company reported $40.2 million in debts and about $24 million in assets.

New Owners: New UPI Inc., 1986–88

In June 1986, New UPI Inc., owned by Mexican businessman Mario Vazquez-Rana and Texas real estate investor Joe Russo, bought the company. New UPI Inc. paid $41 million for UPI, beating out Financial News Network (FNN) in the bidding. Employees took a 25 percent wage cut to keep UPI going, as Vazquez-Rana, who owned 90 percent of the company, pledged to keep it as a general news service.

But after two years, during which UPI lost between $1 million and $2 million a month, Vazquez-Rana sold the company to Infotechnology Inc., which held 46 percent of cable business channel Financial News Network. The agreement transferred operational control, but not ownership, to Infotech, with Vazquez-Rana setting up lines of credit to cover costs.

New Owners: Infotechnology Inc., 1988–91

Infotech planned to make UPI "the cornerstone of a high-tech information network," according to Elizabeth Tucker in a 1988 *Washington Post* article. UPI Chairman Earl Brian envisioned UPI reporters feeding information to FNN and its 30 million viewers, while financial information from FNN correspondents would be available for UPI's print business products.

As part of its strategy, Infotech broke up UPI's generalized wire-service report into specific segments—national sports, business news, photographs, and international news—and concentrated more heavily on covering local and regional news.

By November 1990, Infotech, owing some $160 million to banks and not able to meet daily operating expenses, put UPI and FNN up for sale. The following August, with $65.2 million in liabilities and $22.7 million in assets, UPI sought to reorganize under Chapter 11. The news service was down to 586 employees, and its future was uncertain.

Significant changes had occurred in the way news was gathered and delivered, with compact satellite technology enabling broadcasters to send their own reporters to cover news and specialized wire services offering more comprehensive information. "There's so much information available now that it's difficult for a [general wire service] to prosper, especially one that's number two," business professor Jon Udell told Paul Farhi of the *Washington Post*.

New Owners: Middle East Broadcasting Centre, Ltd., 1992–96

In May 1992, it appeared that religious broadcaster Pat Robertson would buy UPI, but he withdrew his bid for the entire operation, offering instead to buy just the name, UPI's photo archive, and its overseas news photo distribution business. In June the bankruptcy judge selected Middle East Broadcasting Centre, Ltd. (MBC) of London over Robertson and a Dutch foundation. Middle East Broadcasting paid $3.95 million in cash for UPI.

The private communications company, whose principal owner, Sheik Walid Al-Ibrahim, was brother-in-law of King Fahd of Saudi Arabia, broadcast news and entertainment in Arabic to Europe, Africa, and the Middle East. MBC was UPI's fifth owner in a decade, a period that also included two bankruptcies, a court-ordered liquidation, management upheaval, and labor disputes. For the second time in its 85-year history, UPI was foreign-owned.

Over the next 18 months, the new owners reorganized UPI into six regional bureaus, made significant investments to upgrade the company's communications system, and started expanding into new areas. The management team who took over early in 1994 symbolized MBC's new strategic direction for UPI. Headed by CEO L. Brewster Jackson, they came from media and high-tech companies and international businesses. In a 1994 interview, Jean AbiNader, vice-president of operations, told the Canada NewsWire, "Our worldwide technology in-

vestment alone should tell the world that we aren't resting on our laurels. Our new global satellite system, delivering an array of news and information services to desktop computers anywhere in an instant says a lot about our future direction."

The company began selling electronic news services to a wider array of subscribers and created 35 worldwide sales positions to market UPI's products to corporate and government markets as well as to media customers. It also upgraded its photos and other images technologically, so that they could be delivered by satellite. By 1995 UPI had completed a satellite transmission system and no longer needed to send news over telephone lines.

One of UPI's first new services was "World View," a global satellite network to provide information important to corporate clients. "If a country in Latin America decided to nationalize oil refineries, for instance, that information would be instrumental to a company like Mobil or Exxon," UPI Marketing Director Ron MacIntyre explained to the *Washington Times*. Using the network program, clients could access text, audio, photographs, and live video information.

Focus on Broadcast and Online Services, 1996–97

Studies during 1996 found that the company's future lay in broadcasting, not in wire service writing. By the end of the year, UPI had decided to concentrate its efforts on expanding its broadcast and computer online services. In January 1997 the company closed all of its European bureaus except the London office as well as most of its news bureaus in the United States, depending on freelance "stringers" for coverage. It also strengthened its radio broadcast activities, merging the news desk and broadcast desk.

Focusing on broadcasting made sense. UPI Radio Network, with 120 affiliates, accounted for one-half of the company's income. The network's clients included Salem Broadcasting, Skylight, and People's Radio Network, three religious broadcasters, as well as The Armed Forces Radio Network and Bloomberg News Radio. Employment at UPI was down to 300 staff members and 800 "stringers" with about 1,000 broadcast clients and 1,000 newspaper and World Wide Web clients.

Still far from profitable, UPI was developing what the *New York Times*, in a March 1997 article, described as "a kind of niche journalism, selling fragments of news to customers ranging from a San Francisco paging service that puts headlines on pager screens to a Kentucky enterprise that wants to flash headlines in small streaming lights installed in bars to religious broadcasters who have been adding news broadcasts as a way of keeping their listeners tuned in."

The headline service, which UPI called "Short Service," provided two-sentence news summaries. For its news articles, UPI adopted a new writing style limited to 350 words. "We provide details to reporters and editors to use in their own reports," a UPI executive explained in the *Times* article.

Shaping Knowledge: 1997 to the Present

In mid-1997 James Adams was named CEO. Adams, who had been the Washington bureau chief for London's *Sunday*

Times after serving as its defense correspondence and managing editor, greatly accelerated the company's move to becoming an electronic information source. He also aimed UPI at the Internet and at developing ways individual consumers could access the specific "knowledge" they wanted.

One new service was the UPI MEMO, an online joint venture with Meridian Emerging Markets Ltd. of Virginia. For $10,000 a year, a client received comprehensive coverage on 16,000 companies in emerging markets and the software to screen and analyze the data. Reports addressed the political and cultural issues influencing the economic outlook in a market as well as pricing and dividend information, earnings estimates, and historical fundamental financial data on individual companies.

In 1998 Adams announced UPI was getting into the production business, with the formation of UPI Productions to create documentary and news programs for television, video, and the Internet. He also moved to develop new markets and customers for UPI's extensive archives. To that end, he developed a joint venture with Microsoft Corporation, called UPI-Microsoft Knowledge Center, to convert and distribute text, photos, audio, and video/film over the Internet. He also announced the company would launch a new entity to sell its library of films and videos as well as make UPI material available through Media Exchange International's web site on a per-use basis to the general user. In May, Adams announced an agreement with Geoworks Corporation to deliver headlines and news summaries to wireless devices. With Geoworks' software, customers also would be able to use their handsets to search for news by topics, names, or keywords.

As CEO Adams told CNNfn, his strategy was "to move to the Web as fast as possible. All our future lies with the Internet and business through the Web. Our delivery systems must be there. Our products must be put through there. That is where our market is." He predicted that UPI would be profitable in 1999 for the first time in its history and that he hoped to take the company public eventually.

Principal Subsidiaries

UPI Productions.

Further Reading

Bartholomew, Frank H., "Putting the 'I' into U.P.I.," *Editor & Publisher*, September 25, 1982, p. 25.

Berry, John F., "New Hope at Distressed Wire Service; Youthful Owners Set Out To Make UPI Profitable," *Washington Post*, October 3, 1982, p. M1.

Day, Kathleen, "Financial News Network, UPI Are Put Up for Sale," *Washington Post*, November 8, 1990, p. B15.

Farhai, Paul, "UPI's Fate Goes Down to Wire," *Washington Post*, November 16, 1990, p. C11.

Friendly, Jonathan, "U.P.I. To Spend $20 Million To Improve and Expand Operation," *New York Times*, October 3, 1982, p. 40.

"From Threatened to Just Threadbare, U.P.I. Adjusts to Buyout," *New York Times*, July 20, 1992, p. D6.

"Geoworks Enters Agreement with United Press International To License News Content for Wireless Information Service," *PR Newswire*, May 5, 1998.

Jayne, Micah, "UPI Hopes New Information Service Will Do Big Business with Big Business," *Washington Times*, July 27, 1994, p. B7.

Jones, Alex S., "Mideast Broadcaster Acquires U.P.I. in Bankruptcy Court," *New York Times*, June 24, 1992, p. D2.

"Key Dates in UPI History," *The Associated Press*, September 5, 1995.

Lattin, Don, "Robertson Gives Mixed Signals About Religion's Role in UPI," *The San Francisco Chronicle*, May 15, 1992, p. A9.

Lilling, Adam, "UPI's Latest Survival Strategy," *American Journalism Review*, September 1997, p. 15.

Manning, Robert, "When U.P. Had No I," *New York Times*, June 12, 1982, p. 31.

"Pat Robertson Backs Out of UPI Deal," *Star Tribune* (Minneapolis), June 11, 1992, p. 3D.

Peterson, Iver, "In News Business, UPI Plans To Thrive in 350 Words or Less," *New York Times*, March 31, 1997, p. D1.

Quigg, H.D., "UPI's Diamond Anniversary: From Morse Code to Satellites," *U.P.I.*, June 19, 1982.

Schuch, Beverly, "UPI CEO Interview," *CNNfn Business Unusual*, Transcript #98042102FN-112, April 21, 1998.

"Suddenly UPI Is in Demand as 3 Groups Wrestle for Control," *Chicago Tribune*, June 19, 1992, Bus. Sec., p. 2.

Sugawara, Sandra, "UPI Proves Too Much for Vazquez-Rana: Owner Hands Over Operating Control of Troubles Wire Service to Former Rival," *Washington Post*, February 21, 1988, p. A4.

Tharp, Paul, "UPI Upgrades Wires Service to the 'Net,' " *New York Post*, March 20, 1998, p. 034.

Tucker, Elizabeth, "Brian's Aggressive Plans for Troubled UPI," *Washington Post*, November 28, 1988, p. F37.

UPI Corporate Website, United Press International, http://www.upi.com

"UPI Eyes TV, Video Internet," *AP Online*, March 19, 1998.

—Ellen D. Wernick

Universal International, Inc.

5000 Winnetka Avenue North
New Hope, Minnesota 55428
U.S.A.
(612) 533-1169
Fax: (612) 533-1158

Public Company
Incorporated: 1956
Employees: 273
Sales: $62.3 million (1997)
Stock Exchanges: NASDAQ
Ticker Symbol: UNIV
SICs: 5331 Variety Stores

A regional discount retailer, Universal International, Inc., operates a chain of nearly 60 Only Deals stores in the upper Midwest and Texas. For much of its history, Universal was known primarily as a wholesaler of close-out merchandise, operating on a national basis for more than two decades. In 1997, however, the company exited the wholesale business and pinned its future on its growing chain of Only Deals retail outlets, which sold a variety of merchandise, including toys, food, health and beauty aids, housewares, and other items, all priced between $1 and $10. The Only Deals concept was first tested in Minnesota in 1991, followed by a rush of store openings that fanned out from the company's headquarter state of Minnesota. During the late 1990s, Universal also controlled a 40.5 percent stake in Odd's-N-End's, Inc., a New York-based discount retailer that operated more than 20 discount stores in its home state.

1950s Origins

Universal was founded by Norman J. Ravich in 1956 as a small, privately owned chain of retail stores selling discount merchandise. He christened his outlets "Little Big Dollar Stores," and began stocking the shelves with an eclectic array of merchandise including health and beauty aids, household gadgets, and sundry other products all priced under $1. For roughly 15 years, Ravich poured his energies into developing the chain. He opened new stores when profits gleaned from his existing stores gave him the financial means, and he added additional units through franchise agreements, creating a substantial regional retail chain in less than twenty years. By the early 1970s, however, Ravich had resolved to close his retail chain, which at its peak comprised 50 company-owned Little Big Dollar Stores and 25 franchised units, and in its place establish a business focused on the wholesale side of discount merchandise. The turning point arrived in 1972.

Wholesale Operations Started in 1970s

Ravich left behind a successful, firmly established business for the vagaries of starting anew. He quickly registered success in wholesale, transforming Universal into a specialist in close-out merchandise. When close-out merchandise became available through over-production, the discontinuation of a particular product line, or excess inventory, Universal purchased it in large quantities at prices that ranged from 10 to 50 percent of traditional wholesale prices. The company then found retailers to purchase it, and the retailers, in turn, sold the merchandise to the public. The key to success was locating the close-out merchandise in the first place—that is, finding the best bargains—and then developing an ample roster of retailers willing to buy it. In this essential process, Ravich acted as the chief bargain-hunter and buyer for his company. It was a position he held for the next two decades, as Universal matured into one of the nation's leading wholesalers of discount merchandise.

By the mid-1980s, the company had a steady and enviable record of consistent financial growth behind it, but success never bred complacency—or even much satisfaction—at company headquarters in Minnesota. Under Ravich's direction, the company undertook another gradual reorganization, moving back to its retail origins.

The basis for the change was a desire to increase Universal's stature, particularly its financial might. After nearly 30 years of business, Universal's revenue volume stood at a modest $5 million, and the company's management, led by Ravich, was determined to increase that total by developing a retail arm to

510

augment the company's wholesale business. With this as his aim, in 1985 Ravich slowly began laying the groundwork for Universal's re-entry into the retail sector, recruiting new management talent and putting in place an operational structure to support retail activities. By the beginning of the 1990s the pace of change had accelerated, touching off a period of expansion that eventually led to Universal's complete transformation.

1990 Public Offering Finances Retail Expansion

In late 1990 Universal completed its initial public offering of stock. Its debut as a publicly traded company marked the end of 34 years of private ownership and netted the company $4.5 million, capital it would need to fund the establishment of retail outlets. Norman Ravich's son, Mark H. Ravich, took over as chief executive officer in September 1990, working alongside his father, who presided as chairman of the board.

Mark Ravich perceived the imminent move into the retail sector as "synergistic." By developing a retail arm to its wholesale operations, Universal could take advantage of its expertise in purchasing close-out merchandise—a talent honed over the previous four decades—and broaden its business in a complementary direction.

He created a prototype that operated under the banner "Only Deals," a store that drew upon Universal's experience in the health, beauty, and household merchandise once stocked by the chain of Little Big Dollar Stores, as well as men's, women's, and children's wear. Only Deals offering items that ranged between $1 and $10. The first store opened in the Crystal Shopping Center in Crystal, Minnesota, and was followed by five more Only Deals in Minnesota shopping malls. By the end of 1992, there were 30 Only Deals scattered throughout Minne-sota, South Dakota, Iowa, Illinois, and Nebraska, all located in shopping malls or strip shopping centers.

Expansion plans for 1993 called for the opening of 30 to 50 more Only Deals units, a goal the company fell short of. In 1994 Universal entered into a supply agreement with one of its wholesale customers, Odd's-N-End's, Inc., and subsequently acquired 40.5 percent of the company. Odd's-N-End's operated 22 discount retail stores in New York state, which joined Universal's fold in early 1995 when Ravich's company assumed day-to-day control over the retail operator.

Since reentering the retail field, Universal's revenue volume had swelled dramatically, rising to nearly $90 million in 1995, and in early 1997 the company completely divested itself of its wholesale operations. Universal's Only Deals chain had developed into a 56-unit enterprise stretching across six states in the Midwest and in Texas. With Only Deals as its mainstay business, Universal prepared for its future, which had much in common with Ravich's first years as the operator of Little Big Dollar Stores.

Principal Subsidiaries: Only Deals Inc.; Odd's-N-End's, Inc. (40.5%).

Further Reading

Gellers, Stan E., "Closeout King Goes Retail," *Daily News Record,* October 23, 1992, p. 4.

Scally, Robert, "99 Cents Only to Venture Out of LA to Eastern, Midwestern Markets," *Discount Store News,* March 9, 1998, p. 10.

Schafer, Lee, "Universal International Inc.," *Corporate Report-Minnesota,* January 1991, p. 98.

Straumanis, Andris, "Universal's Retail Play," *Corporate Report-Minnesota,* December 1991, p. 17.

—Jeffrey L. Covell

Viatech Continental Can Company, Inc.

One Aerial Way
Syosset, New York 11791
U.S.A.
(516) 822-4940
Fax: (516) 931-6344

Wholly Owned Subsidiary of Suiza Foods Corporation
Incorporated: 1913
Employees: 3,442
Sales: $546.3 million (1997)
SICs: 3081 Unsupported Plastics Film & Sheet; 3089
Plastic Products, Not Elsewhere Classified; 3411
Metal Cans; 3565 Packaging Machinery; 8711
Engineering Services

Viatech Continental Can Company, Inc.—since June 1998 a wholly owned subsidiary of Dallas-based dairy and packaging firm Suiza Foods Corporation—is a packaging company operating through a number of subsidiaries. The company holds an 84 percent stake in Plastic Containers, Inc., which in turn owns Continental Plastic Containers, Inc., a leading manufacturer and marketer of extrusion blow-molded plastic containers for household chemicals, food and beverages, automotive products and motor oil, industrial and agricultural chemicals, and cosmetics and toiletries. Dixie Union GmbH & Company KG is a wholly owned subsidiary of Continental Can based in Germany and makes multilayer shrink bags, composite plastic films, and packaging machines and slicers, primarily for the food and pharmaceutical industries. Continental Can also owns 64 percent of Paris-based Ferembal S.A., the second-largest manufacturer of food cans in France as well as a producer of cans for pet foods and industrial products. In turn, Ferembal holds 96 percent of Obalex A.S., a manufacturer of cans in the Czech Republic. Continental Can also wholly owns Lockwood, Kessler & Bartlett, Inc., an engineering consulting firm with no connection to the packaging field.

The Continental Can Company of the late 20th century represents a second chapter in the use of the company name,

although there is more than just the name connecting the historical periods. The original Continental Can traces its roots to 1913 and enjoyed a long period as a financially stable container company. Engaged in the mature and traditionally slow growth industry of canmaking, its revenues increased every year without interruption from 1923 into the early 1980s. The company overcame the problems endemic to canmaking (small profit margins, shrinking domestic market, large capital outlays for industrial machinery, etc.) through astute and careful management. In 1984, however, the tranquil atmosphere at Continental (by this time known as Continental Group) was disrupted when the company began accepting offers for a possible takeover. It was ultimately purchased by the Omaha, Nebraska, construction firm of Peter Kiewit Sons Inc., which over the succeeding seven years chopped up the company assets and sold them off piece by piece. In 1992 Donald J. Bainton, a former president of the company, bought the rights to the Continental Can name and logo and resurrected the company in name—and, in terms of operations, resurrected the company itself, at least in part, since he had in 1991 acquired one of Continental's units, Continental Plastic Containers.

Early History

Incorporated during 1913 in New York, the company was acquired by the Los Angeles Can Company in 1926 and then merged with the Continental Can Company of California. As cans gradually became the preferred method of packaging and preserving consumer products, Continental's business grew impressively. By the 1930s it was also producing corrugated paper boxes and crown bottle caps and had emerged as the second-largest container company in the United States, behind American Can.

The decade of the 1930s was particularly important for Continental. It expanded outside the United States and began licensing equipment and expertise to affiliate companies in Europe. These holdings were then subsequently increased after World War II, providing Continental a strong foothold in the burgeoning European can market and a large competitive edge over American Can. In fact, Continental went from being just half the size of American Can Company in 1942 to being slightly larger than American Can in 1956, with most of the growth coming in the ten year period between 1945 and 1955 when Europe was experiencing its postwar boom.

Not all the news was good, however. Both Continental and American suffered a setback in 1950. Up until that year these two companies had offered volume discounts to their larger customers, thereby significantly underselling their smaller competitors. In 1950 a Federal Court struck down this practice and also demanded that the two companies offer canmaking machinery for sale. Prior to this, Continental and American would only lease machinery to other canmakers. This also served to weaken the grip of the "big two" on the industry.

Because the business was opened more widely to competition, prices and profit margins began to decrease, and many of the major can customers began to see the benefits of manufacturing their own cans. The most vivid example of this was the Campbell Soup Company, which, despite only making cans for its own products, became the third-largest canmaker in the world.

New Cans and Attempted Diversification in the 1950s

This situation left Continental Can two choices: either invest heavily in research and development to make the technology of competitors and defecting customers obsolete, or diversify into other markets to mitigate the drop in can profits. Company management decided to do both. The traditional three-piece, soldered-seam tin can was gradually being replaced by cans of lighter metals such as aluminum and other steel alloys. While the new cans required a more complex manufacturing process and more expensive materials, their lighter weight made them popular with consumers and less expensive to transport. This represented the future of canmaking, and Continental was quick to prepare for it.

In 1956 the company made its first major ventures outside canmaking. In that year Continental merged with the Hazel-Atlas Glass Company and a few months later purchased the Robert Gair Paper Company. However, no sooner had Continental finalized the agreements than it was charged with an antitrust suit. The litigation lasted for several years, ultimately reaching the Supreme Court where the mergers were declared lawful. The Justice Department could not prove that the Continental-Hazel-Gair agreements adversely affected competition. However, between the court costs and three successive years of subpar performance, both Gair and Hazel-Atlas were proving to be costly financial ventures. Less than a year after the mergers had been pronounced legal, Continental divested itself of both companies.

In 1963 a simple but ingenious feature was introduced to cans—the pop-top tab opener. Though it is unclear who thought of the idea first (both Amcan and Alcoa have patents on somewhat similar designs), it did not take long for most major can producers to introduce the new pop-tab cans. The industry was virtually revolutionized overnight. The era of the "six-pack" had begun. The new cans, which were light, easy to open, easy to store, and unbreakable, helped ward off a challenge from the non-returnable bottle which was so popular at the time. Due in large part to the new can, beer and soda pop

consumption in the United States increased dramatically in the 1960s. Continental, which had always considered itself an industrial container corporation, began to manufacture consumer beverage cans and flourished.

The various brewers and soft drink bottlers were eventually consolidated under a few large companies, thus reviving the trend towards the self-manufacture of cans. A corporation such as beer brewer Schlitz, by building "on-site" can plants instead of contracting a company to make and transport their cans, could save a large amount of money. Container technology was also changing. Aluminum, despite its higher price, was emerging as the canmaking "staple" by replacing the heavier and less popular tin can. Moreover, for the first time the storage and container potential of plastics began to be recognized. To keep up with the shifting topography of the industry, the traditional canmaking companies American Can and Continental were forced to make huge capital outlays for modernization programs in the early 1970s.

1970s Modernization and Diversification

The first thing Continental did was develop the Cono-plan program, under which, in an effort to keep its customers and slow the trend toward self-manufacturing, Continental would construct a canmaking operation within the client's factory, thereby eliminating all transportation costs. In addition, Continental Chief Executive Officer Robert Hatfield closed 15 plants considered too distant from customers. He then spent over $100 million to modify existing plants so that they could produce the newer and more profitable two-piece can which was quickly replacing the older three-piece can.

However, these measures were not enough. In order to achieve more substantial growth, Continental accelerated its diversification program and more firmly established itself in foreign markets. The company developed and marketed its paper products with considerable success and also moved into the non-container fields of oil and gas. In 1969 it established the Europemballage container holding company, which in a matter of years became the largest canmaker in Europe's Common Market. It became so large, in fact, that the Common Market principals sued Europemballage for antitrust violations and succeeded in restricting the holding company from acquiring affiliates in new markets. Despite this setback, Continental was able to take advantage of Europe's move toward supermarkets and canned perishables and reap large financial rewards.

In 1976 the company, reflecting its more diverse corporate personality, adopted the new name of Continental Group, with Continental Can continuing to be the name of the packaging unit within Continental Group. As if to prove its reorientation, the company spent $370 million to purchase the Richmond Corporation, a $1.1 billion life, title, and casualty insurer. The idea behind the acquisition was to integrate the capital intensive packaging sectors with a sector that had low capital requirements but plenty of liquid assets. These assets were then redeployed to such areas as oil and gas exploration.

In 1981 Robert Hatfield retired, and S. Bruce Smart took over as chairman. Smart continued most of Hatfield's programs and procedures and, like his predecessor, regarded energy, not consumer retail goods, as the prime growth industry of the future. He planned to spend $800 million over a five-year period on energy exploration, research, and transportation. (In 1983 Donald J. Bainton, president of the Continental Can unit, took early retirement in frustration over what he felt was a misguided program of diversification.)

Sold in 1984, Dismantled by 1991

Continental continued its slow but steady growth and gradually increased its lead over American Can. Despite its continuing success, however, the company's stock was markedly undervalued. In 1984 British financier James Goldsmith made an offer to buy the Continental Group. Soon Continental had attracted several potential suitors, both foreign and domestic. Smart and the management at Continental ultimately sold the company to Peter Kiewit Sons Inc., a construction firm based in Omaha, Nebraska. Kiewit paid $3.5 billion in cash and assumed debt to finalize the agreement.

Smart apparently thought that a Nebraska construction company one-third the size of Continental would be easier to deal with than financial professionals like Goldsmith. At a banquet dinner given to celebrate the finalization of the sale, Smart said, "I don't think we'll have anyone from Nebraska coming all the way to Connecticut to tell us how to make cans."

The full irony of the statement was not felt until a year later. If the people at Kiewit did not change the way Continental made cans, they changed everything else. Under the direction of Donald Strum, Kiewit dismantled the sprawling Continental Group in an effort to make the operation even more profitable. His two goals were to sell Continental's properties until only the can operations and the timberlands were left, and to eliminate the corporate management "dead wood" which had become conservative and complacent. In the matter of a year Strum sold $1.6 billion worth of insurance, gas pipelines, and oil and gas reserves. Staff at the Stamford, Connecticut, corporate headquarters was reduced from 500 to 40. Among those relieved of their duties was S. Bruce Smart himself, who later accepted a job with the Reagan Administration as Secretary of International Commerce.

Apart from those in higher management, however, not many jobs were lost during the changes brought on by the dismantling and restructuring of the company, and the real winners in the deal were Continental stockholders. The sale to Kiewit raised share prices, and the selling of Continental properties brought impressive dividends.

However, within a few short years, Continental Group was no more, as Kiewit sold off all the remaining packaging units. Philadelphia-based Crown Cork & Seal Co. Inc. bought Continental Can Canada Inc. in late 1989 and the U.S. aluminum can operations of Continental in the following year. German industrial group Viag AG bought Continental Can Europe in 1991.

During this time, in early 1991, Continental Can Company was ordered to pay out $415 million to some 3,700 former employees and members of the United Steel Workers of America, when the courts found that the company had attempted to defraud the employees of pensions during the late 1970s.

Continental Can Resurrected in the 1990s

Also in 1991 Kiewit sold the only remaining Continental unit—Plastic Containers, Inc. (PCI), which owned Continental Plastic Containers, Inc. Purchasing a 50 percent interest in PCI was Syosset, New York-based Viatech Inc., which Donald Bainton had run since leaving Continental Group in 1983. At the time he joined Viatech, the firm owned only Lockwood, Kessler & Bartlett, Inc., an engineering consulting firm with $6 million in annual revenues. This business had no connection to the packaging industry, but Bainton planned to make Viatech his base for bringing Continental Can back to life.

Bainton made Viatech's first move into packaging with the mid-1980s purchase of Dixie Union GmbH & Company KG, a moneylosing German manufacturer of plastic bags used in food packaging, such as in the packaging of hot dogs and lunchmeat. Next was the acquisition of another troubled European firm, Onena Bolsas de Papel, S.A., a printer and laminator of plastic films based in Spain. Bainton quickly turned both companies around. In 1989 he purchased 51 percent of Ferembal S.A., the second-largest food can maker in France. After acquiring the 50 percent interest in PCI in 1991, Bainton purchased the rights to the Continental Can Company name and logo from Kiewit, renamed Viatech Continental Can Company, Inc. in October 1992, and took the company public. With annual revenues of $500 million, the new Continental Can was a mere shadow of the one-time giant $4 billion Continental Can of old, but Bainton was determined to grow the company, mainly through acquisition.

The newly opened markets of Eastern Europe provided one area of growth for Continental Can in the mid-1990s. The company's first move into this region came in the Czech Republic, where a majority stake was purchased in Obalex A.S., a maker of metal cans, most of which were used for food. In 1997 Continental Can, through Ferembal, took a 51 percent stake in Amco S.A. of Romania, a leading manufacturer of metal cans, caps, and crowns. Meanwhile, the company sold Onena Bolsas de Papel in 1996 and increased its stake in PCI from 50 percent to 84 percent, while the stake in Obalex was jumped to 96 percent in 1997. In April 1998 the company boosted its interest in Ferembal to 97 percent.

In June 1998 Suiza Foods Corporation completed its acquisition of Continental Can for about $345 million. Suiza, which was also positioned as one of the leading dairy companies in the United States, had 16 plastic packaging plants in the United States which when added to Continental Can's 15 such plants created a leader in plastic packaging, particularly in the high-density polyethylene (HDPE) segment of the industry. Continental Can's plastic packaging operations were thus clearly what made the acquisition attractive for Suiza. The divestment of Continental's European units became a possible outcome of the deal, although it was also possible that Suiza would use Continental's overseas presence as a base for international expansion in the 21st century.

Principal Subsidiaries

Ferembal S.A. (France; 97%); Lockwood, Kessler & Bartlett, Inc.; Dixie Union GmbH & Company KG (Germany); Plastic

Containers, Inc. (84%); Continental Plastic Containers, Inc.; Continental Caribbean Containers, Inc.; Obalex A.S. (Czech Republic; 96%); Amco S.A. (Romania; 51%).

Further Reading

Khalaf, Roula, ''Field of Dreams,'' *Forbes,* November 9, 1992, pp. 58, 60.

Regan, Bob, ''Crown Cork to Acquire Continental's Can Units,'' *American Metal Market,* March 28, 1990, pp. 1 +.

Scolieri, Peter, ''Continental Can Given $415M Tab,'' *American Metal Market,* January 8, 1991, pp. 4 +.

Sheridan, John H., ''On the Resurrection Trail,'' *Industry Week,* November 16, 1992, pp. 20–22, 24.

—updated by David E. Salamie

Vlasic Foods International Inc.

Vlasic Plaza
6 Executive Campus
Cherry Hill, New Jersey 08002-4112
U.S.A.
(609) 969-7100
Web site: http://www.vlasic.com

Public Company
Founded: 1997
Employees: 9,200
Sales: $1.5 billion (1997)
Stock Exchanges: New York
Ticker Symbol: VL
SICs: 2035 Pickles & Pickle Products; 2038 Frozen
    Specialties, Not Elsewhere Classified; 2099 Food
    Preparations, Not Elsewhere Classified

Spun off from Campbell Soup Company in March 1998, Vlasic Foods International Inc. is an independent public company manufacturing and marketing well-known convenience food products. Its brands in the United States and Canada include Vlasic pickles, Open Pit barbecue sauce, and Swanson pot pies and frozen dinners. Internationally, its holdings include Kattus, a leading specialty foods distributor in Germany; Swift, the number one canned meat pâté in Argentina; and Freshbake frozen foods and SonA and Rowats pickles and canned beans and vegetables, leading brands in the United Kingdom. Vlasic is also the top mushroom producer in the United States and one of Argentina's largest exporters of processed beef products.

Early Days: 1940s to 1969

Joseph Vlasic, a Croatian immigrant who settled in Detroit, started his first business, a creamery, in the 1920s. He built that into Michigan's largest wholesale milk distributorship, expanded to include Polish hams, and, during World War II, added pickles, marketing them to Detroit's Polish community. Eventually he formed Vlasic Food Products, Inc.

Robert J. Vlasic took over the West Bloomfield, Michigan businesses from his father in 1963, when the elder Vlasic retired. From the beginning, the Vlasics produced pickles that were easy to transport. The raw cucumbers were put in jars and covered with hot brine. Once the jars were sealed, they were ready to go. Called hot-pack pickles, they required no refrigeration, unlike cold-pack pickles, and lasted longer than pickles cured in vats. Bob Vlasic bought and expanded three pickle plants, sold off the other businesses, and introduced a bow-tie-wearing cartoon stork in its ads. By 1967, the company had sales of about $10 million.

In 1947, Campbell Soup Company began growing its own mushrooms at Prince Crossing, Illinois. Campbell acquired Omaha-based C.A. Swanson & Sons in 1955, expanding into the relatively new area of frozen foods. Swanson had originated its trademarked TV Dinner the year before, with turkey, cornbread stuffing, gravy, peas, and sweet potatoes served in a three-compartment aluminum tray and packaged in boxes illustrated to look like televisions, complete with knobs. An ad in *Frozen Food Age* in 1954, stressed the convenience of the new dinner: "Revolutionary New Food Trend! Swanson TV Dinners. Just what housewives want—no work, no thawing needed. Out of the box into the oven—25 minutes later a hearty turkey dinner ready to eat on its own aluminum serving tray."

Swanson had introduced its frozen pot pies (chicken, turkey, and beef) in 1951, and in the next three years produced 100 million frozen meat pies. Swanson had sales of about $100 million when Campbell bought it, with its frozen meals accounting for about 60 percent of sales. With Campbell's resources behind it, Swanson soon was producing 25 million TV Dinners a year. During the 1960s, Campbell removed TV Dinners from the packaging, calling them simply Swanson Dinners. In 1969, Campbell developed a line of frozen breakfasts and marketed them under the Swanson name.

Becoming Number One: 1970–77

The decade of the 1970s saw an important advancement in pickle production, with the addition of calcium to the brine, allowing packers to reduce the amount of salt needed by half

516

and still get firm pickles. In 1970, Vlasic and H.J. Heinz Company each had 10 percent of the national pickle market. Seven years later, Vlasic had become the nation's largest pickle maker, with the company's bow-tied cartoon stork mascot delivering one-quarter of all the pickles sold at retail in the United States and bringing in over $100 million in sales a year. Heinz was still at 10 percent of the market.

Bob Vlasic explained his company's growth to *Forbes* in a 1997 article, "Most of our competitors were manufacturing oriented, generations of fine pickle makers and proud of it. We came in exactly the opposite, as marketers who manufactured to have something to sell."

Vlasic may have been more entrepreneurial than his competitors, but his success led to an investigation by the Federal Trade Commission. According to the *Forbes* article, "Vlasic's marketing strategy is to bombard the consumer with pickle power. This year it will spend more than $2 million—more than all its competitors combined—on television advertising. It also has introduced the largest product line, 138 items (including relishes, peppers and sauerkraut) that can be introduced into a store en masse."

The fact was that to succeed in the pickle business, a company had to be willing to spend, making discount deals with stores year-round even though people made most of their pickle purchases during the summer and at holidays. A packer contracted with farmers for cucumbers at least a year in advance. To get shelf space for the next year's supply, he had to reduce the price of a jar to encourage people to buy. Otherwise, inventories would back up in the warehouse or curing tanks.

Vlasic's competitors complained that the company came into a market, dropped the price on its jars to gain distribution, then moved on. Vlasic countered that the competition was good for the business. "We haven't driven anybody out of business nor do we intend to. Our merchandising makes competitors try harder and then overall sales improve," argued Vlasic president Dennis Sullivan in the *Forbes* article. That appeared to be the case, at least in California. Within a year of Vlasic entering the market in 1976, pickle volume had grown eight percent. But the company was not successful in every market. Private regional producers as well as pickle divisions of corporations proved more popular in markets ranging from St. Louis to Seattle to Atlanta.

But things began to slow down in 1977. Vlasic had spent over $20 million since 1970, building two new plants and buying and completely renovating a California operation. The price of cucumbers had increased more than 35 percent since 1973, to almost $4 a bushel, and the company's bank loans to finance the buying of its cuke inventory (a very seasonal buildup) were running as high as $20 million. Earnings on its $100 million in sales were only about $1.3 million, and the company's debt-to-equity ratio stood at over 2-to-1.

Meanwhile, things were beginning to change at conservative Campbell Soup Company. Harold A. Shaub, who was named president of Campbell in 1972, had decentralized the company's operations, organizing it into divisions built around its major product lines and was beginning to hire outsiders to shake up the marketing efforts. In 1973, Swanson introduced a new

line of meals and pot pies under the name Hungry Man, with larger-sized portions of meat and vegetables. "When I came to it, the company was a producer of canned foods," Shaub told *Business Week* in 1980. "Now, I like to think of us as being in a consumer goods business.

Vlasic Joins Campbell and Adds Specialties: 1978–89

In 1978, Campbell Soup Company bought Vlasic Food Products, which had sales the previous year of $102 million. Campbell paid $35 million in capital stock for the company, one of Campbell's largest acquisitions ever. As a wholly owned subsidiary of Campbell, Vlasic Foods, Inc. now had the manufacturing, distribution, and financial backing it needed to keep growing. Campbell had gained the leading pickle producer, a strategic move in its bitter war with Heinz, the number two pickle company.

Two years later, R. Gordon McGovern succeeded Shaub as president of Campbell, and that company acquired Swift-Armour S.A. Argentina, a major beef processor. In 1982, Vlasic bought Win Schuler Foods, a specialty-foods producer, and Campbell reintroduced its Swanson frozen breakfasts using the name "Great Starts."

In 1985 Vlasic made its jars more consumer-friendly, fashioning the jars themselves shorter and easier to store, increasing the size of the jar opening, and adding a "made" date on the lid to emphasize freshness. Even more importantly for its marketing, the company introduced color coded labels on its jars. Surveys, interviews, and taste tests had found that shoppers were confused with all the varieties on the shelf and reluctant to try a new brand when there was no information on the labels about the taste. Under Vlasic's new system dills got green labels, sweets had yellow, and bread and butter pickles were wrapped in orange. And the colors were not the only difference. A flavoring scale at the bottom of each label rated the type of pickle inside from 1 (lightly seasoned) to 4 (highly seasoned).

The cosmetic efforts with its jars may have been a factor in Vlasic's ability to increase its unit sales by two percent that year in what was a flat pickle market. Vlasic was far and away the top pickle company, having increased its share to one-third of the $580-million-a-year pickle market. But that market was not growing.

In an effort to boost revenues, Vlasic and Campbell decided the subsidiary should expand into other specialty food areas. Vlasic's first move, in late 1986, was into olives, with the test marketing of an extensive line, including Spanish and California Ripe olives, under the Vlasic name. Campbell then paid $7.1 million for Bonduel Pickling Co. Inc., a 33-year-old Wisconsin marketer of the "Milwaukee's" brand of pickles. Bonduel had been acquired by Milwaukee Cheese Co. Inc. in 1977 as a wholly owned subsidiary, and was sold when Milwaukee Cheese went into bankruptcy.

Vlasic continued its expansion in 1987, with the purchase of Open Pit barbecue sauce from General Foods Corp. Open Pit, which General Foods introduced in 1960, was a leading brand in the Midwest, but had only about 10 percent of the national market. The purchase pitted Vlasic against Kraft Foods, Inc., which controlled about 51 percent of the $325 million barbecue sauce market.

The following year, Campbell bought some of the assets of San Francisco-based Specialty Brands Inc., including an olive processing plant in Spain and the Early California line of olives. The Early California brand, which was to be marketed by Vlasic, accounted for about 27 percent of the ripe olive market in the United States. The purchase made Campbell and Vlasic number one in ripe olives and in the total U.S. olive market. In 1988, Campbell also acquired Freshbake Foods Group PLC, a British producer of frozen foods.

Meanwhile, Swanson made changes to its frozen dinners in 1986, removing the brownie from the dessert options and replacing the aluminum dinner tray with a microwavable plastic version. The original tray was placed in the Smithsonian Museum of American History. The public raised such an uproar about the missing brownie that the company brought it back the next year. In 1988, Robert J. Vlasic became chairman of Campbell, and in 1989, Swanson introduced the microwavable pot pie with two crusts.

Operating in Mature Markets: 1990–97

At the beginning of the decade, David J. Johnson, from Australia, became president and CEO of Campbell. In 1991, as its sales topped the $6 billion mark, Campbell consolidated key components of Vlasic into its Camden, New Jersey headquarters, eliminating about 140 positions at Vlasic, and relocated Vlasic's marketing and administrative divisions from Michigan to Camden. Two years later, in 1993, Bob Vlasic retired from Campbell. That same year Campbell completed a new $120 million Swift-Armour beef processing plant in Argentina and dedicated a multimillion-dollar expansion of its Omaha, Nebraska frozen food operation.

In an effort to increase the market for pickles, Vlasic introduced two new concepts. To entice more people to eat pickles at non-traditional times, Vlasic came up with the idea of ''Pickles To Go!'' in 1993. Two pickle spears were packaged in a foil laminate pouch for on-the-go eating, without the drips and mess associated with eating pickles.

In 1994, Vlasic introduced Sandwich Stackers. By cutting the pickle lengthwise in broad, flat slices instead of the traditional wedges, Vlasic was going after the huge market of pickle-free sandwiches. About two-thirds of the pickles sold in a year went on sandwiches, but only about four percent of the 35 billion sandwiches eaten in the United States each year came with a pickle. Even without heavy advertising, the new offering increased Vlasic's pickle sales by about seven percent a year and captured 65 percent of the $50 million in new pickle sales in the United States during 1994.

But these and other efforts such as Swanson's Fun Feast kids' meals introduced in 1992, were being made in mature markets with low potential for growth. Swanson faced competition not only from other manufacturers of frozen meals, but from prepared meals available in grocery stores and fast-food restaurants. Making matters more difficult, Campbell practically ignored Vlasic and Swanson during the 1990s, spending little on product development and advertising. Instead, the

company acquired bakery, soup, and sauce operations, began selling soups in China and South America, introduced a new soup label design and glass jars, and launched a new soup advertising campaign, the largest in the company's history. Between 1991 and 1995, Campbell increased sales by one billion dollars, from $6 billion to $7 billion.

By 1997, Campbell was looking for a buyer for Swanson, but was not able to agree on a price with the various candidates. In September, Campbell announced it would create a spinoff company of its ''nonstrategic'' businesses in order to concentrate on its core businesses: soups, sauces, baked goods, and chocolates.

The new company consisted of seven low-growth businesses with combined sales of $1.5 billion, about 18 percent of Campbell's total 1997 sales. Campbell allocated $500 million in debt to the new company, temporarily named Specialty Foods, and received a cash payment of $500 million. After initial positive responses from investors, the *New York Times* raised a basic question: ''Is the spinoff a canny move of tax avoidance that will greatly benefit both Campbell and its new corporate offspring, or is it simply a strategy for dumping Campbell castoffs into a new company that will excite little interest on Wall Street?'' Vlasic Foods International was incorporated in November 1997.

A New Company with a Famous Name: 1998 to the Present

Vlasic Foods International, Inc. became an independent company on March 30, 1998. Campbell shareholders received one share of the new company for every ten Campbell shares they held. Heading Vlasic was Robert F. Bernstock, the Campbell executive responsible for its U.S. grocery business.

Vlasic Foods operated in three segments. Its frozen foods segment accounted for 40 percent of sales in fiscal 1997 and included Swanson and Freshbake, a leading U.K. brand of steak and kidney pies and other frozen meat pies, sausages, pastries, and pies. In addition to pickles and condiments marketed under the Vlasic and Milwaukee brands, the grocery products segment, representing 36 percent of sales, consisted of Open Pit barbecue sauce; SonA and Rowats pickles, canned beans and vegetables in the United Kingdom; Swift canned meat pâtés, cold cuts, hot dogs, and other grocery products in Argentina; and Kattus, a specialty foods distributor in Germany. Finally, in the agricultural products category, with about 24 percent of sales, Vlasic Foods owned and operated eight mushroom farms in the United States, making it the largest producer of fresh mushrooms in the country. The company was also one of Argentina's leading beef processors through its Swift-Armour operations, selling to more than 60 countries. Campbell was a major customer of Vlasic Foods' mushrooms and beef.

In May 1998, Vlasic moved to its new headquarters in Cherry Hill, New Jersey. Earnings were lower than expected, with consumption of Vlasic pickles down seven percent and that of the Swanson line off about six percent. Sales for both brands were down about ten percent. Berstock announced that Vlasic would double advertising spending on the two brands to $10 million, introduce a new dill pickle product in October, and begin distributing its products through Wal-Mart Stores' Sam's Club outlets. He predicted that sales and earnings would improve in fiscal 1999.

Analysts questioned whether Bernstock would be able to deliver, believing that the company needed a complete makeover, according to the Bergen County *Record*. But having turned V8 vegetable juices, a declining brand, into one of Campbell's fastest-growing items, the Vlasic Foods president and CEO hoped he could do the same for pickles and frozen meals by investing in marketing and product development and by cutting costs.

Principal Subsidiaries

Kattus (Germany).

Further Reading

Bloomberg News, "Vlasic Pins Hopes on Pickles, TV Dinners," *Record* (Bergen County, N.J.), March 29, 1998, p. B1.

"Campbell's History," http://www.campbellsoup.com/center/history.

"Campbell Soup Acquires," *Business Week*, June 12, 1978, p. 70.

"Campbell Soup: Widening Its Menu and Looking Beyond Food," *Business Week*, August 11, 1980, p. 85.

"Campbell to Cut Vlasic Payroll," *Nation's Restaurant News*, October 28, 1991, p. 42.

Collins, Glenn, "Marketplace: Seeking Status As Blue Chip, Campbell Sets 7-Unit Spinoff," September 10, 1997, p. D1.

Egan, Cathleen, "Pickle Maker Seeking Turnaround," *Record* (Bergen County, N.J.), June 2, 1998, p. B1.

Fernandez, Bob, "At Vlasic, a Jarring Task Begins," *Philadelphia Inquirer*, April 12, 1998, http://www.phillynews.com/inquirer/98/Apr/12/business/VLAS12.htm.

Jaffe, Thomas, "Who's Got Heinz in a Pickle?" *Forbes*, August 15, 1977, p. 63.

Lazarus, George, "Campbell's Adds to Its Olive Groves," *Chicago Tribune*, January 13, 1988, p. 4 (Business).

——, "Olé! Olé! at Vlasic," *Adweek*, June 23, 1986.

——, "Vlasic Dips Deeper into Condiments," *Chicago Tribune*, August 10, 1987, p. 4 (Business).

Sheridan, Margaret, "Want to Pick a Pack of Pickles? No Need to Puzzle," *Chicago Tribune*, November 14, 1985, p. 10.

Taylor, John, "Campbell's Plant Is Now Vlasic's," *Omaha World-Herald*, March 31, 1998, p. 14sf.

Thayer, Warren, "Most Expect Brighter Future for Swanson Under Vlasic," *Frozen Food Age*, March 1998, p. 1.

"Vlasic Foods International," Camden, N.J.: Campbell Soup Company, March 5, 1998.

"Vlasic Foods to Acquire Bonduel Pickling Co.," *PR Newswire*, June 30, 1986.

"Vlasic Honors Kuralt with Portable Pickles As He Starts Out 'On the Road,' " Cherry Hill, N.J., Vlasic Foods International Inc., April 7, 1994.

"Vlasic Pledges Gain in FY'99 Consumption," Cherry Hill, N.J.: Vlasic Foods International Inc., May 27, 1998.

Waldsmith, Lynn, "Vlasic Makes a New Start on Exchange," *Detroit News*, April 1, 1998, p. B1.

"Whose Pickles on Your Table?" *Economist*, June 10, 1978, p. 57.

—Ellen D. Wernick

Wacoal Corp.

**29 Nakajima-Cho
Kishoin, Minami-Ku, Kyoto 601
Japan
81-7-5682-5111
Fax: 81-7-5682-1183**

Public Company
Incorporated: 1949 as Wako Shoji Co. Ltd.
Employees: 20,000
Sales: US$992.6 million (fiscal 1998)
Stock Exchanges: NASDAQ
Ticker Symbol: WACLY
SICs: 2330 Women's & Misses' Outerwear; 2341
    Underwear & Nightwear—Female; 2342 Brassieres
    Girdles & Allied Garments

Wacoal Corp. was the first and is the leading lingerie maker in Japan. The multinational public company is headquartered in Kyoto, Japan, and manufactures and sells women's intimate apparel and outerwear (such as slips, bra-slips, and briefs) and children's nightwear, sportswear, underwear, outerwear, and other products under a variety of brand names, including the top-priced ''Wacoal'' line of innerwear, the licensed ''Donna Karan Intimates'' line of innerwear, and mid-price label ''Parfage.''

From Jewelry to Innerwear, 1945–49

Following World War II, Koichi Tsukamoto returned home to Japan, got married, and went into business selling crystal necklaces. He opened a tiny shop in Kyoto, took out a buyer's ad in a trade magazine called *Shiire-Annai*, and received a response from Yoshinao Yoda, who had a factory in another part of Japan and who, after manufacturing parts for the Nakajima Airplane Plant during the war, had returned to making crystal products. Tsukamoto sent Yoda ¥3,000, his entire savings, and received ¥3,600 worth of products in return. Eventually, Tsukamoto's sales grew to ¥10,000 per month and then to ¥100,000 per month, and the two men developed a friendship beyond the business, which culminated with Yoda teaching Tsukamoto how to succeed in business.

In October 1947, Tsukamoto discovered jewelry by Hirano-Shoukai which was much more beautiful and of better workmanship than what he was currently selling. Approaching the dealer, Mr. Hirano, he was turned away many times. But, through persistence and the clever use of a disguise, he managed to secure an audience with Hirano. Impressed by Tsukamoto's tenacity, Hirano gave the budding entrepreneur a chance, providing him with nearly ¥100,000 worth of product to sell. By April of the following year, Tsukamoto's monthly turnover was at ¥500,000.

In June 1948, as sales of crystal necklaces were petering out, Tsukamoto looked around, found hair clips were coming into style in Japan, and decided to start manufacturing them in Kyoto. At the same time, he met Takeo Yasuda, who worked in the outerwear division of a department store before World War II. Yasuda produced what Tsukamoto would describe later as ''a curious thing which looked like a small cake made of cloth. On the top of a spiral spring made of aluminum was some cotton stuffing and the whole was covered with cloth. When it was put on a woman's bust, it made it look glamorous.'' Yasuda called it a ''brapad,'' and said that it would sweep through Japan. Tsukamoto, knowing that men already used pads to enhance their shoulders, agreed. Prior to World War II, Japanese women wore ''juban'' or ''kosbimaki,'' or wrap-around undergarments of cotton, wool, or silk.

Traveling to the famous Ginza shopping center in Tokyo, Tsukamoto sold out his first batch of brapads, then selling for ¥100 each, and discovered a rival company, Aoyama Shouten. Having seen brassieres in a U.S. magazine by this time, Tsukamoto rushed home and decided to try putting the pad in a cloth bag that would be held against the breast with straps. Since no one else was making bras in Japan at the time, he tried to devise a paper pattern in the shape of a bowl by fitting it to the bust of his wife. He eventually bought cloth and found a sewing subcontractor, but met with much failure early on. Eventually, he fashioned a workable prototype. Naming his first original product ''No. 101,'' Tsukamoto's product began selling well.

Company Perspectives:

Wacoal Corp. is dedicated to being the world leader in the women's apparel industry.

How the West Was Worn: Founding, 1949

Tsukamoto then began the difficult task of bringing people into his fledgling company. Finally, he found Ikuo Kawaguchi and Iichi Nakamura, both graduates of The Hachiman School of Commerce. Kawaguchi left a steady job working in Mitsubishi Heavy Industry's Kyoto Apparatus Factory. Nakamura, who had moved from Hachiman to Yokohama Commercial School and Tokyo Commercial College (now Hitotsubashi University) to study management and accounting, left his teaching job at Hachiman in March 1949 to join the company as well. Tsukamoto took the name of his father Kumejiro's former company, Wako Shoji.

On October 9 of that year, Wako Shoji exhibited brapads and brassieres at a department store exhibition, which went well. But the same day, Kumejiro, who had taken ill while working for the company and died, was buried. In honor of his father, Tsukamoto incorporated the company on November 1, as Wako Shoji Co. Ltd. and one of his early customers, Hanzawa Shouten, ordered 50 dozen brapads.

But the new company floundered in the seasonal clothing market, which slumped traditionally in the fourth quarter of the year, and Tsukamoto's friends ridiculed his choice of business. However, Yasuda, the brapad designer, provided fabrics and Tsukamoto, driven by a desire to not lay off any of the employees he had attracted, formulated an ambitious series of five 10-year plans toward becoming a global leader in the industry.

The First and Second Ten-Year Plans, 1950–70

During the first ten years, Tsukamoto wanted to concentrate on the domestic market. Sales did begin to grow as Japanese women became more and more conscious of changing fashions and looked to the West for new ideas. Hanzawa ordered a hundred dozen in February 1950, but Tsukamoto, seeing in their warehouse piles of lingerie he had never encountered before, asked to be paid in trade for the new items. He took them back to Kyoto and began selling the items there, while Hanzawa sold the brapads in Tokyo. Also that year, Tsukamoto met Kohiro Kihara, a sewing manufacturer who was looking for civilian contracts. Kihara put up ¥50,000 and began manufacturing brassieres and packaging them with care, infusing Wako Shoji with pride in production that led it to worldwide success.

In June 1950, Tsukamoto met with Takashimaya Department Store's fashion department chief and asked him to take them on as a client. The chief refused, Tsukamoto took it to the chief's boss, and got a one-week trial period in the Kyoto store. Set in an out-of-the-way corner of the building, Tsukamoto packaged goods and ran the cash register while saleswoman Miyo Uchida sold the products. In one week, the company sold five times more lingerie than Takashimaya's larger store in Aoyama had done. Asking to have product included in the Osaka store, Tsukamoto again was turned down. Again, he found a new ear, this time the Osaka store manager, who looked at the products Wako Shoji offered and bought enough to fill three of the four display cases in the Osaka store.

In May 1951, Tsukamoto approached Kihara about merging the two companies. Kihara refused, but Tsukamoto offered him the presidency. Kihara capitulated and Tsukamoto demoted himself to senior managing director. Wako Shoji bought Kihara's factory from the owner, with ¥150,000 of Tsukamoto's money, a ¥1.5 million loan from a bank, using the building title as security, paid ¥1.25 million up front, leveraged the rest on debt, and bought electric sewing machines with the remaining ¥250,000.

By the fall of 1952, Wako Shoji was in most major Japanese department stores except Hankyu, who unexpectedly asked Tsukamoto if they would hold a fashion show. Ensconced in a very traditional society, the company could not find any professional models who were willing to wear such skimpy clothing, especially on the runway, so Tsukamoto was forced to hire strippers in order to hold the company's first fashion show. The second ten years, from 1960 to 1970, the plan was to steadily expand the domestic market in Japan, which the company did very successfully.

The Third and Fourth Ten-Year Plans, 1970–90

The third and fourth ten-year plans were to gradually move into overseas markets. The Thai Wacoal Public Company Ltd. was established in 1970, and entry into Korea, Hong Kong, and Singapore followed, as the company, now called ''Wacoal Ltd.,'' introduced the innovative clothing items for the first time to those countries as well, expanding throughout the Far East during the 1970s.

Tsukamoto set his sights on the United States in the late 1970s, convinced that U.S. women were looking for higher quality and better service than the cluttered department store lingerie counters offered. When the Japanese innerwear giant entered the U.S. market in 1983, it was aiming at the upper end of the market, providing products at a premium price, and marketing them through boutiques in ''classy'' department stores such as Bloomingdale's, Saks Fifth Avenue, and I. Magnin.

Then competition abounded as companies including Victoria's Secret and Frederick's of Hollywood began springing up, eventually becoming huge household names in the lingerie industry. Faced with such competitors, and following the lead of the cosmetics industry, Tsukamoto and the company refused to mark down prices or have ''fire'' sales.

In 1984, the company created Wacoal America Inc., a U.S. subsidiary located in Carlstadt, New Jersey; and Sri Racha Wacoal Co. Ltd. in Thailand, which would run as separate entities from the parent company.

In October 1986, the company released a ''high-tech'' brassiere that ''remembered'' its original shape while tumbling in the clothes dryer. A byproduct of a special metal alloy with so-called ''shape memory'' which was developed in the late

1950s-early 1960s by the U.S. military, the company began marketing the ''Memory Wire Bra'' in the United States. The bras, which retailed for around US$30, avoided a difficulty common to many regular wire bras, which often can become twisted and more rigid after each washing. Total revenue for 1986 reached US$750 million.

The Fifth Ten-Year Plan, 1990–2000

As the company entered the 1990s, it had 14 principal subsidiaries and six joint ventures in Korea, Hong Kong, Taiwan, Thailand, China, and The Philippines and was distributing 64 lingerie brands worldwide. The venture in The Philippines, known as Wacoal Philippines Corp., was created in the spring of 1991 specifically to strengthen the business in Southeast Asia.

In 1990, clothes designer Carlos Falchi, who made his name as a handbag and belt designer, entered the lingerie market in Japan, as his Carlos Falchi Enterprises (who also signed licenses with Pancaldi for shoes, Grandoe for gloves, and Ashear Bros. for scarves) signed a license with Wacoal Corp. Falchi's first entry into designing intimate apparel came in 1972, when he designed a group of kimonos for Henri Bendel.

In-store Falchi innerwear boutiques were opened that year at Seibu, Isetan, Takashimaya, Daimaru, and Mitsukoshi department stores. The first (fall) line for the Japanese market featured seven groups broken into four categories (sleepwear, loungewear, daywear, and bras and panties), as well as slippers and lingerie bags. Two cohesive themes worked throughout the collection—snake-patterned nylon and Lycra spandex lace, and ''croco-patterned'' silks and polyesters, designed to complement Falchi's signature ''whip stitch'' used on the lingerie bags. Colors ranged from jewel brights to black, spice tones, and gold lamé, with prints including foulards, geometrics, tapestry, and Falchi's signature patchworks of solid and printed textures. In addition to Falchi, Wacoal Corp. introduced a second licensed product line in Japan, with Karl Lagerfeld lingerie, launched during the fall season.

About this time, the company was turning its attention toward the markets of Europe, West Asia, and Canada. The first Wacoal Europe S.A. offices were opened in Paris (selected as the European headquarters due to its consideration as a fashion capital and with plans to expand throughout the European Community and into Eastern Europe) in April, with intimate apparel as the primary focus for European sales, although the Kyoto-based parent firm also marketed the textiles and other apparel it manufactured. The European arm was also designed to operate as a separate entity, as its U.S. counterpart did.

In June 1991, the intimate apparel manufacturer reported that profits for the fiscal year ended March 31 declined some 10 percent when earnings were expressed in yen. However, when profits for the year were expressed in dollars, the total net income came to approximately US$54.5 million, some 21 percent more than the previous year. The Kyoto-based company blamed the earnings decline on increased sales and new business development costs, including installation of point-of-sale computer systems. The company also reported that sales in the United States were flat as a result of the recession going on at

the time, but the Southeast Asian market continued to grow in spite of the ongoing Gulf War. Total sales for the company for the year reached US$1 billion.

The Wacoal America branch launched the ''Parfage'' line of products, featuring five bras and three panties, at the fall market in May, with wholesale prices debuting at US$6.72 for bikinis and US$12.48 for bras, and wholesale prices for the ''Wacoal'' brand beginning at US$15.36 for bras and US$6.96 for panties.

In July of that year, the company introduced a computer software system with which retail shoppers could select garments. Following four years of testing and nearly US$3 million in research and development costs, the company created a computer graphic system which enabled women to see how to hide or highlight their curves by using the right undergarment. The process involved the customer stripping down to their underwear and standing in front of a video camera which displayed their outline on a computer screen, allowing the customer to see how her shape compared with one that store consultants considered ideal for her age, weight, and condition. The customer then tried on the lingerie which improved her figure and could see the new outline on the screen. The company reported that nearly 60 percent of women wore underwear which was the wrong size for their body types, but after the so-called ''proportion clinic,'' Wacoal Corp. reported an approximately 10 percent increase in lingerie sales at the 12 stores utilizing the system, including Tokyo Department Store.

Nonetheless, despite continued growth, by November 1991 the company was losing the market lead to its competitors. As sales on luxury goods slumped in late 1991-early 1992, the company reported, for the fiscal year ending March 31, 1992, profits slipping to US$51.1 million on total sales of US$1.2 billion.

As the Japanese economy weakened during the 1992–93 fiscal year, consumer spending declined, and, in women's fashion apparel, consumer orientation shifted from high-quality, high-priced items to reasonably priced value items; the year ending March 31, 1993 yielded earnings of US$57.5 million on sales of US$1.3 billion for the company, making Wacoal Corp. the world's largest manufacturer of intimate apparel. The company was also able to expand in most innerwear markets. That year also saw the company's U.S. subsidiary successfully manufacture and launch the licensed ''Donna Karan Intimates'' collection of innerwear in the United States, with distribution of the collection focusing mainly on high-end specialty stores such as Neiman Marcus, Nordstrom, and Saks Fifth Avenue, and department store flagships like Macy's Herald Square.

By 1994, the latest trend in women's underclothing was smooth underwear which could not be detected beneath tight-fitting clothes. That year, the Japanese underwear manufacturing giant unexpectedly found a hit item on its hands with its ''Body Balance Wear,'' a pair of upholstered underpants that fulfilled a function similar to a woman's girdle. The company also sold a product called ''Good Up,'' a seamless girdle. For the fiscal year ending in March 1994, Wacoal Corp. reported net earnings of US$71.8 million, with total sales of US$1.5 billion.

Helped by the U.S. economic recovery, which bolstered sales of women's innerwear under the ''Wacoal'' and licensed

"Donna Karan" labels, and French sales surging 60 to 70 percent, Wacoal Corp. reported pretax profit for the fiscal year ended March 31, 1995 at US$151 million, as sales rose to US$1.8 billion. That year also marked the first profitable year for the U.S. subsidiary Wacoal America.

By late 1995, the women's fashion merchandise industry was facing difficult times as personal consumption levels slowed down and consumers shifted toward lower-priced goods. But many high quality and high value-added products, such as various brands of women's stockings and panties, performed well and sales grew twice as fast as the previous year for the company. For the fiscal year ended March 31, 1996, the company had pretax profits of US$111.3 million on sales of US$1.24 billion.

Operating in a weak Japanese economy in 1996–97 in which levels of consumer spending were stagnant, the company continued to develop new products in the Japanese market, with its "Make-Up" bra and "Mune-Tsun" bra lines continuing to perform well; the company's new "Slender Bra," "Hip Star" panties, and "Q-T-Up" panties lines were quite successful. Sales in the United States on both the "Wacoal" and the "Donna Karan Intimates" brands grew steadily, and the company continued to have strong growth in other Asian countries, particularly China.

For the year ending March 1997, Wacoal reported net profits of US$52.3 million on sales of US$1.36 billion, some of which was broken into segments as follows: sales of foundations and lingerie at US$903.2 million and nightwear at US$103.4 million.

In May of that year, the company increased its investment in a joint venture in China to strengthen manufacturing and sales there, starting a manufacturing operation in Guandong, China.

In January 1998, the company established a manufacturing subsidiary in Vietnam for use as a production base and began marketing "Wacoal Petites" for small-breasted women (sizes ranging from 30–36, with AA, A, and B cups), retailing for US$30–US$40. For the year ending March 31, 1998, net profits rose to US$60 million, while sales only reached US$992.6 million.

Also early in 1998, in a move to enter an industry already entrenched in a battle between two world-class heavyweights (Warnaco Group's "Calvin Klein Underwear" and Sara Lee Corporation's "Ralph Lauren Intimates"), Donna Karan International signed a second licensing deal with Wacoal Corp., this one for a line of women's intimate apparel and men's underwear, launching the "DKNY" designer label into the competitive innerwear market. The agreement, which called for Wacoal Corp. to manufacture the line and Donna Karan to merchandise the "DKNY" innerwear line at upscale department stores such as Neiman Marcus, Nordstrom, and Saks Fifth Avenue; as well as Macy's; Dillard's; Jacobson Stores' 24 units in the Midwest and Florida; and Jenns, a four-unit specialty chain in Amherst, New York; was merely the latest move in the Karan company's ambitious licensing strategy, following deals with Liz Claiborne Inc. for jeans and activewear and The Estée Lauder Companies for beauty and fragrance products. Donna Karan planned to showcase a full range of women's underwear, sleep-

wear, and at-home wear in 600 to 800 DKNY innerwear in-store shops in the spring of 1999, with distribution initially aimed at stores already selling DKNY apparel in the United States, Canada, and Europe, before moving into about 100 locations in Japan and elsewhere in Asia.

Warnaco's "Calvin Klein" line of men's underwear and women's innerwear debuted in 1995 and, by 1998, was being distributed in some 1,500 specially created in-store shops, bringing in combined yearly wholesale sales figures exceeding US$310 million in 1997. Sara Lee Intimates' licensed "Ralph Lauren Intimates" debuted on the retail market in June 1997 in approximately 1,300 in-store shops, with another 100 opening up by June 1998, bringing in an estimated several hundred million dollars more by the year 2000. The "DKNY" line would also compete against other high-end lingerie labels such as "Chantelle," "Hanro," and "La Perla." To contend with "Calvin Klein" and "Ralph Lauren" innerwear, the "DKNY" bras would be listed at a suggested US$25–US$38 retail, compared to the "Donna Karan Intimate" bras, which listed at between US$40–US$60.

In mid-1998, Wacoal partnered with Damart, the world leader in thermal underwear, who had been selling in Japan since 1979. The alliance created a line of feminine lingerie called "Chaleur et Glamour" for marketing in Japan. As the Japanese lingerie giant moved into the 21st century, an interesting battle between Wacoal and its competitors could be expected to unfold.

Principal Subsidiaries

Wacoal International Corp.; Thai Wacoal Public Company Ltd. (Thailand); Wacoal America Inc. (U.S.A.); Wacoal Europe S.A. (Paris); Wacoal Philippines Corp.

Further Reading

Cohen, Joyce, "Priming for Petites," *WWD*, July 28, 1997, p. S2.
"DKNY Signs Underwear License," *Daily News Record*, February 13, 1998, p. 4.
Do Rosario, Louise, "Frills and Spills," *Far Eastern Economic Review*, November 14, 1991, p. 69.
Hirano, Koji, "Karan Line Spurs Wacoal," *WWD*, June 8, 1998, p. 22.
——, "Wacoal Earnings up 1.5% for Year," *WWD*, May 27, 1997, p. 18.
"Karan Said Nearing Deal for Intimate Apparel Line," *WWD*, February 11, 1998, p. 20.
Katayama, Hiroko, "Western Wear," *Forbes*, November 16, 1987, p. 305.
"Memories Are Made of This," *Time*, October 6, 1986, p. 63.
Monget, Karyn, "Carlos Falchi: Eyeing Lingerie Fame," *WWD*, January 24, 1991, p. 6.
——, "DKNY Aims to Be Key Player," *WWD*, February 23, 1998, p. 13.
——, "Karan Confirms Wacoal Deal," *WWD*, February 13, 1998, p. 2.
——, "Wacoal's World: The Japanese Giant Broadens Its International Appeal with Fashion and Fit," *WWD*, January 3, 1991, p. I12.
"Murray Named Wacoal President in U.S.," *WWD*, May 6, 1993, p. 9.
Nanami, Akito, "Underwear Maker Firms up U.S. Base," *Nikkei Weekly* (Japan), April 17, 1995, p. 10.
——, "Unlimited Market for Unseen Underwear," *Nikkei Weekly* (Japan), July 18, 1994, p. 15.

524   **Wacoal Corp.**

Okabe, ''Wacoal—Company Report,'' Okasan Economic Research Institute Co., Ltd., June 18, 1997.

Sakamaki, Sachiko, ''Tight Fit,'' *Far Eastern Economic Review,* April 4, 1996, p. 64.

Taylor, Craig, and Fredric Frank, ''Assessment Centers in Japan,'' *Training & Development Journal,* February 1988, p. 54.

Terazono, Emiko, ''Japanese Underwear Group Advances 5%,'' *Financial Times,* November 25, 1993, p. 28.

Thornton, Emily, ''Software for Fitting Lingerie,'' *Fortune,* July 29, 1991, p. 18.

''Wacoal Corp.,'' *Wall Street Journal,* June 11, 1998, p. A10.

''Wacoal Earnings Increase 2.9% in Year; Sales Up 0.1%,'' *WWD,* June 25, 1993, p. 15.

''Wacoal Licensed to Create Underwear and Sleepwear,'' *Wall Street Journal,* February 13, 1998, p. B4.

''Wacoal Net Declines 0.7% in 12 Months,'' *WWD,* June 25, 1992, p. 7.

''Wacoal Net Declines 22.4% for Year,'' *WWD,* June 30, 1997, p. 8.

''Wacoal Net Off 10.8% in Year,'' *WWD,* June 24, 1991, p. 6.

''Wacoal Notes '95 Pretax Net Climbed 9.6%,'' *WWD,* May 20, 1996, p. 13.

''Wacoal Posts 8.5% Growth in Yearly Net,'' *WWD,* June 30, 1994, p. 6.

''Wacoal Pretax Profit Up 4.1%,'' *WWD,* June 12, 1995, p. 8.

''Wacoal Profits Up,'' *WWD,* November 20, 1995, p. 6.

''Wacoal Weighs In,'' *WWD,* December 27, 1994, p. 11.

—Daryl F. Mallett

WellPoint Health Networks Inc.

21555 Oxnard Street
Woodland Hills, California 91367
U.S.A.
(818) 703-4000
Web site: http://www.wellpoint.com

Public Company
Incorporated: 1992
Employees: 10,100
Sales: $227.4 million (1996)
Stock Exchanges: New York
Ticker Symbol: WLP
SICs: 6324 Hospital & Medical Service Plans; 6719
    Holding Companies, Not Elsewhere Classified

WellPoint Health Networks Inc. ranks among the largest publicly traded healthcare insurers in the United States. Its approximately 6.6 million members nationwide are served by two subsidiaries: Blue Cross of California and UNICARE. WellPoint offers a comprehensive selection of healthcare products, including health maintenance organizations (HMOs), preferred provider organizations (PPOs), point-of-service plans (POS), self-insured employer sponsored programs, and specialty plans for dental, optical, pharmacy, and mental health coverage. WellPoint's principal products in California are the CaliforniaCare HMO and the Prudent Buyer Plan PPO. The latter is the state's largest PPO with approximately 2.8 million members served by a network of some 42,000 physicians and 443 hospitals. On the national level, WellPoint's most important plans are the UNICARE Classic POS modeled on the Prudent Buyer Plan and the UNICARE Health Plans HMO which as of March 1998 was still in the early start-up stage.

Beginnings in 1986

WellPoint Health Networks Inc. was organized in 1986 as the division responsible for the managed healthcare operations of Blue Cross of California (BCC). BCC was founded in 1937 as a nonprofit corporation whose purpose was to provide resi-dents of California with quality, affordable medical coverage. For nearly 50 years it was successful in this mission. In the mid-1980s, however, after a tumultuous period when the cost of medical care increased rapidly, the group found itself in precarious financial straits. As company CEO Leonard Schaeffer described the situation in *Health Affairs,* "BCC's very existence was threatened." Blue Cross ran a $55 million deficit in 1986. The sale of its Woodland Hills, California headquarters building provided temporary help, balancing out BCC's 1987 stock market and underwriting losses. In April 1988 Schaeffer announced the worst was past. The following August, however, the group reported second quarter losses of $20.5 million and was only able to stave off insolvency at the end of the year when it found a buyer for its TakeCare HMO and was able to book it at an increased value in company books.

Restructuring of Blue Cross of California

In early 1989 BCC completed an initial restructuring implemented by Schaeffer. Within a few months, the group's staff had been cut from 6,500 to 3,825 and BCC could report a fourth quarter profit of $41.9 million. A new California law enacted in the fall of 1990 enabled BCC to be licensed as a healthcare services plan. By 1991 BCC could report a dramatic turnaround. Under Schaeffer's leadership, Blue Cross had earned $159.7 million in profits. It boasted the largest growth in enrollment and earnings of any healthcare plan in California, and of any Blue Cross or Blue Shield plan in the entire country. Nonetheless, as Schaeffer wrote in 1996, "BCC faced significant challenges: uncertainty over future government policy and regulations, limited access to capital markets, and increasing competition in a rapidly growing marketplace. BCC thus began to look for a way to compete on the same regulatory and marketing playing field with its competitors."

Official Incorporation: 1992

Against this background WellPoint was incorporated in 1992. BCC's most profitable operations were concentrated in the new company—the health maintenance organization, the preferred provider organization, and the various specialty plans. Blue Cross of California retained the traditional health insurance plans. In August 1992, BCC management presented a restructuring plan to the California Department of Corporations (DOC). It would create a wholly owned, for-profit subsidiary, WellPoint Health Networks, whose stock would be sold in a public offering. The plan was designed to further improve Blue Cross's financial position by giving it access to the country's capital markets.

Under the plan, Blue Cross of California would retain 80 percent of WellPoint and the BCC board would hold 97.5 percent of the voting shares in the new company. BCC would also restructure but would not convert to for-profit status. An important consideration in that decision was a Blue Cross and Blue Shield Association rule which prevented a for-profit entity from being the primary licensee of the Blue Cross name and trademark.

In January 1993 the California Department of Corporations approved BCC's proposal. The first public offering of WellPoint stock took place in late January 1993. At first BCC planned to sell 15 million shares at a cost of $22 to $24 a share. "Brisk investor demand," reported by the *Wall Street Journal*, led to the sale of some 18 million shares at $28 a share. The strong showing could be traced to WellPoint's large membership base—423,000 HMO members, 1.5 million PPO members—and its healthy 1992 earnings of $142.8 million, an exceptionally good year for a Blue Cross division. WellPoint's performance on the market, the *Journal* said, "underscores growing investor enthusiasm for managed-care companies." Also contributing to investor interest were WellPoint's high-profit services which indicated the company would probably experience quick growth.

WellPoint Public Offering Mires Nonprofit Blue Cross in Controversy

The deal created one of the largest public managed healthcare companies in the United States and brought $517 million to Blue Cross of California. Afterwards, though, the restructuring proved to be extremely controversial. Under California law, when a nonprofit converted to for-profit status it was required to compensate the public for the years it was allowed to operate on a tax-free basis. That normally entailed contributing the full value of the assets of the converted organization to a charitable foundation. In this case, however the nonprofit BCC had not *itself* converted to for-profit status, its subsidiary had, though, and BCC controlled it completely.

There was no provision in California law requiring a contribution in such a case. The Department of Corporation's initial ruling absolved BCC from making any compensation. The decision drew criticism from the California Office of Consumers Union and the California Medical Association. In transferring most of its assets to WellPoint while remaining nonprofit, critics maintained Blue Cross had taken advantage of a loophole in the law and that Blue Cross executives, who also sat on the board of WellPoint, stood to profit personally from the change through stock option plans and the like.

In April members of the California legislature became involved in the dispute. Accusing Blue Cross of ducking its public responsibility, a bill was introduced that would penalize Blue Cross retroactively for hundreds of millions of dollars. Estimates of a fair settlement ranged from $500 million proposed by the California Medical Association to "a reasonable percentage of $2.6 billion" proposed by Gene Erbin, counsel for the Legislature's Judiciary Committee, according to the *San Francisco Chronicle*. Erbin claimed $2.6 billion was the value the stock market had placed on WellPoint. Blue Cross offered $5 million a year for 20 years. Although Blue Cross and legislators negotiated for weeks, the talks did not hurt WellPoint's standing with investors. Even after it was reported that California might demand $10–$20 million over 20 years, WellPoint stock closed up 50 cents. In the summer of 1993 an agreement was reached: BCC would pay a $100 million lump sum to charity as well as increasing its annual charitable contributions by $5 million. Once the issue had been settled, the bill that would have required retroactive payment was allowed to die.

In August 1993, however, Gary S. Mendoza was appointed to head the DOC. In December 1993 the new, more aggressive commissioner informed Blue Cross that he did not consider the agreement with the legislature to be sufficient. According to Leonard Schaeffer, Mendoza did not indicate to Blue Cross what he considered sufficient compensation.

Mendoza told BCC he believed their public benefit activity in 1993 had been minimal. Alfred G. Hagerty reported in *National Underwriter Life & Health* that after months of talks Mendoza finally told Blue Cross that its plan to spend $25 to $35 million in 1994 was "wide of the mark by an order of magnitude." In April 1994 he informed Blue Cross it should commit not less than $100 million to charitable purposes in 1994, and at least 40 percent of Blue Cross of California's WellPoint holdings to a new charitable foundation. By comparison, when Health Net, another California health insurance provider, went for-profit in 1992, it had to endow the California Wellness Foundation with $300 million and 80 percent of its stock; BCC was nearly ten times larger than Health Net.

The DOC's demand took BCC by surprise. Blue Cross countered with an offer that included the original $100 million payment, an additional $25 million in 1994, and 12 million shares of WellPoint stock, equivalent to a 12 percent stake in the company. At the same time, BCC told Mendoza that it did not believe there was any statutory basis to justify the stock turnover or the loss of control of WellPoint that it would entail for BCC. On May 6, 1994, in apparent frustration, Mendoza sent Blue Cross "a stern letter," quoted in part in the *Wall Street Journal,* urging BCC to come to an accommodation. The letter reiterated DOC's previous demands and said the department had "begun to take the necessary steps to initiate an enforcement action . . . if the department concluded that it was necessary to do so."

Leonard Schaeffer wrote later in *Health Affairs* of the "widespread confusion" the controversy caused around WellPoint. WellPoint customers, he said, were surprised that the company had so many surplus funds to distribute. WellPoint employees were uncertain whether they were working for a for-profit or nonprofit company. Company shareholders were concerned that the long, dragged-out dispute would depress the value of their stock and distract WellPoint management from their work.

In May 1994 an event occurred that seemed to offer a way out of the impasse. The Blue Cross and Blue Shield Association amended its bylaws to allow a for-profit organization to hold a primary Blue Cross license. Blue Cross of California drew up a new plan which it presented to DOC in September 1994. Blue Cross would separate its nonprofit and for-profit activities completely by donating all of its remaining assets to two brand new charitable foundations which it would found and then convert itself to for-profit status. All of BCC's insurance activities would be merged into WellPoint, which would also take over the rights to the Blue Cross license and logo. Some analysts observed that Blue Cross was exactly where it would have been if it had acceded to critics demands in 1992. But to go completely for-profit at that time would have entailed surrendering the rights to the company's respected—and valuable—Blue Cross affiliation.

All that remained to be established was WellPoint's actual value as an asset. BCC proposed using the company's publicly traded price as a yardstick—despite a year and a half of wrangling, it had remained remarkably stable at just over $27. "The DOC," according to Schaeffer, "said that the company could be better valued by putting it up for auction through a 'market assessment' process." While disagreeing fundamentally with this approach, WellPoint declined to challenge the position in court, a process that would probably have lasted years. As a result, he wrote, "the company was put up for sale." By February three interested companies had signed confidentiality agreements enabling them to examine WellPoint's books. The following month Blue Shield of California, attempting to develop its HMO business, offered first $4.5 billion, then $4.8 billion, for WellPoint. If its bid were successful, Blue Shield said, it would follow WellPoint's example and convert to for-profit status.

Merger with Health Systems On, Then Off

WellPoint rejected both Blue Shield offers. It had been pursuing negotiations to acquire Health Systems International (HSI), a company headquartered near WellPoint in Woodland Hills, California. On April 4, 1995, the two companies formally announced that they were merging. Terms of the deal entailed the exchange of $1.9 billion in stock. The new company, which would operate under the Blue Cross name, would comprise a California HMO with 4.4 million members and $6 billion in annual revenues, second in the state only to Kaiser Permanente. The deal promised a new healthcare giant, a view Leonard Schaeffer seemed to confirm, telling the *Wall Street Journal,* "We expect this to be a national company." WellPoint also expected the merger to save it approximately $200 million annually.

All that stood in the way was approval by state and federal regulators, a process the *Wall Street Journal* speculated "could be difficult." One, the California Department of Corporations had not yet formally approved the plan for conversion that Blue Cross had presented it the previous September. Commissioner Mendoza favored the Blue Shield takeover and urged WellPoint to reconsider that offer. Although part of the WellPoint-HSI merger proposal called for the transfer of $3 million in cash and stocks to two new foundations, Mendoza continued to stress his concern that any WellPoint merger should benefit the public significantly. "The public is an 80 percent holder in WellPoint, in effect, through an indirect interest in Blue Cross," he told the *San Francisco Chronicle.* "We've been working with Blue Cross for some period of time to make sure the public receives appropriate benefits." Mendoza said he would need two to three weeks to determine whether there were any problems with the HSI plan.

In July Commissioner Mendoza sent BCC an eight-page letter which the *San Francisco Chronicle* obtained. It outlined his "serious concerns" about the "fairness and reasonableness" of the plan for the two new foundations WellPoint wanted to endow. Mendoza was concerned that the foundations be independent charitable entities and not under the control of the WellPoint board. Consumer groups had also criticized the plan for the new charities. Their structure, a Consumers Union spokesperson said, was suspiciously similar to that of lobbying groups like the National Rifle Association. The group told the *San Francisco Chronicle* the plan was "infected with conditions and restrictions" that would make the foundations "a lobbying and research arm" of Blue Cross.

Leonard Schaeffer was impatient with the way DOC seemed to be dragging its feet. Invoking BCC's right under California law to a decision within 20 days, he demanded the DOC act by August 22. Mendoza countered, charging Blue Cross had not been completely forthcoming with information the DOC needed to reach a decision. In the end the merger was approved contingent on the new foundations' refraining from all political activity and changes being made in the foundation's board of directors to weaken its ties to WellPoint.

After Mendoza had given his approval, the WellPoint-Health Systems International merger lingered on inconclusively and as autumn passed the deal seemed less and less likely. Its completion was postponed in November, a delay the *Wall Street Journal* blamed on "unresolved 'contractual interruptions.' " It seemed likely that both WellPoint and HSI would hesitate to pull out on their own—the preliminary agreement stipulated a $50 million penalty if either party reneged.

The deal finally broke down completely when HSI management who had previously supported the merger revoked their approval, saying they had been misled by WellPoint. Outside observers said the deal was ruined when HSI and WellPoint management disagreed about who would have ultimate control over the future direction of the new company. "Over the past couple of weeks, it was harder to imagine how these two managements could have worked together than how they could separate," one analyst was quoted in the *Wall Street Journal*. The California Medical Association speculated that what precipitated the merger was WellPoint's vulnerability to outside takeover after DOC ruled it had to devote $2 billion to charity. "Leonard Schaeffer and his top people feared they could lose their jobs. That is what precipitated the HSI merger," a CMA spokesperson told Rachel Kreier of *American Medical News*. Eventually negotiations were mutually terminated to avoid penalties and costly lawsuits.

In the wake of the failed merger, WellPoint filed a third recapitalization plan with the Department of Corporations in February 1996. It called for the creation of two foundations which would receive about 80 percent of Blue Cross's WellPoint stock. WellPoint would pay out additional monies to acquire remaining Blue Cross commercial assets. The total endowment would amount to approximately $3 billion. Over a five-year period, the foundations would be required to reduce their voting share to less than five percent in WellPoint through sales or transfers. On May 20, 1996, Blue Cross of California and its remaining assets were merged into WellPoint, which assumed the rights to the Blue Cross name and logo.

WellPoint's service plans and networks had been expanding under Leonard Schaeffer's leadership during 1995. In May 1995 WellPoint acquired nine San Francisco Bay Area dental practices with 800,000 patients to form what it called a "dental service organization" (DSO), similar in organization to the management-services organization (MSO) in the medical world. Participating dentists would be part owners of the organization, and in effect pool their resources with WellPoint's to create advantageous economies of scale. WellPoint's DSO was said to be the first of its kind in the country and the company hoped within 18 months to have a network in place that would reach a quarter of all Californians.

Schaeffer's sights were set much higher though: "We are committed to being a national company," he told *Medical Economics*' Cathy Tokarski. A key step in this direction took place in January 1996 when WellPoint acquired the Group Life & Health subsidiary (L&H) of Massachusetts Mutual Life Insurance Company for $380 million. L&H's one million members, combined with WellPoint's 2.8 million, created the second largest publicly held managed health company in the United States. It was WellPoint's first major acquisition outside California and enabled the company to expand its coverage into ten states, including Massachusetts, New York, and New Jersey, and to add Mass Mutual's sizable dental insurance and group life and disability insurance business to its own rosters.

In late 1996 WellPoint bought the Group Benefit Operations of the John Hancock Mutual Life Insurance Company for $86.7 million. The unit, WellPoint announced, would continue to concentrate on serving the needs of large employers. The pur-

chase extended WellPoint's presence to a number of new states, including Michigan, Texas, and the mid-Atlantic area. The purchase of the Hancock and Mass Mutual units, with their more traditional types of policies, reflected WellPoint's unconventional conviction at the time: the popularity of HMOs had peaked and both employers and workers were looking for healthcare plans that offered them greater latitude. WellPoint made its UNICARE subsidiary responsible for the Mass Mutual and Hancock operations. UNICARE continued to expand in 1997. A joint venture was begun with Blue Cross of Idaho in May; in July it won a major contract with the state of Illinois.

A Tarnished Reputation?: The 1990s

Despite WellPoint's healthy profits—even in 1994 during the uncertainty with the Department of Corporations its profit margin was 13 percent—it had a bad reputation among California doctors. Cathy Tokarski wrote in *Medical Economics*, they complained of WellPoint's "bargain-basement reimbursement rates and strong-arm tactics against physicians." One group of doctors complained to DOC that WellPoint had kicked them out of its PPO because they had left its HMO. WellPoint countered it had only excluded the doctors after they signed an exclusive agreement with one of its competitors.

Hospitals also complained, in particular in the summer of 1995 when WellPoint announced it was organizing a two-tiered network of hospitals in California. Hospitals who provided convincing plans for cutting costs and providing increased quality in healthcare would be placed in the first tier. Those institutions would get a higher volume of WellPoint patients, while patients who used tier two hospitals would be required to make higher co-payments. Most hospitals chose to cooperate and complete WellPoint's questionnaire rather than be squeezed out of the extensive WellPoint network altogether.

Studies released by the California Medical Association between 1994 and 1996 claimed that WellPoint's CaliforniaCare HMO spent less of its total revenues on patient care and more on profits and overhead than any other plan in California. For example, the CMA found that WellPoint spent only 73 percent of its revenues on patients in 1995 and that at the same time its CEO Leonard Schaeffer was one of the highest paid healthcare executives in California. By contrast, the nonprofit Kaiser Permanente put 96.8 percent on medical care. WellPoint maintained the CMA's survey was flawed pointing out that it ignored differences in accounting practice in nonprofit and for-profit entities, and the higher overhead required to support independent sales agents.

Other groups gave WellPoint poor ratings as well. The Pacific Business Group, an organization of employers in California, rated 13 HMOs in 14 service categories. WellPoint's CaliforniaCare was the only plan that did not receive a single "A" in any category. In addition, the National Committee for Quality Assurance which evaluates managed healthcare refused to give its accreditation to the WellPoint HMO.

WellPoint's results in 1997 continued to be good. Its operating income at the end of 1997 was up 14 percent while its stock rose 23 percent. Membership that year increased 19 percent, partly because of the Hancock and Mass Mutual acquisitions and also because of strong growth in its co-payment plan. The company hoped to finish the decade on the same strong footing.

Principal Subsidiaries

Blue Cross of California; UNICARE.

Further Reading

Anders, George, "Blue Cross of California Sells Stake in WellPoint Health for $476 Million," *Wall Street Journal*, January 28, 1993.

Barnum, Alex, "Blue Cross IPO Tantalizes Wall Street," *San Francisco Chronicle*, January 28, 1993.

"California Pressing Blue Cross to Give $1 Billion to Charity," *Wall Street Journal*, May 13, 1994.

Connolly, Jim, "California Blue Cross Plans to Start For-Profit Sub," *National Underwriter Life & Health*-Financial Services Edition, September 14, 1992.

Gemignani, Janet, "Stock Market Successes and HMO Growing Pains," *Business & Health*, April 1998.

Hagerty, Alfred G., "California Wants More Funds from Blue Cross for Non-Profit Unit," *National Underwriter Life & Health*-Financial Services Edition, May 30, 1994.

Hall, Carl T., "Big HMO Bickering with State Over Merger," *San Francisco Chronicle*, July 26, 1995.

——, "Deal to Create Huge HMO Dies," *San Francisco Chronicle*, December 15, 1995.

——, "WellPoint Confirms Health Care Merger," *San Francisco Chronicle*, April 4, 1995.

——, "WellPoint Runs Last in Survey," *San Francisco Chronicle*, February 13, 1996.

Louis, Arthur M., "HMO Merger Takes a Turn," *San Francisco Chronicle*, March 28, 1995.

——, "WellPoint Urged to Reconsider Blue Shield Bid," *San Francisco Chronicle*, April 1, 1995.

Niedzielski, Joe, "Plan Set to Recapitalize WellPoint," *National Underwriter Life & Health*-Financial Services Edition, March 4, 1996.

Rauber, Chris, "WellPoint Picks up String of Bay Area Dental Practices," *Business Journal*, May 22, 1995.

Rundle, Rhonda L., "Blue Cross of California to Turn Over Most Assets to New Charity Foundation," *Wall Street Journal*, September 16, 1994.

——, "California in Talks with Blue Cross Over Public Sale, " *Wall Street Journal*, August 23, 1993.

——, "Observers Detect a Health-Care Giant Looming in WellPoint-Health Systems," *Wall Street Journal*, April 4, 1995.

——, "WellPoint Purchase of Health Systems Is Approved by Key California Agency," *Wall Street Journal*, September 8, 1995.

——, "WellPoint's Buying of Health Systems Hits Big Obstacle," *Wall Street Journal*, November 28,1995.

Russell, Sabin, "Blue Cross Spin-Off Under Attack," *San Francisco Chronicle*, April 29, 1993.

Schaeffer, Leonard D., "Health Plan Conversions: The view from Blue Cross of California," *Health Affairs*, Winter 1996, pp. 183–87.

Scism, Leslie, and Rhonda L. Rundle, "WellPoint Is Close to Deal with Hancock," *Wall Street Journal*, October 3, 1996.

Shinkman, Ronald, "Blue Cross, State Bump Heads," *Los Angeles Business Journal*, September 4, 1995.

——, "Blue Cross Submits Plan for Charitable Units," *Los Angeles Business Journal*, March 4, 1996.

Tokarski, Cathy, "Forget Everything You Thought You Knew About the blues," *Medical Economics*, March 25, 1996.

—Gerald Brennan

Western Digital

Western Digital Corp.

8105 Irvine Center Drive
Irvine, California 92618
U.S.A.
(714) 932-5000
Fax: (714) 932-6629
Web Site: http://www.wdc.com

Public Company
Incorporated: 1970
Employees: 15,000
Sales: $4.1 billion
Stock Exchanges: New York
Ticker Symbol: WDC
SICs: 3572 Computer Storage Devices; 3672 Printed
    Circuit Boards

Western Digital Corp. is a leading manufacturer of computer hardware equipment, which is then used by the manufacturers of personal computers (PC's) and network systems to produce their own products. Western Digital not only sells hardware to computer manufacturers, but also serves consumer markets directly through its product replacement items and add-on data storage products, which are sold under the Western Digital brand name. In the late 1990s, Western Digital ranked third behind Seagate and Quantum in terms of numbers of drives shipped and market share. *Fortune* magazine, however, found in 1997 that among its readers, Western Digital was more admired than either Quantum or Seagate in the computer peripherals sector, citing management and investment value as several of the criteria. Over 15,000 people are employed by Western Digital in ten countries, including Singapore and Malaysia. The company is divided into two business units: the Personal Storage Division—responsible for PC memory storage and comprising 90 percent of the company's business—and the Enterprise Storage Group, which makes high-capacity hard drives for servers and workstations.

The Early Years

The invention of the computer microprocessor and all that followed is surely matchless in the history of U.S. manufacture. The computer industry is loaded with sweeping epics like that of the rise and tumble of Steven Jobs and Apple Computer, but the Western Digital saga is reasonably serene. While Western Digital miscalculated the evolutionary direction of the computer industry on several occasions, it has always managed to recover and to maintain a significant presence.

In 1970, Western Digital began producing special semiconductors in its incarnation as Emerson Electric Company of St. Louis. Based in Santa Ana, California, the company was financially backed by the Emerson Electric Company of St. Louis and various other independent investors. A year later, the Western Digital appellation was born and headquarters were shifted to Newport Beach, California. Alvin B. Phillips was the founder and president of Western Digital from its inception until 1976. His technical experience in semiconductors was a critical element of the early formation of the company. The most important company event of the 1970s was the manufacture of a 4K RAM chip. Technological breakthroughs multiplied exponentially in this period.

The 1980s proved to be the least predictable period of growth in the electronics/computer industry. The company underestimated the importance of IBM's PC/XT and its related floppy drives and interfaces. But in 1983, Western Digital engineers produced a wire-wrapped prototype of a hard-drive controller for IBM's PC/AT in only 14 days. Western Digital then elected to concentrate its attention on supplying components for the newly developed PC market.

Of the innovations that President and Chief of Operations Roger W. Johnson brought to Western Digital in the early-1980s, nurturing a stable of engineering innovators was one of the most important. Within four years of Johnson's start, sales doubled and earnings grew to $21 million. Among the achievements at Western Digital in the early 1980s was the first Winchester disk drive controller in 1982. Almost 90 percent of Western Digital's income was coming from storage controller products by 1985. The company was one of the first to choose to provide controllers to the pre-eminent PC manufacturers, such as IBM, Compaq, Hewlett-Packard, and Tandy, thus positioning it for later successes and perhaps foreshadowing Western Digital's later partnership with IBM.

Expansion in the 1980s

By the mid-1980s, Western Digital was in the position to acquire new business and start off in new directions. MIT worked in concert with Western Digital to develop the "Nu machine," an artificial intelligence computer later sold to Texas Instruments. Another result of this hybrid team was the "Nu bus", designed to open Macintosh buses to peripherals. Macintosh had developed several of their own versions of this product, but the Nu bus was chosen over all of them.

The late 1980s brought Kathryn Braun into the administrative spotlight in the Personal Storage Division, and the decisions she made would effect the future success of the company profoundly. In a time of fiscal strength for Western Digital, Braun recommended that the company focus on supplying hard disk storage to Original Equipment Manufacturers, or OEMs—like IBM and its compatibles. By acquiring Tandon drive manufacturers at this time, Western Digital gained a foothold in this growing sector. In Singapore, the Western Digital team labored to convert Tandon's production line into a smoother and more profitably run facility. Braun succeeded in increasing her division's annual income from $15 million to more than $2 billion.

Western Digital went on to buy several other smaller peripheral manufacturers, such as Adaptive Data Systems, Paradise, and Verticom. These companies provided Western Digital with key components to diversify and expand. In 1988, Western Digital became a Fortune 500 company. Two years later, the silicon wafer fabrication facility was opened in Irvine, California, and corporate headquarters, Irvine Spectrum, also transferred to Irvine.

Challenges in the 1990s

The early 1990s saw many changes for the worse at Western Digital, reflecting the woes of the computer industry at large. The company reported that large-scale layoffs, financial write-offs, and debt restructure were necessary to keep Western Digital afloat. A recession similarly affected many other U.S. markets. Charles A. Haggarty was hired at Western Digital in 1992, having come from IBM. At Western Digital, he filled a variety of executive management needs. In 1993, he was first

elected director, then chairman, and then chief executive officer of the company. At IBM, his Rochester, Minnesota, storage products team had won the Malcolm Baldrige National Quality Award in 1990. His years of OEM storage expertise were put to good use at Western Digital.

Under Haggarty's leadership, Western Digital was weaned from stand-alone memory storage to integrated disk drive storage. Western Digital fabricated the first two-platter, 3.5-inch, 340-megabyte drive in 1993. A year later, the first 3.5-inch, 1-gigabyte, 3-platter Enhanced IDE drive was produced. IDE stands for Integrated Drive Electronic, otherwise known as a hard drive interface. An Enhanced IDE was faster, had more expansion options, and handled more material. By 1995, Western Digital's IDE storage capacity was increased by another half gigabyte. These products were members of the well-received Caviar family of hard drives, which were found in Apples, Bull-Zeniths, Compaqs, Gateway 2000s, NECs, IBMs, and many other PCs.

In 1994, Western Digital was proud to announce that it had become the first U.S.-headquartered, multinational company to be awarded ISO 9001 status by the International Standards Organization. The ISO 9001 status linked all of Western Digital's operations with a global standard for high-quality processes.

While Western Digital's revenues increased steadily in the late 1990s, it was still experiencing an industry-wide slump based on increased competition, overproduction of drives that molder in warehouses while inventory values decline, and a struggle to keep up with rapidly advancing technology.

One of Western Digital's sources of technological weakness was the lack of GMR research advancement. The GMR technology was based on a recently discovered property of certain magnetic materials that increase electrical resistance when exposed to a magnetic field. The resulting sensors are extraordinarily sensitive, making it possible to store enormous amounts of data in the disk. It was speculated that this technology could eventually make chip memory storage obsolete. IBM's research scientists announced that they had fit "more than 11.6 billion bits of data in one square inch on the surface of a rotating magnetic disk," according to a February 1998 issue of the *New York Times*.

The Turn of the Century and Beyond

The disastrous declines in Asian markets near the end of the 1990s hurt U.S. technology revenues in general, and compounded Western Digital's woes. Not only did Western Digital manufacture drives in the East, but it sold ten to fifteen percent of those drives there, before selling the remainder in the United States. The declining values of Asian currency had at least one benefit—however temporary—for Western Digital: "Sales in Asia have fallen, but profits are rising," the *New York Times* reported in late 1997. "The disk drives are sold in dollars, while the manufacturing costs are incurred in the weakening Asian currencies." It was predicted that inflation would eventually correct this phenomenon, but Western Digital enjoyed it while it lasted.

Western Digital's struggle to keep up, technology-wise, led industry experts to speculate that the company was perfect for purchase in 1998. The *Orange County Business Journal* quoted David Takata, an analyst with Gruntal & Co., in February 1998: "One of the reasons people are speculating about IBM buying a desktop drive company like Western Digital [is that] IBM would gain manufacturing expertise and Western Digital would gain R&D talent." Takata speculated that Haggarty's previous relationship with IBM might smooth the way for a takeover. As the situation developed, however, market researcher Jim Porter of Disk/Trend Inc., had a different outlook: "My take on the management out there is they would rather do it themselves. I can't imagine Chuck [Haggarty] going back to work for IBM."

Instead of a takeover, IBM and Western Digital entered into an agreement to work together for the very reasons Porter cited. Haggarty told his board of directors that the move was a "major step in changing the game," according to a Western Digital press release. "Last fall we rolled up our sleeves, did a lot of soul searching and seriously examined our business model. We concluded that pursuing a significantly expanded relationship with IBM ... was in the best interests of our company, our employees and shareholders." Haggarty went on to detail the advantages of the agreement, and to emphasize the enthusiasm of company officers in both companies.

Concern had been raised in late 1997 among Western Digital shareholders that the company had misrepresented its assets, and that losses were not taken in a timely fashion. A class action suit was announced against Western Digital on February 2, 1998, alleging that some key insiders had manipulated financial numbers to their benefit, while the average stockholder took a loss. The New York law firm of Stull, Stull & Brody represented what one source called a "handful" of plaintiffs, while Western Digital denied all charges against it.

Western Digital had indeed sustained hard financial blows late in 1997; the company went from debt-free to $513.1 million in debt between December 27, 1997, and March 28, 1998. While Western Digital stock went as high as 54 ¾ and split at 44 in 1997, it had yet to regain its original value a year later, going as low as 14 ½. Funding was tight, and Western Digital raised money the old-fashioned way: they sold $400 million of zero coupon convertible subordinated debentures. The *Dow Jones Newswires* reported on February 12, 1998, that Western Digital "intends to use the net proceeds of the offering for general corporate purposes." A month before, the company had broken ground on a new manufacturing facility in San Jose, California. Meanwhile in Rochester, Minnesota, the new Enterprise Storage Group's headquarters were in the process of being built. The new research and development facility was planned to include a clean room, administrative and engineering offices, and design laboratories.

Western Digital took special measures to recover its financial equilibrium. In mid-1998, the company entered into a special partnership agreement whereby IBM would share its areal-density giant magnetoresistive (GMR) heads with Western Digital, and IBM in turn would have a foothold in the PC peripherals market. It was hoped that this partnership would ensure that Western Digital would be a force to reckon with well into the next century.

Further Reading

"Applied Magnetics Down; IBM-Western Dig Deal Hurts Outlook," *Dow Jones Newswires,* May 5, 1998.

Grimes, Christopher, "Disk Drives' Woes Continues in 1Q; Slow Recovery Seen," *Dow Jones Newswires,* April 13, 1998.

Markoff, John, "Crowding Even More Data Into Even Smaller Spaces," *New York Times,* February 23, 1998.

"Rumors Rife of Western Digital Takeover By IBM," *Orange County Business Journal,* February 23–March 1, 1998, p. 1.

"Technology Brief—Western Digital Corp.: Quarterly Loss Is Posted As Charges Are Recorded," *Wall Street Journal,* January 30, 1998.

Uchitelle, Louis, "Dimming Economies of Asia Cast Shadows on U.S. Firms," *New York Times,* December 14, 1997.

"Western Digital Begins Construction On R&D Center," *Dow Jones Newswires,* May 22, 1998.

"Western Digital Boosts Conv Sub Deb Offering to $400M," *Dow Jones Newswires,* February 12, 1998.

"Western Digital Breaks New Ground," *Business Journal Serving San Jose & Silicon Valley,* January 26, 1998, p. 58.

Twenty-Five Years of Innovation: The History of Western Digital, Western Digital Corp.: Irvine, California, 1995, 10 pp.

—Christine L. Ferran

Wickes Inc.

706 North Deerpath Drive
Vernon Hills, Illinois 60061
U.S.A.
(847) 367-3400
Fax: (310) 452-9509
Web Site: http://www.wickes.com

Public Company
Incorporated: 1854 as Genesee Iron Works
Employees: 3,766
Sales: $884.1 million (1997)
Ticker Symbol: WIKS
Stock Exchanges: NASDAQ
SICs: 5211 Lumber Retail and Building Materials; 5099
    Importers

Wickes Inc., most recently known as Wickes Lumber Company, is a staple in the building supplies retail and wholesale market, operating 101 sales and distribution facilities in 23 states in the Midwest, Northeast, and South. The company also operates 10 component manufacturing plants throughout these regions to produce and distribute pre-hung door units, roof and floor trusses, and framed wall panels. While the company's largest market is in the U.S. Midwest, Wickes has also expanded internationally and does business in the Baltic States, Egypt, Japan, Panama, Poland, Russia, and Turkey. Wickes is 52 percent owned by the Jacksonville, Florida-based Riverside Group Inc.

The Beginning of the Wickes Empire: 1850s to World War I

The first version of the Wickes company was founded by brothers Henry Dunn Wickes and Edward Noyes Wickes, in Flint, Michigan. The Wickes family had left New York state and settled in Flint in 1854, and were soon modestly established in the area's burgeoning lumber business. Michigan possessed some of the thickest and choicest pine forests in the United States, and land could be purchased at the bargain price of only $1.25 per acre. The Wickes brothers, along with H.W. Wood, established the Genesee Iron Works, a foundry and machine shop specializing in repair work and the casting of odd metal parts for equipment used in the logging and lumber business. Yet the pig iron the company used had to be hauled in from Saginaw, Michigan, by ship and wagon; conversely, the equipment the foundry manufactured was being hauled back to Saginaw for shipment. As the company's business increased, it became obvious that the closer the foundry was to Saginaw—a boom town at the time—the more efficient and profitable the operation would be.

Life in Saginaw did not appeal to H.W. Wood, however—the landscape was composed mostly of the swampland and mosquito-infested marshes adjacent to Lake Huron—so in 1864 he sold out to the Wickes brothers. That same year, the company's name was changed to the Wickes Bros. Iron Works. During these years, Henry Wickes developed and marketed the Wickes gang saw, a steam-powered mill saw capable of ripping two or three logs into boards simultaneously. In 1869 the company made some basic improvements to the gang saw's design, which revolutionized the lumber milling business. The new saw had an oscillating motion, allowing the teeth of the machine's parallel saw blades to cut evenly. In addition, the saw's speed was increased and thinner-gauge steel blades were used to cut down on waste. The new design's success created a national market for Wickes Bros. And international saw sales enabled the company to survive as Michigan's lumber business slowly dried up. By 1887 there were more than 300 Wickes saws in operation.

In another move towards diversification, Wickes bought equipment from troubled sawmills, reconditioned it, and resold it to mills in other parts of the country. Wickes also expanded its repair and resale business to include all kinds of machinery. As the new business grew, the Wickes brothers noticed industrial boilers were one of the most frequently bought and resold items. After developing the machinery necessary to manufacture new boilers, the Wickes Boiler Company was founded. At this time, two of Henry's sons, Harry and William, took over management of the family's enterprises. Harry headed Wickes Bros. Foundry, and William led the boiler business.

In 1901 the original founders of the burgeoning Wickes empire died: Edward died first and was followed just a month and a day later by older brother Henry. Henry died in Guadalajara, Mexico, where both brothers had traditionally gone to spend their winters. It was on just such a trip to Guadalajara that the third Wickes business, the United States Graphite Company (U.S. Graphite), had been born.

While vacationing in Mexico, Henry and Edward had heard of a huge graphite deposit not far from where they were staying. Upon further exploration, they discovered an enormous workable vein of about 85 percent pure graphite in the desert mountains below La Colorada, Mexico. They passed the information on to Henry's sons, who incorporated U.S. Graphite in 1891. After acquiring an abandoned shed next to a railroad depot back in Saginaw, and having some luck—both the Mexican government and the Southern Pacific Railroad were in the process of building rail lines that permitted easy and inexpensive shipment of the raw graphite back to Michigan—U.S. Graphite began to mine, import, and sell the black powder as paint coloring, a lead substitute for pencils, and an industrial lubricant. At one point, U.S. Graphite supplied the graphite-based lead substitute for at least 90 percent of the world's pencils; it achieved even greater success in the years preceding World War I as the demand for electricity grew. Graphite was the major component in the manufacture of carbon brushes, or contacts, necessary in the operation of electric motors.

Lumber Takes a Back Seat: World War I to 1959

In the years following World War I, Wickes introduced the straight-tube vertical boiler. These new boilers lasted longer than any previously manufactured boiler and did not require a shutdown to be cleaned. The phenomenal success of the Wickes Vertical Safety Boiler propelled the company to the forefront of the institutional heating and steam-plant business. As orders for hundreds of the new boilers flowed in, the company had trouble keeping up with demand. During the Depression the boiler business, like most others, suffered heavy losses. But the advent of World War II and the resulting increases in production needed to equip the U.S. military helped Wickes pull out of the doldrums. The U.S. Maritime Commission purchased 360 Wickes 1,000-horsepower boiler units for use in Liberty ships. Wickes also built boilers used in many Navy vessels. The company increased its work force to 500, built its first production line, went to three shifts, and in 1944 was awarded the Maritime Commission Award of Merit.

In 1947 the three Wickes operations—Wickes Bros. Foundry, Wickes Boiler, and U.S. Graphite—were merged to form The Wickes Corporation. Under the terms of the merger, the newly-formed corporation had an authorized capitalization of $10 million, consisting of two million shares with a $5 par value. Some 770,000 of these shares were used in the exchange of stock with the companies that had been absorbed. The remaining 1.23 million shares stayed in the company's treasury for use in future purchases of other manufacturing companies. With the end of the war, Wickes capitalized on its newly-acquired production techniques and upgraded capabilities of its bent-tube boilers to 350,000 pounds of steam per hour and experienced great success in selling the redesigned unit to factories, refineries, schools, hospitals, and municipal utility companies.

The company's increased sales volume, however, brought with it new problems: malfunctioning boilers occasionally exploded, and in the late 1950s a spate of damage suits from some of the new, more powerful units resulted in settlements for millions of dollars. This was a major turning point for Wickes, who discontinued pushing the growth of its boiler business and instead concentrated resources toward expanding its highly-profitable lumber division. As a result, Wickes later sold the boiler operation to Combustion Engineering Company in 1959.

Wickes in the 1960s

The post World War II years were typified by a tremendous housing shortage. The lumber business as it existed in the United States was not equipped to handle the increased demand. Lumber was sold by small, independent dealers to builders who completed construction of one dwelling at a time and purchased the materials to build these houses in small quantities, resulting in high prices that were often passed along to the home buyer. Home builders were at the mercy of the local lumberyard owner, and in many instances, lumber stock needed to complete construction was not available when needed. Wickes' lumber division had taken advantage of this tense situation back in 1952, when it fashioned a building supplies retail outlet from part of a former grain terminal in Bay City, Michigan.

Under the supervision of Joseph S. McMullin, who ran Wickes at the time, the Wickes retail outlet carried a full range of lumber and construction materials needed by builders. By always having a healthy supply of product, Wickes created a one-stop store to which builders' simply sent trucks for loads of materials. There were rarely delays in obtaining necessary materials, and there were often lower prices than were found at small independent or neighborhood lumberyards. The new Wickes venture was called the Bay City Cash Way Company. The idea was such an overwhelming success that Cash Way soon found itself selling to independent lumberyards, who found they could buy lumber at Cash Way for less than the cost to mill the lumber themselves. The key to Cash Way's success was high volume, and McMullin realized that as long as the company was willing to turn large amounts of product at relatively low profit margins, high sales would take care of the company's bottom line.

The company opened additional Cash Way stores, and in 1962—the year Cash Way was renamed the Wickes Lumber Company—sales topped $66 million nationwide. The division had become responsible for more than half the business of the entire Wickes organization. A year later, the lumber division was doing about two-thirds of the company's business, and its growth seemed to be out of control. The company pulled Smith Bolton in from U.S. Graphite to head the lumber division and tighten up the Wickes corporate framework. Bolton took a hard look at the lumber division's organization, inventory distribution method, and the process used to decide where new lumber centers were to be located. He discovered that the vast majority of Wickes Lumber profits were being generated by its more established stores in Michigan and other Midwestern states, and that many of the newer ones in the South and Southwest were losing money.

These losses appeared to be twofold—first, all the stores carried identical products, irrespective of climate and local building codes; secondly, a haphazard method was being used to choose new locations. Bolton discovered that location choices were made without any actual market research and believed the existing management team did not realize the complexity of this larger business arena. The changes instituted by Bolton resulted in more than 40 resignations from the lumber division's management team. The first executive to leave was the division's president, Dick Wolohan, who struck out on his own and began a competing company. The remaining resignations were, in most cases, defections to Wolohan's new company. An aggressive internal management promotion program and recruiting from outside the company eventually filled the void created by the mass resignations. By 1966 Wickes had broken the $200 million per year sales mark.

Massive Growth & the Consequences: The 1970s and 1980s

The 1970s brought with it even greater growth for Wickes. In 1971 Wickes Companies, Inc., was formed to be the parent company of the Wickes Corporation. The company expanded its business into Europe and, fueled by the profits generated by the continuing growth of the lumber division, entered into many new enterprises, including the retail furniture, consumer credit, modular housing, and commercial construction businesses. In 1974 the company surpassed $1 billion in annual sales, and in 1978 purchased Builders Emporium, a home-improvement retailer. Another non-core acquisition came in 1980 with Gamble-Skogmo Inc., a Minneapolis, Minnesota-based retail company consisting of supermarkets, drugstores, mail-order houses, and other outlets valued at more than $200 million. This purchase elevated sales to more than $4 billion per year, but Wickes was weighed down by significant debt.

A worldwide recession, coupled with less than sound planning in its building supplies and furniture lines, put the company in a tenuous situation following the Gamble-Skogmo merger. In April 1982, Wickes and most of its domestic subsidiaries filed for protection from creditors under Chapter 11 of the U.S. Bankruptcy Code. In June 1982 the Securities and Exchange Commission (SEC) began investigating some former Wickes officials for allegedly issuing false data and omitting material information about the company's deteriorating financial condition in the year preceding the filing. The investigation was prompted by complaints filed by many former Gamble-Skogmo shareholders. The following year, however, the judge presiding over the company's Chapter 11 case ordered the court-appointed examiner to terminate his investigation, as the cost (already more than $1.5 million) and the sheer volume of

work needed to complete the inquiry did not appear to be justified.

A month before Wickes filed for Chapter 11, Sanford C. Sigoloff had been brought in as the company's new chairman and CEO. Immediately following his appointment, a purge of upper-level Wickes executives occurred as the first step in the new chairman's reorganization plan. After building up enough capital to see the company through the first stages of the Chapter 11 filing, Sigoloff began to sell off practically all of the general retailing operations in an attempt to make the company less vulnerable to cyclical retail sales. Simultaneously, he began a program for several major acquisitions.

In 1985, Wickes emerged from the second-largest bankruptcy proceedings in U.S. history. After divesting many of its interests, including the company's vehicle leasing operations, Wickes Machine Tool Group, and the Wickes Engineered Material Division, it acquired the Consumer and the Industrial Products Group of Gulf + Western Inc. for approximately $1 billion. Then in 1986, Wickes acquired a group of retail stores from W. R. Grace & Co., which it added to its Builders Emporium operations. The company also spent $1.16 billion to acquire the Collins & Aikman Corporation, a manufacturer and distributor of upholstery, fabrics, and wall coverings for the home, as well as carpeting, upholstery, and seat coverings for automobiles. Also in 1986, Wickes made unsuccessful takeover bids for Owens-Corning Fiberglass Corporation and National Gypsum Company. Though the Wickes organization had recovered from bankruptcy, it had no real identity as a leader in one business or industrial sector. As a result, some divisions suffered, others were scuttled, and Sigoloff still continued to buy in what seemed an indiscriminate manner.

Independence in the Late 1980s and Early 1990s

In 1987, Wickes Lumber Company was incorporated in Delaware and the following year was spun off from its parent company. As Wickes Lumber began a life of its own, the only other remaining company with the Wickes name, Wickes Furniture, was also spun off. The remainder of the once-mighty Wickes Companies Inc. was taken private by WCI Holdings Corporation, an investment group jointly owned by Blackstone Capital Partners L.P. and Wasserstein, Perella Partners L.P. Some units were divested, others reborn under new names with no Wickes connection: Collins & Aikman took over the home furnishings arm, Orchard Supply hardware stores were acquired by Sears Hardware, and Builders Emporium went out of business. Wickes Lumber, however, was just beginning its new adventure in independence.

At the time of its spinoff, Wickes Lumber consisted of 223 building centers and 10 manufacturing facilities across the United States. Over the next several years, Wickes streamlined its operations to cut costs, and closed underperforming stores and plants. By 1993, the number of company building centers had been reduced to 124, and its manufacturing plants were slashed by 40 percent to 6 facilities. In the fall of 1993, the company completed a recapitalization plan, retired all debt associated with its spinoff, restructured its existing capital stock, and went public on the NASDAQ market with 2.8 million shares of common stock. Year-end net sales totaled $846.8 million with net income of $8.2 million.

In 1994 and 1995, Wickes went ahead with several acquisitions and mergers. The transactions brought another 15 building centers into play, along with 5 additional manufacturing facilities. This brought the total back to 11 plants and 139 retail centers. Its expansion was ill-timed, however, and during the fourth quarter of 1995, the company was again reorganizing by closing or consolidating 21 building centers and 3 manufacturing plants to reduce overhead. The company also reworked its revolving bank credit in early 1996 and issued another 2 million shares of common stock for $10 million. Net sales for 1994 had risen to $986.9 million with earnings of $28.1 million, while the troubles in 1995 brought sales down slightly to $972.6 million but with a loss of $15.6 million.

While the number of housing starts bounced back up in 1996, the figures fell again slightly in 1997. More significantly—in Wickes' major home market in the Midwest, housing starts were down 5.5 percent for the year. Single-family housing starts, which were the bread-and-butter of the company's primary customers—builders—experienced a 2.4 percent drop from the previous year. These shortfalls, partially due to extreme weather attributed to El Niño, affected not only the overall new home construction market but especially Wickes, as these sales accounted for 57 percent of the company's bottom line.

Though the total market for home improvement/new home construction had run just over $212 billion for 1997, the market continued to be highly fragmented and less prone to the merger-mania and consolidation of the late 1990s. With no competitor accounting for more than 12 percent of the market, few companies were unaffected by the industry slowdown. Wickes year-end net sales reached $884.1 million in 1997, but the company still recorded a loss of $1.6 million.

Still struggling amidst high overhead costs and unremarkable sales, Wickes had again overhauled its operations and its name, changing it from Wickes Lumber Company to a more generic Wickes Inc. Once again, the company began closing centers and manufacturing facilities (8 of the former, 2 of the latter), sold 2 retail centers in Iowa, and reduced its headquarters staff by 25 percent. Yet Wickes also set its sights firmly on the future by initiating several innovations, which were designed to take the company not only through the remainder of the 1990s, but into the next century as well. Among these were the installation of computerized design hardware and software at its building centers, so customers could visualize a new deck,

kitchen, or addition. Short or long-term specialized equipment rentals at 25 of its busiest sales and distributions facilities were also added, and a new home page on the World Wide Web was introduced. In addition, a new Internet site called ''www.toolsonline.com'' made its debut, to sell 65,000 different tools 24-hours a day, 7 days a week. Finally, the company remodeled kitchen and bath showrooms within many of its building centers. The latter improvements immediately made a difference, and helped propel sales by as much as 15 percent in those facilities.

In 1998, Wickes was following the same path that it had followed during the previous few years, closing underperforming building and distribution centers while opening new ones in high-yield areas. The company announced its intention mid-year to buy Eagle Industries Inc., an Indiana-based manufacturer with 1997 sales of $10.5 million. The sales augmented Wickes' own manufacturing and distribution of roof trusses, wall panels and other building materials, and was expected to be complete by the third quarter of the year.

Despite its ups and downs, Wickes was still a force to be reckoned with in the home improvement and new home construction market. A company long known for its dependable products, delivery services—with a fleet of over 770 trucks, many of which were specialized to meet builders' needs as well as lend access to the railway and most of the company's distribution plants—technical and sales help, and the capability to specially build practically anything needed by builders and do-it-yourselfers.

Further Reading

Bush, George, *The Wide World of Wickes,* New York: McGraw-Hill, 1976.

Sansweet, Stephen, ''Salvage Operation,'' *Wall Street Journal,* August 2, 1985.

''Wickes Inc. Reports Increased Sales and Gross Margins; Announces Further Restructuring,'' *FRB (Financial Relations Board) News Bulletin,* February 23, 1998.

''Wickes Inc. Continues to Report Same Store Sales Increases; Begins Servicing New Online Buying Service 'Toolsonline,' '' *FRB News Bulletin,* July 8, 1998.

''Wickes Lumber Company: Third-Period Profit to Trail Projections by Wall Street,'' *Wall Street Journal,* September 21, 1995, p. B4.

''Wickes Inc.: Revamping to Include Sale of Units, Staffing Cutbacks,'' *Wall Street Journal,* October 20, 1997, p. C21.

''Wickes Completes Sale of Iowa Units,'' *Wall Street Journal,* March 24, 1998, p. A8.

—updated by Taryn Benbow-Pfalzgraf

Willis Corroon Group plc

Ten Trinity Square
London EC3P 3AX
England
(44) 171 488 8111
Web site: http://www.williscorroon.com

Public Company
Incorporated: 1828 as Henry Willis & Co.
Employees: 9,400
Total Assets:£692 million (US$1.41 billion) (1997)
Stock Exchanges: London New York Pacific
Ticker Symbol: WCG
SICs: 6411 Insurance Agents, Brokers, & Service; 6719
    Holding Companies, Not Elsewhere Classified

Willis Corroon Group plc. is a world-leading provider of insurance and reinsurance brokerage services. Headquartered in London, England, with U.S. headquarters in Nashville, Tennessee, Willis Corroon operates more than 250 offices in 69 countries around the world. The company offers an extensive range of insurance products to major corporations and public sector organizations, private and public associations, as well as to individuals.

In the late 1990s, Willis Corroon reorganized its operations around six major divisions: Global Reinsurance; Global Specialities; U.K. Brokering; North American Brokering; U.S. Wholesale; and International. A seventh division, Fine Art, Jewellery & Specie, was added in January 1998. The company's global specialities focus on the aerospace, marine, and energy industries, with an emphasis on global reinsurance and global brokerage packages. Included among the company's areas of expertise are industries including: environment; construction; healthcare; mergers and acquisitions; leisure; food and drink; and "unusual and niche" fields such as the company's 1998 launch of its Fine Art, Jewellery & Specie division. The company's International division guides its operations in countries outside of the United Kingdom and North America. In the late 1990s, the company has been moving to increase its position in other European markets, especially Germany and France.

Since the completion of a merger with Corroon & Black in the early 1990s, the formerly British-focused company has become a major insurer in the United States. While England continues to represent some 40 percent of the company's total revenues, North America accounts for approximately 50 percent of annual sales, which totaled £692 million (US$1.4 billion) in 1997.

Willis Corroon is led by Executive Chairman John Reeve, the first outsider to be appointed head of the company. After an extensive reorganization in the mid-1990s, Willis Corroon has posted strong profits in the late 1990s, with net earnings reaching £57.4 million (US$94.7 million) for 1997.

Roots in the Industrial Age

The modern Willis Corroon Group originated in Industrial Era England and grew through a long series of mergers. In the early 19th century, British industrial expertise established that country as the world's leading manufacturer, while the kingdom's merchant fleet continued its long reign over the world's oceans. These factors gave rise to London-based financial and insurance industries that dominated the world market.

One of the founding members of Willis Corroon was Henry Willis & Co., formed in 1828. Henry Willis, then 28, oriented his business primarily towards Britain's shipping industry, operating as a broker and an agent for marine hull insurance offered by Lloyd's, then already one of the world's leading insurers. The mid-19th century saw the appearance of several other later members of the Willis Corroon group. In 1863, another firm, formed by George Henry Smith, began doing business for Lloyd's. Smith's sons, who changed the family name to its Latin form, Faber, set up their own insurance business in 1886. These three firms would form the core of the first development of what would eventually become Willis Corroon.

At the same time, other branches of the future Willis Corroon group had made their appearance. One of these was the merger of two London-based insurers, Galbraith and Henderson, in 1848, which, together with the firm of Fletcher and Welton, would grow into the Stewart Wrightston group of insurers. Another was the formation of C. Wuppesahl & Co. Assekuranzmakler, based in Bremen, Germany. In 1843, Henry Dumas opened the Dumas and Wylie firm, which also brokered for Lloyd's. Yet another branch was represented by the 1865 founding of Gibb & MacIntyre, later known as James Gibb & Son and then Bray Gibb.

The 1890s set the scene for the first wave of Willis Corroon mergers. By then, Willis had begun expanding beyond the United Kingdom, entering especially the Italian market as agents for Italia and Generali. In 1892, Henry Willis & Co. reached an agreement with US-based Johnson & Higgins to broker their marine insurance services through Lloyd's. The growing Willis company soon after merged its business with the Faber family, forming Willis Faber in 1898. Another boost to the company came the following year, when it became an agent for Tokyo Marine & Fire Insurance Company.

Family Tree in the 20th Century

At the turn of the century, Willis Faber opened a new subsidiary, the Cornhill Insurance Company, and moved to increase its international operations, with agencies in Montreal, Canada, and Hamburg, Germany. The period also saw the appearance of several new Willis Corroon branches. One of the principal of these was brokerage specialist R.A. Corroon & Co. Inc., based in New York, as that city's prominence in the world insurance and financial markets grew alongside the overall developing economic power of the entire United States. Two more London companies made their appearance in the first decade of the 20th century: Matthews Wrightson and Arthur Bray & Son, both to become major components of the Stewart Wrightson Group. Stewart Wrightson would later form one of the three principal components of the Willis Corroon Group.

Over the next decades, Willis Faber continued to grow both internally and through acquisitions. The early 1920s were marked by the acquisitions of two British companies, Brodrick, Leitch & Kendall and Henry L. Riseley, enabling Willis Faber to expand its British presence into the cities of Cardiff, Liverpool, Bristol, and Birmingham, while also adding the Riseley subsidiary British & Irish Plate Glass Insurance Company, later known as the Sovereign Insurance Company. Internationally, the company was given the London agency representation for Chile's Caja and for the U.S.'s Atlantic Mutual companies. Willis Faber also formed a treaty with the newly established Soviet State Insurance Organization. At the end of the decade, Willis Faber became Willis Faber & Dumas Limited, after its merger with Dumas & Wylie in 1928.

This move was matched on the U.S. side when R.A. Corroon—which by then had expanded beyond brokerage to include underwriting services as well—merged with another company to form Corroon & Reynolds. In 1929, Corroon & Reynolds became the first insurance broker to obtain a listing on the New York stock exchange. Corroon became the third primary component of the future Willis Corroon Group.

In the 1930s, the final branches of the Willis Corroon Group appeared. In 1931, J. H. Miller founded a construction bonds surety agency in California; that company took on the name Miller & Day in the following year. At the end of that decade, Miller & Day expanded to become Miller Day & Ames. That name was simplified to Miller & Ames in 1947.

While Willis Faber, established as a leading London broker, appeared to rest from its line of acquisitions, the other branches of the later Willis Corroon Group continued the pattern of mergers. In the mid-1960s, Corroon & Reynolds made the decision to sell off its underwriting operations and concentrate on expanding its brokering activities. That move was followed by its consolidation with another prominent New York brokerage house, C.R. Black Jr. Corporation, in 1966, forming the Corroon & Black Corporation. Miller & Ames's operations were added two years later, as Corroon & Black moved to establish a national position. Corroon & Black would continue to build via acquisitions and mergers throughout the 1970s and 1980s. The most prominent of these came in the 1970s, with the reinsurance business of G.L. Hodgson, based in New York in 1970; in 1976 Corroon & Black doubled in size with its merger with Nashville, Tennessee's Synercon Corporation, the largest such merger in the U.S.-based brokering sector at that time. By the late 1980s, Corroon & Black would hold the position as the United States' fifth largest insurance broker.

In the 1970s, Willis Faber went public with a listing on the London stock exchange. By the end of the decade, Willis Faber had established its headquarters at the Ten Trinity Square address. Meanwhile, the formation of Stewart Wrightson—through the consolidation of the activities of Matthews Wrightson, Bray Gibb, and Stewart Smith—brought that company to the London stock exchange as well.

Joining the Branches in the 1980s and 1990s

Willis Faber hit the acquisition trail again in the early 1980s, adding U.K.-based companies Carter Wilkes & Fane, a reinsurance specialist based in London, and Yorkshire-based Rattray Daffern. At the same time, Willis Faber underwent a change in strategy. Traditionally, Willis Faber had built its business around a core of agency brokering and reinsurance operations. In the 1980s, the company sought greater independence, especially in terms of revenues, by repositioning itself further into the direct brokering market. With the shift of the world financial and insurance industries' focus to New York, and the British economic crisis of the 1980s, Willis Faber also recognized the need to establish a presence in the U.S. market.

The merger of Willis Faber with Stewart Wrightson provided the company a strong boost in this direction. Renamed Willis Wrightson, the company became the largest direct broker in the U.K., gave the company a strengthened position among the global reinsurance market, and added a strong entry into the United States. By the end of the decade, the third component was in place: Willis Wrightson merged with Corroon & Black, forming the Willis Corroon Group.

Through the early 1990s, the company worked to restructure its operations, expanding its international presence through the opening of offices worldwide, while building its position throughout Europe with the establishment of a network of subsidiary and related operations. The company's U.S. headquarters was also moved from Corroon & Black's former New York offices to Nashville. Willis Corroon's transition was realized by 1993. The company was then one of the world leaders in risk management and brokering services.

The cost of putting the company's new structure into place—at a time when the worldwide market had gone sour with the extended recession of the first half of the 1990s—cut into the company's profits. The company turned to John Reeves, who became the first company chairman brought in from outside the company. In 1995, the company took steps to reorganize its operations, reforming the company into five primary divisions: U.K. Retail, U.K. Wholesale, International, North American Retail, and Global Specialities. These divisions were later refined into the company's late 1990s structure. The reorganization of the company helped lift profits by 1996.

By then, Willis Corroon had begun to position itself beyond its traditional insurance brokering core into becoming, as stated in its annual report, "a global knowledge-based professional services firm." Beyond simply offering insurance services, Willis Corroon expanded its definition to include problem-solving and other risk management consulting activities. In the late 1990s, the company also began to concentrate on the rapidly opening European market, with a focus on Germany and France. As such, the company concluded an agreement with Germany's Jaspers Wuppesahl to increase Willis Corroon's position in the German company to 30 percent at the beginning of 1998, and to 44.6 percent by the end of 1998—with an option to build a majority position in the early years of the next century. In late 1997, the company also enhanced its position in India, with the joint-venture Willis Corroon Tower (Private) Limited, based in Mumbai.

Principal Subsidiaries

Willis Corroon International Holdings Limited; Willis Faber North America Inc. (U.S.A.); Willis Faber Re; Willis Corroon Limited; Willis Corroon Commercial; Willis Corroon Tower (Private) Limited (India; 50%).

Principal Divisions

Global Reinsurance; Global Specialities; U.K. Broking; North American Broking; U.S. Wholesale; International; Fine Art, Jewellery & Specie.

Further Reading

Willis Corroon Group, "Our History," Internet: http://www.williscorroon.com/history.htm.

—M. L. Cohen

Wilmington Trust Corporation

Rodney Square North
1100 North Market Street
Wilmington, Delaware 19890
U.S.A.
(302) 651-1000
Fax: (302) 651-8010
(800) 441-7120

Public Company
Incorporated: 1901 as Delaware Guarantee and Trust Co.
Employees: 2,418
Total Assets: $5.56 billion (1996)
Stock Exchanges: NASDAQ
Ticker Symbols: WILM
SICs: 6712 Bank Holding Companies

Wilmington Trust Corporation is the holding company for the Wilmington Trust Company and its subsidiaries. It is the largest banking company in Delaware, with a market share of more than 40 percent in that state. Wilmington Trust has branches all across Delaware, several in the neighboring states of Pennsylvania and Maryland, and one branch in Palm Beach, Florida. The core of Wilmington Trust's business long has been personal trust management, and the bank ranks as the eighth largest nationwide in terms of the personal trust assets it manages. The bank also offers a full range of other banking and investment services. It makes business and consumer loans, manages institutional investments, and runs its own mutual funds group, called the Rodney Square Funds. Wilmington Trust also is one of the nation's largest retailers of precious metals. It sells and purchases metals and stores gold and silver bullion, bars and coins.

Early History

Wilmington Trust (under the name Delaware Guarantee and Trust Co.) was incorporated in Delaware in 1901 by members of the du Pont family. The du Ponts held one of the oldest and wealthiest U.S. manufacturing fortunes. Éleuthere Irenee du Pont de Nemours, his company's founder, emigrated from France to the United States in 1797 and subsequently built a gunpowder plant on the banks of Delaware's Brandywine River. Du Pont's company grew to be the largest industry in Wilmington and by the early 1900s was one of the largest corporations in the entire United States. Its assets at that time were believed to be worth around $24 million, a stupendous amount in the economy of that era. The Delaware Guarantee and Trust Co. was founded to handle the banking needs of the growing Du Pont company. The bank changed its name to Wilmington Trust Company in 1903. Wilmington Trust was deeply tied to the du Pont family and their company throughout its early years. Du Pont family members sat on Wilmington Trust's board, and they maintained million dollar checking accounts and even larger trust funds there. As a result Wilmington Trust, which otherwise might have been a typical small-town bank, ranked near the top of banks nationwide for assets.

Leader in Trusts in the 1960s and 1970s

Wilmington Trust extended its influence across the state of Delaware beginning in the 1940s, when it began acquiring smaller banks. It bought up the Union National Bank of Wilmington in 1943 and the Industrial Trust Co. of Wilmington in 1955. It bought up banks in the nearby towns of Newport, Claymont, and Newark between 1943 and 1949 and acquired three other area banks in 1959. It branched out into other businesses in the 1960s and 1970s, forming a subsidiary, the Brandywine Insurance Agency, Inc., in 1964 and acquiring a travel agency in 1974. The bank continued to hold massive amounts of du Pont family fortune, and the Du Pont company also did the bulk of its banking there. Trust handling was the bank's preeminent business. By 1969 Wilmington had the twelfth largest trust department in the United States, with trust assets worth $5.7 billion. Wilmington handled the fortunes of many famously wealthy clients, attracting them through national advertising. The bank stated its expertise in dealing with personal wealth in its publicity. By 1969 Wilmington Trust derived 18 percent of its total income from its trust department, a higher percentage even than the giant Morgan Guaranty Trust in New York, the nation's leader in trust assets.

Because of its unique position as the bank of such a wealthy family, there were ways in which Wilmington Trust did not operate like other banks. It derived very little of its income from loans, either to homeowners or to small businesses. The bank kept a larger percentage of its assets on hand than did other Delaware banks, because it needed money to cover the large demand accounts of its wealthy clients. Whereas in 1969 other Delaware banks kept only between eight and 15 percent of their total assets in cash and short-term notes, Wilmington Trust had 24 percent of its total assets on hand. This meant that there were millions of dollars Wilmington Trust was unable or unwilling to invest or loan out. Because of its need to have large amounts of cash available, it did not put as much of its money to work as did other banks.

More than half of Wilmington Trust's board of directors were du Pont family members in the early 1970s, and this also may have led to operations different from those typical at other banks. For example, in the spectacular bankruptcy of Lammot du Pont Copeland Jr. in 1970, some accused the bank's board of protecting its client with secrecy and not alerting other creditors to Copeland's looming financial disaster. Copeland Jr. ran a holding company, the Winthrop Lawrence Corporation, which amassed a small business empire in the 1960s. He or his company owned a string of California newspapers, a toy company, a van line, and college dormitories at one point. But towering debts led Copeland Jr. to declare bankruptcy in 1970, in one of the biggest personal bankruptcy cases ever up to that time. When Copeland Jr. defaulted on a $3.4 million loan from Wilmington Trust, the bank's judgment against him was carried out quite inconspicuously. Copeland Jr. was able to get a $1 million loan from a Swiss bank a month after Wilmington Trust published its judgment against him for default. Wilmington Trust also made little effort to collect the money owed it by Copeland Jr. Most of the loan, an amount of $3 million, had been guaranteed by his father, Lammot du Pont Copeland Sr., who happened to be a director of Wilmington Trust. This seemed a clear case of preferential treatment by the bank, because of family ties.

Changes in the 1980s

Wilmington Trust began to suffer from some of its policies, and by 1979 it was not doing well. Earnings were sinking, though the fact was masked in 1979 by profits from the sale of the bank's building. Return on assets was much lower than for its peer banks, and its loan-loss reserves were perilously low. A new president and CEO, Bernard J. Taylor, took over the bank in the summer of 1979, coming to Wilmington from a troubled Philadelphia bank. Taylor convinced Wilmington's board that their bank was in a grim situation, and he quickly embarked on a plan to save it. One element of Taylor's plan was to get Wilmington Trust out of bonds. More than half the bank's assets in 1979 were in 30-year bonds, which were low-yielding and had to be financed with short-term money that was priced every 30 or 60 days according to federal interest rates. Taylor sold off a third of the bank's bonds just months before the Federal Reserve began pushing interest rates up, a fortuitous move. He put the bank's money instead into short-term, high-yield investments. With the money gained from these investments, Taylor began to get the bank involved in commercial

lending. This was an area in which Wilmington Trust traditionally did little. In 1978 only a fourth of its assets were in loans. But Delaware was undergoing a building boom, and Taylor determined to take advantage of it. He started the bank lending to small businesses and individuals, and this turned out to be both safe and profitable.

In just three years loans went from 26 percent of assets to 44 percent. And the low-yielding bonds, which had made up more than half of Wilmington Trust's assets when Taylor took over, by 1982 made up only 15 percent of the bank's assets. The attitude of management had changed as well. When Taylor first began working at Wilmington Trust, the bank had an aristocratic atmosphere. Bankers never took their suit coats off, even on the hottest summer days. CEO Taylor himself began appearing around the office in shirtsleeves, provoking alarm and then relief among his colleagues. This seemed to symbolize the bank's new direction. Wilmington Trust was ready to work hard to maintain its profits and was not as bound to patrician tradition. Taylor also staunchly maintained that du Pont family and corporate interests had no influence on bank policy. Wilmington's shares began to shoot up on Wall Street, as the company earned the moniker "the money management firm disguised as a bank" (according to a May 16, 1985 *Wall Street Journal* article). Wilmington Trust was deemed to be more than just a regular bank, and it apparently had many enthusiastic backers in investment circles.

The bank flourished in the 1980s under Taylor's direction. It continued to expand its loan program and held loans of $2 billion—more than two-thirds of its commercial assets—by 1989. Its share of the commercial loan market in Delaware doubled, from less than 20 percent at the start of the decade to almost 40 percent in 1989. In ten years the bank had gone from an ailing, tradition-bound institution to one of the most profitable banks in the nation. For the two benchmark measures, return on assets and return on equity, Wilmington Trust showed percentages almost double the average for other banks its size. Not only had commercial lending added to the bank's profitability, but its traditional business of handling trusts also had grown. By the end of the 1980s more than ten percent of individuals on *Forbes* magazine's list of the 400 richest people in the United States had their trusts at Wilmington.

More Growth in the 1990s

After its amazing turnaround in the 1980s Wilmington Trust planned major expansion over the next decade. As the building boom in Delaware began to slow in 1990, most of the state's banks became unwilling or unable to make new construction loans. But Wilmington Trust was in such a sound financial condition that it continued to make these loans, and the bank picked up a good number of new customers. The bank planned to increase its market share by expansion as well. In 1991 the bank adopted its present holding company structure, with the Wilmington Trust Corporation holding the Wilmington Trust Company. This structure allowed it to meet regulations in the neighboring states of Maryland and Pennsylvania that would allow it to acquire banks there. But first Wilmington Trust turned its attention to acquiring small banks in its home state. In 1992 Wilmington Trust bought the Sussex Trust Company, a

$400 million-asset bank with 20 branches in the southern part of Delaware. That part of the state was growing more quickly than the northern area around Wilmington. Soon after this purchase Wilmington Trust took over $45 million in deposits from a failed Westchester, Pennsylvania bank, the Bank of Brandywine Valley. Because Brandywine Valley's failure was deemed an emergency by Pennsylvania banking authorities, Wilmington Trust was allowed to operate the bank as a branch rather than as a subsidiary. This was contrary to usual practice, but Wilmington used this precedent to convince the state to let it open other branches in Pennsylvania. It soon had branches in Maryland as well.

Wilmington Trust also expanded its role as a precious metal dealer in the early 1990s. In late 1990 Wilmington Trust bought the precious metal program of New York-based Citibank. Citibank was a subsidiary of Citicorp, the nation's largest bank, and one of the largest banks in the world. Wilmington Trust had cleared the way for this transaction in 1987, when it became the first bank outside of New York City approved by the New York Metals Exchange to store gold and silver bullion. With the 1990 deal with Citibank, Wilmington Trust became one of the largest precious metals retailers in the United States. It built this business up even more over the next few years. In 1992 Wilmington Trust bought up the metals depository business of the Bank of Delaware, and in 1993 it acquired the retail sales and service business of Idaho's Sunshine Bullion Co.

Next the bank moved to expand its handling of mutual funds. Wilmington Trust had doubled its sales of mutual funds between 1989 and 1994, and it had several competitive advantages over other banks. Wilmington Trust was a state-chartered bank but not a member of the Federal Reserve system, and this outsider status allowed it to do what few other banks could, namely distribute its own mutual funds. Other banks were required to contract with another agent to distribute its funds, but Wilmington was able to manage all aspects of its mutual fund program, which it called the Rodney Square Funds. The bank traded on its expertise in the trust area and its reputation for handling the fortunes of markedly wealthy clients to build up its mutual fund business.

Wilmington Trust's mutual funds business stumbled in 1994, after taking some losses on risky investments. In July 1994 Standard and Poor's Corp. downgraded Wilmington's triple A rating to A, because the Rodney Square funds held 12 percent of its portfolio in structured and variable-rate notes. Standard and Poor's considered these notes not sufficiently stable, and perhaps they were right, as the Rodney Square fund subsequently lost nearly $4 million. The head of Wilmington's subsidiary Rodney Square Management Corp. resigned in 1995, and the bank reorganized the unit. But two years later Wilmington's money management business seemed to be thriving. The firm acquired a 24 percent stake in a New York money management firm, Clemente Capital Inc., in April 1996. Clemente previously had acted as sub-advisor for Wilmington's trust department, and it was well known for its wealthy clientele. Without revealing minimums, Clemente claimed its mutual funds were basically for people with hundreds of thousands of dollars to invest. This high-end business fit nicely with Wilmington Trust's expertise. And by purchasing a share in Clemente, Wilmington saved itself the sub-advisory fees it had been paying the firm to manage some $15 million for its clients.

In a similar move, Wilmington Trust next made arrangements with the New York investment firm Morgan Stanley Group and Florida's J.W. Charles Financial Services Inc. to generate referrals for its trust business. These two investment firms had hundreds of brokers in their sales forces, and Wilmington wanted to reach their broad client bases by paying for referrals. Then in late 1996 Wilmington Trust created a new structure for its mutual fund administration. The bank changed to a so-called master-feeder structure, where assets of several different mutual funds (the feeders) were managed centrally by a "master." This new structure gave the bank more flexibility in handling different funds and allowed it to convert some of its nonproprietary funds into proprietary ones.

All of these changes led to increasing earnings in the late 1990s. Wilmington Trust's fees from trust and asset management climbed, and its commercial loan department continued to be quite successful. The bank gained income from its newer ventures while continuing to grow in earnings from its core trust management business. At the end of the 1990s Wilmington Trust seemed in a very solid position. It had used its expertise in trusts to branch into the vibrant mutual fund market and was backed up by an excellent commercial loan portfolio. From a lackluster bank that dealt principally in trusts in 1979, Wilmington had become a powerhouse in financial services in the 1990s. Nevertheless, its growth had been well planned and relatively moderate. Aside from the mutual fund bump in 1994, Wilmington Trust had proved itself uncommonly successful in adapting to new markets and services. Its steady growth was predicted to continue over the coming years.

Principal Subsidiaries

Wilmington Trust Company; Wilmington Trust of Pennsylvania; Wilmington Trust FSB.

Further Reading

Bennett, Robert A., "Wilmington Trust: A Little Gem," *United States Banker,* July 1992, pp. 28–31.
Braitman, Ellen, "A Rave Review for Wilmington," *American Banker,* April 22, 1992, p. 6.
Crockett, Barton, "S&P Slashes Its Rating on Wilmington Trust Money Market Fund," *American Banker,* July 5, 1994, p. 1.
Forde, John P., "Delaware Bank's Strategy Is To Put Future in Trust," *American Banker,* June 27, 1985, pp. 3–5.
Fraser, Katharine, "Morgan Stanley, Broker, To Sell Wilmington Trust Services," *American Banker,* August 8, 1996, p. 12.
——, "Wilmington Trust Bolsters Fund Administration Business with New Structure, Clients," *American Banker,* October 9, 1996, p. 10.
Fraust, Bart, "Stocks Top Balanced Funds: Wilmington Trust Has Best Return in Index," *American Banker,* May 25, 1983, pp. 2–4.
Hensley, Scott, "Wilmington's Funds Chief To Call It Quits in Shake-Up," *American Banker,* December 27, 1995, p. 10.
Kapiloff, Howard, "Wilmington Takes Stake in a Money Manager," *American Banker,* April 17, 1996, p. 10.
Munford, Christopher, "Wilmington Trust Set To Acquire Citibank's Precious Metals Unit," *American Metal Market,* November 5, 1990, p. 7.
Newman, A. Joseph Jr., "Wilmington Trust of Delaware Comes In Out of Cold," *American Banker,* March 16, 1983, pp. 2–4.

Novack, Janet, ''They Never Put on Jackets Again,'' *Forbes,* October 2, 1989, pp. 120–23.

Pare, Terence P., ''Bankers Who Beat the Bust,'' *Fortune,* November 4, 1991, pp. 159–63.

Phelan, James, and Pozen, Robert, *The Company State,* New York: Grossman Publishers, 1973.

Piro, Dan, and Stiroh, Kevin, ''Wilmington, Banc One: The Logic Behind Two High-Priced Deals,'' *American Banker,* June 19, 1991, pp. 13–14.

Rundle, Rhonda L., ''Wilmington Trust Plans a Shift in Business, But Surge in Stock's Price Prompts Caution,'' *Wall Street Journal,* May 16, 1985, p. 63.

Talley, Karen, ''Wilmington Trust Expanding in Mutual Funds,'' *American Banker,* January 26, 1994, p. 8.

''Wilmington To Buy Bullion Dealer,'' *American Banker,* July 27, 1993, p. 5.

—A. Woodward

Zapata Corporation

1717 St. James Place
Houston, Texas 77210
U.S.A.
(713) 940-6100
Fax: (713) 226-6084
Web site: http://www.zap.com

Public Company
Incorporated: 1953 as Zapata Petroleum Inc.
Employees: 1,100
Sales: $117.5 million (1997)
Stock Exchanges: New York
Ticker Symbol: ZAP
SICs: 4899 Communications Services, Not Elsewhere
　　　Classified; 2077 Animal and Marine Fats and Oils;
　　　6719 Holding Companies, Not Elsewhere Classified

Slated to become one of the ten largest Internet companies in the world, Zapata Corporation is involved in Internet and electronic-commerce businesses, operating an Internet portal and two on-line magazines, *Word* and *Charged.* Formerly an international oil and gas conglomerate, Zapata suffered profound financial losses during the 1980s, which eventually led the company away from energy-related businesses and toward its new identity, adopted in April 1998, as an Internet-related business. Zapata also maintained a 59.7 percent stake in a former wholly owned subsidiary named Omega Protein Corporation, which caught and processed fish for use as livestock feed.

1980s Spark Change

Zapata got its start in 1953 as an independent oil and gas venture launched by future President of the United States, George Bush. Bush, in his years before entering the national political spotlight, formed the company with the help of another distinguished individual, Pennzoil chairman J. Hugh Liedtke. Together, the pair set in motion a corporate entity that matured into a sprawling force in international energy-processing, with corporate reaches into a spectrum of diversified businesses, including natural-gas compression, off-shore drilling, and coal mining. At its peak as a global conglomerate, Zapata collected as much as $350 million in annual sales, exerting itself as a formidable force in its various industries. However, the most intriguing chapter in the company's history began when its encouraging success started to unravel at an alarming speed, long after both Bush (who cashed in his stake in 1966) and Liedtke had left Zapata to pursue other interests. In the wake of the company's sanguine years, debt accrued to a deleterious magnitude, touching off a two-decade period that saw the company scramble to forestall bankruptcy while it grappled with shaping a new identity for itself over and over again. The search to find a solution to its profound problems steered Zapata far away from its original business, into a field Bush and Liedtke could never had imagined.

Zapata's troubles began in the early 1980s, when long-time leader R.C. Lassiter headed the company. At that time, company executives foresaw an imminent drop in oil prices, the beginning of what proved to be a disastrous decade for the U.S. petroleum industry. In an effort to increase Zapata's market share before oil prices fell, company management directed the construction of 12 offshore drilling rigs, launching one last big push to dominate rival firms before the expected price plunge. The addition of the 12 new rigs did not deliver its intended effect, however. Instead, the imprudent construction of a dozen offshore drilling rigs delivered a blow to Zapata, saddling the company with enormous debt. When the fortunes of oil exploration took a downward turn, Zapata was left exposed to the fiercest effects of the industry-wide slump, unable to maneuver itself in a proper direction under the weight of more than $600 million of debt. In early 1985, Zapata reported a profit for its first quarter of business, but for years afterward the company reported financial losses, all largely because of the misguided decision to expand before the petroleum market contracted. As a Zapata spokesperson later noted in reference to the early 1980s expansion, ''Those rigs turned out to be a turkey.''

While the remainder of the 1980s would be bleak years for Zapata, there was one positive aspect of the company's business during the decade that would provide a glimmer of hope for the future: fishing. With a 57-vessel fleet at its disposal, Zapata caught fish—primarily menhaden—in the Gulf of Mexico and Chesapeake Bay. Menhaden, fish used as a source of fish oil, fertilizer, and bait, were processed and converted into livestock feed, from which the company realized a sizeable profit. To supplement its oil and gas exploration business and its commercial fishing operations, Zapata was also engaged in providing offshore services through Zapata Gulf Marine Corp. Started by Zapata, Houston Natural Gas Corp., and Halliburton Co., Zapata Gulf Marine, 34.7 percent owned by Zapata, made its debut in 1984, roughly a year before the oil drilling losses manifested themselves on Zapata's balance sheet. The subsidiary company, along with the marine protein operations in the Gulf of Mexico and Chesapeake Bay, stood as two potential saviors for Zapata during the latter half of the 1980s, although neither performed well enough to compensate for the deep losses stemming from oil drilling.

As the mid-1980s began, the race to stave off bankruptcy began as well, with Zapata's financial health becoming increasingly grave with each passing year. The company lost money in 1985, 1986, and again in 1987, when losses totaled $156 million on $146 million in revenues. A $600 million debt restructuring saved Zapata from bankruptcy in 1987, giving the company temporary relief, but, for the company to look forward to long-term financial health, Chairman Lassiter and his executive management team needed to find solutions that addressed the fundamental problems the enterprise faced. Lassiter began slashing costs wherever he could, and he began shedding assets that were dragging the company deeper into debt.

Through his efforts, overhead was reduced by 50 percent and more than $200 million worth of oil and gas properties were removed from Zapata's portfolio. These measures, undertaken to create a more efficient and, with hope, profitable company, were enacted roughly at the same time Lassiter's team engineered two shrewdly timed acquisitions. The company acquired two financial services companies and then resold them, netting a quick $65 million profit. This maneuver, coupled with $10 million of cash flow—the one encouraging figure amid a host of plunging financial totals—and the steps taken during the company's restructuring, fanned a modicum of optimism at corporate headquarters, a positive perspective that some industry observers were quick to embrace. *Forbes* magazine, in particular, began pronouncing the potential recovery of the destitute Zapata, citing its encouraging cash flow, the significant reduction of overhead, and Zapata's flourishing commercial fishing business as the ingredients for a successful turnaround. As would be the case during this difficult period in Zapata's existence, however, hopeful expectations frequently were dashed.

Those who hoped for a more positive end to the 1980s for Zapata generally embraced the theory that the company's robust fishing operations and its leaner oil service division would allow it to cover interest payments on its debt and then realize annual gains of 25 percent for 1989 and 1990. They were wrong. Zapata's fishing operations did record great gains, more than doubling operating income in 1988, but the increase was not enough, falling short of pundits' projections. A drought had increased the Gulf of Mexico's saline content, which consequently depressed Zapata's fish catch from an expected 950,000 tons down to 725,000 tons. Moreover, the adverse weather hurt the company in the one area it could ill-afford to suffer any damage. Commercial fishing had become increasingly important to Zapata, accounting for 47 percent of the company's revenues when drought and high levels of saline conspired to reduce the year's fish harvest. This unforeseeable problem, combined with a still-suffering offshore drilling business and a struggling oil service business, crippled the company.

The company's precarious financial position entering the 1990s led to another corporate-wide, comprehensive restructuring, the failure of which, company officials admitted, would likely lead to Zapata seeking protection under federal bankruptcy laws. Zapata teetered on the brink of insolvency, having not declared a profit since the first fiscal quarter of 1985 and having just come off a $42 million loss for the nine months ending June 1990. As the essential restructuring progressed, the company announced in September 1990 that it had signed a definitive agreement to sell its offshore drilling rig fleet for $298 million. The properties were sold to a European investment group in an agreement that stipulated Zapata would continue to oversee the 12 rigs under a management contract. Meanwhile, company officials announced their plan to concentrate on the growth of Zapata's three remaining businesses—offshore services, commercial fishing, and natural gas—until conditions improved for more sweeping, fundamental changes.

By the end of 1991, Zapata officials could at last glance at the company's balance sheet without wincing. After registering a $105 million loss in 1990, the company ended 1991 by posting a $2 million profit. Company executives used the momentum built up to push ahead in 1992, when Zapata found itself in a position to make an acquisition. The company's management contract for the 12 rigs it had built in the early 1980s expired in October 1992, creating a void that was filled the following month when Zapata re-entered the oil business through the acquisition of the Cimmaron Gas Cos. A Tulsa, Oklahoma-based private holding company, Cimmaron owned a variety of natural gas compression, processing, and marketing companies that, combined, generated annual revenues of approximately $180 million. Shortly after the completion of the acquisition, Zapata announced its plans to make further acquisitions and use Cimmaron as the foundation for a deeper presence in the gas-gathering and service industries. Highly fragmented, these two industries were beginning to consolidate, the prospect of which encouraged Zapata executives to make additional acquisitions.

Infighting in the 1990s

The calm that was beginning to settle by the end of 1992 was next interrupted by a shareholder power struggle. At the heart of the power struggle was Florida financier Malcolm I. Glazer, who, among various other business holdings, owned the National Football League's Tampa Bay Buccaneers, for which he paid a record-setting $192 million. Glazer owned roughly 33 percent of Zapata's stock, acquiring the shares in 1990 when Zapata was desperately fighting to avoid bankruptcy, and threatened a proxy fight in mid-1993 to install himself and his two sons to the company's board of directors. With this fight looming by the end of June, Zapata hired a New York-based firm specializing in fighting takeover attempts to assist in its bid to re-elect Lassiter and two other candidates. The struggle ended peacefully after Lassiter and Glazer reached an agreement that resulted in the re-election of Lassiter and the appointment of Glazer and one of his sons, Avram Glazer, to Zapata's board of directors.

At the time of the internal tumult, Zapata was continuing to pursue its new business strategy of increasing its presence in the natural gas processing and marketing segments of the energy industry. However, with Glazer occupying a position of power from mid-1993 forward, the company's strategic objectives would change. Glazer's control over Zapata increased significantly when Lassiter retired in July 1994, vacating positions that Glazer took over when he was elected the company's chairman, president, and chief executive officer. Now fully in command, Glazer began taking actions that promised to change the face of Zapata entirely, as he sought to create a company more in tune with his talents and his business empire, which included real estate, television, health care, and food service companies.

After a plan to sell the company's commercial fishing operations was cancelled in April 1995, Glazer completed the sale of Zapata's gas compression business, operated by a subsidiary named Energy Industries Inc., to Enterra Corp. for $130 million. Glazer also sold the company's five remaining oil and gas leases and a 31-mile natural gas gathering pipeline, further stripping Zapata of its former mainstay business lines. Next to go was Cimmaron, the natural gas compression, processing, and marketing company acquired in 1992, which was sold in April 1996 for $24 million, leaving a 25 percent stake in Bolivian natural gas properties as the only energy concern owned by Zapata. Soon, the Bolivian properties would be sold as well, as Glazer moved forward with his plan to create a new kind of Zapata for the 1990s.

A New Zapata Takes Shape for the Late 1990s

Glazer did not reveal his plans for what type of business Zapata would enter until a merger was announced in early 1996 that would wed Houlihan's Restaurant Group, operator of a chain of nearly 100 casual-theme restaurants, and Zapata. Two Zapata shareholders immediately protested the proposed acquisition, arguing that the deal unfairly benefited Glazer, who owned 35 percent of Zapata and 73 percent of Houlihan's. In response to the suit filed by the two shareholders, the Delaware Court of Chancery ruled that 80 percent of Zapata's shareholders—a "supermajority"—were required to approve the merger before it could be completed, a ruling that prompted Glazer to terminate the deal in October 1996. His plan thwarted, Glazer made his next major move eight months later when he achieved his goal of ridding Zapata of all its energy-related assets.

In July 1997, Glazer sold all of Zapata's Bolivian and oil and gas properties to Tesoro Bolivia Petroleum Company, thereby eliminating all links to the company's past. Next, in November, Glazer bolstered the company's commercial fishing operations by acquiring American Protein, Inc., which operated ten steamers and a menhaden processing plant in the Chesapeake Bay area, and Gulf Protein, Inc., owner of six steamers, five spotter planes, and processing equipment near Morgan City, Louisiana. Although at first it appeared Glazer might be shaping Zapata into a mighty commercial fishing operator, this was not the case. In April 1998 the company's fishing business, controlled through a wholly owned subsidiary named Omega Protein Corporation, was spun-off in an initial public offering of stock (IPO), with Zapata controlling 59.7 percent of the newly independent company's shares. Having distanced himself from Zapata's last remaining business, Glazer was ready to make his most important decision. His next move would determine the future course for Zapata.

Two weeks after completing Omega Protein's IPO, Glazer announced what type of business Zapata would enter. From April 27, 1998 forward, Zapata would compete in Internet and e-mail commerce business, its objective to acquire and consolidate companies involved with Internet and e-mail related ventures. Concurrent with the announcement, Zapata completed its first acquisition in its new industry, purchasing ICON CMT Corp., the owner of *Word* and *Charged,* two on-line World Wide Web magazines. In July 1998, Zapata increased its presence in its new business field by signing letters of intent to acquire or invest in 21 Internet sites and electronic-commerce businesses. Once the transactions were finalized, the company planned to integrate them into an Internet site located at www.zap.com, which was launched on July 6, 1998. Looking forward from this juncture in the company's history, Zapata's future course appeared clear as Glazer's son Avram, who served as president and chief executive officer, led the charge into Internet-related business. Zapata's goal, Avram Glazer explained, "is to become one of the largest Internet companies in world. We have the resources," he continued, "to make [the company's] strategy a reality and to lead the upcoming consolidation of this industry." With this ambitious objective, Zapata prepared for the 21st century, facing a future that would be entirely unlike its past.

Principal Subsidiaries

Zap, Inc.; Omega Protein Corporation (59.7%).

Further Reading

Culbertson, Katherine, "Zapata Managers Plan to Leave Energy Behind with Sale of Gas Assets," *The Oil Daily,* April 10, 1995, p. 1.

Dittrick, Paula, "Zapata Gives Glazer, Son Seat on Board in Peaceful Finale to Threatened Proxy Battle," *The Oil Daily,* July 6, 1993, p. 2.

Papiernik, Richard L., "Houlihan's 2Q Profits Off as Zapata Takeover Looms," *Nation's Restaurant News,* August 26, 1996, p. 12.

Prewitt, Milford, "Zapata Corp. Agrees to Acquire Houlihan's," *Nation's Restaurant News,* May 13, 1996, p. 1.

Schifrin, Matthew, "No Fish Story," *Forbes,* September 19, 1988, p. 218.

"Shareholders Try to Stop Houlihan's Zapata Merger," *Nation's Restaurant News,* May 20, 1996, p. 4.

Shearer, Brent, "Zapata Poised to Sell fish Protein Business," *Chemical Marketing Reporter,* March 6, 1995, p. 10.

Stewart-Gordon, Thomas, "Zapata Takes Another Crack at Petroleum with Purchase of Tulsa-based Gas Company," *The Oil Daily,* November 18, 1992, p. 3.

"Zapata Nears Exit from Energy Industry with Sale of Gas Compression Firm to Enterra," *The Oil Daily,* September 22, 1995, p. 3.

"Zapata Sells Cimmaron Gas," *The Oil Daily,* April 4, 1996, p. 5.

—Jeffrey L. Covell

INDEX TO COMPANIES

Index to Companies

Listings in this index are arranged in alphabetical order under the company name. Company names beginning with a letter or proper name such as Eli Lilly & Co. will be found under the first letter of the company name. Definite articles (The, Le, La) are ignored for alphabetical purposes as are forms of incorporation that precede the company name (AB, NV). Company names printed in bold type have full, historical essays on the page numbers appearing in bold. Updates to entries that appeared in earlier volumes are signified by the notation **(upd.).** Company names in light type are references within an essay to that company, not full historical essays. This index is cumulative with volume numbers printed in bold type.

Pacific Western Oil Co., **IV** 537
Pacific Wine Co., **18** 71
Pacific-Burt Co., Ltd., **IV** 644
Pacific-Sierra Research, **I** 155
PacifiCare Health Systems, Inc., III 85; **11** 378–80; **25** 318
PacifiCorp, V 688–90; **6** 325–26, 328; **7** 376–78
Package Products Company, Inc., **12** 150
Packaged Ice, Inc., **21** 338
Packaging Corporation of America, I 526; **12** 376–78, 397; **16** 191
Packard Bell Electronics, Inc., I 524; **II** 86; **10** 521, 564; **11** 413; **13** 387–89, 483; **21** 391; **23** 471
Packard Motor Co., **I** 81; **8** 74; **9** 17
Packer's Consolidated Press, **IV** 651
Packerland Packing Company, **7** 199, 201
Pacolet Manufacturing Company, **17** 327
PacTel. *See* Pacific Telesis Group.
Paddington Corp., **I** 248
PAFS. *See* Pacific Alaska Fuel Services.
Page, Bacon & Co., **II** 380; **12** 533
Page Boy Inc., **9** 320
PageAhead Software, **15** 492
Pageland Coca-Cola Bottling Works, **10** 222
PageMart Wireless, Inc., **18** 164, 166
Paging Network Inc., 11 381–83
Pagoda Trading Company, Inc., **V** 351, 353; **20** 86
Paid Prescriptions, **9** 346
Paige Publications, **18** 66
PaineWebber Group Inc., I 245; **II** 444–46, 449; **III** 409; **13** 449; **22** 352, 404–07 (upd.), 542; **25** 433
Painter Carpet Mills, **13** 169
Painton Co., **II** 81
La Paix, **III** 273
Pak Arab Fertilizers Ltd., **IV** 364
Pak Mail Centers, **18** 316
Pak Sak Industries, **17** 310; **24** 160
Pak-a-Sak, **II** 661
Pak-All Products, Inc., **IV** 345
Pak-Paino, **IV** 315
Pak-Well, **IV** 282; **9** 261
Pakhoed Holding, N.V., **9** 532
Pakkasakku Oy, **IV** 471
Paknet, **11** 548
Pakway Container Corporation, **8** 268
PAL. *See* Philippine Airlines, Inc.
Pal Plywood Co., Ltd., **IV** 327
Palace Station Hotel & Casino. *See* Station Casinos Inc.
Palais Royal, Inc., **24** 456
Palatine Insurance Co., **III** 234
Palco Industries, **19** 440
Pale Ski & Sports GmbH, **22** 461
Palestine Coca-Cola Bottling Co., **13** 163
Pall Corporation, 9 396–98
Palm Beach Holdings, **9** 157
Palm Shipping Inc., **25** 468–70
Palmafina, **IV** 498–99
Palmer Communications, **25** 418
Palmer G. Lewis Co., **8** 135
Palmer Tyre Ltd., **I** 428–29
Palmolive Co. *See* Colgate-Palmolive Company.
Palo Alto Brewing, **22** 421
Palo Alto Research Center, **10** 510
Palomar Medical Technologies, Inc., 22 408–10
Pamida Holdings Corporation, 15 341–43

Pamour Porcupine Mines, Ltd., **IV** 164
The Pampered Chef, Ltd., 18 406–08
Pamplemousse, **14** 225
Pan American Banks, **II** 336
Pan American Petroleum & Transport Co., **IV** 368–70
Pan American World Airways, Inc., I 20, 31, 44, 64, 67, 89–90, 92, 99, 103–04, 112–13, **115–16**, 121, 124, 126, 129, 132, 248, 452, 530, 547–48; **III** 536; **6** 51, 65–66, 71, 74–76, 81–82, 103–05, 110–11, 123, 129–30; **9** 231, 417; **10** 561; **11** 266; **12** 191, **379–81** (upd.), 419; **13** 19; **14** 73; **24** 397
Pan European Publishing Co., **IV** 611
Pan Geo Atlas Corporation, **18** 513
Pan Ocean, **IV** 473
Pan Pacific Fisheries, **24** 114
Pan-Alberta Gas Ltd., **16** 11
Panacon Corporation, **III** 766; **22** 545
Panagra, **I** 547–48
Panama Refining and Petrochemical Co., **IV** 566
PanAmSat, **18** 211, 213
Panarctic Oils, **IV** 494
Panasonic, **9** 180; **10** 125; **12** 470
Panatech Research & Development Corp., **III** 160
Panavia Aircraft GmbH, **24** 84, 86–87
Panavia Consortium, **I** 74–75
Panavision Inc., 24 372–74
Pandair, **13** 20
Pandel, Inc., **8** 271
Pandick Press Inc., **23** 63
Panhandle Eastern Corporation, I 377, 569; **IV** 425; **V** 691–92; **10** 82–84; **11** 28; **14** 135; **17** 21
Panhandle Oil Corp., **IV** 498
Panhandle Power & Light Company, **6** 580
Panhard, **I** 194
Panhard-Levassor, **I** 149
Panificadora Bimbo, **19** 191
AB Pankakoski, **IV** 274
Panmure Gordon, **II** 337
Pannill Knitting Company, **13** 531
Panocean Storage & Transport, **6** 415, 417
Panola Pipeline Co., **7** 228
Panosh Place, **12** 168
Pansophic Systems Inc., **6** 225
Pantepec Oil Co., **IV** 559, 570; **24** 520
Pantera Energy Corporation, **11** 27
Pantheon Books, **13** 429
Panther, **III** 750
Panther Express International Company, **6** 346
Pantry Pride Inc., **I** 668; **II** 670, 674; **III** 56; **23** 407–08
Pants Corral, **II** 634
Papa John's International, Inc., 15 344–46; **16** 447; **24** 295
Pape and Co., Ltd., **10** 441
Papelera Navarra, **IV** 295; **19** 226
Papeleria Calparsoro S.A., **IV** 325
Papeles Venezolanos C.A., **17** 281
The Paper Factory of Wisconsin, Inc., **12** 209
Paper Makers Chemical Corp., **I** 344
Paper Recycling International, **V** 754
Paper Software, Inc., **15** 322
Paper Stock Dealers, Inc., **8** 476
Paperituote Oy, **IV** 347–48
PaperMate, **III** 28; **23** 54
Paperwork Data-Comm Services Inc., **11** 64

Papeterie de Pont Sainte Maxence, **IV** 318
Papeteries Aussedat, **III** 122
Papeteries Boucher S.A., **IV** 300
Les Papeteries de la Chapelle-Darblay, **IV** 258–59, 302, 337
Papeteries de Lancey, 23 366–68
Les Papeteries du Limousin, **19** 227
Papeteries Navarre, **III** 677; **16** 121
Papetti's Hy-Grade Egg Products, Inc., **25** 332–33
Papierfabrik Salach, **IV** 324
Papierwaren Fleischer, **IV** 325
Papierwerke Waldhof-Aschaffenburg AG, **IV** 323–24
Papyrus Design Group, **IV** 336; **15** 455
Para-Med Health Services, **6** 181–82
Parade Gasoline Co., **7** 228
Paradyne, **22** 19
Paragon, **IV** 552
Paramax, **6** 281–83
Parametric Technology Corp., 16 405–07
Parametrics Corp., **25** 134
Paramount Communications, **16** 338; **19** 403–04
Paramount Oil Company, **18** 467
Paramount Paper Products, **8** 383
Paramount Pictures Corporation, I 451–52; **II** 129, 135, 146–47, **154–56**, 171, 173, 175, 177; **IV** 671–72, 675; **7** 528; **9** 119, 428–29; **10** 175; **12** 73, 323; **19** 404; **21** 23–25; **23** 503; **24** 327; **25** 88, 311, 327–29, 418
Parasitix Corporation. *See* Mycogen Corporation.
Paravision International, **III** 48; **8** 343
Parcelforce, **V** 498
PARCO, **V** 184–85
Parcor, **I** 676
Parfums Chanel, **12** 57
Parfums Christian Dior, **I** 272
Parfums Rochas, **I** 670; **III** 68; **8** 452
Parfums Stern, **III** 16
Pargas, **I** 378
Paribas. *See* Compagnie Financiere de Paribas.
Paridoc and Giant, **12** 153
Paris Corporation, 22 411–13
Paris Group, **17** 137
Paris Playground Equipment, **13** 319
Parisian, Inc., 14 374–76; **19** 324–25
Park Consolidated Motels, Inc., **6** 187; **14** 105; **25** 306
Park Corp., 22 414–16
Park Drop Forge Co. *See* Park-Ohio Industries Inc.
Park Hall Leisure, **II** 140; **24** 194
Park Inn International, **11** 178
Park Ridge Corporation, **9** 284
Park View Hospital, Inc., **III** 78
Park-Ohio Industries Inc., 17 371–73
Parkdale State Bank, **25** 114
Parkdale Wines, **I** 268; **25** 281
Parke, Davis & Co. *See* Warner-Lambert Co.
Parke-Bernet, **11** 453
Parker, **III** 33
Parker Appliance Co., **III** 601–02
Parker Brothers, **II** 502; **III** 505; **10** 323; **16** 337; **21** 375; **25** 489
Parker Drilling Company of Canada, **9** 363
Parker Pen Corp., **III** 218; **9** 326
Parker's Pharmacy, Inc., **15** 524

Tokyo Dairy Industry, **II** 538
Tokyo Denki Kogaku Kogyo, **II** 109
Tokyo Dento Company, **6** 430
Tokyo Disneyland, **IV** 715; **6** 123, 176
Tokyo Electric Company, Ltd., **I** 533; **12** 483
Tokyo Electric Express Railway Co., **IV** 728
Tokyo Electric Light Co., **IV** 153
Tokyo Electric Power Company, IV 167, 518; **V 729–33**
Tokyo Electronic Corp., **11** 232
Tokyo Express Highway Co., Ltd., **IV** 713–14
Tokyo Express Railway Company, **V** 510, 526
Tokyo Fire Insurance Co. Ltd., **III** 405–06, 408
Tokyo Food Products, **I** 507
Tokyo Fuhansen Co., **I** 502, 506
Tokyo Gas and Electric Industrial Company, **9** 293
Tokyo Gas Co., Ltd., IV 518; **V 734–36**
Tokyo Ishikawajima Shipbuilding and Engineering Company, **III** 532; **9** 293
Tokyo Maritime Insurance Co., **III** 288
Tokyo Motors. *See* Isuzu Motors, Ltd.
Tokyo Sanyo Electric, **II** 91–92
Tokyo Shibaura Electric Company, Ltd., **I** 507, 533; **12** 483
Tokyo Steel Works Co., Ltd., **IV** 63
Tokyo Tanker Co., Ltd., **IV** 479
Tokyo Telecommunications Engineering Corp. *See* Tokyo Tsushin Kogyo K.K.
Tokyo Trust & Banking Co., **II** 328
Tokyo Tsushin Kogyo K.K., **II** 101, 103
Tokyo Yokohama Electric Railways Co., Ltd., **V** 199
Tokyu Corporation, IV 728; **V** 199, **526–28**
Tokyu Department Store Co., Ltd., V 199–**202**
Tokyu Electric Power Company, **V** 736
Tokyu Kyuko Electric Railway Company Ltd., **V** 526
Tokyu Land Corporation, IV 728–29
Tokyu Railway Company, **V** 461
Toledo Edison Company. *See* Centerior Energy Corporation.
Toledo Milk Processing, Inc., **15** 449
Toledo Scale Corp., **9** 441
Toledo Seed & Oil Co., **I** 419
Toll Brothers Inc., 15 497–99
Tom Bowling Lamp Works, **III** 554
Tom Doherty Associates Inc., 25 483–86
Tom Huston Peanut Co., **II** 502; **10** 323
Tom Piper Ltd., **I** 437
Tom Thumb-Page, **16** 64
Tomakomai Paper Co., Ltd., **IV** 321
Toman Corporation, **19** 390
Tombstone Pizza Corporation, 13 515–17
Tomei Fire and Marine Insurance Co., **III** 384–85
Tomen Corporation, IV 224–25; **19** 256;
Tomen Corporation, 24 488–91 (upd.)
Tomen Transportgerate, **III** 638
Tomkins plc, 11 525–27
Tomkins-Johnson Company, **16** 8
Tomlee Tool Company, **7** 535
Tommy Hilfiger Corporation, 16 61; **20 488–90; 25** 258
Tomoe Trading Co., **III** 595
Tonami Transportation Company, **6** 346

Tone Brothers, Inc., 21 496–98
Tone Coca-Cola Bottling Company, Ltd., **14** 288
Tonen Corporation, IV 554–56; 16 489–92 (upd.)
Tong Yang Group, **III** 304
Toni Co., **III** 28; **9** 413
Tonka Corporation, 12 169; **14** 266; **16** 267; **25** 380, **487–89**
Tonkin, Inc., **19** 114
Tony Lama Company Inc., **19** 233
Toohey, **10** 170
Tootal Group, **V** 356–57
Tootsie Roll Industries Inc., 12 480–82; 15 323
Top End Wheelchair Sports, **11** 202
Top Green International, **17** 475
Top Man, **V** 21
Top Shop, **V** 21
Top Tool Company, Inc., **25** 75
Top Value Stamp Co., **II** 644–45; **6** 364; **22** 126
Topco Associates, **17** 78
Topkapi, **17** 101–03
Toppan Printing Co., Ltd., IV 598–99, 679–81
Topps Company, Inc., 13 518–20; 19 386
Topps Markets, **16** 314
Tops Appliance City, Inc., 17 487–89
Topy Industries, Limited, **8** 506–07
Tor Books. *See* Tom Doherty Associates Inc.
Toray Industries, Inc., V 380, **383; 17** 287
Torbensen Gear & Axle Co., **I** 154
Torchmark Corporation, III 194; **9** 506–**08; 10** 66; **11** 17; **22** 540–43
Torfeaco Industries Limited, **19** 304
Torise Ham Co., **II** 550
Tornator Osakeyhtiö, **IV** 275–76
Toro Assicurazioni, **III** 347
The Toro Company, III 600; **7 534–36**
Toromont Industries, Ltd., 21 499–501
Toronto and Scarborough Electric Railway, **9** 461
Toronto Electric Light Company, **9** 461
Toronto-Dominion Bank, II 319, **375–77,** 456; **16** 13–14; **17** 324; **18** 551–53; **21** 447
Torpshammars, **IV** 338
Torrey Canyon Oil, **IV** 569; **24** 519
The Torrington Company, III 526, 589–90; **13 521–24**
Torrington National Bank & Trust Co., **13** 467
Torstar Corp., **IV** 672; **7** 488–89; **19** 405
Tosa Electric Railway Co., **II** 458
Toscany Co., **13** 42
Tosco Corporation, 7 537–39; 12 240; **20** 138; **24** 522
Toshiba Corporation, I 221, 507–08, **533–35; II** 5, 56, 59, 62, 68, 73, 99, 102, 118, 122, 326, 440; **III** 298, 461, 533, 604; **6** 101, 231, 244, 287; **7** 529; **9** 7, 181; **10** 518–19; **11** 46, 328; **12** 454, **483–86 (upd.),** 546; **13** 324, 399, 482; **14** 117, 446; **16** 5, 167; **17** 533; **18** 18, 260; **21** 390; **22** 193, 373; **23** 471
Toshin Kaihatsu Ltd., **V** 195
Toshin Paper Co., Ltd., **IV** 285
Tostem. *See* Toyo Sash Co., Ltd.
Total Audio Visual Services, **24** 95
Total Beverage Corporation, **16** 159, 161

Total Compagnie Française des Pétroles S.A., I 303; **II** 259; **III** 673; **IV** 363–64, 423–25, 466, 486, 498, 504, 515, 525, 544–47, **557–61; V** 628; **7** 481–84; **13** 557; **21** 203
Total Exploration S.A., **11** 537
Total Global Sourcing, Inc., **10** 498
Total Petroleum Corporation, **21** 500
TOTAL S.A., 24 492–97 (upd.), 522; **25** 104
Total System Services, Inc., 12 465–66; **18** 168, 170, **516–18**
Totem Resources Corporation, 9 509–11
Totino's Finer Foods, **II** 556; **13** 516
Toto Bank, **II** 326
Toto, Ltd., III 755–56
Totsu Co., **I** 493; **24** 325
Touch-It Corp., **22** 413
Touche Remnant Holdings Ltd., **II** 356
Touche Ross. *See* Deloitte & Touche.
Touchstone Films, **II** 172–74; **6** 174–76
Tour d'Argent, **II** 518
Tourang Limited, **7** 253
Touristik Union International GmbH. and Company K.G., II 163–65
Touron y Cia, **III** 419
Touropa, **II** 163–64
Toval Japan, **IV** 680
Towa Nenryo Kogyo Co. Ltd., **IV** 554–55
Tower Automotive, Inc., 24 498–500
Tower Records, **9** 361; **10** 335; **11** 558
Towers, **II** 649
Towle Manufacturing Co., **14** 482–83; **18** 69
Town & City, **IV** 696
Town & Country Corporation, 7 372; **16** 546; **19 451–53; 25** 254
Town Investments, **IV** 711
Townsend Hook, **IV** 296, 650, 652; **19** 226
Toxicol Laboratories, Ltd., **21** 424
Toy Biz, Inc., 10 402; **18 519–21**
Toy Liquidators, **13 541–43**
Toy Park, **16** 390
Toyad Corp., **7** 296
Toyo Bearing Manufacturing, **III** 595
Toyo Cotton Co., **IV** 224–25
Toyo Kogyo, **I** 167; **II** 361; **11** 139
Toyo Marine and Fire, **III** 385
Toyo Menka Kaisha Ltd. *See* Tomen Corporation.
Toyo Microsystems Corporation, **11** 464
Toyo Oil Co., **IV** 403
Toyo Pulp Co., **IV** 322
Toyo Rayon, **V** 381, 383
Toyo Sash Co., Ltd., III 757–58
Toyo Seikan Kaisha Ltd., I 615–16
Toyo Soda, **II** 301
Toyo Tire & Rubber Co., **V** 255–56; **9** 248
Toyo Toki Co., Ltd., **III** 755
Toyo Tozo Co., **I** 265; **21** 319
Toyo Trust and Banking Co., **II** 347, 371; **17** 349
Toyoda Automatic Loom Works, Ltd., I 203; **III** 591, 593, 632, **636–39**
Toyokawa Works, **I** 579
Toyoko Co., Ltd., **V** 199
Toyoko Kogyo, **V** 199
Toyomenka (America) Inc., **IV** 224
Toyomenka (Australia) Pty., Ltd., **IV** 224
Toyota Gossei, **I** 321
Toyota Motor Corporation, I 9–10, 174, 184, **203–05,** 507–08, 587; **II** 373; **III** 415, 495, 521, 523, 536, 579, 581, 591–93, 624, 636–38, 667, 715, 742; **IV**

INDEX TO INDUSTRIES

Index to Industries

ENGINEERING & MANAGEMENT SERVICES

ENTERTAINMENT & LEISURE

FINANCIAL SERVICES: BANKS

INSURANCE

LEGAL SERVICES

MANUFACTURING

United Paper Mills Ltd. (Yhtyneet
Paperitehtaat Oy), IV
Universal Forest Products Inc., 10
UPM-Kymmene Corporation, 19
West Fraser Timber Co. Ltd., 17
Westvaco Corporation, IV; 19 (upd.)
Weyerhaeuser Company, IV; 9 (upd.)
Wickes Inc., 25 (upd.)
Willamette Industries, Inc., IV
WTD Industries, Inc., 20

PERSONAL SERVICES

ADT Security Systems, Inc., 12
CUC International Inc., 16
Educational Testing Service, 12
Franklin Quest Co., 11
Goodwill Industries International, Inc., 16
KinderCare Learning Centers, Inc., 13
The Loewen Group, Inc., 16
Manpower, Inc., 9
Regis Corporation, 18
Rollins, Inc., 11
Rosenbluth International Inc., 14
Service Corporation International, 6
SOS Staffing Services, 25
Stewart Enterprises, Inc., 20
Weight Watchers International Inc., 12
Youth Services International, Inc., 21

PETROLEUM

Abu Dhabi National Oil Company, IV
Agway, Inc., 21 (upd.)
Alberta Energy Company Ltd., 16
Amerada Hess Corporation, IV; 21 (upd.)
Amoco Corporation, IV; 14 (upd.)
Anadarko Petroleum Corporation, 10
ANR Pipeline Co., 17
Anschutz Corp., 12
Apache Corp., 10
Ashland Inc., 19
Ashland Oil, Inc., IV
Atlantic Richfield Company, IV
Baker Hughes Incorporated, 22 (upd.)
BJ Services Company, 25
The British Petroleum Company plc, IV; 7
(upd.); 21 (upd.)
Broken Hill Proprietary Company Ltd., 22
(upd.)
Burlington Resources Inc., 10
Burmah Castrol plc, IV
Caltex Petroleum Corporation, 19
Chevron Corporation, IV; 19 (upd.)
Chiles Offshore Corporation, 9
Chinese Petroleum Corporation, IV
CITGO Petroleum Corporation, IV
The Coastal Corporation, IV
Compañia Española de Petróleos S.A., IV
Conoco Inc., IV; 16 (upd.)
Cooper Cameron Corporation, 20 (upd.)
Cosmo Oil Co., Ltd., IV
Crown Central Petroleum Corporation, 7
DeepTech International Inc., 21
Den Norse Stats Oljeselskap AS, IV
Deutsche BP Aktiengesellschaft, 7
Diamond Shamrock, Inc., IV
Egyptian General Petroluem Corporation,
IV
Elf Aquitaine SA, 21 (upd.)
Empresa Colombiana de Petróleos, IV
Energen Corporation, 21
Enron Corporation, 19
Ente Nazionale Idrocarburi, IV
Enterprise Oil plc, 11
Entreprise Nationale Sonatrach, IV
Exxon Corporation, IV; 7 (upd.)
FINA, Inc., 7
Flying J Inc., 19

Forest Oil Corporation, 19
General Sekiyu K.K., IV
Giant Industries, Inc., 19
Global Marine Inc., 9
Halliburton Company, 25 (upd.)
Helmerich & Payne, Inc., 18
Holly Corporation, 12
Hunt Oil Company, 7
Idemitsu Kosan K.K., IV
Imperial Oil Limited, IV; 25 (upd.)
Indian Oil Corporation Ltd., IV
Kanematsu Corporation, IV
Kerr-McGee Corporation, IV; 22 (upd.)
King Ranch, Inc., 14
Koch Industries, Inc., IV; 20 (upd.)
Kuwait Petroleum Corporation, IV
Libyan National Oil Corporation, IV
The Louisiana Land and Exploration
Company, 7
Lyondell Petrochemical Company, IV
MAPCO Inc., IV
Maxus Energy Corporation, 7
Mitchell Energy and Development
Corporation, 7
Mitsubishi Oil Co., Ltd., IV
Mobil Corporation, IV; 7 (upd.); 21 (upd.)
Murphy Oil Corporation, 7
Nabors Industries, Inc., 9
National Iranian Oil Company, IV
Neste Oy, IV
NGC Corporation, 18
Nigerian National Petroleum Corporation,
IV
Nippon Oil Company, Limited, IV
Noble Affiliates, Inc., 11
Occidental Petroleum Corporation, IV; 25
(upd.)
Oil and Natural Gas Commission, IV
ÖMV Aktiengesellschaft, IV
Oryx Energy Company, 7
Patina Oil & Gas Corporation, 24
Pennzoil Company, IV; 20 (upd.)
PERTAMINA, IV
Petro-Canada Limited, IV
Petrofina, IV
Petróleo Brasileiro S.A., IV
Petróleos de Portugal S.A., IV
Petróleos de Venezuela S.A., IV
Petróleos del Ecuador, IV
Petróleos Mexicanos, IV; 19 (upd.)
Petroleum Development Oman LLC, IV
Petronas, IV
Phillips Petroleum Company, IV
Qatar General Petroleum Corporation, IV
Quaker State Corporation, 7; 21 (upd.)
Repsol S.A., IV; 16 (upd.)
Royal Dutch Petroleum Company/ The
''Shell'' Transport and Trading Company
p.l.c., IV
Sasol Limited, IV
Saudi Arabian Oil Company, IV; 17 (upd.)
Schlumberger Limited, 17 (upd.)
Seagull Energy Corporation, 11
Shanghai Petrochemical Co., Ltd., 18
Shell Oil Company, IV; 14 (upd.)
Showa Shell Sekiyu K.K., IV
Société Nationale Elf Aquitaine, IV; 7
(upd.)
Sun Company, Inc., IV
Talisman Energy, 9
Tesoro Petroleum Corporation, 7
Texaco Inc., IV; 14 (upd.)
Tonen Corporation, IV; 16 (upd.)
Tosco Corporation, 7
Total Compagnie Française des Pétroles
S.A., IV
TOTAL S.A., 24 (upd.)
Travel Ports of America, Inc., 17

Triton Energy Corporation, 11
Türkiye Petrolleri Anonim Ortakliği, IV
Ultramar PLC, IV
Union Texas Petroleum Holdings, Inc., 9
Unocal Corporation, IV; 24 (upd.)
USX Corporation, IV; 7 (upd.)
Valero Energy Corporation, 7
Vastar Resources, Inc., 24
Wascana Energy Inc., 13
Western Atlas Inc., 12
Western Company of North America, 15
The Williams Companies, Inc., IV
YPF Sociedad Anonima, IV

PUBLISHING & PRINTING

A.H. Belo Corporation, 10
Advance Publications Inc., IV; 19 (upd.)
Affiliated Publications, Inc., 7
American Greetings Corporation, 7, 22
(upd.)
Arnoldo Mondadori Editore S.p.A., IV; 19
(upd.)
The Atlantic Group, 23
Axel Springer Verlag AG, IV; 20 (upd.)
Banta Corporation, 12
Bauer Publishing Group, 7
Berlitz International, Inc., 13
Bertelsmann A.G., IV; 15 (upd.)
Big Flower Press Holdings, Inc., 21
Book-of-the-Month Club, Inc., 13
Bowne & Co., Inc., 23
Burda Holding GmbH. & Co., 23
The Bureau of National Affairs, Inc., 23
Butterick Co., Inc., 23
Cadmus Communications Corporation, 23
CCH Inc., 14
Central Newspapers, Inc., 10
The Chronicle Publishing Company, Inc.,
23
Commerce Clearing House, Inc., 7
The Condé Nast Publications Inc., 13
The Copley Press, Inc., 23
Cowles Media Company, 23
Cox Enterprises, Inc., IV; 22 (upd.)
Crain Communications, Inc., 12
Dai Nippon Printing Co., Ltd., IV
Daily Mail and General Trust plc, 19
Day Runner, Inc., 14
DC Comics Inc., 25
De La Rue PLC, 10
Deluxe Corporation, 7; 22 (upd.)
Dorling Kindersley Holdings plc, 20
Dow Jones & Company, Inc., IV; 19 (upd.)
The Dun & Bradstreet Corporation, IV; 19
(upd.)
Duplex Products Inc., 17
The E.W. Scripps Company, IV; 7 (upd.)
Edmark Corporation, 14
Elsevier N.V., IV
EMI Group plc, 22 (upd.)
Encyclopedia Britannica, Inc., 7
Engraph, Inc., 12
Enquirer/Star Group, Inc., 10
Essence Communications, Inc., 24
Farrar, Straus and Giroux Inc., 15
Flint Ink Corporation, 13
Follett Corporation, 12
Franklin Electronic Publishers, Inc., 23
Gannett Co., Inc., IV; 7 (upd.)
Gibson Greetings, Inc., 12
Graphic Industries Inc., 25
Gray Communications Systems, Inc., 24
Grolier Inc., 16
Groupe de la Cite, IV
Groupe Les Echos, 25
Hachette, IV
Hachette Filipacchi Medias S.A., 21

REAL ESTATE

RETAIL & WHOLESALE

UTILITIES

WASTE SERVICES

NOTES ON CONTRIBUTORS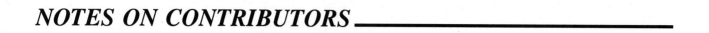

Notes on Contributors

AZZATA, Gerry. Freelance writer, researcher, and editor based in Medford, Massachusetts; former academic reference librarian with graduate degrees in law and library science. She has published numerous materials in the areas of law, business, health, and online research.

BENBOW-PFALZGRAF, Taryn. Freelance editor, writer, and consultant in the Chicago area.

BIANCO, David. Freelance writer.

BRENNAN, Gerald. Freelance writer living in Arcata, California; former editor of the bowling journal *HareLip*.

BROWN, Susan Windisch. Freelance writer and editor.

COHEN, M. L. Novelist and freelance writer living in Paris.

COVELL, Jeffrey L. Freelance writer and corporate history contractor.

DERDAK, Thomas. Freelance writer and adjunct professor of philosophy at Loyola University of Chicago.

DORGAN, Charity Anne. Detroit-based freelance writer.

FELDMAN, Heidi. Freelance writer, arts management consultant, and doctoral student in ethnomusicology.

FERRAN, Christine L. Freelance writer.

FIERO, John W. Freelance writer, researcher, and consultant; Professor of English at the University of Southwestern Louisiana in Lafayette.

HALASZ, Robert. Former editor in chief of *World Progress* and *Funk & Wagnalls New Encyclopedia Yearbook*; author, *The U.S. Marines* (Millbrook Press, 1993).

HAUSER, Evelyn. Marketing specialist and writer based in Arcata, California.

INGRAM, Frederick C. South Carolina-based business writer who has contributed to *GSA Business, Appalachian Trailway News,* the *Encyclopedia of Business,* the *Encyclopedia of Global Industries,* the *Encyclopedia of Consumer Brands,* and other regional and trade publications.

JACOBSON, Robert R. Freelance writer and musician.

JONES, Allison A. Freelance writer.

KNIGHT, Judson. Freelance writer.

LEMIEUX, Gloria A. Freelance writer and editor living in Nashua, New Hampshire.

MALLETT, Daryl F. Freelance writer and editor; actor; contributing editor and series editor at The Borgo Press; series editor of SFRA Press's *Studies in Science Fiction, Fantasy and Horror*; associate editor of Gryphon Publications and for *Other Worlds Magazine*; founder and owner of Angel Enterprises, Jacob's Ladder Books, and Dustbunny Productions.

MOZZONE, Terri. Iowa-based freelance writer specializing in profile essays.

PASSAGE, Robert Alan. Freelance writer.

PEIPPO, Kathleen. Minneapolis-based freelance writer.

ROTHBURD, Carrie. Freelance technical writer and editor, specializing in corporate profiles, academic texts and academic journal articles.

SALAMIE, David E. Co-owner of InfoWorks Development Group, a reference publication development and editorial services company; contributor to such reference works as *Encyclopedia of American Industries* and *Encyclopedia of Global Industries.*

UHLE, Frank. Ann Arbor-based freelance writer; movie projectionist, disc jockey, and staff member of *Psychotronic Video* magazine.

WALDEN, David M. Freelance writer and historian in Salt Lake City; adjunct history instructor at Salt Lake City Community College.

WERNICK, Ellen D. Freelance writer and editor.

WEST, Melissa. Freelance writer.

WOODWARD, A. Freelance writer.